The Law of Restitution

BUTTERWORTHS COMMON LAW SERIES

The Law of Restitution

SERIES EDITOR

Andrew Grubb MA (Cantab), LLD (Lond), FMedSci, Barrister Professor of Medical Law and Head of Department Cardiff Law School.

GENERAL EDITORS

Steve Hedley
University Lecturer, Faculty of Law, Cambridge

Margaret Halliwell
Senior Lecturer, City University, London

CONTRIBUTORS

Neil Allen
Barrister, Young Street Chambers, Manchester

Dr Joanna Bird
Australian Securities and Investments Commission

Dr Paula Giliker
Lecturer, Faculty of Law, Queen Mary & Westfield College, London

David Howarth
University Lecturer, Department of Land Economy, Cambridge

Dr Peter M McDermott
Senior Lecturer, The University of Queensland Law School, Australia

Dr Craig Rotherham
College Lecturer, Gonville & Caius College, Cambridge

Gregory Tolhurst
Faculty of Law, University of Sydney, Australia

Butterworths
LexisNexis™

Members of the LexisNexis Group worldwide

United Kingdom	LexisNexis Butterworths Tolley, a Division of Reed Elsevier (UK) Ltd, Halsbury House, 35 Chancery Lane, LONDON, WC2A 1EL, and 4 Hill Street, EDINBURGH EH2 3JZ
Argentina	LexisNexis Argentina, BUENOS AIRES
Australia	LexisNexis Butterworths, CHATSWOOD, New South Wales
Austria	LexisNexis Verlag ARD Orac GmbH & Co KG, VIENNA
Canada	LexisNexis Butterworths, MARKHAM, Ontario
Chile	LexisNexis Chile Ltda, SANTIAGO DE CHILE
Czech Republic	Nakladatelství Orac sro, PRAGUE
France	Editions du Juris-Classeur SA, PARIS
Hong Kong	LexisNexis Butterworths, HONG KONG
Hungary	HVG Orac, BUDAPEST
India	LexisNexis Butterworths, NEW DELHI
Ireland	Butterworths (Ireland) Ltd, DUBLIN
Italy	Guiffrè Editore, MILAN
Malaysia	Malayan Law Journal Sdn Bhd, KUALA LUMPUR
New Zealand	LexisNexis Butterworths, WELLINGTON
Poland	Wydawnictwo Prawnicze LexisNexis, WARSAW
Singapore	LexisNexis Butterworths, SINGAPORE
South Africa	Butterworths SA, DURBAN
Switzerland	Stämpfli Verlag AG, BERNE
USA	LexisNexis, DAYTON, Ohio

A CIP Catalogue record for this book is available from the British Library.

ISBN 0-406-98261-9

9 780406 982612

Typeset by Columns Design Ltd, Reading, England
Printed and bound in Great Britain by Clays Ltd, St Ives Plc

Visit Butterworths LexisNexis *direct* at www.butterworths.com

Series Preface

The common law is justifiably seen as a jewel in the crown of English Law. The common law has travelled far afield to many other countries where it has been adopted and developed by the local courts. No longer the sole preserve of the judges in London (or Edinburgh and Cardiff), its durability and richness has been due in no small way to the diversity of approach that exists between the common law countries throughout the world. Many of the great judges in England, such as Mansfield, Blackburn, Atkin, Devlin, Reid and Denning, and those from overseas such as Oliver Wendell Holmes, Benjamin Cardozo and Owen Dixon, have been masters of the common law. As we enter the new Millenium, the common law continues to influence the development of law elsewhere. It will remain a major export, but now also an import, of this country.

Butterworths Common Law Series conceives of the common law in broad terms, providing analysis of the principles informing the frameworks of the law derived from judicial decisions and legislation. The *Series* seeks to provide authoritative accounts of the common law for legal practitioners, judges and academics. While providing a clear and authoritative exposition of the existing law, the *Series* also aims to identify and examine potential developments in the common law drawing on important and significant jurisprudence from other common law jurisdictions. Judges have increasingly looked to academic works for guidance on the accepted view of the law but also when contemplating a reformulation or change of direction in the law. The *Series* may, it is hoped, provide some assistance such that the law is less likely to be left undeveloped 'marching... in the rear limping a little', to quote a famous judicial aphorism (*Mount Isa Mines v Pusey* (1970) per Windeyer J).

Andrew Grubb

Foreword

For some of us restitution has emerged as a structured subject only during our professional lifetime. With the guidance and assistance of Lord Goff and Professor Gareth Jones, it has been developed from disparate sources in the common law and equity. These sources included both strict liabilities and ones which were based upon more flexible principles. The common law action for money had and received has become largely obsolete and been replaced by innominate causes of action which are open to essentially equitable defences based on such considerations as whether there has been unjust enrichment or change of position. However, the proprietary remedies still govern in equity and, it may be thought, have handicapped the same beneficial developments there and the desired assimilation of law and equity. The most critical development in the last few years has been the recognition of mistake as a ground for recovery. Welcome as it is, there has not yet been the examination of its character and implications which will provide satisfactory rules for its use.

The law of restitution, therefore, continues to be a subject where the authors of texts have a special contribution to make. The judge is at the mercy of the cases which happen to come before him or her. The authors can create their own structures, pose their own questions and, even, provide their own answers in accordance with what they opine the law should be. Thus, this addition to Butterworths' Common Law Series will be of value to both academics and practitioners. It is a pleasure to see that this volume does not shrink from asking some awkward questions and discussing frankly the merits of some of the decisions of the courts. One of the valuable messages of this volume is that, without attempting to conquer the territory of others or extend the subject beyond what is properly within the scope of the restitutionary remedy, the subject is still a frontier subject requiring the rigorous and accurate identification and refinement of the underlying principles.

This volume completes the trilogy of volumes covering contract, tort, and now restitution. Butterworths are to be congratulated and one can express the hope that this will be the first of a number of editions.

Lord Hobhouse of Woodborough
July 2002

Preface

Restitution is now a well-established, if occasionally baffling, member of the legal family. The topics it covers are diverse, though with an overall distinctly commercial flavour. The cases on which it is based are sometimes disconcertingly ancient, as we come across shards and splinters from the old forms of action; but also sometimes shockingly up-to-date, as it deals with novel situations and arguments in public law, in intellectual property, in the consequences of high-tech fraud, and in the contemporary conflict of laws. Its importance to modern business law is now undoubted.

Yet it is also mysterious, for the subject is surrounded by a dense cloud of academic theory, which repels many, and sows confusion amongst the rest. Indeed, simply to keep track of which theories are on offer would be a full-time pursuit. However, while the writers of this book have derived much inspiration and illumination from these academic sources (and, indeed, most are academics themselves), the goal of the book is much more oriented towards legal practice. Its aim is no more and no less than to give an account of the English law as it currently is, invoking theory as a tool whenever it seems useful. How well we have succeeded in that goal, we leave it to our readers to judge.

The production of this book, which was the brainchild of Steve Hedley, has been delayed due to unforeseen personal circumstances affecting several of the contributors. Whilst Margaret Halliwell has kept the ship afloat during turbulent times, Steve Hedley has undertaken the substantial editorial work. Heartfelt thanks go to all the contributors, who have all made substantial sacrifices to bring it to completion. Thanks also to the staff at Butterworths, for their hard work, competence, and, on occasion, patience.

Steve Hedley & Margaret Halliwell

Contents

Part I
Introduction

Part II
Property and Equity

TABLE OF STATUTES

References in the right-hand column are to paragraph numbers

TABLE OF STATUTORY INSTRUMENTS

References in the right-hand column are to paragraph numbers

TABLE OF CASES

References in the right-hand column are to paragraph numbers

A

B

C

D

E

F

G

H

I

J

K

O

P

S

T

U

V

W

Part I
Introduction

CHAPTER 1

Restitution and Unjust Enrichment

Steve Hedley

A   Introduction

1.1   The word 'restitution' is used in statutes and in cases in a bewildering variety of different, though related, senses.

- **The root meaning** is the return of something which the defendant wrongly acquired from the claimant, or (at least) wrongly retains. So an action for the return of specific items of personal property is an action for 'specific restitution'. Similarly, a claimant who seeks to set aside a transaction, so that each side returns what they have received from the other, is said to claim *restitutio in integrum*.
- **By extension**, the word can also refer to any remedy for the defendant's wrongful taking or retention of something the claimant was entitled to. It seems to make little difference which measure is used to reduce the claimant's entitlement to a precise amount in money. So 'restitution' can refer to a sum representing property taken, or the equivalent value, or representing its proceeds. It can also refer to a remedy representing the value of a profit made on a wrongful taking by the defendant, or the loss suffered by the claimant. While usually used in relation to property, it has also been used in respect of the protection of non-proprietary interests. So the victim of a criminal assault may seek an order for restitution from the attacker (meaning an order to pay the equivalent of civil damages), and a claimant who has performed valuable services at the defendant's request may seek restitution for them (meaning a remedy of the payment of a fair price). So used, the word overlaps substantially with (though is not identical to) 'compensation'.
- **By convention**, however, use of the word 'restitution' is restricted to cases where the remedy claimed is not easily referable to the traditional notions of contract, tort or property. So, for example, where a claimant has voluntarily transferred goods to the defendant in the expectation that they will be paid for, it is usual to refer to the liability claimed as restitutionary *only where it cannot be justified on contractual grounds*.

Obviously, while the word 'restitution' is useful enough in a non-technical sense, some caution is needed before it is used in technical contexts, if its precise significance is to be clear.

1.2   For the purposes of this book, the conventional meaning is used throughout. While there is an occasional (and unavoidable) overlap with doctrines in contract law, damages law, and property law, nonetheless the core of the book covers doctrines which are understood to be outside those areas. It is plainly disadvantageous that the boundaries of restitution shift with every fluctuation in neighbouring legal doctrines. However, in a legal system that grows slowly and organically, there is no obvious alternative.

1.3   Is restitution, so defined, based on unjust enrichment? Many writers suggest that *some* liabilities in restitution are based on an underlying legal obligation to restore enrichments unjustly acquired, or which it would be unjust not to restore to the claimant. This suggestion has been made at varying times, and with varying force. It has many implications, which are considered at appropriate places throughout this work.

It has even been suggested in recent years that *all* restitutionary liabilities might be based on unjust enrichment. On this view, the expressions 'unjust enrichment' and 'restitution' reflect a perfect theoretical symmetry or 'quadration'. Unjust enrichment is remedied by restitution (and *only* by restitution), and restitution is a response to unjust enrichment (and *only* to unjust enrichment)[1]. However, the writer who proposed this view with the greatest rigour has now abandoned it, and it seems to have little support today[2]. A trap for the unwary reader is the careless reference to particular liabilities as 'restitutionary', where the writer means that the liabilities are grounded on unjust enrichment. This usage seems impossible to defend (except of course if it is used by a member of the quadrationist tendency), but is common nonetheless.

1   This is the general approach of Goff and Jones *Law of Restitution* (5th edn, 1998), especially ch 1, though the proposition is not there subjected to close logical analysis. The proposition was enunciated with far greater rigour in Birks *An introduction to the law of restitution* (revised edn, 1989), especially chs 1–3.
2   See Birks 'Misnomer' in Cornish, Nolan, O'Sullivan and Virgo (eds) *Restitution past present and future – Essays in honour of Gareth Jones* (1998), p 1. For a recent defence of 'quadration' see Burrows 'Quadrating restitution and unjust enrichment: A matter of principle?' [2000] RLR 257.

B   Subject matter

1.4   Restitution has a tendency to gather to itself odds and ends of law and equity, which do not seem to fit elsewhere. Nonetheless, systematic treatment shows certain broad patterns in the material.

1.5   Much of restitution covers important doctrines in commercial equity, particularly those relating to the consequences of breach of equitable obligations and the payment of another's debt. These doctrines form the core of proprietary notions in restitution, though in some cases equity was building on a (somewhat slender) common law foundation. Successive chapters therefore consider the role of modern equity[1], proprietary claims[2] and tracing[3], liability for receipt of trust property or assistance with breach of trust[4], recoupment[5], contribution[6], subrogation[7], the liability of fiduciaries to disgorge profits wrongly made[8], and various equitable doctrines based on unconscionability[9].

1   See below, ch 2.
2   See below, ch 3.
3   See below, ch 4.
4   See below, ch 5.
5   See below, ch 6.
6   See below, ch 7.
7   See below, ch 8.
8   See below, ch 9.
9   See below, ch 10.

1.6   Another recurrent theme is the treatment of certain exceptional situations or remedies in the law of contract and tort.

   So successive chapters deal with the recovery of profits from breach of contract[1] and from other wrongs[2].

1   See below, ch 11.
2   See below, ch 12.

1.7   The book then proceeds to other exceptional cases either in contract, or in near-contract situations: cases of uncertain or merely anticipated contracts[1], illegality[2], incapacity[3], and necessity and emergency situations[4]. It then proceeds to cases of mistaken payments in cases in pure private law[5] and in cases with a public law element[6]. That section concludes with the case where a valid contract was subsequently discharged by breach[7] or by frustration[8].

1   See below, ch 13.
2   See below, ch 14.
3   See below, ch 15.
4   See below, ch 16.
5   See below, ch 17.
6   See below, ch 18.
7   See below, ch 19.
8   See below, ch 20.

1.8   A final section covers matters common to all the doctrines discussed: general defences[1], liability to pay interest on restitutionary claims[2], and the conflict of laws[3].

1   See below, ch 21.
2   See below, para 21.70ff.
3   See below, ch 22.

C   History of restitution

1.9   Much of the terminology used in the area is still antique, deriving from the forms of action which characterised the common law before 1852. This language reflects a simple remedial common law scheme. The principal action was the 'action for money had and received', for the restitution of money paid by the claimant to the defendant. The other three actions, in practice of lesser importance, were the 'action for money paid' (where the claimant had paid money to a third party, seeking reimbursement from the defendant); the 'action for a quantum meruit' (for services rendered to, or for the benefit of, the defendant); and the 'action for a quantum valebat' (for goods supplied to or for the benefit of the defendant).

   These remedies were, for most of their history, barely distinguishable from the remedies on informal contracts. For example, it is natural today to ask whether a claimant on a quantum meruit is relying on a contract implied in fact (ie a genuine, if tacit, agreement to pay a fair price) or a contract implied in law (ie an obligation imposed despite the absence of agreement). But in the early days of the common law, before the establishment of modern contractual theory, this distinction would have been hard to make. Indeed, there was no *point* in making it at the stage of the pleadings; if the distinction needed to be made before a jury, counsel could still do so. Despite the abolition of the system of pleading to which it refers, this terminology has survived, and is used to this day. Restitution is also taken today to include much that is of equitable origin[1].

1   See below, ch 2.

1.10   Most of what we now think of as common law restitution was, in the mediaeval period, handled by the law of debt. 'Debt' is to modern eyes a rather expansive concept, drawing no firm distinction between debts arising by agreement and debts arising for other reasons. Nonetheless, by the fifteenth century it carried substantial procedural disadvantages, not the least of which being that it allowed the defendant to 'wage his law', escaping liability if twelve persons could be found who would swear an oath to his non-liability. The action of debt was gradually superseded by the action of assumpsit, which initially required an actual promise by the defendant to acknowledge the indebtedness, but which was expanded to allow for a fictitious promise. While the history is not entirely clear, it is usually considered that some sort of milestone was reached in *Slade's case*, which holds that a promise to pay could be implied from the mere fact of the indebtedness[1]. The action of assumpsit could therefore take on the whole of the work previously done by the action of debt, with a markedly more modern procedure – including the substitution of a jury in place of 'wager of law'. The seventeenth century therefore saw a great rise in the importance of this action. The beginnings of important equitable developments can also be seen at this period, particularly in relation to commercially important areas such as contribution, subrogation and tracing, areas where equity was (and still is) considerably in advance of the common law.

1   See especially Ibbetson 'Sixteenth century contract law: *Slade's case* in context' (1984) 4 OJLS 295.

1.11   By the middle of the eighteenth century, restitutionary recovery was well developed[1]. A very important figure here is Lord Mansfield, who did much to foster a commercial orientation for the civil law. Among his many enthusiasms in commercial law, a particular favourite was the action for money had and received. In a famous passage, he expounded its virtues, stressing that the action was broad in scope, but was also subject to sensible limits; and he listed a variety of circumstances where it would be available[2].

However, from a modern point of view it is hard to know what to make of his enthusiasm for the action. Some take it as an important precursor to more modern notions of unjust enrichment, stressing the Roman sources on which Mansfield was evidently drawing[3]. Others agree that it is an important statement of liability, but argue that the root ideas were equitable[4]. Yet others, while not doubting the importance of the statement in its day, doubt that it was meant to promote any substantive principle at all. Mansfield did not mention unjust enrichment, and may not have been suggesting that the many instances he mentioned had anything in common *doctrinally*, but only in that they all deserved rapid and efficacious solution. Mansfield's focus was on procedure, not doctrine, and it may be a mistake to treat him as commenting on doctrinal matters. Whatever may be the truth of this, the law of restitution remained very disparate for many years afterwards[5].

1   Baker 'The use of assumpsit for restitutionary money claims 1600–1800' in Schrage (ed) *Unjust enrichment: The comparative legal history of the law of restitution* (1995), p 31.
2   *Moses v Macferlan* (1760) 2 Burr 1005 at 1012, 97 ER 676 at 680–681. For another report of the case see *Moses v Macpherlan* (1760) 1 Black W 219, 96 ER 120. The core of the passage is quoted below, para 2.16.
3   Birks 'English and Roman learning in *Moses v Macferlan*' [1984] CLP 1. See also Birks and McLeod 'The implied contract theory of quasi-contract: Civilian opinion current in the century before Blackstone' (1986) 6 OJLS 46.
4   See below, para 2.16.
5   See especially Evans *An essay on the action for money had and received* (1802), reprinted in [1998] RLR 1.

1.12   Over the course of the nineteenth century, the foundations were laid for much of the modern law[1]. Abolition of the forms of action in 1852 led writers to concentrate more on the substance of the actions, and less on the procedure through which they were brought. The fusion of law and equity in 1875 took this process further, forcing writers to consider which of the many differences between the two systems represented genuine differences of approach, and which were mere historical accidents. And the emergence, in the final decades of the century, of a general theory of contract law, proved an insuperable hurdle to rational discussion of quasi-contract. The 'implied contract' of which the cases spoke sounded like an archaic fiction, to a generation of lawyers that took 'contract' to be based on the actual will of real parties to an undeniable agreement. Thus the language of the cases seemed impossible, and, having no other, all tended to neglect the subject.

Whether the 'implied contract' can really be dismissed so easily is a controversial question. In many areas, the function of the law of restitution is precisely to make for the parties the contract they have not or cannot make for themselves. So in cases of the supply of necessary goods to those too ill to buy them, it is entirely appropriate to 'imply' a contract that the recipient should pay at the going rate[2]. Both history and the practicalities of the situation point to an analogy with contractual liability, which cannot be simply brushed aside. Yet the truth is that the notion of contract itself in the early twenty-first century is profoundly unsatisfactory; we have outgrown the Victorian concept of contract, but have yet to find one that is better. Dissatisfaction with notions of contract seems to be behind many restitutionary developments[3].

1   Ibbetson *A Historical Introduction to the Law of Obligations* (1999), ch 14.
2   See below, chs 15 and 16.
3   See Hedley *Restitution: Its Division and Ordering* (2001), especially chs 3 and 8.

1.13   There was a slow revival of interest in restitution in scholarly writings over the course of the twentieth century. Most of the writers involved were of the opinion that restitution cases could be explained by postulating a principle against 'unjust enrichment'. Much interest was stimulated by the American Law Institute's *Restatement of Restitution* (1937), which was discussed in detail in English journals. This led to a heated academic debate over whether 'unjust enrichment' could or should replace 'implied contract', with Winfield strongly favouring unjust enrichment[1], Landon favouring implied contract[2], and Holdsworth adopting a position which was more nuanced, but which essentially favoured implied contract[3].

Matters rested there until the 1960s, when Goff and Jones published their *Law of Restitution*[4], powerfully arguing for a principle against unjust enrichment, though providing little by way of detailed theoretical justification for such a principle, or argument as to why other possible explanations for the cases were inadequate or wrong. A more theoretical approach was then taken in Birks's *An Introduction to the Law of Restitution*[5], which remains highly influential today, albeit increasingly subject to qualifications[6].

1   Winfield 'The province of the law of tort: A reply' (1932) 9 Bell Yard 32.
2   Landon, review of Winfield *Province of the law of tort* (1931) 8 Bell Yard 19.
3   Holdsworth 'Unjustifiable enrichment' (1939) 55 LQR 37.
4   (1st edn, 1966). The current edition is the 5th (1998).
5   (Revised edn, 1989).
6   Birks's views on certain points have changed since he wrote *An introduction to the law of restitution* (revised edn, 1989). For a more modern statement of his position see Birks 'The law of restitution at the end of an epoch' (1999) 28 Western Australian Law Review 13.

1.14   The years following Birks's *Introduction* have seen the provisional acceptance by the judiciary that there is a principle against unjust enrichment; but they have also seen the accumulation of academic attacks on that principle. The detailed exposition of the law has turned up numerous points of difficulty, and it is a matter of opinion how well the theory of unjust enrichment has been able to tackle them. The overall result to date is that, while plainly there is significant judicial support for a principle against unjust enrichment, it is by no means clear what subject-matter that principle applies to, or what it requires in cases to which it applies. Unjust enrichment is not, as will become clear, a theory that can be adequately summed up in a single paragraph, let alone a single sentence. It is a complex theory with many ramifications. The working-through of those ramifications, on which the success or otherwise of the theory must ultimately depend, is exemplified throughout this book.

D   'Unjust enrichment' today: the theory

1.15   Talk of 'unjust enrichment' has often suffered from a degree of vagueness. In reaction to this, a very precise terminology was adopted in Birks's *An introduction to the law of restitution*. Opinions are sharply divided on the merits of this terminology: for some it provides a key to the entire area, for others it is only occasionally useful, for yet others it is an attempt to squeeze the law into a mould it patently does not fit. But whatever we make of it, much of the scholarly writing in the field employs its jargon, and for that reason alone, an understanding of it is of value.

1.16   Using this terminology, to say that a particular claimant is entitled to a remedy from a particular defendant on the ground of unjust enrichment involves four distinct arguments. Firstly, that the defendant was enriched; secondly, that this enrichment was unjust; thirdly, that the unjust enrichment was at the expense of the claimant; and fourthly, that there is no relevant defence open to the defendant. There are no additional requirements – in particular, there is no requirement that the defendant be at fault[1]. Each of these requirements requires distinct consideration. Detailed discussion will follow in later chapters, in the context where each discussion is relevant.

1   For a more extended discussion see Birks 'The role of fault in the law of unjust enrichment' in Swadling and Jones (eds) *The search for principle – Essays in honour of Lord Goff of Chieveley* (1999), p 235.

1.17   The requirement that the defendant be enriched may be satisfied in a variety of ways. Receipt of an economic benefit, such as money or other property, is a relatively straightforward example. Most writers are prepared to regard the receipt of services as a benefit as well, though some regard this as a mistake except in cases where there is a tangible, valuable end-product or residuum of some kind. Further examples of valuable benefits are the payment of a debt which the defendant should have paid, and saving the defendant an expense which would, but for the claimant's intervention, have been inevitable.

1.18   Assuming that a benefit is received, what value is to be placed on it? In general, receipt of a sum of money by the defendant is unproblematic, and may be valued as equivalent to that precise sum. Again, a benefit of the saving of an (otherwise inevitable) expense may be valued as equivalent to the expense saved.

But what of other types of benefit? In practice, the measure adopted is that of the market value of the benefit. However, a sale in the market usually presupposes both a willing seller and a willing buyer, and so it is not thought appropriate to value a benefit at the market rate without some indication that the defendant placed that value on it. Hence the notion of 'subjective devaluation': that the courts will not make the defendant liable for the market value of a benefit, if the defendant in fact did not place that value on the benefit. This is thought to explain why a claimant who makes improvements to a defendant's property cannot, without more, recover anything from the defendant for the value of the improvements. The claimant must go further, and establish either that the defendant did in fact value the improvements (as where the defendant requested them), or that the defendant cannot reasonably deny that they have value (as where the improvements prevented the destruction of the property). In the latter case the benefit is said to be 'incontrovertible', and the defendant's attitude to it is irrelevant[1].

1   See further below, para 13.46.

1.19   A further complication in the notion of 'enrichment' is the role of post-receipt events. Suppose, firstly, that the defendant receives an undoubted benefit, but by the time of the claim it has gone – perhaps spent by the defendant, or perhaps lost through accident. Is the defendant still 'enriched' for the purposes of an action in unjust enrichment? It appears that there is, at least in some circumstances, a defence that the defendant changed his or her position in reliance on the enrichment. It is a matter of debate whether that defence can be rationalised as an attempt to define those circumstances in which the defendant is no longer enriched[1]. The good faith or otherwise of the defendant is clearly crucial: no defendant can rely on disposal of the benefit where, at the time of the disposal, he or she was aware that it should be returned to the claimant.

Suppose, secondly, the converse case: the defendant acquires a benefit, which then increases in value. This may be due to fortuitous circumstances (as where the defendant acquires property, the market value of which then rises) or to deliberate action (as where the defendant receives money, and invests it profitably). May the claimant recover the increased value, or is the claim limited to the value received? It seems clear that the claim will usually be limited to the measure of value received. There are two principal exceptions: that the claimant is usually entitled to recover his or her own property, even if it is now more valuable than it was when lost; and that certain wrongs against claimants entitle them to the value the defendant acquired it as a result. Neither exception is entirely clear, however, and each exception is limited in the case of a good-faith defendant, who will be entitled to some sort of allowance for beneficial work done.

1   See eg Birks 'Change of position and surviving enrichment' in Swadling (ed) *The limits of restitutionary claims: A comparative analysis* (1997), p 36.

1.20   The requirement that the benefit be an 'unjust' one is taken to mean either that it was acquired in an unjust manner, or that its retention is unjust. This requirement has further been elaborated by Birks as capable of being satisfied in one of three ways:

  (i) by showing that the claimant did not genuinely mean the defendant to have the benefit;
 (ii) by showing that the defendant's receipt of the benefit was unconscientious; or
(iii) by demonstrating that public policy requires the return of the benefit.

This scheme is capable of considerable expansion[1].

1   A fuller version, adapted from Birks and Chambers *Restitution Research Resource* (2nd edn, 1997) [1997] RLR (supp), is as follows: (i) No genuine intention to give, comprising (a) Absence of intention (comprising 1. Ignorance, 2. Helplessness, 3. Incapacity, 4. Non-beneficial transfer (a Proven, ß Presumed)), (b) Vitiated intention (comprising 1. Spontaneous mistakes, 2. Induced mistakes, 3. Duress, 4. Legal compulsion, 5. Moral compulsion in emergencies, and 6. Inequality), and (c) Qualified intention (which comprises 1. Outside contract, 2. Invalid contracts, 3. Anticipated contracts which fail to arise, 4. Frustrated contracts, and 5. Breach of contract); (ii) Unconscientious receipt, comprising (a) Free acceptance, (b) Acquiescence, (c) Knowing receipt, and (d) Exploitation of disadvantage; and (iii) Policies calling for restitution, comprising (a) Constitutional legality, (b) Private legality, (c) Encouraging help, (d) Sensitive transactions (1. Penalties and forfeitures, 2. Credit, 3. Expectant heirs, 4. Others), and (e) Protection of certain classes of persons.

1.21   The requirement that the benefit be received 'at the expense of' the claimant may be satisfied in a number of ways. Most straightforwardly, the claimant may transfer the benefit directly to the defendant. Other, indirect, ways in which a benefit may be transferred are when the defendant acquires property belonging to the claimant; or the claimant pays a debt owed by the defendant; or the defendant acquires a benefit by means of a legal wrong against the claimant.

1.22   The requirement of the absence of a defence does not break much new ground. Some of the defences to restitutionary claims are familiar from other heads of private law: consent, illegality, and limitation. Others are either unique to restitution, or lead to unusual problems there: change of position, estoppel by representation, and bona fide purchase. There are also some defences which have been suggested in academic writings, but for which there is so far little judicial support: principally 'passing on' and 'ministerial receipt'.

1.23   All of the cases so far discussed are ones where the benefit gained by the defendant is precisely balanced by the loss suffered by the claimant ('unjust enrichment by subtraction'). It seems clear that liability for enrichments obtained by means of a legal wrong against the claimant ('unjust enrichment by wrong') are very hard to fit into the framework of concepts so far described. Birks at one point suggested that they might be fitted in, provided those concepts were modified somewhat[1], but this view has since been retracted[2]. Most regard it as at best misleading, and at worst a solecism, to treat such claims as based on unjust enrichment.

1   *An Introduction to the Law of Restitution* (revised edn, 1989), ch 10.
2   'Misnomer' in Cornish, Nolan, O'Sullivan and Virgo (eds) *Restitution past present and future – Essays in honour of Gareth Jones* (1998), p 1.

1.24   The principles so far discussed relate principally to personal claims. Are proprietary claims on the same facts governed by restitutionary principles also, or not? Suppose that a claimant paid money to the defendant, which can now be recovered on the ground that the consideration for the payment wholly failed. However, the defendant is bankrupt, and has numerous other creditors. What criteria must the claimant satisfy to establish a *proprietary* claim to the money? Birks suggests that this enquiry is still essentially an unjust enrichment one, so that the claimant would have to show not only that the four ordinary criteria of unjust enrichment were satisfied, but also that an additional criterion, appropriate for proprietary claims, were present. This aspect of the theory is still under development[1].

1   See generally below, ch 3.

E 'Unjust enrichment' today: is it law?

1.25 Birks's account of the law of unjust enrichment is complex, and certain aspects of it are as yet imperfectly developed. It is so far an influential achievement; however, it is far from the only influence on the courts. In this section, it is considered whether this theory, or something like it, can be said to be part of the law.

1.26 A basic dilemma for the theory of unjust enrichment is that the academics who proposed it were so doing with an eye to providing a good *classification* of legal claims. The courts are occasionally concerned with these questions, for example when characterising a dispute to determine which jurisdiction's law to apply to it[1]. But, in general, the classificatory scheme is unimportant. It is results which matter, not the precise label applied to those results. For that reason Lord Millett, while a supporter of the theory of unjust enrichment, has nonetheless declared that the courts are 'profoundly uninterested' in issues of classification[2]. The courts have no mission to confirm or to refute academic theories, except where these theories have a bearing on the case before them. Proponents of unjust enrichment would no doubt argue that good classification is a necessary precursor to adequate determination of actual cases. But in fact the courts have managed, and continue to manage, to dispose of cases while making relatively little reference to the classificatory scheme. Whether the courts will eventually be convinced that this is an error remains to be seen.

1 See for example *Kleinwort Benson Ltd v Glasgow City Council* [1999] 1 AC 153, [1997] 4 All ER 641; discussed below, para 22.11ff.
2 'The Law of Restitution: Taking Stock' (1999) 14 Amicus Curiae 4.

1.27 A related point is that the highest courts exist to deal with difficult questions, unusual circumstances or exceptionally innovative arguments. A case which can adequately be resolved on established principles is unlikely to reach those heights. Accordingly, a scheme aimed principally at systematising past results will not always be seen as relevant in resolving the disputes which reach those higher courts. It is therefore not surprising to find the most recent cases criticised by the academics, for the difficulties which become apparent when they try to slot new precedents into the classificatory scheme. And controversial cases are often ones on which different academics have different views; so, close attention to the academic sources may put the court in the position of having to decide between rival academic arguments[1].

1 See eg *Westdeutsche Landesbank Girozentrale v Islington London Borough Council* [1996] AC 669, [1996] 2 All ER 961.

1.28 There is now a respectable body of authority supporting a principle of unjust enrichment in English law[1]. Further, a few eminent judges at least have specifically endorsed the four-fold enquiry into unjust enrichment[2]. However, the implications of accepting the theory of unjust enrichment in full can hardly be said to have been spelled out in these cases, and it remains to be seen whether they will prove acceptable. It seems over-simplistic to ask whether the courts have or have not accepted the theory of unjust enrichment. Certainly many judicial statements have been made on these issues, some of which fit well with the theory of unjust enrichment, and some of which do not. The higher courts now regularly make reference to academic discussions of unjust enrichment, which they have sometimes found useful, and sometimes have not. Meanwhile, the academics themselves have not stood still, and so the unjust enrichment viewpoint is continually evolving new theories, not all of which have so far been put to the judges. So for example the *Lipkin Gorman* decision[3] was hailed by many academics, at the time it was decided, as signalling a major advance[4], but is now increasingly the subject of academic doubts whether it did not oversimplify important issues[5]. The picture is therefore a very mixed one.

1   See particularly *Lipkin Gorman v Karpnale Ltd* [1991] 2 AC 548, [1992] 4 All ER 512; *Banque Financière de la Cité v Parc (Battersea) Ltd* [1999] 1 AC 221, [1998] 1 All ER 737; *Kleinwort Benson Ltd v Lincoln City Council* [1999] 2 AC 349, [1998] 4 All ER 513.
2   See eg *Banque Financière de la Cité v Parc (Battersea) Ltd* [1999] 1 AC 221 at 227, [1998] 1 All ER 737 at 740, per Lord Steyn.
3   *Lipkin Gorman v Karpnale Ltd* [1991] 2 AC 548, [1992] 4 All ER 512.
4   See especially Birks 'The English recognition of unjust enrichment' [1991] Lloyds Maritime and Commercial Law Quarterly 473.
5   See eg Virgo 'What is the law of restitution about?' in Cornish, Nolan, O'Sullivan and Virgo (eds) *Restitution past present and future – Essays in honour of Gareth Jones* (1998), pp 315–316.

'Enrichment'

1.29   Both practically and historically, the emphasis of the subject is on the recovery of money. This is fitted into the theory of unjust enrichment, as noted above[1], by saying that while in money cases it is rather easy to value the benefit, nonetheless in principle the grounds of recovery are identical whatever the form of the benefit. As a matter of history, however, this is simply wrong. There never was an action for 'goods and services had and received', and recovery under a quantum valebat or quantum meruit was never stated in terms approaching the breadth of the action for money had and received. Is it possible that the courts will, at some future date, expand the causes of action for non-money benefits, to the same extent as the money actions? Perhaps, but there is no very obvious sign of this happening; and there seems to be no very obvious consideration of justice, as opposed to theoretical symmetry, why it should. Recovery of money is, and remains, at a far broader extent than recovery for other types of benefit.

1   Above, para 1.17.

1.30   Some mention was made above of the theoretical apparatus for the valuing of benefits[1]. Little of this however has so far filtered down to the courts. There was a significant discussion of valuation of benefits in Robert Goff J's judgement in *BP v Hunt*[2], including a discussion of when it would be appropriate to value services for themselves, and when it was necessary to look for a valuable end-product[3]. However, this discussion was in the context of a particular statute, under which 'enrichment' defined not the claimant's remedy, but the *upper limit* of the remedy which the court might, in its discretion, award the claimant. So while the discussion by Robert Goff J is a masterpiece of its type, it is of only limited general importance. Other discussions, or references to concepts such as 'subjective devaluation' or 'incontrovertible benefit', are hard to locate, and relatively unilluminating once located.

1   Above, para 1.18.
2   *British Petroleum Co (Libya) Ltd v Hunt (No 2)* [1979] 1 WLR 783. For the case see below, para 20.10ff.
3   *British Petroleum Co (Libya) Ltd v Hunt (No 2)* [1979] 1 WLR 783 at 801–802.

'Unjust'

1.31 Even amongst academic expositors of unjust enrichment, there is little agreement on the precise list of the 'unjust factors' justifying recovery. Rival lists abound[1]. Most such lists include the factors of 'mistake' and varieties of unfair pressure such as 'duress' and 'undue influence'. Beyond that, controversy reigns. A particular academic controversy concerns the status of 'free acceptance' originally proposed as an unjust factor[2], but then heavily criticised[3], with its proponent eventually retreating to a more modest version[4]. However, the implications of this debate have largely concerned the structure of the theory of unjust enrichment, and so have not been much commented on in the courts. A later dispute has been over the supposed factor that a benefit was conferred for 'no consideration', and the boundary between that factor and 'mistake' (if indeed both exist, which is disputed)[5]. A further dispute is whether mere 'failure of consideration' is a factor in itself, or whether it must be qualified by demanding a *total* failure[6].

1 Compare and contrast the different factors postulated in Burrows *Law of Restitution* (1993); Virgo *Principles of the law of restitution* (1999); McMeel *Modern law of restitution* (2000).
2 Birks *An Introduction to the Law of Restitution* (revised edn, 1989), ch 8.
3 Burrows 'Free acceptance and the law of restitution' (1988) 104 LQR 576.
4 Birks 'In defence of free acceptance' in Burrows (ed) *Essays on the law of restitution* (1991), p 105.
5 See especially Birks 'No consideration: Restitution after void contracts' (1993) 23 Western Australian Law Review 195.
6 See especially Birks 'Failure of consideration' in Rose (ed) *Consensus ad idem – Essays in the law of contract in honour of Guenter Treitel* (1996), p 179; McKendrick 'Total failure of consideration and counter-restitution: Two issues or one?' in Birks (ed) *Laundering and tracing* (1995), p 217.

1.32 A particular problem, with pronounced practical implications, concerns a succession of cases involving a public law element. In the *Woolwich* case[1], the House of Lords declared (contrary to the previous understanding) that sums paid in consequence of a wrongful demand by tax authorities could be recovered by the payor. Most of the language of the opinions suggested that this was on a special public law ground, possibly related to the principle of the Bill of Rights 1689, art 4, that there should be no taxation without Parliamentary authority[2]. The academic orthodoxy of the time supported this interpretation of the case as well, and the facts of the case do not fit very well into any recognised private law ground such as duress or mistake[3]. Since that time, however, doubts have emerged whether the result might not be explicable on grounds analogous to, or even identical with, those employed in private law. Some weight has been placed on the point that one member of the court postulated an additional, and quite different, ground, namely that the payment was made for no consideration[4]. Yet others seek to preserve the ancient notion of 'duress *colore officii*', which bases recovery on the private law principle of duress, but introduces a presumption that a demand from a public official involves illegitimate pressure[5]. It is therefore quite unclear what the true ground is. This debate has obvious implications for the scope of liability, particularly on the question whether or when a payer can be said to have waived the right to be repaid should the demand turn out to be invalid. This question is considered below[6].

1 *Woolwich Equitable Building Society v IRC* [1993] AC 70, [1992] 3 All ER 737; see below, para 18.3ff.
2 See especially [1993] AC 70 at 171, per Lord Goff, and at 178, per Lord Jauncey.
3 For factual findings on the (rather complex) motives of the payors, see the judgement at first instance [1989] 1 WLR 137 at 142–143, per Nolan J.
4 [1993] AC 70 at 197, per Lord Browne-Wilkinson.

5   See Goff and Jones *Law of Restitution* (5th edn, 1998), pp 320–327.
6   See below, para 18.6ff.

1.33   A related dispute, which again has practical implications, concerns the scope of 'mistake'. A decision of Robert Goff J in 1979 placed 'restitution for mistake' on a firm footing[1]. However, doubts are now emerging as to whether the concept is not over-extended. It has tended to be used as the 'explanation' of last resort, for cases which do not mention it as such[2]. It is out of tune with the actual case law on mistaken gifts, which make it plain that a gift cannot be recovered on proof merely that the donor was mistaken[3]. And the cases reveal a distressing tendency to extend the notion of 'mistake' by means of fictions, such as by deeming those whose views on the law were ultimately rejected by the courts to have been making a 'mistake of law'. It is perhaps unfortunate that the House of Lords in the *Kleinwort Benson* case[4] appeared to endorse the unjust factor of 'mistake', in a case where liability was not in issue, and had not been based on 'mistake' by the lower courts. The issue before the House of Lords was whether there was a 'mistake' for the purpose of Limitation Act 1980, s 32, though the opinions show an awkward tendency to confuse that issue with questions of liability. It was never, in fact, established whether the facts of the cases (part of the 'swaps litigation', discussed below[5]) involved a 'mistake' or not. Any reasonably well informed individual involved in the payment in the case would have realised that there were doubts as to its legality; it was never established whether any of the individuals involved in fact had such doubts, or how well informed they were[6]. The idea of mistake is now increasingly being elaborated upon in legal journals, and no doubt in time these new ideas will be tested in the courts[7].

1   *Barclays Bank Ltd v WJ Simms Son and Cooke (Southern) Ltd* [1980] QB 677.
2   See eg *Banque Financière de la Cité v Parc (Battersea) Ltd* [1999] 1 AC 221, so explained by Villiers 'A path through the subrogation jungle' [1999] Lloyds Maritime and Commercial Law Quarterly 223 at 232.
3   See below, para 17.50ff.
4   *Kleinwort Benson Ltd v Lincoln City Council* [1999] 2 AC 349; on which see below, para 18.24ff.
5   See below, para 18.18ff.
6   On the difficult question of the unjust factor in the swaps cases see below, paras 18.23; also Birks and Rose (eds) *Lessons of the swaps litigation* (2000), especially chs 1, 2, 4, 5 and 6.
7   See for example Sheehan 'What is a mistake?' (2000) 20 Legal Studies 538. On mistake liability generally, see below, ch 17.

1.34   There is a distinct risk that certain judges, keen to listen to what the academics have to say, but necessarily not aware of the latest research, may end up endorsing academic arguments which are soon afterwards shown to be wrong, or at best misleading. It is therefore not irrelevant to note that the very idea of 'unjust factors' has recently been brought into question, by a number of academics who are otherwise committed to 'unjust enrichment'. The argument is, in essence, based on a comparison with German law, which gets by without requiring an 'unjust factor' but conversely, by asking whether there was any good legal ground (such as contract or gift) for the transfer of the benefit. 'Unjustified enrichment' (*ungerechtfertigte Bereicherung*) therefore consists of those transfers for which no good legal ground exists[1]. Would this be a desirable innovation for English law? The merits of this view are still a matter of debate[2]; it seems premature to commit English law to the notion of 'unjust enrichment' while its merits are still being debated.

1   See especially Meier *Irrtum und Zweckverfehlung (Mistake and failure of purpose)* (1999); Krebs 'Review article: A German contribution to English enrichment law' [1999] RLR 271. See also (on

Canadian law) Smith 'The mystery of "juristic reason"' (2000) 12 Supreme Court Law Review (2d) 211.

2 For discussion see especially Chen-Wishart 'Unjust factors and the restitutionary response' (2000) 20 OJLS 557; and Krebs *Restitution at the crossroads: A comparative study* (2001).

'At the claimant's expense'

1.35 This relatively straightforward concept has not received much commentary in the courts. Academic controversies there have been, but they have related mostly to structural concerns. Some have proposed a notion of 'interceptive subtraction', whereby a defendant who appropriates gains which would otherwise have come to the claimant may be said to have profited at the claimant's expense[1]. Others have rejected the notion[2]. The courts have yet to pronounce. General reviews of this area reveal that the very different senses of 'at the claimant's expense' in fact relate to quite different areas of law, with even active proponents of harmonisation of unjust enrichment across these areas seeing it only as an aspiration, not a currently attainable goal[3]. Most academic writers on unjust enrichment recognise a 'general privity restriction', which entails that benefits transferred directly from claimant to defendant are rewarded more generously than those transferred 'at the claimant's expense' in some more indirect sense[4].

1 Birks *An introduction to the law of restitution* (revised edn, 1989), p 133ff.
2 Smith 'Three-Party Restitution: A Critique of Birks's theory of interceptive subtraction' (1991) 11 OJLS 481.
3 Birks 'At the expense of the claimant: Direct and indirect enrichment in English law' (2000) Oxford University Comparative Law Forum 1 (at http://ouclf.iuscomp.org); Hedley *Restitution: Its division and ordering* (2001), ch 8.
4 See eg Burrows *Law of Restitution* (1993), pp 45–54; Virgo *Principles of the law of restitution* (1999), pp 106–113.

Defences

1.36 Most of the defences to restitutionary claims are, as noted above, uncontroversial, and are treated in detail below[1]. However, controversy has attended some defences.

1 See below, ch 21.

1.37 An early and repeated suggestion was that there was, or should be, a defence of 'change of position' to restitutionary claims. The House of Lords in the *Lipkin Gorman* case adopted this suggestion[1], where it was stated in principle to apply to any restitutionary claim, though its precise limits were left to later cases to determine[2]. However, Lord Goff emphasised that the defence was in fact 'likely to be available only on comparatively rare occasions'[3]. Later cases have confirmed this, there being few actual examples of its successful use[4]. Meanwhile, continuing theoretical controversy has suggested a number of different approaches to the doctrine. A vague suggestion that the defence is not available to a 'wrongdoer'[5] suggests to some that the defence might never be available in cases of restitution for wrongdoing. Some writers have tried to rationalise the defence as a denial that the defendant was, in the events which happened, enriched; none of this rationalising theory has yet been accepted by the courts. Further, a number of writers have suggested that if the defence is available for the restitutionary recovery of the claimant's personal property, then it ought equally to be available for the tortious recovery of that property in conversion[6]. It seems well-established for now that this defence is not available in conversion, but while that denial may have been based on sound policy when it was established in the eighteenth century, it is not obvious that it reflects current needs. If so, the defence of change of position may turn out not to be exclusively restitutionary.

1   *Lipkin Gorman v Karpnale Ltd* [1991] 2 AC 548; discussed below, para 21.39ff.
2   See especially [1991] 2 AC 548 at 580, per Lord Goff.
3   [1991] 2 AC 548 at 580, per Lord Goff.
4   See generally below, para 21.37ff.
5   [1991] 2 AC 548 at 580, per Lord Goff.
6   See eg Hedley *Restitution: Its division and ordering* (2001), p 156.

1.38   The interpretation recently placed by the House of Lords on s 32 of the Limitation Act 1980 has extended the defence of limitation to a surprising extent[1]. As a result of that interpretation, the law now is that the limitation period for sums paid under mistake only runs from the date on which the mistake could reasonably have been discovered. So where sums are paid in the belief that the law requires them, but a later and novel precedent holds that the sums were not in fact payable, then the limitation period begins to run from the date of that novel precedent. It does not matter how far in the past the payment was made. This is a surprising result; it was reached only by a bare majority, and many would say that there has to be something wrong with such a ruling where members of the majority as well as the minority call for immediate statutory reform[2]. As noted above, the case leaves a measure of confusion as well, for the statutory provision in question applies to claims 'for relief from the consequences of a mistake'[3], which is usually assumed to mean claims where a mistake is a vital ingredient of the cause of action. However, it is quite unclear whether the case involves such a claim – liability was established not on the basis of mistake, but for absence of consideration[4] – nor is it clear that there was, in fact, a mistake of any kind on the facts. The controversy continues.

1   *Kleinwort Benson Ltd v Lincoln City Council* [1999] 2 AC 349; on which see below, para 17.88ff.
2   See [1999] 2 AC 349 at 364, per Lord Browne-Wilkinson, and at 389, per Lord Goff.
3   See the Limitation Act 1980, s 32(1)(c).
4   See below, para 18.23ff.

1.39   A number of defences have been proposed in the public law context, for cases where a payment has been made following a demand which was in fact ultra vires. These defences include 'payment under a settled view of the law', 'honest receipt', 'disruption of public finances', and 'passing on' (ie that as the taxpayer was able to pass on to others the burden of the illegal tax, it would be inappropriate to allow recovery). There is no significant support for these defences, none of which were accepted in the *Kleinwort Benson* case. Attempts to apply the defence of 'change of position' in public law cases have also met with little success, largely because the effect of the defence is usually to give an ultra vires transaction the same incidents as an intra vires one, and thus to subvert the ultra vires principle[1]. However, the matter is still unsettled. Many cases of wrongly-paid taxes are dealt with by statute, which provides for a *defence* of unjust enrichment, that granting the remedy claimed would entail the unjust enrichment of the claimant[2]. As applied in practice, most cases where the statutory defence is invoked are examples of passing on; the tribunals in these cases are evidently not impressed with the defence unless it can be shown that the wrongly-demanded tax will in fact be refunded to those who have in fact paid it.

1   See below, para 18.36ff.
2   See below, para 18.2.

The treatment of wrongs

1.40   For some decades now, a number of writers have urged the recognition of a broad principle that profits received in consequence of an actionable wrong should be recoverable in an action of restitution[1]. However, while there are certainly many cases that can be explained in that way, it is not obvious that this is the only or the best explanation of them. And in any event, it would be a distinct step for the courts to recognise a general principle, which could be applied to novel circumstances. So far, this is a step which the courts have on several occasions declined to take[2]. Moreover, while broad provision has been made for profits made from *crime*[3], there seem to be no plans to extend this to merely civil wrongs.

1   See eg Goff and Jones *Law of restitution* (5th edn, 1998), chs 32–38.
2   See especially *Stoke-on-Trent City Council v W&J Wass Ltd* [1988] 3 All ER 394; *Halifax Building Society v Thomas* [1996] Ch 217. For further discussion see below, ch 12.
3   See below, para 12.70ff.

1.41   The initial academic enthusiasm for a broad doctrine seems now to be mellowing. It is now generally accepted that, if there is such a broad doctrine, it is no part of the law of unjust enrichment[1]. It is also increasingly being accepted that such a doctrine has too readily been invoked as the explanation of unusual cases: while there may be such a doctrine, it is narrower than has been supposed[2]. Ironically, after these developments had been absorbed by academia, the House of Lords proposed a broad doctrine under which profits from breach *of contract* were recoverable by the victim, in cases where justice seemed so to demand[3]. However, the scope of that case is very unclear. The facts are highly atypical, and it may be that the courts will subsequently hold the doctrine entirely inapplicable to ordinary commercial cases[4].

1   See eg Birks 'Restitution for wrongs' in Schrage (ed) *Unjust enrichment – The comparative legal history of the law of restitution* (1995), p 171.
2   See eg Edelman *Gain-based damages* (2002), especially ch 3.
3   *A-G v Blake* [2001] 1 AC 268, [2000] 4 All ER 385.
4   See discussion below, para 11.21.

Proprietary claims

1.42   In what circumstances may a restitutionary claim be asserted not merely against the defendant personally, but also against the enrichment in the defendant's hands, so that the claimant is actually claiming his or her own property? It was initially hoped that the additional facts necessary to justify a proprietary claim could be stated in simple terms, to fit in with the theory of unjust enrichment. Hopes rose especially after the *Lipkin Gorman* case, where the House of Lords used notions of unjust enrichment when tracing the proceeds of stolen money into funds held by the casino where the thief had staked them[1]. However, further academic analysis has thrown the reasoning in the case into doubt, and it is now a distinct puzzle.

1   *Lipkin Gorman v Karpnale Ltd* [1991] 2 AC 548.

1.43   Less difficult to understand is *A-G v Reid*, where a bribe taken by a public prosecutor was traced into foreign property he subsequently bought with it[1].

However, this result, while satisfactory in itself, has nonetheless been severely criticised for its implications. A proprietary claim was there asserted for jurisdictional reasons: unless the funds could be traced, it was hard to see how they could be reclaimed from the defendant at all. It would be very different, however, if the funds were traced for other reasons, such as to assert priority in bankruptcy. There is no obvious justice in preferring the claim by his employer to that of the defendant's other honest creditors. As this emphasises, claimants may wish to convert personal claims into proprietary ones for a variety of reasons[2], and it may be that no satisfactory doctrine will emerge until doctrine is sophisticated enough to distinguish between these reasons.

1   *A-G for Hong Kong v Reid* [1994] 1 AC 324, discussed below, para 9.13.
2   See generally below, ch 3.

1.44   Subsequent cases have been less willing to recognise novel proprietary restitution claims. In the *Westdeutsche* case, where a claim to restitution of sums paid under an invalid interest rate swap was said to be a proprietary claim, in order to claim compound interest on it, the House of Lords refused to allow the argument[1]. And again in *Foskett v McKeown*[2], where a trustee stole trust money and used it to pay premiums on a life policy, it was sought to trace the funds into the eventual payment on maturity, the proportionate share of the maturity payment being far greater than mere restitution of the stolen money. Interestingly, the House of Lords allowed the claim for the greater sum, but denied that unjust enrichment had anything to do with it: the case was rather one about property rights. The argument from unjust enrichment is therefore not one which is currently finding much favour from the courts.

1   *Westdeutsche Landesbank Girozentrale v Islington London Borough Council* [1996] AC 669, [1996] 2 All ER 961; discussed below, para 3.34ff.
2   [2001] 1 AC 102, [2000] 3 All ER 97; discussed further below, para 4.36ff.

F   Conclusion

1.45   It might be tempting to argue that either English law either accepts the principle of unjust enrichment, or it does not. However, the theory of unjust enrichment has many ramifications, some of which have been accepted by the courts, some of which have been rejected, and still more of which (perhaps the majority) have yet to be put to them. Those ramifications will sufficiently appear throughout the course of this book.

CHAPTER 2

Modern Equity

Margaret Halliwell

A Introduction

2.1 A significant proportion of the law of restitution is concerned with the righting of equitable wrongs. That is what the decided case law says. Causes of action in equity generate a substantial amount of litigation. The hallmarks of equity – flexibility, fairness and issues of conscience – do not make life easier for a practitioner who, in general, wishes to make an assessment of the current law with enough confidence to afford a certain and predictable outcome for a client. Bearing this in mind, terminological analysis is not necessarily of much value to practitioners, nor is a rarefied discussion of conceptual categories. Rather, the practitioner wishes to have a detailed discussion of what the law actually is.

2.2 Unfortunately, treatises on the law of restitution tend, on the whole, to aspire to describe what the law ought to be, often ignoring the reality of judicial decisions. The aim of this chapter is, therefore, to highlight the principles triggering restitutionary remedies which the courts have endorsed, to evaluate recent developments, and to dispel some of the myths which surround this subject. In attempting to achieve this aim, I hope to avoid some of the pithy criticisms made by Fred Rodell in 'Goodbye to Law Reviews'[1]. This article is highly recommended for its amusement value, although practitioners might not find the assessment of their role in the final four paragraphs quite as amusing as the rest of the article. Bearing in mind Rodell's observation that:

> So far as I can make out, there are two distinct types of footnote. There is the explanatory or if-you-didn't-understand-what-I-said-in-the-text-this-may-help-you-type and there is the probative or if-you're-from-Missouri-just-take-a-look-at-all-this-type ...
> ... In any case the footnote foible breeds nothing but sloppy thinking, clumsy writing and bad eyes[2].

I shall confine my footnote references as far as possible to citations only.

1 Rodell 'Goodbye to Law Reviews' (1936) 23 Virginia Law Review 38.
2 (1936) 23 Virginia Law Review 38 at 40–41.

2.3 The modern emphasis on theories of restitution has tended to obscure the traditional equitable emphasis on unconscionability. It is mythical, however, to insist that courts will not effect restitution in the context of an underpinning category of unconscionability. The courts do so often and explicitly. The first point to note is that the courts have always been prepared to provide restitutionary remedies within well established categories of liability. Those treated in subsequent chapters include duress[1], unconscionable bargains and undue influence[2], dishonest assistance[3], knowing receipt in breach of trust[4], fiduciaries[5] and confidence[6]. Equity may impose personal or proprietary remedies[7], the latter including a lien, the return of property, or a proprietary remedy via the tracing process[8]. Restitution is, essentially, about restoration to a particular position, but in some areas at least the remedy given in equity might also be the disgorgement of profits acquired as a result of legally recognised wrongdoing[9]. The categories of liability so described are those within judicial parlance in decided cases, and it is within the language of judicial decisions that modern equity must speak.

1   See below, para 10.51ff.
2   See generally below, ch 10.
3   See below, para 5.4ff.
4   See below, para 5.49ff.
5   See below, ch 9.
6   See below, para 10.18ff.
7   See generally below, ch 3.
8   See generally below, ch 4.
9   See generally below, ch 9.

B   Unconscionability – myth and reality

2.4   To suggest, as one writer does, that a category of law relating to unconscionable behaviour is useless, and, therefore 'the lawyer who deals in "unconscionable behaviour" is rather like the ornithologist who is content with "small brown bird"'[1], is to ignore the fact that judges and courts very often deal with such a categorisation. A recent LEXIS database search revealed 1,440 cases which included the word 'unconscionable'[2]. Moreover, it is not uncommon for judges to seek to do justice in a broader equitable sense. Even when judges disagree as to the precise circumstances of application of broader equitable principles, the role of such principles in the real world of litigation is beyond doubt.

1   Birks 'Equity in the Modern Law: An Exercise in Taxonomy' (1996) 26 Western Australian Law Review 1 at 16.
2   Search for text 'unconscionable' in UK Cases (Combined Courts file, 1 May 2002).

An illustration – Foskett v McKeown

2.5   The differing opinions of the members of the House of Lords in *Foskett v McKeown*[1] serve to illustrate the practical impact of judicial disagreement as to this role. The facts of the case raised the question, which was put succinctly by Lord Browne-Wilkinson, as to which of two innocent parties was to benefit from the activities of a fraudster. Murphy was trustee of £2,645,000 paid by prospective purchasers of land in the Algarve. On 5 November 1986, he effected a whole-life policy, in the sum of £1,000,000. The beneficial interest in the policy was vested in members of Murphy's family, including his three children. Murphy paid the first and second premiums. There was a dispute as to the source of the third premium, but the fourth and fifth premiums were paid from the purchasers' trust money. Murphy then committed suicide. The sum of £1,000,580.04 was paid to the trustees of the insurance policy for the benefit of Murphy's children. When it was discovered that all the purchasers' trust money had been dissipated, one of the purchasers claimed that they could trace their money into the proceeds of the policy, on the grounds that their money had been used to keep the policy on foot; and therefore they were not, as was contended on behalf of the children, limited to a charge in respect of the premiums. The purchasers, therefore, claimed a 40% share in the proceeds. It was accepted that the first and second premiums, paid from Murphy's own money, had been sufficient to keep the policy on foot until his death, and that the fourth and fifth premiums paid out of the purchasers' money had not been necessary to keep the policy on foot. That, however, did not impress the majority.

1 [2001] 1 AC 102; considered below, para 4.36ff.

2.6   The majority of the House of Lords considered that the purchasers were entitled to a 40% share in the proceeds of the policy, and differed very sharply from the minority in their perception of the role of equitable principles. In the minority, Lord Steyn outlined four considerations, which materially affected his approach to the claims of the purchasers. The first was the relative moral claim of the children and the purchasers. He concluded that the proprietary claim of the purchasers was not underpinned by any consideration of fairness or justice[1]. Lord Hope, also in the minority, considered the question as to whether it was equitable for the purchasers to recover a share in the proceeds. In 'balancing the equities', he took into account the fact that the purchasers had recovered land in the Algarve in specie, and had received some monetary compensation in satisfaction of their claims for the misappropriation[2]. He concluded that, even without attaching any weight to those factors, the equities lay with the children, and that it was fair, just and reasonable to restrict the purchasers' remedy to a lien. Lords Browne-Wilkinson, Hoffman and Millett disagreed. Lord Browne-Wilkinson described the cases as one of 'hard-nosed property rights'[3]. He did not consider that there was any room for consideration of whether it was equitable, in a moral sense, that the purchasers' claim should succeed. Lord Millett's view on this was equally explicit. He said:

> Property rights are determined by fixed rules and settled principles. They are not discretionary. They do not depend upon ideas of what is 'fair, just and reasonable'. Such concepts, which in reality mask decisions of legal policy, have no place in the law of property[4].

However, it was somewhat inconsistent for Lord Millett to go on to say that:

> It is morally offensive as well as contrary to principle to subordinate the claims of the victims of a fraud to those of the objects of the fraudster's bounty on the ground that he concealed his wrongdoing from both of them[5].

The object of this discussion is not to analyse the merits of the outcome of the case. That, in any event, can only be done in the context of the process of tracing[6]. The object is to emphasise that the function and role of broad equitable principles is very much an issue before our courts. The intensity of the debate is very clear. The majority view very narrowly prevailed, because Lord Browne-Wilkinson had, at the conclusion of the hearing, considered that the majority of the Court of Appeal had been correct. He changed his mind in allowing the appeal only after having read the draft speech of Lord Millett[7]. Moreover, unlike in *Foskett v McKeown*, equitable principles very often prevail. Lord Millett's observation on the law of property should not therefore be taken out of the factual context of the case, because it is too broad a generalisation.

1 [2001] 1 AC 102 at 115.
2 See his discussion [2001] 1 AC 102 at 125.
3 [2001] 1 AC 102 at 109.
4 [2001] 1 AC 102 at 127.

Another illustration – proprietary estoppel

2.7   The principle of unconscionability, which by its nature imports a discretionary element into judicial decision-making, is at the very heart of proprietary estoppel cases. Although concerning expectations rather than restitution, the recent case of *Gillett v Holt*[1] amply demonstrates the effect of such an equitable principle in a property law case. Put shortly, the case concerned a gratuitous promise to leave property by will, where the promisor wished to resile from the promise, and the promisee wanted the promise enforced. The Court of Appeal held in favour of the promisee under the doctrine of proprietary estoppel. Robert Walker LJ said in respect of that doctrine:

> Moreover the fundamental principle that equity is concerned to prevent unconscionable conduct permeates all the elements of the doctrine. In the end the court must look at the matter in the round[2].
>
> The requirement [of detriment] must be approached as part of a broad inquiry as to whether repudiation of an assurance is or is not unconscionable in all the circumstances[3].

1   [2001] Ch 210.
2   [2001] Ch 210 at 225.
3   [2001] Ch 210 at 232.

2.8   Property rights were similarly affected in *Yaxley v Gotts*[1]. That case involved a dispute concerning an oral agreement. The defendant's father was about to buy a house. He represented to the claimant, a builder, that if the claimant would convert the house into flats, and act as managing agent for the flats, then he (the claimant) would get the ground floor flat. The house was, ultimately, purchased in the name of the defendant. The claimant carried out his part of the oral agreement but, after an argument the defendant refused to grant the claimant an interest in the property. It was contended before the Court of Appeal that the oral agreement was void by virtue of section 2 of the Law of Property (Miscellaneous Provisions) Act 1989[2], which required all contracts for the sale of land to be in writing, and that the doctrine of proprietary estoppel could not operate to give effect to such an agreement. It was held that, as a result of the conduct of the parties, which could equally found a constructive trust or a proprietary estoppel, the defendant was constructive trustee of a 99 year lease of the flat on behalf of the defendant under the saving provisions of s 2(5) of the Act[3].

The Court of Appeal accepted that, at a high level of generality, there is much common ground between the doctrines of proprietary estoppel and the constructive trust. Robert Walker LJ suggested two areas where the concepts do not overlap:

> when a landowner stands by while his neighbour mistakenly builds on the former's land the situation is far removed (except for the element of unconscionable conduct) from that of a fiduciary who derives an improper advantage from his client[4].

Beldam LJ was prepared to reach the same conclusion on the facts, by way of either constructive trust or proprietary estoppel. This was on the basis that he did not think it inherent in a social policy of simplifying conveyancing, by requiring the certainty of a written document, that unconscionable conduct or equitable fraud should be allowed to prevail[5].

1   [2000] Ch 162.
2   See the Law of Property (Miscellaneous Provisions) Act 1989, s 2(1).
3   Section 2(5) of the Act provides that nothing in s 2 is to affect the creation of resulting, implied or constructive trusts.
4   [2000] Ch 162 at 176.
5   [2000] Ch 162 at 193.

C   Is the idea of unconscionability too vague?

2.9   This is not to say that decisions within the field of equity do not yield a predictive outcome. Sir Anthony Mason, in explaining that unconscionability has been at the heart of equitable doctrine in Australia, acknowledges that unconscionability incorporates ingredients of fact, degree and value judgment. He goes on, however, to suggest that general guidance will arise from an array of decisions on particular facts[1]. Even when judges, as the minority in *Foskett v McKeown*[2], think that broader equitable principles ought to prevail, they do not measure such principles according to the length of the Chancellor's foot, but by closely reasoned analysis. Moreover, from all of the judgments in *Foskett v McKeown*, the law has acquired a certainty which it did not have before. We now know that, whenever a dishonest trustee or fiduciary mixes his own and trust money to purchase property which increases in value, the defrauded beneficial owners are not restricted to recovering a charge, but can trace into a pro rata share of the profit. Prior to *Foskett v McKeown*, an obiter dictum of Sir George Jessel MR in *Re Hallett's Estate*[3] had left this point in some doubt, but the issue is now resolved for the future[4].

1   Sir Anthony Mason 'The Place of Equity and Equitable Remedies in The Contemporary Common Law World' (1994) 110 LQR 238 at 254–255.
2   See above, para 2.6.
3   (1880) 13 Ch D 696 at 709.
4   See below, para 4.12.

2.10   Practitioners can also take heart that, in some areas of equity, the courts are striving to provide guidelines, which will promote clarity and certainty. There are notable examples of this. The opinion of Lord Nicholls in the Privy Council in *Royal Brunei Airlines v Tan*[1] clarified the basis of liability of third party assistance in a breach of trust[2]. Similarly, in the consolidated appeals *Royal Bank of Scotland v Etridge (No 2)*[3] an attempt was made to delineate and clarify the important decision in respect of undue influence of the House of Lords in *Barclays Bank v O'Brien*[4].

1   [1995] 2 AC 378.
2   See below, ch 5.
3   [1998] 4 All ER 705, CA; on appeal [2001] 4 All ER 449, HL.
4   [1994] 1 AC 180. See below, ch 10.

D   Correction of unsatisfactory precedents

2.11   There has, also, been an increasing tendency for judges to overturn equity cases which have long been perceived to be bad law. The absence of a proprietary remedy against a fiduciary who has accepted bribes, established by the long standing precedent of *Lister & Co v Stubbs*[1], has now been overturned, albeit in a somewhat controversial manner, in *A-G for Hong Kong v Reid*[2].

Similarly, the majority of the House of Lords in *Westedeutsche Landesbank Girozentrale v Islington London Borough Council*[3] were prepared to depart from the unsatisfactory findings of the existence of a fiduciary relationship in both *Sinclair v Brougham*[4] and *Chase Manhattan Bank NA v Israel-British Bank Ltd*[5].

In the *Westdeutsche* case, Lord Browne-Wilkinson addressed, albeit obiter, the problem whereby an equitable proprietary claim was unavailable to someone who had simply been swindled without the involvement of a trustee or fiduciary. Lord Browne-Wilkinson suggested that:

> Although it is difficult to find clear authority for the proposition, when property is obtained by fraud equity imposes a constructive trust on the fraudulent recipient; the property is recoverable and traceable in equity[6].

That dictum has subsequently been approved of and applied by the Court of Appeal in *Twinsectra Ltd v Yardley*[7].

Developments as to the basis of equitable liability, and as to the provision of equitable liabilities, continue apace. Several trends which practitioners need to take note of have been discernible in the way in which developments in modern equity have taken place.

1 (1890) 45 Ch D 1.
2 [1994] 1 AC 324. See below, para 9.13ff.
3 [1996] AC 669.
4 [1914] AC 398.
5 [1981] Ch 105.
6 [1996] AC 669 at 716.
7 [1999] Lloyd's Rep Bank 438. This point is not affected by the appeal to the Lords ([2002] 2 All ER 377). See below, para 5.31.

2.12   First, the courts have shown increasing concern, in a number of cases, to promote certainty in commercial transactions. Amongst many examples which may be cited, the decision in *Re Goldcorp Exchange* provides one illustration. The Privy Council refused to countenance the elevation, in the context of insolvency, of a contractual commercial relationship into a fiduciary relationship giving rise to an equitable proprietary remedy at the expense of general creditors and of the holder of a floating charge[1].

1 [1995] 1 AC 74. See below, para 9.3.

2.13   Second, particularly in the higher courts, there has been a growing tendency in the process of decision-making to take into account both law reform proposals and developments in the law in other jurisdictions, particularly Commonwealth jurisdictions. A recent example of this took place in the House of Lords decision in *Kleinwort Benson Ltd v Lincoln City Council*[1]. In deciding that the rule of law bar to mistaken payments should be abrogated, their Lordships considered the law in other jurisdictions, both Commonwealth and civilian, and the Law Commission's recommendations in *Restitution: Mistakes of law and Ultra Vires Public Authority Receipts and Payments*[2].

1 [1999] 2 AC 349.
2 Law Com no 227 (1994). The rejection, by the majority, of the Law Commission's recommendation, paras 5.1–5.3 and cl 3 of the Restitution (Mistakes of Law) Draft Bill, is controversial. See below, para 17.90ff.

2.14   Third, opinions of academic writers are increasingly canvassed in the courts, and have had an extremely pervasive influence on developments, not only within modern equity but within the whole of the area of the law of restitution. Indeed this phenomenon has become so widespread that it is difficult to choose one example from amongst so many. Consideration of the competing views of Birks[1] and Swadling[2] as to the nature, extent and role of the resulting trust in the *Westdeutsche* case perhaps provides one of the most notable examples in modern equity[3]. There is, therefore, an increasing requirement on practitioners to familiarise themselves not only with existing law, but also with academic proposals as to development of the law of modern equity and of restitution in general. This is even further emphasised by the current contribution of the higher judiciary to academic debate. Lord Nicholls and Lord Millett submitted substantial contributions to a recent collection of essays on restitution[4]. Moreover, these contributions to academic debate may well herald changes in the law when the opportunity presents itself to the House of Lords. This is because both of their Lordships advocate the importation of strict liability into an area of equity where, up to now, fault and unconscionability have been the driving forces behind equitable decisions[5].

1   Birks 'Restitution and Resulting Trusts' in Goldstein (ed) *Equity and Contemporary Legal Developments, Papers Presented at the First International Conference on Equity* (1992), p 335.
2   Swadling 'A New Role for Resulting Trusts' (1996) 16 Legal Studies 110.
3   See [1996] AC 669 especially at 689–690, per Lord Goff.
4   Lord Nicholls 'Knowing Receipt: The Need For A New Landmark' and Lord Millett 'Restitution and Constructive Trusts', both in Cornish, Nolan, O'Sullivan and Virgo (eds) *Restitution past present & future – essays in honour of Gareth Jones* (1998), pp 119–217 and 231–245.
5   See below, para 5.54ff.

2.15   This leads to an uncomfortable conclusion for the practitioner. As noted earlier, such academic debate needs to be rooted within the dominant adversarial system that produces our law[1]. Restitution for equitable wrongs may easily be explained in terms of identifiable categories of fiduciaries, breach of confidence, duress, undue influence, unconscionability, receipt and dishonest assistance. Equitable remedies may be adequately described in terms of concepts such as 'proprietary remedies' and 'the tracing process'. Clarity of language would be best served if restitution in equity were to be perceived, as suggested by one academic writer[2], to distinguish between disgorgement of profits occasioned by equitable wrongs, which forms one aspect of restitution in equity, and the alternative function of equity, such as in undue influence, of reversing enrichment which is perceived in equity as being unjust. Clarity of language in an area as fluid and as flexible as modern equity has never been readily attainable, but an even bigger threat is posed by a newcomer on the English scene: the cause of action based on unjust enrichment.

1   See above, para 2.1.
2   Smith 'The Province of the Law of Restitution' (1992) 71 Canadian Bar Review 672.

E   Unjust enrichment and equity

2.16   For the benefit of pragmatic analysis, this book seeks to interpret this newcomer into specific, accessible and readily understood causes of action. In the context of the relationship between equitable causes of action and unjust enrichment as a general cause of action, clarity of explanation is not, however, easy to attain. It is not entirely inappropriate to hold academic writers responsible for this.

It is sometimes acknowledged that an academic thesis, demonstrating that there is a coherent and principled English law of restitution based on reversing unjust enrichment, has gained acceptance amongst practitioners and judges[1].

The origins of the principle are, however, clearly rooted in judicial decisions, and in the notion of unconscionability. The origins of claims underpinned by the general principle of unjust enrichment lie, first of all, in Lord Mansfield CJ's judgment in *Moses v Macferlan*[2]. He said that the action for money had and received lay in some typical instances:

> ... for money paid by mistake; or upon a consideration which happens to fail; or for money got through imposition, (express, or implied); or extortion; or oppression; or an undue advantage taken of the plaintiff's situation, contrary to laws made for the protection of persons under those circumstances. In one word, the gist of this kind of action is, that the defendant, upon the circumstances of the case, is obliged by the ties of natural justice and equity to refund the money[3].

Lord Mansfield's interpretation of the unifying general principle of equity underpinning a number of circumstances was, therefore, stated in terms of where it been unconscionable for a defendant to retain money. In 1760, according to him, the law already recognised specific circumstances where it would be inequitable, unfair or unjust to allow a defendant to retain money. Lord Mansfield's doctrinal analysis has been described by Baker as 'a common law reincarnation of pristine equity'[4].

The next most important endorsement of the principle came from Lord Wright in both an extra-judicial and judicial capacity. Lord Wright, in a very favourable review of the American *Restatement of the Law of Restitution*, noted the broad general principle that restitution should be made where there has been an unjust enrichment. His review, however, identified the six central chapters of the substantive law as covering:

(1)   Mistake including Fraud;
(2)   Coercion;
(3)   Benefits Conferred at Request;
(4)   Benefits Voluntarily Conferred without Mistake, Coercion or Request (eg necessaries supplied under certain conditions);
(5)   Benefits Lawfully Required which are not conferred by the person claiming restitution (eg where the claimant's property has been lawfully appropriated to satisfy the defendant's debt, as in distress or legal attachment); and
(6)   Benefits Tortiously Acquired.

He found it interesting to compare this list with the types of claim enumerated by Lord Mansfield in 'his famous sketch of the action for money had and received'[5]. Again, the implicit reference to unconscionability is plain.

1   See for example Burrows and McKendrick *Cases and Materials on the Law of Restitution* (1997), p 1.
2   (1760) 2 Burr 1005, 97 ER 676.
3   (1760) 2 Burr 1005 at 1012, 97 ER 676 at 681. See above, para 1.11.
4   Baker 'The History Of Quasi-Contract In English Law' in Cornish, Nolan, O'Sullivan and Virgo (eds) *Restitution past present & future – essays in honour of Gareth Jones* (1998), p 56.
5   Lord Wright 'A review of the American *Restatement Of The Law Of Restitution*' (1937) 51 Harvard Law Review 369 at 379.

2.17   When utilising the concept of unjust enrichment in a judicial capacity, in *Fibrosa Spolka Akayjna v Fairbairn Lawson Combe Barbour Ltd*[1], Lord Wright's view of the concept was abundantly clear, and does not deviate from anything said by Lord Mansfield two centuries earlier. His speech in the *Fibrosa* case is the second most important contribution to the development of the principle of unjust enrichment in English law, and merits close analysis. The *Fibrosa* case concerned a claim from a Polish company to recover a deposit from an English company under a contract, which had been frustrated by the outbreak of war. The House of Lords allowed the claim on the basis that there had been a total failure of consideration. Two elements of Lord Wright's speech need to be emphasised. First, his explanation of the principle of unjust enrichment:

> It is clear that any civilized system of law is bound to provide remedies for cases of what has been called unjust enrichment or unjust benefit, that is to prevent a man from retaining the money of or some benefit derived from another which it is against conscience that he should keep[2].

Again the emphasis here was on the underpinning principle of unconscionability. Second, Lord Wright recognised that there were identifiable categories within that general principle, very much in keeping with Lord Mansfield's explanation. Lord Wright said: 'The standard of what is against conscience in this context has become more or less canalized or defined, but in substance the juristic concept remains as Lord Mansfield left it'[3].

The causes of action in contemporary times are, however, becoming gradually more ill defined and with equally ill consequences.

1   [1943] AC 32. On the case see below, para 20.19.
2   [1943] AC 32 at 61.
3   [1943] AC 32 at 63.

2.18   The authority of *Banque Financière de la Cité v Parc (Battersea)*[1] serves to demonstrate this. Parc owned land over which the Royal Trust Bank held a first charge for money lent. In 1990 Parc needed to refinance its borrowing. Banque Financière agreed to refinance the borrowing but, knowing that there was also a second charge over the land in favour of OOL, a company in the same group as Parc, obtained a letter of postponement, ranking OOL's claim behind its own. That letter was valueless, having been issued without OOL's authority. All the companies in the group became insolvent, and Banque Financière argued that it could be subrogated to the rights of the Royal Trust Bank, whose charge against Parc it had partly paid off, being treated as a loan to Parc. The Court of Appeal had rejected Banque Financière's claim for a number of reasons. Amongst these were:

- the failure to obtain the security for which it stipulated, which was an agreement binding on all the companies of the group that they would postpone their demands against Parc. Such failure was due entirely to the failure of Banque Financière to take normal and elementary precautions;
- there had been no sharp practice or misrepresentation on the part of OOL;
- subrogation would give Banque Financière rights for which it had never bargained. The possibility of a second charge had been considered and rejected;
- the loan was specifically structured to avoid disclosure under Swiss banking laws.

1   [1999] 1 AC 221. On the case see further below, para 8.47ff.

2.19   Unfortunately these factors held little, if any, significance when the case came before the House of Lords. Ultimately, the House of Lords ruled in favour of Banque Financière, because it had mistakenly believed that it was protected in respect of intra-group indebtedness, and would not, otherwise, have proceeded with the refinancing. It is difficult to see why these, as opposed to the above factors, rendered any enrichment unjust. Moreover, although the majority of their Lordships considered the case to lie within the category of providing a restitutionary remedy of subrogation to prevent unjust enrichment, Lord Steyn and Lord Clyde treated the principle of unjust enrichment as providing a category of claim in its own right.

2.20   Lord Steyn analysed the case by endorsing the central concepts of the principle of unjust enrichment precisely according to the conceptual definition given by Goff and Jones in 1966. He reached the conclusions that:

(1)   OOL had been enriched;
(2)   the enrichment had been at the expense of Banque Financière; and
(3)   that enrichment had been unjust.

On the latter issue, in the context of Parc and OOL not being guilty of sharp practice or misrepresentation, Lord Steyn suggested that restitution is not a fault based remedy, and that the case must 'in the vivid terminology of Professor Peter Birks, *An Introduction to the Law of Restitution* (1985), be unjust enrichment by subtraction'[1]. This does not, however, clarify what the unjust factor was in the case.

Lord Clyde took a somewhat different view. He explained that the principle of unjust enrichment is more fully expressed in the Latin formulation, *nemo debet locupletari aliena jactura*. He continued by stating that the principle is not entirely discretionary so as to enable a court in any case to withhold a remedy where all the necessary elements for its satisfaction have been established. The principle, he suggested, is equitable, in the sense that it seeks to secure a fair and just determination of the rights of the parties concerned in the case[2].

Lord Hutton's opinion is even more confusing as to the relationship between the principle of unjust enrichment and conscience. Lord Hutton advanced BFC's case on an 'equitable' principle that, where a lender advances a sum of money to another person intended to be a secure loan, and the money is used by that person to discharge a debt owed to him by a secured creditor, the lender is entitled to be subrogated to the charge of that creditor if his security proves to be defective. He went on to point out that one of the elements which gives rise to the right of subrogation is the unjust enrichment of the defendant at the expense of the claimant. Lord Hutton explained that the doctrine of subrogation applies in a variety of different circumstances where the defendant has been unjustly enriched at the expense of the claimant, and 'where equity considers that it would be unconscionable for the defendant to retain that enrichment'[3]. He concluded that BFC were entitled to the relief sought, because OOL was enriched at the expense of BFC, and it would be unconscionable to permit OOL to retain that enrichment.

Lord Hoffmann's opinion was, admittedly, more tightly reasoned, but his blunt conclusion that OOL's entitlement was 'unjust'[4] is no more satisfactory than in any other of their Lordships' judgments.

Clearly this will not do. McMeel describes Lord Steyn's adoption of the analytical methodology to the structure of the unjust enrichment, which had been promoted in leading scholarly works, as helpful[5]. A more robust and pragmatic approach yields a different conclusion:

> The leniency shown by the House of Lords towards careless impoverished parties ... makes one yearn for a return to nominate categories of restitutionary recovery ...
>   ... it is highly questionable for the law of restitution to come to the aid in this way of a large financial institution that neglects to take proper precautions. It is hardly an inducement to the application of the highest professional standards in the City of London for restitution to serve as a crutch for those injured because they do not look where they are going[6].

If it is correct to say that 'Disorderly law is no more than an alibi for illegitimate power'[7], such an amorphous principle of unjust enrichment as was utilised in *Banque Financière de la Cité v Parc (Battersea) Ltd* must not be allowed to prevail. The terminological analysis is confused and unhelpful. Scrutton LJ's description of the history of the action for money had and received as a 'history of well-meaning sloppiness of thought'[8] might now apply to the history of the principle of unjust enrichment.

1   [1999] 1 AC 221 at 226.
2   [1999] 1 AC 221 at 237.
3   [1999] 1 AC 221 at 245.
4   [1999] 1 AC 221 at 234.
5   McMeel *Modern Law of Restitution* (2000), p 5.
6   Bridge 'Failed Contracts, Subrogation and Unjust Enrichment: *Banque Financière de la Cité v Parc (Battersea) Ltd and Others*' [1998] Journal of Business Law 323 at 328 and 333.
7   Birks 'Equity in the Modern Law: An Exercise in Taxonomy' (1996) 26 Western Australian Law Review 1 at 99.
8   *Holt v Markham* [1923] 1 KB 504 at 514.

2.21   The principle of unconscionability is much less vague for several reasons. A primary reason is that there already exists a substantial array of decisions on particular facts[1]. This reason is reinforced by the fact that the principle underpins explicit sub-categories such as undue influence and proprietary estoppel. Even where the principle stands alone, as for example in equity's jurisdiction to set aside unconscionable bargains (described as a 'venerable' jurisdiction by Nourse LJ in *Crédit Lyonnais Bank Nederland NV v Burch*[2]), there is still room for analogy with existing case law. Thus in applying an 1888 decision, *Fry v Lane*[3], in *Cresswell v Potter*, in 1978, Megarry J was able to adapt the antique phrasing of that older case to modern circumstances[4].

1   See above, para 2.9ff.
2   [1997] 1 All ER 144 at 151. On this case see below, para 10.16.
3   (1888) 40 Ch D 312.
4   [1978] 1 WLR 255n at 257–258. See below, para 10.8.

2.22   The principle of unjust enrichment, by contrast, has no such historical pedigree, except in the sense that it arguably underpins the categories of claims as originally outlined by Lord Mansfield[1]. If the categories of claims is to be extended, which (given the comment by Lord Nicholls in *CTN Cash and Carry Ltd v Gallaher* that ' ... the categories of unjust enrichment are not closed'[2]) seems likely to occur, it is hoped that it is not along the lines of *Banque Financière de la Cité v Parc (Battersea) Ltd*. All of this is not to suggest that critical, academic discussion of the law has no utility. It is merely to highlight that, where the law is developed and reformed in the substantive law of equity, it should be done on the basis of detailed analysis of existing cases, and not on the basis of academic conceptualisations.

1   See above, para 2.16. Cf above, para 1.11.
2   [1994] 4 All ER 714 at 720. On the case see below, para 10.62.

F   The substantive law of equity and restitution

2.23   Critical analysis of the law is essential. The staple diet of English law is argument and advocacy. A treatise which is merely descriptive of the law has limited value. Critical analysis must, however, be conducted in the terminology which is used in litigation and judicial decisions. There are inherent dangers in resorting to conceptualisations from outside of the realm of existing law. As a result of this occurring in *Banque Financière de la Cité v Parc (Battersea) Ltd*, the case, at least in my opinion and Bridge's opinion[1], was wrongly decided. Similarly, if the courts undo bargains because of unconscionable conduct, it is of no value if academic treatises replace the words 'unconscionable conduct' with 'discreditable behaviour'[2].

Discourse and development of the law is a matter of contributions from the judiciary and academics, but it is the former rather than the latter who should retain the dominant role. It is, for example, of value to discuss the requirement of 'manifest disadvantage' for a successful plea of presumed undue influence. Such a requirement was imposed by the House of Lords in *National Westminster Bank v Morgan*[3]. This was doubted by Lord Browne-Wilkinson in *CIBC Mortgages v Pitt*[4]. He suggested that the exact limits of the requirement may have to be considered in the future, because the requirement was inconsistent with abuse of confidence cases. The Court of Appeal in *Royal Bank of Scotland v Etridge (No 2)* appear to suggest that it is an evidential and not a substantial requirement[5]. More recently, in *Barclays Bank v Coleman*[6], the Court of Appeal accepted that *CIBC Mortgages v Pitt* had put a serious question mark over the future of the requirement of manifest disadvantage in cases of presumed undue influence, and that the House of Lords had signalled that it might not continue to be a necessary ingredient indefinitely.

This issue will be discussed below[7], but it is raised here to make a fundamental point. This issue has not been finally resolved by the judiciary, and it is of fundamental importance. If females, as is the predominant situation, use their share of a home to stand as surety for the indebtedness of male partners, they will, normally, secure some manifest advantage in ensuring the continuation of their partners' businesses. The question, which remains to be resolved, is whether this precludes them from any remedy in equity where the relationship with their male partners raises a presumption of undue influence. Homes may be lost or retained according to the answer to this question. Questions such as these, whether relating to family, commercial or public transactions, are at the root of restitution in modern equity. The answer to such questions depends upon a close examination of what the law, how it came to be, and how the judiciary is likely to develop it.

1   See above, para 2.20.
2   Birks 'Equity in the Modern Law: An Exercise in Taxonomy' (1996) 26 Western Australian Law Review 1 at 65.
3   [1985] AC 686.
4   [1994] 1 AC 200 at 209.
5   [2000] 1 All ER 385.
6   [2001] QB 20.
7   See below, para 10.37ff.

Part II
Property and Equity

CHAPTER 3

Proprietary Claims and Remedies

Craig Rotherham

A   Introduction

3.1   The law often responds to unjust enrichment by holding that the defendant is under a personal obligation to make restitution by paying a specified sum of money that reflects a benefit gained at the expense of the claimant. However, in some circumstances, the law grants claimants proprietary rights. The provision of these rights has been recognised as giving rise to some of the most difficult questions in the law of restitution[1]. This is understandable, given that restitution can be effected by the provision of personal rights alone. Some additional rationale is needed to justify the award of proprietary remedies. However, the jurisprudence on the distribution of property rights in English law remains undeveloped, and is often clouded in fiction and metaphor. This chapter examines the availability of proprietary claims at common law and proprietary remedies in equity, and endeavours to make some basic conceptual distinctions that will assist an understanding of the area.

1   See for example Millett, Book Review (1995) 111 LQR 517 at 518; Burrows *Law of Restitution* (1993), p 35.

The distinction between enforcing existing property rights and creating new property rights

3.2   It can be difficult to distinguish between proprietary rights that have the effect of reversing unjust enrichment and those that do not[1]. Generally a line is drawn between the enforcement of existing property rights and the creation of new rights. Thus, in some circumstances, the law holds that a defendant in possession of an asset is liable because the claimant has at all times retained title to it. The most obvious example involves a defendant obtaining possession of the claimant's property, in circumstances in which the law provides for specific recovery of the asset in question. While the enforcement of such property rights may allow the claimant to regain physical possession of an asset, it does not effect restitution of any enrichment gained at the expense of the claimant. Rather, the property right ensures that the defendant is never legally enriched.

1   See for example Grantham and Rickett 'Property and Unjust Enrichment: Categorical Truths or Unnecessary Complexity?' [1999] NZLR 668. Virgo, in contrast, rejects the significance of this distinction, arguing that all remedies arising in response to interference with property rights are part of the law of property, and have nothing to do with notions of unjust enrichment. See Virgo *Principles of the Law of Restitution* (1999), p 596.

3.3   The difficulties in this aspect of the classification of proprietary claims are apparent in *Macmillan Inc v Bishopsgate Investment Trust plc (No 3)*[1]. The issue arose in relation to conflicts of law questions – one context in which such matters of characterisation are practically relevant. The claimant, which was registered in New York, sought to recover shares in England that it beneficially owned, but which were pledged by its trustee as security in breach of trust and subsequently sold to the defendants with the agreement of the trustee's creditors. The defendant resisted the claim arguing that it was a bona fide purchaser. The characterisation of the basis for the action was important for the choice of law. Some members of the court took the view that the 'claim' could be characterised as restitutionary[2]. What should follow from this is not clear, given that 'restitution' can describe the relief given in response to a wide range of causative events. More important and convincing was the Court of Appeal's conclusion that the 'issue' to be resolved was one of property rights rather than unjust enrichment, and that, as a result, the lexus situs was to be determined by the proprietary and not the restitutionary choice of law rules[3].

1   [1996] 1 All ER 585, [1996] 1 WLR 387; discussed below, para 22.32.
2   [1996] 1 All ER 585 at 596, per Staughton LJ and at 605, per Auld LJ.
3   [1996] 1 All ER 585 at 615, per Aldous LJ. See below, para 22.44.

3.4   Proprietary rights that reverse unjust enrichment can also be distinguished from rights that are generated by consent. Property rights are very often transferred pursuant to contract. For example, title passes under a contract for sale of goods when the parties intend it[1]. Elsewhere, conveyance of title documents is often required before legal title is transferred. On the other hand, equity provides that property passes as soon as there is a specifically enforceable contract[2].

1   See the Sales of Goods Act 1979, s 17.
2   See for example *Lysaght v Edwards* (1876) 2 Ch D 499; *Oughtred v IRC* [1960] AC 206.

3.5   In contrast, the law may effect restitution by granting property rights without regard to the intention of the parties. It is instances of relief of this type that are referred to here as proprietary remedies. Such remedies arise in several contexts. First, the law may give relief by finding that, while the defendant took title to property received from the claimant, that title is voidable. Where this is so, the claimant is entitled to rescind the transaction and revest title in himself[1]. Secondly, it may be held that property that the defendant received from a third party, either belonged to the claimant the moment title passed from its former owner[2], or that the defendant received a title to that property that is defeasible at the election of the claimant[3]. Thirdly, a claimant may, by subrogation, be allowed to exercise a right of security over another's property. Such a right arises where the debt secured by the right in question was discharged using money that belonged to the claimant[4]. Similarly, proprietary subrogation will be available where money is advanced by the claimant on the understanding that it would be secured by a charge, and ultimately a charge was not or could not be granted[5] or for some reason the charge granted proved to be ineffective[6].

1   *Twinsectra Ltd v Yardley* [1999] Lloyd's Rep Bank 438. This point is not affected by the appeal to the Lords ([2000] 2 All ER 377), on which see below, para 5.36.
2   For example, *A-G for Hong Kong v Reid* [1994] 1 AC 324.
3   This is true of tracing: see *Lipkin Gorman v Karpnale Ltd* [1991] 2 AC 548 at 573, per Lord Goff.
4   For example, *Boscawen v Bajwa* [1995] 4 All ER 769, [1996] 1 WLR 328; below, para 8.43.
5   For example, *Butler v Rice* [1910] 2 Ch 277; below, para 8.45.
6   For example, *Ghana Commercial Bank v Chandiram* [1960] AC 732; below, para 8.46.

Which claims and remedies are part of the law of restitution?

3.6   In some circumstances, breaches of property rights may be vindicated through the provision of personal remedies. However, where personal relief is given, it can be difficult to determine whether the basis of the relevant claim is properly characterised as proprietary, or whether it should be regarded as restitutionary[1]. One distinction is clear enough. A claim can only be characterised as proprietary in nature if it vindicates a right that is enforceable against all the world or at least a broad class of people[2]. Thus, a distinction must be made, between remedies given to vindicate a personal right against a particular defendant, and remedies given to vindicate a property right. Claims for money had and received may be maintained in the context of a mistaken payment when title has passed. Because the claimant no longer has any proprietary interest in the money, no action will be available against any third party who receives the money from the initial recipient. Thus, such a claim enforces a personal right to restitution. It may be distinguished from a claim for conversion that is enforceable against any party that takes possession of the claimant's property, and is, to that extent, properly characterised as a proprietary claim.

1   See for example Burrows 'Proprietary Restitution: Unmasking Unjust Enrichment' (2001) 117 LQR 412.
2   Tony Honoré 'Rights of Exclusion and Immunities against Divesting' (1960) 34 Tulane Law Review 453 at 466.

3.7   So a question that needs to be resolved in this context concerns the extent to which proprietary claims form part of the law of restitution. Here we face a difficulty with the ambiguous nature of the term 'restitution'. Almost all relief given for wrongs might be characterised as restitutionary, in the sense that it is designed to compensate the claimant for loss suffered. If we are to distinguish meaningfully between the various branches of private law, it makes sense to draw a distinction between relief that is granted to reverse unjust enrichment, and that which is given to vindicate property rights or to enforce consensually undertaken obligations. In other words, a more helpful means of categorisation will be provided by focusing on the event that gives rise to the remedial response, rather than on the response itself. Thus, our focus is on those proprietary claims that are concerned with the reversal of unjust enrichment.

3.8   It might be argued that claims that respond to interferences with property rights are essentially concerned with unjust enrichment. Whether this can really be maintained depends in part on our definition of unjust enrichment. However, while a claim for conversion, for example, will often reverse unjust enrichment, this will not always be so. For defendants will be liable even if they are bona fide purchasers of assets (at least of assets other than money). It is difficult in these circumstances to conclude that a defendant can be characterised as being unjustly enriched if he gave value for the property[1]. Thus, the only party that has been unjustly enriched at the expense of the claimant is the party that initially took the property. The rule that subsequent purchasers are liable reflects a decision to attach particular importance to the owner's interest in having security of title – it has nothing to do with the reversal of unjust enrichment.

1   See *Macmillan Inc v Bishopsgate Investment Trust plc (No 3)* [1996] 1 All ER 585 at 605, per Auld LJ.

3.9   This might lead us to argue that the reason for protection in these circumstances is not unjust enrichment but property[1]. However, this does not necessarily tell us much, as property is a slippery concept[2]. While we enforce pre-existing rights of property, we do not always do so to the same degree. There is a balance to be made between the interests of an owner and of others who have come into possession of (and/or purported to purchase an interest in) the assets in question. In striking that balance, owners' security of title is sometimes limited by reference to notions of fault and unjust enrichment. We cannot explain the compromise that is struck by reference to some abstract notion of property; for, ultimately, our law of property is nothing more than the sum total of such compromises. Yet, nor can such compromises be simply explained in terms of unjust enrichment; for there are too many other considerations involved. This can be seen in the case of equitable proprietary rights. In comparison with the common law, the level of protection provided is less exclusively motivated by a concern for owners' rights to the use and enjoyment of their assets. The rule that bona fide purchasers take free from beneficiaries' rights can be seen as qualifying property rights, according to a mixture of considerations of good faith and unjust enrichment. Similarly, the rule that recipients who are no longer in possession of trust property are liable to account only if their dealing with that property was unconscionable[3] means that an owner's rights are enforced only against those who were at fault.

1   Grantham and Rickett 'Property and Unjust Enrichment: Categorical Truths or Unnecessary Complexity?' [1999] NZLR 668.
2   See for example Rotherham 'Conceptions of Property in Common Law Discourse' (1998) 18 Legal Studies 41.
3   *Bank of Credit and Commerce International (Overseas) Ltd v Akindele* [2001] Ch 437, [2000] 4 All ER 221; on which see below, para 5.52ff.

3.10   Relief given following a breach of property rights might meaningfully be described as part of the law of restitution if the availability of relief is limited according to considerations of unjust enrichment. This will most obviously be so where, in addition to the defence of bona fide purchase, the defence of change of position is available. Yet, even where this is so, liability is not determined solely by reference to considerations of unjust enrichment; for defendants who have purchased the property in question, or changed their position, will be liable if they did not act in good faith.

B   Common law proprietary claims

3.11   Property rights are enforced in various ways depending on the type of assets involved. The common law provided remedies for the specific recovery of land, but limited owners of chattels to compensation[1]. In addition to providing proprietary claims for the breach of pre-existing property rights[2], the common law effects a reversal of unjust enrichment in certain circumstances, by allowing for the revesting of property rights or for their extension to substituted assets.

1   This was altered by the Torts (Interference with Goods) Act 1977, s 3, which gives the courts the discretion to require defendants to deliver up chattels.
2   For example, through an action for conversion.

3.12   Certain forms of vitiation of intention render contracts voidable at common law. The right arises in respect of contracts induced by a fraudulent misrepresentation[1]. In addition, although it is difficult to support such a distinction, it has been suggested that, while duress to the person renders a contract voidable, other forms of duress give rise only to a claim in quasi-contract[2]. On the other hand, the common law takes a strict approach to rescission. It is possible to rescind contracts at law only if *restitutio in integrum* is possible without judicial assistance. Thus, rescission will be denied to claimants who have received any consideration pursuant to the transaction in question, or cannot take possession of the assets in question without resort to legal process.

1   The courts of common law offered no relief for contracts induced by an innocent misrepresenta-tion, see *Kennedy v Panama, New Zealand, and Australian Royal Mail Co Ltd* (1867) LR 2 QB 580.
2   *Pao On v Lau Yiu Long* [1980] AC 614 at 635, per Lord Scarman.

3.13   In addition, in some circumstances, an owner who enjoys title to one asset may elect to assert the same rights over its exchange product. *Lipkin Gorman v Karpnale Ltd*[1] provides a recent analysis of the relevant principles. Cass, a partner in a firm of solicitors, fraudulently withdrew money from his firm's client account and gambled it at a casino operated by the defendant. The House of Lords held that the firm was able to trace from the chose in action represented by the debt owed to it by the bank into the funds withdrawn from the client account. On Lord Goff's analysis, while Cass initially took legal title to the money, that interest was defeasible in that it was liable to be lost in the event that the firm elected to claim title to the money in place of its original chose in action[2]. Moreover, once the money had come into the hands of the defendant, the claimant could elect to bring an action against it for money had and received.

1   [1991] 2 AC 548.
2   [1991] 2 AC 548 at 574.

3.14   There is some confusion as to the nature of the action in *Lipkin Gorman*[1]. On the one hand, Lord Goff indicated that the claimant needed to demonstrate that the defendant had received money to which the claimant could have asserted title[2]. On the other hand, he indicated that the claim was founded upon unjust enrichment and subject to the defence of change of position[3]. Strictly speaking, the action in question was not a proprietary claim. The only claim that may be brought in respect of money that may reasonably accurately be described as proprietary in nature is one for conversion. Often a claimant who could sue for conversion of money would have the right to elect to bring an action for money had and received instead. However, in *Lipkin Gorman*, the claimant had no choice but to maintain an action for money had and received because authorities precluded a claim of conversion[4]. Lord Goff explained this on the basis that the claimant could not, by electing to trace, turn the defendant into a wrongdoer[5]. While the claim in question required that the claimant demonstrate that it had the right to assert title to the assets in question at the time the defendant received them, it did not demand that the claimant retained that right. Thus, it was not a proprietary claim but a personal action for restitution.

1   See below, para 4.10.
2   [1991] 2 AC 548 at 572.
3   [1991] 2 AC 548 at 577–583.
4   Such a claim was prevented by authorities that hold that a partner of a firm with apparent authority to make a withdrawal gains title to money withdrawn from the firm's account, despite an absence of actual authority. See *Union Bank of Australia Ltd v McClintock & Co* [1922] 1 AC 240; *Commercial Banking Co of Sydney Ltd v Mann* [1961] AC 1.
5   [1991] AC 548 at 573.

3.15   While the action for money had and received that is available in conjunction with tracing at common law is essentially a personal claim for restitution, it may often bring with it some of the advantages associated with proprietary remedies. For example, if the defendant is in possession of money identifiable as belonging to the claimant at the time that the defendant's estate vests in a trustee in bankruptcy, the claimant will have an action against the trustee based on the trustee's receipt of the claimant's property[1]. Such a claim will be available only if, as in *Lipkin Gorman,* the claimant retains title to the assets in question. It would not be available, for example, with respect to the proceeds of assets given to the defendant by the claimant as the result of a non-fundamental mistake[2]. In addition, a claimant may be able to claim, through an action for money had and received, any profits made by the defendant where the value of the proceeds exceeds that of the property for which they were exchanged[3].

1 *Tooke v Hollingworth* (1793) 5 Term Rep 215, 101 ER 121. See Scott 'Tracing at Common Law' (1965–1966) 7 University of Western Australia Law Review 463; Fox 'Common Law Claims to Substituted Assets' [1999] RLR 55 at 72–73; cf Cuthbertson 'Tracing at Common Law – Myth or Reality?' (1967–1968) 8 University of Western Australia Law Review 402.
2 Thus, in most cases of mistake where an action is available for money had and received, property will have passed to the defendant. See *Barclays Bank Ltd v WJ Simms Son and Cooke (Southern) Ltd* [1980] QB 677 at 689, per Robert Goff J.
3 See for example *Jones & Sons (Trustee) v Jones* [1997] Ch 159, [1996] 4 All ER 721; below, para 4.3.

C   Equitable proprietary remedies

Revesting property rights and creating new proprietary interests

Rescission

3.16   Rescission is more readily granted in equity than it is at common law[1]. The requirement that rescission be allowed only if the status quo can be restored is interpreted less strictly in equity, in that rescission may be granted on terms. In addition, rescission is allowed in equity in a wider range of circumstances than it is at common law. Most importantly, equity permits rescission of a contract where the consent of one party has been induced by an innocent misrepresentation[2]. In addition, equity provides for the rescission of contracts vitiated by a common mistake 'that renders the subject matter of the contract essentially and radically different from the subject matter which the parties believed to exist'[3]. Similarly, a claimant may rescind a contract on the grounds of undue influence or unconscionable bargain[4]. Perhaps because the area was well-developed at common law at an early stage, it is less clear whether equity makes rescission available to the victim of duress. However, in principle, there is much to be said for the view that the remedy should be available in that context.

1 On common law rescission see above, para 3.12.
2 *Redgrave v Hurd* (1881) 20 Ch D 1, [1881–1885] All ER (Rep) 77.
3 *Associated Japanese Bank (International) Ltd v Crédit du Nord SA* [1989] 1 WLR 255 at 268, per Steyn J. See also *Solle v Butcher* [1950] 1 KB 671, [1949] 2 All ER 1107.
4 See Beatson *Anson on Contracts* (27th edn, 1998), p 284. See generally below, ch 10.

3.17   Where a transaction is voidable, the transferee obtains a defeasible title, and may give good title to bona fide purchasers[1]. Like equitable interests, the equity of rescission has important effects in insolvency: because trustees in bankruptcy take the property of bankrupts subject to any equities, they are bound by rights of rescission[2].

1   *Babcock v Lawson* (1880) 5 QBD 284; *Bainbrigge v Browne* (1881) 18 Ch D 188.
2   *Johnson v Smiley* (1853) 17 Beav 223, 51 ER 1019; *Re Beeston* [1899] 1 QB 626.

3.18   Where a contract is rescinded, it is clear enough that the underlying transaction is thereafter treated as if it were void ab initio. However, it is less certain what effect, if any, this has on the passing of title to money, goods or land transferred pursuant to such a transaction. Two important questions have emerged in this context. The first concerns the extent to which a constructive or resulting trust might arise prior to or following rescission. The second relates to the availability of tracing in the aftermath of rescission. These issues are dealt with subsequently in this chapter in a broader examination of the constructive trust[1].

1   See below, para 3.44ff.

THE CREATION OF NEW PROPRIETARY RIGHTS

3.19   In addition to enforcing existing rights to trust assets and revesting rights through rescission, equity provides for the creation of new rights in a number of situations. Rights enjoyed over one asset can be transferred to another asset by the process of tracing[1], or another person's rights to particular assets may be acquired by the process of subrogation[2]. In addition, a constructive trust or equitable lien may be imposed to give a claimant an equitable interest in property where it would be unconscionable for the defendant to have an unencumbered title to property received from the claimant[3] or a third party[4].

1   See generally below, ch 4.
2   See generally below, ch 8.
3   See for example *Chase Manhattan Bank v Israel-British Bank* [1981] Ch 105; *Neste Oy v Lloyds Bank plc* [1983] 2 Lloyd's Rep 658 at 666; *Westdeutsche Landesbank Girozentrale v Islington London Borough Council* [1996] AC 669, [1996] 2 All ER 961. See generally below, ch 5.
4   See for example *A-G for Hong Kong v Reid* [1994] 1 AC 324, [1994] 1 All ER 1.

The advantages of proprietary remedies

3.20   Proprietary remedies offer a number of advantages, the most obvious of which include the following:

● The most significant benefit they bring relates to the distribution of entitlements in bankruptcy. Claimants who are able to enforce only personal rights are obliged to line up with other unsecured creditors to share pari passu in the distribution of what remains of a bankrupt defendant's estate after the claims of secured and preferential creditors have been satisfied[1]. In contrast, the effect of awarding a constructive trust over particular assets is that, in the event of the defendant's bankruptcy, those assets are not available for distribution among unsecured creditors[2]. Similarly, a claimant who is granted a lien, or allowed to assume the rights of a secured creditor by subrogation, will be able to have recourse to particular assets in order to satisfy the debt owed to him before those assets will be made available for distribution among other creditors.

- Equitable proprietary rights are good against all the world except bona fide third party purchasers for value. As a result, the recognition that assets that have come into the hands of a third party are impressed with a constructive trust may allow a claimant to bring a claim (whether proprietary or personal) against a defendant who would otherwise not be liable[3].
- In equity, claimants who are able to identify their property or its proceeds in the defendant's possession will be able to take advantage of a stricter standard of liability than the personal liability that is imposed on defendants for having received such property[4].
- Obtaining a right to specific assets rather than a personal right to compensation may allow a claimant to take advantage of any appreciation in value of those assets, or from the fact that the exchange product of those assets is worth more than the original assets. In this way claimants may recover more than they have lost[5].
- Rather than being limited to simple interest, claimants who can establish a proprietary right to money are entitled to compound interest[6].

1   See *Re Polly Peck (No 2)* [1998] 3 All ER 812.
2   See the Insolvency Act 1986, s 283(3)(a) and (5); Goff and Jones *Law of Restitution* (5th edn, 1998), p 73.
3   See for example *El Ajou v Dollar Land Holdings plc* [1993] 3 All ER 717; *Banque Belge pour L'Etranger v Hambrouck* [1921] 1 KB 321.
4   Thus, it would seem that only those who were unconscionable in their receipt or subsequent retention of the claimant's property will be personally liable to account for it. See *Bank of Credit and Commerce International (Overseas) Ltd v Akindele* [2001] Ch 437, [2000] 4 All ER 221; below, para 5.62.
5   *Re Tilley's Will Trust* [1967] Ch 1179, [1967] 2 All ER 303; *Foskett v McKeown* [2001] 1 AC 102, [2000] 3 All ER 97; see generally below, para 4.25.
6   See for example *Westdeutsche Landesbank Girozentrale v Islington London Borough Council* [1996] AC 669, [1996] 2 All ER 961; *Lonrho v Export Credit Guarantee Department* [1996] 2 Lloyd's Rep 649; *Stearns v Village Main Reef Gold Mining Co* (1905) 10 Com Cas 89. See below, para 3.49, and on interest see below, para 21.70ff.

Justifying proprietary relief

3.21   The most important effect of proprietary remedies relates to their capacity to put the claimant in the position of a secured creditor. However, this comes at a cost. Proprietary remedies – whether they are awarded in the wake of vitiated transactions, over profits for which defendants were obliged to account, following tracing, or as the result of subrogation – are apt to cause confusion. For one thing, these remedies threaten the utility of devices designed to provide protection against the risks of bankruptcy, such as the floating charge and the negative pledge. In addition, they make it difficult for those administering bankrupt estates 'to determine whether property which is, on the face of it, divisible among the creditors is truly so divisible'[1]. For these reasons, the consequences of proprietary relief in insolvency need to be justified.

1   Per Pincus J in *Re Osborn* (1989) 91 ALR 135.

3.22   The effect of proprietary remedies in conferring priority in bankruptcy points to the importance of property, not just for the parties to the action, but also for third parties. Justification of this priority must focus not just on the claimant's case for a remedy from the defendant, but also on the contest between the claimant and others seeking a share of the defendant's assets in bankruptcy. Thus, a proprietary remedy can be justified only if there is something in the nature of a claim that indicates that the claimant should be given priority over the defendant's general creditors[1].

1   See for example Waters 'The English Constructive Trust: A Look into the Future' (1966) 19 Vanderbilt Law Review 1215 at 1250; Sherwin 'Constructive Trusts in Bankruptcy' [1989] University of Illinois Law Review 297 at 329.

3.23   Some might argue that cases of enrichment by subtraction are regarded as the most compelling of private law claims[1]. For, where a claim is based upon the defendant's being enriched as a result of a subtraction from the claimant's wealth, restitution does no more than return the parties to the position they enjoyed before the enrichment[2]. This characteristic of unjust enrichment suggests a basis for giving restitution actions priority over other claims in the event of a defendant's insolvency. According to the 'swollen assets' rationale, according unjust enrichment claims priority will effect corrective justice between the claimant and the defendant's unsecured creditors. For, where the claimant's loss is matched by a corresponding gain in the pool of assets available for distribution in the defendant's bankruptcy, to give the claimant priority to the extent of that gain will do no more than return all the interested parties to the situation that they would have enjoyed but for the defendant's enrichment.

1   See for example Fuller and Purdue 'The Reliance Interest in Contract Damages' (1936) 46 Yale Law Journal 52 at 56.
2   Of course, this is only true if the defendant's estate continues to be enriched by the subtraction in question. Where this is not the case, we might require some degree of fault before we demand restitution from a defendant, or we might allow defendants to avail themselves of the defence of change of position. Consider, for example, the doctrine of knowing receipt, where a debate rages as to which of these alternatives should be favoured. For a discussion, see Gardner 'Knowing Assistance and Knowing Receipt: Taking Stock' (1996) 112 LQR 56.

3.24   On the other hand, this rationale cannot in itself explain why restitution claims are generally thought to merit priority over contract claims. It is generally thought that it would be unjustified to grant proprietary remedies to contract claimants who have failed to avail themselves of the opportunity to obtain some form of security to protect themselves against the possibility of the debtor's insolvency. Consequently, unsecured contract creditors are said to have assumed the risk of their debtors' bankruptcy. On this view, proprietary relief should be available only to involuntary creditors who did not have the opportunity to protect themselves in this way[1]. This is generally true of restitution claimants[2].

1   On the notion that priority is justified where a restitutionary claimant is an involuntary creditor: see for example Sherwin 'Constructive Trusts in Bankruptcy' [1989] University of Illinois Law Review 297 at 335. For judicial recognition of its importance: see for example *Westdeutsche Landesbank Girozentrale v Islington London Borough Council* [1996] AC 669 at 683, per Lord Goff, and at 704, per Lord Browne-Wilkinson (a claim for restitution for failure of consideration in the aftermath of an unsecured ultra vires loan did not merit priority, as the claimant had chosen to be an unsecured creditor); *Re Kountze Bros* 79 F 2d 98 at 102 (2d Cir, 1935) (a claimant seeking restitution for mistake viewed as a voluntary creditor).
2   An exception is claims that arise from invalid contracts, where the claimant had not negotiated for security: see for example *Westdeutsche Landesbank Girozentrale v Islington London Borough Council* [1996] AC 669, [1996] 2 All ER 961.

3.25   The 'assumption of risk' might be a necessary condition, but it is certainly not a sufficient one. If the fact that voluntary creditors had the opportunity to safeguard their position and failed to do so were a sufficient justification in itself for giving non-voluntary creditors priority, it would justify giving tort claimants preference over contract creditors. In *Space Investments Ltd* *v Canadian Imperial Bank of Commerce*[1], Lord Templeman made the error of assuming that the fact that a claimant was an involuntary creditor was a sufficient justification for conferring priority in bankruptcy. In his view, it would have been appropriate to give beneficiaries of a trust a charge over all the assets of a bank to secure their claim if the bank had failed in its obligation to keep trust assets separate from its own assets. Even if it were reasonable to characterise the beneficiaries as involuntary creditors, such a priority could only be warranted if it could also be justified in terms of the 'swollen assets' rationale. This would require limiting such a charge to the extent that it could be demonstrated that a trustee's estate continued to be enriched at the expense of the beneficiaries so that, without the charge, unsecured creditors would enjoy a greater dividend in the defendant's bankruptcy. It is only this requirement that would provide a basis for distinguishing between aggrieved beneficiaries and other involuntary creditors, such as tort victims.

1   [1986] 3 All ER 75, [1986] 1 WLR 1072.

3.26   Thus, neither the 'swollen assets' nor the 'assumption of risk' rationales are sufficient in themselves to justify priority in bankruptcy. In combination, however, they offer a plausible justification for conferring such preferential treatment. Thus, the paradigm case of a situation thought to justify priority involves a claimant who has involuntarily enriched the defendant's estate so that there is an increase in the value of the assets that would be available for distribution in bankruptcy were a proprietary remedy not given.

Two processes of generating proprietary rights – tracing and subrogation

ACQUIRING PROPERTY RIGHTS BY TRACING

3.27   Proprietary rights can be acquired as a consequence of 'tracing': a process that is examined at length in chapter 4. Where a claimant has title to an asset, he may elect to 'trace' the proceeds of any exchange transactions involving that asset made without his consent. In these circumstances, a claimant has a choice of either claiming a constructive trust over those proceeds, or asserting a lien over them to secure the defendant's obligation to account for the value of the original asset[1]. The underlying rationale for permitting tracing lies in the instinct that involuntary creditors who have enriched the defendant's estate should be preferred ahead of general creditors who have accepted the risks of the defendant's bankruptcy. However, courts tend to take a rigid approach to the notion of tracing and permit claimants to assert their rights to the exchange product of their property regardless of its value[2]. While this has the advantage of ensuring that defendants cannot profit from their use of property obtained at the expense of the claimant, it is difficult to justify achieving this result at the expense of general creditors.

1   *Re Hallett's Estate* (1880) 13 Ch D 696, [1874–1880] All ER Rep 793.
2   See especially *Foskett v McKeown* [2001] 1 AC 102, [2000] 3 All ER 97.

ACQUIRING RIGHTS OF SECURITY BY SUBROGATION[1]

3.28   Proprietary rights may also be obtained by subrogation, whereby a claimant is permitted to 'step into the shoes' of a secured creditor. Generally, but not always[2], the acquisition of proprietary rights by subrogation is permitted in situations where the claimant cannot readily be characterised as a voluntary creditor. Thus, it is available where a charge has been discharged by the defendant using money which belonged to the claimant at law or in equity[3]. Subrogation is also available as a response to mistake, for instance, where the debt was discharged using money that the claimant had lent in the mistaken belief that the borrower had in return granted an effective right of security[4]. In addition, a claimant may acquire a creditor's rights by subrogation where he has been compelled to discharge the debt secured[5]. In all these cases, given that there was already a security interest in existence, allowing the claimant to exercise this interest means that general creditors are in no worse position than they would have been had the transaction that resulted in the defendant's unjust enrichment never taken place. Nonetheless, the courts have struggled to provide a formal explanation for permitting the acquisition of proprietary rights through subrogation, and have tended to justify it (rather implausibly) in terms of consent[6].

1   On subrogation generally see below, ch 8.
2   See for example sureties' rights, below, para 8.30.
3   See for example *Boscawen v Bajwa* [1995] 4 All ER 769, [1996] 1 WLR 328.
4   *Butler v Rice* [1910] 2 Ch 277.
5   See for example where claimants in order to preserve an interest in land discharged a mortgage of an interest upon which their own interest is derivative. See for example *Tarn v Turner* (1888) 39 Ch D 456.
6   See for example *Butler v Rice* [1910] 2 Ch 277; *Boscawen v Bajwa* [1995] 4 All ER 769 at 781. See below, para 8.3ff.

The notion of the remedial constructive trust

3.29   Analysis of the nature of the constructive trust is commonly framed in terms of whether the device is an 'institution' or a 'remedy'. While this distinction has been in vogue in this context for the last forty years[1], the meaning of these terms remains unclear. Nonetheless, it is possible to identify certain key distinctions upon which courts and commentators have focused, when discussing the notion of the remedial constructive trust.

1   The expression was first used in this area by Roscoe Pound, who commented that the constructive trust was a remedial institution rather than a substantive institution. Thus he evidently assumed that, regardless of the function of the trust, it was indeed an institution. Pound 'The Progress of Law' (1920) 33 Harvard Law Review 420 at 420–421. Maudsley observed that 'English law has always thought of the constructive trust as an institution, a type of trust': 'Proprietary Remedies for the Recovery of Money' (1959) 75 LQR 234 at 237. The institutional/remedial dichotomy was further entrenched in Waters' challenging work, *The Constructive Trust* (1964).

THE CONSTRUCTIVE TRUST AS A DEVICE FOR PROTECTING FIDUCIARY RELATIONSHIPS

3.30   There is a tendency in English legal thought to assume that the constructive trust's only legitimate function is in the context of express trusts and other fiduciary relationships[1]. Thus, in Re Polly Peck (No 2)[2], Mummery LJ argued that one of the features that distinguishes the Canadian remedial constructive trust from the English institutional constructive trust is that the Canadian courts do not require a pre-existing fiduciary relationship[3]. As a result of this emphasis, there is a tendency to envisage the proper route to making proprietary remedies more widely available as depending on the courts' being 'more ready to categorise wrongdoers as fiduciaries'[4].

1   For analyses of this tendency, see Maddaugh and McCamus *Law of Restitution* (1990), pp 82, 87–93; Waters *The Constructive Trust* (1964), p 2; *Rathwell v Rathwell* [1978] 83 DLR (3d) 289 at 305, per Dickson J. This is not true of other jurisdictions. See for example *Newton v Porter* 69 NY 133 (1877); *Elders Pastoral Ltd v BNZ* [1989] 2 NZLR 180.
2   [1998] 3 All ER 812.
3   [1998] 3 All ER 812 at 825. Similarly, the perceived importance of fiduciary relationships and the constructive trust was emphasised by Gault J in *Liggett v Kensington* [1993] 1 NZLR 257 at 281.
4   Sir Peter Millett 'Equity – The Road Ahead' (1995) 9 Trust Law International 35 at 40.

3.31   The controversy that is generated by the use of constructive trusts outside the context of fiduciary relationships is apparent in several cases in which claimants have claimed an equitable interest after having transferred legal title in circumstances in which their intention to do so was vitiated in some way[1]. Signs of the understanding that constructive trusts are inextricably linked to fiduciary relationships are also apparent in recent enrichment-for-wrongs case law. This can be seen, for example, in *A-G for Hong Kong v Reid*[2], where the Privy Council concluded that an employer became the beneficial owner of a bribe accepted by an employee. What seemed to be a remedial constructive trust, in that it neither reflected the parties' intentions nor protected existing property rights, was justified on the basis that it enforced a fiduciary relationship[3]. Subsequently, in *Halifax Building Society v Thomas*[4], the Court of Appeal distinguished the facts in *Reid* from a claim brought by a bank asserting a constructive trust over the profits made by a fraudulent borrower on the basis that the defendant in *Halifax* was not a fiduciary[5]. Lord Millett has recently suggested extra-judicially that, apart from rescinded transactions where there is a right to recover a specific asset, constructive trusts arise only in response to breaches of fiduciary duty[6].

1   The possibility that a constructive trust might arise in these circumstances has been raised in the High Court decisions of *Chase Manhattan Bank v Israel-British Bank* [1981] Ch 105, [1979] 3 All ER 1025, and *Neste Oy v Lloyds Bank Plc* [1983] 2 Lloyd's Rep 658 at 666, the House of Lords' decision in *Sinclair v Brougham* [1914] AC 398, [1914–1915] All ER Rep 622, and Lord Browne-Wilkinson's controversial analysis in *Westdeutsche Landesbank Girozentrale v Islington London Borough Council* [1996] AC 669 at 714–715. For a fuller account of the issues arising in this area, see below, para 3.44ff.
2   [1994] 1 AC 324; on which see below, para 9.13.
3   [1994] 1 AC 324 at 331, per Lord Templeman.
4   [1996] Ch 217; on which see below, para 12.54ff.
5   [1996] Ch 217 at 229, per Peter Gibson LJ. See below, para 12.56.
6   Millett 'Restitution and Constructive Trusts' (1998) 114 LQR 399 at 416.

3.32   On the other hand, even if the constructive trust is generally limited to regulating fiduciary relationships, it is hardly obvious that it should be so restricted. Certainly Lord Browne-Wilkinson's analysis of the constructive trust in *Westdeutsche Landesbank Girozentrale v Islington London Borough Council*[1] suggests a shift in perspective whereby the constructive trust is seen as a remedial response to unconscionability in general rather than to breaches of fiduciary duty alone[2].

1   [1996] AC 669, [1996] 2 All ER 961.
2   See below, para 3.39ff.

IS THE REMEDY DISCRETIONARY?

3.33   A central issue in the remedial constructive trust debate is whether the trust 'arises ... in defined circumstances and in accordance with settled principles of equity, or ... is imposed by the court in its discretion whenever it is considered just to do so'[1]. Thus, several commentators have argued that what distinguishes remedial constructive trusts from other constructive trusts is the degree of discretion that the courts exercise in deciding whether proprietary relief is appropriate[2]. On this view, English courts decline to exercise discretion in awarding proprietary relief[3]. Yet, a discretionary approach to the determination of proprietary rights is hardly something foreign to English law – as the flexibility exercised in determining the appropriate remedy in proprietary estoppel attests[4].

1   Millett 'Restitution and Constructive Trusts' (1998) 114 LQR 399 at 399.
2   See, especially, Gardner 'The Element of Discretion' in Birks (ed) *Frontiers of Liability Vol II* (1994), pp 186 at 190–192; Birks 'The End of the Remedial Constructive Trust?' (1998) 12 Trust Law International 202 at 203.
3   Millett 'Restitution and Constructive Trusts' (1998) 114 LQR 399 at 399.
4   For a recent example, see *Campbell v Griffin* [2001] EWCA Civ 990, (2001) 82 P & CR D 43. See also Gardner 'The Remedial Discretion in Proprietary Estoppel' (1999) 115 LQR 438.

REMEDIAL CONSTRUCTIVE TRUSTS ARISING ONLY WHEN DECLARED

3.34   In *Westdeutsche Landesbank Girozentrale v Islington London Borough Council*[1], Lord Browne-Wilkinson remarked that 'an institutional constructive trust ... arises by operation of law as from the date of the circumstances which give rise to it: the function of the court is merely to declare that such trust has arisen in the past'[2]. In contrast, the remedial constructive trust has pejoratively been described as being 'created by the court after the event'[3]. One reason why so much importance may have been placed on the timing of interests arising under constructive trusts relates to the objection to discretionary proprietary remedies. If an interest arises automatically, this indicates that its award is not discretionary. However, it does not follow that the obverse is true. It would be perfectly possible to establish a rule that provides the requisite certainty by holding that a claimant is entitled to relief on the proof of particular defined facts, but which still provides that the remedy given takes effect prospectively from the time of its declaration[4]. Thus, the notion that the constructive trust arises automatically may have been emphasised more for its capacity to suggest that the courts are not involved in redistributing property than for any other reason[5].

1   [1996] AC 669.
2   [1996] AC 669 at 714. See also *Muschinski v Dodds* (1985) 160 CLR 583 at 614, per Deane J; and *Fortex Group Ltd (in receivership and liquidation) v MacIntosh* [1998] 3 NZLR 171 at 172, per Tipping J (Gault and Keith JJ concurring).
3   *Re Polly Peck (No 2)* [1998] 3 All ER 812 at 824, per Mummery LJ.
4   Something that was contemplated by Deane J in *Muschinski v Dodds* (1985) 160 CLR 583 at 614.
5   See generally Rotherham *Proprietary Remedies in Context: A Study in the Judicial Redistribution of Property Rights* (2002).

REMEDIAL CONSTRUCTIVE TRUSTS AS REDISTRIBUTIVE

3.35   In *Re Polly Peck (No 2)*[1] Nourse LJ defined the remedial constructive trust in terms that provide an indication of why the notion causes so much anxiety in English legal culture. In his view, the remedial constructive trust involves 'an order of the court, granting, by way of remedy, a proprietary right to someone, who, beforehand, had no proprietary right'[2]. He argued that:

> You cannot grant a proprietary right to A who has not had it beforehand, without taking some proprietary right away from B. No English Court has ever had the power to do that, except with the authority of Parliament[3].

Similarly, Mummery LJ noted with concern that in Canada the constructive trust had developed in such a way that the remedy could now be awarded 'even though there is no pre-existing right of property'[4].

1   [1998] 3 All ER 812.
2   [1998] 3 All ER 812 at 830.
3   [1998] 3 All ER 812 at 831.
4   [1998] 3 All ER 812 at 825.

3.36   Thus, the more difficult it is to characterise relief given in a particular context as merely enforcing existing rights or a consensual transfer, the more likely it is that the court's response will be characterised as 'remedial'. This does indeed point to an important difference between North American and English constructive trust jurisprudence. On the other side of the Atlantic, judges and jurists have openly accepted that constructive trusts might give a claimant a new proprietary right[1]. In contrast, in England, in some instances the constructive trust has been denied as a remedy on the basis that it would be redistributive[2]. Moreover, in other contexts, English courts have conceptualised what appear to be redistributive constructive trusts in a manner that suggests that they involve the enforcement of existing proprietary rights or consensual transfers of property[3].

1   See for example *LAC Minerals v Corona Ltd* (1989) 61 DLR (4th) 14 at 50, per La Forest J.
2   See for example *Gissing v Gissing* [1971] AC 886.
3   See for example *Lord Napier and Ettrick v Hunter* [1993] AC 713, [1993] 1 All ER 385; *A-G for Hong Kong v Reid* [1994] 1 AC 324, [1994] 1 All ER 1. See Rotherham 'Restitution and Property Rites: Reason and Ritual in the Law of Proprietary Remedies' [2000] 1 Theoretical Inquiries in Law 205.

Situations in which constructive trusts are granted

3.37   Constructive trusts are sometimes granted to enforce existing equitable interests where third parties come into possession of trust property, to give effect to agreements to transfer property rights[1] or to regulate consensual relationships[2]. More controversially, in other situations the constructive trust is used as a restitutionary remedy. These are examined below.

1   See for example *Lysaght v Edwards* (1876) 2 Ch D 499.
2   Consider the constructive trust over any surplus realised from a sale by a mortgagee. See *Banner v Berridge* (1881) 18 Ch D 254; Oakley *Constructive Trusts* (3rd edn, 1997), p 308. Another example is provided by the use of constructive trusts to enforce mutual will arrangements: see *Dufour v Pereira* (1769) Dick 419 at 421, 21 ER 332 at 333; *Re Cleaver* [1981] 2 All ER 1018 at 1024. See Oakley *Constructive Trusts* (3rd edn, 1997), p 263.

VITIATED CONSENT AS BASIS FOR PROPRIETARY RELIEF

3.38   Constructive trusts and vitiated transfers   The possibility that a trust might arise by operation of law where a transferor's intention to pass property is vitiated in some way came to the fore in *Chase Manhattan plc v Israel-British Bank*[1]. The claimant bank mistakenly paid £2,000,000 to another bank for the account of the defendant bank. Because the defendant was insolvent, the only way the claimant would have been able to obtain a satisfactory remedy was if it could demonstrate that it had an equitable interest in the money transferred and it could identify the traceable proceeds of that money. Goulding J concluded that, because the defendant could not have retained the money in good conscience, a trust arose as soon as it was received[2]. This proprietary interest enabled the claimant to trace in equity.

1   [1981] Ch 105.
2   [1981] Ch 105 at 118–120. While Goulding J treated the claimant's proprietary interest as a constructive trust, others have since characterised it as a resulting trust. Whatever label is attached to it, the practical implications of awarding proprietary relief are the same.

3.39   The House of Lords subsequently considered the question of the proprietary consequences of vitiated transfers in *Westdeutsche Landesbank Girozentrale v Islington London Borough Council*[1]. The case arose in the aftermath of an interest swap arrangement that, because it was ultra vires the local authority, was void ab initio[2]. The bank argued that a proprietary remedy arose in its favour, so entitling it to compound rather than simple interest. While their Lordships accepted that the bank was entitled to bring an action for money had and received to recover the value of the money it had transferred, they rejected the suggestion that the failure of consideration generated an equitable interest in that money in the bank's favour. The case is notable for a lengthy analysis of the juridical basis of the constructive trust by Lord Browne-Wilkinson, that has proved both influential[3] and controversial[4].

1   [1996] AC 669.
2   See further below, para 18.18ff.
3   Thus, on the basis of Lord Browne-Wilkinson's analysis Aikens J recently concluded that *Chase Manhattan* could not be regarded as good law: see *Bank of America v Arnell* [1999] Lloyd's Rep Bank 399 at 405. See also below, para 4.22.
4   Indeed, Lord Goff made it clear that he thought that it was inappropriate for Lord Browne-Wilkinson to enter into such a wide-ranging analysis of the constructive trust in these circumstances: [1996] AC 669 at 685.

3.40   Lord Browne-Wilkinson and Lord Goff were sensitive to the fact that awarding a resulting or constructive trust would have meant that neither the property transferred nor its proceeds would be available for distribution in bankruptcy among the defendant's general creditors[1]. In their view, it was not appropriate to award a proprietary remedy, given that the bank had chosen to be an unsecured creditor under the interest swaps arrangement[2].

1   [1996] AC 669 at 704, per Lord Browne-Wilkinson. In addition, he suggested that a beneficiary's rights under a resulting trust would bind third party transferees, other than bona fide purchasers for value of the legal title without notice, including those who might purchase an equitable interest from the initial transferee.
2   [1996] AC 669 at 704, per Lord Browne-Wilkinson, and at 683–684, per Lord Goff.

3.41   In Lord Browne-Wilkinson's view, a constructive trust would have arisen only if the bank had knowledge of the local authority's rights[1]. In light of this premise, he offered a new interpretation of the controversial decision in *Chase Manhattan v Israel-British Bank*[2]. According to Lord Browne-Wilkinson, Goulding J's analysis in *Chase Manhattan* that a constructive trust arose immediately on the bank's receipt of the mistaken payment was unsupportable. Nevertheless, because the bank became aware of the claimant's mistake only two days after the transfer, he concluded that the case was rightly decided. In his view, once the defendant in *Chase Manhattan* became aware of the mistake, a constructive trust arose in the claimant's favour.

1   [1996] AC 669 at 705.
2   [1996] AC 669 at 714–715.

3.42   There is little to be said for this reinterpretation. On Lord Browne-Wilkinson's analysis, a constructive trust would have arisen, and the bank would have been permitted to trace the proceeds of the money paid, once the local authority became aware that the transaction was ultra vires. Thus, Lord Browne-Wilkinson explained that the bank was not entitled to a constructive trust because the money transferred had become untraceable before the defendant had the requisite knowledge[1]. Accordingly, if at any time the bank had been made aware of the mistake in question when it was in possession of any traceable proceeds of the payments, the local authority would have been entitled to trace and claim a constructive trust. This conclusion is completely at odds with his Lordship's analysis that it would have been unjust to have allowed proprietary relief, given that the claimant had chosen to be an unsecured creditor.

1   [1996] AC 669 at 707.

3.43   Lord Browne-Wilkinson mistakenly equated the merits of the claim in *Chase Manhattan* with the claim in *Westdeutsche*. There are, however, important distinctions between the two claims. Where, as in *Westdeutsche*, there was a mistake that was relevant to the formation of a contractual relationship, it is appropriate to discern whether the claimant had the opportunity to protect himself against the risk of the defendant's insolvency. Where a claimant in entering into a transaction failed to avail himself of such an opportunity, it would be inappropriate to give him a remedy that would confer priority over the defendant's unsecured creditors. In contrast, in circumstances such as those in *Chase Manhattan*, it may be argued that the claimant had not accepted the risk of the defendant's bankruptcy, and therefore was deserving of a proprietary remedy[1].

1   On the conditions justifying proprietary relief, see above, para 3.21.

3.44   The right of rescission and constructive/resulting trusts[1]   While it is sometimes assumed otherwise, the orthodox view is that the right to rescind is not indicative of an existing equitable interest; rather, such an interest arises, if at all, only if and when a claimant actually elects to rescind. Elaborating this view recently in the Court of Appeal in *Twinsectra Ltd v Yardley*[2], Potter LJ observed that:

> ... the transferor may elect whether to avoid or affirm the transaction and, until he elects to avoid it, there is no constructive (resulting) trust ... The result ... is that, before rescission, the owner has no proprietary interest in the original property; all he has is the mere equity of his right to set aside the voidable contract[3].

1   See also below, para 5.31ff.
2   [1999] Lloyd's Rep Bank 438. This point is not affected by the appeal to the Lords ([2000] 2 All ER 377), on which see below, para 5.36. See also *Daly v Sydney Stock Exchange Ltd* (1986) 160 CLR 371 at 390; *Lonrho plc v Fayed (No 2)* [1992] 1 WLR 1 at 11–12; *El Ajou v Dollar Land Holdings plc* [1993] 3 All ER 717 at 734.
3   [1999] Lloyd's Rep Bank 438 at 463. This point is not affected by the appeal to the Lords ([2000] 2 All ER 377), on which see below, para 5.36.

3.45   What is the significance of the distinction between an equity of rescission and an equitable interest? First, there is a small difference in the extent of protection afforded against third party purchasers. In addition to being unenforceable against bona fide purchasers of the legal title in the same way as an equitable interest, mere equities are defeasible by a third party's bona fide purchase of the equitable title of the assets in question[1]. Secondly, and potentially more importantly, a distinction might arise from the requirement that a fiduciary relationship or equitable interest must exist before claimants may trace.

1   *Phillips v Phillips* (1862) 4 De GF & J 208, 45 ER 1164; *Latec Investments Ltd v Hotel Terrigal Pty Ltd* (1965) 113 CLR 265. See Birks 'Property and Unjust Enrichment: Categorical Truths' [1997] NZLR 623 at 638.

3.46   The view might be taken that the absence of an equitable proprietary interest or a fiduciary relationship prevents a claimant from tracing through exchange transactions that took place prior to any purported election to rescind. However, in cases such as *Lonhro v Fayed*[1] and *El Ajou v Dollar Land Holdings plc*[2], Millett J favoured an account of the relationship of rescission and tracing that countered this objection[3]. In his view, where a transfer is induced by fraud, claimants

> are entitled to rescind the transaction and revest the equitable title to the purchase money in themselves ... and ... [such a claimant] can then invoke the assistance of equity to follow property of which he is the equitable owner[4].

1   *Lonhro plc v Fayed (No 2)* [1991] 4 All ER 961, [1992] 1 WLR 1.
2   [1993] 3 All ER 717.
3   This analysis was developed by Brennan J in *Daly v Sydney Stock Exchange* (1986) 160 CLR 371 at 388.
4   *El Ajou v Dollar Land Holdings plc* [1993] 3 All ER 717 at 734. For a similar analysis by the same judge, see *Lonrho plc v Fayed (No 2)* [1991] 4 All ER 961, [1992] 1 WLR 1. In addition, in *Halifax Building Society v Thomas* [1996] Ch 217 at 226, Peter Gibson LJ suggested that, if the building society had not affirmed the mortgage that it had been induced to enter into by the defendant's fraud, it could have rescinded the transaction and traced any proceeds of the money advanced. On *Halifax* see below, para 12.54ff.

3.47   This analysis proceeds on the basis that, because rescission operates retrospectively to avoid the contract in question, the parties will be treated on the basis that any property transferred under the contract was held for the benefit of the transferor from the moment of receipt. It is thought to follow from this premise that transferors may elect to 'trace' and assert their property rights in the exchange product of the assets they initially owned.

3.48   Despite the emergence of this analysis, it is not clear that constructive and/or resulting trusts have much, if any, role to play in the aftermath of rescission. Typically, a court in granting rescission gives orders declaring the contract void, to deliver up or reconvey specific property and execute any documents required for that purpose, to deliver up any formal instruments of transfer, and to repay money transferred pursuant to the rescinded contract. The courts have not tended to declare that the defendant holds property transferred under the rescinded contract on trust. With respect to specific property that the claimant seeks to have delivered up, this is hardly surprising. Given that the order that such property be delivered up or reconveyed will bind third party volunteers who have received the property, including trustees in bankruptcy, it is not obvious that a constructive trust is needed in this context.

3.49   It is even less probable that the constructive trust has any role with respect to monetary restitution ordered in the context of rescission. This was certainly the view taken by the Privy Council in *Re Goldcorp Exchange Ltd*[1]. The purchasers of unallocated gold claimed that they were the victims of a misrepresentation. They argued that it followed from this that they could rescind their contracts of purchase and reassert title to the money they had advanced. It was held that, because they had affirmed the contract, the purchasers were not able to rescind. However, Lord Mustill concluded that, even if this had not been the case, a proprietary interest would not have arisen in the claimants' favour following rescission. He observed that:

> Whilst it is convenient to speak of the customers 'getting their moneys back' this expression is misleading. Upon payment by the customers the purchase money became, and rescission or no rescission remained, the unencumbered property of the company. What the customers would recover on rescission would not be 'their' money, but an equivalent sum ... [2]

There is much to be said for this view. According to the contrary understanding, a claimant who was induced into giving an unsecured loan by a misrepresentation or common mistake would, by rescinding the arrangement, revest in himself property in the money transferred or its proceeds. In doing so, in the event of the transferee's bankruptcy, the claimant would put himself ahead of the transferee's general creditors. It would, however, be difficult to reconcile this result with the House of Lords' decision in *Westdeutsche Landesbank Girozentrale v Islington London Borough Council*[3]. It would indeed be peculiar if those seeking to recover payments made in the aftermath of transactions that were void ab initio, such as the interest swap arrangement in *Westdeutsche*, were to find themselves in a worse position than they would have been in had the transaction been merely voidable. This suggests that the availability of rescission cannot provide a basis for proprietary relief in respect of transfers of property made pursuant to a rescinded transaction. At the very least, the court must consider whether the claimant had assumed the risks of the defendant's insolvency[4].

1   [1995] 1 AC 74.
2   [1995] 1 AC 74 at 102.
3   [1996] AC 669, [1996] 2 All ER 961. On the other hand, Lord Browne-Wilkinson's analysis would seem to suggest that once the defendant was aware of the grounds of the rescission, it would hold any money transferred (or its traceable proceeds) as a constructive trustee. This would seem to suggest that a constructive trust would inevitably arise in the context of fraudulent misrepresentation. However, as mentioned, an analysis that predicates the existence of a proprietary remedy on the defendant's state of mind is fundamentally flawed. See above, para 3.38ff.
4   It was such considerations that in *Daly v Sydney Stock Exchange* (1986) 160 CLR 371 at 379, led Gibbs CJ to reject the analysis that Brennan J had offered in the same case. In his view: 'In deciding whether or not the money should be held to have been subject to a constructive trust it is not unimportant that the ordinary legal remedy of a creditor would have been adequate to prevent the firm from being benefited at the expense of the appellant'.

3.50   Recently, extra-judicially, Lord Millett substantially modified his position on proprietary remedies[1]. He now takes the view that a resulting trust will arise only where a claimant had no intention to pass title. In addition, he argues that a constructive trust will arise in only two circumstances. First, it arises in response to breaches of fiduciary duty. Secondly, a constructive trust arises in the aftermath of a vitiated transaction 'where the original transfer is rescinded and special retransfer is ordered because monetary restitution would not be an adequate remedy'[2]. On this analysis, there is no scope for tracing the proceeds of unique property if it happens to have been disposed of prior to rescission.

1   Millett 'Restitution and Constructive Trusts' (1998) 114 LQR 399.
2   Millett 'Restitution and Constructive Trusts' (1998) 114 LQR 399 at 417.

CONSTRUCTIVE TRUSTS OVER PROPERTY OBTAINED IN BREACH OF FIDUCIARY DUTY

3.51   In some circumstances, a claimant may be allowed to assert a proprietary interest over assets that were obtained in breach of a fiduciary duty.

In *Keech v Sandford*[1] a trustee acquired a lease of a property for his own benefit after the lessor had declined the trustee's request to renew a lease of the same property enjoyed by the beneficiary. It was held that, because of a conflict of interest, the trustee was obliged to hold the lease on trust for the beneficiary. Here the remedy was sought, not in order to acquire priority in bankruptcy, but because the claimant wanted the right to the possession and control of the land over which he had previously enjoyed an interest. In these circumstances an account of profits would generally be ineffectual; for the trustee purchased the property in question at market value, and it would in all likelihood have been impossible to point to any objective profit made by the trustee. Nonetheless, it would have been an affront to the claimant had the trustee been allowed to retain the property. Moreover, there is a danger that fiduciaries who might attach a value to an asset over and above its market worth will not be deterred by the threat of damages from acquiring the asset for themselves[2]. Consequently, the constructive trust is an appropriate remedy in these circumstances.

1   (1726) Sel Cas Ch 61, 22 ER 629; considered further below, para 9.29ff.
2   This justification might also explain the Canadian Supreme Court decision in *LAC Minerals Ltd v International Corona Resources Ltd* (1989) 61 DLR (4th) 14. In that case, La Forest J argued that the restoration of the asset would serve to deter breaches of fiduciary duty and to strengthen 'the social fabric those duties are imposed to protect': (1989) 61 DLR (4th) 14 at 48.

3.52   It is unlikely that the policy considerations concerning the granting of priority in bankruptcy, which are frequently so relevant in proprietary remedies cases, arose in *Keech v Sandford*[1]. In particular, it was unlikely that the defendant's creditors would have been prejudiced by the granting of a constructive trust. The effect of the remedy was that the claimant had to pay for the lease of the property. Thus, the defendant's estate did not suffer a net loss that might have undermined the position of his creditors in the event of his insolvency.

1   (1726) Sel Cas Ch 61, 22 ER 629; considered further below, para 9.29ff.

3.53   In other instances, the granting of proprietary rights over property obtained in breach of a fiduciary duty is indeed likely to have a prejudicial effect on the defendant's creditors. It is for this reason that the decision in *A-G for Hong Kong v Reid*[1] attracted so much controversy. The Privy Council concluded that a bribe, accepted by an employee in breach of the fiduciary obligation owed to his employer, was held on constructive trust. In delivering the advice of the Judicial Committee, Lord Templeman argued that it must be presumed that the fiduciary received the bribe for the benefit of his principal. When the equitable maxim 'equity regards as done that which ought to have been done' was applied to this, it was said to follow that: 'As soon as the bribe was received ... the false fiduciary held the bribe on a constructive trust for the person injured'[2]. This explanation is far from convincing. Not only does it rely on a fictional attribution of intent, but it is not clear why relief was not limited to a personal obligation to account.

1   [1994] 1 AC 324; on which see further below, para 9.11ff.
2   [1994] 1 AC 324 at 331.

3.54   On the other hand, profits obtained from wrongdoing will not always be held on constructive trust[1]. In *Halifax Building Society v Thomas*[2] the claimant, a building society that had been defrauded into lending a mortgage, claimed a constructive trust over the surplus generated by a sale of the property in question. In addition to rejecting the claim on the basis that the claimant had affirmed the mortgage transaction, the Court of Appeal distinguished the case from *A-G for Hong Kong v Reid* on the basis that the rogue in the case before it was not a fiduciary of the building society[3]. In the course of his judgment, Sir Peter Gibson LJ noted with apparent approval the conclusion reached by Auld J in the court below, that 'in many instances to strip a wrongdoer of his property will serve only to deprive other creditors'[4].

1   Outside the context of breaches of fiduciary duty, it is sometimes argued that a constructive trust might arise to prevent killers acquiring the beneficial interest in property that has devolved to them by will, intestacy or survivorship. See Hanbury and Martin *Modern Equity* (15th edn, 1997), pp 315–317; Oakley *Constructive Trusts* (3rd edn, 1997), p 50. However, thus far, English courts have done without the constructive trust in this field. Thus, in the context of property devolving by will or intestacy, the courts have seemed to assume that a killer cannot inherit even a legal interest in the deceased's estate: *In the Estate of Crippen* [1911] P 108, [1911–1913] All ER Rep 207; *Re Sigsworth* [1935] 1 Ch 89. Nor has the constructive trust been used to deal with difficulties arising in the context of survivorship; instead, the courts have treated unlawful killing as an act severing a joint tenancy: see *Re K* [1985] Ch 85; affd [1986] Ch 180. However, the analysis has been used in this context in other jurisdictions: See for example *Bradley v Fox* 129 NE 2d 699 (1955); *Re Pechar* [1969] NZLR 574; *Re Stone* [1989] 1 Qd R 351 at 352. It is possible that there is some use for the concept in the context of registered land, at least where the killer has become the registered proprietor.
2   [1996] Ch 217. See Watts 'Halifax Building Society v Thomas' (1996) 112 LQR 219. On other aspects of the case see further below, para 12.54ff.
3   [1996] Ch 217 at 229.
4   [1996] Ch 217 at 324.

THE AWARD OF CONSTRUCTIVE TRUSTS AND EQUITABLE LIENS OVER SUMS DUE TO A DEFENDANT BY A THIRD PARTY, TO PREVENT THE DEFENDANT'S OVER-INDEMNIFICATION

3.55   In some circumstances a constructive trust or equitable lien is imposed upon a defendant who is entitled to a payment from a third party tortfeasor but is obliged to account to the claimant for any sum that would go beyond compensating the defendant for his loss.

3.56   Insurers' rights to sums paid to an indemnified assured
Proprietary rights arise in favour of an insurer where damages or settlement money paid to an indemnified assured would go beyond compensating him for his loss. This principle was established in *Lord Napier and Ettrick v Hunter*[1], where certain Lloyds names had been indemnified by underwriters for their losses except to the extent of an agreed excess. Thereafter, the names settled a negligence claim that they had against their syndicate manager. The House of Lords held that the underwriters were entitled to an equitable lien over any settlement money that went beyond compensating the names for their loss. Lord Browne-Wilkinson explained the rights recognised as arising as a result of an implied term of the insurance contract that was converted into a proprietary interest because 'equity regards as done that which ought to be done'[2].

1   [1993] AC 713. The decision is examined in more detail, below, para 8.18ff.
2   [1993] AC 713 at 752.

3.57   This analysis is not without its problems. It depends upon the rather questionable implication of a term into the contract. Nor is it obvious why such a term should be treated as akin to a contract to assign future property, rather than an obligation to account. These and other difficulties are discussed below[1].

1   See below, para 8.25.

3.58   An assured's rights against an over-indemnified insurer Insurers who have the right to pursue actions against those liable to the assured are not entitled to keep any sums that go beyond what is necessary to recoup loss that has resulted from indemnifying the assured pursuant to the contract of insurance. In *Lonhro v Export Credit Guarantee Department*[1] the court considered whether an insurer's obligation to make restitution to the assured in these circumstances was personal or proprietary. The defendant department had guaranteed the claimant company for 95% of various foreign debts that included obligations incurred by Zambian buyers in respect of sale of goods contracts. Payment under the contracts was not made, as a result of currency restrictions introduced by the Zambian government. After meeting its obligations under the guarantee arrangement, the defendant successfully negotiated with the Zambian government for the recovery of the money due under the contracts. It was accepted that, after recovering the debts and recouping its own loss, the defendant was obliged to account to the claimant for any additional sums. The claimant argued that it had a proprietary interest in the sums in question, with the result that the defendant was also obliged to account for compound interest on such sums for the period between its receipt of the money and its payment to the claimant.

1   [1996] 2 Lloyd's Rep 649.

3.59   In Lightman J's view, it followed from the rule established in *Lord Napier and Ettrick v Hunter*[1] that, where an insurer brought an action against a third party to recoup losses resulting from indemnifying the assured, the insurer has no more than a right of security over the proceeds recovered. Accordingly: 'The moneys in the hands of the insurer belong to the assured, subject only to the right of the insurer to retain the sum secured in his own favour'[2]. As a result, Lightman J argued, the parties' rights in this context could be determined by analogy with the rule that mortgagees who have exercised their rights of sale hold any surplus money on trust for the mortgagor[3].

1   [1993] AC 713. The decision is examined in more detail below, para 8.18ff.
2   [1996] 2 Lloyd's Rep 649 at 661.
3   [1996] 2 Lloyd's Rep 649 at 661.

3.60   Lightman J justified his conclusion in part on considerations of justice in the distribution of entitlements in insolvency. In his view:

> There is no reason why the assured's part of recoveries in the hands of the insurer should form part of the cash flow of the insurer available for the insurer's creditors. Equity has intervened to lend assistance to the insurer, not to deny the assured his equitable proprietary title to recoveries[1].

There is something to be said for this. Insurers' rights of subrogation are an exceptional remedy provided to assist them to recoup payments made under insurance policies. There is no reason why these rights should give insurers a proprietary interest in money recovered in excess of their losses.

1   [1996] 2 Lloyd's Rep 649 at 661.

3.61   Constructive trusts over sums recovered for the benefit of another   The general rule is that claimants are allowed to recover only in respect of their own loss. This causes problems where a party, to whom contractual duties are owed, suffers no loss from a breach of contract because the subject matter of the contract has been assigned to another, or is otherwise at the risk of a third party. To prevent a legitimate claim disappearing into 'a legal black hole'[1], the courts have in some cases permitted claimants to sue for losses ensuing from a breach in the performance of a contract, despite the fact that the risk of such losses were borne by a third party. One such exception to the general rule can be found in the context of shipping contracts. Thus, in *The Albazero*[2], Lord Diplock concluded that:

> the consignor may recover substantial damages against the shipowner if there is privity of contract between him and the carrier for the carriage of goods; although, if the goods are not his property or at his risk, he will be accountable to the true owner for the proceeds of his judgment[3].

1   *GUS Property Management Ltd v Littlewoods Mail Order Stores Ltd* 1982 SC (HL) 157 at 166, per Lord Stewart; *McAlpine Construction v Panatown* [2000] 3 WLR 946 at 955, per Lord Clyde. See Unberath 'Third Party Losses and Black Holes: Another View' (1999) 115 LQR 535.
2   [1977] AC 774.
3   [1977] AC 774 at 844.

3.62   This rule has been attributed at times to the intentions of the contracting parties[1]. Recently, in *McAlpine Construction Ltd v Panatown Ltd*[2], Lord Clyde was sceptical that it was necessary that the matter be within the contemplation of the parties to the contract. In his view, it was 'preferable to regard it as a solution imposed by the law and not as arising from the supposed intention of the parties, who may in reality not have applied their minds to the point'[3].

1   [1977] AC 774 at 847.
2   [2000] 3 WLR 946.
3   [2000] 3 WLR 946 at 955.

3.63   There is some support for the view that the claimants hold money recovered in these circumstances subject to a constructive trust. Thus, in the context of consignors' rights to bring an action against a carrier for the loss suffered by the owner of goods, Lord Ellenborough suggested that consignors 'will hold the sum recovered as trustees for the real owner'[1]. On the other hand, in *The Albazero*, Lord Diplock apparently assumed that the basis for liability would be an action for money had and received[2].

1   *Joseph v Knox* (1813) 3 Camp 320 at 322, 170 ER 1397 at 1397.
2   [1977] AC 774 at 845–846.

3.64   A rule that provides that a constructive trust arises in this context is unlikely to cause any injustice to third parties. Rather, such a rule is likely to function in much the same way as subrogation does for indemnity insurers, allowing the party beneficially entitled to the proceeds of the action to control the litigation. As a result, the proceeds of the litigation are never likely to come into the hands of the party that is nominally the claimant and, consequently, problems of ostensible ownership should not arise.

3.65   Constructive trusts arising in favour of carers of tort victims over damages due from tortfeasors   Another example of such proprietary rights arises in relation to those who provide voluntary care to those who suffer accidents. A tort victim is entitled 'to recover as ... damages the reasonable value of services rendered to him gratuitously by a relative or friend in the provision of nursing care or domestic assistance of a kind rendered necessary by the injuries ... suffered'[1]. The rationale of this rule is to provide for the compensation of the voluntary caregiver, who is apparently not permitted to claim against the tortfeasor directly. In order to ensure that the carer is duly compensated, any damages recovered under this head are to be held by the victim on a trust for the carer[2].

1   *Hunt v Severs* [1994] 2 AC 350 at 355, per Lord Bridge.
2   *Cunningham v Harrison* [1973] QB 942; *Hunt v Severs* [1994] 2 AC 350 at 363, per Lord Bridge. In *Hunt*, the voluntary care had been rendered by the tortfeasor himself, and the court concluded that, to avoid any circuity, the tortfeasor's obligation to compensate the victim should be reduced to reflect the value of care provided. See Degeling 'Carers' Claims: Unjust Enrichment and Tort (Law Com no 262)' [2000] RLR 172.

CHAPTER 4

Tracing

Craig Rotherham

A   The nature of tracing

Tracing as a remedial process

4.1   Where an owner has not given legally effective consent to transfer title to his property, he may elect to assert rights to the proceeds of any exchange transaction involving that property. The process of asserting rights to such proceeds is known as tracing. It is often insisted that tracing is not a remedy but merely a neutral process of identification[1]. One reason tracing might not be thought of as a remedy, in the conventional sense, is that it is not the end of the matter for the claimant. Instead, tracing places claimants in a position to bring actions in respect of proceeds and it is through these actions that claimants ultimately obtain the remedies they are seeking. At common law tracing enables claimants to bring personal actions such as money had and received. In equity, a claimant may seek a personal remedy through actions such as knowing receipt or knowing assistance to obtain relief for interference with his proprietary rights. Alternatively, where a claimant's property or its proceeds remain identifiable in the defendant's hands, the claimant might seek a proprietary remedy such as a declaration of a constructive trust or an equitable lien.

1   *Boscawen v Bajwa* [1996] 1 WLR 328 at 334. For similar statements, see also *Jones & Sons (Trustee) v Jones* [1997] Ch 159 at 169–170, per Millett LJ; *Foskett v McKeown* [2001] 1 AC 102 at 128, per Lord Millett.

4.2   It is in this light that tracing tends to be characterised as a process whereby existing rights are transferred from one thing to another[1]. Understood in this way, tracing might properly be characterised as an intermediate remedy that allows a claimant the right to assert title to substitutes, and as a result to bring various claims. In this respect tracing may be compared with rescission, where claimants who ask that assets or documentary title be delivered up to them are exerting property rights that are analytically separate from, but contingent upon, the process of rescinding the underlying transaction. Structurally, tracing also bears a strong resemblance to subrogation. Both are methods of readjusting rights: subrogation allows claimants to assume the rights of another; whereas tracing allows claimants to assert rights they already enjoy over one thing in respect of something else. As with tracing, subrogation does not provide a final remedy in itself; for, claimants must still exercise the rights they have obtained. Yet, by contrast with tracing, we do not hesitate to refer to rescission and subrogation as remedies[2].

1   See for example Smith *Law of Tracing* (1997), p 3.
2   Indeed, this view recently received the endorsement of the House of Lords in *Banque Financière de La Cité v Parc (Battersea) Ltd* [1999] 1 AC 221 at 231, per Lord Hoffman. Similarly, in *Boscawen v*

Bajwa [1995] 4 All ER 769 at 777, after stating that tracing was not a remedial in nature, Millett LJ observed that subrogation was indeed a remedy.

A continuing property right, or a power in rem?

4.3   At what point does the claimant's interest in traceable assets arise? On one view, the owner has a fully-fledged title to traceable proceeds automatically from the moment of the exchange transaction in question. There is some judicial support for this perspective[1]. Such an understanding seems to be implicit in Millett LJ's analysis of tracing in *Boscawen v Bajwa*[2], where he explained that the 'claim is based on the *retention* by him of a beneficial interest in the property which the defendant handled or received'[3]. Equally, this understanding is apparent in Millett LJ's judgment in *Jones & Sons (Trustee) v Jones*[4]. In that case, the wife of a partner of a firm withdrew money from the firm's bank account, and invested it. Because the firm had, prior to the withdrawal, committed an act of bankruptcy, title to the firm's assets passed retrospectively to the trustee in bankruptcy by virtue of the doctrine of relation back. Millett LJ concluded that, because the firm's assets had vested in the trustee in bankruptcy, Mrs Jones at no time gained any title to the fruits of the investment[5].

1   *Cave v Cave* (1880) 15 Ch D 639; *Jones & Sons (Trustee) v Jones* [1997] Ch 159, [1996] 4 All ER 721.
2   [1995] 4 All ER 769.
3   [1995] 4 All ER 769 at 776 (emphasis added).
4   [1997] Ch 159.
5   [1997] Ch 159 at 167.

4.4   On the other hand, tracing is often described as a process involving an election between rights[1]. This is true of some of the most seminal tracing decisions. For example, in *Re Hallett's Estate*, Jessel MR observed that, 'If the sale was wrongful, you can take the proceeds of sale, in a sense adopting the sale for the purpose of taking the proceeds'[2]. More recently, in *Lipkin Gorman v Karpnale Ltd*[3], Lord Goff commented, 'Of course, tracing or following property into its product involves a decision by the owner of the original property to assert his title to the product in place of his original property'[4].

1   See Goode 'The Right to Trace in Commercial Transactions – II' (1976) 92 LQR 528 at 543.
2   (1880) 13 Ch D 696 at 708.
3   [1991] 2 AC 548.
4   [1991] 2 AC 548 at 573. Millett LJ quoted this dictum in the course of his judgment in *Jones v Jones* [1997] Ch 159 at 169. This is of course difficult to reconcile with his conclusion that the defendant never had legal title to the property in question.

4.5   The view that tracing involves an election between rights has much to recommend it. There are real difficulties with the notion that the rights generated by tracing are fully-fledged property rights that arise automatically. In particular, there is the problem of what has been termed the 'geometric multiplication of the plaintiff's property'[1]. An advantage of tracing claims is that they allow claimants a cause of action against more than one defendant. Claimants may assert their title against anyone holding the very assets that were taken from them. Alternatively, claimants may 'trace' their title into the exchange product of subsequent transactions. However, an owner cannot simultaneously have title to both the original thing and its exchange-proceeds. It follows from this that it cannot be plausibly argued that, prior to the claimant's exercise of this power of election, a full-blown proprietary interest arises in respect of the proceeds of sale held by the defendant. Prior to tracing, one holding traceable proceeds has a defeasible title to those proceeds – a title that is liable to be lost if the claimant elects to trace. The interest that arises automatically in the claimant's favour is an 'inchoate' property right, analogous to a 'mere equity' – rather like that enjoyed by one who has the power to elect to revest title by rescinding a transfer of property[2].

1   Birks *An Introduction to the Law of Restitution* (revised edn, 1989), pp 92 and 394.
2   This view was taken, for example, by Porter MR in *Re Ffrench's Estate* (1887) 21 LR Ir 283, the effect of this being that a subsequent purchaser of an equitable interest in the traceable proceeds was not bound by the equity.

Rights exercisable over traceable proceeds

4.6   While Sir Peter Millett has stated that, 'The effect of a successful tracing exercise is to confer on the parties the same rights and obligations *mutatis mutandis* in respect of the substituted asset as they ... had in the original asset'[1], this is not always so. For one thing, it is increasingly accepted that legal owners should be able to trace in equity[2]. If this is indeed possible, it is obvious that the interest in the proceeds is not the same as the interest enjoyed in the initial asset: for the right in the proceeds is limited to equitable ownership. The two interests vary in provenance: for it is well established that an absolute legal owner has no separate equitable interest because such interests arise only where the conscience of the legal owner is affected[3]. More importantly, the equitable interest conferred also differs in content from the legal interest that the owner previously enjoyed. Rather than being good against all the world, this interest is liable to be defeated by a bona fide third party purchaser for value.

1   Millett 'Restitution and Constructive Trusts' (1998) 114 LQR 399 at 409. On the other hand, in *Foskett v McKeown* [2001] 1 AC 102 at 128, Lord Millett was more tentative in suggesting that a claimant 'will normally be able to maintain the same claim to the substituted asset as he could have maintained to the original asset'.
2   *Westdeutsche Landesbank Girozentrale v Islington London Borough Council* [1996] AC 669 at 716, per Lord Browne-Wilkinson.
3   *Stamp Duties Comr (Queensland) v Livingston* [1965] AC 694 at 712, per Viscount Radcliffe; *DKLR Holdings Co (No 2) Pty Ltd v Stamp Duties Comr (NSW)* (1982) 149 CLR 431 at 463, per Aickin J; *Westdeutsche Landesbank Girozentrale v Islington London Borough Council* [1996] AC 669 at 706, per Lord Browne-Wilkinson.

4.7   Secondly, even in instances where the interest initially enjoyed by the claimant was an equitable one, it is difficult to conclude that, upon tracing, he has the same right that he had previously enjoyed. For the claimant who has successfully traced has the option of asserting a lien over the asset in question[1]. Where a claimant elects to claim a lien, his right to be compensated for a violation of an interest in one asset is secured by new rights over a second asset. Rather than transferring a right enjoyed in one object to another, the lien allows for the creation of a new property right, to secure a personal obligation to account arising from a violation of another property right.

1   *Re Hallett's Estate* (1880) 13 Ch D 696, [1874–1880] All ER Rep 793.

B   Tracing at Common Law

The notion of common law tracing

4.8   Tracing at common law has generally been assumed to be governed by principles that are different from those which apply in equity. This is largely based on an interpretation of *Taylor v Plumer*[1]. In that case, the defendant had given his broker money to buy Exchequer bills. The broker instead used the money to buy gold doubloons and securities for his own benefit, and then absconded. The defendant apprehended the broker, who then handed over the gold and securities. Subsequently, the assignee in bankruptcy of the broker sought to recover this property from the defendant. The Court held that the defendant could resist the assignee's claim, because the defendant had title to the property. Lord Ellenborough commented that:

> ... it should seem that if the property in its original state and form was covered with a trust in favour of the principal, no change of that state and form can divest it of such trust, or give the factor, or those who represent him in right, any more valid claim in respect to it, than they respectively had before such change[2].

The case came to be understood as establishing a right to trace at common law. Moreover, Lord Ellenborough's reference to property no longer being identifiable 'when turned into money and confounded in a mass of the same description' was thought to indicate that at common law it was not possible to trace proceeds after they had been deposited in a mixed fund. In fact, it has recently been established that the court was considering *equitable* rights[3]. Thus, while the understanding that common law and equity favoured different tracing rules is often attributed to Lord Ellenborough's judgment in *Taylor v Plumer*, this is a misconception. In fact, at the time *Taylor v Plumer* was decided, a doctrine of tracing had not been developed at common law.

1   (1815) 3 M & S 562, 105 ER 721.
2   (1815) 3 M & S 562 at 574, 105 ER 721 at 725.
3   Khurshid and Matthews 'Tracing Confusion' (1979) 95 LQR 78; Smith 'Tracing in *Taylor v Plumer*, Equity in the Court of King's Bench' [1995] Lloyd's Maritime and Commercial Law Quarterly 240. See below, para 4.12.

4.9   In *Jones & Sons (Trustee) v Jones*[1], Millett LJ recognised that *Taylor v Plumer* was not, as later courts had generally assumed, a case of common law tracing. However, he was understandably of the view that it was too late to question the availability of tracing at common law, given that it had been recognised by English appellate courts in cases such as *Banque Belge pour l'Etranger v Hambrouck*[2] and *Lipkin Gorman v Karpnale Ltd*[3]. In his view, this recognition of common law tracing could be best reconciled with the English doctrine of *stare decisis* by concluding that 'in recognising claims to substituted assets, equity must be taken to have followed the law, even though the law was not declared until later'[4]. While this would appear to be an unnecessarily convoluted way of explaining the matter, it is clear that common law tracing has been recognised for too long for it to be rejected now.

1   [1997] Ch 159.
2   [1921] 1 KB 321.
3   [1991] 2 AC 548.
4   [1997] Ch 159 at 169.

Common law claims in respect of traceable proceeds

4.10   Tracing is utilised to enable a claimant to bring an action in respect of the exchange product of his property. The type of action that may be brought will vary according to the nature of the assets in question, depending on whether the exchange product takes the form of land, money or other chattels. An important recent consideration of the principles governing common law claims to proceeds was provided by the House of Lords in *Lipkin Gorman v Karpnale Ltd*[1]. Cass, a partner in a firm of solicitors, withdrew money from his firm's client account and lost much of it gambling in the defendant's casino. The firm sought to hold the defendant liable for its receipt of the money. Authorities indicated that title to the money withdrawn passed to Cass, and that consequently an action for conversion was not available to the claimant[2]. However, their Lordships concluded that the title that passed to Cass was a qualified one[3]. In their view, the claimant could elect to trace from the chose in action represented by the bank's debt to it and into the money withdrawn from the client account. Lord Goff explained the unavailability of an action for conversion on the basis that a claimant could not by electing to trace turn the defendant into a wrongdoer[4]. Instead, the only action that was available at law was one for money had and received. This action is not, strictly speaking, proprietary. While the action will be available in some circumstances in which a claimant continues to enjoy title to the money received by the defendant, it will equally be available in some circumstances where title has passed to the defendant[5]. The action is premised on the defendant's receipt of money in circumstances in which the law imposes a personal right to repayment that we would now generally describe as restitutionary. One consequence of this is that the claimant's right is weakened, in that it is susceptible to the defence of change of position. This was apparent in *Lipkin Gorman* where the defendant was able to rely on the defence to reduce its liability to the net enrichment it had received from Cass, after taking into account winnings that Cass had collected from the casino[6].

1   [1991] 2 AC 548.
2   *Union Bank of Australia Ltd v McClintock & Co* [1922] 1 AC 240; *Commercial Banking Co of Sydney Ltd v Mann* [1961] AC 1.
3   [1991] 2 AC 548 at 573, per Lord Goff.
4   [1991] 2 AC 548 at 573, per Lord Goff.
5   For example, the action will be available to provide restitution where property has passed in the context of a non-fundamental mistake: *Barclays Bank Ltd v WJ Simms, Son and Cooke (Southern) Ltd* [1980] QB 677 at 689, per Robert Goff J.
6   For the defence of change of position, see below, para 21.37ff.

Tracing out of a mixed bank account

4.11   The supposed limitations of common law tracing emerge primarily where money is deposited in a bank account containing money belonging to others. The action for money had and received merely requires that the defendant has received the claimant's money; it is irrelevant whether that money remains identifiable in the defendant's hands[1]. Consequently, there is nothing to prevent a claimant bringing such an action against a defendant who deposited traceable proceeds in a mixed account. However, difficulties do arise if the claimant seeks to trace his money out of a mixed account and into the hands of another. In *Re Diplock*[2] Greene MR took the view that tracing at common law was not possible in these circumstances. He attributed this limitation to 'the materialistic approach of the common law' and contrasted this with the 'more metaphysical approach' favoured by equity[3]. The existence of this limitation was subsequently affirmed by the Court of Appeal in *Agip (Africa) Ltd v Jackson*[4].

1   *Lipkin Gorman v Karpnale* [1991] 2 AC 548 at 572, per Lord Goff.
2   [1948] Ch 465.
3   [1948] Ch 465 at 520.
4   [1991] Ch 547 at 566, per Fox LJ.

4.12   Ultimately, the notion that the common law takes a more rigid approach to tracing than does equity is attributable to a misunderstanding of *Taylor v Plumer*[1], where Lord Ellenborough remarked that:

> ... the product of or substitute for the original thing still follows the nature of the thing itself, as long as it can be ascertained to be such, and the right only ceases when the means of ascertainment fail, which is the case when the subject is turned into money, and mixed and confounded in a general mass of the same description[2].

Subsequently, this was taken to indicate the limitations of tracing at common law. However, as mentioned, in recognising the defendant's claim to the gold and securities, the Court was actually applying equitable principles[3]. Moreover, Lord Ellenborough's reference to the limits of tracing preceded the development of presumptions in *Clayton's case*[4] and *Re Hallett*[5] that would subsequently allow for the tracing of money after mixing. Thus, these remarks reflected the received wisdom of the time as to the limits of tracing in equity, and need to be considered in the light of subsequent developments[6].

1   (1815) 3 M & S 562, 105 ER 721.
2   (1815) 3 M & S 562 at 575, 105 ER 721 at 726.
3   See above, para 4.8.
4   (1816) 1 Mer 572, 35 ER 781.
5   (1880) 13 Ch D 696, [1874–1880] All ER Rep 793.
6   On the (rather broader) limits of equitable tracing, see below, para 4.24ff.

4.13   In any event, if it is thought that it should be possible for an owner to assert title to proceeds, it is surprising that an owner's ability to identify his property should be lost by mixing. For, there are well established rules that allow for the identification of fungible assets after they are 'confounded in a general mass of the same description'[1]. It is not clear why the matter should be thought to be so different where money is involved.

1   For an account, see Smith *Law of Tracing* (1997), pp 70–104.

Tracing through clearing systems

4.14   The perceived limitations of common law tracing have also been thought to preclude tracing through the clearing systems, by which there is a setting-off of credits and debits between banks so that payments are only made by one bank to another if there is a net liability. In *Agip (Africa) Ltd v Jackson*[1] the Court of Appeal accepted the conclusion of Millett J in the court below[2] that transfers made through the New York clearing system resulted in mixing that precluded tracing at common law[3].

1   [1991] Ch 547.
2   [1990] Ch 265 at 286.
3   [1991] Ch 547 at 566, per Fox LJ. See also *Bank Tejarat v Hong Kong and Shanghai Banking Corpn (CI) Ltd* [1995] 1 Lloyd's Rep 239 at 245, per Tuckey J.

4.15   The courts have not taken a consistent approach in their treatment of this issue. If they had, it is difficult to see how tracing would ever be possible where payments are made by cheques issued by one bank and deposited with another. In *Jones & Sons v Jones*[1] the Court of Appeal was willing to allow money to be traced from an account in one bank to an account in another via several cheques. As Millett LJ analysed the matter:

The trustee does not need to follow money from one recipient to another or follow it through the clearing system; he can follow the cheques as they pass from hand to hand[2].

Yet, analytically, the medium that A uses to ask a bank to credit the account of B should be irrelevant: it should make no difference whether payment is made by cheque or by electronic transfer. In either case the clearing system will come into play. Nonetheless, this should not matter. Ultimately, the claimant is seeking, not to trace money as it passes from one bank to another, but to trace from one chose in action to another. Where A instructs his bank to transfer funds to B's account at another bank, A's bank will ask B's bank to credit B's account, and will debit A's account. The chose in action thereafter owned by B is the product of the chose in action formerly owned by A. How the banks of A and B choose to settle their liabilities inter se is a completely different matter. We merely need to be concerned with the choses in action created, and not with any movement of money between the banks[3].

1   [1997] Ch 159.
2   [1997] Ch 159 at 169.
3   Smith *Law of Tracing* (1997), pp 252–255.

4.16   Another decision that has to be considered in this context is *R v Preddy*[1]. At issue was whether the defendant fraudsters, who had their bank accounts credited as a result of an electronic transfer, could be said to have obtained 'property belonging to another' for the purposes of the Theft Act 1968, s 15(1). Lord Goff concluded that in the process that involved the lender's account being debited and the borrower's account credited, the lender:

> ... does not obtain the lending institution's chose in action. On the contrary that chose in action is extinguished or reduced pro tanto, and a chose in action is brought into existence representing a debt in an equivalent sum owed by a different bank to the defendant or his solicitor. In these circumstances, it is difficult to see how the defendant thereby obtained *property belonging to another*, ie to the lending institution[2].

At first sight, it might seem difficult to reconcile this terse analysis with principles of common law tracing that provide for property rights in substitutes. However, it is arguably consistent with Lord Goff's own analysis of tracing in *Lipkin Gorman Ltd v Karpnale*[3]. The borrower did not receive the lender's property, but the proceeds of the lender's property. Even if the lender was entitled to assert its title to those proceeds, this does not alter the fact that those proceeds did not at belong to the lender at the point of receipt.

1   [1996] AC 815.
2   [1996] AC 815 at 834 (emphasis in original).
3   [1991] 2 AC 548, [1992] 4 All ER 512. See above, para 4.10.

The future of common law tracing

4.17   The courts have not always accepted that the common law has a set of tracing principles that are more limited than those found in equity. A different view is apparent in some of the judgments in *Banque Belge pour L'Etranger v Hambrouck*[1]. The defendant, Hambrouck, drew cheques on his employer's account with Banque Belge. He deposited these into his own account in a different bank. As Atkin LJ put it: 'In substance no other funds were paid into the account than the proceeds of these forged cheques'[2]. Hambrouck subsequently withdrew a sum of money and paid it into an account that his mistress had with a third bank. She was held to be liable to the bank for money had and received. Much attention has focused upon the view expressed emphatically by Atkin LJ, and more tentatively by Bankes LJ, that Banque Belge could have traced into Hambrouck's mistress's account even if there had been other money in Hambrouck's account. In Atkin LJ's view there was no reason why the principles of identification developed in equity in *Re Hallett's Estate* should not equally apply at common law[3].

1   [1921] 1 KB 321.
2   [1921] 1 KB 321 at 331.
3   [1921] 1 KB 321 at 335.

4.18   While in *Agip (Africa) Ltd v Jackson*, Fox LJ rejected Atkin LJ's view as contrary to the weight of precedent[1], it may yet be accepted. Thus, recently in *Foskett v McKeown*[2], Lord Millett observed obiter that: 'There is ... no sense in maintaining different rules for tracing at law and in equity'[3]. While the issue awaits an authoritative statement from the House of Lords, indications suggest that the supposed limitations on bringing common law claims in respect of proceeds will be case aside.

1   [1991] Ch 547 at 566.
2   [2001] 1 AC 102.
3   [2001] 1 AC 102 at 128; see also below, para 4.23.

C   Tracing in equity

Claims maintainable in respect of proceeds

4.19   As at common law, tracing will assist a claimant to obtain a remedy in equity only if he can demonstrate that the defendant has received property to which the claimant may elect to assert title. If this can be shown, the proper form of action will vary depending on whether the defendant has retained the assets in question. Where the defendant has retained the traceable proceeds of the claimant's assets, the claimant may seek a declaration that the defendant holds the assets in question on constructive trust. Alternatively, the claimant may elect to claim a lien over those assets to secure his personal right to have the defendant account for the value of the original assets[1]. If, in contrast, the defendant no longer retains traceable proceeds, the proper action is for knowing receipt, requiring the defendant to account for the property in question[2].

1   *Re Hallett's Estate* (1880) 13 Ch D 696, [1874–1880] All ER Rep 793.
2   See for example *El Ajou v Dollar Land Holdings plc* [1993] 3 All ER 717.

The need for a fiduciary relationship

4.20   There is a longstanding view in English law that the availability of tracing in equity 'depends on there having existed at some stage a fiduciary relationship of some kind ... sufficient to give rise to the equitable right of property'[1]. This view is largely the result of an interpretation of the House of Lords' decision in *Sinclair v Brougham*[2] by the Court of Appeal in *Re Diplock*[3]. There are, however, difficulties in this interpretation. First, it is difficult to distill majority support for such a view from the rather confusing judgments given in the House of Lords in *Sinclair v Brougham*. And, secondly, it is far from obvious why, on the facts of that case, the money that a company had borrowed ultra vires should be said to be held by the company in a fiduciary capacity for the borrowers. Nonetheless, this interpretation has been accepted as authoritative by the Court of Appeal in later cases[4]. Moreover, the House of Lords in *Westdeutsche Landesbank Girozentrale v Islington London Borough Council*[5], while overruling *Sinclair v Brougham* in other regards, did not choose to reject the fiduciary duty requirement[6].

1   *Re Diplock* [1948] Ch 465 at 540, per Greene MR.
2   [1914] AC 398, [1914–1915] All ER (Rep) 622.
3   [1948] Ch 465, [1948] 2 All ER 318.
4   See for example *Westdeutsche Landesbank Girozentrale v Islington London Borough Council* [1994] 4 All ER 890.
5   [1996] AC 669.
6   [1996] AC 669 at 714, per Lord Browne-Wilkinson.

4.21   The fiduciary relationship precondition provides that a right to trace arises in at least two situations. Firstly, and most obviously, where the property belongs in equity to the claimant and is misappropriated, equity will assist the claimant to trace the proceeds of that property into the hands of the fiduciary or third parties. It is not necessary for there to have been a fiduciary relationship between the claimant and a defendant who is a third party recipient of property, provided that the claimant and the party that misappropriated the property had such a relationship[1]. Secondly, a claimant will also be able to trace where property that was legally owned by the claimant is misappropriated by one who owed the claimant a fiduciary duty. Thus, a principal may trace where his agent disposes of his property without authority[2].

1   See for example *Re Diplock* [1948] Ch 465, [1948] 2 All ER 318.
2   *Re Hallett* (1880) 13 Ch D 696 at 710, per Jessel MR.

4.22   More controversial is the suggestion that in situations where there was no fiduciary relationship that pre-existed the transaction in question, such a relationship might arise as the result of the receipt of property to which the defendant cannot in good conscience claim beneficial title. First, it has been held that a constructive trust may arise in the context of a transaction in which legal title passes. This conclusion was reached in the controversial decision of *Chase Manhattan NA v Israel-British Bank (London) Ltd*[1], where the recipient of a mistaken double payment of a debt was said to be a constructive trustee. Similarly, it has been suggested that a resulting or constructive trust might arise and permit tracing where a claimant exercises a power to rescind a transaction[2]. Secondly, it is unclear whether a legal owner may trace the proceeds of his property and claim a constructive trust after that property is stolen. In *Westdeutsche Landesbank Girozentrale v Islington London Borough Council*[3], Lord Browne Wilkinson suggested that a legal owner would be able to claim a constructive trust against a thief[4]. Yet, it makes little sense to say that a constructive trust arises at the time of the theft. The victim of the theft retains his legal title, and the thief gains no interest in the asset in question. Thus, there is no separation of legal and equitable title, and it follows that, at this point, the thief cannot be a constructive trustee[5]. However, as the law stands, the victim is subsequently liable to lose his legal interest if the property in question or its proceeds is placed in a mixed bank account[6]. It may be that at this point the victim will be permitted to trace the proceeds of his legal property in equity and enforce a constructive trust[7].

1 [1981] Ch 105.
2 *El Ajou v Dollar Land Holdings plc* [1993] 3 All ER 717 at 734, per Millett J. See above, para 3.46, and below, para 5.31ff.
3 [1996] AC 669.
4 [1996] AC 669 at 716. A similar conclusion was reached by the Australian High Court in *Black v Freeman and Co* (1910) 12 CLR 105. While this view has been accepted in the United States since the decision in *Newton v Porter* 69 NY 133 (1877), that case is widely regarded as rejecting the requirement of a fiduciary relationship as a pre-requisite for tracing.
5 For a similar observation in a different context, see *Jones & Sons (Trustee) v Jones* [1997] Ch 159 at 167, per Millett LJ.
6 It should be noted however that the inability of the claimant to identify his money as a result of its being deposited in a mixed bank account would not prevent him from bringing an action for money had and received. Generally, equity's assistance would become crucial only if the claimant sought to trace out of the mixed account and into the hands of a third party.
7 A possibility which Lord Browne-Wilkinson recognised in *Westdeutsche Landesbank Girozentrale v Islington London Borough Council* [1996] AC 669 at 716.

4.23   Again, the issue as to whether a fiduciary relationship is a precondition for tracing in equity has assumed significance largely because of the perception that, while at common law it is not possible to trace after money is deposited in a mixed fund, equity is not so restricted. However, the tide appears to be turning against this perspective. Thus, in *Foskett v McKeown*[1], Lord Millett concluded that:

> There is certainly no logical justification for allowing any distinction between them [ie equitable and common law tracing principles] to produce capricious results in case of mixed-substitutions by insisting on the existence of a fiduciary relationship as a precondition for applying equity's tracing rules[2].

If, as is likely, the supposed restrictions on common law tracing comes to be rejected[3], the issue of the ability of a legal owner to trace in equity will probably cease to attract interest.

1 [2001] 1 AC 102.
2 [2001] 1 AC 102 at 128.
3 See above, para 4.17.

Tracing after mixing – equity's presumptions[1]

4.24   Where a trustee mixes trust property, or its traceable proceeds, with other assets, the question arises whether the identity of the property is lost. There is authority for the view that where a trustee mixes trust property or its traceable proceeds with his own property, so that it is no longer identifiable, the beneficiary can claim the entire mass[2]. However, while there was support for a similar approach at common law, this was rejected in *Indian Oil Corpn v Greenstone Shipping Co*[3], where a defendant had mixed a cargo of crude oil with their own oil. The court concluded that because it was possible to identify the amount of the claimant's oil that was mixed with that of the defendant's, the proper approach was to declare them to be tenants in common of the mixture[4]. In all likelihood, the drastic response of allowing a claimant exclusive ownership of a mixture would only be taken in cases where, as a result of the defendant's wrongdoing, it is impossible either to identify the quantity of the claimant's property mixed with that of the defendant or to separate the resultant mass[5]. Thus, when discussing the principles governing the identification of property in mixtures in *Foskett v McKeown*, Lord Millett concluded that the law 'does not ... exclude a pro rata division where this is appropriate as in the case of money and other fungibles like grain, oil or wine'[6]. It is in this light that we should interpret the remark of Sir William Page Wood VC in *Frith v Cartland*[7] that, 'if a man mixes trust funds with his own, the whole will be treated as the trust property, except so far as he may be able to distinguish what is his own'[8].

1   For a discussion of the area, see Smith *Law of Tracing* (1997), ch 2.
2   *Lupton v White* (1808) 15 Ves 432, 33 ER 817; *Sandeman & Sons v Tyzack and Branfoot Steamship Co Ltd* [1913] AC 680 at 695, per Lord Moulton.
3   [1988] QB 345.
4   [1988] QB 345 at 369, per Staughton J.
5   For a discussion, see *Foskett v McKeown* [2001] 1 AC 102 at 132, per Lord Millett (discussing a Canadian case, *Jones v De Marchant* (1916) 28 DLR 561).
6   [2001] 1 AC 102 at 132.
7   (1865) 2 H & M 417, 71 ER 525.
8   (1865) 2 Hem & M 417 at 420, 71 ER 525 at 526.

4.25   Consistently with this analysis, where a claimant's money is mixed in a bank account, equity treats the contributors as tenants in common of the chose in action represented by the bank's obligation to pay the sum credited to the defendant[1]. The claimant is entitled to an interest in the nature of a charge against the bank to enforce this right[2]. However, more difficult questions arise if money is thereafter withdrawn from a mixed bank account. One approach that the law could have taken is to hold that, following mixing, any money withdrawn should be treated as belonging to the tenants in common in proportion to their interest in the fund. However, equity has not generally favoured this approach, and has instead developed a series of presumptions that allow money withdrawn from a mixed bank account to be identified as belonging to only one of the tenants in common. Different presumptions apply depending upon whether the claimant's money has been mixed with the money of other innocent parties, or it has been mixed by a culpable trustee with the trustee's money alone.

1   *Re Tilley's Will Trusts* [1967] Ch 1179.
2   *Re Hallett's Estate* (1880) 13 Ch D 696 at 711.

CLAIMANTS' MONEY MIXED WITH THAT OF ONE OR MORE INNOCENT PARTIES

4.26   Different presumptions apply depending on whether or not the fund is held in a current account[1]. Where the money is in an unbroken deposit account, the parties share rateably in proportion to their contributions. In contrast, where money of two innocents is mixed in a current account, the 'first in, first out' rule developed in *Clayton's case*[2] applies. That is to say, the presumption is that money is withdrawn in the order in which it was deposited. This can be illustrated by an example whereby a trustee of two trust funds misappropriates £10,000 from Trust A, which he then deposits in a current account that he opened for the purpose, before depositing in the same account a further £5,000 misappropriated from Trust B. Thereafter, the trustee withdraws £10,000 from the account and dissipates it. The rule in *Clayton's case* dictates that the money withdrawn was the proceeds of the money misappropriated from Trust A. As a result, the beneficiaries of Trust B would be in a position to identify the £5,000 in the account as their own; while the beneficiaries of Trust A would be left to bring a personal claim against the trustee for the money misappropriated from them. This would, of course, leave the beneficiaries of Trust A vulnerable to the risk that the trustee might be insolvent.

1   *Cory Bros & Co Ltd v Turkish SS Mecca (Owners), The Mecca* [1897] AC 286 at 290, per Lord Halsbury LC.
2   (1816) 1 Mer 572, 35 ER 781.

4.27   The same rule applies if trust money is mixed with the money of an innocent volunteer. This is illustrated by *Re Diplock*[1], where the defendants were executors who had wrongly distributed a deceased's estate to various charities. The deceased's next of kin were permitted to bring a proprietary claim in respect of the traceable proceeds of the deceased's estate in the hands of the charities. While an innocent volunteer in this position can probably be properly described as a constructive trustee[2], the Court of Appeal indicated that 'the volunteer is innocent and cannot be said to act unconscionably if he claims equal treatment for himself'[3]. Thus, in attempting to identify the money withdrawn, the proper presumption to apply was the 'first in, first out' rule from *Clayton's case*, rather than the harsher presumption against errant trustees developed in *Re Hallett*[4].

1   [1948] Ch 465, [1948] 2 All ER 318.
2   Although some doubt is thrown on this by Lord Browne Wilkinson's suggestion that a constructive trust arises only where a recipient's conscience is affected: *Westdeutsche Landesbank Girozentrale v Islington London Borough Council* [1996] AC 669 at 705.
3   *Re Diplock* [1948] Ch 465 at 539.
4   (1880) 13 Ch D 696, [1874–1880] All ER Rep 793.

4.28   The 'first in, first out' rule has been widely criticised as arbitrary. In the view of Judge Learned Hand it 'apportions a common misfortune through a test which has no relation whatever to the justice of the case'[1]. Recently, the Court of Appeal considered the application of the rule in *Barlow Clowes International Ltd v Vaughan*[2], in the aftermath of the liquidation of an investment company that had misappropriated and dissipated much of the assets of two investment funds. The court considered alternative methods of attributing ownership in these circumstances. Some attention was paid to the 'North American solution', according to which a withdrawal from a mixed account is attributed to the parties in proportion to the extent of their interest in the account at the time of the particular withdrawal. In addition, the Court considered the 'pari passu ex post facto solution', whereby the remaining assets would simply be divided amongst those who had contributed to the fund at any point, in proportion to their contributions, without taking into account the timing of the particular contributions or withdrawals.

1   *Re Walter J Schmidt & Co* 298 F 314 at 316 (1923). While Learned Hand was disposed to reject the rule altogether, he acknowledged that precedent prevented this.
2   [1992] 4 All ER 22.

4.29   Not surprisingly, those who had invested their money at a relatively early stage objected to the application of the rule in *Clayton's case*. The Court of Appeal affirmed that 'decisions of this court ... establish and recognise a general rule of practice that *Clayton's case* is to be applied where several beneficiaries' moneys have been blended in one bank account and there is a deficiency'[1]. On the other hand, Lord Woolf indicated that 'the use of the rule is a matter of convenience and if its application in particular circumstances would be impracticable or result in injustice between the investors it will not be applied if there is a preferable alternative'[2]. He concluded that it was not appropriate to apply the presumption to the facts before him, because it would have been 'contrary to either the express or inferred or presumed intention of the investors'[3]. In his view, the fact that the claimants had invested into a common pool meant that it would have been contrary to their intention to apply the 'first in, first out' rule. The court took the view that, while the 'North American solution' had much to recommend it, it would have been impracticable to apply in the circumstances in question. Consequently, the court accepted that the proceeds of the investments should be divided pari passu among the investors, without regard to the timing of investments and withdrawals, subject only to 'lowest intermediate balance' rule established in *Roscoe v Winder*[4].

1   [1992] 4 All ER 22 at 33, per Dillon LJ.
2   [1992] 4 All ER 22 at 42, per Lord Woolf.
3   [1992] 4 All ER 22 at 42, per Lord Woolf. See also *Re British Red Cross Balkan Fund, British Red Cross Society v Johnson* [1914] 2 Ch 419, where Astbury J concluded that it would have been contrary to the intention of those contributing to a war relief fund to apply the rule in *Clayton's case* to determine ownership of surplus money.
4   [1915] 1 Ch 62. See below, para 4.34.

4.30   While the result in *Barlow Clowes* was probably the right one, the reasoning is not entirely convincing. It is implausible to suggest that investors have a particular intention as to how their property should be traced in the event of misappropriation. However, the resort to such fictional justifications is understandable, given the precedents that prevented the court rejecting the rule in *Clayton's case* outright.

CLAIMANTS' MONEY MIXED WITH THAT OF A CULPABLE TRUSTEE

4.31   The second crucial presumption that allows for tracing out of a mixed fund was developed in *Re Hallett's Estate*[1]. A solicitor wrongfully sold bonds that he was holding for a client, and paid the proceeds into his own current account. He later made withdrawals, but at the time of his death the account was in credit to a sum that exceeded the proceeds of the wrongfully sold stock. An application of the rule in *Clayton's case* would have meant that some of the traceable proceeds had been withdrawn and dissipated. However, Jessel MR held that, where a trustee mixes trust money with his own money, it is presumed prima facie that rather than dissipating trust moneys, he withdraws his own money first.

1   (1880) 13 Ch D 696, [1874–1880] All ER Rep 793.

4.32   The rule in *Re Hallett* is designed to ensure that the trustee bears any loss first. However, it is liable to work an injustice if money withdrawn earlier is wisely invested while money withdrawn subsequently is frittered away. This problem arose in *Re Oatway*[1]. There, a trustee had mixed £3,000 of trust money with £4,000 of his own. The money in the account was subsequently withdrawn and dissipated, apart from £2,137 that was used to purchase shares, later sold for £2,475. The claimant was allowed to trace into the money used to purchase the shares, and to claim an equitable lien over the proceeds of those shares to secure the trustee's obligation to account for the misappropriated money. Joyce J explained the result on the basis that, regardless of the order of withdrawals, the fiduciary should be debited with any withdrawals from a mixed bank account that were subsequently dissipated[2].

1   [1903] 2 Ch 356.
2   [1903] 2 Ch 356 at 360.

4.33   The presumption in *Re Hallett* is said to be premised on an assumption that trustees act honestly. Alternatively, both the rule in that case and that in *Re Oatway* can be explained on the basis that a wrongdoer's interest in a mixture will be subordinated to that of any innocent contributor[1]. The consequence of this approach is that an innocent contributor's claim will have to be satisfied before the wrongdoer is allowed to make any claim to a mixture or its proceeds.

1   Smith *Law of Tracing* (1997), pp 77–80.

THE LOWEST INTERMEDIATE BALANCE RULE

4.34   All presumptions providing for the attribution of ownership of money withdrawn from mixed funds are subject to what is known as the 'lowest intermediate balance' rule, established in *Roscoe v Winder*[1]. A claimant's share of a mixed fund is limited with reference to the lowest balance of that fund subsequent to the deposit of the claimant's money. The effect of the rule can be illustrated by the facts of *Roscoe v Winder*, where the defendant collected book debts of £455 that were due to the claimant. The defendant then wrongly put the money in his own account. Subsequently he made withdrawals from the account, until only £25 was left. Thereafter, he made deposits that meant that at his death the account was £358 in credit. While the claimant sought to trace into the £358, Sargant J held that it could identify only £25 of that balance as the proceeds of the book debts. In his view, 'when the drawings out had reached such an amount that the whole of [the trustee's] private money part had been exhausted, it necessarily followed that the rest of the drawings must have been against trust moneys'[2]. Given that at one stage there was only £25 'standing to the credit of the debtor's account, it is quite clear that on that day [the trustee] ... must have denuded his account of all the trust moneys there ... except to the extent of £25'[3]. While in *Roscoe v Winder*, the rule was being applied in the conjunction with the rule in *Re Hallett's Estate*, it applies equally to the rule in *Clayton's case* that is applied where the claimant's money is mixed with that of another innocent party.

1   [1915] 1 Ch 62.
2   [1915] 1 Ch 62 at 68.
3   [1915] 1 Ch 62 at 68.

A claimant's interest in property acquired with trust property

4.35   In *Re Hallett's Estate*[1], Jessel MR suggested that where a trustee purchased property using both trust money and his own money, the beneficiary would be limited to a lien over the property to secure the repayment of the trust money expended on it[2]. In contrast, in *Re Tilley's Will Trust*[3], Ungoed Thomas J took the view that the beneficiary was entitled to claim a share of the equitable ownership of the asset, in proportion to the extent to which trust money had contributed to its purchase[4].

1   (1880) 13 Ch D 696.
2   (1880) 13 Ch D 696 at 709.
3   [1967] Ch 1179.
4   [1967] Ch 1179 at 1189.

4.36   The latter view was preferred recently by the House of Lords in *Foskett v McKeown*[1], a case involving a claim by beneficiaries whose money had been used by a trustee to pay premiums on a life insurance policy. Their Lordships all agreed that, if the policy had been an ordinary life policy, such that the payment of the annual premiums was necessary to provide life cover for the following year, the beneficiaries would have been entitled to a pro rata share of the benefit payable on the assured's death[2]. In reaching this conclusion, Lord Millett rejected unequivocally the suggestion that the beneficiaries might be limited to a lien to secure the trustee's obligation to account for trust money spent on the premiums[3].

1   [2001] 1 AC 102.
2   While the majority explained this outcome in terms of tracing, the minority viewed it as a consequence of the trustee's obligation not to profit from his position.
3   [2001] 1 AC 102 at 131.

4.37   In fact, the policy in *Foskett v McKeown* was not a standard life cover policy. Premiums contributed to a notional savings element and, after the first year, life cover was maintained by 'internal premiums' whereby units previously allocated to the investment component of the policy were cancelled in return for the provision of life cover for the following year. Moreover, if premiums went unpaid, the life cover would be maintained, so long as there were sufficient units previously allocated to the investment element of the policy to fund the necessary internal premiums. On the facts of the case, even if the premiums paid for with trust money had not been met, the death benefit would have been unaffected. Lords Steyn and Hope thought that the lack of causation between the contributions and the death benefit ultimately payable indicated that the beneficiaries of the policy could not be said to have been enriched at the claimant's expense. In their view, this was fatal to the claimant's action for a beneficial share of the death benefit[1]. However, the majority argued that the payments of premiums to an existing life insurance policy were akin to the payment of money into a mixed bank account and gave the claimants a pro rata share of any entitlement arising under the policy. Those in the majority dismissed as irrelevant the lack of causation between the premiums in question and the level of death benefit payable. In their view, 'The transmission of a claimant's property rights from one asset to traceable proceeds is part of the law of property, not part of the law of unjust enrichment'[2].

1   [2001] 1 AC 102 at 114–115, per Lord Steyn, and 125, per Lord Hope.
2   [2001] 1 AC 102 at 127, per Lord Millett.

The need for identifiable assets

4.38   Considerable interest was generated by comments made obiter by Lord Templeman, in giving the advice of the Privy Council in *Space Investments Ltd v Canadian Imperial Bank of Commerce*[1], that suggested a very flexible approach to proprietary claims. He indicated that it would be appropriate to give beneficiaries of a trust a charge over all the assets of a defendant bank to secure their claim, if the bank had failed in its obligation to keep trust assets separate and not to use them for its own purposes. He justified this conclusion on the basis that, while other creditors of the bank 'voluntarily accept the risk that the trustee bank might become insolvent ... the settlor of the trust and the beneficiaries interested under the trust never accept any risks involved in the possible insolvency of the trustee bank'[2]. However, it is difficult to accept that this explanation alone can justify Lord Templeman's conclusion that:

> Where a bank trustee is insolvent, trust money wrongfully treated as being on deposit with a bank must be repaid in full so far as may be out of the assets of the bank in priority to any payment of customers' deposits and other unsecured debts[3].

It might be reasonable to characterise the beneficiaries as not having assumed the risks of the bank's insolvency. Nonetheless, the provision of such a priority could be justified only to the extent that it could be demonstrated that a trustee's estate has been enriched at the expense of the beneficiaries so that, without the charge, unsecured creditors would enjoy a greater dividend in the defendant's bankruptcy than they otherwise would. It is only this requirement that would provide a basis for distinguishing between aggrieved beneficiaries and other claimants, such as tort victims, who are also involuntary creditors[4].

1   [1986] 1 WLR 1072.
2   [1986] 1 WLR 1072 at 1074.
3   [1986] 1 WLR 1072 at 1074.
4   See above, para 3.21ff.

4.39   Subsequently, Lord Templeman's remarks in *Space Investments* have meet with little approval. The dictum was discussed in *Re Goldcorp Ltd*[1]. The customers of Goldcorp Ltd had made advance payments for gold, pursuant to contracts that did not provide for gold to be allocated to individual orders, but obliged the company to maintain adequate reserves of gold to meet all its orders. After the company failed to meet this obligation, the customers sought a proprietary interest over the assets of the company as a whole. Lord Mustill, who gave the Privy Council's advice, distinguished the facts before the Judicial Committee from those in *Space Investments* on the basis that in *Re Goldcorp* there never was an identifiable trust fund. However, more generally, the decision reaffirmed the identification of specific assets as a precondition for a proprietary claim. Similarly, in *Bishopsgate Investment Management Ltd v Homan*[2], the Court of Appeal affirmed the conventional view and declined to grant a lien over the assets of a company that had dissipated trust money by paying it into its own overdrawn bank account. Thus, even if a case arose with the same facts as the hypothetical example envisaged by Lord Templeman in *Space Investments*, it is unlikely that an English court would think it appropriate to grant an interest over property not identified as the proceeds of property initially owned by the claimant.

1   [1995] 1 AC 74. The case is discussed below, para 9.3.
2   [1995] Ch 211.

Tracing into already acquired assets – 'backwards tracing'

4.40   A considerable amount of attention has been focused recently on the question of 'backwards' tracing or tracing into the 'proceeds of debt'[1]. Where a claimant's money is paid into an overdrawn bank account, the question arises whether the claimant may trace into the prior withdrawal that had put the account into overdraft and to any assets acquired with the money withdrawn. Similarly, if a defendant acquires assets on credit, and subsequently a claimant's money is used to discharge that debt, the question again arises whether those assets represent the traceable proceeds of the claimant's money.

1   See for example Smith 'Tracing into the Payment of a Debt' [1995] CLJ 290.

4.41   The possibility of 'backwards tracing' was apparently rejected in *Re Diplock*[1], where charities had used money wrongly paid to them to pay debts. Similarly, in *Bishopsgate Investment Management v Homan*[2], Leggatt LJ took the view that the payment of claimants' money into an overdrawn account would prevent any possibility of a tracing claim. Equally, he argued that 'there can be no equitable remedy against an asset acquired before misappropriation of money takes place, since ex hypothesi it cannot be followed into something which existed and so had been acquired before the money was received and therefore without its aid'[3].

1 [1948] Ch 465, [1948] 2 All ER 318.
2 [1995] Ch 211.
3 [1995] Ch 211 at 221.

4.42 In contrast with the conventional view, Dillon LJ in *Bishopsgate Investment Management* suggested that a claimant might trace after his money was paid into an overdrawn account or used to discharge a debt. Dillon LJ concurred with the statement of Vinelott J in the court below that this should be possible where 'there was an inference that when the borrowing was incurred it was the intention that it should be repaid by misappropriations of [the claimant's] money'[1]. Similarly, in *Foskett v McKeown*[2], while his colleagues in the Court of Appeal disagreed, Scott VC thought that it was still an open question as to whether it was possible to trace assets acquired from money withdrawn from an overdrawn bank account. He argued that: 'The availability of equitable remedies ought ... to depend upon the substance of the transaction in question and not upon the strict order in which associated events happen'[3]. On the other hand, Scott VC's obiter dictum suggests that 'backwards tracing' might be available only in rather limited circumstances. Thus, he remarked:

> ... I do not regard the fact that an asset is paid for out of borrowed money with the borrowing subsequently repaid out of trust money as being necessarily fatal to an equitable tracing claim by the trust beneficiaries. If, in such a case, it can be shown that it was always the intention to use the trust money to acquire the asset, I do not see why the order in which the events happen should be regarded as critical to the claim[4].

Thus, on this analysis, the availability of 'backwards tracing' might be dependent upon the defendant's intentions. Quite what would be required as sufficient evidence to justify drawing the necessary inference is unclear. Presumably it will relatively seldom be the case that a defendant would have formed a clear view at the time that he incurred a debt that he would subsequently discharge that debt using trust moneys.

1 [1995] Ch 211 at 216.
2 [1998] Ch 265.
3 [1998] Ch 265 at 283.
4 [1998] Ch 265 at 283–284.

4.43 As long as orthodoxy is against 'backwards tracing', it is obviously crucial to identify what amounts to an already acquired asset. While subrogation may provide a similar remedy in some circumstances[1], it is not possible to trace money used to discharge a mortgage into the property secured. A similar issue arises in relation to the proceeds of life insurance policies. In *Foskett v McKeown*[2] a majority in the Court of Appeal and a minority in the House of Lords took the view that the use of the claimants' money to pay premiums 'did not "buy" any part of the death benefit'[3]. The majority of their Lordships disagreed, maintaining that the payments of the premium were more akin to a payment into a mixed bank account than money used to maintain an already acquired asset[4].

1 See for example *Boscawen v Bajwa* [1995] 4 All ER 769, [1996] 1 WLR 328; discussed below, para 8.43.
2 [2001] 1 AC 102.
3 [2001] 1 AC 102 at 114, per Lord Steyn. See also at 118, per Lord Hope. For the Court of Appeal judgments see [1998] Ch 265 at 289, per Hobhouse LJ, and at 296, per Morritt LJ.
4 [2001] 1 AC 102 especially at 110, per Lord Browne-Wilkinson.

Defences to proprietary claims in respect of traceable proceeds

4.44   It is well established that, like all equitable proprietary rights, those rights contingent upon tracing are liable to be defeated by a bona fide purchaser for value without notice[1].

1   See below, para 21.3ff.

4.45   What is less clear is the extent to which proprietary rights arising from tracing are subject to the change of position defence[1]. A good deal of attention has been focused on the Court of Appeal's decision in *Re Diplock*[2]. One of the innocent volunteers who received money from the Diplock estate was a hospital that had used the money to build a new ward. The court took the view that it would have been inequitable to give the claimant a lien over the hospital's land to secure its personal claim against the hospital. This has been viewed as akin to an application of the change of position defence[3]. This raises some interesting questions. One of the concerns that the court had was that it was unclear to what extent the improvements in question had actually increased the value of the hospital. This points to a difficulty in tracing in these circumstances; for the traceable proceeds of an investment in property will be the increase in value generated. If no increase can be identified, tracing simply is not possible and a proprietary remedy is out of the question. Thus, the issue should be whether the innocent volunteer should be entitled to plead a change of position to escape personal liability. If, on the other hand, there is an identifiable increase in value of the asset at issue, the question that arises is why the defendant should be regarded as having changed his position in a manner that would render a proprietary claim inequitable. The concern expressed in *Re Diplock* was that innocent volunteers should not be placed in the position where they might be forced to sell the assets in question[4].

1   See below, para 21.58ff.
2   [1948] Ch 465, [1948] 2 All ER 318. On another aspect of the case see above, para 4.27.
3   See for example Goff and Jones *Law of Restitution* (5th edn, 1998), p 110; *Boscawen v Bajwa* [1995] 4 All ER 769 at 782, per Millett LJ.
4   [1948] Ch 465 at 546. See Virgo *Principles of the Law of Restitution* (1999), p 729.

4.46   In *Re Diplock*, the effect of the decision not to grant the claimant a lien did not affect the defendant's personal liability. What is not clear is whether an innocent volunteer who has spent money on improving his property can be said to have changed his position sufficiently to excuse him from any obligation to make restitution altogether. It may seem unfair to require one who has spent money he has received in good faith to find the money to make restitution. Yet it might be thought equally unsatisfactory to allow such a defendant to make no restitution for the extent to which he has increased the value of his property.

4.47   The question of whether a defendant should be able to rely on the change of position defence to excuse him of proprietary and possibly even personal liability might be thought to depend on whether the defendant has sufficient assets to meet the liability in question. While on the facts in *Re Diplock*, it might have been reasonable to deny the claimant a lien, would it have been appropriate to deny this remedy if the defendant had had adequate liquid assets to obviate any danger that it might be forced to sell the property charged[1]? Perhaps the availability of such assets should merely go to the question of whether the expenditure in question was made in reliance on the receipt of the enrichment at issue. While it might be tempting to take the view that the application of the change of position defence should be moulded according to the facts, it would be difficult to reconcile such an approach with the judicial hostility toward discretion in the provision of proprietary remedies[2].

1   Goff and Jones *Law of Restitution* (5th edn, 1998), p 111.
2   See above, para 3.33.

4.48   Finally, the view that the change of position defence should apply to proprietary claims is at odds with the view expressed by the House of Lords in *Foskett v McKeown*[1] that tracing claims are about property rights and not unjust enrichment[2]. Given that the availability of the change of position defence was justified in terms of unjust enrichment in *Lipkin Gorman*[3], it is difficult to see how it could have any application to actions that are seen to have nothing to do with this rationale. Indeed, in his judgment in *Foskett v McKeown*, Lord Millett indicated that the only defence to a proprietary claim brought in respect of traceable proceeds would be that of bona fide purchase[4].

1   [2001] 1 AC 102.
2   [2001] 1 AC 102 at 108 and 109, per Lord Browne-Wilkinson, 115, per Lord Hoffmann, 127 and 129, per Lord Millett.
3   [1991] 2 AC 548.
4   [2001] 1 AC 102 at 129.

4.49   On the other hand, in recognising the change of position defence as part of English law in *Lipkin Gorman*, Lord Goff expressed the hope that its introduction might lead to 'a more consistent approach to tracing claims, in which common defences are recognised as available to such claims, whether advanced at law or in equity'[1]. Moreover, in *Boscawen v Bajwa*[2], Millett LJ, as he was then, discussed the change of position defence in terms that suggested that the defence would be generally available in the context of claims contingent on tracing[3].

1   [1991] 2 AC 548 at 581.
2   [1995] 4 All ER 769.
3   [1995] 4 All ER 769 at 776–777.

4.50   The better view is that the dichotomy drawn by the majority of the House of Lords in *Foskett v McKeown* is misconceived. We allow property rights to be extended by tracing in large part because of considerations of unjust enrichment, and it would be surprising if the factors that underlie the change of position defence were not equally relevant in this context.

CHAPTER 5

Assistance in a Breach of Trust and Receipt of Trust Property

Margaret Halliwell

A Introduction

5.1   The liability of third parties, usually referred to in this context as strangers, who become involved in a breach of trust either by knowingly receiving money obtained by breach of trust or by dishonestly assisting in such a breach, is not easily encompassed within the law of restitution. Although a recipient found to be liable would be compelled to effect restitution to a defrauded owner, it is difficult to describe an assistor's liability in terms of restitution, because the assistor never receives the property of the defrauded owner and, therefore, has nothing to restore. The liability of the assistor is to compensate for the loss. Nevertheless, the two forms of liability are inextricably intertwined, both in the factual circumstances of cases and in the judicial and extra-judicial debate as to the basis of liability under both heads.

5.2   It is not uncommon for both forms of liability to be alleged against the same person. Although the origin of both forms of liability lies and still operates within the realm of the express trust, allegations of liability in the context of a constructive trust, arising as a result of commercial fraud, have dominated recent litigation. It is in this latter category of constructive trust, in particular, that the basis of liability under both heads has caused profound judicial agreement. It is perhaps merely coincidental that the clearest statements of principle appear to be found in the context of express trusts where, for example, the seminal authority on dishonest assistance, albeit a case of Privy Council advice, is now *Royal Brunei Airlines Sdn Bnd v Tan Philip Kok Ming*[1]. As will be seen later in the chapter[2], this authority has recently been fully endorsed by the House of Lords.

1 [1995] 2 AC 378.
2 See below, paras 5.43–5.47.

5.3   In *Royal Brunei Airlines* Lord Nicholls of Birkenhead delivered the opinion of the Privy Council. Yet even this impressive enunciation of the correct basis of liability has been subject to further interpretation and refinement. As yet, there has been no authoritative resolution of the ingredients of liability for receipt. As Nourse LJ recently remarked in *Bank of Credit and Commerce International (Overseas) Ltd v Akindele*:

> With the proliferation in the last 20 years or so of cases in which the misapplied assets of companies have come into the hands of third parties, there has been a sustained judicial and extra-judicial debate as to the knowledge on the part of the recipient which is required in order to found liability in knowing receipt[1].

Nourse LJ undertook a thorough review of the receipt cases, and it is necessary to do so in order to examine the problems that have, historically, bedevilled the courts, before determining the current state of affairs. This will be examined below[2].

1   [2000] 4 All ER 221 at 231.
2   See below, para 5.49ff.

B   Assistance in a breach of trust

Royal Brunei Airlines – The first comprehensive review of the law

5.4   The first comprehensive review of dishonest assistance cases occurred in the *Royal Brunei Airlines* case[1]. Lord Nicholls, in delivering the advice of the Privy Council in *Royal Brunei Airlines*, was clearly of the opinion that the existing judicial debate stemmed from lack of analysis of underlying concepts. He considered a notable exception to this to be the judgment of Thomas J in the New Zealand case of *Powell v Thompson*[2]. Thomas J had based his decision on the principle of unconscionability:

> Once a breach of trust has been committed, the commission of which has involved a third party, the question which arises is one as between the beneficiary and that third party. If the third party's conduct has been unconscionable, then irrespective of the degree of impropriety in the trustee's conduct, the third party is liable to be held accountable to the beneficiary as if he or she were a trustee[3].

The Privy Council in *Royal Brunei Airlines* (correctly in my opinion, as will be explained[4]), did not rely on unconscionability in determining the issue of liability of an assistor or procurer to a breach of trust. The issue of unconscionability has, however, as a result of the decision in *BCCI International (Overseas) Ltd v Akindele*, now become critical to the knowing receipt head of liability. That decision and its implications are discussed at length later in the chapter[5].

1   [1995] 2 AC 378.
2   [1991] 1 NZLR 597.
3   [1991] 1 NZLR 597 at 613.
4   See below, para 5.26ff.
5   See especially below, para 5.52.

The authorities before Royal Brunei Airlines

5.5   In *Royal Brunei Airlines*, Lord Nicholls observed that the proper role of equity in commercial transactions is a topical question. In the context of the pre-existing case law, his Lordship identified a number of reasons which accounted for the unsatisfactory state of the law. He concluded that, fundamentally, the difficulties stemmed from the courts' failure to examine the underlying reason as to why a third party who has received no trust property should be made liable at all.

5.6   Lord Nicholls identified this process as having occurred since the decision in *Selangor United Rubber Estates v Cradock (No 3)*[1] highlighted the potential uses of equitable remedies in connection with misapplied company funds. In that case, the claimant company was seeking to recover the monies misapplied by its directors in financing the purchase of its own shares. There were two circular cheque transactions, each involving a different bank. The allegation against the bank in the first transaction, the District Bank, was that it paid out monies of the claimant's in circumstances in which it ought to have known that the payment was to finance a purchase of the claimant's shares. It was not alleged that the bank was under a duty to inquire. It was held that, even though the officials of the bank did not realise that the payment was being made for the purpose of purchasing the claimant's own shares, a reasonable banker, knowing what the District Bank did know, would have known that was the purpose. Accordingly, the Bank was held liable as a constructive trustee. Ungoed-Thomas J, holding the bank liable for knowing assistance in the fraudulent breach of trust, said:

> The knowledge required to hold a stranger liable as constructive trustee in a dishonest and fraudulent design, is knowledge of circumstances which would indicate to an honest, reasonable man that such a design was being committed or would put him on inquiry, which the stranger failed to make, whether it was being committed[2].

1   [1968] 1 WLR 1555.
2   [1968] 1 WLR 1555 at 1590.

5.7   Rather than addressing the fundamental question, Lord Nicholls concluded that, after that decision, there had been a tendency to cite and interpret Lord Selborne's formulation of liability in *Barnes v Addy*[1] as though it were a statute. In so doing the courts had wrestled with interpretation of the individual ingredients of liability, especially 'knowingly'.

In *Barnes v Addy* a solicitor, who took the precaution of obtaining a deed of indemnity because of the doubtful appointment of a sole trustee, was held not to be liable in respect of the subsequent breach of trust by that trustee. Lord Selborne emphasised that a third party should not be liable if he acts honestly and without fraud. James LJ gave a very clear warning in the case:

> I have long thought, and more than once expressed my opinion from this seat, that this Court has in some cases gone to the very verge of justice in making good to the *cestuis que trust* the consequences of the breaches of trust of their trustees at the expense of persons perfectly honest, but who have been in some more or less degree, injudicious. I do not think it is for the good of *cestuis que trust*, or the good of the world, that those cases should be extended[2].

1   (1874) 9 Ch App 244.
2   (1874) 9 Ch App 244 at 255–256.

5.8   Lord Selborne's formulation of liability was:

> ... responsibility may no doubt be extended in equity to others who are not properly trustees, if they are found ... actually participating in any fraudulent conduct of the trustee to the injury of the *cestui que trust*. But, on the other hand, strangers are not to be made constructive trustees merely because they act as the agents of trustees in transactions within their legal powers, transactions, perhaps of which a Court of Equity may disapprove, unless those agents receive and become chargeable with some part of the trust property, or unless they assist with knowledge in a dishonest and fraudulent design on the part of the trustees[1].

1   (1874) 9 Ch App 244 at 251–252.

5.9   Liability was, subsequently, catch-phrased into two categories, viz 'knowing receipt' and 'knowing assistance'. Although the categories of liability applied in the context of an express trust, as a direct result of the proliferation of commercial fraud a variety of factual scenarios have been subsequently forced to fit into one category or the other. Moreover, as Harpum points out, principles relevant to one category have been indiscriminately applied to cases belonging to the other category[1]. Concentration on the individual ingredient of knowledge has proved to be particularly unhelpful.

1   Harpum 'The Stranger As Constructive Trustee' (1986) 102 LQR 114 at 162.

5.10   *Baden Delvaux and Lecuit v Société General pour Favoriser le Développment du Commerce et de l'Industrie en France SA*[1] demonstrates the concentration of the courts on this individual ingredient of liability, at the expense of recourse to the underlying principles behind the two forms of liability. The case is one of a series of High Court decisions[2] which borrowed principles from cases of knowing receipt, and applied them to cases of assistance. The claimant liquidator argued that the defendant was liable to account as constructive trustee for over $4,000,000 of IOS Fund Money. The Fund Money was held in an account designated as a trust account by its customer, a Bahamian bank, BCB. BCB ordered the transfer of the monies to an account, not designated as a trust account, with a Panamanian bank. The monies were then dissipated. The defendant had relied on a Bahamian court order apparently releasing the monies from the trust, but the order had been obtained by fraud. It was alleged that in all the circumstances the defendant ought to have known the monies were still trust monies.

1   (1982) [1993] 1 WLR 509n.
2   *Selangor United Rubber Estates v Cradock (No 3)* [1968] 1 WLR 1555; *Karak Rubber Co Ltd v Burden (No 2)* [1972] 1 All ER 1210; *Rowlandson v National Westminster Bank* [1978] 3 All ER 370.

5.11   Peter Gibson J categorised five mental states that would constitute the knowledge necessary to fix the stranger with liability for knowing assistance, as follows:

  (i)   actual knowledge;
 (ii)   wilfully shutting one's eye to the obvious;
(iii)   wilfully and recklessly failing to make such inquiries as an honest and reasonable man would make;
(iv)   knowledge of circumstances which would indicate the facts to an honest and reasonable man; and
 (v)   knowledge of circumstances which would put an honest and reasonable man on inquiry[1].

Clearly (i)–(iii) involve a want of probity, being party or privy to the dishonesty in actually knowing of the dishonest breach or of turning a blind eye to it (the latter often referred to as 'Nelsonian knowledge'). If you wilfully turn a blind eye to some factor then you are clearly aware of that factor. Categories (iv) and (v), however, confuse the issue of participation in dishonesty with mere negligence, in the sense of failing to make inquiries.

1   (1982) [1993] 1 WLR 509n at 575–576.

5.12   Peter Gibson J went on to describe four essential elements of knowing assistance as: a trust or other fiduciary relationship; a dishonest design on the trustee's part; assistance by the stranger in that design; and the stranger's knowledge. He went on to say, somewhat inconsistently, that the court must be satisfied that the alleged constructive trustee was a party or privy to dishonesty on the part of the trustee. The defendant was held not to be liable. Following this, even before the decision in *Royal Brunei Airlines*, there was some dissatisfaction with concentration on the individual ingredients of liability, especially knowledge.

5.13   Millett J warned in *Agip (Africa) Ltd v Jackson*[1] against over-refinement of 'knowledge'. In that case the claimant company was systematically defrauded of millions of US dollars over a period of time by its chief accountant, a Mr Zdiri. He achieved this fraud by altering the name of a payee on a payment order after it had been signed by the authorised signatory, and thereby diverted the payment to a recipient of his own choosing. The payees were all companies registered in England, and managed by the defendants from the Isle of Man. At first instance, the defendants were held liable on the grounds of knowing assistance. Millett J, in warning against over-refinement of the concept of 'knowledge', emphasised that knowing assistance cases are concerned with the furtherance of fraud. He perceived the necessary distinction to be between honest and dishonest conduct. The Court of Appeal dismissed an appeal against Millett J's finding of liability[2]. Unfortunately, in the judgment delivered by Fox LJ, the degree of knowledge as described by Ungoed-Thomas J in *Selangor United Rubber Estates v Cradock (No 3)*[3] was adopted. Fox LJ also accepted the formulation of Peter Gibson J in the *Baden Delvaux* case[4]; although he noted that it was merely an explanation of the general principle, and was not necessarily comprehensive.

1   [1990] Ch 265.
2   [1991] Ch 547.
3   [1968] 1 WLR 1555.
4   (1982) [1993] 1 WLR 509n; see above, para 5.11.

5.14   A further problem stemming from concentration on knowledge is that it has resulted in the importation of constructive notice in commercial transactions. In determining whether a defence of bona fide purchase succeeds in receipt cases, this was inevitable. There would be an anomaly if the burden of diligence which is placed on the bona fide purchaser was not similarly placed on the recipient of trust property. The problem, however, is to what extent the doctrine of notice should correspond to the duty to make inquiries associated with land transactions. In the *Baden Delvaux* case, Peter Gibson J referred to the case of *Carl Zeiss Stiftung v Herbert Smith & Co (No 2)*[1]. In that case, there was a dispute between the Carl Zeiss company of Jena ('the East German Foundation') and the Carl Zeiss company of Würtemberg ('the West German foundation'). In the main action, the East German foundation claimed that the assets of the West German foundation, including its property in England, were held by that foundation in trust for the East German foundation. The East German foundation later issued a writ against the current and former solicitors of the West German foundation, claiming that when they were put in funds by their client, they had notice, via the East German foundation's pleadings in the main action and from other material, that such money belonged to the East German foundation, and it was said that the solicitors were accountable accordingly. This submission failed, on the basis that the solicitors only had knowledge of a *disputed claim* that the assets of the West German foundation were trust property; they did not have knowledge that such assets were in fact trust property. Obiter, Sachs LJ said ' ... negligent, if innocent, failure to make inquiry is not sufficient to attract constructive trusteeship'. An element of 'dishonesty or consciously acting improperly' is required, which would entail the stranger having 'actual knowledge' of, or 'wilfully shutting his eyes' to, the breach of trust[2]. Peter Gibson

J suggested that Sachs LJ had been wrong to imply that inquiries are inappropriate unless dealing with land.

1   [1969] 2 Ch 276.
2   [1969] 2 Ch 276 at 298.

5.15   This issue remains under debate under the knowing receipt head of liability[1] but, in the context of the liability of a third party who has merely been an accessory to a breach of trust by a fiduciary, the guidance given by Lord Nicholls in *Royal Brunei Airlines* has done much to alleviate the confusion created by the emphasis on knowledge and notice.

1   See below, para 5.50 et seq.

The Royal Brunei Airlines decision

5.16   *Royal Brunei Airlines* came before Lords Goff, Ackner, Nicholls, Steyn and Sir John May[1]. Given that this was the first time in many years that the issue had come before the Law Lords, Lord Nicholls laudably attempted to present a resolution of the conflicting views of liability on the basis of rejecting semantic analysis of individual ingredients of liability. Rather, as above, the judgment concerns itself with analysis of the underlying concept of accessory liability. By addressing this fundamental question of principle, the Privy Council was able to conclude that liability should exist when a third party has acted dishonestly in assisting or procuring a fiduciary to commit a breach of trust. This major development was achieved in the context of the breach of an express trust.

1   [1995] 2 AC 378, PC.

5.17   Royal Brunei Airlines, the claimant, sought to recover B$335,160 from Mr Tan on the basis that he had assisted a company, Borneo Leisure Travel Sdn Bnd, in a breach of trust. The company was a travel agent, which, under an agreement with the airline, was a trustee for the airline for the money it received from the sale of passenger and cargo transportation by the airline. Mr Tan was the managing director and principal shareholder in the company, but he was not a party to the trust agreement between the company and the airline. Mr Tan authorised the use of the trust money by the company for its ordinary business purposes. The Court of Appeal of Brunei Darussalam reached the conclusion that, because the trustee company had not been dishonest in the handling of the trust funds in breach of trust, Mr Tan was not liable. This doubtful conclusion was based on citation, interpretation and application of Lord Selborne's formulation of liability in *Barnes v Addy*[1]. Before the Privy Council, the claimant relied upon the knowing assistance head of liability, and the particular point in issue before the Privy Council arose from the expression 'a dishonest and fraudulent design on the part of the trustees'.

1   (1874) 9 Ch App 244; on which see above, para 5.7.

5.18   Lord Nicholls' criticism of the earlier approach of the courts is undoubtedly correct; and it is in this sense, of reducing the issue of liability to a linguistic and semantic exercise, that Lord Selborne's convenient shorthand catch-phrasing has had unfortunate effects. Moreover, as Lord Nicholls pointed out, different considerations apply to the two heads of liability, whereas the distinction has been blurred by the inadequacy of attention paid to underlying principle. Millett J had reached this conclusion in the earlier case of *Agip (Africa) Ltd v Jackson*:

The basis of liability in the two types of cases is quite different; there is no reason why the degree of knowledge required should be the same, and good reason why it should not. Tracing claims and cases of 'knowing receipt' are both concerned with rights of priority in relation to property taken by a legal owner for his own benefit; cases of 'knowing assistance' are concerned with the furtherance of fraud[1].

The Privy Council had no difficulty in concluding that Mr Tan was liable even though the company had not acted with a fraudulent and dishonest design. Mr Tan's conduct had been dishonest, and it made no difference that misapplied funds were not confined to his personal gain. More importantly, according to Lord Nicholls, the trustee's state of mind is irrelevant to the question whether the third party should be made liable to the beneficiaries for the breach of trust. Lord Nicholls emphasised that the issue concerned, for want of a better compendious description, the liability of an 'accessory' to a trustee's breach of trust. He emphasised that the test of liability applied should be the same if, instead of procuring the breach, the third party dishonestly assisted in the breach, and he gave practical illustrations of both situations[2]. As Nolan points out[3], to distinguish between cases by distinguishing between 'assistance' and 'procurement' is neither practicable nor justifiable. The critical issue is that there is no difference in culpability. Liability ought not to resolve around the manner of the third party's involvement in the breach, but on the nature of the involvement.

On the fundamental issue of whether accessory liability should be restricted to circumstances when the breach has been made fraudulently by the trustees, Lord Nicholls' response was an unequivocal 'No':

> The alternative view would mean that a dishonest third party is liable if the trustee is dishonest, but if the trustee did not act dishonestly that of itself would excuse a dishonest third party from liability[4].

1   [1990] Ch 265 at 292–293.
2   [1995] 2 AC 378 at 384–385.
3   Nolan 'From Knowing Assistance To Dishonest Facilitation' [1995] CLJ 505.
4   [1995] 2 AC 378 at 385.

5.19   Lord Nicholls examined precedent by way of three cases to support his proposition, *Fyler v Fyler*[1], *A-G v Leicester Corpn*[2], and *Eaves v Hickson*[3]. Of these, the latter is the strongest case, because trustees, acting in good faith, paid over to William Knibb's adult children on the strength of a forged marriage certificate produced to them by William Knibb. Sir John Romilly MR held that William Knibb was liable to replace the fund, to the extent that it was not recovered from his children, and to do so in priority to the undoubted liability of the trustees. Far from this being a case of fraud by the trustees, the Master of the Rolls described it as a very hard case on the trustees, who were deceived by a forgery which would have deceived anyone who was not looking out for forgery or fraud.

1   (1841) 3 Beav 550, 49 ER 216.
2   (1844) 7 Beav 176, 49 ER 1031.
3   (1861) 30 Beav 136, 54 ER 840.

5.20   Similarly, Mr Tan's conduct had been dishonest, and it made no difference that misapplied funds were not confined to personal gain. It was, therefore, plainly unnecessary to establish any dishonest breach of trust by BLT. Lord Nicholls was clearly of the opinion that this could, in any event, be established under the 'directing mind and will' doctrine[1]. Mr Tan *was* the company, and his state of mind could, therefore, be imputed to BLT. The 'directing mind and will' doctrine exposes companies to considerable risk, as was evidenced by the Court of Appeal decision in *El Ajou v Dollar Land Holdings plc*[2]. Although that case concerned the knowing receipt category of third party liability for breach of trust, the trend of recent cases has shown that the 'directing mind and will' theory has added another weapon to be used against companies by defrauded owners[3].

1   Considered below, paras 5.63–5.64.
2   [1994] 2 All ER 685; see below, para 5.61.
3   See *Meridian Global Funds Management Asia Ltd v Securities Commission* [1995] 2 AC 500; Sealy 'The Corporate Ego and Agency Untwined' [1995] CLJ 507.

The nature of the liability

5.21   Having identified the abuse of Lord Selborne's apothegm[1] as a cause of what has gone wrong in this area of the law, Lord Nicholls went to some lengths to answer the more fundamental question, as to why a dishonest third party who has never received trust property should be liable.

1   See above, para 5.7.

5.22   As noted earlier, Lord Nicholls described this head of liability as that of an accessory to a trustee's breach of trust. It arises even though no trust property has reached the hands of the accessory, and is a form of secondary liability, in the sense that it only arises where there has been a breach of trust. Lord Nicholls considered the three alternative propositions of no liability, strict liability, and fault-based liability. He summarily dismissed the possibility of no liability. According to him, a trust, in its simplest terms, is a relationship which exists when one person holds property on behalf of another. If, for his own purposes, a third party deliberately interferes in that relationship by assisting the trustee in depriving the beneficiary of the property held for him or her by the trustee, the beneficiary should be able to look for recompense to the third party as well as the trustee. The rationale for this is that beneficiaries are entitled to expect that third parties will refrain from intentionally intruding in the trustee-beneficiary relationship, and thereby hindering a beneficiary from receiving his or her entitlement in accordance with the terms of the trust. Affording the beneficiary a remedy thus serves a dual purpose. It allows the beneficiary's loss to be made good should the trustee lack financial means, and it discourages others from behaving in a similar fashion.

5.23   The other extreme possibility of strict liability was also rejected summarily. Within defined limits, proprietary rights, whether legal or equitable, endure against third parties who are unaware of their existence. Accessory liability, however, is not property-based. It is concerned with interference with the due performance by the trustee of personal fiduciary obligations. Every-day business would be impossible if third parties were to be held liable for unknowingly interfering in the due performance of such personal obligations. After a careful review of the existing case law and of academic commentary, Lord Nicholls considered standards of fault-based liability, which might apply. Negligence was conclusively rejected as being insufficient to found liability. It was decided that dishonesty is an essential ingredient. There is no room for the proposition that a third party owes a duty of care to the beneficiaries to, in effect, check that a trustee is not misbehaving.

5.24   Lord Nicholls went on to carefully try to explain what dishonesty means in this context, but acknowledged that it was impossible to be more specific. The judgment essentially echoes the opinion of Millett J in *Agip (Africa) Ltd v Jackson*, where he suggested that the true distinction between honesty and dishonesty is essentially a factual question[1]. In the context of accessory liability, Lord Nicholls explained that acting dishonestly (or with a lack of probity, which is synonymous), means not acting as an honest person would in the circumstances. Although this is an objective standard, he said that:

> ... it has a strong subjective element in that it is a description of a type of conduct assessed in the light of what a person actually knew at the time, as distinct from what a reasonable person would have known or appreciated[2].

He went on to say that honesty, and its counterpart dishonesty, are mostly concerned with advertent conduct, not inadvertent conduct. Carelessness is not dishonesty. Dishonesty should be equated with conscious impropriety. He acknowledged that applying the test might not always be particularly straightforward, but that to enquire in the cases, whether a person dishonestly assisted in what is later held to be a breach of trust, is to ask a meaningful question, which is capable of being given a meaningful answer. He went on to explain that if a person knowingly appropriates another's property, he will not escape a finding of dishonesty simply because he sees nothing wrong in such behaviour; honesty is not an optional scale. Happily, he went on to say that framing the question in the form of knowledge is inapt as a criterion, when applied to a gradually darkening spectrum where the differences are of degree and not kind.

1   [1990] Ch 265 at 293–295.
2   [1995] 2 AC 378 at 389.

5.25   Thus tortuous convolutions about the 'sort' of knowledge required should be avoided in future cases. Indeed, in this context, he suggested that the scale of knowledge established in the *Baden Delvaux* case[1] best be forgotten. *Royal Brunei Airlines* appears to have restored the law, at least in the context of the accessory liability of strangers, to its proper reasoned course.

1   See above, para 5.11.

5.26   In so doing, the Privy Council also rejected the test of unconscionable behaviour favoured by Thomas J in *Powell v Thompson*[1]. The case under consideration in *Powell v Thompson* was a case of both knowing receipt and dishonest assistance, and Thomas J undertook an extensive review of the law. He asserted the need for equity to retain as much flexibility as possible, and specifically rejected the notion that dishonesty was required on the part of an accessory to a breach of trust. He considered it to be clearly repugnant to raise the threshold of equity's tolerance to meet some perceived commercial need, the commercial need referred to being the need to transact at speed, and without obligations transferred from the lengthy proceedings associated with land transactions[2]. According to Thomas J, equity's conscience has been entrusted to the courts and it is not to be equated with the supposed conscience of the commercial community. Whenever, therefore, in all the circumstances, a court finds the conduct of an accessory to be unconscionable, this should be sufficient to found liability. Thomas J suggested that, if a Court of Equity disapproves of a transaction, it should be prepared to say so. Although the approach of Thomas J was recognised as providing a notable exception from the general judicial approach, Lord Nicholls was unable to agree with him that liability for assistance is founded on unconscionable conduct. This is because, as Thomas J clearly intended, equity recognises 'unconscionable' conduct which is less reprehensible than conduct which can be described as 'dishonest'. This more general principle of unconscionability is, according to Lord Nicholls, too wide a principle of liability in this context. This must be correct because, if the view of Thomas J had prevailed, the jurisdiction in equity to make accessories liable for another's breach of trust would arguably be too extensive, and a narrower test of liability is preferable when a third party has received no beneficial interest in the property. As a matter of description, Lord Nicholls added that on the narrower requirement of dishonesty, although unconscionable conduct clearly encompasses dishonesty, dishonesty is the preferable label. Lord Nicholls referred to a number of New Zealand cases which took a different view from that of Thomas J[3], and concluded that, as Henry J had recently observed in *Springfield Acres Ltd (In liquidation) v Abacus (Hong Kong) Ltd*[4], the law in New Zealand could not be regarded as settled.

1   [1991] 1 NZLR 597; above, para 5.4.
2   Judicial warnings in English law against extending the boundaries of constructive notice to commercial transactions, unconnected with land, have been common. An example often cited is the warning by Lindley LJ in *Manchester Trust v Furness* [1895] 2 QB 539 at 545: 'In dealing with estates in land title is everything, and it can be leisurely investigated; in commercial transactions possession is everything, and there is no time to investigate title; and if we were to extend the doctrine of constructive notice to commercial transactions we should be doing infinite mischief and paralyzing the trade of the country'. (Cited by Nourse LJ in *Bank of Credit and Commerce International (Overseas) Ltd v Akindele* [2000] 4 All ER 221 at 234, and by Vinelott J in *Eagle Trust Plc v SBC Securities* [1993] 1 WLR 484 at 504; see below, para 5.61.)
3   *Equiticorp Industries Group Ltd v Hawkins* [1991] 3 NZLR 700; *Marshall Futures Ltd v Marshall* [1992] 1 NZLR 316; *Nimmo v Westpac Banking Corpn* [1993] 3 NZLR 218.
4   [1994] 3 NZLR 502.

5.27   As a result of *Royal Brunei Airlines*, the principles underlying accessory liability became much clearer and, as a matter of intellectual clarity, accessory liability has subsequently been referred to as 'dishonest assistance in a breach of trust'. Unfortunately, it cannot be said that earlier semantic distinctions have been forgotten, as suggested by Lord Nicholls. Because of the large sums of money that are usually involved in these types of cases, aggrieved parties will, inevitably, continue to seek to take advantage of artificial distinctions.

5.28   An example of this swiftly occurred in a subsequent case, *Brinks Ltd v Abu-Saleh (No 3)*[1], where, despite Lord Nicholls' comments, the *Baden Delvaux* case was cited yet again in the context of dishonest assistance[2]. The case arose as a consequence of the Brinks bullion robbery at Heathrow in 1983. Brinks brought civil proceedings against 57 defendants, allegedly involved either in the robbery or in the laundering of the money. The breach of trust enabling Brinks to commence such proceedings was by a security guard, Anthony Black. He facilitated the robbery by, amongst other things, providing a key to, and photographs of, the warehouse in which the bullion was stored. The particular defendant in the case in hand, Mrs Elcombe, had, between August 1984 and February 1985, helped her husband in the part he had played in laundering the money, by carrying £3 million cash for one of the convicted robbers, Mr Parry, from England to Zurich by car. An argument was put forward by counsel on behalf of Brinks that an individual could be liable as an accessory to a breach of trust, even though unaware of the breach of trust. Counsel for Brinks argued that, as a direct result of the decision in *Royal Brunei Airlines*, in order to fix Mrs

Elcombe with liability in equity as an accessory, all that was required was to prove:

(1)   that she had rendered assistance in what, objectively assessed, was a dishonest transaction;

(2)   that the transaction involved a breach of trust.

Rimer J was content to conclude that Mrs Elcombe went on the trips simply in the capacity of Mr Elcombe's wife. An answer to the second point was not, therefore, necessary. Nevertheless he concluded, albeit obiter, that the decision in *Royal Brunei Airlines* provided sound authority against the imposition of liability against an accessory who dealt with a trustee in ignorance that he was a trustee, or who knew that he was a trustee but had no reason to know or suspect that the transaction in which he was assisting was a breach of trust. Rimer J held that both Mr and Mrs Elcombe believed the source of the money to be derived from Mr Parry's business empire and was the subject of a tax evasion scheme. They did not, therefore, know that the source of the money was the breach of trust by Anthony Black.

1   [1996] CLC 133.
2   On *Baden Delvaux* see above, para 5.11.

5.29   This, in my opinion, is a correct interpretation of the *Royal Brunei Airlines* case, and addresses a criticism of the case by Wright, whereby he suggests that the case does not shed much light on those situations where the third party does not actually know that a breach of trust is being committed or, possibly, even that trust property is involved[1]. Lord Nicholls was, however, unequivocal on this issue in *Royal Brunei Airlines*. Not only did he reject the imposition of liability when a third party is wholly unaware of the existence of a trust, but he specifically addressed the question of whether an honest third party who receives no trust property should be liable if he procures or assists in a breach of trust of which he would have become aware had he exercised reasonable diligence. Again, in keeping with the rejection of negligence as a standard of liability, his answer was unequivocal: the essence of culpability is dishonesty, and negligence is not a sufficient basis for liability.

1   Wright '*Royal Brunei Airlines v Tan Kok Ming*: A Commentary' [1995] 15 Insolvency Lawyer 9. See Halliwell 'Liabilities Of Companies And Directors For Dishonest Assistance In A Breach Of Trust' [1996] Insolvency Lawyer 9.

5.30   This, however, has been subject to some refinement in subsequent cases. Because of the continuing problems facing the courts in cases of complicated commercial frauds, involving large casts of characters and financial transactions in respect of vast sums of money, this and a number of other issues have had to be addressed. These include whether defrauded owners can recover in equity when they have simply been 'swindled' without any involvement by a fiduciary; how to apply the dishonesty test; and finally, whether a firm can be vicariously liable for the dishonest assistance of a partner in a fraudulent scheme.

Application to resulting and constructive trusts – mere 'swindling'

5.31   Millett J suggested in *El Ajou v Dollar Land Holdings*[1] that defrauded owners can recover in equity when they have simply been 'swindled', without any involvement by a fiduciary, on the basis that they could establish an interest by way of resulting trust. Although this argument has not prevailed, the dictum of Lord Browne-Wilkinson in *Westdeutsche Landesbank Girozentrale v Islington London Borough Council*[2] has paved the way for recovery by way of constructive trust. Lord Browne-Wilkinson said 'when property is obtained by fraud equity imposes a constructive trust on the recipient'[3]. That dictum was approved of by Mance LJ in *Grupo Torras SA v Al-Sabah*[4] and by the Court of Appeal in *Twinsectra v Yardley*[5]. On the constructive trust analysis Potter LJ said, in the latter case:

> It seems to me that, whatever the legal distinctions between 'theft' and 'fraud' in other areas of the law, the distinction of importance here is that between non-consensual transfers and transfers pursuant to contracts which are voidable for misrepresentation. In the latter case, the transferor may elect whether to avoid or affirm the transaction and, until he elects to avoid it, there is no constructive (resulting) trust; in the former case, the constructive trust arises upon the moment of transfer[6].

The point was not decisive, since the dishonest assistance claim rested on the breach of a primary, *Quistclose*[7], type of trust. It is now clear, however, that when owners of property are defrauded, without the involvement of a fiduciary, they may make claims against third parties on the basis of dishonest assistance or knowing receipt as a result of a constructive trust being found in their favour. Because of the finding of a *Quistclose* type of trust, it was relevant in the *Twinsectra* case as to whether the assistor has to know of the existence of a trust or fiduciary relationship, which was the issue raised before Rimer J in *Brinks Ltd v Abu-Saleh (No 3)*, discussed above[8].

1   [1993] 3 All ER 717.
2   [1996] AC 669.
3   [1996] AC 669 at 716.
4   [1999] CLC 1469.
5   [1999] Lloyd's Rep Bank 438. On the decision of the Lords ([2002] 2 All ER 377), see below, para 5.36.
6   [1999] Lloyd's Rep Bank 438 at 461.
7   *Barclays Bank v Quistclose Investments* [1970] AC 567.
8   [1996] CLC 133; discussed above, para 5.28.

5.32   Twinsectra agreed to advance £1,000,000 to Mr Yardley for the acquisition of property. This was subject to a provision that the money was advanced to a solicitor, on the latter's professional undertaking that the funds would be retained by him until such time as they were applied in the acquisition of property by his client, Mr Yardley, and would in any event be repaid with the interest by the solicitor personally. Mr Yardley's own solicitor, Mr Leach, refused to give such an undertaking. It was given by another solicitor, Mr Sims, who owed Mr Yardley money as a result of some dubious dealings with Nigerian government officials, involving putting up money to bribe the officials to induce the government to pay fees under a completed engineering contract. Mr Yardley obtained the money to acquire the property from another source and Mr Sims simply paid the money away according to Mr Yardley's instructions, mostly to Mr Leach, acting also on behalf of Mr Yardley. Twinsectra sought to recover the loan with interest from Mr Yardley in contract or in deceit or, alternatively, in equity under the batteries of the tracing process for an equitable proprietary claim, dishonest assistance and knowing receipt.

5.33   In the Court of Appeal, the common law claims against Mr Yardley were upheld[1]. The court held that the loan had been induced by a fraudulent misrepresentation as to the purposes for which the funds would be used. The funds advanced were held to have been subject to a *Quistclose* trust, and that trust had been breached by the utilisation of the funds for purposes other than the acquisition of property. Both solicitors, Mr Sims and Mr Leach, were liable for dishonest assistance. Potter LJ analysed the *Quistclose* type of trust as a primary trust in favour of the creditors (characterised as an express 'purpose trust' enforceable by the lender), and, in the event of the failure of that trust, a secondary trust in favour of the lender.

1   [1999] Lloyd's Rep Bank 438.

5.34   He added that the mere declaration of a specified purpose would not, however, be sufficient to establish such a trust. According to Potter LJ, there must be some additional indication that the borrower is not to have the full beneficial interest in the fund. He said that this conclusion could usually be drawn from the requirement that the borrower keeps the loan monies separate from his other assets. Such segregation, coupled with the expressed purpose, is regarded as indicating an intention to create/retain a proprietary interest in the loan monies to support a right to repayment on failure of the purpose. Whilst the *Quistclose* type cases have generally concerned loans for the payment of specific debts or classes of debt, Potter LJ saw no inherent reason as to why the imposition of a wider special purpose, as on the facts of the case, should not impose a trust as long as the terms of the restraint on the borrower's use of the money are sufficiently certain to be enforceable by the lender. The meaning of the words 'acquisition of property' was a sufficiently clear statement of purpose. Segregation of the fund was achieved by the Solicitor's Accounts Rules 1986, rr 3 to 7 relating to the keeping of a client account. The strict obligations imposed by the Rules as to payments proper to be made into and out of Mr Sims's client account would ensure the preservation of the fund once paid in. The question whether or not an express purpose trust existed depended upon the proper construction of Sims's undertaking, in the light of the surrounding circumstances, and without regard to the private and unexpressed intentions of the parties. While, in principle, when dealing with the question of whether or not the terms of the undertaking were apt to create a fiduciary obligation, one may have regard to the communications between the parties which preceded it, Potter LJ concluded that those communications should be judged objectively, in the sense of what one party might reasonably have inferred from the statements of the other.

5.35   Under these circumstances, whereby it was held that there was a *Quistclose* type of resulting trust, it was argued that, whereas in *Royal Brunei Airlines* there was a clear misapplication of trust assets, here the second solicitor, Mr Leach, could not have known of the existence of the trust, let alone a breach of such trust. That argument was rejected by the Court of Appeal. In order to fix Mr Leach with accessory liability the standard of honesty required was that of a reasonably prudent and honest solicitor. That test applied to the effect that Mr Leach had deliberately closed his eyes to the inherent problems in the relationship between Mr Yardley and Mr Sims. He deliberately closed his eyes to the rights of Twinsectra, whether legal or equitable, as the beneficiary of the undertaking.

5.36   In the House of Lords[1], however, the formulation of the *Quistclose/Twinsectra* type of trust was explained differently. Although Lord Millett dissented on the test of accessory liability, his reformulation of this type of trust was accepted by the other members of the House, all of whom accepted that, on the facts, there was such a trust. The reformulation must now, therefore, be regarded as settled law and is worth quoting in full. Lord Millett said:

> [I] hold the *Quistclose* trust to be an entirely orthodox example of the kind of default trust known as a resulting trust. The lender pays the money to the borrower by way of loan, but he does not part with the entire beneficial interest in the money, and in so far as he does not it is held on a resulting trust for the lender from the outset. Contrary to the opinion of the Court of Appeal, it is the borrower who has a very limited use of the money, being obliged to apply it for the stated purpose or return it. He has no beneficial interest in the money, which remains throughout in the lender subject only to the borrower's power or duty to apply the money in accordance with the lender's instructions. When the purpose fails, the money is returnable to the lender, not under some new trust in his favour which only comes into being on the failure of the purpose, but because the resulting in his favour is no longer subject to any power on the part of the borrower to make use of the money. Whether the borrower is obliged to apply the money for the stated purpose or merely at liberty to do so, and whether the lender can countermand the borrower's mandate while it is still capable of being carried out, must depend upon the circumstances of the particular case[2].

1   *Twinsectra Ltd v Yardley* [2002] UKHL 12, [2002] 2 All ER 377.
2   [2002] 2 WLR 802 at 830.

5.37   That being so, how is the test of dishonesty to be applied in cases of a resulting or constructive trust? A suitable solution to this problem lies, in my opinion, in the analysis by Mance LJ, when discussing the *Brinks* case, in *Grupo Torras SA v Al-Sabah*:

> The problem with which Rimer J was concerned was the not uncommon problem that, if she had assisted at all, the defendant would plainly have been dishonest in a general sense, since it was clear that the whole purpose of the trips was dishonest tax invasion. But the answer to this problem seems to lie in recognising that, for dishonest assistance, the defendant's dishonesty must have been towards the plaintiff in relation to property held or potentially held on trust or constructive trust, rather than in the introduction of a separate criterion of knowledge of any such trust[1].

1   [1999] CLC 1469 at 1665–1666.

5.38   This analysis provides a clear rationale for reconciliation of the above cases. Mr Leach undoubtedly knew the source of the property with which he dealt, unlike Mrs Elcombe in the *Brinks* case. Mance LJ clearly wished to keep within the spirit of Lord Nicholl's opinion in *Royal Brunei Airlines* by avoiding recourse to states of knowledge. Mance LJ's finding was not disturbed on this issue when his finding of liability for dishonest assistance was appealed to the Court of Appeal[1]. The Court of Appeal also, however, was inclined to agree with Rimer J in the *Brinks* case.

1   *Grupo Torras SA v Al-Sabah (No 5)* [2001] Lloyd's Rep Bank 36.

5.39   When Mr Leach's appeal was heard before the House of Lords, this particular point was not discussed at length. It appears from their Lordships' speeches that it was wholly accepted that Mr Leach knew of the trust. The only salient comment was made by Lord Hoffmann, who said that a person can be dishonest without a full appreciation of the legal analysis of the transaction. He said that a person may dishonestly assist in the commission of a breach of trust without any idea of what a trust means. The necessary dishonest state of mind may be found to exist simply on the fact that he knew perfectly well that he was helping to pay away money to which the recipient was not entitled[1]. This seems entirely consistent with the view taken by Mance LJ. The test of dishonesty is being consistently applied although, as the next section demonstrates, there is some inconsistency in the formulation of the test, and the courts may well have to be careful in the future to avoid the very over-refinement, which Lord Nicholls had wished to jettison.

1   *Twinsectra v Yardley* [2002] UKHL 12, [2002] 2 WLR 802 at 808.

Is the test of dishonesty subjective or objective?

5.40   The standard applied according to the circumstances of Mr Leach by the Court of Appeal in the *Twinsectra* case has already been discussed. The standard of honesty required was that of a reasonably prudent and honest solicitor. Mr Leach, according to the Court of Appeal, deliberately closed his eyes to the inherent problems in the relationship between Mr Yardley and Mr Sims. He deliberately closed his eyes to the rights of Twinsectra. In allowing Mr Leach's appeal, the House of Lords held that it was not open for the Court of Appeal to reach this conclusion because the judge at first instance, Carnworth J, had held that Mr Leach had not been dishonest. The House of Lords declined to order a retrial.

5.41   However, there is still some confusion as to the objective/subjective nature of the test of dishonesty:

- Mance LJ in *Grupo Torras SA v Al-Sabah* after re-defined the ingredients of this form of liability as:
  '(i)   A breach of trust or fiduciary duty by someone other than the defendant;
  (ii)   in which the defendant assisted;
  (iii)   dishonestly, together with;
  (iv)   resulting loss'[1].
  He concluded that dishonesty is an objective standard. The individual is expected to attain the standards which would be observed by an honest person placed in the circumstances he was, but those circumstances include subjective considerations like the defendant's experience and intelligence, and what he actually knew at the time;
- the formulation of Colman J in the Court of Appeal decision in *Heinl v Jyske Bank (Gibraltar) Ltd*[2], was somewhat different. Colman J suggested that: 'It is important in this analysis to be very clear that the material question is not the objective test whether he ought as a reasonable businessman to have appreciated that the funds subject to his control had been fraudulently procured from the Bank or that there was a real probability that they had been, but the subjective test whether he did indeed appreciate that the funds had been or probably been so procured'[3]. He went on to suggest that, if third parties are to be held accountable for breaches of trust committed by others, the standard of proof of dishonesty, although not as high as the criminal standard, should involve a high level of probability;
- in *Satnam Investments Ltd v Dunlop Heywood & Co Ltd*[4] the Court of Appeal was content to equate dishonesty with conscious impropriety;
- in *Houghton v Fayers*[5] Nourse LJ was content to say that 'dishonesty ... is based, as in comparable cases it nearly always is, on inference'[6].

1 [1999] CLC 1469 at 1664.
2 [1999] Lloyd's Rep Bank 511.
3 [1999] Lloyd's Rep Bank 511 at 546.
4 [1999] 3 All ER 652. For a fuller discussion of the case see below, para 9.38.
5 [2000] Lloyd's Rep Bank 145.
6 [2000] Lloyd's Rep Bank 145 at 149.

5.42   The Court of Appeal in *Grupo Torras SA v Al-Sabah (No 5)*[1] tried to reconcile all of the various cases. It is worthwhile to quote Lord Nicholls *Royal Brunei Airlines* in full to understand the Court of Appeal decision in *Grupo Torras*. Lord Nicholls said:

> Before considering this issue further it will be helpful to define the terms being used by looking more closely at what dishonesty means in this context. Whatever may be the position in some criminal or other contexts (see, for instance, *R v Ghosh*[2]), in the context of the accessory liability principle acting dishonestly, or with a lack of probity, which is synonymous, means simply not acting as an honest person would in the circumstances. This is an objective standard. At first sight this may seem surprising. Honesty has a connotation of subjectivity, as distinct from the objectivity of negligence. Honesty, indeed, does have a strong subjective element in that it is a description of a type of conduct assessed in the light of what a person actually knew at the time, as distinct from what a reasonable person would have known or appreciated. Further, honesty and its counterpart dishonesty are mostly concerned with advertent conduct, not inadvertent conduct. Carelessness is not dishonesty. Thus for the most part dishonesty is to be equated with conscious impropriety. However, these subjective characteristics of honesty do not mean that individuals are free to set their own standards of honesty in particular circumstances. The standard of what constitutes honest conduct is not subjective. Honesty is not an optional scale, with higher or lower values according to the moral standards of each individual. If a person knowingly appropriates another's property, he will not escape a finding of dishonesty simply because he sees nothing wrong in such behaviour.
>
> In most situations there is little difficulty in identifying how an honest person would behave. Honest people do not intentionally deceive others to their detriment. Honest people do not knowingly take others' property. Unless there is a very good and compelling reason, an honest person does not participate in a transaction if he knows it involves a misapplication of trust assets to the detriment of the beneficiaries. Nor does an honest person in such a case deliberately close his eyes and ears, or deliberately not ask questions, lest he learn something he would rather not know, and then proceed regardless ...
>
> ... The only answer to these questions lies in keeping in mind that honesty is an objective standard. The individual is expected to attain the standard which would be observed by an honest person placed in those circumstances. It is impossible to be more specific. Knox J captured the flavour of this, in a case with a commercial setting, when he referred to a person who is 'guilty of commercially unacceptable conduct in the particular context involved': see *Cowan de Groot Properties Ltd v Eagle Trust plc*[3]. Acting in reckless disregard of others' rights or possible rights can be a telltale sign of dishonesty. An honest person would have regard to the circumstances known to him, including the nature and importance of the proposed transaction, the nature and importance of his role, the ordinary course of business, the degree of doubt, the practicability of the trustee or the third party proceeding otherwise and the seriousness of the adverse consequences to the beneficiaries. The circumstances will dictate which one or more of the possible courses should be taken by an honest person. He might, for instance, flatly decline to become involved. He might ask further questions. He might seek advice, or insist on further advice being obtained. He might advise the trustee of the risks but then proceed with his role in the transaction. He might do many things. Ultimately, in most cases, an honest person should have little difficulty in knowing whether a proposed transaction, or his participation in it, would offend the normally accepted standards of honest conduct.

Likewise, when called upon to decide whether a person was acting honestly, a court will look at all the circumstances known to the third party at the time. The court will also have regard to personal attributes of the third party, such as his experience and intelligence, and the reason why he acted as he did.

Before leaving cases where there is real doubt, one further point should be noted. To inquire, in such cases, whether a person dishonestly assisted in what is later held to be a breach of trust is to ask a meaningful question, which is capable of being given a meaningful answer. This is not always so if the question is posed in terms of 'knowingly' assisted. Framing the question in the latter form all too often leads one into tortuous convolutions about the 'sort' of knowledge required, when the truth is that 'knowingly' is inapt as a criterion when applied to the gradually darkening spectrum where the differences are of degree and not kind ...

'Knowingly' is better avoided as a defining ingredient of the principle, and in the context of this principle the *Baden* scale of knowledge[4] is best forgotten[5].

1   [2001] Lloyd's Rep Bank 36.
2   [1982] QB 1053.
3   [1992] 4 All ER 700 at 761.
4   (1982) [1993] 1 WLR 509n at 575–576; above, para 5.11.
5   [1995] 2 AC 378 at 389–392.

5.43   The issue before the Court of Appeal in *Grupo Torras* was whether Mance LJ had applied this test correctly at first instance, and whether he would have decided differently if he had been aware of the Court of Appeal decision in *Heinl v Jyske Bank (Gibraltar) Ltd*[1] (which was decided a month after Mance LJ handed down his judgment). Put shortly, counsel for the appellant in the case argued that Mance LJ in imposing liability for assistance had, incorrectly, applied a test of negligence. The Court of Appeal disagreed. Having stated that Lord Nicholls's test in *Royal Brunei Airlines* is neither difficult nor complicated to apply, they proceeded to summarise the different tests of dishonesty. The case presupposes liability for 'subjective' dishonesty, 'blind eye' dishonesty and 'Robin Hood' dishonesty. The latter presupposes purely objective dishonesty in that the alleged assistor believes that he is not doing anything wrong, but no honest person would have held such a belief. The Court of Appeal acknowledged, as is indeed implicit in Lord Nicholls's explanation, that different tests may apply in different circumstances, and called, correctly in my opinion, for trial judges to be absolutely explicit as to what test of dishonesty was being applied on the facts before them. The Court of Appeal suggested, for example, that the less stringent test of subjective dishonesty should apply in an ordinary commercial transaction[2].

1   [1999] Lloyd's Rep Bank 511. It is perhaps rather unfortunate that in that case Nourse LJ doubted whether *Royal Brunei Airlines* had been correct in respect of the *Baden* scale of knowledge, although Nourse LJ was very specific as to the scope and utility of the scale. He said: 'I believe that [the *Baden* classification] will sometimes continue to be helpful in identifying different states of knowledge which may or may not result in a finding of dishonesty' ([1999] Lloyd's Rep Bank 511 at 523).
2   [2001] Lloyd's Rep Bank 36.

5.44   The House of Lords in *Twinsectra* reached the same conclusion, particularly in the context of 'Robin Hood' dishonesty. Lord Hutton's speech contains the main analysis of the test of dishonesty: he defined the 'Robin Hood' test of dishonesty as a purely subjective standard, whereby a person is only regarded as dishonest if he transgresses his own standard of dishonesty, even if that standard is contrary to that of reasonable and honest people. With only a minimal explanation, he baldly asserted that this test has been rejected by the courts. His explanation was that:

A person may in some cases act dishonestly, according to the ordinary use of language, even though he genuinely believes that his action is morally justified. The penniless thief, for example, who picks the pocket of the multi-millionaire is dishonest even though he genuinely considers that theft is morally justified as a fair redistribution of wealth and that he is therefore not being dishonest[1].

1   [2002] 2 WLR 802 at 809, quoting Sir Christopher Slade stated in *Walker v Stones* [2001] QB 902 at 939.

5.45   Lord Hutton went on to identify a second possible test of dishonesty, where there is a purely objective standard whereby a person acts dishonestly if his conduct is dishonest by the ordinary standards of reasonable and honest people, even if he does not realise this. This test he also rejected as insufficient to escape liability.

His preference was for a more comprehensive test of dishonesty where there is a standard, which combines an objective test and a subjective test. This type of dishonesty requires that before there can be a finding of dishonesty it must be established that the defendant's conduct was dishonest by the ordinary standards of reasonable and honest people and that he himself realised that by those standards his conduct was dishonest. He termed this 'the combined test'. This combined test was accepted by the majority of the House. The resulting test of dishonesty, as stated by Lord Hutton, is that dishonesty requires knowledge by the defendant that what he was doing would be regarded as dishonest by honest people, although he should not escape a finding of dishonesty because he sets his own standards of honesty and does not regard as dishonest what he knows would offend the normally accepted standards of honest conduct.

5.46   This is now the binding precedent on the courts, but this current test is not without difficulty. In the first place it is not clear what the distinction is between 'Robin Hood' dishonesty and the second, purely objective standard of dishonesty. Moreover, the second limb of the combined test seems to incorporate 'Robin Hood' dishonesty entirely. It would be very surprising if it did not. If I assisted an accountant in a multi-millionaire company in embezzling the company's money in order to fund an operation for one of the accountant's seriously ill relatives, it cannot really be said that I would not be liable for dishonest assistance because I thought my actions to be morally justified? The application of the test of dishonesty appears, therefore, to remain problematic.

5.47   However the test is formulated, it can only be perceived as beneficial that the question being addressed is one of honesty/dishonesty, rather than one of over-refined categories of knowledge, and that Lord Nicholls's seminal analysis has prevailed. Given that a serious allegation is being made with the less onerous civil balance of proof, it appears entirely appropriate that trial judges pinpoint the precise manner of dishonesty, if found on the facts.

Imputed knowledge

5.48   The majority of the Court of Appeal in *Dubai Aluminium Co Ltd v Salaam*[1] held that under the Partnership Act 1890, s 10[2], partners in a firm would not be liable for a fellow partner whose dishonest assistance in a fraudulent scheme went outside the ordinary course of business between the firm and its clients. Although Turner J agreed on the ordinary course of business point, he did not agree that dishonest assistance cases fell within s 10 but that, alternatively, it fell within ss 11 and 13[3]. He considered that the concept of a breach of trust within those sections was wide enough to embrace conduct of the description 'knowing assistance' by a person who thereby made himself a constructive trustee. The accepted single test of dishonesty, as a prerequisite of liability for assistance or procurement in a breach of trust, was also applied in that case. It appears that there is now some temptation to import the same test into knowing receipt cases.

1 [2001] QB 113.
2 'Where, by any wrongful act or omission of any partner acting in the ordinary course of the business of the firm, or with the authority of his co-partners, loss or injury is caused to any person not being a partner in the firm, or any penalty is incurred, the firm is liable therefor to the same extent as the partner so acting or omitting to act.'
3 **11.** In the following cases; namely–
    (a) Where one partner acting within the scope of his apparent authority receives the money or property of a third person and misapplies it; and
    (b) Where a firm in the course of its business receives money or property of a third person, and the money or property so received is misapplied by one or more of the partners while it is in the custody of the firm;
    the firm is liable to make good the loss.
        13. If a partner, being a trustee, improperly employs trust-property in the business or on the account of the partnership, no other partner is liable for the trust property to the persons beneficially interested therein:
        Provided as follows–
    (1) This section shall not affect any liability incurred by any partner by reason of his having notice of a breach of trust; and
    (2) Nothing in this section shall prevent trust money from being followed and recovered from the firm if still in its possession or under its control.

C   Receipt of trust property

The requirements of liability

5.49   The requisites of enforcing a receipt claim were conveniently summarised in the Court of Appeal decision in *El Ajou v Dollar Land Holdings*[1] by Hoffmann LJ:

> For this purpose the plaintiff must show, first, a disposal of his assets in breach of fiduciary duty; secondly, the beneficial receipt by the defendant of assets which are traceable as representing the assets of the plaintiff; and thirdly, knowledge on the part of the defendant that the assets he received are traceable to a breach of fiduciary duty[2].

1 [1994] 2 All ER 685.
2 [1994] 2 All ER 685 at 700.

Is dishonesty required?

5.50   In *Bank of America v Arnell*[1], Aikens J said that the fundamental question that the court has to ask now is:

> Was the recipient acting honestly when he received the funds?

He based this on the authority of Potter LJ, who delivered the judgment of the Court of Appeal in *Twinsectra v Yardley*[2]. In commenting on *Houghton v Fayers*[3], the editor of Lloyd's Law Reports similarly asserts that the Court of Appeal decision in *Twinsectra v Yardley* appears to require dishonesty for a claim to succeed in knowing receipt[4].

1 [1999] Lloyd's Rep Bank 399.
2 [1999] Lloyd's Rep Bank 438.

3   [2000] Lloyd's Rep Bank 145.
4   [2000] Lloyd's Rep Bank 145 at 151–152.

5.51   In my opinion, this interpretation of Potter LJ's judgment is incorrect. There were two personal actions against Mr Leach in respect of different amounts of money. As well as the dishonest assistance claim discussed above, there was, as explained, a claim in knowing receipt in respect of three transactions which were identified as [F], [J] and [K][1]. It is somewhat unfortunate that Potter LJ pursued a discussion under the heading '"knowing" receipt or assistance'. It was, also, unfortunate that he used the terminology of 'Nelsonian' dishonesty to establish liability in the accessory category. Nevertheless, he found the necessary ingredient of dishonesty so as to prove the assistance claim. On the knowing receipt claim in respect of the three transactions, he was succinct and to the point: 'In relation to the receipt-based claim, it is plain that Mr Leach received the trust property for his own benefit with notice of the trust, took subject to it and is liable personally to account for it to *Twinsectra*'[2]. That appears to me to unequivocally apply a test of notice, with no requirement of dishonesty. Unfortunately, the knowing receipt claim was not heard before the House of Lords on appeal, and this issue remains unresolved.

1   See above, para 5.32.
2   [1999] Lloyd's Rep Bank 438 at 466.

5.52   More recently Nourse LJ, in delivering the judgment of the Court of Appeal in *Bank of Credit and Commerce International (Overseas) Ltd v Akindele*[1], stated that dishonesty has never been a prerequisite of liability in knowing receipt. The authority which Nourse LJ heavily relied upon was *Belmont Finance Corpn Ltd v Williams Furniture Ltd*[2]. He used this authority to demonstrate that there is no requirement of dishonesty in knowing receipt cases. In *Belmont Finance* the defendant company owned all the shares in City Industrial Finance Ltd, which in turn owned all the shares in the claimant company. A scheme was arranged under which Belmont would purchase all the shares in a fourth company for a sum greatly in excess of its asset value, and that the Chairman of Maximum would buy from City all the shares in Belmont. The transaction was held unlawful under the Companies Act 1948[3]. On Belmont's subsequent insolvency, the receiver claimed to recover from City and its directors the money received by City on the sale of the Belmont shares, on the ground that it had been received by the directors in breach of their fiduciary duty respecting the funds of the company. The Court of Appeal held City liable as constructive trustee. There was no need to prove fraud or dishonesty. Liability arose by receipt of trust money in circumstances whereby the state of the recipient's knowledge meant that the funds could not conscientiously be retained[4]. Nourse LJ went on to cite three other authorities supporting the view that dishonesty is not a requirement of liability for knowing receipt, Millett J in *Agip (Africa) Ltd v Jackson*[5], Vinelott J in *Eagle Trust plc v SBC Securities Ltd*[6] and Scott LJ in the Court of Appeal in *Polly Peck International plc v Nadir (No 2)*[7].

1   [2000] 4 All ER 221.
2   [1979] Ch 250.
3   See the Companies Act 1948, s 54.
4   [2000] 4 All ER 221 at 235.
5   [1990] Ch 265.
6   [1993] 1 WLR 484 at 497.
7   [1992] 4 All ER 769 at 777.

5.53   It would seem, therefore, on the preponderance of authority, that it is not necessary to prove fraud or dishonesty in order to establish liability in knowing receipt. Clearly, there is an even stronger case here than with that discussed above[1], of a third party who has merely assisted with a breach of trust for some form of liability. Here the third party has had the benefit of the property received through a breach of trust. It is appropriate, therefore, to apply a more stringent test than dishonesty.

1   See above, para 5.23.

Is liability strict?

5.54   Lord Nicholls acknowledged in *Royal Brunei Airlines* that this limb of Lord Selborne's formulation[1] is concerned with the liability of a person as a recipient of trust property or its traceable proceeds. Recipient liability is, according to him, restitution-based. In an extra-judicial capacity he has advocated a principle of strict liability, subject to a change of position defence, on the basis that the recipient of trust property has been unjustly enriched at the expense of the beneficial owner[2]. Other commentators, such as Birks, agree that liability should be strict[3]. The common law position, authoritatively countenanced by the decision of the House of Lords in *Lipkin Gorman v Karpnale Ltd*[4], is one of strict liability. Referring to this decision in an essay, Lord Nicholls said:

> In this respect equity should now follow the law. Restitutionary liability, applicable regardless of fault but subject to a defence of change of position, would be a better-tailored response to the underlying mischief of misapplied property than personal liability which is exclusively fault-based. Personal liability would flow from having received the property of another, from having been unjustly enriched at the expense of another. It would be triggered by the mere fact of receipt, thus recognising the endurance of property rights. But fairness would be ensured by the need to identify a gain, and by making change of position available as a defence in suitable cases when, for instance, the recipient had changed his position in reliance on the receipt[5].

1   See above, para 5.8.
2   'Knowing Receipt: The Need for a New Landmark' in Cornish, Nolan, O'Sullivan and Virgo (eds) *Restitution past present and future – Essays in honour of Gareth Jones* (1998), p 231.
3   See for example Birks *Restitution – The Future* (1992), pp 26–42.
4   [1991] 2 AC 548.
5   'Knowing Receipt: The Need for a New Landmark' in Cornish, Nolan, O'Sullivan and Virgo (eds) *Restitution past present and future – Essays in honour of Gareth Jones* (1998), p 238.

5.55   So far, this has not been the position in decided cases. It was specifically rejected by Nourse LJ in *Bank of Credit and Commerce International (Overseas) Ltd v Akindele*. Nourse LJ said:

> While in general it may be possible to sympathise with a tendency to subsume a further part of our law of restitution under the principles of unjust enrichment, I beg to leave to doubt whether strict liability coupled with a change of position defence would be preferable to fault-based liability in many commercial transactions ... [1]

1   [2000] 4 All ER 221.

5.56   Nourse LJ relied heavily on another decision, *Re Montagu's Settlement Trust*[1], in reaching his conclusions. *Re Montagu's Settlement Trust* entails a very different perception of liability than strict liability. That case, again, differs from the usual cases in that it concerned a classic institutional trust, rather than a commercial transaction. Trustees transferred settled chattels to the beneficiary, the tenth Duke, absolutely. The transfer, which was the result of an honest mistake, was in breach of trust. The Duke's solicitor had, at an earlier stage, known of the terms of the settlement. Sir Robert Megarry VC considered that not to be relevant, in the sense that a person should not be treated as having knowledge of a fact which the person has genuinely forgotten. The Duke disposed of a number of the chattels during his lifetime. After his death, the eleventh Duke claimed that his predecessor had become a trustee of the chattels, and was therefore personally accountable for the value of any chattels which had been disposed of. Sir Robert Megarry VC held that the tenth Duke's estate must return any remaining chattels or their traceable proceeds, but that the Duke had incurred no personal liability as constructive trustee. He reached this conclusion on the basis that there should be a distinction between rights of priority and constructive trusteeship. Megarry VC regarded a trust in the circumstances of a recipient who has parted with the trust property as a remedial constructive trust, imposing personal liability, and, therefore, only appropriate when the conscience of the recipient is affected by the original breach to the extent of involving a 'want of probity'. He perceived a fundamental difference between the questions that can arise in respect of the doctrine of purchaser without notice and constructive trusts:

> The former is concerned with the question whether a person takes property subject to or free from some equity. The latter is concerned with whether or not a person is to have imposed upon him the personal burdens and obligations of trusteeship. I do not see why one of the touchstones for determining the burdens on property should be the same as that for deciding whether to impose a personal obligation on a man. The cold calculus of constructive and imputed notice does not seem to me to be an appropriate instrument for deciding whether a man's conscience is sufficiently affected for it to be right to bind him by the obligations of a trustee[2].

He went on to say:

> (2) In considering whether a constructive trust has arisen in a case of the knowing receipt of trust property, the basic question is whether the conscience of the recipient is sufficiently affected to justify the imposition of such a trust.

> (3) Whether a constructive trust arises in such a case primarily depends on the knowledge of the recipient, and not on notice to him; and for clarity it is desirable to use the word 'knowledge' and avoid the word 'notice' in such cases[3].

1   [1987] Ch 264.
2   [1987] Ch 264 at 273–273.
3   [1987] Ch 264 at 285.

5.57   There are now strong grounds for believing, on the basis of the opinion of Lord Browne-Wilkinson in *Westdeutsche Landesbank Girozentrale v Islington London Borough Council*[1], that strict liability will not, at least for the time, being, be the test of liability in English law. Lord Browne-Wilkinson stated, albeit obiter, three relevant principles of trust law: A constructive trust is imposed because of unconscionable conduct; a person cannot be a trustee if ignorant of the facts alleged to affect his conscience; and there must be identifiable trust property, the only apparent exception to this rule being where a constructive trust is imposed on a person who *dishonestly* assists in a breach of trust[2].

He then went on to cite both *Re Montagu's Settlement Trust*[3] and *Re Diplock*[4], to conclude that innocent receipt by a third party of property subject to an existing equitable interest does not by itself make the third party a trustee. Taken in conjunction, the tenor of his statements reaffirms the position that equity will not countenance strict liability as the basis for liability in knowing receipt, although the position may change when an appeal comes before the House of Lords.

1   [1996] AC 669.
2   [1996] AC 669 at 705 (emphasis added).
3   [1987] Ch 264; above, para 5.56.
4   [1948] Ch 465.

5.58   In my opinion, it would be contrary to equitable principles to make an innocent recipient strictly liable for the breach of trust on the part of the person in whom equitable owners have reposed trust and confidence in the handling of their affairs. To pursue the suggestion of Lord Nicholls, that a mere act of receipt is an 'unjust factor' which triggers restitution[1], leads to a *petitio principii*. Why does the mere fact of receipt by an innocent third party, who knows nothing of an earlier breach of trust or fiduciary relationship, render such receipt unjust? If the rationale, as suggested by Lord Nicholls, is the endurance of property rights, the value in the eyes of the law of such a conservative principle needs to be discussed in a case at the highest judicial level. Put shortly, is this area of equitable liability underpinned by the endurance of property rights and, if so, why so? There are many areas of equity, proprietary estoppel for example, where endurance of property rights is subsumed by equity's prevention of unconscionable conduct, and there are good reasons why this should be so. As Thomas J said in *Powell v Thompson*, 'No single formulation will suffice to embrace all the factual circumstances which calling for an equitable response which will arise in the course of human affairs'[2]. It seems inconceivable that equity will impose strict liability indiscriminately, so that a defendant described as 'naqve' and 'duped'[3] would be treated in exactly the same way as another defendant described as a 'highly prominent businessman of [Nigeria]'[4]. Megarry VC's observations in *Re Montagu's Settlement Trust*[5] about the concept of equity (' ... this would in no way be equity as I know it') seems entirely apposite in this context. As discussed above in relation to the test of dishonesty[6], it may be appropriate to have a more flexible test which can apply to a variety of factual circumstances.

1   See above, para 5.54.
2   [1991] 1 NZLR 597 at 608.
3   Viz Miss Haddon in *Bank of America v Arnell* [1999] Lloyd's Rep Bank 399 at 407, per Aikens J.
4   Viz Chief Akindele in *Bank of Credit and Commerce International (Overseas) Ltd v Akindele* [2000] 4 All ER 221 at 223, per Nourse LJ.
5   [1987] Ch 264 at 284; above, para 5.56.
6   See above, para 5.47.

Requisite degree of fault

5.59   The remaining question is, in the absence of a requirement of dishonesty and the rejection of strict liability as the basis of liability, what degree of fault is required to establish liability for knowing receipt with such an element of flexibility? In my view, the appropriate standard is not that of 'constructive notice', but rather of unconscionability.

5.60   Nourse LJ also pointed out in *Bank of Credit and Commerce International (Overseas) Ltd v Akindele* that, in *Belmont Finance Corpn Ltd v Williams Furniture Ltd*[1], actual knowledge was found to exist on the part of the recipient[2]. He then went on to discuss a number of cases. These cases adopt Megarry VC's suggestion to use the word 'knowledge' and, generally speaking, suggest that constructive knowledge is not enough to establish liability.

1   [1979] Ch 250.
2   [2000] 4 All ER 221 at 232, per Nourse LJ.

5.61   In *Eagle Trust plc v SBC Securities Ltd*[1], Mr Ferriday, in gross breach of his duty as director, misappropriated Eagle's money and, in contravention of the Companies Act 1985, s 151, used the company's property to defray costs of underwriting a take-over. Eagle Trust alleged that the underwriter should have been aware that assets of the company were being used to pay the underwriting expenses, and should, accordingly, be liable as constructive trustee of £13.5 million. Vinelott J struck out the claimant's claim, on the following basis. Before a stranger to whom money had been paid in breach of trust could, after he had parted with it, be held liable as a constructive trustee to account for it to its defrauded owner, knowledge falling within category (i) (ii) or (iii) on the *Baden Delvaux* scale was essential; constructive knowledge was not enough[2].

In *Cowan de Groot v Eagle Trust*[3], Ferriday deliberately and in breach of trust procured the sale of five properties at an undervalue to Cowan de Groot. It was argued by Eagle Trust that Cowan de Groot was liable as constructive trustee on the basis of knowing receipt of trust property and on the basis of knowing assistance in a fraudulent breach of fiduciary duty. Independent of the constructive trust claims, a tracing claim was advanced on the footing that Cowan de Groot was not a bona fide purchaser for value without notice of the breach of fiduciary by directors of Eagle. Knox J held that Cowan de Groot was not liable, and followed the decision of Vinelott J in *Eagle Trust plc v SBC Securities Ltd (No 2)*. Both of these decisions were then followed by Arden J in the trial of the action in the latter case[4]. Millett J in *El Ajou v Dollar Land Holdings*[5] also agreed with Vinelott J in *Eagle Trust plc v SBC Securities Ltd* that, in commercial transactions, even where the claim is a proprietary one and the defendant raises the defence of bona fide purchaser for value without notice, there is no room for the doctrine of constructive notice, in a strict conveyancing sense, in a factual situation where it is not the custom and practice to make inquiry.

Before the Court of Appeal[6], the contested issue turned around the actual knowledge of an ex Director of Dollar Land Holdings (hereafter DLH), Mr Ferdman. The crucial issue in the case had, therefore, now become a question of company law, as to whether the knowledge of Mr Ferdman could be attributed to DLH. Mr Ferdman had candidly admitted that he knew that the Canadians who were providing investment money for DLH were the persons who had been behind a fraudulent scam. The Court of Appeal held that DLH were liable to the claimant as constructive trustee, because Mr Ferdman's actual knowledge was imputed to the company, on the grounds that the 'directing mind and will' of DLH in relation to the transactions under consideration was the mind and will of Mr Ferdman and none other[7].

1   [1993] 1 WLR 484.
2   On the *Baden Delvaux* scale see above, para 5.11.
3   [1992] 4 All ER 700.
4   [1996] 1 BCLC 121.
5   [1993] 3 All ER 717.
6   *El Ajou v Dollar Land Holdings plc* [1994] 2 All ER 685.
7   Millett J had concluded that Mr Ferdman's knowledge could not constitute ipso facto the knowledge of DLH, because he was a non-executive director who was not responsible for the business of DLH. According to Millett J, Mr Ferdman's only executive responsibilities extended

merely to the paperwork of DLH. Moreover, Millett J treated the acquisition by DLH of the Canadians' interest as an entirely separate transaction. By that time, Mr Ferdman had ceased to be a director of DLH for nine months, and he had nothing at all to do with the transaction. Thus, even if Mr Ferdman's knowledge could be attributed to the company, the company could properly be said to have 'lost its memory'. Millett J relied on observations made by Megarry VC in *Re Montagu's Settlement Trusts* to reach this conclusion (see above, para 5.56).

All three members of the Court of Appeal disagreed with Millett J on this vital element of the case, and held that DLH were liable to the claimant as constructive trustee, because Mr Ferdman's knowledge was imputed to the company on the grounds that the 'directing mind and will' of DLH in relation to the transactions was the mind and will of Mr Ferdman. It made no difference that Mr Ferdman had no involvement with the business activities of DLH, because the doctrine of 'directing mind and will' was not something to be considered generally or in the round. The authorities showed clearly that different persons may for different purposes satisfy the requirements of being a company's directing mind and will. It was necessary to apply the doctrine in relation to the act or omission in point. Moreover, although all three Lord Justices agreed with the 'loss of memory' point made by Millett J, they all concurred that it did not apply on the facts because the imputed knowledge applied to any subsequent stages of the same transaction. It was, therefore, immaterial that Mr Ferdman had resigned well before DLH's acquisition of the disputed funds.

5.62   None of these cases suggest that constructive knowledge will suffice to impose liability on a third party recipient. Nourse LJ in *Bank of Credit and Commerce International (Overseas) Ltd v Akindele*, eventually, came to the conclusion that, in the context of knowing receipt, there is no purpose to be served by a categorisation of knowledge. He suggested that all that is necessary is that the recipient's state of knowledge should be such as to make it unconscionable for him to retain the benefit of the receipt. He went on to add:

> I have come to the view that, just as there is now a single test of dishonesty for knowing assistance, so ought there to be a single test of knowledge for knowing receipt. The recipient's state of knowledge must be such as to make it unconscionable for him to retain the benefit of that receipt. A test in that form, though it cannot, any more than any other, avoid difficulties of application, ought to avoid those of definition and allocation to which the previous categorisations have led. Moreover, it should better enable the courts to give common-sense decisions in the commercial context in which claims in knowing receipt are now frequently made ...[1]

There is a clear echo here of Thomas J in *Powell v Thompson*[2]. The test advocated by Thomas J is undoubtedly wide, in that he said that liability is founded on the third party gaining a material advantage at the claimant's expense which is regarded as 'unconscionable' – in the sense of unreasonable or inequitable. It is clear from his judgment overall, however, that he intended some measure of fault sufficient to shock the conscience of a court of equity. Whilst this test is at too high a threshold of liability for making an accessory liable, it does not necessarily mean that, linked with knowledge in the factual circumstances of the cases, it is not the correct threshold of liability for knowing receipt cases. There is a strong case for having a higher threshold of liability in receipt cases. The recipients have, after all, had the benefit of the property.

1   [2000] 4 All ER 221 at 235–236, per Nourse LJ.
2   [1991] 1 NZLR 597; above, para 5.4.

Vicarious liability and ministerial receipt

5.63   As outlined above, vicarious liability may arise under both heads of liability via the 'directing mind and will' theory or via the Partnership Act 1890[1].

1   See above, paras 5.20, 5.48 and 5.61.

5.64 One important feature in formulating the requisites of enforcing a constructive trust on the grounds of knowing receipt in such a way as to insist upon beneficial receipt of assets by the defendant, is to preclude circumstances of purely *ministerial* receipt, by third parties such as banks, who act in the capacity of agents for the equitable owners of funds from facing liability under this head[1]. Thomas J in *Powell v Thompson*[2], following the distinction identified by Sir Clifford Richmond in *Westpac v Savin*[3], considered that the conduct of an agent who comes into possession of trust property on his or her principal's instructions, and not for their own benefit, falls to be judged under the knowing assistance category of liability. Following *Royal Brunei Airlines*, liability in such circumstances should only be imposed where the conduct has been dishonest. It must also follow from the general re-assertion in English law of the rule, that there must be identifiable funds in order for a proprietary claim to succeed[4], that, where agents such as banks use funds to discharge the overdrafts of the fiduciary involved in the breach of trust, the relevant test of liability will relate to personal liability. The test here for recipient based liability remains subject to the problems enunciated above.

1 On 'ministerial receipt' see further below, para 21.26ff.
2 [1991] 1 NZLR 597; above, para 5.4.
3 [1985] 2 NZLR 41.
4 Recent authorities (*Re Goldcorp Exchange* [1995] 1 AC 74 and *Bishopgate Investment Management v Homan* [1995] Ch 211) have confirmed that there can be no tracing into an overdrawn account (above, para 4.34). The *Westdeutsche* case ([1996] AC 669), similarly, highlights the necessity for identifiable trust property.

CHAPTER 6

Recoupment

Craig Rotherham

A Introduction

6.1   Where a claimant is legally compelled to make a payment that has the effect of discharging a defendant's liability, a right to restitution will often arise. The identification of an enrichment presents no difficulties: the defendant has been relieved of a liability. In addition, rights to recoupment depend upon on an underlying obligation, the breach of which renders the enrichment unjust. This can be characterised as a responsibility to bear the burden of obligations for which one is primarily liable.

6.2   While the basis of contribution is a common liability[1], the right to recoupment arises from the defendant's obligation to the claimant to discharge the obligation in its entirety. The right arises in a number of circumstances. First, a claimant is entitled to be indemnified by the defendant where the claimant has discharged the defendant's liability in order to recover goods held by the third party[2]. Secondly, the right similarly arises where the claimant has paid a debt owed by the defendant in order to preserve rights in land that is subject to a charge securing the debt in question[3]. Thirdly, the right arises where the claimant discharges an obligation for which the defendant is primarily liable and the claimant is only secondarily liable[4].

1   On rights of contribution see below, ch 7.
2   See below, para 6.5ff.
3   See below, para 6.8.
4   See below, para 6.9ff.

6.3   The right to recoupment is generally enforced through an action for money paid to the defendant's use. However, recoupment may also give rise to rights of set-off. Thus, where there is a liability accrued or accruing between the claimant and the defendant at the date at which the claimant discharges a debt for which the defendant was primarily liable, the claimant may deduct a sum equal to his payment from the amount he owes the defendant.

6.4   Some of the most difficult issues in this area centre on the question as to whether payments are officious and/or have the effect of discharging the liability in question[1]. The English judiciary is traditionally suspicious of volunteers, and has at times insisted that only the compulsory discharge of another's liability gives rise to a right to recoupment.

1   See below, para 6.15ff.

B   Situations in which a right of recoupment arises

Discharge of another's liability in order to recover goods

6.5   A number of early recoupment cases involved claimants who were seeking to be indemnified for a payment that was made in order to recover goods lawfully held by a third party and which had the effect of discharging a debt owed by the defendant. Thus in *Exall v Partridge*[1] a claimant was unfortunate enough to have a carriage, that he had left in the care of the defendant, distrained by the defendant's landlord. It was held that, after paying the landlord the rent owed, the claimant was entitled to be indemnified by the defendant and two co-owners. Similarly, in *Johnson v Royal Mail Steam Packet Co*[2], a mortgagee was held to be entitled to be reimbursed for a payment it had made to discharge a debt owed by the mortgagor in order to take possession of mortgaged ships that were subject to a maritime lien for wages unpaid to the crew.

1   (1799) 8 Term Rep 308, 101 ER 1405.
2   (1867) LR 3 CP 38 at 45.

6.6   There is some suggestion that a claimant should be denied a right of recoupment if he 'by his own voluntary act, and without any request of the defendant ... placed his goods in a position to enable the [defendant's] landlord to seize them'[1]. Thus, in *England v Marsden*[2], the defendant mortgaged certain goods to the claimant. After the defendant was arrested for failing to pay his debts, the claimant took constructive possession of those goods, leaving them on the defendant's premises. Apparently, the defendant did not consent to the goods being left in this way, but neither did he object to it. After the defendant's landlord distrained the goods in question, and the claimant paid the outstanding rent in order to obtain the release of the goods, the claimant sought to be indemnified by the defendant. However, the Court of Common Pleas concluded that recoupment should be unavailable because the claimant had placed the goods in a position that enabled the defendant's landlord to lawfully distrain them[3]. Perhaps it was thought relevant that the claimant 'was not ignorant of the accruing claim of the landlord'[4]. Nonetheless, the decision seems a harsh one. It is difficult to see that the claimant's payment of the rent could meaningfully be characterised as voluntary or that it would have been unfair to the defendant to require him to indemnify the claimant.

1   *England v Marsden* (1886) LR 1 CP 529 at 533, per Montague Smith J.
2   (1886) LR 1 CP 529.
3   (1886) LR 1 CP 529 at 533.
4   (1886) LR 1 CP 529 at 533.

6.7   In *Edmunds v Wallingford*[1] the Court of Appeal reconsidered this issue. Lindley LJ, delivering the court's judgment, noted that *England v Marsden* had been subject to a good deal of adverse criticism, and remarked that the court thought that it should not be followed[2]. In his discussion of the earlier decision, he remarked that: 'The evidence did not shew that the plaintiff's goods were left in the defendant's house against his consent'[3]. Thus, it seems that his view was that relief should be denied if a claimant's goods had been distrained after being left on the defendant's premises against the defendant's will. It is not obvious why this should preclude a claim for indemnification. If it was unlikely that the claimant would have considered the danger of the defendant's goods being distrained, it would be odd to conclude that he has accepted this risk. Perhaps the better explanation is that without the defendant's consent, goods remaining on the defendant's premises could not be said to be in the constructive possession of the claimant.

1   (1885) 14 QBD 811.
2   (1885) 14 QBD 811 at 816.
3   (1885) 14 QBD 811 at 816.

Discharge of a liability in order to safeguard an interest in property

6.8   A right to reimbursement may also arise where a claimant pays a debt owed by the defendant so as discharge an encumbrance over property in which the claimant enjoys an interest. This was the case in *Kleinwort Benson Ltd v Vaughan*[1], where the claimants were able to trace into an interest in land that had been acquired with money stolen from them. However, the land was encumbered by a prior mortgage which the claimants chose to redeem in order to safeguard their own interest. If they had declined to act in this way, the value of the claimants' interest would have been difficult to realise. Moreover, the claimants would have been liable to lose their right of possession of the land and even find that their interest was worthless if the mortgagee had acted to repossess the property and sold it at a relatively low price. The right that arises in this context can be justified by the degree of practical necessity that motivates an owner to act to safeguard his interest[2]. The right of reimbursement accorded in these circumstances may be compared with the rights of subrogation that arise where one with a partial interest in a property repays a debt that is secured by a charge over that property[3]. In that context, the claimant is thereafter allowed to exercise the rights formerly enjoyed by the charge holder against others who have an interest in the property. Subrogation to real rights was not a possibility in *Kleinwort Benson Ltd v Vaughan*, as the defendant possessed at most a bare legal interest in the property. Nonetheless, rather than claiming a direct right of recoupment, the claimants could equally have sought to be indemnified by being subrogated to the mortgagee's personal rights against the defendant.

1   [1996] CLC 620. See McMeel *Modern Law of Restitution* (2000), p 270.
2   See, for example, *Tarn v Turner* (1888) 39 Ch D 456 (a lessee paid a debt owed by his landlord in order to safeguard his own interest in the property). See also Mitchell *Law of Subrogation* (1994), p 169.
3   See for example *Countess of Shrewsbury v Earl of Shrewsbury* (1790) 1 Ves 227, 30 ER 314; *Morley v Morley* (1855) 5 De GM & G 610, 43 ER 1007. See below, paras 8.67 and 8.68.

Payment of a common debt for which the defendant is primarily liable

6.9   A second class of cases in which recoupment is available involve claimants who have discharged a debt for which they were only secondarily liable. In these circumstances such claimants are entitled to be indemnified by the party principally liable.

At first sight perhaps the most straightfoward example of this principle involves the right of a surety to be indemnified by the principal debtor after being called upon to meet the debt. Since the early seventeenth century, sureties have had a right in equity to be indemnified by a principal debtor after being required to pay the creditor[1]. Subsequently, a similar right was recognised in quasi-contract at common law[2]. It is surprising that this right is often not analysed as an example of a right of recoupment arising by operation of law[3]. Instead, judges and commentators often characterise this right as arising from an implied term in surety contracts[4]. Yet it is difficult to accept that the orthodox principles regarding the implication of contractual terms support this analysis. Consequently, it is preferable to conclude that the right is primarily restitutionary[5]. On the other hand, it is true that because the surety is also entitled to recover expenses incurred in meeting his liability under the guarantee, these rights cannot be readily be described as purely restitutionary[6]. However, this is not a serious objection. We should not be perturbed if quasi-contractual or equitable doctrines do not neatly coincide with a single conceptual basis for relief.

1   *Ford v Stobridge* (1633) Nels 24, 21 ER 780.
2   *Morrice v Redwyn* (1731) 2 Barn KB 26, 94 ER 333.
3   For an analysis of this issue, see Mitchell *Law of Subrogation* (1994), p 55.
4   Goff and Jones *Law of Restitution* (5th edn, 1998), p 454.
5   Birks *An Introduction to the Law of Restitution* (revised edn, 1989), pp 185 189.
6   Mitchell *Law of Subrogation* (1994), p 55.

6.10   Claimants are also entitled to recoupment where they have had to meet a liability that arises because of a proprietary interest they have acquired or by statutory imposition. Thus, in *Moule v Garrett*[1], the claimant assigned a lease to one party who later conveyed it to the defendant. The defendant breached a term of the lease, for which he was liable to the landlord as a consequence of the rule that the burden of covenants that touch and concern the land 'run with the land' on assignment[2]. However, the landlord chose to sue the claimant, who was also liable for the breach because of his contractual relationship with the landlord[3]. The claimant asserted the right to be indemnified by the defendant. The claim for reimbursement could not be based on an express or implied term of a contract; for there was no privity of contract between the claimant and the defendant. Cockburn CJ found that the claimant had an independent right to be indemnified that we would now characterise as restitutionary. In order to explain this right, the Chief Justice cited the following passage from *Leake on Contracts*:

> Where the plaintiff has been compelled by law to pay, or being compellable by law, has paid money which the defendant was ultimately liable to pay, so that the latter obtains the benefit of the payment by the discharge of his liability, under such circumstances the defendant is held indebted to the plaintiff in the amount[4].

1   (1872) LR 7 Exch 101.
2   *Spencer's Case* (1583) 5 Co Rep 16a, 77 ER 72.
3   This rule recognised in *Walker's Case* (1587) 3 Co Rep 22a, 76 ER 676. As a result of the Landlord and Tenant (Covenants) Act 1995, s 5(2), the rule will generally not apply to assignments taking place after 1 January 1996.
4   (1872) LR 7 Exch 101 at 104.

6.11   Of course, in order to apply this principle, a court must first determine who is 'ultimately' or primarily liable to meet the obligation in question. At first sight it is not obvious why in *Moule v Garrett* the defendant, rather than the claimant, should have been characterised as primarily liable to the landlord. Both the original tenant and the assignee of the lease were, because of their different legal relationships with the landlord, obliged to ensure that the covenant in question was observed. However, it is manifestly fair to conclude that the tenant in possession should be viewed as primarily liable. If the original tenant remains liable for breaches, those breaches are not in any sense that tenant's fault. In addition, only the tenant in possession is in a position to ensure that covenants regarding the physical condition of the premises are observed. Moreover, it reflects the reality of tenancies that the landlord will first look to the current tenant to pay rent and make good any breach of the lease[1].

1 In any event, the reform enacted by Landlord and Tenant (Covenants) Act 1995, s 5(2), whereby a tenant's liability to a landlord ends upon assignment of the lease, means that the issue is less likely to arise in these circumstances today.

6.12 The principle is equally applicable where statute makes a claimant secondarily liable for an obligation for which the defendant alone would otherwise be responsible. This was the case in *Brook's Wharf and Bull Wharf Ltd v Goodman Bros*[1]. The claimant stored in its bonded warehouse a consignment of squirrel skins imported by the defendants. The skins were stolen from the warehouse without any fault on the part of the claimant, who was not liable for their loss. Despite the loss, the defendants remained liable to pay import duties on the skins. However, the customs authorities demanded payment of the import duties from the claimant, pursuant to statutory powers that allowed them to make such a demand where imported goods had left the warehouse prior to duty being paid. After paying duty, the claimant sought to be indemnified by the defendant. Lord Wright MR characterised the claimant's liability to the demand as 'ancillary to and by way of security for' the defendant's liability[2]. He analogised the claim before him to the surety's right to reimbursement from the principal debtor, and applied *Moule v Garrett*[3] in finding for the claimant. In his view: 'The defendant would be unjustly benefited at the cost of the plaintiffs if the latter ... should be left out of pocket by having to discharge what was the defendant's debt'[4].

1 [1937] 1 KB 534.
2 [1937] 1 KB 534 at 543.
3 (1872) LR 7 Exch 101.
4 [1937] 1 KB 534 at 545.

6.13 There is no reason why a right of reimbursement on this principle might not involve performance of a duty involving something other than making a monetary payment. *Gebhardt v Saunders*[1] illustrates the point. There, a tenant abated a nuisance, following a notice from the local sanitary authority. In the course of carrying out the necessary work, it transpired that the cause of the nuisance was a structural problem for which the landlord was liable. The court held that the tenant had been legally compelled to do the work for which the defendant was primarily liable, and consequently was permitted to recover the cost of the work as money paid to the defendant's use.

1 [1892] 2 QB 452.

6.14 One difficulty with this decision is that it is far from clear that the regulations in question imposed any liability on the claimant in these circumstances. Charles J found that the tenant was 'legally compellable' to do the work, on the basis that a notice had been served against it[1]. Yet it is difficult to imagine that the tenant would not have had a defence to the proceedings for failing to comply with the notice if they could have demonstrated that they were not liable for the nuisance under the statute. Consequently, it has been argued that mistake would offer a more satisfactory explanation for the outcome of the case[2]. However, it does not seem that tenant was necessarily under the mistaken belief that it was statutorily liable for the problem. Indeed, it was aware the landlord had also been served with a notice to abate the nuisance, and thus would seem to have understood that there was some doubt as to which party was actually liable. Nonetheless, given that it could not readily determine that it was not liable, and was faced with a penalty if it did not act, its actions were entirely reasonable. Given that the tenants were compelled to pay a debt by a threat of legal action that they could not readily discount, the basis for their payment might be characterised in terms of necessity.

1   [1892] 2 QB 452 at 457.
2   Birks *An Introduction to the Law of Restitution* (revised edn, 1989), p 191; Burrows *Law of Restitution* (1993), p 213.

C   Issues of voluntariness

6.15   It is easy enough to see why the law insists that the payment in question must have the effect of discharging a liability of the defendant. If the defendant were not released from his obligation to another, he could hardly be said to have been enriched by the payment. On the other hand, it is not so clear when a payment by one party should be said to discharge a liability owed by another. After all, it would be possible to conclude that a voluntary payment of a debt by a third party has the effect of discharging the debt, but the law concludes that it does not[1]. This rule effectively puts the interest that a debtor has in controlling his own affairs ahead of the claimant's interest in gaining restitution. In contrast, a payment by one legally compelled to pay another's debt does discharge that debt. This reflects an understanding that the absence of voluntariness means that the claimant's interest in gaining restitution is more important than that which the defendant has in having the right to determine who pays the debt. Thus, it can be seen that the questions of whether the payment is voluntary and whether the debt is discharged are often deeply interrelated[2].

1   See *Owen v Tate* [1976] QB 402.
2   The area is a difficult one. See below, para 6.23; Birks and Beatson 'Unrequested Payment of Another's Debt' (1976) 92 LQR 188; Hedley *Restitution: Its division and ordering* (2001), pp 140–144.

6.16   The difficulties that arise in this context are best examined in terms of those reasons for which a claim for recoupment is sometimes denied.

Where the liability discharged is not one owed by the defendant

6.17   In some circumstances, apart from issues of voluntariness, there is a real difficulty in concluding that a debt has been discharged. *Bonner v Tottenham and Edmonton Permanent Investment Building Society*[1] illustrates this. The claimants assigned their leasehold interest in a property and the assignee in turn mortgaged his interest to the defendants. When the assignee became bankrupt, the mortgagees took possession of the property; however, they failed to pay rent as they were obliged to under the mortgage. The claimants, despite having assigned their interest, remained contractually liable for any breaches of the lease and were called upon to pay the rent arrears by the landlord of the property. Thereafter, the claimants brought an action against the mortgagees seeking to be reimbursed for their payment of the rent. However, the claim was rejected on the basis that, as the landlord did not enjoy privity of estate or contract with the mortgagees, the claimants could not have discharged a debt due by the mortgagees to the landlord. According to this view, given their absence of privity with the mortgagee, the proper person from whom the claimant should have sought an indemnity was the assignee – although insolvency obviously meant that he was not a very attractive defendant. On the other hand, other cases focusing on such problems arising from a lack of privity suggest that, at least today, the claimant's position might not be regarded as dire as might appear at first sight. Arguably, after the claimant had discharged its debt, the assignee would have held any sums recovered from the mortgagees on trust for the claimant and, more arguably, could have been compelled by the claimant to bring an action against the mortgagees[2]. In any event, following the enactment of the Landlord and Tenant (Covenants) Act 1995, the issue is unlikely to arise in these circumstances[3].

1   [1899] 1 QB 161.
2   Cf *Jones v Broadhurst* (1850) 9 CB 173, 137 ER 858 (rights of an indorser of a bill of exchange, who has partially paid the holder, with respect to sums subsequently recovered against the acceptor); *Cunningham v Harrison* [1973] QB 942 (rights of a carer to damages recovered by an victim from a tortfeasor); *Joseph v Knox* (1813) 3 Camp 320 at 322, 170 ER 1397 (rights against assignee in affreightment context).
3   See above, para 6.11, n 1.

Where the payment in question is said not to have the effect of reducing the defendant's liability

6.18   In *Metropolitan Police District Receiver v Croydon Corpn*[1] the Court of Appeal considered a recoupment action brought by a police authority which was statutorily required to pay one of its employees throughout a period during which he unable to work, as the result of an accident caused by the defendant's negligence. The claimant argued that, in paying the officer in question, it had reduced the amount of compensation that the defendant would otherwise have been liable to pay in damages for loss of wages. The court rejected the claim, concluding that the defendant was not enriched at the expense of the claimant. Curiously, Morris LJ concluded that 'the real position in this case is that what has been lost, probably not by the plaintiff but by someone else, is the benefit of the services that the police officer would have rendered during the time when he was incapacitated'[2]. This is difficult to follow. What was lost might be said to be the benefit of the services, but the cost of those services is precisely the wages that the authority had to pay during the officer's incapacity. And, if it was not the claimant who suffered this loss, who was it?

1   [1957] 2 QB 154.
2   [1957] 2 QB 154 at 166.

6.19   Perhaps this problem could be dealt with in a similar way to other instances involving what can be characterised as an incidental or collateral benefit. In the context of voluntary care given to an injured party, the problem has been dealt with by holding that while the victim is entitled 'to recover as ... damages the reasonable value of services rendered to him', such damages are to be held by the victim on trust for the carer[1].

1   *Hunt v Severs* [1994] 2 AC 350 at 355, per Lord Bridge. See also *Cunningham v Harrison* [1973] QB 942. See above, para 3.65.

Where a liability is said not to be discharged, but claimants are allowed restitution by other means

6.20   The law is rather arbitrary on the question of whether the payment of an obligation owed by another has the effect of discharging that obligation. Thus, in the context of bills of exchange, the position is taken that payment by a drawer or indorser does not have the effect of discharging the obligation of the acceptor[1]. Instead, the law demands that an indorser who wishes to bring an action against the acceptor must first exercise his right to become holder of the bill, and then exercise the rights arising under the bill[2]. Problems arise, however, if an indorser has paid the holder only in part, and so cannot require the surrender of the bill. In these circumstances, the indorser's only recourse is to persuade the holder to sue the acceptor for the full amount due under the bill. Should a holder who has recovered from a drawer or indorser thereafter recover from the acceptor for the full amount due under bill, he will hold on trust for indorser a sum equal to that which the holder had previously received from the indorser[3]. What is less clear is whether an indorser in this position is entitled to require the holder to sue the acceptor on his behalf.

1   *Jones v Broadhurst* (1850) 9 CB 173, 137 ER 858. This position is now statutorily entrenched in the Bills of Exchange Act 1882, s 59(2). In contrast, in *Pownal v Ferrnad* (1827) 6 B & C 439, 108 ER 513, an indorser who had partially paid the holder was permitted to recover from the acceptor in an action for money paid. In the light of subsequent developments in case law and legislation, this can hardly be regarded as good law today.
2   See *Duncan Fox & Co v North and South Wales Bank* (1880) 6 App Cas 1 at 18, per Lord Blackburn.
3   *Jones v Broadhurst* (1850) 9 CB 173, 137 ER 858.

6.21   The difficulties relating to the discharge of a debt are well illustrated by the decision in *The Esso Bernicia*[1]. The case concerned the aftermath of a discharge of oil from a tanker that caused substantial pollution to the Scottish coastline and left a ship builder, Hall Russell, liable in negligence to local crofters. Esso, along with other tanker owners, was party to an agreement whereby they had undertaken to compensate those who suffered damage from such accidents. Pursuant to this arrangement, Esso made a substantial payment to the crofters. However, Esso did not require that the crofters assign any rights they had against Hall Russell in return. Subsequently, Esso claimed the right to be subrogated to the position of the crofters, so allowing them a right to sue Hall Russell and/or a direct right to be indemnified by Hall Russell. The House of Lords denied the claim on the basis that the payment was not compelled by law but only by a voluntary agreement that Esso had with third parties and did not have the effect of discharging Hall Russell's liability to the crofters[2]. The consequence of this was that Esso could not sue Hall Russell in their own name. On the other hand, Lord Goff indicated that subrogation might have entitled Esso to bring a claim against Hall Russell by suing in the name of the crofters[3]. In any event, it is likely that, had they sued, to the extent that they recovered a sum that exceeded their loss, the crofters would have held damages recovered on trust for Esso[4].

1   *Esso Petroleum Ltd v Hall Russell & Co* [1989] AC 643.
2   [1989] AC 643 at 662, per Lord Goff, and at 678, per Lord Jauncey.
3   [1989] AC 643 at 662–663. See also below, para 8.2.
4   Cf *Linden Gardens Trust Ltd v Lenesta Sludge Disposals Ltd* [1994] 1 AC 85 at 115, per Lord Browne-Wilkinson.

Where recoupment is denied for officiousness

6.22   There is authority that a claimant might be legally compelled to make a payment owed by the defendant and yet not be entitled to reimbursement if he 'officiously' put himself in that position[1]. This was the view taken in *Owen v Tate*[2]. Without consulting the defendant debtor, the claimant entered into an agreement with the defendant's creditor, whereby he agreed to guarantee the debt in question, in return for the existing surety's release. After he was subsequently called upon to meet his obligation under the guarantee, the claimant brought an action against the defendant for recoupment. The Court of Appeal rejected the claim. This is sometimes explained on the basis of the principle that a debt cannot be discharged without the debtor's consent. Yet, it seems that the Court of Appeal advanced on the basis that the payment did indeed discharge the debt[3]. Thus, it seems that the decision is based purely on a policy against the officious payment of another's debt.

1   See also *England v Marsden* (1886) LR 1 CP 529; discussed above, paras 6.6 and 6.7.
2   [1976] QB 402.
3   See for example [1976] QB 402 at 413, per Stephenson LJ.

6.23   It is sometimes said that the surety in *Owen v Tate* might have had an alternative claim against the creditor for failure of consideration. It is argued that a creditor who accepts a voluntary surety must be aware the surety intends that, should he be called on to pay the debt, he will be able to seek reimbursement from the debtor[1]. This is difficult to accept. It is artificial to assume that voluntary sureties have this expectation, and doubly artificial to assume that creditors must be aware of it. If the surety actually wants this right, would he not negotiate for it by seeking the debtor's approval of the arrangement, or by seeking an assignment of the debt? Moreover, the right to reimbursement enjoyed by non-officious sureties arises without the need for any agreement. This reflects judicial recognition of the fact that, while those accepting the responsibilities of suretyship will not necessarily consider the matter, it is only fair that they have the right to be indemnified in the event they are called upon to meet the debt.

1   Birks and Beatson 'Unrequested Payment of Another's Debt' (1976) 92 LQR 188 at 211.

CHAPTER 7

Contribution

Craig Rotherham

A   Introduction

The basis of rights of contribution

7.1   A right of contribution arises in a variety of circumstances where two or more parties are under a common liability to a creditor and the creditor compels one of them alone to discharge the liability. Perhaps the most straightforward example of the doctrine involves the right of contribution that a co-surety has from other co-sureties after being called upon to pay a debt for which all co-sureties are liable. In *Dering v Earl of Winchelsea*[1], Eyre CB commented that, 'If we take a view of the cases both in law and equity, we shall find that contribution is bottomed and fixed on general principles of justice, and does not spring from contract ... '[2]

1   (1787) 1 Cox Eq Cas 318, 29 ER 1184. The decision was also reported as *Deering v Earl of Winchelsea* 2 Bos & P 270, 126 ER 1276 when, after it was referred to in *Cowell v Edwards* (1800) 2 Bos & P 268, 126 ER 1275, the reporters took the opportunity to print a manuscript they had of the earlier decision. Given that it was reported at the time of the decision and is somewhat fuller and bearing in mind the high reputation in which these reports were held (see John William Wallace, *The Reporters* (Boston: Sale and Bugbee, 1882) 517), the version from Cox's Chancery Cases is preferred here.
2   (1787) 1 Cox Eq Cas 318 at 321, 29 ER 1184 at 1185.

7.2   But what is the nature of these 'general principles of justice'? While contribution is generally characterised as restitutionary, the question that needs to be determined is why the defendant's enrichment in not being required to meet the liability in question should be characterised as unjust. Some commentators have identified the basis for contribution as legal compulsion[1]. However, it is not obvious why co-sureties, for example, should be able to plead compulsion when they put themselves under this liability. The right of contribution is perhaps instead best explained as motivated by a policy that liabilities should be borne fairly[2].

1   See for example Virgo *Principles of the Law of Restitution* (2000), p 239.
2   Dietrich *Restitution: A New Perspective* (1998), p 157.

Sources of rights of contribution

7.3   Contribution has been considerably extended by the Civil Liability (Contribution) Act 1978. The Act has made a right of contribution available to 'any person liable in respect of any damage suffered by another person ... from any other person liable in respect of the same damage (whether jointly with him or otherwise)'[1]. While the common law required co-obligors to bear losses equally, the Act gives the courts the discretion to apportion contribution as is 'just and equitable having regard to the extent of that person's responsibility for the damage in question'[2]. The Act makes it clear that the statutory right 'supersedes any right, other than an express contractual right, to recover contribution'[3]. It follows that it is important to distinguish between those situations that are to be regulated pursuant to the Act and those which fall outside it and are left to be dealt with according to principles developed in case law.

1   See the Civil Liability (Contribution) Act 1978, s 1(1).
2   See the Civil Liability (Contribution) Act 1978, s 2(1).
3   See the Civil Liability (Contribution) Act 1978, s 7(3).

ARE RESTITUTIONARY CLAIMS THEMSELVES WITHIN THE CIVIL LIABILITY (CONTRIBUTION) ACT 1978?

7.4   Claims for damage suffered   One question is whether a restitutionary claim is one for damage suffered. The position taken in *Friends' Provident Life Office v Hillier Parker May & Rowden*[1] was that an action for money had and received based on mistake or failure of consideration could come within the Act. The position has been criticised by some restitution scholars who would draw a strict line between compensatory and restitutionary actions[2]. On this view, one who is liable to make restitution in the wake of a mistake or failure of consideration is liable because of their enrichment rather than the claimant's loss, and the claim is more in the nature of a debt rather than for damages. The contrary view is that the wording of the Act is wide enough to cover restitutionary claims where a claimant is seeking to recover loss.

1   [1997] QB 85, [1995] 4 All ER 260.
2   See Goff and Jones *Law of Restitution* (5th edn, 1998), p 396.

7.5   In general however, it is difficult to see that a defendant who is liable to an action based on his unjust enrichment should be entitled to seek contribution from anyone who is liable simply for causing the claimant loss and has obtained no benefit at the expense of the claimant. The nature of liability for restitution and the defence of change of position is such that a good faith restitution defendant should never be left out of pocket. To the extent that the defendant no longer retains an enrichment obtained at the expense of the claimant, he will be entitled to a defence provided he has changed his position in good faith. To the extent that one liable to make restitution remains enriched at the expense of the claimant, his making restitution will do no more than restore the status quo. It follows that he should not be entitled to seek contribution from any other party.

7.6   Liability in respect of the same damage   It is not enough that parties incur a liability that arises out of the same event. The Court of Appeal decision in *Birse Construction Ltd v Haiste Ltd*[1] illustrates the point. Anglia Water commissioned Birse to construct a reservoir. The work was poorly done and the reservoir had to be rebuilt. Birse sought compensation from Haiste, the consultant engineer on the project. Haiste in turn sought contribution from another consultant who had issued certificates to the effect that the work was progressing satisfactorily at different stages of the project. The difficulty was that the second consultant was liable only to Anglia Water, as there was no privity of contract between the second consultant and either Birse or Haiste. In the view of the Court of Appeal, the fact that Haiste was liable to Birse, while the second consultant was liable to Anglia Water, precluded Haiste's claim for contribution.

1   [1996] 2 All ER 1, [1996] 1 WLR 675.

CLAIMS OUTSIDE THE CIVIL LIABILITY (CONTRIBUTION) ACT 1978

7.7   On the other hand, actions for debt are not claims for compensation or damage within the terms of the Act[1]. As a result these actions are to be dealt with pursuant to equitable contribution principles.

1   This was the position favoured by the Law Commission who produced the report upon which the legislation is based: Law Commission Working Paper no 59 (1975), para 45(a). More equivocal are statements by the Court of Appeal in *Friends' Provident Life Office v Hillier Parker May & Rowden* [1995] 4 All ER 260 at 271 and 273, per Auld LJ.

B   Contribution claims at common law and in equity

7.8   Co-obligers are subject to contribution if they are liable in respect of the same demand. Liability will arise where an obligor has paid more than his share of the common liability. In addition, a right of contribution arises when judgment is obtained against an obligor or the estate of a deceased obligor for more than his or its share of that liability. The right of contribution ensures that co-obligors bear the loss resulting from a common debt equally by dividing the amount of the liability by the number of solvent co-obligors still bound at the date of the contribution action.

Co-sureties

DEVELOPMENT OF RIGHTS OF CONTRIBUTION AT LAW AND IN EQUITY

7.9   Since early in the seventeenth century, equity assumed a broad jurisdiction to hold co-sureties liable for contribution[1]. Similarly, from the early nineteenth century, the common law recognised a limited right to contribution through an action at law for quasi-contract[2]. Subsequently, this obligation to meet a share of the common liability was explained as 'inferred upon the implied knowledge of' the right to contribution in equity[3]. Lord Eldon stated that the action was available 'if there are co-sureties by the same instrument' and, given that it was based on an implied contractual term, it may be limited to situations to this context where there can be said to be privity of contract between the sureties[4]. In addition, the common law required a greater degree of certainty as to the content of the obligation than did equity. Consequently, the claim of a surety to contribution at law is limited by reference to the total amount owed by the principal debtor, divided by the number of sureties[5]. The surety's share is not adjusted if one or more of the sureties becomes insolvent before the action is brought. The limitation of sureties' rights at law was never likely to be a cause of injustice, given the availability of an action in equity. After the Judicature Act the common law action fell into obsolescence. As a result, the orthodox avenue for contribution is an action brought in the Chancery Division. All co-sureties should be parties, allowing the court to settle the rights of all in the same inquiry.

1   See for example *Fleetwood v Charnock* (1629) Nels 10, 21 ER 776; *Peter v Rich* (1629) 1 Rep Ch 34, 21 ER 499; *Morgan v Seymour* (1638) 1 Rep Ch 120, 21 ER 525.

2   An action in assumpsit was allowed, but not explained, in *Cowell v Edwards* (1800) 2 Bos & P 268,
     126 ER 1275 and *Davies v Humphreys* (1840) 6 M & W 153, 151 ER 361.
3   *Craythorne v Swinburne* (1807) 14 Ves 160 at 164, 33 ER 482 at 484, per Lord Eldon LC.
4   *Craythorne v Swinburne* (1807) 14 Ves 160 at 164, 33 ER 482 at 483, per Lord Eldon LC.
5   *Cowell v Edwards* (1800) 2 Bos & P 268, 126 ER 1275.

MODIFICATION OR EXCLUSION OF DUTY TO CONTRIBUTE

7.10   The nature of the equitable rights and obligations pertaining to co-sureties was described by Eyre CB in *Dering v Earl of Winchelsea*[1] in 1787:

> sureties have a common interest, and a common burthen; they are joined by the
> common end and purpose of their several obligations, as much as if they were joined
> in one instrument, with this difference only, that the penalties [ie the common
> liabilities] ascertain the proportion in which they are to contribute, whereas if they
> had joined in one bond, it must have depended on other circumstances[2].

1   (1787) 1 Cox Eq Cas 318, 29 ER 1184.
2   (1787) 1 Cox Eq Cas 318 at 322, 29 ER 1184 at 1186.

7.11   Prima facie the parties are equally bound to contribute toward the common liability. However, they can agree among themselves to be bound for different amounts and thereby alter their rights to, and obligations for, contribution[1]. For example, in *Swain v Wall*[2], because sureties contracted to pay fixed proportions of the common debt, their liability could not thereafter be altered by the insolvency of one of the sureties.

1   *Swain v Wall* (1641) 1 Rep Ch 149, 21 ER 534; *Pendlebury v Walker* (1841) 4 Y & C Ex 424 at
     441, 160 ER 1072 at 1079, per Alderson B.
2   (1641) 1 Rep Ch 149, 21 ER 534.

7.12   Indeed, a surety may contract to exclude liability to other sureties altogether. This occurs where a contract of suretyship indicates that the promisor is obliged to meet the liability in question only in the event that other sureties fail to meet their obligations. In such a case, the surety in question is not properly speaking a co-surety but is merely a 'sub-surety'[1] for those from whom the creditor is obliged to seek payment first[2]. Such exclusions are more often inferred than explicit.

In *Scholefield Goodman & Sons Ltd v Zyngier*[3] the respondent had by mortgage covenanted to pay the Commercial Bank of Australia in respect of bills of exchange on which Z Ltd was liable. Z Ltd dishonoured bills that it had accepted and indorsed and which the bank had discounted in its favour. The bank chose to present the bills to the appellants who were liable to indemnify it as drawers. After paying the debt, the appellants claimed a contribution from the respondent as co-surety. Their Lordships indicated that the availability of contribution depended upon the 'true construction of the contract which created the suretyship'[4]. In their view, in the absence of a contrary intention, the proper inference was that the respondent did not intend to place herself 'on the same level of liability' as the drawer and any indorsers of any bill upon which Z Ltd was liable[5]. Their Lordships concluded that the respondent was not liable on the mortgage unless there was default by both the acceptor and the drawer. While it was difficult to see that there was anything in the mortgage arrangement that required the bank to exhaust its remedies against other parties to the bill before requiring payment from the respondent, it would have been harsh if the bank had not done so. Thus, according to their Lordship's construction of the contract of suretyship, in relation to Z Ltd's liability on any bills of exchange, the respondent had contracted to be a sub-surety with respect to other parties to the bill.

1   See Goode *Commerical Law* (2nd edn, 1995), p 841.
2   See for example *Craythorne v Swinburne* (1807) 14 Ves 160, 33 ER 482; *Scholefield Goodman & Sons Ltd v Zyngier* [1986] AC 562 at 574–575.
3   [1986] AC 562.
4   [1986] AC 562 at 574.
5   [1986] AC 562 at 575.

7.13   There is authority to indicate that where a party becomes a surety at the request of another surety, 'there is no pretence for saying that he shall be liable to be called upon by the person at whose request he entered into the surety'[1]. While it might be difficult to justify such a broad conclusion, it seems that the inference generally to be drawn in such circumstances is that a party who was induced to act as surety by another guarantor was intended to act merely as a sub-surety.

1   *Turner v Davies* (1796) 2 Esp 478, 170 ER 425; *Batard v Hawes* (1853) 2 E & B 287, 118 ER 775.

7.14   Co-sureties' rights and obligations arise without the need for agreement. Indeed, they arise even if a co-surety agreed to be bound prior to and independently of other co-sureties and even if a co-surety is unaware that there are other co-sureties[1].

1   *Scholefield Goodman & Sons Ltd v Zyngier* [1986] AC 562 at 571, per Lord Brightman.

7.15   For the right of contribution to arise the liability must be a common one. This means that there is no right to demand a contribution from one who has guaranteed a different debt of the same principal debtor.

WHEN DOES THE RIGHT OF CONTRIBUTION BECOME EXERCISABLE?

7.16   The right to contribution arises where certain preconditions are satisfied. First, sureties must be able to establish either that they have paid more than their proportion of the debt in question or that the creditor has obtained judgment against them. Secondly, sureties must utilise their rights to be indemnified by principal debtors before seeking contribution.

7.17   Requirement that a surety has been required to meet more than his share of a common debt   The right to contribution enjoyed by a surety who has paid more than his share of a debt may arise even if the creditor has not obtained judgment or even brought and filed a claim against him. This right was considered recently in *Stimpson v Smith*[1]. The claimant and the defendant were company directors who had jointly and severally guaranteed payment of the company's liability to a bank on written demand up to a maximum of £25,000. Under pressure from the bank, the claimant agreed to pay £20,000 in reduction of the company's overdraft, in return for releasing him and the defendant from any further liability under the guarantee. Thereafter, the claimant requested the defendant to pay £10,000 as his share under the guarantee. The defendant refused on the basis that the bank had made no written demand to the company and the co-sureties. It was already well established that a surety could in some circumstances claim an indemnity from his principal debtor after paying a debt even though the debtor had not made a formal demand[2]. In the Court of Appeal's view, the same principle applied to rights of contribution between co-sureties. In its view, the making of a demand was a procedural requirement and not a precondition of liability, and this requirement could be waived by a surety without affecting its rights to contribution from co-sureties. A right to contribution would arise provided that: the amount of the liability was ascertainable; in the absence of a settlement, a formal demand could be expected to follow; and the arrangement made with the creditor was not disadvantageous to the co-surety[3].

1   [1999] Ch 340.
2   *Thomas v Nottingham Incorporated Football Club Ltd* [1972] Ch 596, per Goff J.
3   [1999] 2 WLR 1292 at 1300, per Peter Gibson LJ, and 1303, per Judge LJ.

7.18   Where a creditor has obtained judgment against one co-surety, the latter is entitled to a declaration that he would be entitled to contribution from any co-sureties once, in meeting the judgment, he has paid more than his share[1].

1   *Wolmershausen v Gullick* [1893] 2 Ch 514 at 529, per Wright J.

7.19   Payments of instalments   Difficulties arise in relation to payments of instalments of a debt. Unless the instalments are regarded as separate debts, the payment of more than one's share of an instalment will not give rise to a right of contribution. This is illustrated by *Stirling v Burdett*[1], where several parties had jointly and severally guaranteed the repayment of £15,000 secured by a mortgage. At the time of action, the claimant had contributed more than his share of mortgage instalments and interest then due, but less than his share of the entire debt. Warrington J noted that, if any co-surety were ordered to contribute at this point, he might ultimately be called upon by the mortgagee to meet more than his share of the debt as a whole. Consequently, he determined that the debt should be treated as indivisible. Thus, the claim for contribution failed.

1   [1911] 2 Ch 418.

7.20   Exhaustion of rights against the principal debtor   The requirement that the surety make use of his right to be indemnified by the principal debtor means that the right to contribution arises only after the principal debtor is joined as a party to the action or has become insolvent. If the claimant does not have formal proof that the principal debtor is insolvent, such as declaration of bankruptcy, the right to contribution will nevertheless arise provided that there is sufficient evidence to indicate that the principal debtor is in fact insolvent[1].

1   *Hay v Carter* [1935] Ch 397 at 405–406, per Lord Hanworth MR; *Lawson v Wright* (1786) 1 Cox Eq Cas 275 at 275, 29 ER 1164 at 1164, per Sir Lloyd Kenyon. See Goff and Jones *Law of Restitution* (5th edn, 1998), p 402.

THE EXTENT OF THE OBLIGATION TO MAKE CONTRIBUTION

7.21   Difficult issues arise where co-sureties have agreed to stand surety for different sums. For example, we might ask what the co-sureties' respective shares of the common debt are where the principal debtor is liable for £1,000 and A has contracted to stand surety for the full amount of the debt while B has contracted so as to limit his liability to £500. The difficulty is that it is not clear whether the fact that a limit has been set on B's liability should be determinative of the co-sureties' rights of contribution inter se. In *Pendelbury v Walker*[1], Alderson B stated that the law requires that 'all contribute equally, if each is a surety to an equal amount; and if not equally, then proportionately to the amount for which each is a surety'[2]. This suggests that, in terms of the example offered above, if the principal debtor defaulted owing £500 and A was called upon to pay this, B would be obliged to contribute only $\frac{1}{3}$ of the common debt. Nonetheless, the matter is not entirely resolved. A different approach has been favoured in the context of liability insurance[3]. And while the approach endorsed in *Pendelbury* is binding at High Court level, the Court of Appeal is not bound by any ruling on the matter[4].

1   (1841) 4 Y & C Ex 424, 160 ER 1072.
2   (1841) 4 Y & C Ex 424 at 441, 160 ER 1072 at 1079, per Alderson B.
3   *Commercial Union Assurance Co Ltd v Hayden* [1977] QB 804. See below, para 7.39.
4   [1977] QB 804 at 815, per Cairns LJ.

7.22   In the absence of an agreement to the contrary among themselves, each solvent surety is liable to contribute in proportion to his share of the common debt. In addition, in deciding co-sureties' liability, any benefits that a co-surety has recovered from the principal debtor must be taken into account. An illustration of this is provided by *Re Arcedeckne*[1], where the principal creditor had taken out a policy on the life of the principal debtor and assigned it to a surety in return for payment of the debt. Pearson J held that the matter had to be treated as if the surety had 'purchased those rights ... not for the benefit of himself only, but for the benefit of his co-sureties'[2]. Consequently, the surety held the benefit of the life policy for all the solvent co-sureties as tenants in common. The imputation of intention introduces an unnecessary fiction. The matter is better explained in terms of the duty of co-sureties to share their burden of what the law treats as a common debt. Given the uncertainty of the value of benefits such as securities or policies on the life of the debtor, the most efficacious method of ensuring that all co-sureties bear their share of their common liability is to provide that such assets are held for the benefit of all co-sureties.

1   (1883) 24 Ch D 709.
2   (1883) 24 Ch D 709 at 716.

7.23   It might be that a creditor accepts a payment from one co-surety as discharging the entire debt even though the payment would represent only that surety's share of the common debt were the creditor to insist on the full amount. It follows from the principle that the burden of a common debt should be equally shared that the surety will be able to claim a rateable contribution from his co-sureties[1]. Similarly, any contribution made by the principal debtor will reduce the share of all the co-sureties rateably[2].

1   *Ex p Snowdon* (1881) 17 Ch D 44.
2   *Stirling v Forrester* (1821) 3 Bligh 575, 4 ER 712.

DISCHARGE OF SURETIES BY CREDITORS

7.24   In certain circumstances, the act of a creditor may have the effect of discharging the debt in question, thereby rendering the issue of contribution moot. If a creditor simply releases a principal debtor from a debt, he thereby also discharges the debtor's sureties. However, a creditor may covenant not to sue the principal debtor, but reserve his rights against any sureties. In these circumstances, the debt is not discharged and the sureties remain liable[1]. This rule has been justified on the basis that the sureties are not unduly prejudiced by the arrangement between the creditor and the debtor because they retain the right to sue the debtor[2].

1   *Bateson v Gosling* (1871) LR 7 CP 9 at 17, per Brett LJ.
2   Glanville Williams *Joint Obligations* (1949), p 121.

7.25   More controversial is the view that a creditor's giving a principal debtor time to pay the debt has the effect of releasing any sureties. Early in the nineteenth century, Best CJ justified this rule on the basis of a concern for the danger that the debtor's financial position might further deteriorate during the additional time allowed by the creditor. Thus, if the principal debtor became insolvent in this period, the creditor's delay might have had the effect of undermining the effectiveness of a surety's right to be indemnified by the principal debtor[1]. While this is a legitimate concern, it is also no doubt the case that sureties would generally prefer that a creditor gave the principal debtor additional time rather than seeking payment from them. Moreover, even if, in retrospect, a surety's decision to give a principal debtor time undermines the position of other sureties, this does not mean that the risk entailed in the decision was not a sensible one to take at the time. While Lord Eldon noted this reality in *Samuell v Howarth*[2], he remarked that: 'The creditor has no right – it is against the faith of his contract – to give time to the principal, even though manifestly for the benefit of the Surety, without the consent of the Surety'[3]. However, later that century, Blackburn J suggested that this rule was misconceived, noting that he was 'not aware of any instance in which a surety ever in practice exercised this right'[4]. Nonetheless, he was of the view that the rule was 'so long firmly established that it can only be altered by the legislature'[5]. Perhaps this conclusion reflects an unduly static understanding of the common law that was prevalent at the time. It might be that today the House of Lords might consider that it could legitimately reverse this rule, if it were ever offered the opportunity. Ultimately, the question that needs to be asked is whether it is unreasonable to expect creditors to seek permission of any sureties before extending principal debtors extra time to meet their obligations.

1   *Philpot v Briant* (1828) 4 Bing 717 at 719, 130 ER 945 at 946.
2   (1817) 3 Mer 272, 36 ER 105.
3   (1817) 3 Mer 272 at 279, 36 ER 105 at 107.
4   *Swire v Redman* (1876) 1 QBD 536 at 541.
5   (1876) 1 QBD 536 at 542.

7.26   What is the effect of a decision by a creditor to release one co-surety? In the absence of an express condition in the contract of guarantee to the contrary[1], other sureties will be released only if they have contracted jointly, or jointly and severally. In this case, 'the joint suretyship of the others being part of the consideration of the contract of each', the discharge of one surety releases the others[2]. Where sureties' liability is merely several, one surety will not be automatically released by the creditor's decision to release another surety. However, remaining sureties may have their liability wholly or partially limited to the extent that the release has the effect of depriving them of their remedy of contribution[3]. This principle was applied in *Ward v National Bank of New Zealand Ltd*[4], where one co-surety was released from a guarantee it had given to stand surety for the principal debtor's obligations up to £600 in return for executing a guarantee for up to £1,400. The defendant was a surety who had separately guaranteed the principal debtor's obligations to the bank. Clearly, the defendant's right to contribution had not been adversely affected by the release, as the other surety remained liable to make a contribution as a result of the substituted guarantee. Consequently, the Privy Council held that the defendant's obligation was not discharged.

1   See for example *Ellesmere Brewery Co v Cooper* [1896] 1 QB 75.
2   *Ward v National Bank of New Zealand Ltd* (1883) 8 App Cas 755 at 764–765.
3   *Ward v National Bank of New Zealand Ltd* (1883) 8 App Cas 755 at 765–767.
4   (1883) 8 App Cas 755.

7.27   By consenting to give time to a surety to meet his obligation, a creditor does not release other sureties[1]. It has been argued that such a concession inures to the benefit of sureties by postponing a claim for contribution and giving the principal debtor more time to pay[2]. This may not always be the case; giving time to one surety might have effect of undermining other sureties' ability to seek contribution, thanks to the first surety's financial state's deteriorating. Again, the question is whether it would be reasonable to insist that a creditor seek the consent of other sureties before giving one surety time to meet his obligations. In any event, while the rule may be on balance a sensible one, it is obviously difficult to reconcile with the approach taken toward creditors' giving principal debtors time[3].

1   *Dunn v Slee* (1816) Holt NP 399, 171 ER 284.
2   Goff and Jones *Law of Restitution* (5th edn, 1998), p 408.
3   See above, para 7.25.

7.28   A secured creditor is said not to owe his surety any duty of care to exercise at any particular time, or even at all, the power of sale conferred by a mortgage securing the principal debt. While it is said that equity provides that a surety may be discharged if the creditor acts in a way that is injurious to the surety's rights, the restrictions placed on the creditor appear to be very limited indeed[1].

1   *Watts v Shuttleworth* (1860) 5 H & N 235 at 247–248, 157 ER 1171 at 1176–1177, per Pollock
    CB; *China and South Sea Bank Ltd v Tan* [1990] 1 AC 536.

LOSS OF RIGHTS OF CONTRIBUTION

7.29   By the act of the surety   One matter that has yet to be resolved is whether a surety who, after meeting his obligation under a guarantee, gives the principal debtor time to meet his obligation to indemnify the surety thereby discharges any co-sureties. By analogy with the rule that releases sureties where creditors give principal debtors time, it might be argued that the same result should apply to sureties who delay enforcing their remedies against the debtor. According to this approach, because the debt in question is a common one, the creditor should seek the approval of sureties before taking a decision that might affect their position. However, equally it could be argued that the proper approach to take is that adopted where a creditor gives one co-surety time, whereby other co-sureties are not released from their obligation to contribute to the common debt[1].

1   *Dunn v Slee* (1816) Holt NP 399, 171 ER 284.

7.30   A different problem arises where a surety who has been called upon by the creditor to pay the debt in question thereafter releases another co-surety from his obligation to make a contribution. Where the sureties are jointly, or jointly and severally, liable, following the approach taken in relation to creditors releasing sureties[1], such an action will also release other co-sureties. Following *Ward v National Bank of New Zealand Ltd*[2], where the sureties are severally liable, if the release of a surety affects their rights to seek a contribution from the released surety[3], the remaining sureties should also be released pro tanto to the extent that their position has been undermined.

1   *Ward v National Bank of New Zealand Ltd* (1883) 8 App Cas 755. See above, para 7.26.
2   (1883) 8 App Cas 755.
3   See above, para 7.26.

7.31   Finally, there is the question as to the effect of a surety's paying the creditor without the agreement of a co-surety. Where the effect of a failure to inform a co-surety is that a compromise was reached in circumstances where none should have been conceded, or at least not on such burdensome terms, the co-surety will be released[1].

1   *Smith v Compton* (1832) 3 B & Ad 407, 110 ER 146.

7.32   Death   A creditor's rights against a joint surety comes to an end in the event of the latter's death[1]. On the other hand, the independent joint and several equitable obligations owed by sureties to their co-sureties, arising as they do by operation of law rather than out of contract, will bind a deceased surety's estate[2].

1   *Ashby v Day* (1886) 54 LT 408,
2   *Ashby v Ashby* (1827) 7 B & C 444, 108 ER 789; *Batard v Hawes* (1853) 2 E & B 287, 118 ER 775; *Prior v Hembrow* (1841) 8 M & W 873, 151 ER 1294; Glanville Williams *Joint Obligations* (1949), pp 165–166; Goff and Jones *Law of Restitution* (5th edn, 1998), p 409.

Insurers

WHEN DOES THE RIGHT OF CONTRIBUTION ARISE?

7.33   Where more than one insurer has insured a person against a loss, the insurers' liabilities are treated as a common debt. One who is insured against the same loss by more than one policy is entitled to recover against any of the insurers to the full extent of his loss provided the policy allows it. An insurer who has been called upon to meet the assured's loss may thereafter seek contribution from the other insurers who are liable for the same loss. As with other rights of contribution, the entitlement arises independently of contract but may be modified by contract among the insurers.

7.34   Strictly speaking, notice by an assured of his loss is a condition precedent to an insurer's liability under a policy. Does this mean that, if an assured fails to give one co-insurer notice, this will prevent that insurer from being liable to a claim for contribution after the assured has recovered against another co-insurer? In *Legal and General Assurance Society Ltd v Drake Insurance Co Ltd*[1], the Court of Appeal held that contribution was to be determined according to the potential liability at the date of the loss in question. It noted that to conclude otherwise would mean that a co-insurer's right of contribution would be dependent upon the actions of an assured. The court, therefore, drew a sharp distinction between such procedural steps with which an assured needed to comply in order to enforce a valid claim and more substantive matters such as misrepresentation or non-disclosure that would give the insurer a good defence to a claim.

1   [1992] QB 887.

7.35   However, the Privy Council in *Eagle Star Insurance Co Ltd v Provincial Insurance plc*[1] declined to make such a distinction. Two insurers were both statutorily liable to the victim of an accident caused by the assured. Both were in the position that they could have resisted a claim made by the assured. First, Eagle Star had cancelled the assured's policy before the accident, but thanks to a Bahamian statute, remained liable to third parties because it had failed to take steps to obtain surrender of the policy from the assured. Secondly, the assured had failed to notify Provincial Insurance within the period required under its policy, although that did not affect the insurer's statutory liability to third parties. Eagle Star argued that, because only Provincial's policy was in existence at the time of the accident, it was entitled to be fully indemnified by Provincial. The approach taken in *Legal and General* would have suggested that there was an important distinction to be drawn between the different bases on which the co-insurers could have resisted a claim made by the assured. In terms of the earlier case, Provincial was 'potentially liable' to the insured under its policy at the date of the loss, while Eagle Star was not. However, the Privy Council took a different view. In its view, the basis on which an insurer could resist a claim from the assured was irrelevant. In this case, given that both insurers remained statutorily liable to a third party but would have been able to repudiate liability to the assured, there was no distinction between their positions and they were required to contribute equally towards the liability in question.

1   [1994] 1 AC 130.

7.36   The Privy Council dismissed the notion that the co-insurers' liability to contribute arose at the date of the loss in question. Rather it held that the proper basis on which to determine co-insurers' obligations inter se was in accordance with their liability to the insured under the contracts of insurance. If applied to the facts of *Legal and General*, the implications of this conclusion are stark. It would mean that one co-insurer that had been called upon to meet the assured's loss would have no right to claim contribution from a co-insurer who had not been given due notice under its policy. Thus, a right of contribution might be lost due to no fault of a co-insurer. Lord Woolf, delivering the Board's advice, made light of this implication by noting that this was unlikely to frustrate insurers' expectations, because 'it is unlikely that the existence of the other insurer would have been known at the time the contract of insurance was made'[1]. Yet, it is difficult to see that this really answers the objection. While the proposed rule may not disappoint expectations formed at the time at which the insurance contract in question was entered into, it is liable to prove inconsistent with intuitions about fairness commonly formed after the event. After all, the courts have seen fit to make a right of contribution available whether or not co-sureties or co-insurers knew of one another's existence. It is difficult to escape the conclusion that the Privy Council's approach allows one co-insurer to escape a common liability on a technicality.

1   [1994] 1 AC 130 at 141.

7.37   An insurer will not be entitled to contribution if a payment is regarded as voluntary in that it was not required under its policy with the assured. If the policies of co-insurers contain rateable proportion clauses and one of the insurers pays a claim in full, despite being aware of the presence of co-insurers, a payment will be treated as voluntary to the extent that it is in excess of the insurer's rateable proportion[1].

1   *Legal and General Assurance Society Ltd v Drake Insurance Co Ltd* [1992] QB 887 at 896–897, per Lloyd LJ.

7.38   Insurers will be treated as subject to a common liability if their policies insure against a common peril and cover the same interest. Thus, there will be no right of contribution between those who insure different parties against the same peril[1].

1   See for example *North British and Mercantile Insurance Co Ltd v London, Liverpool and Globe Insurance Co Ltd* (1877) 5 Ch D 569.

CALCULATING CO-INSURERS' RATEABLE SHARES

7.39   In *Godin v London Assurance Co*[1], Lord Mansfield CJ indicated that, in cases of double insurance, 'the several insurers shall all of them contribute pro rata'[2]. However, this of course raises the question, in proportion to what? As mentioned, the method favoured in surety cases is to fix shares with reference to the maximum liability that each surety has assumed[3]. However, this is not the only basis according to which insurers' relative liabilities might be fixed. In *Commercial Union Assurance Co Ltd v Hayden*[4], the Court of Appeal contrasted the 'maximum liability' approach favoured in surety cases with one calculated on an 'independent liability basis', whereby insurers' contributions are fixed according to 'the liability of each insurer if it had been the only insurer'[5]. In *Hayden* there were two insurers, one of whom was liable up to a maximum of £100,000 and the other for up to £10,000. If a 'maximum liability' approach were taken, the second insurer would be liable for only an $1/_{11}$ share of the common liability. Cairns LJ reasoned that, according to the 'independent liability' approach:

> any claim up to £10,000 would be borne equally, but on a claim for, say, £40,000 the plaintiff's independent liability would be £40,000 and the defendant's independent liability would be limited to £10,000 so that the apportionment would be in the ratio of 4:1, i.e. £32,000 to be paid by the plaintiffs and £8,000 by the defendant[6].

Cairns LJ noted that, apart from the surety context, it seemed that the maximum liability was also taken in property cases, although, at least outside the domestic context, policies generally provide pro rata average clauses that apply the independent liability basis[7]. On the other hand, he observed that it is unclear whether the same approach was to be applied in relation to marine insurance. The Marine Insurance Act 1906, s 80(1), obliges insurers to contribute rateably in proportion to the amount of their liability under their respective policies. However, it is unclear whether this refers to the maximum liability assumed under the policy or the 'actual liability in the particular case'[8].

1   (1758) 1 Burr 489, 97 ER 419.
2   (1758) 1 Burr 489 at 492, 97 ER 419 at 420.
3   *Pendlebury v Walker* (1841) 4 Y & C Ex 424, 160 ER 1072. See above, para 7.21.
4   [1977] QB 804.
5   [1977] QB 804 at 811.
6   [1977] QB 804 at 811.
7   [1977] QB 804 at 811–812.
8   [1977] QB 804 at 813. See also at 819, per Stephenson LJ

7.40   Ultimately, the Court in *Hayden* favoured the independent liability basis for determining the insurers' share of the common liability. Cairns LJ observed that the purpose of stipulating a maximum level of liability was to safeguard the insurer from having to bear exceptionally heavy claims. Consequently, he reasoned that it would be 'artificial to use the limits under two policies to adjust liability in respect of claims which are within the limits of either policy'[1]. Thus, the court concluded that the independent liability approach would better fulfil the expectations of the parties in the context of liability insurance.

1   [1977] QB 804 at 816.

7.41   Following *Hayden*, it is likely that an independent liability approach will be taken in relation to liability policies in marine insurance[1]. A justification might be made for favouring a maximum liability approach in relation to valued policies, where premiums are more likely to be based on the value insured. In contrast, in liability cases, premiums do not necessarily bear a direct relationship to the maximum liability assumed by the insurer. However, it is more difficult to distinguish the function that the designation of a maximum level of liability performs in the surety context from the role it plays in liability insurance[2].

1   Mustill and Gilman (eds) *Arnould's Law of Marine Insurance and Average* (16th edn, 1997), vol 1, para 438.
2   Burrows *Law of Restitution* (1993), p 222.

Partners

7.42   Partners are jointly liable for the partnership's liabilities[1]. This liability to a common demand gives a partner who has paid more than his share of a liability the right to claim contribution from other partners[2]. Claims for contribution that arise out of damage caused to a third party by the wrongful act of a fellow partner are now subject to the Civil Liability (Contribution) Act 1978[3]. However, other claims continue to be governed by principles developed in case law.

1   A common liability now found in the Partnership Act 1890, ss 10–12.
2   *Re the Royal Bank of Australia, Robinson's Executors* (1856) 6 De GM & G 572, 43 ER 1356.
3   See the Civil Liability (Contribution) Act 1978, s 7(3). On the Act, see below, para 7.47ff.

7.43   The share of the common liability that the partners bear inter se depends on the terms of the partnership agreement. In the absence of any indication to the contrary, the proper inference is that partners intend to share benefits and losses equally[1]. Where the partnership agreement provides that benefits are to be shared unequally, the proper inference in the absence of any indication to the contrary, is that the parties intend to contribute in the same unequal proportions to any losses[2]. During the currency of the partnership, rights of contribution are properly enforced through an action for a general partnership account[3].

1   See the Partnership Act 1890, s 24(1).
2   See the Partnership Act 1890, s 44.
3   *Boulter v Peplow* (1850) 9 CB 493, 137 ER 984; *Sedgwick v Daniell* (1857) 2 H & N 319, 157 ER 132.

Mortgagors

7.44   Do rights of contribution arise where A, an owner of land subject to a charge, first subdivides the land and transfers part of the land to B while retaining the rest and, secondly, pays off the charge on the whole land? This depends on whether one of the parties has assumed primary liability for the debt. Most obviously, where A has personally covenanted to pay the mortgage debt, no such right will arise[1]. Any rights A has against B must arise out of a contract between them, and will be in the nature of an obligation to indemnify, and not a common debt. A right to contribution is likely to arise only where A's land was subject to a mortgage liability that he did not create himself and he transferred the land subject to this charge[2].

1   *Re Best* [1924] 1 Ch 42.
2   *Ker v Ker* (1869) IR 4 Eq 15; *Re Mainwaring's Settlement Trusts* [1937] Ch 96; Goff and Jones *Law of Restitution* (5th edn, 1998), p 414.

Joint tenants

7.45   Claims for contribution by a joint tenant who has incurred an expense on behalf of fellow joint tenants happened from time to time before 1926[1]. Since the 1925 legislative revolution, property will generally be held on trust (formerly a trust for sale[2] and now a trust of land[3]). Consequently, joint tenants who incur expenses will generally be trustees and entitled to reimbursement pursuant to normal principles of trust law. As a result, contribution claims are now unlikely to arise in this context.

1   Goff and Jones *Law of Restitution* (5th edn, 1998), p 414.
2   Under the Law of Property Act 1925.
3   Under the Trusts of Land and Appointment of Trustees Act 1996, s 5.

Joint contractors

7.46   Joint contractors who are called upon to perform more than their share of a common liability are entitled to a contribution from other joint contractors. For this purpose, joint contractors are treated in the same way as co-sureties but for two important exceptions. First, the courts have long held that a covenant of a creditor not to sue one joint contractor does not release other joint contractors from their liability to contribute their proper share of a debt[1]. Secondly, the courts have also declined to extend to this context the rule that by giving time to a principal debtor a creditor discharges the debtor's sureties[2].

1   *Lacy v Kynaston* (1701) 2 Salk 575, 91 ER 484; *Hutton v Eyre* (1815) 6 Taunt 289, 128 ER 1046; *Walmesley v Cooper* (1839) 11 Ad & El 216, 113 ER 398.
2   *Swire v Redman* (1876) 1 QBD 536 at 542, per Cockburn CJ.

C   Contribution claims under the Civil Liability (Contribution) Act 1978

7.47   The Civil Liability (Contribution) Act 1978 provides that:

> ... any person liable in respect of any damage suffered by another person may recover contribution from any other person liable in respect of the same damage (whether jointly with him or otherwise)[1].

The Act only applies to 'damage' that occurred after 1979. As mentioned, 'damage' has been interpreted widely so as to include claims for restitution of benefits received as well as compensation for loss suffered. One is 'a person liable for damage' if liable to compensate for damage suffered 'whatever the legal basis of his liability, whether tort, breach of contract, breach of trust or otherwise'[2].

1   See the Civil Liability (Contribution) Act 1978, s 1(1).
2   See the Civil Liability (Contribution) Act 1978, s 6(1).

The effect of cesser of liability

7.48   Section 1(2) of the Act provides that a claimant has a right of contribution, 'notwithstanding that he has ceased to be liable in respect of the damage in question since the time when the damage occurred, provided that he was so liable immediately before he made or was ordered or agreed to make the payment in respect of which the contribution is sought'. Thus, a claimant who at the time he made or was ordered to make or agreed to make a payment, was liable to make that payment, may claim contribution, even if his liability is subsequently removed, for instance, by the expiration of a limitation period.

7.49   Section 1(3) provides that a right of contribution will not be lost merely because a limitation period regarding the damage for which both parties were initially liable has run. Rather, a right of contribution will be lost only if the Statute of Limitation has run against that right itself. A right to contribution accrues from the date a judgment is made against the person who has suffered loss, or from the date of a settlement or compromise between the person claiming contribution and the person who has suffered loss[1].

1   See the Civil Liability (Contribution) Act 1978, s 10(4).

7.50   Section 1(5) provides that the determination of issues in a judgment by a United Kingdom court, in an action brought by the party who has suffered damage against a person from whom contribution is sought, will be conclusive in a subsequent action for contribution. The effect of this is that one who has successfully defended an action brought by the person who has suffered the damage in question will not subsequently be liable to a claim for contribution by another who is found liable for that damage.

Bona fide settlement or compromise

7.51   Section 1(4) provides that one who reaches a bona fide settlement or compromise with respect to the damage in question may claim contribution from another who is liable for the same damage. A claimant need not prove that he 'is or ever was liable in respect of the damage' provided that 'he would have been liable assuming that the factual basis of the claim against him could be established'[1]. On the other hand, no right of contribution will arise if a claimant cannot establish that he would have been legally liable if the factual basis of the claim could have been established.

1   See the Civil Liability (Contribution) Act 1978, s 1(4).

7.52   The burden will lie on a claimant seeking contribution after a settlement or compromise to establish that the party from whom the claimant seeks contribution would have been liable to the person who suffered damage if he had been sued. In all likelihood, the party from whom the contribution is sought will have the burden of establishing that the settlement was not bona fide[1]. Any contribution recoverable will be a proportion of the amount paid or agreed under the compromise, even if the liability of the party from whom contribution is sought would have exceeded this figure.

1   Goff and Jones *Law of Restitution* (5th edn, 1998), p 418.

The discretion of the court

7.53   The 1978 Act gives the court the power to determine the amount of contribution as is 'just and equitable having regard to that person's responsibility for the damage in question'[1]. The language follows that of the 1935 Act[2], and decisions interpreting the earlier legislation remain relevant to the interpretation of the 1978 Act.

1   See the Civil Liability (Contribution) Act 1978, s 2(1).
2   Law Reform (Married Women and Tortfeasors) Act 1935, superseded as to contribution by the 1978 Act.

7.54   The courts have developed some guidelines on the proper exercise of the discretion under the Act. Particular factors identified as relevant are the relative 'causative potency' and 'blameworthiness' of the parties' actions[1]. These considerations were raised in *Madden v Quirk*[2], which concerned the question of contribution between two negligent drivers who were in a collision that resulted in the claimant's being injured. As well as driving negligently, the first defendant was the driver of a vehicle in which the claimant was being carried in an unsafe manner. In addition to taking account of the extent to which the parties' negligent driving contributed to the accident, Simon Brown J took into consideration the fact that the first defendant failed in his statutory duty to carry his passenger in a safe manner. In his view, this failure made the first defendant more blameworthy for the claimant's injuries[3]. As a result, the first defendant's liability to contribute toward the damages due to the claimant was assessed at 85%.

1   See for example *Madden v Quirk* [1989] 1 WLR 702 at 707, per Simon Brown J; *Downs v Chappell* [1996] 3 All ER 344 at 363, per Hobhouse LJ. See Mitchell *Law of Subrogation* (1994), p 34.
2   [1989] 1 WLR 702.
3   [1989] 1 WLR 702 at 709.

7.55   How might these considerations apply where a court has to allocate contribution between one party who was a conscious wrongdoer and another who was merely careless? The issue arose in *Downs v Chappell*[1], where the first defendant was liable for deceit for giving a false account of his business's profitability and the second defendant was an accountant who had negligently verified the misstated figures. While the first defendant's actions were obviously more blameworthy than those of the second defendant, the Court of Appeal was swayed by the fact that the claimant placed greater reliance on the second defendant's judgement. As a result, it upheld the lower court's decision to fix the responsibility of each to contribute at 50%. The result might appear lenient on the fraudulent first defendant. It obviously reflects the court's displeasure at the recklessness of a professional upon whom the claimant had relied. Yet, the second defendant's liability to the claimant for any injury caused should provide a sufficient deterrent for such actions. Perhaps the decision could also be justified on the basis that the second defendant should have saved the first defendant, his client, from his own dishonesty.

1   [1997] 1 WLR 426.

7.56   A question that has yet to be resolved is how the Act applies to relationships in respect of which the courts had developed special rules regarding rights to contribution. The issue has particular relevance for trustees, directors and partners.

7.57   Trustees are, of course, liable jointly and severally for any breach of trust. Equity has long recognised rights of contribution between trustees. However, prior to the 1978 Act, the courts were reluctant to apportion liability between trustees so that those who were not actively involved in a breach bore less of a burden than trustees who actively perpetrated the breach. It was thought that apportionment would provide a disincentive for trustees to be vigilant. However, in certain circumstances, equity provided that trustees who were not actively involved in a breach were entitled to be indemnified. This was true where one trustee misapplied trust funds entirely for his own use, where trustees were led to commit a breach as a result of following the advice of a solicitor trustee, and where only one of the trustees acted fraudulently. In addition, trustees who were also beneficiaries of the fund were under an obligation to indemnify any co-trustees to the extent of their beneficial interest[1]. It is unclear whether the courts will continue to follow these principles. It is perhaps more likely that they will consider that the 1978 Act, directing them as it does to determine contribution as is 'just and equitable, having regard to the extent of ... [trustees'] responsibility for the damage in question'[2], envisages a more flexible approach.

1   *Chillingworth v Chambers* [1896] 1 Ch 685 at 698, per Lindley LJ.
2   See the Civil Liability (Contribution) Act 1978, s 2(3).

7.58   Similar issues arise in the context of directors, where equity has also developed special rules to govern contribution claims[1]. Directors are liable to indemnify the company against losses caused by their breaches of duty. Equity provided a right of contribution between directors liable for a breach[2]. However, contribution was denied to those directors who had been the sole beneficiaries of a particular breach[3]. Again, given the broad statutory discretion to apportion any loss resulting from a breach as is just and equitable having regard to a director's responsibility for the damage in question, it may be that the courts will not consider themselves to be bound by this rule.

1   See Mitchell *Law of Subrogation* (1994), p 37, and Goff and Jones *Law of Restitution* (5th edn, 1998), p 424.
2   *Spottiswoode's Case* (1855) 6 De GM & G 345, 43 ER 1267. Directors were not invariably liable for ultra vires transactions. In contrast to trustees, who are obliged to act unanimously, directors must abide by the decision of the majority of the board. Individual directors who did not attend the meeting at which the breach was sanctioned, or who attended the meeting but voted against a particular breach, are not treated as parties to that breach. See for example *Land Credit Co of Ireland v Lord Fermoy* (1870) 5 Ch App 763; *Spottiswoode's Case* (above). Such directors are not liable to indemnify the company against the consequences of the breach; nor, it follows, are they liable for any contribution to those who are so liable.
3   *Walsh v Bardsley* (1931) 47 TLR 564.

7.59   The issue also arises in relation to damage caused to third parties by partners in the course of the business of the partnership. The courts held that partners were liable to contribute equally towards losses caused by the action of one of the partners alone, provided he was bona fide and did not act with culpable negligence[1]. However, contribution will be denied where a partner has acted fraudulently or has been culpably negligent[2]. It is, again, unclear to what extent the courts will consider themselves bound by these rulings.

1   *Cragg v Ford* (1842) 1 Y & C Ch Cas 280 at 284, 62 ER 889 at 891, per Knight Bruce VC; I'Anson Banks (ed), *Lindley & Banks on Partnership* (17th edn, 1995), p 570.
2   *Bury v Allen* (1845) 1 Coll 589 at 604, 63 ER 556 at 563, per Knight Bruce VC; *Robertson v Southgate* (1848) 6 Hare 536 at 540, 67 ER 1276 at 1278, per Knight Bruce VC; *Thomas v Atherton* (1878) 10 ChD 185 at 199, per James LJ.

7.60   Section 2(3) determines the effect on a right of contribution where the amount of damages that was or might have been awarded against the person from whom contribution is being sought was or would have been reduced because of contributory negligence[1], a contractual exclusion clause[2], or a limitation imposed by domestic legislation[3] or foreign law[4]. Where this is the case, the amount of any contribution awarded will not exceed the amount of damages that was or would have been awarded as result of such a reduction.

1   See the Civil Liability (Contribution) Act 1978, s 2(3)(b).
2   See the Civil Liability (Contribution) Act 1978, s 2(3)(a).
3   See the Civil Liability (Contribution) Act 1978, s 2(3)(a).
4   See the Civil Liability (Contribution) Act 1978, s 2(3)(c).

EX TURPI CAUSA

7.61   It is unclear whether a person whose conduct was unlawful will be entitled to claim contribution from someone liable for damage caused to another. The 1935 Act expressly provided for a right of contribution where 'damage is suffered by any person as a result of a tort (whether crime or not)'[1]. While the 1978 Act is less clear on the question, it does provide that contribution is available 'whatever the legal basis of ... [the claimant's] liability, whether tort, breach of contract, breach of trust or otherwise'. This has been interpreted as allowing, for example, a fraudulent tortfeasor to claim contribution from a tortfeasor who was merely negligent[2]. However, the relative blameworthiness of the parties will obviously be an important factor in the court's decision as to the level of contribution that would be appropriate.

1   Law Reform (Married Women and Tortfeasors) Act 1935, s 6.
2   *K v P (J, third party)* [1993] Ch 140 at 148, per Ferris J.

CHAPTER 8

Subrogation

Craig Rotherham

A   Introduction

8.1   The term subrogation is used to describe a remedial process by which a claimant is permitted to 'step into the shoes' of another and exercise that person's rights against other parties. The term provides a 'convenient way of describing the transfer of rights from one person to another, without assignment or the assent of the person from whom the rights are transferred'[1]. Typically the right arises in one of two situations. First, where A has indemnified B against a loss B has suffered for which C is liable, A is permitted to assume B's rights to recover from C. Secondly, where A discharges an obligation for which B is principally liable to C, A is permitted to assume C's rights against B.

1   *Orakpo v Manson Investments Ltd* [1978] AC 95 at 112.

Subrogation, recoupment and contribution

8.2   In the situations in which subrogation arises, claimants will typically have a direct claim for restitution. Claimants who have indemnified another or discharged another's debts will have a claim for recoupment[1]. Similarly, claimants who have discharged more than their share of a common liability may bring an action for contribution[2]. This raises the question, if the payment of a debt for which another is primarily or jointly liable gives rise to an independent right of recoupment or contribution, what is the need for the more convoluted notion of subrogation? There are at least two reasons why a claimant might seek subrogation. First, and most importantly, subrogation has a role because it may enable a claimant to acquire proprietary rights. Secondly, it may be that subrogation is available in circumstances in which recoupment or contribution is not. In particular, there is some suggestion that, unlike recoupment[3], subrogation may be available where A's payment or assumption of B's liability is characterised as voluntary. This is apparent in *The Esso Bernicia*[4], where Esso, pursuant to an agreement made with other tanker owners, indemnified local crofters for loss resulting from an oil spill for which a shipbuilder was liable to the crofters in negligence. Subsequently, Esso brought an action directly against the shipbuilder, seeking to be indemnified for the payment it had made to the crofters. The House of Lords denied the claim on the basis that the payment was voluntary and did not have the effect of discharging the shipbuilder's liability to the crofters[5]. While it was held that Esso could not sue the shipbuilders in its own name, Lord Goff indicated that it would have been entitled to be subrogated to the crofters' claim against the shipbuilders and to have sued in their name[6].

1   See above, ch 6.
2   See above, ch 7. Indeed, the right of contribution is said to carry with it a right of subrogation. Thus Lord Eldon concluded that the surety's right of subrogation rests upon the same 'principle of natural justice ... upon which one surety is entitled to contribution from another': *Craythorne v Swinburne* (1807) 14 Ves 160 at 169, 33 ER 482 at 485. For similar remarks, see *Stirling v Forrester* (1821) 3 Bligh 575 at 590, 4 ER 712 at 717, per Lord Redesdale, and *Duncan Fox & Co v North and South Wales Bank* (1880) 6 App Cas 1 at 19, per Lord Blackburn.
3   Cf *Owen v Tate* [1976] 7 QB 402. See above, para 6.22.
4   *Esso Petroleum Ltd v Hall Russell & Co* [1989] AC 643.
5   *Esso Petroleum Ltd v Hall Russell & Co* [1989] AC 643 at 662, per Lord Goff, and 678, per Lord Jauncey.
6   *Esso Petroleum Ltd v Hall Russell & Co* [1989] AC 643 at 662–663.

Explaining subrogation

8.3   The doctrine of subrogation is rather odd in its portrayal of the relief provided as a process by which the claimant stands in the position of another in order to exercise existing rights, including rights that have apparently been extinguished. Perhaps it is favoured because of its capacity to obscure. After all, where the rights in question do not arise out of contract, subrogation appears to conflict with one of the basic axioms of the common law – the understanding that individuals should not be subject to obligations to which they have not consented[1]. Moreover, where subrogation results in the redistribution of proprietary rights, it is liable to be doubly controversial. The idea of the claimant standing in the shoes of another obscures this by suggesting that no new rights or obligations are being created.

1   See *Gillies v Keogh* [1989] 2 NZLR 327 at 347, per Richardson J.

8.4   However, the resort to such a metaphoric mode of reasoning has its hazards. One difficulty is that, taken literally, the notion of subrogation, and the metaphor associated with it of stepping into the shoes of another, suggest that subrogated parties should be placed in precisely the same position that was enjoyed by the person whose shoes they now fill. Thus, in *Castellain v Preston*[1], Brett LJ stated that, 'In order to apply the doctrine of subrogation, it seems to me that the full and absolute meaning of the word must be used, that is to say, the insurer must be placed in the position of the assured'[2]. In particular, there has been a tendency to assume that, if a claimant is subrogated to the position of a creditor, he must be permitted to exercise any security that the creditor might have enjoyed, and not simply any personal claim that the creditor had against the defendant[3]. In some instances this has led to claimants' being awarded proprietary rights with little consideration as to whether this was appropriate[4]. In other cases, when courts have been disinclined to allow claimants to assume another's proprietary rights, they have tended to deny relief altogether[5].

1   (1883) 11 QBD 380.
2   (1883) 11 QBD 380 at 388.
3   Goff and Jones *Law of Restitution* (5th edn, 1998), p 125.
4   See for example an indorser's rights to acquire any securities held by the holder of a bill of exchange (below, para 8.36), and the subrogation of creditors of a trust business to the trustee's lien (below, para 8.39).
5   See for example *Thurstan v Nottingham Permanent Building Society* [1902] 1 Ch 1 at 12, per Romer J (refusing to allow the claimant to exercise a vendor's lien, without considering whether it should be permitted to exercise the vendor's personal rights). The issue arises predominately in the context of invalid contracts. Elsewhere a direct personal remedy is generally available as an alternative to subrogation. See below, para 8.51.

8.5 This problem was apparent in *Re Wrexham Mold and Connah's Quay Rly Co*[1]. A loan was void because it was ultra vires the company to which it was advanced. The company had used some of the money advanced to discharge legitimate debts, and the lender asked to be subrogated to the position of the discharged creditors. However, while the ultra vires loan was unsecured, the discharged debts had been secured. Ultimately, the court was prepared to give the lender a personal claim by treating the loan as valid to the extent that the money advanced had been spent on legal debts. However, it characterised the outcome, not as the result of allowing a claimant to assume another's rights, but as an independent personal remedy. For, in the court's view, subrogating the bank to the position of the creditors would have inevitably given it all the creditor's rights, and so given the bank rights of security for which it had never bargained. Lindley MR suggested that, while subrogation rhetoric had been used in earlier ultra vires lending cases:

> that theory was not really wanted in order to justify them. It was, however, adequate for the purposes for which it was used, and as applied to the cases before the Courts it led to just results. But, if logically followed out in other cases, it leads to consequences not only not foreseen by those who had recourse to it, but to results so startling that I cannot accept the theory as sound[2].

Lindley MR's assessment effectively represents a recognition that relief could be provided, where it is needed, without recourse to subrogation analysis. Nonetheless, the concept of subrogation did not disappear from legal discourse. The courts have continued to use it opportunistically wherever it seems to endorse a just outcome.

1 [1899] 1 Ch 440.
2 [1899] 1 Ch 440 at 447.

8.6 An overly literal understanding of the notion of subrogation was one of the reasons why the Court of Appeal denied relief in *Banque Financière de la Cité v Parc (Battersea) Ltd*[1]. The Court concluded that, if subrogation were allowed, it would inevitably have the effect of allowing the claimant to assume, not merely personal rights, but also secured rights for which it had not bargained[2]. However, the House of Lords rejected this view on appeal[3]. Lord Hoffman examined the notion that, in some circumstances, where a claimant had advanced money that was used to pay a debt secured by a charge, the charge might be 'kept alive' for the claimant's benefit. He concluded that the phrase 'is not a literal truth but rather a metaphor or analogy'[4]. Furthermore, he continued:

> When judges say that the charge is 'kept alive' for the benefit of the plaintiff, what they mean is that his legal relations with a defendant ... are regulated as if the benefit of the charge had been assigned to him. It does not by any means follow that the plaintiff must for all purposes be treated as an actual assignee of the benefit of the charge[5].

1 (29 November, 1996, unreported). See Mitchell [1998] Lloyd's Maritime and Commercial Law Quarterly 14 at 18.
2 (29 November, 1996, unreported).
3 *Banque Financière de La Cité v Parc (Battersea) Ltd* [1999] 1 AC 221. For the facts of the case and further analysis of the decision see below, para 8.47ff.
4 *Banque Financière de La Cité v Parc (Battersea) Ltd* [1999] 1 AC 221 at 236.
5 *Banque Financière de La Cité v Parc (Battersea) Ltd* [1999] 1 AC 221 at 236.

8.7 This is a rather different approach to that taken by Lindley MR in *Re Wrexham Mold and Connah's Quay Rly Co*[1]. Rather than accepting that the concept had to be applied strictly and recognising the unfortunate results it could generate if taken to logical extremes, Lord Hoffman suggested that it was nothing more than a metaphor, and need not be taken too seriously. Yet, if this view is accepted the need to identify the rationale for, and the limitations upon, intervention in 'subrogation' cases becomes all the more pressing.

1   [1899] 1 Ch 440.

Subrogation as a remedy for unjust enrichment

8.8   The rationale and precise limits of subrogation are notoriously difficult to identify[1]. While a right of subrogation may be conferred expressly by contract, in some circumstances it arises without agreement. Even so, in these circumstances, the remedy is sometimes described, rather unhelpfully, as a quasi-assignment or implied assignment[2]. On the other hand, attempts at a more open justification of the remedy tend to feature vague references to natural justice[3]. In the past, English courts generally eschewed any attempt at justifying subrogation that went beyond references to general notions of fairness and reliance on precedent. Thus, in *Orakpo v Manson Investments Ltd*[4], Lord Salmon argued that:

> The test as to whether the courts will apply the doctrine of subrogation to the facts is entirely empirical. It is, I think, impossible to formulate any narrower principle than that the doctrine will be applied only when the courts are satisfied that reason and justice demand that it should be[5].

1   See for example Burrows *Law of Restitution* (1993), p 77.
2   See for example *Re McMyn* (1886) 33 Ch D 575. See also *Baroness Wenlock v River Dee Co* (1887) 19 QBD 155 at 165, per Fry LJ.
3   See for example *Craythorne v Swinburne* (1807) 14 Ves 160 at 162, 33 ER 482 at 483, per Sir Samuel Romilly.
4   [1978] AC 95.
5   [1978] AC 95 at 110.

8.9   In recent years, much attention has focused on explaining subrogation in terms of unjust enrichment. There was a time when the disorderly law of subrogation appeared to provide a stumbling block to the recognition of a relatively discrete and systematic law of restitution. Thus, in *Orakpo*, Lord Diplock observed that:

> [T]here is no general doctrine of unjust enrichment in English law. What it does is to provide specific remedies in particular cases of what might be classified as unjust enrichment in a legal system that is based upon the civil law ...

> This makes particularly perilous any attempt to rely upon analogy to justify applying to one set of circumstances which would otherwise result in unjust enrichment a remedy of subrogation which has been held to be available for that purpose in a different set of circumstances[1].

After the House of Lords' recourse to the concept of unjust enrichment in *Lipkin Gorman v Karpnale*[2], it was perhaps inevitable that the courts would eventually attempt to explain subrogation in these terms, as indeed commentators had been doing for some time[3]. So it was that recently, in *Banque Financière de la Cité v Parc (Battersea) Ltd*[4], the House of Lords endorsed the view that subrogation is concerned with the reversal of unjust enrichment[5].

1   [1978] AC 95 at 104.
2   [1991] 2 AC 548.
3   See for example Goff and Jones *Law of Restitution* (1st edn, 1966), p 376.

4   [1999] 1 AC 221.
5   This is so at least where the right is not expressly or impliedly provided for by contract between the claimant and the defendant: see [1999] 1 AC 221 at 231, per Lord Hoffman.

8.10   The analysis that unjust enrichment is at the heart of subrogation is rather unhelpful. For one thing, while many instances of subrogation can be relatively easily analysed as effecting the reversal of an enrichment, there will often be difficulties in identifying a satisfactory 'unjust factor'[1]. Moreover, a claimant asking to be subrogated to the position of another will generally have ample other causes of action, apart from subrogation, to reverse any enrichment that another has received at his expense[2]. In these circumstances, the purpose of subrogation is to enable the claimant to obtain the advantages that come with the acquisition of another's proprietary rights. In common with other examples of proprietary remedies, where subrogation has the effect of allowing a claimant to assume another's proprietary rights, the result cannot be justified purely in conventional bilateral restitutionary terms[3].

1   See for example the difficulty in identifying an unjust factor that would justify allowing sureties to assume lender's securities: below, para 8.38.
2   An exception may be invalid contracts. See below, para 8.50ff.
3   See above, para 3.6ff.

Justifying the acquisition of proprietary rights by subrogation

8.11   The decision to allow the acquisition of proprietary rights by subrogation involves a redistribution of property rights and, as a result, is inevitably controversial. Traditionally, the formal explanation offered for permitting a claimant to take advantage of a creditor's rights of security is that the claimant intends to keep the original security alive for his own benefit[1]. At best, this fiction is rather unhelpful. The only good indication that a claimant had such an intention would be if he expressly contracted for the assignment of the creditor's rights. Moreover, the notion that the claimant intended to keep any security alive is hardly consistent with the fact that a claimant will acquire the creditor's rights even if he were unaware of the circumstances that give rise to the right of subrogation[2].

1   See for example *Morley v Morley* (1855) 5 De GM & G 610 at 620, 43 ER 1007 at 1011; *Butler v Rice* [1910] 2 Ch 277; *Ghana Commercial Bank v Chandiram* [1960] AC 732; *Boscawen v Bajwa* [1995] 4 All ER 769 at 781.
2   See for example *Butler v Rice* [1910] 2 Ch 277; *Chetwynd v Allen* [1899] 1 Ch 353. For discussion, see *Banque Financière de la Cité v Parc (Battersea) Ltd* [1999] 1 AC 221 at 232, per Lord Hoffman.

8.12   Some advance in the judicial analysis of this area was made in *Banque Financière de la Cité v Parc (Battersea) Ltd*[1]. Lord Hoffman argued that:

it is a mistake to regard the availability of subrogation as a remedy to prevent unjust enrichment as turning entirely upon the question of intention. Such an analysis has inevitably to be propped up by presumptions which can verge on outright fictions more appropriate to a less developed system than we now have[2].

Some attempts to explain proprietary subrogation have focused on the relationship of the claimant and the owner of assets secured by a charge that the claimant is seeking to exercise[3]. This makes little sense. After all, the claimant will generally have a direct remedy that is sufficient to reverse any unjust enrichment.

1   [1999] 1 AC 221.
2   [1999] 1 AC 221 at 234. Similar observations are made by Lord Hutton at 241.
3   See for example *Boscawen v Bajwa* [1995] 4 All ER 769 at 777, per Millett LJ.

8.13   A different attempt to explain the acquisition of proprietary rights by subrogation in terms of unjust enrichment has seen it analysed on the basis that the remedy is required to prevent the unjust enrichment of third party creditors. This shift in analysis is apparent in *Banque Financière*, where a claimant sought to be subrogated to the position of a first mortgagee in order to take priority over a second mortgagee[1]. Their Lordships' analysis proceeds on the premise that the subrogation of the claimant to the position of the first mortgagee requires an explanation of why the second mortgagee would be unjustly enriched if the remedy were not given. This was clearest in the judgment of Lord Steyn, who argued that the matter could be dealt with in terms of a direct claim of unjust enrichment by the claimant against the second mortgagee. Applying Birks's analysis to the case, Lord Steyn concluded that the following questions arose:

(1)   Has [the second mortgagee] benefited or been enriched?
(2)   Was the enrichment at the expense of [the claimant]?
(3)   Was the enrichment unjust?
(4)   Are there any defences?[2].

1   For a fuller account see below, para 8.47ff.
2   [1999] 1 AC 221 at 231. For a similar analysis see per Lord Hoffman at 234.

8.14   In cases in which a claimant is allowed to assume another's proprietary rights, it makes sense to focus on the claimant's position, not in relation to the owner of the assets which are affected by the charge in question, but in relation to the owner's creditors. According to this analysis, relief should be given to reflect the extent to which the claimant did not assume the risk of the defendant's bankruptcy and has enabled a defendant to discharge a secured debt. In these circumstances, from the perspective of any other creditors, provided the claimant is permitted to do no more to assume the same rights enjoyed by the discharged creditor, subrogation does no more than to restore the status quo. According to this analysis, subrogation in these circumstances has the effect of denying the defendant's creditors an unmerited windfall[1].

1   See above, para 3.20.

B   Circumstances in which a right of subrogation arises

8.15   Before a systematic theory of unjust enrichment had gained wide currency, remedial responses developed incrementally and were justified in a variety of ways. Thus, subrogation developed in an ad hoc fashion where it seemed just. Today we must make as much sense of this legacy as we can, without expecting it to fit neatly into some preconceived theoretical framework. Consequently, subrogation is best analysed in the specific contexts in which it has been made available.

Indemnity insurers' rights of subrogation

THE INSURER'S RIGHTS AGAINST AN INDEMNIFIED ASSURED

8.16   It has long been held that an insurer is entitled to acquire the rights of an indemnified assured by subrogation. Where insurers have fully indemnified the assured for any loss suffered, they have the right to bring an action, in the name of assured, for their own benefit against any third party liable for the assured's loss[1]. If the assured, of his own accord, settles a claim against a third party after this point, the insurer will be bound only if the third party had no notice that the right to pursue the claim had vested in the insurer[2]. In any event, such an action by an assured may give the insurer a right to damages for breach of contract[3].

1   *Mason v Sainsbury* (1782) 3 Doug KB 61, 99 ER 358; *Dickenson v Jardine* (1868) LR 3 CP 639; *H Cousins & Co Ltd v D & C Carriers Ltd* [1971] 2 QB 230.
2   *West of England Fire Insurance Co v Isaacs* [1897] 1 QB 226.
3   *Commercial Union Assurance Co v Lister* (1874) 9 Ch App 483; *West of England Fire Insurance Co v Isaacs* [1897] 1 QB 226; *Phoenix Assurance Co v Spooner* [1905] 2 KB 753; *Horse, Carriage & General Insurance Co Ltd v Petch* (1916) 33 TLR 131; *Andrews v Patriotic Insurance Co* (1886) 18 LR Ir 355.

8.17   In addition to policies that are characterised as indemnity policies, these principles apply to valued policies in marine insurance. Even if the agreed value proves to be less than the actual value of the asset insured, the insurer will be entitled to be subrogated to the position of the assured[1]. This may be justified on the basis that the parties have agreed the value of the asset, thereby precluding difficult inquiries after the event that would be needed to determine whether the assured had indeed been fully indemnified. However, dicta suggest that the same principle does not apply in respect of fire policies[2]. Such a distinction between marine and fire policies is difficult to justify.

1   *North of England Iron Steamship Insurance Association v Armstrong* (1870) LR 5 QB 244.
2   *Re Driscoll* [1918] 1 IR 152; *Page v Scottish Insurance Corpn* (1929) 140 LT 571 at 576, per Scrutton LJ.

8.18   Where an assured is not fully indemnified, he retains the right to choose to sue any party responsible for his loss and to control the litigation. Pursuant to a term implied into contracts of insurance, an assured in such a position must have due regard to the interests of the insurer. Subject to this, the assured is at liberty to settle any claim or to bring it to court. However, assured parties in this position must account to the insurer for any amount received by way of damages or settlement that goes beyond indemnifying them for their loss (taking into consideration any prior insurance payout). In addition, the House of Lords held in *Lord Napier and Ettrick v Hunter*[1] that any moneys received from a third party by the assured must be applied to reimburse the insurer, before it can be applied to compensate any loss borne by the assured as the result of an excess provided for in the contract of insurance. It was formerly thought that the insurer would not be subrogated to the position of the assured where an indemnity policy carried an excess clause and that the assured would retain the right to control the proceedings. However, given the attitude taken towards excess clauses by the House of Lords in *Lord Napier and Ettrick v Hunter*, possibly the courts will hold insurers to be entitled to be subrogated to an assured's rights once the assured has been indemnified under the terms of such a policy[2].

1   [1993] AC 713.
2   See Mitchell *Law of Subrogation* (1994), pp 42–43.

8.19   The rights of insurers have been explained on the basis that 'the contract of insurance contained in a marine or fire policy is a contract of indemnity and of indemnity only, and ... the assured ... shall be fully indemnified, but never more than fully indemnified'[1]. Thus, the rule ensures that the assured is not overcompensated for his loss, to the detriment of the insurer. If, on the other hand, the assured is overcompensated as a result of a third party's making a payment that exceeded the assured's loss, the assured need not account for the windfall[2].

1   *Castellain v Preston* (1883) 11 QBD 380 at 386, per Brett LJ.
2   *Yorkshire Insurance Co v Nisbet Shipping Co Ltd* [1962] 2 QB 330.

8.20   The insurer's rights to subrogation have sometimes been attributed to an implied term in the contract of indemnity[1]. At other times, the courts have explained the right as arising from 'the very nature of the contract of indemnity in itself'[2], or as 'giving effect to the underlying nature of a contract of insurance'[3]. However, it might be argued that the attempt to ground the right of subrogation in the intention of the parties is unnecessary and that the right could be better explained as an independent restitutionary right arising by operation of law in the same way as rights of contribution and recoupment.

1   See for example *Yorkshire Insurance Co v Nisbet Shipping Co Ltd* [1962] 2 QB 330 at 339–340, per Diplock J; *Hobbs v Marlowe* [1978] AC 16 at 39, per Lord Diplock; *Lord Napier and Ettrick v Hunter* [1993] AC 713 at 752, per Lord Browne-Wilkinson. Similarly, in *Banque Financière de la Cité v Parc (Battersea) Ltd* [1999] 1 AC 221 at 231, Lord Hoffman took the view that 'the doctrine of subrogation in insurance rests upon the common intention of the parties and gives effect to the principle of indemnity embodied in the contract'.
2   *Morris v Ford Motor Co* [1973] QB 792 at 805, per Stamp LJ.
3   *Lord Napier and Ettrick v Hunter* [1993] AC 713 at 743, per Lord Goff.

8.21   It is clear that the right of subrogation may be excluded impliedly or expressly by a contract of indemnity. However, such instances are likely to be rare indeed. One case in which it was suggested that such an exclusion could be inferred was *Morris v Ford Motor Co Ltd*[1]. A contractor had agreed to indemnify Ford against any loss or injury arising from the cleaning work it was doing on Ford's premises. One of the contractor's employees was injured as a result of the negligence of one of Ford's employees. While accepting its obligation to indemnify Ford, the contractor claimed the right to be subrogated to Ford's right to sue its employee for the loss in question. This caused considerable consternation. While the right of an employer to sue an employee is well established[2], the right is not in practice exercised by employers or insurers. James LJ concluded that the right to be subrogated to the assured's rights against its employee was impliedly excluded by the contract of insurance[3]. More broadly, Lord Denning MR was willing to deny the insurer the right to sue the assured's employee because it was not 'just and equitable' to permit it[4].

1   [1973] QB 792.
2   See *Lister v Romford Ice & Cold Storage Ltd* [1957] AC 555.
3   [1973] QB 792 at 815.
4   [1973] QB 792 at 801.

PROPRIETARY REMEDIES AVAILABLE TO AN INSURER

8.22   Until recently, the nature of an indemnity insurer's rights against the assured with respect to money paid to an assured by a third party liable for a fully or partially indemnified assured's loss was not entirely clear. However, there were dicta from various cases referring to an assured as holding on trust for the insurer any sums that would result in the assured's being overcompensated[1]. Recently the matter arose in *Lord Napier and Ettrick v Hunter*[2]. The litigation developed out of losses of £160,000 suffered by certain Lloyd's names (the assured) in the late 1980s. Underwriters (the insurers) paid out under a contract of insurance with the names that provided for an excess of £25,000 and limited the names' cover to £100,000. Given that they had not been fully indemnified, the names were entitled to control the litigation against any third parties responsible for their loss. In pursuing this right, the names settled a negligence action that they had brought against the manager of their syndicates for £130,000. Subsequently, a dispute arose between the names and the underwriters that eventually found its way to the House of Lords. One matter at issue was whether the underwriters had any proprietary interest in sums paid pursuant to this settlement. Their Lordships accepted the underwriters' claim that they were entitled to an equitable lien over the settlement money securing the names' obligation to account to the insurers.

1   For example, *Commercial Union Assurance Co v Lister* (1874) 9 Ch App 483, per Sir George Jessel MR; *Re Miller, Gibb & Co Ltd* [1957] 1 WLR 703.
2   [1993] AC 713. See Luey 'Proprietary Remedies in Insurance Subrogation' (1995) 25 Victoria University of Wellington Law Review 449.

8.23   Lords Browne-Wilkinson, Templeman and Goff all placed considerable reliance on authorities that had described the relationship between insurers and the assured in these circumstances in terms of trusteeship[1]. In addition, Lord Browne-Wilkinson explained the result by first conceptualising the assured's obligations as arising out of contract and, secondly, converting those contractual rights into a proprietary interest by use of the maxim 'equity regards as done that which ought to be done'[2]. This analysis presents several difficulties. First, it depends upon the rather questionable implication of a term into the contract. Certainly, the extent of the obligation imposed in *Napier v Hunter*, requiring the assured to account to the insurer before recovering any loss resulting from bearing an excess, is one that would hardly satisfy the tests for implying contractual terms[3]. Secondly, it is difficult to understand why the maxim that 'equity regards as done that which ought to be done' should be thought to have operated to convert the assured's obligation into a proprietary right. Lord Browne-Wilkinson's analysis appears to follow from his view that this particular contractual term was enforceable 'in just the same way as are other contracts to assign or charge specific property'[4]. Thus, it seems that the term implied was one to assign future property. Yet, it is hardly obvious why the term implied should be seen as one to assign rather than to account; and, if the obligation assumed was merely to account, there is no reason why ensuring that this is done need result in a proprietary interest[5].

1   The decisions relied upon were *Randal v Cockran* (1748) 1 Ves Sen 98, 29 ER 916; *White v Dobinson* (1844) 14 Sim 273, 60 ER 363; *Commercial Union Assurance Co v Lister* (1874) 9 Ch App 483; *Re Miller, Gibb & Co Ltd* [1957] 2 All ER 266.
2   [1993] AC 713 at 752.
3   The difficulties with reconciling the implication of rights are reflected in Lord Templeman's rather tentative view that: 'It may be that the common law invented and implied in contracts of insurance ... a promise by the insured person to account to the insurer for moneys recovered from a third party in respect of the insured loss' ([1993] AC 713 at 736).
4   [1993] AC 713 at 752.
5   The same criticism may be made of the decision in *A-G for Hong Kong v Reid* [1994] 1 AC 324.

8.24   The question that remains unanswered is why an insurer should receive rights that would give it priority in bankruptcy over the assured's general creditors. In *Napier v Hunter* only Lord Templeman tackled this issue directly. He apparently took the view that the insurer could be regarded as an involuntary creditor. Thus, he remarked that:

> The ... insurers will be in a worse position than an unsecured creditor because the insurers could not resist payment under the policy whereas an unsecured creditor may choose whether to advance money or not[1].

Yet, the insurers were only liable to pay under the policy because they had agreed that they should be liable to make good the assured's loss if a particular contingency arose. If they had wanted priority over general creditors they could have bargained for it when entering into the insurance contract. Consequently, commentators have generally taken the view that the insurers' priority was unmerited[2].

1   [1993] AC 713 at 737.
2   Mitchell *Law of Subrogation* (1994) p 83; Goff and Jones *Law of Restitution* (5th edn, 1998), p 86; Burrows *Law of Restitution* (1993), p 83.

8.25   The explanation offered by Lord Browne-Wilkinson is difficult to reconcile with the precise remedy given in *Napier v Hunter*. If the implied term in question were really in the nature of an assignment of the proceeds of the claim, the application of the maxim 'equity regards as done that which ought to be done' should have resulted in the assured's holding the fund in question on trust for the insurer. However, their Lordships restricted the insurer to an equitable lien: a charge over the settlement money, securing the assured's obligation to account[1].

1   The decision to award a lien in *Napier v Hunter* is difficult to reconcile with the decision in *A-G for Hong Kong v Reid* [1994] 1 AC 324 where the application of the same maxim led the Privy Council to award to a constructive trust.

8.26   A further argument advanced by Lord Templeman in favour of giving proprietary relief was that many of the underwriters were overseas, and that it would be much more difficult to enforce a personal as opposed to a proprietary claim[1]. Yet difficulties of enforcement may arise on occasion for any type of claim. Something more should be required before a proprietary remedy is preferred to a personal obligation to account.

1   [1993] AC 713 at 737.

RIGHTS ARISING FROM AN OVERPAYMENT BY THE INSURER

8.27   Issues of insurers' rights also arise where an assured has already received compensation from a third party, and the insurer, in ignorance of this, makes a payment that has the effect of overcompensating the assured. The issue arose in *Stearns v Village Main Reef Gold Mining Co*[1]. The claimant insurers indemnified the defendant under a contract of insurance for the full value of gold expropriated by the Transvaal Government in the Boer War. Thereafter, the claimants discovered that the defendant had already received a substantial payment from the expropriator. The claimants not only argued that their payment was motivated by a mistake of fact that gave rise to an action for money had and received, but claimed a trust over '[t]hat portion, which was in fact an over-payment'[2]. The primary motivation for the claimants' argument that the overpayment was held on trust was that it would have meant that the defendant was liable to pay compound interest[3].

1   (1905) 10 Com Cas 89.
2   (1905) 10 Com Cas 89 at 92.
3   On the necessity to establish a proprietary interest in order to claim compound interest, see *Westdeutsche Landesbank Girozentrale v Islington London Borough Council* [1996] AC 669. On interest see below, para 21.70ff.

8.28   Only Stirling LJ considered the question of whether the claimants had a proprietary right. It is not surprising that he found against them on this point. At least before *Chase Manhattan NA v Israel-British Bank (London) Ltd*[1], the received wisdom was that the proper action for a mistaken overpayment was for money had and received, and that this gave rise to personal liability alone.

1   [1981] Ch 105. See above, para 3.31.

8.29   On the other hand, the result reached in *Stearns* would seem to suggest that the underwriter in *Napier v Hunter* should have been restricted to a personal remedy. Lord Browne-Wilkinson evidently thought otherwise, arguing that in *Stearns*, '[s]o far as trusteeship was concerned, there was no fund capable of being the subject matter of the trust ... '[1]. However, it is difficult to see why this should be so. For one thing, if the reasoning in *Chase Manhattan* were followed, a proprietary remedy would be available in a case with the facts of *Stearns*. However, even if it were not, the question would then arise whether the approach taken in *Napier v Hunter* would produce the same result in a case where the overcompensation came from the insurer rather than a third party. There seems little reason why a court should not conclude that the implied contractual term that the court relied upon in *Napier v Hunter* should not apply to any overcompensation, regardless of its source. Equally, there is no reason to think that the maxim 'equity regards as done that which ought to be done' should not apply to create a property right on the facts of *Stearns*, in the same as it did in *Napier v Hunter*.

1   [1994] AC 713 at 751.

Subrogation of sureties to the position of secured creditors

SURETIES' RIGHTS TO SUBROGATION

8.30   Where sureties are called on to meet a loan, the law allows them to seek redress from the principal debtor. Since the eighteenth century, sureties have been able to bring an action at common law in quasi-contract against a principal debtor to recoup any sum paid for which the principal debtor was primarily liable[1]. In addition, sureties who have been called upon to meet a debt that they have guaranteed are, by virtue of subrogation, entitled to the benefit of securities given by the principal debtor[2], and equally to any securities granted by co-sureties who have not contributed their due proportion of the debt[3]. While the surety's entitlement to be subrogated to the rights of the principal debtor might be specified in the contract of guarantee, even in the absence of such a term, this right has been recognised in equity since the seventeenth century[4]. The surety's right to be subrogated to the position of a secured creditor vis-à-vis the principal debtor and co-sureties arises regardless of whether the surety was aware of the existence of those securities[5] and applies equally to securities given after the surety has given his guarantee[6]. While the surety's rights of subrogation do not depend on contract, they may be altered by contractual agreement.

1   *Morrice v Redwyn* (1731) 2 Barn KB 26, 94 ER 333. See Mitchell *Law of Subrogation* (1994), p 55.
2   *Morgan v Seymour* (1637) 1 Rep Ch 120, 21 ER 525; *Hole v Harrison* (1675) Cas temp Finch 203, 23 ER 111; *Parsons v Briddock* (1708) 2 Vern 608, 23 ER 997; *Wright v Morley* (1805) 11 Ves 12, 32 ER 992; *Craythorne v Swinburne* (1807) 14 Ves 160, 33 ER 482.
3   *Stirling v Forrester* (1821) 3 Bligh 575 at 590, 4 ER 712 at 717, per Lord Redesdale. See also *Duncan Fox & Co v North and South Wales Bank* (1880) 6 App Cas 1 at 19, per Lord Blackburn.
4   See n 2.
5   *Aldrich v Cooper* (1803) 8 Ves 382 at 389, 32 ER 402 at 405, per Lord Eldon; *Mayhew v Crickett* (1818) 2 Swan 185 at 191, 36 ER 585 at 587, per Lord Eldon; *Newton v Chorlton* (1853) 10 Hare 646, 68 ER 1087.

6 *Lake v Brutton* (1854) 18 Beav 34, 52 ER 14; *Pledge v Buss* (1860) John 663 at 668, 70 ER 585 at 587, per Page Wood VC; *Campbell v Rothwell* (1877) 38 LT 33; *Forbes v Jackson* (1882) 19 Ch D 615.

8.31   The right to subrogation arises where a surety has discharged the whole of the debt in question. Where the surety reaches an accommodation with the creditor to discharge the debt at a discount, he is entitled to be subrogated to the securities only to the extent of the sum paid, rather than the original debt[1].

1 *Reed v Norris* (1837) 2 My & Cr 361 at 375, 40 ER 678 at 683, per Lord Cottenham.

8.32   The law obliges creditors to transfer to sureties who have met the principal debtor's obligation any documents of security relating to the debt in question[1]. Prior to 1856, a surety was entitled to be subrogated only to those securities that were not discharged by the surety's payment. Thus, sureties were able to exercise only securities such as mortgages, which had to be reconveyed to the principal debtor before they were extinguished[2]. However, since the Mercantile Law Amendment Act 1856, a surety has been able to exercise any securities enjoyed by the creditor, including those that were technically extinguished by the surety's payment[3].

1 *Copis v Middleton* (1823) Turn & R 224, 37 ER 1083.
2 *Copis v Middleton* (1823) Turn & R 224, 37 ER 1083. See Mitchell *Law of Subrogation* (1994), p 57.
3 See the Mercantile Law Amendment Act 1856, s 5.

JUSTIFYING THESE RIGHTS

8.33   Today this form of subrogation tends to be characterised as restitutionary. According to this view, the principal debtor is enriched by the discharge of his liability to the creditor and the 'unjust factor' arises from the legal compulsion on the surety to meet the obligation[1]. However, this view ignores the fact that the legal compulsion in question is the consequence of the enforcement of an obligation that was assumed voluntarily and that it might be argued that if a surety wants rights to repayment he should bargain for them[2].

1 See for example Burrows *Law of Restitution* (1993), p 82; Birks *An Introduction to the Law of Restitution* (revised edn, 1989), p 21.
2 Thus Lord Blackburn wondered whether 'it would not have been better to say that every one should have the full extent of his rights given by contract, express or implied and no more'. See *Duncan, Fox, & Co v North and South Wales Bank* (1880) 6 App Cas 1 at 20–21.

8.34   It is doubly difficult to justify sureties' rights to any securities given to the creditor. The right has rather unhelpfully been described as standing 'upon a principle of natural justice'[1]. In addition, it is sometimes said that the surety is presumed to keep the security alive for his own benefit[2]. However, the presumption is plainly counterfactual. It has been recognised that the surety 'seldom if ever stipulates for the benefit of the security which the principal debtor has given'[3]. Moreover, as mentioned, sureties are entitled to enforce both securities of which they were unaware at the time they entered into the guarantee and securities that were given after the guarantee was made[4]. Thus, these rights are better understood as being conferred by operation of law.

1 *Craythorne v Swinburne* (1807) 14 Ves 160 at 169, 33 ER 482 at 485, per Lord Eldon, adopting the argument of counsel Sir Samuel Romilly.
2 *Re Davison's Estate* (1893) 31 LR Ir 249 at 255, affirmed at [1894] 1 IR 56; Goff and Jones *Law of Restitution* (5th edn, 1998), p 134.

3   *Yonge v Reynell* (1852) 9 Hare 809 at 818, 68 ER 744 at 748, per Turner VC.
4   *Craythorne v Swinburne* (1807) 14 Ves 160 at 169, 33 ER 482 at 485.

8.35   In terms of the justification offered elsewhere for proprietary remedies, the surety is a voluntary creditor[1]. Consequently, some scholars suggest that the sureties' acquisition of proprietary rights is unjustified[2]. Certainly, the initial decision to give rights of security to those who have not demanded them (especially in situations in which the parties are commercially sophisticated) is difficult to justify. Nonetheless, this rule has now been part of the landscape of commercial law for so long now that its removal could not be contemplated. The personal and proprietary rights of a surety are well-established incidents of surety arrangements, and they may sometimes implicitly form part of the terms of the parties' negotiations. Thus, the law as it stands provides a useful default rule that the parties can bargain around if they choose to do so.

1   See generally above, ch 3.
2   Burrows *Law of Restitution* (1993), p 83; Mitchell *Law of Subrogation* (1994), p 59.

Bills of exchange – an indorser's rights to a holder's securities

8.36   It is uncontroversial that an indorser of a bill of exchange who has been required to pay out on the bill following the acceptor's failure to honour it is entitled to take possession of the bill and sue as a holder[1]. In addition, the indorser is entitled to the benefit of any securities that the acceptor had given the holder. The indorser's right to compel the holder to surrender the bill arises only where the indorser has paid the bill in full. However, an indorser who has paid the bill in part may be able to bring a direct personal action against the acceptor for money paid[2].

1   Mitchell *Law of Subrogation* (1994), pp 86–96; Goff and Jones *Law of Restitution* (5th edn, 1998), pp 135–137.
2   *Pownal v Ferrand* (1827) 6 B & C 439, 108 ER 513.

8.37   *Duncan Fox & Co v North & South Wales Bank*[1] illustrates the operation of subrogation in this context. In that case, Radford & Sons deposited title deeds for freehold property with the defendant bank in order to secure any debts it owed the bank. Subsequently, the claimant agreed to accept a bill from Radford & Sons as consideration for a consignment of wheat, after reaching an arrangement with the bank whereby the bank would discount the bills after the claimant had indorsed them. Subsequently, the bills were dishonoured, and the bank as holder demanded payment from the claimant as the indorser. Thereafter, the claimant learned of the securities held by the bank, which took on a greater significance as Radford & Sons (the acceptor) went bankrupt. In the context of a dispute that developed between the claimant and certain unsecured creditors, the House of Lords held that the claimant was entitled to take possession of the title deeds that the acceptor had deposited with the bank.

1   (1880) 6 App Cas 1.

8.38   The rule that gives the indorser a right to recover from the acceptor is hardly controversial. Given that it is hardly likely that anyone would indorse bills of exchange without this right, the rule can be justified, both because it reflects the parties' understanding of their mutual rights and obligations, and because it serves to encourage the negotiation of bills of exchange. On the other hand, subrogation to proprietary rights is more difficult to justify. In *Duncan Fox*

& Co, Lord Selborne LC and Lord Watson justified the indorser's rights by analogy with a surety's entitlement to assume any rights of security that the creditor enjoyed against the principal debtor[1]. However, it is very difficult to see that there can be any justification for allowing claimants to acquire securities that they were unaware of at the time they indorsed a bill of exchange. Given that such claimants have taken the risk that they will have to line up with the acceptor's unsecured creditors in the event that the bill should be dishonoured, it is not obvious that the law should come to their aid merely because it transpires, quite fortuitously, that the acceptor has deposited securities with the holder.

1   (1880) 6 App Cas 1 at 12 and 22. In addition, Lord Selborne LC justified the outcome by analogy
    with the doctrine that permits a creditor of a trust business to exercise the trustee's lien: (1880) 6
    App Cas at 13. For a critique of that doctrine see below, para 8.40.

Subrogation of creditors of a trust business to the trustees' lien

8.39   On occasion, a trustee may run a trust business – for example, where executors manage the business of a deceased trader prior to its sale or liquidation. While trustees are personally liable for their acts and omissions, they enjoy the right to be indemnified by the trust estate for any costs incurred in carrying out their duties, and any liability that arises in this way is secured by a lien over the trust assets[1]. On the other hand, creditors dealing with a trust business do not have any direct recourse against trust assets. However, if in administering a trust business in an authorised fashion, a trustee incurs debts, the creditors in question are entitled to be subrogated to the trustee's rights against the trust estate – both personal and proprietary[2].

1   See for example in *Re Beddoe* [1893] 1 Ch 547 at 558, per Lindley LJ.
2   On creditors' rights to exercise the trustee's lien, see *Farhall v Farhall* (1871) 7 Ch App 123; *Owen
    v Delamere* (1872) LR 15 Eq 134.

8.40   In *Re Johnson*[1], Sir George Jessel MR explained the rule giving creditors personal rights against the trust estate in these circumstances on the basis that '[t]he trust assets having been devoted to carrying on the trade, it would not be right that the *cestui que trust* should get the benefit of the trade without paying the liabilities'[2]. On the other hand, this explanation in no way indicates that these creditors should be entitled to exercise the trustee's lien over trust assets. It is difficult to see that there can be any justification for allowing those who have voluntarily become unsecured creditors in a commercial context to acquire a better right through subrogation. To hold otherwise raises difficult questions as to the order of priority among subrogated creditors and the beneficiaries' other secured and unsecured creditors. In *Re Johnson*, Sir George Jessel MR suggested that the provision of proprietary rights in this context was 'a mere corollary to those numerous cases in equity in which persons are allowed to follow trust assets'[3]. This explanation appears to be based on a very tenuous analogy. While similar justifications might be offered for tracing and some instances of subrogation, this hardly indicates that the one is 'a mere corollary' of the other. In addition, this form of subrogation has been supported by drawing a parallel with the right of sureties to assume the securities of a creditor after discharging the liability of the principal debtor[4]. Once again, the analogy is not a strong one. There is little similarity between the transactions that give rise to the right to subrogation in these different contexts.

1   (1880) 15 Ch D 548.
2   (1880) 15 Ch D 548 at 552.

3   (1880) 15 Ch D 548 at 552.
4   *Yonge v Reynell* (1852) 9 Hare 809 at 819, 68 ER 744 at 749, per Sir GJ Turner VC. See Burrows
      Law of Restitution (1993), p 84.

Where a debt has been discharged, or land purchased, using the claimant's money

8.41   Where a defendant discharges a debt owed by another using money obtained from the claimant, in circumstances in which title has not passed at law or in which title has not passed in equity, the claimant will be entitled to exercise the creditors' remedies against the debtor. Apart from subrogation, the claimant will typically have a direct personal claim against the debtor for recoupment or contribution. Consequently, in general, subrogation is sought because it may enable a claimant to acquire proprietary rights enjoyed by a third party creditor.

8.42   The principle operates where a claimant retains legal title to property: for example, where the defendant uses money stolen from the claimant, or its traceable proceeds, to discharge a mortgage, the claimant is entitled to be subrogated to the position of the mortgagee[1]. The principle also applies where a debt is discharged using money that belongs to the claimant in equity: for example, where a debt is discharged using misapplied trust money.

1   See for example the Canadian decision of *McCullough v Marsden* (1919) 45 DLR 645. See also
      Mitchell *Law of Subrogation* (1994), pp 114–115.

8.43   *Boscawen v Bajwa*[1] provides a recent example of subrogation in these circumstances. A prospective purchaser had exchanged contracts for the sale of a property with the defendant, Bajwa. The sale was to be financed by a loan from the Abbey National Building Society that was to be secured by a mortgage over the property. The Abbey National transferred to the purchaser's solicitor the sum that was payable on completion of the sale. However, the purchaser's solicitor initially sent a cheque for slightly less than the required amount. When asked to forward the balance, the purchaser's solicitor sent a further cheque. Before the latter cheque had cleared, the defendant's solicitors used the proceeds of the first cheque to discharge a mortgage over the property in question enjoyed by the Halifax Building Society. However, this proved to be rather premature, as the second cheque was dishonoured. The defendant's solicitors' actions were found by the court to amount to a misappropriation of trust money. Subsequently, it transpired that the purchaser's solicitor was insolvent and the sale was never completed. As a result, the Abbey National never received the charge over the property for which it had bargained. As Bajwa himself became financially embarrassed, a contest emerged between the Abbey National and a judgment creditor who had obtained a charging order on the property. Was the Abbey National entitled to exercise Halifax's mortgage by virtue of subrogation? Or was it to be left with an unsecured debt, along with claims against the two firms of solicitors?

1   [1995] 4 All ER 769.

8.44   The Court of Appeal agreed with the court below that the bank was entitled to be subrogated to the position of the mortgagee, thereby giving it priority over the judgment creditor. On its analysis, the fact that the money transferred by the building society was affected with a trust, combined with the effect of subrogation, meant that, in equity, Mr Bajwa never obtained an unencumbered freehold interest in the property. Instead, when the mortgage was ostensibly discharged, the building society immediately acquired an equitable right to enforce the mortgagee's interest for its own benefit[1]. This is a defensible result. The bank had bargained for a first charge over the property in question, and the money that they had advanced was used to discharge an existing mortgage. In these circumstances, if the claimant, who had not assumed the risk of the defendant's bankruptcy, had not been permitted to assume a security that was discharged using an enrichment gained at the claimant's expense, the defendant's unsecured creditors would have enjoyed an unmerited windfall.

1   [1995] 4 All ER 769 at 784.

Subrogation where a claimant has been induced by mistake to give a loan that has been used to repay a secured debt

8.45   Subrogation may also be available in response to a mistake. *Butler v Rice*[1] provides an illustration. Rice borrowed money from Butler for the purpose of discharging a charge over certain real estate. Rice had represented that the property in question was his own and promised to grant Butler a new security. In fact, the property belonged to Rice's wife, and he was not entitled to grant such an interest. After Rice used the advance to pay off the first mortgagee, his wife refused to grant a new charge in Butler's favour. Warrington J held that Butler was entitled to be subrogated to the position of the first mortgagee. The result is best explained on the basis that the claimant's advance was induced by a mistake[2] and because Mrs Rice's position would not be unfairly prejudiced by the remedy given. As Warrington J explained: 'The only alteration in her position is that instead of owing the money to A she will in future owe it to B'[3]. Similarly, subrogation has been permitted in the context of co-owned land, where one co-owner has fraudulently obtained a loan in order to pay off an existing mortgage and purported to grant a new mortgage by forging the signature of the other co-owner[4].

1   [1910] 2 Ch 277. See also *Chetwynd v Allen* [1899] 1 Ch 353.
2   Mitchell *Law of Subrogation* (1994), p 135.
3   [1910] 2 Ch 277 at 282–283.
4   *National Guardian Mortgage Corpn v Roberts* [1993] NPC 149. See also Mitchell *Law of Subrogation* (1994), pp 123–124.

8.46   A similar analysis explains the relief given when claimants are mistaken in believing that they are acquiring an interest free of any prior encumbrance. This problem arises where one purchases property, thereby enabling the vendor to discharge an existing mortgage, only to find that there is an additional encumbrance (such as a second charge or a charging order) on the title, which, though ranking lower in priority than the discharged mortgage, would bind the purchaser[1]. In such situations, the purchaser will be permitted to take advantage of the (ostensibly discharged) mortgage by subrogation. The rationale of the rule stems from the fact that the claimant obtained a less valuable security than that for which he bargained and was thereby exposed to a higher level of risk than he intended to assume. To allow the claimant to acquire the earlier mortgage not only fulfils the claimant's expectations, it does no more than return the holder of the later encumbrance to the position that he would have enjoyed but for the claimant's loan[2]. If, in contrast, subrogation were denied, the holders of the encumbrances in question would be enriched as a result of the claimant's mistake.

1 See for example *Carlisle Banking Co v Thompson* (1884) 28 Ch D 398; *Re Mutual Trust Co and Creditview Estate Homes Ltd* (1997) 149 DLR (4th) 385 (second charges); *Ghana Commercial Bank v Chandiram* [1960] AC 732 (charging order).
2 Palmer *Law of Restitution* (1978), v 4, para 22.1.

8.47 *Banque Financière de la Cité v Parc (Battersea) Ltd*[1] provides another example of subrogation. The claimant gave a loan to Parc to enable it to repay part of a prior loan that had been secured by a mortgage over real estate owned by Parc. The loan was negotiated by the chief financial officer of Parc's holding company, who gave an undertaking that another subsidiary company would not enforce a second charge it enjoyed over the same real estate before the claimant had been repaid in full. However, neither Parc nor the second mortgagee knew of this undertaking. After Parc became insolvent, and when it became clear to the claimant that the letter of postponement that it had received was unenforceable, it sought be subrogated to the rights of the first mortgagee.

1 [1999] 1 AC 221.

8.48 The Court of Appeal had denied the claim, concluding that it would hardly be fair on third party creditors if the claimant were subrogated to the position of the first mortgagee, given that the claimant had never bargained for a charge. However, the House of Lords allowed the appeal, on the basis that subrogation was acceptable, provided that the claimant was permitted to obtain only a personal right to rank in priority to the second mortgagee, effective only as between the claimant and the second mortgagee[1]. The first mortgagee was permitted to enforce its first charge to recoup the money it was still owed by Parc. Thereafter, before the second mortgagee could have recourse to any money realised by the sale of the land in question, a sum representing the money advanced by the claimant would be set aside. The claimant would have a right to prove for this sum along with all other creditors (including the second mortgagee, if its second charge proved to be insufficient to ensure recovery of that which was owed to it).

1 [1999] 1 AC 221 at 237, per Lord Hoffman.

8.49 *Banque Financière* raises the question as to whether subrogation should be made available to those whose misfortune is attributable to their own carelessness. The claimant chose to be an unsecured creditor and to attempt to protect itself only by a subordination arrangement because it did not want to subject itself to the disclosure requirements that Swiss banking regulations demand when security is taken. It was manifestly careless in its failure to ensure that the officer of the holding company with which it dealt had the authority to bind the second mortgagee to the subordination arrangement that it negotiated. Given that the claimant was a large institutional lender, it is difficult to have much sympathy for its plight. Nonetheless, the House of Lords was prepared to hold that the second mortgagee was bound by the arrangement between the claimant and Parc. Lord Steyn disposed with the point by remarking that 'restitution is not a fault based remedy ... In any event, the neglect of [the claimant] is akin to the carelessness of a mistaken payor: it does not by itself undermine the ground of restitution'[1]. It is true that negligence does not undermine the claim of a mistaken payor to recover from a payee[2]. Yet it is not clear that it should follow that negligence should not preclude an attempt by a mistaken payor to obtain rights against third parties. Where a claim is brought against the recipient of a mistaken payment, acts of detrimental reliance can be protected through the change of position defence. In contrast, the defence may prove unworkable in cases where rights are claimed against third parties, such as unsecured creditors, who may not be parties to the action.

1   [1999] 1 AC 221 at 227.
2   *Kelly v Solari* (1841) 9 M & W 54, 152 ER 24.

Subrogation in the context of invalid loans

8.50   In some circumstances, a claimant who has advanced money pursuant to an invalid or unenforceable loan that has been used to discharge a debt may be entitled to be subrogated to the position of the creditor. However, the extent to which subrogation is available in this context remains controversial. This question must be considered in the light of the treatment of the issues raised by restitution in the context of invalid loans more generally.

THE AVAILABILITY OF DIRECT PERSONAL CLAIMS

8.51   The view has long been taken that to make a direct restitutionary claim available in the aftermath of an unenforceable loan would amount to little more than the enforcement of the loan by other means[1]. There has, however, often been a judicial willingness to give a claimant a remedy by way of subrogation, to the extent that any money advanced has been spent on discharging the borrower's legitimate liabilities[2]. Moreover, the tide appears to have turned against the view that the recognition of direct restitutionary claims in this the context would be contrary to the policy of legislation that provides that particular types of loans are invalid or unenforceable. In *Westdeutsche Landesbank Girozentrale v Islington London Borough Council*[3], Lord Goff suggested (obiter) that a restitution claim would not indirectly enforce an invalid contract. He reached this conclusion on the basis that 'such an action would be unaffected by any of the contractual terms governing the borrowing, and moreover would be subject (where appropriate) to any available restitutionary defences'[4]. If this perspective were to be accepted, there would be no necessity to use subrogation in this context to obtain personal rights. A direct restitutionary action would be available if the invalidity meant that there was a failure of consideration or if it could be said that the claimant, in being unaware of the invalidity, was the victim of a mistake of fact or law[5].

1   See for example *Re Wrexham Mold and Connah's Quay Rly Co* [1899] 1 Ch 440; *Sinclair v Brougham* [1914] AC 398.
2   See for example *Re Wrexham Mold and Connah's Quay Rly Co* [1899] 1 Ch 440.
3   [1996] AC 669.
4   [1996] AC 669 at 688.
5   See *Kleinwort Benson Ltd v Lincoln City Council* [1999] 2 AC 349, discussed below, para 17.40ff.

8.52   If, on the other hand, the courts continue to follow the authorities that preclude direct personal claims for restitution, it is not obvious that subrogation should be any more acceptable. Thus in *Orakpo v Manson Investments Ltd*[1], the House of Lords thought that a claimant that was unable to enforce a loan because of a failure to comply with requirements of writing imposed by the Moneylenders Act 1927 was equally precluded by reasons of public policy from acquiring creditors' rights by subrogation[2].

1   [1978] AC 95.
2   See below, para 8.60.

ASSUMPTION OF THE RISK OF UNENFORCEABILITY

8.53   While subrogation is likely to be denied where a lender makes a loan in the knowledge that it is irredeemably void or unenforceable, it is less clear whether the remedy will be available where a loan was made in the expectation that it would subsequently be ratified. The issue arose in *Re Cleadon Trust*[1]. The appellant was a company director who purported to discharge a debt that was owed by the company's subsidiaries and guaranteed by the company itself. While the payments were made without the company's authorisation, the appellant was assured by fellow company officers that the matter would be ratified at a later point. In fact, a subsequent resolution confirming the payments was invalid. After the company went into liquidation, the majority of the Court of Appeal denied the appellant's claim for subrogation on the basis that he had taken the risk that the company might not ratify the payment[2].

1   [1939] Ch 286.
2   [1939] Ch 286 at 312, per Scott LJ.

8.54   On the other hand, the courts have not taken a consistent approach to such matters. Relief has been allowed where money advanced to an agent by a lender who was aware that the agent did not have his principal's authority to take the loan was then applied to pay valid debts owed by the principal[1]. Similarly, the issue of voluntariness has never been thought to be relevant to the ability of lenders to be subrogated in cases where those who lack legal capacity use the money advanced to purchase necessaries[2]. Perhaps this simply demonstrates the impossibility of attempting to fit subrogation into a preconceived conceptual framework of unjust enrichment that is premised on the view that relief will be available only where a claimant is able to adduce some 'unjust factor'.

1   *Reversion Fund and Insurance Co Ltd v Maison Cosway Ltd* [1913] 1 KB 364 at 379, per Buckley LJ.
2   See below, para 8.55.

INSTANCES OF SUBROGATION IN THE CONTEXT OF LOANS THAT ARE ILLEGAL, UNAUTHORISED, OR OTHERWISE UNENFORCEABLE

8.55   Where money loaned to those lacking legal capacity is used to purchase necessaries   In the past, when wives lacked the legal capacity to contract, those who lent money to them could rely on subrogation for relief. To the extent that the money advanced was used to purchase necessaries, the lender was entitled to be subrogated to the position of the supplier of those necessaries, who at common law was entitled to a direct claim against the husband[1]. Similarly, by analogy, where money is lent to minors or the mentally infirm, lenders have been able to recover money advanced to the extent that it has been spent on necessaries[2].

1   *Harris v Lee* (1718) 1 P Wms 482, 24 ER 482; *Jenner v Morris* (1861) 3 De GF & J 45, 45 ER 795.
2   *Marlow v Pitfield* (1719) 1 P Wms 558, 24 ER 516.

8.56   The justification for subrogation in the context of the provision of necessaries is somewhat obscure. In *Jenner v Morris*[1], Lord Campbell LC suggested that the basis of the right to be subrogated to the position of one who sold necessaries to a wife:

> may possibly be that equity considers that the tradespeople have for valuable consideration assigned to the party who advanced the money the legal debt which would be due to them from the husband on furnishing the necessaries ... [2]

This seems a rather unhelpful fiction. The common law rule that allowed wives to pledge their husbands' credit for the purchase of necessaries reflected a concern for wives' welfare that overrode conventional restrictions on their legal capacity. Similarly, the willingness to give a remedy to claimants who have advanced money for the same purposes to those who lack legal capacity recognises that such assistance deserves to be rewarded and encouraged. The doctrines relating to the provision of necessaries represent a principled departure from the rules on legal capacity, as they serve to further the fundamental objective pursued in this context: the protection of the vulnerable.

1   (1861) 3 De GF & J 45, 45 ER 795.
2   (1861) 3 De GF & J 45 at 52, 45 ER 795 at 798.

8.57   Unauthorised borrowings by agents and partners   Where an agent has borrowed money without authorisation, to the extent that the money is applied to pay the principal's debts, the lender will be subrogated to the remedies of the relevant creditors. This principle was established in *Bannatyne v D & C MacIver*[1], a case in which the claimant was under the misapprehension that the agent was acting within his authority. Of course, even where an agent does not have actual authority, a lender will often be able to enforce a loan directly by relying on the agent's apparent authority. Given that the doctrine of apparent authority protects third parties who have reasonably relied on the acts of agents, it is perhaps difficult at first sight to explain why it is thought appropriate to allow equitable intervention to enforce a loan in this context. Moreover, there has been some criticism of the willingness of the Court of Appeal in *Reversion Fund and Insurance Co Ltd v Maison Cosway Ltd*[2] to permit subrogation in this context where the lender was aware that the agent did not have authority[3]. This once again emphasises that the law does not take a uniform approach to the issue of voluntariness in restitution. It is unlikely that the claimant's action could be countered with an objection sometimes raised elsewhere where claimants make a payment to a defendant's creditors, whereby it is asserted that the debt in question was not discharged by the payment[4]. It will almost inevitably be within the apparent authority of an agent to pay the debt in question[5].

1   [1906] 1 KB 103.
2   [1913] 1 KB 364.
3   See for example Mitchell *Law of Subrogation* (1994), p 134.
4   Cf *Owen v Tate* [1976] QB 402. See above, para 6.22.
5   The outcome has been explained on the basis that the principal should not be allowed to take the benefit after he has adopted his agent's acts without paying for it. See for example *Rolled Steel Products (Holdings) Ltd v British Steel Corpn* [1986] Ch 246; Goff and Jones *Law of Restitution* (5th edn, 1998), p 162. However, it is difficult to see that there is any need for the principal to adopt the agent's act in this context. Thanks to the doctrine of apparent authority, as between the creditor and the principal, the debt will generally be discharged without any positive act on the principal's part.

8.58   While there is no authority precisely on the point, the received wisdom is that subrogation is also available in the context of unauthorised borrowings by partners when the money advanced is used to pay off partnership debts[1].

1   I'Anson Banks (ed) *Lindley and Banks on Partnership* (17th edn, 1995), paras 12–194 and 12–196; Goff and Jones *Law of Restitution* (5th edn, 1998), p 162.

8.59   Where money advanced pursuant to void or voidable loans is used to purchase land: acquiring a vendor's lien by subrogation
Subrogation is likely to remain relevant in the aftermath of invalid contracts,

despite the availability of direct personal actions, if it enables claimants to obtain the benefit of a discharged creditor's proprietary rights. A claimant was permitted to obtain such an advantage in *Thurstan v Nottingham Permanent Building Society*[1], where the claimant had given the defendant a loan which was to be secured by a mortgage over land that the defendant was purchasing. Thanks to the Infants Relief Act 1874[2], the loan was voidable and the charge void as a consequence of the borrower's youth. Nonetheless, the claimant was permitted to assume the equitable lien that arises in favour of an unpaid vendor of land after the making of a specifically enforceable contract for sale[3]. According to the analysis favoured by the Court of Appeal, it was crucial that the claimant was acting as the borrower's agent when it paid the money in question to the vendor – a rather dubious interpretation of events. In the view of the Court, the claimant was entitled to a remedy because it was not permissible for the principal to adopt an agent's acts without incurring any obligation to repay that agent[4]. However, the Court did not consider whether it might have been more appropriate to limit the claimant to a personal remedy. Perhaps this was the result of the tendency to assume that subrogation *must* mean that the claimant acquires all the rights enjoyed by the person into whose shoes he steps[5]. Nonetheless, the outcome is consistent with the approach taken in cases involving valid loans, where claimants are permitted to obtain proprietary relief where they had negotiated for a security that proves to be defective[6].

1   [1902] 1 Ch 1; affirmed on another point by the House of Lords [1903] AC 6.
2   See the Infants Relief Act 1874, s 1. This has now been repealed by the Minors' Contracts Act 1987.
3   See *Lysaght v Edwards* (1876) 2 Ch D 499.
4   [1902] 1 Ch 1 at 9, per Vaughan Williams LJ.
5   See above, paras 8.4 and 8.5.
6   See above, para 8.45ff.

8.60   By contrast, in *Orakpo v Manson Investments Ltd*[1], the House of Lords refused to allow the claimant even a personal remedy when the agreement pursuant to which it advanced money was rendered unenforceable by a failure to comply with the formalities requirements imposed by the Moneylenders Act 1927, s 6[2]. Lord Edmund Davies concluded that a different approach would have been in conflict with the policy of the Act. In his view, *Thurstan* could be distinguished because the security given in that case was void, while the contract in the case before their Lordships was valid but unenforceable. Yet it is difficult to see that this really provides a sound basis for distinguishing between the cases. In each case, as a result of legislation, the lender was unable to obtain the security for which it had bargained. If anything, given that the Infants Relief Act 1874 was more protective of the class of borrower in question than is the Moneylenders Act 1927[3], there should have been more concern about giving relief in *Thurstan* than in *Orakpo*.

1   [1978] AC 95.
2   See the Moneylenders Act 1927, s 6(1).
3   Burrows *Law of Restitution* (1993), p 90.

8.61   Lord Keith, with whom Lord Salmon concurred, placed considerable emphasis on the notion that the right of subrogation was a creature of contract. It followed in his view that the right sought was essentially a security 'given by the borrower' and consequently was void if not mentioned in writing[1]. This hardly provides a sound basis for determining the matter. Clearly the understanding that any security obtained by subrogation was 'given by the borrower' relies on the fiction that subrogation is a product of common intention – an understanding that was subsequently criticised by Lord Hoffman in *Banque Financière de la Cité v Parc (Battersea) Ltd*[2].

1 [1978] AC 95 at 119–120.
2 [1999] 1 AC 221 at 234.

8.62   In addition, Lord Keith argued that any attempt to enforce the rights acquired by subrogation 'would be an attempt to enforce the contract for repayment of the money lent'[1]. Yet subsequently, in *Westdeutsche Landesbank Girozentrale v Islington London Borough Council*, Lord Goff denied that direct restitutionary actions would amount to the enforcement of an invalid loan by other means[2]. If this view were to be accepted, the further question that would arise would be whether there are any policy reasons against allowing subrogation to proprietary rights where invalid loans had been given in the expectation of the lender's being granted a valid security.

1 [1978] AC 95 at 120.
2 See above, para 8.51.

8.63   One context in which the courts have been unwilling to allow subrogation is where security has been granted but is unenforceable because of the lender's failure to register it. Thus, the remedy was denied to a mortgagee in *Burston Finance Ltd v Speirway Ltd*[1], where a mortgage was void against the liquidator because of a failure to register the security as required by company law[2]. Walton J argued that the lender had received what it had bargained for under the loan contract and its subsequent inability to enforce the security was entirely its own doing. It is difficult to argue with this conclusion: to allow subrogation in these circumstances would be contrary to the policy that promotes registration as the most fair and efficient basis for the protection of rights of security.

1 [1974] 1 WLR 1648.
2 See the Companies Act 1948, s 95(1).

8.64   Ultra vires loans[1]   In the context of ultra vires loans, the courts have taken the view that to recognise a personal action that required the company to repay the money lent 'would simply be to allow them to carry through an ultra vires transaction'[2]. On the other hand, in a number of cases lenders were allowed a remedy to the extent that the moneys advanced had been used to pay valid debts. It was argued that, given that the level of the company's liabilities remained the same, the policy behind limitations on borrowing would not be subverted by allowing this form of relief[3]. Thus, in a number of nineteenth century cases, claimants were permitted to assume the rights of an unsecured creditor in this way[4].

1 Most of the cases giving rise to this issue have occurred in the context of company law. By the Companies Act 1985, s 35(1), 'the validity of an act done by a company shall not be called into question on the ground of lack of capacity by reason of anything in the company's memorandum'. As a result, this issue is unlikely to arise in a corporate context today; see below, para 15.26. However, this issue might still arise elsewhere in the context of other bodies with limited capacity, as the recent interest swaps litigation involving public authorities demonstrates: see below, para 18.18ff.
2 *Re Wrexham Mold and Connah's Quay Rly Co* [1899] 1 Ch 440 at 457, per Vaughan Williams LJ.
3 *Re Wrexham Mold and Connah's Quay Rly Co* [1899] 1 Ch 440 at 451, per Rigby LJ.
4 See for example *Re German Mining Co* (1853) 4 De GM & G 19, 43 ER 415; *Re Norwich Yarn Co* (1856) 22 Beav 143, 52 ER 1062; *Re Cork and Youghal Rly Co* (1869) 4 Ch App 748; *Baroness Wenlock v River Dee Co* (1887) 19 QBD 155; *Blackburn Building Society v Cunliffe, Brooks & Co* (1882) 22 Ch D 61.

8.65   On the other hand, it is clear that a claimant who intended to give an unsecured loan will not be permitted to assume the secured rights of creditors repaid with the money advanced. This was made apparent in *Re Wrexham Mold and Connah's Quay Rly Co*[1], where a company's borrowing was ultra vires because it took it beyond the levels of debt that it was permitted to assume. While the court permitted the claimant lender a personal remedy to the extent that the money was used to discharge the company's valid debts[2], it was not allowed to acquire the rights of security enjoyed by the company's creditors.

1   [1899] 1 Ch 440.
2   See above, paras 8.5 and 8.51.

8.66   The approach taken elsewhere suggests that a claimant who had advanced money pursuant to a secured ultra vires loan should be entitled to be subrogated to any securities enjoyed by creditors of the company repaid using the loan[1]. However, there is no authority directly on the point. More controversial is the outcome in *Blackburn Building Society v Cunliffe, Brooks & Co*[2]. A building society gave its bank certain title deeds to secure its overdraft. While the overdrawing of the account was ultra vires, the Court of Appeal held that the bank could hold the deeds as security for any moneys that the building society had applied to repay existing debts. This result cannot readily be conceptualised as subrogation. In any event, it is difficult to justify. If the advance had not been used to repay secured debts, the result of the bank's being allowed to exercise these rights of security in this context would be to put general creditors in a worse position than they would have been in had the ultra vires loan not been made.

1   Cf the advantages given to those who advance money in the expectation of receiving an enforceable security. See for example *Butler v Rice* [1910] 2 Ch 277; *Ghana Commercial Bank v Chandiram* [1960] AC 732.
2   (1882) 22 Ch D 61. See also *Re Durham County Permanent Investment Land and Building Society* (1871) LR 12 Eq 516; *Re Harris Calculating Machine Co* [1914] 1 Ch 920.

Subrogation to creditors' rights where payment is made by one with a partial interest in property

8.67   Where claimants with a partial interest in a property repay a debt that is secured by a charge over that property, they are thereafter allowed to exercise the rights formerly enjoyed by the charge holder against others who have an interest in the property[1]. This remedy was often granted to provide relief for life tenants who repaid secured debts over the property in which they had their interest and subsequently sought some contribution from those with reversionary interests. While the courts in these cases do not describe this relief as subrogation, it takes effect in the same way, and commentators sometimes analyse it in those terms[2].

1   See for example *Countess of Shrewsbury v Earl of Shrewsbury* (1790) 1 Ves 227, 30 ER 314; *Morley v Morley* (1855) 5 De G M & G 610, 43 ER 1007; *Burrell v Earl of Egremont* (1844) 7 Beav 205, 49 ER 1043; *Re Harvey* [1896] 1 Ch 137. For discussion see Sutton 'Payment of Debts Charged Upon Property' in Burrows (ed) *Essays on the Law of Restitution* (1991), p 82.
2   Mitchell *Law of Subrogation* (1994), pp 112 and 169.

8.68   Occasionally, a payment by one with a partial interest in land might have been induced by a mistake[1]. In addition, some of the cases in this context might perhaps be explained on the basis that the claimant was effectively compelled to pay the debt in order to protect his interest in the property[2]. However, in many cases, it is difficult to explain the payment as involuntary in any meaningful sense. At times in these cases the courts have adopted fictions of implied intent[3], arguing that the claimant intended to keep the security alive for his own benefit and thereby suggesting that there was an implied assignment of the rights in question. These fictions are implausible; for, in many, if not most cases, it is clear that the claimant gave this matter no thought. Thus, subrogation in this context is best regarded as a sui generis dispensation given to those with a partial interest in property. The courts have essentially favoured a default rule whereby 'something is required to manifest an intention to exonerate' the successors in title from liability[4]. Thus, if the claimant has positively disclaimed the rights of security, subrogation will not be permitted[5]. Otherwise, 'A simple payment of the charge without more, is sufficient to establish the right of a tenant for life to have the charge raised out of the estate'[6].

1   See for example *Earl of Buckinghamshire v Hobart* (1818) 3 Swan 186, 36 ER 824 (tenant in tail paid off mortgage in the belief that he was tenant in fee simple, when in fact another had been given a life tenancy under the former owner's will).
2   This might be said to be the case where a lessee meets a debt owed by his landlord in order to safeguard his own interest; see *Tarn v Turner* (1888) 39 Ch D 456. See Mitchell *Law of Subrogation* (1994), p 169; Burrows *Law of Restitution* (1993), p 210.
3   See for example *Morley v Morley* (1855) 5 De GM & G 610 at 619, 43 ER 1007 at 1011.
4   *Burrell v Earl of Egremont* (1844) 7 Beav 205 at 232, 49 ER 1043 at 1054, per Lord Langdale MR.
5   *Parry v Wright* (1823) 1 Sim & St 369 at 379, 57 ER 148 at 152, per Sir J Leach VC; Mitchell *Law of Subrogation* (1994), p 169.
6   *Burrell v Earl of Egremont* (1844) 7 Beav 205 at 232, 49 ER 1043 at 1054, per Lord Langdale MR.

Banks' rights of subrogation after an unauthorised payment of a customer's creditor

8.69   Where a bank transfers money to a third party in the mistaken belief that it has been authorised to do so by a customer and the transfer has the effect of discharging the customer's debt to a creditor, the bank is subrogated to the rights that the creditor had against its customer. This principle was established in *B Liggett (Liverpool) Ltd v Barclays Bank Ltd*[1]. Wright J justified the bank's right to subrogation by analogy to the cases involving invalid loans. In his view, 'The customer in such a case is really no worse off because the legal liability which has to be discharged is discharged'[2]. Of course, this conclusion depends upon the premise that the debt in question is actually discharged by the payment. The law does not take a consistent approach to this question, as the cases examining the legal effect of a payment of a debt by a third party demonstrate[3]. Indeed, in *Barclays Bank Ltd v WJ Simms, Son and Cooke (Southern) Ltd*[4], Robert Goff J suggested that a customer's debt is not discharged in these circumstances, and that, as result, the bank should sue the creditor and not the customer. If this view were taken, the use of subrogation to provide relief in this context might appear to be an unnecessary complication. However, the process of subrogation will be attractive to banks who would like to acquire any rights of security enjoyed by the discharged creditor.

1   [1928] 1 KB 48.
2   [1928] 1 KB 48 at 64.
3   See above, para 6.20ff.
4   [1980] QB 677.

8.70   A difficult issue concerns the remedies of a bank that has made a payment that is invalid because the customer's bankruptcy means that his assets have vested in the trustee in bankruptcy. The issue arose in *Re Byfield*[1], where the bank followed a customer's instructions to transfer money to her mother after the notice of the customer's bankruptcy had been gazetted. While the trustee in bankruptcy was able to recover some of the money, the customer's mother had used part of it to pay off some of the customer's creditors. The bank was obliged to account to the trustee in bankruptcy for this shortfall. It then asked to be subrogated to the remedies of the creditors in question. Goulding J concluded that this remedy would have been contrary to the policy of the Bankruptcy (Amendment) Act 1926, s 4, that protected the position of those transferring a bankrupt's money up to the point the notice of bankruptcy is gazetted. On the other hand, it might be argued that, if the money in question had been used to pay other creditors, subrogation would merely replace one creditor with another, leaving the remaining creditors in no worse a position.

1   [1982] Ch 267.

8.71   One reason why Goulding J declined the bank's claim was because it had not paid the creditors directly. This might seem understandable; for, if the bank pays money to its customer or its agent, property passes, and the bank cannot thereafter claim that creditors were paid with the bank's money[1]. Yet, if this reasoning were pursued consistently it would prevent subrogation in many contexts in which it is allowed. After all, where money has been advanced in circumstances in which the lender was operating under the influence of a mistake, orthodox opinion would have it that property passes to the recipient both at law and in equity. Nonetheless, subrogation is often allowed in these circumstances[2].

1   Cf *Boscawen v Bajwa* [1995] 4 All ER 769.
2   Consider, for example, *Butler v Rice* [1910] 2 Ch 277; *Ghana Commerical Bank v Chandiram* [1960] AC 732.

Subrogation and marshalling

8.72   In *Webb v Smith*[1] Cotton LJ explained the doctrine of marshalling on the basis that,

> If A has a charge upon Whiteacre and Blackacre, and if B also has a [second] charge upon Blackacre only, A must take payment of his charge out of Whiteacre, and must leave Blackacre, so that B the other creditor, may follow it and obtain payment of his debt out of it[2].

If a secured creditor fails to observe this rule, subrogation will ensure that the rights of other secured creditors are not undermined. If, pursuant to the example offered by Cotton LJ, A exercises his charge over Blackacre to realise the debt owed to him, B will be subrogated to position of A, thereby allowing B to rely on the charge that A enjoyed over Whiteacre[3]. The doctrine of marshalling represents a decision to privilege the position of secured creditors (mainly institutional lenders) over that of unsecured creditors (generally, smaller contract creditors) for reasons that have never been satisfactorily explained.

1   (1880) 30 Ch D 192.
2   (1880) 30 Ch D 192 at 200.
3   *Lanoy v Duke and Duchess of Atholl* (1742) 2 Atk 444, 26 ER 668; *Wallis v Woodyear* (1855) 2 Jur NS 179; *Noyes v Pollock* (1886) 32 Ch D 53. See Cleaver 'Marshalling' (1991) 21 Victoria University of Wellington Law Review 275; Mitchell *Law of Subrogation* (1994), p 143.

CHAPTER 9

Fiduciaries

Margaret Halliwell

A   Introduction

9.1   As will be seen throughout this chapter, forms of relief for breach of a fiduciary relationship are not always restitutionary in nature. Equitable compensation and injunctive orders may be available. This chapter would not, however, provide a full picture if it were to be restricted to circumstances where a breach of a fiduciary relationship gives rise to the restitutionary remedies by way on an account of profits or the imposition of a constructive trust.

B   Which relationships are fiduciary?

9.2   The classification of a relationship as being of a fiduciary nature has been subject to continuing developments both in this country and abroad.

A recent trend, as mentioned above[1], has been for the judiciary to refuse to elevate an ordinary commercial contract into a fiduciary relationship at the expense of general creditors in an insolvency situation[2]. The clear policy issue behind this is that, under normal circumstances, commercial contractors run the risk of ranking with general creditors in insolvency. An exceptional case occurred in Canada in *LAC Minerals Ltd v International Corona Resources Ltd*[3] where the Supreme Court of Canada expressed a willingness to impose fiduciary obligations in favour of any party to a commercial transaction who is vulnerable to the other, even where the vulnerability has arisen only by virtue of the relative sizes and resources of the two commercial enterprises involved. However, even in that case it was emphasised that such vulnerability will only rarely be found to exist, and there is little possibility of that case being followed by English courts.

1   See above, para 2.12.
2   See *Re Goldcorp Exchange (in receivership)* [1995] 1 AC 74; below, para 9.3.
3   (1989) 61 DLR (4th) 14.

9.3   In *Re Goldcorp Exchange (in receivership)*[1] the Privy Council considered an appeal from the decision of the Court of Appeal of New Zealand[2]. That court had imposed fiduciary obligations on a gold-dealer, which had offered its purchasers the option of leaving their bullion in its custody on the purchasers' behalf as 'non-allocated bullion'. Purchasers who did so were issued with a certificate of ownership, and were entitled to take physical possession of their bullion on seven days' notice. The Court of Appeal decided that the company was a fiduciary, because it was bound to protect the interests of the purchasers and, also, because it was free from control and supervision by them. The Privy Council rejected these arguments, and the current position can be summarised in the words of Lord Mustill:

> No doubt the fact that one person is placed in a particular position vis-à-vis another through the medium of a contract does not necessarily mean that he does not also owe fiduciary duties to that other by virtue of being in that position. But the essence of a fiduciary relationship is that it creates obligations of a different character from those deriving from the contract itself ... Many commercial relationships involve just such a reliance by one party on the other, and to introduce the whole new dimension into such relationships which would flow from giving them a fiduciary character would (as it seems to their Lordships) have adverse consequences far exceeding those foreseen by Atkin LJ in *In re Wait* [3].

1   [1995] 1 AC 74.
2   [1993] 1 NZLR 257.
3   [1995] 1 AC 74 at 98, referring to *Re Wait* [1927] 1 Ch 606.

9.4   Other limitations have been imposed, in that a duty imposed by statute to perform certain functions does not, as a general rule, impose fiduciary obligations, and that the presumption is, in the absence of indications to the contrary in the statute, that no such obligations are imposed. So, for example, it was held by the House of Lords, in *Swain v Law Society* [1], that the Law Society was not in a fiduciary relationship with respect to members of the solicitors' profession. Furthermore, in *Tito v Waddell (No 2)* [2] it was held that the Crown will not become a fiduciary unless it deliberately chooses to do so.

1   [1983] 1 AC 598.
2   [1977] Ch 106.

9.5   Beyond these specific limitations, the circumstances when a relationship will be treated as fiduciary are far from closed. As a general description, a fiduciary relationship will arise when one person reposes trust and confidence in another person in the management of the first person's affairs. There is, therefore, considerable overlap between the law relating to restitution for a breach of the fiduciary duty of loyalty and the abuse of confidence cases discussed below [1]. There have been four relationships that have, traditionally, been treated as fiduciary relationships: trustee and beneficiary, agent and principal, director and company, and partner and co-partner. The relationship between solicitor and client is also classified as fiduciary, in *Brown v IRC* [2] for example, although again the relationship with this classification and the early abuse of confidence cases such as *Walmsley v Booth* [3] has never been fully explored. More recently, fiduciary relationships have been discerned to exist between senior management employee and company in *Sybron Corpn v Rochem Ltd* [4] and *Canadian Aero Service Ltd v O'Malley* [5], and between a member of the Security Services and the Crown in *A-G v Guardian Newspapers (No 2)* [6] and *A-G v Blake* [7].

1   See below, ch 10.
2   [1965] AC 244.
3   (1741) 2 Atk 25, 26 ER 412; below, para 10.18.
4   [1984] Ch 112.
5   (1973) 40 DLR (3d) 371 at 381.
6   [1990] 1 AC 109.
7   [2001] 1 AC 268.

9.6   Developments have been even more extensive in other jurisdictions. Other jurisdictions have added the relationships between doctor and patient (*Norberg v*

Wynrib[1], *McInerney v MacDonald*[2], and *SEC v Willis*[3]), and between parent child-abuser and abused child (*M (K) v M (H)*[4]). The particular facts of almost any circumstances may give rise to the establishment of a fiduciary relationship where key elements exist of trust and confidence reposed in one person, who is then relied on to control some aspect of property rights. The fiduciary is then expected to act completely selflessly in respect of the property rights and, as a concomitant of this, the courts stringently assert the duty of loyalty, which the fiduciary owes to his or her principal.

1   (1992) 92 DLR (4th) 449.
2   (1992) 93 DLR (4th) 415.
3   787 Fed Supp 58 (1992).
4   (1993) 96 DLR (4th) 289.

9.7   The classification of fiduciaries for the purposes of recovering secret profits has been cast extraordinarily wide.

In *A-G v Goddard*[1] a fiduciary relationship was found when a police officer had received bribes not to report brothel keepers. In *Reading v A-G*[2], somewhat controversially, a fiduciary relationship was found to exist between an army sergeant and the Crown. The sergeant had obtained large bribes from smugglers for riding, in his uniform, through Cairo in lorries in which smuggled goods were being transported, so as to enable the lorries to pass the civil police without search. £19,000 had been found in his possession and confiscated when he was eventually caught, and he was attempting to recover this sum of money. In the Court of Appeal[3] Asquith LJ held that a fiduciary relationship was necessary in order to defeat his claim against the Crown, and that such a relationship arose from the use of his uniform and the opportunities attached to it. He acknowledged that this was using the concept of fiduciary relationship 'in a very loose sense', but the House of Lords ultimately confirmed his view.

1   (1929) 45 TLR 609.
2   [1951] AC 507.
3   [1949] 2 KB 232.

9.8   More recently, in *A-G v Blake*[1], a rather more restrictive approach was applied in the context of a former fiduciary. The *Blake* case arose because of the publication of the book, *No Other Choice*, by Jonathan Cape on 17 September 1990. The book is the autobiography of the convicted spy, George Blake, and contains information relating to his employment in the Secret Intelligence Service, his activities on behalf of the KGB, his trial, imprisonment and subsequent escape to Moscow. A sum of £90,000 remained payable to the defendant by the publishers. The Attorney-General was seeking to deprive the defendant of any financial benefit derived from publication of the book. The Court of Appeal[2] accepted that the relationship between an employer and employees is of a fiduciary nature and that Blake, therefore, owed duties of trust and confidence to his employer. Such fiduciary duties, however, last only as long as the relationship which gives rise to them lasts. A former employee owes no such duties to a former employer. As to the fiduciary relationship of confidentiality, the duty to respect confidence subsists only as long as the information remains confidential. The Crown's equitable claim against the defendant was, therefore, tenable on neither basis. These particular findings were undisturbed by the House of Lords. It is suggested that the first finding should be restricted to circumstances, as in the case itself, where a considerable period of time has elapsed since the termination of the fiduciary relationship. To hold otherwise would allow a dishonest fiduciary to defer obtaining secret profits as a result of the relationship until that relationship has come to an end.

1   [2001] 1 AC 268.
2   [1997] Ch 84.

C   The duty of loyalty

9.9   Lord Herschell made the classic statement of fiduciary responsibility in respect of the latter two propositions in *Bray v Ford*[1]. Lord Herschell espoused two principles: a fiduciary cannot be permitted to profit from his fiduciary position, and a fiduciary must not allow his personal interest to prevail over his duty of loyalty to his principal. Although the two principles are similar, they are distinct in that a fiduciary cannot profit from his fiduciary position even when there is no real conflict of interest and duty. Within these principles, the attitude of English law towards fiduciaries has been severely strict, and consistently so. Not only is it irrelevant that the principal has suffered no loss, it is also irrelevant that the principal receives a gain as a result of the fiduciary's conduct, when it is necessarily unlikely that there will be a real conflict of interest and duty. Lord Herschell acknowledged this in *Bray v Ford*[2] by saying that the principles 'might be departed from in many cases, without any breach of morality, without any wrong being inflicted, and without any consciousness of wrong-doing'. The reason for the strictness of the principles is clearly on policy grounds to deter any possible abuse of the fiduciary relationship by the fiduciary.

As was made clear in *Sargeant v National Westminster Bank*[3], if the making of a profit by the fiduciary is either authorised by the instrument originally creating the fiduciary relationship or has received the fully informed consent of the principal, then clearly *Bray v Ford* will not apply. Other than that, there have been very limited examples of any relaxation of the very strict principles.

1   [1896] AC 44.
2   [1896] AC 44 at 52.
3   (1990) 61 P & CR 518.

D   Duty to act without remuneration

9.10   A trustee is, prima facie, under a duty to act without remuneration, even where a considerable amount of time and trouble is deployed in managing the trust business. Moreover, if by virtue of his position as trustee, he holds an office of profit, such as a directorship in a company in which the trust has a shareholding, he will prima facie be liable to account to the trust for any remuneration which he receives as a result of holding that office.

9.11   Where a fiduciary has received unauthorised remuneration, remedies will be available either via the imposition of a constructive trust, or by liability to account to the principal for its value. Prior to the Privy Council decision in *A-G for Hong Kong v Reid*[1], the situation was somewhat different in respect of remuneration in the form of secret profits.

1   [1994] 1 AC 324.

9.12   Until the decision of the Privy Council in *A-G for Hong Kong v Reid*[1], the decided cases appeared to draw a distinction between bribes and other secret profits. In *Lister & Co v Stubbs*[2], the defendant was the claimant's foreman, and was responsible for buying in whatever was needed in his employer's business. He regularly gave orders to a third party in return for a secret large commission. In an action to recover this bribe, the claimant sought an order restraining the defendant from dealing with certain investments, purchased with the money received, on the basis that the defendant was a constructive trustee of the bribes, and so the claimant would be entitled to follow the money into its product and recover the investments. The Court of Appeal declined to grant this order, holding that the only obligation of the defendant was to pay over the sums received to the claimant. The relationship between the defendant and the claimant was held to be that of debtor-creditor rather than trustee-beneficiary. This decision was much criticised in academic literature, and sat uneasily along cases such as *Williams v Barton*[3]. In the latter case, a trustee used a firm of which he was a member to value trust securities. His action was absolutely bona fide but he was nevertheless held liable to account to the trust as a constructive trustee for the commission that he had made out of the introduction of the trust business. The defendant in *Williams v Barton* was, therefore, liable as a constructive trustee of a commission which he had earned in good faith, whereas the defendant in *Lister & Co v Stubbs* was held not to have been a constructive trustee of a dishonestly obtained bribe.

1   [1994] 1 AC 324.
2   (1890) 45 Ch D 1.
3   [1927] 2 Ch 9.

9.13   The issue was resolved by the Privy Council in *A-G for Hong Kong v Reid*[1]. This case concerned a Hong Kong Public Prosecutor, who was convicted of having accepted bribes as an inducement to exploit his official position to obstruct the prosecution of certain criminals. He was ordered to pay the Crown the sum of HK$12,400,000, the value of assets then controlled by him which could only have been derived from the bribes. No payments having been made, the Attorney-General for Hong Kong brought proceedings in New Zealand, claiming that three freehold houses which the bribes had been used to purchase were held on constructive trust for the Crown. The Court of Appeal of New Zealand applied *Lister & Co v Stubbs* and dismissed this claim[2]. The Privy Council reversed this decision, holding that *Lister & Co v Stubbs* had been wrongly decided. Lord Templeman, delivering the opinion of the Privy Council, held that as soon as any bribe is received, the fiduciary becomes in equity the debtor of his principal for the amount of the bribe, which should immediately be transferred to his principal. Because equity considers as done that which ought to have been done, the bribe therefore becomes subject to a constructive trust in favour of the principal as soon as it is received. As a result of this authority, the liability of a fiduciary who receives a bribe will be identical to that of a fiduciary who receives any other type of secret profit.

1   [1994] 1 AC 324.
2   [1992] 2 NZLR 385.

When is remuneration allowed?

9.14   The basic principle is that no remuneration is available unless expressly stipulated for in the trust instrument. However, the position of express fiduciaries is usually favourable. Normally, such fiduciaries are unlikely to have agreed to act without first having provided for the payment of appropriate remuneration.

The Articles of Association of a company, for example, generally provide for the payment of remuneration to its directors[1]; a Partnership Deed will provide for the payment of remuneration to the partners; and a contract of agency will make provision for the payment of appropriate remuneration to the agent.

1   The Table A Articles of Association recommended by statute reserve to the company in general meeting by ordinary resolution the right to determine the remuneration of the directors of the company.

9.15   The House of Lords has held, however, in *Guinness plc v Saunders*[1], that where the formula by which authorisation has to be obtained has not been complied with, the fiduciary will not be entitled either to remuneration or to the benefits of any other office to which he has been appointed by virtue of his fiduciary position, and will be liable to account to his principal for any sums received. In such circumstances, the House of Lords also held that the court has no inherent jurisdiction to award remuneration to the fiduciary in question[2]. This was because the articles of association vested in the board of directors the specific power to award special remuneration.

1   [1990] 2 AC 663. The remuneration of the director in question had not, as required by the Articles of Association, been approved by the board of directors.
2   [1990] 2 AC 663 at 700–702.

9.16   In certain exceptional circumstances, the courts will exercise the inherent jurisdiction, where neither the trust instrument nor the beneficiaries have authorised remuneration[1].

1   See *Re Duke of Norfolk's Settlement Trusts* [1982] Ch 61; *Foster v Spencer* [1996] 2 All ER 672. See also below, para 9.42.

9.17   The Trustee Act 2000, ss 28 and 29, introduces a right for a trust corporation or a trustee acting in a professional capacity to receive remuneration out of the trust funds[1]. The Act, which came into force on 1 February 2001[2], introduces a right to receive reasonable remuneration even if the services rendered are capable of being provided by a lay trustee. As this is a very recent reform of the law and the statutory provisions are not particularly clear, the provisions are set out in full:

28.   Trustee's entitlement to payment under trust instrument
    (1) Except to the extent (if any) to which the trust instrument makes inconsistent provision, subsections (2) to (4) apply to a trustee if–
    (a) there is a provision in the trust instrument entitling him to receive payment out of trust funds in respect of services provided by him to or on behalf of the trust, and
    (b) the trustee is a trust corporation or is acting in a professional capacity.
    (2) The trustee is to be treated as entitled under the trust instrument to receive payment in respect of services even if they are services which are capable of being provided by a lay trustee.
    (3) Subsection (2) applies to a trustee of a charitable trust who is not a trust corporation only–
    (a) if he is not a sole trustee, and
    (b) to the extent that a majority of the other trustees have agreed that it should apply to him.
    (4) Any payments to which the trustee is entitled in respect of services are to be treated as remuneration for services (and not as a gift) for the purposes of–
    (a) section 15 of the Wills Act 1837 (gifts to an attesting witness to be void), and
    (b) section 34(3) of the Administration of Estates Act 1925 (order in which estate to be paid out).

(5) For the purposes of this Part, a trustee acts in a professional capacity if he acts in the course of a profession or business which consists of or includes the provision of services in connection with–
  (a) the management or administration of trusts generally or a particular kind of trust, or
  (b) any particular aspect of the management or administration of trusts generally or a particular kind of trust,
and the services he provides to or on behalf of the trust fall within that description.
  (6) For the purposes of this Part, a person acts as a lay trustee if he–
  (a) is not a trust corporation, and
  (b) does not act in a professional capacity.

29.   Remuneration of certain trustees

  (1) Subject to subsection (5), a trustee who–
  (a) is a trust corporation, but
  (b) is not a trustee of a charitable trust,
is entitled to receive reasonable remuneration out of the trust funds for any services that the trust corporation provides to or on behalf of the trust.
  (2) Subject to subsection (5), a trustee who–
  (a) acts in a professional capacity, but
  (b) is not a trust corporation, a trustee of a charitable trust or a sole trustee,
is entitled to receive reasonable remuneration out of the trust funds for any services that he provides to or on behalf of the trust if each other trustee has agreed in writing that he may be remunerated for the services.
  (3) 'Reasonable remuneration' means, in relation to the provision of services by a trustee, such remuneration as is reasonable in the circumstances for the provision of those services to or on behalf of that trust by that trustee and for the purposes of subsection (1) includes, in relation to the provision of services by a trustee who is an authorised institution under the Banking Act 1987 and provides the services in that capacity, the institution's reasonable charges for the provision of such services.
  (4) A trustee is entitled to remuneration under this section even if the services in question are capable of being provided by a lay trustee.
  (5) A trustee is not entitled to remuneration under this section if any provision about his entitlement to remuneration has been made–
  (a) by the trust instrument, or
  (b) by any enactment or any provision of subordinate legislation.
  (6) This section applies to a trustee who has been authorised under a power conferred by Part IV or the trust instrument–
  (a) to exercise functions as an agent of the trustees, or
  (b) to act as a nominee or custodian,
as it applies to any other trustee.

In the absence, as yet, of any judicial interpretation of the section, it is too early to assess to what extent this encroaches on the prima facie principle of no remuneration.

1   Different provision is made for charity trustees in s 30, which allows for the promulgation of relevant rules by statutory instrument. At the time of writing (April 2002) no such statutory instrument has been promulgated.
2   SI 2001/49.

E   Transactions into which a fiduciary has entered in a double capacity

9.18   This second group of cases concerns transactions in which a fiduciary has purported to represent the interests of both his principal and himself. The transactions can be classified as the purchase of property by a fiduciary from his principal, the sale of property by a fiduciary to his principal and, in a recent case, the provision of a loan from a fiduciary to his principal. It does not matter how fair such transactions are. Because such transactions involve a conflict between the personal interest of the fiduciary and his duty of loyalty towards the principal, the principal has the right to have the transaction set aside unless fully aware of the facts.

Purchases of property by a fiduciary from the principal – the 'self-dealing rule' and the 'fair dealing rule'

9.19   Megarry VC, in *Tito v Waddell (No 2)*[1], described the rules that relate to transactions of this nature as the 'self-dealing rule' and the 'fair-dealing rule'. The 'self-dealing rule' applies to purchases by trustees from their trusts. The 'fair-dealing rule' applies to purchases by trustees of the interests of their beneficiaries. In *Ex p Lacey*[2] Lord Eldon LC explained the undesirability of the first of these transactions in the context of a trustee not being in a position where there is a conflict of interest and duty. He held that, in a purchase by a trustee from the trust, the trustee is both vendor and purchaser. This renders it impossible to determine from the evidence whether or not the purchase has been made on advantageous terms, and so there is necessarily a conflict of interest and duty and the transaction must be set aside at the suit of any beneficiary.

1   [1977] Ch 106 at 224–225.
2   (1802) 6 Ves 625, 31 ER 1228.

9.20   In *Tito v Waddell (No 2)*[1], Megarry VC went further and added that any beneficiary may have the sale set aside, however fair the transaction is considered to be. The strictness of this interpretation is easily demonstrated. In *Wright v Morgan*[2], for example, property was devised to two trustees on trust for sale for one of them, with a provision in the will to offer the trustee-beneficiary the land at a price to be fixed by independent valuers. The trustee-beneficiary assigned his beneficial interest to the other trustee, who bought the property at the price fixed by the independent valuers in accordance with the terms of the will. The Privy Council held that this sale had to be set aside, since only a sale to the trustee-beneficiary had been authorised by the will. The fact that the price was to be fixed independently was not sufficient. In theory at least, the trustees could themselves fix the time at which the property was to be sold, and thus influence the valuation.

1   [1977] Ch 106 at 224–225.
2   [1926] AC 788.

9.21   The same attitude was taken in respect of trust property for sale at auction in *Whelpdale v Cookson*[1], in which it was held that a trustee is in a position to discourage bidders. In all cases, however, it is axiomatic that the trust instrument can specifically authorise a purchase of trust property by trustees, and *Sargeant v National Westminster Bank*[2] is direct authority on this point. It is, of course, open to a court to authorise a purchase of trust property[3], and it is possible, in the absence of a provision in the trust instrument, for beneficiaries to authorise a purchase of trust property by trustees.

1   (1747) 1 Ves Sen 9, 27 ER 856.
2   (1990) 61 P & CR 518.
3   *Farmer v Dean* (1863) 32 Beav 327, 55 ER 128; and *Campbell v Walker* (1800) 5 Ves 678, 31 ER 801.

9.22   In one controversial case, *Holder v Holder*[1], the Court of Appeal upheld such a transaction. In *Holder v Holder* one of the executors of a will renounced his executorship after carrying out certain acts which, it was conceded, were fiduciary in nature. The executor was the tenant of certain farms, which the other executors offered for sale by auction subject to his tenancy. At the auction he purchased the farms at a substantial price, well above the independently valued reserve price. The Court of Appeal refused to set aside the sale at the request of one of the other beneficiaries. The case is controversial, because of the comments of Danckwerts LJ and Sachs LJ to the effect that the rule in *Ex p Lacey*[2] was no more than a rule of practice, which could be departed from at the discretion of the judges. All three members of the Court of Appeal, in any event, agreed that all the beneficiaries had acquiesced in the purchase and could not now seek to set it aside; but Harman LJ took a more conservative view of the law. He fully accepted the principle in *Ex p Lacey*, but distinguished it on the facts before him because the executor had played no real part in the administration of the estate, and had renounced his executorship long before the sale. All the beneficiaries were aware of this, and so could not have been expecting him to act towards them in a fiduciary capacity in respect of the transaction. The mischief, which the principle was intended to prevent, did not arise and, given the extent of the acquiescence there was no reason to set aside the sale. Although this still encompasses a more lenient interpretation than that taken in *Wright v Morgan*[3], it is much less radical than that taken by the other two members of the Court, and is the judgment that has been followed so far.

1   [1968] Ch 353.
2   (1802) 6 Ves 625, 31 ER 1228.
3   [1926] AC 788.

9.23   Vinelott J, in a subsequent case, *Re Thompson's Settlement*[1], held that two leases in favour of a company and a partnership (of which the two trustees were respectively a shareholder and a partner) were not valid. In so doing, he took the view that *Holder v Holder* was decided on the basis of the reasons given by Harman LJ, and that, save in the exceptional circumstances of that case, the self-dealing rule should be applied stringently.

1   [1986] Ch 99.

9.24   The only remaining way by which trustees can purchase trust property is by way of acquiring beneficial interests in the trust property, and this is governed by the somewhat less stringent fair-dealing rule. The fair-dealing rule applies to purchases by trustees of the interests of their beneficiaries[1], and to purchases by other fiduciaries from their principals[2]. Again the requirements, which need to be met for these transactions to be upheld, are very similar to the requirements, outlined below[3], to establish that there has not been an abuse of a confidence. *Coles v Trescothick*[4] provides authority to the effect that a trustee/fiduciary must show that there was no abuse of the fiduciary relationship, that no material facts were concealed, that the price was fair, and that the beneficiary/principal did not rely solely on his advice. Provided that all these requirements are met, transactions will not be set aside.

1   *Chalmer v Bradley* (1819) 1 Jac & W 51, 37 ER 294.
2   *Edwards v Meyrick* (1842) 2 Hare 60, 67 ER 25.
3   See below, para 10.20ff.
4   (1804) 9 Ves 234, 32 ER 592.

9.25   Obviously, as discussed earlier, in the context of *A-G v Blake*[1], there must be a period of time after the fiduciary relationship has come to an end, when the ex-fiduciary will be safely able to purchase the beneficial interest free from the fair-dealing rule. An example (which concerns land rather than confidential information) is *Re Boles and British Land Co's Contract*[2], where there was an interval of twelve years between retirement and purchase. The sale was upheld. This can be contrasted with *Re Mulholland's Will Trusts*[3]. Here a sale was not upheld where a trustee retired with the intention that the property would be conveyed to him after his retirement. Plainly, the distance in time between the termination of the relationship and the dealing with the property is a crucial factor, though it is unlikely to be regarded as the only one.

1   [2001] 1 AC 268; discussed above, para 9.8.
2   [1902] 1 Ch 244.
3   [1949] 1 All ER 460.

Sales of property by a fiduciary to the principal

9.26   There is no direct authority in English law as to the purchase of a trustee's property on behalf of the trust, but the cases in respect of other fiduciaries will clearly be applied by analogy. The general rule is again strict, since the courts police fiduciary relationships very firmly in order to discount any possibility of abuse ever arising.

* In *Gillett v Peppercone*[1] it was acknowledged that sales from a fiduciary to a principal will be set aside at the instance of the principal, unless the fiduciary has fully disclosed the nature of his interest in the transaction, irrespective of the honesty of the fiduciary or the fairness of the price.
* In *Armstrong v Jackson*[2] a sale was set aside even where the fiduciary purchased the property in question before he entered into the fiduciary relationship. In that case, a stockbroker did not disclose to his client that, ever since the formation of a company, he had owned the shares, which he was persuading his client to buy. Five years later, the client discovered the true facts and, as the shares had fallen in value to less than $1/_5$ of the purchase price, the client successfully applied to the court to have the transaction set aside. Where the subject matter of the sale has, alternatively, increased in price, the fiduciary will be forced to disgorge the relevant profits if the fiduciary relationship existed at the time of the sale.
* In *Bentley v Craven*[3] the defendant operated a business as a sugar dealer. He was also, however, responsible for the purchase of sugar for a partnership of sugar refiners. In the former capacity, he purchased a quantity of sugar, which he later resold to the partnership. Although he made a personal profit in the transaction, the price was the fair market price. He was held liable to account for his profit to the partnership, because he had been a fiduciary at the date of purchase, and so should have purchased for the partnership rather than for himself.
* If, however, the profit was clearly made before the fiduciary relationship arose, no liability will arise in respect of the profits made. This was clearly the case in *Re Cape Breton Co*[4], where a director of a company acquired a beneficial interest in certain mining claims two years before the company and concomitant fiduciary relationship came into existence. He later sold his interest in the mining claims to the company and, after the property had been sold on at a loss, the company's claim to the profit made by him failed.

1   (1840) 3 Beav 78, 49 ER 31.
2   [1917] 2 KB 822.
3   (1853) 18 Beav 75, 52 ER 29.
4   (1885) 29 Ch D 795.

Loans from a fiduciary to a principal

9.27   In *Swindle v Harrison*[1], Mrs Harrison wished to obtain a bridging loan in order to purchase another property. The claimants, members of a firm of solicitors, provided the loan. The judge, at first instance, had found that the claimants were negligent and in breach of fiduciary duty in failing to disclose two material facts. The claimants had not disclosed that Mrs Harrison's son's bank was unwilling to provide a reference, which meant that he was unable to secure a loan to assist with the purchase. The claimants also failed to disclose that they would profit from the bridging loan agreement. The equity in the property purchased by Mrs Harrison fell in value, and the argument put before the court on her behalf was that, because of the claimants' breach and her inability to repay the loan, they were liable to restore her financially to the position she was in when the breach occurred, under the equitable compensation principle in *Nocton v Lord Ashburton*[2].

1   [1997] 4 All ER 705.
2   [1914] AC 932.

9.28   The Court of Appeal decided that there was a breach of fiduciary duty. In the absence of fraud, the common law causation test of compensation applied: that is, the 'but for' test. It was held that, even if full disclosure had been made to Mrs Harrison, she would have accepted the loan and completed the purchase. She would, therefore, have lost the value in her home in any event. She could not recover damages for the loss claimed except on proof that the claimants acted in a manner equivalent to fraud, or on proof that she would not have completed the purchase if full disclosure had been made. She could prove neither. The decision is entirely consistent on the causation point with the decision reached, on different facts, by the House of Lords in *Target Holding Ltd v Redferns*[1]. In that case counsel had argued that common law principles of causation did not apply to breach of trust. That proposition was firmly rejected by their Lordships. A crucial point in both cases is the absence of fraud, actual or constructive. A fraudulent breach of fiduciary duty will still attract the full extent of equity's relief.

1   [1996] AC 421.

Utilisation of opportunities by a fiduciary for his or her own benefit

9.29   The final category of cases which may be said to fall within the ambit of the rationale in *Bray v Ford*[1] actually arises because of the much earlier decision of *Keech v Sandford*[2]. In *Keech v Sandford* a lease of a market was held on trust for an infant. The trustee sought, unsuccessfully, to renew the lease for the benefit of the trust. However, the landlord, although not prepared to renew the lease to the trust, was prepared to grant a renewal to the trustee in his personal capacity, and the trustee duly took up the lease in his own right. Lord King LC held that any trustee who abuses his position by entering into a transaction with a third party must account for the benefit of the transaction as a constructive trustee.

Consequently the trustee held the benefit of the lease on constructive trust for the infant.

The rationale of the rule was stated very clearly, and is perfectly consistent with prevailing social and economic provisions prevailing at the time[3]. As Lord King LC said:

> I very well see, if a trustee, on the refusal to renew, might have a lease to himself, few trust-estates would be renewed to [the beneficiary] ... [T]he trustee is the only person of all mankind who might not have the lease[4].

The rule in *Keech v Sandford* has, however, led to some very harsh decisions in more modern times, where fiduciaries have utilised their position, no matter how honestly and in good faith, to make a profit for themselves.

1   [1896] AC 44.
2   (1726) Sel Cas Ch 61, 25 ER 223.
3   For a fuller explanation see Oakley *Constructive Trusts* (3rd edn, 1997), p 157.
4   (1726) Sel Cas Ch 61 at 62, 25 ER 223 at 223.

9.30   Where there is a clear abuse of a fiduciary position, it is uncontroversial that a principal can recover property. This occurred in *Cook v Deeks*[1]. Three of the four directors and shareholders of a company, with the intention of excluding the fourth member, arranged for a contract which they had negotiated on behalf of the company to be made with them in their private capacities. The excluded member claimed successfully before the Privy Council that the company was entitled to the benefit of this contract.

1   [1916] 1 AC 554.

9.31   Such a case of actual abuse of a fiduciary relationship clearly poses no problem. The real difficulty arises when the stringent rule applies to situations where the conduct of the fiduciary falls very much short of improper conduct. A stringent application of the rule has resulted in some highly controversial cases where the principal in question has, for a variety of reasons, failed to utilise an opportunity to make a profit and, as a direct consequence of this, the fiduciary has been able to utilise the opportunity for personal profit.

9.32   The rule in *Keech v Sandford*, subject to one possible exception, has been extended to other fiduciaries in a variety of factual circumstances. It has been extended, as in *Protheroe v Protheroe*[1], to cases where the fiduciary has acquired the reversion in property of which the principal is lessee. The one possible exception is in the context of purchase of a reversion on a lease by a partner or partners of a firm. Dicta in the Court of Appeal in *Re Biss*[2] suggested that partners were only caught by the rule in *Keech v Sandford* if it could be shown that an advantage had actually been obtained by virtue of their position. Those dicta have not, however, been followed in subsequent cases. In both *Thompson's Trustee v Heaton*[3] and *Popat v Shonchhatra*[4] it was held that *Keech v Sandford* applied strictly, and that partners could not acquire the reversion for their sole benefit. The rule in *Keech v Sandford* has also been applied where a fiduciary makes a profit by speculating with the property of the principal, as in *Reid-Newfoundland Co v Anglo-American Telegraph Co*[5], and, as in *Re Thomson*[6] to restrain a trustee from commencing any business which competes with business carried out on behalf of the trust.

1   [1968] 1 WLR 519.
2   [1903] 2 Ch 40.
3   [1974] 1 WLR 605.

4   [1995] 1 WLR 908 (decided on a different ground on appeal: [1997] 1 WLR 1367).
5   [1912] AC 555.
6   [1930] 1 Ch 203.

9.33   In *Regal (Hastings) Ltd v Gulliver*[1], Regal's board of directors formed a subsidiary company for the purpose of acquiring the leases of two cinemas. The subsidiary was to have a share capital of £5,000, with £2,000 paid up. The landlord would not grant the leases unless all the shares were paid up. As Regal could not find more than the £2,000, four of the directors and the company solicitor put up £500 each for shares, and the company chairman found friends to put up the remaining £500. Regal was eventually taken over by another company, and as a result the shares in the subsidiary were sold at a substantial profit. The purchasers of Regal brought proceedings against the four directors, the solicitor and the chairman, to recover the profits they had made on the subsidiary's shares, on the ground they had made an unauthorised profit. The chairman escaped liability, as he had not subscribed for any shares, and had clearly not made any unauthorised profit. The solicitor escaped liability because those to whom he owed a fiduciary duty as agent, namely the board of directors, had approved of his purchase. But the other four directors had to account: they had acted in breach of their fiduciary duty in purchasing the shares in the subsidiary, and the company had not approved of this, as it could have, by ratifying the matter in a general meeting. As Lord Russell of Killowen said:

> I am of the opinion that the directors standing in a fiduciary relationship to Regal in regard to the exercise of their powers as directors, and having obtained these shares by reason and only by reason of the fact that they were directors of Regal and in the course of the execution of that office, are accountable for the profits which they have made out of them. The equitable rule laid down in *Keech v Sandford* ... applies to them in full force[2].

This case shows the application of a constructive trust in a rigid manner. The breach of fiduciary relationship was in many respects a technical one, since the directors could have called a shareholders' meeting at any time and had their breach of fiduciary duty ratified by the company. This had not been done before they sold the shares. Further, the purchasers of the shares were obtaining an undeserved reduction in the price they had agreed to pay.

1   [1942] 1 All ER 378.
2   [1942] 1 All ER 378 at 389.

9.34   The decision in *Regal (Hastings)* must be contrasted with the conclusion reached by the Privy Council in *Queensland Mines v Hudson*[1]. In that case, the board of the claimant company, being fully informed of all relevant facts, decided to renounce all interest in the exploitation of certain mining exploration licences, which it had obtained. The board assented to the venture being taken over by the defendant, a director of the company who had been its managing director until a shortage of finance had prevented the claimant company from exploiting the licences itself. The claimant subsequently claimed to be entitled to the profit obtained by the defendant. The Privy Council held that the defendant had obtained the opportunity to make this profit by virtue of his position as managing director of the claimant company. He was, therefore, in principle liable. It was held, however, that the fully informed decision of the board amounted to sufficient consent to enable him to retain the profit. This conclusion is clearly inconsistent with the decision in *Regal (Hastings)*, where, because all the members of the board had taken part in the impeached transaction, they must necessarily have consented to it. Despite the inconsistencies between the two cases, the principle remains clear that the courts are not prepared to countenance a fiduciary exploiting an opportunity for his personal benefit irrespective of whether there has, in reality, been a conflict between the duty of loyalty to the principal and the fiduciary's own self-interest.

1   [1978] 18 ALR 1.

9.35   On this particular point, the Canadian courts also have taken a very different view. In *Peso Silver Mines v Cropper*[1] several directors of Peso took up prospecting claims, which the company had itself turned down because it considered them to be highly speculative, and financially unattractive. After the company had rejected the claims, Cropper and some other directors, who had unsuccessfully urged the company to take up the claims, formed a company to take them up. Peso's board was informed of this. The claims proved highly profitable, and Peso's board demanded an account. The Canadian Supreme Court refused to apply the strict rule in *Regal (Hastings)*. Rather, it was held that the company's deliberate act in refusing to take up the claims released the directors, so that they could form a separate company to exploit the claims themselves. This seems a much fairer interpretation.

1   (1966) 58 DLR (2d) 1.

9.36   There remains the question, however, as to whether English law will follow the Canadian example in *Peso Silver Mines*, and utilise some discretion in future cases where, in reality, there is no conflict of interest and duty. This was certainly the case in both *Regal Hastings v Gulliver*[1] and *Boardman v Phipps*[2]. One commentator has suggested that there has been some relaxation of the rules in the context of pension schemes[3]. As, however, statutory provisions are relevant in that context, it would seem that this is a very limited exception. Thus Scott VC in *Edge v Pensions Ombudsman*[4] held that, as statute now requires pension schemes to have member-nominated trustees[5], trustees were entitled to exercise their powers to reduce employee contributions and enhance pensions in payment. The real difficulty in relaxation of, admittedly, very harsh rules, is one of what may be described as 'preventative medicine'. Any relaxation of the rules might countenance abuse of the fiduciary relationship of loyalty.

1   [1942] 1 All ER 378.
2   [1967] 2 AC 46; below, para 9.39.
3   Parker and Mellows *Modern Law of Trusts* (7th edn, 1997), p 287.
4   [1999] 4 All ER 546.
5   See the Pensions Act 1995, ss 16–21.

9.37   A more flexible approach than has been taken so far in English law may also be more desirable where a fiduciary has utilised confidential information.

If a fiduciary has acquired information in such circumstances that it would be a breach of confidence to disclose it to another, it is axiomatic that there will be a conflict of interest and duty. This occurred in *Industrial Development Consultants v Cooley*[1]. The defendant was the managing director of the claimant company. In that capacity, he had been attempting to obtain a contract with the Eastern Gas Board. The Gas Board, for a variety of reasons, was not prepared to contract with the claimant company. Subsequently, the Gas Board initiated a meeting with the defendant in his private capacity, and suggested that, if he disassociated himself from the company, he had a very good chance of obtaining the contract for himself, in a personal capacity. As a consequence of this, the defendant falsely represented to the claimant that he was on the verge of a nervous breakdown, thereby releasing himself from his contract with the claimant. He then entered into a contract with the Gas Board to do the work, which he had unsuccessfully attempted to obtain for the claimant. The claimant argued that the defendant was a trustee of that contract. The claimant succeeded in obtaining an account of the defendant's profits, because there was a clear conflict of interest and duty. The only capacity in which the defendant received the information that he could obtain the contract for himself was as managing director of the claimant. His failure to pass on to the claimant any information which reached him while in that capacity, and subsequent use of the information for his own benefit, was a breach of fiduciary duty.

1   [1972] 1 WLR 443.

9.38   Utilisation of confidential information in breach of trust may also give rise to a claim for equitable compensation. This occurred recently in *Satnam Investment Ltd v Dunlop Heywood & Co Ltd*[1]. To summarise the rather complicated facts, a property development company acquired an option to purchase a site. The site's owners were entitled to terminate the option if the company, Satnam Investments Ltd, went into receivership. Because of temporary cash flow problems, Satnam was placed in administrative receivership by its banks. Satnam's surveyors sent a letter to a rival development company, Morbaine, behind Satnam's back. Ultimately, Morbaine put in a rival, and successful, bid for the purchase of the site. Satnam contended that the surveyors had breached their fiduciary duty by revealing confidential information to Morbaine, and that Morbaine had been aware of that breach. As a result, it was argued that Morbaine was liable to Satnam in a number of ways, and that the surveyors were liable to pay equitable compensation. Nourse LJ, delivering the judgment of the Court of Appeal, held that the surveyors owed a fiduciary duty, and the disclosure of confidential information constituted a breach of such duty. It was held, however, that Morbaine did not act dishonestly, dishonesty being acquainted with conscious impropriety, and therefore could not be liable for dishonest assistance. It was, also, held that there was an insufficient nexus between the disclosure to Morbaine and the purchase of the site as to establish liability by way of knowing receipt or an account of profits and, further, that the confidential information could not be traced into the site. In principle, it was accepted that the surveyors could be liable to pay equitable compensation, but the Court of Appeal was not satisfied that the findings of fact at first instance were sufficient to establish the necessary causation of loss test[2]. A new trial was ordered to resolve this issue. There was a clear breach of fiduciary duty in any event.

1   [1999] 3 All ER 652.
2   Discussed in relation to *Swindle v Harrison* [1997] 4 All ER 705; above, para 9.28.

9.39   The leading case on abuse of confidential information is *Boardman v Phipps*[1]. The estate of a testator, which was held on trust for his wife for life with remainders over to his children, included a substantial minority holding of shares in a textile company, Lester & Harris Ltd. The trustees were dissatisfied with the returns on the shares in this company, and considered this was due to bad management. Boardman, the trustees' solicitor, and Phipps, a beneficiary, both of whom supported the trustees' view, attended an annual general meeting of the company. They expressed their dissatisfaction with the company's affairs, and tried unsuccessfully to have Phipps elected as a director. Boardman and

Phipps then decided to acquire the shares in the company, and on this they had the approval of two of the trustees, but not the third, who was the widow of the deceased and senile at the time. An offer was made for the outstanding shares, but it was only partly successful. Afterwards, Boardman entered into negotiations with the directors of the company, apparently as representative of the trustees, for a division of the assets between the trust and the majority shareholders. These negotiations were not authorised by the trustees and, although unsuccessful, Boardman gained much information from them about the company's business and the value of its assets. On the basis of this information, Boardman and Phipps made another offer for the outstanding shares in the company. A letter to all the beneficiaries informing them of the proposal, and seeking their consent, preceded this offer. The offer was successful, and enabled Boardman, Phipps and the trustees to take full control of the company, which Phipps then reorganised. Substantial distribution of surplus capital was made to themselves as shareholders, so they all made handsome profits. However, a beneficiary entitled to a share in remainder brought an action, claiming that Boardman and Phipps held the shares they acquired in the company as constructive trustees, and that they were liable to account for the profits they had made.

1   [1967] 2 AC 46.

9.40   The House of Lords, by a majority of three to two, upheld the claim. The majority (Lords Cohen, Hodson and Guest) applied the conflict of duty and interest rule very strictly, and it seems that the minority (Viscount Dilhorne and Lord Upjohn) differed in that they were prepared to take a more flexible approach towards fiduciary duties. All were agreed that Boardman stood in a fiduciary capacity to the trustees, as he was called upon from time to time to give them advice. Phipps was a fiduciary because he had been a co-adventurer with Boardman. The case turned on whether, as fiduciaries, they were liable to account, because they had represented themselves as acting for the trustees in the negotiations for a division of the assets, and had obtained information in so doing which had prompted them to acquire more shares in the company, ultimately for themselves. This information gave them the opportunity to make a profit. Lord Cohen admitted that information is, of course, not property in the strict sense of the word. Lord Upjohn, dissenting, went much further, saying:

> In general, information is not property at all. It is normally open to all who have eyes to read and ears to hear. The true test is to determine in what circumstances the information has been acquired. If it has been acquired in such circumstances that it would be a breach of confidence to disclose it to another then courts of equity will restrain the recipient from communicating it to another ... I protest at the idea that information acquired by trustees in the course of their duties as such is necessarily part of the assets of the trust which cannot be used by the trustees except for benefit of the trust[1].

1   [1967] 2 AC 46 at 127–128.

9.41   Yet there seems little between the majority and the minority on the issue of whether information can be property. The judgements differ on when a trustee or fiduciary will be accountable as a constructive trustee when he uses information acquired as such. Lord Cohen took a strict view:

> ... the mere use of any knowledge or opportunity which comes to the trustee or agent in the course of his trusteeship or agency does not necessarily make him liable to account. In the present case had the company been a public company and had the

appellants bought the shares on the market, they would not, I think, have been accountable. But the company is a private company and not only the information but the opportunity to purchase these shares came to them through the introduction which Mr Fox [the active trustee] gave them to the board of the company[1].

This judgment suggests that, as Boardman and Phipps got the information and could only have got it in acting for the trust, they were liable to account in this particular case. Lord Upjohn, alternatively, said that a conflict of interest only arose where the reasonable man, looking at all the relevant circumstances, would think that there was a real sensible possibility of conflict, and not where the only possibility of conflict arose from events not contemplated as real sensible possibilities by any reasonable person. He said:

> ... there was no question whatever of the trustees contemplating the possibility of a purchase of further shares in the company ... The reasons for this attitude are worth setting out in full: (a) The acquisition of further shares in the company would have been a breach of trust, for they were not authorised by the investment clause in the will; (b) ... it must have been obvious to those concerned that no court would sanction the purchase of further shares in a small company which the trustees considered to be badly managed ... (c) the trustees had no money available for the purchase of further shares[2].

1   [1967] 2 AC 46 at 100–101.
2   [1967] 2 AC 46 at 119.

9.42   A crucial aspect of this case was that, as a result of the fiduciaries' actions, the trust itself benefited by £47,000. Boardman and his colleague made a profit of about £75,000. In effect, the trust obtained the whole of the profit made on the take-over, less an allowance, which the House awarded to Boardman under its inherent jurisdiction by way of remuneration for the work which he had done.

In the opinion of the majority, it was no defence that that the defendants had acted honestly and openly, in a manner highly beneficial to the trust. However, in such a case the court has an inherent jurisdiction to grant remuneration, and in fact this was done in *Boardman* itself. This jurisdiction is well-established, but rarely used. It is not enough merely that the fiduciaries were honest and that their activities benefited the trust. In a recent first instance decision, *Badfinger Music v Evans*[1], Lord Goldsmith QC considered that, although this was an important factor, it was not necessarily a determinative factor. He relied heavily on the undue influence case of *O'Sullivan v Management Agency*[2], where remuneration was awarded by the court to the parties who had actually exercised undue influence. Lord Goldsmith added that the existence or absence of conflict of interest was also, although an important factor, again not necessarily determinative. In awarding remuneration to a former member of a pop band who, in somewhat dubious circumstances in relation to other interested parties, produced a remixed record album, he took two other factors into account. He said that it was relevant that the work done could only realistically have been done by the fiduciary, and was of a special character calling for the exercise of a particular kind of professional skill. Lord Goldsmith QC added (obiter) that, in appropriate circumstances, the court's jurisdiction might extend to awarding a share of profits as part of the remuneration. The case constitutes a wide interpretation of the inherent jurisdiction to award remuneration, which may herald a more generous interpretation in the future for honest fiduciaries who find themselves in breach of the strict interpretation of the conflict of interest and duty rule.

1   [2001] WTLR 1.
2   [1985] 1 QB 428.

F   Conclusion

9.43   The range and scope of fiduciary relationships is open to development. It is clear from cases in this area and in other areas (such as the refusal by the House of Lords to elevate an ordinary commercial contractual relationship into an equitable relationship in respect of compound interest in *Westdeutsche Landesbank Girozentrale v Islington London Borough Council*[1]), that the definition of a fiduciary relationship will not extend to such relationships. This is clearly entirely fair in the context of the ranking of claims in insolvency. Once a fiduciary relationship has been found to exist, it is equally clear from the above that the courts police fiduciary relationships very strictly.

1   [1996] AC 669. See above, para 3.39.

9.44   A final and recent case puts the discussion of *A-G v Blake*[1] in perspective. In *Longstaff v Birtles*[2] the claimants, in 1987, instructed solicitors to act on their behalf in the purchase of an inn as a business venture. Negotiations in respect of this purchase broke down. Subsequently, at the suggestion of the solicitors, the claimants entered into a partnership agreement with the solicitors and two others to buy into a hotel business. The solicitors referred the claimants to a valuer, but did not recommend that the claimants took independent advice. The claimants paid £40,000 for a half-share in the partnership. The venture proved to be a disaster. The claimants sued the solicitors for professional negligence, but the Court of Appeal allowed the statement of claim to be amended to add a claim of breach of fiduciary duty. The Court of Appeal held that the claimants were entitled to equitable compensation for loss suffered as a result of breach of fiduciary duty. The duty to insist on independent advice could endure beyond the termination of the retainer which originally formed the relationship of solicitor and client. That relationship was a fiduciary relationship of trust and confidence, and the duty of loyalty requires that a principal can never be in a position of conflict of interest and duty.

1   [2001] 1 AC 268; discussed above, para 9.8.
2   [2001] EWCA Civ 1219, [2002] 1 WLR 470.

9.45   The consistency of the law in this area is demonstrated by the fact that a very similar decision was reached as early as 1903 in *Wright v Carter*[1]. It remains open to debate as to whether the current strict interpretation will continue to apply when there is no de facto conflict of interest and duty. Some relaxation of the rules would be a welcome development in circumstances similar to either *Regal (Hastings) v Gulliver*[2] or *Boardman v Phipps*[3].

1   [1903] 1 Ch 27.
2   [1942] 1 All ER 378; above, para 9.33.
3   [1967] 2 AC 46; above, para 9.39.

CHAPTER 10

Unconscionability – Abuse of Confidence, Undue Influence and Duress

Margaret Halliwell

A   Introduction

10.1   It has been argued elsewhere[1] that the restitutionary categories of abuse of confidence, undue influence and duress are merely sub-species of the general principle of unconscionability. The only relevance of this argument to this chapter is whether or not a requirement of 'manifest disadvantage' is necessary for a successful claim of presumed undue influence[2]. My ordering of this chapter does, however, reflect my view.

1   Halliwell *Equity & Good Conscience In A Contemporary Context* (1997), ch 3.
2   On which see below, para 10.34ff.

10.2   The starting point of discussion must be unconscionability as an independent cause of action. Although unconscientious conduct may be established through the taking advantage of an objective weakness such as illiteracy or drunkenness, it has, at least since *Walmsley v Booth*[1], included taking advantage of a superior position. That has led to a stricter application of the principle of unconscionability in the context of abuse of confidence cases[2]. Analysis of the abuse of confidence cases leads, inevitably in my opinion, to the conclusion that manifest disadvantage should not be required for a successful claim of presumed undue influence. Judicial opinion in recent cases suggests that a change in this area is likely to occur[3]. The final issue to be discussed is the concept of duress, which shares the same characteristic of the unconscientious application of pressure, physically or otherwise, in order to obtain some advantage[4].

1   (1741) 2 Atk 25, 26 ER 412; below, para 10.18.
2   See below, para 10.18ff.
3   See below, para 10.38.
4   See below, para 10.51ff.

B   Unconscionability as an independent ground of relief

10.3   Several issues are made clear in the early cases. First, once a claimant has established that a transaction, of contract or gift, is prima facie oppressive and extortionate, an onus is placed upon the defendant to prove that there has not been unconscionable conduct. The prima facie burden can be met by the claimant showing either that weakness has been abused, or by establishing that the consideration for a bargain is so inadequate as to shock the conscience, or by demonstrating a combination of both of these factors. So, for example, in *Earl of Aylesford v Morris*[1], the circumstances of the particular transaction gave the stronger party domination over the weaker, and the defendant did not discharge the burden of proving that the transaction was not unconscionable. Lord Selborne LC elaborated on the nature of the cause of action:

> Fraud does not here mean deceit or circumvention; it means an unconscientious use of the power arising out of these circumstances and conditions; and when the relative position of the parties is such as prima facie to raise this presumption, the transaction cannot stand unless the person claiming the benefit of it is able to repel the presumption by contrary evidence, proving it to have been in point of fact fair, just, and reasonable[2].

1   (1873) LR 8 Ch 484.
2   (1873) 8 Ch App 484 at 490–491.

10.4   Inadequacy of consideration will often be a specially important element in cases of this type. It may support the inference that a position of disadvantage existed, and may also show that an unfair use was made of the occasion. Thus in *Blomley v Ryan*[1] a contract for inadequate consideration was set aside because, to the defendant's knowledge, the claimant, by reason of his intoxication due to a rum addiction, was in no condition to negotiate intelligently. Similarly, in *Clark v Malpas*[2], where a poor and illiterate man was induced to enter a transaction in great haste, whereby the defendant obtained property at 'not very far short of one-fourth' its value, the defendant failed to discharge the obligation of proving that the bargain was not unconscientious. In *Blachford v Christian*[3], Lord Wynford set aside deeds entered into by a man aged 74, whose health was declining, and whose mind 'evidently sympathized with his body'[4]. He did so on the basis that a consideration of the deeds themselves would not lead a reasonable man to conclude that they were the deeds of a man of sound intellect, freely exercising his mind, uninfluenced by falsehood and unswayed by deceit. The ultimate onus on defendants in such circumstances is, as in *Fry v Lane*[5], to show that the transaction was 'in point of fact fair, just, and reasonable'.

1   (1956) 99 CLR 362.
2   (1862) 4 De GF & J 401, 45 ER 1238.
3   (1829) 1 Knapp 73, 12 ER 248.
4   (1829) 1 Knapp 73 at 78, 12 ER 248 at 250.
5   (1888) 40 Ch D 312.

10.5   The early cases emphasise that the defendant can only really discharge this burden of proof if the claimant has had competent and disinterested advice or assistance. Independent legal advice satisfies this requirement.

There have not been a significant number of successful cases on the grounds of unconscionability in more modern times, simply because the prerequisites of the cause of action have not always been made out. The cause of action has, however, been explained in modern parlance both here and in Australia.

10.6   In *Commercial Bank of Australia v Amadio*[1] the High Court of Australia set aside a transaction involving a mortgage and guarantee, made between the bank and an elderly couple. Mason J, as he then was, concluded that courts have exercised jurisdiction to set aside contracts and other dealings on a variety of equitable grounds. Nevertheless, he went on to explain that these grounds all constitute species of unconscionable conduct on the part of a party who stands to receive a benefit under a transaction which cannot be consistent with equity and good conscience. On the facts, the bank had acted unconscientiously in taking advantage of the 'weakness' of Mr and Mrs Amadio. That weakness constituted a special disability from the combination of their age, their limited grasp of written English, the circumstances in which the bank presented the document to them for their signature, and, most importantly, their lack of knowledge and understanding of the contents of the document. The width of the equitable principle of relieving against unconscionable conduct is such that:

> The circumstances adversely affecting a party, which may induce a court of equity either to refuse its aid or to set a transaction aside, are of great variety and can hardly be satisfactorily classified. Among them are poverty or need of any kind, sickness, age, sex, infirmity of body or mind, drunkenness, illiteracy or lack of education, lack of assistance or explanation where assistance or explanation is necessary. The common characteristic seems to be that they have the effect of placing one party at a serious disadvantage vis-à-vis the other[2].

1   (1983) 151 CLR 447.
2   *Blomley v Ryan* (1956) 99 CLR 362 at 405, per Fullager J. This passage was cited with approval by Mason J in *Amadio* (1983) 151 CLR at 462.

10.7   *Louth v Diprose*[1] serves as another, more recent, Australian example. In that case a woman was held to have taken unconscientious advantage of a man, who expended a large part of his assets in purchasing a house which was conveyed to her, because she had taken advantage of his infatuation with her by manufacturing a crisis, including suicide threats. It is important to note that there was no cause of action in undue influence in *Louth v Diprose*, as the man was a solicitor who did not repose any sort of trust and confidence in the woman. It was expressly held that the woman did not have any form of undue influence over the man. The transaction was set aside on the sole cause of action of unconscionability.

1   (1992) 175 CLR 621.

10.8   A similar development had occurred earlier in England in striking down an unconscientious transaction. In applying the 1888 decision *Fry v Lane*[1] in *Cresswell v Potter*, Megarry J was able to say:

> The plaintiff has been a van driver for a tobacconist, and is a Post Office telephonist ... In those circumstances I think the plaintiff may properly be described as 'poor' in the sense used in *Fry v Lane*, where it was applied to a laundryman who, in 1888, was earning £1 a week ... Further, although no doubt it requires considerable alertness and skill to be a good telephonist, I think that a telephonist can properly be described as 'ignorant' in the context of property transactions in general and the execution of conveyancing documents in particular[2].

1   (1888) 40 Ch D 312.
2   (1968) [1978] 1 WLR 255n at 257–258.

10.9   Subsequent events led to little application of the principle of unconscionability as an independent cause of action in the English courts. In particular, as noted above[1], in cases where the cause of action was pleaded, the necessary prerequisites were often not made out. Writing extra-judicially in 1994, Sir Anthony Mason suggested that, given the reasons by the House of Lords in rejecting the case based on undue influence in *National Westminster Bank plc v Morgan*[2], unconscionability, as an independent ground of relief, did not loom large on the English scene[3]. This, however, is not the current position, although the revival of the cause of action in unconscionability began only with the advice of the Privy Council in *Boustany v Pigott*.

1   See above, para 10.5.

2   [1985] AC 686.
3   Sir Anthony Mason 'The Place of Equity and Equitable Remedies in The Contemporary Common
    Law World' (1994) 110 LQR 238.

10.10   In *Boustany v Pigott*[1], the Privy Council cited and applied the
Australian decision in *The Commercial Bank of Australia v Amadio*[2], and reviewed
those English cases where the prerequisites of the cause of action in
unconscionability had not been made out. The Privy Council set aside a lease on
the grounds that it was an unconscionable bargain.

In 1976 Miss Pigott leased a building to Mrs Boustany for five years at a
monthly rent of $833.33, with an option to renew for a further period of five
years, at a rent to be agreed or fixed by a qualified person as the fair market rent.
From 1977 onwards Mr George Pigott, a cousin of Miss Pigott, took over the
management of family properties, and Mrs Boustany was aware that Mr George
Pigott was the agent of Mrs Pigott. In September 1980, when Mr George Pigott
was temporarily absent from the state, Miss Pigott appeared in the chambers of
Mr Kendall, a barrister, with a copy of the 1976 lease with amendments
providing, inter alia, for the grant of a new lease for ten years at a rent of $1,000.
Mr Kendall was unhappy with the hurry, since the existing lease still had a year
left to run and, also, because the increase in rent was very small, and he
considered the transaction to be improvident as a commercial transaction. He,
therefore, insisted on seeing all parties to the transaction, and Mrs Boustany, her
husband, and Miss Pigott subsequently attended a meeting in his chambers. Mrs
Boustany said nothing at this meeting, and Miss Pigott insisted that Mr Kendall
carry out her instructions, which he duly did. When in due course Mr George
Pigott discovered the existence of the new lease, he obtained a power of attorney
from Miss Pigott, and asked for a declaration that the 1980 lease was an
unconscionable bargain. The circumstances alleged on behalf of Miss Pigott were
that, on a number of occasions before the 1980 lease was signed, Mrs Boustany
had collected her from her home and taken her to tea parties, lavishing attention
and flattery upon her, that Mr George Pigott was absent at this time and that
Miss Pigott had no advice of any nature when she entered into the lease
agreement and was unaware of the true market value of the property.

1   (1993) 69 P & CR 298.
2   (1983) 151 CLR 447.

10.11   The trial judge inferred unconscionable conduct by Mrs Boustany, after
consideration of a number of features. Lord Templeman, delivering the advice of
the Privy Council, put the conclusion in short that Mrs Boustany must have
taken advantage of Miss Pigott before, during and after the lease transaction,
with full knowledge that her conduct was unconscionable. He thought the trial
judge was entitled to draw the inference that Mrs Boustany had prevailed upon
Miss Pigott to agree to grant a lease, on terms which she knew she could not
extract from Mr George Pigott or anyone else.

As well as citing the *Amadio* case, Lord Templeman agreed with a number of
submissions based on English decisions. Lord Templeman approved of the
following submissions[1]:

(1)   It is not sufficient to attract the jurisdiction of equity to prove that a
      bargain is hard, unreasonable or foolish; it must be proved to be
      unconscionable, in the sense that 'one of the parties to it has imposed the
      objectionable terms in a morally reprehensible manner, that is to say, in a
      way which affects his conscience' – *Multiservice Bookbinding v Marden*[2].

(2) 'Unconscionable' relates not merely to the terms of the bargain but to the behaviour of the stronger party, which must be characterised by some moral culpability or impropriety – *Alec Lobb (Garages) Ltd v Total Oil (Great Britain) Ltd*[3].

(3) Unequal bargaining power or objectively unreasonable terms provide no basis for equitable interference in the absence of unconscientious or extortionate abuse of power where exceptionally, and as a matter of common fairness, 'it was not right that the strong should be allowed to push the weak to the wall' – *Alec Lobb (Garages) Ltd v Total Oil (GB) Ltd*[4].

(4) A contract cannot be set aside in equity as 'an unconscionable bargain' against a party innocent of actual or constructive fraud. Even if the terms of the contract are 'unfair' in the sense that they are more favourable to one party than the other ('contractual imbalance'), equity will not provide relief unless the beneficiary is guilty of unconscionable conduct – *Hart v O'Connor*[5].

1 *Boustany v Pigott* (1993) 69 P & CR 298 at 303.
2 [1979] Ch 84 at 110, per Browne-Wilkinson J.
3 [1983] 1 WLR 87 at 94, per Peter Millett QC.
4 [1985] 1 WLR 173 at 183, per Dillon LJ.
5 [1985] AC 1000.

10.12 The modern authorities have fully followed the principle as enunciated in the early cases. It is clear that the propositions relating to burdens of proof and independent advice remain good. Once the comparative weakness of the elderly couple in the *Amadio* case was established, the onus was cast upon the bank to show that the transaction was fair, just and reasonable. The bank could not discharge this onus, because independent legal advice and assistance was necessary to achieve any reasonable degree of equality between itself and the Amadios. Following this case, in *Boustany v Pigott*[1], it was deemed necessary to show that the claimant, Miss Pigott, had been unconscientiously taken advantage of, because of her circumstances, by the defendant, Mrs Boustany. Once this was demonstrated by the facts, Miss Pigott was entitled to relief in equity by setting aside the lease, because Mrs Boustany could not prove that the lease transaction was fair, just and reasonable.

1 (1995) 69 P & CR 298.

10.13 In *Hart v O'Connor*[1], the Privy Council had made a distinction between this form of unconscionability, based on procedural unfairness in entering into a contract, and a contract which is 'unfair' in the sense that the terms of a contract are more favourable to one party than to the other. Whilst acknowledging that the latter form of 'contractual imbalance' might be so extreme as to raise a presumption of procedural unfairness, Lord Brightman considered it not to do so on the facts before him. In the absence of any evidence of procedural imbalance, because the defendant had contracted with a person ostensibly mentally fit, but actually ill, the court concluded that the contract was not an unconscionable bargain.

1 [1985] AC 1000.

10.14 Again, in *Multiservice Bookbinding Ltd v Marden*[1], contractual imbalance, although acknowledged by Browne-Wilkinson J to exist because the defendants had made a bad bargain, was not sufficient per se to necessitate equitable relief. The claimants in this case, entered into a loan agreement whereby the debt was to be inflation-proofed by reference to the Swiss franc, and, at the same time, provided for a rate of interest 2% above the bank rate. The bank rate reflected, at least in part, the unstable state of the pound sterling. Crucially, the claimants were businessmen who went into the transaction with the benefit of independent advice, without any compelling necessity to accept a loan on these terms, and without any sharp practice by the defendants. The contract was not, therefore, an unconscionable bargain.

1   [1978] 2 All ER 489.

10.15   In *Alec Lobb (Garages) Ltd v Total Oil GB Ltd*[1], judges at first instance and in the Court of Appeal followed the decision in *Multiservice Bookbinding Ltd v Marden* in requiring the claimant to show that the objectionable contractual terms had been imposed in a morally reprehensible manner. The claimant failed to do this, as he had been independently advised and also, far from pressurising him to enter into the transaction, the defendants had been reluctant to enter into it. Millett J, at first instance in *Alec Lobb*, reiterated the grounds of relief as:

> In the development of the equitable jurisdiction to relieve against fraud and oppression, there was a natural tendency to categorise cases by reference to the relationship between the parties or the special situation of the weaker party. Thus equity frequently intervened to protect the expectant heir, the reversioner, and the mortgagor. As the law has progressed, however, it has become possible to analyse the basis of the court's jurisdiction and the criteria for its exercise. It can now be seen that all those cases are merely particular examples of situations in which one party may be unfairly exploited by the other[2].

1   [1983] 1 All ER 944 (Peter Millett QC); on appeal [1985] 1 All ER 303, CA.
2   [1983] 1 All ER 944 at 965.

10.16   A clear illustration of this arose on the facts of a case which came before the Court of Appeal in 1997, *Crédit Lyonnais Bank Nederland NV v Burch*[1]. This case concerned, as many modern cases do, the giving of surety for a debt. Miss Burch was an employee of the debtor. She had a modest salary of £12,000 to £14,000, and owned a flat worth £100,000 with an outstanding mortgage of £30,000. The debtor wished to increase his company's overdraft limit from £250,000 to £270,000. While the point was not directly in issue, it is important that Nourse LJ considered it to be 'very well arguable' that Miss Burch could have had the legal charge set aside against the bank as an unconscionable bargain. Although he noted that equity's jurisdiction to relieve against such transactions is rarely exercised in modern times, he perceived it to be 'at least as venerable as its jurisdiction to relieve against those procured by undue influence'[2]. He felt constrained from resting his decision on the ground of unconscionability as an independent cause of action, because this had not been argued at first instance.

1   [1997] 1 All ER 144.
2   [1997] 1 All ER 144 at 151.

10.17   The Court of Appeal has asserted the jurisdiction even more recently in *Portman Building Society v Dusangh*[1]. The facts of that case were, however, entirely distinguishable from the *Burch* case, and were not sufficient as to 'shock the conscience' of the court so as to prompt the Court of Appeal to set aside the transaction with the third party. The principle of unconscionability as an independent cause of action is well established, but there remains some confusion over the interrelationship of causes of action based on undue influence and the less familiar action of restitution for abuse of confidence.

1   [2000] Lloyd's Rep Bank 197.

C   Abuse of confidence

10.18   The origins of this head of restitutionary liability appear to be in the decision in 1739 in *Walmsley v Booth*[1]. Lord Hardwicke LC struck down a transaction between an attorney and his client, even though there was no possibility of the attorney exercising any influence over the client. He grounded his decision on public utility. The client, Japhet Cook, was, according to Lord Hardwicke LC, more likely to impose than be imposed upon:

> ... it would be an extraordinary thing if the representatives of *Japhet Cook* should prevail to set aside a bond fraudulently obtained, and by imposition upon a man, whose character for art and cunning was so well established in the world[2].

He nonetheless awarded relief without requiring particular evidence of actual imposition, because of the great power and influence that an attorney has over his client. In *Newman v Payne*[3], Lord Loughborough LC concluded that the ruling in *Walmesley v Booth* constituted a distinct principle: transactions between an attorney and client could be impeached irrespective of misconduct or actual influence, because no advantage could be taken over his client by an attorney. He extended the principle in *Newman v Payne* to the circumstances of an attorney undertaking to act as confidential agent for another in the management of the affairs of that other. *Taylor v Obee*[4] extended liability to a builder who was in a position of trust and confidence with a recently bereaved widow, whose husband had been a close friend of the builder's.

Clearly, from these early cases liability arose simply because of the *potential* for abuse of confidence. There is no necessity to prove any actual abuse. As with unconscionability, this cause of action arises independently of undue influence. There was, also, no requirement of manifest disadvantage. Subsequent case law has established, however, that liability may be avoided if there is both independent advice and full disclosure of facts.

1   (1741) 2 Atk 25, 26 ER 412.
2   (1741) 2 Atk 25 at 27, 26 ER 412 at 413.
3   (1793) 2 Ves 199, 30 ER 593.
4   (1816) 3 Price 83, 146 ER 180.

10.19   The formulation of this head of liability is clearly stated by Lord Chelmsford LC in *Tate v Williamson*[1]:

> Wherever two persons stand in such a relation that, while it continues, confidence is necessarily reposed by one, and the influence which naturally grows out of that confidence is possessed by the other, and this confidence is abused, or the influence is exerted to obtain an advantage at the expense of the confiding party, the person so availing himself of his position will not be permitted to retain the advantage, although the transaction could not have been impeached if no such confidential relation had existed[2].

Such a relationship existed in *Tate v Williamson* because the claimant, Tate, asked one Hugh Williamson for assistance and advice as to the payment of his debts. Hugh Williamson, owing to ill health, was unable to attend to the matter in person and, therefore, deputed the defendant, Robert Williamson, to do so.

Robert Williamson undertook to see how the claimant's liabilities could be discharged. It was held that the defendant had placed himself in a de facto relation of confidence with Tate, by undertaking the office of arranging Tate's debts by means of a mortgage of his property. He therefore placed himself in a position of responsibility, which rendered it incumbent upon him to give the best advice as to how the claimant could relieve himself from his debts. This being so, the defendant was prevented from becoming a purchaser of the property without disclosing the fullest communication of all material information which he had obtained as to its value. The court, therefore, struck down the transaction. Counsel for the claimant made several related assertions, but the primary argument was that the jurisdiction of the courts of equity rests on the principle of correcting the abuse of influence founded on confidence. Lord Chelmsford was careful to state the relevant principle in wide enough terms to avoid fettering the jurisdiction by defining the exact nature of the confidential relationship.

1   (1866) 2 Ch App 55.
2   (1866) 2 Ch App 55 at 61.

10.20   Could the defendant discharge the onus therefore placed on him? It was held that he could not. Clear principles applied in this case to two issues. First, that the defendant needed to show not only the receipt of independent and disinterested advice but, also, that he had made a full and frank disclosure of all material facts. Second, that manifest disadvantage was completely irrelevant. Moreover, the defendant had to justify the transaction between himself and the claimant before the Court of Equity. Lord Chelmsford held that the defendant, pending the contractual agreement, was bound to communicate all the information he acquired, which it was material for the claimant to know in order to enable him to judge the value of his property. Once it was established that there was a concealment of a material fact, which the defendant was bound to disclose, it was immaterial that the defendant could have shown that the price given was a fair one.

Admittedly, there were strong grounds for thinking that the price agreed to be paid by the defendant was quite inadequate to the value of the claimant's property. Nonetheless, the judgment is unequivocal on this point. Even if the defendant could show that the price was a fair one, Lord Chelmsford answered that:

> You had the means of forming a judgment of the value of the property in your possession, you were bound, by your duty to the person with whom you were dealing, to afford him the same opportunity which you had obtained of determining the sufficiency of the price which you offered; you have failed in that duty, and the sale cannot stand[1].

1   (1866) 2 Ch App 55 at 66.

10.21   It is clear from the reasoning in *Tate v Williamson* that the decision was based on public policy, rather than on proof of actual abuse. The transaction could not have been impeached but for the confidential relationship. The case follows the general principle of equitable intervention based on 'constructive fraud', but goes slightly further. Public policy, in the context of transactions in such circumstances of trust and confidence, dictates that a transaction cannot stand, even if it is proved to be fair, if the defendant has concealed material facts. This is reinforced by a number of other authorities.

10.22   In *Demerara Bauxite Co Ltd v Hubbard*[1], in the context of a purchase by a solicitor from a client of an option over land, the solicitor was unable to prove full disclosure of the material facts within his knowledge. The transaction could not, therefore, stand. Lord Parmoor explained that the defendant would have to prove that he advised the claimant as diligently as he should have done, had the transaction been one between the claimant and a stranger, and that the transaction was as advantageous to the client as it would have been if he had been endeavouring to sell the property to a stranger.

1   [1923] AC 673.

10.23   Stirling LJ in *Wright v Carter*[1] expressed the firm view that the principle is founded on important reasons of public policy. Again, in the context of transactions between a solicitor and client, Stirling LJ considered that such transactions are watched and scrutinised by the court with utmost jealousy. He went on to require that 'The client must be fully informed; secondly, he must have competent advice; and thirdly, the price which is given must be a fair one'[2]. Vaughan Williams LJ, in the same case, cited with approval the judgment of Lord Eldon in *Huguenin v Baseley*[3]. In the latter case Lord Eldon LC was considering a transaction of gift between a woman and her religious advisor. Lord Eldon represented the crux of his judgment as:

> ... I represent the question thus: whether she executed these instruments not only voluntarily, but with that knowledge of all their effect, nature and consequences, which the Defendants *Baseley* and the attorney were bound by their duty to communicate to her ... [4]

1   [1900–1903] All ER Rep 706.
2   [1900–1903] All ER Rep 706 at 718.
3   (1807) 14 Ves 273, 33 ER 526.
4   (1807) 14 Ves 273 at 300, 33 ER 526 at 536.

10.24   In considering a similar transaction in *Allcard v Skinner*[1], Cotton LJ explained that the basis of the court's interference is not on the ground that any wrongful act has in fact been committed by the defendant, but on the ground of public policy, and to prevent the relations which existed between the parties from being abused. Kekewich J, Cotton LJ and Bowen LJ agreed that, on the facts of *Allcard v Skinner*, the burden of proving that the gift was free rested on the confidant.

1   (1887) 36 Ch D 145 (Kekewich J and CA).

10.25   One case, which makes it clear beyond any doubt that in such circumstances, it is not necessary to prove any actual undue influence, is *Tufton v Sperni*[1]. In *Tufton v Sperni*, the Court of Appeal applied *Tate v Williamson*[2] to conclude that a contract of sale, by Tufton in favour of Sperni, should be set aside. Sperni had been introduced as advisor to Tufton in regard to the matter of repairs to Tufton's property. Thereafter, the relationship was concerned with the purpose of furthering some charitable object. Tufton did not repose anything like blind and uncritical confidence in Sperni. Moreover, the trial judge had found as a fact that there had been no actual undue influence. Sir Raymond Evershed MR concluded that it was immaterial that no such domination was proved. The jurisdiction to relieve from the transaction stemmed from the relationship whereby Tufton reposed confidence in Sperni. Jenkins LJ explained that there is no distinction for this purpose between a gift, a purchase at an undervalue, and a value at an excessive price, where the donee or the person making the purchase or affecting the sale, as the case may be, stands in a relationship of trust and confidence to the person making the gift to him, selling to him, or buying from him. It was incumbent on the defendant to show that the transaction was not brought about by an abuse of that relationship. Manifest disadvantage was discussed in the case as being useful in establishing whether there was prima facie such a relationship of trust and confidence. It is important that, in this context, Jenkins LJ was careful to warn against the temptation of working backwards from the undeniable fact of an unconscionable bargain, and endeavouring to construct some such relationship. This serves to emphasise the very secondary role which manifest disadvantage plays.

1   [1952] 2 TLR 516.
2   (1866) 2 Ch App 55; above, para 10.19.

10.26   A slightly different point arose in *Alec Lobb (Garages) Ltd v Total Oil GB Ltd*[1]. In that case Peter Millett QC was able to conclude that, if the claimant, was in a relationship of confidentiality, even if he was in fact in receipt of independent advice, this would have been of no consequence once it was established that there was a concealment of a material fact which the defendant was bound to disclose. Millett J, however, distinguished *Tufton v Sperni*[2], on the basis that the defendant did not stand in a relationship of confidentiality with the claimant. He was also prepared to hold that, in any event, there could have been no breach of duty in failing to disclose a valuation which actually supported the offer made by the defendants to the claimant. This seems to be uncontroversial. A fact which supports a confidant's role in the transaction can hardly be said to be described as an abuse of the relationship.

1   [1983] 1 All ER 944; discussed above, para 10.15.
2   [1952] 2 TLR 516; above, para 10.25.

10.27   *Allcard v Skinner*[1] is the only case cited so far in which a duty of disclosure was not explicitly required and, as far as the facts of that case are concerned, the issue of concealment of material facts was simply not relevant to the proceedings. In *Moody v Cox*[2], it was argued that the requirement of disclosure is not applicable in transactions between a client and solicitor when the solicitors are not dealing with their own property. The solicitors here were under a duty to beneficiaries to get as much as they could for the property sold to the client. Nevertheless, this contention was firmly rejected by Lord Cozens-Hardy MR, who held that a solicitor, selling to a client or buying from a client, is bound to disclose everything that is material or may be material to the judgment of his client before the transaction is completed. Lord Cozens-Hardy MR also made plain that this requirement arises out of the duty of confidentiality which is implicit in the fiduciary relationship of solicitor and client.

1   (1877) 36 Ch D 145.
2   [1917] 2 Ch 71.

10.28   A requirement of manifest disadvantage has, therefore, never been necessary in abuse of confidence cases. Rather, it was only used, if at all, as evidence to support the de facto existence of a relationship of trust and confidence. An unusual illustration of this arose in the Court of Appeal decision in *Wright v Carter*[1] where Vaughan Williams LJ treated the issue of manifest disadvantage as relevant to whether a relationship of confidentiality continued to exist between a solicitor and his client. He considered that where a gift, which manifestly a prudent man would not have given, is shown to have been made, then, notwithstanding the solicitor's own view of the matter, the relationship of confidence has not ceased, but has continued. On the other hand, the fact that the gift is a trifling gift, or is made by a man with so ample a fortune that it must have been trifling to him, is a matter which may fairly be taken into consideration in considering whether the relationship of confidence continues.

1   [1900–1903] All ER Rep 706.

10.29   It necessarily follows from the above that more than one cause of action may arise on the facts of some cases, if there has been an abuse of confidence and, also, a wrongful act has been committed. This is illustrated by *Rhodes v Bate*[1]. It is clear from the judgment of Sir John Stuart VC that there were two possible grounds of action against the defendant in the case. One was that he stood in a relationship of confidence to the claimant; but, even if he were not her confidential legal adviser, he was well aware of the actual undue influence exercised over the claimant by her brother-in-law, for whose debts she had been rendered liable. Even if the defendant had not (which was disputed) been liable because he was not in such a relationship of confidence, he would have been liable on the second ground of obtaining, with notice, an advantage derived because of the actual undue influence of the claimant's brother-in-law.

1   (1865) 1 Ch App 252.

10.30   The question which remains to be addressed is whether these propositions have any relevance to undue influence cases. Lord Browne-Wilkinson pointed out in *CIBC Mortgages v Pitt*[1] that the law of undue influence as articulated by Lord Scarman in *National Westminster Bank v Morgan*[2] had never been reconciled with long-standing principles in the abuse of confidence cases, and the next section on undue influence will suggest the appropriate reconciliation for the future.

1   [1994] 1 AC 200.
2   [1985] AC 686.

10.30A   In conclusion, the authorities on abuse of confidence establish a number of propositions:
* A claimant may impugn a transaction between a defendant by proving that there was a relationship of trust and confidence reposed in the defendant.
* Manifest disadvantage inherent in the transaction may help to establish such a cause of action, but is not a requisite component of the cause of action.
* Once the relationship is established, the burden is on the defendant to prove that the transaction should be upheld.
* There need be no actual wrongdoing on the part of the defendant; the cause of action is founded on public policy grounds.
* The defendant can only discharge the burden of proof if there has been both independent legal advice and a full disclosure of material facts.

D   Undue influence

10.31   The law of undue influence has been the subject of much recent litigation, in the context of females acting as surety for the debts of their partners. The complex arguments necessitate extensive judicial quotation to reflect the current position.

The starting point of the law of undue influence must be the seminal House of Lords authority in *Barclays Bank v O'Brien*[1], which, strictly speaking, involved an equitable wrong of misrepresentation rather than undue influence. The House of Lords had to decide whether Barclays Bank could succeed in possession proceedings in respect of the matrimonial home of Mr and Mrs O'Brien. The possession proceedings were being brought to enforce payment under a guarantee of Mr O'Brien's indebtedness. The matrimonial home, which was jointly owned by the O'Briens, had been charged to the bank in order to secure an overdraft facility of £135,000 for Mr O'Brien's company. Mrs O'Brien argued that the bank could not enforce the surety obligation, because her husband had put pressure on her to sign the legal charge in favour of the bank and, also, that he had misrepresented to her the effect of the legal charge. The House of Lords held that Mrs O'Brien was entitled to have the legal charge in the matrimonial home set aside against the bank.

1   [1994] 1 AC 180.

10.32   The principles of undue influence were explained by Lord Browne-Wilkinson as follows:

- **Class 1: Actual undue influence** – In these cases it is necessary for the claimant to prove affirmatively that the wrongdoer exerted undue influence on the complainant to enter into the particular transaction which is impugned;
- **Class 2: Presumed undue influence** – In these cases the complainant only has to show, in the first instance, that there was a relationship of trust and confidence between the complainant and the wrongdoer, of such a nature that it is fair to presume that the wrongdoer abused that relationship in procuring the complainant to enter into the impugned transaction. However, somewhat controversially, Lord Browne-Wilkinson added that a transaction in class II would be set aside only if it is shown that the transaction was to the manifest disadvantage of the person influenced. Class II comprises:
  - **Class 2A** – Certain relationships (for example solicitor and client, medical advisor and patient) as a matter of law raise the presumption that undue influence has been exercised;
  - **Class 2B** – Even if there is no relationship falling within class 2A, if the complainant proves the de facto existence of a relationship under which the complainant generally reposed trust and confidence in the wrongdoer, the existence of such relationship raises the presumption of undue influence.

In relation to the case before the court, he concluded that there was no presumption of undue influence between a husband and wife. He rejected the theory, put forward by Scott LJ in the Court of Appeal[1], to the effect that wives were awarded special protection by the law. He conceded that a wife might raise such a presumption by proving a de facto relationship with her husband whereby she reposed trust and confidence in him with regard to her financial affairs.

1   [1993] 1 QB 109 at 139.

10.33   However, the later case of *Royal Bank of Scotland v Etridge (No 2)*[1], while generally following Lord Browne-Wilkinson in *Barclays Bank v O'Brien*, the House of Lords concluded that the categorisation of presumed undue influence was not a useful forensic tool. Lord Clyde, for example, said:

I question the wisdom of the practice which has grown up, particularly since *Bank of Credit and Commerce International SA v Aboody*[2] of attempting to make classifications of cases of undue influence. That concept is in any event not easy to define. It was observed in *Allcard v Skinner* that 'no Court has ever attempted to define undue influence'[3]. It is something which can be more easily recognised when found than exhaustively analysed in the abstract. Correspondingly the attempt to build up classes or categories may lead to confusion. The confusion is aggravated if the names used to identify the classes do not bear their actual meaning. Thus on the face of it a division into cases of 'actual' and 'presumed' undue influence appears illogical. It appears to confuse definition and proof. There is also room for uncertainty whether the presumption is of the existence of an influence or of its quality as being undue. I would also dispute the utility of the further sophistication of subdividing 'presumed undue influence' into further categories. All these classifications to my mind add mystery rather than illumination[4].

The merits of Lord Browne-Wilkinson's classification therefore remain a matter of controversy.

Two difficult questions remain, the answers to which are in practice bound together. Firstly, what is the precise relevance of 'manifest disadvantage'? And secondly, when will a third party involved in the transaction (such as the bank in *O'Brien*) be treated as having notice of the undue influence, and therefore liable to have the transaction set aside?

1   [2001] UKHL 44, [2001] 4 All ER 449.
2   [1990] 1 QB 923.
3   (1887) 36 Ch D 145 at 183, per Lindley LJ.
4   [2001] UKHL 44, [2001] 4 All ER 449 at 477.

The relevance of manifest disadvantage

10.34   So far as the finding of undue influence is concerned, manifest disadvantage remains relevant only to presumed undue influence, according to a decision in relation to actual undue influence in the decision in *CIBC Mortgages v Pitt*[1].

The Court of Appeal, in *Bank of Credit and Commerce International SA v Aboody*[2], denied a remedy to a victim of actual fraud, Mrs Aboody. Mrs Aboody, under the actual undue influence of her husband, had entered into transactions with the bank, which, in essence, secured the husband's company's borrowings against the matrimonial home, which was owned by Mrs Aboody. Mrs Aboody's action to have the transaction with the bank set aside failed, because she could not demonstrate that the transaction was to her manifest disadvantage. The Court of Appeal first considered the decision of the House of Lords in *National Westminster Bank plc v Morgan*[3]. In that case, a wife executed a mortgage to the bank over the matrimonial home in order to avert possession proceedings being taken. She subsequently contended that she had signed the charge because of undue influence from the bank and that, therefore, it should be set aside. Relationships between customers and banks do not, ordinarily, encompass a relationship of trust and confidence, and it was necessary for the wife to raise a class 2B presumption. Lord Scarman, in delivering the opinion of the House, had introduced a requirement of manifest disadvantage as a constituent element of the cause of action based on presumption of undue influence. The Court of Appeal in *Aboody* decided to extend the requirement of manifest disadvantage to cases of actual undue influence.

1   [1994] 1 AC 200; below, para 10.35.
2   [1992] 4 All ER 955.
3   [1985] AC 686.

10.35   In *CIBC Mortgages v Pitt* Lord Browne-Wilkinson unequivocally disagreed with the decision of the Court of Appeal in *Aboody*[1]. His Lordship held that a claimant who proved actual undue influence was not under the further burden of proving that the transaction induced by undue influence was manifestly disadvantageous: he or she was entitled as of right to have it set aside. As Lord Browne-Wilkinson explained, a person guilty of fraud is not entitled to argue that the transaction was beneficial to the person defrauded. The effect of the wrongdoer's conduct is to prevent the wronged party from bringing a free will and properly informed mind to bear on the proposed transaction which, accordingly, must be set aside in equity as a matter of justice. It follows, therefore, that there is now clearly no requirement to show that a transaction was of manifest disadvantage in order to establish liability for actual undue influence.

Lord Browne-Wilkinson also questioned whether manifest disadvantage was a necessary ingredient in establishing liability in cases of presumed undue influence. He pointed out that the law of undue influence as articulated *National Westminster Bank v Morgan*[2] had never been reconciled with long-standing principles in the abuse of confidence cases[3]. For the present, however, this point remains highly controversial.

1   [1994] 1 AC 200 at 208–209.
2   [1985] AC 686.
3   See above, para 10.30.

10.36   In *National Westminster Bank v Morgan*, Lord Scarman had approved of the approach taken by Sir Eric Sachs in *Lloyds Bank Ltd v Bundy*[1]. Sir Eric Sachs considered a vital element needed to exist before the Court of Appeal would grant relief to the claimant, Mr Bundy, in respect of the transaction with the bank. He referred to this vital element, as a matter of convenience, as of 'confidentiality'. This he found was impossible to define, and described the issue to be a matter for the judgment of the court on the fact of any particular case. He adopted the word 'confidentiality', with some hesitation, to avoid the possible confusion that can arise through referring to 'confidence'. Reliance on advice can, in many circumstances, be said to import that type of confidence which only exists in a common law duty to take care – a duty which may co-exist with, but is not conterminous with that of importing equitable obligations:

> 'Confidentiality' is intended to convey that extra quality in the relevant confidence that is implicit in the phrase 'confidential relationship' ... and may perhaps have something in common with 'confiding' and also 'confidant' when, for instance, referring to someone's 'man of affairs'[2].

Following the cases of *Tate v Williamson*[3] and *Tufton v Sperni*[4], Sir Eric Sachs concluded that Lloyds Bank had gone further than advising on more general matters germane to the wisdom of the transaction. In so doing, the bank had crossed the line into the area of confidentiality. On a meticulous examination of the particular facts, the bank was under this duty of confidentiality, and was in breach of that duty. Lord Scarman, in *Morgan*, stated this to be good sense and good law, although he would prefer to avoid the term 'confidentiality' as a description of the relationship which has to be proved. Lord Scarman, however, denied that public policy provided the rationale behind the striking down of transactions procured by undue influence[5].

This is, in the light of earlier authorities, undoubtedly incorrect. Lord Browne-Wilkinson pointed out[6] that the cases of *Demerara Bauxite Co Ltd v Hubbard*[7] and *Moody v Cox*[8] were not brought to the attention of Lord Scarman in *Morgan*. Lord

Browne-Wilkinson also refers to an article[9] in which Tiplady, correctly in my opinion, points out that the House of Lords in *Morgan* overlooked both the Court of Appeal decision in *Wright v Carter*[10] and the categorical opinion of Lord Chelmsford LC in *Tate v Williamson*[11]. It is, therefore, preferable to accept the interpretation adopted by Lord Browne-Wilkinson in *CIBC Mortgages v Pitt*. That is to say no more than that manifest disadvantage may be necessary to discharge the prima facie burden on the claimant to show a de facto relationship, capable of being abused[12].

1   [1975] QB 326.
2   [1975] QB 326 at 341. Note the similarity in expression with the early extension in *Newman v Payne* (1793) 2 Ves 199, 30 ER 593 (above, para 10.18) to 'managing affairs'.
3   (1866) 2 Ch App 55; above, para 10.19.
4   [1952] 2 TLR 516; above, para 10.25.
5   [1985] AC 686 at 708.
6   *CIBC Mortgages v Pitt* [1994] 1 AC 200 at 209.
7   [1923] AC 673.
8   [1917] 2 Ch 71.
9   Tiplady 'The Limits of Undue Influence' (1985) 48 MLR 579.
10 [1900–1903] All ER Rep 706; above, para 10.23.
11 (1866) 2 Ch App 55; above, para 10.19.
12 See above, para 10.28.

10.37   Subsequent authorities seemed to suggest that this view would be the approach taken by the House of Lords on hearing appeals from the Court of Appeal's finding in the context of the nine consolidated appeals in *Royal Bank of Scotland v Etridge (No 2)*[1] and from the Court of Appeal decision in *Barclays Bank v Coleman*[2]. Obiter dicta in the first of these Court of Appeal decisions indicate that manifest disadvantage may be used, as suggested by Lord Browne-Wilkinson, in establishing a presumption of a de facto relationship of undue influence, and not as a prerequisite of a successful cause of action[3].

In *Barclays Bank v Coleman*, there was an appeal against a possession order in favour of the bank in respect of a matrimonial home. A wife alleged that the execution of the mortgage of the matrimonial home was procured by the undue influence of her husband. The main point in the case was whether the bank's rights were affected by the undue influence of her husband over her, and on this point she ultimately lost[4]. The Court of Appeal noted in passing, however, that the authorities on manifest disadvantage were in a very unsatisfactory state. According to the court, the observations by Lord Browne-Wilkinson in *CIBC Mortgages plc v Pitt*[5] had put a serious question mark over the future of the requirement of manifest disadvantage in cases of presumed undue influence. The House of Lords had signalled that it might not continue to be a necessary ingredient indefinitely. Whilst, on the authority of *National Westminster Bank v Morgan*[6], it did remain a necessary ingredient, the Court of Appeal went on to suggest a low threshold of manifest disadvantage. Where, as in this case, the form of the legal charge had resulted in the house being subjected to much greater financial risk than the wife could have ever known, there was a clear and obvious disadvantage to the wife[7].

However, the House of Lords in *Royal Bank of Scotland v Etridge (No 2)*[8], while recognising that there are difficulties, have declined to remove the requirement of 'manifest disadvantage' in cases of presumed influence. In this context, the House of Lords rejected the suggestion made in the Court of Appeal in *Barclays Bank plc v Coleman*[9] that it should depart from the decision of the House of Lords in *National Westminster Bank plc v Morgan*[10] in respect of the requirement of manifest disadvantage. Lord Nicholls explained that, in *Morgan*, Lord Scarman attached the label 'manifest disadvantage' to the second ingredient necessary to raise the evidential presumption of undue influence. Lord Nicholls accepted that this label has been causing difficulty. In respect of the disputed surety transactions, he acknowledged that manifest disadvantage could occur in both a narrow and a wide sense. In a narrow sense, such a surety transaction plainly is disadvantageous to the wife. She undertakes a serious financial obligation, and in return she personally receives nothing. However, in the case of husband and wife there are inherent reasons why such a transaction may well be for her benefit. According to Lord Nicholls, ordinarily, the fortunes of husband and wife are bound up together. If the husband's business is the source of the family income, the wife has a lively interest in doing what she can to support the business. A wife's affection and self-interest run hand-in-hand in inclining her to join with her husband in charging the matrimonial home, usually a jointly-owned asset, to obtain the financial facilities needed by the business. The finance may be needed to start a new business, or expand a promising business, or rescue an ailing business.

In consequence, Lord Nicholls concluded that neither the narrow approach or the wider approach should be used. The 'manifest disadvantage' label should be discarded[11]. Instead the courts should adhere more directly to the test outlined by Lindley LJ in *Allcard v Skinner*[12]. Lindley LJ had pointed out that where a gift of a small amount is made to a person standing in a confidential relationship to the donor, some proof of the exercise of the influence of the donee must be given. The mere existence of the influence is not enough. He went on to say:

> But if the gift is so large as not to be reasonably accounted for on the ground of friendship, relationship, charity, or other ordinary motives on which ordinary men act, the burden is upon the donee to support the gift[13].

It is difficult to see how adherence to this test will provide any clarification in future disputes. Moreover, yet again there was no attempt to reconcile undue influence and abuse of confidence cases.

1   [1998] 4 All ER 705.
2   [2000] 1 All ER 385.
3   See especially [2000] 1 All ER 385 at 397–399, per Nourse LJ.
4   On this point see below, para 10.39ff.
5   [1994] 1 AC 200; see above, para 10.35.
6   [1985] AC 686.
7   [2000] 1 All ER 385 at 400–401, per Nourse LJ.
8   [2001] UKHL 44, [2001] 4 All ER 449.
9   [2000] 1 All ER 385.
10 [1985] AC 686.
11 [2001] 4 All ER 449 at 462.
12 (1887) 36 Ch D 145.
13 (1887) 36 Ch D 145 at 185.

10.38   However, in my view it remains arguable that manifest disadvantage should not be a requirement of liability in presumed undue influence cases. Abuse of confidence and presumed undue influence cases are species of the same cause of action, but under different names. The principles outlined in respect of abuse of confidence cases should, therefore, apply equally to cases of presumed undue influence. The appropriate reconciliation of the two strands of case law would mean that in cases of presumed undue influence:

- a claimant may impugn a transaction with a defendant by proving that there was a relationship of trust and confidence reposed in the defendant;
- manifest disadvantage inherent in the transaction may help to establish

such a cause of action, but is not a requisite component of the cause of action;

- once the relationship is established, the burden is on the defendant to prove that the transaction should be upheld;
- some qualification on the latter point of the burden of proof has been given recently by the House of Lords[1] but, before turning to that point, the very difficult question has to be addressed, as to what quality of advice will be sufficient to discharge a third party involved in the transaction from liability.

1   See below, para 10.42ff.

What quality of legal advice will be sufficient to discharge liability?

10.39   Assuming that undue influence can be proved or presumed, what is the position of a third party to the transaction? Third parties who are not themselves guilty of undue influence may enforce the transaction, unless it can be said that they are fixed with notice of the undue influence. The issue of when they will be so fixed has been one of the most difficult and controversial in this area.

In *Barclays Bank plc v O'Brien*[1] Lord Browne-Wilkinson acknowledged that he was extending the law in so far as creditors would now be put on inquiry by the risk of undue influence or misrepresentation, whereas earlier authorities had suggested that creditors must actually know of the circumstances giving rise to undue influence or misrepresentation. He rejected however the suggestion, put by counsel for the bank, that the result of his decision would be to impose too heavy a burden on financial institutions. A common feature of today's society, is that a high proportion of privately-owned wealth is invested in the matrimonial home. It is usual, therefore, for the home to be used as a means of security, in order to raise finances for the business enterprises of one or other of the spouses. The parties in such circumstances are not always married and sometimes not even cohabiting in the home in question, but are linked by an emotional and sexual relationship. It is still, unfortunately, a common feature of such relationships that one of the parties acts unconscionably in persuading the other party to use the home as a means of security[2]. Given these economic and social conditions, the House of Lords attempted to lay down clear guidelines as to how creditors can avoid being fixed with notice of such unconscionable pressure. This obligation would be discharged where the creditor warned the surety, at a meeting not attended by the principal debtor, of the risks involved, and advised the surety to take independent legal advice. The House of Lords deliberately and overtly tried to draw a balance between the interests of financial institutions and the interests of sureties, in the context of economic realities[3]. Presumably, the House of Lords hoped, by so doing, to stem the flood of litigation. Unfortunately this has not proved to be the case. A number of issues arose in subsequent cases[4], such as whether legal advice was independent if the solicitor of the alleged wrongdoer gave it.

1   [1994] 1 AC 180.
2   [1994] 1 AC 180 at 188.
3   [1994] 1 AC 180 at 188.
4   See for example the strong dissenting judgment of Hobhouse LJ in *Banco Exterior Internacional v Mann* [1995] 1 All ER 936 at 945–949, where he objected to the fact that the bank had not complied with the criteria as being necessary, according to Lord Browne-Wilkinson, in order not to be fixed with constructive notice.

The guidelines of the Court of Appeal in Royal Bank of Scotland v Etridge (No 2)

10.40   The various issues which had arisen before the courts post *Barclays Bank v O'Brien* were considered before the Court of Appeal in the nine consolidated appeals in *Royal Bank of Scotland v Etridge (No 2)*[1]. All of the appeals involved circumstances whereby it was alleged that transactions against financial institutions should be set aside on the basis that they had been procured by undue influence or misrepresentation on the part of a male partner. A critical issue at stake in each of the appeals was as to the quality of the legal advice given.

The following, very detailed, propositions were established by the Court of Appeal after a full review of existing authority:

(a)   Where the wife deals with the bank through a solicitor, whether acting for her alone or for her and her husband, the bank is not ordinarily put on inquiry. The bank is entitled to assume that the solicitor has considered whether there is a sufficient conflict of interest to make it necessary for the bank to ask the solicitor to carry out his professional obligation to give proper advice to the wife, or to confirm that he has done so. The bank is ordinarily not required to take any steps at all.

(b)   Where the wife does not approach the bank through a solicitor, it is normally sufficient if the bank has urged her to obtain independent legal advice before entering into the transaction. This is especially the case if the solicitor provides confirmation that he has explained the transaction to the wife and that she appears to understand it.

(c)   When giving advice to the wife, the solicitor is acting exclusively as her solicitor. It makes no difference whether he is unconnected with the husband or the wife, or is also the husband's solicitor, or that he has agreed to act in a ministerial capacity as the bank's agent at completion. Whoever introduces the solicitor to the wife and asks him to advise her, and whoever is responsible for his fees, the bank is entitled to expect the solicitor to regard himself as owing a duty to the wife alone when giving her advice. If the solicitor accepts the bank's instructions to advise the wife, he still acts as her solicitor and not the bank's solicitor when he interviews her.

(d)   It follows that the bank is not fixed with imputed notice of what the solicitor learns in the course of advising the wife, even if he is also the bank's solicitor. Such knowledge does not come to him in his capacity as the bank's solicitor.

(e)   The bank is entitled to rely on the fact that the solicitor undertook the task of explaining the transaction to the wife as showing that he considered himself to be sufficiently independent for this purpose. The bank is not required to question the solicitor's independence, even if it knows that he is also the husband's solicitor.

(f)   The bank is not concerned to question the sufficiency of the advice, and is not put on further inquiry by the fact that the solicitor was asked only to explain the transaction to the wife and ensure that she understood it, and not to see that she was sufficiently independent of her husband. Nor is the bank put on inquiry by the fact that the confirmation provided by the solicitor is similarly limited.

(g)   Only one decision is inconsistent with these authorities, viz the decision of Hobhouse and Mummery LJJ at an interlocutory stage of the proceedings in *Royal Bank of Scotland plc v Etridge*². They held that, where a bank instructed a solicitor to act on its behalf for the purposes of ensuring that a wife received independent advice in respect of her liabilities under a proposed collateral charge to support her husband's indebtedness to the bank, it was arguable that the solicitor was acting as the bank's agent in carrying out his instructions, with the result that the bank would be fixed, presumably with imputed notice, if, notwithstanding his certificate to the contrary effect, he had not in fact carried them out. That decision was considered to have been *per incuriam*.

(h)   It follows from the need to avoid subtle distinctions that no importance is to be attached to the fact that the solicitor may not provide the bank with a full or adequate confirmation that he has followed his instructions. Where the bank has asked him to explain the transaction to the wife and confirm that she appeared to understand it, the bank is not put on inquiry by the fact that the solicitor has confirmed that he has explained the transaction to her but not that she appeared to understand it. In any case such confirmation is not considered to be an essential requirement. Where the bank has asked a solicitor to explain the transaction to the wife and he fails to confirm that he has done so, the bank is not entitled to assume that he has: see *Cooke v National Westminster Bank plc*³. But at most this should put the bank on inquiry whether the solicitor has in fact advised the wife. If it fails to make further inquiry, then it takes the risk that he has not done so; but if he has and merely omitted to confirm the fact, then the bank should not be affected by its failure to obtain confirmation before completing the transaction.

(i)   When advising the wife, the solicitor obviously owes her a duty of care. It does not necessarily follow, however, from the fact that he is not also acting for the bank that he owes the bank no corresponding duty of care. Although in many respects the bank and the wife have conflicting interests, they share a common interest in ensuring that the wife should not enter into the transaction without her informed consent, and free from the undue influence of her husband.

(j)   While the bank is normally entitled to assume that a solicitor who is asked to advise the wife will discharge his duties fully competently, and that he will not have restricted himself to giving an explanation of the transaction and satisfying himself that she appears to understand it, it cannot make any such assumption if it knows or ought to know that it is false. If the bank is in possession of material information which is not available to the solicitor, or if the transaction is one into which no competent solicitor could properly advise the wife to enter, the availability of legal advice is insufficient to avoid the bank being fixed with constructive notice.

(k)   Ultimately the issue is whether, at the time when value is given, and in the light of all the information in the bank's possession, including its knowledge or the state of the account, the relationship of the parties, and the availability of legal advice for the wife, there is still a risk that the wife has entered into the transaction as a result of her husband's misrepresentation or undue influence.

1   [1998] 4 All ER 705.
2   [1997] 3 All ER 628.
3   [1998] 3 FCR 643.

10.41   The Court of Appeal appear to have redrawn the balance between sureties and financial institutions in favour of the latter. The approach seems inconsistent with the opinion of the House of Lords in *Barclays Bank v O'Brien*[1], particularly in the rejection of the principle that the creditor should warn the surety, at a meeting not attended by the principal debtor, of the risks involved. Lord Browne-Wilkinson there relied heavily on a report on a Review Committee on *Banking Services: Law and Practice*[2] and on the *Code of Banking Practice*, adopted by banks and building societies in determining that the burden placed on financial institutions was not too onerous[3]. The Court of Appeal in *Royal Bank of Scotland v Etridge (No 2)* appear to flagrantly contradict the precedent in *Barclays Bank v O'Brien*.

Drawing the right balance is, ultimately, a difficult task for the courts to achieve. In an empirical study by Fehlberg[4], it is clear that even with the benefit of legal advice, many women would not have refused to act as security for their husband or partner. On the other hand, it is clear that financial institutions must have some safeguard against a third party abusing a relationship of trust and confidence.

1   [1994] 1 AC 180.
2   (1989) (Cmnd 622).
3   [1994] 1 AC 180 at 197.
4   Fehlberg *Sexually Transmitted Debt: Surety Experience and English Law* (1997).

The burden of proof – Barclays Bank v Boulter

10.42   *Barclays Bank v Boulter* concerned a possession action by Barclays Bank as mortgagee of freehold property. The wife counterclaimed that her half of the property was free of the bank's legal charge because the bank, as creditor, had the burden of proving that it had no constructive notice of the misrepresentation by her husband which had procured her consent to the charge in favour of the bank. When the Court of Appeal[1] considered the effect of *Barclays Bank v O'Brien*[2] in order to determine Mrs Boulter's position, the speech of Lord Browne-Wilkinson was interpreted as introducing the same approach to pleading and proof of constructive notice in this type of case as in the standard case of the bona fide purchaser for value of the legal estate without notice of an equitable estate or interest. Once, therefore, the wife had alleged the facts supporting her claim, the bank had to prove that it did not have constructive notice. She had raised the necessary facts, and it was for the bank to prove either that there was nothing to put it on inquiry as to the potential existence of the claim or that, if there was, it took reasonable steps to avoid being fixed with notice.

1   [1997] 2 All ER 1002.
2   [1994] 1 AC 180.

10.43   On appeal, the House of Lords[1] held that, where a wife relied on the doctrine of constructive notice to resist a bank's action on a legal charge, the bank was not required to prove that it had no notice of the husband's undue influence or misrepresentation. The burden was on the wife to show why her husband's act should render the transaction invalid as between her and the bank. That burden could be easily discharged by the wife demonstrating that the bank knew that she was living with her husband, and that the transaction was not on its face to her financial advantage. Lord Hoffmann, in delivering the leading opinion of the House, acknowledged that this was an unusual issue of pleading to come before the House of Lords. This was because the Court of Appeal, in upholding Mrs Boulter's claim, had said that it was for the bank to prove that it did not have constructive notice. Mummery LJ, in the Court of

Appeal, had relied on the analogy of the defence of purchaser in good faith for value without notice. But, according to Lord Hoffmann, that defence enables a purchaser to defeat a prior interest which burdened the title. In this case, however, the bank took a charge directly from Mrs Boulter, and she had the necessary title to grant it. There was no prior interest that the bank needed to defeat. Lord Hoffmann considered a better analogy is the case of the purchaser of a chattel whose vendor's title is vitiated by fraud. In such a case it is for the defrauded owner to prove that the purchaser had actual or constructive notice of the fraud. The result is, however, entirely consistent with *Barclays Bank v O'Brien*, in the sense that the creditor is put on inquiry by the two factors of financial disadvantage and cohabitation. As is illustrated by *Crédit Lyonnais Bank Nederland NV v Burch*[2], where the financial disadvantage is so extreme as to clearly give notice of some improper influence over the surety, the financial institution will not be saved from liability by satisfying the independent advice criterion. This is also made clear in point (i) of the Court of Appeal's observations in *Royal Bank of Scotland v Etridge (No 2)*[3].

1   [1999] 4 All ER 513.
2   [1997] 1 All ER 144; above, para 10.16.
3   See above, para 10.40.

10.44   Importantly, Mummery LJ, delivering the judgment of the Court of Appeal in the *Boulter* case, had added that in cases like *O'Brien*, it was irrelevant whether the land was registered or unregistered; the question was whether the creditor had actual or constructive notice of the facts on which the equity to set aside the transaction was founded[1]. Thompson[2] has argued that the principles laid down in *O'Brien* applied only to unregistered land. His argument rested on the foundation that the nature of the right in question is proprietary. This view, however, has been challenged by Dixon and Harpum[3]. They conclude, correctly in my opinion, that the right of the claimant is a personal equity. Clearly, this construction avoids any difficulty in applying the doctrine to registered land. The *Boulter* case has resolved this controversy, and the overriding issue is that of notice.

1   [1997] 2 All ER 1002 at 1010.
2   Thompson 'Mortgages and Wives: Proceed With Caution' [1992] Conv 443.
3   Dixon and Harpum 'Fraud, Undue Influence and Mortgages of Registered Land' [1994] Conv 421.

The current position – The House of Lords decision in Royal Bank of Scotland v Etridge (No 2)[1]

10.45   In summary, only some points of the law on undue influence were beyond dispute before the House of Lords heard the appeals in *Etridge*. Issues such as the relationship between presumed undue influence and the abuse of confidence cases, with the consequential impact on manifest disadvantage, remained unresolved. Similarly, the issue as to the quality of independent advice necessary to discharge liability remained open for further consideration. It is hardly surprising, in the current contextual circumstances in which disputes on undue influence arise, that the courts are grappling to find the fairest solution for all. In the author's opinion, the ratio decidendi and the obiter dicta in both *Barclays Bank v O'Brien* and *CIBC Mortgages v Pitt* signified a sound and rational way forward, but others have an entirely different perspective[2].

The House of Lords in the consolidated appeals in *Royal Bank of Scotland v Etridge (No 2)*[3] tried yet again to provide clear guidelines for the future, although some of their Lordships' observations are likely to prove controversial. The report of the judgment is over one hundred pages in length and cannot be dealt with succinctly. As Lord Bingham commented, there is a paramount need in this important field for minimum requirements, which should be clear, simple and practically operable.

1   [2001] UKHL 44, [2001] 4 All ER 449.
2   See for example Auchmuty 'The Fiction Of Equity' in Scott-Hunt and Lim (eds) *Feminist Perspectives On Equity and Trusts* (2001).
3   [2001] UKHL 44, [2001] 4 All ER 449.

10.46   The House of Lords carried out an extensive review of the law of undue influence. Lord Scott gave a useful summary as to their Lordships' conclusions[1]. Lord Nicholls' restatement of the applicable principles was accepted by the majority of the House.

Lord Nicholls said that proof that the complainant received advice from a third party before entering into the impugned transaction is one of the matters a court takes into account when weighing all the evidence. According to him, the weight, or importance, to be attached to such advice depends on all the circumstances. In the normal course, advice from a solicitor or other outside adviser can be expected to bring home to a complainant a proper understanding of what he or she is about to do. However, a person may understand fully the implications of a proposed transaction, for instance, a substantial gift, and yet still be acting under the undue influence of another.

1   [2001] UKHL 44, [2001] 4 All ER 449 at 509–510. It is not however entirely clear that his point (3) ('If the wife's consent has in fact been procured by undue influence or misrepresentation, the bank may not rely on her apparent consent unless it has good reason to believe that she understands the nature and effect of the transaction') was accepted by all members of the House. Something more than the bank's mere belief is surely required.

10.47   Lord Nicholls concluded, therefore, that proof of outside advice does not, of itself, necessarily show that the subsequent completion of the transaction was free from the exercise of undue influence. He added that, whether it will be proper to infer that outside advice had an emancipating effect, so that the transaction was not brought about by the exercise of undue influence, is a question of fact to be decided having regard to all the evidence in the case[1].

1   [2001] UKHL 44, [2001] 4 All ER 449 at 460.

10.48   All of their Lordships agreed that, for the future a bank satisfies minimum requirements if it insists that the wife attend a private meeting with a representative of the bank at which she is told of the extent of her liability as surety, warned of the risk she is running and urged to take independent legal advice. Their Lordships accepted, however, that this will not occur in practice.

It was held not to be unreasonable for the banks to prefer that this task should be undertaken by an independent legal advisor. Their Lordships were sceptical, however, as to how this practice was currently operated. Lord Hobhouse pointed out for example that:

> The involvement of a solicitor has too often been a formality or merely served to reinforce the husband's wishes and undermine any scope for the wife to exercise an independent judgment whether to comply[1].

Lord Hobhouse went on to stress that the guidance given in Lord Nicholls' speech should not be treated as optional, to be watered down when it proves inconvenient. He was not encouraged by the amount of litigation which has resulted from what he perceived as a carefully crafted scheme of Lord Browne-Wilkinson in *Barclays Bank v O'Brien*[2].

Lord Nicholls' guidance provided that:

> Since the bank is looking for its protection to legal advice given to the wife by a solicitor who, in this respect, is acting solely for her, I consider the bank should take steps to check *directly with the wife* the name of the solicitor she wishes to act for her. To this end, in future the bank should communicate directly with the wife, informing her that for its own protection it will require written confirmation from a solicitor, acting for her, to the effect that the solicitor has fully explained to her the nature of the documents and the practical implications they will have for her. She should be told that the purpose of this requirement is that thereafter she should not be able to dispute she is legally bound by the documents once she has signed them. She should be asked to nominate a solicitor whom she is willing to instruct to advise her, separately from her husband, and act for her in giving the necessary confirmation to the bank. She should be told that, if she wishes, the solicitor may be the same solicitor as is acting for her husband in the transaction. If a solicitor is already acting for the husband and the wife, she should be asked whether she would prefer that a different solicitor should act for her regarding the bank's requirement for confirmation from a solicitor. The bank should not proceed with the transaction until it has received an appropriate response directly from the wife.
>
> Representatives of the bank are likely to have a much better picture of the husband's financial affairs than the solicitor. If the bank is not willing to undertake the task of explanation itself, the bank must provide the solicitor with the financial information he needs for this purpose. Accordingly it should become routine practice for banks, if relying on confirmation from a solicitor for their protection, to send to the solicitor the necessary financial information. What is required must depend on the facts of the case. Ordinarily this will include information on the purpose for which the proposed new facility has been requested, the current amount of the husband's indebtedness, the amount of his current overdraft facility, and the amount and terms of any new facility. If the bank's request for security arose from a written application by the husband for a facility, a copy of the application should be sent to the solicitor. The bank will, of course, need first to obtain the consent of its customer to this circulation of confidential information. If this consent is not forthcoming the transaction will not be able to proceed.
>
> Exceptionally there may be a case where the bank believes or suspects that the wife has been misled by her husband or is not entering into the transaction of her own free will. If such a case occurs the bank must inform the wife's solicitors of the facts giving rise to its belief or suspicion.
>
> The bank should in every case obtain from the wife's solicitor a written confirmation to the effect mentioned above[3].

1   [2001] UKHL 44, [2001] 4 All ER 449 at 487.
2   [2001] UKHL 44, [2001] 4 All ER 449 at 480.
3   [2001] UKHL 44, [2001] 4 All ER 449 at 473 (emphasis in original).

10.49   Lord Nicholls also outlined the core minimum of advice that a solicitor should give before providing the conformation required by the bank:

> Typically, the advice a solicitor can be expected to give should cover the following matters as the core minimum. (1) He will need to explain the nature of the documents and the practical consequences these will have for the wife if she signs them. She could lose her home if her husband's business does not prosper. Her home may be her only substantial asset, as well as the family's home. She could be made bankrupt. (2) He will need to point out the seriousness of the risks involved. The wife should be told the purpose of the proposed new facility, the amount and principal terms of the new facility, and that the bank might increase the amount of the facility, or change its terms, or grant a new facility, without reference to her. She should be told the amount of her liability under her guarantee. The solicitor should discuss the

wife's financial means, including her understanding of the value of the property being charged. The solicitor should discuss whether the wife or her husband has any other assets out of which repayment could be made if the husband's business should fail. These matters are relevant to the seriousness of the risks involved. (3) The solicitor will need to state clearly that the wife has a choice. The decision is hers and hers alone. Explanation of the choice facing the wife will call for some discussion of the present financial position, including the amount of the husband's present indebtedness, and the amount of his current overdraft facility. (4) The solicitor should check whether the wife wishes to proceed. She should be asked whether she is content that the solicitor should write to the bank confirming he has explained to her the nature of the documents and the practical implications they may have for her, or whether, for instance, she would prefer him to negotiate with the bank on the terms of the transaction. Matters for negotiation could include the sequence in which the various securities will be called upon or a specific or lower limit to her liabilities. The solicitor should not give any confirmation to the bank without the wife's authority.

The solicitor's discussion with the wife should take place at a face-to-face meeting, in the absence of the husband. It goes without saying that the solicitor's explanations should be couched in suitably non-technical language. It also goes without saying that the solicitor's task is an important one. It is not a formality.

The solicitor should obtain from the bank any information he needs. If the bank fails for any reason to provide information requested by the solicitor, the solicitor should decline to provide the confirmation sought by the bank[1].

1   [2001] UKHL 44, [2001] 4 All ER 449 at 470.

10.50   *Etridge* has redrawn the balance between women and banks in surety transactions. Lord Hobhouse, in particular, was scathing about past practices and used a National Westminster Bank 'Action Sheet' to demonstrate that the new guidelines will not be burdensome for lending institutions to comply with[1]. The guidelines constitute a welcome development. Ironically, in some circumstances they may give greater protection to lending institutions. As Lord Scott points out, in most of the cases before the House, the husband was supporting the wife in her attempt to prevent the bank from enforcing its security in order to save the family home. The guidelines for future conduct are now very clear, but general observations in the case as to undue influence may well not have clarified the law.

What is certain, by way of conclusion, is that the procedures laid down by the House of Lords will have to be followed whenever the surety is standing in a non-commercial relationship with the principal debtor, whether heterosexual or homosexual and, as per *Massey v Midland Bank plc*[2], cohabitation is not essential.

1   [2001] UKHL 44, [2001] 4 All ER 449 at 488–489.
2   [1995] 1 All ER 929.

E   Duress

10.51   The concept of equitable fraud discussed in this chapter is wide enough to encompass restitution in one final area, duress. Although duress is often referred to as a common law cause of action, the interplay between this and other causes of action based on unconscionable conduct is very strong.

10.52   The early case of *Williams v Bayley*[1] is, for example, often cited both as an authority on undue influence and as an authority on duress. Even the ratio decidendi of this case is, as will be explained, somewhat imprecise. A son gave to his bank several promissory notes, upon which he had forged the endorsement of his father. At a subsequent meeting, the bank made it clear that, if some arrangement were not reached, the son would be prosecuted. The father, described by Lord Westbury as a 'defenceless old man'[2], feared the possible transportation of his son, and agreed to make an equitable mortgage to the bank in consideration of the return of the promissory notes. This agreement was held to be invalid.

Lord Cranworth LC considered the relevant question to be what sort of influence the bank exercised on the mind of the father to induce him to take on himself the responsibility of paying these notes. He observed that the parties were not standing in any fiduciary relation to one another. He reached the conclusion that the agreement could not be upheld because it was substantially an agreement to stifle a prosecution. He would have been prepared to hold that such an agreement would still have been invalid even if it had been made without any pressure on the father. Lord Chelmsford, alternatively, made the fact that the agreement had been extorted from the father by undue pressure the foundation of his opinion. He held, therefore, that the fears of the father were stimulated to the extent of depriving him of free agency, and to extort an agreement from him for the benefit of the bankers. Lord Westbury was prepared to hold the agreement invalid for two reasons. First, under the circumstances, he could not accept that the father entered into the transaction as a voluntary arrangement. Second, the conduct of the defendants, in violating policy grounds of not making a trade of a felony, was a departure from principles of fair dealing. The case remains good authority for the proposition that, where someone is pressured into making a payment to avoid the prosecution of a third party, the payment will be recoverable.

1   (1866) LR 1 HL 200.
2   (1866) LR 1 HL 200 at 219.

10.53   Whether or not the origins of duress lie at common law or in equity, it is clear that there are several forms of duress which may give rise to restitution, duress to the person, duress to goods and economic duress.

Duress to the person

10.54   The leading authority on duress to the person is *Barton v Armstrong*[1]. Barton, the managing director of a company, executed on its behalf a deed by which the company agreed to pay a sum of money to Armstrong, its chairman, and to buy Armstrong's shares from him, in order to get him off the board of the company. Barton had commercial reasons for this, but he argued that the main reason why he executed the deed was because Armstrong had threatened to have him killed if he did not make the arrangements. Barton later succeeded in having the deed set aside for duress.

The Privy Council held that, if the defendant's threat was 'a' reason for the claimant, Barton, executing the deed, the claimant was entitled to relief even though he might well have entered into the contract if the claimant had uttered no threats to induce him to do so. No onus lay on the claimant in this respect. On the contrary, it was for the defendant to establish, if he could, that the threat, which he was making, and the unlawful pressure, which he was exerting in fact, contributed nothing to the claimant's decision to sign the agreement. In this context, the onus of proof mirrors the situation in the context of the other causes of action discussed in this chapter. Aside from this issue of the burden of proof, the concept of duress was traditionally employed in the well established category of duress to goods, considered next.

1   [1975] 2 All ER 465. Note however a dissenting opinion by Lords Wilberforce and Simon.

Duress to goods

10.55   In the early case of *Astley v Reynolds*[1], a payment made as a result of duress of goods was recoverable in restitution. A pawnbroker claimed interest over the maximum permitted amount, and refused to deliver up the pledgor's goods unless the interest was paid. The pledgor duly paid, but subsequently succeeded in recovering his money.

1   (1731) 2 Stra 915, 93 ER 939.

10.56   In a subsequent case Lord Reading CJ, in *Maskell v Horner*, stated the relevant principle to be that 'If a person pays money, which he is not bound to pay, under the compulsion of urgent and pressing necessity or of seizure, actual or threatened, of his goods he can recover it as money had and received'[1]. The claimant in that case had repeatedly paid market tolls, but always under protest that the defendant was not entitled to receive the amounts of money. A critical feature, which has come to dominate the modern law of duress, is that he had no choice but to make the payments. If he had not done so, the defendant would have seized his goods. This critical feature was prominent in the case, which was probably the forerunner of the development of a more general category of economic duress, considered next.

1   [1915] 3 KB 106 at 118.

Economic duress

10.57   In *D & C Builders v Rees*[1] the defendant owed a small firm of builders the sum of £482. The builders were in severe financial difficulties, with the possibility of bankruptcy, and the defendant and his wife were aware of this. The defendant's wife offered the builders a cheque for £300 on an 'all-or-nothing' basis. Under their current financial difficulties, the builders accepted the cheque, but then sued for the outstanding balance. Amongst other things, counsel for the defendant argued that it would be inequitable for the builders to be able to enforce their strict legal rights. The Court of Appeal rejected this argument, and Lord Denning MR clearly based his judgment on a general conception of economic duress. He said:

> The debtor's wife held the creditor to ransom. The creditor was in need of money to meet his own commitments, and she knew it ... [S]he was putting undue pressure on the creditor. She was making a threat to break the contract (by paying nothing) and she was doing it so as to compel the creditor to do what he was unwilling to do (to accept £300 in settlement): and she succeeded. He complied with her demand. That was on recent authority a case of intimidation[2].

1   [1966] 2 QB 617.
2   [1966] 2 QB 617 at 625, citing *Rookes v Barnard* [1964] AC 1129 and *JT Stratford & Son Ltd v Lindley* [1964] 2 All ER 209.

10.58   This early case established a link between the issue of whether there may be a 'finding' of consideration for an agreement to vary a pre-existing legal agreement and the concept of economic duress, which was reinforced by the Court of Appeal decision in *Williams v Roffey Bros & Nicholls (Contractors) Ltd*[1]. That case concerned the promise of a main contractor to pay more for a sub-contractor to finish the job at hand. The main contractor had realised that the sub-contractor was in financial difficulties and, therefore, offered the extra payment. Technically, the Court of Appeal held that there was a practical benefit to the main contractor and the obviation of a disbenefit, which constituted good consideration for the promise to make the extra payment. The court made it abundantly clear, however, that its decision was dependent upon the absence of any element of duress on the part of the sub-contractor. The Court of Appeal, in refusing to apply the strict consideration rule in *Stilk v Myrick*[2], expressly did so on the basis of the absence of duress on the facts before them. The finding of the court, as was made clear, would have been very different if the sub-contractor had approached the main contractor for the extra payment.

1 [1991] 1 QB 1.
2 (1809) 2 Camp 317, 170 ER 1168. On this case see Furmston (ed) *Law of Contract* (1999), paras 2.70–2.72.

10.59   In the 25 years that separate *D & C Builders v Rees* and *Williams v Roffey*, both cases concerning variation of existing legal agreements, a doctrine of economic duress had become established, in the slightly different context of threats to break contracts. The elements of this cause of action have been variously described but, aside from the absence of choice, the essential point to note is that commercial pressure is not sufficient to substantiate a claim.

This point was made very clear by Lord Scarman in *Pau On v Lau Yiu Long*[1]. Whilst rejecting an argument of economic duress on the facts, the opinion of the Privy Council in this case, following developments in American law, recognised the existence of such a cause of action. Lord Scarman's exposition of the ingredients of the cause of action has since been refined by him in a later case[2] but, whilst refined in certain ways, the point about commercial pressure remains valid. Lord Scarman said:

> Duress, whatever form it takes, is a coercion of the will so as to vitiate consent ... [I]n a contractual situation commercial pressure is not enough. There must be present some factor which could in law be regarded as a coercion of his will so as to vitiate his consent ... [3]
>
> ... The commercial pressure alleged to constitute such duress must, however, be such that the victim must have entered the contract against his will, must have had no alternative course open to him, and must have been confronted with coercive acts by the party exerting the pressure ... American judges pay great attention to such evidential matters as the effectiveness of the alternative remedy available, the fact or absence of protest, the availability of independent advice, the benefit received, and the speed with which the victim has sought to avoid the contract[4].

1 [1980] AC 614.
2 See below, para 10.60.
3 Quoting with approval *Occidental Worldwide Investment Corpn v Skibs A/S Avanti* [1976] 1 Lloyd's Rep 293 at 336, per Kerr LJ.
4 [1980] AC 614 at 635–636.

10.60   Lord Scarman refined his own exposition of the principle of economic in a subsequent decision of the House of Lords, *Universe Tankships Inc of Monrovia v International Transport Workers' Federation, The Universe Sentinel*[1]. On this occasion, the claimant's argument for restitution of a sum of money succeeded. The claimant's ship was blacked by the defendant union, International

Transport Workers Federation ('ITF'). To secure its release the claimants, amongst other things, acquiesced in a demand to pay $6,480 to ITF's welfare fund. They later succeeded in recovering this sum, on the grounds that it had been paid under economic duress. On this occasion Lord Scarman said:

> There must be pressure, the practical effect of which is compulsion or the absence of choice. Compulsion is variously described in the authorities as coercion or the vitiation of consent. The classic case of duress is, however, not the lack of will to submit but the victim's intentional submission arising from the realisation that there is no other practical choice open to him ...
>
>   The absence of choice can be proved in various ways, eg by protest, by the absence of independent advice ... But none of these evidential matters goes to the essence of duress. The victim's silence will not assist the bully, if the lack of any practicable choice but to submit is proved[2].

1   [1983] 1 AC 366.
2   [1983] 1 AC 366 at 400.

10.61   The practical application of this statement of substantive principle (rather than evidential issues) can be aptly illustrated by two further cases.

In *B & S Contracts and Designs Ltd v Victor Green Publications Ltd* the claimants agreed to erect stands for the defendants for an exhibition at Olympia. The claimants were involved in an industrial dispute with their employees, and informed the defendants that they would not complete their contractual obligations unless they received a further sum in excess of the contract price. The money was paid, but the defendants later deducted the sum from the balance of the contract price. The Court of Appeal rejected the claim for the extra sum, on the ground that the promise had been extracted under economic duress. The claimants had been aware that the defendants would incur serious financial losses, as well as loss of reputation, from exhibitors to whom they had let space[1]. The Court of Appeal accepted that the absence of choice had been tantamount to the defendants' being held 'over a barrel'[2].

A similarly straightforward application of the principle of economic duress occurred in *Atlas Express Ltd v Kafco (Importers and Distributors) Ltd*[3]. Kafco, a small company, had secured a very important contract to supply its products for sale in Woolworths. Atlas agreed to deliver the goods at a rate of £1.10 per carton, but then discovered that the price was not as profitable as expected, because of their own mistake as to the number of cartons they could carry. In the full knowledge on Atlas's part that Kafco was entirely dependent on the Woolworth's contract, they sent a lorry to Kafco's premises with new terms, specifying a minimum price of £440 per trailer, and refusing to deliver goods unless that enhanced price was paid. Unsurprisingly, Tucker J held that the agreement to pay more had been extracted under economic duress.

These two cases are clear examples of economic duress whereby illegitimate threats to break contracts left the other parties with no other practicable choice than to accede to the pressure to pay money.

1   [1984] ICR 419 at 428.
2   [1984] ICR 419 at 424, per Eveleigh LJ.
3   [1989] QB 833.

10.62   The Court of Appeal in *CTN Cash and Carry Ltd v Gallaher Ltd*[1] refused, however to give redress for 'lawful act duress'. The claimants purchased cigarettes from the defendants under various separate contracts of sale. The defendants mistakenly delivered a consignment to the wrong warehouse and, before the claimants could arrange to transfer the cigarettes, the consignment was stolen. In the belief that the risk had passed to the claimants, the defendants threatened to withdraw future credit facilities unless the claimants paid for the stolen cigarettes. The claimants were heavily reliant on the credit facilities, and made the payment. It was later discovered that the risk had not, in fact, passed to the claimants; but their claim to recover the money on the basis of economic duress failed before the Court of Appeal. The defendants were legitimately entitled to withdraw future credit facilities entirely as they saw fit, and did so in pursuit of a bona fide claim. The Court of Appeal refused to extend the category of duress to cover these circumstances, even though the result was unpalatable.

Interestingly, Sir Donald Nicholls VC opined that, had it been argued, he would have been prepared to allow the claimants' claim on the basis of unjust enrichment. He suggested that 'the categories of unjust enrichment are not closed' and, on the facts, it seems that the defendants were unjustly enriched at the expense of the claimants because the risk had not passed[2]. For the time being, however, the parameters of economic duress have developed in a coherent form.

1   [1994] 4 All ER 714.
2   [1994] 4 All ER 714 at 720.

Part III
Profits from Wrongs

CHAPTER 11

Profits from Breach of Contract

David Howarth

A   Contract damages

11.1   The basic principle governing the measure of damages for breach of contract is well known:

> The rule of the common law is, that where a party sustains a loss by reason of a breach of contract, he is, so far as money can do it, to be placed in the same situation, with respect to damages, as if the contract had been performed[1].

That principle is subject to two equally well known qualifications: the mitigation rule, that the claimant cannot claim for losses which would not have occurred had the claimant acted reasonably to mitigate the loss[2]; and the remoteness rule, that the claimant cannot recover for any unusual loss, unless the possibility of that loss was within the contemplation of the parties when they made the contract[3].

In many ordinary commercial circumstances, the effective version of these rules is to be found in their embodiment in the Sale of Goods Act 1979, ss 50 and 51: that the measure of damages for both buyers and sellers in sale of goods cases is 'the estimated loss directly and naturally resulting, in the ordinary course of events, from the ... breach of contract'; and that 'where there is an available market for the goods in question the measure of damages is prima facie to be ascertained by the difference between the contract price and the market or current price at the time or times when the goods ought to have been' accepted or delivered.

1   *Robinson v Harman* (1848) 1 Exch 850 at 855, 154 ER 363 at 365, per Parke B; *British Westinghouse Electric and Manufacturing Co Ltd v Underground Electric Rlys Co of London Ltd* [1912] AC 673 at 688–689, per Viscount Haldane LC. See generally Furmston (ed) *Law of Contract* (1999), para 8.40ff.
2   *British Westinghouse Electric and Manufacturing Co Ltd v Underground Electric Rlys Co of London Ltd* [1912] AC 673.
3   *Hadley v Baxendale* (1854) 9 Exch 341, 156 ER 145.

The primacy of contractual expectations

11.2   The fundamental measure of damages for breach of contract is thus the expected benefit the claimant has lost as a result of the breach, with the mitigation rule and the remoteness rule helping to determine what should count as 'lost as a result of the breach'.

Even where the contract is shown to have been a losing one, the claimant can still recover damages if, had the contract been performed properly, the claimant would have made a smaller loss than the loss sustained in the event[1]. In addition, if the claimant cannot establish that it would have benefited from the deal overall (for example if it is unclear whether the claimant would have made a profit on the deal), the law will presume, albeit rebuttably, that the claimant would not have made an overall loss, so that, effectively, the claimant can in such cases claim for wasted expenditure incurred as a result of the breached contract[2]. Wasted expenditure damages (or 'reliance interest' damages) are, however, an alternative way of calculating the claimant's lost expected benefits in particular circumstances. They are not a completely different kind of damages.

1   *Milburn Services Ltd v United Trading Group (UK) Ltd* (1995) 52 Con LR 130.
2   *Anglia Television Ltd v Reed* [1972] 1 QB 60; *C & P Haulage (a firm) v Middleton* [1983] 3 All ER 94; *CCC Films (London) v Impact Quadrant Ltd* [1985] QB 16. According to an obiter remark of Clarke J in *Bem Dis A Turk Ticaret S/A TR v International Agri Trade Co Ltd, The 'Selda'* [1998] 1 Ll 416 the claimant can proceed on this basis even if the lost profits can be proved. *Sed quaere*, for the claimant would only choose to proceed on the wasted expenditure basis in such a case if the wasted expenditure exceeded the lost profits, and if that were so, it is unclear how the excess wasted expenditures could count as arising out of the contract, as opposed to arising out of the claimant's own lack of judgment and thus failure to mitigate.

11.3   Contracts may thus be conceived of as exchanges or deals which both parties expect will do them some good. The contract can be seen as creating a pool of benefits, which the contract also distributes between the parties. The law protects each side's expectation, for that is what induces that party to enter into the contract. In normal circumstances, the size of the other side's expected benefit is irrelevant to the decision to enter into the contract. Since contract damages are designed to protect the claimant's contractual expectations of benefit, there is no prima facie reason why the defendant's actual (or expected) benefits from breach should be relevant to the measure of damages for breach of contract.

11.4   There might exceptionally be contracts according to the terms of which the parties are allowed to choose as their consideration either a set price or the other side's profits (one might imagine a joint venture contract in this form, for example). In such a contract, to award the defendant's profit, if it was greater than the set price, would be to enforce the contract in its own terms, and thus would be to award the claimant's lost expectation as established by the contract itself. It is also possible that the courts might find an implied term in contracts establishing particular forms of relationship, such as employer and employee, that in certain circumstances, for example bribery[1] or improper use by an employee of the employer's property or, more generally, his position as an employee[2], the employee will have to pay over the benefit made by breaching the term to the employer[3]. But otherwise, there is usually no obvious connection between the claimant's lost expectation and the defendant's profit[4].

1   *Boston Deep Sea Fishing & Ice Co v Ansell* (1888) 39 Ch D 339, 59 LT 345.
2   See eg *Reading v A-G* [1951] AC 507 (in exchange for a fee, a soldier improperly used his uniform to help other engage illegal activities – required to pay his fees for this assistance to his employer). See discussion above, para 9.7.
3   See further *A-G for Hong Kong v Reid* [1994] 1 AC 324 (bribe itself is held on trust, so that the defendant is accountable for profits made using the bribe, not just for the bribe itself – *Lister & Co v Stubbs* (1890) 45 Ch D 1 disapproved), discussed above, para 9.12ff.
4   See Megarry V-C in *Tito v Waddell (No 2)* [1977] Ch 106 at 332, and Kerr J in *Occidental Worldwide Investment Corpn v Skibs A/S Avanti* [1976] 1 Lloyd's Rep 293. It is sometimes claimed that *British Motor Trade v Gilbert* [1951] 2 All ER 641, [1951] WN 454 (below, para 11.20), forms an exception to this rule (see eg the remarks of Lord Nicholls in *A-G v Blake* [2001] 1 AC 268 that in *Gilbert* 'the plaintiff suffered no financial loss but the award of damages for breach of contract effectively stripped the wrongdoer of the profit he had made from his wrongful venture

into the black market for new cars'). This is plainly not so on the facts of the case, for the court set the damages at the difference between the price paid by the defendant (£1,263 3s 11d) and the market price of the car (£2,100), which was different from the actual selling price of the car (£2,200) obtained by the defendant. *Gilbert* is an application of the Sale of Goods Act rules on damages for non-delivery, not an example of an account of profits for breach of contract. Lord Nicholls is not alone in this error – see Birks 'Restitutionary Damages for Breach of Contract' (1987) Lloyd's Maritime and Commercial Law Quarterly 421 at 431. The damages awarded were £836 16s 1d (see [1951] 2 All ER at 645), not £936 16s 1d as stated by Birks. Another case which is sometimes said to support a measure of damages derived from the defendant's profit from the breach is *East Ham Corpn v Bernard Sunley & Sons Ltd* [1966] AC 406 on the basis of a passing remark in the dissenting speech of Lord Cohen, that in a construction case, in addition to the cost of repair measure and the lost value of the property measure, the damages might be measured by 'the difference in cost to the builder of the actual work done and work specified'. This is a very flimsy basis for a change in a fundamental principle. All four of the other Law Lords treat the case as a matter of remoteness, and treat the cost of repair measure as primary. Moreover, counsel for the losing side had used the possibility of 'difference in cost' damages to establish that the damages should be measured at the time of breach, not at the time of repair. This was precisely the argument the court rejected.

11.5   It is sometimes claimed that the existence of specific remedies for breach of contract, such as injunctions and specific performance, shows that protection of contractual expectations is not always the primary purpose of contract remedies, and that such damages are sometimes found to be 'inadequate'. But the inadequacy of contractual damages occurs precisely when damages would be inadequate to protect contractual expectations[1]. Thus, in the 'monopoly supplier' cases[2], the expectation that the claimant will be able to carry on in business at all is protected by injunction or specific performance because, if the contract is not performed according to its terms, there will be no-one to compensate in damages[3]. The 'uniqueness' rule, to the extent that it is different from the 'monopoly supplier' rule[4] (that damages will be inadequate where there is failure to supply goods or services which are of 'peculiar and practically unique value to the plaintiff'[5]), is also oriented to putting the claimant in the position the claimant would have been in if the contract had been performed[6].

It is also sometimes alleged that the availability of specific remedies shows that the law is capable of taking breach of contract more seriously than the expectation measure appears to take it, and that, although damages are the primary remedy for breach of contract and specific remedies are 'exceptional'[7], it is an open question for the courts how large to make the exception[8]. Removing the defendant's profits, it is said, is a monetary, ex post facto version of an injunction[9], aimed at removing all incentive to breach, and thus capable of forming part of the exception which takes breach of contract more seriously than the expectation measure[10]. The difficulty with this line of reasoning, however, is that it ignores the close connection, via the concept of 'adequacy', between the availability of specific remedies and expectation losses. It also cannot explain the clear rule that exemplary damages are not available for breach of contract – if the law were desperate to make people carry out their bargains, it would either make it a crime not to carry out contractual obligations, or at least set damage awards at clearly deterrent levels. It does not do so[11].

1   *Société des Industries Métallurgiques SA v Bronx Engineering Co Ltd* [1975] 1 Lloyd's Rep 465. See generally Mitchell 'Remedial Inadequacy in Contract and the Role of Restitutionary Damages' (1999) 15 Journal of Contract Law 133.
2   *Sky Petroleum Ltd v VIP Petroleum Ltd* [1974] 1 WLR 576; *Worldwide Dryers Ltd v Warner Howard Ltd* (1982) Times, 9 December.
3   It should be mentioned, however, that both *Sky Petroleum Ltd v VIP Petroleum Ltd* [1974] 1 WLR 576; and *Worldwide Dryers Ltd v Warner Howard Ltd* (1982) Times, 9 December gloss over the issue of remoteness. Why on *Hadley v Baxendale* principles should a monopoly supplier be held responsible for the insolvency of its customer as a consequence of failure to supply? One can,

admittedly, construct an argument that a monopoly supplier and a customer of a monopoly supplier will have in their contemplation, or at least should be presumed to have in their contemplation, that the customer will go out of business if supply ceases, but such an argument makes no appearance in these cases. On the other hand Goff and Jones *Law of Restitution* (5th edn, 1998), pp 518ff imply that expectation damages can be said to be 'inadequate' simply because they rule out some damages on remoteness grounds. Such a notion implies that the remoteness rules have no rationale, even though their rationale as recognising the allocation of risk established between the parties and ensuring optimal use of the information available to each of the parties is well-known. See eg Posner 'Contract Remedies: Foreseeability, Precaution, Causation and Mitigation' *Encyclopedia of Law and Economics* (1999), para 4620.

4   Lord Edmund-Davies in *Société des Industries Métallurgiques SA v Bronx Engineering Co Ltd* [1975] 1 Lloyd's Rep 465 seems to hint that the rules are the same.

5   *Behnke v Bede Shipping Co Ltd* [1927] 1 KB 649 at 661, per Wright J.

6   Admittedly it is difficult to explain the uniqueness rule as a consequence of protecting contractual expectations if one accepts literally the view of Buckley LJ in the Court of Appeal in *Société des Industries Métallurgiques SA v Bronx Engineering Co Ltd* [1975] 1 Lloyd's Rep 465 at 470, that 'mere difficulty in quantification is not, in my judgment, a matter which really affects the principle at all', but, it is submitted, Buckley LJ was adverting to the difficulties there might be in calculating damages for consequential loss. Similarly, Parker J said in *CN Marine Inc v Stena Line A/B* [1982] 2 Lloyd's Rep 323: 'In many cases there are items of inconvenience which may not be capable of quantification or which the law regards as too remote to sound in damages but such matters do not, without more, justify the granting of an order for specific performance', which also seems to suggest that there is more to the uniqueness rule than remoteness – but Parker J might have been referring to matters such as anxiety and distress. The central issue is rather the difficulty in cases of unique goods in saying what would count as a close enough substitute that its value could be used to estimate the loss of expectation, so that specific performance becomes the most accurate way to protect the claimant's expectation. See Kronman 'Specific Performance' (1978) 45 University of Chicago Law Review 352.

7   *Co-operative Insurance Society Ltd v Argyll Stores (Holdings) Ltd* [1998] AC 1, per Lord Hoffmann.

8   Cf Chen-Wishart 'Restitutionary Damages for Breach of Contract' (1998) 114 LQR 363.

9   Cf Beatson *Use and Abuse of Unjust Enrichment* (1991), p 17.

10 See the Israeli case *Adras Building Material Ltd v Harlow & Jones GmbH* [1995] RLR 235 for the consequences of the view that the starting point of the law of contract remedies is that contracts ought to be performed. *Adras* is explained and criticised by Dagan 'Restitutionary Damages for breach of contract: An exercise in private law theory' (2000) 1 Theoretical Inquiries in Law 115. Cf Chen-Wishart 'Restitutionary Damages for Breach of Contract' (1998) 114 LQR 363.

11 See *Addis v Gramophone Co* [1909] AC 488; *Perera v Vandiyar* [1953] 1 WLR 672; and *Kenny v Preen* [1963] 1 QB 499. Some academics regret this position: McBride 'A Case for Awarding Punitive Damages in Response to Deliberate Breach of Contract' (1995) 24 Anglo-American Law Review 369, but see Mitchell 'Remedial Inadequacy in Contract and the Role of Restitutionary Damages' (1999) 15 Journal of Contract Law 133, and Weinrib 'Restitutory Damages as Corrective Justice' (2000) 1 Theoretical Inquiries in Law 1. See further Beale 'Exceptional Measures of Damages in Contract' in Birks (ed) *Wrongs and Remedies in the 21st Century* (1996), p 217; Jaffey 'Restitutionary Damages and Disgorgement' [1995] RLR 30 at 37–38; and Jaffey *Nature and Scope of Restitution* (2000), pp 374ff.

11.6   In addition, recent cases such as *Ruxley Electronics and Construction Ltd v Forsyth*[1] and *McAlpine (Alfred) Construction Ltd v Panatown Ltd*[2] show that English law takes the promisee's expectation interest in the performance of the contract increasingly seriously.

In *Ruxley*, contractors made a swimming pool nine inches shallower than was specified in the contract. The problem was that the cost of repairing the pool was practically the same as the original cost of making it, but the effect on the market value of the claimant's property was virtually nil. The former measure seemed too much, but the latter seemed too little. The House of Lords awarded a compromise £2,500 for 'loss of amenity', which the court equated to loss of 'consumer surplus'[3].

In *Panatown*[4], the defendant contracted with the claimant for the construction of an office block, on a site owned by another company in the same group as the claimant. The building itself became the property of the other company. The defendant had entered into a deed with the owner of the site, under which the owner acquired a direct remedy against the contractor for any failure by the contractor to exercise reasonable skill in the execution of the contract. Serious defects were discovered in the building, and the claimant sued for damages. The issue was whether the claimant was entitled to substantial, as opposed to nominal, damages under the contract. The contractor said that the client had suffered no loss, because the defective building was owned by the owner of the site, not by the claimant. In the House of Lords, three of the five law lords were prepared to accept that, as a matter of principle, the claimant had a substantial interest in the performance of the contract, and should therefore be entitled to receive substantial damages. Building on earlier remarks of Lord Griffiths[5] and Steyn LJ[6], these three lords were prepared to accept that the fact that the innocent party did not receive the bargain for which it contracted is itself a loss. In the event, however, one member of those three, Lord Browne-Wilkinson, decided that the existence of the direct remedy, the action on the deed in favour of the owner, defeated the general principle in this particular case, and he voted with the two dissentients in favour of nominal damages[7]. The overall result was therefore that no remedy was available.

These cases are an important move forward in English contract law. They move away from the idea that, for claimants to be entitled to substantial damages, they have to show they have suffered a specific 'loss' 'caused by' the breach. That idea was the result of confusing the mitigation and remoteness rules with the damage itself. The damage suffered by the claimant is the fact that the contract is not performed. The mitigation and remoteness rules are merely subsidiary limiting principles, used principally at the stage of measuring the damage. The importance of these cases for present purposes, however, is that they throw into very serious doubt claims[8] that damages measures based on the defendant's profits are necessary to establish that English contract law takes seriously a failure to perform a contract as promised regardless of 'loss'[9]. Although Lord Millett says in *Panatown* that he believes there is room for both the 'performance interest' approach and the 'defendant's profits' approach[10], it can no longer be said that the absence of the former makes the adoption of the latter necessary[11].

1   [1996] AC 344. See O'Sullivan 'Loss and Gain at Greater Depth: The implications of the *Ruxley* decision' in Rose (ed) *Failure of Contracts – Contractual, Restitutionary and Proprietary Consequences* (1997), p 1.

2   [2001] 1 AC 518. See Coote 'The Performance Interest, *Panatown* and the Problem of Loss' (2001) 117 LQR 81.

3   [1996] AC 344 at 360, per Lord Mustill. The 'consumer surplus' is the difference between the price the buyer paid for a good or service and the maximum price the buyer would have been prepared to pay for that good or service.

4   *McAlpine (Alfred) Construction Ltd v Panatown Ltd* [2001] 1 AC 518.

5   *St Martins Property Corpn Ltd v Sir Robert McAlpine Ltd* [1994] 1 AC 85 at 96–97.

6   *Darlington Borough Council v Wiltshier Northern Ltd* [1995] 1 WLR 68 at 80.

7   The view of the other two on the point of principle was that there was only a substantial interest if the claimant intended to pay for the necessary repairs.

8   See Goff and Jones *Law of Restitution* (5th edn, 1998), pp 518ff; Virgo *Principles of the Law of Restitution* (1999), p 500; and Friedmann 'The Performance Interest in Contract Damages' (1995) 111 LQR 628. Against these see Mitchell 'Remedial Inadequacy in Contract and the Role of Restitutionary Damages' (1999) 15 Journal of Contract Law 133. See further Coote 'Contract Damages, *Ruxley*, and the Performance Interest' [1997] CLJ 537.

9   See further below, para 11.20ff.

10   [2001] 1 AC 518 at 587–588.

11   See O'Sullivan 'Loss and Gain at Greater Depth: The implications of the *Ruxley* decision' in Rose (ed) *Failure of Contracts – Contractual, Restitutionary and Proprietary Consequences* (1997), p 1.

B   The decision of the House of Lords in *A-G v Blake*

11.7   Despite these considerations, the House of Lords ruled in *A-G v Blake*[1] that exceptionally, an account of profits may be the most appropriate remedy for breach of contract even where, by the terms of the contract itself, no such measure of damages seems to have been contemplated. Lord Nicholls, who spoke for a majority of the court, declined to say what circumstances would count as appropriately 'exceptional':

> No fixed rules can be prescribed. The court will have regard to all the circumstances, including the subject matter of the contract, the purpose of the contractual provision which has been breached, the circumstances in which the breach occurred, the consequences of the breach and the circumstances in which relief is being sought. A useful general guide, although not exhaustive, is whether the plaintiff had a legitimate interest in preventing the defendant's profit-making activity and, hence, in depriving him of his profit[2].

A-G v Blake concerned George Blake, 'a notorious, self-confessed traitor'[3] who had been sent to prison for 42 years for spying for the Soviet Union while employed as a member of the British security and intelligence services. He had escaped from prison and fled to Moscow where he wrote his autobiography, parts of which related to his adventures as a secret intelligence officer. By the time the book was written, the information in it was no longer confidential, and its disclosure was not damaging to the public interest. Blake contracted to have the book published by Jonathan Cape Ltd under the title *No Other Choice*. Blake did not seek any prior authorisation from the Crown about the contents of the book, and the Government was not otherwise aware of the book until its publication was announced. The Crown sought to stop Jonathan Cape making any further payments to Blake under the publishing contract. By the time the case reached the House of Lords, one of the points put forward by the Crown was that Blake was bound in contract by an undertaking to which he had agreed when he was first employed by British Intelligence, that he would not 'divulge any official information gained ... as a result of [his] employment, either in the press or in book form'. The undertaking went on, 'I also understand that these provisions apply not only during the period of service but also after employment has ceased'. The Crown argued that as a consequence of his breach of contract, Blake should be condemned to pay damages to the Crown, and those damages should be set (as 'restitutionary damages' or, as Lord Nicholls preferred in the event, as 'an account of profits'), at the same sum as Blake's royalties from Jonathan Cape.

1 [2001] 1 AC 268. See Hedley '"Very Much the Wrong People": The House of Lords and the publication of spy memoirs' [2000] 4 Web Journal of Current Legal Issues, and notes by Jaffey [2000] RLR 578 and Edelman 'Profits and Gains from Breach of Contract' [2001] Lloyds Maritime and Commercial Law Quarterly 9. See also Worthington and Goode 'Commercial Law: Confining the Remedial Boundaries' in Hayton (ed) *Law's Future(s) – British Legal Developments in the 21st Century* (2000), p 281.
2 [2001] 1 AC 268 at 285.
3 [2001] 1 AC 268 at 275.

11.8   The court held that Blake's breach fell within the new general, if vague, principle. Lord Nicholls said:

> The Crown had and has a legitimate interest in preventing Blake profiting from the disclosure of official information, whether classified or not, while a member of the service and thereafter. Neither he, nor any other member of the service, should have a financial incentive to break his undertaking. It is of paramount importance that members of the service should have complete confidence in all their dealings with

each other, and that those recruited as informers should have the like confidence. Undermining the willingness of prospective informers to co-operate with the services, or undermining the morale and trust between members of the services when engaged on secret and dangerous operations, would jeopardise the effectiveness of the service. An absolute rule against disclosure, visible to all, makes good sense[1].

The obvious retort to this point is that the information concerned was no longer confidential, and so revealing it broke no fiduciary duty. The law of confidential information would be undermined if its remedies were available even if the conditions for applying it are not fulfilled. Lord Nicholls dealt with this point as follows:

> The undertaking, if not a fiduciary obligation, was closely akin to a fiduciary obligation, where an account of profits is a standard remedy in the event of breach. Had the information which Blake has now disclosed still been confidential, an account of profits would have been ordered, almost as a matter of course. In the special circumstances of the intelligence services, the same conclusion should follow even though the information is no longer confidential. That would be a just response to the breach. I am reinforced in this view by noting that most of the profits from the book derive indirectly from the extremely serious and damaging breaches of the same undertaking committed by Blake in the 1950s[2].

It is not clear how this passage relates to Lord Nicholls's more general statement of principle. It does not relate to the 'subject matter' of the contract, since the relevant subject matter is the confidentiality of the information, and we know that the information was no longer confidential. Similarly, the 'purpose of the contractual provision which has been breached' was to preserve secrets – but those secrets had already been revealed. The 'circumstances in which the breach occurred' are by no means exceptional for a breach of a confidentiality clause. The 'consequences of the breach' are merely that Blake and Jonathan Cape make a profit, not that the Crown makes any kind of loss or that any secret is revealed. And 'the circumstances in which relief is being sought' are ones in which no injunction appears to be justified, so why should an account of profits be justified?[3]

1   [2001] 1 AC 268 at 287.
2   [2001] 1 AC 268 at 287. Lord Steyn in his separate speech in *Blake* used very similar language: 'The distinctive feature of this case is, however, that Blake gave an undertaking not to divulge any information, confidential or otherwise, obtained by him during his work in the intelligence services. This obligation still applies to Blake. He was, therefore in regard to all information obtained by him in the intelligence services, confidential or not, in a very similar position to a fiduciary. The reason of the rule applying to fiduciaries applies to him': [2001] 1 AC 268 at 292. See above, paras 9.8.
3   See Jaffey 'Restitutionary Damages and Disgorgement' [1995] RLR 30 at 47–48. See further below, para 11.26.

11.9   Lord Nicholls appeals also to the nature of the claimants, the security and intelligence services, and the fact that Blake's revelations of state secrets to the Soviet Union were extremely damaging at the time. The reasoning behind of the former point is obscure. Obviously the security and intelligence services need to be secure if they are to do their work, but it was Blake's treachery which threatened to undermine the basis of trust which a high level of security brings, not his publishing a book many years later[1]. If by the latter Lord Nicholls means only that Blake was a very bad man[2], it is not at all clear that this should mean that he should be subjected to a different measure of damages in contract law from other people.

It could be, however, that Lord Nicholls means that Blake's own crimes were ultimately responsible for the revelation of the secrets which were contained in the book, for example at his criminal trial. If so, the effect of *Blake* is somewhat limited. It is that the law of confidentiality has been extended to include information which would be confidential except for the defendant's own wrong. In other words *Blake* creates a law of constructive confidentiality.

1   It would now in any case be more difficult to make a case on the facts for the proposition that the publication of formerly confidential information would undermine the security and intelligence services in the light of the public pronouncement of the former head of the Security Service that it is 'unrealistic' to maintain a blanket confidentiality regime in the security and intelligence services. See Norton-Taylor 'Former MI5 chief blasts secrets act': (2001) Guardian, 8 September.

2   See Hedley '"Very Much the Wrong People": The House of Lords and the Publication of spy memoirs' [2000] 4 Web Journal of Current Legal Issues.

Conditions insufficient to trigger an account of profits

11.10   Lord Nicholls in *Blake* emphasised the exceptional nature of a resort to an account of profits for breach of contract. In doing so he listed a number of circumstances which he believed would be insufficient in themselves to trigger an account of profits. They were:

(a)   The mere fact that 'the defendant has obtained his profit by doing the very thing he contracted not to do'. Lord Nicholls said: 'This category is defined too widely to assist. The category is apt to embrace all express negative obligations. But something more is required than mere breach of such an obligation before an account of profits will be the appropriate remedy'[1].

(b)   '[T]he fact that the breach was cynical and deliberate'[2]. This is not sufficient in itself, because, as the Law Commission has commented: '[M]any breaches of contract are made for commercial reasons and it is difficult to draw the line between 'innocent' breach, for which there would be only compensation, and 'cynical' breach ... This would lead to greater uncertainty in the assessment of damages in commercial and consumer disputes'[3].

(c)   '[T]he fact that the breach enabled the defendant to enter into a more profitable contract elsewhere'[4]. In the Court of Appeal Lord Woolf referred to *Teacher v Calder*[5] in support of the proposition that this factor is insufficient in itself to trigger an account. In the House of Lords, Lord Nicholls approves of Lord Woolf's assertion, but, somewhat oddly, seems to approve *Lake v Bayliss*[6], in which it was held that a vendor who contracted to sell a property to the claimant and then sold it to another person was accountable as a trustee to the original purchaser for the proceeds of sale[7]. This apparent contradiction is left hanging by the majority in *Blake*. Perhaps the resolution of the contradiction is that contractual rights can be treated as proprietary rights only where there is something akin to the transfer of property (as in *Lake*), but not when all that happens is that the defendant takes his or her services elsewhere for more money[8].

(d)   '[T]he fact that by entering into a new and more profitable contract the defendant put it out of his power to perform his contract with the plaintiff'[9]. Lord Woolf MR said in the Court of Appeal that this point is indistinguishable from (c) above. Lord Nicholls apparently agrees. The obvious distinction, however, is that this factor concentrates on the *effects* of the defendant's acts (that the defendant can no longer perform) as opposed to the defendant's *motives* for acting (to profit from the breach).

The 'consequences of breach' is, of course, one of the factors which Lord Nicholls says is admissible in deciding whether the claimant had sufficient legitimate interest to justify an account of profits. We are forced to conclude, therefore, that the consequence of breach that the defendant is not able to perform the contract is not a relevant consequence for these purposes, and that when Lord Nicholls refers to the 'consequences of breach' he must be referring to the consequences of non-performance rather than to the fact of non-performance.

1   [2001] 1 AC 268 at 286. Applied in *World Wide Fund for Nature v World Wrestling Federation Entertainment Inc* (LEXIS Transcript 1 October 2001); affd [2002] EWCA Civ 196, [2002] NLJR 363. Lord Steyn in his separate speech in *Blake* seemed, however, more favourable to this condition.
2   [2001] 1 AC 268 at 286, agreeing on this point with Lord Woolf MR in *Blake* in the Court of Appeal [1998] Ch 439 at 457. To the contrary see Birks 'Restitutionary Damages for Breach of Contract' [1987] Lloyd's Maritime and Commercial Law Quarterly 421.
3   Law Com no 247 *Aggravated, Exemplary and Restitutionary Damages*, Pt III, para 1.47 (p 42).
4   [2001] 1 AC 286.
5   [1899] AC 451.
6   [1974] 1 WLR 1073. See below, para 11.30.
7   [2001] 1 AC 268 at 284.
8   See below, para 11.20. This would not be an easy distinction to make, however. Cf the question of whether using a corporate opportunity is the same as improperly using the company's property: *CMS Dolphin Ltd v Simonet* [2001] 2 BCLC 704, discussing eg *Cook v Deeks* [1916] 1 AC 554, *Regal (Hastings) Ltd v Gulliver* [1942] 1 All ER 378, *Industrial Development Consultants Ltd v Cooley* [1972] 2 All ER 162, [1972] 1 WLR 443, and *Canadian Aero Service Ltd v O'Malley* [1974] SCR 592, 40 DLR (3d) 371. See also *Peso Silver Mines Ltd v Cropper* (1966) 58 DLR (2d) 1; on which see above, para 9.35.
9   [2001] 1 AC 268 at 286.

Relationship with adequacy of damages and availability of specific performance and injunctions

11.11   Some commentators have suggested that an account of profits should be available when damages would not be an adequate remedy[1], or, along the same line of thought, when an injunction would be available[2]. In *Blake*, Lord Nicholls points to the availability of injunctions and specific performance in cases in which damages would not be 'adequate', but instead of transferring the rules for the availability of these remedies to the account of profits, he comments:

> But [injunctions and specific performance] are not always available. For instance, confidential information may be published in breach of a non-disclosure agreement before the innocent party has time to apply to the court for urgent relief. Then the breach is irreversible. Further, these specific remedies are discretionary. Contractual obligations vary infinitely. So do the circumstances in which breaches occur, and the circumstances in which remedies are sought. The court may, for instance, decline to grant specific relief on the ground that this would be oppressive[3].

This suggests that the account of profits becomes available only when *both* damages *and* specific remedies are not 'adequate' or when damages are not 'adequate' and specific remedies are *not* available[4]. Both aspects of this rule – the damages aspect and the specific remedy aspect – require further comment.

1   See eg Maddaugh and McCamus *Law of Restitution* (1990), pp 432–438.
2   Nolan 'Remedies for Breach of Contract: Specific Performance and Restitution' in Rose (ed) *Failure of Contracts – Contractual, Restitutionary and Proprietary Consequences* (1997), p 35, Law Com no 247 *Aggravated, Exemplary and Restitutionary Damages*, Pt III, para 1.46 (p 41). See also Beatson *Use and Abuse of Unjust Enrichment* (1991), pp 15–17; Waddams 'Restitution as Part of Contract Law' in Burrows (ed) *Essays on the Law of Restitution* (1991), p 208ff.

3   [2001] 1 AC 268 at 282.
4   Cf the argument of the Solicitor-General in *Blake*, as laid out in the speech of Lord Steyn; discussed below, para 11.19.

11.12   It should be noted that the notion of the 'adequacy' of a remedy begs the question of what it is supposed to be adequate for[1]. Contract damages increasingly protect the claimant's expectation interest in performance of the contract in flexible and responsive ways[2]. In consequence, there are surely fewer sets of circumstances in which damages are 'inadequate' for the purposes of protecting the claimant's expectation interest in the performance of the contract[3]. But if the purpose of contract damages is taken to be much broader, to deter all breaches of contract, for example, or to correct 'unjust enrichment', expectation of performance damages will often look 'inadequate'[4].

1   See above, para 11.2.
2   *Ruxley Electronics and Construction Ltd v Forsyth* [1996] AC 344; *McAlpine (Alfred) Construction Ltd v Panatown Ltd* [2001] 1 AC 518. See above, para 11.2.
3   See above, para 11.2. Cf O'Sullivan 'Loss and Gain at Greater Depth: The implications of the *Ruxley* decision' in Rose (ed) *Failure of Contracts – Contractual, Restitutionary and Proprietary Consequences* (1997), p 1; Friedmann 'The Performance Interest in Contract Damages' (1995) 111 LQR 628; Coote 'Contract Damages, *Ruxley* and the Performance Interest' [1997] CLJ 537.
4   This is essentially the position of Goff and Jones *Law of Restitution* (5th edn, 1998), pp 518ff, and of McGregor 'Restitutionary Damages' in Birks *Wrongs and Remedies in the 21st Century* (1996). Cf Chen-Wishart 'Restitutionary Damages for Breach of Contract' (1998) 114 LQR 363; and Virgo *Principles of the Law of Restitution* (1999), p 500.

11.13   The circumstances in which granting specific relief, such as an injunction, will be refused even to enforce a negative obligation are generally taken to be set out by AL Smith LJ in *Shelfer v City of London Electric Co*:

> (1) If the injury to the plaintiff's legal rights is small, (2) And is one which is capable of being estimated in money, (3) And is one which can be adequately compensated by a small money payment, (4) And the case is one in which it would be oppressive to the defendant to grant an injunction: – then damages in substitution for an injunction may be given[1].

AL Smith LJ adds that:

> It is impossible to lay down any rule as to what, under the differing circumstances of each case, constitutes either a small injury, or one that can be estimated in money, or what is a small money payment, or an adequate compensation, or what would be oppressive to the defendant[2].

Nevertheless, in *Jaggard v Sawyer*[3] Millett LJ pointed out that usually 'oppression' meant that the harm to the defendant consequent on granting the injunction would be 'out of all proportion to that which would be suffered by the plaintiff if it were refused, and would indeed deliver him to the plaintiff bound hand and foot to be subjected to any extortionate demands the plaintiff might make'[4]. In the same case, Sir Thomas Bingham MR emphasised that 'oppression' is not the same as a mere 'balance of convenience' test, even though it 'must be judged as at the date the court is asked to grant an injunction'. Sir Thomas Bingham MR also said that 'It is relevant that the plaintiff could at an early stage have sought interlocutory relief ... [and that] it is also relevant that the defendants could have sought a declaration of right' but, he added, 'These considerations are not decisive'. Finally he said that 'It would weigh against a finding of oppression if the defendants had acted in blatant and calculated disregard of the plaintiff's rights'[5].

In the case of mandatory injunctions, which are more likely to be 'oppressive', the discretionary element in the court's decision looms larger and the conditions under which they will be refused are somewhat easier to satisfy[6]. Mandatory injunctions will be refused unless the claimant shows that:

(a) there is a 'very strong probability upon the facts that grave damage will accrue to him in the future'[7];

(b) 'damages will not be a sufficient or an adequate remedy if such damage does happen'[8];

(c) 'the remedy must be reasonably proportional to the wrong'[9] (which is another way of saying that it must not be 'oppressive'); and

(d) the injunction must be capable of being precisely formulated both as to the ends to be achieved and the means used to achieve it[10].

The court may also take into account the wider public interest in deciding whether to grant a mandatory injunction[11].

1   [1895] 1 Ch 287 at 322–323. See further para 12.26 below.
2   [1895] 1 Ch 287 at 323.
3   [1995] 2 All ER 189. See generally Grubb (ed) *Law of Tort* (2002), para 8.52ff.
4   [1995] 2 All ER 189 at 208. These words are taken from Lord Westbury's speech in *Isenberg v East India Housing Estate Co Ltd* (1863) 3 De GJ & Sm 263 at 273, 46 ER 637 at 641.
5   [1995] 2 All ER 189 at 203.
6   Grubb (ed) *Law of Tort* (2002), para 8.20.
7   *Redland Bricks Ltd v Morris* [1970] AC 652 at 665, per Lord Upjohn.
8   *Redland Bricks Ltd v Morris* [1970] AC 652 at 665, per Lord Upjohn.
9   *Jordan v Norfolk County Council* [1994] 1 WLR 1353 at 1358, per Sir Donald Nicholls V-C.
10 *Redland Bricks Ltd v Morris* [1970] AC 652 at 666, per Lord Upjohn.
11 *Harold Stephen & Co Ltd v Post Office* [1978] 1 All ER 939, [1977] 1 WLR 1172. See Grubb (ed) *Law of Tort* (2002), para 8.29.

11.14   Thus it appears that an account of profits will potentially be available under *Blake* if any of the reasons mentioned above apply for refusing a specific remedy and, in addition, damages would be 'inadequate'. But this set of conditions is bound to generate difficulties. For example, if a specific remedy would have been refused because it would have been disproportionate to the wrong, why should not the account of profits also strike the court as disproportionate[1]? Similarly, if a prohibitory injunction would be refused because the harm to the claimant is small and easily compensated, what room is there for an account of profits?

In addition, if the defendant has acted in 'blatant and calculated disregard of the plaintiff's rights', that is a reason for issuing an injunction, and thus a reason against an account of profits. *Blake* goes further than simply rejecting the 'cynical breach' rule[2]. In some circumstances it has produced the opposite – a rule which says that cynical breaches should be dealt with by injunction, not by an account of profits.

These considerations bring the interpretation of *Blake* back to constructive confidentiality[3]. In a breach of confidence case, the reason an injunction will not be issued when the information is already in the public domain is nothing to do with the *Shelfer* conditions or the mandatory injunction rules, but is rather that to issue an injunction in such conditions is simply pointless. The effect of *Blake* is to create a damages remedy broadly equivalent to the now pointless injunction.

1   For discussion, see Jaffey 'Restitutionary Damages and Disgorgement' [1995] RLR 30 at 47–48.
2   See above, para 11.10.
3   See above, paras 11.8 and 11.9.

The earlier case law

11.15   The House of Lords in *Blake* also discussed the status of three previous breach of contract cases, in which the question had arisen of the place of restitutionary concepts in cases where injunctions are not issued in circumstances in which injunctions would normally be issued: *Wrotham Park Estate Co Ltd v Parkside Homes Ltd*[1], *Surrey County Council v Bredero Homes Ltd*[2] and *Jaggard v Sawyer*[3]. In *Wrotham Park*, Brightman J refused to grant a mandatory injunction to pull down a number of houses which had been built in violation of a restrictive covenant. He decided instead to grant damages in lieu under the Lord Cairns Act jurisdiction[4]. In reaching the sum to be paid under the Act, Brightman J referred to the 'wayleave' cases[5], to the patent case *Watson, Laidlaw & Co Ltd v Pott, Cassels and Williamson*[6] and to the interference with goods cases *Strand Electric and Engineering Co Ltd v Brisford Entertainments Ltd*[7] and *Penarth Dock Engineering Co Ltd v Pounds*[8]. In all these cases the court awarded damages on a 'reasonable fee' (or 'reasonable price' or 'reasonable hire') basis. They form the basis of the 'user principle' under which defendants who without authorisation use the claimant's property must pay damages based on a reasonable fee for that use[9]. Brightman J went on to say that he thought that a reasonable fee in the circumstances of the case would be a royalty of '5% of [the defendant's] anticipated profit' from the infringing acts.

1   [1974] 1 WLR 798.
2   [1993] 3 All ER 705.
3   [1995] 1 WLR 269.
4   See generally below, para 12.24ff.
5   See below, para 12.35.
6   (1914) 31 RPC 104. See below, paras 12.35, 12.45 and 12.61.
7   [1952] 2 QB 246, [1952] 1 All ER 796.
8   [1963] 1 Lloyd's Rep 359.
9   See below, para 12.35ff.

11.16   In *Bredero*[1], the claimant councils sold land subject to a restrictive covenant that no more than a certain number of houses should be built on it, a number which was further entrenched in the planning permission granted by one the claimants, the relevant district council. The defendant, the buyers of the land, applied for and obtained a new planning permission from the district council to build more than the number of houses specified in the covenant[2]. At that stage the claimants could have applied for a prohibitory injunction to prevent the development at the new higher density. They chose not to do so, for reasons which do not appear in the first instance judgment[3], but which seem to be connected with their statement to the Court of Appeal, that 'their sole purpose in imposing the covenants at all ... was that the defendant would have to apply for and pay for a relaxation if it wanted to build anything more'[4]. They chose instead to wait until the houses had been built and sold and to sue the defendants for damages, claiming that they had lost at least a share in the extra profits generated by the sale of the extra houses. The councils submitted to the Court of Appeal that where:

(a)   the breach is deliberate, in the sense that the defendant is deliberately doing an act which he knows or should know is plainly or arguably in breach of contract;

(b)   the defendant, as a result of the breach, has profited by making a gain or reducing a loss; [and]

(c)   at the date of the breach it is clear or probable that damages under the conventional measure will either be nominal or much smaller than the profit to the defendant from the breach[5],

damages 'for loss of bargaining power' can be awarded, as long as the following condition is fulfilled:

(d)   [Damages for loss of bargaining power can be awarded if, but only if, the party in breach could have been restrained by injunction from committing the breach of contract or compelled by specific performance to perform the contract. Where no such possibility existed there was no bargaining power in reality and no right to damages for loss of it. Hence damages for loss of bargaining power cannot be awarded where there is for example a contract for the sale of goods or generally a contract of employment[6].]

The Court of Appeal refused to accept this submission, and ordered nominal damages only. Dillon LJ rejected the whole notion of damages for 'loss of bargaining power':

> ... in theory every time there is a breach of contract the injured party is deprived of his 'bargaining power' to negotiate for a financial consideration a variation of the contract which would enable the party who wants to depart from its terms to do what he wants to do. In addition it has been held in *Walford v Miles*[7], that an agreement to negotiate is not an animal known to the law and a duty to negotiate in good faith is unworkable in practice – and so I find it difficult to see why loss of bargaining or negotiating power should become an established factor in the assessment of damages for breach of contract[8].

Other than 'loss of bargaining power', Dillon LJ said, the claimants had suffered no loss. They could not apply the principles of Lord Cairns' Act[9] because they did not want an injunction, but only damages 'at common law'. *Wrotham Park* did not apply because the case at hand was not a case under the Lord Cairns' Act jurisdiction.

Rose LJ agreed with Dillon LJ, but added that it was also a significant distinction between the case at hand and *Wrotham Park*, that not only had the claimants never wanted to enforce the covenant by injunction, they had also waited five years to attempt to enforce it by an action for damages. It was therefore 'inconceivable' that they would have been granted an injunction if they had asked for one, and so damages in lieu were equally inconceivable.

Steyn LJ said that *Wrotham Park* was rightly decided, and that it 'is only defensible on the basis of the ... restitutionary principle'[10], describing the claimants' 'loss of bargaining opportunity' theory as 'a fiction'[11]. Steyn LJ, however, characterised *Wrotham Park* as case in which there had been an invasion of property rights[12], and he refused to extend the 'restitutionary' principle in contract damages into cases in which no invasion of property rights was involved. In particular, Steyn LJ said that he could not accept the claimants' fourth condition that the application of the restitutionary principle should depend on the availability of specific remedies such as injunctions and specific performance. He did not want the restitutionary principle to apply to contracts such as charterparties and affreightment, where negative injunctions are available, and in any case:

> ... why should the availability of a restitutionary remedy, as a matter of legal entitlement, be dependent on the availability of the wholly different and discretionary remedies of injunctions specific to performance? If there is merit in the argument I cannot see any sense in restricting a compensatory remedy which serves

to protect the restitutionary interests to cases where there would be separate remedies of specific performance or injunction, designed directly and indirectly to enforce payment, available[13].

He added an attack on the very idea that restitutionary concepts should have wide application in damages for breach of contract:

The introduction of restitutionary remedies to deprive cynical contract breakers of the fruits of their breaches of contract will lead to greater uncertainty in the assessment of damages in commercial and consumer disputes[14].

Further:

[A] widespread availability of restitutionary remedies will have a tendency to discourage economic activity in relevant situations. In a range of cases such liability would fall on underwriters who have insured relevant liability risks. Inevitably underwriters would have to be compensated for the new species of potential claims. Insurance premiums would have to go up. That, too, is a consequence which militates against the proposed extension[15].

1   [1993] 3 All ER 705.
2   The granting of the new planning permission in contradiction of the council's own contractual rights might seem surprising, but planning law does not permit the council to take into account non-planning matters, such as the existence of covenants, in deciding whether to grant or refuse planning permission.
3   [1992] 3 All ER 302.
4   [1993] 3 All ER 705 at 709, per Dillon LJ. There was probably more to it than this. It is clear that the claimants were embarrassed politically by any suggestion that they should support the demolition of the houses. At first instance, the judge invited the councils to change their claim to one for a mandatory injunction. Counsel replied that he was reluctant to do so, and said that, 'if leave to amend were granted, the plaintiffs would undertake not to pursue the claim for mandatory relief embodied in the new prayer'. The councils insisted throughout that their claim was for 'common law' damages and not for damages 'in equity' under the Lord Cairns' Act jurisdiction, presumably because they did not want to be seen to be asking, even in theory, for an injunction forcing the demolition of the houses. The judges at all levels seem airily unaware of the political dimensions of the case – Rose LJ in the Court of Appeal, for example said that the reason the councils did not seek an injunction was simply that 'there [was] no harm to their adjoining land'. Whether the judges were really unaware of the political dimensions of the case is, of course, a different question.
5   [1993] 3 All ER 705 at 712, per Dillon LJ.
6   The words in square brackets were a late substitution for the original submission which read: 'if the profit results from the avoidance of expenditure, the expenditure would not have been economically wasteful or grossly disproportionate to the benefit which would have resulted from it'.
7   [1992] 2 AC 128.
8   [1993] 3 All ER 705 at 713, per Dillon LJ. For the theoretical underpinnings of the 'loss of bargaining opportunity' view, see Sharpe and Waddams 'Damages for Lost Opportunity to Bargain' (1982) 2 OJLS 290.
9   See above, para 11.5.
10   Steyn LJ cited *MacGregor on Damages* and Birks 'Civil Wrongs: A New World' in *Butterworths Lectures 1990–1991* (1992), p 71 in support of this proposition.
11   [1993] 3 All ER 705 at 714.
12   Citing *Tito v Waddell (No 2)* [1977] Ch 106 at 335; and *Bracewell v Appleby* [1975] Ch 408.
13   [1993] 3 All ER 705.
14   [1993] 3 All ER 705 at 715. Not surprisingly, Steyn LJ's views were not well-received in some quarters. See Birks 'Profits of Breach of Contract' (1993) 109 LQR 518 and Goff and Jones *Law of Restitution* (5th edn, 1998), p 518ff. Counsel for the defeated side in *Bredero* itself was, however, more equivocal on some of Steyn LJ's points – see Goodhart 'Restitutionary Damages for Breach of Contract' [1995] RLR 3 at 10.
15   [1993] 3 All ER 705 at 715. Goff and Jones state that there is no evidence for the view that the introduction of restitutionary damages will disrupt commercial life. It is true that many in business pay scant regard to contract law in their day-to-day dealings (see eg Macaulay 'Non-contractual relations in business' (1963) 55 American Sociological Review 5), so that not much subjective disruption would occur in business whatever changes to contract doctrine were introduced. But the effects of a change in the damages measure would make itself felt sooner or later, as Steyn LJ

points out, through liability insurance, whether that of contractors themselves or that of their professional advisers. Increased damages means increased insurance premiums. Increases in insurance premiums, being increases in the costs of production, can have any number of effects on the quality, quantity and prices of goods and services. See further below, para 11.20.

11.17   In *Jaggard v Sawyer*[1], a Lord Cairns' Act jurisdiction case concerning restrictive covenants which, if specifically enforced, would have made the defendant's property unusable and worthless, the Court of Appeal criticised Steyn LJ's view of *Wrotham Park*. Sir Thomas Bingham MR said:

> I cannot, however, accept that Brightman J's assessment of damages in *Wrotham Park* was based on other than compensatory principles. The defendants had committed a breach of covenant, the effects of which continued. The judge was not willing to order the defendants to undo the continuing effects of that breach. He had therefore to assess the damages necessary to compensate the plaintiffs for this continuing invasion of their right. He paid attention to the profits earned by the defendants, as it seems to me, not in order to strip the defendants of their unjust gains, but because of the obvious relationship between the profits earned by the defendants and the sum which the defendants would reasonably have been willing to pay to secure release from the covenant[2].

Millett LJ said, in similar vein:

> It is plain from his judgment in the *Wrotham Park* case that Brightman J's approach was compensatory, not restitutionary. He sought to measure the damages by reference to what the plaintiff had lost, not by reference to what the defendant had gained. He did not award the plaintiff the profit which the defendant had made by the breach, but the amount which he judged the plaintiff might have obtained as the price of giving its consent. The amount of the profit which the defendant expected to make was a relevant factor in that assessment, but that was all[3].

Millett LJ was also critical of Dillon LJ's approach in *Bredero* to the Lord Cairns' Act jurisdiction. He did not agree with Dillon LJ if Dillon LJ meant that there could be no claim under the Lord Cairns' Act jurisdiction just because the claimants had failed to include a claim for an injunction in their writ. But Millett LJ said that the claimants in *Bredero* could not have claimed a mandatory injunction anyway because at the time of trial the defendants no longer owned the houses in question[4]. Millett LJ also criticised Dillon LJ's approach to *Wrotham Park* for failing to appreciate that the point of damages in lieu, because they were a substitute for an injunction, was to compensate for the future as well as for the past, which was why Brightman J's 'capitalised royalty' approach made sense as compensation for loss[5].

1   [1995] 2 All ER 189. See below, para 12.32. Criticised by Goodhart 'Restitutionary Damages for Breach of Contract' [1995] RLR 3 at 7–8.
2   [1995] 2 All ER 189 at 202.
3   [1995] 2 All ER 189 at 211–212.
4   [1995] 2 All ER 189 at 210. Millett LJ does not, however, deal with the suggestion in *Bredero* that the defendant could have complied with an injunction to buy back the houses and demolish them.
5   [1995] 2 All ER 189 at 212.

11.18   In *Blake*, Lord Nicholls approves of *Wrotham Park* and disapproves of *Bredero*, in so far as it might be inconsistent with *Wrotham Park*[1]. He also mentions without disapproval the criticisms made of *Bredero* in *Jaggard v Sawyer*. But his view of *Wrotham Park* is deeply ambiguous:

> The *Wrotham Park* case ... still shines, rather as a solitary beacon, showing that in contract as well as tort damages are not always narrowly confined to recoupment of

financial loss. In a suitable case damages for breach of contract may be measured by the benefit gained by the wrongdoer from the breach. The defendant must make a reasonable payment in respect of the benefit he has gained[2].

This passage seems to conflate the *Jaggard v Sawyer* view of *Wrotham Park*, in which the relevance of the benefit gained by the defendant is only as an aid in setting the reasonable payment the defendant must make, and the Steyn LJ view of *Wrotham Park* in *Bredero* that *Wrotham Park* is about 'restitutionary' concepts. Lord Nicholls, of course, goes on to say that an account of profits should sometimes be available for breach of contract, and so one might say that therefore his analysis of *Wrotham Park* is more likely to mean that the *Wrotham Park* remedy is 'restitutionary'. But it is also clear that Lord Nicholls in the passage quoted is discussing a 'reasonable payment' remedy, and that if he thought that that *Wrotham Park* should be explained on a basis different from that put forward by the Court of Appeal in *Jaggard v Sawyer*, he would have openly criticised *Jaggard v Sawyer*, something he did not do. In addition, there is the obvious point that the award of a 5% royalty on profits is not the same as an account of profits, and that there is nothing in the accepted methods for taking an account which leads to a royalty measure.

In his separate speech in *Blake*, Lord Steyn refers without regret to his criticism in *Bredero* of attempts to broaden the scope of restitutionary damages for breach of contract beyond the proprietary cases[3], but, surprisingly, those criticisms fail to prevent his agreeing with Lord Nicholls's speech. Lord Steyn appears attracted to the Solicitor-General's four stage test[4] but he does not explain how this test would meet the point he made in *Bredero* that 'widespread availability' of restitutionary remedies for breach of contract would 'discourage economic activity in relevant situations'. We must conclude that Lord Steyn believes that such a test would not lead to 'widespread' restitutionary liability. Lord Steyn's endorsement of Lord Nicholls's approach suggests that Lord Steyn envisages that Lord Nicholls's approach will also not lead to the 'widespread' availability of restitutionary damages.

1   [2001] 1 AC 268 at 283.
2   [2001] 1 AC 268 at 283–284.
3   [2001] 1 AC 268 at 291.
4   See below, para 11.19.

The Solicitor-General's argument

11.19   The Solicitor-General argued in *Blake* that an account of profits should be available for breach of contract where:

(1)   There has been a breach of a negative stipulation.
(2)   The contract breaker has obtained the profit by doing the very thing which he promised not to do.
(3)   The innocent party (in this case the Crown as represented by the Attorney-General) has a special interest over and above the hope of a benefit to be assessed in monetary terms.
(4)   Specific performance or an injunction is an ineffective or virtually ineffective remedy for the breach[1].

Lord Steyn appears to approve of the Solicitor-General's submission, but he does not say so explicitly, commenting only that the Solicitor-General had satisfied him that each condition applied in the case at hand. Lord Steyn then went on to justify his decision to order an account of profits in more general terms[2]. Lord Nicholls does not mention the Solicitor-General's conditions for the application of an account of profits in terms, but he does express disapproval of the 'very thing which he promised not to do' condition at least as a ground in itself for ordering an account of profits[3]. Lord Nicholls, however, does seem to approve of the Solicitor-General's third condition, at least in the form of the 'legitimate interest' test, and the Solicitor-General's fourth condition seems to be reflected in his remarks on the relevance of the non-availability of specific remedies.

1   [2001] 1 AC 268 at 291.
2   [2001] 1 AC 268 at 291.
3   [2001] 1 AC 268 at 286.

Lord Hobhouse's dissent and the 'expropriation' of personal rights

11.20   In a powerful dissent in *Blake*, Lord Hobhouse points out that it is remarkable to order an account of profits when the defendant has not made the relevant profits at the claimant's expense, and has not in any way used the claimant's property[1]. In response, Lord Nicholls appears to support the view expressed by some academics[2] and the Israeli judges[3] that breach of contract can amount to expropriating the victim's contractual rights, in a way similar to the expropriation of the victim's property rights in a 'user principle' case, or a Lord Cairns' Act case, or an intellectual property case[4]. But even laying to one side the important point that the remedy in user principle cases, Lord Cairns' Act cases and even in many intellectual property cases is not an account of profits, but the quite different 'reasonable fee' measure[5], Lord Nicholls's response cannot explain the Sales of Goods Act position, that damages for breach are expectation-based as qualified by the mitigation and remoteness rules, not account of profits-based. In particular, the policy of the Sale of Goods Act is clearly that when the market moves in favour of the victim of a breach of contract, the defendant's liability to pay compensation for breach is reduced to the same extent, thus permitting the defendant to profit from a breach of contract[6]. The defendant is thus permitted to 'expropriate' the victim's contractual rights in the central example of a contract in English law – namely the contract of sale – a fact which should give theorists and Lord Nicholls some cause for concern. Furthermore, the commercial logic of the Sale of Goods Act is very different from that of the account of profits remedy. The Sale of Goods Act logic is that of the mitigation rule itself – that there is rarely any point allowing victims of breaches of contract to make the situation worse when they are in the better position to stop further losses[7]. The account of profits remedy deals with the mitigation problem in a very different way, that since there is no connection between the victim's loss and the amount of compensation, and the victim will receive the same amount regardless of the loss, the victim has an incentive to mitigate merely because the victim will bear any greater loss[8]. Lord Nicholls's position requires a radical separation of the Sale of Goods Act from the rest of contract law, which would be a wrenching break with the history of the law.

Moreover, Lord Nicholls's view would mean that the law would no longer offer more protection to property owners than it offers to contractors; it would be the ultimate stage in securitisation[9]. The law presently offers more protection to property ownership largely because property ownership carries expectations which do not vary according to the identities of people who might infringe them – the right to exclude others, for example, and the discretion to use or not to use the property[10] – they are expectations backed by rights which are good against the world; whereas contractual expectations relate only to a specific other person or set of persons, the risks of dealing with whom (including the risk that they will renege), are part of the risks the contractor has to take into account whether deciding to enter into the particular contract.

1   [2001] 1 AC 268 at 297.
2   See eg Smith 'Disgorgement of the profits of breach of contract: Property, contract and "efficient breach"'(1995) 24 Canadian Business Law Journal 121. But see contra Worthington 'Reconsidering disgorgement for wrongs' (1999) 62 MLR 218.
3   *Adras Building Material Ltd v Harlow & Jones GmbH* [1995] RLR 235, per Barak J.
4   See below, para 12.57ff.
5   See below, para 12.31ff. See also Chen-Wishart 'Restitutionary Damages for Breach of Contract' (1998) 114 LQR 363 and Mitchell 'Remedial Inadequacy in Contract and the Role of Restitutionary Damages' (1999) 15 Journal of Contract Law 133.
6   See eg *British Motor Trade v Gilbert* [1951] 2 All ER 641, [1951] WN 454, and see above, para 11.4, n 4.
7   See generally Goetz and Scott 'The Mitigation Principle: Toward a General Theory of Contractual Obligation' (1983) 69 Virginia Law Review 967; Posner 'Contract Remedies: Foreseeability, Precaution, Causation and Mitigation' *Encyclopedia of Law and Economics* (1999), para 4620.
8   Posner 'Contract Remedies: Foreseeability, Precaution, Causation and Mitigation' *Encyclopedia of Law and Economics* (1999), para 4620. The Law Com no 247 *Aggravated, Exemplary and Restitutionary Damages*, Pt III, para 1.47 (p 42), suggests that a reason for refusing to allow an account of profits is that it allows to claimant to evade the duty to mitigate. Economic analysis suggests that this would not be a problem, for the reason mentioned in the text.
9   There is a parallel between this issue and the different treatment in tort of negligently caused pure economic loss and negligently caused property damage. See Grubb (ed) *Law of Tort* (2002), para 12.187ff.
10   See below, para 12.24ff.

11.21   The 'expectation of performance' measure protects the promisee insofar as the promisee can rely on receiving either performance or compensation equivalent to performance, and the promisor can choose between performance and paying compensation. The 'account of profits' remedy transfers risk to the promisor, because it substantially reduces any incentive to renege, in the same way that the threat of an injunction or an order for specific performance reduces the incentive to renege. The obvious effect of the account of profits remedy is that it creates an incentive for promisors to add a premium to the contract, to cover the risk that circumstances might change, with the result that the promisor would find paying compensation cheaper than performance[1]. This is why Lord Hobhouse says 'if some more extensive principle of awarding non-compensatory damages for breach of contract is to be introduced into our commercial law the consequences will be very far reaching and disruptive'[2]. The lack of precision in the conditions of the application of the account of profits remedy makes the situation worse.

1   See Steyn LJ in the Court of Appeal in *Surrey County Council v Bredero Homes Ltd* [1993] 3 All ER 705 at 715. See above, para 11.15.
2   [2001] 1 AC 268 at 299. It is so far unclear whether *Blake* will be put to use in a commercial context; see for example the rather inconclusive *Esso Petroleum Co v Niad* (22 November 2001, unreported).

11.22   The ultimate test of a contract law doctrine is commercial practice. If the commercial reaction to the availability of an account of profits for breach is the growth of attempts to exclude that remedy by contractual terms, we will know that the introduction of the new remedy was a mistake, for all it will have achieved is a small addition to transaction costs. Indeed, the apparent rarity of contracts containing provisions for an account of profits in case of breach might suggest that, in commercial terms, the remedy is not thought to be worth the candle[1].

1   Admittedly another explanation for such an absence might be that accounts of profits clauses are thought to amount to penalties.

Envy and skimping

11.23   There are some situations in which A's beliefs about the degree of profit B will derive from the deal are relevant to whether A agrees to the deal with B. To discover the other side's bottom line is an important advantage in any negotiation. Moreover, there might be people whose concern for their dignity is such that they would prefer to lose all the benefits they could derive from a deal, if it brings the other side more benefits than they regard as fair.

But such considerations, if they should be relevant at all in contract law – for they seem to legitimise envy – seem to be most immediately relevant to misrepresentation rather than to the measure of damages for breach. If the defendant induced the claimant to enter into a contract by misrepresenting the profit the defendant expected to derive from the contract, it would seem that there has been a misrepresentation of fact (the defendant's state of mind) which might justify rescission.

11.24   What if, however, the circumstances are such that a representation about profitability counts as having been incorporated into the contract, in the form, for example, of a term that the defendant promises not to make more than a certain level of profit out of the deal (one might imagine a contract between a utility supplier and a governmental body in such a form)? In that case, one might be able to argue that the position in which the contract would have placed the claimant, had the contract been performed according to its terms, would have been one in which the defendant would have made less profit.

It is not clear, however, why all the extra profit in such a case should go to the claimant, since that would mean that the claimant in turn receives a benefit greater than that which the contract envisaged. The underlying reality seems to be that the pool of benefits produced by the contract has turned out to be greater than that which (at least one of) the parties anticipated. In such circumstances, one can argue just as readily for a distribution of the unanticipated benefits based on the proportions expected by the contract as for an account of profits. The argument for using the contractual proportions is that the parties agreed those proportions, and that there is no better estimate of what was acceptable to them. This solution would also be in line with the rule in the Sale of Goods Act 1979, s 30, that where the seller delivers the wrong quantity, one of the options the buyer has is to accept the wrong quantity at the contract price per item. The argument for the 'account of profits' measure is that it might act as a 'penalty default', inducing parties in the position of the defendant to reveal more of the information they hold about profitability in the process of negotiation, and thus facilitating 'fairer' deals[1].

1   See Ayres and Gertner 'Filling Gaps in Incomplete Contracts: An Economic Theory of Default Rules' (1989) 99 Yale Law Journal 87.

11.25   Examples of this kind of case are, however, lacking in English case law. The nearest to it has been the discussion of cases of 'skimping' in *A-G v Blake*[1]. In the Court of Appeal in *Blake*, Lord Woolf MR referred to an old Louisiana case, *City of New Orleans v Firemen's Charitable Association*[2]. Lord Woolf said:

> The defendant contracted with the plaintiff to provide a firefighting service and was paid the full contract price. After the expiry of the contract the plaintiff discovered

that the defendant had not provided the stipulated number of firemen or horses or the promised length of hosepipe. The defendant had saved itself substantial expense by the breach, but had not failed to put out any fires in consequence. The court ruled that the plaintiff had not proved that it had suffered any loss and was unable to recover more than nominal damages. Justice surely demands an award of substantial damages in such a case, and the amount of expenditure which the defendant has saved by the breach provides an appropriate measure of damages. This could be achieved by presuming that the plaintiff has suffered a loss of an amount corresponding to the amount by which he has been overcharged for the service actually provided; and the presumption could be justified by invoking the notion of 'the consumer surplus'. But it would surely be preferable, as well as simpler and more open, to award restitutionary damages[3].

'Skimping' is an example of unanticipated additional profits. Lord Woolf MR would hand all the additional profits to the claimant/buyer. But in the House of Lords in the same case Lord Nicholls responded:

> Nor does an account of profits seem to be needed in this context. The resolution of the problem of cases of skimped performance, where the plaintiff does not get what was agreed, may best be found elsewhere. If a shopkeeper supplies inferior and cheaper goods than those ordered and paid for, he has to refund the difference in price. That would be the outcome of a claim for damages for breach of contract. That would be so, irrespective of whether the goods in fact served the intended purpose. There must be scope for a similar approach, without any straining of principle, in cases where the defendant provided inferior and cheaper services than those contracted for[4].

That is, Lord Nicholls opts for the 'contractual proportions' approach rather than the 'account of profits' approach.

1   [2001] 1 AC 268.
2   9 So 486 (1891).
3   [1998] Ch 439 at 458.
4   [2001] 1 AC 268 at 286.

11.26   Some commentators say that *Ruxley Electronics and Construction Ltd v Forsyth*[1] is another example of skimping[2]. But *Ruxley* is not a case in which there is necessarily an unanticipated increase in the total benefits created by the contract. The benefit for the contractor might have increased, but the benefit for the buyer has decreased. The point is that the contractor has been overpaid *for what it supplied*[3]. The buyer has therefore undoubtedly lost compared to his expectation under the contract, because the buyer has paid the original price for less than the buyer expected. The question is, how to measure that loss. The House of Lords' view, that the decrease in the value of the swimming pool to the buyer is to be measured neither by the cost of repair nor the loss in value, but has to be represented by a sum which roughly reflects the buyer's disappointment, is perfectly in line with principle. Similarly, if a claimant has paid £100 for a luxury meal made with the freshest ingredients, but is served a meal made out of inferior tinned ingredients[4], it is not artificial to say that the claimant has made a loss. He has not received what he expected to receive, which is what constitutes loss in contract[5]. The question is, how to measure that loss. It does not seem unreasonable to measure it either by the market value of the dinner supplied[6] (as illustrated by the price of such dinners at inferior restaurants), or by the price a reasonable person in the position of the claimant would pay for such a dinner. There is no need at all to use the defendant's gain in profits by using the inferior ingredients.

1   [1996] AC 344.
2   See Virgo *Principles of the Law of Restitution* (1999), p 501ff. See also *White Arrow Express v Lamey's Distribution Ltd* [1995] NLJR 1504 (Beale 'Damages for Poor Service' (1996) 112 LQR 205).

3   Cf O'Sullivan 'Loss and Gain at Greater Depth: The implications of the *Ruxley* decision' in Rose (ed) *Failure of Contracts – Contractual, Restitutionary and Proprietary Consequences* (1997), p 1.
4   The example is that of Virgo *Principles of the Law of Restitution* (1999), p 503.
5   *McAlpine (Alfred) Construction Ltd v Panatown Ltd* [2001] 1 AC 518. See above, para 11.6.
6   Cf *White Arrow Express v Lamey's Distribution Ltd* [1995] NLJR 1504.

Imbalance in knowledge of benefits

11.27   Another set of circumstances in which defendants' profits on the deal might be relevant to claimants is where the claimants, but not the defendants, have no way of knowing what level of benefits they will derive from the contract. In other words, the claimant, but not the defendant, does not know what the size of the pool of benefits will be, and therefore cannot tell whether or not the distribution of benefits between the parties proposed in the contract is fair.

These situations are in practice usually characterised as giving rise to 'fiduciary duties' and, as such, have already been dealt with above[1]. As Lord Nicholls says in *Blake*:

> Equity reinforces the duty of fidelity owed by a trustee or fiduciary by requiring him to account for any profits he derives from his office or position. This ensures that trustees and fiduciaries are financially disinterested in carrying out their duties. They may not put themselves in a position where their duty and interest conflict. To this end they must not make any unauthorised profit. If they do, they are accountable. Whether the beneficiaries or persons to whom the fiduciary duty is owed suffered any loss by the impugned transaction is altogether irrelevant[2].

1   See above, ch 9.
2   [2001] 1 AC 268 at 280.

11.28   There are, however, relationships which are said not to give rise to fiduciary duties, which might also fall within the category of case in which the imbalance between the parties is such that the claimant does not know the size of the total pool of benefits to be created by the contract, and therefore cannot know whether the distribution of benefits is fair. For example, the relationship between doctors and patients is generally accepted in normal circumstances not to give rise to fiduciary duties[1]. But the patients of doctors in private practice do not really know what improvement in their situation is possible, and how likely each degree of improvement is, given different courses of treatment. Patients therefore cannot really judge whether the fees they are asked to pay are fair. It is possible to construct an argument that, where a doctor chooses a method of treatment which is more profitable for the doctor but less effective for the patient than another method of treatment (a method which the doctor does not mention to the patient), the patient should be able to recover the doctor's increased profits as damages for the breach of an implied contractual term that the doctor will take all reasonable care to act in the best interests of the patient's physical well-being[2] even if the patient is in no way made worse off by the treatment received[3].

1   *Sidaway v Board of Governors of Bethlem Royal Hospital* [1985] AC 871 at 884, per Lord Scarman. See also *Breen v Williams* (1995–1996) 186 CLR 71, 43 ALD 481. Of course doctors may receive confidential information from patients, and may be subject to the law of undue influence. See above, para 9.6.
2   The possibility of such an implied term is accepted even in *Breen v Williams* (1995–1996) 186 CLR 71, 43 ALD 481.
3   The field of cosmetic surgery seems the most likely to give rise to such a case in England. Cf *O'Keefe v Harvey-Kemble* (1998) 45 BMLR 74; *Williamson v East London and City Health Authority* (1997) 41 BMLR 85.

11.29   The speeches of the House of Lords in *A-G v Blake* can be interpreted in two ways on the question of whether an account of profits should be available in these circumstances. On the one hand, it could be argued that 'the subject matter of the contract, the purpose of the contractual provision which has been breached, the circumstances in which the breach occurred [and] the consequences of the breach' point in the direction of the claimant having 'a legitimate interest' in the doctor's not making an excessive profit. In addition, the effect of allowing an account of profits in such circumstances would be similar to that in *Blake* itself – just as *Blake* slightly extends the law of confidentiality, the extension discussed here would slightly extend the law of fiduciary relationships. On the other hand the claimant's interest, unlike in *Blake*, would not be in preventing the defendant making any profit at all, only in preventing an excessive profit. In addition, Lord Nicholls's point about 'skimping' appears to apply. The doctor has provided worse services than those contracted for, and so a proportional approach might be the appropriate solution, rather than an account of profits. The difference, however, is that the problem of the imbalance of information is paramount in the doctor-patient relationship, and so the information-forcing properties of the account of profits remedy are more attractive than in the *Ruxley* situation.

Breach of contract amounting to a breach of trust

11.30   It is possible for a breach of contract to amount to a breach of trust, and thus to give rise to an account of profit. For example, if the seller of land in breach of contract sells the land to a second purchaser, the seller must account for the profits in the second sale to the first purchaser[1]. Similarly, if the defendant uses the claimant's property in ways which go beyond the authorisation for such use in a contract between the parties, but the defendant nevertheless has lawful possession of the property, the defendant counts as a trustee of the property, and the breach of the contract in using the property in an unauthorised way amounts to a breach of trust for which the defendant must account[2].

1   *Lake v Bayliss* [1974] 1 WLR 1073.
2   *Reid-Newfoundland Co v Anglo-American Telegraph Co Ltd* [1912] AC 555. Distinguished in *Henry v Hammond* [1913] 2 KB 515. The defendants in *Reid-Newfoundland* were held to be constructive trustees (*Taylor v Davies* [1920] AC 636), which is why an account of profits was the appropriate remedy, not just reasonable fee damages under the 'user principle'. See above, para 9.32, and below, para 12.34ff.

11.31   More generally, some of the relationships which give rise to fiduciary duties, for example agent and principal, director and company, partner and co-partner, will often also be governed by a contract and the acts which constitute breaches of their fiduciary duties may also constitute breaches of contract[1].

In all these cases, however, it is the fiduciary nature of the relationship, whether or not created by contract, which gives rise to the obligation to account, not the contractual obligation alone. Theorists have objected that the use of the fiduciary concept in these circumstances is so unclear, that it must be the case that it is being used merely to disguise the use of restitutionary damages when it would be better openly to recognise what is happening[2]. Yet there is no sign in the positive law of the abandonment of the fiduciary concept. The House of Lords in *Blake* has, however, allowed the use of a fiduciary remedy in a situation which is close to, but which is not, a fiduciary relationship. As in other boundary problems in the law, for example the problem of pure economic loss at the boundary between contract and tort, the similarities in the nature of the underlying disputes produce a constant temptation to reach across the boundary for concepts to use in making decisions about those disputes. This process can in time lead to a reclassification of certain disputes from one side of the boundary to the other, but it need not do so, especially if there are significant pressures in the opposite direction, for example differences in procedure and limitation.

1   See above, ch 9. See further Oakley *Constructive Trusts* (3rd edn, 1997), p 87ff.
2   Birks 'Restitutionary Damages for Breach of Contract' (1987) Lloyd's Maritime and Commercial Law Quarterly 421.

CHAPTER 12

Torts and Miscellaneous Other Wrongs

David Howarth

A   Torts

12.1   Tort law and restitution law are not, in English law, integrated into a single system. Tort law 'has yet to recognise a general principle requiring the defendant to account for profit derived from his tortious conduct'[1]. Moreover, an action for money had and received is not itself an 'action in tort'[2]. Whatever the position in other legal systems or in the hopes of legal theorists, the practical position remains that tort law and restitution law should be treated as intersecting circles, not as parts of the same universe.

1   Grubb (ed) *Law of Tort* (2002), para 6.33. But see the discussion below, para 12.54ff.
2   *Chesworth v Farrar* [1967] 1 QB 407, [1966] 2 All ER 107.

'Waiver of tort'

12.2   Discussion of the relationship between tort law and restitution is sometimes dogged by the elegant but misleading term 'waiver of tort'. Use of the phrase 'waiver of tort' can give the impression that a claimant can, by ignoring or forgiving a tort, create a restitutionary right, such as a right to an action for money had and received. For the most part[1], such usage is nonsensical. As Lord Atkin said,

> ... in the ordinary case the plaintiff has never the slightest intention of waiving, excusing or in any kind of way palliating the tort. If I find that a thief has stolen my securities and is in possession of the proceeds, when I sue him for them I am not excusing him. I am protesting violently that he is a thief and because of his theft, I am suing him ... [2]

Instead the situation is, ex hypothesi, one in which the claimant has both a right to compensation for loss *and* a restitutionary right.

> The substance of the matter is that on certain facts [the plaintiff] is claiming redress either in the form of compensation ie, damages as for a tort, or in the form of restitution of money to which he is entitled, but which the defendant has wrongfully received. The same set of facts entitles the plaintiff to claim either form of redress[3].

1   An exception is where there has been a real, as opposed to a notional, ratification in an agency case, see *Verschures Creameries v Hull & Netherlands Steamship Co* [1921] 2 KB 608 as explained in *United Australia Ltd v Barclays Bank Ltd* [1941] AC 1 at 51–52, [1940] 4 All ER 20 at 51–52, per Lord Porter.
2   *United Australia Ltd v Barclays Bank Ltd* [1941] AC 1 at 28–29, [1940] 4 All ER 20 at 36–37.
3   *United Australia Ltd v Barclays Bank Ltd* [1941] AC 1 at 19, [1940] 4 All ER 20 at 30, per Viscount Simon LC.

12.3   The right to the two remedies can either arise out of the tort itself or from two separate legal doctrines – with a tort giving rise to the compensatory remedy and some other doctrine giving rise to the restitutionary remedy. Where the right to the two remedies arises from the same tort, 'waiver of tort' simply means that the claimant cannot add the proceeds of the two remedies together, but must choose, or 'elect', between them[1]. The remedies are incompatible, even though there is no inconsistency in asserting the underlying right[2]. Where the two remedies arise out of two different legal rules, there may be an inconsistency in asserting the two rights, in the sense, for example, that to win on one basis the claimant has to assert a fact which would defeat its claim on the other basis[3]. But where there is no such inconsistency of rights, 'waiver of tort' still means merely that there is an incompatibility of remedies, and that the claimant cannot add together the proceeds of the two causes of action, but must choose one or the other. 'What was waived by the judgment was not the tort, but the right to recover damages for the tort'[4].

1   *United Australia Ltd v Barclays Bank Ltd* [1941] AC 1 at 28, [1940] 4 All ER 20 at 36, per Lord Atkin; *Tang Man Sit v Capacious Investments Ltd* [1996] AC 514, [1996] 1 All ER 193, PC.
2   *Tang Man Sit v Capacious Investments Ltd* [1996] AC 514, [1996] 1 All ER 193, PC.
3   For the distinction between an inconsistency of rights and an inconsistency of remedies see Lord Atkin in *United Australia Ltd v Barclays Bank Ltd* [1941] AC 1 at 29–30; Lord Wilberforce in *Johnson v Agnew* [1980] AC 367 at 396; Lord Nicholls in *Tang Man Sit v Capacious Investments Ltd* [1996] AC 514 at 521–522; Robert Walker LJ in *Oliver Ashworth (Holdings) Ltd v Ballard (Kent) Ltd* [2000] Ch 12 at 27–28.
4   *United Australia Ltd v Barclays Bank Ltd* [1941] AC 1 at 34, [1940] 4 All ER 20 at 40, per Lord Romer

12.4   Where there is an inconsistency of rights[1], the position is more complicated, but, in the context of torts, there is often no practical difference from the position in the other possibilities already considered, since the claimant can be counted as not having elected between the two rights until judgment. The choice between the rights is effectively counted as a choice between remedies[2]. Alternatively, and more radically than is perhaps strictly necessary, in *Lissenden v CAV Bosch Ltd*[3] Viscount Maugham implied that cases of 'waiver of tort' are 'mainly' to be treated as choices between remedies, rather than choices between rights in the first place. Lord Atkin in the same case, alluding perhaps to *Verschures Creameries v Hull & Netherlands Steamship Co*[4], points out that election between the liability of principal and agent is possibly an exception to any such general rule, for in that case where the 'person to whom the choice belongs irrevocably and with knowledge adopts the one, he cannot afterwards assert the other'. As the Law Commission comments, 'In this situation, the tort is truly extinguished'[5].

1   See eg *Oliver Ashworth (Holdings) Ltd v Ballard (Kent) Ltd* [2000] Ch 12.
2   'At some stage of the proceedings the plaintiff must elect which remedy he will have. There is, however, no reason of principle or convenience why that stage should be deemed to be reached until the plaintiff applies for judgment': per Viscount Simon LC, [1941] AC 1 at 19, [1940] 4 All ER 20 at 30. 'On a question of alternative remedies, no question of election arises until one or other claim has been brought to judgment. Up to that stage the plaintiff may pursue both remedies together, or pursuing one, may amend and pursue the other, but he can take judgment only for the one ... ': per Lord Atkin, [1941] AC 1 at 30, [1940] 4 All ER 20 at 38.
3   [1940] AC 412, [1940] 1 All ER 425.
4   [1921] 2 KB 608. See above, para 12.2, n 1.
5   Law Com no 247 *Aggravated, Exemplary and Restitutionary Damages*, Pt III, para 1.7 (p 30).

12.5   The conclusion that 'waiver of tort', in the usual sense of claiming a restitutionary remedy such as money had and received in the place of damages, does not involve a conflict of rights, but merely a conflict of remedies, is supported by Viscount Simon's important remark in *United Australia Ltd v Barclays Bank Ltd* that:

> When the plaintiff 'waived the tort' and brought assumpsit, he did not thereby elect to be treated from that time forward on the basis that no tort had been committed; indeed, if it were to be understood that no tort had been committed, how could an action in assumpsit lie? It lies only because the acquisition of the defendant is wrongful and there is thus an obligation to make restitution[1].

This remark shows that in these cases, the underlying 'right' (the 'right' that the defendant not commit the relevant 'wrong') is the same for the two remedies. The claimant is not saying that the 'wrong' did not take place, for otherwise there would be no basis for the claim to a restitutionary remedy.

1   [1941] AC 1 at 18, [1940] 4 All ER 20 at 29.

12.6   Whether the relevant elections occur at judgment or later, at the point of recovery for example, has not always been entirely clear. In *Tang Man Sit v Capacious Investments Ltd*[1], however, the Privy Council attempted a clarification. Lord Nicholls said that normally the claimant has to elect at judgment, but the court had jurisdiction to require further disclosure by the defendant, to assist the claimant in making the choice[2], and if the situation was plausibly one in which the claimant was still investigating the magnitude of the larger measure, but had accepted a payment based on the lower measure as an interim payment, it was inequitable to treat the claimant as having elected the lower measure. Similarly, in *Johnson v Agnew*[3] the House of Lords allowed an order for specific performance to be discharged where it had failed to be brought to fruition, and ordered an inquiry as to damages. Lord Wilberforce said, 'Election, though the subject of much learning and refinement, is in the end a doctrine based on simple considerations of common sense and equity'[4].

Lord Nicholls further explained in *Tang Man Sit v Capacious Investments Ltd*[5], that confusion had arisen by failing to distinguish between cases in which the remedies were incompatible ('alternative remedies'), such as compensatory damages and an account of profits, and cases in which the remedies claimed were perfectly compatible ('cumulative remedies'), such as claims against different people for the damages for the same wrong[6]. In the latter type of case, there was no need for 'election' at all[7], but where damages had actually been recovered from one defendant, it will often be right to deduct those damages from the damages claimable from other defendants. In cases of compatible remedies, therefore, satisfaction was the important event, rather than judgment[8].

1   [1996] AC 514, [1996] 1 All ER 193.
2   See eg *Island Records Ltd v Tring International plc* [1995] 3 All ER 444.
3   [1980] AC 367, [1979] 1 All ER 883.
4   [1980] AC 367 at 398, [1979] 1 All ER 883 at 894.
5   [1996] AC 514, [1996] 1 All ER 193.
6   'The law frequently affords an injured person more than one remedy for the wrong he has suffered. Sometimes the two remedies are alternative and inconsistent. The classic example, indeed, is (1) an account of the profits made by a defendant in breach of his fiduciary obligations and (2) damages for the loss suffered by the plaintiff by reason of the same breach. The former is measured by the wrongdoer's gain, the latter by the injured party's loss. Sometimes the two remedies are cumulative. Cumulative remedies may lie against one person. A person fraudulently induced to enter into a contract may have the contract set aside and also sue for damages. Or there may be cumulative remedies against more than one person. A plaintiff may have a cause of action in negligence against two persons in respect of the same loss': *Tang Man Sit v Capacious Investments Ltd* [1996] AC 514 at 521, [1996] 1 All ER 193 at 197.
7   'Faced with alternative and inconsistent remedies a plaintiff must choose between them. Faced

with cumulative remedies a plaintiff is not required to choose. He may have both remedies. He may pursue one remedy or the other remedy or both remedies, just as he wishes. It is a matter for him. He may obtain judgment for both remedies and enforce both judgments. When the remedies are against two different people, he may sue both persons. He may do so concurrently, and obtain judgment against both. Damages to the full value of goods which have been converted may be awarded against two persons for successive conversions of the same goods. Or the plaintiff may sue the two persons successively. He may obtain judgment against one, and take steps to enforce the judgment. This does not preclude him from then suing the other': *Tang Man Sit v Capacious Investments Ltd* [1996] AC 514 at 522, [1996] 1 All ER 193 at 198, PC.

8 '[A] plaintiff cannot recover in the aggregate from one or more defendants an amount in excess of his loss. Part satisfaction of a judgment against one person does not operate as a bar to the plaintiff thereafter bringing an action against another who is also liable, but it does operate to reduce the amount recoverable in the second action. However, once a plaintiff has fully recouped his loss, of necessity he cannot thereafter pursue any other remedy he might have and which he might have pursued earlier. Having recouped the whole of his loss, any further proceedings would lack a subject matter. This principle of full satisfaction prevents double recovery': *Tang Man Sit v Capacious Investments Ltd* [1996] AC 514 at 522, [1996] 1 All ER 193 at 199. The court also pointed out some other limitations on the freedom of the claimant to pursue these remedies separately: 'One limitation is the so-called rule in *Henderson v Henderson* (1843) 3 Hare 100, [1843–60] All ER Rep 378. In the interests of fairness and finality a plaintiff is required to bring forward his whole case against a defendant in one action. Another limitation is that the court has power to ensure that, when fairness so requires, claims against more than one person shall all be tried and decided together': [1996] AC 514 at 522, [1996] 1 All ER 193 at 198–199.

12.7   The existence of third parties in 'waiver' cases is another possible complication. In *United Australia Ltd v Barclays Bank Ltd*[1] the House of Lords held that, where the claimant had started an action for a restitutionary remedy against one defendant, it was not thereby precluded from bringing an action for compensatory damages against a second defendant. The main reason for the result was that merely beginning an action does not count as 'waiving' the tort – the case against the first defendant would have had to proceed at least to judgment for that to have happened. But Lord Atkin went further:

> I think it necessary to add that even if the tort had been waived, or the plaintiff had made any final election against [the first defendant], I fail to see why that should have any effect upon their claims against the [second defendant]. If a thief steals the plaintiff's goods worth 500*l* and sells them to a receiver for 50*l* who sells them to a fourth party for 400*l*, if I find the thief and he hands over to me the 50*l*, or I sue him for it and recover judgment I can no longer sue him for damages for the value of the goods, but why should that preclude me from suing the two receivers for damages[2].

Lord Porter said in support of the same conclusion:

> [T]he substance is the right of the plaintiff to recover property or its proceeds from one who has wrongfully received them and if the realities of the matter are kept in mind I see no reason why the party deprived of his property should be precluded from suing a second wrongdoer either in trover or for money had and received because he had previously sued another wrongdoer in assumpsit, nor do I see any difference in substance between a case where the plaintiff sues successive wrongdoers in conversion (in which he can admittedly recover judgment against each) and a case in which he proceeds against the first defendant in assumpsit and not trover[3].

In *Tang Man Sit v Capacious Investments Ltd*[4], Lord Nicholls explains that these passages are explicable in terms of the distinction between incompatible ('alternative') and compatible ('cumulative') remedies[5]. Lord Nicholls said:

> [T]he remedies of [the claimant] against [the first defendant] on the one hand and the [second defendant] on the other hand were cumulative, not alternative. Accordingly the earlier proceedings against [the first defendant] could not bar the company subsequently bringing fresh proceedings against the bank unless the company had recouped the whole of its loss in the earlier proceedings[6].

Thus, even if there has been a waiver with regard to one defendant, there will be no effect on other defendants against whom compatible or 'cumulative' remedies can be claimed unless there has been some form of execution.

1   [1941] AC 1, [1940] 4 All ER 20.
2   [1941] AC 1 at 31, [1940] 4 All ER 20 at 38.
3   [1941] AC 1 at 54, [1940] 4 All ER 20 at 53.
4   [1996] AC 514, [1996] 1 All ER 193.
5   'The leading authority on the subject of election is the decision of the House of Lords in *United Australia Ltd v Barclays Bank Ltd*. Contrary to the view sometimes expressed, there is no inconsistency between the various speeches in that case if the different considerations applicable to alternative remedies and cumulative remedies are kept firmly in mind': Lord Nicholls in *Tang Man Sit v Capacious Investments Ltd* [1996] AC 514 at 522–523, [1996] 1 All ER 193 at 199.
6   [1996] AC 514 at 523, [1996] 1 All ER at 200.

12.8   Regardless of these complications, it should be noted that nothing in them removes the necessity for the claimant to show that, on at least one interpretation of the facts before the court, there is a legal doctrine, whether as part of tort law or otherwise, which gives rise to a right to a restitutionary remedy. If there is only a right to compensatory damages in the first place, no amount of 'waiving' it can give rise to a right to a restitutionary remedy[1]. The right to a restitutionary remedy must be justified separately, either as arising out of the tort itself or on some other basis. In this chapter we consider examples of the former, where the right to a restitutionary remedy arises out of the tort itself[2]. The combination of a tort with the latter, where the right to a restitutionary remedy arises independently of the tort, lies strictly outside the scope of this chapter.

1   *Stoke-on-Trent City Council v W & J Wass Ltd* [1988] 3 All ER 394, [1988] 1 WLR 1406. Similarly, a right to one restitutionary remedy does not automatically establish that there is a right to a different restitutionary remedy.
2   Cf Law Com no 247 *Aggravated, Exemplary and Restitutionary Damages*, Pt III, paras 1.1 and 1.8.

Tort damages – general

12.9   The standard remedy for torts in English law is the award of damages. Exceptionally, for example in the tort of nuisance, the standard remedy is the award of an injunction. The measure of damages is normally compensatory, which is to say that claimants are to be put back, so far as a monetary award can achieve this, into the position they were in before the tort damaged them[1]. Compensation can also include sums to recompense the claimant not only for the fact the tort caused the claimant loss, but also, in the form of 'aggravated damages', for the way in which the defendant inflicted the harm[2]. Compensation can also include amounts which attempt to anticipate future losses as well as amounts for losses which have already occurred. (Where injunctions are awarded, however, at least as a matter of principle, the injunction itself is taken to prevent future additional losses, so that only losses which the injunction itself cannot now prevent are eligible for compensation.) But compensation is not without more taken to include benefits taken by the defendant as a result of the tort. 'Damages are measured by the plaintiff's loss, not by the defendant's gain'[3].

The rest of this section therefore considers not a general principle, but a set of particular circumstances, cases in which, exceptionally, torts can give rise to restitutionary remedies of one form or other[4].

1   See eg *Livingstone v Rawyards Coal Co* (1880) 5 App Cas 25 at 39, per Lord Blackburn.
2   Grubb (ed) *Law of Tort* (2002), para 6.29.

3 Lord Nicholls in *A-G v Blake* [2001] 1 AC 268 at 278, [2000] 4 All ER 385 at 391.
4 See *Stoke-on-Trent City Council v W & J Wass Ltd* [1988] 1 WLR 1406; and *Halifax Building Society v Thomas* [1996] Ch 217, [1995] 4 All ER 673.

EXEMPLARY DAMAGES

12.10   Exceptionally, damages beyond the amount necessary to compensate the claimant, namely exemplary or punitive damages, can be awarded in tort cases[1]. Currently, English law takes a restrictive view of the circumstances in which exemplary damages may be awarded[2]. Except where there is explicit statutory authorisation[3], exemplary damages may be awarded only where there has been 'oppressive, arbitrary or unconstitutional action' by a servant of the state, or where the defendant's wrongful conduct was 'calculated by him to make a profit for himself which may well exceed the compensation payable to the plaintiff'[4]. It should be noted, however, that in *Kuddus v Chief Constable of Leicestershire Police*[5], at least one of their Lordships was prepared to widen the scope of exemplary damages[6]. The Law Commission also favours the widening of the availability of exemplary damages (or 'punitive damages', as it prefers). The formula favoured by the Law Commission is that punitive damages should be available in all cases in which the defendant has 'deliberately and outrageously disregarded' the claimant's rights. The Law Commission also favours the availability of restitutionary damages on the same basis.

1 Grubb (ed) *Law of Tort* (2002), para 6.21ff.
2 Grubb (ed) *Law of Tort* (2002), para 6.22.
3 Whether there are any such statutes is a matter of dispute. See Grubb (ed) *Law of Tort* (2002), para 6.22, and Law Commission Consultation Paper 132 *Aggravated, Exemplary and Restitutionary Damages* (1993), p 65.
4 *Rookes v Barnard* [1964] AC 1129 at 1226.
5 [2001] UKHL 29, [2001] 3 All ER 193, [2001] 2 WLR 1789.
6 Viz Lord Nicholls: 'On occasion conscious wrongdoing by a defendant is so outrageous, his disregard of the claimant's rights so contumelious, that something more is needed to show that the law will not tolerate such behaviour': [2001] 3 All ER 193 at 210, [2001] 2 WLR 1789.

12.11   The second of the two currently established categories gives rise to a form of restitution, although its basis is not merely the defendant's profit motive, but rather the defendant's 'outrageous conduct' in having such a motive in the circumstances.

The second category has been applied, for example, to cases of wrongful eviction of tenants[1] and to cases of defamation[2].

The existence of the category itself was doubted by Lord Scott in *Kuddus v Chief Constable of Leicestershire Police*[3]. Lord Scott said:

> Lord Devlin's second category, cases in which the defendant's wrongful conduct has made a profit for himself which exceeds the compensation payable to the victim of the conduct, has been largely overtaken by developments in the common law. Restitutionary damages are available now in many tort actions as well as those for breach of contract. The profit made by a wrongdoer can be extracted from him without the need to rely on the anomaly of exemplary damages: see the discussion of the topic in *A-G v Blake*[4] ...

These remarks are, however, puzzling. Lord Scott refers to Lord Nicholls' speech in *Blake*, but at no point in that speech does Lord Nicholls refer to exemplary or punitive damages, or to tort law in general. The nearest Lord Nicholls comes to discussing tort law is when he refers to 'Interference with rights of property'. It is not clear, for example, what relevance Lord Nicholls' speech would have to a defamation case, which is one of the main areas of the application of Lord Devlin's second category. Is Lord Scott saying that 'restitutionary damages' are not to be available in defamation cases, on the ground that Lord Nicholls' speech in *Blake* could not apply to such cases? Or is he saying that such damages are available in defamation cases on some other ground, which he does not need to discuss? Moreover, Lord Scott gives the impression that Lord Nicholls' speech in *Blake* has set out clear and specific criteria for the award of restitutionary damages in contract, criteria which are applicable to tort. This is far from the case[5]. It should be noted that Lord Scott's remarks were not endorsed by the rest of the court, and were not pertinent to the case at hand.

1   See eg *Drane v Evangelou* [1978] 2 All ER 437, [1978] 1 WLR 455; *Francis v Brown* (1997) 30 HLR 143; *Mehta v Royal Bank of Scotland* [1999] 3 EGLR 153.
2   See eg *John v MGN Ltd* [1997] QB 586; *Rantzen v Mirror Group Newspapers (1986) Ltd* [1994] QB 670, [1993] 4 All ER 975; *Riches v News Group Newspapers Ltd* [1986] QB 256.
3   [2001] UKHL 29, [2001] 3 All ER 193, [2001] 2 WLR 1789.
4   [2001] 3 All ER 193 at 222, [2001] 2 WLR 1789 at 1819, referring to [2000] 4 All ER 385 at 391–394, [2001] 1 AC 268 at 278–280, per Lord Nicholls of Birkenhead.
5   See discussion above, para 11.7ff.

12.12   The exact formulation of the second category is however in some doubt, since, as Lord Nicholls pointed out in *Kuddus v Chief Constable of Leicestershire Police*[1], it is not clear why there should have to be specifically an intention to *profit*, as opposed to any sort of malicious motive. Even in its original formulation, the purpose of the rule is said to be 'to teach a wrongdoer that tort does not pay'[2], a lesson the need for which is not to confined to cases in which there is a specific monetary motive. The gaining of property was therefore covered from the start[3]. The rule has subsequently been said to apply to all cases in which defendants were 'seeking to gain some object at the expense of the claimant', which either they 'could not properly or lawfully gain at all', or which they 'could only get at a price in excess of what they were prepared to pay'[4]. Only the latter is clearly a form of 'profit'. The former is much wider, and seems to potentially to include acting on any wrongful motive. It will also be noticed that there is some slippage here, from 'object' in the sense of a thing or specific piece of property, to 'object' in the sense of an 'objective', that is any state of affairs preferred or found valuable by the defendant.

Intention, or even motive, is, however, crucial. It is not enough that the defendant did in fact profit from the tort. The claimant must show that the defendant was motivated by a desire to benefit from the violation of the claimant's rights[5]. Material advantage must have been *a reason* for committing the tort[6]. Thus, the fact that the tort took place in the course of a commercial activity, such as publishing a newspaper, is not in itself enough to ground an award of exemplary damages[7]. On the other hand it is not necessary, when attempting to demonstrate that the defendant acted on a desire to benefit, to show that the defendant went through the kind of mathematical calculation to be found on a balance sheet[8]. It is also not necessary to show that the defendant specifically thought that the compensatory damages a court would normally award would be less than the defendant's gain. The defendant might equally have been relying on the claimant's lack of resources to launch an action, or the claimant's fear of extra-judicial reprisals or loss of reputation[9].

1   [2001] UKHL 29, [2001] 3 All ER 193, [2001] 2 WLR 1789.
2   *Cassell & Co Ltd v Broome* [1972] AC 1027 at 1130, per Lord Diplock.
3   Lord Devlin in *Rookes v Barnard* [1964] AC 1129 at 1227.

4 See also Stuart-Smith LJ in *AB v South West Water Services Ltd, Gibbons v South West Water Services Ltd* [1993] QB 507, [1993] 1 All ER 609.
5 *John v MGN Ltd* [1997] QB 586 at 618–619, per Sir Thomas Bingham MR.
6 *Cassell v Broome* [1972] AC 1027 at 1079, per Lord Hailsham LC.
7 *Cassell v Broome* [1972] AC 1027 at 1079, per Lord Hailsham LC.
8 *Cassell v Broome* [1972] AC 1027 at 1078, per Lord Hailsham LC.
9 *Cassell v Broome* [1972] AC 1027 at 1079, per Lord Hailsham LC.

12.13   In addition, regardless of the general rules for the tort concerned, intention or recklessness is required in the commission of the tort. The defendant must have either consciously violated the claimant's rights, or not cared whether the claimant's rights were being violated or not[1]. Carelessness is not enough[2].

It is not clear whether intentionally continuing a tort is enough for the purposes of the requirement of intentionality or recklessness. In *AB v South West Water Services Ltd*[3], Stuart-Smith LJ said that where the defendants had deliberately continued the tort of nuisance in an attempt to disguise their conduct, the second rule did not apply[4]. *AB* was overruled on other grounds in *Kuddus v Chief Constable of Leicestershire Police*[5], and so the status of Stuart-Smith LJ's remarks is now uncertain. It is submitted that, in a continuing tort such as nuisance, it makes no sense to separate 'committing' the tort and 'continuing' it. Continuing the tort *is* committing the tort. It follows that Stuart-Smith LJ's view should not now be treated as authoritative[6]. Stuart-Smith LJ's remarks might be attributed to an excess of zeal in hostility to the very concept of exemplary damages, a point of view which only one judge in the House of Lords, Lord Scott, appears unequivocally to share in *Kuddus v Chief Constable of Leicestershire Police*.

1 *Cassell v Broome* [1972] AC 1027 at 1079, per Lord Hailsham LC. See also *Riches v News Group Newspapers Ltd* [1986] QB 256; and *John v MGN Ltd* [1997] QB 586.
2 *Riches v News Group Newspapers Ltd* [1986] QB 256. In the context of jury trials in defamation cases it is necessary for the judge to take care lest the jury misunderstand 'not caring' as 'careless', and so another formulation involving the defendant's genuine belief of what it had published ought to be used. See per Sir Thomas Bingham in *John v MGN Ltd* [1997] QB 586 at 618.
3 Aka *Gibbons v South West Water Services Ltd* [1993] QB 507.
4 [1993] QB 507 at 526.
5 [2001] UKHL 29, [2001] 3 All ER 193, [2001] 2 WLR 1789.
6 In this I have the misfortune to disagree with my colleague Alistair Mullis in Grubb (ed) *Law of Tort* (2002), para 6.25.

12.14   The fact that intention or recklessness is a *requirement* for an award of exemplary damages in tort does not justify the conclusion that intentional or reckless wrongdoing automatically authorises the award of exemplary damages. If the law were otherwise, every intentional tort would give rise to exemplary damages without proof of loss. Exemplary damages are a remedy for situations in which torts have been committed in a certain way. The availability of such damages cannot affect the question of what has to be proved to establish that the tort has been committed. That the defendant profited by doing wrong intentionally or recklessly is not enough without proof of such loss.

As long ago as *Pasley v Freeman* Ashhurst J said in relation to deceit or fraud:

> ... the gist of the action is the injury done to the plaintiff, and not whether the defendant meant to be a gainer by it: what is it to the plaintiff whether the defendant was or was not to gain by it; the injury to him is the same[1].

The requirement of there being a loss is important. If a fraud in the event leads to no loss to the claimant, the fact that the defendant made a profit is not actionable in itself[2].

But note that this line of argument does not necessarily rule out restitutionary damages, in the form of compensatory damages plus exemplary damages, where there is both loss and benefit in excess of the loss. Such a situation is rare, however. Normally in frauds the situation is one of zero sum. The gains of the fraudsters are equal to the losses of the victims. Exceptionally, as anticipated by Ashhurst J, the victims' losses can outweigh the fraudsters' gains, if, for example, the fraudster is motivated by spite and simply wishes to see the victim suffer harm. Situations in which the gains to the fraudster are greater than the losses to the victims are more rare still, especially if one calculates the gain carefully. Let us suppose that D fraudulently induces P to buy shares at price £X by saying that there were other bidders for the shares, bidders who did not in fact exist. The real market value of the shares was $£(X - Y)$. Because of the revelation of unexpected good news, the price of the shares rises to a price between £X and $£(X - Y)$, viz $£(X - Z)$ where $Z < Y$. One might say, therefore, that D's gain was greater than P's loss, because D gains £Y but P loses only £Z. But note that one might instead say that the value of D's shares turned out to be $£(X - Z)$, not $£(X - Y)$, so that D's profit was really £Z, not £Y, which therefore still matches P's loss[3].

On this interpretation, for the claimant's loss to be less than the fraudster's gain requires a very odd combination of events, in which the asset which is the subject of the fraud is inherently worth more to the claimant than it is to the fraudster, but less than the claimant thought it was worth and hence less than the claimant paid the fraudster for it. One example might be where the claimant already holds an exclusive and non-transferable licence to do something with the asset (a personal planning permission, for example)[4], so that the asset is worth more to the claimant than to anyone else, including the fraudster. In such a case, it might be argued that the defendant was motivated by a desire to profit from the tort, and that the tort was committed intentionally or recklessly, so that an award of exemplary damages might be open to the court. On the other hand, it seems odd that a defendant who causes a victim less harm than one would normally expect should have to pay as much as a defendant who causes the normally expected amount of harm[5].

1   (1789) 3 Term Rep 51 at 62, 100 ER 450 at 456.
2   *Halifax Building Society v Thomas* [1996] Ch 217, [1995] 4 All ER 673.
3   This hypothetical is an adaptation of the facts in *Smith New Court Securities Ltd v Scrimgeour Vickers (Asset Management) Ltd* [1996] 4 All ER 769, where, in contrast, the subsequent event was the revelation of a separate fraud which caused the market value of the shares to fall below even their fair market value at the time of the fraud. In *Smith New Court*, therefore, at first sight the claimant's losses were greater than the defendant's gains, but one should perhaps argue, in parallel to the argument in the main text, that the defendant's gains were, in fact, equal to the claimant's losses, since if the defendant had held on to the shares, the defendant would have suffered the subsequent market fall.
4   Cf *Allied Maples v Simmonds and Simmonds* [1995] 4 All ER 907, [1995] 1 WLR 1602.
5   There are some more features of this hypothetical which merit comment. First, it could be argued that the motivation to profit from the tort should be a motivation which relates to the excess profit the defendant would make given the chances of the claimant successfully suing for the *loss*, not just that the defendant aimed generally to profit from the fraud. That would require that the defendant knew about the special circumstance which gave rise to the asset's being worth more to the claimant than to the defendant, otherwise the defendant would expect the claimant's loss to be equal to the defendant's gain. But if that was the case, a further question arises as to what to make of the fact that in those circumstances the defendant could have come to an honest and voluntary deal with the claimant at any price between the defendant's valuation and the claimant's valuation. It will be seen that in those circumstances, what the defendant achieves by the fraud depends on what price the defendant believed the parties would have arrived at voluntarily. At one extreme, if the defendant expected the voluntary price to be little above the defendant's own valuation, the defendant has gained almost the full difference between the value of the asset to the defendant and the fraudulent price. At the other extreme, if the defendant

expected the voluntary price to be almost the claimant's valuation, the defendant has gained only slightly more than what the claimant has lost – viz the difference between the fraudulent price and the value of the asset to the claimant. It would therefore be much easier to say that exemplary damages should in principle be awarded (because in both extremes one can say that the defendant expected compensatory damages to be less than the defendant's gain) than to say what the award should be – at one extreme it is nearly the whole of the difference between the defendant's valuation of the asset and the fraudulent price, in the other it is almost nothing.

QUANTUM

12.15   The principle controlling the exact amount to be awarded by the court under Lord Devlin's second category should be reasonably clear. Since the purpose of the award is 'to teach a wrongdoer that tort does not pay' the amount should be sufficient to teach that lesson, but no more than is necessary to teach it. As Sir Thomas Bingham said in *John v MGN Ltd*, 'principle requires that an award of exemplary damages should never exceed the minimum sum necessary to meet the public purposes underlying such damages'. On the other hand, it seems that simply to strip away the defendant's profit is not enough in the eyes of some judges to produce the desired deterrent effect. As Lord Diplock remarked in *Cassell & Co Ltd v Broome*:

> [T]o restrict the damages recoverable to the actual gain made by the defendant if it exceeded the loss caused to the plaintiff, would leave a defendant contemplating an unlawful act with the certainty that he had nothing to lose to balance against the chance that the plaintiff might never sue him or, if he did, might fail in the hazards of litigation. It is only if there is a prospect that the damages may exceed the defendant's gain that the social purpose of this category is achieved ... [1]

It is not at all clear by how much the court must exceed the defendant's profit while not exceeding 'the minimum sum necessary to meet the public purposes' of the award. But we can at least say that the careful calculations characteristic of an account of profits are not appropriate in the setting of an exemplary award on the basis of Lord Devlin's second rule.

1   [1972] AC 1027 at 1130.

12.16   In addition to the profit or the value of the benefit the defendant would otherwise obtain, which is clearly relevant if not always decisive, it is also said to be relevant to take into account defendants' means, and their degree of fault[1]. Taking into account the defendant's means seems odd, since it seems to give defendants an incentive to rid themselves quickly of their ill-gotten gains so that they can claim no longer to be able to afford to pay them over to the claimant. Taking into account the degree of fault also seems odd, since exemplary damages may not be awarded in the first place unless there was conscious wrongdoing. It is submitted that a certain amount of confusion has entered the law at this point. The criteria for permitting an award of exemplary damages under this head have been partially merged with the rules for deciding the amount of such an award, a result, perhaps, of judicial reluctance to appear to interfere with the jury's discretion in matters of quantum.

1   Per Sir Thomas Bingham MR in *John v MGN Ltd* [1997] QB 586 at 619.

12.17   A separate issue is whether any of the rules developed in the context of Lord Devlin's first rule, that which concerns 'oppressive, arbitrary or unconstitutional action' by a servant of the state, should apply in his second category. It is not clear why, for example, the exact status of the person who committed the tort should be a relevant consideration in the second category, although it is relevant in cases in the first category[1].

1   *Thompson v Metropolitan Police Comr* [1998] QB 498, [1997] 2 All ER 762.

VICARIOUS LIABILITY

12.18   There is some judicial support for the proposition that exemplary damages may not be awarded in cases where liability relies on the doctrine of vicarious liability[1]. Even if such a proposition does apply to Lord Devlin's first category, it is submitted that it is a separate matter whether it should apply to his second category[2]. In defamation cases, for example, the extra profit made from publishing a scurrilous story about a well-known personality normally accrues to the newspaper, that is to the employer, rather than to the editor, the journalist or other relevant employee. Lord Scott's comment that 'the defendant should not be liable to pay exemplary damages unless he has committed punishable behaviour' seems excessively to limit the possibilities of exemplary damages being awarded against organisations even where it is the organisation's illegitimate profit which is the object of the law's attention. It is noticeable that the point was not taken in the leading cases concerning the exemplary damages liability of publishers in defamation, namely *Cassell & Co Ltd v Broome*[3] and *John v MGN Ltd*[4] and that in *Riches v News Group Newspapers Ltd* Stephenson LJ took it for granted that:

> [I]t was the state of mind of the defendants' servants which the jury had to decide if their conduct was to justify punitive damages and that must be mainly if not entirely inferred from what they said or did[5].

It may be that Lord Scott meant his strictures to apply only to what he called 'pure vicarious liability', by which he appears to mean cases in which employers or their equivalent are liable for the torts of their employees even when the employer has explicitly forbidden the conduct which constituted the tort. But even so, should the fact that the board of a company which owns a newspaper has issued a memorandum to the editor saying that the editor should not publish libels, be enough to exempt the company itself from having to pay exemplary damages to the victims of the editor's libels? The company accepts the profits generated by the editor, and the board will presumably judge the editor on the level of profit he or she generates for the company.

It might be possible to avoid this difficulty entirely by careful application of the principle enunciated by the Privy Council in *Meridian Global Funds Management Asia Ltd v Securities Commission*[6], that the mental state of an organisation is to be determined not by looking to any 'directing mind or will', but to the mental state of the individual or individuals in the organisation who make the relevant decisions on behalf of the organisation. Thus an editor's decision to publish, on the basis of increasing the circulation of the newspaper, will be enough to fix the company which owns the newspaper with the relevant reason for acting.

1   Lord Scott in *Kuddus v Chief Constable of Leicestershire Police* [2001] UKHL 29, [2001] 3 All ER 193 at 228, [2001] 2 WLR 1789 at 1825. The other Law Lords explicitly reserved their position on this point.
2   See eg *Mehta v Royal Bank of Scotland* [1999] 3 EGLR 153, where exemplary damages were awarded on the second basis for the acts of a landlord's representatives in unlawfully evicting a tenant.
3   [1972] AC 1027.
4   [1997] QB 586.
5   [1986] QB 256 at 270, [1985] 2 All ER 845 at 851.
6   [1995] 2 AC 500, [1995] 3 All ER 918.

Damages under the Housing Act 1988, ss 27 and 28

12.19   One particular example of restitutionary damages under statute should be mentioned. Under the Housing Act 1988, s 27, where any landlord or a person acting on behalf of a landlord:

(a)   attempts unlawfully to deprive the residential occupier of any premises of his occupation of the whole or part of the premises, or

(b)   knowing or having reasonable cause to believe that the conduct is likely to cause the residential occupier of any premises–
     (i)   to give up his occupation of the premises or any part thereof, or
    (ii)   to refrain from exercising any right or pursuing any remedy in respect of the premises or any part thereof,
does acts likely to interfere with the peace or comfort of the residential occupier or members of his household[1], or persistently withdraws or withholds services reasonably required for the occupation of the premises as a residence, and, as a result, the residential occupier gives up his occupation of the premises as a residence[2]

the landlord[3] commits a statutory tort[4] the remedy for which, as laid out in s 28, is that the landlord has to pay damages equivalent to the difference in value of the landlord's interest with and without the presence of the tenant. The effect of s 28 is that the landlord must hand over to the tenant the entire increase in value of the property achieved by ousting the tenant. The restitutionary nature of the remedy is reinforced by the fact that only the landlord whose interest increases in value is liable for the statutory damages. Others, such as the landlord's agents, are not liable even though they might have taken part in the eviction[5].

1   See, on this part of the section, *Abbott v Bayley* (1999) 32 HLR 72.
2   'Residential occupier' means 'a person occupying the premises as a residence, whether under a contract or by virtue of any enactment or rule of law giving him the right to remain in occupation or restricting the right of any other person to recover possession of the premises'. See the Housing Act 1988, s 1, and *Mehta v Royal Bank of Scotland* [1999] 3 EGLR 153.
3   On who counts as a landlord for these purposes see *Jones v Miah* (1992) 24 HLR 578.
4   See Housing Act 1988, s 27(4)(a).
5   *Sampson v Wilson* [1996] Ch 39, doubting remarks by Dillon LJ in *Jones v Miah* (1992) 24 HLR 578 at 586.

12.20   Section 28 mandates the court to award the difference between, on the one hand, the value of the landlord's interest as of the point in time just before the tenant left and on the assumption that the tenant would have continued to have had the same right to occupy the premises, and, on the other hand, the value of that interest assuming that the tenant has ceased to have that right. It also provides that for the purposes of the valuation, the court should assume that the landlord is selling his interest on the open market to a willing buyer, that neither the tenant nor any member of his family wishes to buy, and that it is unlawful to carry out any substantial development of any of the land in which the landlord's interest subsists or to demolish the whole or part of any building on that land[1]. The valuation should be made on the basis of the actual situation in the premises being valued, rather than on the basis of the assumed vacant possession value[2]. But the actual situation includes the parties' obligations, so that if the tenant was under a duty to leave the premises at a certain date, damages under s 28 should assume that the tenant would fulfil his or her duty[3].

1   See the Housing Act 1988, s 28(3).
2   *Melville v Bruton* (1996) 29 HLR 319, [1996] 13 LS Gaz R 26; *Tinker v Potts* (LEXIS Transcript, 30 July 1996).
3   *King v Jackson* [1998] 03 EG 138, 30 HLR 541.

12.21   The statutory damages are not payable if the tenant is reinstated in the premises 'in such circumstances that he becomes again the residential occupier of them', or the court orders his reinstatement in such circumstances[1]. But an interim injunction for a limited period which does not restore the tenant to his or her rights is not sufficient to oust the right to statutory damages[2].

1   See the Housing Act 1988, s 27(6).
2   *Mehta v Royal Bank of Scotland* [1999] 3 EGLR 153.

12.22   The court may reduce the statutory damages if it appears reasonable to do so in the light of the conduct of the tenant (or that of 'any person living with him in the premises'), or if the tenant acted unreasonably in declining an offer from the landlord to be re-instated[1]. It is also a defence for the defendant to prove that he believed, and had reasonable cause to believe, that the tenant had ceased to reside in the premises at the time the tenant was put out, or that, where the allegation was that liability arose by virtue only of the doing of acts or the withdrawal or withholding of services, the landlord had reasonable grounds for doing the acts or withdrawing or withholding the services in question[2].

1   See the Housing Act 1988, s 27(7). See further *Regalgrand Ltd v Dickerson & Wade* (1996) 29 HLR 620; *Osei-Bonsu v Wandsworth London Borough Council* [1999] 1 All ER 265, [1999] 1 WLR 1011.
2   See the Housing Act 1988, s 27(8). See *Osei-Bonsu v Wandsworth London Borough Council* [1999] 1 All ER 265, [1999] 1 WLR 1011 for the meaning of 'reasonable cause'.

12.23   Liability under s 28 is in addition to any tortious or contractual liability[1], but the claimant cannot recover damages twice in respect of the same loss[2]. The award of exemplary damages is a common occurrence in tenant eviction cases[3]. It is clear that exemplary damages as well as compensatory damages (which include aggravated damages) have to be set off against the statutory damages under s 28[4].

1   See the Housing Act 1988, s 27(4)(b).
2   See the Housing Act 1988, s 27(5).
3   See eg *Francis v Brown* (1997) 30 HLR 143; *Mehta v Royal Bank of Scotland* [1999] 3 EGLR 153.
4   *Francis v Brown* (1997) 30 HLR 143; *Mehta v Royal Bank of Scotland* [1999] 3 EGLR 153.

Damages in lieu of an injunction – the 'Lord Cairns' Act' jurisdiction

12.24   Although injunctions are theoretically 'discretionary' remedies, successful claimants in tort actions have a prima facie right to an injunction to enjoin further commission of the tort[1]. Exceptionally, however, the court may award damages in lieu of an injunction. The court's power arises out of the Supreme Court Act 1981, s 50, a section which originated in the Chancery Amendment Act 1858 (otherwise known as Lord Cairns' Act). The section says:

> Where the Court of Appeal or the High Court has jurisdiction to entertain an application for an injunction or specific performance, it may award damages in addition to, or in substitution for, an injunction or specific performance.

The section applies, in terms, where the court 'has jurisdiction to entertain an application for an injunction', not just where, in the exercise of its ultimate discretion, it would have issued an injunction. In *Surrey County Council v Bredero Homes Ltd*[2], Dillon LJ appears to accept that where there was no 'practical possibility' of a court issuing an injunction, the power to award damages in lieu does not arise. In *Jaggard v Sawyer*, however, Millett LJ pointed out that the reason the Lord Cairns' Act jurisdiction could not arise in *Surrey County Council v Bredero Homes Ltd* was not merely a matter of 'practical possibility', but because the subject matter of the dispute was no longer under the control of the defendant, and the persons who now had control of the subject matter of the dispute had not been made parties to the dispute. There was thus no 'jurisdiction to entertain an application for an injunction' within the terms of the Act[3].

The jurisdiction applies not only to prohibitory injunctions but also to mandatory injunctions[4], even though there is no equivalent to the prima facie right to an injunction in the case of a mandatory injunction[5].

1   *Redland Bricks Ltd v Morris* [1970] AC 652 at 664, per Lord Upjohn. See generally Grubb (ed) *Law of Tort* (2002), para 8.11.
2   [1993] 3 All ER 705, [1993] 1 WLR 1361.
3   *Jaggard v Sawyer* [1995] 2 All ER 189 at 210, [1995] 1 WLR 269 at 289–290.
4   *Isenberg v East India Housing Estate Co Ltd* (1863) 3 De GJ & SM 263, 46 ER 637.
5   *Isenberg v East India Housing Estate Co Ltd* (1863) 3 De GJ & SM 263, 46 ER 637; *Redland Bricks Ltd v Morris* [1970] AC 652.

12.25   The section gives a power to award damages, not a duty to do so, so that the court may refuse to award damages on grounds similar to those on which courts may deny an injunction, for example delay or acquiescence[1]. But the loss of the right to an injunction on such a ground does not in itself entail the loss of damages in lieu[2]. The court retains a discretion to award damages nevertheless.

The relevant time for judging the existence of the jurisdiction appears to be the commencement of proceedings, rather than the time of trial[3]. On the other hand, the jurisdiction applies not merely to ordinary final injunctions, but also to quia timet injunctions in advance of the claimant's suffering any actionable harm[4].

1   *Smith v Smith* (1875) LR 20 Eq 500.
2   *Sayers v Collyer* (1884) 28 Ch D 103, *Gafford v Graham* [1999] 41 EG 159. See further Grubb (ed) *Law of Tort* (2002), para 8.51.
3   *Jaggard v Sawyer* [1995] 2 All ER 189, [1995] 1 WLR 269; *City of London Brewery Co v Tennant* (1873) 9 Ch App 212.
4   *Leeds Industrial Co-operative Society Ltd v Slack* [1924] AC 851. Cited in *Jaggard v Sawyer* [1995] 2 All ER 189, [1995] 1 WLR 269. To the contrary, but per incuriam, *Midland Bank plc v Bardgrove Property Services Ltd* [1992] 2 EGLR 168.

12.26   The Lord Cairns' Act jurisdiction is only invoked with great care. The denial of an injunction where the claimant's rights are acknowledged to have been violated tends to undermine the right itself, and, where that right is a property right, can even be said to tend towards undermining the institution of property[1]. Admittedly, as Millett LJ says in *Jaggard v Sawyer*, Lord Cairns' Act can be seen as improving the claimant's position over that in a case in which an injunction is simply refused, because at least the claimant receives some money[2]. But there are two points which nevertheless give cause for concern about the exercise of the jurisdiction under the Act: that the existence of the jurisdiction might increase the temptation to refuse an injunction in the first place; and that the exercise of the jurisdiction removes the claimant's power to set his or her own price for giving up the right concerned, and substitutes a price set by the court[3]. The Act gives rise to a form of compulsory purchase[4], and should therefore not be invoked lightly.

For these reasons, since *Shelfer v City of London Electric Co*[5], the courts have limited the circumstances in which the jurisdiction will be invoked. In *Shelfer*, in a passage which is often cited, though should be treated as a statement of principle rather than as a legislative text[6], AL Smith LJ said:

> In any instance in which a case for an injunction has been made out, if the plaintiff by his acts or laches has disentitled himself to an injunction the Court may award damages in its place. So again, whether the case be for a mandatory injunction or to restrain a continuing nuisance, the appropriate remedy may be damages in lieu of an injunction, assuming a case for an injunction to be made out. In my opinion, it may be stated as a good working rule that – (1) If the injury to the plaintiff's legal rights is small, (2) And is one which is capable of being estimated in money, (3) And is one which can be adequately compensated by a small money payment, (4) And the case is one in which it would be oppressive to the defendant to grant an injunction: – then damages in substitution for an injunction may be given[7].

AL Smith LJ warned against any attempt to reduce these principles to specific rules[8]:

> It is impossible to lay down any rule as to what, under the differing circumstances of each case, constitutes either a small injury, or one that can be estimated in money, or what is a small money payment, or an adequate compensation, or what would be oppressive to the defendant. This must be left to the good sense of the tribunal which deals with each case as it comes up for adjudication[9].

AL Smith LJ also said, however, that even where the principles applied, the defendant's conduct might nevertheless justify the issuance of an injunction:

> There may also be cases in which, though the four above-mentioned requirements exist, the defendant by his conduct, as, for instance, hurrying up his buildings so as if possible to avoid an injunction, or otherwise acting with reckless disregard to the plaintiff's rights, has disentitled himself from asking that damages may be assessed in substitution for an injunction[10].

1 See eg Lindley LJ in *Shelfer v City of London Electric Lighting Co* [1895] 1 Ch 287 at 312ff, and Lord Donaldson in *Elliott v Islington London Borough Council* [1991] 1 EGLR 167 at 168.
2 [1995] 2 All ER 189 at 207, [1995] 1 WLR 269 at 286–287.
3 See generally Calabresi and Melamed 'Property Rules, Liability Rules and Inalienability: One View of the Cathedral' (1972) 85 Harvard Law Review 1089.
4 *Elliott v Islington London Borough Council* [1991] 1 EGLR 167 at 168, per Lord Donaldson MR.
5 [1895] 1 Ch 287.
6 *Jaggard v Sawyer* [1995] 2 All ER 189 at 208, [1995] 1 WLR 269 at 287, per Millett LJ.
7 [1895] 1 Ch 287 at 322–323.
8 For consideration in detail of each of AL Smith LJ's four principles, see Grubb (ed) *Law of Tort* (2002), paras 8.53–8.56.
9 [1895] 1 Ch 287 at 323.
10 [1895] 1 Ch 287 at 323.

12.27   The central point in the present context about damages in lieu under Lord Cairns' Act is that, because they are in substitution for an injunction, they must go beyond compensation for past harm, but must also in some way account for the future[1]. The question for the court is therefore how to account for the future in the calculation of damages.

1 *Leeds Industrial Co-operative Society Ltd v Slack* [1924] AC 851; *Jaggard v Sawyer* [1995] 2 All ER 189, [1995] 1 WLR 269.

12.28   In *Wrotham Park Estate Co v Parkside Homes Ltd*[1] Brightman J calculated damages in lieu of an injunction for breach of a covenant by taking 5% of the profits which the defendants could reasonably expect from their continuing breach of the covenant. In *Surrey County Council v Bredero Homes Ltd*[2], Steyn LJ remarked that damages on that basis could only be justified as restitutionary damages in the form of an account of profits. 'The object of the award in *Wrotham Park* was not to compensate the plaintiff for financial injury, but to deprive the defendants of an unjustly acquired gain.' But in *Jaggard v Sawyer*[3] a differently constituted Court of Appeal rejected the idea that Lord Cairns' Act had introduced any new principle for the assessment of damages[4]. The court re-asserted the customary view that damages in lieu under the Act represented the price at which the claimant might reasonably have sold the right in question to the defendant[5], and that such a measure of the damages due should be seen as essentially compensatory – either as compensation for the claimant's loss of opportunity to bargain, or as compensation in the sense in use in compulsory purchase[6]. The Court of Appeal interpreted Brightman J's use of the defendant's profits in *Wrotham Park* as merely an attempt to measure the loss, not to strip the defendant of profits:

> He had therefore to assess the damages necessary to compensate the plaintiffs for this continuing invasion of their right. He paid attention to the profits earned by the defendants, as it seems to me, not in order to strip the defendants of their unjust gains, but because of the obvious relationship between the profits earned by the defendants and the sum which the defendants would reasonably have been willing to pay to secure release from the covenant[7].

1   [1974] 2 All ER 321, [1974] 1 WLR 798.
2   [1993] 3 All ER 705, [1993] 1 WLR 1361.
3   [1995] 2 All ER 189, [1995] 1 WLR 269.
4   See also *Johnson v Agnew* [1980] AC 367 at 400, per Lord Wilberforce.
5   *Bracewell v Appleby* [1975] Ch 408, [1975] 1 All ER 993. But see below, para 12.36, for the perhaps better view that such damages are neither purely compensatory nor purely restitutionary.
6   In *Surrey County Council v Bredero Homes Ltd*, Steyn LJ said that he thought that the 'loss of opportunity to bargain' conception of damages under the Act was 'a fiction' [1993] 1 WLR 1361 at 1369, [1993] 3 All ER 705 at 714. The Court of Appeal in *Jaggard v Sawyer* [1995] 2 All ER 189, [1995] 1 WLR 269 disagrees. Perhaps the way to resolve this difference of view is to observe that loss of the opportunity to bargain is not so much a principle which is meant to determine the amount of compensation payable, but rather a justification for why compensation should be paid at all. The determination of the amount could then be determined quite consistently in line with the principles of compulsory purchase.
7   [1995] 2 All ER 189 at 202, [1995] 1 WLR 269 at 281–282, per Sir Thomas Bingham MR.

12.29   In *A-G v Blake*[1] Lord Nicholls seems to confirm the approach taken by the Court of Appeal in *Jaggard v Sawyer*. He says, citing *Johnson v Agnew*[2], that 'the Act did not alter the measure to be employed in assessing damages'. He also says:

> The measure of damages awarded in this type of case is often analysed as damages for loss of a bargaining opportunity or, which comes to the same, the price payable for the compulsory acquisition of a right. This analysis is correct[3].

But Lord Nicholls goes on to remark that *Jaggard v Sawyer* shows that 'under Lord Cairns' Act damages may include damages measured by reference to the benefits likely to be obtained in future by the defendant'. He also appears to assert that cases such as *Jaggard v Sawyer*[4] and *Bracewell v Appleby*[5], and not just *Wrotham Park*, show that the courts habitually 'assess the damages by reference to the defendant's profit obtained from the infringement' even 'when no financial loss flows from the infringement'. It is far from clear how any of this is so. *Jaggard* maintains that the relevance of the defendant's profits is only in the assessment of the proper price, and that the reasonable price measure itself is a measure of loss, not a measure of a gain to be disgorged. There is, it submitted, an irreconcilable tension in Lord Nicholls' view as expressed in *A-G v Blake*[6].

1 [2001] 1 AC 268, [2000] 4 All ER 385.
2 [1980] AC 367 at 400, per Lord Wilberforce.
3 [2001] 1 AC 268 at 281, [2000] 4 All ER 385 at 394.
4 [1995] 2 All ER 189, [1995] 1 WLR 269.
5 [1975] Ch 408, [1975] 1 All ER 993.
6 [2001] 1 AC 268, [2000] 4 All ER 385.

12.30   In line with the premise that damages in lieu under Lord Cairns' Act are in the nature of compensation for the compulsory purchase of the claimant's rights, in inquiring into the appropriate 'price' the court should treat the seller neither as 'eager to sell' nor as holding out for a 'ransom price'[1].

1 *Jaggard v Sawyer* [1995] 2 All ER 189 at 203, [1995] 1 WLR 269 at 282, per Sir Thomas Bingham MR.

FUTURE DEVELOPMENT

12.31   It might be argued that an account of profits measure should replace the reasonable price measure in Lord Cairns' Act cases, and that Lord Nicholls' speech in *Blake* leaves that path open. The account of profits measure is arguably a closer equivalent to the missing injunction than the reasonable price measure, at least in the sense that if calculated properly it should result in the removal of all incentive, in advance of the wrong, for defendants to violate the claimant's rights. The reasonable fee measurement might not be such a deterrent. On the other hand, one might doubt whether these subtle differences in remedy are likely to have much of an ex ante effect on behaviour.

12.32   One might also ask why it should be any less oppressive to order an account of profits than it would be to issue the injunction. In *Jaggard v Sawyer*[1], for example, the claimants complained about the defendants' use of part of their garden as a drive for a new house which the defendants had constructed at the rear of their house. The claimants established that use of the drive would violate a covenant which said that gardens in the street had to remain as gardens. They also established that, since the road was a private road, it would constitute a trespass for the defendants to use the road outside the claimants' house to gain access to their new drive. The court decided that it would be oppressive to grant an injunction, and that it should award damages on the basis of a reasonable price for the right to use the drive and the road. What if the court had awarded damages on the basis of an account of profits? Let us assume that the claimants were unreasonable people who would prefer to see the defendants suffer rather than accept any amount of money for their assent to the use of the drive. In such circumstances, the entire value of house would be payable in damages, for its market value would be zero in the absence of the claimants' assent. Is this any less oppressive to the defendants than issuing an injunction?

1 [1995] 2 All ER 189, [1995] 1 WLR 269.

12.33   Indeed the potential effects of the account of profits remedy to deal with future damage in the absence of an injunction are, to say the least, peculiar[1]. If the right is valuable in the sense of productive (a right of access which allows a factory to operate, for example – a right which is more valuable to the defendant than to the claimant), the court would take away the *expected* returns to the defendant of that right. What happens if the returns turn out to be higher than expected? If the court permits the claimant to come back to the court for a further account, the effect will be that the defendant has an incentive to exploit the right no more effectively than the court assumed that the defendant would in its original award. And what if the returns turn out to be lower than expected? Would the court permit the defendant to go back the court, to recoup some of the profit? The case would never be closed. On the other hand, if, as is more likely, the claimant is not allowed to come back to court to capture the extra gains, the 'account of profits' remedy effectively turns into the equivalent of a 'reasonable fee' remedy, with the fee set to the highest value for the fee as appeared plausible at the time of the award[2].

This peculiar result, however, seems to be precisely the result produced in the context of breach of contract by the majority of the House of Lords in *A-G v Blake*[3]. The House of Lords lifted the injunction imposed by the Court of Appeal on the basis of the 'public law' argument[4], but it reversed the Court of Appeal on the 'private law' argument and ordered an account of profits. Thus the court seems to envisage either the possibility of an order for an account of profits which includes future profits, not just past profits or, which seems just as unlikely, the possibility of future profits encumbered neither by an order to account nor by an injunction[5].

1   It might make sense to order an account of profits without an injunction where there is no prospect of further actionable harm. Cf *A-G v Guardian Newspapers Ltd (No 2)* [1990] 1 AC 109, [1988] 3 All ER 545; *Proctor v Bayley* (1889) 42 Ch D 390. Liability under the Housing Act 1988, ss 27 and 28, is limited to an estimate of the change in value of the property at a particular time, the point just before the tenant is evicted, and therefore does not apply to as yet unknown future profits.
2   It is relevant to note that in intellectual property law it is said that the court deals with the situation of damages combined with no injunction by measuring damages on the basis of a capitalised royalty – ie a 'reasonable fee' measure. See Cornish *Intellectual Property* (4th edn, 1999), para 2–43.
3   [2001] 1 AC 268, [2000] 4 All ER 385.
4   See below, para 12.71.
5   See below, para 12.47. The precise form of the order in *Blake* muddies the waters further. The order was 'a declaration that the Attorney-General is entitled to be paid a sum equal to whatever amount is due and owing to Blake from Jonathan Cape under the publishing agreement of 4 May 1989'. But the House of Lords also ordered that the Court of Appeal's injunction should remain in force, on a basis which is deeply obscure, 'until Jonathan Cape duly makes payment to the Attorney-General'. It is very unclear what the effect of this combination of orders is. Does 'is due and owing' refer to the time of judgment, or to any time at which such an amount becomes due? Lord Nicholls in the course of his discussion of the public law argument says that the injunction cannot be of confiscatory effect, so that it cannot be the intention of the court that the injunction should continue indefinitely. That means that there must come a point in time at which payment has 'duly' been made, but at which Cape might still become further indebted to Blake (or Blake's estate). But what happens thereafter, when no injunction is in force so that more sales might be made and more royalties will fall due, is unclear.

The user principle

12.34   Another exception to the rule that damages in tort are measured solely by the claimant's loss, an exception described by Lord Nicholls in *A-G v Blake* as 'pragmatic'[1], is the 'user principle'. Where a trespasser enters another's land, it may cause the landowner no measurable financial loss. Nevertheless, damages can be awarded to represent an amount due to the landowner for using the claimant's land. Similarly, using the claimant's land as a waste dump, or as a path, or in the form of underground passage-ways, also give rise to an obligation to pay damages based on the same 'user principle'. The amount due is the price a reasonable person would pay for the relevant use[2]. The same principle has been used in cases of the wrongful detention of goods[3] and, beyond tort law, has also been used in analogous cases concerning confidential information[4] and breaches of covenants[5]. It is also analogous to the way in which damages are calculated in some intellectual property cases[6].

1   [2001] 1 AC 268 at 278, [2000] 4 All ER 385 at 391.
2   *Whitwam v Westminster Brymbo Coal and Coke Co* [1896] 2 Ch 538; *Martin v Porter* (1839) 5 M & W 351, 151 ER 149; *Jegon v Vivian* (1871) 6 Ch App 742; *Penarth Dock Engineering Co Ltd v Pounds* [1963] 1 Lloyd's Rep 359. See Lord Nicholls in *A-G v Blake* [2001] 1 AC 268 at 278.
3   *Strand Electric and Engineering Co Ltd v Brisford Entertainments Ltd* [1952] 2 QB 246.
4   *Seager v Copydex (No 2)* [1969] 2 All ER 718, [1969] 1 WLR 809 (although note that the reasonable price in that case was based on that which a willing buyer and a willing seller would have reached – the seller in most user principle cases is ex hypothesi not 'willing').
5   *Jaggard v Sawyer* [1995] 2 All ER 189, [1995] 1 WLR 269; *Wrotham Park Estate v Parkside Homes* [1974] 2 All ER 321, [1974] 1 WLR 798.
6   See below, para 12.61.

THE PURPOSE OF THE USER PRINCIPLE

12.35   The user principle is traceable to the 'wayleave' cases[1], the characteristic facts of which were that the defendant trespassed by carrying coals along an underground way through the claimant's mine. Although the value of the claimant's land had not been affected by the trespass, the claimant recovered damages equivalent to what he would have received if he had been paid for a wayleave. The basis of the wayleave cases is obscure. In *Phillips v Homfray, Fothergill v Phillips*[2] Lord Hatherley LC said that he had had doubts about wayleave claims, but was persuaded otherwise because, 'Here is a man doing a surreptitious act'[3], suggesting that some kind of fraud is necessary. But in *Jegon v Vivian*, Lord Hatherley LC awarded wayleave damages in a case in which the defendant acted in good faith[4].

A principle begins to emerge in *Whitwham v Westminster Brymbo Coal & Coke Co*[5], in which the defendant had trespassed on the claimant's land by dumping on it waste from the defendant's mine. The Court of Appeal said that because the defendant had used the claimant's land, the defendant should be charged for that use. The court was not concerned with the profit (or loss) taken by the defendant, but it was concerned that the defendant had taken a benefit without paying for it. A form of benefit and burden principle seemed to be in play.

In *Strand Electric and Engineering Co Ltd v Brisford Entertainments Ltd*[6], the court added that the principle had something in common with the rule about common law damages, expressed in *Mediana (Owners of Steamship) v Comet (Owners of Lightship)*[7], that damages for negligent damage to property should not be limited to the nominal merely because the property was not profit-bearing, or because the claimant already owned a substitute for the damaged property. As the Earl of Halsbury LC had said in that case, it is no answer for a wrongdoer who has deprived the plaintiff of his chair to point out that he does not usually sit in it, or that he has plenty of other chairs in the room[8].

The *Mediana* rule is explicable in terms of the standard purpose of tort damages, to put the claimant back into the position he or she was in before the tort[9]. If, before the tort, the claimant had a spare ship, the claimant should receive the value of a spare ship in damages for the tort. In *A-G v Blake*[10], however, Lord Nicholls linked the *Mediana* rule to a remark of Lord Shaw in the patent case *Watson, Laidlaw & Co Ltd v Pott, Cassels and Williamson* that:

wherever an abstraction or invasion of property has occurred, then, unless such abstraction or invasion were to be sanctioned by law, the law ought to yield a recompense under the category or principle ... either of price or of hire.

Lord Shaw illustrated his principle thus:

If A, being a liveryman, keeps his horse standing idle in the stable, and B, against his wish or without his knowledge, rides or drives it out, it is no answer to A for B to say: 'Against what loss do you want to be restored? I restore the horse. There is no loss. The horse is none the worse; it is the better for the exercise'[11].

Lying behind these remarks is the idea that if the law did not recognise the user principle, the defendant would have appropriated the claimant's property with impunity[12]. The user principle therefore protects property rights in themselves. The claimant's property right is protected not because of what the claimant might or could have done with the property, but because the claimant had the right to exclude others from using the property at the claimant's own discretion. The concept of property protected by the user principle is one in which what is important is the owner's *exclusion* of others from use and the owner's *discretion* to use or not to use, rather than the owner's *enjoyment* of the use. The defendant's wrong consists of disregarding the claimant's right to exclude. The damages recognise the nature of the wrong.

1   *Martin v Porter* (1839) 5 M & W 351, 151 ER 149; *Jegon v Vivian* (1871) 6 Ch App 742; and *Phillips v Homfray, Fothergill v Phillips* (1871) 6 Ch App 770.
2   (1871) 6 Ch App 770.
3   (1871) 6 Ch App 770 at 780.
4   (1871) 6 Ch App 742.
5   [1896] 2 Ch 538.
6   [1952] 2 QB 246.
7   [1900] AC 113.
8   [1900] AC 113 at 117; approved in *Inverugie Investments Ltd v Hackett* [1995] 3 All ER 841, [1995] 1 WLR 713.
9   *Livingstone v Rawyards Coal Co* (1880) 5 App Cas 25 at 39, per Lord Blackburn.
10   [2001] 1 AC 268 at 279, [2000] 4 All ER 385 at 391.
11   (1914) 31 RPC 104 at 119.
12   *Dormeuil Frères SA v Feraglow Ltd* [1990] RPC 449 at 459, per Knox J, quoting *MacGregor on Damages*, that otherwise 'the law, when appealed to, would be standing by and allowing the invader or abstractor to go free'. See also *Penn v Jack* (1867) LR 5 Eq 81; *Shelfer v City of London Electric Lighting Co* [1895] 1 Ch 287 at 312ff, per Lindley LJ; and *Elliott v Islington London Borough Council* [1991] 1 EGLR 167 at 168, per Lord Donaldson.

REASONABLE FEES, RENTS AND PRICES

12.36   The precise amount to be paid under the user principle has caused controversy. The starting point is that the defendant must pay a 'reasonable rent' or a 'reasonable fee'. The claimant is not bound to show that he has suffered an actual loss, and is not therefore bound to show that he would otherwise have rented or hired out the property concerned, or even have used the property for any valuable purpose[1]. As Romer LJ explained in *Strand Electric Co Ltd v Brisford Entertainments Ltd*:

[A] defendant who has wrongfully detained and profited from the property of someone else cannot avail himself of a hypothesis such as this. It does not lie in the mouth of such a defendant to suggest that the owner might not have found a hirer, for in using the property he showed that he wanted it and he cannot complain if it is assumed against him that he himself would have preferred to become the hirer rather than not have had the use of it at all[2].

The measure is therefore not purely compensatory. On the other hand, the measure is also not an account of profits. It is no answer for the defendant that he has, in the event, failed to make any profit from his tort[3]. The measure is hence not fully restitutionary either. In *Inverugie Investments Ltd v Hackett*[4], the Privy Council said: 'The principle need not be characterised as exclusively compensatory, or exclusively restitutionary; it combines elements of both'. It might be even more accurate to say that it stands apart from both[5].

1 *Swordheath Properties Ltd v Tabet* [1979] 1 WLR 285 at 288, per Megaw LJ. Approved in *Inverugie Investments Ltd v Hackett* [1995] 3 All ER 841 at 845, [1995] 1 WLR 713 at 717.
2 [1952] 2 QB 246 at 257, [1952] 1 All ER 796 at 802.
3 *Stoke-on-Trent City Council v W & J Wass Ltd* [1988] 1 WLR 1406, per Nicholls LJ. Approved in *Inverugie Investments Ltd v Hackett* [1995] 3 All ER 841, [1995] 1 WLR 713.
4 [1995] 3 All ER 841 at 845, [1995] 1 WLR 713 at 718.
5 Note that in the context of the Lord Cairns Act' jurisdiction (above, para 12.29) the courts tend toward the 'compensatory' view of reasonable fee damages. The *Inverugie* view might well be a better view in that context as well.

QUANTUM AND THE ROLE OF BENEFITS GAINED

12.37 In *Strand Electric Co Ltd v Brisford Entertainments Ltd*[1] the Court of Appeal referred to the 'full' or 'recognised' hiring value of the property used, without any deduction for hypothetical events such as the possibility that the property would have been damaged has it remained in the hands of the claimant.

1 [1952] 2 QB 246, [1952] 1 All ER 796.

12.38 But where the property has unique characteristics, such as most types of land, the determination of the 'recognised' value might not be easy. In an ordinary case of trespass to land where a tenant has overstayed the lease period, the measure of damages, known in that context as 'mesne profits', is normally the rent reserved under the expiring lease[1]. In other cases, such as where the claimant is a tenant who has been kept out of his tenancy by the defendant reversioner[2], the claimant is entitled to the market rent, or, where there is no ready market, to 'a fair and proper price'[3]. The measure is 'objective' in the double sense that the damages 'must be ... ascertained by reference to what would be likely to have been agreed between persons who were not only reasonable but also properly informed'[4].

But such phrases sometimes merely disguise further difficulties. In *Inverugie*[5], for example, the court had to decide whether, in a case in which the defendant had used 30 of the claimant's holiday apartments as part of its own hotel, the correct approach was to take the wholesale rate (the rate at which holiday tour operators would taken the apartments en bloc), or the retail rate (the rate at which the claimant could have rented out the apartments to individual holiday-makers)[6]. The court chose the former, and furthermore deducted a sum which the claimant would have to had pay out to the defendant in management fees, a sum which would have been, it was claimed, deductible from such a wholesale rent. But there was no deduction for general running expenses, which would not have been deductible from a wholesale rent, but would have been a general business expense of the claimant.

But that was not the end of the difficulty. In deciding what the wholesale rent would have been, the court in *Inverugie* was invited to look to how much profit the defendant made per apartment, and thence to how much the defendant would have offered in rent. The Privy Council rejected that approach. It was too close to an account of profits, a remedy the court rejected because it would have meant that the claimant would have received no damages at all if the defendant had made a loss on the entire transaction[7]. The measure chosen looked as far as it could to the market beyond the two parties themselves, to the conditions of supply in the market for holiday apartments rather than the defendant's place in that market. No doubt the profitability of the industry as a whole, in which the defendant was a participant, heavily influenced the rents chargeable for holiday apartments, but it was industry-wide demand which mattered, not the particular circumstances of the defendant[8].

1   *Inverugie Investments Ltd v Hackett* [1995] 3 All ER 841, [1995] 1 WLR 713.
2   *Inverugie Investments Ltd v Hackett* [1995] 3 All ER 841, [1995] 1 WLR 713.
3   Cf *Jaggard v Sawyer* [1995] 2 All ER 189, [1995] 1 WLR 269; and *Bracewell v Appleby* [1975] 1 All ER 993, [1975] Ch 408.
4   *National Provident Institution v Avon County Council* [1992] EGCS 56.
5   [1995] 3 All ER 841, [1995] 1 WLR 713.
6   It was irrelevant, of course, whether the claimants could have dealt with the tour operators in this way.
7   Cf the application of the account of profits remedy in intellectual property cases, below, para 12.62.
8   Cf the similar view expressed in the context of the Lord Cairns' Act jurisdiction, above, para 12.27ff (*Wrotham Park Estate Co v Parkside Homes Ltd* [1974] 2 All ER 321, [1974] 1 WLR 798 as explained in *Jaggard v Sawyer* [1995] 2 All ER 189 at 202, [1995] 1 WLR 269 at 281–282, per Sir Thomas Bingham MR).

12.39   Other complications occurred in *Ministry of Defence v Ashman*[1], in which, because the defendant's husband, an air force serviceman, had left their service quarters, the defendant had ceased to be entitled to live there. The accommodation had been available to the defendant and her husband at a heavily subsidised below-market rent. When she was served with notice to quit, she had nowhere else to go, her only distant prospect being social housing at a rent higher than the one she was paying to the claimant, though at less than full market rent. She therefore stayed on as a trespasser until she finally obtained social housing. The question was what damages were payable for the period of the trespass. The claimant would not have rented the property on the open market had it become free, but would have retained it for use as subsidised accommodation. The judge at first instance noted that the heavy subsidy was calculated by deducting from average local authority rents a figure designed to represent the disadvantages of service life. The judge reasoned that since the defendant had lost the right to live in service quarters because she had lost her service connection, viz her husband, the best way to calculate the damages was to remove the 'service' element from the subsidised rent and to charge the average local authority rent. The Court of Appeal disagreed.

- Kennedy LJ said that it was appropriate to look to the benefit the defendant had obtained, and that the benefit was related not to the average local authority rent as used by the air force in its calculations, but the actual local authority rent which the defendant would have been required to pay had she been able to obtain such accommodation.
- Hoffmann LJ agreed, but he added that he reached this result by explicitly restitutionary reasoning: that the claimant could normally claim the defendant's gain, that the defendant's gain was normally measured by the open market value, but in a case such as this, in which the defendant could never plausibly have dealt at market values, the question could be asked in the form 'what was the value of the gain *to the defendant*', that is, a version of the question which takes into account 'subjective devaluation'[2].

- Lloyd LJ, however, relying on *Phillips v Homfray*[3], rejected the view that restitutionary reasoning could be applied directly to trespass to land. Instead, he said that the claim was to be treated as analogous to the established principles of mesne profits, and that although the matter was not subject to decisive authority, the best approach was that where the case was not one in which the parties normally dealt on market principles, the measure of damages depended on 'the terms which would in practice form the terms on which the landlord would let'[4]. In the case at hand, that meant a rent at service terms[5].

In *Inverugie*, the Privy Council purported to pass no comment on *Ashman*, using the argument that in *Inverugie* counsel had not suggested a restitutionary form of reasoning to the court, and that therefore the issue did not come up for decision. In *Blake*, however, Lord Nicholls, in distinguishing clearly between the 'reasonable fee' basis of the 'user principle' cases and the 'account of profits' basis used in other parts of the law, might be said to have given comfort to the Lloyd view of *Ashman*, or at least not to have backed the Hoffmann view to the extent that its supporters might have hoped.

There is some evidence, however, that in cases similar to *Ashman* lower courts are allowing claimants to opt for what they call a 'restitutionary' measure of damages, and that they assess this 'restitutionary' measure by reference solely to the defendant's benefit[6]. In *Gondal v Dillon Newsagents Ltd*[7] the Court of Appeal appears to have endorsed this approach, although the court notes that the 'objective' nature of the reasonable rent measure produces very similar results to the 'benefits' measure.

In contrast, in *Lewisham London Borough Council v Masterson*[8] the Court of Appeal, while citing Hoffmann LJ's approach in *Ashman* 'with respect', makes three decisions which are clearly incompatible with an account of profits approach. First, an award for trespass is made even though the defendant's venture was a failure and made no profit. Secondly, the defendant was not allowed to deduct from the award any amount to represent his own expenditure in the venture[9]. And thirdly, and most importantly, the court said that where the parties had reached agreement on a rent, but the defendant entered the property prematurely without authorisation, the measure of damages is prima facie to be based on the rent agreed, and is not affected by the fact that what the defendant 'received' through the trespass was not the full lease itself (on which the rent was based), but a tenancy at will. The measure is thus not the actual 'benefit' accruing to the particular defendant in the particular circumstances, but the market value of what the claimant gave up as evidenced by the deal itself.

1   (1993) 66 P & CR 195, [1993] 2 EGLR 102, 25 HLR 513. See also *Ministry of Defence v Thompson* [1993] 2 EGLR 107.
2   On 'subjective valuation' see above, para 1.30.
3   (1883) 24 Ch D 439. Both the correctness and the scope of the authority of this case have come in for a good deal of, mainly adverse, academic comment. See eg Gummow 'Unjust Enrichment, Restitution and Proprietary Remedies' in Finn (ed) *Essays on Restitution* (1990), pp 60–67, Birks 'Civil Wrongs: A New World' in *Butterworths Lectures 1990–1991* (1992), pp 65–67, Virgo *Principles of the Law of Restitution* (1999), pp 481–484. The judicial approach to it (see *Inverugie Investments Ltd v Hackett* [1995] 3 All ER 841, [1995] 1 WLR 713) is that, whatever it means, it does not stand in the way of the user principle.
4   Citing *Woodfall on Landlord and Tenant*.
5   Lloyd LJ's conclusion should in turn have meant that he would have set it at zero, since the defendant had continued to pay the claimants at the original rate. Mysteriously, however, Lloyd LJ opted to vote for Kennedy LJ's version of 'the benefit to Mrs Ashman' on the ground that 'it would not make much difference in terms of money'.
6   See eg *Gondal v Dillon Newsagents Ltd* (LEXIS Transcript, 29 July 1998). See also *City Securities*

(London) Ltd v Berkshire Car Parks Ltd (LEXIS Transcript, 8 December 1998), in which the Court of Appeal disallowed a 'restitutionary' claim for the benefits accruing to the defendant, but only on the ground that the benefits had accrued to someone other than the defendant who was liable. The Court did not question the exact meaning of the 'restitutionary' basis itself, although it is not clear that the point was argued. But cf *Dean and Chapter of the Cathedral and Metropolitan Church of Christ Canterbury v Whitbread plc* [1995] 24 EG 148, [1995] 1 EGLR 82 (referring to the reasonable rent measure).

7   LEXIS Transcript, 29 July 1998.
8   [2000] 1 EGLR 134.
9   See below, para 12.65, for the practice in intellectual property cases.

12.40   It is submitted that, notwithstanding *Ashman*, the correct measure, at least for the time being, is the *Inverurgie* reasonable rent measure, not an account of profits (or some other pure 'benefit' measure); and that the relevance of the defendant's benefit is only as one factor in gauging a reasonable level for the rent. The reasonable fee measure fully recognises the purposes of the user principle, namely the vindication of the rights of property owners to exclude others and to preserve their discretion whether to use their property or not[1].

1   See below, para 12.47 for possible future developments.

NUISANCE

12.41   In *Carr-Saunders v Dick McNeil Associates Ltd*[1] the court effectively awarded reasonable price damages, in a nuisance case in which the claimant had abandoned a claim for a mandatory injunction but had pursued a claim for an injunction in lieu. The court took into account the bargaining positions of the parties as they would have been had the defendant sought to buy the right from the claimant, and added that, as part of that consideration, it could, if the evidence had been available, have used the defendant's expectation of profit from the purchase of the right. As we have seen[2], the relevance of the profit to be made by the defendant is to the amount of the reasonable fee, not, at least yet, to an account of profits.

1   [1986] 2 All ER 888.
2   See above, paras 12.28, 12.36, and 12.40.

12.42   Nuisances often consist essentially of the wrongful 'use' of someone else's property, in the sense that the defendant 'uses' the claimant's property as a kind of dumping ground for the adverse consequences of the defendant's activities[1]. This is most clear in 'physical interference' cases, such as the 'dust' claim in *Hunter v Canary Wharf*[2]. But it might also apply in a more metaphorical way to other forms of interference.

1   Cf *Whitwham v Westminster Brymbo Coal & Coke Co* [1896] 2 Ch 538.
2   [1997] AC 655, [1997] 2 All ER 426.

12.43   The possibility of reasonable fee damages in nuisance was confirmed by the Court of Appeal in *Stoke-on-Trent City Council v W & J Wass Ltd*[1], at least where the claimant had suffered a substantial loss.

1   [1988] 1 WLR 1406; below, para 12.44.

12.44   In *Stoke-on-Trent City Council v W & J Wass Ltd*[1] the question for the Court of Appeal was whether the user principle should apply to rights to prohibit competing markets held on the same date (same-day market rights), where there was no proof of loss. Infringement of same-day market rights, unlike infringement of other market rights, is actionable without proof of loss. Customarily, however, where no loss has been established, the remedy for infringement of a same-day market right is the combination of an injunction and nominal damages.

1   [1988] 1 WLR 1406.

12.45   The argument for the extension of the user principle to same-day market rights was that since the facts established that the defendant had committed the tort, the only question was whether the claimant could use the user principle as a measure of the damages. The objective of user principle damages, as explored in *A-G v Blake*[1], citing in *Watson Laidlaw & Co Ltd v Pott, Cassels and Williamson*[2] and *Mediana (Owners of Steamship) v Comet (Owners of Lightship)*[3], is to protect the claimant's property rights and to vindicate a certain concept of property itself[4]. Same-day market rights are property rights and, it was argued for the claimant, should therefore be protected in the same way.

The Court of Appeal rejected the claim. Nourse LJ said that, apart from the wayleave cases, the user principle applied only where the claimant had suffered a substantial loss. In trespass cases, the defendant had deprived the claimant of the opportunity to use the claimant's own property, which counted as such a substantial loss[5]. In patent cases, the loss was presumed from the claimant's established willingness to licence the right. As for the wayleave cases, Nourse LJ said:

> Although I would accept that there may be a logical difficulty in making a distinction between the present case and the wayleave cases, I think that if the user principle were to be applied here there would be an equal difficulty in distinguishing other cases of more common occurrence, particularly in nuisance. Suppose a case where a right to light or a right of way had been obstructed to the profit of the servient owner but at no loss to the dominant owner. It would be difficult, in the application of the user principle, to make a logical distinction between such an obstruction and the infringement of a right to hold a market. And yet the application of that principle to such cases would not only give a right to substantial damages where no loss had been suffered but would revolutionise the tort of nuisance by making it unnecessary to prove loss. Moreover, if the principle were to be applied in nuisance, why not in other torts where the defendant's wrong can work to his own profit, for example in defamation? As progenitors of the rule in trespass and some other areas, the wayleave cases have done good service. But just as their genus is peculiar, so ought their procreative powers to be exhausted[6].

It is not clear that Nourse LJ's reasoning will stand the test of time. It is not necessary in nuisance to show 'loss'. It is necessary, rather, to show 'damage', which usually consists of a substantial interference in the enjoyment of the relevant right. There is no necessity to show any specific financial loss flowing from such a substantial interference[7]. Furthermore, even though the purpose of the tort of nuisance is to protect the value of land, it is not necessary for the claimant to show, at least in a case of interference with enjoyment, that there has been a loss in market value. The loss of 'amenity' value (its value to the claimant) inherent in 'substantial interference' is enough[8]. The application of the user principle to nuisance would not 'revolutionise' the tort, as long as it was remembered that the user principle cannot affect whether there is liability in the first place. As for the defamation example, Nourse LJ does not explain how the user principle could apply at all in a case in which the defendant in no sense of the word 'uses' the claimant's property. It is submitted that Nourse LJ has confused the application of the user principle with a more general claim that an account of profits should be available as a remedy in tort, a claim which is in no way furthered by admitting the user principle in the tort of nuisance, or indeed the protection of same-day market rights.

1   [2001] 1 AC 268, [2000] 4 All ER 385.
2   (1914) 31 RPC 104, HL (Sc).
3   [1900] AC 113 at 117.
4   See above, para 12.35.
5   '[T]he trespass cases really depend on the fact that the defendant's use of the plaintiff's land deprives the plaintiff of any opportunity of using it himself': *Stoke-on-Trent City Council v W & J Wass Ltd* [1988] 1 WLR 1406 at 1414, per Nourse LJ.
6   [1988] 1 WLR 1406 at 1415.
7   *Nicholls v Ely Beet Sugar Refinery* [1936] Ch 343 at 356, per Romer LJ. Buckley *Law of Nuisance* (2nd edn, 1996), p 123 says that nuisance by interference with a servitude requires no proof of *damage*, not just no proof of *financial loss*. If true, this point would further undermine Nourse LJ's reasoning in *Stoke-on-Trent City Council v W & J Wass Ltd* [1988] 1 WLR 1406. It is not, however, universally accepted. See Grubb (ed) *Law of Tort* (2002), para 22.14.
8   *Hunter v Canary Wharf Ltd* [1997] AC 655 at 696, [1997] 2 All ER 426 at 442, per Lord Lloyd.

12.46   Nicholls LJ follows a somewhat different course in *Stoke-on-Trent City Council v W & J Wass Ltd*[1]. Nicholls LJ concentrates on the analogy between market rights and patents[2], pointing out that market rights are only protected against 'disturbance', whereas in patents the protection is of the property right itself. The difficulty with this line of thought is that same-day market rights are actionable without proof of loss, which is difficult to explain without conceding that such rights protect against more than 'disturbance'. Nicholls LJ's point of view seems, at the end of his judgment, to reduce to declaring that holders of same-day market rights have always in the past received only nominal damages, and there should be no change.

1   [1988] 1 WLR 1406.
2   [1988] 1 WLR 1406 at 1418. See below, para 12.58ff.

FUTURE DIRECTION OF THE LAW

12.47   Lord Nicholls in *A-G v Blake* says that the only explanation, in his view, for the law using the 'reasonable fee' measure in some circumstances and the account of profits in others, is the historical divide between common law and equity, 'an accident of history'[1]. The question whether the reasonable fee remedy should be replaced by an account of profits therefore remains open[2].

To meet the problem identified in *Inverugie*[3], that an account of profits in a case in which profits were low or non-existent would leave the claimant worse off than the reasonable fee basis, it is possible that the suggestion might be made that the claimant should have an option to choose the reasonable fee basis or the account of profits basis[4], an option which exists in intellectual property law[5].

Where no injunction is granted to prevent future wrongful use, the better view is surely that the reasonable fee basis should be used, or that, if the account of profits basis is used, the criteria employed by the courts in deciding whether to refuse an injunction[6] might also need to apply to the possibility of refusing an account of profits. But that would still leave open the possibility of an option for an account of profits in other cases.

It is worth asking, however, whether there is any need for such a development. Exemplary damages are available in cases in which defendants would otherwise escape with deliberately making profits out of torts, and the reasonable fee measure deals with the *excess* profits made by defendants because the commission of the tort meant that their costs were artificially low. The account of profits remedy seems to target only the profit an innocent or merely negligent defendant would have made anyway. But in intellectual property cases, which might be thought to be operating in a similar context, the account of profits remedy is not usually available unless the defendant knows about the claimant's rights[7]. Additionally, in many contexts, the account of profits is subject to allowances for the defendant's efforts and also to apportionment[8], so that profits beyond those produced by the reduction in costs the defendant achieved by the infringement are often not claimable. It is therefore far from clear that there is much to gain by extending the account of profits remedy to the user principle cases, even as an option.

1   [2001] 1 AC 268 at 280, [2000] 4 All ER 385 at 393.
2   This is true at least at House of Lords level. Whether it is true in the lower courts depends on the view taken of *Phillips v Homfray* (1883) 24 Ch D 439. In *Ministry of Defence v Ashman* (1993) 66 P & CR 195 at 200–201, [1993] 2 EGLR 102 at 105, (1993) 25 HLR 513 at 519, Hoffmann LJ was prepared to say that an account of profits was recoverable in trespass to land. The other judges were not prepared to say this (see above, para 12.39). See also the works cited at para 12.39, n 3 above, and Cooke 'Trespass, Mesne Profits and Restitution' (1994) 110 LQR 420. No progress was made down the route from reasonable fee to account of profits in *Re Polly Peck International plc (No 4)* [1997] 2 BCLC 630 (see Jaffey 'Restitution and Trespass to Land' [1997] RLR 79).
3   *Inverugie Investments Ltd v Hackett* [1995] 3 All ER 841, [1995] 1 WLR 713.
4   It might be argued that there are the beginnings of such a development in *Gondal v Dillon Newsagents Ltd* (LEXIS Transcript, 29 July 1998), which the Court of Appeal treats the 'benefit' measure as one optional measure with the user principle reasonable fee damages as the other option.
5   See below, para 12.58ff.
6   See above, para 12.26: '(1) ... the injury to the plaintiff's legal rights is small, (2) And is one which is capable of being estimated in money, (3) And is one which can be adequately compensated by a small money payment, (4) And the case is one in which it would be oppressive to the defendant to grant an injunction': *Shelfer v City of London Electric Lighting Co* [1895] 1 Ch 287 at 322–323, per AL Smith LJ; approved in *Jaggard v Sawyer* [1995] 2 All ER 189 at 208, [1995] 1 WLR 269 at 287, per Millett LJ.
7   See below, para 12.59.
8   See below, para 12.63.

Torts (Interference with Goods) Act 1977

12.48   Two situations analogous to the user principle should be mentioned in the specific contexts of the torts concerning interference with goods, especially the tort of conversion (or trover), namely the torts which are governed by the Torts (Interference with Goods) Act 1977[1].

1   See generally Grubb (ed) *Law of Tort* (2002), ch 11.

12.49   Under the Torts (Interference with Goods) Act 1977, s 3(2), the remedies available for wrongful interference with goods are:

(a)   an order for delivery of the goods, and for payment of any consequential damages, or

(b)   an order for delivery of the goods, but giving the defendant the alternative of paying damages by reference to the value of the goods, together in either alternative with payment of any consequential damages, or

(c)   damages.

Only one of the three forms of remedy can apply. The first remedy, which is, of course, a restitutionary remedy, is at the discretion of the court[1]. The claimant has the power to choose between the second and third remedies[2], and the second remedy itself contains a choice which the defendant may make.

1   See the Torts (Interference with Goods) Act 1977, s 3(3)(b).
2   See n 1.

12.50   Damages in conversion are generally compensatory. Consequential damages are measured according to ordinary tort principles of remoteness[1]. Damages for the conversion of the goods themselves are based on the market value of the goods[2]. Market value is generally taken to be the value of the goods at the time of the conversion[3], so that it makes no difference if the value of the goods falls after the conversion but before trial[4]. If the value of the goods rose between conversion and trial, the claimant may only claim the additional value as consequential loss if the claimant can show that the goods would have been sold in the period and the extra value realised[5], a rule explicable only in terms of the compensatory nature of the measure of damages[6]. There is some lack of clarity, however, because the Torts (Interference with Goods) Act 1977 abolished the tort of detinue, integrating it into conversion, without saying whether its somewhat different rule, that the value of the goods is their value at the time of trial, should carry over into the post-1977 era. In *IBL Ltd v Coussens*[7] the Court of Appeal said that, where the evidence shows that the claimant would have sold the goods before trial had they been returned, the correct value is the value at the time of the conversion, but if the evidence is that the claimant would not have sold on the goods, the correct value is the 'detinue' measure, viz the value at the time of trial. An approach which seems to flow naturally from a purely compensatory view of the measure of damage.

1   *Hillesden Securities v Ryjack Ltd* [1983] 1 WLR 959; *Kuwait Airways Corpn v Iraqi Airways Co (No 3)* [2001] Lloyd's Rep 161.
2   *Henderson v Williams* [1895] 1 QB 521; *Solloway v McLaughlin* [1938] AC 247.
3   *Henderson v Williams* [1895] 1 QB 521; *Solloway v McLaughlin* [1938] AC 247.
4   *BBMB Finance (Hong Kong) Ltd v Eda Holdings* [1990] 1 WLR 409; *Solloway v McLaughlin* [1938] AC 247.
5   *The Playa Larga* [1983] 2 Lloyd's Rep 171.
6   See also *Sachs v Miklos* [1948] 2 KB 23, [1948] 1 All ER 67 (the claimant knew that the defendant was going to sell the claimant's furniture, the value of which then rose, but the claimant did nothing to intervene – the claimant was denied the enhanced value of the furniture).
7   [1991] 2 All ER 133.

12.51   But in one circumstance, the measure of damages has been said to have a restitutionary element[1]. In conversion (though not in the abolished tort of detinue[2]), where there is a judgment for damages, if the defendant delivers the same or equivalent goods, the delivery only goes to mitigate the damages, and the claimant is entitled to claim any difference between the value of the goods at the time of conversion and the value at the time of their return. For example, if the defendant converts the goods when they are worth £1,000, but returns equivalent goods later when the market value has fallen to £750, the claimant is entitled to £250 in damages. This rule applies regardless of whether the claimant would have sold the goods or not, or even whether the claimant would have used the goods or not[3]. It is argued that, since a claimant who would not have sold the goods, or who would not have used them, is returned by the mere return of the goods to the position he or she would have been in if the tort had not been committed, there is in these cases no real loss. It is furthermore argued that the effect of the rule is to measure the damages by reference to the defendant's gain, at least in the case in which the defendant sells the goods at the higher price, buys them back (or buys equivalent goods) at the lower price, and hands over the lower-priced goods to the claimant, leaving the defendant with the difference[4].

1   See Grubb (ed) *Law of Tort* (2002), para 11.121; Tettenborn 'Damages in Conversion – the Exception or the Anomaly?' [1993] CLJ 128.
2   *Crossfield v Such* (1852) 8 Ex Ch 159, 155 ER 1301.
3   See *BBMB Finance (Hong Kong) Ltd v Eda Holdings* [1990] 1 WLR 409; *Solloway v McLaughlin* [1938] AC 247; *Rhodes v Moules* [1895] 1 Ch 236.
4   *Rhodes v Moules* [1895] 1 Ch 236; *Solloway v McLaughlin* [1938] AC 247.

12.52   But the principle lying behind the rule is arguably simply the same as that which lies behind the user principle. Recall, for example the Earl of Halsbury LC's remark in *Mediana (Owners of Steamship) v Comet (Owners of Lightship)*[1] that it is no answer for a wrongdoer who has deprived the claimant of his chair to point out that he does not usually sit in it, or that he has plenty of other chairs in the room[2]. Even if the claimant would not have sold the goods at the higher price, the defendant has deprived the claimant of the opportunity to decide what to do with his or her own property. If the defendant had been obliged to travel a long way to find the replacement goods, so that the defendant's profit on the deal is considerably less than the difference between the market value at conversion and the market value on restoration, it would be very surprising indeed if the claimant were only entitled to claim the defendant's profit[3].

1   [1900] AC 113 at 117.
2   Approved in *Inverugie Investments Ltd v Hackett* [1995] 3 All ER 841 at 845, [1995] 1 WLR 713 at 717–718.
3   Cf *Glasspoole v Young* (1829) 9 B & C 696, 109 ER 259. Note that if the claimant would have sold the goods, the claimant's transaction costs are deductible from the damages because they would have been incurred anyway, a rule consistent with the compensatory measure of damages: *Whitmore v Black* (1844) 13 M & W 507, 153 ER 211.

12.53   The other example of non-compensatory damages for wrongful interference with goods is simply the application of the user principle itself to consequential damages in such torts. If the defendant has made use of the claimant's chattels, the claimant is entitled to a reasonable fee for that use regardless of whether the claimant can show that the goods would have been put to productive use[1].

The damages are based on the reasonable hire measure, not the defendant's profit[2]. It does not avail the defendant to show that because, for example, the goods were damaged, the defendant failed to put the goods to any valuable use[3]. On the other hand, although conversion itself may be brought against someone who is not in possession of the goods, user principle damages can only be claimed against those who have possession[4].

1   *Strand Electric Co Ltd v Brisford Entertainments Ltd* [1952] 2 QB 246, [1952] 1 All ER 796. But note that where the defendant was not making actual use of the goods, it seems that the claimant has to show that he or she was in fact deprived of use. Accordingly, where substitute goods are supplied by the defendant (as in *Mediana (Owners of Steamship) v Comet (Owners of Lightship)* [1900] AC 113), or even by a third party (*Dimond v Lovell* [2000] 2 All ER 897), no user principle damages are payable. It was further suggested by Denning LJ in *Strand Electric Co Ltd v Brisford Entertainments Ltd* (see also *Brandeis Goldschmidt & Co Ltd v Western Transport Ltd* [1981] QB 864, [1982] 1 All ER 28) that in the absence of actual use or damage by the defendant there can be no

damages under the user principle. There is thus no liability under this head for a warehouseman who detains goods without using or damaging them. But the distinction is not entirely clear. If I take your goods and then happen to do nothing with them, why should I not have to pay a reasonable fee for having them? How is that situation different from where I use them unsuccessfully? Is my intention to use them decisive? What if I do not know what purpose I will put them to, and in the event do nothing with them? Can it count as holding the goods for my purposes that I simply want to have them (eg works of art which I put in a bank vault)? Is the extra point about the warehouseman really non-use, or is it that having acquired the goods legitimately he merely refuses to hand them back? Is it that there might be no element of depriving the claimant of an opportunity to negotiate with the defendant?

2   *Strand Electric Co Ltd v Brisford Entertainments Ltd* [1952] 2 QB 246, [1952] 1 All ER 796.
3   *Mediana (Owners of Steamship) v Comet (Owners of Lightship)* [1900] AC 113.
4   *Farid v Theodorou and Blacklake Securities* (LEXIS Transcript, 30 January 1992, CA).

Beyond the user principle?

12.54   Attempts to extend restitutionary remedies beyond the user principle cases in English tort law have not so far been successful. The leading case is *Halifax Building Society v Thomas*[1]. Thomas perpetrated a mortgage fraud on the Halifax Building Society. The Society sold the mortgaged property for more than the amount it was owed, thus creating the surplus which was the subject matter of the dispute. The society held on to the profit while its status was decided. Thomas was convicted of fraud in a criminal court, and the criminal court ordered that his profit from the fraud should be confiscated for the benefit of the Crown Prosecution Service. The Society moved for a declaration that the surplus was the property of the Society, not of Thomas, and that therefore the Crown Prosecution Service could not enforce the confiscation order against the Society. The Court of Appeal, agreeing with the judge below, dismissed the Society's application.

The Society argued for the recognition of a general rule that the principle of unjust enrichment as laid out in the American Law Institute's 1st *Restatement of the Law of Restitution, Quasi-Contract and Constructive Trusts* should be adopted as part of English law, and applied to the case of tortfeasors regardless of whether the user principle applied. The relevant principle is that: 'A person who has been unjustly enriched at the expense of another is required to make restitution to the other'[2]. The Society accepted that the principle of subtractive unjust enrichment[3] could not apply, because the surplus did not represent property which the Society had lost. It argued instead for a general rule that gains arising from wrongs gave rise to a duty to make restitution. The Court of Appeal decisively rejected this approach. The law remained as Ashhurst J understood it in *Pasley v Freeman*[4]: 'what is it to the plaintiff whether the defendant was or was not to gain by it; the injury to him is the same'[5].

1   [1996] Ch 217, [1995] 4 All ER 673. Followed in *MacDonald v Myerson* [2001] EWCA Civ 66, [2001] NPC 20; and *Mortgage Express v McDonnell* [2001] EWCA Civ 887, (2001) 82 P & CR 39.
2   At para 1.
3   On 'unjust enrichment by subtraction' see above, para 1.23.
4   (1789) 3 Term Rep 51 at 62, 100 ER 450 at 456.
5   Virgo *Principles of the Law of Restitution* (1999), p 494 cites *Hill v Perrott* (1810) 3 Taunt 274, 128 ER 109, and *Abbotts v Barry* (1820) 2 Brad & Bing 369, 129 ER 1009, as contrary authorities, although these cases seem to concern restitution for mistake or as vindicating the claimant's continuing proprietary interests.

12.55   There have been attempts to explain away *Halifax Building Society v Thomas* by pointing to the fact that the confiscation order had already taken the profits away from Thomas, so that he was not, at the time of the hearing on the

Society's application, 'enriched' at all[1]. This interpretation is not borne out by a close reading of the case. Peter Gibson LJ, with whose judgment both the other members of the court agreed, says that the fatal objection to the Society's case was that the Society had affirmed the mortgage to enforce the charge, and recovered all that it was entitled to under the original contract, so that it would be inconsistent to allow the Society to claim even more[2].

One might argue that, in the light of *Blake*[3], Peter Gibson LJ's point might now be met by saying that there might be a restitutionary remedy for breach of the contract, so that electing to enforce the mortgage is not necessarily inconsistent with the existence of a restitutionary right. But, whatever *Blake* means, it seems unlikely that it would cover cases of mortgage fraud[4].

In any case, even if *Blake* might cover mortgage fraud, Peter Gibson LJ puts his point in a second way which would still be fatal to the Society's position, namely that he would not be prepared to say that the 'unjust enrichment' was 'at the expense' of the Society, since the Society has suffered no relevant loss[5].

1 See eg Law Com no 247 *Aggravated, Exemplary and Restitutionary Damages*, Pt III, para 1.27 (p 36).
2 [1996] Ch 217 at 228, [1995] 4 All ER 673 at 681.
3 [2001] 1 AC 268, [2000] 4 All ER 385; above, para 11.17ff.
4 Note also that Lord Nicholls in his review of the law in *Blake* mentions various kinds of restitutionary claims, but does not take the clear opportunity provided by undertaking such a review to cast any doubt whatsoever on *Halifax Building Society v Thomas*.
5 Virgo *Principles of the Law of Restitution* (1999), p 496 suggests that Peter Gibson LJ is here 'right for the wrong reason' – the right reason allegedly being that the surplus proceeds of sale were only 'an indirect result of the wrong once the house had been sold'.

12.56 It is also worth remarking that, when discussing whether it would be offensive to concepts of justice to allow a fraudster such as Thomas to take a profit derived from his fraud, Peter Gibson LJ does not leap into a discussion of the effects of the criminal law confiscation order, but rather points to the House of Lords decision in *Tinsley v Milligan*[1], where the court rejected the 'public conscience' test for illegality in contract and spoke instead of whether the claimant was relying on an illegality to establish her claim. Since it was the Society, not Thomas, that was making the claim, the 'concept of justice' point was said not to arise.

Peter Gibson LJ only mentions the confiscation point in the context of the Society's second way of putting its case, namely that the court should say that there was a constructive trust with regard to the surplus. Peter Gibson LJ says that the confiscation order is Parliament's answer to the question of whether the constructive trust should be used to stop wrongdoers benefiting from their own wrongs, which reinforces him in his conclusion, arrived at on other grounds, that the law of constructive trusts itself does not apply to situations such as these. In a subsequent case, *Box v Barclays Bank plc*[2], Ferris J, admittedly obiter, said that *Halifax* precludes the conclusion that where the defendant induces the claimant to deposit money with the defendant by means of a fraud, the defendant holds the money on the basis of a constructive trust. Ferris J also relied on *Lonrho plc v Fayed (No 2)*[3], *El Ajou v Dollar Land Holdings plc*[4] and *Re Goldcorp Exchange Ltd*[5] to establish the proposition that fraud does not create fiduciary relationships, a line of reasoning independent of the criminal compensation point in *Halifax*.

1 [1994] 1 AC 340, [1993] 3 All ER 65; on which see below, para 14.56ff.
2 [1998] Lloyd's Rep Bank 185.
3 [1991] 4 All ER 961, [1992] 1 WLR 1 (no fiduciary relationship exists between representor and representee in a case of fraudulent misrepresentation).

4   [1993] 3 All ER 717, [1993] BCLC 735 (no fiduciary relationship created with third parties in a case of fraudulent misrepresentation); above, para 5.61ff.
5   [1995] 1 AC 74, [1994] 2 All ER 806; see above, para 9.3.

12.57   Another objection to Peter Gibson LJ's approach is that the claimant's affirming of the mortgage should not have affected the question of whether the defendant had to pay over the surplus funds. The objection is that the claimant's failure to rescind the transaction could not have waived any restitutionary rights the claimant might have had, because any such waiver would also have affected the claimant's right to sue on the original tort if the proceeds of sale had failed to cover the loss, an effect it could not possibly have had[1]. One suspects, however, that the court's response to such a point would be to say that the claimant did not have any restitutionary rights in the absence of a rescission. By affirming the contractual rights under the mortgage, the claimant asserted a right to apply the funds to any loss, and to sue for a shortfall if there was one. In doing so, the claimant chose not to go down a route along which any restitutionary rights lay.

1   Mitchell 'No Account of Profits for a Victim of Deceit' [1996] Lloyd's Maritime and Commercial Law Quarterly 314; Virgo *Principles of the Law of Restitution* (1999), p 495. See also Birks 'The Proceeds of Mortgage Fraud' (1996) 10 Trust Law International 2.

B   Intellectual property rights

12.58   Where the defendant has violated the claimant's intellectual property rights – whether the form of the infringement of a patent, a design right, a copyright or a trademark or in the form of an action for passing off – the claimant, in addition to seeking an injunction to prevent future violations, may choose either damages or an account of profits. The latter remedy has been described as 'a laborious and expensive procedure and ... infrequently resorted to'[1], but it is nevertheless available.

Although the claimant must choose one basis or the other[2], the courts allow the claimant to delay the choice until after it has obtained sufficient information from the defendant on which to make an informed choice. The court may, however, not only order the defendant to supply the necessary information, but also order the claimant to choose within a specified period after receipt of the information[3].

The two measures are capable of producing very different results. Only where the claimant's and defendant's anticipated profits are the same will the defendant's gain be the plaintiff's loss, and this will usually not be the case. In particular, although in many cases the defendant's profits might exceed the claimant's losses, there is no obvious upper limit to damages (especially where there are a number of possible claimants), whereas the upper limit of the profits measure does have an obvious limit – the total profits of the defendant[4].

1   Cornish *Intellectual Property* (4th edn, 1999), para 2–43.
2   *Neilson v Betts* (1871) LR 5 HL 1; and *De Vitre v Betts* (1873) LR 6 HL 319. See the Copyright Designs and Patents Act 1988, s 102. See further *Spring Form Inc v Toy Brokers Ltd* [2001] All ER (D) 09. See also *Redrow Homes Ltd v Bett Bros plc* [1999] 1 AC 197, [1998] 1 All ER 385 ('additional damages' under the Copyright Designs and Patents Act 1988, s 97, form part of the 'damages' option, and therefore cannot be claimed in addition to an account of profits).
3   *Island Records Ltd v Tring International plc* [1995] 3 All ER 444, [1996] 1 WLR 1256, [1995] FSR 560.
4   *Celanese International Corpn v BP Chemicals Ltd* [1999] RPC 203.

Innocence[1]

12.59   A complication of intellectual property law, which distinguishes it from some of the other principles of liability under consideration in this chapter, is the relevance of the defendant's innocence or otherwise when violating the claimant's rights.

In the statutes about patents, designs and copyrights there are explicit provisions to the effect that no damages are payable for any period in which the infringer did not know, and had no reasonable grounds for supposing, that the right existed[2]. The rule specifically concerns the existence of the right, however, not whether the defendant's act amounted to a infringement. A genuine belief that there was no infringement, or that the right had been properly licensed, is no excuse[3].

In types of intellectual property case in which statute has not intervened, the law is less certain. Damages are apparently payable for innocent infringements of a trade mark, whether registered or unregistered[4], even where an account of profits might be limited or refused[5].

There is also an 'innocence' rule specifically with regard to the account of profits remedy, but its range of application is different. Where statute has not explicitly intervened, the innocence rule appears to apply as it does generally[6]. Windeyer J explained in *Colbeam Palmer Ltd v Stock Affiliates Pty Ltd* that in an account of profits in an intellectual property case:

> [A] defendant is made to account for, and is then stripped of, profits he has made which it would be unconscionable that he retain. These are profits made by him dishonestly, that is by his knowingly infringing the rights of the proprietor ... This explains why the liability to account is still not necessarily coextensive with acts of infringement. The account is limited to the profits made by the defendant during the period when he knew of the plaintiff's rights[7].

An account of profits will thus only be awarded for infringement of a trade mark, for example, if the defendant deliberately interfered in the claimant's rights[8]. Similarly, in passing off, an account of profits will not be awarded unless the defendant deliberately passed off the claimant's goods[9]. Moreover, under the Patents Act 1977[10] that statute's innocence rule applies also to an account of profits[11].

But, for copyright infringements under the Copyrights Designs and Patents Act 1988[12], the rule applies only to 'damages', and is explicitly said to be 'without prejudice to any other remedy'[13]. In the predecessor provision to this part of the 1988 Act, the Copyright Act 1956, s 17, the innocence rule did not apply to accounts of profits, and the 1988 Act provides that changes in expression between its predecessors and itself are not to be taken to indicate changes in the law[14]. It seems likely that the courts will take a similar view of the provisions which apply to infringements of design rights[15], even though there were no corresponding predecessor sections[16].

The burden is on the claimant to show that the defendant had the relevant knowledge[17].

1   Cornish *Intellectual Property* (4th edn, 1999), para 2–42.
2   See the Patents Act 1977, s 62(1); the Registered Designs Act 1949, s 9(1); and the Copyrights Designs and Patents Act 1988, ss 97(1) and 233 (also affecting 'secondary infringement').
3   *Byrne v Statist Co* [1914] 1 KB 622.
4   *Spalding v Gamage* [1915] RPC 273.
5   *Spalding v Gamage* (1915) 32 RPC 273; *Gillette UK Ltd v Edenwest* [1994] RPC 279.
6   *Colbeam Palmer Ltd v Stock Affiliates Pty Ltd* [1972] RPC 303.
7   [1972] RPC 303 at 310.

8 *Edelsten v Edelsten* (1863) 1 De GJ & Sm 185, 46 ER 72; *Slazenger & Sons v Spalding & Bros* [1910] 1 Ch 257. A remedy in damages might nevertheless still be possible: *Gillette UK Ltd v Edenwest* [1994] RPC 279.

9 *My Kinda Town Ltd v Soll* [1982] FSR 147.

10 See the Patents Act 1977, s 62.

11 See the Registered Designs Act 1949, s 9, refers only to 'damages' and 'an injunction', which, it is submitted, allows room for the rule to apply.

12 See the Copyrights Designs and Patents Act 1988, ss 96 and 97. See *Redrow Homes Ltd v Bett Bros plc* [1999] 1 AC 197, [1998] 1 All ER 385.

13 See the Copyrights Designs and Patents Act 1988, s 97(1).

14 Section 172. See *Redrow Homes Ltd v Bett Bros plc* [1999] 1 AC 197, [1998] 1 All ER 385.

15 See eg s 229(2).

16 Cf *Redrow Homes Ltd v Bett Bros plc* [1999] 1 AC 197, [1998] 1 All ER 385.

17 *Moet v Couston* (1864) 33 Beav 578, 55 ER 493; *Colbeam Palmer Ltd v Stock Affiliates Pty Ltd* [1972] RPC 303.

Damages[1]

12.60   It is recognised that infringements of intellectual property rights amount to torts, albeit in some cases (such as that of patents), torts with a statutory basis[2]. The starting point for the measure of damages is therefore the loss suffered by the claimant as a result of the infringement, and that the object of damages is to return the claimant to the position which would have obtained but for the commission of the tort[3]. Such damages largely consist of the claimant's lost profits arising from the infringement[4], or, perhaps more accurately, the claimant's lost income minus any expenses the claimant would have incurred in generating that income[5].

1 For extensive treatment of the measure of damages in this context, see Cornish *Intellectual Property* (4th edn, 1999), para 2–43.

2 *Gerber Garment Technology Inc v Lectra Systems Ltd* [1997] RPC 443.

3 *General Tire and Rubber Co v Firestone Tyre and Rubber Co Ltd* [1976] RPC 197; *Gerber Garment Technology Inc v Lectra Systems Ltd* [1997] RPC 443. It is irrelevant that the defendant might have inflicted the same loss on the claimant by a different, non-infringing course of action. See *Gerber Garment Technology Inc v Lectra Systems Ltd* [1997] RPC 443; and *Celanese International Corpn v BP Chemicals Ltd* [1999] RPC 203.

4 These damages are not limited to the lost profits arising from the lost sales of the protected items themselves, but include the profits lost on the sales of associated items and on associated services such as repair contracts. See *Gerber Garment Technology Inc v Lectra Systems Ltd* [1997] RPC 443.

5 *Gerber Garment Technology Inc v Lectra Systems Ltd* [1997] RPC 443. Thus, according to the Court of Appeal in *Gerber*, the correct approach deducts from the lost income only the claimant's marginal costs, not the claimant's average costs.

12.61   It is important to note, however, that where the claimant cannot establish loss in the ordinary way, the measure of damages in intellectual property cases is a reasonable fee (a 'royalty'), just as if the user principle applied[1]. The reasonable fee measure is mostly used where the claimant would have licensed the right to the defendant had the defendant sought such a licence[2], and where, although the claimant would not have licensed the right, the parties were not in competition[3]. There is no rule of law, however, which restricts the claimant to the royalty measure in such cases, and the claimant may claim lost profits if it is possible to establish what they were[4].

1 See eg *Watson Laidlaw & Co Ltd v Pott, Cassels and Williamson* (1914) 31 RPC 104, HL (Sc); *General Tire and Rubber Co v Firestone Tyre and Rubber Co Ltd* [1976] RPC 197; *Gerber Garment Technology Inc v Lectra Systems Ltd* [1997] RPC 443.

2 See eg *General Tire and Rubber Co v Firestone Tyre and Rubber Co Ltd* [1976] RPC 197.

3 *Watson Laidlaw & Co Ltd v Pott, Cassels and Williamson* (1914) 31 RPC 104 at 119–120, HL (Sc). See also *Penn v Jack* (1867) LR 5 Eq 81; *Dormeuil Frères v Feraglow* [1990] RPC 449 (a trademark case).

4   *Gerber Garment Technology Inc v Lectra Systems Ltd* [1997] RPC 443. Lost chances in the manner
    of *Allied Maples Group Ltd v Simmons and Simmons* [1995] 4 All ER 907, [1995] 1 WLR 1602 may
    be used to establish the loss.

Account of profits

12.62   An account of profits in this context is 'a restitutionary remedy whose
purpose is to deprive the defendant of the profits which he has improperly made
by wrongful acts committed in breach of the plaintiff's rights and to transfer
those profits to the plaintiff'[1]. Although, clearly, a primary target of the remedy
is any additional profits the defendant has made as a result of the infringement, it
is important to note that 'If the defendant's wrong merely enables him to save
expense in production, the plaintiff may only be entitled to the amount by which
the saving increases the profit'[2].

Unrealised profits are recoverable[3], but, apparently, reductions in losses are
not[4]. The remedy is regarded as personal, not proprietary, and does not give rise
to a constructive trust[5].

1   Per Pumfrey J in *Spring Form Inc v Toy Brokers Ltd* [2001] All ER (D) 09. See also *My Kinda Town v
    Soll* [1983] RPC 15, [1982] 8 FSR 147; *United Horsenail Co v Stewart & Co* (1886) 3 RPC 139;
    Cartier v Carlile (1862) 31 Beav 292, 54 ER 1151. Note that the principle implies that the
    relevant profit is that after tax, not pre-tax. See *O'Sullivan v Management Agency & Music Ltd*
    [1985] 1 QB 428, [1985] 3 All ER 351; and *Celanese International Corpn v BP Chemicals Ltd*
    [1999] RPC 203.
2   *United Horsenail Co v Stewart & Co* (1886) 3 RPC 139, and on appeal (1888) 13 App Cas 401.
3   *Potton Ltd v Yorkclose Ltd* [1990] FSR 11.
4   *Celanese International Corpn v BP Chemicals Ltd* [1999] RPC 203. This is a consequence of the
    rejection of the 'marginal' or 'incremental' approach. See below, para 12.63.
5   Cornish *Intellectual Property* (4th edn, 1999), para 2–44.

12.63   The 'profit' is not always calculated on the same basis. In fraudulent
passing off, the profit is the actual profit made in selling the goods in question.
But in patent or trade mark cases, the relevant profit is limited to the part of the
total profit which is 'attributable' to the infringement of the mark or patent[1].
Where a person makes profits by the use or sale of some thing, and that whole
thing came into existence by reason of the wrongful use of a patent design or
copyright, the whole of the profit is attributable to the infringement[2]. But in
other cases there should be an apportionment[3].

Apportionment takes place on the basis of 'legal' causation, analogous to that
used in deciding whether damages are recoverable in tort[4]. There is liability for
profits 'caused' by the infringement, but not for profits merely 'occasioned' by the
infringement[5]. These principles apply, however, in ways peculiar to intellectual
property infringements. For example, in a reversal of the tort damages rule,
claimants have to take *defendants* as they find them, and cannot complain that the
defendant should have generated greater profits by acting differently. The
question is what profit was made by the defendant, not what profit the defendant
could have made[6].

The precise method of apportionment to be adopted is not, however, entirely
clear. A purely marginal (or 'incremental') approach has not found favour,
because of the problem that the infringement might have improved the efficiency
of other aspects of the infringer's business[7]. One method which has received
judicial approval is, at least in the absence of special reasons to the contrary, to
attribute the profits of a single project to different parts or aspects of that project
in the same proportion as the costs and expenses were contributed by them[8]. But
this procedure gives only a 'base allocated profit'[9] and it is possible, if the

evidence clearly so shows[10], to make adjustments to allow for the possibility that particular cost elements added more than average value[11].

1   *Cartier v Carlile* (1862) 31 Beav 292, 54 ER 1151; *United Shoe and Nail v Stewart* (1888) 13 App Cas 401; *Colbeam Palmer Ltd v Stock Affiliates Pty Ltd* [1972] RPC 303; See also per Pumfrey J in *Spring Form Inc v Toy Brokers Ltd* [2001] All ER (D) 09, citing Meagher Gummow and Lehane *Equity: Doctrines and Remedies* (3rd edn, 1992).
2   *Celanese International Corpn v BP Chemicals Ltd* [1999] RPC 203; and *Spring Form Inc v Toy Brokers Ltd* [2001] All ER (D) 09, both using the analogy of *Peter Pan Manufacturing Corpn v Corsets Silhouette* [1963] 3 All ER 402, [1964] 1 WLR 96. See also *Dart Industries Inc v Decor Corp Pty Ltd* [1994] FSR 567.
3   Note that the issue of whether to apportion or not is said to be an issue of fact: 'In deciding whether the defendant has to account for all or only a part of the profits made on a particular venture, I respectfully agree with the view expressed by the Canadian Federal Court of Appeal in *Imperial Oil v Lubrizol* (1996) 71 CPR (3d) 26 that this is a matter of fact and that form must not be allowed to triumph over substance': per Laddie J in *Celanese International Corpn v BP Chemicals Ltd* [1999] RPC 203.
4   *Celanese International Corpn v BP Chemicals Ltd* [1999] RPC 203. See also *Imperial Oil v Lubrizol* (1996) 71 CPR (3d) 26.
5   *Celanese International Corpn v BP Chemicals Ltd* [1999] RPC 203, citing *Galoo v Bright Grahame Murray* [1994] 1 WLR 1360; and *Imperial Oil v Lubrizol* (1996) 71 CPR (3d) 26 at 30.
6   *Celanese International Corpn v BP Chemicals Ltd* [1999] RPC 203, approving *Dart Industries Inc v Decor Corpn Pty Ltd* [1994] FSR 567 (HC of Australia). Similarly it is not relevant that the defendant could have made the same profits in a different way which would have avoided infringing the claimant's rights: *Celanese International Corpn v BP Chemicals Ltd* [1999] RPC 203, citing *Potton Ltd v Yorkclose Ltd* [1990] FSR 11; *Peter Pan Manufacturing Corpn v Corsets Silhouette* [1963] RPC 45; and *Baker Energy Resources Corpn v Reading & Bates Construction* (1994) 58 CPR (3d) 359.
7   *Celanese International Corpn v BP Chemicals Ltd* [1999] RPC 203, following *Imperial Oil v Lubrizol* (1996) 71 CPR (3d) 26. See apparently contra, *Siddell v Vickers* (1888) 5 RPC 416 and *My Kinda Town Ltd v Soll* [1983] RPC 15 at 49. These cases were explained in *Celanese International Corpn v BP Chemicals Ltd* [1999] RPC 203 at 228, per Laddie J: *Siddell* is 'unclear' and in *My Kinda Town*: 'The comparative inquiry ... was designed only to discover what proportion of the defendant's customers were confused. In other words it was only intended to distinguish non-infringing from infringing activities. It was not an incremental assessment of the profits made in respect of sales to diners who were confused'.
8   *Celanese International Corpn v BP Chemicals Ltd* [1999] RPC 203; *Potton Ltd v Yorkclose Ltd* [1990] FSR 11.
9   *Celanese International Corpn v BP Chemicals Ltd* [1999] RPC 203.
10 The evidence must apparently relate to additional profitability, not to speculative assessments of importance: *Celanese International Corpn v BP Chemicals Ltd* [1999] RPC 203.
11 See n 9.

12.64   The maximum amount which can be awarded is the total profit made by the defendant. If different claimants seek accounts in respect of different infringing activities of a defendant within a single business, the total profits payable cannot exceed the total profits made by the defendant in that business[1]. Where the defendant carries on multiple businesses or sells different products, only one of which infringes, he has only to account for the profits made by the infringements.

1   *United Horse Shoe & Nail Co Ltd v Steward & Co* (1888) 5 RPC 260; *Celanese International Corpn v BP Chemicals Ltd* [1999] RPC 203.

12.65   The court has an additional discretion to allow expenses for the exercise of skill and labour in bringing the infringing item to the market at all. The costs of research and development incurred (including abortive research) are deductible on this basis, although a different approach might be necessary if where there is a massive imbalance between research and development costs in the years of infringement as compared with other years[1]. Financing costs specifically attributable to the project are also deductible[2], but there can be no deduction for internal financing costs, which would amount to making a deduction for the profits themselves[3].

1   *Celanese International Corpn v BP Chemicals Ltd* [1999] RPC 203. Note that the court also says that income from the exploitation of the resultant technology through licensing has to be deducted from the total costs.
2   *Celanese International Corpn v BP Chemicals Ltd* [1999] RPC 203.
3   *Potton Ltd v Yorkclose Ltd* [1990] FSR 11; *Re United Merthyr Collieries Co* (1872) LR 15 Eq 46.

12.66   There is a further distinction to be made, between patent and copyright cases on the one hand and trade mark cases on the other:

> It was suggested that the defendant's profit should be measured by the difference between the amount it received for painting sets bearing the trade mark and the amount it had paid to obtain them. The account taken when a patent has been infringed was suggested as an analogy. But to my mind there is an important distinction. If the infringer of a patent sells an article made wholly in accordance with the invention and thereby obtains more than it cost him to make or acquire it, he is accountable for the difference as profit. That is because he has infringed the patentee's monopoly right to make, use, exercise and vend the invention. But in the case of a registered trade mark, infringement consists in the unauthorised use of the mark in the course of trade in relation to goods in respect of which it is registered. The profit for which the infringer of a trade mark must account is thus not the profit he made from selling the article itself but, as the ordinary form of order shews, the profit made in selling it under the trade mark[1].

Thus in *Colbeam Palmer Ltd v Stock Affiliates Pty Ltd*[2] the defendant could deduct from the selling price not just the cost of acquiring the goods, but also all the 'direct' (ie marginal) costs of selling and delivering the goods. But no deduction was made to represent contributions to overheads or general managerial expenses, since, on the facts, there was no evidence that such costs had increased at the margin[3].

1   *Colbeam Palmer Ltd v Stock Affiliates Pty Ltd* [1972] RPC 303 at 312, High Court of Australia.
2   [1972] RPC 303.
3   *Colbeam Palmer Ltd v Stock Affiliates Pty Ltd* [1972] RPC 303; *Spring Form Inc v Toy Brokers Ltd* [2001] All ER (D) 09.

C   Crimes

12.67   Defendants may commit crimes in the course of acting in ways which, quite independently, give rise to restitutionary rights. For example where there is a claim for the restoration of money paid under duress, it will often be the case that in the course of the same events the defendant will have committed a crime, for example blackmail or false imprisonment[1]. Similarly, claims for money had and received can arise from circumstances in which someone has committed a theft or the crime of handling stolen goods[2]. Moreover, some of the torts discussed in the preceding sections of this chapter also amount to crimes, or amount to crimes in certain circumstances.

1   See eg *Duke de Cadaval v Collins* (1836) 4 Ad & El 858, 111 ER 1006.
2   Cf *Lipkin Gorman (a firm) v Karpnale Ltd* [1991] 2 AC 548; on which see above, para 3.13.

12.68   In addition, several statutes that establish criminal liability also provide for the restoration of property. For example the Powers of Criminal Courts (Sentencing) Act 2000, s 148, provides that where goods have been stolen and a person has been convicted of any offence 'with reference to the theft':

(a)   the court may order anyone having possession or control of the stolen goods to restore them to any person entitled to recover them from him; or

(b)   on the application of a person entitled to recover from the person convicted any other goods directly or indirectly representing the stolen goods (as being the proceeds of any disposal or realisation of the whole or part of them or of goods so representing them), the court may order those other goods to be delivered or transferred to the applicant; or

(c)   the court may order that a sum not exceeding the value of the stolen goods shall be paid, out of any money of the person convicted which was taken out of his possession on his apprehension, to any person who, if those goods were in the possession of the person convicted, would be entitled to recover them from him.

There is, however, no general common law doctrine that victims of crime are entitled to restitutionary remedies, such as an account of profits, from defendants guilty of those crimes[1]. This doctrine follows from the general approach of English law to the relationship between civil and criminal liability. In England crimes do not automatically create torts[2]. The right to sue in tort on the breach of a statute which does not explicitly provide for such an action can only be established on the basis of a finding that Parliament intended there to be such a remedy[3], a finding which is difficult to extract from the courts since the issue is subject to a number of presumptions in the opposite direction[4]. Indeed there are some judicial pronouncements to the effect that the existence of a criminal penalty tends by itself to exclude the existence of any civil remedy[5]. Even if such pronouncements are the subject of just criticism[6], the fact remains that it would prima facie be inconsistent for English law to accept the existence of restitutionary rights on the basis of breaches of the criminal law alone when it denies compensatory damages in the same circumstances. At the very least, such a doctrine should be subject to the same tests as those used to determine whether there should be a private right to compensation on a statute[7].

1   *Halifax Building Society v Thomas* [1996] Ch 217. This fact is regretted by several commentators, eg Virgo *Principles of the Law of Restitution* (1999), pp 556–568; see also 'The Law of Restitution and the Proceeds of Crime – A Survey of English Law' [1998] RLR 34, and Birks 'The Proceeds of Mortgage Fraud' (1996) 10 Trust Law International 1. The essence of the argument in favour of a different rule is that there is a principle that a criminal 'should not profit from his crime', and that this principle should be supplemental to the sentencing options allowed to the court by statute. The contrary argument is that the sentencing disposals established by statute must be taken to be the instantiation of that principle currently favoured by Parliament with regard to that crime, and that civil liabilities based on that principle should have to be established separately. Both Virgo and Birks also say that it is just that where X pays Y £1,000 to assault Z, Z should get the £1,000. This is extremely puzzling. Z can sue X and Y as joint tortfeasors (in assault and in conspiracy) for compensatory damages and, if appropriate, exemplary damages. The Offences Against the Person Act 1861, s 45, is no bar if the civil proceedings are initiated first and in case might not apply to the conspiracy action, and if the Act did apply, it would be an illegitimate attempt to frustrate the policy of the statute to allow a restitution action. Why should the amount X paid Y be any more relevant in itself (as 'profit') to Z than the wages an employee has received from an employer in an ordinary vicarious liability case? The answer appears to be that the wages are 'enrichment' but they are not 'unjust', whereas the £1,000 is both 'unjust' and 'enrichment'. But all this points to is the fact that X and Y are engaged in an inherently unlawful enterprise, whereas that is not the case in the ordinary vicarious liability case. The inherent unlawfulness of an enterprise is not in itself, in the absence of fiduciary duties, a ground for the award of an account of profits against those who participate in that enterprise, where no-one has suffered any loss. It might, however, be relevant to the question of exemplary damages where someone has suffered any loss.

2   *O'Rourke v Camden London Borough Council* [1998] AC 188, [1997] 3 All ER 23.

3   See generally Grubb (ed) *Law of Tort* (2002), para 15.9.

4   Grubb (ed) *Law of Tort* (2002), para 15.10; Howarth *Textbook on Tort* (1995), p 338ff.

5 Grubb (ed) *Law of Tort* (2002), para 15.17.
6 Grubb (ed) *Law of Tort* (2002), para 15.17.
7 It might be argued that the alleged principle that a criminal should not profit from the crime is more important than the parallel principle in tort that people who are injured by the fault of others should receive compensation by those who are at fault; but it is not clear why this should be so. Another possible line of argument is that the main purposes of the presumptions against the establishment of tort liability on statutes are to prevent the accidental creation of strict liability torts and the extension of tort liability to forms of loss which otherwise tort does not protect against (see Howarth *Textbook on Tort* (1995), p 345); whereas restitution is already more strict in its form of liability, and covers the form of loss concerned. But there is a counter-argument, that the deeper underlying point of the breach of statutory duty presumptions is to hold separate civil and criminal liability, so the development of the former is considered separately and distinctly, and is not led into confusion by the often contradictory policies of the criminal law as expressed in statute.

12.69 Admittedly, a principle that no-one should be allowed to benefit from his own crime operates in insurance law[1] and in the form of the forfeiture rule[2] to deny property and other benefits to criminals who would otherwise be entitled to them. But these doctrines do not operate to transfer the benefit gained by the criminal to the victim of the crime. The effect of the forfeiture rule, for example, is to transfer the criminal's interest to the person otherwise entitled to residue of the victim's estate.

1 See eg *Cleaver v Mutual Reserve Fund Life Association* [1892] 1 QB 147; *Beresford v Royal Insurance Co* [1938] AC 586; *Haseldine v Hoskin* [1933] 1 KB 822; *Geismar v Sun Alliance and London Insurance Ltd* [1978] QB 383, but also note *Hardy v Motor Insurers' Bureau* [1964] 2 QB 745.
2 The forfeiture rule is 'rule of public policy which in certain circumstances precludes a person who has unlawfully killed another from acquiring a benefit in consequence of the killing' (Forfeiture Act 1982, s 1). See *Re Crippen's Estate* [1911] P 108. The rigours of the rule are relaxed in all cases, except those of murder, by the Forfeiture Act 1982 s 2 (s 5 excludes murder). For the application of the Act see *Dunbar v Plant* [1998] Ch 412 (the forfeiture rule applies to all unlawful killing, including assisting suicide, but the relief available under the Act is potentially total). See also *Re Royse* [1985] Ch 22; *Re K* [1986] Ch 180, [1985] 2 All ER 833; *Davitt v Titcumb* [1990] Ch 110, [1989] 3 All ER 417; *Re H* [1990] 1 FLR 441; *Francisco v Diedrick* (1998) Times, 3 April.

12.70 Where a statutory tort exists on the same basis as a crime, either explicitly or through construction of the statute, the rules are those which apply generally to torts – there is no need, without more, for there to be special rules simply because the conduct also amounts to a crime[1].

1 See *Halifax Building Society v Thomas* [1996] Ch 217 at 229, [1995] 4 All ER 673 at 682, per Glidewell LJ ('The proposition that a wrongdoer should not be allowed to profit from his own wrongs has an obvious attraction. The further proposition, that the victim or intended victim of the wrongdoing who has in the event suffered no loss is entitled to retain or recover the amount of the profit is less obviously persuasive').

Restitutionary claims by the state

12.71 Although the point did not technically arise for decision, the House of Lords in *A-G v Blake* went out of its way, in discussing what was called 'the public law claim', to say that there was no jurisdiction outside statute under which the public authorities can apply to strip a criminal of the proceeds of a crime. Lord Nicholls was emphatic that the courts should not attempt to create such a jurisdiction:

An attempt to do so would offend the established general principle, of high constitutional importance, that there is no common law power to take or confiscate property without compensation ... [1]

In similar vein, the Court of Appeal decided in *Webb v Chief Constable of Merseyside Police*[2] that, outside statute, there was no legal basis for a refusal by the police to restore to alleged criminals money the police claimed represented the proceeds of crime. May LJ said:

> [T]he court should not extend the law in the way suggested. Although from the chief constable's perspective the money is the proceeds of crime, from another perspective the court should not, in my view, countenance expropriation by a public authority of money or property belonging to an individual for which there is no statutory authority[3].

1   [2001] 1 AC 268 at 289, [2000] 4 All ER 385 at 402. On this point he referred to *A-G v De Keyser's Royal Hotel Ltd* [1920] AC 508; *Burmah Oil Co Ltd v Lord Advocate* [1965] AC 75; and *Malone v Metropolitan Police Comr* [1980] QB 49 at 61–63, per Stephenson LJ.
2   [2000] QB 427, [2000] 1 All ER 209. Approved by Lord Steyn in *A-G v Blake* [2001] 1 AC 268 at 292.
3   [2000] QB 427 at 446, [2000] 1 All ER 209 at 223–224.

12.72   There is, however, a statutory scheme for seizure and confiscation of the proceeds of crime. The law originates as a sentencing option in, for example, the Criminal Justice Act 1988, s 71[1], the Proceeds of Crime Act 1995, s 1, and the Drug Trafficking Act 1994, s 3[2]. The law is now on the verge of being extended and developed in the Proceeds of Crime Bill 2002[3]. Under the Bill, where there has been a Crown Court conviction for any offence[4], or a conviction for an offence triable either way or even for a summary only offence covered by the Powers of Criminal Courts (Sentencing) Act 2000, s 6 and the prosecutor has referred the conviction for such an offence from the Magistrates' Court to the Crown Court[5], the Crown Court *must*, if told to do so by the prosecutor or the new 'Assets Recovery Agency', proceed as follows[6]:

(a)   it must decide whether the defendant has a criminal lifestyle;
(b)   if it decides that he has a criminal lifestyle, it must decide whether he has benefited from his general criminal conduct;
(c)   if it decides that he does not have a criminal lifestyle, it must decide whether he has benefited from his particular criminal conduct.

If the court concludes that (b) or (c) applies, it must[7] make a confiscation order for the 'recoverable amount', which is defined as the amount by which the defendant has benefited from his crimes up to a maximum (the 'available amount') of all his property, including 'tainted gifts'[8], except for other financial penalties imposed by the court, preferential debts in bankruptcy, and property already subject to other forfeiture or confiscation orders under other legislation[9]. All these matters are to be decided 'on the balance of probabilities'[10].

1   The provisions of the Criminal Justice Act 1988, s 71ff, survived a Human Rights Act challenge in *R v Rezvi* [2002] UKHL 1, [2002] 1 All ER 801, on the ground that confiscation proceedings forming part of the sentencing process did not amount to a new criminal charge, cf *Phillips v United Kingdom* ECtHR 5 July 2001, (2001) Times, 13 August; and *HM Advocate v Macintosh* [2001] UKPC D1.
2   The provisions of the Drug Trafficking Act 1994 survived a human rights challenge in *Phillips v United Kingdom* ECHR 5 July 2001, (2001) Times, 13 August, as a justified control on the use of property, and because art 6 does not apply to sentencing. See also *R v Rezvi* [2002] UKHL 1, [2002] 1 All ER 801; and *HM Advocate v McSalley* (10 April 2001, unreported), High Court of Justiciary.
3   At the time of writing (April 2002), the Bill has almost completed its passage through Parliament, but some of the details of its provisions are still matters of Parliamentary debate.
4   See cl 6.
5   See cl 70.
6   See cl 6.
7   Except that if civil proceeding by victims of the crimes are in prospect, the court's duty becomes a power to make an order for an amount it believes is just: cls 6(6) and 8(3).

8 See cl 77.
9 See cl 82.
10 See cl 6(7).

12.73 The phrase 'if ... he has a criminal lifestyle' is defined in cl 75 as meaning that any of the offences concerned involved drug trafficking[1], or money laundering[2], or 'constitutes conduct forming part of a course of criminal activity', or is an offence committed over a period of more than six months. 'Conduct forming part of a course of criminal activity' means that the criminal has 'benefited' from the conduct and either the defendant has been convicted in the current proceedings of three or more offences from which he has benefited, or he has been convicted, in two or more separate proceedings, of at least two more such offences in the six years preceding the start of the current proceedings[3].

'General criminal conduct' means conduct which constitutes an offence, or would constitute an offence if it happened in the jurisdiction, and includes conduct before the commencement of the Bill[4]. 'Particular criminal conduct' includes all the offences relevant to the current proceedings, including offences taken into account[5]. Benefiting from criminal conduct means obtaining property wholly or partly 'as a result of or in connection with' the conduct[6].

In deciding the amount by which the defendant benefited from his criminal lifestyle, unless 'it is shown to be incorrect' or 'there would be a serious risk of injustice', the court must assume that any property obtained by the defendant in the six years preceding the start of the current proceedings was obtained as a result of his general criminal conduct, that any property obtained after conviction was also obtained as a result of his general criminal conduct, that any expenditure made by the defendant in the six year period was made out of funds obtained a result of his general criminal conduct, and that for the purposes of valuing property the defendant obtained it free of other interests[7].

1 Defined in cl 88.
2 Defined in cl 89.
3 See cl 75.
4 See cl 76.
5 See cl 76.
6 See cl 76.
7 See *R v Rezvi* [2002] UKHL 1, [2002] 1 All ER 801, for the human rights aspects of similar provisions in the predecessor legislation.

12.74 But the Bill goes beyond mere sentencing. First, if the defendant absconds after proceedings are started, after two years the court must make a confiscation order. Secondly, under Part 5, the authorities are empowered to recover in civil proceedings before the High Court property which is or which represents the proceeds of 'unlawful conduct', regardless of whether any criminal proceedings have been brought or whether anyone has been convicted of any crime[1]. Part 5 also enables the forfeiture in civil proceedings in the Magistrates Court of any cash 'obtained through unlawful conduct' or 'intended to be used in unlawful conduct' similarly regardless of whether any criminal proceedings have been brought or whether anyone has been convicted of any crime[2]. 'Unlawful conduct' means any criminal conduct in any part of the world, whether under British or local law (and including conduct which would be criminal in Britain which happens not to be criminally locally[3]). The existence of 'unlawful conduct' does not have to have been proved in criminal proceedings. The civil court merely has to believe 'on the balance of probabilities' that there has been such conduct[4]. The 'unlawful conduct' does not need to have been that of the defendant, merely that the defendant obtained the property 'by or in return for the conduct'. All such property can be made subject to an order, except where victims prove that the property belongs to them[5].

Part 5 of the Bill sets up a statutory tracing regime[6], deals with mixing of property on a proportional basis[7], includes profits made by use of recoverable property as themselves recoverable[8] and provides for a statutory version of the rules of equity in declaring that the property ceases to be recoverable if comes into the hands of a good faith purchaser for value without notice[9].

1   And also regardless of whether anyone has been acquitted of the relevant offences. There is an element of double jeopardy in these sections, and also an element of imposing a penalty without full due process. A Human Rights Act challenge can be expected to these provisions.
2   See cl 249.
3   See cl 250.
4   See cl 250(3). This provision may be subject to a Human Rights Act challenge. Forfeiture to the state is a penalty (see eg *Welch v United Kingdom* (1995) 20 EHRR 247) – the fact that there is no penalty of imprisonment in default in the 2002 Bill may not be enough to save it if the motives in introducing it are deterrent and punitive – see eg *Schmautzer v Austria* (1995) 21 EHRR 511. To impose a penalty without convincing proof might be held to be a violation of art 6, although there is not much case law on the point (see Buxton 'The Human Rights Act and the Substantive Criminal Law' [2000] Criminal Law Review 331); but note *Barberà, Messegué and Jabardo v Spain* (1988) 11 EHRR 360.
5   See cl 285. For other exemptions see cl 286 (eg property held by the Financial Services Authority).
6   See cl 308.
7   See cl 309.
8   See cl 310.
9   See cl 311.

Part IV
Contract and Near-Contract

CHAPTER 13

Uncertain or Anticipated Contracts

Paula Giliker

A   Introduction

13.1   In this chapter, I examine the role of restitution in relation to contracts which are too uncertain to be enforced, and where the claimant has acted in anticipation of a contract. The two situations overlap. In the typical case, the claimant will allege, first, that a valid contract exists, and, secondly, that if this argument fails, that he or she should be awarded a restitutionary remedy. The restitutionary claim is therefore generally treated as one of secondary concern, arising when the rules of contractual certainty exclude the prospect of a contract. Any consideration of this area of law must therefore commence with an examination of these rules. English law has certain minimum requirements which parties must satisfy if they wish to establish that a contract has been formed. In addition to an intention to create legal relations, consideration and correspondence of offer and acceptance, the terms of the contract must be certain and complete. English law will not recognise vague and incomplete agreements: the parties must show 'a concluded bargain ... which settles everything that is necessary to be settled and leaves nothing to be settled by agreement between the parties'[1]. When a contract fails to meet this standard, the claimant will be forced to turn to the law of restitution to find a remedy.

1   *May and Butcher v R* (1929) [1934] 2 KB 17n at 21, per Viscount Dunedin.

13.2   In a number of cases, the courts have used restitution to award a remedy to the claimant[1]. This case law will be examined in detail and will be accompanied by an analysis of the basis for the award and whether restitution is the only means by which a claimant can recover damages. This is a difficult area of law, on which there is very limited authority, but a number of guiding principles can be identified which will assist future claimants. These are set out in the conclusion[2].

1   As in the leading case of *British Steel Corpn v Cleveland Bridge and Engineering Co Ltd* [1984] 1 All ER 504; considered below, para 13.38ff.
2   See below, para 13.63ff.

13.3   The first half of this chapter therefore sets out the rules of certainty of contracts and identifies when the parties, despite the informality of their agreement, may obtain a contractual remedy. This leads on to a wider discussion of the role of restitution, and the ability of claimants to obtain a restitutionary remedy.

B   The requirement of certainty

13.4   As stated earlier, in addition to the primary requirements for formation of a contract, English law requires that the contract is sufficiently certain. The court must be able to identify clearly the terms of the agreement, and ascertain whether such terms have been breached. Only then may a court judge whether a remedy is appropriate in the circumstances. This aspect of English law, which derives largely from the classical view of contract law, dictates a largely objective approach to construction of a contract. It is also presumed (rightly or wrongly) that businessmen require predictability and certainty to ensure that their transactions are secure. The courts therefore feel justified in demanding a minimum level of certainty before a claimant can seek to assert any contractual rights.

13.5   In setting a standard to ensure transactional certainty for the business community, whereby parties can be confident that a court will enforce their contract or award contractual damages should the agreement be subject to challenge, the courts face a dilemma. Businessmen frequently do not set out their agreement in detailed terms. They may wish for flexibility, for example, if the price of raw materials is particularly volatile at the time of contracting, or they are unsure of the availability of certain goods. Such matters may be left for future resolution, or to be re-assessed at set periods during the agreement, or 'to be negotiated at a future date'. Equally, parties may shake hands on a deal, leaving matters to be settled by their lawyers or according to usage or previous dealings. The traditional rules of contract law do not respond easily to such common commercial practice. As will be seen below, whilst some informal arrangements may be fitted within the rules of contractual certainty, others cannot be construed to satisfy the strict rules applied by the court. In such circumstances, a claimant may turn to restitution, and seek at least financial recognition of the benefit received by the defendant. The likely success of such claims are examined in the second half of this chapter[1].

1   See below, para 13.27ff.

The minimum requirements of certainty

13.6   The courts recognise, pragmatically, that the most that can be required is a minimum level of certainty, that is agreement on the *essential* elements of the contract[1]. These essential terms must be expressed in a *clear and unambiguous way* to enable the courts to enforce them if necessary. In *G Scammell & Nephew Ltd v Ouston*, for example, an agreement to buy goods on 'hire purchase' terms, when there were many such kinds of terms, was considered too vague by the House of Lords[2]. Non-essential or minor terms of the contract may, however, be supplied by the court. In this sense, the court cannot be said to make the contract for the parties, but preserves agreements intended by their parties to govern their working relationship, which would otherwise fail due to incomplete agreement[3].

1   *Rossiter v Miller* (1878) 3 App Cas 1124 at 1151, per Lord Blackburn.
2   [1941] AC 251. See also *Bishop & Baxter Ltd v Anglo-Eastern Trading Co* [1944] KB 12; *Love & Stewart Ltd v S Instone & Co* (1917) 33 TLR 475; *British Electrical etc Industries Ltd v Patley Pressings Ltd* [1953] 1 WLR 280.
3   See Fridman 'Construing, without Constructing, a Contract' (1960) 76 LQR 521.

What is an 'essential' term of the contract?

13.7   This, of course, is the key issue in relation to certainty. The courts cannot assist the parties by providing essential terms. Yet, what is 'essential' remains an open question[1]. It will vary according to the nature of the contract[2]. The approach taken by the courts will now be examined.

1   Samek (1970) 48 Canadian Bar Review 203 at 212 notes that 'This qualification is plausible only because it contains an ambiguity'. See also *Pagnan SpA v Feed Products* [1987] 2 Lloyd's Rep 601 at 619, per Lloyd LJ.
2   For example, the courts have found matters such as the date on which a lease commences (*Harvey v Pratt* [1965] 2 All ER 786) or the amount of land to be conveyed on payment of each instalment (*Bushwall v Vortex* [1976] 2 All ER 283, [1976] 1 WLR 591) to amount to essential terms of the contract.

Judicial guidance on 'essential' terms

13.8   Although each transaction will be assessed on its own facts, it is possible to identify certain criteria used by the courts in deciding whether agreement exists on the essential terms to the agreement[1]. An objective approach is adopted, whereby the courts consider all that has passed between the parties, and ascertain whether, in such circumstances, the parties intended to be legally bound[2]. Yet, this may give an unduly inflexible impression of English contract law, which is far from the case in practice. In spite of requiring a settled agreement, the courts are also aware that '[b]usiness men often record the most important agreements in crude and summary fashion ... [I]t is accordingly the duty of the court to construe such documents fairly and broadly without being too astute or subtle in finding defects'[3]. Hence the maxim *certum est quod certum reddi potest* (that which is capable of being made certain is to be treated as certain). The courts may construe a contract to implement the parties' intentions, provided they do not go so far as to construct the agreement for them[4]. The courts have recognised that, realistically, a more flexible approach is required if the very aim of security of transactions is not to be undermined, and undue prejudice suffered by one or both of the parties.

1   See generally Fox 'Certainty in Business Contracts' (1982) 126 Solicitors Journal 91.
2   *Hussey v Horne-Payne* (1879) 4 App Cas 311; *Scammell v Ouston* [1941] AC 251 at 255.
3   *Hillas v Arcos* (1932) 147 LT 503 at 514, per Lord Wright.
4   See *Hillas v Arcos* (1932) 147 LT 503 at 514, per Lord Wright. Contrast Samek 'The Requirement of Certainty of Terms in the Formation of Contract' (1970) 48 Canadian Bar Review 203, who questions whether the courts are able to maintain this distinction in practice.

13.9   The courts therefore possess a considerable discretion in determining whether a contract is sufficiently clear and certain to be enforced. Two dominant factors influence their reasoning: the commercial nature of the parties' relationship[1], and whether the agreement has been (fully or partially) executed[2]. As Lord Steyn commented in *G Percy Trentham Ltd v Archital Luxfer Ltd*[3], the courts seek to meet the 'reasonable expectations of sensible businessmen ... [T]he fact that the transaction is executed makes it easier to imply a term resolving any uncertainty, or, alternatively, it may make it possible to treat the matter not finalised in negotiations as inessential'[4]. In the absence of these factors, where there is no settled agreement as to all the relevant terms, the courts will not enforce the contract. In failing to ensure that the agreement was expressed with sufficient clarity, the claimant is left to the risks of the market.

The following techniques have been used by the courts to counter uncertainty and vagueness in contractual agreements.

1   See for example Viscount Maugham in *Scammell v Ouston* [1941] AC 251 at 255; *Halsbury's Law of England* (4th edn, reissue, 1998), vol 9(1), para 674.
2   See *British Bank for Foreign Trade Ltd v Novinex Ltd* [1949] 1 KB 623 at 630, per Cohen LJ, and *G Percy Trentham Ltd v Archital Luxfer Ltd* [1993] 1 Ll 25 at 27, per Steyn LJ; *Halsbury's Law of England* (4th edn, reissue, 1998), vol 9(1), para 675.
3   [1993] 1 Lloyd's Rep 25 at 27.
4   See also the comments of the Lord Denning MR in *Sykes (Wessex) Ltd v Fine Fare Ltd* [1967] 1 Lloyd's Rep 53, approved in *The Didymi (Didymi Corpn v Atlantic Lines and Navigation Co)* [1988] 2 Lloyd's Rep 108 and applied in *Voest Alpine v Chevron* [1987] 2 Lloyd's Rep 547. For a recent example, see *Northern Foods plc v Focal Foods Ltd* [2001] All ER (D) 306, CA.

REFERENCE TO ACCEPTED BUSINESS PRACTICE

13.10   This is a familiar contractual tool, and lies at the heart of the 'business efficacy'[1] test used in relation to implied terms. The courts will examine evidence of trade usage[2], or the practice within a certain market, to support a contract. In *Hillas v Arcos*[3], for example, the court referred to the familiarity of both parties with the Russian softwood timber trade. It is entirely dependant, however, on the ability of the court to identify 'usual' terms, and where there are a variety of possible terms which could be used by the parties, the courts will be unable to intervene[4].

1   *The Moorcock* (1888) 13 PD 157 and (1889) 14 PD 64.
2   See *British Crane Hire Corpn Ltd v Ipswich Plant Hire Ltd* [1975] QB 303.
3   (1932) 147 LT 503. See also *Sweet & Maxwell v Universal News Service* [1964] 2 QB 699 ('the usual covenants') and *Shamrock Steamship Co v Storey & Co* (1899) 81 LT 413 ('the usual colliery guarantee').
4   *Scammell and Nephew Ltd v Ouston* [1941] AC 251 (no settled form of hire purchase terms); *Love & Stewart Ltd v S Instone & Co* (1917) 33 TLR 475 (no settled form of strike and lock-out clause); *Lee-Parker v Izzet (No 2)* [1972] 2 All ER 800, [1972] 1 WLR 775 (no settled meaning of 'satisfactory mortgage').

REFERENCE TO PREVIOUS DEALINGS BETWEEN THE PARTIES

13.11   Where the parties have a pre-existing business relationship, the courts will refer to their prior practice to determine remaining issues of uncertainty. This has been applied generously, and indicates the willingness of the court to support agreements which have been executed fully or in part. A much-cited example is that of the House of Lords in *Hillas v Arcos*[1], where an option to enter into a contract to purchase 100,000 'standards' for delivery was deemed sufficiently certain by reference to the timber contract of the previous year. The court was prepared to imply that the contract related to timber 'of fair specification' and that this could be understood by reference to the output of the previous season. The court adopted a presumption of validity, seeking 'to exclude as impossible all reasonable meanings which would give certainty to the words'[2]. Whilst so generous an approach may not be adopted in all cases[3], the courts are generally wary of any attempt to circumvent a claim for damages for breach of contract by belatedly challenging the validity of the contract, and will respond by a generous application of its powers to imply terms to support the parties' agreement.

1   (1932) 147 LT 503.
2   (1932) 147 LT 503 at 512, per Lord Tomlin. Samek (1970) 48 Canadian Bar Review 203 at 225 comments that 'In the present case, the court obviously went far beyond construing. If it had not

done so, the decision would have lost its commercial value which lay precisely in the recognition that business men need flexibility in their arrangements'. See also *Foley v Classique Coaches Ltd* [1934] 2 KB 1.
3 Particularly in non-commercial cases or where the parties' arrangement is clearly aleatory. See *The John S Darbyshire (Albion Sugar Co Ltd v William Tankers Ltd)* [1977] 2 Lloyd's Rep 457 at 465, per Mocatta J.

SETTLEMENT OF TERMS BY MACHINERY EXTERNAL TO THE CONTRACT

13.12 Although the courts will not permit parties to determine essential terms at a later date, the courts will allow parties to agree a mechanism by which such terms may be determined at a later date, *provided* that it is not by the parties themselves[1]. By this means, the courts recognise that in many long-term commercial agreements, it may be a commercial necessity to review matters such as price or costs allowances as the contract progresses. It would, for example, usually make little sense for the parties to decide the price of the goods to be delivered over a 15 year period *on formation*, taking no account of the changes which may take place during that period. In the sale of goods, it has long been accepted that the price may be fixed by the valuation of a third party. This is set out in the Sale of Goods Act 1979, s 9. In relation to the sale of land, in the leading case of *Sudbrook v Eggleton*[2] the House of Lords demonstrated a particularly flexible approach in this context. A lease gave the tenant the option to purchase the premises 'at such price as may be agreed upon by two valuers, one to be nominated by the lessor and the other by the lessee and in default of such agreement by an umpire appointed by the ... valuers'. The landlord refused to appoint a valuer. There was no provision for the landlord failing to appoint a valuer, but this did not prevent the House of Lords overcoming precedent[3] to enforce the contract. It was held that it was, on its true construction, an agreement to sell at a fair and reasonable price. The machinery to ascertain the price was a subsidiary and non-essential part of the contract and, if it broke down, the court could substitute its own machinery to ascertain a fair and reasonable price. It would be different, however, if a particular valuer or arbitrator was required. The identity of the third party would be of essential importance, and the court would not substitute its view for that of a specific third party[4].

1 Even where the machinery specified is not very precise: see *Brown v Gould* [1972] Ch 53. The courts will, however, enforce an agreement where a term will be determined at a future date by *one* party to the transaction: see *Lombard Tricity Finance Ltd v Paton* [1989] 1 All ER 918 (interest rate on credit agreement variable on notification by the creditor, although this will now be subject to the Unfair Terms in Consumer Contracts Regulations 1999 SI 1999/2083, see Sch 2, paras 1(j) and 2(b) and the Court of Appeal decision in *Paragon Finance plc v Nash* [2002] 1 WLR 685 which imposed an implied term that any such variation would not be exercised for an improper purpose, dishonestly, capriciously, arbitrarily, or so unreasonably that no reasonable lender would have acted in that way). See also *David T Boyd & Co v Louis Louca* [1973] 1 Lloyd's Rep 209 (port of shipment at buyer's option); *The Star Texas (Star Shipping AS v China National Foreign Trade Transportation Corpn* [1993] 2 Lloyd's Rep 445 (one party to choose place of arbitration).
2 [1983] 1 AC 444 (Lord Russell dissenting). For comment see Harpum and Lloyd Jones 'Certainty at one fell swoop' [1982] CLJ 233.
3 See *Milnes v Gery* (1807) 14 Ves 400, 33 ER 574 (as set out in the judgment of Templeman LJ below [1983] 1 AC 444 at 451, CA).
4 See also the Sale of Goods Act 1979, s 9(1): 'Where there is an agreement to sell goods on the terms that the price is to be fixed by the valuation of a third party, and he cannot or does not make the valuations, the agreement is avoided'.

13.13 There is some authority that an agreement may be supported by reference to arbitration clauses. For example, in *F & G Sykes (Wessex) Ltd v Fine*

Fare Ltd[1], the Court of Appeal was more willing to support an agreement where there was an arbitration clause 'which, liberally construed, is sufficient to resolve any uncertainties which the parties have left'[2]. It must be doubted, however, whether the presence of an arbitration clause alone could provide sufficient certainty[3].

1   [1967] 1 Lloyd's Rep 53.
2   [1967] 1 Lloyd's Rep 53 at 58, per Lord Denning MR. The agreement had provided after the first year for 'such other figures as may be agreed between the parties hereto'. Referring to the arbitration clause, the court interpreted this to signify agreement to a reasonable figure, which could be determined by an arbitrator if necessary.
3   In *Sykes* (previous note), the agreement had been in operation for over a year, and the court was clearly motivated by the previous dealings of the parties and the fact that the parties had clearly intended a five year agreement. Equally, whilst an arbitration clause was used in *Foley v Classique Coaches Ltd* [1934] 2 KB 1 to support an agreement which had been in operation for three years, it did not assist the claimants in *May and Butcher v R* (1929) [1934] 2 KB 17n where the agreement had not yet been performed. The clause in *Foley* was additionally very broad in dealing with 'any dispute or *difference* [which] shall arise on the *subject matter* or construction of this agreement the same shall be submitted to arbitration' (emphasis supplied).

A TEST OF REASONABLENESS

13.14   A further technique used by the courts is to imply a requirement of reasonableness. For example, in *Hillas v Arcos*[1], an agreement for the sale of timber of 'fair specification' was interpreted according to a standard of reasonableness. Equally in *Sudbrook v Eggleton*[2] a primary obligation to appoint valuers (or in default an umpire) to fix a purchase price was interpreted as an agreement to fix a 'fair and reasonable' price. This has been criticised for disregarding the true nature of the parties' relationship. Lord Russell, dissenting in *Sudbrook*, commented that 'Vendors and purchasers are normally greedy' and therefore may not desire a 'reasonable' price[3].

1   (1932) 147 LT 503. See also *British Bank for Foreign Trade Ltd v Novinex Ltd* [1949] 1 KB 623; *Foley v Classique Coaches Ltd* [1934] 2 KB 1; *Sweet & Maxwell v Universal News Service* [1964] 2 QB 699.
2   [1983] 1 AC 444; above, para 13.12.
3   [1983] 1 AC 444 at 486.

STATUTORY ASSISTANCE

13.15   Section 8 of the Sale of Goods Act 1979 provides:

(1) The price in a contract of sale may be fixed by the contract, or may be left to be fixed in a manner agreed by the contract, or may be determined by the course of dealing between the parties.
(2) Where the price is not determined as mentioned in subsection (1) above the buyer must pay a reasonable price.
(3) What is a reasonable price is a question of fact dependent on the circumstances of each particular case.

A buyer must therefore pay a reasonable price where the price has not been determined by the contract. Section 15(1) of the Supply of Goods and Services Act 1982 makes similar provision for services.

13.16   It should be noted, however, that where the parties have agreed that the price will be fixed by further agreement, the statutory provisions will not apply. Parties may only rely on the statutory provisions where no such provision has been made[1].

1   *May and Butcher v R* (1929) [1934] 2 KB 17n, which states that such an agreement to agree is void for uncertainty (see below, para 13.18).

SEVERANCE OF MEANINGLESS TERMS

13.17   So far, the courts have implied additional terms to ensure the formation of a valid contract. However, there may be agreed terms within the contract which obstruct formation. For example, in *Nicolene Ltd v Simmonds*[1], it was stated that 'the usual conditions of acceptance apply', in circumstances in which there were no such conditions. The court was unable to find any meaning for the clause[2], and chose to sever this clause as meaningless. A distinction was drawn between a term which is meaningless, and a term which is yet to be agreed. In the view of Denning LJ, 'it would be strange indeed if a party could escape from every one of his obligations by inserting a meaningless exception from some of them'[3]. This technique is limited, however, to minor terms, which may be severed without affecting performance of the contract.

1   [1953] 1 QB 543. See also *EJR Lovelock v Exportles* [1968] 1 Lloyd's Rep 163.
2   *The Tropwind (Tropwood AG of Zug v Jade Enterprises Ltd)* [1982] 1 Lloyd's Rep 232 demonstrates the efforts the courts will undertake to find a meaning for such terms.
3   [1953] 1 QB 543 at 551.

Agreements which are too uncertain[1]

AGREEMENTS TO AGREE

13.18   An agreement to agree an essential term of the contract will have no contractual force. In *May and Butcher Ltd v R*[2], an agreement for the sale of tentage provided that the price to be paid and the dates of payment 'shall be agreed upon from time to time ... as the quantities of the said old tentage become available for disposal'. Lord Buckmaster in the House of Lords held that 'It has long been a well-recognised principle of contract law that an agreement between two parties to enter into an agreement in which some critical part of the contract matter is left undetermined is no contract at all'[3].

1   See Dugdale and Lowe 'Contracts to contract and contracts to negotiate' [1976] Journal of Business Law 28.
2   (1929) [1934] 2 KB 17n.
3   (1929) [1934] 2 KB 17n at 20. See also *Von Hatzfeldt-Wildenberg v Alexander* [1912] 1 Ch 284 at 289, per Parker J; *Ridgway v Wharton* (1856) 6 HL Cas 238. Note McLauchlan 'Rethinking agreements to agree' (1998) 18 New Zealand University Law Review 77, who advocates the abandonment of the *May and Butcher* principle. The principle does not, however, extend to the situation where the parties agree to incorporate their agreed terms in a formal contract. Such a 'contract to make a contract' is perfectly valid, the terms being already settled: *Morton v Morton* [1942] 1 All ER 273.

13.19   However, the fact that a term is 'to be agreed' will not always obstruct contract formation. The Court of Appeal decision in *Foley v Classique Coaches Ltd*[1] demonstrates the willingness of the courts to intervene to assist commercial parties. The claimant had agreed to supply petrol 'at a price to be agreed by the parties in writing and from time to time'. The arrangement had been performed for three years before any dispute arose, and had been part of a larger transaction, by which the claimant agreed to sell some land to the defendants for a coach station. In such circumstances, the Court was willing to imply a term that the petrol would be supplied at a reasonable price, and be of reasonable quality and that, failing agreement, the price would be determined under the arbitration clause[2].

Equally, in *The Didymi*[3], the Court of Appeal upheld an agreement containing a clause that 'hire shall be equitably decreased by an amount to be mutually agreed between the owners and charterers'. The parties had been in a close and continuing contractual relationship for five years, and the subsequent dispute had arisen on a relatively minor aspect of their relationship[4]. The majority held that use of the term 'equitably' was sufficient to establish agreement to a 'fair and reasonable' level of hire[5]. The determination of this level was a matter of subsidiary machinery, which could, in the light of *Sudbrook v Eggleton*[6], be established if necessary by the court. An objective standard had thus been set. It mattered little whether the objective standard would be determined by valuers, or by the parties themselves, provided the term was not to be decided by the future *subjective* determination of the parties[7]. Again, the commercial nature of the relationship and the ongoing contractual relationship of the parties would appear to have influenced the court in finding a valid, enforceable agreement.

1   [1934] 2 KB 1. Note by RSTC (1933) 49 LQR 316.
2   *Foley* has also been distinguished from *May and Butcher* on the basis that the agreement in *Foley* was contained in a stamped document. This is unlikely to have had much influence on the court.
3   *Didymi Corp v Atlantic Lines and Navigation Co* [1988] 2 Lloyd's Rep 108.
4   See [1988] 2 Lloyd's Rep 108 at 112, per Bingham LJ.
5   Dillon LJ held that the arbitration clause in the agreement was capable of resolving any dispute.
6   See above, para 13.12.
7   See *Pagnan SpA v Feed Products* [1987] 2 Lloyd's Rep 601, followed by Judge Esyr Lewis QC in *Mitsui Babcock Energy Ltd v J Brown Engineering Ltd* (1996) 51 Con LR 129, where performance tests 'to be discussed and agreed' did not bar formation of a binding contract which was workable and certain in practice. See also *Queensland Electricity Generating Board v New Hope Collieries Pty Ltd* [1989] 1 Lloyd's Rep 205, PC.

AGREEMENTS TO NEGOTIATE

13.20   In spite of dicta to the contrary[1], the courts will not enforce a 'mere' agreement to negotiate. In *Courtney and Fairbairn Ltd v Tolaini Bros (Hotels) Ltd*[2], the Court of Appeal firmly rejected such a contract. In this case, the parties had reached agreement that, once financing had been obtained for a proposed development, Tolaini would negotiate with Courtney 'fair and reasonable contract sums in respect of ... three projects'. Although finance was arranged and negotiations took place, the parties could not agree, and Tolaini eventually employed another contractor. The Court of Appeal rejected Courtney's claim for breach of contract. All had been left to be agreed in the future. Lord Denning remarked that '[the agreement] is too uncertain to have any binding force. No court could estimate the damages because no one could tell whether the negotiations would be successful or would fall through; or if successful what the result would be. It seems to me that a contract to negotiate, like a contract to enter into a contract, is not a contract known to law'[3].

1   *Hillas & Co Ltd v Arcos Ltd* (1932) 147 LT 503 at 515, per Lord Wright; *Chillingworth v Esche* [1924] 1 Ch 97 at 113. Lord Diplock in *Courtney and Fairbairn Ltd v Tolaini Bros (Hotels) Ltd* [1975] 1 WLR 297 at 302 regarded Lord Wright's dictum in *Hillas* as 'bad law'.
2   [1975] 1 WLR 297. Contrast with the less rigid views of the Canadian and Australian courts: *Coal Cliff Collieries Pty Ltd v Sijehama Pty Ltd* (1991) 24 NSWLR 1; *Empress Towers Ltd v Bank of Nova Scotia* (1990) 73 DLR (4th) 400. For comment see Buckley 'False certainty about uncertainty – an Australian perspective' (1993) 6 Journal of Contract Law 58.

3 *Courtney & Fairbairn Ltd v Tolaini Bros (Hotels) Ltd* [1975] 1 WLR 297 at 301. This dictum has been followed by the Court of Appeal in *Mallozzi v Carapelli SpA* [1976] 1 Lloyd's Rep 407 and at first instance: *Albion Sugar Co Ltd v Williams Tankers Ltd* [1977] 2 Lloyd's Rep 457; *Scandinavian Trading Tanker Co AB v Flota Petrolera Ecuatoriana, The Scaptrade* [1981] 2 Lloyd's Rep 425; *Trees Ltd v Cripps* (1983) 267 Estates Gazette 596; *Nile Co for the Export of Agricultural Crops v H & JM Bennett (Commodities) Ltd* [1986] 1 Lloyd's Rep 555; *Voest Alpine Intertrading GmbH v Chevron International Oil Co Ltd* [1987] 2 Lloyd's Rep 547; *Star Steamship Society v Beogradska Plovidba* [1988] 2 Lloyd's Rep 583.

13.21 Such authority has been supported more recently by the House of Lords in *Walford v Miles*[1]. In this case, the House of Lords refused to enforce a contract to negotiate in good faith, on the ground that it lacked certainty. Such an agreement was 'inherently repugnant to the adversarial position of the parties when involved in negotiations' who must be free to advance their own interests during the negotiations, subject to the law of misrepresentation[2]. Lord Ackner reiterates the criticism made in *Courtney*: such agreements could not be policed by the judiciary, which is not in a position to determine whether a proper reason existed for the termination of negotiations. Although such arguments may be criticised[3], they represent a firm rejection of the contract to negotiate in good faith in English law[4].

1 [1992] 2 AC 128.
2 [1992] 2 AC 128 at 138, per Lord Ackner. However, empirical research would seem to question such assumptions: see Macaulay 'Non-contractual relations in business: a preliminary study' (1963) 28 American Sociological Review 45; Beale and Dugdale 'Contracts between businessmen: planning and the use of contractual remedies' (1975) 2 British Journal of Law and Society 18; Macneil 'The many futures of contracts' (1974) 47 South California Law Review 691.
3 See Treitel *Law of Contract* (10th edn, 1999), pp 57–58; Neill 'A key to lock-out agreements?' (1992) 108 LQR 405; Cumberbatch 'In freedom's cause: the contract to negotiate' (1992) 12 OJLS 586; Jamieson 'Lock-out agreement is unenforceable' [1992] Lloyds Maritime and Commercial Law Quarterly 186; Brown 'The contract to negotiate: a thing writ in water?' [1992] Journal of Business Law 353; Shaw 'Pre-contractual negotiations in English law: *Walford v Miles* and its aftermath' [1994] European Review of Private Law 269. One particular area of criticism has been Lord Ackner's distinction between an obligation to negotiate in good faith (too uncertain to be enforceable) and an obligation to use best endeavours (sufficiently certain to be enforceable). The United States Court of Appeals in *Channel Home Centers, Division of Grace Retail Corpn v Grossman* 795 F 2d 291 (1986) found no distinction between the two. Treitel *Law of Contract* (10th edn, 1999), p 57 suggests that the former applies to formation of a contract, and the latter to performance, different rules applying where the contract is already in operation. There is clear authority to support obligations to use 'one's best endeavours to agree' in English law: see *Queensland Electricity Generating Board v New Hope Collieries Pty Ltd* [1989] 1 Lloyd's Rep 205, PC; *Lambert v HTV Cymru (Wales) Ltd* [1998] EMLR 629; but note the comments of Millett LJ in *Little v Courage* (1994) 70 P & CR 469 at 476 and Lloyd J in *The Scaptrade* [1981] 2 Lloyd's Rep 425 at 432.
4 On good faith negotiating, generally, see Beatson and Friedmann (eds) *Good faith and fault in contract law* (1997), and note the comment of Bingham LJ in *Interfoto Library Ltd v Stilletto Ltd* [1989] QB 433 at 439: 'In many civil law systems, and perhaps in most legal systems outside the common law world, the law of obligations recognises and enforces an overriding principle that in making and carrying out contracts parties should act in good faith ... It is in essence a principle of fair and open dealing ... English law has, characteristically, committed itself to no such overriding principle but has developed piecemeal solutions to demonstrated problems of unfairness'. The classic article is that of Farnsworth 'Precontractual liability and preliminary agreements: fair dealing and failed negotiations' (1987) 87 Columbia Law Review 217. See also Carter and Furmston 'Good faith and fairness in the negotiation of contracts' (1994) 8 Journal of Contract Law 1 and 93, and, most recently, Mason 'Contract, good faith and equitable standards in fair dealing' (2000) 116 LQR 66.

PRELIMINARY AGREEMENTS

13.22 The House of Lords in *Walford v Miles*[1] recognised the existence and validity of preliminary agreements in English law. The courts are prepared to enforce such agreements where the parties have reached a consensus on a number of preliminary matters with a sufficient degree of certainty. By this means, contract law can support, at least to a limited extent, the parties' agreement. The key issue is what the parties *intended* to do. If the parties intended their preliminary agreement to be contractually enforceable, then the courts will enforce the preliminary or interim agreement. Alternatively, the parties may expressly state their intention that the agreement is not enforceable, for example, by making a 'gentleman's agreement'[2] or by the use of the term 'subject to contract'[3]. In the latter case, the agreement will be deemed incomplete, until the details of a formal contract have been settled and agreed by the parties[4]. However, the question of intention will not always be clear[5].

1   [1992] 2 AC 128.
2   See *Milner (J H) & Son v Percy Bilton Ltd* [1966] 2 All ER 894 at 898, per Fenton Atkinson J.
3   See *Winn v Bull* (1877) 7 Ch D 29.
4   Treitel *Law of Contract* (10th edn, 1999), p 50; *Pym v Campbell* (1856) 6 E & B 370, 119 ER 903; *Winn v Bull* (1877) 7 Ch D 29; *Munton v Greater London Council* [1976] 1 WLR 649; *Henderson Group v Superabbey* [1988] 39 EG 82.
5   Compare for example the approach of differently constituted sittings of the Court of Appeal in *Pagnan SpA v Granaria BV* [1986] 2 Lloyd's Rep 547; and *Pagnan SpA v Feed Products* [1987] 2 Lloyd's Rep 601. On interim agreements, see also *Malcolm v Chancellor, Masters and Scholars of the University of Oxford* [1994] EMLR 17.

13.23   In *Walford*, it had been argued that the parties had reached a 'lock-out' agreement, that is, a preliminary agreement whereby an individual agrees to refrain from negotiating with a third party[1]. The defendants had, in fact, continued to negotiate with a third party, to whom they ultimately sold their business. The House of Lords accepted the validity of lock-out agreements in English law, provided they applied for a defined period of time. Lord Ackner recognised that there were often good commercial reasons for a party to agree to such agreements; for example, a party might not be prepared to risk spending time and money preparing an offer without some sign of commitment from the other party[2]. However, no time limit had been agreed between the parties in *Walford*, and thus any lock-out agreement was unenforceable in any event[3]. In the subsequent case of *Pitt v PHH Asset Management*, the Court of Appeal determined that a lock-out agreement for a period of two weeks was enforceable[4].

1   Although in the House of Lords, this claim was amended to add an implied obligation to continue to negotiate in good faith. Halson *Contract Law* (2001), p 88 suggests that this was necessary to circumvent the argument that under a mere lock-out agreement, if the defendants had decided not to sell, the claimants would have suffered no consequential loss.
2   [1992] 2 AC 128 at 139.
3   The House of Lords rejected the view of Bingham LJ in the Court of Appeal that the validity of the lock-out agreement might be saved by reading it as enduring 'for such time as is reasonable'. This would, in the House's view, impose indirectly a duty to negotiate in good faith on the defendants ([1992] 2 AC 128 at 140).
4   [1994] 1 WLR 327. See Chan 'Lock-out agreements – consideration and enforceability' (1994) 8 Journal of Contract Law 84 and Sengrove 'Lock-out agreements: the new legal landscape' (1993) 38 EG 139. Applied in *Tye v House* (1997) 76 P & CR 188.

13.24   Such preliminary agreements must also satisfy the ordinary rules of contract formation. Whilst the lock-out agreement failed in *Walford v Miles* for lack of certainty, consideration had been provided by the Walfords' obtaining a comfort letter from their bankers. In *Pitt*, it was argued that Mr Pitt had failed to provide consideration to support the lock-out agreement. The Court of Appeal held that Mr Pitt, by agreeing not to apply for an injunction or cause trouble with the other buyer and to progress to exchange of contracts within two weeks, had provided valuable consideration sufficient to support the lock-out agreement. It was irrelevant that the threat of an injunction had no substance and was of nuisance value only[1]. It has been questioned whether it is consistent with authority that refraining from being a 'nuisance' can amount to good consideration[2].

1   [1994] 1 WLR 327 at 332.
2   Macmillan 'How to lock out a gazumper' [1993] CLJ 392 at 393, citing *White v Bluett* (1853) 23 LJ Ex 36.

13.25   The courts have therefore shown themselves ready to enforce preliminary agreements where there is sufficient evidence to show that the parties intended to create enforceable agreements. On this basis, letters of intent[1] and comfort letters[2] may be enforceable if the court is satisfied that this is what the parties intended in the circumstances of the case[3]. Whilst the English courts continue to refuse to enforce contracts to negotiate in good faith, the enforceability of preliminary agreements represents a limited acknowledgement of the informality, in practice, of agreement during the negotiation process[4].

1   In *British Steel Corpn v Cleveland Bridge and Engineering Co Ltd* [1984] 1 All ER 504, Robert Goff J at 508–509 explores the prospect of a letter of intent giving rise to an ordinary executory contract (see *Turriff Construction Ltd v Regalia Knitting Mills* (1971) 222 Estates Gazette 169), or a unilateral contract where the letter amounts to a standing offer which will result in a binding contract if acted on by the offeree before it lapses or is validly withdrawn. Examples of the former will be rare. See Ball 'Work carried out in pursuance of letters of intent – contract or restitution?' (1983) 99 LQR 572, who argues for greater contractual regulation of letters of intent. See also *Wilson Smithett & Cape (Sugar) Ltd v Bangladesh Sugar Industries Ltd* [1986] 1 Lloyd's Rep 378; and *Chemco Leasing SpA v Rediffusion* [1987] 1 FTLR 201.
2   The leading case is that of *Kleinwort Benson Ltd v Malaysia Mining Corpn Bhd* [1989] 1 WLR 379. See Brown 'The letter of comfort: placebo or promise?' [1990] Journal of Business Law 281; Murdoch 'Letter of intent and comfort' (1992) 4 EG 143; Ramsay [1995] International Banking and Finance Law 74.
3   See generally Furmston Norisada and Poole *Contract formation and letters of intent* (1998) particularly ch 9; Lake and Draetta *Letters of intent and other pre-contractual documents: comparative analysis and forms* (2nd edn, 1994).
4   See *Blackpool and Fylde Aero Club v Blackpool Borough Council* [1990] 1 WLR 1195 (duty to consider tenders, but not to consider it in good faith). The limits of this precedent are highlighted in the subsequent case of *Fairclough Building v Port Talbot Borough Council* (1992) 62 BLR 82.

13.26   In the remaining part of this chapter, I examine what options remain for a claimant who fails to establish a sufficiently certain and complete contract: can restitution provide an alternative basis for recovery?

C   A restitutionary remedy?

13.27   Where a contract fails for uncertainty, the claimant may have incurred a number of costs, for example, in preparatory work, products made, money expended on investment and planning, and so forth. Where the parties have been acting on the basis that a contract is in force, the courts, as seen above, are unlikely to find the parties' agreement void for uncertainty. The courts will look to the operation of the agreement and imply non-essential terms to support its operation. Once a contract is found, it will generally cover any expenses incurred prior to formation. Failing this, a court may imply a term which provides that the contract shall be retrospectively applicable to work performed prior to formation of the contract[1]. The problem generally lies, therefore, in situations where the parties are still at the negotiation stage, and any agreement has not reached the level of certainty necessary to form a valid contract. Here, on the classical view of contract, any costs incurred will lie at the foot of the party concerned. A risk has been undertaken with an expectation of profit under a contract. If the contract fails to eventuate, such a risk has materialised, and the risk-taker is left with the consequences[2]. Such a result is not 'unjust' or 'inequitable', but a risk undertaken by the would-be contractor which has materialised[3].

1   See *Trollope & Colls Ltd v Atomic Power Constructions Ltd* [1963] 1 WLR 333.
2   See Barry J in *William Lacey (Hounslow) Ltd v Davis* [1957] 1 WLR 932 at 934.
3   See Rattee J in *Regalian Properties plc v London Dockland Development Corpn* [1995] 1 WLR 212 at 231.

13.28   This section will therefore concentrate on the ability of litigants to claim such pre-contractual expenses in the law of restitution. Whilst it is clear from the above paragraph that the courts will generally resist such claims, there is a developing line of authority which is prepared to permit claims for restitution in limited circumstances. These are examined below. It will be seen that there are two lines of authority currently operating in English law: one in which the 'risk' argument is dominant; the other where the courts are prepared to use concepts of 'restitution' or 'estoppel' to protect the claimant against financial loss[1].

1   Although the two can be reconciled: see Carter 'Restitution and contract risk' in McInnes (ed) *Restitution: Developments in unjust enrichment* (1996), pp 147–150.

The 'risk' argument

13.29   This argument is clearly presented in the judgment of Rattee J in *Regalian Properties plc v London Docklands Development Corpn*[1]. In this case, Regalian had undertaken preparatory works to the value of £2.89 million in relation to a proposed development in the London Docklands. Regalian's tender had been accepted 'subject to contract', but, due to intervening delays and a subsequent fall in the property market, no final contract had been reached. In view of the fact that the project was no longer profitable, Regalian did not attempt to claim in contract, but sought to bring a claim in the law of restitution for preparatory work. As will be seen, there is some limited authority which grants a restitutionary remedy in such circumstances, but this was distinguished by Rattee J, who rejected the claim:

> [W]here, however much the parties expect a contract between them to materialise, both enter negotiations expressly (whether by use of the words 'subject to contract' or otherwise) on terms that each party is free to withdraw from the negotiations at any time ... pending the conclusion of a binding contract any cost incurred by [either party] in preparation for the intended contract will be incurred *at his own risk*, in the sense that he will have no recompense for those costs if no contract results[2].

1   [1995] 1 WLR 212. See also Lord Templeman in *A-G for Hong Kong v Humphreys Estate (Queen's Gardens) Ltd* [1987] AC 114 at 124.
2   [1995] 1 WLR 212 at 231 (emphasis supplied).

13.30   The court therefore took the view that the expenditure had been undertaken by Regalian to place itself in a position where it could obtain and comply with the terms of the proposed contract. In so doing, it took the risk that such a contract would not materialise. This would have been apparent to its advisers[1] and, particularly, in the light of the clear use of the term 'subject to contract'.

1   Rattee J [1995] 1 WLR 212 at 231 noted that Regalian was acting under the leadership of a very experienced operator in the property development market.

13.31   However, in two subsequent decisions, the courts chose to distinguish *Regalian*, and find that the claimant was no longer acting at his or her own risk. In *Countrywide Communications Ltd v ICL Pathway Ltd*[1], the claimants (a public relations and communications company) had assisted ICL in obtaining a contract, on the basis that, if the bid was successful, they would be appointed public relations consultants on the project. The bid was successful, but ICL appointed a different company in place of the claimants. Nicholas Strauss QC held that this was an exceptional case where the court would impose an obligation to pay, despite the fact that no contract had been reached between the parties. ICL had assured the claimants that they would negotiate a contract with them should their bid succeed. This assurance led the claimants to perform work beyond that normally expected of a potential sub-contractor, and was enough to take the work outside the normal risk process. The court listed four factors to be considered in deciding whether to grant a restitutionary remedy:

(i)   Were the services performed of a kind normally provided free of charge?
(ii) The terms on which the claimant performed. For example, were the negotiations 'subject to contract'? Had the defendants given any assurance that they would not withdraw from negotiations?
(iii) Did the defendants receive any real benefit from the claimants' work?
(iv) Had the defendants been at fault?

1   [2000] CLC 324, [1999] All ER(D) 1192. Comment by Jaffey 'Restitution, reliance and quantum meruit' [2000] RLR 270.

13.32   Again, in *Easat Antennas Ltd v Racal Defence Electronics Ltd*[1], Hart J supported a claim for expenses for work undertaken to assist a contract bid by the defendant. Although the exclusive supply agreement, whereby the claimant would be awarded a sub-contract should the defendant's bid be successful, was void for uncertainty, the judge held that the claimant could bring a claim for quantum meruit. On the facts, while prepared to take the risk that the defendant's bid would fail, the claimant was *not* prepared to run the risk that, if the defendant's bid succeeded, it would not be rewarded. The claimant thus had a good claim for the cost of its services.

1   (28 March 2000, unreported), [2000] All ER (D) 845.

13.33   In both *Countrywide* and *Easat*, despite the obvious risks involved in the bidding process for sub-contractors, the courts were prepared to find that the claimants were not acting at their own risk. While the courts found the contractual claims to fail for uncertainty, the claimants succeeded on the basis of restitution.

The restitution argument

13.34   In rejecting the claim in contract, the court will nevertheless proceed to consider whether the claimant has an alternative claim in restitution to recover any benefits transferred to the defendant[1]. Where the claimant seeks to recover money paid to the other party prior to contract, the law is fairly straightforward. A claimant will be able to recover the monies paid, provided that there has been a total failure of consideration. On this basis, in *Chillingworth v Esche*[2], potential purchasers were able to recover the deposit paid when negotiations for the purchase of the premises failed. Partial performance will, however, obstruct any claim[3]. The courts have, however, been prepared to circumvent this problem. In a number of cases, the courts have ignored certain benefits received by the claimant on the basis that they did not form part of the 'bargained-for' benefit, and thus permitted the claimant to recover monies paid[4]. The claimant may also be able to recover on the basis of mistake[5].

1   Rattee J has been criticised for failing to adopt restitutionary analysis in *Regalian* (above, para 13.29), although it is generally accepted that, due to problems in ascertaining enrichment (see below, para 13.44), the case was correctly decided in any event: see McKendrick 'Negotiations "Subject to Contract" and the Law of Restitution' [1994] 3 RLR 100; Virgo 'Anticipatory Contracts – Restitution Restrained' [1995] CLJ 243; Mannolini 'Restitution where an Anticipated Contract fails to Materialise' (1996) 59 MLR 111.
2   [1924] 1 Ch 97.
3   See *Whincup v Hughes (Executrix)* (1871) LR 6 CP 78, although the decision itself is no longer good law (see below, para 20.20).
4   See *Rover International Ltd v Cannon Film Sales Ltd (No 3)* [1989] 1 WLR 912 at 924–925, per Kerr LJ; *Rowland v Divall* [1923] 2 KB 500; *Warman v Southern Counties Car Finance Corpn Ltd* [1949] 2 KB 576; *Butterworth v Kingsway Motors* [1954] 1 WLR 1286. See further below, para 19.14ff.
5   See below, ch 17. See also *Rover International Ltd v Cannon Film Sales Ltd* [1989] 1 WLR 912. Comment by Beatson 'Restitutionary remedies for void and ineffective contracts' (1989) 105 LQR 179.

13.35   The law, however, remains unclear where the claimant has commenced work or produced goods during the pre-contractual period. Authority is scarce and it is difficult to ascertain any clear principles as to when recovery will be permitted[1]. For example, the doctrine of total failure of consideration has yet to be applied to work performed or goods delivered in this context and it must therefore be questioned whether, as a matter of law, a claimant can rely on this doctrine. Equally, whilst some cases may be able to be decided on the basis of mistake, in most cases, the parties will be found not to be mistaken, but to have simply wrongly 'anticipated' formation of a contract. If a restitutionary claim exists, it must be questioned on what basis this claim should lie. Indeed, it has been challenged whether such claims lie in restitution at all, or whether it is more convincing to view such cases in terms of fault or estoppel. I now examine the relevant case law.

1   Consider for example *Peter Lind & Co v Mersey Docks and Harbour Board* [1972] 2 Lloyd's Rep 234, where no attempt is made to explain the award of payment on a quantum meruit basis.

THE LEADING CASES IN RESTITUTION

13.36   This line of authority has developed largely from the post-war case of *William Lacey (Hounslow) Ltd v Davis*[1]. In this case, the claimants were a firm of builders, who had successfully tendered for rebuilding premises which had been damaged during the war. At the defendant's request, and in the belief that they would be awarded the contract, they undertook a considerable amount of preparatory work, which included the preparation of estimates and various calculations. When the defendant later sold the premises instead of proceeding with its reconstruction, the builders brought a claim, inter alia, for payment on a quantum meruit. This claim succeeded. Their work had gone beyond the normal work which a builder would perform gratuitously when asked to submit a tender, both parties had expected that the firm would be awarded the contract; and, in such circumstances, 'the court should imply a condition or imply a promise that the defendant should pay a reasonable sum to the plaintiffs for the whole of these services which were rendered by them'[2].

1   [1957] 1 WLR 932.
2   [1957] 1 WLR 932 at 940, per Barry J.

13.37   Unfortunately, the basis for recovery is not particularly clear. Barry J relied on the Court of Appeal decision in *Craven-Ellis v Canons Ltd*[1] where the Court had permitted a claim for remuneration for services rendered under an ineffective contract. The Court held that there was no 'valid distinction between work done which was to be paid for under the terms of a contract erroneously believed to be in existence, and work done which was to be paid for out of the proceeds of a contract which both parties erroneously believed was about to be made'[2]. This may be criticised for failing to recognise that generally, in the latter situation, the parties still appreciate that they are acting at their own risk[3]. More convincing is the emphasis placed on distinguishing the relationship between the parties from the ordinary aleatory nature of the negotiation process. Where there is a mutual belief that the contract will eventuate, work has been requested by the defendant, who obtains some benefit[4], it is clear that Barry J would consider it 'a denial of justice' if a claim for quantum meruit did not exist[5].

1   [1936] 2 KB 403.
2   [1957] 1 WLR 932 at 939.
3   See Goff and Jones *Law of Restitution* (5th edn, 1998), pp 668 and 669 and Birks *An Introduction to the Law of Restitution* (revised edn, 1989), p 274, who regards it as a 'misprediction' case.
4   In this case, Barry J noted ([1957] 1 WLR at 935) that the defendant had used some of the claimants' estimates to negotiate compensation from the War Damage Commission, which had 'at least some influence' on the price for which the building was subsequently sold.
5   [1957] 1 WLR 932 at 936. Applied recently in *Yule v Little Bird* (5 April 2001, unreported, Buckley J).

13.38   The leading case in restitution is currently *British Steel Corpn v Cleveland Bridge and Engineering Co Ltd*[1]. In this case, the defendants had successfully tendered for the fabrication of steelwork to be used in the construction of a building. In the course of negotiation of a sub-contract for the supply of cast-steel nodes, the defendants had sent the claimants a letter of intent, which requested the claimants to start work 'pending the preparation and issuing to you of the official form of sub-contract'. The claimants manufactured and delivered the nodes requested, but the parties failed to reach agreement on a number of contract terms, including progress payments and liability for loss arising from late delivery. When the defendants refused to pay for the nodes, claiming damages for late delivery or delivery of the nodes out of the sequence envisaged, the claimants sued for the value of the nodes on a quantum meruit.

1   [1984] 1 All ER 504.

13.39   Robert Goff J, as he then was, rejected the argument that a unilateral contract had come into existence. The court held that, since the parties were still negotiating over material contractual terms such as price and delivery dates, any contract was too uncertain to be enforced. Nevertheless, the claimants could bring a claim in restitution for payment for the nodes. Where both parties confidently expected a formal contract to eventuate and, to expedite performance, one party had been requested to commence the contract work, the law imposed an obligation on the party who made the request to pay a reasonable sum for that work. Such an obligation arose, according to Robert Goff J, 'in quasi-contract or, as we now say, in restitution'[1].

1   [1984] 1 All ER 504 at 511, citing *William Lacey (Hounslow) Ltd v Davis* [1957] 1 WLR 932;
     Sanders & Forster Ltd v A Monk & Co Ltd [1980] CA Transcript 35; *OTM Ltd v Hydranautics* [1981]
     2 Lloyd's Rep 211 at 214, per Parker J.

13.40   Both Goff J and Barry J rejected the argument that the claimants in
both cases had worked on the basis that they would be remunerated under the
contract and therefore could not be said to have expected to be remunerated
otherwise. Barry J held that the actual views or intentions of the parties were
irrelevant in deciding whether to impose an obligation to pay[1].

1   [1957] 1 WLR 932 at 936. See also per Robert Goff J [1984] 1 All ER 504 at 511.

13.41   One potential problem arising from *British Steel Corpn v Cleveland Bridge
and Engineering Co Ltd* should be noted at this stage. Robert Goff J rejected the
defendants' counterclaim for damages for late delivery of the nodes or delivery
out of sequence. Such claims could only be brought in contract, and therefore
failed when the court found no contract to exist[1]. This would appear to leave the
defendant at a particular disadvantage when facing a restitutionary claim, if the
court can disregard any deficiencies in the claimant's performance. Ball argues
that this throws the whole risk of negotiations breaking down after performance
on the buyer, who has to pay for everything he actually receives but gets no
protection in relation to any expectations he had of greater or better
performance[2]. It may be, however, that this point has limited practical
importance in that a defendant who receives a deficient performance can always
argue that the quantum meruit should be assessed at a correspondingly low
level.

1   Although Robert Goff J held at [1984] 1 All ER 504 at 510–511 that, in any event, such claims
     would not have been successful.
2   Ball 'Work carried out in pursuance of letters of intent – contract or restitution?' (1983) 99 LQR
     572 at 577. Note, however, the response of McKendrick in 'The battle of the forms and the law of
     restitution' (1988) 8 OJLS 197 at 211–218, who argues for a more sensitive analysis of the
     buyer's request.

The theoretical basis of the case law

13.42   The cases examined above expressly award a remedy on the basis of
restitution. They give little explanation, however, as to the basis for the
restitutionary claim. In this section, I examine whether such cases fit within
accepted restitutionary principles. Generally, it has been held that a claim for
restitution (or unjust enrichment) will exist when a claimant can show that a
defendant has been unjustly enriched at his or her expense[1]. It has been disputed
whether the above cases manifest these characteristics, or whether they may be
better interpreted on the basis of contractual, tortious or estoppel principles[2]. I
now examine this question.

1   See per Lord Goff in *Lipkin Gorman (a firm) v Karpnale Ltd* [1991] 2 AC 548 at 572.
2   Contrast for example McKendrick 'Work done in anticipation of a contract which does not
     materialise' and Hedley 'Work done in anticipation of a contract which does not materialise: a
     response' in Cornish Nolan O'Sullivan and Virgo *Restitution past present and future – Essays in
     honour of Gareth Jones* (1998), chs 11 and 12. Note also J Dietrich 'Classifying precontractual
     liability: A comparative analysis' (2001) 21 Legal Studies 153 who develops Hedley's analysis by
     analogy with the German doctrine of *culpa in contrahendo* to suggest that the remedy lies in a grey
     area between contract and tort.

Restitution

THE UNJUST GROUND

13.43   In adopting restitutionary analysis, it is necessary to identify the basis on which the defendant has been *unjustly* enriched. A number of possible 'unjust' grounds exist. For example, it may be possible to argue that the claimant performed in the mistaken belief that a contract was in existence. This will be strengthened by the fact that mistake of law now appears to be a valid ground for recovery[1]. This will only apply, however, where the parties believe a contract to be in existence, and that they are no longer subject to the risks of the negotiation process. If it is clear that certain essential matters have yet to be agreed, then such a ground cannot be relied upon. In such circumstances, any restitutionary claim must rest on the grounds of free acceptance[2] or failure of consideration[3]. The scope, or even existence, of these grounds is a matter of dispute amongst restitution lawyers themselves[4]. The case-law provides little assistance. In *William Lacey (Hounslow) Ltd v Davis*[5] and *British Steel Corpn v Cleveland Bridge and Engineering Co Ltd*[6], the courts merely recognise that, in these circumstances, the law should imply an obligation. There is therefore no clear authority at present on the 'unjust' basis for a claim in restitution.

1   *Kleinwort Benson Ltd v Lincoln City Council* [1999] 2 AC 349; on which see below, para 17.40ff.
2   See below, para 13.45. See Birks *An Introduction to the Law of Restitution* (revised edn, 1989), p 115; Goff and Jones *Law of Restitution* (5th edn, 1998), p 19; Ball 'Work carried out in pursuance of letters of intent – contract or restitution?' (1983) 99 LQR 572 at 575; and McKendrick 'The battle of the forms and the law of restitution' (1988) 8 OJLS 197.
3   See Burrows and McKendrick *Cases and Materials on the Law of Restitution* (1997), pp 268 and 269; Burrows 'Free acceptance and the law of restitution' (1988) 104 LQR 576; Virgo *Principles of the Law of Restitution* (1999), p 361.
4   Whilst Birks *An Introduction to the Law of Restitution* (revised edn, 1989), pp 281–283 advocates free acceptance as an explanation for pre-contractual liability, this has been criticised: see, in particular, Burrows 'Free acceptance and the law of restitution' (1988) 104 LQR 576. Birks 'In defence of free acceptance' in Burrows (ed) *Essays on the Law of Restitution* (1991), p 114 accepts that in relation to work in anticipation of a contract, Burrows is correct to identify failure of consideration as the unjust factor, except where it happens to be possible to prove initially unconscientious behaviour on the part of the defence. See also Birks *Restitution – the future* (1992), pp 53–60.
5   [1957] 1 WLR 932 at 935.
6   [1984] 1 All ER 504.

BENEFIT AT THE CLAIMANT'S EXPENSE

13.44   A further, and more significant, difficulty in these claims is to show that a benefit has, in fact, been received by the other party. Whilst this may not be a problem, for example, in *British Steel*, where the nodes manufactured by the claimant had a clear value to the defendants, this is not always the case. There is an obvious problem in showing that the defendant has benefited from preparatory work for a project with which the defendant has decided not to proceed[1]. Yet, as recognised by McKendrick, 'the absence of an enrichment is fatal to the existence of a restitutionary claim'[2]. Indeed, absence of benefit was one of the grounds given by Rattee J for rejecting Regalian's claim in *Regalian Properties plc v London Docklands Development Corpn*. Regalian had incurred expenses in preparation for the expected contract, but did not, in the view of Rattee J, render any benefit to LDDC[3]. In contrast, Rattee J argued that the defendant in *William Lacey* had obtained the benefit of estimates and calculations to negotiate a grant from the War Damage Commission for the project[4]. This is a fine line. The receipt of a 'benefit' in *William Lacey* was not central to the decision, and of minimal impact where the defendant had chosen not to proceed with the rebuilding and sell the premises instead[5].

1   See for example the controversial decision in *Marston Construction Co Ltd v Kigass Ltd* (1989) 15 Con LR 116, which is now generally regarded as incorrect: see *Regalian Properties plc v London Dockland Development Corpn* [1995] 1 WLR 212 at 229, per Rattee J, commentary in (1989) 46 BLR 110–113.
2   McKendrick 'Work done in anticipation of a contract which does not materialise' in Cornish, Nolan, O'Sullivan and Virgo *Restitution past present and future – Essays in honour of Gareth Jones* (1998), p 172 notes the difficulties experienced by restitution lawyers in defining 'enrichment'.
3   [1995] 1 WLR 212.
4   See per Rattee J, [1995] 1 WLR 212 at 224. On *William Lacey* see above, para 13.36ff.
5   Goff and Jones *Law of Restitution* (5th edn, 1998), p 668 suggest that: 'The reality is that the award concealed a claim for loss suffered in anticipation of a contractual agreement which never materialised'.

13.45   To resolve difficulties in ascertaining enrichment, restitution lawyers have proposed a number of tests to identify receipt of a benefit. Goff and Jones have promoted the concept of 'free acceptance': if the defendant chooses to accept the claimant's performance in the full knowledge that this performance is not intended to be gratuitous, this is a sufficient indicator that a benefit has been received[1]. It is not essential that the defendant should have requested such performance. This concept remains controversial[2], and arguably contravenes the English version of the principle of freedom of contract, which does not require good faith in negotiations and therefore permits parties to take advantage of the claimant's premature performance.

1   'In our view, [the defendant] will be held to have benefited from the services rendered if he, as a reasonable man, should have known that the plaintiff who rendered the services expected to be paid for them, and yet he did not take a reasonable opportunity open to him to reject the proffered services': Goff and Jones *Law of Restitution* (5th edn, 1998), p 18. There is also very limited authority that the mere request for performance is sufficient to demonstrate a benefit: see *Planché v Colburn* (1831) 8 Bing 14, 131 ER 305, although doubt has been cast on its authority, see Goff and Jones (above), pp 20–21, 670.
2   See for example Burrows (1988) 104 LQR 576 and *Law of Restitution* (1993), pp 11–16; Mead 'Free acceptance: some further considerations' (1989) 105 LQR 460; Garner 'The role of subjective benefit in the law of unjust enrichment' (1990) 10 OJLS 42; Simester 'Unjust free acceptance' [1997] Lloyds Maritime and Commercial Law Quarterly 103.

13.46   A further, and perhaps more convincing, argument is that of 'incontrovertible benefit', that is, the defendant has received a benefit if, due to the claimant's performance, he or she has received an immediate and realisable financial gain, or has been saved necessary expense[1]. This is an objective test, and merely expands the ordinary notion of benefit to include positive and negative benefits. It will not, however, apply in all cases, and there is an ongoing dispute whether the gain must be realised or merely realisable[2].

1   The leading cases are generally accepted to be *Craven–Ellis v Canons Ltd* [1936] 2 KB 403; and *Greenwood v Bennett* [1973] QB 195.
2   'There is much to be said for the view that a person has been incontrovertibly benefited if a reasonable person would conclude that he had been saved an expense which he otherwise would necessarily have incurred or where he has made, in consequence of the plaintiff's acts, a realisable financial gain': Goff and Jones *Law of Restitution* (5th edn, 1998), p 22. Birks *An Introduction to the Law of Restitution* (revised edn, 1989), pp 121–124 argues that the benefit must not merely be realisable, but realised.

13.47   An additional complication is whether 'pure services', that is, services which do not leave a valuable end-product or save necessary expense[1], can be regarded as a benefit[2]. Beatson adopts an 'exchange-value' test. On this basis, cases such as *Brewer Street Investments Ltd v Barclays Woollen Co Ltd*[3], where it is difficult to see any increase in wealth, should not be regarded as based on unjust enrichment, but rather on injurious reliance. Such reasoning is inconsistent with any test based on free acceptance, which Beatson dismisses as based on an 'overinclusive' concept of unjust enrichment[4]. Predictably, this view has been criticised by the main proponents of free acceptance[5].

1 For example, a teacher who has given a lesson to an able pupil or given a lecture to an unresponsive audience.
2 Beatson 'Benefit, reliance and the structure of unjust enrichment' (1987) 40 CLP 71, reprinted in Beatson (ed) *Use and Abuse of Unjust enrichment* (1991), ch 2.
3 [1954] 1 QB 428; below, para 13.51.
4 'These cases are concerned with "consent", "acquiescence", "reliance", "fault", and "risk" rather than "enrichment" or "benefit"': Beatson (ed) *Use and Abuse of Unjust enrichment* (1991), p 35.
5 Goff and Jones *Law of Restitution* (5th edn, 1998), p 21; Birks *An Introduction to the Law of Restitution* (revised edn, 1989), pp 449–451; Birks 'In defence of free acceptance' in Burrows (ed) *Essays on the Law of Restitution* (1991), pp 132–135.

13.48 Virgo has also suggested that the defendant may, in certain circumstances, be estopped from denying enrichment, where the defendant has represented to the claimant that he or she wishes to receive the benefit and will pay for it, the claimant acts to his or her detriment in reliance upon the representation, and the defendant falsifies the representation in some way[1]. This view runs very close to the concept of fault, examined immediately below.

1 Virgo *Principles of the Law of Restitution* (1999), pp 88–91.

13.49 The main problem with these tests, which is freely admitted by the textbook writers[1], is that they are not utilised by the courts[2]. However, in the light of recognition in the highest courts of the main texts on restitution, this may be merely a matter of time. Nevertheless, at present, these concepts operate at a theoretical level only, and it is difficult to see any consistent approach for the courts, if they so choose, to adopt.

1 Goff and Jones *Law of Restitution* (5th edn, 1998), pp 19 and 23.
2 Even where the courts have referred to these concepts, their application may be questioned: see *Marston Construction Co Ltd v Kigass Ltd* (1989) 15 Con LR 116 at 129, per Peter Bowsher QC (on incontrovertible benefit).

Alternative explanations for recovery

FAULT

13.50 It has been suggested that the real basis for recovery is one of fault. The leading authority is the judgment of Sheppard J in *Sabemo Pty Ltd v North Sydney Municipal Council*[1]. Again, the court faced the familiar scenario of work performed in anticipation of a contract. Sabemo had incurred expenses of A$426,000, in undertaking detailed work on plans for a proposed development, before the council finally decided to abandon the scheme altogether. Sheppard J held that the unilateral withdrawal of the council amounted to fault, which would entitle Sabemo to compensation for expenses incurred:

> To my mind, the defendant's decision to drop the proposal is the determining factor. If the transaction had gone off because the parties were unable to agree, then I think it would be correct ... to say that each party had taken a risk, in incurring the expenditure which it did, that the transaction might go off because of a bona fide

failure to reach agreement on some point of substance in such a complex transaction. But I do not think it right to say that the risk should be so borne when one party has taken it upon itself to change its mind about the entirety of the proposal[2].

Sheppard J expressly stated that this was not a case of unjust enrichment[3].

1   [1977] 2 NSWLR 880, Supreme Court of New South Wales. Considered further in *Brenner v First Artists' Management Property Ltd* [1993] 2 VR 221 at 258–259. Comment by Davies 'What's in a title?' (1981) 1 OJLS 300. Contrast the view of Carter 'Contract, restitution and promissory estoppel' (1989) 12 University of New South Wales Law Journal 30, who prefers to interpret *Sabemo* on the basis of promissory estoppel.
2   [1977] 2 NSWLR 880 at 901.
3   [1977] 2 NSWLR 880 at 897.

13.51   There is some support for this approach in English law. In *Brewer Street Investments Ltd v Barclays Woollen Co Ltd*[1], landlords had undertaken certain alterations to the premises at the request of prospective lessees, who had accepted responsibility for the costs. When negotiations for the lease broke down, the landlords sought remuneration for the works[2]. The Court of Appeal kept the defendants to their initial acceptance of responsibility. They had been aware of the risk of negotiations failing[3], and yet nevertheless had requested that alterations to the premises be performed prior to contract. All three judges considered the relative fault of the parties, and indicated that if the negotiations had failed due to the fault of the landlords, the case may have been decided differently[4]. In the view of Somervell and Romer LJJ (but not Denning LJ[5]), the prospective tenants had been at fault and should therefore pay for services rendered under a collateral contract.

1   [1954] 1 QB 428.
2   The works, which were stopped when negotiations failed, were not found to benefit the landlords: see Denning LJ [1954] 1 QB 428 at 437.
3   Agreement on principal matters had been reached 'subject to contract'.
4   See, for example, per Romer and Denning LJJ, in argument, [1954] 1 QB 428 at 431.
5   Denning LJ found (at 436) that neither party had been at fault, and that the claim should lie in restitution. One might question what benefit the prospective tenants had received in this case.

13.52   The use of fault reasoning may also be seen in the earlier judgment of the same Court of Appeal in *Jennings and Chapman Ltd v Woodman, Matthews & Co*[1]. The facts were similar to those of *Brewer*. The landlords had undertaken alterations at the request of a prospective tenant, who had agreed to pay for the cost of the works, and take a sublease of the offices as soon as the work was completed. The Court found here that the landlords could not claim for the cost of the alterations. On the facts, only the landlords could have foreseen the problem which led to the contract failing to materialise and therefore must bear the risk of the tenant withdrawing[2].

Fault was also relied on more recently in *Countrywide Communications Ltd v ICL Pathway Ltd*[3]. Here, Countrywide had been induced to perform work in anticipation of a contract, on the firm assurance from ICL that, if their bid was successful, Countrywide would be rewarded with a sub-contract; an assurance ICL later dishonoured.

If such fault-based reasoning is adopted, any benefit to the defendant becomes incidental. It is therefore difficult to view such cases as having a restitutionary basis, without adopting a very broad interpretation of 'benefit' to include any work done at the defendant's request.

1   [1952] 2 TLR 409.
2   It was also found that the landlord was the only person who could possibly benefit from the works undertaken.

3   [2000] CLC 324, [1999] All ER (D) 1192; above, para 13.31, where the element of fault which
    deprived Countrywide of its promised subcontract was regarded as pivotal. See Sarker 'Paying for
    work done without a contract' (2000) 144 Solicitors Journal 12.

13.53   Nevertheless, the concept of 'fault', in this context, does not fit easily into
English law, which has rejected the civil law concept of *culpa in contrahendo*[1]. As we
have seen, the courts have refused to enforce an obligation to negotiate in good
faith[2]. The English courts place considerable emphasis on freedom of contract, and
refuse to regulate the negotiation process by concepts of fault. Rattee J stated
clearly that *Sabemo*[3] is not established by any English authority, and that there is
nothing 'inequitable' in allowing the loss to lie where it falls when negotiations
fail[4]. There is, at present, little support for fault-based liability in English law.

1   See Beatson and Friedmann (eds) *Good faith and fault in contract law* (1997), particularly ch 2;
    Kessler and Fine 'Culpa in contrahendo, bargaining in good faith and freedom of contract: a
    comparative study' (1964) 77 Harvard Law Review 401.
2   See *Walford v Miles* [1992] 2 AC 128; above, para 13.21. Fault has also been criticised as
    productive of uncertainty: '"Fault" is a shadowy sign-post which may point in more than one
    direction': Goff and Jones *Law of Restitution* (5th edn, 1998), p 671.
3   See above, para 13.50.
4   *Regalian Properties plc v London Docklands Development Corpn* [1995] 1 WLR 212 at 231.

E<small>QUITABLE ESTOPPEL</small>

13.54   It has also been argued that the case law can be best explained by
reference to the doctrine of estoppel. A number of influential academics have
identified the claimant's action as being, in reality, one of reliance: the claimant
has incurred costs in reliance on the belief, induced by the defendant, that a
contract would eventuate[1]. Whilst the current edition of Goff and Jones suggests
equitable estoppel as the basis for a restitutionary claim[2], it may be argued that it
should stand as a basis for recovery in its own right[3]. On this basis, the
identification of a 'benefit' to the defendant would be irrelevant, and the courts
should concentrate on the doctrine of estoppel in ascertaining whether the
claimant has any remedy at law.

1   See in particular Jones 'Claims arising out of anticipated contracts which do not materialise'
    (1980) 18 University of Western Ontario Law Review 447; Beatson 'Benefit, reliance and the
    structure of unjust enrichment' in Beatson *Use and Abuse of Unjust enrichment* (1991), pp 21–44,
    Beale (ed) *Chitty on Contracts* (28th edn, 1999), vol 1, para 30–019; and Carter 'Contract,
    restitution and promissory estoppel' (1989) 12 University of New South Wales Law Journal 30.
    See also Carter 'Services rendered under ineffective contracts' [1990] Lloyds Maritime and
    Commercial Law Quarterly 495 at 499–506 and 'Ineffective transactions' in Finn (ed) *Essays on
    restitution* (1990), ch 7.
2   Goff and Jones *Law of Restitution* (5th edn, 1998), pp 670–673 ('The restitutionary claim
    conceals a claim for reliance loss, where no claim for damages for breach of contract can lie').
    Note criticism of such reasoning: McKendrick 'Work done in anticipation of a contract which
    does not materialise' in Cornish Nolan O'Sullivan and Virgo *Restitution past present and future –
    Essays in honour of Gareth Jones* (1998), p 180.
3   See, for example, Liew 'Restitution and contract risk: Commentary' in McInnes (ed) *Restitution:
    Developments in unjust enrichment* (1996), p 163.

13.55   This argument falters, however, in the light of the current complex
rules relating to estoppel. As has been noted:

> There are the divisions between common law and equitable estoppel, between
> estoppel by conduct and estoppel by representation, and the distinction between
> present and future fact. There are titles such as promissory estoppel, proprietary
> estoppel and estoppel by acquiescence[1].

In relation to a belief that a contract would eventuate, the applicable estoppel would, on conventional reasoning, be promissory estoppel. Promissory estoppel has a number of characteristics, which are as follows[2]:

(i)   a clear and unambiguous representation is necessary[3];
(ii)   reliance must be proved[4];
(iii) detriment must be proved[5];
(iv)   it must be inequitable to go back on the promise[6];
(iv)   the remedy is suspensory in nature[7];
(v)   a pre-existing relationship is required[8]; and
(vi)   the remedy may only be used in a defensive capacity[9].

Such limitations would, at present, appear to limit the potential of estoppel to assist claimants performing in anticipation of a contract.

1   *Commonwealth of Australia v Verwayen* (1990) 170 CLR 394 at 409, per Mason CJ.
2   See Treitel *Law of Contract* (10th edn, 1999), pp 99–113; Turner *Spencer-Bower and Turner: The law relating to estoppel by representation* (3rd edn, 1977), ch 14.
3   See *Woodhouse AC Israel Cocoa Ltd SA v Nigerian Produce Marketing Co Ltd* [1972] AC 741.
4   See *Tool Metal Manufacturing Co Ltd v Tungsten Electric Co Ltd* [1955] 1 WLR 761.
5   See n 4, but contrast *W J Alan & Co Ltd v El Nasr Export and Import Co* [1972] 2 QB 189.
6   See *The Post Chaser (Société Italo-Belge pour le Commerce et l'Industrie v Palm and Vegetable Oils (Malaysia) Sdn Bdh* [1982] 1 All ER 19 and *D & C Builders v Rees* [1966] 2 QB 617.
7   See n 4.
8   See *Durham Fancy Goods Ltd v Michael Jackson (Fancy Goods) Ltd* [1968] 2 QB 839.
9   See *Combe v Combe* [1951] 2 KB 215.

13.56   However, there is a line of authority in English law which supports a broader interpretation of estoppel. In a number of cases, the courts have accepted the concept of 'equitable estoppel', that is, a broader notion of estoppel based on unconscionability[1]. These cases derive mainly from authority concerning *proprietary* estoppel[2]. In cases such as *Crabb v Arun District Council*[3] and *Taylors Fashions Ltd v Liverpool Victoria Trustees Co Ltd*[4], the courts have demonstrated a willingness to support equitable intervention on the basis of unconscionability, and move away from the rigidity of earlier authority[5]. The potential for such developments to assist the pre-contractual performer can be illustrated by examining *Salvation Army Trustee Co v West Yorkshire Metropolitan County Council*[6]. In this case, faced with the compulsory purchase of their meeting hall for road widening purposes, the Salvation Army had negotiated an agreement with the local council, whereby the council would purchase the old site, and sell to the Salvation Army a new site on terms which reflected their receiving compensation under the Land Compensation Act 1961. This was agreed 'subject to contract' and, with the knowledge of the council, the Salvation Army had entered upon the new site and constructed a hall in preparation for the move. Unfortunately, the road widening scheme was subsequently abandoned, and the council withdrew from the purchase of the old site. Woolf J held that, nevertheless, the conduct of the city council had encouraged the Salvation Army to believe that they would not resile from the arrangements. On this basis, the council would be required to proceed with their purchase of the old site.

1   See Halliwell 'Estoppel: unconscionability as a cause of action' (1994) 14 Legal Studies 15, although her formulation would exclude promissory estoppel from any unified doctrine on the basis that it amounts to an exceptional contractual response. Similarly, Cooke, who in *Modern law of estoppel* (2000) proposes a framework for a unified estoppel (see particularly, chs 4 and 8), would limit any cause of action to interests in land. For a broader view, see Spence *Protecting reliance: The emergent doctrine of equitable estoppel* (1999).
2   Note however *Amalgamated Investment & Property Co Ltd v Texas Commerce International Bank Ltd* [1982] QB 84 at 122, per Lord Denning MR (estoppel by convention).

3   [1976] Ch 179.
4   (1978) [1982] QB 133n at 151–152, per Oliver J, noted by Jackson 'How many kinds of estoppel?' [1982] Conv 450. See also *Habib Bank Ltd v Habib Bank AG Zurich* [1981] 1 WLR 1265 at 1285, per Oliver J; *Sledmore v Dalby* (1996) 72 P & CR 196 at 207, per Hobhouse LJ; and Lord Bingham in Johnson v Gore Wood & Co [2001] 1 All ER 481.
5   Such as *Willmott v Barber* (1880) 15 Ch D 96 at 105–106, where Fry J set out the 'five probanda' test to establish whether a claim for proprietary estoppel existed.
6   (1980) 41 P & CR 179. See also *Holidays Inns Inc v Broadhead* (1974) 232 Estates Gazette 951; and *JT Developments v Quinn* (1990) 62 P & CR 33 (where the defendants were held to be entitled to a new lease by virtue of proprietary estoppel).

13.57   The case is important, in that proprietary estoppel is being used to force a defendant to enter a contract. Its limitations must, however, be noted. First, Woolf J emphasised that the sale of the land was inextricably woven into the Salvation Army's purchase of the new site, to which it was conceded that the principles of proprietary estoppel would apply[1]. Secondly, the judge acknowledged that it was a novel case, which was unlikely to have a wide application, and should not interfere with the ordinary conduct of negotiations 'subject to contract'[2].

1   (1980) 41 P & CR 179 at 192.
2   (1980) 41 P & CR 179 at 198–199.

13.58   This last point is illustrated by the Privy Council decision in *A-G of Hong Kong v Humphreys Estate (Queen's Gardens) Ltd*[1]. Here, the defendants had entered into negotiations with the claimant group of companies, to exchange a Crown lease of government property for 83 flats in premises owned by the group. An agreement in principle was reached 'subject to contract'. The government took possession of the flats, fitted them out, moved civil servants in, and disposed of the residences they formerly occupied. Equally, the group was given a licence to enter the Crown land and demolish the existing buildings on it, in preparation for redevelopment, and had, as agreed, paid the difference in value between the two properties. Some three years after the agreement in principle, the group withdrew from the negotiations, and required the defendants to give up possession of the flats.

Lord Templeman, giving the opinion of the Privy Council, rejected the defendants' claim that the claimants should be estopped from withdrawing at this stage. The defendants themselves had insisted that the terms of the agreement in principle could be varied or withdrawn prior to formal execution of the transaction. Where the parties had proceeded on the basis that either party might suffer a change of mind and withdraw, estoppel would not intervene[2]. It was necessary to establish an expectation or belief, created or encouraged by the other party, which was relied upon; and this had not occurred in this case. The Court distinguished the *Salvation Army* case as one where the term 'subject to contract' was irrelevant. The council had specifically represented that it would go ahead with the transaction, and was estopped from changing its expressed intention. This contrasted with the ordinary situation where parties acting 'subject to contract' are fully aware of the non-binding nature of their relationship. Lord Templeman conceded that:

> ... it is possible but unlikely that in circumstances at present unforeseeable a party to negotiations set out in a document expressed to be 'subject to contract' would be able to satisfy the court that the parties had subsequently agreed to convert the document into a contract or that some form of estoppel had arisen to prevent both parties from refusing to proceed with the transactions envisaged by the document[3].

This would appear to limit the authority of *Salvation Army* to a situation where, due to the defendant's representation, the claimant has a firm belief that the contract will eventuate despite the fact that negotiations are 'subject to contract'. This will be rare. The courts have also in recent years expressed reluctance to embrace the concept of a unified estoppel. In *The Indian Endurance and The Indian Grace*, for example, the House of Lords rejected the possibility of an overarching principle governing estoppel by convention and proprietary estoppel, fearing that 'to restate the law in [these] terms ... might tend to blur the necessarily separate requirements, and distinct terrain of application, of the two kinds of estoppel'[4]. In *Baird Textile Holdings Ltd v Marks & Spencer plc*[5], the Court of Appeal struck out a claim framed in terms of a broad notion of estoppel and maintained a conservative approach. Nevertheless, the court recognised that it was open to the House of Lords to develop or correct the existing legal position and that 'the principles of the law of estoppel have not yet been fully developed'[6].

1   [1987] AC 114, PC. See generally Pawlowski 'New limits on proprietary estoppel doctrine' (1998) 114 LQR 351.
2   [1987] AC 114 at 127, per Lord Templeman.
3   [1987] AC 114 at 127–128, per Lord Templeman.
4   *Republic of India v India Steamship Co Ltd (No 2)* [1998] AC 878 at 914, per Lord Steyn. See also *First National Bank v Thompson* [1996] Ch 231 at 236, per Millett LJ: '[the] valiant attempt to demonstrate that all estoppels ... are now subsumed in the single and all embracing estoppel by representation and that they are all governed by the same requirements has never won general acceptance'.
5   [2001] CLC 999. The Court of Appeal also rejected the contractual claim for lack of certainty.
6   [2001] CLC 999 at 1011, per Judge LJ. The case itself concerned estoppel by convention.

13.59   Greater support for estoppel has come from the High Court of Australia. In a number of decisions, the High Court adopted a radical approach towards promissory estoppel, which moved towards a broad unified concept of equitable estoppel[1]. In *Waltons Stores (Interstate) v Maher*[2], negotiations for a lease had advanced to a stage where contracts were about to be exchanged. Under the terms of the proposed lease, the lessors were obliged to demolish existing premises, and construct new buildings to Waltons' specifications, with a strict deadline for completion. In the light of an assurance that approval would be forthcoming, Maher forwarded the necessary documents and commenced work, thus ensuring completion within the stated time. Waltons, however, chose a more cautious approach and, without informing Maher, reviewed the situation and resolved not to proceed. At this point, approximately 40% of the construction work had been performed, for which Maher claimed compensation.

1   See *Waltons Stores (Interstate) v Maher* (1988) 164 CLR 387; and *Commonwealth of Australia v Verwayen* (1990) 170 CLR 394, and particularly the judgments of Deane J in those cases. See generally Spence *Protecting reliance: the emergent doctrine of equitable estoppel* (1999), pp 87–106. However, not all Australian writers take the same view: see Robertson 'Reliance, conscience and the new equitable estoppel' (2000) 24 Melbourne University Law Review 218. The United States courts have also used promissory estoppel in a flexible way to permit a claimant to recover reliance loss: see most famously *Hoffman v Red Owl Stores Inc* 26 Wis 2d 683, 133 NW 2d 267 (1965).
2   (1988) 164 CLR 387. For comment see Duthie 'Equitable estoppel, unconscionability and the enforcement of promises' (1988) 104 LQR 362; Phillips and Proksch '*Waltons Stores (Interstate) Ltd v Maher*: Implications for the law of contract' (1989) 19 University of Western Australia Law Review 171; Bagot 'Equitable Estoppel and Contractual Obligations in the light of *Waltons v Maher*' (1988) 62 ALJ 926; Sutton 'Contract by Estoppel' (1988) 1 Journal of Contract Law 205.

13.60   The High Court of Australia rejected the company's argument that there was a valid enforceable agreement. Although the parties had reached agreement, they had yet to exchange the necessary documents, and a valid contract had not been formed. Nevertheless, the Court held that Waltons were estopped from denying that they were bound by reason of their unconscionable conduct. They had stood by in silence whilst Maher had undertaken work in the belief that exchange of contracts was a formality. On this basis, Waltons would not be permitted to withdraw from the contract, although equity would be satisfied by ordering damages in lieu of specific performance.

13.61   Whilst the judges in *Waltons Stores* differed on a number of points[1], the whole court favoured a broader interpretation of equitable estoppel. In its subsequent decision in *Commonwealth of Australia v Verwayen*[2], the Court again favoured a broad concept of equitable estoppel which paid no regard to the traditional boundaries between different types of estoppel. Whilst the Australian courts have recognised such authority, the exact status of promissory estoppel in Australian law is difficult to specify[3]. Additional problems arise in determining what remedy a claimant might expect. The clearest statement is that of Brennan J who, influenced by *Crabb v Arun District Council*[4], limits the remedy to that necessary to avoid the detriment which will be suffered if the assumption of the claimant goes unfulfilled[5]. Nevertheless, it has been suggested that the doctrine may go beyond protecting detrimental reliance and protect the parties' expectations[6]. This does not appear to be the intention of the High Court of Australia and risks a serious conflict with the rules of contract law[7]. It is perhaps inevitable that the doctrine has been criticised for causing 'deplorable uncertainty'[8].

1   Most significantly on the applicability of common law estoppel to the case.
2   (1990) 170 CLR 394.
3   See Spence *Protecting reliance: the emergent doctrine of equitable estoppel* (1999), p 17; *Giumelli v Giumelli* (1999) 196 CLR 101 at 112–113.
4   [1976] Ch 179.
5   *Waltons Stores (Interstate) v Maher* (1988) 164 CLR 387 at 423. See also *Commonwealth of Australia v Verwayen* (1990) 170 CLR 394.
6   See Robertson 'Satisfying the minimum equity: Equitable estoppel remedies after *Verwayen*' (1996) 20 Melbourne University Law Review 805, who notes a continuing tendency to award expectancy relief. See also Cooke 'Estoppel and the protection of expectations' (1997) 19 Legal Studies 258 and *Modern law of estoppel* (2000).
7   See Giliker *Pre-contractual liability in English and French law* (2002), ch 5.
8   Birks *An Introduction to the Law of Restitution* (revised edn, 1989), p 291.

13.62   The limitations of such authority must also be stressed. First, a court cannot utilise estoppel to force a party to enter a contract which is too uncertain to be enforced[1]. This would be pointless. Secondly, the High Court recognised the validity of *A-G of Hong Kong v Humphreys Estate (Queen's Gardens) Ltd*[2]. Brennan J in *Waltons* stated expressly that the doctrine has no application where the parties appreciate that they are acting at their own risk: 'it is only if a party induces the other party to believe that he ... is already bound and his freedom to withdraw has gone that it could be unconscionable for him subsequently to assert that he is legally free to withdraw'[3]. This broader doctrine of estoppel would therefore only apply where the conduct of the parties induces another to believe, to his or her detriment, that the other will not withdraw from the negotiation process.

1   *Austotel Pty Ltd v Franklyns Selfservice Pty Ltd* (1989) 16 NSWLR 582 (New South Wales Court of Appeal). For comment see Parkinson 'Equitable estoppel: developments after *Waltons Stores v Maher*' (1990) 3 Journal of Contract Law 50. Equally, a promise to make a gift will not give rise to an estoppel, because the promisee at no stage regards the promise as binding: see *Waltons Stores (Interstate) v Maher* (1988) 164 CLR 387 at 402–403, per Mason CJ and Wilson J.
2   [1987] AC 114, PC, above, para 13.58.

D   Conclusion

The role of restitution

13.63   The question of money paid in advance of a contract is fairly clear. If the claimant cannot rely on a contract because its terms are too uncertain or incomplete, recovery of monies paid in advance will depend on the concept of total failure of consideration[1]. If the claimant has received no benefit in return for the payment, he or she will have a right to recover any sums paid. In contrast, the courts at present appear unclear as to the exact basis of the case law permitting a party to recover compensation for works performed or goods delivered in anticipation of a contract[2]. It is clear that in Australia, the courts favour estoppel and there is some academic support in England for this approach. Yet, the dicta in the cases expressly refer to restitution. As we have seen, academics have experienced considerable difficulties in ascertaining the exact nature of the restitutionary remedy, for example, is it based on 'free acceptance', 'failure of consideration', 'failure of condition' or simply 'mistake'? More significantly, problems have also been experienced in identifying receipt of benefit, which is an essential element in any claim for unjust enrichment[3]. In this light, it is difficult to accept an explanation of the case law based solely on restitutionary principles.

1   The claimant may also, depending on the facts of the case, be able to rely on other grounds, such as mistake.
2   Consider, for example, *Way v Latilla* [1937] 3 All ER 759 in which it is difficult to ascertain the basis on which the House of Lords awarded payment for services rendered on a quantum meruit basis.
3   See above, para 13.43ff.

13.64   A number of conclusions may be reached, however, in surveying the case law. First, the imposition of liability would appear to reflect the allocation of risks between the parties. If an agreement is expressly stated to be 'subject to contract', a court is very unlikely to intervene. In contrast, if one party has expressly or impliedly accepted responsibility, for example by requesting the works, he or she is likely to be found liable to pay. Secondly, performance in excess of that ordinarily undertaken at the pre-contract stage seems to suggest to the courts that the party performing is no longer acting at his or her own risk, particularly where such performance is at the request of the other negotiating party. Thirdly, where performance is by way of accelerated performance of an anticipated contract, and yet the court cannot intervene due to the absence of essential terms, the court will be at its most willing to intervene: the classic example being *British Steel Corpn v Cleveland Bridge*[1]. Fourthly, the conduct of the parties appears relevant. Where one party is at fault, the court may intervene to prevent an inequitable result. Finding a theoretical basis which encapsulates these four overlapping guidelines is a challenge still to be met, and it must be questioned whether restitution provides the answer. In view of the equity-based arguments used by the courts, an explanation resting on estoppel appears the preferable explanation, namely that the behaviour of the other party to the negotiations encouraged the claimant to believe that he or she was no longer acting at his or her own risk, and therefore would be paid for any performance.

There is, as yet, little support in English law for this explanation, which, it is suggested, would require the English courts to recognise the validity of developments by the Australian courts. This has yet to occur.

1   [1984] 1 All ER 504, above, para 13.38. The *Waltons* cases (above, para 13.59) is also of this type.

The continuing role of contract law

13.65   It must be recognised that the courts will attempt, whenever possible, to find a contract, if they are satisfied that this is the intention of the parties[1]. Where performance has already taken place, and the parties are in a long-term business relationship, the courts will attempt to support the agreement by means of implied terms if necessary. Only where the agreement is executory and there is no clear evidence of contractual intent will the courts refuse to assist and the question of restitution become relevant.

1   See *G Percy Trentham Ltd v Archital Luxfer Ltd* [1993] 1 Lloyd's Rep 25.

CHAPTER 14

Illegality

Paula Giliker

A   Introduction

14.1   This chapter examines the effect of illegality on a claim for restitution in English law[1]. Traditionally, illegality has been treated as a bar or defence to the restitutionary claim. The courts will not assist the claimant in an action to recover money, property or the value of services where the claimant is forced to rely on the illegal transaction to substantiate his or her claim. The reason for this is said to be public policy[2]. The courts will not assist a party who founds his or her claim on an illegal or immoral act (*ex turpi causa non oritur actio*). It would be contrary to the dignity of the court to assist such claimants. It is equally hoped that by refusing assistance to parties to an illegal transaction, this may have some deterrence effect in dissuading parties against entering such transactions[3]. This latter aim must, however, be questioned in the light of the second Latin maxim which dominates this area of law: *in pari delicto potior est conditio defendentis* (where the parties are equally guilty, the defendant is in the stronger position). By refusing to intervene to assist the claimant's action in restitution, the defendant, whatever his or her blame, retains any benefit received. From the point of view of the defendant, this is hardly a disincentive to enter illegal transactions. As a result of the doctrine, the defendant may receive a windfall as a result of the doctrine, but this has been held to be irrelevant in the light of the wider goals of public policy, which require that illegal transactions should be treated as void and unenforceable[4].

1   See generally Enonchong *Illegal Transactions* (1998) and RA Buckley *Illegality and public policy* (2002). For an examination of the civil law approach to illegality, see Danneman 'Illegality as Defence against unjust enrichment claims' (2000) Oxford University Comparative Law Forum 4 (at http://ouclf.iuscomp.org), and Enonchong 'Effects of illegality: a comparative study in French and English law' (1995) 44 ICLQ 196. For Scottish law, see Macgregor 'Illegal contracts and unjustified enrichment' (2000) 4 Edinburgh Law Review 19.
2   On this basis, the court may raise the issue of illegality of its own motion: *North-Western Salt Co Ltd v Electrolytic Alkali Co Ltd* [1914] AC 461; *Scott v Brown, Doering, McNab & Co* [1892] 2 QB 724 at 728. This is an exception to the ordinary pleading rules.
3   The policy grounds for the illegality defence are examined and approved by the Law Commission in their Consultation Paper No 154 *Illegal transactions: the effect of illegality on contracts and trusts* (1999), Pt VI.
4   Devlin J in *St John Shipping Corpn v Joseph Rank Ltd* [1957] 1 QB 267 at 288 questions how far such a windfall contributes to public morality. For a detailed analysis of the policy reasons see Wade 'Benefits obtained under illegal transactions – Reasons for and against allowing restitution' (1946) 25 Texas Law Review 31.

14.2   The classic policy statement is given by Lord Mansfield in *Holman v Johnson*[1]:

The objection, that a contract is immoral or illegal as between plaintiff and defendant, sounds at all times very ill in the mouth of the defendant. It is not for his sake, however, that the objection is ever allowed; but it is founded in general principles of policy, which the defendant has the advantage of, contrary to the real justice, as between him and the plaintiff, by accident, if I may so say. The principle of public policy is this; *ex dolo malo non oritur actio*. No Court will lend its aid to a man who founds his cause of action upon an immoral or an illegal act. If, from the plaintiff's own stating or otherwise, the cause of action appears to arise *ex turpi causa*, or the transgression of a positive law of this country, there the Court says he has no right to be assisted. It is upon that ground the Court goes; not for the sake of the defendant, but because they will not lend their aid to such a plaintiff. So if the plaintiff and defendant were to change sides, and the defendant was to bring his action against the plaintiff, the latter would then have the advantage of it; for where both are equally in fault, *potior est conditio defendentis*.

This raises a number of points which will be examined in more detail in this chapter. First, the doctrine only applies where the claimant *founds* his or her cause of action upon an immoral or an illegal act and, as will be seen, this does not apply if the claimant can bring an action on another basis, which does not rely on the illegal transaction[2]. Secondly, Lord Mansfield accepts that the demands of policy may lead to an unjust result between claimant and defendant 'by accident'. This is emphasised by Lord Goff more recently in *Tinsley v Milligan*[3], who remarked that 'the principle is not a principle of justice: it is a principle of policy, whose application is indiscriminate and so can lead to unfair consequences as between the parties to litigation'. In view of these unfair consequences, the courts have been willing to adopt a more flexible approach to the public policy rules, both in terms of defining illegality, and in interpreting the three main exceptions to the defence of illegality[4]. Whilst there is clear authority against any discretion in this area of law[5], the courts in a number of decisions have found ways to distinguish the defence, or extend the exceptions to situations where the claimant is attempting to recover damages from an unmeritorious defendant.

The unfortunate result of such cases is that illegality now consists of a set of complex and contradictory rules, which render analysis extremely difficult. Whilst this chapter will attempt to state the main rules clearly, few would dispute that it is an area of law badly in need of reform. The recent Consultation Paper of the Law Commission[6], which sensibly advocates a structured discretion as a preferable alternative to the current complex public policy rules, is therefore welcomed as an overdue attempt to bring coherence to this area of law[7].

This chapter deals with illegality as a defence. It is suggested that illegality may form a basis for a restitutionary claim, and this will be examined in the course of this chapter[8]. It is the author's view that there is at present limited authority to support such claims[9]. It has therefore been preferred to adopt a 'traditional' analysis of illegality, whilst noting suggestions for an alternative approach to this topic.

1   (1775) 1 Cowp 341 at 343, 98 ER 1120 at 1121.
2   See eg below, para 14.46.
3   [1994] 1 AC 340 at 355.
4   See below, para 14.24ff.
5   *Tinsley v Milligan* [1994] 1 AC 340 at 355, per Lord Goff.
6   Law Commission Consultation Paper No 154 *Illegal transactions: the effect of illegality on contracts and trusts* (1999), paras 9.4–9.20.
7   On reform see below, para 14.65ff.
8   Especially below, para 14.61ff.
9   See Swadling 'The role of illegality in the English law of unjust enrichment' (2000) Oxford University Comparative Law Forum 5 (at http://ouclf.iuscomp.org).

B   What is illegality?

14.3   Although claims for restitution are primarily concerned with the *effect* of illegality – can the claimant recover the benefit passed under the illegal transaction? – the first stage in any analysis must be to determine what is meant by 'illegality'[1]. The authority on this point is largely contractual, and there is unfortunately no clear definition. 'Illegality' would appear to signify conduct under a contract which is contrary to public policy[2]. Whilst this may seem vague, it reflects the absence of any clear authority. Illegality is therefore best illustrated by example. Case law indicates that the transaction may be deemed illegal where it involves conduct which amounts to a crime or a civil wrong, or simply conduct regarded as immoral. This latter category is obviously broad, for example Treitel defines 22 heads of public policy[3]. To assist classification, illegality may be helpfully divided into statutory and common law illegality. Statutory illegality lists the situations where a contract is rendered void by statutory provision. This may be express or implied. The courts are required to construe the statute, and identify whether Parliament intended to render contracts contravening the statutory provisions in question void. In view of the large amount of legislation (primary and delegated) in the twentieth and undoubtedly the twenty-first century, the potential for illegality is enormous. The courts have faced difficult questions of construction in identifying whether the intention of the statute is simply to penalise the parties in criminal law, or to go further and render any associated transactions void.

1   See Furmston 'The Analysis of Illegal Contracts' (1966) 16 University of Toronto Law Journal 267 at 283–286.
2   The Law Commission adopts a very broad definition in their Consultation Paper No 154 *Illegal transactions: the effect of illegality on contracts and trusts* (1999), para 1.4: 'any transaction which involves (in its formation, purpose or performance) the commission of a legal wrong (other than the mere breach of the transaction in question) or conduct which is otherwise contrary to public policy'. This definition has been criticised as unduly wide: see Enonchong 'Illegal transactions: the future?' [2000] RLR 82.
3   See Treitel *Law of Contract* (10th edn, 1999), pp 393–415, in addition to contracts in restraint of trade. Beatson *Anson's Law of Contract* (27th edn, 1998), pp 349–359 proposes nine different types of illegality.

14.4   Common law illegality involves even greater uncertainty. A contract whose nature is illegal or immoral will not be enforced by the courts. The courts have developed a number of categories of illegal or immoral transactions which reflect society's disapproval of these transactions. These categories have developed over time and must inevitably be viewed in accordance with changes in economic and social conditions[1]. The courts have also shown a reluctance to develop new categories of public policy[2], although it must be said that this does not prevent them modifying existing categories of common law illegality in the light of social change.

1   'The law relating to public policy cannot remain immutable. It must change with the passage of time. The wind of change blows upon it': *Nagle v Feilden* [1966] 2 QB 633 at 650, per Danckwerts LJ.
2   See Earl of Halsbury LC in *Janson v Driefontein Consolidated Mines Ltd* [1902] AC 484 at 491.

14.5   A further distinction is apparent from the case law on this topic. The courts, in trying to minimise the impact of illegality, have drawn a distinction between contracts which are illegal *ex facie*, ie on formation, and contracts which are legal *ex facie* but rendered illegal by performance[1]. It is frequently unclear whether the statute in question intends to render void transactions which are legal *ex facie*, but which one or both parties have performed in an illegal manner. In the case of illegality in performance, the courts have shown themselves willing to examine the intention and knowledge of the parties respectively. Where one party is unaware of the illegal performance, the courts have refused to apply the defence and allowed the party to enforce the contractual agreement. In such situations, the courts have even been prepared to assist claimants, who knowingly have committed a minor breach of a statute in the course of their contractual performance, by construing the statute in such a way that it does not render the transaction illegal. This is a complex area of law, which I examine in more detail below.

1   The distinction between contracts which are 'illegal as formed' and those which are 'illegal as performed' may be found in a number of cases: see for example *Re Mahmoud and Ispahani* [1921] 2 KB 716 at 725, per Bankes LJ, and at 729, per Scrutton LJ; *Anderson Ltd v Daniel* [1924] 1 KB 138 at 144, per Bankes LJ, and at 149, per Atkin LJ; *Edler v Auerbach* [1950] 1 KB 359 at 367, per Devlin J. It has been criticised by Treitel *Law of Contract* (10th edn, 1999), p 448.

14.6   It should be noted that this chapter will not deal with the effect of 'supervening illegality', ie the effect of a transaction subsequently becoming illegal, for example by declaration of war[1]. This is properly classified as frustration[2].

1   See *Fibrosa Spolka Akcyjna v Fairbairn Lawson Combe Barbour Ltd* [1943] AC 32, on which see below, para 20.19.
2   On the effect of frustration see below, ch 20.

Statutory illegality

14.7   Here, the courts face a situation where either or both parties to the transaction have acted in breach of a statutory provision. This will usually amount to a criminal offence[1], but the question for the courts is whether this also affects the parties' remedies in contract and restitution. A transaction may either be expressly or impliedly illegal under a particular statutory provision or regulation and if so, regardless of the intent of the parties, the claimant has no remedy in contract or restitution[2]. In contract law at least[3], it is no defence that the parties are ignorant of the legal provisions – if the contract is illegal, then no remedy will lie. The courts have developed various rules of statutory construction where the statute fails to state expressly the consequences of breach of its provisions[4]. The case may be straightforward, as in *Re Mahmoud and Ispahani*[5]. Here, the claimant had agreed to sell linseed oil to the defendant, having been falsely informed by the defendant that he had a licence as required by the Seeds, Oils and Fats Order 1919. The sale of linseed oil without a licence was prohibited, and the Court of Appeal held that the wording of the Order, which stated that 'a person shall not ... buy or sell ... certain articles ... except under and in accordance with the terms of a licence', clearly prohibited any contracts. The court therefore refused to assist the claimant in such circumstances[6]. In less obvious cases, the court will consider the purpose of the statute, and whether it seeks to protect or regulate a particular class of persons or activity.

1   Although it would seem that this is not essential: *Fuji Finance Inc v Aetna Life Insurance Co Ltd* [1997] Ch 173.
2   See *St John Shipping Corpn v Joseph Rank Ltd* [1957] 1 QB 267 at 283, per Devlin J.
3   See below, para 17.40ff.
4   Certain statutes deal with this expressly: the Road Traffic Act 1988, s 65(4), which provides that 'nothing in [s 65(1): offence to supply certain vehicles which do not comply with specified safety

requirements] shall affect the validity of any contract or any rights arising under or in relation to a contract'. See also the Fair Trading Act 1973, s 26. Note that the Gaming Acts 1845 and 1892 render gaming contracts void without being illegal, and so will not be dealt with in this chapter. Such contracts are therefore ineffective to create any rights in the parties concerned.

5   [1921] 2 KB 716.
6   See also *J Dennis & Co Ltd v Munn* [1949] 2 KB 327.

14.8   The leading case in this field is that of *St John Shipping Corpn v Joseph Rank Ltd*[1], in which Devlin J gave valuable guidance as to how the courts should approach such cases. The case itself involved illegality in performance (overloading a ship contrary to the Merchant Shipping (Safety and Load Line Convention) Act 1932) for which the shipowners were prosecuted, and had received a nominal fine. Devlin J advised that in determining whether the Act rendered the contract illegal, the court should ask itself two questions[2]:

- Does the statute mean to prohibit contracts at all?
- If so, does this contract belong to the class which the statute intends to prohibit?

In his Lordship's view, contracts for the carriage of goods were not within the ambit of the statute at all, and so no question of illegality arose. The statute intended the criminal penalty to be the only consequence of breach of the statutory provisions. The object of the statute was to prevent overloading and not to prohibit contracts, which object could be achieved by imposing a fine and not by subjecting shipowners to additional financial loss.

1   [1957] 1 QB 267. Noted by Grunfeld (1957) 20 MLR 172. See also *Hughes v Asset Managers plc* [1995] 3 All ER 669; and *Cope v Rowlands* (1836) 2 M & W 149, 150 ER 707.
2   [1957] 1 QB 267 at 287.

14.9   Devlin J also expressed concern that the increased volume of statutory provisions could lead to the undermining of commercial transactions by the doctrine of illegality and advised a cautious approach: 'Caution in this respect is, I think, especially necessary in these times when so much of commercial life is governed by regulations of one sort or another, which may easily be broken without wicked intent'[1].

1   [1957] 1 QB 267 at 288. See also *Shaw v Groom* [1970] 2 QB 504 at 522–523, per Sachs LJ.

14.10   This decision was applied by the Court of Appeal in *Archbolds (Freightage) Ltd v S Spanglett Ltd*[1]. This again involved licensing difficulties. The defendants had, contrary to the Road and Rail Traffic Act 1933, transported goods under an incorrect licence, which entitled them to carry their own goods, but not the goods of others for reward. The claimants had been told, however, that the defendants possessed the requisite licence, and employed them to carry a load of whisky from London to Leeds. The load was stolen en route due to the negligence of the defendants' driver. The claimants brought an action for damages for the loss of the whisky. The Court of Appeal found for the claimants. Pearce LJ, giving the leading judgment, held that the first question was to find whether the contract was forbidden by statute, expressly or by necessary implication. Whereas in *Mahmoud*[2], the object of the Order had been to prevent a person buying or selling except under licence, here the statute sought to regulate the means by which the carriers should carry the goods. Its object was therefore not to interfere with the owner of goods or his facilities for transport, but to control those who provided the transport, with a view to promoting transport efficiency by means of penalties. On this basis, the contract was not prohibited, expressly or by implication, under the 1933 Act.

Equally, in *Bloxsome v Williams*[3], the object of Sunday trading laws was found to be aimed at traders and not consumers. In deciding whether the transaction is impliedly prohibited, the courts will also consider on whom the statute places the duty to observe the statutory requirement and whether the object of the statute is to protect the public or a particular class of persons[4].

1   [1961] 1 QB 374. Noted by Furmston (1961) 24 MLR 394.
2   See above, para 14.7ff.
3   (1824) 3 B & C 232, 107 ER 720.
4   See *Cope v Rowlands* (1836) 2 M & W 149; *St John Shipping Corpn v Joseph Rank Ltd* [1957] 1 QB 267; but contrast the Court of Appeal decision in *Phoenix General Insurance Co of Greece SA v Halvanon Insurance Co Ltd* [1988] QB 216 at 273. In this case, the court interpreted the Insurance Companies Act 1974, which provided that it was an offence to undertake certain insurance business without authorisation ('effecting and carrying out contracts of insurance') to render all such insurance contracts illegal and unenforceable. On this basis, the assured could not enforce, either directly or indirectly, any contract of insurance or reinsurance. The relevant provision has since been amended by the Financial Services Act 1986, s 132, to enable the assured, but not the insurer, to enforce the insurance contract. This provision came into force on 12 January 1987, and has, in turn, been replaced by the Financial Services and Markets Act 2000, Pt II, ss 26–28 (the 1986 Act was repealed by the Financial Services and Markets Act 2000 (Consequential Amendments and Repeals) Order 2001, SI 2001/3649, Pt 1, Art 3(1)(c) on 1 December 2001).

ILLEGALITY IN PERFORMANCE

14.11   These rules of construction have been applied particularly generously where the transaction is legal, but the breach of the statutory provision occurs during performance. For example, in *Shaw v Groom*[1], despite the landlord's clear breach of the Landlord and Tenant Act 1962, s 4 (which made it a criminal offence for a landlord to fail to provide certain statutory information in the rent book), the Court of Appeal refused to permit this breach to bar the landlord's claim for arrears of rent. The court held that the true question was whether the statute impliedly forbade the contract, and this entailed consideration of public policy. In this situation, the object of the statute was simply to impose a fine, and the legislature did not intend to impose on the landlord any forfeiture beyond the prescribed penalty[2]. Here, the court is clearly influenced by the injustice of depriving the landlord of his right to rent because of a minor breach[3]. In spite of the public policy aim of protecting tenants, the court was nevertheless prepared to assist the landlord in his claim for rent.

1   [1970] 2 QB 504.
2   Harman LJ ([1970] 2 QB 504 at 518) dismissed as no longer conclusive previous authority which held that while statutes which imposed penalties to protect the Revenue did not bar the claim (see *Smith v Mawhood* (1845) 14 M & W 452, 153 ER 552), statutes which imposed penalties to protect the public would render all contracts illegal (see *Anderson Ltd v Daniel* [1924] 1 KB 138).
3   See Sachs LJ [1970] 2 QB 504 at 525.

14.12   It should further be noted that where one party does not know, and could not have known, that the contract, which is not *ex facie* illegal, would be performed illegally, the courts will permit the claimant to bring a claim for contractual damages. In *Archbolds (Freightage) Ltd v S Spanglett Ltd*[1], the Court of Appeal held that in such cases, public policy did not constrain the court to refuse aid to such claimants, who did not know that the contract would be performed illegally. Pearce LJ clearly indicated[2], however, that this would not apply where the contract is expressly or by necessary implication forbidden by statute or is otherwise illegal, or, if *ex facie* legal, both parties know that it can only be performed illegally or is intended to be performed illegally[3].

1   [1961] 1 QB 374. Arguably there is authority in *Bloxsome v Williams* (1824) 3 B & C 232, 107 ER 720, to permit an innocent party to withdraw even where the contract is *ex facie* illegal, although this was doubted by Parker J in *Bedford Insurance Co Ltd v Instituto de Resseguros do Brasil* [1985] QB 966 at 985.
2   [1961] 1 QB 374 at 384. See also Devlin J in *St John Shipping Corpn v Joseph Rank Ltd* [1957] 1 QB 267.
3   See for example *Pearce v Brooks* (1866) LR 1 Exch 213; *Taylor v Bhail* [1996] CLC 377.

Common law illegality

14.13   As stated above, in addition to statutory illegality, there are a number of heads of illegality at common law[1]. The courts will not assist in a transaction which is illegal, or which is associated with, or furthers, an illegal purpose. The most important examples are listed below:

- Contracts to commit a crime or civil wrong[2];
- Contracts prejudicial to the administration of justice[3];
- Contracts prejudicial to marriage[4];
- Contracts prejudicial to sexual morality[5];
- Contracts prejudicial to foreign relations[6];
- Contracts which lead to public corruption[7].

1   I do not include contracts in restraint of trade in my analysis. They are generally treated as unenforceable rather than illegal. For further discussion, see Beale (ed) *Chitty on Contracts* (28th edn, 1999), vol 1, paras 17–075 to 17–139, and Furmston (ed) *Law of Contract* (1999), paras 5.93–5.126.
2   See below, para 14.14.
3   See below, para 14.15.
4   See below, para 14.16.
5   See below, para 14.17.
6   See below, para 14.18.
7   See below, para 14.19.

CONTRACTS TO COMMIT A CRIME OR CIVIL WRONG

14.14   This is the most obvious example: where both parties set out to deliberately commit a crime[1] or civil wrong[2]. Here, the illegality defence will bar any claim by either party. Again, this category is applied flexibly, and will include agreements to defraud another[3].

1   See *Cowan v Milbourn* (1867) LR 2 Ex Ch 230.
2   *Clay v Yates* (1856) 1 H & N 73, 156 ER 1123 (contract to publish libellous material); *Allen v Rescous* (1676) 2 Lev 174, 83 ER 505 (agreement to commit trespass to the person). See also *Brown Jenkinson & Co Ltd v Percy Dalton (London) Ltd* [1957] 2 QB 621 (agreement to make fraudulent misrepresentations); *Taylor v Bhail* [1996] CLC 377 (conspiracy to defraud insurance company); and *Birkett v Acorn Business Machines Ltd* [1999] 2 All ER (Comm) 429 (contract intended to deceive finance company).
3   *Cockshott v Bennett* (1788) 2 Term Rep 763, 100 ER 411; *Alexander v Rayson* [1936] 1 KB 169. But see Furmston 'The Analysis of Illegal Contracts' (1966) 16 University of Toronto Law Journal 267 at 286–290.

CONTRACTS PREJUDICIAL TO THE ADMINISTRATION OF JUSTICE

14.15   This is a broad category, the aim of which is protect the judicial system. Consequently, contracts to give false evidence in criminal proceedings[1] and to compromise or stifle a prosecution[2] will be regarded as illegal. A recent example may be seen in the case of *Mohamed v Alaga & Co*[3]. Here, the court held that an agreement whereby a solicitor had agreed, in breach of the Solicitors' Practice Rules 1990, to share his fees in return for Mohamed (a professional translator and prominent member of the Somali community) introducing to the solicitor Somali asylum-seekers and assisting in their cases was illegal as contrary to public policy[4].

1   *R v Andrews* [1973] QB 422.
2   *Keir v Leeman* (1844) 6 QB 308; affd 9 QB 371; *Windhill Local Board of Health v Vint* (1890) 45 Ch D 351. This is subject to the Criminal Law Act 1967, s 5(1), which provides that it is no longer an offence to withhold information which might secure a conviction of an arrestable offence, if it is withheld in return for reasonable compensation for the loss or injury caused by the offence or making good any such injury. 'Arrestable offences' are defined in the Police and Criminal Evidence Act 1984, s 24(1). See also *R v Panayiotou* [1973] 3 All ER 112. On duress generally see above, paras 10.51ff.
3   [1999] 3 All ER 699, [2000] 1 WLR 1815. See also Lightman J at first instance [1998] 2 All ER 720 at 724. Noted by McBride [1998] CLJ 449.
4   Note that the Solicitors' Practice Rules were treated in any event as having the force of subordinate legislation. On differential fees rates contrary to Solicitors' Practice Rules 1990, rr 8(1), 18(2)(c), see *Swain v Law Society* [1983] 1 AC 598, and, more recently, *Awwad v Geraghty & Co (a firm)* [2001] QB 570, which refused to follow the more liberal decision in *Thai Trading Co v Taylor* [1998] QB 781. See also *Hughes v Kingston upon Hull City Council* [1999] QB 1193. Such cases are subject, of course, to the provisions in the Access to Justice Act 1999. Maintenance and champerty are no longer treated per se as crimes or torts (Criminal Law Act 1967, ss 13 and 14), but such agreements may still be found to be contrary to public policy.

CONTRACTS PREJUDICIAL TO MARRIAGE

14.16   This category may seem questionable in view of modern acceptance of cohabitation and stable relationships outside marriage, but remains part of English law[1]. For example, it has been held that a contract of marriage brokage (namely, an agreement for reward for the procurement of marriage) is illegal[2]. In *Hermann v Charlesworth*[3], the court held that a contract by which one party contracts to find a spouse for another is deemed illegal. This is difficult to justify in view of the plethora of dating agencies in modern society. Equally, one may wish to challenge whether an agreement by a married person to marry[4] or separation agreements (where the parties are currently cohabiting or prior to marriage)[5] should still be considered illegal, although in the light of the Law Reform (Miscellaneous Provisions) Act 1970 this is likely to be of only theoretical concern[6]. This is a good example of changing economic and social trends challenging established heads of common law public policy, and this head may require further consideration.

1   See Dwyer 'Immoral contracts' (1977) 93 LQR 386.
2   See Powell 'Marriage brocage agreements' (1953) 6 CLP 254.
3   [1905] 2 KB 123. See also *Cole v Gibson* (1750) 1 Ves Sen 503, 27 ER 1169.
4   See *Wilson v Carnley* [1908] 1 KB 729 (agreement by married man to marry another woman illegal and void). However, a promise to marry, made by a married man between the decree nisi and decree absolute, is not contrary to public policy: *Fender v St John-Mildmay* [1938] AC 1.
5   For agreements between husband and wife for future separation, see *St John v St John* (1805) 11 Ves 526, 32 ER 1192; *Brodie v Brodie* [1917] P 271; *Westmeath v Westmeath* (1831) 1 Dow & Cl 519, 6 ER 619. However, the contract will not be illegal if the agreement is made after or immediately before separation.
6   This statute abolishes the action for breach of promise of marriage. Some possible application of these cases is considered by Beale (ed) *Chitty on Contracts* (28th edn, 1999), vol 1, para 17–070; and Furmston (ed) *Law of Contract* (1999), paras 5.82–5.87.

CONTRACTS PREJUDICIAL TO SEXUAL MORALITY

14.17   This category, again, arguably reflects attitudes from a previous century and, in particular, disapproval of sexual relationships outside marriage[1].

Nevertheless, modern society continues to draw a line at a certain level of sexual morality, and the cases on prostitution will no doubt still apply. A contract which either directly or indirectly supports prostitution will be deemed illegal. An example of indirect support may be found in *Pearce v Brooks*[2]. The claimants here were coach-builders who had hired a coach to the defendant, whom they knew to be a prostitute. In view of the fact that they could, at least, be presumed to know that she would use the coach to attract customers, the contract was found to be illegal.

1   For example see *Feret v Hill* (1854) 15 CB 207, 139 ER 400 (using leased premises for brothel); *Taylor v Chester* (1869) LR 4 QB 309 (security for money spent in brothel); *Re Vallance* (1884) 26 Ch D 353 (bond in consideration of future non-marital cohabitation was said to be contrary to public policy and void, although in that case there was no evidence that the bond was given in consideration of future cohabitation).
2   (1866) LR 1 Exch 213.

CONTRACTS PREJUDICIAL TO FOREIGN RELATIONS

14.18   Contracts which involve trading with the enemy or an alien enemy (that is, a person of whatever nationality, who is carrying on business in, or is voluntarily resident in, the enemy's country[1]) are unenforceable in English law[2]. This also extends to the performance of illegal acts in friendly foreign states[3].

1   *Porter v Freudenberg* [1915] 1 KB 857 at 869.
2   *Sovfracht (V/O) v Van Udens Scheepvaart en Agentuur Maatschappij (NV Gebr)* [1943] AC 203; *Ertel Bieber & Co v Rio Tinto Co* [1918] AC 260; *Branigan v Saba* [1924] NZLR 481.
3   *Foster v Driscoll* [1929] 1 KB 470 (importing liquor into United States during prohibition); *Regazzoni v KC Sethia (1944) Ltd* [1958] AC 301 and, more recently, *Soleimany v Soleimany* [1999] QB 785 (refusal to enforce arbitration award). The English courts will not refuse to enforce a contract governed by foreign law which is not illegal, but contrary to public policy of that country, unless the public policy argument also applies in England: *Lemenda Trading Co Ltd v African Middle East Petroleum Co Ltd* [1988] QB 448.

CONTRACTS WHICH LEAD TO PUBLIC CORRUPTION

14.19   Contracts detrimental to the sanctity of public office will be found to be illegal. For example, in *Parkinson v College of Ambulance Ltd*[1], the claimant was induced to make a large donation to a certain charity, by the secretary's fraudulent representation that he or the charity was in a position to undertake that the claimant would receive a knighthood. The claimant paid £3,000 to the charity, but no title was forthcoming. The court refused the claimant's action for money had and received, and in contract. The contract was contrary to public policy, and the claimant could not recover his £3,000[2].

1   [1925] 2 KB 1. See also *Montefiore v Menday Motor Components Co* [1918] 2 KB 241.
2   See now Honours (Prevention of Abuses) Act 1925.

C   The effect of illegality

14.20   So far I have examined when a transaction will be deemed 'illegal' and the courts will apply the illegality defence. In this part of the chapter, I examine the consequences of this decision. If the contract is deemed illegal, when will it bar a claim for restitution? Not all illegal contracts bar a claim for restitution. It may be that the illegality only bars the claim of one party, for example on the basis of statutory interpretation[1] or because of the *in pari delicto* rule[2].

Alternatively, the claimant may be rewarded for withdrawing from the illegal transaction. Further, the claimant may be able to establish proprietary rights outside the transaction which he or she can enforce without relying on the illegal transaction. This section examines the nature of these rules, and how far they permit restitutionary claims for money, property and services in English law.

1   See above, para 14.7ff.
2   See below, para 14.24ff.

When a claim for restitution will fail

14.21   The general rule is that illegal contracts will not found a claim in English law. A claimant will not succeed if his or her claim is based on an illegal contract[1]. This includes situations where the claimant intends to perform the contract in an illegal way, where the claimant knows the contract will involve an illegal act or where the illegality must be pleaded to establish his or her claim. Such a claimant will be deemed a 'guilty party', and a guilty party will only succeed in recovering any benefit passing under the illegal transaction if he or she can satisfy one of the exceptions to the rule set out below.

If the claimant is unaware of the illegality, the situation is more complicated. Such an 'innocent party' may still be able to sue, depending on the nature of the illegality. If the contract is illegal by its very nature (illegal *ex facie*), it would seem that, the defence will operate to bar a claim, subject to the exceptions below. There is also authority that even if the claimant is unaware of the breach due to ignorance of the law, then the claimant is to be treated as equally guilty as ignorance of the law is no defence[2]. This would appear to be confined to cases where the claimant 'participates' in the unlawful purpose in full knowledge of the facts which render the transaction illegal and where the contract could not be carried out without a violation of the law[3], but may need to be reviewed in the light of the developments relating to mistake of law outlined below. If the contract is legal but has, unknown to the claimant, been performed illegally by the other party (illegality in performance), then the innocent party may be able to bring a claim in contract[4].

1   For recent authority, see *Shanshal v Al-Kishtaini* [2001] EWCA Civ 264, [2001] 2 All ER (Comm) 601; *Soleimany v Soleimany* [1999] QB 785 at 794–795; and *Royal Boskalis Westminster NV v Mountain* [1999] QB 674 at 691–692.
2   See *J M Allan (Merchandising) Ltd v Cloke* [1963] 2 QB 340 at 348, per Lord Denning MR: 'where two people together have the common design to use a subject-matter for an unlawful purpose, so that each participates in the unlawful purpose, then that contract is illegal in its formation and it is no answer for them to say that they did not know the law on the matter'.
3   [1963] 2 QB 340 at 348, per Lord Denning MR, thereby distinguishing *Waugh v Morris* (1873) LR 8 QB 202. See also *Hindley and Co Ltd v General Fibre Co Ltd* [1940] 2 KB 517.
4   See *Re Mahmoud and Ispahani* [1921] 2 KB 716 at 729, per Scrutton LJ. Treitel *Law of Contract* (10th edn, 1999), pp 447–449 argues that the same rule applies to initial illegality, and cites in support *Bloxsome v Williams* (1824) 3 B & C 232, 107 ER 720 (contract illegal as formed) and *Archbolds (Freightage) Ltd v S Spanglett Ltd* [1961] 1 QB 374 (no distinction between contracts illegal as formed/performed). For a contrary view see Beale (ed) *Chitty on Contracts* (28th edn, 1999), vol 1, para 17–007.

14.22   There is also a line of authority supporting restitutionary claims for services rendered under an illegal contract by an innocent party. In *Clay v Yates*[1], a printer had published a book prior to discovering its dedication to be libellous. He had withdrawn from the contract as soon as he had noticed the libel, and was permitted to recover for work undertaken in printing the text to that date[2]. In this case, the printer had been innocent of the illegal conduct, having withdrawn as soon as the illegality came to light.

In the more recent case of *Mohamed v Alaga & Co*[3], the claimant had participated in the illegal transaction. Nevertheless, the Court of Appeal permitted the claimant to recover a reasonable sum for services rendered. In this case, a professional translator had contracted with a firm of solicitors to introduce asylum-seekers and provide a translating service and other assistance, in return for half of any fee received from the Legal Aid Board in respect of these clients. Such a fee-sharing arrangement was contrary to the Solicitors' Practice Rules 1990 and therefore unenforceable. The court nevertheless permitted him to bring a claim for a reasonable sum for professional services rendered. Lord Bingham CJ held that where the blameworthiness of the parties is not equal, the court should permit a claim for reasonable remuneration of professional services rendered, provided the claimant does not sue on the contract[4]. However, a restitutionary claim would not lie where both parties were equally culpable[5]. The Court of Appeal overturned the view of Lightman J at first instance that permitting a restitutionary claim on such facts would contradict and circumvent the statutory provisions[6].

This decision, which was on an application to strike out, was considered by a differently constituted Court of Appeal in *Awwad v Geraghty & Co*[7] four months later. In this case, a solicitor had agreed to act for the claimant in libel proceedings on the basis that the claimant would be charged the normal hourly rate if successful, but a lower rate if unsuccessful. This differential fee arrangement was contrary to the Solicitors' Practice Rules 1990, rr 8(1) and 8(2)(c). Schiemann LJ held that such agreements were unlawful and unenforceable, but additionally refused to permit an alternate claim by the solicitor for restitution. His Lordship distinguished *Alaga* on the basis that the interpreter in that case was blameless, and no public policy had been infringed by allowing him to recover a fair fee for interpreting, which was not contrary to the Solicitors' Practice Rules. Public policy solely prohibited the payment of a fee for the introduction of clients. On this basis, the translator's claim would have failed if he had claimed a fee for introducing clients: 'If the court, for reasons of public policy refuses to enforce an agreement that a solicitor should be paid it must follow that he cannot claim on a quantum meruit'[8]. In *Awwad*, the solicitor was claiming a differential fee, which was directly contrary to the Rules, and the court would not in such circumstances grant a restitutionary remedy. Additionally, the claimant solicitor, a partner in her own firm, was clearly aware of the rules governing fees, and could by no means claim to be an innocent party or to be of lesser fault in entering the transaction. *Awwad* clearly demonstrates a more restrictive approach than *Alaga*, which is closer to the traditional approach of *Clay v Yates*[9].

1   (1856) 1 H & N 73, 156 ER 1123. See also *Branigan v Saba* [1924] NZLR 481.
2   No claim was made for the printing of the libellous dedication.
3   [1999] 3 All ER 699 (*Clay v Yates* was not cited in the case). See above, para 14.15.
4   [1999] 3 All ER 699 at 706.
5   This line of authority could therefore be seen as consistent with the *non in pari delicto* exception set out below, para 14.24ff.
6   The court relied on the House of Lords' opinions in *Westdeutsche Landesbank Girozentrale v Islington London Borough Council* [1996] AC 669 (above, para 3.44ff), which overturned previous House of Lords' authority in *Sinclair v Brougham* [1914] AC 398 that a claim for restitution would undermine the invalidity of an ultra vires borrowing contract. One might question, however, the application of *Westdeutsche* outside ultra vires claims: see *Mohamed v Alaga* [1998] 2 All ER 720 but, to the contrary, McCamus 'Restitutionary Recovery of Benefits Conferred under Contracts in Conflict with Statutory Policy – the New Golden Rule' (1987) 25 Osgoode Hall LJ 787.

7   [2001] QB 570.
8   [2001] QB 570 at 596.
9   (1856) 1 H & N 73, 156 ER 1123, see above. See also *Branigan v Saba* [1924] NZLR 481. Birks
    has suggested that *Alaga* may be interpreted as a mistake of law case: see 'Recovering value
    transferred under an illegal contract' (2000) 1 Theoretical Inquiries in Law 155 at 174.

When a claim for restitution will succeed despite the illegality – the exceptions[1]

14.23   Three exceptions need consideration: where the illegality only bars the
claim of one party[2], withdrawal from the illegal transaction[3], and independent
proprietary rights[4].

1   See the classic article of Wade 'Restitution of benefits acquired through illegal transactions'
    (1947) 95 University of Pennsylvania Law Review 261.
2   See below, para 14.24ff.
3   See below, para 14.35ff.
4   See below, para 14.46ff.

THE ILLEGALITY ONLY BARS THE CLAIM OF ONE PARTY – THE 'NON IN PARI DELICTO' RULE

14.24   This is an important exception to the illegality bar, by which, despite
the illegality, the claimant may nevertheless be able to bring a claim in
restitution on the basis that the parties are not equally at fault, or '*non in pari
delicto*'. Much has been made of the fact that the grounds for finding the parties
not equally at fault resemble the modern grounds (or 'unjust factors') for
restitution, namely mistake, oppression, deceit. There is a further ground where
the courts find that the statute itself seeks to protect a particular class of
individual whose claim will succeed despite breach of its provisions. These
categories overlap considerably and a claim may succeed under two different
headings[1]. At present, there is very limited evidence to support suggestions of
further heads based on actual or potential exploitation[2] or vulnerability[3].

1   See for example *Kiriri Cotton Co Ltd v Dewani* [1960] AC 192 (mistake of law/class protecting
    statute) (below, paras 14.26 and 14.31).
2   See Virgo *Principles of the Law of Restitution* (1999), pp 746 and 747 (treated as duress/undue
    influence and class protection below, paras 14.29–14.30).
3   See for example Burrows and McKendrick *Cases and Materials on the Law of Restitution* (1997), pp
    520–522 and Burrows *Law of Restitution* (1993), pp 341–344.

14.25   Mistake   The clearest examples arise under mistake. The leading
case is *Oom v Bruce*[1] where the claimants were found to be labouring under a
mistake of fact. The claimants had agreed to act as the agent for a Russian
subject and had paid the insurance premiums for goods on the ship 'Elbe' on his
behalf. It is unclear, but it appears that both parties were unaware that, at the
time the contract was made, war had broken out between Russia and England,
rendering the contract illegal. The court nevertheless permitted the claimants to
recover the premiums paid, as the claimants had no knowledge of the outbreak
of war when the contract was made. As Lord Ellenborough CJ commented:

> [T]he plaintiffs had no knowledge of the commencement of hostilities by Russia
> when they effected this insurance; and, therefore, no fault is imputable to them for
> entering into the contract; and there is no reason why they should not recover back
> the premiums which they have paid[2].

Unfortunately this case raises an obvious criticism: if both parties were
unaware of the outbreak of war, they were equally guilty or innocent depending

on one's point of view. This has led some authors to suggest that the case supports a separate exception, outside the *non in pari delicto* framework based simply on the claimant's mistake[3]. At best, it forms an uneasy basis for a rule of recovery where the parties are *not* equally guilty, and suggests that the claimant may claim for mistake regardless of the state of mind of the defendant[4].

1   (1810) 12 East 225, 104 ER 87.
2   (1810) 12 East 225 at 226, 104 ER 87 at 88.
3   Burrows *Law of Restitution* (1993), p 465.
4   See the Law Commission Consultation Paper No 154 *Illegal transactions: the effect of illegality on contracts and trusts* (1999), para 2.39: 'This would mean that in cases of restitution based on mistake of fact where the mistake is such as to mask the illegality, that in itself is sufficient to defeat a defence based on illegality, regardless of the state of mind of the defendant'.

14.26   A further complication arises with the abolition of the much-criticised rule that a claim for unjust enrichment could not be founded on a mistake of law. This rule was finally overturned by the House of Lords in *Kleinwort Benson Ltd v Lincoln City Council*[1]. On the basis that mistake of law and fact should no longer be distinguished, it would seem by implication that the *non in pari delicto* doctrine must also now apply to cases of mistake of law. This is supported by common law authority which applied the rule as an exception to the mistake of law bar in any event. In *Kiriri Cotton Co Ltd v Dewani*[2], Lord Denning held that while:

> ... money paid under a mistake of law, by itself and without more, cannot be recovered back ... If there is something more in addition to a mistake of law – if there is something in the defendant's conduct which shows that, of the two of them, he is the one primarily responsible for the mistake – then it may be recovered back. Thus, if as between the two of them the duty of observing the law is placed on the shoulders of the one rather than the other – it being imposed on him specially for the protection of the other – then they are not in pari delicto and the money can be recovered back[3].

Here, the Privy Council upheld the claim by a tenant for recovery of a premium charged by the landlord on taking a sublease of a flat, which, unknown to both parties, was contrary to the Ugandan Rent Restriction Ordinance. It can be argued that *Kiriri* was actually decided on the basis of class protection: the breach was under a statute which protected a particular class of individuals, which included the claimant[4]. However, in view of *Kleinwort Benson*, there would now be no need to rely on this argument. If the claimant can establish that, despite the contract's illegality, he or she was less guilty because the illegality was masked by their mistake of fact or of law, then he or she should be able to claim. However, if the mistake does not mask the illegality (for example in *Morgan v Ashcroft*[5] where the mistake of fact did not mask the illegality of the wagering contract) the exception cannot be evoked.

1   [1999] 2 AC 349; considered below, para 17.40ff.
2   [1960] AC 192.
3   [1960] AC 192 at 204.
4   See below, para 14.31.
5   [1938] 1 KB 49; on which see below, para 17.23ff. See also *Edler v Auerbach* [1950] 1 KB 359.

14.27   Fraud   The courts have shown themselves sympathetic towards claims for restitution by victims of fraud. Where the claimant is unaware of the illegality of the transaction due to the fraud of the defendant, there is clear authority that the claimant can recover any sums paid. The leading authority is that of *Hughes v Liverpool Victoria Friendly Society*[1]. Here, an innocent claimant had been induced by the fraudulent misrepresentations of one of the defendants' insurance agents to take up five policies, although she had no insurable interest in the lives in question. The policies were in fact illegal, and the claimant sued to recover the premiums paid. The Court of Appeal held that the claimant was not *in pari delicto* with the defendants. She could therefore recover the premiums paid.

1   [1916] 2 KB 482.

14.28   However, there is authority that this will not extend to negligent or innocent misrepresentation. In *Harse v Pearl Life Assurance Co*[1], the claimant had entered into two illegal contracts of insurance, in reliance of a mistaken statement by the insurance agent that such contracts were legal. The Court of Appeal found the claimant to be *in pari delicto* with the defendant, on the basis that both parties had simply been mistaken and no fraud was involved[2]. It is arguable, however, that today the claimant could have succeeded by framing his claim as one of mistake of law[3]. The fraud must also mask the illegality of the transaction. In *Parkinson v College of Ambulance Ltd*[4], for example, the claimant had paid £3,000 in reliance on a fraudulent misrepresentation that a knighthood could be arranged by the charity. The fraud did not mask the illegal character of the transaction, and the claimant was unable to recover his money. It made no difference that the claimant sued on a total failure of consideration. Although it is now generally regarded as one of the grounds for restitution, this was not considered sufficient to establish a claim for restitution.

1   [1904] 1 KB 558.
2   Note criticism of the case by Grodecki '*In pari delicto potior est conditio defendentis*' (1955) 71 LQR 254 at 264. Neither *Oom v Bruce* (1810) 12 East 225, 104 ER 87, nor *Hentig v Staniforth* (1816) 5 M & S 122, 105 ER 996, were cited to the Court of Appeal.
3   See above, para 14.26.
4   See above, para 14.19. See also *Berg v Sadler and Moore* [1937] 2 KB 158.

14.29   Duress, oppression and undue influence   The court, in such cases, will adopt the same approach to that seen in relation to mistake and fraud above. It will examine whether the illegality of the contract is masked by the fact that the claimant entered the contract because of illegitimate pressure placed on him or her by the defendant, and so cannot be deemed *in pari delicto* with the defendant. The leading case is *Smith v Cuff*[1]. Here, the claimant sought a composition with his creditors. One of his creditors (the defendant) refused to enter the arrangement unless he was paid in full. This illegally favoured one creditor over the others[2]. In a later action, the claimant was held to be able to recover the extra sum paid to the defendant. Lord Ellenborough CJ remarked that:

> This is not a case of par delictum: it is oppression on one side, and submission on the other: it never can be predicated as par delictum, when one holds the rod, and the other bows to it. There was an inequality of situation between these parties: one was creditor, the other debtor, who was driven to comply with the terms which the former chose to enforce[3].

This will not extend, however, to parties who enter a contract due to anxiety or distress, such as concern as to a daughter's health in *Bigos v Bousted*[4].

1   (1817) 6 M & S 160, 105 ER 1203. See also *Smith v Bromley* (1760) 2 Doug KB 696n, 99 ER 441; and *Atkinson v Denby* (1862) 7 H & N 934, 158 ER 749. See also *Williams v Bayley* (1866) LR 1 HL 200 (on which see above, para 10.52) and *Davies v London and Provincial Marine Insurance Co* (1878) 8 Ch D 469 (money paid to stifle prosecution).
2   Such an agreement has been held to be illegal as a fraud on the other creditors: *Cockshot v Bennett* (1788) 2 Term Rep 763, 100 ER 411.

3   (1817) 6 M & S 160 at 165, 105 ER 1203 at 1205.
4   [1951] 1 All ER 92. This case is discussed in more detail below, para 14.40ff.

14.30   Class protecting statutes   The remit of this exception is unclear, but it rests on a dictum of Lord Mansfield in *Browning v Morris*[1]:

> But, where contracts or transactions are prohibited by positive statutes, for the sake of protecting one set of men from another set of men; the one, from their situation and condition, being liable to be oppressed or imposed upon by the other; there, the parties are not *in pari delicto*; and in furtherance of these statutes, the person injured, after the transaction is finished and completed, may bring his action and defeat the contract.

1   (1778) 2 Cowp 790 at 792, 98 ER 1364 at 1364.

14.31   His Lordship clearly places this head within the '*non in pari delicto*' exception, although the court could alternatively determine that the transaction is not illegal as a matter of construction. This latter option may seem preferable in view of the Court of Appeal decision in *Green v Portsmouth Stadium Ltd*[1] which dictates a very narrow line should be taken under this head. In refusing a bookmaker's claim for recovery of course charges, which had been paid in contravention of the Betting and Lotteries Act 1934, the court held the vital question to be the intention of the statute. The 1934 Act had clearly not been enacted with the intention of protecting bookmakers, but was intended to regulate racecourses and other such matters in the interest of the general public. The claim failed because there was 'nothing in this statute to authorise such an action'[2].

However, claims have been allowed under the provisions of the Rent Act 1977[3]. In *Kiriri Cotton Co Ltd v Dewani*[4], the Privy Council supported interpretation of Ugandan landlord and tenant legislation as protecting the tenant and thereby permitting his claim. Lord Denning held, distinguishing his own judgment in *Green*, that the Ordinance placed the duty on the landlord to observe the law, and so the parties were not *in pari delicto*[5]. In his Lordship's view, the statute in *Green* was of a different kind, which was not intended to protect any particular party involved. Where recovery is permitted, it is irrelevant that the claimant was aware of, and participated in, the illegality. In *Gray v Southouse*[6], the sub-tenants were permitted to recover a premium paid even though they had been aware that what they were doing was prohibited by law, and had disguised the payment by representing it as money paid for the cost of re-decoration of the flat. Devlin J held that 'The cases of innocent tenants must be rare, and I can hardly believe that Parliament intended the wide words of the statute to be restricted to those exceptional cases ... I am satisfied that public policy puts no impediment in the way of their obtaining judgment'[7].

1   [1953] 2 QB 190.
2   [1953] 2 QB 190 at 196, per Denning LJ.
3   See s 119, as interpreted in *Farrell v Alexander* [1977] AC 59 (although decided under an earlier section of the Rent Act 1968, s 85).
4   [1960] AC 192. See also *Re Cavalier Insurance Co Ltd* [1989] 2 Lloyd's Rep 430 at 449–450, per Knox J.
5   [1960] AC 192 at 205.
6   [1949] 2 All ER 1019.
7   [1949] 2 All ER 1019 at 1020.

14.32   There is some authority that the claimant, to succeed under this head, must give counter-restitution of any benefits received[1], but this has largely been discredited[2]. The question remains that of statutory interpretation: is the intention of the statute to protect a class of individuals to which the claimant belongs?

1 *Lodge v National Union Investment Co Ltd* [1907] 1 Ch 300 (breach of Money–lenders Act 1900).
2 *Chapman v Michaelson* [1908] 2 Ch 612; affd [1909] 1 Ch 238; *Cohen v J Lester Ltd* [1939] 1 KB 504; *Kasumu v Baba-Egbe* [1956] AC 539 (which all concern breach of moneylending legislation). *Kasumu* was applied by Goulding J in *Barclay v Prospect Mortgages Ltd* [1974] 1 WLR 837 at 845. The High Court of Australia recently distinguished *Kasumu v Baba-Egbe* in *Nelson v Nelson* (1995) 184 CLR 538, on the basis that counter-restitution in *Kasumu* would have been contrary to the policy of the legislation: see per McHugh J at 196, and per Deane and Gummow JJ at 153.

14.33   Further examples   Inevitably there are further examples in case law, where the court has sought to grant a remedy to a claim on the basis that the defendant is more at fault, and should therefore not retain the benefit received. These defy classification, and are generally treated as ad hoc exceptions to the illegality defence[1].

1 See for example *Re Thomas* [1894] 1 QB 747 (refusal to allow solicitor and officer of the Supreme Court to rely on illegal contract to resist client's claim), although it should be contrasted with *Kearley v Thomson* (1890) 24 QBD 742; below, para 14.37.

14.34   One further line of authority is that relating to agents[1]. There is authority that an agent, who receives money from a third party under an illegal contract, cannot raise the illegality if the money is claimed by his or her principal[2]. The courts have held that the fiduciary duty of the agent to the principal has nothing to do with the illegality of the contract[3]. There are also dicta to the effect that the result should not differ whether the agent knows or is ignorant of the illegality, on the basis that it would be 'monstrous' if the agent with guilty knowledge could resist the principal's claim[4]. However, it is unlikely that recovery will be permitted where the agency itself is illegal, because the principal would be forced to rely on an illegal contract[5].

1 Logically the rule should apply to all persons liable to account, for example partners in a firm.
2 *Tenant v Elliott* (1797) 1 Bos & P 3, 126 ER 744 (broker who effected an illegal insurance contract for the claimant, and later received the policy monies, held accountable for them to principal). See also *Farmer v Russell* (1798) 1 Bos & P 296, 126 ER 913.
3 *Farmer v Russell* (1798) 1 Bos & P 296 at 298, 126 ER 913 at 914.
4 *Farmer v Russell* (1798) 1 Bos & P 296 at 299–301, 126 ER 913 at 915–916.
5 See *Harry Parker Ltd v Mason* [1940] 2 KB 590; and *Sykes v Beadon* (1879) 11 Ch D 170 at 195–196, per Jessel MR.

WITHDRAWAL FROM THE ILLEGAL TRANSACTION[1]

14.35   The reason for this second exception is that the court wishes to encourage parties to withdraw from illegal transactions. It therefore ensures that the party who withdraws is not penalised for his or her involvement in the illegal transaction, and thereby deters involvement in such transactions[2]. This is a well established exception. In the eighteenth century case of *Lowry v Bourdieu*[3], Buller J commented (obiter) that claimants could not recover money paid when the contract had been executed before they sought to withdraw from it. Logically, however, such claimants could recover if they had withdrawn while the contract had been executory. Following somewhat unclear authority[4], the exception was restated by the Court of Appeal in *Taylor v Bowers*[5] in 1876. In this case, the claimant was in debt and, in an attempt to prevent his creditors from seizing his business assets, he agreed with his nephew, Alcock, to transfer his assets to him in return for fictitious bills of exchange. This was illegal, in that it was an agreement to defraud the claimant's creditors. Despite two meetings with his creditors, no compromise was reached. Alcock later sold the goods to the defendant (a creditor with full knowledge of the transaction), without the claimant's consent. The Court of Appeal held that the claimant was entitled to recover the goods because he had withdrawn from the illegal contract before any settlement had been reached. Mellish LJ commented that '[i]f money is paid or goods delivered for an illegal purpose, the person who had so paid the money or delivered the goods may recover them back before the illegal purpose is carried out; but if he waits till the illegal purpose is carried out, or if he seeks to enforce the illegal transaction, in neither case can he maintain an action; the law will not allow that to be done'[6].

1   This is also known as the '*locus poenitentiae*' (space for repentance) exception.
2   See Millett LJ in *Tribe v Tribe* [1996] Ch 107 at 134.
3   (1780) 2 Doug KB 468 at 471, 99 ER 299 at 300.
4   See for example *Tappenden v Randall* (1801) 2 Bos & P 467, 126 ER 1388; and *Aubert v Walsh* (1810) 3 Taunt 277, 128 ER 110.
5   (1876) 1 QBD 291.
6   (1876) 1 QBD 291 at 300, Baggallay JA, concurring. James LJ found for the claimant on the different ground that property had not passed under the illegal contract (see Gooderson 'Turpitude and Title in England and India' [1958] CLJ 199 at 209, who approves such reasoning). Such reasoning has, however, since been discredited – see below, paras 14.46ff, and Millett LJ in *Tribe v Tribe* [1996] Ch 107 at 125.

14.36   This decision is open to criticism[1]. At best, it lacks clarity as to when the court will find the illegal purpose to have been carried out. In *Taylor*, the property had been transferred to the nephew and two meetings of creditors had taken place, but the claimant was still permitted to withdraw and reclaim his property.

1   See Beatson *Anson's Law of Contract* (27th edn, 1998), pp 389–390; Goff and Jones *Law of Restitution* (5th edn, 1998), p 617. Note also Millett LJ in *Tribe v Tribe*, who argues ([1996] Ch 107 at 125) that it is too late in any event to criticise the decision, which was cited without disapproval by the House of Lords in *Tinsley v Milligan* [1994] 1 AC 340.

14.37   Further doubt was thrown on *Taylor* by the subsequent decision of the Court of Appeal in *Kearley v Thomson*[1]. Here, the claimant (a friend of the bankrupt) had reached an agreement with the solicitors for the petitioning creditor that, in return for £40, they would not appear at the bankrupt's public examination, and would not oppose his discharge. Such an agreement was clearly illegal, as tending to pervert the course of justice. The solicitors took the money, did not appear at the public examination; then, before any application for discharge had been made, the claimant sought to recover back his £40. The Court of Appeal, however, found that on the facts, it was too late for him to recover it. The exception would not apply where the contract had been partly performed in a substantial manner, even though there remained something to be performed. Fry LJ (with whom Lord Coleridge CJ agreed) doubted expressly whether *Taylor v Bowers* was correct[2].

1   (1890) 24 QBD 742.
2   (1890) 24 QBD 742 at 746.

14.38   Whilst such doubts have not been followed, the Court of Appeal in *Tribe v Tribe*[1] re-examined the exception in more detail. It was held that the court will only assist the claimant if he or she has withdrawn before the illegal purpose has been wholly or partly carried into effect. A distinction was drawn, between carrying out the illegal purpose and merely carrying an illegal transaction into effect[2]. In *Tribe*, a father had executed a share transfer to his son with the intent of deceiving his creditors, but in the event the dispute with his creditors was resolved and the share transfer proved unnecessary. In such circumstances, the Court of Appeal held that the father could withdraw from the transaction, as the illegal purpose (deceiving his creditors) had not been carried into effect. It was irrelevant that the share transactions had been executed and registered. In contrast, in *Kearley* the illegal purpose had clearly been substantially achieved. The solicitors had stayed away from bankrupt's public examination, and so he could proceed to discharge as planned.

1   [1996] Ch 107, below, para 14.58. See Virgo 'Withdrawal from illegal transactions – a matter for consideration' [1996] CLJ 23.
2   See Nourse LJ at [1996] Ch 107 at 121–122.

14.39   Voluntary withdrawal   However, it is not enough merely that the claimant has withdrawn in time; the withdrawal must also be *voluntary*. By 'voluntary', the courts appear to mean that the claimant must choose to withdraw. At one time, to rely on this exception the claimant would have to show that the decision to withdraw was due to repentance. The need for genuine repentance placed this exception on a clear moral ground – those who repent of their illegal purpose will find mercy in the courts. However, the courts now seem to be content with the sole requirement of voluntariness. Indeed it is hard to view *Taylor v Bowers* as a genuine repentance case in any event[1].

1   Birks *An Introduction to the Law of Restitution* (revised edn, 1989), pp 302 and 303 argues that there must be a spontaneous change of mind and a change of heart, ie *genuine* repentance. He explains *Taylor v Bowers* as an exception to this rule, where the illegal purpose had not been achieved, and only recovery could prevent it being achieved. Genuine repentance is therefore required to prevent the claimant from using the right to withdraw as a lever with which to compel performance and to deprive the other party of his incentive to abstain from the illegality. This has been validly criticised for assuming that illegality always requires moral turpitude: see Burrows *Law of Restitution* (1993), p 340.

14.40   The requirement of repentance may be seen in *Bigos v Bousted*[1]. Here, the claimant had agreed to supply the defendant's wife and daughter with £150-worth of Italian lire. In return, the defendant agreed to pay the claimant in sterling in England, and gave the claimant a share certificate as security for repayment of loan. Such an agreement was illegal under the Exchange Control Act 1947. The claimant failed to supply the lire as promised and, in a subsequent action[2], the defendant counter-claimed for the return of his share certificate, on the basis that the contract, although illegal, was still executory.

1   [1951] 1 All ER 92. See also *Parkinson v College of Ambulance Ltd* [1925] 2 KB 1 at 16, per Lush J; and *Harry Parker Ltd v Mason* [1940] 2 KB 590.
2   The claimant had sued to recover £150 from the defendant, but had abandoned her claim at the commencement of the hearing.

14.41   Pritchard J refused to apply the withdrawal exception. The illegal purpose was not fulfilled because the defendant wished to withdraw, but because the claimant refused to produce the money as promised. This would not suffice:

[The authorities] show ... that there is a distinction between what may, for convenience, be called the repentance cases, on the one hand, and the frustration cases, on the other hand. If a particular case may be held to fall within the category of repentance cases, I think the law is that the court will help a person who repents, provided his repentance comes before the illegal purpose has been substantially performed ... [T]his case falls within the category of cases which I call the frustration cases[1].

1   [1951] 1 All ER 92 at 100. The 'frustration cases' to which Pritchard J referred were *Alexander v Rayson* [1936] 1 KB 169; and *Berg v Sadler and Moore* [1937] 2 KB 158. In *Berg v Sadler and Moore* the court refused to assist the claimant, whose attempt to obtain goods from the defendants by false pretences had been frustrated by the defendants' refusal to complete the transaction.

14.42   A requirement of genuine repentance reduced the doctrine to a limited exception to the illegality defence based on morality. In most cases, claimants will withdraw because circumstances have changed due to events beyond their control. The requirement of genuine repentance does not, however, appear to have survived the re-examination of this exception by the Court of Appeal in *Tribe v Tribe*[1], in which the whole court rejected the need for genuine repentance by the claimant. Although the case dealt with the effect of illegality on trusts, Millett LJ at least intended his reasoning to apply to all restitutionary claims[2] and held that:

> Justice is not a reward for merit; restitution should not be confined to the penitent. I would also hold that voluntary withdrawal from an illegal transaction when it has ceased to be needed is sufficient. It is true that this is not necessary to encourage withdrawal, but a rule to the opposite effect could lead to bizarre results[3].

On this reasoning, the defendant in *Bigos* could have recovered his money if he had withdrawn, because the money was no longer needed by his family or exchange controls had been abolished. In contrast, it is still doubtful whether he could have recovered if the arrangement had been terminated by the conduct of the other party. The withdrawal must be voluntary, and Millett LJ held that it is not sufficient that the claimant withdraws simply because his or her plan had been discovered[4].

1   [1996] Ch 107. This case is discussed in more detail below. However, Beale (ed) *Chitty on Contracts* (28th edn, 1999), vol 1, para 17–181 still states that the claimant must genuinely repent and not merely seek recovery because the illegal purpose of the contract has been frustrated.
2   His Lordship uses the term 'restitution' throughout. In contrast, Nourse LJ (at [1996] Ch 107 at 121) confines his comments to property transfer cases (see below, para 14.46ff). Otton LJ agreed with both judges.
3   [1996] Ch 107 at 135. Nourse LJ, however, preferred not to become embroiled in the debate in relation to withdrawal generally: [1996] Ch 107 at 121.
4   [1996] Ch 107 at 135.

14.43   This decision has been generally welcomed[1]. Nevertheless the exact limits of the doctrine, despite extensive academic debate[2], remain open to discussion.

1   Goff and Jones *Law of Restitution* (5th edn, 1998), p 619 welcomes the decision as a step towards ensuring that justice is done; and also doubts (at p 620) whether the exception applies to marine insurance following the Marine Insurance Act 1906, s 84.
2   See for example Beatson 'Repudiation of Illegal Purpose as a Ground for Restitution' (1975) 91 LQR 313, who argues that recovery should only be allowed where the application of the general rule would increase the probability of the illegal purpose being achieved; Merkin 'Restitution by Withdrawal From Executory Illegal Contracts' (1981) 97 LQR 420; and the classic article of Grodecki '*In pari delicto potior est conditio defendentis*' (1955) 71 LQR 254, arguing for a more flexible approach.

14.44   Court-sanctioned withdrawal?   One further line of authority remains, which is difficult to integrate with the cases discussed above. It has been suggested that the courts retain an equitable discretion to permit withdrawal from a transaction[1], although such a discretion has only been used in more recent times in relation to *marriage brokage contracts*[2]. These contracts, by which a party agrees for reward to arrange or at least attempt to arrange for the party to marry a specified or unspecified individual, are illegal as contrary to public policy[3]. In *Hermann v Charlesworth*[4], a woman who had entered such a contract was permitted to recover her fee, even though she had been introduced to several prospective suitors, and trouble and expense had been incurred by the defendant. Yet, the case may be explained simply as a matter of construing the illegal purpose to be the arrangement of a marriage and that the introductions were merely preparatory[5], thereby rendering it consistent with *Taylor v Bowers*[6]. On this basis, it is difficult to see any real ground for equitable intervention beyond the limits of the exception, as stated above.

1   Treitel *Law of Contract* (10th edn, 1999), p 464.
2   See Goff and Jones *Law of Restitution* (5th edn, 1998), p 621 for further examples, although they concede that it is doubtful whether such authority would be applied today.
3   See above, para 14.16.
4   [1905] 2 KB 123; above, para 14.16.
5   See Collins MR [1905] 2 KB 123 at 135: 'the object being to bring about a marriage, it could not be performed in part'.
6   (1876) 1 QBD 291; above, para 14.35.

14.45   Bars to withdrawal?   It has been suggested that the courts will not permit the exception to be relied upon where the contract involves a serious crime, for example, where one person has paid another to murder a third party[1].

1   See *Tappenden v Randall* (1801) 2 Bos & P 467 at 471, 126 ER 1388 at 1390, per Heath J; *Kearley v Thomson* (1890) 24 QBD 742 at 747, per Fry LJ.

INDEPENDENT PROPRIETARY RIGHTS

14.46   Under this exception, the claimant's action will succeed if it is based not on the illegal transaction, but property rights gained under the illegal transaction. The exception rests on the principle that property rights can pass under an illegal contract; a principle which has not escaped extensive criticism[1]. In the leading case of *Singh v Ali*[2], Lord Denning justified the principle as follows:

> The reason is because the transferor, having fully achieved his unworthy end, cannot be allowed to turn round and repudiate the means by which he did it – he cannot throw over the transfer. And the transferee, having obtained the property, can assert his title to it against all the world, not because he has any merit of his own, but because there is no one who can assert a better title to it. The court does not confiscate the property because of the illegality – it has no power to do so – so it says, in the words of Lord Eldon 'Let the estate lie where it falls'[3].

The House of Lords more recently in *Tinsley v Milligan*[4] has accepted that illegality would not prevent claims based on independent property rights[5]. There is a fine line, however, between enforcing the contract, and enforcing proprietary rights irrespective of the illegality of the contract. The rights claimed under this exception can only be understood in the light of the contract in question. While not enforcing the contract, the courts must acknowledge its presence, but this is not found to conflict with the illegality defence[6]. It has been questioned whether this fine line withstands detailed examination and whether in reality 'as far as proprietary rights and remedies are concerned ... the law simply ignores the illegality'[7].

1   See Higgins 'The transfer of property under illegal transactions' (1962) 25 MLR 149, and Goo 'Let the estate lie where it falls' (1994) 45 NILQ 378.
2   [1960] AC 167 at 176.
3   See *Muckleston v Brown* (1801) 6 Ves 52 at 69, 31 ER 934 at 942. Rose also argues that '[t]he principal reason why proprietary claims succeed is that, regardless of the claimant's merits, there

is no one with a better title, and to hold otherwise would cause uncertainty and sanction confiscation by anyone with impunity': 'Restitutionary and proprietary consequences of illegality' in Rose (ed) *Consensus ad idem: Essays on the Law of Contract in honour of Guenter Treitel* (1996), p 218.
4   [1994] 1 AC 340.
5   Equally, the claimant could logically found a collateral claim in contract (see *Strongman (1945) v Sincock* [1955] 2 QB 525) or in tort (see *Shelley v Paddock* [1980] QB 348).
6   See per Lord Browne-Wilkinson in *Tinsley v Milligan* [1994] 1 AC 340 at 370 and 377; and per Millett LJ in *Tribe v Tribe* [1996] Ch 107 at 129.
7   Burrows *Law of Restitution* (1993), p 469. See also Virgo *Principles of the Law of Restitution* (1999) p 641, and Enonchong 'Title Claims and Illegal Transactions' (1995) 111 LQR 135, who argues that the courts in reality allow claimants to rely on the illegal transaction in relation to title claims.

14.47   The current state of the law is summarised by Lord Browne-Wilkinson in *Tinsley v Milligan*[1]:

(1)   Property in chattels and land can pass under a contract which is illegal and therefore would have been unenforceable as a contract;
(2)   A claimant can at law enforce property rights so acquired provided that he does not need to rely on the illegal contract for any purpose other than providing the basis of his claim to a property right;
(3)   It is irrelevant that the illegality of the underlying agreement was either pleaded or emerged in evidence: if the claimant has acquired legal title under the illegal contract that is enough.

This applies to both legal and equitable rights to property.

1   [1994] 1 AC 340 at 370.

14.48   On this basis, the transferee under an illegal contract retains rights to property transferred under the contract and can retain his or her property, despite being party to an illegal contract. There are three main classes of case when this argument will be raised:

● the claimant has received property under an illegal contract, and wishes to retain it or recover it from another[1];
● the claimant has transferred a lesser interest in the property to the defendant, this interest has been terminated and the claimant now wishes to recover the property in question[2]; and
● the claimant seeks recognition of an equitable interest in the property[3].

1   See below, para 14.49ff.
2   See below, para 14.53ff.
3   See below, para 14.56ff.

14.49   The claimant has received property under an illegal contract and wishes to retain it or recover it from another   The classic authority is *Singh v Ali*[1]. In this case, regulations in Malaysia required that persons using or selling vehicles for the carriage of goods must obtain a haulage permit. The claimant was not entitled to a permit, but entered into a contract with the defendant by which the defendant would purchase a vehicle on his behalf (the defendant being entitled to a permit). Such a contract was illegal. The defendant later took back the lorry, and the claimant sued for return of the lorry or its value. The Privy Council supported his claim. Lord Denning held that although the contract was illegal, the claimant was entitled to sue for detinue: 'Although the transaction between the plaintiff and the defendant was illegal, nevertheless it was fully executed and carried out: and on that account it was effective to pass the property in the lorry to the plaintiff'[2].

1 [1960] AC 167. See also *Feret v Hill* (1854) 15 CB 207, 139 ER 400; *Simpson v Nicholls* (1838) 3 M & W 240 at 244, 150 ER 1132 at 1134; *Elder v Kelly* [1919] 2 KB 179.
2 [1960] AC 167 at 176, relying on *Scarfe v Morgan* (1838) 4 M & W 270 at 281, 150 ER 1430 at 1435.

14.50   Whilst this reasoning is consistent with the doctrine of illegality, in that the loss lies where it falls, it is clearly taken a step further when the transferee is permitted to assert his or her rights to recover the property from the transferor or a third party. Nevertheless, this exception has been supported by a number of authorities, which allow the transferee to assert his or her rights. An extreme example may be seen in *Belvoir Finance Co Ltd v Stapleton*[1]. In this case, the claimants had purchased three cars from motor dealers under illegal contracts of sale. The cars were hired out to the Belgravia Car Hire Co Ltd under illegal hire purchase agreements. The cars were delivered directly to Belgravia, and were never in the claimants' possession. The Court of Appeal held that, even so, the illegal contracts of sale were fully executed and the claimants obtained title to the cars. They could therefore sue for conversion when the cars were sold without their knowledge or consent by Belgravia, and it was immaterial that they had never taken possession of the cars[2].

1 [1971] 1 QB 210.
2 See per Lord Denning MR [1971] 1 QB 210 at 217.

14.51   One further point should be noted at this stage. In both cases, the claimant obtained title despite the contract being illegal. If, however, the seller fails to deliver goods as promised under the contract, the buyer's claim is one for breach of contract relying on the precise terms of the contract and, in such circumstances, the court will not support the buyer's claim.

14.52   It is clear that this exception applies to property, be it personal or real. It will also apply to claims for money paid under an illegal contract, where the property in the money clearly passes to the payee[1], subject to rare exceptions, for example payment of a deposit or to a stakeholder[2]. It also applies to copyright[3] and securities[4].

1 See *Gordon v Metropolitan Police Chief Comr* [1910] 2 KB 1080; *Chief Constable of the West Midlands v White* reported in [1992] NLJR 455. See also above, para 3.38ff.
2 See for example *Smith v Bickmore* (1812) 4 Taunt 474, 128 ER 413; and *Bate v Cartwright* (1819) 7 Price 540, 146 ER 1054.
3 *Instone v A Schroeder Music Publishing Co Ltd* [1974] 1 All ER 171.
4 *Taylor v Chester* (1869) LR 4 QB 309.

14.53   The claimant has transferred a lesser interest in the property to the defendant, which he or she has now terminated   This raises a different proprietary issue. Here, the claimant has transferred a proprietary interest, less than full legal ownership, under an illegal contract, and seek to recover the property. As stated earlier, the proprietary interest will pass to the defendant despite the illegality. This does not mean, however, that when the interest ends, for example by passage of time, the claimant cannot recover the property. Such lesser interests include leases[1], bailment[2] and pledges[3]. The crucial issue is whether the interest has been terminated. If so, the claimant asserts his or her right to recover the property or chattel independent of any illegal transaction[4].

1 A lease will vest a term of years certain in the tenant: *Lace v Chantler* [1944] KB 368. Therefore, at the end of the term the landlord will recover possession, regardless of whether the lease is legal or illegal. It must be doubted, however, whether the landlord could recover the premises for non-

payment of rent during the course of the lease. This would appear to rely on the forfeiture terms of the lease (failure to pay rent does not automatically terminate the lease), and the courts will not support a claim which is founded on the terms of an illegal contract: see *Alexander v Rayson* [1936] 1 KB 169 at 186–187; and *Feret v Hill* (1854) 15 CB 207, 139 ER 400. A contrary view was held by Hamson 'Illegal Contracts and Limited Interests' (1949) 10 CLJ 249 at 256–257.

2 *Belvoir Finance Co Ltd v Stapleton* [1971] 1 QB 210, [1970] 3 All ER 664.

3 See *Taylor v Chester* (1869) LR 4 QB 309. Although the claim was refused when he sought to recover a half bank-note pledged at a brothel (see per Mellor J at 314), it has been suggested that the claimant would have succeeded if he had tendered the amount due under the pledge and then claimed back the note on the basis of his revived property rights: Treitel *Law of Contract* (10th edn, 1999), pp 457–458.

4 See Coote 'Another Look at *Bowmakers v Barnet Instruments*' (1972) 35 MLR 38 at 48 and Gooderson, 'Turpitude and Title in England and India' [1958] CLJ 199 at 209. See also Stewart 'Contractual Illegality and the Recognition of Proprietary Interests' (1988) 1 Journal of Contract Law 134 at 142–144.

14.54   Much confusion arises, however, from the leading case of *Bowmakers Ltd v Barnet Instruments Ltd*[1]. Here the defendants had hired machine tools from the claimant finance company under three separate hire-purchase agreements. The agreements were in fact illegal, in that they breached orders of the Ministry of Supply. The defendants paid some, but by no means all, of the agreed payments, and, in breach of the agreements, sold the machines hired under the first and third agreement, and refused to return on demand the machines under the second agreement. They alleged that the claimants had no remedy, due to the illegality of all three agreements.

Du Parcq LJ (giving the judgment of the court) held that the claimants could recover the property which had been converted or detained on the basis of their rights to possession:

> In our opinion, a man's right to possess his own chattels will as a general rule be enforced against one who, without any claim of right, is detaining them, or has converted them to his own use, even though it may appear either from the pleadings, or in the course of the trial, that the chattels in question came into the defendant's possession by reason of an illegal contract between himself and the plaintiff, provided that the plaintiff does not seek, and is not forced, either to found his claim on the illegal contract or to plead its illegality in order to support his claim[2].

1 [1945] KB 65. See Hamson 'Illegal Contracts and Limited Interests' (1949) 10 CLJ 249 and Stewart 'Contractual Illegality and the Recognition of Proprietary Interests' (1988) 1 Journal of Contract Law 134.

2 [1945] KB 65 at 71.

14.55   Some difficulty has been experienced in understanding the basis for the Court of Appeal's decision in this case. The remedy given to the claimants is predicated on their right to possess their own chattels, but, as has been noted, this would seem to clash with the previous class of cases, which dictate that property can pass to the defendant even under an illegal contract[1]. It is therefore necessary to identify the basis for the claimants' right to possession. If the property in the machines has passed to the defendants under the illegal hire purchase contracts, this interest must have been terminated, thereby allowing the claimants to assert their reversionary interest in the machines. It may be argued that by selling the goods, the defendants had automatically terminated their rights under the hire purchase agreement, and that the interest in the goods would revert back to the claimants. Yet, this cannot explain why *merely refusing to pay* the instalments due under the second agreement would give the claimants a right to possession of the goods[2]. This would amount, of course, to breach of contract, but this is not generally sufficient to determine a proprietary interest in the goods. This throws into doubt the distinction between enforcing rights under an illegal contract, and enforcing property rights retained by the transferor after entering an illegal contract. This is not assisted by the fact that the transferor can only evidence his or her reversionary right to possession by the terms of the illegal contract. Whilst this aspect of *Bowmakers* remains questionable, the general *Bowmakers* approach has received approval from the House of Lords in *Tinsley v Milligan*[3]. As the Law Commission has commented recently, 'the picture that seems to be emerging here is that the courts simply ignore the illegality when considering the proprietary consequences of an illegal contract'[4].

1 See above, para 14.49ff. It should be noted that the claimants had themselves purchased the machine tools under illegal contracts. Counsel for the defendants, however, conceded (in the court's view correctly) that the claimants had received good title to the goods: [1945] KB 65 at 70, per Du Parcq (per curiam).
2 See, for example, Law Commission Consultation Paper no 154 *Illegal transactions: the effect of illegality on contracts and trusts* (1999), para 2.64. Treitel *Law of Contract* (10th edn, 1999), p 458 suggests that the agreements might have provided that the non-payment of hire amounted to repudiatory breach, which determined the defendants' interest in the goods. Unfortunately, this is hypothetical (the case report merely states that 'a familiar form' of hire purchase agreement was used: [1945] KB 65 at 66, although Coote 'Another Look at *Bowmakers v Barnet Instruments*' (1972) 35 MLR 38 at 38 suggests that it is reasonable to suppose that this would include such a clause). Again, this appears to leave the claimants relying on the particular terms of the agreement: see Enonchong 'Title Claims and Illegal Transactions' (1995) 111 LQR 135 at 140–144.
3 [1994] 1 AC 340.
4 Law Commission Consultation Paper no 154 *Illegal transactions: the effect of illegality on contracts and trusts* (1999), para 2.66.

14.56   The claimant seeks recognition of an equitable interest in the property   The House of Lords has recently found the rules just stated to apply to equitable interests in land. *Tinsley v Milligan*[1] involved a claim by Ms Milligan for recognition of her equitable interest in a property, towards which she had contributed purchase money, on the basis that there was a common intention between herself and Ms Tinsley that the property belonged to them equally. The women had bought the property as a lodging house, but to enable Ms Milligan to make claims for social security benefit, the legal title had been placed solely in Ms Tinsley's name. The arrangements between the parties had therefore been undertaken with the intention of achieving an illegal purpose, ie to defraud the DSS.

The majority of the House was of the opinion that, on the facts, a resulting trust arose in favour of Ms Milligan, which would entitle her to an equitable interest in the property. The rules governing proprietary claims applied to equitable interests, which required the courts to analyse the difficult questions of trust law which arose. They rejected the view of the minority (Lords Goff and Keith) that the illegal purpose of the parties should bar the claim, on the basis that Ms Milligan did not come to equity with clean hands[2]. Lord Browne-Wilkinson found that the same principles should apply in common law and equity, and if Ms Milligan could establish a proprietary right without relying on the illegal transaction, then her claim would stand:

> If the law is that a party is entitled to enforce a property right acquired under an illegal transaction, in my judgment the same rule ought to apply to any property right so acquired, whether such right is legal or equitable[3].

Here, the property right could be established by means of a resulting trust. The presumption of a resulting trust could not be displaced by Ms Tinsley, because to do so she would be forced to raise the illegal arrangement to defraud the DSS, which the court refused to acknowledge. The illegality therefore only emerged when raised by Ms Tinsley herself.

1   [1994] 1 AC 340. Comment by Stowe 'The "Unruly Horse" has Bolted: *Tinsley v Milligan*' (1994) 57 MLR 441 at 447; Buckley 'Social security fraud as illegality' (1994) 110 LQR 3; Berg 'Illegality and equitable interests' (1993) Journal of Business Law 513.
2   [1994] 1 AC 340 at 357–358, per Lord Goff. The position of Goff and Jones *Law of Restitution* (5th edn, 1998), p 624 should be noted: 'The clean hands rule may be a good reason for denying equitable relief, but arguably not for denying the existence of equitable title. Ms Milligan had established the resulting trust by demonstrating that she had contributed to the purchase price of the house and that the common understanding of the parties was that they owned the house equally'. See also Virgo *Principles of the Law of Restitution* (1999), pp 743–744.
3   [1994] 1 AC 340 at 371.

14.57   It may be doubted, however, whether this case leaves this area of the law in a satisfactory state. The House recognised that the resulting trust could be displaced by the presumption of advancement, ie a presumption that a transfer to certain family members (such as husband to wife or parent to child), is intended to be a gift unless the contrary is shown[1]. Where the presumption of advancement applies, the transferor faces a dilemma, in that to rebut the presumption that he or she has made a gift, he or she will be obliged to explain the illegal purpose underlying the transaction, and thereby rely on the illegality to rebut the presumption. This will not be permitted by the courts. On this basis, the decision whether one party has obtained an equitable interest is entirely dependant on the relationship between the parties. If they are father and son, no equitable interest will arise in the father's favour (the presumption of advancement dictates a gift)[2]. In contrast, if they are cohabitees, a resulting trust arises[3]. In neither case can this be contradicted by evidence of the real arrangement if it had an illegal purpose[4].

1   See eg McGhee *Snell's Equity* (30th edn, 2000), pp 206–211.
2   See *Palaniappa Chettiar v Arunasalam Chettiar* [1962] AC 294 (father's claim against son failed due to presumption of advancement, which could not be rebutted without relying upon the illegal transaction). Virgo and O'Sullivan are highly critical of the elevation of the presumption of advancement to conclusive status: 'Resulting trusts and illegality' in Birks and Rose (eds) *Restitution and Equity* (2000), pp 103–107.
3   See for example the application of *Tinsley* in *Lowson v Coombes* [1999] Ch 373. Comment by Thompson [1999] Conv 242; Cotterill 'Property and impropriety – The *Tinsley v Milligan* problem again' [1999] Lloyds Maritime and Commercial Law Quarterly 465.
4   However, note that in *Silverwood v Silverwood* (1997) 74 P & CR 453 Peter Gibson LJ was prepared to allow a claimant to rely on illegality to disprove a spurious defence.

14.58   This problematic distinction was highlighted in the Court of Appeal decision in *Tribe v Tribe*[1]. In this case, a father had transferred shares in his company to his son to safeguard his assets from his creditors. The consideration for the transfer was never paid. As circumstances turned out, this device was unnecessary, and the father later requested that the shares be transferred back. His son refused. The father therefore brought an action for recovery of the shares, claiming that the son was a bare trustee. The son, following *Tinsley*, perhaps predictably relied on the presumption of advancement and alleged that the father could not raise his illegal purpose to rebut this argument. The Court of Appeal held that this argument was correct. Despite a finding by the trial judge that the father did not intend to give the shares to his son, this would be the effect of the *Tinsley* judgment. However, this did not mean that justice could not be done. As noted earlier, the Court of Appeal took a broad view of the withdrawal exception, and held that the father had withdrawn from the illegal transaction before the illegal purpose had been carried into effect. No creditors had been deceived by the transaction. On this basis, he would be entitled to the return of his share certificates despite the presumption of advancement, which was rebutted.

1 [1996] Ch 107; above, para 14.38. In reaching its decision, the Court relied heavily on the decision of the High Court of Australia in *Perpetual Executors and Trustees Association of Australia Ltd v Wright* (1917) 23 CLR 185. Note criticism of the application of the *locus poenitentiae* exception in relation to resulting trusts: Enonchong 'Illegality and the presumption of advancement' [1996] RLR 78.

14.59   *Tribe* does little to resolve the problem left by *Tinsley*. Such arbitrary reasoning, which is entirely dependent on the technical rules of property and trust law, seems a considerable distance from the illegality defence itself[1]. It has been criticised as 'a triumph of procedure over substance ... [which] pays no regard to the nature or seriousness of the illegality'[2]. The decision in *Tribe* may be compared with that of the High Court of Australia in *Nelson v Nelson*[3]. In this case, a mother had transferred a property to her son and daughter, to enable her to obtain a government subsidy to purchase a second house. She now sought the court's assistance to recover the proceeds of sale of the property when her daughter refused to relinquish her share. Her daughter argued that, under the presumption of advancement, she would be entitled to an interest in the property conveyed. The High Court of Australia refused to follow *Tinsley v Milligan*. Despite the fact that the presumption of advancement was held to operate between mother and daughter, the court supported the mother's claim. The majority suggested that instead of a strict proprietary approach, the courts should adopt a discretionary approach which examined the underlying policy of the Act in question. Recovery would, however, be subject to repayment of the government subsidy, suggesting a requirement of counter-restitution in Australian law. It is doubtful whether such a requirement exists in English law. Whilst counter-restitution in fact occurred on the facts of *Tinsley* (Ms Milligan had reached a settlement with the DSS), the more recent case of *Anzal v Ellahi*[4] suggests that the courts will not make this a condition for recovery. In that case, the Court of Appeal held that in a *Tinsley* situation, the court may choose at full hearing to order that a transcript of its judgment be prepared at the public expense, and sent to the DSS for them to consider whether, in the light of all the circumstances, it should seek any repayment from the claimants. By this means, the court has the option of encouraging parties who have been defrauded to pursue their own action for recovery.

1 Note the comments of Nourse LJ and the trial judge in *Tribe* ([1996] Ch 107 at 118), of Millett LJ ([1996] Ch 107 at 134), and of Nourse LJ in *Silverwood v Silverwood* (1997) 74 P & CR 453 at 458. See also Law Commission Consultation Paper no 154 *Illegal transactions: the effect of illegality on contracts and trusts* (1999), para 3.22.
2 Toohey J in *Nelson v Nelson* (1995) 132 ALR 133 at 176.
3 (1995) 132 ALR 133, 184 CLR 538. See also Rose 'Reconsidering illegality' (1996) 10 Journal of Contract Law 271.
4 (21 July, 1999, unreported).

14.60   Limits to the exception   Du Parcq LJ in *Bowmakers Ltd v Barnet Instruments Ltd*[1] stated that the rule of recovery would not always apply. For example, in his Lordship's view, it was obvious that a court would not permit recovery of goods which were of such a kind that it was unlawful to deal in them at all, for example obscene books. This is generally treated as excluding recovery by the claimant when the contract is grossly immoral[2]. A second possible exception is that the court will not permit the property to pass under an illegal contract where the legislation in question not only renders the contract unenforceable, but also ineffective. This would appear to be one of two grounds for the decision in *Amar Singh v Kulubya*[3].

1   [1945] KB 65 at 72; on the case see above, para 14.54ff.
2   It has also been suggested that the rule of recovery will not apply where the property is being used to commit a serious crime, for example, A seeks to recover a dagger lent to B to murder C: see Glanville Williams 'The legal effect of illegal contracts' (1942) 8 CLJ 51 at 62. Recent case-law indicates, however, that the fact that the claimant is seeking to recover the proceeds of sale of properties obtained by mortgage fraud will *not* obstruct recovery: *MacDonald v Myerson* [2001] EWCA Civ 66, [2001] EGCS 15, applied in *Mortgage Express v Robson* [2001] EWCA Civ 887, [2001] 2 All ER (Comm) 886; see also *Halifax Building Society v Thomas* [1996] Ch 217, on which see above, para 12.54ff.
3   [1964] AC 142, PC. See Hamson 'Contract – illegality – *in pari delicto*' [1964] CLJ 20 and Enonchong 'Title Claims and Illegal Transactions' (1995) 111 LQR 135 at 144–145. The second ground for the decision was that the relevant legislation had as its object the protection of Africans as a class, and the lessor was a member of that class, and therefore entitled to claim possession of the lands in question.

Do the exceptions amount to a ground for restitution or unjust enrichment?

14.61   Some academics have argued that the exceptions to the illegality defence are in fact capable of forming an independent basis for a claim in restitution[1]. For example, it has been argued that the withdrawal exception could form a ground for restitution, and this view has been accepted by the Law Commission in their Consultation Paper[2]. Birks has argued that a claim for restitution could lie on the basis of the claimant's penitence, which reflects the policy aim of discouraging unlawful conduct[3]. Burrows agrees that withdrawal should be a separate ground[4], but disagrees with Virgo[5] that it is based on total failure of consideration. Whilst accepting that the claimant cannot withdraw if he or she has received part of the benefit, which resembles a requirement of total failure of consideration, Burrows asserts that as a matter of strict law, there cannot be a total failure of consideration if the defendant is still ready and able to perform[6]. In his view:

> ... the law wishes to discourage illegal conduct and hence wishes to encourage the abandonment of illegal contracts. There would be no incentive for the claimant to withdraw if the defendant were allowed to retain, without payment, the benefits received at the claimant's expense[7].

It has also been suggested that the *non in pari delicto* exception is based on restitutionary grounds[8].

1   See for example McCamus 'Restitutionary Recovery of Benefits Conferred under Contracts in Conflict with Statutory Policy – the New Golden Rule' (1987) 25 Osgoode Hall Law Journal 787; Burrows *Law of Restitution* (1993), ch 11; Goff and Jones *Law of Restitution* (5th edn, 1998), ch 24; Rose 'Illegality limited' (1997–1998) 8 King's College Law Journal 69.
2   Law Commission Consultation Paper no 154 *Illegal transactions: the effect of illegality on contracts and trusts* (1999), paras 2.49–2.56.
3   Birks *An Introduction to the Law of Restitution* (revised edn, 1989), pp 301–303, although this leads to a more restrictive definition than that adopted by the Court of Appeal in *Tribe v Tribe* [1996] Ch 107 (see above, para 14.39ff). In a recent article, Birks has gone further to suggest that illegality could be better explained in terms of stultification, and that claims for restitution should be permitted where the claim does not undermine the refusal to enforce the contract: see 'Recovering value transferred under an illegal contract' (2000) 1 Theoretical Inquiries in Law 155.
4   See Burrows *Law of Restitution* (1993), pp 333–335; Burrows and McKendrick *Cases and Materials on the Law of Restitution* (1997), pp 511–523. See now also Law Commission Consultation Paper No 154 *Illegal transactions: the effect of illegality on contracts and trusts* (1999), para 7.69.

5   Virgo *Principles of the Law of Restitution* (1999), pp 747 and 372. See also by the same author
    'Withdrawal from illegal transactions – a matter for consideration' [1996] CLJ 23 and 'The effect
    of illegality on claims for restitution in English law' in Swadling (ed) *The Limits of Restitutionary
    Claims: A comparative analysis* (1997), ch 7.
6   See *Thomas v Brown* (1876) 1 QBD 714 (there is only a total failure of consideration if the
    defendant is unable or unwilling to perform as promised); see below, para 19.8.
7   Burrows *Law of Restitution* (1993), p 335.
8   See Birks *An Introduction to the Law of Restitution* (revised edn, 1989), p 300, Burrows *Law of
    Restitution* (1993), pp 333 and 334, Virgo 'The effect of illegality on claims for restitution in
    English law' in Swadling (ed) *The Limits of Restitutionary Claims: a comparative analysis* (1997),
    ch 7.

14.62   There has also been some discussion whether the third exception
(independent proprietary rights) is capable of forming a ground of restitution.
Millett LJ in *Tribe v Tribe*[1] held that the claimant's action was based on
restitution[2]. Rose has advised that 'confusion from use of the word "restitution"
can be avoided if recovery of property by enforcement of an existing right is not
confused with restitution in the stricter sense of reversing unjust enrichment'[3]. A
distinction should therefore be drawn between 'pure proprietary claims', which
are not based on restitution, and 'restitutionary proprietary claims'[4]. The third
exception would appear to belong to the former. It can therefore not realistically
be categorised as a restitutionary claim.

1   [1996] Ch 107.
2   His Lordship used the term 'restitution' throughout. In contrast, Nourse LJ ([1996] Ch 107 at
    121) confined his comments to property transfer cases (above, para 14.46ff). Otton LJ agreed
    with both judges.
3   Rose 'Restitutionary and proprietary consequences of illegality' in Rose (ed) *Consensus ad idem:
    Essays on the Law of Contract in honour of Guenter Treitel* (1996), p 204, n 7. See also Swadling
    [1995] All ER Review 456.
4   To use the terminology of Goff and Jones. On the extent to which claims for restitution can be
    regarded as proprietary, see above, ch 3.

D   The Human Rights Act 1998

14.63   It was perhaps inevitable that the illegality defence would be
challenged under the Human Rights Act 1998 ('the 1998 Act'), which came
into force on 2 October 2000. In *Shanshal v Al-Kishtaini*[1], the claimant alleged
that if illegality was found to bar his right to recovery, it would amount to a
deprivation of his right to possession of the money claimed, which would be
incompatible with Article 1 of the First Protocol to the European Convention of
Human Rights (as set out in Sch 1 to the 1998 Act). This states that:

> Every natural or legal person is entitled to the peaceful enjoyment of his possessions.
> No one shall be deprived of his possessions except in the public interest and subject to
> the conditions provided for by law and by the general principles of international law.
> The preceding provisions shall not, however, in any way impair the right of a State
> to enforce such laws as it deems necessary to control the use of property in
> accordance with the general interest or to secure the payment of taxes or other
> contributions or penalties.

The Court of Appeal unanimously rejected this claim. The transaction was in
breach of Directions which prohibited transactions with persons normally
resident in Iraq following its invasion of Kuwait, and had implemented
resolutions of the United Nations Security Council. Further, the prohibition had
not been absolute: the Bank of England had been given a discretion to grant
permission for any proposed transaction, although no such application had been

made in this case. On the facts, it could not be suggested that recovery would be in the 'public interest'.

1   [2001] EWCA Civ 264, [2001] 2 All ER (Comm) 601.

14.64   Their Lordships expressly left open the question whether a claimant was indeed 'deprived of his possessions' when illegality barred his right of action to recover money paid under a transaction[1]. Assuming this hurdle could be overcome, the court refused to accept that the policy justification for the illegality defence would always meet the 'public interest' requirement. Quoting Lord Goff in *Tinsley v Milligan*[2], Rix LJ remarked that 'It may be necessary to justify the rule's application in the instant case as representing that "fair balance", between the demands of the general interest and the requirements of the protection of an individual's fundamental rights ... '[3]. There would therefore still seem to be some prospect of challenge of the illegality defence under the 1998 Act[4].

1   As property passes under an illegal contract (see above, paras 14.46ff), such doubts would seem justified in that the claimant is not deprived of funds which passed under the illegal transaction, but of his or her right of action for the money. Rix LJ [2001] 2 All ER (Comm) at 619 also queried whether convention rights had horizontal effect. On claims for restitution as 'possessions' within the Human Rights Convention see further *National Provincial Building Society v United Kingdom* [1997] STC 1466, noted by Tiley [1998] CLJ 269.
2   *Tinsley v Milligan* [1994] 1 AC 340 at 355: 'the principle is not a principle of justice: it is a principle of policy, whose application is indiscriminate and so can lead to unfair consequences as between the parties to litigation'.
3   [2001] 2 All ER (Comm) 601 at 620, para 96.
4   See also Law Commission Consultation Paper no 154 *Illegal transactions: the effect of illegality on contracts and trusts* (1999), para 1.23, which notes the possibility of a challenge under the 1998 Act.

E   The need for reform

14.65   Few would argue that this area of law is not in need of reform. It is technical, requires fine distinctions, and following *Tinsley v Milligan*[1] it is most unclear to what extent a claimant may refer to the terms of an illegal contract and still succeed in his or her claim. The rule, as qualified by the exceptions raised above, evokes exceptional uncertainty in the name of public policy, which has long since relinquished any hope of achieving justice.

Three proposals for reform should be noted, however, whereby the courts, and now the Law Commission, have attempted to bring some coherence to this area of law.

1   [1994] 1 AC 340.

A test of public conscience

14.66   This test was developed in tort in relation to the defence of *ex turpi causa*, although it received a mixed reception by the Court of Appeal in the now leading tort authority of *Pitts v Hunt*[1]. It was founded on the test stated by Hutchinson J in *Thackwell v Barclays Bank plc*[2]: whether, in all the circumstances, it would be an affront to public conscience if, by affording the claimant relief, the court was seen to be indirectly assisting or encouraging the claimant in his or her criminal act (or encouraging others in similar criminal acts[3])? This line of authority was enthusiastically adopted by Nicholls LJ in the Court of Appeal in

Tinsley v Milligan[4], who stated the test broadly: 'The court must weigh, or balance, the adverse consequences of granting relief against the adverse consequences of refusing relief. The ultimate decision calls for a value judgement'[5]. On the facts of *Tinsley*, Nicholls LJ held that it would be an affront to public conscience not to grant relief in this case.

1   [1991] 1 QB 24 at 44–46, where only Beldam LJ used this argument as the basis for his Lordship's decision. Balcombe and Dillon LJJ preferred other grounds for their decision.
2   [1986] 1 All ER 676 (claim against bankers for damages for negligence and for conversion of a cheque). This was subsequently developed by the Court of Appeal in decisions such as *Saunders v Edwards* [1987] 2 All ER 651, [1987] 1 WLR 1116. See also *Euro-Diam Ltd v Bathurst* [1990] 1 QB 1 and *Howard v Shirlstar Container Transport Ltd* [1990] 3 All ER 366, [1990] 1 WLR 1292.
3   Added by Nicholls LJ in *Saunders v Edwards* [1987] 1 WLR 1116 at 1132.
4   [1992] Ch 310. Lloyd LJ also adopted the test, albeit with some reluctance (at 339), but also based his decision on the ground that the illegality was collateral and incidental to the agreement.
5   [1992] Ch 310 at 319. See also Dickson 'Restitution and illegal transactions' Burrows (ed) *Essays on the Law of Restitution* (1991), ch 7.

14.67   This test was firmly rejected, however, by the House of Lords in *Tinsley v Milligan*[1]. Lord Browne-Wilkinson highlighted the uncertainty of the test, and that the effect of illegality cannot depend on such 'an imponderable factor'[2] as the extent to which the public conscience would be affronted by recognising rights created by illegal transactions. Lord Goff (although dissenting on the final decision) agreed. In his Lordship's view, the test was contrary to authority which had developed over 200 years, and such a reform should only be undertaken by the legislature after a full inquiry into the matter by the Law Commission[3].

1   [1994] 1 AC 340 at 364. Note comments also in *Nelson v Nelson* (1995) 184 CLR 538, particularly McHugh J who finds the Nicholls approach to be too broad and leaves the matter at large. McHugh J favoured an approach whereby the courts exercised a discretion subject to a number of guiding principles, see 184 CLR at 611–614.
2   [1994] 1 AC 340 at 369.
3   [1994] 1 AC 340 at 363. Lord Goff also refers ([1994] 1 AC at 364) to the more drastic reforms in New Zealand under the New Zealand Illegal Contracts Act 1970, s 7, which grants the court the power to grant relief by way of restitution as the court in its discretion thinks just. See below, para 14.68ff.

A discretionary approach

14.68   This approach has been adopted in New Zealand and Israel. The Illegal Contracts Act 1970 (NZ) grants the courts a wide discretion in dealing with the illegality defence. Whilst illegal contracts are unenforceable[1], the courts may grant relief 'by way of restitution, compensation, variation of the contract, validation of the contract in whole or part or for any particular purpose, or otherwise howsoever the Court in its discretion thinks just'[2]. Section 7(3) provides that:

In considering whether to grant relief under subsection (1) of this section the Court shall have regard to–

(a) the conduct of the parties; and
(b) in the case of a breach of an enactment, the object of the enactment and the gravity of the penalty expressly provided for any breach thereof; and
(c) such other matters as it thinks proper

but shall not grant relief if it considers that to do so would not be in the public interest.

This permits the courts a wide discretion to reach a just result in each case[3]. No hierarchy is set between the different provisions, and much is left for case-law development.

1   Illegal Contracts Act 1970 (NZ), s 6(1).
2   Illegal Contracts Act 1970 (NZ), s 7(1).
3   See generally Furmston 'The Illegal Contracts Act 1970 – An English View' (1972) 5 New Zealand Universities Law Review 151; and Beck 'Illegality and the courts' discretion: the New Zealand Illegal Contracts Act in action' (1989) 13 New Zealand Universities Law Review 389.

14.69   Similarly the Israeli Contracts (General Part) Act 1973, s 31, permits restitutionary claims where a contract is void for illegality, but the court may 'if it deems it just to do so and on such conditions as it sees fit, relieve a party [to the illegal contract] of the whole or part of the duty' to make restitution[1].

1   See further Cohen 'Illegality: the case for discretion' in Swadling (ed) *The Limits of Restitutionary Claims: A comparative analysis* (1997), ch 7; Friedmann 'Consequences of illegality under the Israeli Contract Law (General Part) Act 1973' (1984) 33 ICLQ 81; Cohen 'The quiet revolution in the enforcement of illegal contracts' [1994] Lloyds Maritime and Commercial Law Quarterly 163.

14.70   In the light of the dicta of the House of Lords in *Tinsley v Milligan*[1], such an approach is unlikely to find favour in the English courts. Many have expressed concern as to the uncertainty likely to result from such a broad discretion, although it has recently been suggested that the New Zealand model, after thirty years of operation, is working well and has not led to the uncertainty anticipated by many commentators[2]. Nevertheless, such models have not at present found favour with the English courts or legislature.

1   [1994] 1 AC 340 at 364; above, para 14.67.
2   See Buckley 'Illegal transactions: chaos or discretion?' (2000) 20 Legal Studies 155.

A structured discretion: Law Commission Consultation Paper no 154 'Illegal transactions – the effect of illegality on contracts and trusts' (1999)

14.71   This leaves a third option: reform following a study by the Law Commission. At present, the Law Commission are preparing the final report, but its Consultation Paper did recommend reform in this area of law. The Commission found that there was a need to retain an illegality doctrine of some kind[1], but proposed a structured discretion, which would guide the courts by requiring that, in reaching a decision on the effect of illegality, they should take into account[2]:

(1)   the seriousness of the illegality involved;
(2)   the knowledge and intention of the claimant;
(3)   whether denying relief will act as a deterrent;
(4)   whether denying relief will further the purpose of the rule which renders the contract illegal; and
(5)   whether denying relief is proportionate to the illegality involved.

On this basis, a court could decide that it was appropriate for the claimant to recover money or property despite the fact that it was transferred under an illegal transaction. Although a distinction is drawn between contracts which involve the commission of legal wrongs and contracts which are contrary to public policy in the context of enforcement[3], no such distinction applies in relation to claims for restitution.

1   See Law Commission Consultation Paper no 154 *Illegal transactions: the effect of illegality on contracts and trusts* (1999), para 6.12.
2   See Law Commission Consultation Paper no 154 *Illegal transactions: the effect of illegality on contracts and trusts* (1999), para 7.43. See generally Enonchong 'Illegal transactions: the future?' [2000] RLR 82.
3   The Law Commission found that there was no scope for a discretion to permit enforcement of a contract contrary to public policy, on the basis that the court in classifying the contract in this category would have already resolved that it was against the public interest to enforce such a contract: see Law Commission Consultation Paper no 154 *Illegal transactions: the effect of illegality on contracts and trusts* (1999), para 7.13.

14.72   The Law Commission also made proposals concerning the transfer or creation of property rights under illegal contracts, and in relation to the withdrawal exception. It proposes that a structured discretion would determine whether illegality would act as a defence to recognition of transferred or created property rights[1], but that it would not invalidate the disposition of property to a third party purchaser for value without notice of the illegality[2]. Withdrawal should only be permitted 'where allowing the party to withdraw would reduce the likelihood of an illegal act being completed or an illegal purpose being accomplished'[3].

1   See Law Commission Consultation Paper no 154 *Illegal transactions: the effect of illegality on contracts and trusts* (1999), para 7.26.
2   See Law Commission Consultation Paper no 154 *Illegal transactions: the effect of illegality on contracts and trusts* (1999), para 7.25. Such a provision is also present in the New Zealand Illegal Contracts Act 1970.
3   In deciding this question, courts are directed to consider the genuineness of any repentance (although it is not a necessary condition for the exercise of the discretion), and the seriousness of the illegality. Under the enforcement provisions recommended by the Law Commission, the claimant would also have to satisfy the court that the contract could not be enforced against him: see para 7.69.

14.73   Not all academic opinion, however, is in favour of such a discretion. It has been suggested, for example, that a discretion contains its own problems, and may be 'an inadequate substitute for the certainty in legal rules required by lawyers advising their clients'[1]. The final report of the Law Commission is expected in 2002. Such delay is due to the Law Commission expanding its remit to the effect of illegality in tort[2].

1   Rose 'Restitutionary and proprietary consequences of illegality' in Rose (ed) *Consensus ad idem: Essays on the Law of Contract in honour of Guenter Treitel* (1996), p 218. See also Virgo and O'Sullivan 'Resulting trusts and illegality' in Birks and Rose (eds) *Restitution and Equity* (2000), pp 103 at 118; but contrast Giliker 'Restitution, reform and illegality: an end to transactional uncertainty?' [2001] Singapore Journal of Legal Studies 102.
2   The Law Commission Consultation Paper no 160 was published recently: *The illegality defence in tort* (2001).

CHAPTER 15

Incapacity

Paula Giliker

A Introduction

15.1   Incapacity raises a number of important questions concerning the treatment of contracting parties who lack the ability to give real consent to a transaction. First, to what extent should such incapacity invalidate an agreement, particularly where the other party is unaware of the problem? Secondly, if the agreement is invalid, when may either the person lacking capacity or the other contracting party recover money paid or services rendered under the putative agreement? This raises a conflict between the policy of the courts in enforcing agreements which have the appearance of validity, and that of protecting those who lack the capacity to enter such agreements.

This chapter will discuss the conclusions reached by the courts and the legislature in dealing with these problems, and the extent to which restitution is possible in this context. Although there is some overlap, incapacity divides traditionally into three main categories: minors (ie children below the age of 18), persons suffering from a mental disorder (and, by analogy, persons under the influence of alcohol), and corporations. These three categories will thus be examined in turn. The case of the *public* corporation is briefly considered[1].

1   The case of public law ultra vires is considered in greater depth below, ch 18.

B Minors[1]

What is a minor?

15.2   A minor is defined by the Family Law Reform Act 1969, s 1, as a 'natural person who has not yet reached the age of 18'[2]. This overturned the earlier common law rule which set the age of majority at 21.

1   For an approach to this problem from a different angle see below, para 16.31.
2   As recommended by the Latey Committee (*Report of the Committee on the Age of Majority*, Cmnd 3342) and taking effect from 1 January 1970. Section 9 explains that: 'The time at which a person attains a particular age expressed in years shall be the commencement of the relevant anniversary of his birth'.

General rule[1]

15.3   The general rule is that a minor is not bound by a contract unless he or she chooses to ratify it when of age, or within a reasonable time of reaching majority[2]. It is therefore voidable at his or her option[3]. On this basis, the other contracting party cannot enforce the contract, for example, by suing for contractual damages. The other contracting party remains, however, bound by the contract[4]. The clear aim is to prevent the minor from exploitation. Yet the non-enforceability of the contract does not necessarily prevent property passing under an executed transaction[5]. Such property may only be recovered by an action for restitution.

1   For comparative studies, see Hartwig 'Infants' contracts in English law: With Commonwealth and European comparisons' (1966) 15 ICLQ 780; Valero 'The contractual capacity of minors in the English and French law of employment' (1978) 27 ICLQ 215.
2   *Nash v Inman* [1908] 2 KB 1 at 12. Ratification may be express or implied. It has been doubted whether a contract entered into by a very young child who is unable to understand the nature of the transaction would ever be enforceable: see *R v Oldham Metropolitan Borough Council, ex p Garlick* [1993] 1 FLR 645 at 662, per Scott LJ (affirmed without comment, [1993] AC 509).
3   Note that 'voidable' in this context does not signify that the transaction is valid unless rescinded, but that it will only be valid against the minor if he or she chooses to ratify the transaction. This should be contrasted with the exception for contracts valid until repudiation, discussed below, para 15.8.
4   *Bruce v Warwick* (1815) 6 Taunt 118, 128 ER 978. The courts would, however, be very unlikely to grant the minor specific performance: *Flight v Bolland* (1818) 4 Russ 298, 38 ER 817; and *Lumley v Ravenscroft* [1895] 1 QB 683.
5   *Chaplin v Leslie Frewin (Publishers) Ltd* [1966] Ch 71; *Stocks v Wilson* [1913] 2 KB 235 at 242. This is supported by the Minors' Contract Act 1987, s 3(1) (below, para 15.13).

Exceptions

NECESSARIES[1]

15.4   It would not be in the minor's interest to invalidate contracts providing necessary goods and services, and such contracts are thus valid[2]. 'Necessaries' are defined widely, and include not only basic goods and services such as food, clothing and accommodation, but those appropriate to the condition in life of the minor[3]. The Sale of Goods Act 1979, s 3(3), defines 'necessaries' as:

> Goods suitable to the condition in life of the minor or other person concerned and to his actual requirements at the time of the sale and delivery.

Although confined to goods, it is clear that the court must consider both the lifestyle of the minor and his *actual* requirements at the time of 'sale and delivery'[4]. In *Nash v Inman*[5], the court seemed to consider that waistcoats could in principle amount to necessaries for a Cambridge undergraduate. In contrast in *Ryder v Wombwell*[6], a pair of diamond ruby and gold cufflinks and an antique silver goblet were not necessaries, even though the minor was the younger son of a deceased baronet who moved in the 'highest society'. The burden is on the other contracting party to prove that the goods supplied are 'necessaries'[7]. Thus on the facts of *Nash v Inman*, a student who had purchased from the claimant clothing which included 11 fancy waistcoats, at two guineas each, was held not liable to pay. Although clothing may amount to a necessary good, the trader had not produced evidence which proved that the goods were suitable for the student's lifestyle, or that he was not already supplied with suitable clothing[8].

1   This section expounds the basic rules; for the basis of liability, see below, para 15.15ff.
2   Thereby ensuring that traders will deal with minors in relation to necessaries. The whole contract will not, however, be binding on the minor merely because the goods include certain necessary items, where the bulk of the goods are not necessaries (*Stocks v Wilson* [1913] 2 KB 235), although the courts have not always been willing to address this issue: see *Ryder v Wombwell* (1868) LR 3 Ex Ch 90.
3   *Peters v Fleming* (1840) 6 M & W 42, 151 ER 314.

4   The term 'sale and delivery' has caused some difficulties, in that it suggests that the court must assess the minor's actual needs both at the time of sale and the time of delivery – which may be some time apart. The general view is that no such significance should be placed on this term, which is probably derived from the formal action for goods sold and delivered: see Winfield 'Necessaries under the Sale of Goods Act 1893' (1942) 58 LQR 82 at 91. It would seem that the time of delivery is the appropriate time of assessment.

5   [1908] 2 KB 1. See also *Elkington & Co Ltd v Amery* [1936] 2 All ER 86 (diamond engagement and wedding rings for son of a former cabinet minister were considered necessaries).

6   (1868) LR 3 Ex Ch 90; revsd LR 4 Ex Ch 32. See also *Stocks v Wilson* [1913] 2 KB 235 (snuff-boxes, candlesticks, weapons from various countries and two gongs were not necessaries for a minor due to inherit £3,000 in 12 months time).

7   *Nash v Inman* [1908] 2 KB 1 at 5. This is a mixed question of fact and law. The court will not take account of the difficulties experienced by the tradesman in proving that the minor does not have an adequate supply (thereby reversing the general rule that the court will not impose a burden to prove a negative: *Joseph Constantine Steamship Line Ltd v Imperial Smelting Corpn Ltd* [1942] AC 154, HL). It is irrelevant that the trader had no knowledge of the minor's existing supplies: *Barnes & Co v Toye* (1884) 13 QBD 410; and *Johnstone v Marks* (1887) 19 QBD 509.

8   [1908] 2 KB 1.

15.5   The contract must also be beneficial to the minor if it is to be upheld[1]. The courts take a broad view, and consider the contract as a whole. They will not therefore consider particular clauses of the contract out of context. In *Clements v London and North Western Rly Co*[2], a minor was employed on terms that he would relinquish his rights to sue for personal injuries under the Employers' Liability Act 1880, and agree to join the employers' insurance scheme. The Court of Appeal ruled that the contract, taken as a whole, was for his benefit. Although the damages under the scheme were likely to be less than those available under the Act, the scheme was not confined to accidents for which the employer would be liable at law, and compensation was automatic, thereby avoiding the risks and delays of litigation. In contrast, in *De Francesco v Barnum*[3], an apprenticeship deed provided that for seven years, the minor would be taught stage dancing on strict terms which forbade her from undertaking any professional engagement (or even to marry) without the defendants' consent, and which made no provision for payment save for professional engagements, which the master was under no obligation to provide. The Court of Appeal held that such provisions conferred inordinate power on the master without any correlative obligations, and were thus not for the benefit of the minor. The contract was unenforceable.

1   *Fawcett v Smethurst* (1914) 84 LJKB 473 (the contract will not be enforced if it contains harsh or onerous terms). See also *Flower v London and North Western Rly Co* [1894] 2 QB 65.

2   [1894] 2 QB 482.

3   (1890) 45 Ch D 430.

15.6   These last two cases additionally highlight the fact that contracts for necessaries cannot be restricted to the supply of goods and services[1], but will also include contracts of employment or education which provide the minor with a living, or the means to earn a living. The courts again take a broad view, and such contracts extend to analogous contracts such as that between a boxer and the British Boxing Board of Control, under which the minor was given a licence to box[2], and a minor whose memoirs were to be ghost-written and his publisher[3]. This category does not, however, extend to trading contracts, which, even if beneficial to the minor, will not be treated as contracts for necessaries, and are therefore not binding on the minor[4].

1   Examples of services include medical services (*Dale v Copping* (1610) 1 Bulst 39, 80 ER 743; and *Huggins v Wiseman* (1690) Carth 110, 90 ER 669, although free provision under the NHS may render these cases defunct); funeral services (*Chapple v Cooper* (1844) 13 M & W 252, 153 ER 105: burial of husband of minor widow); legal services (*Helps v Clayton* (1864) 17 CB NS 553,

144 ER 222); and even the hire of a car to fetch the minor's luggage from a station (*Fawcett v Smethurst* (1914) 84 LJKB 473).

2 *Doyle v White City Stadium Ltd* [1935] 1 KB 110, where a licence was required to box professionally. The rule applies even where the contract, on the facts of the case, operated to the detriment of the minor.

3 *Chaplin v Leslie Frewin (Publishers) Ltd* [1966] Ch 71 (on the basis that it would enable him to make a start as an author and support his family).

4 *Cowern v Nield* [1912] 2 KB 419; *Mercantile Union Guarantee Corpn v Ball* [1937] 2 KB 498. The reason for this distinction is said to be that, by engaging in trade, the minor necessarily risks his or her capital: Treitel *Law of Contract* (10th edn, 1999), p 504. There is no precise definition of a 'trading contract' in the case law.

15.7   Where an adult has provided a loan to a minor to purchase necessaries, liability will depend on the use to which the money has been put. Where the infant has actually spent the money on necessaries, he or she will be liable in equity to repay the money lent, and the lender will stand in the place of the tradesman who has supplied the necessaries[1]. Where the money has been lent for this purpose, but used otherwise, the minor will not be liable[2].

1 *Marlow v Pitfeild* (1719) 1 P Wms 558, 24 ER 516; and *Re National Permanent Benefit Building Society* (1869) 5 Ch App 309 at 313, thereby invoking the principles of subrogation, on which see above, ch 8. Equally, if necessaries are purchased for the minor at his or her request, a claim will lie: *Ellis v Ellis* (1698) Comb 482, 90 ER 605. The same principles would appear to apply to those suffering under a mental disorder (and by analogy drunkenness) discussed below (see below para 15.19ff): see *Re Beavan* [1912] 1 Ch 196 (bank advancing money for necessaries to pay off the creditors of a person suffering from mental incapacity may stand in the shoes of the creditors paid by son).

2 *Darby v Boucher* (1693) 1 Salk 279, 91 ER 244; and *Marlow v Pitfeild* (1719) 1 P Wms 558, 24 ER 516. See above, para 8.54.

CONTRACTS VALID UNTIL REPUDIATION

15.8   Contracts which confer on the minor property of a permanent nature, with continuous or recurring obligations attached, are valid unless repudiated before or within a reasonable time of coming of age[1]. Examples include a contract to acquire shares in a company whereby the minor is liable for calls[2], or an interest in land with continuing obligations, such as a lease[3]. If the minor wishes to repudiate, he or she must act within a reasonable period of time after the age of 18 (to be judged on the facts of the case)[4], and disclaim any property received under the agreement. Any obligations arising after repudiation will not be enforceable, but it would appear that the minor is liable for obligations arising prior to this date[5].

1 *North Western Rly Co v M'Michael* (1850) 5 Ex Ch 114, 155 ER 49; affd 5 Exch 855, 155 ER 374. For the law relating to partnerships, see *Goode v Harrison* (1821) 5 B & Ald 147 at 157, 106 ER 1147 at 1150; and *Lovell and Christmas v Beauchamp* [1894] AC 607 at 611, per Lord Herschell LC (a minor will not become liable to partnership creditors, but if he or she chooses to repudiate the agreement, the minor will not be entitled to any share in the profits until all debts and liabilities to third parties have been met).

2 See for example *Steinberg v Scala (Leeds) Ltd* [1923] 2 Ch 452.

3 See *Ketsey's Case* (1613) Cro Jac 320, 79 ER 274. Although a minor may not hold a legal estate in land (Law of Property Act 1925, s 1(6)), he or she may hold an equitable estate.

4 *Edwards v Carter* [1893] AC 360 (marriage settlement).

5 *Steinberg v Scala (Leeds) Ltd* [1923] 2 Ch 452, although this is a matter of dispute: see Hudson 'Contracts relating to property of a permanent nature' (1957) 35 Canadian Bar Review 1213; and *North Western Rly v M'Michael* (1850) 5 Ex 114 at 125, 155 ER 49 at 54.

Restitution by the minor

15.9   It is clear that a minor may recover money paid under an unenforceable contract, provided he or she can show a total failure of consideration. A number of examples may be used to illustrate this. In *Steinberg v Scala (Leeds) Ltd*[1], the minor had been allotted shares, but 18 months later, while still a minor, she sought to repudiate the contract and recover the money paid. It was held that she had received due performance of the contract (ie the receipt of shares), and could not show total failure of consideration.

Equally in *Pearce v Brain*[2], a minor had exchanged his motorcycle and sidecar for the defendant's second hand car. The car broke down after about 70 miles due to a defect in the back axle, and the minor then sought to repudiate the contract and recover his motorbike and sidecar, or their value. The Divisional Court again found no total failure of consideration, and held the same rule applied to both money and goods.

1   [1923] 2 Ch 452. See also *Austen v Gervas* (1703) Hob 77, 80 ER 226; *Holmes v Blogg* (1818) 8 Taunt 508, 129 ER 481 (no total failure of consideration); *Corpe v Overton* (1833) 10 Bing 252, 131 ER 901 (total failure of consideration); *Re Burrows, ex p Taylor* (1856) 8 De GM & G 254, 44 ER 388; *Everitt v Wilkins* (1874) 29 LT 846.
2   [1929] 2 KB 310.

15.10   It has been questioned whether a minor should be able to recover in a case where he or she has received property but is able and willing to return it[1]. Some support for this proposition may be derived from *Valentini v Canali*[2]. Here, a minor had entered a lease for a furnished property, which he had occupied for several months. Lord Coleridge CJ rejected his claim to recover money paid on account on the basis that under the lease, the minor had obtained the use of the house and furniture, and that: 'He could not give back this benefit or replace the defendant in the position in which he was before the contract'[3]. Such a comment may be taken in two ways: first, to support a requirement of total failure of consideration (as it was taken in *Pearce v Brain*), or secondly, as favoured by modern restitution writers, as an indication that *if* the minor could have returned the benefits received, he could have recovered his money[4].

This somewhat tenuous second argument received little support from the majority in *Chaplin v Frewin*[5]. Here, the son of Charlie Chaplin, whilst still a minor, had contracted with a firm of publishers to produce his memoirs, which would be ghost-written on his behalf, and for which he received advance royalties of £400[6]. Having assigned his rights to the publisher and approved the proofs, he later experienced a change of heart, and sought to restrain publication, on the grounds that the contract was not for his benefit, and that the copyright of the manuscript was still vested in him. The majority of the Court of Appeal found the contract to be, as a whole, for his benefit, and therefore binding, and that the copyright had in any event passed under the contract. Lord Denning, dissenting, held that, despite the receipt of benefits, the minor should be able to recover the copyright for the work[7]. His Lordship distinguished *Steinberg* and *Pearce v Brain* on the basis that they related to transfers by delivery, and not transfers, as in the present case, which required deed or writing to be effective. With all due respect, this seems artificial, and it is unlikely that a modern court would justify recovery on this basis. It does raise important questions, however, as to whether a modern court *should* continue to require total failure of consideration as a condition for recovery[8].

1   Note the debate between Treitel and Atiyah: Treitel 'The Infants Relief Act, 1874' (1957) 73 LQR 194, Atiyah 'The Infants Relief Act, 1874 – A reply' (1958) 74 LQR 97 at 101–103, and Treitel 'The Infants Relief Act, 1874 – A short rebutter' (1958) 74 LQR 104.
2   (1889) 24 QBD 166.
3   (1889) 24 QBD 166 at 167.
4   See for example Goff and Jones *Law of Restitution* (5th edn, 1998), pp 641 and 642; and Virgo *Principles of the Law of Restitution* (1999), p 418.
5   *Chaplin v Leslie Frewin (Publishers) Ltd* [1966] Ch 71.
6   A further £200 was paid to the ghost-writers.
7   He also found that the contract was not beneficial in any event, arguing ([1966] Ch 71 at 88) that it purveyed scandalous information, brought shame and disgrace on others, invaded the privacy of family life and exposed the minor to the risk of claims for libel.
8   For example, Goff and Jones *Law of Restitution* (5th edn, 1998), p 643 support Denning's judgment on the basis that, provided the minor returned the money received, he could prove failure of consideration. Note challenges to the requirement of *total* failure of consideration (*Goss v Chilcott* [1996] AC 788) and subversion of this rule in cases such as *Rowland v Divall* [1923] 2 KB 500 and *Butterworth v Kingsway Motors Ltd* [1954] 2 All ER 694: see further below, para 19.14ff.

15.11   One further point to note is that the fact that the adult is willing and able to perform under the contract, and that the failure was due to the act of the minor in repudiating the contract, does not affect the availability of this remedy for the minor. This is in contrast to the ordinary rule applying to claims based on total failure of consideration[1].

1   *Thomas v Brown* (1876) 1 QBD 714; see below, para 19.8, and Burrows *Law of Restitution* (1993), p 325.

Restitution by the other contracting party

NO CLAIM FOR TOTAL FAILURE OF CONSIDERATION

15.12   There is clear authority that only a minor may recover money or goods transferred for a total failure of consideration. In *Cowern v Nield*[1], the claimant ordered some clover and hay from a minor, and paid him in advance. Although the clover was delivered, it was rightfully returned as rotten; and the hay was never delivered. The court rejected the claimant's action for money paid as a total failure of consideration. It was held that the contract was unenforceable, and this would obstruct any claim unless it was based solely in tort[2]. This was supported two years later by the Court of Appeal in *R Leslie Ltd v Sheill*[3].

Such reasoning is based on the assumption that total failure of consideration is a contractual remedy, and that any remedy would be inconsistent with the general rule that a contract cannot be enforced against a minor. In view of House of Lords authority overturning the view of restitution as based on an implied contract[4], it must be questioned whether a claim would now lie in the modern law of unjust enrichment. At present, no clear answer exists. Some authors have favoured a position in which recovery should be permitted only if it restores the status quo, and does not indirectly enforce the contract[5]. Other authors have been more forthright, and argued that a claim for restitution should lie subject to the defence of change of position[6]. Although there is much to be said for the former, less radical, option, the fact remains that unless a court accepts one of these arguments, no claim will lie under this head.

1   [1912] 2 KB 419.
2   Relying on *Bristow v Eastman* (1794) 1 Esp 172 at 173, 170 ER 317 at 317–318, per Lord Kenyon (which allows 'waiver of tort' where it would not indirectly enforce the contract). On 'waiver of tort' see above, para 12.2ff.
3   [1914] 3 KB 607.

4   See in particular *Westdeutsche Landesbank Girozentrale v Islington London Borough Council* [1996] AC 669 at 710, and contrast it with Lord Sumner in *Leslie Ltd v Sheill* [1914] 3 KB 607 at 613: 'To money had and received and other indebitatus counts infancy was a defence just as to any other actions in contract.' See above, para 1.12.
5   See Goff and Jones *Law of Restitution* (5th edn, 1998), pp 645 and 646 and adopted by Beale (ed) *Chitty on Contracts* (28th edn, 1999), vol 1, para 8–046.
6   For example, Virgo *Principles of the Law of Restitution* (1999), pp 759 and 760 argues that a claim for restitution should lie subject to the defence of change of position, which would adequately protect the minor, particularly if applied flexibly. On the change of position defence see below, para 21.37ff.

Minors' Contracts Act 1987

15.13   This Act, which followed from Law Commission Report No 134 (*Minors' Contracts*) in 1984, repealed[1] the Infants Relief Act 1874, by which contracts with minors were, subject to certain exceptions, rendered void. Section 3(1) provides for restitutionary relief in favour of a claimant dealing with a minor:

Where–

(a)   a person ('the plaintiff') has after the commencement of this Act entered into a contract with another ('the defendant'), and

(b)   the contract is unenforceable against the defendant (or he repudiates it) because he was a minor when the contract was made,

the court may, if it is just and equitable to do so, require the defendant to transfer to the plaintiff any property acquired by the defendant under the contract, or any property representing it.

This provides the court with a discretion to transfer to the other contracting party 'property acquired'. The wording is less than helpful. 'Property' is not defined, but would seem to include goods transferred under the contract, or property representing the original property (for example, the minor exchanges a car for a motorbike, or sells the car for £500[2]). There is also little indication how the court should exercise its discretion[3]. Where the property obtained has been dissipated by the minor, no remedy will exist[4].

1   See the Minors' Contracts Act 1987, s 4(2): in force 9 June 1987.
2   It is more contentious whether 'property acquired' includes money paid. This is certainly not the impression given by the Law Commission Working Paper no 81 *Minors' Contracts* (1982), para 6.12. Nevertheless, the Working Paper does accept that 'any property representing' the property passing under the contract will include the proceeds of sale, and this has encouraged Treitel to argue for a broader meaning (*Law of Contract* (10th edn, 1999), p 512).
3   This reflects a deliberate decision by the Law Commission not to fetter too closely the courts' powers to do justice according to the circumstances of each case: see Law Commission Report no 134, para 4.20. Treitel *Law of Contract* (10th edn, 1999), p 513 suggests that the courts will refer to the equity cases (discussed below, paras 15.16–15.18) and to the fairness of the original contract.
4   The Law Commission finding in its Report (no 134) at para 4.23 that granting a remedy in such circumstances would amount to indirect enforcement of the contract against the minor.

15.14   The section also leaves the common law intact[1]. Thus any common law grounds for recovery (for example, necessaries[2] and equity[3]) may also be used by the contracting party.

1   Section 3(2): 'Nothing in this section shall be taken to prejudice any other remedy available to the plaintiff'.
2   See below, para 15.15.
3   See below, paras 15.16–15.18.

NECESSARIES

15.15 Whilst it is not contested that a minor will be liable to the other contracting party for necessaries supplied[1], it is a matter of contention whether recovery is based on restitution or contract law. Most commentators in this field are divided[2], although the traditional view is that liability is restitutionary in nature. This question is not purely academic. If liability is based on restitution[3], no claim will lie under an executory contract. Where a defendant has yet to receive goods or services, it will be impossible to argue that he or she has been unjustly enriched. A mere promise does not give rise to enrichment, performance is required.

The authority which exists may be used to support both arguments. The classic example is that of *Nash v Inman* in which Lord Justice Fletcher Moulton supports an explanation in restitution[4], whilst Lord Justice Buckley is equally convinced that recovery is based on the rules of contract law[5]. The Sale of Goods Act 1979, s 3(2), also gives limited assistance. This section states that 'Where necessaries are sold and delivered to a minor ... he must pay a reasonable price for them'. The requirement of a 'reasonable price', rather than the price stipulated by the contract, would suggest a restitutionary claim[6], but it has been argued that the term merely refers to the fact that the contract must be beneficial to the minor, ie he or she may only be charged a 'reasonable price'[7]. Equally, other terms of the Sale of Goods Act imply a 'reasonable price' into a valid contract[8], and interference with one term of a transaction does not necessarily signify the invalidity of the contract as a whole[9].

The main obstacle to the restitutionary explanation is the existence of authority which supports a claim under an executory contract. In *Roberts v Gray*[10], Roberts, a professional billiards player, had agreed to take Gray on a world tour and pay all hotel and travelling expenses. As a contract of 'education', it was thus a contract for necessaries. Gray withdrew before the tour began, but not before Roberts had incurred costs in preparing for the tour. The Court of Appeal found the contract to be binding as a contract for necessaries, and expressly questioned why a contract should 'cease to be binding merely because it is still executory'[11]. This would appear to support a contractual analysis. Subsequent attempts to draw distinctions between contracts for services (contractual) and contracts for goods (restitutionary), or simply to distinguish contracts of employment as a separate category[12], have been far from convincing. Yet, the case itself is of limited authority. Due to Roberts' preparatory work, some performance had already taken place and so the contract had been partially executed. Equally, it is an isolated case with limited case-law support[13]. It must be questioned whether a modern court would be willing to intervene to enforce an executory contract for necessaries.

1 See above, para 15.4ff.
2 For example, Goff and Jones *Law of Restitution* (5th edn, 1998), p 639 give some support for a contractual explanation, whilst Birks *An Introduction to the Law of Restitution* (revised edn, 1989), p 436; and Miles 'The infant's liability for necessaries' (1927) 43 LQR 389 argue that it is restitutionary.
3 For example on an unjust ground of 'necessity' or 'moral compulsion', although it must be stated that the existence of these heads of liability is far from established in English law, which arguably consists of a series of ad hoc circumstances in which the courts have chosen to intervene. This contrasts with the more principled approach adopted in civil law systems based on the Roman law doctrine of *negotiorum gestio*: see, for example, Arts 1372–1375 of the French *Code civil*. See above, para 16.7.
4 *Nash v Inman* [1908] 2 KB 1 at 8. See also his judgment in *Re J* [1909] 1 Ch 574 at 577, relying on *Re Rhodes* (1890) 44 Ch D 94, on which see below, paras 15.21 and 16.39ff.

5 *Nash v Inman* [1908] 2 KB 1 at 12. See also per Lord Hanworth MR in *Doyle v White City Stadium Ltd* [1935] 1 KB 110 at 123–124.
6 See *Pontypridd Union v Drew* [1927] 1 KB 214 at 220, per Scrutton LJ.
7 Goff and Jones *Law of Restitution* (5th edn, 1998), p 639.
8 See ss 8–9 for example, although admittedly in a very different context (where a price has not been determined).
9 See Treitel *Law of Contract* (10th edn, 1999), p 501.
10 [1913] 1 KB 520.
11 [1913] 1 KB 520 at 530, per Hamilton LJ.
12 See for example Furmston *Cheshire Fifoot and Furmston's Law of Contract* (14th edn, 2001), pp 480 and 481; and Winfield 'Necessaries under the Sale of Goods Act 1893' (1942) 58 LQR 82.
13 See *Ive v Chester* (1619) Cro Jac 560, 79 ER 480; and *Delaval v Clare* (1625) Lat 156, 82 ER 323.

EQUITY AND FRAUD[1]

15.16   Whilst it is often difficult for the contracting party to gauge the age of the other party, this is made particularly problematic when the minor falsely claims to be of age. This naturally raises questions as to the level of protection a fraudulent minor should receive from the courts. Although the case-law lacks clarity, in a number of cases the courts have been prepared to assist adults in equity, although such intervention will only take place where the court is satisfied that any remedy given will not amount to indirect enforcement of the contract. This is consistent with the general rule stated above and applied in relation to parallel claims in tort, as illustrated by cases such as *Jennings v Rundall*[2] and *Burnard v Haggis*[3]. Recovery of money or goods passing under the contract will thus be dependent on the *effect* of intervention. Where the claim is to restore goods acquired under the contract, the courts will generally intervene[4], but claims for money passing under a contract of loan have generally received a hostile reception, on the basis that allowing recovery here would amount to indirect enforcement of the contract[5]. As Lord Sumner explained in *Leslie Ltd v Sheill*[6], equity 'scrupulously stopped short of enforcing against [the minor] a contractual obligation entered into while he was an infant, even by means of a fraud ... Restitution stopped where repayment began'.

A decision more favourable to recovery may be found in the judgment of Lush J in *Stocks v Wilson*[7]. Here, a minor had claimed to be of full age, and had obtained various non-necessary goods on credit, some of which he had then resold for £30 and, with the consent of the claimant's agents, the remainder had been used as security for a loan of £100. Lush J held the defendant liable in equity to return both the £30 and the £100, holding that 'this is a very different thing from making him liable to pay damages or compensation for the loss of the other party's bargain'[8]. The judge took no notice of the fact that the goods in question had been sold, and that the claim was in fact for the proceeds of this sale[9]. More controversially, the judge at no stage considered whether the defendant still retained those funds. This aspect of the decision was doubted (although not overruled) in *R Leslie Ltd v Sheill*[10]. There, a minor had defaulted on a loan obtained by falsely claiming to be of full age, and the Court of Appeal, applying the rule stated above, refused to force the minor to return the money in question. Lord Sumner challenged the view of Lush J that a general jurisdiction existed to permit the return of any benefits fraudulently received[11], and this latter view seems to have prevailed in modern law.

1 See Atiyah 'The liability of infants in fraud and restitution' (1959) 22 MLR 273.
2 (1799) 8 Term Rep 335, 101 ER 1419 (no liability for wrongful and injurious riding of a horse under a contract of hire, as this would amount to indirect enforcement of the contract). See also *Johnson v Pye* (1665) 1 Sid 258, 82 ER 1091.

3 (1863) 14 CBNS 45, 143 ER 360 (liable in tort where defendant's conduct was expressly prohibited by contract, and could not be said to be within the object and purpose of the contract). See also authority permitting recovery on the basis of 'waiver of tort': *Bristow v Eastman* (1794) 1 Esp 172 at 173, 170 ER 317 at 317–318, where the court ordered a minor to return money embezzled from his employer, where the tort was not connected with his contract. On 'waiver of tort' see above, para 12.2ff.
4 See *Clarke v Cobley* (1789) 2 Cox Eq Cas 173, 30 ER 80; and *Lemprière v Lange* (1879) 12 Ch D 675.
5 See *Leslie Ltd v Sheill* [1914] 3 KB 607 at 613; *Clarke v Cobley* (1789) 2 Cox Eq Cas 173, 30 ER 80; and *Levene v Brougham* (1908–1909) 25 TLR 265.
6 [1914] 3 KB 607 at 618.
7 [1913] 2 KB 235.
8 [1913] 2 KB 235 at 242.
9 This was acknowledged to be correct by Lord Browne-Wilkinson in *Westdeutsche Landesbank Girozentrale v Islington London Borough Council* [1996] AC 669 at 716, on the principles of equitable tracing.
10 [1914] 3 KB 607.
11 [1914] 3 KB 607 at 619; his Lordship drawing a distinction between 'restoring' property in one's possession, and 'refunding' monies, which would amount to indirect enforcement of the contract (see also above, para 15.13, n 4). Note that Lord Browne-Wilkinson ([1996] AC 669 at 716) also confines his approval of *Stocks v Wilson* to the 'restoration' of property.

15.17   Equity will also intervene to relieve the other contracting party of any obligations undertaken as a result of the minor's fraudulent misrepresentation, provided of course that this does not require the court to enforce the contract. Thus in *Clarke v Cobley*[1], where the minor had given a bond to a creditor in return for the delivery of certain promissory notes signed by his wife, the court ruled that, although the bond was void for incapacity, the notes should be returned. It refused, however, to order repayment of the money due, on the basis that this would amount to indirect enforcement of the contract.

1 (1789) 2 Cox Eq Cas 173, 30 ER 80. See also *Lemprière v Lange* (1879) 12 Ch D 675 (lease cancelled and possession to be given up).

15.18   This is a complicated area of law, and it is unfortunate that the Minors' Contracts Act 1987 has yet to be relied upon[1]. A broad interpretation of s 3 would avoid significant injustice in this area of law. Its neglect, however, does suggest that there is little interest in litigation in this field – a fact no doubt accentuated by the lowering of the age of majority in 1970. Such difficulties may thus, in practice, be simply of theoretical interest.

1 A search of LEXIS in April 2002 revealed no cases under the Act.

C   Persons suffering a mental disorder[1]

What is a mental disorder?

15.19   A 'patient', as defined the Mental Health Act 1983, Pt VII[2], will obviously fall within this category. It would seem that such a person is incapable per se of entering a contract, in that it would be inconsistent with the management of his or her property by the Court of Protection[3].

Otherwise it is a question whether, at the time of contracting, the person was capable of understanding the nature and quality of the actions in question[4].

1 For an approach to this problem from a different angle, see below, para 16.32ff.
2 See the Mental Health Act 1983, s 94(2): 'The functions of the judge ... shall be exercisable where, after considering medical evidence, he is satisfied that a person is incapable, by reason of

mental disorder, of managing and administering his property and affairs; and a person as to whom the judge is so satisfied is referred to in this Part of this Act as a patient'.

3 *Re Walker* [1905] 1 Ch 160 (even where the contract is made during a lucid interval). The case was applied in *Re Marshall* [1920] 1 Ch 284, but contrast *Baldwyn v Smith* [1900] 1 Ch 588.

4 *Boughton v Knight* (1873) LR 3 PD 64 at 72, per Sir J Hannen; *Ball v Mannin* (1829) 3 Bli NS 1, 4 ER 1241; and *Re Beaney* [1978] 1 WLR 770, in which the court held that the degree of understanding would vary according to the circumstances, from a low degree for a contract or gift where the subject matter and value were trivial, to as high a degree as was required for a will, where the effect of the gift was to dispose of the donor's only asset of value, thus pre-empting its devolution as part of the donor's estate under his will or on intestacy.

General rule

15.20   This is stated by Lord Esher in *Imperial Loan Co Ltd v Stone*[1]:

> When a person enters into a contract, and afterwards alleges that he was so insane at the time that he did not know what he was doing, and proves the allegation, the contract is as binding on him in every respect, whether it is executory or executed, as if he had been sane when he made it, unless he can prove further that the person with whom he contracted knew him to be so insane as not to be capable of understanding what he was about.

It is therefore not enough for the claimant to state that he or she lacked capacity at the time the contract was made. The claimant must also prove that, at that time, the other contracting party knew or ought to have known of his or her incapacity. This appears a harsh rule[2], which differs from the rules applying to minors, and places security of transactions ahead of protection of the weaker party[3]. The rule has been challenged in New Zealand[4], but the Privy Council, faced with such authority, chose in *Hart v O'Connor*[5] to confirm the rule in *Imperial*. Their Lordships rejected the argument that the court should intervene to protect persons with a mental incapacity from transactions which were substantively 'unfair'. As stated by Lord Brightman[6]:

> The validity of a contract entered into by a lunatic who is ostensibly sane is to be judged by the same standards as a contract by a person of sound mind, and is not voidable by the lunatic or his representatives by reason of 'unfairness' unless such unfairness amounts to equitable fraud which would have enabled the complaining party to avoid the contract even if he had been sane.

On this basis, any contract will be valid unless proved otherwise, in which case the claimant may seek to rescind the contract.

1 [1892] 1 QB 599 at 601. See also *Molton v Camroux* (1848) 2 Exch 487, 154 ER 584; on appeal 4 Exch 17, 154 ER 1107; *York Glass Co Ltd v Jubb* (1924) 131 LT 559; on appeal 134 LT 36; *Manches v Trimborn* (1946) 115 LJKB 305; Fridman 'Mental incompetency' (1963) 79 LQR 502 and (1964) 80 LQR 84; *Hart v O'Connor* [1985] AC 1000.

2 See Goudy 'Contracts by lunatics' (1901) 17 LQR 147 at 151: 'if of two innocent parties one must suffer, surely the courts ought to favour that one who is least capable of guarding his own interests'; but note Wilson 'Lunacy in relation to contract, tort and crime' (1902) 18 LQR 21. The claimant may, however, be able to utilise the law relating to undue influence (above, para 10.31ff) or *non est factum* (Furmston (ed) *Law of Contract* (1999), para 4.111f).

3 It has been suggested that it can be justified on the basis that whilst a businessman can verify the age of a minor, he would find it difficult to verify the mental status of the other contracting party by mere inquiry: see Burrows *Law of Restitution* (1993), p 327.

4 *Archer v Cutler* [1980] 1 NZLR 386. For comment see Beatson 'Unconscionability: placebo or pill?' (1981) 1 OJLS 426 and Hudson 'Mental incapacity in the law of contract and property' [1984] Conv 32.

5 [1985] AC 1000. For comment see Hudson 'Mental incapacity revisited' [1986] Conv 178, arguing that this places the insane at a very serious disadvantage to their sane equivalent.

6 [1985] AC 1000 at 1027.

Exception for necessaries[1]

15.21   In common with minors above, it would seem that the person suffering due to mental incapacity will be liable to pay for necessaries[2]. The Sale of Goods Act 1979, s 3(2), provides that:

> Where necessaries are sold and delivered ... to a person who by reason of mental incapacity or drunkenness is incompetent to contract, he must pay a reasonable price for them.

Common law authority prior to the Act, viz the Court of Appeal in *Re Rhodes*[3], held that, in this context at least[4], liability was founded on the principles of restitution, not contract, and, on this basis, it would seem that no remedy would lie under an executory contract[5]. The claim for necessaries failed in *Re Rhodes* due to the failure of the claimants to establish an intention to be repaid. Assuming this applies to the statute, this will exclude claims by those providing necessaries out of pity for the plight of the individual in question.

1   Necessary goods are defined in the Sale of Goods Act 1979, s 3(3). For discussion see above, para 15.4.
2   And see above, para 15.7, n 1, on the possibility of subrogation.
3   (1890) 44 Ch D 94.
4   Cotton LJ refers ((1890) 44 Ch D at 105) to 'a person who by reason of disability cannot himself contract', which suggests support for a restitutionary explanation beyond those suffering from mental incapacity.
5   Winfield argues that the decision was made 3 years before the Sale of Goods Act 1893, and was therefore likely to be in the mind of the drafters of the Act: 'Necessaries under the Sale of Goods Act 1893' (1942) 58 LQR 82 at 87. See also Matthews 'Contracts for necessaries and mental incapacity' (1982) 33 NILQ 148.

D   Persons under the influence of alcohol

General rule

15.22   The *Imperial* rule[1] applies equally to those acting under the influence of alcohol[2]. The claimant must thus prove (a) that he or she was not capable of understanding the nature of the actions in question, and (b) that the other party knew or ought to have realised his or her condition to render the contract voidable. Here the question of knowledge would appear to be easier to prove, in that the fact that a person is so drunk as to be incapable is likely to be obvious to the other contracting party. It would seem logical that the same rules should apply to those under the influence of drugs.

Although there is limited authority in this area of law, a good example may be found in *Matthews v Baxter*[3]. Here the defendant, while drunk, had agreed at an auction to purchase certain houses and land. Afterwards, when sober, he ratified and confirmed the contract. It was held that 'a drunken man when he recovers his senses might insist on the fulfillment of his bargain, and therefore that he can ratify it so as to bind himself to a performance of it[4].

1   See above, para 15.20.
2   See *Gore v Gibson* (1845) 13 M & W 623, 153 ER 260; and *Moulton v Camroux* (1849) 4 Ex Ch 17 at 19, 154 ER 1107 at 1108 (in which the court treats mental incapacity and drunkenness as subject to the same legal rules). Note also the comments of Millett LJ in *Barclays Bank plc v Schwartz* [1995] CLY 2492. Beale (ed) *Chitty on Contracts* (28th edn, 1999), vol 1, para 8–077, also suggests that authority exists which supports a wider equitable jurisdiction to set aside unfair or unconscionable transactions, although the English authority cited is old: *Cory v Cory* (1747) 1 Ves Sen 19, 27 ER 864; *Cooke v Clayworth* (1811) 18 Ves 12, 34 ER 222; *Butler v Mulvihill*

(1823) 1 Bligh 137, 4 ER 49; *Wiltshire v Marshall* (1866) 14 LT 396; and *Blomley v Ryan* (1956) 99 CLR 362 (on which see above, para 10.4).
3   (1873) LR 8 Ex 132.
4   (1873) LR 8 Ex 132 at 134, per Martin B, although in the case the party was seeking to avoid the agreement in question.

Exception for necessaries

15.23   Section 3(2) of the Sale of Goods Act 1979 equally applies to those acting under the influence of alcohol and the provisions applying to necessaries described above[1] apply equally in this context.

1   See above, para 15.21.

E   Corporations

What is a corporation?

15.24   In this section we will concentrate on statutory corporations, that is, principally companies incorporated under the Companies Act 1985. Corporations created by charter have the power to bind themselves in the same manner as ordinary individuals, and no specific difficulties arise[1].

1   *Baroness Wenlock v River Dee Co* (1883) 36 Ch D 675 at 685, per Bowen LJ (affirmed (1885) 10 App Cas 354, HL). The courts may intervene, however, where the corporation acts outside its charter, either by granting a member an injunction, or where the corporation has persistently acted outside its charter, by welcoming an application from the Attorney-General for revocation of the charter: see *Jenkins v Pharmaceutical Society of Great Britain* [1921] 1 Ch 392 and, generally, Farrar and Hannigan *Farrar's Company Law* (4th edn, 1998), p 99. It should also be noted that unincorporated associations have no legal identity, and hence no contractual capacity. Actions may therefore only be brought against individual members found to be acting in their own right: see *Bradley Egg Farm Ltd v Clifford* [1943] 2 All ER 378.

The common law position

15.25   Where a corporation acts outside its powers stated by statute or the objects stated in its memorandum of association, it is acting ultra vires. At common law, such contracts are void, and may not be ratified subsequently by the shareholders of the company[1]. It would seem, however, that either or both parties may bring a claim for total failure of consideration[2].

The aim is to protect those dealing with these institutions[3]. In practice, however, it places these third parties at a particular disadvantage, in that they cannot realistically be expected to appreciate, or verify, the limits of the corporation's powers, and they run the constant risk of such transactions subsequently being declared void.

1   *Ashbury Railway Carriage and Iron Co Ltd v Riche* (1875) LR 7 HL 653; and *City of Sydney v Chappell Bros & Co* (1910) 43 SCR 478.
2   See *Phoenix Life Assurance Co, Burges and Stock's Case* (1862) 2 John & H 441, 70 ER 1131, where a company was found liable for premiums obtained under ultra vires marine insurance policies; and *Brougham v Dwyer* (1913) 108 LT 504, 29 TLR 234, where a building society was entitled to recover money loaned under ultra vires lending contracts. See also *Flood v Irish Provident Assurance Co Ltd* [1912] 2 Ch 597n, 46 ILT 214, and the obiter comments of Mocatta J in *Bell Houses Ltd v City Wall Property Ltd* [1966] 1 QB 207 at 226 (point left open on appeal, [1966] 2 QB 656 at 694). Some confusion has been caused by *Sinclair v Brougham* [1914] AC 398, in which the House of Lords rejected personal claims by depositors where the building society had

carried out an ultra vires banking business. However, this decision has now been discredited by Lord Browne-Wilkinson in *Westdeutsche Landesbank Girozentrale v Islington London Borough Council* [1996] AC 669 at 710: 'In my judgment, your Lordships should now unequivocally and finally reject the concept that the claim for moneys had and received is based on an implied contract. I would overrule *Sinclair v Brougham* on this point. It follows that in *Sinclair v Brougham* the depositors should have had a personal claim to recover the moneys at law based on a total failure of consideration' (cf above, para 3.44ff). For a discussion of the policy issues involved, see Arrowsmith 'Ineffective transactions, unjust enrichment and problems of policy' (1989) 9 LS 307.

3   For companies, see *Ashbury Railway Carriage and Iron Co Ltd v Riche* (1875) LR 7 HL 653 at 678, per Lord Chelmsford, and *Cotman v Brougham* [1918] AC 514 at 520, per Lord Parker, and at 522, per Lord Wrenbury. For local authorities, see Lord Templeman in *Hazell v Hammersmith and Fulham London Borough Council* [1992] 2 AC 1 at 36.

Statute

15.26   Reforms to the Companies Act 1985 ('the 1985 Act') drastically diminish the importance of the ultra vires rule in relation to third parties contracting with companies under the Companies Act. Following amendments introduced by the Companies Act 1989, third parties contracting with a company in good faith should experience few difficulties in enforcing their contract[1].

1   In addition to the provisions discussed below, the third party will also be protected if the company adopts a general object of carrying on a business as a general commercial company: see s 3A (as inserted by the Companies Act 1989, s 110(1)). In such circumstances, there are unlikely to be any ultra vires problems. For pre-incorporation contracts, see s 36C(1) of the 1985 Act, which provides that a party entering a contract with an unformed company will be entitled to enforce the contract against the person purporting to act for or as the agent of the unformed company. The Court of Appeal has recently confirmed that such a person or agent may enforce the contract against the third party unless enforcement is precluded by the ordinary rules of contract law: *Braymist Ltd v Wise Finance Co Ltd* [2002] 2 All ER 333.

THE THIRD PARTY

15.27   Section 108 of the Companies Act 1989 amended the 1985 Act and introduced two new sections: 35A and 35B[1]. The amended s 35(1) overruled the ultra vires rule in this context:

> The validity of an act done by a company shall not be called into question on the ground of lack of capacity by reason of anything in the company's memorandum.

On this basis, neither the company nor the other contracting party would be able to challenge the contract on the basis of the ultra vires rule. Section 35A(1) permits the third party to enforce the contract, provided he or she acted in good faith:

> In favour of a person dealing with a company in good faith, the power of the board of directors to bind the company, or authorise others to do so, shall be deemed to be free of any limitation under the company's constitution.

A person will be presumed to have acted in good faith unless the contrary is proved. The burden will be on the company to prove bad faith[2].

The 1985 Act thus overcomes one of the great problems of the previous law, in that the third party was expected to know or discover the powers of the company, and if not, acted at his or her peril. This was obviously unrealistic, and the 1985 Act acknowledges this explicitly, in determining that 'a party to a transaction with a company is not bound to inquire as to whether it is permitted by the company's memorandum or as to any limitations on the powers of the board of directors to bind the company or authorise others to do so'[3]. The previous law will only be relevant where the company can show that the third party acted in bad faith, which, due to the statutory provisions, will be very difficult to prove. The third party is presumed to be acting in good faith, and it is not enough to prove that he or she knew that the company was acting outside its powers[4]. Further evidence of bad faith must be shown, for example, malicious intent or collusion by the third party in the breach by the directors. It is questionable whether the courts would assist such a contracting party, either in equity or the law of restitution[5].

1 Thus seeking to implement EC 1st Directive on Company Law: 68/151/EEC (as amended), Art 9. The operation of ss 35 and 35A is restricted in relation to companies which are charities, by the Charities Act 1993, s 65(1), and the Companies Act 1989, s 112(3).
2 See the Companies Act 1985, s 35A(2)(c).
3 See the Companies Act 1985, s 35B.
4 See the Companies Act 1985, s 35A(2)(b): 'A person shall not be regarded as acting in bad faith by reason only of his knowing that an act is beyond the powers of the directors under the company's constitution'.
5 Goff and Jones *Law of Restitution* (5th edn, 1998), p 653 find it (in my view correctly) 'inconceivable' that either party could make a successful claim, and assert that the most likely result would be to find the directors and the other party constructive trustees of any identifiable gain. See *International Sales and Agencies Ltd v Marcus* [1982] 3 All ER 551, Martin 'Recipient liability after *Westdeutsche*' [1998] Conv 13.

SHAREHOLDERS

15.28 The ultra vires rule is still applicable to shareholders, whose rights to bring proceedings to restrain an act beyond the company's capacity are protected, but are subject to the rights of any third party[1]. Section 35(3) imposes a duty on directors of the company to observe any limitations on their powers imposed by the memorandum of association, although acts which would be, but for s 35(1), beyond the capacity of the company may be ratified by special resolution.

1 Section 35(2): 'no .. proceedings shall lie in respect of an act to be done in fulfillment of a legal obligation arising from a previous act of the company'. See also the Companies Act 1985, s 35A(4).

F   Public authorities[1]

15.29 The ultra vires rule also applies to public bodies, such as local authorities, whose powers are defined by statute[2]. Such corporations are not subject to the Companies Acts, and thus the provisions considered above will not protect third parties. Any party contracting with a public authority is expected to appreciate the limited capacity and competence of such institutions[3].

The effect of these limitations is illustrated clearly in the so-called 'swaps' cases, in which local authorities were found to have acted beyond their powers in undertaking interest rate swap agreements with banks to circumvent government spending restrictions[4]. Banks which had contracted with local authorities thus found the contracts to be void ab initio, and wholly unenforceable. In subsequent litigation, the banks sought to recover sums paid under these transactions. In the leading case of *Westdeutsche Landesbank Girozentrale v Islington London Borough Council*[5], the House of Lords accepted that the law of restitution would intervene to prevent unjust enrichment at the bank's expense. This case is significant in recognising intervention based on unjust enrichment reasoning, in relation to a contract void for incapacity. The full implications of this decision will be discussed below[6]. It should be noted, however, that such authority – dealing with *void* transactions by public bodies – does not affect our analysis of the other heads of incapacity set out above.

1   For fuller consideration of the position of public authorities see below, ch 18.
2   Note however the Local Government (Contracts) Act 1997, in which if a contract for the provision of services for the purposes of, or in connection with, the discharge of any of the functions of the local authority which operates, or is intended to operate, for a period of at least five years is certified under s 2, the contract shall have effect as if the local authority had had the power to enter it: see ss 2, 3 and 4(3).
3   See per Hobhouse LJ in *Crédit Suisse v Allerdale Borough Council* [1997] QB 306 at 348.
4   See *Hazell v Hammersmith and Fulham London Borough Council* [1990] 2 QB 697 (QBD and CA), [1992] 2 AC 1, HL; *Crédit Suisse v Allerdale Borough Council* [1997] QB 306; and *Crédit Suisse v Waltham Forest London Borough Council* [1997] QB 362.
5   [1996] AC 669. The lower court judgment is also significant in this case: see Hobhouse J at [1994] 4 All ER 890. See also *South Tyneside Metropolitan Borough Council v Svenska International plc* [1995] 1 All ER 545; *Guinness Mahon & Co Ltd v Kensington and Chelsea Royal London Borough Council* [1999] QB 215 (comment by White 'Restitution and the doctrine of ultra vires' (1999) 115 LQR 380); and *Kleinwort Benson Ltd v Lincoln City Council* [1999] 2 AC 349. These cases indicate recovery on the basis of (total) failure of consideration and mistake of law (see below, para 18.23ff).
6   See below, ch 18.

G   Conclusion – A need for reform?

15.30   Incapacity raises a conflict of policy for the courts. Whilst the courts wish to protect vulnerable parties, security of transaction indicates that such contracts should be enforceable. As seen above, the courts have resolved this conflict in a number of ways.

In relation to minors, the law is needlessly complicated. A 'voidable' contract may be valid at the option of the minor, or valid unless repudiated – two completely different concepts. Equally, it seems harsh to continue to deny the adult a remedy based on total failure of consideration, although this may be circumvented by a broad interpretation of the Minors' Contracts Act 1987.

The law in relation to those suffering from mental incapacity also seems unduly severe. It offers little protection for such vulnerable parties, except where they are subject to the provisions of the Mental Health Act 1983. At a time where, due to the advantages of modern medicine and better social and economic conditions, individuals are likely to live longer, and therefore a larger proportion of the population is likely to suffer from mental incapacity, this seems to offer inadequate protection and give undue prominence to the policy of security of transactions.

The law relating to statutory corporations at least seems settled. Due to reforms, few problems are now likely to arise in relation to companies incorporated under the Companies Act 1985.

The only remaining area of dispute is that of public authorities, which, due to the particular issues involved and recent intervention in this area, is best dealt with in its own specific chapter[1].

1   See below, ch 18.

CHAPTER 16

Necessity, Incapability and Emergency

Neil Allen

A Introduction

16.1   In modern commercial practice the most common method of obtaining goods and services is the traditional contract. The law governing contractual liability and quantum is today voluminous, and supplemented by statute, providing a comprehensive body of coherent principles. However, there are many instances where those most in need of goods and services are incapable of entering into the relevant contract. There may be legal difficulties inhibiting one's capacity to form contractual relations, or practical difficulties preventing one party from contacting the other. Indeed, the one common thread running through the legal precedents on necessity is this: that there is no unifying principle or theory to rationalise them *all*.

16.2   As a general rule, there is no *legal* obligation in English law on any member of the public to intervene in an emergency situation. It does not matter how simple the exercise would be; still there is no civil duty upon any passer-by[1]. Moreover, if a qualified doctor walks past on the other side of the road, provided he is not acting in the course of his employment, he will incur no liability to an injured person for failing to provide necessary medical treatment. In fact, the law almost discourages the Good Samaritan[2]. For if someone does decide to intervene, a common law duty of care may arise if it can be reasonably foreseen that their conduct may cause some harm to the person they assist. Similarly, the law will require an intervening doctor to act in accordance with a responsible and competent body of relevant professional opinion when providing medical assistance at the scene[3].

1   Unlike the French Civil System of law, under which there is a limited duty to rescue.
2   Dawson 'Rewards for Rescue of Human Life' in Nadelmann (ed) *20th Century Comparative and Conflicts law: Legal Essays presented to Hessel E Yntema* (1961), p 142.
3   As set down in *Bolam v Friern Hospital Management Committee* [1957] 1 WLR 582.

16.3   The emergence of the welfare state with its publicly funded institutions has gone some way in assisting vulnerable members of society. In most circumstances, when one's health or property is in imminent danger one is thankfully able to rely upon the emergency services of the State, financed by the taxpayer. Those employed in the public sector are thereby contractually remunerated for these 'services rendered out of necessity'.

The approach of restitution

16.4   Before the Judicature Acts 1873–1875, there were two distinct streams of law flowing parallel to one another. One of them provided for the development of the common law and the other related to the doctrine of equity. Such a divided legal system consequently led to divided legal reasoning on the part of the judiciary, dependent upon the jurisdiction of the Court in which they were sitting. In analysing the law on necessity I suggest that it is most important to consider the legal authorities in their proper historical context with this former procedural division in mind.

16.5   Over the centuries many Judges have struggled to rationalise this area of law, and its theoretical basis remains a matter of some dispute. Traditionally, the legal authorities have been seen either as sui generis, or as based on a contract implied between the parties. Some theorists argue that this is still an appropriate way of determining liability and quantum, whereas others would prefer the common law to develop a doctrine of *negotiorum gestio* akin to many continental legal systems. Moreover, restitution lawyers have theorised this branch of the law in terms of unjust enrichment.

16.6   This chapter focuses upon those situations in which an 'intervener' has conferred a benefit on another – referred to hereafter as the 'intervenee' – in circumstances where a contract cannot be formed because of some practical or legal incapability. The case law on necessity falls into two categories. The first relates to necessary intervention resulting from some *legal incapability*: for example, the intervenee may not have the capacity to contract owing to their age or level of understanding[1], or mental health[2]. In the second part of this chapter, by contrast, I analyse those situations in which the necessity to intervene is derived from some *practical incapability*: for example, the intervenee was impossible to contact and the circumstances required intervention on an emergency basis. Maritime law and international trade frequently come within this category as distance and peril on the high seas often make communications troublesome. In all of these cases, a claim by the intervener for a reasonable remuneration is possible, although the courts have always been wary of those seeking to exploit the vulnerable. Whilst there is great diversity in the subject matter considered below, there is also an underlying notion of 'necessity' which should be explained at the outset.

1   See below, para 16.31.
2   See below, paras 16.32–16.39.

B   The principle of necessity

16.7   In order to clarify the case law in this area, it is important to draw a distinction between the concepts of 'necessity' and 'emergency'. The historical origins of the principle of necessity do not rely upon an emergency, as such, as providing the criterion for lawful intervention. 'The old Roman doctrine of *negotiorum gestio* presupposed not so much an emergency as a prolonged absence of the *dominus* from home as justifying intervention'[1]. Similarly, the ancient maritime cases discussed below found their origin in the difficulty experienced by professional salvors in communicating with the cargo owner over a prolonged period of time. The conclusion of Lord Goff was this:

Emergency is however not the criterion or even a prerequisite; it is simply a frequent origin of the necessity which impels intervention. The principle is one of necessity not of emergency[2].

1   *F v West Berkshire Health Authority* [1989] 2 All ER 545 at 565, per Lord Goff.
2   See n 1.

16.8   Indeed, when canvassed in this way it becomes clear that the principle of necessity is much wider in its scope than the concept of 'emergency', and is therefore capable of governing those situations in which an intervener acts over a prolonged period. Furthermore, many of the legal precedents in this area do not concern emergencies in the true sense of the word. And so it is the necessitous intervention on the part of the intervener, rather than the emergency itself, that gives rise to a cause of action.

Analysis of Falcke v Scottish Imperial Insurance Co

16.9   At this juncture it may be convenient to discuss what has been regarded as an authoritative statement of the law on necessity, in order to understand its proper historical context. This legal precedent was decided soon after the sweeping changes brought about in 1875, the main object of which was the procedural fusion of the two streams of law and equity. By the date of the Court of Appeal's decision in *Falcke v Scottish Imperial Insurance Co*[1], the fusion of legal thought was still in its infancy, which may explain the brief reference to equitable doctrine in their Lordships' judgments.

1   (1886) 34 Ch D 234.

16.10   In 1883 Emanuel, through Davis, paid a premium on a life assurance policy in Falcke's name that became due in July of that year. In 1885 Falcke died, and Davis absconded having been declared bankrupt. Falcke's widow initiated legal proceedings against the insurance company in order to recover the payout on the policy. However, Emanuel also claimed for the payment he had made to keep the policy going.

16.11   The Court of Appeal was clearly concerned with the public policy issues behind the appeal. The proposition that had been laid before the Bench was this: that when one person makes an outlay upon property, and another person takes the benefit of that outlay, a request should be implied, and the person taking the benefit is therefore liable to repay the money, or submit to a lien over the property benefited for the repayment of the money. This was certainly a very general submission by counsel in the case, which was unsupported by judicial authority. Fry LJ observed that to turn that proposition into a rule of law would be tantamount to saying that:

> the mortgagor remaining in possession would be entitled to a lien against his mortgagee, and in priority of the mortgage money, for every sum which is expended in the repair or the improvement of the estate, and of which the mortgagee, by entering into possession, might take the benefit.

That would have set a most unsatisfactory legal precedent. So with these concerns in mind, the two leading judgments will now be examined.

16.12   Cotton LJ began by reiterating the general rule that governs necessitous intervention by a stranger[1]. The common law issue before the Court of Appeal was whether the intervener, Emanuel, had been requested by Falcke to pay the insurance premium. His Lordship stated the following:

> It is not disputed that if a stranger pays a premium on a policy that payment gives him no lien on the policy. A man by making a payment in respect of property belonging to another, if he does so without request, is not entitled to any lien or charge on that property for such payment. If he does work upon a house without request he gets no lien on the house for the work done. If the money has been paid or the work done at the request of the person entitled to the property, the person paying the money or doing the work has a right of action against the owner for the money paid or for the work done at his request[2].

1   In this chapter, the term 'stranger' is intended to refer to those that intervene in the absence of any contractual obligation.
2   34 Ch D 234 at 241.

16.13   The substance of the above proposition is that, at common law, an intervener will have a right of action where a request was made, but in the absence of such a request will be denied any claim. This general rule accords with the law on voluntary payments which cannot normally be recovered[1]. But is it really as simple as that? If so, how can one reconcile the right of action provided to those who intervene to maintain relatives with mental illnesses[2], often in the absence of any express request? Cotton LJ went on to say:

> I think that in a case of this sort, when money is paid in order to keep alive property which belongs to another, a request to make that payment might be implied from slight circumstances, but in my opinion there is no circumstance here in evidence from which such a request can be implied[3].

1   For example see *Stokes v Lewis* (1785) 1 Term Rep 20, 99 ER 949; *Bates v Townley* (1847) 2 Ex Ch 152, 154 ER 444. See also below, para 17.45ff.
2   See below, para 16.32ff.
3   34 Ch D 234 at 241.

16.14   This passage foreshadows the developments which followed the case. In order to correct the general law and to do justice between the parties, the reformed Victorian Courts of law began to imply those requests on behalf of intervenees whose health or property was protected by virtue of the necessitous intervention. Yet this is where we enter the realms of judicial fiction, with the concept of 'implied request'. It is submitted that the need for such artificial concepts shows that the rigid, universal nature of the common law can only go so far. That is to say, the blunt tool of common law is ill-equipped to determine the issue of restitution within the field of necessity. It proved to be a most troublesome judicial exercise.

16.15   The judgment of Bowen LJ is of particular interest, as it is more often referred to by academics and Judges alike[1]. His Lordship began by stating:

> The general principle is, beyond all question, that work and labour done or money expended by one man to preserve or benefit the property of another do not according to English law create any lien upon the property saved or benefited, nor, even if standing alone, create any obligation to repay the expenditure. Liabilities are not to be forced upon people behind their backs any more than you can confer a benefit upon a man against his will.

There is an exception to this proposition in the maritime law [which] differs from the common law. That has been so from the time of the Roman law downwards[2].

1   For example, see *Re Cleadon Trust Ltd* [1939] Ch 286 at 322, per Clauson LJ; *Sorrell v Paget* [1950] 1 KB 252 at 260, per Bucknill LJ.
2   34 Ch D 234 at 248.

16.16   He went on to say that the liability afforded to maritime law 'is a special consequence arising out of the character of the mercantile enterprises, the nature of sea peril, and the fact that the thing saved was saved under great stress and exceptional circumstances'. His Lordship refused to entertain any suggestion that a similar doctrine applied to events taking place on land. There does not seem to be any reason why this should be so. Indeed, as the judgment of Sir John Donaldson MR in *The Goring* case[1] quite properly states, there can be no logical distinction between sea and soil. Surely good conscience requires a right of action where similar exceptional circumstances leading to necessitous intervention have taken place on land? Sadly, at the time of the *Falcke* decision, the Court of Appeal seemed to be unfamiliar with the stream of equitable precedents that had flowed from the Court of Chancery, and was therefore unprepared to openly adopt their rationale.

1   'In the end I believe that I have to seek a rational basis of confining the cause of action to tidal waters and I can find none. It is, of course, a maritime remedy and the public policy considerations which support it are directed at commercial shipping and seagoing vessels. But that said, I can see no sense in a cause of action which will remunerate the salvors of an ocean-going vessels inward bound for Manchester up to the moment when the vessel enters the Manchester Ship Canal, but no further. Some of the perils facing the vessel in the canal may be different from those facing it at sea, but many, such as fire, will be the same. The need to encourage assistance otherwise than under contract may be greater at sea, but the skills required of the salvors will be the same or at least similar. The vessel is not intended to sail only on tidal waters. The voyage over tidal and non-tidal waters is a single maritime adventure and should not attract wholly different rights and obligations by reference to the tidality of the water in which the vessel is for the time being sailing': [1987] 2 All ER 246 at 253–254. On *The Goring* see below, para 16.41.

16.17   Bowen LJ analysed the proper basis for recovering damages:

With regard to ordinary goods upon which labour or money is expended with a view of saving them or benefiting the owner, there can, as it seems to me, according to the common law be only one principle upon which a claim for repayment can be based, and that is where you can find facts from which the law will imply a contract to repay or to give a lien. It is perfectly true that the inference of an understanding between the parties – which you may translate into other language by calling it an implied contract – is an inference which will unhesitatingly be drawn in cases where the circumstances plainly lead to the conclusion that the owner of the saved property knew that the other party was laying out his money in the expectation of being repaid. In other words, you must have circumstances from which the proper inference is that there was a request to perform the service. It comes to the same thing, but I abstain the using the word 'request' more than is necessary, for fear of plunging myself into all the archaic embarrassments connected with the cases about requests[1].

1   34 Ch D 234 at 249.

16.18   It must be emphasised that this statement of principle related solely to the position at common law; it does not affect the rights of interveners in equity. This was most apparent from the structure of his Lordship's judgment; separate consideration was given to each juridical doctrine. Clearly, the two parallel streams of legal thought, though fused in terms of their procedure, were still flowing independently of one another in the minds of the appellate Judges. It was well-established by 1886 that in order to recover damages at common law, the circumstances must be such that the law will imply a contract to repay the money, or to give the intervener a lien over the property. But what are those circumstances? Well, it seems that a contract will be implied where:

(a)   the intervenee has expressly requested the services of the intervener; or
(b)   the intervenee knows that the intervener is expecting to be repaid for his services.

In the latter instance, the request is implied from the circumstances surrounding the knowledge of the intervenee. On the face of his Lordship's judgment, the test of knowledge is subjective, requiring the intervenee to have actually known of the intervener's expectation. But either way, the rigid nature of the common law requires an express or implied request as a precondition to recovery.

16.19   To some extent this authoritative decision went against the leading case of *Great Northern Rly Co v Swaffield*[1] in which Kelly CB drew an analogy with maritime law in granting restitution for necessary intervention on land. His Lordship held that a carrier was entitled to recover the stable costs that he had paid out of necessity when the consignee refused to take delivery of his horse and stated:

> ... it has been held that a shipowner who, through some accidental circumstance, finds it necessary for the safety of the cargo to incur expenditure, is justified in doing so, and can maintain a claim for reimbursement against the owner of the cargo. That is exactly the present case. The plaintiffs were put into much the same position as the shipowner occupies under the circumstances I have described. They had no choice, unless they would leave the horse at the station or in the high road to his own danger and the danger of other people, but to place him in the care of a livery stable keeper, and as they are bound by their implied contract with the livery stable keeper to satisfy his charges, a right arises in them against the defendant to be reimbursed those charges which they have incurred for his benefit[2].

1   (1874) LR 9 Exch 132.
2   (1874) LR 9 Exch 132 at 136.

A broader equitable approach

16.20   The appellate Judges in the *Falcke* decision gave separate consideration to the respective positions of common law and equity. By the date of their decision the stream of equity had only recently been procedurally fused with that of the common law, and was given somewhat brief attention by their Lordships. Cotton LJ held:

> It is very true that if a man who has a title to property sees another expending money upon it in the erroneous belief that he has a title to it when he has no title, there is an important doctrine of Equity which will prevent the real owner from insisting on his title so as to deprive the person who was acting on the supposition of his title of the benefit of his expenditure. But in order to make this doctrine applicable, there must be not only knowledge on the part of the person having the real title that the man whom he sees so acting believes he has a title and acts in consequence of that belief, but also a knowledge that the title on the faith of which he is acting is a bad one[1].

1   34 Ch D 234 at 242–243.

16.21   This was a most important development by the Court of Appeal. This extract provides a practical illustration of the way in which the equitable concept of unconscionability can be applied, as envisaged by Lord Mansfield CJ. That principle requires the Court to provide a right of action in equity where the intervenee knows that the intervener is acting in the mistaken belief that he has a good title to the property he helped to preserve.

16.22   What may be described as Cotton LJ's equitable 'test of knowledge' is two-limbed in its nature. An intervener must establish that the intervenee knew:

(a)   that he, the intervener, was acting in consequence of a belief that he had a title to the property; and
(b)   that the title on the faith of which he was acting was a bad one.

This test, derived from the general principle of unconscionability, is sufficiently precise to govern the circumstances in which intervening *strangers* are entitled to recover damages against intervenees. Furthermore, any such claim in equity will be subject to the strict equitable maxims.

16.23   In Cotton LJ's judgment, therefore, the doctrine of equity did not require any request – be it express or implied – to have been made by the intervenee. This approach avoids the artificial reasoning inherent in any contractual analysis. Furthermore, it enables a simple test of knowledge to be used in order to determine whether the intervenee is liable to the intervener. In the present case the intervener, Emanuel, was a stranger to the intervenee, Falcke, who was totally unaware of the former's intervention to preserve his life assurance policy. Emanuel's claim therefore failed the equitable test of knowledge.

16.24   Regrettably, Bowen LJ dealt with the position in equity only summarily. After referring to Fry LJ's analysis in *Re Leslie*[1], his Lordship simply noted that the general rule was the same in equity as at common law. That is entirely correct, but does little to clarify those exceptional circumstances in which restitution will be granted. Bowen LJ continued:

> Here the simple question is whether there are any facts from which we can say that it is unjust or inequitable that Mr Falcke's representatives should be allowed to have that which is their own? If you state the case in that way the answer is obvious, that one cannot see anything of the kind[2].

On the facts of the case there was nothing unjust, inequitable or unconscionable in dismissing the intervener's cause of action as Falcke had no knowledge of Emanuel's actions. The law of necessity cannot impose liabilities behind people's backs.

1   (1883) 23 Ch D 552.
2   34 Ch D 234 at 251.

16.25   In my view, this legal precedent illustrates the way in which the doctrine of equity is capable of rectifying that which it is against good conscience to keep. Following the reasoning in *Falcke*, the state of mind of the intervenee is clearly an important consideration to take into account in determining the equities in the case. However, it is submitted that Cotton LJ's two-limbed knowledge test does not constitute a condition precedent to recovery; it is but one equitable appliance from the toolbox of unconscionability[1]. In deciding what is just and reasonable, all of the circumstances of the case should be taken into account.

1   On unconscionability see above, ch 10.

16.26   In *Owen v Tate*[1] Scarman LJ held that there might be a right of recovery if the intervener is able to show that in the particular circumstances of the case there was 'some necessity for the obligation to be assumed', and that such reimbursement was 'just and reasonable'. In the same case, Stephenson LJ held that there may be circumstances where an intervener could recover if 'it is obviously unjust that a debtor should be enriched by accepting the benefit'[2].

1 [1976] QB 402; on which see above, para 6.22.
2 [1975] 2 All ER 129 at 136.

16.27   Similarly in the *Brook's Wharf* case, a warehouseman had paid the import duties on goods for which their owner was primarily liable. He did so because of an obligation imposed by statute, and without any prior request from the owner. In allowing the warehouseman a right of restitution, Lord Wright summarised the law as follows:

> These statements of the principle do not put the obligation on any ground of implied contract or a constructive or notional contract. The obligation is imposed by the Court simply under the circumstances of the case and on what the Court decides is just and reasonable, having regard to the relationship of the parties. It is a debt or obligation by the act of the law, apart from any consent or intention of the parties or any privity of contract[1].

1 *Brook's Wharf and Bull Wharf Ltd v Goodman Bros* [1937] 1 KB 534 at 545. On the case see above, para 6.12.

16.28   Concentrating on the intervener's initial decision to confer a benefit on the assisted person, I suggest that it may be helpful to consider the following spectrum of decision-making. At one extreme, an intervener may have voluntarily assumed an obligation to benefit the intervenee, in effect, behind his back; it is highly likely that the principle of unconscionability will not provide him with a remedy. At the other extreme, an intervener may have been compelled by law to benefit the intervenee[1]; in those circumstances it would clearly be just and reasonable to order restitution of the derived benefit. The core question for any Judge determining an equitable cause of action of this nature is whether the intervenee has been unjustly benefited or enriched by the necessary intervention.

1 For a good example of such compulsion see *Moule v Garrett* (1872) LR 7 Exch 101. On the case see above, para 6.10.

16.29   It is also apparent from the case law that even if a necessitous intervener is able to bring his claim within the exception to the general rule, the action is likely to be defeated where he has derived a possible benefit from the intervention. A good example is to be found in *Saunders v Dunman*, where Fry J felt unable to imply a request for intervention because the intervener 'derived a possible benefit from making these payments, and I cannot measure the extent of that benefit'[1]. It is submitted that the rationale behind this restriction is twofold. Firstly, it goes against good conscience to order restitution where the intervener has benefited from his own intervention. From a public policy standpoint, the courts must be wary of self-rewarding intervention in other people's affairs. Secondly, on a more practical level, it may be impossible for a Judge to quantify precisely the extent to which the intervener has benefited.

1 (1878) 7 Ch D 825.

16.30   With this spectrum in mind, it is submitted that the doctrine of equity is far more appropriate to deal with cases of necessitous intervention than is the common law. The following statement of principle by Scarman LJ in *Owen v Tate* reflects the true essence of the principle of unconscionability. His Lordship held:

> In my judgment, the true principle of the matter can be stated very shortly, without reference to volunteers or to the compulsions of law, and I state it as follows. If without an antecedent request a person assumes an obligation or makes a payment for the benefit of another, the law will, as a general rule, refuse him a right of indemnity. But if he can show that in the particular circumstances of the case there was some necessity for the obligation to be assumed, then the law will grant him a right of reimbursement if in all the circumstances it is just and reasonable to do so[1].

1   [1976] QB 402 at 411–412.

C   Legal incapability

Age[1]

16.31   Natural persons below the age of eighteen are severely restricted in their capacity to enter contracts. Indeed, the earliest authorities on necessity concerned necessary payments that were made to support children[2]. In *Manby v Scott* three Judges held that an infant might be bound for necessaries provided to him and said, obiter, 'what has been said of an infant is applicable to an idiot in a case of housekeeping'[3]. It is not entirely clear which goods should be regarded as 'necessaries' in modern conditions, and the case law is mostly too antiquated to be of much use. But the core idea is clear – that the goods should be necessary for everyday living and not ones which can be seen as luxuries.

1   For an approach to this problem from another angle, see above, para 15.2ff.
2   Today the Children Act 1989, s 9(6) and (7), and the Child Support Act 1991, s 1, place a statutory duty upon parents to maintain their children until they reach the age of 16.
3   (1659) 1 Sid 109 at 112, 82 ER 1000 at 1002, per Mallett and Twisden JJ and Terrill B; or, in the language the court actually used, 'Et come ad estre dit de infant issint poit estre dit de ideot in case de housekeeping ... '

Those with mental illness[1]

16.32   Much of the case law on necessity dating from the approach set out earlier related to money spent on, or services rendered towards, the upkeep and maintenance of people with mental illnesses, sometimes referred to as 'lunatics' by the Victorian Judges. It was not unknown for family members to pay to have their relatives maintained in mental health institutions, or 'asylums', only to then claim the cost from their estate. In *Howard v Digby* Lord Brougham confidently held:

> Upon what ground are all these allowances made? Not from kindness, not from charity, not for the convenience of the parties; but because they are debts; because in the eye of that Court, be it a Court of Law or a Court of Equity, or the Chancellor sitting in lunacy, they are valid debts incurred by the insane person, and are discharged by the justice of the Court[2].

1   For an approach to this problem from another angle, see above, para 15.19ff.
2   (1834) 2 Cl & Fin 634 at 663.

16.33   The importance of this general statement of principle cannot be overstated. For in Lord Brougham's view, the legal reasoning behind his decision was to be applied to the whole judicial system and was, therefore, to come within both the common law and equitable jurisdiction of the Courts. Note that there is no mention of a contract justifying restitution. Instead the emphasis is on the assisted party – or 'intervenee' – being *indebted* to the intervener. His Lordship's reference to the courts of equity is most important. The doctrine of equity has played – and to this day continues to play – a vital role in the law of necessity. On the facts of the case before him, Lord Brougham held that payments made for the maintenance of a 'lunatic' were debts payable out of the 'lunatic's' estate.

16.34   Lord Brougham's decision in *Howard v Digby* reflected the 'common law reincarnation of pristine equity'[1] of Lord Mansfield CJ in *Moses v Macferlan*[2]. The decision in *Howard v Digby* was followed by Lord Langdale MR in *Williams v Wentworth* in which he held:

> ... I am of opinion, that in the case of money expended for the necessary protection of the person and estate of the lunatic, the law will raise an implied contract, and give a valid demand or debt, against the lunatic or his estate ... [3]

1   So described by Baker in 'The History of Quasi-Contract in English Law' in Cornish, Nolan, O'Sullivan and Virgo *Restitution past present and future – Essay in honour of Gareth Jones* (1998) 56. See above, para 2.16.
2   (1760) 2 Burr 1005, 97 ER 676.
3   (1842) 5 Beav 325 at 329, 49 ER 603 at 605.

16.35   His Lordship was thereby attempting to impose a contractual analysis to the facts before him. It will become apparent from subsequent case law that this was not the most appropriate way of disposing of this type of claim. It led to legal fiction and overstretched definitions. However, the Master of the Rolls was clearly contemplating the application of such an analysis to cases where either the health or the property of those that are mentally ill had been necessarily protected. The potential scope of this contractual analysis was broadened by his Lordship in *Nelson v Duncombe*:

> It is, I think, true, that in all cases of implied contract which have been decided, there has been a lunacy actually found; but it has not been determined, that this Court will not take notice of what is done, in respect of the property of persons lunatic though not so found, or that a contract may not be implied for the supply of necessaries to such person[1].

1   (1846) 9 Beav 211 at 231, 50 ER 323 at 332, per Lord Langdale MR.

16.36   Despite the problems that resulted from the terminology used in this extract, it nonetheless marked an important legal development. For it follows that there may be a claim for the recovery of such necessary payments even where the intervenee is not found to be a 'lunatic' in the strict sense of the word.

16.37   In the first half of the nineteenth century, it was clear to both the Bench and the Bar that those litigants afflicted by mental illness were unable to form legal relations, and could not therefore contract with others. Nonetheless, justice had to be done and had to be seen to be done in the Superior Courts of Common Law. Hence the Judiciary vainly tried to ground their decisions in this fictitious theory of implied contract. For example, Mellish LJ said '[a] lunatic cannot contract for his maintenance, so whoever maintains him becomes a creditor by implied contract'[1].

1   *Re Gibson* (1871) 7 Ch App 52 at 53–54.

16.38   In 1889 Cotton LJ handed down an important judgment in *Re Rhodes* that clarified some of the law. His Lordship was called upon to determine the issue of whether there can be an implied contract on the part of a mentally unwell lady, who was kept in a private asylum, to repay out of her property money necessarily spent by interveners on her maintenance. Thankfully Cotton LJ stated:

> Now the term 'implied contract' is a most unfortunate expression, because there cannot be a contract by a lunatic ... The answer is, that what the law implies on the part of such a person is an obligation, which has been improperly termed a contract, to repay money spent in supplying necessaries[1].

1   (1890) 44 Ch D 94 at 105.

16.39   The Court of Appeal decided that the intervening family members never intended for their payments to constitute an obligation on the part of their sick relative to repay the money. Hence their appeal was dismissed. This broad approach is to be warmly welcomed, as it requires the Court to take all of the circumstances of the case into account. So, in considering whether there is a cause of action against an intervenee, it will be necessary to examine the way in which the obligation to intervene came to be assumed.

Burying the deceased

16.40   It has been held to be just and reasonable to order restitution from the estate of the deceased where an intervener has voluntarily incurred expense in burying the corpse. So in *Tugwell v Heyman*[1] the executors of the deceased were held liable to repay the reasonable funeral expenses. Case law also establishes that a husband is liable for the cost of his wife's funeral, if others arrange it[2]. This rule can be invoked by a relative, or by anyone who reasonably acts in the matter[3]. Interestingly, in the Canadian case of *Matheson v Smiley*[4] a surgeon who intended to charge for his services was entitled to be paid for his professional services in his reasonable, though unsuccessful, attempt to revive the intervenee who had committed suicide. It is unclear whether this would be followed in England.

1   (1812) 3 Camp 298, 170 ER 1389; see also *Rogers v Price* (1829) 3 Y & J 28, 148 ER 1080, and the Public Health (Control of Diseases) Act 1984, ss 46–48.
2   *Jenkins v Tucker* (1788) 1 Hy Bl 90, 126 ER 55.
3   *Rogers v Price* (1829) 3 Y & J 28, 148 ER 1080.
4   [1932] 2 DLR 787.

D   Practical incapability

Intervening salvors

16.41   The law on maritime salvage is voluminous, and can only be outlined here[1]. Prior to 1875, the jurisdiction over salvage claims in maritime law was exercised exclusively by the High Court of Admiralty[2], independent of the common law courts. Historically, the court's jurisdiction was restrained by statute from hearing matters arising within the realm, whether or not they concerned the sea[3]. It was frequently called upon to determine claims by professional salvors who had to intervene on behalf of others as a result of the perils on the high sea. Over time, the law on salvage was extended to include the saving of life[4] and aircraft[5], irrespective of whether the ship or vessel were 'within the body of a county' or on the high seas at the time the salvage operation was undertaken[6]. With the ratification of the London Salvage Convention 1989, the salvage jurisdiction was extended to include non-tidal waters, provided that a seagoing vessel performed the salvage services[7].

1   For a more detailed discussion on maritime law see Rose (ed) *Kennedy and Rose – Law of Salvage* (6th edn, 2002); and Brice *Maritime Law of Salvage* (3rd edn, 1999).
2   In 1875 this specialised jurisdiction was incorporated into the Probate, Divorce and Admiralty Division of the High Court. However, that division was abolished in 1970 and all admiralty business has now been transferred to the Queen's Bench Division under the Administration of Justice Act 1970. See Aitken '*Negotiorum gestio* and the common law: A jurisdictional approach' (1988) 11 Sydney Law Review 566.
3   See Stat 13 Ric II, c 5 (1389), 15 Ric II, c 3 (1391).
4   See the Merchant Shipping Act 1894, s 544(1). See today the Merchant Shipping Act 1995, s 224.
5   See today the Civil Aviation Act 1982, s 87.
6   See the Admiralty Court Act 1840, s 6.
7   See the Merchant Shipping Act 1995, Sch 11, Pt II, para 2. The common law position, established in *The Goring* [1988] AC 831, was that the jurisdiction extended only to the open sea, and to rivers at points where they were tidal.

16.42   In most salvage cases, there is a contractual relationship between the intervener and the intervenee. Owing to the well-organised nature of the international salvage industry, professional salvors usually have a standard form available for use as the circumstances demand. The Lloyds' Open Form (LOF) is an example of the industry's attempt to encapsulate the accepted customary principles. However, there are occasions when salvage teams are compelled to act without prior contractual authorisation. As unforeseen events unfold, it may not be practicable to communicate in advance with all interested parties, be they shipowners, charterers, cargo-owners (and their respective insurers!). Salvors may – out of necessity – have to intervene first and discuss liability later.

16.43   In the absence of a governing contract, the Admiralty judges have had to ground their decisions on some non-contractual basis. In the judgment of Sir Francis Jeune P it was held[1]:

> To rest the jurisdiction of the Admiralty Court upon an implied request from the owner of the property in danger to the salvors, or on an implied contract between the salvors and owner with the relinquishment of the res for consideration, is, I think, to confuse two different systems of law and to resort to a misleading analogy. The true view is, I think, that the law of Admiralty imposes on the owner of property saved an obligation to pay the person who saves it simply because in the view of that system of law it is just he should ...

1   *The Port Victor, ex Cargo* [1901] P 243 at 249.

16.44   In my view, although the law of salvage is subject to international conventions, particularly the London Salvage Convention 1989[1], the obligation to pay a salvage award following necessitous intervention is derived from the principles of equity.

The main rules for liability on a salvage claim are as follows.

1   This Convention is part of the law by virtue of the Merchant Shipping Act 1995, s 224. It is reproduced as Sch 11, Pt I to the Act.

THE SHIP OR CARGO SALVED MUST HAVE BEEN IN DANGER

16.45   A salvage award will be refused where the danger was not real, or could easily have been avoided without the salvors' assistance[1]. There can be no necessity to intervene without this element of danger being present. Accordingly, the claimant salvor must satisfy the Court that no experienced person in charge of the ship to be salved, knowing that a reward will be expected for the services, could reasonably refuse them. Thus in considering the circumstances prevailing at the relevant time, the question is whether there was any objective basis for refusing the salvage services[2]? Salvage can however be claimed where the services were objectively necessary, even if performed over the protests of the master of the salved vessel, who wrongly considered them unnecessary[3]. However, if the master expressly and reasonably refuses help, there is no right to a salvage award, even if the vessel was demonstrably in danger[4].

1   *The North Goodwin No 16* [1980] 1 Lloyd's Rep 71.
2   See eg *The Hamtun (Owners) v The St John (Owners)* [1999] 1 All ER (Comm) 587.
3   See eg *The Kangaroo* [1918] P 327; *The Flore* (1929) 34 Ll L Rep 172.
4   London Salvage Convention 1989, art 19.

THE DANGER MUST HAVE OCCURRED AT SEA

16.46   It is the location, rather than the type of vessel, which determines jurisdiction. If a yacht is being transported by road, someone who saves it from danger will not be entitled to a salvage award. Conversely, the salvage jurisdiction applies to aircraft just as it does to ships, so long as the aircraft is 'in, on or over the sea or any tidal water'[1]. As noted above, the somewhat illogical distinction drawn by the House of Lords in *The Goring*[2] between tidal and non-tidal waters has now been superseded by the 1989 Convention[3].

1   See the Civil Aviation Act 1982, s 87.
2   [1988] AC 831.
3   See above, para 16.41.

PROPERTY MUST BE SALVED

16.47   The value of any property salved – the ship, its cargo or both – provides the ceiling to any possible salvage award. Therefore, if no property is salved there can be no award. In *The Zephyrus* it was held:

> ... I apprehend that, upon general principles, a mere attempt to save the vessel and cargo, however meritorious that attempt may be, or whatever degree of risk or danger may have been incurred, if unsuccessful, can never be considered in this Court as furnishing any title to a salvage reward. The reason is obvious, viz that salvage reward is for benefits actually conferred, not for a service attempted to be rendered[1].

1   (1842) 1 Wm Rob 329 at 330–331, 166 ER 596 at 596, per Dr Lushington.

16.48   The English courts have yet to accept any doctrine of 'emergency assistance' that would justify an award for saving life alone[1]. However, where an award is made, it may reflect other matters than simply the saving of property. So where both property *and* life are saved, the saving of life can justify an enhanced award, though the total cannot exceed the value of the property salved[2].

1 Compare *Peninsular & Oriental Steam Navigation Co v Overseas Oil Carriers Inc* 553 F 2d 830 (CA 2nd Circuit, 1977, cert denied 434 US 859) (a case of emergency help to the victim of a heart attack). See Friedell 'Salvage' (2000) 31 Journal of Maritime Law and Commerce 31.
2 London Salvage Convention 1989, art 16.

SALVAGE SERVICES MUST BE RENDERED VOLUNTARILY

16.49   Salvage remuneration cannot be claimed by someone merely for doing a job they have already contracted to do[1]. So if a tug has already agreed to tow a vessel, the tug's owners cannot claim for salvage merely because they turn out to have been towing the vessel away from danger. Where danger unexpectedly appears in the course of contracted work, it may be a difficult question whether continuation of the work merits a salvage award. If the contractor merely completes the contracted work, no extra pay is due; but 'if the services rendered are beyond what can be reasonably supposed to have been contemplated by the parties entering into such a contract'[2], they can claim a salvage award for the extra salvage work undertaken.

1 London Salvage Convention 1989, art 17.
2 *Five Steel Barges* (1890) 15 PD 142 at 144, per Sir James Hannen.

Quantifying the salvage award

16.50   The salvage award is payable by those who have benefited from the salvage services. Thus if a ship has been salved, the ship-owner must pay; if cargo has been salved, the cargo-owners are liable. In practice, the insurance on the vessel and cargo covers payment of any salvage award. Those whose lives have been saved by salvors are *not* liable to pay salvage, though the fact that life has been saved is a factor justifying an enhanced award against the owners of the property saved[1].

1 London Salvage Convention 1989, art 16.

16.51   The amount of the award 'shall be fixed with a view to encouraging salvage operations'[1]. A variety of circumstances may be taken into account, including the value of the salved property, the quality of the services employed, the time the operation took, the degree of risk run by all concerned, and the extent of efforts to minimise danger to the environment. Professional salvors are usually entitled to a more generous award than amateurs[2], though amateurs can be rewarded generously if their efforts warrant it[3]. Misconduct by the salvors may diminish their award, or even reduce it to nothing; though if in fact they have nonetheless saved valuable property, the courts traditionally take a lenient view. The total award, coupled with recoverable legal costs, cannot exceed the value of the salved property, except where a salvor has 'prevented or minimised damage to the environment'. In that case, a special award may exceed the value of the salved property[4].

1 London Salvage Convention 1989, art 13. This is true also of the common law measure: see eg *The Telemachus* [1957] P 47 at 49, per Willmer J. See generally 'Calculating and allocating salvage liability' (1986) 99 Harvard Law Review 1896.
2 *The Queen Elizabeth* (1949) 82 Ll L Rep 803.
3 *The Yolaine* [1995] 2 Lloyd's Rep 7.
4 London Salvage Convention 1989, art 14. On the calculation of the special award under that article see *The Nagasaki Spirit* [1997] 1 Lloyd's Rep 323.

16.52 Salvage law has traditionally been grounded explicitly in considerations of justice[1]. Some argue that there is a better explanation of salvage law, that it is designed to avoid the unjust enrichment of salvees at the expense of salvors. There is usually no duty to pay unless there is an enrichment – in the form of salved property – and so the payment can be seen as correcting an unjust enrichment.

However, there are difficulties with this. No doubt the owner of salved property is enriched by the value of the property – but the court does not usually award the value of the property. It gives an award which *cannot exceed* that value, but is usually a great deal less than it. So the court's response does *not* consist of returning the unjust enrichment.

An alternative approach is to say that the salvee is 'enriched' by the commercial value of the services performed by the salvor, and accordingly the salvor should receive the commercial value of the services. But this is just an elaborate way of saying that the salvee must pay the same amount as if there had been a contract for the services. The reference to 'unjust enrichment' adds nothing. It is perhaps for this reason that Birks doubts whether the claim can truly be said to be based on unjust enrichment, and that this will remain unclear unless considerable advances are made in the methods for calculation of the 'enrichment'[2].

1   See above, para 16.43.
2   Birks *An introduction to the law of restitution* (revised edn, 1989), pp 307 and 308.

General average

16.53 Closely related to salvage is the doctrine of general average, which again relates to emergencies at sea. However, this doctrine has a slightly different emphasis. It concerns the situation where it is necessary to make some emergency sacrifice to ensure the successful conclusion of the voyage. Perhaps part of the cargo must be jettisoned to lighten the ship in a storm, or perhaps part of the vessel or cargo must be deliberately destroyed in the course of putting out a fire on board. The basic rule is that the cost of these losses ('general average sacrifices') should be divided fairly between all concerned. So the owner of cargo destroyed in this way will not be expected to bear the whole of the loss, but can demand that the ship-owner and other cargo-owners pay their fair share. All have benefited by the saving of the ship; so all must pay, in proportion to the value of the interest saved.

16.54 The rules regulating this area of law are complex, and only a brief summary can be given here[1]. These rules apply only to 'maritime ventures'; it is unclear to what extent a voyage on inland waters can be a 'maritime venture'. The sacrifice must have been deliberate; it must have been intentional; it must have been made to avert a danger to the entire venture; it must have been reasonable in all the circumstances; and it must have been 'extraordinary', that is, going beyond the ordinary risks of sea transit (which the ship-owner is expected to bear). Rules on the various contributing parties are broad, designed to pull in everyone who benefited from the successful conclusion of the voyage.

1   For further detail see eg Rose *General average: Law and practice* (1997).

16.55 Like salvage, general average is usually a contractual matter, dealt with by standardised contract terms. There is no relevant international convention, but most parties work on the basis of the York-Antwerp Rules 1974 (revised 1990 and 1994). These rules are therefore incorporated into relevant contracts of sea carriage and contracts of marine insurance, and accordingly form the basis of the law in practice.

16.56   Attempts have been made to argue that general average is ultimately based on the prevention of unjust enrichment. But these attempts have run into the same difficulties as they do in the law of salvage[1]. It may be very hard to locate an 'enrichment', especially if the damage was severe, or if the general average sacrifice, while reasonable, was nonetheless unsuccessful. And where there is a clear enrichment, as where cargo is saved from a peril which would otherwise have destroyed it, the measure of recovery is nonetheless not the value of this enrichment. Rather, it is the product of a precise calculation, in which the enrichment is only one element. If there is a single governing idea, it seems not to be enrichment, but rather the equitable sharing of losses[2]. Rose has commented that the law relating to general average 'is a fairly self-contained area of practice with a number of, sometimes obscure or controversial, detailed rules which appear irrelevant to terrestrial situations'[3]. But, as he rightly adds, its peculiarities are not so severe as to justify its exclusion from the law of restitution altogether.

1   See above, para 16.52.
2   Dietrich *Restitution – A new perspective* (1998), pp 154–156. Dietrich also uses his principle to justify cases of contribution, on which see above, ch 7.
3   Rose 'General average as restitution' (1997) 113 LQR 569 at 573.

Agency of necessity

16.57   Parker LJ emphasised in the *Choko Star* case[1] that the cargo owner is not obliged to reward the intervener for preserving his property unless a term giving the latter authority to act is expressed, or can be implied, in the contract of carriage. The one exception to this contractual rule is the principle of necessity. It is well-established that, in the absence of contractual authority to intervene, a salvor must prove that he was acting as an agent of necessity before being entitled to the salvage reward for his professional services. Indeed, the concept of 'agency of necessity' is derived from maritime law, but it has now been extended to cover intervention on land[2].

1   *Industrie Chemiche Italia Centrale v Alexandra G Tsavliris Maritime Co* [1990] 1 Lloyd's Rep 516, CA.
2   See the leading case of *Great Northern Rly Co v Swaffield* (1874) LR 9 Exch 132; discussed above, para 16.19.

16.58   No-one can be an 'agent of necessity' unless, *before* the necessity manifested itself, they already had some kind of legal responsibility in respect of the goods. Applying the dicta of McCardie J[1], to come within the definition of an 'agent of necessity' the intervener must satisfy three further requirements.

1   *Prager v Blatspiel Stamp & Heacock Ltd* [1924] 1 KB 566.

COMMUNICATION WITH THE OWNER MUST HAVE BEEN IMPOSSIBLE AS A PRACTICAL MATTER

16.59   The test seems to be whether there is any sensible alternative to acting without instructions from the owner. An agent may be justified in acting if communication is technically possible, but in practice too slow to help. In *The*

Onward[1] Sir Robert Phillimore held that 'the master is always the agent for the ship and in special cases of necessity the agent for the cargo also. He is the appointed agent to the former, the involuntary agent of the latter'. In very many salvage situations the urgency at sea will often preclude communication with the intervenee. It has been suggested that action may be justified even if the owner *has* been contacted, if the owner then makes no meaningful response[2].

1   (1873) LR 4 A & E 38 at 51.
2   *China-Pacific SA v Food Corpn of India, The Winson* [1982] AC 939 at 961, per Lord Diplock.

THERE MUST BE A PRACTICAL NECESSITY TO INTERVENE

16.60   The courts have never committed themselves to any very definite formula here, and the cases go largely on their own facts[1]. Proof of practical necessity will involve examination of reasonable alternatives to the action taken. Such generalisations as can be made are fairly obvious, such as that it is easier to justify the disposal of perishable goods than of durable ones[2]. This requirement was clarified in the broad statement of maritime principle of Sir Montague Smith in *Australasian Steam Navigation Co v Morse*[3] where he held that:

> ... when by the force of circumstances a man has the duty cast upon him of taking some action for another, and under that obligation, adopts the course which, to the judgment of a wise and prudent man, is apparently the best for the interest of the persons for whom he acts in a given emergency, it may properly be said of the course so taken, that it was, in a mercantile sense, necessary to take it.

1   See eg *Surrey Breakdown Ltd v Knight* [1999] RTR 84; below, para 16.65.
2   Compare: *Sims & Co v Midland Rly Co* [1913] 1 KB 103 (butter); *Springer v Great Western Rly Co* [1921] 1 KB 257 (tomatoes); *Prager v Blatspiel, Stamp and Heacock Ltd* [1924] 1 All ER 524 (non-perishable furs).
3   (1872) LR 4 PC 222 at 230.

THE INTERVENTION MUST BE REASONABLE, PRUDENT, AND TAKEN BONA FIDE IN THE INTERESTS OF ALL CONCERNED

16.61   It is certainly not enough merely to show that the action was reasonable in the agent's own interests. So someone who has agreed to look after another person's property cannot simply sell it when it becomes inconvenient to continue to do so[1].

1   *Sachs v Miklos* [1948] 2 KB 23; though by Torts (Interference with Goods) Act 1977, ss 12 and 13 and Sch 1, there is a power of sale provided that certain specified steps have been taken to contact the owner first.

THE EFFECT OF THE AGENCY

16.62   Where the agent has complied with these rules, then his or her legal rights and liabilities are the same as if the owner of the goods had specifically authorised them to act as they did. So an agent of necessity who justifiably destroys part of a consignment, to preserve the rest, will have a defence to any action by the owner. If the agent justifiably sells goods, then this contract binds the owner. And as an authorised agent, the 'agent of necessity' will be entitled to reimbursement of reasonable expenses, and perhaps to remuneration as well.

If an 'agency of necessity' exists, then, it closely resembles an agency created expressly. This will often entail that there is a *contract* of agency, with the mutual rights and obligations between owner and agent that we would expect under such a contract. It is sometimes suggested that the term 'agency of necessity' should only be applied to cases where the right to act as *agent* – that is, the right to bind the owner to contracts with others – is in issue. On that view, the issue of remuneration or reimbursement should be kept distinct, for these are not unique to contracts of agency[1]. However, it is not clear what this conceptual division would achieve. Either side of the line, some test of necessity needs to be applied, and it seems to make sense to say that it is the same test on both sides.

1   *China-Pacific SA v Food Corpn of India, The Winson* [1982] AC 939 at 958, per Lord Diplock.

16.63   Some argue that to talk of there being an 'agency' or 'contract' in cases of this kind is to engage in fictions. The owner of the goods is by definition uncontactable, and so cannot create an agency, or agree to a contract. There may at one time have been a contract between the two, but (by definition) it did not cover this situation, and it may indeed have been frustrated by the very same events as gave rise to the necessity[1]. However, this proves only that an 'agency of necessity' is not created by express agreement. It does not alter the point that the rights and liabilities are exactly the same *as if* there had been such contract; as if the owner *had* been contactable and had said, 'Yes, I agree that you should take whatever action seems most reasonable'. And someone who tries to insist that a 'genuine' agency is different from a 'fictitious' agency will soon find themselves in difficulties. No clear distinction has been drawn in the case law between cases of genuinely inferred powers of an agent to act in an emergency, and cases of necessitous intervention[2].

1   Goff and Jones *Law of Restitution* (5th edn, 1998), p 466.
2   Maddaugh and McCamus *Law of Restitution* (1990), pp 681–692.

16.64   A proposed alternative explanation, that the agent is entitled to remuneration for acting because this removes the 'unjust enrichment' of the owner of the goods, seems less satisfactory. At best, this only explains one aspect of the liability – that the agent is entitled to remuneration – while saying nothing about other aspects, such as whether the agent's acts bind the owner. And it is not a very good explanation even of that limited aspect. How much remuneration the agent is entitled to, is governed by the contract of agency which the court imposes. The amount may not bear much relation to the enrichment of the owner. It may even be that, though the agent's conduct is entirely justifiable, the goods are through bad luck lost or destroyed. In that situation it is hard to see how the owner is 'enriched' at all, yet the agent may be still entitled to remuneration if he or she has acted properly. While 'unjust enrichment' sometimes happens to fit the facts, it does not do so consistently, or provide any deeper insight into the workings of the law.

Miscellaneous cases

16.65   It is interesting to contrast the following two cases. In *JD White v Troups Transport*[1] a lorry became jammed under a bridge on a busy urban road at 5.30am. The police were unable to contact the haulage company and therefore requested the intervener (a crane hire company) to free the lorry. The basis for the claim was that the intervener was an agent of necessity, and the company were held to be entitled to recover a reasonable fee for the necessitous intervention. However, a similar claim was rejected in *Surrey Breakdown Ltd v*

Knight[2]. Knight's car was stolen and left in a pond, where it was found by the police, who instructed the claimants to remove it. A few days later Knight went to pick up his vehicle but refused to pay the recovery and storage charges, believing them to be excessive. Consequently the Austin 1300 remained in storage for over a year, with £3,470 payable in storage costs. Staughton J held that the interveners did not remove the car from the pond at 4.30am because necessity compelled them to do so; the intervention had been at the request of the police[3]. They were therefore unable to recover any costs incurred.

1 [1976] CLY 33 (County Court).
2 [1999] RTR 84.
3 His Lordship referred to the Road Traffic Regulation Act 1984, ss 101 and 102, but the claim was not based upon any statutory duty to intervene as Knight was not the person responsible for the abandonment; the car had been stolen.

16.66 How can these authorities be reconciled? Both sets of facts are similar in that:

(a) the intervenee was not contactable;
(b) the police requested the intervention; and
(c) expenses were incurred and work was carried out by each intervener.

However, they can be distinguished by reference to the principle of unconscionability. In the former case there was clearly an element of urgency; it was a busy road and the intervention can fairly be described as 'necessary' to protect motorists. However, in the latter case there was no such necessity to justify the intervention, and it would have been against good conscience to order recovery.

16.67 On the other hand, an intervener who acted to preserve some timber that had been carried downstream by the tide was denied a lien over the property for his trouble and expense. Eyre CJ left open the possibility that he might be entitled to a personal, as opposed to a proprietary, remedy and stated:

> ... perhaps it is better for the public that these voluntary acts of benevolence from one man to another, which are charities and moral duties, but not legal duties, should depend altogether for their reward upon the moral duty of gratitude[1].

The key phrase is 'voluntary acts of benevolence'. Where the intervention is purely voluntary the general rule will prevail and a restitutionary remedy will be denied to the intervener. So where a highway authority repairs a road bridge over a canal, in the absence of a legal liability to do so, it will be treated as a mere volunteer and, therefore, will be unable to recover for the work undertaken[2].

1 *Nicholson v Chapman* (1793) 2 Hy Bl 254 at 259, 126 ER 536 at 539.
2 *Macclesfield Corpn v Great Central Railway* [1911] 2 KB 528.

E Conclusion

16.68 From the somewhat diverse subject matter discussed above, it should now be clear that there is no single unifying concept behind the authorities on necessity. Various theories have attempted to bring them under the one umbrella but, it seems, to no avail. With the introduction of the Civil Procedure Rules and the overriding objective at its core, the courts may now be better equipped to rationalise their decisions relating to services rendered out of necessity. By examining *Falcke's case* in its proper historical context, it should be viewed as an example of the general rule rather than a comprehensive statement of the law.

It has been suggested in this chapter that the common law principles can only go so far in determining claims in this field. The judiciary should be encouraged by the thriving development of equitable principles, with the core concept of unconscionability, to remedy those exceptional cases which fall outside the general rule.

CHAPTER 17

Mistaken Payments

Peter McDermott

A   Introduction

17.1   Restitution scholars have referred to the 'voluminous'[1] case law on mistaken payments. There is also considerable academic literature on the subject of mistaken payments. Until comparatively recently, practitioners who sought guidance on this subject would consult works on quasi-contract. As Jones points, out the utilisation of quasi-contract made recovery dependant upon a fiction – the fiction of 'implied contract', imposed because of the fear of uncontrolled judicial discretion, such as what Hamilton LJ referred to as the vague jurisprudence of 'justice between man and man'[2]. The fiction was: 'if A paid B money under a mistake of fact, B was required to repay the money to A'[3]. In 1972, the subject of mistaken payments was still firmly regarded as part of quasi-contract, as Birks then wrote:

> The obligation to repay money received as the result of the payer's mistake is a well-established head of quasi-contract, that is to say, of that species of obligation which is imposed by law in the absence of either tort or contract simply in order to redress what would otherwise be an unjust enrichment of the recipient[4].

1   See Burrows *Law of Restitution* (1993), p 95; Grantham and Rickett 'Restitution, Property and Mistaken Payments' [1997] RLR 83 at 85.
2   *Baylis v Bishop of London* [1913] 1 Ch 127 at 140. On 'implied contract' see above, para 1.12.
3   Jones *Anglo-American Trends in Restitution* (1978), p 3.
4   Birks 'The Recovery of Carelessly Mistaken Payments' (1972) 25 CLP 179.

17.2   Since the publication of the seminal work on restitution by Goff and Jones[1], much of the learning relating to mistaken payments is now to be found in restitution texts. This is because quasi-contract is 'the most ancient and significant part of restitution'[2]. More recently, it was stated: 'A claim to recover money mistakenly paid by the plaintiff to the defendant is often regarded as the paradigm example of a restitutionary claim founded on the principle of unjust enrichment'[3].

1   The influence of the work by Goff and Jones is discussed by Birks 'Misnomer' in Cornish, Nolan, O'Sullivan and Virgo (eds) *Restitution past present and future – Essays in honour of Gareth Jones* (1998), p 2.
2   Goff and Jones *Law of Restitution* (5th edn, 1998), p 3.
3   Virgo *Principles of the Law of Restitution* (1999), p 134. Chapter 8 of that work contains an excellent discussion of the general principles underlying the law of mistake.

17.3   Yet the mere fact that a payment has been mistakenly made does not necessarily mean that the payment can be recovered in an action for restitution[1]. As Virgo points out, there are 'complex policy issues which arise in determining whether the defendant's enrichment really can be considered to be unjust'[2].

Important matters that need to be considered include the type of payment, the nature of the mistake, and any effect of the payment[3]. Another matter that needs to be considered is the increased availability of restitutionary defences by the recipient of the money. This is because in some cases it would be inequitable to require the recipient of the money to repay the money.

1 See *University of Canterbury v A-G* [1995] 1 NZLR 78 at 84, per Williamson J.
2 Virgo *Principles of the Law of Restitution* (1999), p 134.
3 See *University of Canterbury v A-G* [1995] 1 NZLR 78 at 84.

17.4   It should also be appreciated that a claim for restitution of a mistaken payment is sometimes also made on the ground of failure of consideration[1]. It is now accepted that the basis of recovery of a mistaken payment on the ground of failure of consideration is quite distinct from the recovery of a payment under a mistake[2].

1 Birks *An Introduction to the Law of Restitution* (revised edn, 1989), pp 219–264; *Rover International Ltd v Cannon Film Sales Ltd (No 3)* [1989] 1 WLR 912 at 923; *Roxborough v Rothmans of Pall Mall Australia Ltd* (2001) 76 ALJR 203.
2 *David Securities Pty Ltd v Commonwealth Bank of Australia* (1992) 175 CLR 353 at 390, per Brennan J. On failure of consideration see below, para 19.8ff.

Procedural matters

17.5   Where a claimant seeks to recover money that has been mistakenly paid to the defendant, the main remedy that has been traditionally available to a claimant is to make a common law claim for that money. This common law claim is traditionally made by claiming a mistaken payment as money had and received[1]. Lord Mansfield in *Moses v Macferlan*[2] said 'the gist of this kind of action is that the defendant, upon the circumstances of the case, is obliged by the ties of natural justice and equity to refund the money'[3]. Similarly in *R v Brown*[4] Griffith CJ said that the cause of action 'lay whenever the defendant had received money which in justice and equity belonged to the plaintiff and when nothing remained to be done except pay over the money'[5].

1 See *Paul v Pavey & Matthews Pty Ltd* (1985) 3 NSWLR 114 at 120ff, per McHugh JA.
2 (1760) 2 Burr 1005, 97 ER 676.
3 (1760) 2 Burr 1005 at 1012, 97 ER 676 at 681.
4 (1912) 14 CLR 17.
5 (1912) 14 CLR 17 at 25.

17.6   In *Lipkin Gorman v Karpnale Ltd*[1] Lord Goff clarified a number of aspects of the common law claim for money had and received. In contradistinction to equitable remedies that are discretionary, a claim to recover money at common law by a claim for money had and received is made as a matter of right. Lord Goff observed: 'The recovery of restitution is not, as a general rule, a matter of discretion for the court'[2]. Lord Goff also pointed out that the claim for money had and received is 'a personal claim: it is not a proprietary claim'[3]. The fact that specific money received can no longer be identified in the hands of the recipient does not constitute an answer to a claim for restitution[4]. In *Agip (Africa) Ltd v Jackson*[5] Millett J, in discussing the common law claim for money had and received, said: 'It does not depend on the continued retention of the money by the defendant. Save in strictly limited circumstances it is no defence that he has parted with it'[6]. However, as a personal claim this remedy may prove worthless against an insolvent defendant.

1 [1991] 2 AC 548.
2 [1991] 2 AC 548 at 578.
3 [1991] 2 AC 548 at 572.
4 *Australia and New Zealand Banking Group Ltd v Westpac Banking Corpn* (1988) 164 CLR 662 at 673, per curiam.
5 [1990] Ch 265.
6 [1990] Ch 265 at 282. In *Agip (Africa) Ltd v Jackson* [1991] Ch 547 at 566, Fox J remarked: 'The common law remedy attaches to the recipient of the money and its subsequent transportation does not alter this liability'.

17.7   Where the claimant can establish that he still retains title to the money, it can be followed at common law into and out of a bank account and into the hands of a subsequent transferee[1]. In the event that the money is in the hands of a third party, the personal claim of money had and received can be maintained against a third party[2]. This personal claim is made on the basis that the claimant has title to the money that is in the possession of the third party. In *Lipkin Gorman v Karpnale Ltd*[3] Lord Goff has observed that a claim for money had and received against a third party is founded simply on the fact that 'for the third party to retain the money would result in his unjust enrichment at the expense of the owner of the money'[4]. Lord Goff also emphasised that a restitution claim against a third party is not founded upon any wrong by the third party such as conversion or any waiver of tort[5]. However, Lord Goff has observed that the circumstances where such a claim has succeeded against a third party are rare, 'probably, because at common law, property in money, like other fungibles, is lost as such when it is mixed with other money'[6]. There have been a number of cases, including where there was payment to a clearing house[7], where the common law claim for money had and received was not available to recover money in a mixed fund[8]. It is for that reason that equitable tracing claims are generally made against third parties.

1 *Agip (Africa) Ltd v Jackson* [1990] 1 Ch 265 at 285, per Millett J. On this process of following (or 'tracing') see above, ch 4.
2 *Bank Belge pour l'Etranger v Hambrouck* [1921] 1 KB 321; *Agip (Africa) Ltd v Jackson* [1990] 1 Ch 265 at 287, per Millett J. Where a customer's bank has mistakenly paid money from that customer's account to another bank to the credit of another, the customer has been permitted to sue for the restitution of that money: see Bryan 'The Liability of Banks to Make Restitution for Wrongful Payments' (1998) 26 Australian Business Law Review 93 at 95.
3 [1991] 2 AC 548.
4 [1991] 2 AC 548 at 572.
5 On 'waiver of tort' see above, para 12.2ff.
6 [1991] 2 AC 548 at 572.
7 Clearing house rules may provide that in the case of a fraudulent transfer the loss incurred by the clearing house has to be borne by the originating bank: see *State Bank of New South Wales v Swiss Bank Corpn* (1995) 39 NSWLR 350 (New York Clearing House Inter Bank Payment System (CHIPS), r 16(a)).
8 *Re Diplock* [1948] Ch 465 at 518; *Agip (Africa) Ltd v Jackson* [1990] 1 Ch 265 at 285, per Millett J, [1991] Ch 547 at 563; *Nimmo v Westpac Banking Corpn* [1993] 2 NZLR 218 at 238; *Bank Tejarat v Hong Kong and Shanghai Banking Corpn (CI) Ltd* [1995] 1 Lloyd's Rep 239 at 245. However, see McKendrick 'Tracing Misdirected Funds' [1991] LMCLQ 378.

17.8   Lord Mansfield observed in *Clarke v Shee and Johnson*[1] that a claim for money had and received 'is a liberal action in the nature of a bill in equity'[2]. In *Roxborough v Rothmans of Pall Mall Australia Ltd*[3] Gummow J pointed out that Lord Mansfield 'sought to translate equitable principles, doctrines, and procedures into the trial of actions at law; this reflected his appreciation of equitable doctrine for its flexibility and adaptability to modern needs, particularly commercial law'[4]. The views of the Lord Mansfield have been supported in Canada[5] but disapproved in England[6]. Lord Mansfield in *Moses v Macferlan*[7] emphasised that the recipient may 'plead every equitable defence upon the general issue'[8]. It is submitted that one manifestation of that 'equitable nature' of the action is in the flexibility of the defences that are available, such as defence of position[9]. It has been seen that this defence is not automatically available in all cases where the defendant has disposed of the money claimed. In such circumstances the defendant cannot successfully raise a defence merely on the simple basis that he is not presently in possession of any money of the claimant.

1   (1774) 1 Cowp 197, 98 ER 1041.
2   (1774) 1 Cowp 197 at 199, 98 ER 1041 at 1042.
3   (2001) 76 ALJR 203.
4   (2001) 76 ALJR 203 at 220.
5   *Bank of Montreal v R* (1907) 38 SCR 258 at 280; *Dominion Bank v Union Bank of Canada* (1908) 40 SCR 366 at 381–382.
6   See eg *Holt v Markham* [1923] 1 KB 504 at 513; *Morgan v Ashcroft* [1938] 1 KB 49 at 62.
7   (1760) 2 Burr 1005, 97 ER 676.
8   (1760) 2 Burr 1005 at 1010, 97 ER 676 at 679.
9   On the defence of change of position, see below para 21.37ff.

17.9   The claim of money had and received may be available to recover money paid contrary to statute. The omission of a statutory remedy for the recovery of such money does not preclude the recovery of that money[1]. The claim of money had and received has also been available where because of a mistake there has been a failure to deduct tax from rental payments, the statutory right of deduction not being an exclusive remedy[2].

1   *Kiriri Cotton Co Ltd v Dewani* [1960] AC 192 at 205.
2   *Turvey v Dentons (1923) Ltd* [1953] 1 QB 218 at 227, per Pilcher J.

17.10   Where a mistaken payment is induced by an innocent misrepresentation, the claimant may prefer to recover damages under statute[1] rather than pursue a claim for restitution. The fact that the claimant received consideration does not prevent the grant of statutory relief[2]. Where the misrepresentation is negligent or fraudulent, then tortious remedies are clearly available[3]. Moneys mistakenly paid as a result of a fraudulent representation can be recovered[4]. The advantage of having a claim based on tort, rather than restitution where fault is not generally an element of the cause of action, is that a claimant in a case of fraud may sometimes be awarded exemplary damages[5], or costs on an indemnity basis.

1   See the Misrepresentation Act 1967, s 2.
2   See the Misrepresentation Act 1967, s 1(b). Cf *Seddon v North Eastern Salt Co* [1905] 1 Ch 326.
3   Birks, *An Introduction to the Law of Restitution* (revised edn, 1989), p 170.
4   *Hughes v Liverpool Victoria Legal Friendly Society* [1916] 2 KB 482.
5   On exemplary damages see above, para 12.10ff, and more generally Grubb (ed) *Law of Tort* (2002), para 6.21ff.

No NEED FOR A PRIOR DEMAND FOR PAYMENT BEFORE AN ACTION CAN BE COMMENCED

17.11   A claimant who seeks to recover a mistaken payment does not first have to demand that the payee repay the money. This has the consequence that the making of a demand for payment is not an element of the cause of action that the claimant must plead and prove. There is authority that in cases of shared mistake of fact, the giving of notice is not a necessary preliminary to the bringing of an action[1]. This principle also applies in cases where the mistake is only that of the payer. This is because the obligation to repay the mistaken payment arises upon the receipt of the mistaken payment. In *Agip (Africa) Ltd v Jackson*[2] Millett J in discussing the common law claim for money had and received, pointed out that 'the cause of action is complete when the money is received'[3]. The reason why a demand is not a necessary element of the cause of action is because the essence of the action is unjust enrichment, and the cause of action arises at the moment when a recipient is unjustly enriched.

1   *Baker v Courage & Co* [1910] 1 KB 56; *Anglo-Scottish Beet Sugar Corpn v Spalding UDC* [1937] 2 KB 607. Peculiar circumstances were present in *Freeman v Jeffries* (1869) LR 4 Exch 189, where the payment was made with knowledge of the mistake.
2   [1990] Ch 265.
3   [1990] Ch 265 at 282. See also *Baker v Courage & Co* [1910] 1 KB 56 at 62; *Re Mason* [1928] Ch 385 at 393.

17.12   This principle applies whether the mistaken payment is made because of a mistake of fact or a mistake of law. In *David Securities Pty Ltd v Commonwealth Bank of Australia*[1] Brennan J stated the modern learning on this subject: 'If under a mistake, money is paid to and unjustly enriches a payee, the payee's right to recover the money accrues at the moment when the payee received the money'[2]. In the *David Securities* case the High Court of Australia confirmed that restitution was available where moneys are paid under a mistake of law. It was also confirmed in this case that the existence of a cause of action in the case of a payment caused by a mistake of law does not depend upon the giving of notice. In *Kleinwort Benson Ltd v Lincoln City Council*[3] Lord Hope said: 'I agree with Brennan J's observation in the *David Securities* case ... that the right to recover the amount paid by mistake accrues at the moment when the sum is received by the payee'[4].

1   (1992) 175 CLR 353.
2   (1992) 175 CLR 353 at 389. See also *Nimmo v Westpac Banking Corpn* [1993] 2 NZLR 218 at 238.
3   [1999] 2 AC 349.
4   [1999] 2 AC 349 at 409.

17.13   There are some old cases that suggest that there may be a need in some cases to give notice where the payee is ignorant of the mistake in question. For example in *Kelly v Solari*[1] Parke B said: 'a demand may be necessary in those cases where the party receiving it may have been ignorant of the mistake'[2]. In the Victorian case of *Peck v Mayor of Hawthorn*[3] it was held where the defendants know of the mistake under which moneys were paid, the claimant is entitled to maintain an action without any previous demand for payment. In this case it was, however, suggested that there is 'a rule' that notice is required where a payee is unaware that the money has been paid under mistake. However, in the light of the modern learning on this subject, it is now clear that there is no need for a claimant to perfect an action by demanding the repayment of the mistaken payment.

1   (1841) 9 M & W 54, 152 ER 24. See also *Freeman v Jeffries* (1869) LR 4 Ex Ch 189.
2   (1841) 9 M & W 54 at 58, 152 ER 24 at 26.
3   (1892) 18 VLR 24.

17.14   The issue concerning whether it is necessary for a demand to be made before a cause of action arises also has relevance in the context of the operation of limitation legislation. If the giving of notice were necessary to perfect a cause of action, it would have the consequence that a payer could postpone the making of his demand and yet not have the statute run against him[1]. Difficulties occur where a mistake of law has caused a payment to be made. In many cases the parties may be quite unaware of the mistake of law until an authoritative pronouncement is made. However, there is no support for the view that for the purpose of limitation legislation a cause of action for moneys paid under a mistake of law does not accrue until the courts finally acknowledge that the facts alleged give rise to a cause of action[2].

1 See *Baker v Courage & Co* [1910] 1 KB 56 at 65, per Hamilton J.
2 See *Torrens Aloha Pty Ltd v Citibank NA* (1997) 72 FCR 581. On limitation generally see below paras 17.85ff and 21.63ff.

17.15 Notice of the mistake may have relevance in respect of the right of the claimant to claim costs of an action. It might also be relevant in considering the application of defences. A payee who has received notice of a mistake could not thereafter claim that any subsequent expenditure was made in good faith for the purpose of relying upon the change of position defence. This is because Lord Goff has emphasised that an essential element of the defence of change of position is that a defendant has 'acted in good faith throughout'[1].

1 See *Lipkin Gorman v Karpnale Ltd* [1991] 2 AC 548 at 580. On change of position see below, para 21.37ff.

B   General principles

17.16 There has now developed what can, perhaps, be described as some general principles that apply to cases of mistaken payments. It is important to emphasise that Robert Goff J in his principled judgment in *Barclays Bank Ltd v W J Simms, Son & Cooke (Southern) Ltd*[1] has restated the fundamental principles. One important principle is that a payment, which is made by mistake, can prima facie be recovered in an action for restitution. Robert Goff J summarised the law as follows[2]:

> 1.   If a person pays money to another under a mistake of fact which causes him to make the payment, he is prima facie entitled to recover it as money paid under a mistake of fact.
> 2.   His claim may however fail if:
> (a)   the payer intends that the payee shall have the money at all events, whether the fact be true or false, or is deemed in law so to intend[3];
> (b)   the payment is made for good consideration, in particular if the money is paid to discharge, and does discharge, a debt owed to the payee (or a principal on whose behalf he is authorised to receive the payment) by the payer or by a third party by whom he is authorised to discharge the debt[4];
> (c)   the payee has changed his position in good faith, or is deemed in law to have done so[5].

Another important principle, which has been recently clarified, is that the mistake may either be a mistake of fact or a mistake of law. In *Kleinwort Benson Ltd v Lincoln City Council*[6] Lord Goff said 'there should be a general right of recovery of money paid under a mistake, whether of fact or law, subject to appropriate defences'[7]. Where it is sought to recover a mistaken payment, a claimant must show that the payment caused the defendant to be unjustly enriched and that the mistake in question has caused the mistaken payment to be made.

1 [1980] QB 677.
2 [1980] QB 677 at 695.
3 See below, para 17.45ff.
4 See below, para 17.57ff.

5   See below, para 21.37ff.
6   [1999] 2 AC 349.
7   [1999] 2 AC 349 at 373.

Necessity to show unjust enrichment

17.17   A claimant who seeks to recover a mistaken payment from a defendant must show that the defendant has been benefited or unjustly enriched. There must be some evidence of unjust enrichment to enable the recovery of restitution[1]. The receipt of money is ordinarily a clear case of a defendant receiving a benefit[2]. The Court of Appeal in *Portman Building Society v Hamlyn Taylor Neck*[3] emphasised that the mere fact that a payment might have been made by mistake is not by itself sufficient to justify a restitutionary remedy. It is also necessary to show that the defendant has been unjustly enriched by the payment. Where a bank has authority to pay a creditor of a customer and pays that creditor under the mistaken assumption that there are funds in the account of the customer, the creditor has not been unjustly enriched by the payment that has been made to discharge the debt[4]. This is because the payee had a right to receive the payment. The point is considered in more detail below[5].

1   See eg *Crantrave Ltd v Lloyd's Bank plc* [2000] QB 917 at 924, per Pill LJ. The requirement that there be unjust enrichment has been recognised in earlier mistaken payment cases: see *Morgan v Ashcroft* [1938] 1 KB 49 at 76; *Turvey v Dentons (1923) Ltd* [1953] 1 QB 218 at 226.
2   Burrows *Law of Restitution* (1993), p 8.
3   [1998] 4 All ER 202.
4   *Lloyds Bank v Independent Insurance Co Ltd* [2000] QB 110 at 132, per Peter Gibson LJ.
5   See below, para 17.64ff.

Mistake must cause the mistaken payment to be made

17.18   Before a court will order the restitution of a mistaken payment it is necessary to show that the mistake is the operative cause of the mistaken payment. In *Barclays Bank Ltd v W J Simms, Son & Cooke (Southern) Ltd*[1] Robert Goff J remarked: 'If a person pays money to another under a mistake of fact which causes him to make the payment, he is prima facie entitled to recover it as money paid under a mistake of fact'[2]. It is not necessary to show that the payee caused or contributed to the mistake[3]. Restitution will not be granted where the mistake in question was not a cause of the payment. In some mistake of law cases, it is difficult to apply a causation test to say that the mistake caused the payment of money paid under a mistake of law[4].

1   [1980] QB 677.
2   [1980] QB 677 at 695.
3   *Bunge (Australia) Pty Ltd v Ying Sing* (1928) 28 SRNSW 265 at 271–272.
4   See eg *Nurdin & Peacock plc v DB Ramsden & Co Ltd* [1999] 1 WLR 1249 at 1273, per Neuberger J.

Types of mistake

17.19   It is now accepted that any kind of mistake, which caused the mistaken payment to be made, will enable an action of restitution to be maintained[1]. In *Barclays Bank Ltd v W J Simms, Son & Cooke (Southern) Ltd*[2] Robert Goff J made reference to 'a mistake of fact which causes him to make the payment'[3]. What was important in this formulation is the causative effect of the mistake and not how the mistake can be characterised. The function of mistake in the field of restitution on the ground of unjust enrichment is to show that the benefit that was received was an unintended benefit[4].

1   *Barclays Bank Ltd v W J Simms, Son & Cooke (Southern) Ltd* [1980] QB 677; *David Securities Pty Ltd v Commonwealth Bank of Australia* (1992) 175 CLR 353.
2   [1980] QB 677.
3   [1980] QB 677 at 695.
4   *Kleinwort Benson Ltd v Lincoln City Council* [1999] AC 349 at 408, per Lord Hope.

17.20   Lord Hope made some observations in *Kleinwort Benson Ltd v Lincoln City Council*[1] as to what has to be shown in order to establish the requisite mistake of fact:

> The inquiry will not be a difficult one, where the mistake is said to have been one of fact, if the facts have not changed since the date of the payment and the payer is able to show that he paid due to a misunderstanding of them, to incorrect information or to ignorance. Nor is it difficult to deal with the case where the facts have changed. In such a case proof that that the alleged state of the facts at the time did not emerge until afterwards will usually be sufficient to show that there was, at the time of payment, no mistake[2].

In some of the older commentaries there will be found statements that restitution is only available where a mistaken payment is made under a mistake of fact, and not law. Since the decision of the House of Lords in *Kleinwort Benson Ltd v Lincoln City Council*[3] there is now a general right of recovery whether that mistake is a mistake of fact or of law.

1   [1999] 2 AC 349.
2   [1999] 2 AC 349 at 409.
3   [1999] 2 AC 349.

17.21   There is a respectable line of authority that the mistake must be a common mistake between the person paying and the person receiving the money[1]. The modern position is that whilst these are cases of mistake in which restitution is available, this test does not limit the cases in which restitution will be allowed. The test no longer has any authority in modern formulations of principle[2]. In *Barclays Bank Ltd v W J Simms, Son & Cooke (Southern) Ltd*[3] Robert Goff J pointed out that the House of Lords in *R E Jones v Waring & Gillow Ltd*[4] did not impose such a test. Robert Goff J remarked that in that case Viscount Cave 'considered it sufficient for the plaintiff to show that he suffered under a mistake of fact which caused the payment'[5].

1   *Chambers v Miller* (1862) 13 CBNS 125, 143 ER 50; *Morton v Smith* (1912) 34 ALT 79; *Weld-Blundell v Synott* [1940] 2 KB 107; *Bank of New South Wales v Deri* (1963) 80 WNNSW 1499; *Platemaster Pty Ltd v M & T Investment Pty Ltd* [1973] VR 93 at 97; *National Australia Westminster Bank Ltd v Barclays Bank International Ltd* [1975] QB 654.
2   See Goff and Jones *Law of Restitution* (5th edn, 1998), p 210, n 41 and p 211, n 49.
3   [1980] QB 677 at 693.
4   [1926] AC 670.
5   [1980] QB 677 at 693.

Mistake need not be 'fundamental'

17.22   It is now clear that it is not necessary that a mistake that has caused the mistaken payment to be made should be characterised as fundamental. There are statements in some cases that suggest that it is necessary that a mistake must be of a fundamental nature before restitution can take place[1]. For instance, a number of such statements are to be found in *Morgan v Ashcroft*[2]. Sir

Wilfred Greene MR made reference to a 'payment under a mistake of fact which can be described as fundamental or basic'[3]. Scott LJ also said: 'the mistake must be in some aspect or another fundamental to the transaction'[4]. However, it may be questioned whether these statements are central to the ratio of the case, in which relief was refused on the ground that a bookmaker could not recover an overpayment on the ground of statutory illegality.

1   See eg *Norwich Union Fire Insurance Society Ltd v William H Price Ltd* [1934] AC 455; *Platemaster Pty Ltd v M & T Investment Pty Ltd* [1973] VR 93 at 97; *Commercial Bank of Australia v Younis* [1979] 1 NSWLR 444; *Bank of New South Wales v Murphett* [1983] 1 VR 489.
2   [1938] 1 KB 49.
3   [1938] 1 KB 49 at 66.
4   [1938] 1 KB 49 at 77.

17.23   Scott LJ also referred to a number of cases on mistaken payment[1]. In none of these cases is a test of fundamental mistake imposed by the court. In *Kelly v Solari*[2] Parke B said:

> I think that where money is paid to another under the influence of a mistake, that is, upon the supposition that a specific fact is true, which would entitle the other to the money, but which fact is untrue, and the money would not have been paid if it had been known to the payer that the fact was untrue, an action will lie to recover it back ...[3]

In *Aiken v Short*[4] Bramwell B said:

> It seems to me that the right to recover money paid under a mistake of fact must have reference to a belief of the existence of a fact which, if true, would have given the person receiving a right against the person paying the money; and it can never be applicable to a case where the fact mistaken is a fact which would merely have made it desirable for the person paying it to pay to the person receiving it. I do not know whether that is a sufficiently comprehensive principle, but is one which has existed throughout in my mind[5].

1   [1938] 1 KB 49 at 72–73.
2   (1841) 9 M & W 54, 152 ER 24.
3   (1841) 9 M & W 54 at 58, 152 ER 24 at 26.
4   (1856) 25 LJ Ex 321, 1 H & N 210, 156 ER 1180.
5   (1856) 25 LJ Ex 321 at 324. This passage does not appear as such in what appears to be an edited passage in 1 H & N 210 at 215 (156 ER 1180 at 1182) which was cited in *Barclays Bank Ltd v W J Simms, Son & Cooke (Southern) Ltd* [1980] QB 677. In *Morgan v Ashcroft* [1938] 1 KB 49 at 77, Scott LJ pointed out that the Law Journal report was a fuller report.

17.24   It is now settled that there is no need to characterise a mistake as fundamental in the contractual law sense, because a claimant will only seek the recovery of money and not the setting aside of title[1], although it is clear that a fundamental mistake in contract law will certainly enable a mistaken payment to be recovered[2]. In *Barclays Bank Ltd v W J Simms, Son & Cooke (Southern) Ltd*[3] Robert Goff J, after a careful review of all of the authorities, formulated the following authoritative proposition: 'If a person pays money to another under a mistake of fact which causes him to make the payment, he is prima facie entitled to recover it as money paid under a mistake of fact'[4]. There is no need for such a mistake to be characterised as 'fundamental', although Robert Goff J later used that term to refer to a mistake as to the identity of the payee[5]. Robert Goff J also pointed out that in *Kelly v Solari*[6], 'Parke B did not place any restriction on the nature of the mistake which would ground recovery'[7].

1   See Grantham and Rickett 'Restitution, Property and Mistaken Payments' [1997] RLR 83 at 88.
2   Goff and Jones *Law of Restitution* (5th ed, 1998), pp 177, 178 and 189; Virgo *Principles of the Law of Restitution* (1999), p 151.

3   [1980] QB 677.
4   [1980] QB 677 at 695.
5   [1980] QB 677 at 697.
6   (1841) 9 M & W 54, 152 ER 24.
7   [1980] QB 677 at 687.

17.25   In Australia the notion that restitution would only be available where a mistake is 'fundamental' has also been finally repudiated. In *David Securities Pty Ltd v Commonwealth Bank of Australia*[1] the High Court of Australia ruled that there was no place for the view that a causative mistake be fundamental. The High Court remarked:

> The notion of fundamentality is, however, extremely vague and would seem to add little, if anything, to the requirement that the mistake cause the payment. If the payer has made the payment because of a mistake, his or her intention to transfer the money is vitiated and the recipient has been enriched. There is therefore no place for a further requirement that the causative mistake be fundamental; insistence upon that factor would only serve to focus attention in a non-specific way on the nature of the mistake, rather than the fact of enrichment[2].

Previously in *Porter v Latec Finance Pty Ltd*[3] Barwick CJ appeared to use the term 'fundamental' in a causative sense, 'properly identifying the transaction and the relationship of the mistake to it'[4].

1   (1992) 175 CLR 353.
2   (1992) 175 CLR 353 at 377–378, per Mason CJ, Deane, Toohey, Gaudron, and McHugh JJ.
3   (1964) 111 CLR 177 at 187.
4   (1992) 175 CLR 353 at 377–378. See also *Commercial Bank of Australia Ltd v Younis* [1979] 1 NSWLR 444.

Categories of mistake

17.26   The categories in which restitution of a mistaken payment will be allowed are not closed. Goff and Jones have developed the following useful categories: where money is paid under a mistaken belief that there is a present liability; where money is paid under a mistaken belief that a liability will accrue in the future; where the payer mistakenly believed that he was under a moral obligation to make the payment; mistake in gifts[1].

In this chapter a number of distinct categories that have been the subject of litigation concerning mistaken payments are discussed. In some cases a claim for restitution did not succeed, because the mistake in question was not the operative cause of the making of the payment.

1   Goff and Jones *Law of Restitution* (5th edn, 1998), pp 181–191.

SUPPOSED LIABILITY TEST

17.27   One of the paradigm categories in which restitution will be allowed is where the payer has paid money under a mistake of fact (or now since the decision in *Kleinwort Benson Ltd v Lincoln City Council*[1], a mistake of law), that he was liable to pay the money. This is the situation in the leading case of *Kelly v Solari*[2] where an insurance company honoured a life insurance policy on the mistaken assumption that the policy was current. It has been pointed out that, in the vast majority of reported cases on mistaken payments, the mistake in question was one as to supposed liability. Restitution has also been allowed in the case where it was thought that a liability would occur in the future[3].

1   [1999] 2 AC 349.
2   (1841) 9 M & W 54, 152 ER 24.
3   *Kerrison v Glyn, Mills, Currie & Co* (1911) 81 LJKB 465, HL.

17.28   In *Re Bodega Co Ltd*[1] Farwell J said: 'If you are claiming to have money repaid on the ground of mistake, you must show the mistake is one which lead you to suppose you were legally liable to pay'[2].

1   [1904] 1 Ch 276.
2   [1904] 1 Ch 276 at 286.

17.29   However, it is no longer necessary to show that a payment was made because of a supposed liability. Burrows pointed out that in *Barclays Bank Ltd v W J Simms, Son & Cooke (Southern) Ltd*[1] Robert Goff J 'took the opportunity to launch a full-scale attack on the traditional supposed liability rule and attempted to move the law to a new prima facie causation test for mistakes of law'[2]. It is now sufficient to ground a claim for restitution on the following test that was formulated by Robert Goff J: 'If a person pays money to another under a mistake of fact which causes him to make the payment, he is prima facie entitled to recover it as money paid under a mistake of fact'[3]. There is no need to justify a claim for restitution on the ground that the payer had assumed that he was liable to the payee (or even to a third party[4]) before the claim for restitution can succeed.

1   [1980] QB 677.
2   See Burrows *Understanding the Law of Obligations* (1998), p 99.
3   [1980] QB 677 at 695.
4   Cf *R E Jones Ltd v Waring & Gillow Ltd* [1926] AC 670.

17.30   The High Court of Australia in *David Securities Pty Ltd v Commonwealth Bank of Australia*[1] rejected the supposed liability test on the basis that 'it is illogical to concentrate upon the type of mistake made when the crucial factor is that the recipient has been enriched'[2].

1   (1992) 175 CLR 353.
2   (1992) 175 CLR 353 at 376.

PAYMENTS UNDER AN EXISTING AGREEMENT

17.31   The courts have ample jurisdiction, by an appropriate order for restitution, to ensure that the defendant does not receive more than he is entitled to under a contract. Where a mistake has been made in the working out of an existing agreement, the recovery of money paid under a mistake will be allowed[1]. In one case, the agreed charge under a supply contract was varied to provide for a lower quarterly instalment to be paid. After the variation of the contract, the demand notes for the quarterly instalments continued to be made at the higher original amount. It was held that any overpayments made in response to these demand notes could be recovered[2]. In *David Securities Pty Ltd v Commonwealth Bank of Australia*[3] Brennan J remarked: 'If the defendant receives more than his due, he may be unjustly enriched to the extent of the excess and restitution can be ordered pro tanto'[4]. Accordingly the court by an appropriate order may prevent unjust enrichment and ensure that payments that are made in excess of the contract price can be recovered[5].

1   *Cox v Prentice* (1815) 3 M & S 344, 105 ER 641; *Townsend v Crowdy* (1860) 8 CBNS 477, 141 ER 1251; *Newell v Tomlinson* (1871) LR 6 CP 405; *Meadows v Grand Junction Waterworks Co* (1905)

21 TLR 538; *Turvey v Dentons (1923) Ltd* [1953] 1 QB 218; *Prudential Assurance Co Ltd v CM Breedon Pty Ltd* [1994] 2 VR 452 at 457.
2   *Anglo-Scottish Beet Sugar Corpn v Spalding UDC* [1937] 2 KB 607.
3   (1992) 175 CLR 353.
4   (1992) 175 CLR 353 at 392.
5   *Devaux v Conolly* (1849) 8 CB 640, 137 ER 658; *Anglo-Scottish Beet Sugar Corpn v Spalding UDC* [1937] 2 KB 607; *York Air Conditioning & Refrigeration Pty Ltd v Commonwealth* (1949) 80 CLR 11.

17.32   Under this jurisdiction, the court can order restitution if there is patently a mistake as to the interpretation of a contract. In *Phillip Collins Ltd v Davis*[1] the royalties payable to musicians were to be prorated according to the number of tracks on the album in which they had participated. This was held to be the true construction of a music-recording contract. Instead the defendant musicians had been mistakenly paid royalties on the assumption that they had participated in all tracks on the album. In these circumstances the claimants were, subject to the application of the change of position defence, allowed by the court to effectively recover the overpaid royalties by setting off the overpayment against future royalties.

1   [2000] 3 All ER 808.

CARELESSNESS

17.33   In a number of cases, restitution has been allowed where the mistaken payment was made through carelessness[1]. A number of cases have concerned overpayments by banks[2]. In one New Zealand case, because of an internal accounting error by a bank, the debits and credits were reversed in a customer's account[3]. A number of cases have concerned insurance companies making payments, in circumstances where the companies have mistakenly assumed that the policy was current, or that they were under a misapprehension as to the liability of the company to the insured or investor.

1   Birks 'The Recovery of Carelessly Mistaken Payments' (1972) 25 CLP 179.
2   See eg *Lloyd's Bank Ltd v Brooks* (1950) 6 Legal Decisions affecting Bankers 161.
3   See *National Bank of New Zealand v Waitaki International Processing (NI) Ltd* [1997] 1 NZLR 724 discussed by Grantham and Rickett 'Restitution, Property and Mistaken Payments' [1997] RLR 83.

17.34   The leading case is *Kelly v Solari*[1], which Robert Goff J in *Barclays Bank Ltd v W J Simms, Son & Cooke (Southern) Ltd* regarded as the basis of the modern law on the subject of the recovery of money payable under a mistake of fact[2]. An insurance company had paid out to a widow under an insurance policy, which had been taken out on the life of her late husband. However, the policy had lapsed for the non-payment of a premium, and the insurance company had overlooked the fact that the policy had lapsed. The insurance company recovered the mistaken overpayment in proceedings for money had and received. Parke B said: 'where money is paid to another under the influence of a mistake, that is, upon the supposition that a specific fact is true, which would entitle the other to the money, but which fact is untrue, and the money would not have been paid if it had been known to the payer that the fact was untrue, an action will lie to recover it back, and it is against conscience to retain it'[3]. Parke B also pointed out that if money 'is paid under the impression of the truth of a fact which is untrue, it may, generally speaking, be recovered back, however careless the party paying may have been ... '[4]

1   (1841) 9 M & W 54, 152 ER 24.
2   [1980] QB 677 at 686. Birks has referred to the 'great case of *Kelly v Solari*': see 'The Recovery of Carelessly Mistaken Payments' (1972) 25 CLP 179 at 180.
3   (1841) 9 M & W 54 at 58, 152 ER 24 at 26.
4   (1841) 9 M & W 54 at 59, 152 ER 24 at 26.

17.35   A modern example is *Scottish Equitable plc v Derby*[1], where the defendant had invested in a pension policy with the claimant life insurance company, and subsequently exercised an option to take early retirement benefits. The exercise of that option was not recorded because of an administrative error. The defendant was then later overpaid what he was entitled under the policy, because the exercise of his option to take early retirement benefits had not been recorded. It was held that, subject to the application of the defence of change of position, the overpayment could be recovered. Harrison J remarked: 'I am satisfied that the general rule is that mere carelessness by itself does not preclude recovery of the money'[2]. The Court of Appeal confirmed this approach, as well as the application of the observations of Lord Goff in *Lipkin Gorman v Karpnale Ltd*[3], that the recovery of money in restitution is not, as a general rule, a matter of discretion by the court.

1   [2000] 3 All ER 793 (Harrison J), [2001] 3 All ER 818, CA.
2   [2000] 3 All ER 793 at 800.
3   [1991] 2 AC 548.

17.36   The failure by a claimant to use due diligence before making a payment has long been held to be no obstacle to the recovery of a mistaken payment. In *Kelly v Solari*[1] Parke B emphasised that restitution was not precluded by the party paying 'omitting to use due diligence to inquire into the fact'[2]. In *Secretary of State for Employment v Wellworthy Ltd (No 2)*[3] Nield J remarked: 'if money is paid under the impression that a certain state of affairs was true when in reality it was not true, nevertheless, the plaintiff may recover however careless he may have been in omitting to use due diligence in making enquiries'[4].

1   (1841) 9 M & W 54, 152 ER 24.
2   (1841) 9 M & W 54 at 59, 152 ER 24 at 26.
3   [1976] ICR 13.
4   [1976] ICR 13 at 25.

OVERPAYMENTS

17.37   A common instance of a mistaken payment is where a defendant has been paid twice. In *Barclays Bank Ltd v W J Simms, Son & Cooke (Southern) Ltd*[1] Robert Goff J gave a number of examples of overpayment where restitution is available: '(1) A man, forgetting that he has already paid his subscription to the National Trust, pays it a second time. (2) A substantial charity uses a computer for the purpose of distributing small benefactions. The computer runs mad, and pays one beneficiary the same gift one hundred times over'[2]. Robert Goff J mentioned that they were 'by no means far-fetched situations'[3].

1   [1980] QB 677.
2   [1980] QB 677 at 697.
3   [1980] QB 677 at 697.

17.38   An overpayment, which is made because of a failure to make a deduction in accordance with some statutory provision, may be recovered in an action for restitution. In one case concerning a long-term lease, the tenant had failed to exercise the right to deduct income tax, because one of the tenant's agents had wrongly assumed that the lease was for a shorter term. In such a case, the amount of the overpayment can be recovered in a claim for money had and received[1].

1   *Turvey v Dentons (1923) Ltd* [1953] 1 QB 218.

17.39   A personal remedy to recover an overpayment may not be effective in the event that the defendant is insolvent. This was the situation in *Chase Manhattan Bank NA v Israel-British Bank Ltd*[1], in which it was held that where money was paid under a mistake, the receipt of such money, without more, constituted the recipient a trustee, because the payer retains an equitable property interest and the conscience of the recipient 'is subjected to a fiduciary duty to respect his proprietary right'[2]. In *Westdeutsche Landesbank Gironzentrale v Islington London Borough Council*[3] it was pointed out that the mere receipt of the moneys in the *Chase Manhattan* case was insufficient to create a trust where the recipient was ignorant of the mistake. However, in a case where the recipient retained the money after learning of the mistake, the court may have grounds for the imposition of a constructive trust[4]. Lord Browne-Wilkinson pointed out that the Court of Appeal in *Metall und Rohstoff AG v Donaldson Lufkin & Jenrette Inc*[5] had ruled that there was a good arguable case that circumstances may arise in which the court would be prepared to impose a constructive trust de novo as a foundation for the grant of an equitable remedy[6].

1   [1981] Ch 105.
2   [1981] Ch 105 at 119.
3   [1996] 2 All ER 961.
4   On this point see above, para 4.22. In such a case an equity would supervene by reason of the conduct of the recipient: see *Kelly v R* (1902) 27 VLR 522.
5   [1990] 1 QB 391 at 478–479.
6   [1996] 2 All ER 961 at 997.

MISTAKE OF LAW

17.40   Until the long-standing decision in *Bilbie v Lumley*[1] was overruled by the House of Lords in *Kleinwort Benson Ltd v Lincoln City Council*[2], the fact that moneys were paid under a mistake of law was generally a bar to an action for the restitution. The reporters who compiled the *Restatement* had appreciated that the decision in *Bilbie v Lumley*[3] was not always the law: 'Until the nineteenth century no distinction was made between mistake of fact and mistake of law and restitution was freely granted both in law and equity to persons who had paid money to another because of a mistake in law'[4]. The rule against recovery of payments made in mistake of law was never absolutely strict[5]. One well-known exception related to the high standard of conduct expected of a trustee in bankruptcy as an officer of the court, so that mistakes of law relating to payments to or by the trustee can be reviewed[6]. Trustees can recover overpayments made as a mistake of law from beneficiaries[7].

1   (1802) 2 East 469, 102 ER 448.
2   [1999] 2 AC 349.
3   (1802) 2 East 469, 102 ER 448.
4   American Law Institute *Restatement of the Law of Restitution Quasi Contracts and Constructive Trusts* (1937) 179, cited in *David Securities Pty Ltd v Commonwealth Bank of Australia* (1992) 175 CLR 353 at 370. See also *Farmer v Arundel* (1772) 2 Wm Bl 824 at 825.
5   *R v Tower Hamlets London Borough Council, ex p Chetnik Developments Ltd* [1988] AC 858 at 874–877.

6   *Re Condon, ex p James* (1874) 9 Ch App 609.
7   *Re Musgrave* [1916] 2 Ch 417.

17.41   In practice, it is often difficult to distinguish between questions of law and fact[1]. Birks has mentioned that the courts often fought against the absoluteness of the bar against recovery in a case of mistake of law by leaning against the conclusion that the mistake was a mistake of law[2]. It is suggested that the cases of *Secretary of State for Employment v Wellworthy Ltd (No 2)*[3] and *Rover International Ltd v Cannon Film Sales Ltd (No 3)*[4] may be explained by such an attitude.

1   Winfield *Law of Quasi-Contracts* (1952), p 38.
2   Birks *An Introduction to the Law of Restitution* (revised edn, 1989), pp 164 and 165.
3   [1976] ICR 13.
4   [1989] 1 WLR 912.

17.42   Now, since the decision of the House of Lords in *Kleinwort Benson Ltd v Lincoln City Council*[1], it is clear that a payment made by mistake, whether it is a mistake of fact or a mistake of law, will enable an action of restitution to be maintained. In that case Lord Goff considered that there 'should be a general right of recovery of money paid under a mistake, whether of fact or law'[2]. Lord Hope also made some observations in *Kleinwort Benson Ltd v Lincoln City Council*[3] as to what has to be shown in order to establish the requisite mistake of law:

> A question of law may be as capable of being answered as precisely and with as much certainty as a question of fact, or it may be – as are some questions of fact – a matter of opinion.
>
> Nor is it there any essential difference as between fact and law in regard to the payer's state of mind. This may vary from one of complete ignorance to a state of ample knowledge but a misapplication of what is known to the facts. The mistake may have been caused by a failure to take advice, by omitting to examine the available information or by misunderstanding the information which has been obtained. Or it may be due to a failure to predict correctly how the court would determine issues which were unresolved at the time of payment, or even to foresee that there was an issue which would have to be resolved by the court. As Mason CJ said in the *David Securities* case[4], the concept of mistake includes cases of sheer ignorance as well as of positive but incorrect belief[5].

In Australia, since the decision in *David Securities Pty Ltd v Commonwealth Bank of Australia*[6], it is now accepted that 'money is recoverable in restitution proceedings even though the mistake was one of law'[7].

1   [1999] 2 AC 349.
2   [1999] 2 AC 349 at 373.
3   [1999] 2 AC 349.
4   (1992) 175 CLR 353 at p 374.
5   [1999] 2 AC 349 at 409–410.
6   (1992) 175 CLR 353.
7   *Marshall v Marshall* [1999] 1 Qd R 173 at 178, per McPherson JA.

17.43   A recent example of a claim for the recovery of money that was paid under a mistake of law is *Nurdin & Peacock plc v DB Ramsden & Co Ltd*[1]. Overpayments of rent were made. There had been an erroneous explanation to the tenant of the operation of rent review clauses. As the truth began to emerge, the tenant had also paid the rent that was demanded, to avoid the risk that the lease would be forfeited, and under the belief that any overpayments of rent would be recoverable following successful litigation. The case was decided just after the decision in *Kleinwort Benson Ltd v Lincoln City Council*[2], in which their

Lordships recognised that restitution was available in the case of a mistake of law, and so the trial judge had relisted the case for further argument. It was held that all overpayments of rent were recoverable. Neuberger J said:

> it does seem to me clear that in order to found a claim for repayment of money paid under a mistake of law it is necessary for the payer to establish not only that the mistake was made but also that, but for the mistake, he would not have paid the money[3].

He added:

> It may be said that the mistake did not 'cause' the payment, and it is fair to say that the concept of causation is one of which the courts and writers have had much to say in many areas of the law. As I have mentioned already, I consider that the 'but for' test (possibly coupled with a requirement for a close and direct connection between the mistake and the payment and/or a requirement that the mistake impinges on the relationship between payer and payee) is sufficient, in my judgment, to found a claim based on mistake[4].

In Australia, it has been held since the decision of the High Court of Australia in *David Securities Pty Ltd v Commonwealth of Australia*[5] that there is a prima facie right to the restitution of overpayments of rent that are made because of a mistake in interpreting a lease[6].

1   [1999] 1 WLR 1249.
2   [1999] 2 AC 349.
3   [1999] 1 WLR 1249 at 1272.
4   [1999] 1 WLR 1249 at 1273.
5   (1992) 175 CLR 353.
6   *Sydney City Council v Burns Philp Trustee Co Ltd* (Supreme Court of New South Wales, Rogers CJ Comm D, 13 November 1992, unreported), cited in *Palmer v Blue Circle Southern Cement Ltd* (1999) 48 NSWLR 318 at 323, per Bell J.

17.44   One consequence of the decision in *Kleinwort Benson Ltd v Lincoln City Council*[1] is that some thought had been given to the situation where there is a change in the law caused by an appellate decision. The Law Commission had previously recommended that a payment should not be recoverable merely because it was made in accordance with a settled view of the law, which was later departed from by subsequent judicial decisions[2]. One of the Law Lords considered that there is no mistake if a payment is made under a settled view of the law[3]. However, this raises the question of what constitutes a 'settled view' of the law. The Law Commission appreciated that this aspect required definition, and recommended the following partial definition of what is a 'settled view' of the law: 'A view of the law may be regarded for the purposes of this section as having being settled at any time notwithstanding that it was not held unanimously or had not been the subject of a decision by a court or tribunal'[4]. In the *Kleinwort Benson* case Lord Browne-Wilkinson stated that a settled view of the law was 'the practice and understanding of lawyers skilled in the field'[5]. In Australia, it has been held that overpayments of tax made under a mistake of law are refundable only when made from the date of a change in the law[6].

1   [1999] 2 AC 349.
2   *Restitution: Mistakes of Law and Ultra Vires Public Authority Receipts and Payments* (Cm 2731, Law Com no 227, 1994) 190.
3   [1999] 2 AC 349 at 441, per Lord Hope.
4   *Restitution: Mistakes of Law and Ultra Vires Public Authority Receipts and Payments* (Cm 2731, Law Com no 227, 1994) 196, cl 3(2).
5   [1999] 2 AC 349 at 363.
6   *Torrens Aloha Pty Ltd v Citibank NA* (1997) 72 FCR 581.

VOLUNTARY PAYMENTS

17.45 A payment is regarded as voluntary where it is made with full knowledge of the facts and the payment has not been influenced by any mistake[1]. Voluntary payments are generally not recoverable: this has been recognised in a number of cases. In *Cartwright v Rowley*[2], in proceedings for money had and received Lord Kenyon CJ remarked that where money 'has been paid by the plaintiff voluntarily ... it must be taken to be properly and legally paid; nor can money be recovered back again by this form of action, unless there are some circumstances to shew that the plaintiff paid it through mistake, or in consequence of coercion'[3]. In *Barclays Bank Ltd v W J Simms, Son & Cooke (Southern) Ltd*[4] Robert Goff J stated that the claim would fail if 'the payer intends that the payee shall have the money at all events, whether the fact be true or false'[5]. In *Woolwich Equitable Building Society v IRC*[6] Lord Goff said: 'Where a sum has been paid which is not due, but it has not been paid under a mistake of fact or under compulsion ... it is generally not recoverable. Such a payment has often been called a voluntary payment'[7].

1 See eg *Kelly v R* (1902) 27 VLR 522.
2 (1799) 2 Esp 722, 170 ER 509.
3 (1799) 2 Esp 722 at 723, 170 ER 509 at 510.
4 [1980] QB 677.
5 [1980] QB 677 at 695.
6 [1993] AC 70.
7 [1993] AC 70 at 165.

17.46 Often voluntary payments are made in response to demands for payment or threats to take legal action. If the payment is not influenced by any mistake, it will generally be not recoverable. A voluntary payment will often be made under circumstances in which the validity of the payment is not challenged[1].

1 *David Securities Pty Ltd v Commonwealth Bank of Australia* (1992) 175 CLR 353 at 373–374. See further below, para 17.71ff.

17.47 If a person makes a payment that he is not bound to make, and intends to close a transaction, that payment cannot be recovered[1]. This is so if the payer is aware of all of the facts, or is quite indifferent to whether or not he is liable in law[2]. In *Bilbie v Lumley*[3] an underwriter, who had paid out a claimant under an insurance policy, was aware of facts that would have justified him in refusing the claim on the ground of non-disclosure of material facts. Lord Ellenborough justified the denial of recovery of the maxim *ignorantia juris non excusat*, which had only doubtful relevance. *Bilbie v Lumley* was subsequently overruled by the House of Lords in *Kleinwort Benson Ltd v Lincoln City Council*[4] which held that mistake of law was no longer a bar to restitution[5]. However, the High Court of Australia has suggested that *Bilbie v Lumley* 'was probably correct [on its own facts] because the payment appears to have been made voluntarily and not under any mistake at all'[6]. It may well be that *Brisbane v Dacres*[7] is also explicable as being a voluntary payment. In that case a naval captain had paid his Admiral a share of freight revenue in accordance with a custom. Some time later, he unsuccessfully sought to recover that payment when he discovered that the Admiral could not lawfully demand payment of that share.

1 *Maskell v Horner* [1915] 3 KB 106 at 118, per Lord Reading CJ; *Westdeutsche Landesbank Gironzentrale v Islington London Borough Council* [1994] 4 All ER 890 at 933, per Hobhouse J.
2 *Mason v New South Wales* (1959) 102 CLR 108 at 143.

3 (1802) 2 East 469, 102 ER 448.
4 [1999] 2 AC 349.
5 See above, para 17.40.
6 *David Securities Pty Ltd v Commonwealth Bank of Australia* (1992) 175 CLR 353 at 371.
7 (1813) 5 Taunt 143, 128 ER 641.

17.48   In some cases recovery has been denied to a person who has made a payment 'voluntarily', with full knowledge of the facts under a mistake of law[1]. However, after the decision in *Kleinwort Benson Ltd v Lincoln City Council*[2] payments that have been made under a mistake of law are now be recoverable.

1 See eg *Ord v Ord* [1923] 2 KB 432.
2 [1999] 2 AC 349.

17.49   There are cases where a claimant has paid money under the compulsion of pressing necessity, such as where the seizure of his goods has been threatened. In such circumstances the money is regarded as not being paid voluntarily and can be recovered as money had and received[1]. In *Maskell v Horner*[2] Lord Reading CJ remarked: 'There are numerous instances in the books of successful claims in this form of action'[3].

1 *Valpy v Manley* (1845) 1 CB 594 at 602–603, 135 ER 673 at 677; *Atlee v Backhouse* (1838) 3 M & W 633 at 646 and 650, 150 ER 1298 at 1303–1305; *Maskell v Horner* [1915] 3 KB 106 at 118.
2 [1915] 3 KB 106.
3 [1915] 3 KB 106 at 118.

GIFTS

17.50   Gifts cannot generally be recovered[1]. A voluntary payment that is made as a gift, where the payer is quite indifferent to the truth of the facts, is not recoverable. Even where a donor is under a misapprehension of the true state of facts, a court will still be reluctant to order the refund of a gift of money. In *Morgan v Ashcroft*[2] Sir Wilfred Greene MR remarked: 'If a father, believing that his son has suffered a financial loss, gives him a sum of money, he surely could not claim repayment if he afterwards discovered that no such loss had occurred'[3]. Where the recipient of a gift is aware of that the gift is given in circumstances of mistake, it would be inequitable for the recipient to be allowed to retain the gift. In certain classes of gift, the courts will be more cautious in giving restitutionary relief. A court would require clear evidence before a donation to a charitable trust could be retrieved on the ground of mistake. A donor must show that he would not have made the gift but for the mistake of fact[4].

1 *Maskell v Horner* [1915] 3 KB 106 at 118.
2 [1938] 1 KB 49.
3 [1938] 1 KB 49 at 66.
4 See *University of Canterbury v A-G* [1995] 1 NZLR 78 at 81, per Williamson J.

AGENCY

17.51   A number of cases concerning mistaken payments have concerned payment to an agent, and the issue has arisen as to whether the agent or the principal is liable to make restitution. The general principle is: 'The prima facie liability to make restitution is imposed by the law on the person who has been unjustly enriched'[1]. Accordingly, the agent who has received the money has a prima facie responsibility to make restitution, and is liable in an action for restitution[2]. In such an action the agent can be directly sued without the need to join the principal as a party[3].

1 *Australia and New Zealand Banking Group Ltd v Westpac Banking Corpn* (1988) 164 CLR 662 at 673, per curiam.
2 *Kleinwort Sons & Co v Dunlop Rubber Co* (1907) 97 LT 263 at 265; *Australia and New Zealand Banking Group Ltd v Westpac Banking Corpn* (1988) 164 CLR 662.
3 *Cary v Webster* (1721) 1 Stra 480, 93 ER 647.

17.52 Where the agent has paid the money to the principal, then this prima facie responsibility of the agent to make restitution is displaced, and the agent can rely on the defence of 'payment over'[1]. To invoke this defence, the agent must have effectively passed on the money to or on behalf of the principal[2]. Merely allowing the principal to have a credit would be insufficient, unless something equivalent to payment to the principal has occurred[3]. Where the defence of payment over is established, the agent is regarded as 'a mere conduit pipe'[4], and not liable to make restitution[5]. In such a case the principal will have to make restitution of the mistaken payment[6]. There are, however, a number of circumstances in which the defence of payment over will not succeed, such as where the agent had notice of the claim of the payer before the money was paid to the principal[7]. An important aspect of the defence of payment over is that the agent has acted in good faith and paid the money to the principal, or otherwise acted to his detriment with the principal, in the belief that the original payment was good and valid[8].

1 For a different angle on this problem, see below, para 21.26ff. This defence is also known as 'ministerial receipt': see Bryan 'The Liability of Banks to Make Restitution for Wrongful Payments' (1998) 26 Australian Business Law Review 93.
2 Mason and Carter *Restitution Law in Australia* (1995), p 137.
3 *Bowstead & Reynolds on Agency* (17th edn, 2001), p 520.
4 *Australia and New Zealand Banking Group Ltd v Westpac Banking Corpn* (1988) 164 CLR 662 at 674; *Agip (Africa) Ltd v Jackson* [1990] Ch 265 at 288, per Millett J.
5 *Metropolitan Assurance Co v Samuel & Co* [1923] 1 KB 348 at 354.
6 *Gowers v Lloyds and National Provincial Foreign Bank Ltd* [1938] 1 All ER 766; *Australia and New Zealand Banking Group Ltd v Westpac Banking Corpn* (1988) 164 CLR 662 at 682.
7 *Holland v Russell* (1861) 1 B & S 424, 121 ER 773; *Kleinwort Sons & Co v Dunlop Rubber Co* (1907) 97 LT 263 at 265; *Nizam of Hyderabad and State of Hyderabad v Jung* [1957] Ch 185 at 239; *Australia and New Zealand Banking Group Ltd v Westpac Banking Corpn* (1988) 164 CLR 662 at 682.
8 *Bowstead & Reynolds on Agency* (17th edn, 2001), p 520, art 113.

17.53 Claims for the recovery of money mistakenly paid have succeeded even where another agent of the payer has full knowledge of the facts[1]. This principle is apparent in the seminal case of *Kelly v Solari*[2]. In *Simos v National Bank of Australasia Ltd*[3] a bank was only authorised to pay upon cheques that were signed by both customers. The bank could recover money that was paid by mistake, upon a cheque that was signed by only one customer. The fact that at least one of the officers of the bank was aware that cheques required the signatures of both customers did not preclude the recovery of money paid under a mistake of fact.

1 *Anglo-Scottish Beet Sugar Corpn v Spalding UDC* [1937] 2 KB 607; *Purity Dairy Ltd v Collinson* (1966) 58 DLR (2d) 67; *Rural Municipality of Storthoaks v Mobil Oil Canada Ltd* (1975) 55 DLR (3d) 1.
2 (1841) 9 M & W 54, 152 ER 24. See *R E Jones Ltd v Waring & Gillow Ltd* [1926] AC 670 at 627.
3 (1976) 10 ACTR 4.

17.54   In most cases where a principal is a company or corporate body, the activities of that company will be carried out through agents. The principal will be able to recover money paid under a mistake of fact by an agent[1].

1   *Lloyd's Bank Ltd v Brooks* (1950) 6 Legal Decisions Affecting Bankers 161 at 164, per Lynskey J.

C   Defences

17.55   There may be cases where it would be unjust to the defendant to permit recovery of money paid under a mistake by the claimant. As long ago as in 1760 Lord Mansfield in *Moses v Macferlan*[1] recognised that a claim for money had and received, a species of assumpsit, would lie 'for money paid by mistake'[2], and that in such an action the defendant 'may defend himself by every thing which shews that the plaintiff, *ex aequo et bono*, is not intitled to the whole of his demand, or to any part of it'[3]. Without the availability of any defences, the action for money had and received has potential to do injustice to the recipient of a payment[4]. This is why in *Kleinwort Benson Ltd v Lincoln City Council*[5] Lord Goff remarked: 'there should be a general right of recovery of money paid under a mistake, whether of fact or law, subject to appropriate defences'[6]. In an action for restitution the onus of proof of establishing a defence lies clearly on the defendant[7]. Defences generally are considered below[8], but some aspects are peculiar to mistaken payments and are accordingly considered here.

1   (1760) 2 Burr 1005, 97 ER 676.
2   (1760) 2 Burr 1005 at 1012, 97 ER 676 at 681.
3   (1760) 2 Burr 1005 at 1010, 97 ER 676 at 679.
4   Birks 'The Recovery of Carelessly Mistaken Payments' (1972) 25 CLP 179.
5   [1999] 2 AC 349.
6   [1999] 2 AC 349 at 373.
7   See eg *United Overseas Bank v Jiwani* [1976] 1 WLR 964 at 968, per MacKenna J; *David Securities Pty Ltd v Commonwealth Bank of Australia* (1992) 175 CLR 353 at 383; *Phillip Collins Ltd v Davis* [2000] 3 All ER 808 at 827, per Jonathan Parker J.
8   See below, ch 21.

17.56   Recognised categories of defence to an action for the restitution of a mistaken payment include the defence of change of position[1], estoppel[2], the defence that the payment was made for good consideration[3], the defence that the payment was made to discharge an existing liability[4], or that the payment was made in submission or compromise on an honest claim[5]. Defences may also be based on illegality or public policy. In *Kleinwort Benson Ltd v Lincoln City Council*[6] the House of Lords rejected a proposed defence of honest receipt that would only operate in mistake of law cases[7].

1   See below, para 21.37ff. A bank could not act on the faith of the receipt of funds from a clearing house if it did not act in accordance with the authorisation of the payer but on the basis of information from another source: see *State Bank of New South Wales v Swiss Bank Corpn* (1995) 39 NSWLR 350.
2   See below, para 21.16ff.
3   See below, paras 17.57–17.61 and 21.3ff
4   See below, paras 17.62–17.70.
5   See below, paras 17.71–17.74.
6   [1999] 2 AC 349.
7   See below, paras 17.79 and 17.80.

Good consideration and discharge of a payee's existing liabilities

17.57   This defence will not be generally raised, because in the typical mistaken payment case the defendant has not given value[1]. The defence of good consideration is another manifestation of the defence of bona fide purchaser that is not subsumed in the defence of change of position[2]. An early case in which this is recognised is *Aiken v Short*[3], where a payment made to discharge the liability of a third party to the payee was held to be not recoverable, because the payee provided valuable consideration for the payment in accepting that money as discharging that liability. This decision[4] was relied upon in *Barclays Bank v WJ Simms, Son & Cooke (Southern) Ltd*[5] by Robert Goff J who, in his formulation of Proposition 2(b)[6], stated that a mistaken payment is not recoverable if it has been made 'for good consideration, in particular if the money is paid to discharge, and does discharge, a debt owed to the payee (or a principal on whose behalf he is authorized to receive the payment) by the payer or by a third party by whom he is authorised to discharge the debt'[7]. This formulation of Lord Goff is authoritative in Australia[8].

1   See Grantham and Rickett 'Restitution, Property and Mistaken Payments' [1997] RLR 83 at 89.
2   *Lloyds Bank v Independent Insurance Co Ltd* [2000] QB 110 at 132, per Peter Gibson LJ. See also Birks 'The Law of Restitution at the End of an Epoch' (1999) 28 University of Western Australia Law Review 13 at 61.
3   (1856) 25 LJ Ex 321, 1 H & N 210, 156 ER 1180.
4   As well as dicta in *Kerrison v Glyn, Mills, Currie & Co* (1911) 81 LJKB 465, HL.
5   [1980] QB 677.
6   See above, para 17.16.
7   [1980] QB 677 at 695.
8   *David Securities Pty Ltd v Commonwealth Bank of Australia* (1992) 175 CLR 353 at 380.

17.58   In *Lloyds Bank v Independent Insurance Co Ltd*[1] a customer of a bank had instructed the bank to make a transfer of funds to a creditor of the customer as soon as possible. The bank agreed to transfer the funds provided that there was clearance of incoming cheques. The bank then came the mistaken belief that the cheques had in fact cleared, having received a CHAPS statement to that effect, whereas in actual fact the cheques had not cleared. The bank then transferred funds electronically to discharge a debt owed to the customer. The Court of Appeal held that the bank was not entitled to restitution of the funds mistakenly transferred as this was the discharge of a debt owed to the payee by a third party by whom it was authorised to discharge the debt.

1   [2000] QB 110.

17.59   There have been a number of cases where the defence of good consideration has provided a defence to the recovery of money paid under a mistake. The defence of good consideration is available where the mistaken payment is made in satisfaction of a debt that is due and owing under a contract[1]. The payment of a debt to discharge a mortgage would constitute consideration[2]. So that where mortgagors paid off a mortgage, under a mistake as to their liability to do so under the instrument of mortgage, they were precluded from recovering their payment under a claim for money had and received because the payment resulted in good consideration, consisting of the removal from the title of the mortgagee's interest and the delivery up of an unencumbered certificate of title[3]. The defence has even been applied in cases where there was no bargain between the parties[4].

1   *Platemaster Pty Ltd v M & T Investment Pty Ltd* [1973] VR 93 at 96; *Australia and New Zealand Banking Group Ltd v Westpac Banking Corpn* (1988) 164 CLR 662 at 673; *Griffiths v Commonwealth Bank of Australia* (1994) 123 ALR 111 at 123. See also *Krebs v World Finance Co Ltd* (1958) 14 DLR (2d) 405.
2   *Krebs v World Finance Co Ltd* (1958) 14 DLR (2d) 405.
3   *Porter v Latec Finance (Qld) Pty Ltd* (1964) 111 CLR 177 at 185; *Keith Murphy Pty Ltd v Custom Credit Corpn Ltd* (1992) 6 WAR 332 at 341.
4   See eg *National Mutual Life Association of Australasia Ltd v Walsh* (1987) 8 NSWLR 585 at 599. This difficult case, in which consideration was applied as a complete defence, would now be resolved by the application of the change of position defence, on which see below, para 21.37. See also Birks 'Modernising the Law of Restitution' (1993) 109 LQR 164 at 167.

17.60   The defence will not apply when the payee was responsible for the mistake, or received the money with knowledge of it. In *Barclays Bank v WJ Simms, Son & Cooke (Southern) Ltd*[1], as a footnote to his Proposition 2(b)[2], Robert Goff J pointed out that even if the payee has given consideration for the payment, for example, by accepting the payment in discharge of a debt owed to him by the third party on whose behalf the payer is authorised to discharge it, repayment may nonetheless be ordered if the payer's mistake is induced by the payee, or possibly even where the payee being aware of the payer's mistake, did not receive the money in good faith[3]. In one case, the defence was not available where the plaintiff mistakenly overpaid a debt[4]. The defence was also not available where an employee, who had received a payment upon the termination of his employment, had failed to disclose the fraudulent conduct of a subordinate employee, thus inducing the employee to believe that the employment of that subordinate employee could only be terminated by agreement[5].

1   [1980] QB 677.
2   [1980] QB 677 at 695; above, para 17.16.
3   [1980] QB 677 at 695.
4   *Commonwealth of Australia v McCormack* (1982) 45 ALR 355 (Federal Court of Australia, Full Court).
5   *Sybron Corpn v Rochem Ltd* [1983] 2 All ER 707.

17.61   The defence of bona fide purchaser applies where the holder of a cheque has received payment where the drawee has mistakenly assumed that he has sufficient funds of the drawer. In 1937 the *Restatement*[1] recognised that restitution was not available in such circumstances, providing that: 'The holder of a check or other bill of exchange who, having paid value in good faith therefor, receives payment from the drawee without reason to know that the drawee is mistaken, is under no duty of restitution to him although the drawee pays because of a mistaken belief that he has sufficient funds of the drawer or that he is otherwise under a duty to pay'[2].

1   American Law Institute *Restatement of the Law of Restitution Quasi Contracts and Constructive Trusts* (1937).
2   American Law Institute *Restatement of the Law of Restitution Quasi Contracts and Constructive Trusts* (1937) 33 138–139, cited by Peter Gibson LJ in *Lloyds Bank v Independent Insurance Co Ltd* [2000] QB 110 at 133.

17.62   Restitution will generally not lie where a mistaken payment is made which in fact discharges an existing liability on the part of the payee. In most cases the defence of good consideration will preclude recovery of the mistaken payment. But in some cases where a mistaken payment may be made which discharges a liability, which is not founded on contract, the liability may be based on statute. In such cases the general principle laid down by Brennan J in *David Securities Pty Ltd v Commonwealth Bank of Australia*[1] is applicable:

If a defendant has a right to receive a payment, whether under a statute, in discharge of a liability owing to him or pursuant to a contract, a mistake by the plaintiff in making the payment does not convert the receipt into an unjust enrichment[2].

1   (1992) 175 CLR 353.
2   (1992) 175 CLR 353 at 392.

17.63   A debtor who mistakenly pays one creditor instead of another will not be permitted to recover that mistaken payment from the creditor, who was legally entitled to receive that payment[1]. Even where a mistaken payment is made in discharge of a debt that is not legally enforceable (whether because it is statue barred, non-compliance with statute, infancy etc), it is irrecoverable if it is an honest debt[2].

1   *Platt v Bromage* (1854) 24 LJ Ex 63 at 65; *Aiken v Short* (1856) 1 H & N 210, 156 ER 1180 (as explained in Mason and Carter *Restitution Law in Australia* (1995), p 140).
2   *Moses v Macferlan* (1760) 2 Burr 1005, 97 ER 676.

MISTAKEN PAYMENTS BY BANKS, DISCHARGING A DEBT OWED BY THEIR CUSTOMER

17.64   A number of mistaken payment cases have concerned the discharge of another's debts by the claimant. In some cases in which restitution has been claimed the claimant, usually a banker, has paid the debts of a debtor by mistake[1].

Ordinarily, a bank cannot debit the account of a customer without a mandate. Where a bank paid money on the mistaken assumption that a confirmed credit was at the free disposal of the bank and the defendant, whereas the credit was given on to the bank on terms stipulated by a supplier company, the bank could recover the funds mistakenly paid out[2]. A bank cannot pay a debtor of a customer in the absence of authorisation or ratification by the customer[3]. Where that authority has been revoked, by a stop payment order, a bank has no mandate to debit the account of a customer. In such circumstances, any payment that is made after the stop payment order will be recoverable by the bank as having been made in excess of authority[4]. Such a mistaken payment can be recovered from the payee[5].

1   *Crantrave Ltd v Lloyds Bank plc* [2000] QB 917 at 925.
2   *Westminister Bank Ltd v Arlington Overseas Trading Co* [1952] 1 Lloyd's Rep 211. However, in a case where the *Uniform Customs and Practice for Documentary Credits* (ICC, 1993 Revision) applies the issuing and confirming banks would now be precluded by art 14(e) from making a claim where notice of rejection of the documents has not been made.
3   See eg *Crantrave Ltd v Lloyds Bank plc* [2000] QB 917 at 924, per Pill LJ.
4   *Bank of New South Wales v Deri* (1963) 80 WNNSW 1499; *Commercial Bank of Australia Ltd v Younis* [1979] 1 NSWLR 444; *K J Davies (1976) Ltd v Bank of New South Wales* [1981] 1 NZLR 262; *Bank of New South Wales v Murphett* [1983] 1 VR 489. See also *Justin Seward Pty Ltd v Comrs of Rural and Industries Bank* (1980) 1 SR (WA) 272; *RCL Operators Ltd v National Bank of Canada* [1997] 6 Bank LR 195.
5   Virgo *Principles of the Law of Restitution* (1999), p 151.

17.65   The leading case on this question is *Barclays Bank Ltd v W J Simms, Son & Cooke (Southern) Ltd*[1] where a housing association drew a cheque in favour of a building company that was subsequently placed into receivership. On the day that the receiver was appointed, the housing association had instructed the bank to stop payment on the cheque. The bank had entered the stop instruction into its computer, but that fact was overlooked when the receiver presented the cheque for payment. The bank was successful in recovering the payment from the receiver. The ground that Robert Goff J gave for enabling the bank to recover payment was that 'the bank was acting without mandate and so the payment was not effective to discharge the drawer's obligation on the cheque; from this it follows that the payee gave no consideration for the payment, and the claim cannot be defeated on this ground'[2].

1   [1980] QB 677.
2   [1980] QB 677 at 703.

17.66   Where a bank pays a cheque that is not signed by the customer, but is forged, the bank cannot debit the customer's account; nor will its payment be effective to discharge the obligation (if any) of the customer on the cheque, because the bank had no authority to discharge such an obligation[1]. This principle applies where a cheque is not signed in accordance with the authority granted by the customer of the bank, and so any payment that is made on the cheque is made in excess of the mandate given to the bank by the customer. In such circumstances the customer's bank can recover money that has been paid under the mistake of fact that the cheque form represented a valid and subsisting order by the customer to the bank to make payment[2].

1   *Barclays Bank Ltd v W J Simms, Son & Cooke (Southern) Ltd* [1980] QB 677 at 699. See also *Motis Exports Ltd v Dampskibsselskabet AF 1912* [1999] 1 Lloyd's Rep 837 at 842–843; Bills of Exchange Act 1882, s 24.
2   *Simos v National Bank of Australasia Ltd* (1976) 10 ACTR 4 at 9–10; *Westpac Banking Corpn v ATL Pty Ltd* [1985] 2 Qd R 577.

17.67   However, where the bank has the necessary authority to pay on a cheque, and pays the cheque from insufficient funds from the account of the customer, it is clear that the only remedy of the bank will be against the customer. The bank will not be permitted to recover the amount of the payment from the payee or drawee. The reason is that the bank is not required to pay a cheque where the account is insufficient. A customer who draws a cheque for an amount in excess of the funds in the customer's account is regarded as making a request to provide overdraft facilities to meet the cheque. In such a case 'the payment is made within the bank's mandate ... and the bank's payment discharges the customer's obligation to the payee on the cheque'[1].

1   *Barclays Bank Ltd v W J Simms, Son & Cooke (Southern) Ltd* [1980] QB 677 at 699.

17.68   The mere fact that the payment by a bank may have enured to the benefit of a customer does not establish an equity in favour of the bank against the customer[1]. There is no automatic right of recoupment[2] or subrogation[3]. It is suggested that the bank can debit the account of a customer if the bank has authority to pay the debts of its customer[4]. In this context it is important to emphasise that it is insufficient merely to assert that a debt has been discharged, there must, at least, be evidence that the payment had the effect of discharging the debts of a customer[5].

1   *Re Cleadon Trust Ltd* [1939] Ch 286.
2   *Re Cleadon Trust Ltd* [1939] Ch 286 at 321.
3   *Crantrave Ltd v Lloyds Bank plc* [2000] QB 917 at 923–924, per Pill LJ.
4   *B Liggett (Liverpool) Ltd v Barclays Bank Ltd* [1928] 1 KB 48 is a difficult case to rationalize, and appears to be based on the inference that one of the directors was conducting the customer's business: see Goff and Jones *Law of Restitution* (5th edn, 1998), p 156. See above, para 8.69.
5   See *B Liggett (Liverpool) Ltd v Barclays Bank Ltd* [1928] 1 KB 48; *Crantrave Ltd v Lloyds Bank plc* [2000] QB 917 at 924, per Pill LJ. See above, para 8.69.

17.69 It is difficult for a bank to recover a payment from a creditor of a customer who is entitled to receive the payment from the customer. In *Lloyds Bank v Independent Insurance Co Ltd*[1] it was pointed out where a payment has been mistakenly paid to a creditor of a customer and the bank had the authority from the customer to make the payment, restitution of the payment could not be made as the creditor was entitled to the payment. Even where the payer does not have the requisite authority to pay the debts of a third party, it would be difficult to recover payment from a payee that is mistakenly made in discharge of a debt owed to a third party. In *Kleinwort Benson Ltd v Lincoln City Council*[2] Lord Goff posed as the third of three questions raised by a claim of restitution of money paid under a mistake:

> The third question arises because the payee cannot be said to have been unjustly enriched if he was entitled to receive the sum paid to him. The Payer may have been mistaken as to the grounds on which the sum was due to the payee, but his mistake will not provide a ground for its recovery if the payee can show that he was entitled to it on some other ground[3].

This principle is not dependent upon the payment being made by an agent of the debtor[4].

1 [2000] QB 110.
2 [1999] 2 AC 349.
3 [1999] 2 AC 349 at 408.
4 *Lloyds Bank v Independent Insurance Co Ltd* [2000] QB 110 at 132, per Peter Gibson LJ.

17.70 Even where a debt is discharged, restitution may be available where the payee induced the mistake in question. Restitution would be available where the payee is aware that the payment is made by mistake. In such cases the payee would not be receiving the payment in good faith. In *Barclays Bank Ltd v W J Simms, Son & Cooke (Southern) Ltd*[1] Robert Goff J said:

> ... even if the payee has given consideration for the payment, for example by accepting the payment in discharge of a debt owed to him by a third party on whose behalf the payer is authorized to discharge it, that transaction may itself be set aside (and so provide a defence to the claim) if the payer's mistake was induced by the payee, or possibly even where the payee, being aware of the payer's mistake, did not receive the money in good faith[2].

1 [1980] QB 677.
2 [1980] QB 677 at 695, cited by Beldam LJ in *The Trident Beauty* [1993] 1 Lloyd's Rep 443 at 453–454.

Submission, or settlements and compromises of honest claims

17.71 A payment that is made in submission to an honest claim is an example of a voluntary payment, which cannot be recovered[1]. Where municipal authorities have made charges on erroneous bases through misinterpretation of statutory powers, any attempt to recover any overcharges have failed where the charges were paid without question. Such a case is *South Australian Cold Stores Ltd v Electricity Trust of South Australia*[2], where a consumer paid for electricity in accordance with demands that were issued by the defendant. The consumer had assumed that the demands were valid. In actual fact the charges were made at a higher rate than authorised by law, because some formal requirements for approval not been observed. The High Court of Australia held that the claimant could not recover the amount of the overpayment. The main reason was that the consumer entertained no belief concerning the existence or non-existence of facts. The High Court observed: 'This seems to fall outside the reason of the rule under which an action for money had and received lies in payment by mistake'[3].

1   On voluntary payments see above, para 17.45ff.
2   (1957) 98 CLR 65.
3   (1957) 98 CLR 65 at 75.

17.72   A payment that is made in settlement of a claim generally is not recoverable in an action for restitution. There are a number of reasons why a court will not order restitution of a sum paid in settlement of a claim. Foremost, the policy of the law is to prevent unnecessary litigation[1]. This policy may explain some hard cases where restitution was denied where overpayments were made in response to demands for payment: in some of these cases the payment was not made under a mistake[2]. From a contractual perspective, forbearance to sue in respect of a claim will constitute good consideration[3]. It is quite beside the point that a settlement is made because of some mistake as to the liability of a party. In *David Securities Pty Ltd v Commonwealth Bank of Australia*[4] Brennan J remarked: 'Where a claim is settled by accord and satisfaction, a payment made in satisfaction is made in discharge of an obligation created by the accord: it is unaffected by any mistake as to the validity of the claim compromised'[5].

1   *Longridge v Dorville* (1821) 5 B & Ald 117 at 123, 106 ER 1136 at 1138. See Butler 'Mistaken Payments, Change of Position and Restitution' in Finn *Essays on Restitution* (1990), pp 102 and 103.
2   See eg *Brown v M'Kinally* (1795) 1 Esp 279, 170 ER 356; *Marriott v Hampton* (1797) 2 Esp 546, 170 ER 450; *Gower v Popkin* (1817) 2 Stark 85, 171 ER 581; *Hamlet v Richardson* (1833) 9 Bing 644, 131 ER 756; *Moore v Vestry of Fulham* [1895] 1 QB 399.
3   *Longridge v Dorville* (1821) 5 B & Ald 117 at 123, 106 ER 1136 at 1138–1139; *Callisher v Bischoffsheim* (1870) LR 5 QB 449.
4   (1992) 175 CLR 353.
5   (1992) 175 CLR 353 at 395.

17.73   Nonetheless, there are a number of situations where restitution is available, essentially because in such cases there is really no settlement. A payment that is made in response to a mistaken demand may be recovered for there is no accord in such a case as well as no genuine claim[1]. There is similarly no accord where a payment is made in response to duress[2]. A release that is granted in ignorance of relevant facts may not be successfully pleaded as a defence to a claim for restitution. This is because equity will give relief in respect of a general release that extends to all claims where the releasor was unaware of the facts giving rise to a particular claim[3].

1   *Baylis v Bishop of London* [1913] 1 Ch 127.
2   *Keegan (TD) Ltd v Palmer* [1961] 2 Lloyd's Rep 449. On duress see above, para 10.51ff.
3   *Bank of Credit and Commerce International SA (in liquidation) v Ali* [2000] 3 All ER 51.

17.74   It is classic to treat cases where a defendant has made a submission or compromise of an honest claim as being a separate restitutionary ground of defence, although in truth this defence can be seen to rest on the defence of good consideration[1]. In the Australian case of *Prudential Assurance Co Ltd v CM Breedon Pty Ltd*[2], as well as having an insurance policy with an insurance company, the assured was indebted to the insurance company under an outstanding loan. The assured sought to surrender the insurance policy. The insurance company then prepared a form for his signature, which provided that he agreed that all claims would be fully discharged and satisfied upon the insurance company remitting an amount of $97,813.16, which was described as 'surrender value[3] – net of any outstanding debts'. The assured signed the form, and was sent a cheque for that amount. However, in calculating that amount the insurance company had by mistake deducted too little for the outstanding loan, resulting in an alleged overpayment of $36,343.40. It was held that the insurance company could not recover the amount of the alleged overpayment from the assured. The parties had concluded a new and binding contract when the insured accepted the offer from the insurance company to pay the insured the sum of $97,813.16, in return for the assured agreeing to release the insurance company from all claims under the policy.

1   *Prudential Assurance Co Ltd v CM Breedon Pty Ltd* [1994] 2 VR 452 at 461, per curiam. On the defence of good consideration see above, para 17.57ff.
2   [1994] 2 VR 452.
3   The policy or legislation did not specify how the cash surrender value was to be calculated; in practice this was left to the insurance company to determine.

Deliberate waiver of enquiry

17.75   A payment cannot be recovered if the payer intended to pay the defendant irrespective of the truth of a fact of which he was mistaken. This was recognised as early as 1841 in *Kelly v Solari*[1]. Lord Abinger CB said: 'There may also be cases in which, although he might by investigation learn the state of facts more accurately, he declines to do so, and chooses to pay the money notwithstanding; in that case there can be no doubt that he is equally bound'[2]. Parke B remarked: 'If, indeed, the money is intentionally paid, without reference to the truth or falsehood of the fact, the plaintiff meaning to waive all inquiry into it, and that the person receiving shall have the money at all events, whether the fact be true or false, the latter is certainly entitled to retain it'[3].

1   (1841) 9 M & W 54, 152 ER 24.
2   (1841) 9 M & W 54 at 58, 152 ER 24 at 26, applied in *South Australian Cold Stores Ltd v Electricity Trust of South Australia* (1957) 98 CLR 65 at 74.
3   (1841) 9 M & W 54 at 59, 152 ER 24 at 26.

17.76   In *Home & Colonial Insurance Co Ltd v London Guarantee and Accident Co Ltd*[1] the liquidator of an insurance company had made payment under unstamped (and therefore invalid) marine policies. Had the liquidator known that the policies were not stamped, he would have regarded that fact as irrelevant. The court ruled that the payment could not be recovered.

1   (1928) 45 TLR 134.

Existing enforceable contract between the parties

17.77   In cases where the parties are in a contractual relationship, the claimant may be precluded from making a claim in restitution. There is a general principle that the contract should apply to any dispute between the parties rather than a restitutionary claim. In *Foran v Wight*[1] Mason CJ remarked: 'so long as the contract continued on foot, it governed the relations between the parties and there is no basis in these circumstances for an appeal to the law of quasi-contract'[2]. In *Update Constructions Pty Ltd v Rozelle Child Care Centre Pty Ltd* Priestley JA remarked: 'I know of no cases (except possibly in one area of law[3]) where an existing enforceable contract governs specific relations between two parties and yet one has recovered against the other in respect of a matter governed by the contract, on the basis of quantum meruit, quasi contract, or restitution'[4].

1 (1989) 168 CLR 385.
2 (1989) 168 CLR 385 at 413.
3 Employee entitled to recover on a quantum meruit, but not under the contract of employment for working in accordance with union's directive: see *Miles v Wakefield Metropolitan District Council* [1987] AC 539, and below, para 19.77.
4 (1990) 20 NSWLR 251 at 275, in footnote.

17.78 Where a contract imposes specific machinery for resolving a contractual dispute, that machinery must be applied in resolving a dispute. In *Soules CAF v Louis Dreyfus Negoce SA*[1] an international community sales contract provided for the resolution of a dispute in respect of the analysis of a sample to be resolved by a new analysis, to be called for within 14 days of receipt of a second analysis certificate. A seller had not invoked this provision within the stipulated 14 day period, but the original analysis was questioned some months later. The question arose whether the seller could claim the difference between the contract price that was determined in accordance with the original documentation, and a price that was determined with the benefit of a later analysis. Under the contract of sale, the seller had to give an allowance against the specific prices where the combined protein and fat content of the soya bean pellets was less than 48%. The original documentation was issued with an admitted clerical error, and the seller had given allowances that should not have been granted. It was held that the seller could not later rely on the corrected analysis certificate. David Steel J said: 'in international commodity sale contracts where a chain of sales is commonplace, it is desirable that the contractual machinery for resolving mistakes should not be vulnerable to challenge in the Courts'[2].

1 [2000] 2 Lloyd's Rep 307.
2 [2000] 2 Lloyd's Rep 307 at 311.

Honest receipt in a mistake of law case

17.79 In Australia, in *David Securities Pty Ltd v Commonwealth Bank of Australia*[1] Brennan J proposed that a defendant should have a defence to an action for restitution in a mistake of law case where he believes that he was entitled to keep the money that was given to him. Brennan J formulated the following defence:

> It is a defence to a claim for restitution of money paid or property transferred under a mistake of law that the defendant honestly believed, when he learnt of the payment or transfer, that he was entitled to receive and retain the money or property[2].

Brennan J considered that this defence should operate when the payee should discharge 'the onus of proving that, when he learnt of the payment, he had a "ground to claim in conscience"'[3]. However, the other justices of the High Court of Australia did not concur in the proposal of such a defence.

1 (1992) 175 CLR 353.
2 (1992) 175 CLR 353 at 399, quoted by Lord Goff in *Kleinwort Benson Ltd v Lincoln CC* [1999] 2 AC 349 at 398.
3 (1992) 175 CLR 353 at 399.

17.80 In *Kleinwort Benson Ltd v Lincoln City Council*[1] Lords Goff and Hope expressly disapproved of this proposed defence of honest receipt. Lord Goff thought that if the proposed defence 'is so wide' that if it were accepted other defences (such as change of position and submission to an honest claim) would cease to have any relevance. Lord Goff said: 'before so novel and far-reaching defence as the one now proposed can be recognised, a very strong case for it has to be made out'[2]. Lord Hope said:

> I have some difficulty in seeing why this defence, if there is merit in it as a means of preventing recovery where this would be unjust, should be confined to mistake of law cases'. He thought that it would 'also tend to perpetuate the distinction between mistakes of law and mistakes of fact ... [3]

1   [1999] 2 AC 349.
2   [1999] 2 AC 349 at 385.
3   [1999] 2 AC 349 at 413.

Illegality and public policy[1]

17.81   There have been cases where the courts have denied recovery of mistaken payments under transactions that are contrary to statute. Clear cases where the courts would not facilitate the recovery of mistaken payments are where gaming legislation would be infringed[2]. So a bookmaker who has, because of a clerical error, mistakenly overpaid the defendant on a betting account cannot recover that overpayment[3].

1   See more generally above, ch 14.
2   See eg the Gaming Act 1845, s 18.
3   *Morgan v Ashcroft* [1938] 1 KB 49.

17.82   In some cases legislation may preclude a claim for restitution or any monetary benefit for services. In Queensland, the legislation relating to work done by unregistered builders is wide enough to exclude a restitutionary or a quantum meruit claim by an unregistered builder[1]. In one Queensland case, a person made a payment to an unregistered builder under the mistaken belief that she was liable to pay that payment. It was held that she could recover that payment, which was made in mistake of law, in a restitution action[2].

1   Queensland Building Services Authority Act 1991, s 42(3). See *Zullo Enterprises Pty Ltd v Sutton* (1998) 15 Build and Constr Law 283.
2   *Marshall v Marshall* [1999] 1 Qd R 173 at 178, per McPherson JA.

17.83   Whilst the courts will not enforce illegal contracts, the recovery of mistaken payments by weaker parties would generally not infringe the policy of legislation. Where legislation is intended to protect a particular class of persons, the policy of that legislation would not be infringed where recovery is permitted to protected persons or where the parties are not *in pari delicto* with each other[1]. Lord Mansfield certainly thought that money paid contrary to a statute which is intended to protect weaker parties could be recovered where the parties are not *in pari delicto*, such as persons who were 'over-reached, defrauded, or oppressed'[2]. The classic case is the decision of the Privy Council in *Kiriri Cotton Co v Dewani*[3] that concerned tenancy legislation that prohibited landlords from requiring tenants to pay premiums. Lord Denning said that whilst a tenant might be technically an aider or abettor, 'he can hardly be said to be *in pari delicto* with the landlord'[4]. The tenant could recover a premium paid by the remedy of money had and received.

1   On the *in pari delicto* maxim, see above, ch 14.
2   *Clarke v Shee and Johnson* (1774) 1 Cowp 197 at 200, 98 ER 1041 at 1043. See above, para 14.30ff. See also Jackson *History of Quasi-Contract in English Law* (1936), p 91.
3   [1960] AC 192; on which see above, para 14.26.
4   [1960] AC 192 at 205.

17.84   There are other examples where mistaken payments have been recovered under illegal contracts where the parties are not *in pari delicto* with each other. Policyholders for whose protection legislation has been passed have recovered premiums under illegal insurance contracts[1]. Some cases have concerned insurance policies that were void owing to a lack of an insurable interest. Policyholders who were fraudulently informed that the policies were valid have recovered the premiums paid under the policies[2]. However, where a wrong representation by an agent of an insurance company was innocently made the parties were held to be *in pari delicto* with each other, and the premiums could not be recovered[3]. Similarly, in *Oom v Bruce*[4] where an insurance policy was illegal because it related to the transit of goods between Great Britain and Russia, which countries were at war, the claimant could recover the premiums paid. The ignorance of the claimant that a state of war existed was a mistake that was sufficient to ground the restitutionary claim[5].

1   See eg *Hughes v Liverpool Victoria Legal Friendly Society* [1916] 2 KB 482.
2   *British Workman's and General Assurance Co v Cunliffe* (1902) 18 TLR 502; *Hughes v Liverpool Victoria Legal Friendly Society* [1916] 2 KB 482.
3   *Harse v Pearl Life Assurance Co* [1904] 1 KB 558
4   (18010) 12 East 225, 104 ER 87. See above, para 14.25.
5   Goff and Jones *Law of Restitution* (5th edn, 1998), p 626, n 38.

Limitation of actions[1]

17.85   At the time when many of the provisions that are now to be found in the Limitation Act 1980 were originally drafted, restitution was not a well developed body of law. In *Portman Building Society v Hamlyn Taylor Neck*[2] Brooke LJ remarked: 'the law of limitation has grown up piecemeal over the last 450 years before the modern remedy of restitution was properly developed'[3]. It is therefore not surprising that the Limitation Act 1980 does not expressly refer to actions for restitution. It also does not, unlike the position in Australia, refer to quasi-contract[4]. Nevertheless, it has been held that s 5 of the Act, which applies a six-year limitation for actions 'founded on simple contract' must be taken to apply to a claim for an action for money had and received[5].

1   See more generally below, para 21.63ff; see also McLean 'Limitation of Actions in Restitution' [1989] CLJ 472.
2   [1998] 4 All ER 202.
3   [1998] 4 All ER 202 at 209.
4   In New South Wales a limitation period is prescribed for a cause of action founded on 'quasi-contract': see the Limitation Act 1969, s 14(1)(1a). Whilst the language of quasi-contract is not apt to refer to actions for restitution which are based on unjust enrichment, it has been applied to a cause of action for the recovery of money paid under a mistake: see *Torrens Aloha Pty Ltd v Citibank NA* (1997) 72 FCR 581 at 593.
5   *Re Diplock* [1948] Ch 465 at 21; *Kleinwort Benson Ltd v South Tyneside Metropolitan Borough Council* [1994] 4 All ER 972. See also *Maskell v Horner* [1915] 3 KB 106.

17.86   In an equitable action, the periods of limitation for common law actions may also apply by analogy by virtue of the Limitation Act 1980, s 36(1). In *Kleinwort Benson Ltd v South Tyneside Metropolitan Borough Council*[1] Hobhouse J remarked: 'the six-year limit provided for in s 5 of the Limitation Act 1980 applies to an action for money had and received and by analogy to an equivalent equitable action'[2]. One example of a period of limitation applying by analogy is an action for an account against a fiduciary[3]. The Act provides that the period of limitation does not apply to cases of fraud by a trustee (s 21(1)) or persons under a disability (s 28). The Act also provides that the period of limitation does not apply in cases of fraud and concealment or mistake (s 32).

1 [1994] 4 All ER 972.
2 [1994] 4 All ER 972 at 978.
3 *Paragon Finance plc v DB Thakerar & Co* [1999] 1 All ER 400. See below, para 21.68.

17.87 Originally limitation legislation only applied to actions at law, and not bills for equitable relief. The equitable doctrine of laches would not apply until after the mistake was discovered, irrespective of whether the mistake was a mistake of fact or law[1]. This rule of equity did not apply to a case that fell within the exclusive jurisdiction of a court of law[2]. Such a claim would be a common law claim for money had and received[3]. In the case of one such claim, the period of limitation applied where both the party paying and the party receiving the money paid money, under a mistake of fact that was shared[4]. In 1936 the Law Revision Committee considered this position to be unsatisfactory, and recommended that the equitable rule should prevail in all cases where relief was sought from the consequences of a mistake[5]. This is the reason why s 26(c) of the Limitation Act 1939 and s 32(1)(c) of the Limitation Act 1980, which is in identical terms to s 26(c), was passed.

1 *Earl Beauchamp v Winn* (1873) LR 6 HL 223 at 232–235; *Kleinwort Benson Ltd v Lincoln City Council* [1999] 2 AC 349 at 389, per Lord Goff.
2 *Kleinwort Benson Ltd v Lincoln City Council* [1999] 2 AC 349 at 388, per Lord Goff.
3 See *Baker v Courage & Co* [1910] 1 KB 56 at 60, per Boxall QC (in argument).
4 *Baker v Courage & Co* [1910] 1 KB 56.
5 *Fifth Interim Report of the Law Revision Committee* (1936, Cmd 5334) para 23; *Kleinwort Benson Ltd v Lincoln City Council* [1999] 2 AC 349 at 388, per Lord Goff.

17.88 In particular, s 32(1)(c) of the Limitation Act 1980 provides that where an action is for relief from the consequences of a mistake[1], the period of limitation shall not begin to run until the claimant has discovered the fraud, concealment or mistake (as the case may be), or could with reasonable diligence have discovered it. This exemption may prove useful in actions for restitution. In *Kleinwort Benson Ltd v Lincoln City Council*[2], where payments had been made on the strength of a particular interpretation of local authority powers, the House of Lords held that the limitation period did not commence until there was a judicial ruling that this interpretation was wrong[3]. Lord Goff recognised that the effect of s 32(1)(c) is that the cause of action 'may be extended for an indefinite period of time'[4]. In *Kleinwort Benson* their Lordships do not appear to have had their attention drawn to the fact that in Australia a contrary conclusion had been taken in the case of similar legislation[5].

1 See *Phillips-Higgin v Harper* [1954] 1 QB 411. See also *Bank Tejarat v Hong Kong and Shanghai Banking Corpn (CI) Ltd* [1995] 1 Lloyd's Rep 239 at 244.
2 [1999] 2 AC 349.
3 On this litigation see below, para 18.18ff.
4 [1999] 2 AC 349 at 389.
5 In *Torrens Aloha Pty Ltd v Citibank NA* (1997) 72 FCR 581 at 596 Sackville J remarked: 'Neither the rule of equity nor the language of the Limitation Act is apt to postpone the commencement of the limitation period until the courts recognize a novel cause of action for recovery of payments made under a mistake. The authorities to which I have referred suggest strongly that a cause of action for recovery of moneys paid under a mistake of law accrues on the day of payment'.

17.89 Where a defendant can establish that the claimant was aware of facts upon which a person could, with reasonable diligence, have discovered a mistake, that defendant can rely upon s 32(1)(c) of the Limitation Act 1980, so that time will run from the moment that the mistake could have been discovered had the claimant been exercising reasonable diligence. However, where any fact relevant to the claimant's cause of action has been concealed from him by the defendant, then the period of limitation does not begin to run until the claimant has discovered the fraud, concealment or mistake (as the case may be), or could with reasonable diligence have discovered it[1].

1   See the Limitation Act 1980, s 31(1)(b).

17.90   There have been calls to reform the law relating to limitation of actions in the case of restitutionary actions. In *Portman Building Society v Hamlyn Taylor Neck*[1], Brooke LJ considered that there was a 'need for Parliament to bring limitation rules relating to restitutionary remedies within a coherent, principled limitation statute as recommended by the Law Commission'[2]. Since then the Law Commission has completed a review of the law on limitation periods. It is proposed that a core regime, which prescribes a primary limitation period of three years from the time when a claimant discovers or ought to have known the facts on which the cause of action was based, should apply to restitutionary claims[3]. The Law Commission has also proposed a long-stop limitation period of ten years. The draft Bill that was contained in the report of the Law Commission expressly defines a 'civil claim' to include a claim made in civil proceedings in which a claimant seeks 'restitution'[4].

1   [1998] 4 All ER 202.
2   [1998] 4 All ER 202 at 209.
3   *Limitation of Actions* (HC 23, Law Com no 270, 2001) 119–120.
4   *Limitation of Actions* (HC 23, Law Com no 270, 2001) 226, cl 1(4)(b).

17.91   There has also been a suggestion of the need for law reform in respect of the limitation period for the recovery of money paid under a mistake of law. In *Kleinwort Benson Ltd v Lincoln City Council*[1] Lord Goff considered that there was a need for legislative reform 'as a matter of urgency'[2], to provide for some time limit for right to recover money that has been paid under a mistake of law. In some jurisdictions, strict short time limits apply for the recovery of overpaid taxes even where the taxes are unconstitutional. However, the Law Commission had earlier recommended that short time limits for the bringing of claims for repayment of tax overpaid as a result of a mistake should not be enacted as a means of dealing with the problem of disruption of public finances[3].

1   [1999] 2 AC 349.
2   [1999] 2 AC 349 at 389.
3   On mistakes made in a public law context, see below, ch 18.

17.92   The Law Commission favoured the retention of the existing six-year time limit that commenced from the date of payment. It was also recognised that, as a consequence of the Limitation Act, s 32(1)(c), time will not run against a claimant until he discovers the mistake, or could with reasonable diligence have discovered it. In such circumstances it has been pointed out that it would be a defence to actions based on mistake that the claimant could have raised the mistake as a defence against the assessment at the appropriate time, and failed to do so[1].

1   *Restitution: Mistakes of Law and Ultra Vires Public Authority Receipts and Payments* (Cm 2731, Law Com no 227, 1994) 198.

17.93   On payments made under mistake of law, the Law Commission commented: 'the long-stop limitation period, of ten years, will run from the date of the accrual of the cause of action. In a claim to recover money paid under mistake of law this will be the date on which the defendant is enriched. No enrichment received by the defendant over ten years before the date of judgment could therefore be recovered'[1]. In considering transitional matters, the Law Commission considered that the existing limitation regime should apply for only six years after the commencement of the new Limitation Act. The Law Commission stated:

> We consider that it would be unfortunate if, for example, if the claimant had made a payment in reliance on a mistake of law shortly before the new Act came into force but only discovered the mistake twenty or more years later was still able to rely on the old law[2].

1   *Limitation of Actions* (HC 23, Law Com no 270, 2001) 120.
2   *Limitation of Actions* (HC 23, Law Com no 270, 2001) 226, cl 1(4)(b).

CHAPTER 18

Restitution in Public Law

Steve Hedley

A   Introduction[1]

18.1   Lawyers have been slow to catch up with the growth of the state. The great rise in the powers and resources of government over the last two centuries seems to have made relatively little mark on the way lawyers think. To be sure, administrative law is now recognised as a subject in its own right, with its own terminology and ethos. Nonetheless there is still a high degree of borrowing from private law, of using rules and concepts by analogy. Governmental bodies are still treated principally as property-owners, or as trustees for their voters, or as contractors providing services for which their tax-payers have paid.

Yet governmental bodies are not, when all is said and done, private individuals. Still less are they real people. And the extent to which it makes sense to treat them as if they were, may be a political hot potato as well as a conceptual one. The many controversies here have certainly touched the law of restitution. If you over-pay your income tax by accident, is the law then the same as if you accidentally overpaid a private law debt? Or if you enter into a contract with a local authority, but then you discover that the authority had no power to make the contract, what restitutionary rights do you have? These are the questions this chapter addresses. The private law doctrines discussed in the earlier chapters are certainly relevant by analogy. But how useful the analogy is in each case, may be a matter of some debate. There has been an unfortunate tendency to assume that it is more relevant than it actually is, or to call clear conclusions in public law cases into doubt simply because the same conclusions would make no sense in private law cases. Some differences at least are very clear: especially in that the doctrine of ultra vires, which is on its uppers in private law, is still a principle of great importance in relation to public bodies.

1   On the principles of ultra vires in this connection, see above, para 15.29.

B   Payments to public bodies

Statutory rights

18.2   Perhaps surprisingly, there is no general statutory entitlement to repayment of sums wrongly paid to a public authority. What statute provides is very piecemeal. There is a general right to recover wrongly-paid VAT[1], though it is subject to a rather open-ended defence (called 'unjust enrichment'; which is confusing, as 'unjust enrichment' is usually thought of as a principle of liability, not a ground of defence[2]). There is also a provision covering income tax, corporation tax, capital gains tax and petrol vehicle duty, but this has stringent limits. In particular, the overpayment must have been due to an error or mistake in the tax return, and no recovery is allowed where the error was part of the revenue's settled practice at the time. The provision in any event does not give a clear right of recovery, but simply directs the court to do whatever is reasonable and just in the light of the mistake[3]. A general provision for restitution of wrongly-paid tax has been proposed by the Law Commission, but not implemented[4].

1   See the Value Added Tax Act 1994, s 80, as amended by the Finance Act 1997, ss 46 and 47.
2   See further below, para 18.38; and Virgo 'Restitution of overpaid VAT' [1998] British Tax Review 582.
3   See the Taxes Management Act 1970, s 33.
4   *Restitution: Mistakes of law and ultra vires public authority receipts and payments* (Law Com no 227, 1994, Cm 2731). It seems unlikely to be implemented: 'Mistakes of law' (1999) 330 Parl Deb (6th series) 245w (29 April 1999).

Woolwich Equitable Building Society v IRC[1]

18.3   The common law was similarly fragmentary and vague before the *Woolwich* case. However, this seminal decision (by a bare majority) set the common law on a different path. The case concerned the implementation of a new scheme for taxing interest on building society accounts, bringing them in line with bank accounts. The old scheme had been based on the building societies' own accounting years, whereas the new statutory scheme was based on the revenue's fiscal year. As a result, there was a period of a few months covered by neither scheme.

Whether that period should be taxed at all was a matter of some debate when the legislation was enacted. The building societies said that taxing it would mean that the revenue would receive 14 or 15 months' worth of tax in respect of a 12 month period, which seemed excessive. The revenue insisted that *not* to tax it would be to grant a wholly undeserved tax holiday for that period. In the event, Parliament followed the revenue's line, and the revenue introduced transitional regulations covering that period, under which they made various demands for payment from the building societies.

The Woolwich Building Society, ordered to pay some £57m in this way, doubted whether these regulations were valid. In the event, they paid, but almost immediately started proceedings to have the regulations quashed. Their proceedings were successful[2]. The revenue repaid the £57m, though they refused to pay interest; they also procured the passage of retroactive legislation validating the transitional scheme, though they exempted Woolwich from the effect of this. (This was challenged, unsuccessfully, by other building societies in the European Court of Human Rights[3].)

1   [1993] AC 70, [1992] 3 All ER 737.
2   *Woolwich Equitable Building Society v IRC* [1991] 4 All ER 92, [1990] 1 WLR 1400.
3   *National & Provincial Building Society v United Kingdom* [1997] STC 1466, criticised by Tiley 'Human rights and taxpayers' [1998] CLJ 269.

18.4   The live issue was whether Woolwich would have been able to sue for their £57m, had the revenue refused to pay it. For if they could have recovered it as of right, and not by the grace of the revenue, then they were entitled to £6#fm interest[1]. The House of Lords ruled that they were indeed so entitled[2]. The case therefore clearly established a right to a refund, where a payment is made following a wrongful tax demand.

1   On the entitlement to interest in restitution cases see below, para 21.70ff.
2   *Woolwich Equitable Building Society v IRC* [1993] AC 70, [1992] 3 All ER 737.

THE GROUND OF LIABILITY

18.5   However, the actual basis of the liability is not entirely straightforward. A variety of grounds have been suggested. Most of them, it is clear, are too narrow. Before coming on to the more plausible grounds, consider two grounds which are clearly under-inclusive.

18.6   Duress is a ground often suggested. And there is no doubt that duress will actually be present in many of these cases. A taxing authority can bring considerable pressure to bear on those it considers to be defaulters. This has long been recognised at common law, in the notion of duress *colore officii* (ie by pretext of public office), where duress is presumed from the fact that the demand was made by someone holding public office.

However, from a restitutionary angle this all seems to miss the point, for either the sum was due, or it was not. If it was not, then it should be recoverable, no matter how politely or deferentially it was demanded. If it *was* due, it is hard to see that the coercive way in which it was demanded can matter. In an extreme case, an official extracting tax by coercive means might be liable in damages or even criminally; but if the tax was in fact due, then surely it should not be repaid. So the presence or absence of duress seems irrelevant here, and *Woolwich* seems to consign the old cases on 'duress *colore officii*' to the scrap-heap[1].

As a matter of fact, it is most unclear whether there was duress on the facts of the *Woolwich* case. The pressure to pay was strong, but the motives of the payors were complex, and certainly not simply a matter of submission to an irresistible demand[2]. Yet the right to recover was clear.

1   But for a contrary view see Goff and Jones *Law of Restitution* (5th edn, 1998), pp 322 and 686.
2   Various commercial considerations featured in the eventual decision to pay. See below, para 18.8, and detailed factual discussion in *Woolwich Equitable Building Society v IRC* [1989] 1 WLR 137, 142–143 (Nolan J). The lords did not agree whether it could be said that there was duress here: see [1993] AC 173, per Lord Goff, [1993] AC 198, per Lord Browne-Wilkinson, [1993] AC 204, per Lord Slynn. For an argument that there was duress here see Jaffey *Nature and scope of restitution* (2000), pp 204 and 205.

18.7   Can the ground of recovery be 'mistake'? Mistake again will very often be present, but it too focuses attention on the motive for the payment, when the real question is whether the money was due at all. Of course, if a payment is made in full knowledge that the demand for it was illegal, the court might have to ask whether the payor was abandoning the right to recover[1]. But most sets of facts are murkier, and there can still be reasons to pay even if the illegality is perfectly well appreciated. The facts of *Woolwich* neatly illustrate this. The payors there knew all along that the demand to pay was flawed. But they also knew that proceedings to demonstrate that flaw were risky; that those who had received similar demands had paid; and that the markets might conclude that any refusal to pay meant they *could* not pay, which might start a run on Woolwich's shares. So they paid, while being in no material sense mistaken. And so we can be sure that the right to recover does not depend on mistake[2].

1   See below, para 18.33.
2   See also Kremer 'Recovering money paid under void contracts: "Absence of consideration" and failure of consideration' (2001) 17 Journal of Contract Law 37.

18.8   The explanation of the recovery must therefore be some more general ground. There are two general suggestions, each of which draws on analogies from private law. Firstly, we might rely on public policy: the unlawful demand conflicts with the policy of the law against ultra vires actions, and one response to that illegality is to order repayment. An order for repayment furthers the policies which lie behind the ultra vires rule. Secondly, we might draw an analogy with wrongly-paid debts. If I say 'Pay me the £1000 you owe me!' and you do so, then you can recover on proof that nothing was owed. *Woolwich* is perhaps simply the application of that principle in a public law context.

Either of these explanations seems to account for the liability. That is not to say that there is nothing to choose between them, but what is at stake will not appear until later in the chapter.

18.9   As to the first theory, that the recovery is based on the ultra vires rule, there was considerable support for it in *Woolwich*. Three of the five law lords mentioned it as a possible ground. The principle that taxes cannot be legal without specific statutory authorisation is of fundamental importance, and so is in itself a sufficient basis for recovery[1]. Yet while it is easy to assert that ultra vires demands contravene the policy of the law, there must be more to it, for it does not follow that the law will *always* react by ordering repayment. After *Woolwich*, it seems clear that if a tax is wrongly demanded, and the payor protests but pays, then there is a liability to refund. But what if the payor never did protest? Or if the sum cannot be said to be a 'tax' at all, being demanded on a quite different basis? Or if the body making the demand is only marginally 'public' anyway, such as a utility company[2]? It was considerations like this that led the Supreme Court of Canada to reject any general public law principle that all money wrongly demanded is recoverable. Ordering repayment of every such sum causes a great strain on public administration and on those who fund it; it is not obvious that the public interest requires correction of every error[3]. While the *Woolwich* rule is clearly more generous, nonetheless it is not obvious that it applies to *every* payment to a public authority following an ultra vires demand.

1   See Bill of Rights 1689 2 Ja 2 c 2 art 4; *A-G v Wilts United Dairies Ltd* (1921) 37 TLR 884, CA; on appeal 127 LT 822, HL.
2   Cf *South of Scotland Electricity Board v British Oxygen Co Ltd (No 2)* [1959] 2 All ER 225, [1959] 1 WLR 587, where the Lords were prepared to hold that overpayments for electricity were recoverable, though the basis of the liability is unclear.
3   *Air Canada v British Columbia* (1989) 59 DLR (4th) 161, criticised by Fridman 'No justice for taxpayers: The paucity of restitution' (1990) 19 Manitoba Law Review 303.

18.10   The other route to recovery equally has significant judicial support[1]. It is usually called 'absence of consideration': the payment was meant to discharge a liability to pay tax, but did not do so, and is therefore recoverable. 'Absence of consideration' is not a perfect phrase, for it suggests to the unwary that *any* payment is recoverable if there was no consideration for it – which would mean that there could be no such thing as a valid gift of money! It has to be understood as shorthand, meaning 'absence of a consideration which everyone had assumed to be present'. Once this is cleared up, it seems an adequate explanation of the *Woolwich* type of case. But it runs into difficulties with other, analogous cases which are considered below[2].

1   *Woolwich Equitable Building Society v IRC* [1993] AC 70 at 197–199, per Lord Browne-Wilkinson; *Steele v Williams* (1853) 8 Ex Ch 625 at 632–633, 155 ER 1502 at 1505, per Martin B; *Campbell v Hall* (1774) 1 Cowp 204 at 205, 98 ER 1045 at 1045, per Lord Mansfield.
2   See below, para 18.29.

European Union law

18.11   How does the liability apply in the special case of a demand which is unlawful due to a breach of EU law? Provided that the law in question is directly effective, and so can be relied on as affecting the parties' rights, it seems that there is a general right to a refund of the money. Indeed, this has been said to flow from the very concept of 'direct effect':

> The right to reimbursement of sums unduly levied by the authorities is ... rooted in the direct effect of the relevant provisions of Community law and the effectiveness of the protection of the legal positions created by those provisions. It is quite clear that that protection would not be effective if a judgement declaring a charge to be unlawful because it was levied in breach of a Community rule having direct effect were not accompanied by the possibility for individuals to obtain reimbursement[1].

So the general rule is clear, and has been stated on a number of occasions[2]. However, this general principle needs to be set alongside the similarly important principle of national procedural autonomy. So cases which have stated the general principle of recovery have also emphasised that it is for national courts to say 'whether, and to what extent' recovery is available in any one instance[3].

The potential for conflict between these two principles is obvious, though equally obviously it would have been far greater if the *Woolwich* principle had not been adopted at common law. (Indeed, the analogy of EU law was one ground on which *Woolwich* itself was decided[4].)

1   *Société Comateb v Directuer Général des Douanes et Droits Indirects* (Case C–192–218/95) [1997] ECR I-165 at 172, per Tesauro AG.
2   See eg *Comet BV v Produktschap voor Siergewassen* (Case 45/76) [1976] ECR 2043.
3   See eg *Pigs and Bacon Commission v McCarren & Co Ltd* (Case 177/78) [1979] ECR 2161 at 2192, per curiam.
4   *Woolwich Equitable Building Society v IRC* [1993] AC 70 at 177, [1992] 3 All ER 737 at 763–764, per Lord Goff.

18.12   The practical answer seems to be that a payor on a demand which was illegal by EU law can recover *either* by showing that they are within the *Woolwich* principle, *or* that a refusal to refund would be a denial of their directly effective EU rights. The latter state of affairs will be found to exist where domestic law makes it impossible or excessively difficult to claim a refund[1]. Put another way, there is a general right of recovery, which can only be limited where *both* (i) the national legal system would equally have refused a claim based on illegality under its own domestic laws, *and* (ii) the refusal is for specific reasons which do not undermine the general principle of recovery.

1   *Amministrazione delle Finanze dello Stato v SpA San Giorgio* (Case 199/82) [1983] ECR 3595.

Conclusion

18.13   The *Woolwich* principle is therefore clear, though its precise limits are not. In particular, careful analysis is needed as to the reason why a demand might be illegal, and the role of legal action in establishing that illegality. Take *Woolwich* itself. The tax in question was designed to prevent an unjustified tax holiday when the system of accounting changed. Whether there really would have been such a holiday was a matter of controversy, but it is clear that Parliament was the right place for that controversy to be settled, and that Parliament meant to settle it in the revenue's favour. That being so, what was the role of Woolwich's legal action? It pointed to an error in the implementation of Parliament's will, in that the tax regulations were internally inconsistent. And since it is surely valuable for such errors to be pointed out, it is appropriate that Woolwich should be rewarded for this, by a refund of the tax they paid. But it is not so clear that others who paid the tax equally deserve a refund, and the decision of the European Court of Human Rights is useful for pointing out the difference. The case was not one where the tax should clearly never have been imposed; an error was made in the way the tax was implemented, but there was no doubt that it would have been legitimate if slightly different wording had been used. Arguably therefore a *general* right of recovery is too broad, and we should distinguish more between those who take active steps to establish an illegality and those who passively accept it.

C   Payments by public bodies

18.14   There has been relatively little litigation on payments by, rather than to, public authorities. Statute provides for the common case of the overpayment of social security benefits[1]. As to the common law, the clearest statement was in a case where a payment was wrongly made to the Auckland Harbour Board, which the Privy Council held was recoverable. Viscount Haldane, speaking for the Privy Council, pronounced as follows:

> Any payment out of the consolidated fund made without Parliamentary authority is simply illegal and ultra vires, and may be recovered by the Government if it can, as here, be traced ... To invoke analogies of what might be held in a question between subject and subject is hardly relevant[2].

1   See the Social Security Administration Act 1992, s 71. Misrepresentation must be shown before recovery is allowed.
2   *Auckland Harbour Board v R* [1924] AC 318 at 327.

18.15   However, while clear enough in relation to its own facts, there are a number of difficult questions here, which (surprisingly) have not been resolved, or even squarely addressed, in later litigation.

Firstly, was Haldane's reference to 'the consolidated fund' meant merely as an example, or does it have greater significance? It would be strange if different rules applied to different funds, or to different governmental bodies, and it has often been assumed that the rule is quite general[1]. But the matter is not settled.

Secondly, it is not clear what Haldane had in mind when he said that the money could be recovered 'if it can ... be traced'. If he was using the word 'traced' in a technical sense, that would suggest that he saw the claim as one to *ownership* of the money, which would certainly distinguish it from the personal *Woolwich* claim. And he has indeed been taken in this sense[2]. But others have assumed that this was merely loose use of terminology, and he meant rather that a personal claim would lie[3]. This latter approach certainly fits better with the swaps cases[4], which assume that recovery from and by public authorities is of the same nature, and merely personal.

Finally, it is not at all clear that the analogy of private law claims can be dismissed as brusquely as Haldane tried to do, especially in matters of defence[5].

1   See eg *Woolwich Equitable Building Society v IRC* [1993] AC 70 at 172, [1992] 3 All ER 737 at 759, per Lord Goff ('the simple call of justice').
2   See eg *Woolwich Equitable Building Society v IRC* [1993] AC 70 at 177, [1992] 3 All ER 737 at 763, per Lord Goff. On 'tracing' in this strict technical sense, see above, ch 4.
3   See eg *Commonwealth of Australia v Burns* [1971] VR 825.

4   See below, para 18.18ff.
5   On defences see below, para 18.31ff.

18.16   EU law has similarly little authority on the point. However, such authority as there is states clearly not only that money wrongly paid is recoverable, but that state organs which wrongly pay out money have a *duty* to recover it insofar as they can[1]. However, examples of this type of liability are hard to find[2].

1   *EC Commission v Germany* (Case 70/72) [1973] ECR 813.
2   For discussion see Jones *Restitution and European Community Law* (2000), pp 143 and 144.

D   Complex transactions

18.17   So in the case of one-off payments, there is clear authority that they may be recovered, though there are still some areas of doubt and uncertainty in the law, and there are various defences (which are considered later in the chapter). What if the payments were part of some wider transaction, which then proves to have been ultra vires? This area is dominated by the 'swaps' litigation, which concerned illegal financial derivatives transactions entered into by local authorities in the 1980s. To provide background for considering those cases, a short description of the litigation and the issues in it must be given.

The 'swaps' cases

INTRODUCTION AND BACKGROUND

18.18   These cases occurred against a background of conflict between central and local government. To meet their own targets for control of all government expenditure, central government imposed significant cuts and restrictions on local government finances over the course of the 1980s. However, as autonomous institutions, which did not necessarily share central government's objectives, local authorities became more and more adept at 'off-balance-sheet' transactions, which adhered to the letter of local government law, while in fact giving the local authorities substantial financial freedom of action. The increasing use of interest-rate swaps and other financial derivatives was part of that financial ingenuity.

18.19   In its simplest form, an interest rate swap is a contract under which one party promises to pay the other interest as if they had borrowed a substantial sum at a fixed rate of interest. The other party agrees in return to pay interest as if they had borrowed a similar sum, but at a floating rate, varying with the movement of interest rates generally. The contract is thus one for the payment of differences, and from one point of view can be seen as a succession of gambles on how the money markets will move.

Local authorities used swaps with a variety of motives: some simply as a tool in managing their existing debt; others as a covert way of borrowing money at market rates; others still as a method for speculating on market movements. The banks with whom they contracted had more straightforward motives. The precise terms of the swap would be selected so as to build in a profit for the bank providing it. And a bank that did not care to carry the considerable risks involved could 'hedge', by purchasing a 'back-to-back' swap from another bank. In that situation, every payment to or by the bank would be precisely cancelled out by a payment made under the 'hedge' swap, and so the bank would not in fact bear any financial risk – or so it was thought.

18.20   The legality of all these swaps was, however, soon called into question. There was no explicit statutory basis in local authority law for transacting in this way. Local authorities were by statute generally permitted to enter any transaction 'which is calculated to facilitate, or is conducive or incidental to, the discharge of any of their functions'[1]. This is the provision the local authorities relied on. But which local authority 'functions' were the swaps designed to 'discharge'? At least three views were possible. The first was that one 'function' of a local authority was managing its own debt, and that the general use of swaps could be seen as an aspect of that. A second and more restrictive view was that, while managing existing debt was indeed a local authority function, the legislation could only justify swaps where their use was directly and clearly connected to debt-management. A third view, narrowest of all, was that debt management was not a local authority 'function' at all, but only as a matter incidental to their other functions. As such, the use of swaps was not justified in any circumstances at all.

1   See the Local Government Act 1972, s 111(1).

18.21   In the event, when a challenge came, different courts took different views. The court of appeal took the second view: that the use of swaps could be justified, so long as it was clearly connected to the management of exiting debt[1]. But the House of Lords disagreed, taking the third view, with the result that all local authority swap transactions were held ultra vires[2].

In many ways, it is unfortunate that the test case concerned the local authority that had engaged in the most reckless use of swaps. The London Borough of Hammersmith and Fulham was by far the worst offender amongst local authorities. They had started in 1983, initially in a modest way as part of a debt management scheme. The swaps bug bit them in May 1987, and over the next year or more they entered into a large number of transactions – indeed, they made more swaps than all the other local authorities combined. In all, they contracted for 592 distinct swap transactions, with a total notional value in excess of £6bn. (This was about 20 times their total debt, and more than 100 times their annual turnover. At one point, they were responsible for more than $0 \cdot 5\%$ of all swap transactions, world-wide.) So reckless was this authority, that it was hopeless to argue that all of their transactions were valid. Nonetheless, the ruling that *no* swaps by *any* authority were valid can certainly be seen as an over-reaction. And Lord Templeman's comment that 'a swap contract ... is more akin to gambling than insurance'[3] seems embarrassingly unsophisticated, given that there is nothing in the least suspicious about a swap transaction as such. But however this may be, it set the scene for the subsequent litigation.

1   *Hazell v Hammersmith & Fulham London Borough Council* [1990] 2 QB 697, [1990] 3 All ER 33.
2   *Hazell v Hammersmith & Fulham London Borough Council* [1992] 2 AC 1, [1991] 1 All ER 545.
3   [1992] 2 AC 1 at 34–35, [1991] 1 All ER 545 at 559. See to the contrary *Morgan Grenfell & Co Ltd v Welwyn Hatfield District Council* [1995] 1 All ER 1, rejecting arguments that the transactions fell foul of the Gaming Act 1845 or the Financial Services Act 1986.

18.22   The illegality of the swaps being clearly established, nearly 200 actions were started to recover payments made. Sometimes it was local authorities demanding their money back, sometimes banks; on the whole it seems that the banks had lost more than the local authorities under the swaps, and so most of the cases are banks suing local authorities. In some cases, the ruling that swaps were illegal came while the swap was running its course (the 'open swaps' cases), in others the swap had already been completed before the ruling (the 'closed swaps' cases). The local authorities included Scottish as well as English authorities, and the banks were from various jurisdictions, though mostly they were UK companies. Obviously many of the issues were common to a number of cases, and a certain amount of consolidation and joint hearings were organised. Roughly speaking, the issues were of four sorts:

(i)   jurisdictional issues[1];
(ii) the question of liability to refund;
(iii) questions of defences; and
(iv) interest[2].

This chapter focuses on (ii) and (iii).

1   On which see below, para 22.44.
2   See below, para 21.70ff.

THE GROUND OF LIABILITY

18.23   While much is still obscure about the cases, there is at least a clear answer on liability. This is that all sums paid were recoverable. This is so whether or not the swap was 'closed', and whether or not it was the local authority, rather than the bank, that lost out as a result of the swap. And (to anticipate the discussion of defences below) only one defence was clearly available, namely set-off. So if the Ambridge Borough Council entered into a swap arrangement with the Borcestershire Bank, under which each side made payments, then the party which ended up paying less in total was liable to refund the difference to the other party.

All this is now clear, though it took a great deal of clients' money and judicial time to resolve it. And there is considerable doubt as to the ground of recovery. The main ground given by the courts was 'absence of consideration' (or that there was 'no consideration' or a 'failure of consideration' – it seems to make little difference which, though a great deal of ink has been spilled in trying to say[1]). But not everyone had found this satisfactory, and various others grounds have been suggested. Yet, just as in the case of one-off payments considered above, most of the grounds suggested are too narrow, explaining liability in some cases while failing to explain it in others. Consider first some of these under-inclusive grounds.

1   Different views on which formulation is preferable were expressed at all levels in *Westdeutsche Landesbank Girozentrale v Islington London Borough Council* [1994] 4 All ER 890 at 924–930, per Hobhouse J; [1994] 4 All ER 890 at 960, per Dillon LJ, and at 968, per Leggatt LJ); [1996] AC 669 at 682–683, per Lord Goff, and at 710–711, per Lord Browne-Wilkinson. See also the views of individual members of the court of appeal in *Guinness Mahon & Co Ltd v Kensington and Chelsea Royal London Borough Council* [1999] QB 215, [1998] 2 All ER 272. Academic arguments over which formulation is better rely largely on drawing parallels with purely private law cases, which are however of doubtful relevance. See Birks 'No consideration: Restitution after void contracts' (1993) 23 Western Australian Law Journal 195; Virgo *Principles of the law of restitution* (1999), pp 396–408; McMeel *Modern law of restitution* (2000), pp 172–178.

18.24   'Mistake' will certainly have been present in many of the cases. And the House of Lords were prepared to assume that this was at least a possible ground of recovery, which is why it was discussed in the *Kleinwort Benson* case[1]. Yet that case was only concerned with a preliminary point – whether, if 'mistake' was relevant at all, it mattered that the mistake was one of law not fact. In all the fuss over how that point was resolved, the issue *whether there was a mistake at all* was lost sight of. Indeed, the swaps cases illustrate the great difficulties in asking whether complicated organisations like public authorities or banks can rationally be said to be 'mistaken'. No doubt the particular officials who authorised each swap, or each payment, had long forgotten that the legality of the transaction was in doubt, if indeed they ever knew. Yet it is notorious that local authorities have only limited powers, and anyone who looked for chapter-and-verse on the matter would quickly have realised that there was a problem. No court which investigated the matter ever concluded that a 'mistake' had occurred, and it is not a conclusion to be jumped at – however convenient that would be for the officials on both sides[2].

1   *Kleinwort Benson Ltd v Lincoln City Council* [1999] 2 AC 349, [1998] 4 All ER 513. See below, para 18.40
2   For discussion see McKendrick 'The reason for restitution' in Birks and Rose (eds) *Lessons of the swaps litigation* (2000), pp 97–99.

18.25   'Incapacity' is often mentioned as a possible ground. Local authorities have only limited legal powers, like private companies and children, and so an analogy can clearly be drawn[1]. But it seems a loose parallel only, which cannot be pushed very far. The rules for children bend everything round to protecting *their* interests: ultimately children can enforce if the contract benefits them, and it is certainly not easy or straightforward for the other party to recover what they have supplied under it[2]. Yet the swaps cases allow recovery by *both* sides, without distinguishing the interests of the authority from that of the bank. So this analogy is not very close. The analogy of ultra vires private companies is perhaps closer; but this begs important questions, for the operation of the ultra vires principle in that context has been progressively whittled away by statute, precisely because it is so unsatisfactory[3]. All in all, while a parallel can be drawn with cases of incapacity, it seems to raise more questions than it answers.

1   See especially O'Dell 'Incapacity' in Birks and Rose (eds) *Lessons of the swaps litigation* (2000), p 113.
2   See above, paras 15.2–15.18.
3   See above, paras 15.24–15.28.

18.26   This leaves two grounds which seem general enough to explain the liability. One is 'absence of consideration'; the other is 'illegality'. Both seem to have played a role in the judicial reasoning, up to a point. Neither is however wholly satisfactory, particularly when we ask why recovery was allowed not only in cases of the uncompleted ('open') swaps but also in the completed ('closed') swaps.

18.27   'Illegality' is an obviously relevant principle, and clearly explains why the court did not *enforce* the swap transactions. The difficult question is, why we conclude that the transactions should actually be unravelled, and the money returned. After all, the general presumption in case of illegality is the reverse, that parties to an illegal transaction can expect the loss to lie where it falls (*in pari delicto potior est conditio defendentis*[1]). The answer, if there is one, must lie in the policy behind the illegality. Policy very often dictates not merely that the transaction should be stopped in its tracks, but that one side or the other be allowed to recover money paid under it. This might explain why local authorities could recover from banks: the policy is designed to protect authorities, or at least those whose interests they represent. But it does not seem to explain why banks could recover. As sophisticated market actors, it is not clear that banks need protection from anyone, still less that it was the policy of *this* legislation to protect them. This ground therefore leaves a great deal to be explained.

Much has been made here of the 'annuities cases', where payors paid lump sums in return for periodical payments from the defendant, originally envisaged as continuing for the rest of their lives. It then emerged that these annuity transactions were void by statute[2]. The remedy allowed was usually complete recovery of payments, subject to set-off, just as was found in the swaps cases[3]. However, it is not entirely clear why these cases are considered a useful guide. They are antique. They conflict with one another. There is no obvious public law element to the cases. And given how little we know about the policy of the legislation involved, it seems rather bold to assume that it is of relevance to the problems of local authorities over two centuries later. Rather, to modern eyes the cases appear to be ones where a policy protective of those who paid for the annuities resulted in a remedy in their favour, but subject to set-off. The connection to the problems of local authority finance does not precisely leap to the eye. All in all, the analogy is a very unhelpful one.

1   See above, ch 14.
2   Annuity Act 17 Geo III c 26 (1777), re-enacted as Annuity Act 53 Geo III c 141 (1813); repealed by Usury Laws Repeal Act 17&18 Vict c 90 (1854). The long title of the Act suggests that its basic policy was protective of a special class: 'An Act for registering the Grants of Life Annuities; and for the better Protection of Infants against such Grants'.
3   See eg *Hicks v Hicks* (1802) 3 East 16 at 17, 102 ER 502 at 502, per Lord Ellenborough CJ; *Holbrook v Sharpey* (1812) 19 Ves 131, 34 ER 467.

18.28   So while the 'illegality' theory can explain why the court intervenes at all, it is incomplete on why its intervention takes the form of ordering complete recovery of all sums paid. In particular, this response seems incomprehensible in the case of a 'closed' swap under which the local authority happened to end up in profit. What conceivable policy is served by removing this profit? To 'protect' local authorities from having too much money? To 'protect' banks from signing contracts under which they may lose money? Neither reason seems very plausible. If there is an answer to this, it must presumably be that the policy against ultra vires transactions is a very broad-brush one, at all costs discouraging parties from entering into them, even if in fact no-one's legitimate interests were harmed as a result. But this comes awfully close to mandating financial terrorism, deliberately procuring whatever result will most disconcert and shake up the parties, and flouting the public interest in the stability of local authority finances.

18.29   'Absence of consideration' is a more straightforward and precise ground here. And in the case of the 'open' swaps, it seems to provide a convincing explanation. The payments are recoverable because the transaction under which they were paying was not valid, and was never fully concluded. So the payors can fairly say that they did not get what they were paying for.

But in the case of the 'closed' swaps, it fares no better than the 'illegality' theory. For surely if the transaction was finished on both sides, then each *did* get what they were paying for. It is hard to see how either can say that consideration was absent merely on the ground that the payments, when made, were made illegally. If there is an answer to this, it is presumably that the court is not allowed to conclude that each side got what they paid for, as this amounts to giving effect to the ultra vires transaction. The court shies away from the conclusion that consideration was present, as this allows performance of the illegal contract to validate it. Yet why the policy behind the ultra vires principle requires this conclusion is not spelled out[1].

1   For criticism of this ground see Birks 'No consideration: Restitution after void contracts' (1993) 23 Western Australian Law Journal 195.

18.30   Ultimately, then, we have the clear conclusion that the court will unravel the transaction and order repayment; but we have no entirely satisfactory account of why this is. The right conclusion may be that public law is still developing, and perhaps it will only be with a clearer understanding of the purpose of the ultra vires rule that the consequences of infringing it will be understood. Nor is the rule static: since the time of the swaps cases, not only have local authority powers been substantially rewritten, but a procedure has been introduced to give effect to transactions on the borderline of illegality, so long as their status is clearly acknowledged and recorded[1]. As a comparison, company law developed from a policy emphasising the interests of shareholders (and hence the ultra vires principle) to one emphasising the interests of those with whom the company deals (and hence down-grading the ultra vires principle). Perhaps administrative law is starting down the same road.

1   Local Government (Contracts) Act 1997, on which see above, para 15.29, n 2, and Bamforth 'Public law' in Birks and Rose (eds) *Lessons of the swaps litigation* (2000), pp 59 and 60.

E   Defences[1]

18.31   The courts have been very reluctant to admit any defences to the liabilities discussed in this chapter, once established. It is not entirely clear why this is. Certainly there is a feeling that we should not be too subtle in detecting arguments for allowing the state to retain payments which it demanded ultra vires. Yet this reluctance to find defences has extended also to cases where the state is claimant, as it was in many of the swaps cases. Whatever the reason, the courts are unlikely to allow any defence where its practical effect is the same as converting an ultra vires payment into a lawful one.

1   For defences generally see below, ch 21.

Failure to exhaust alternative remedies

18.32   No action lies at common law if statute provides an alternative remedy to recover the ultra vires payment. So a common law action to claim wrong-paid tax lies only if the case falls outside one of the statutory mechanisms for correcting errors[1]. An allegation that EU law has been broken will entail an application to the European Court, unless the application of community law is so obvious that this is unnecessary (under the doctrine of *acte claire*).

In the *Woolwich* case itself, the claim was made in two stages. First, the claimant started public law proceedings to demonstrate that the payment had been demanded unlawfully. Second, a private law action in restitution was commenced to recover it back (or at least, to recover interest, the revenue having refunded the sum paid). Does the principle of exhaustion in fact *require* such a two-stage procedure, or can a claimant simply proceed straight to the restitutionary claim, dealing with the public law point in the course of that action? It seems that it is not necessary to use two stages in most cases. Naturally it is better to deal with the matter in one action if possible; but it is not entirely settled whether this can done through public law proceedings. The relevant rule of procedure allows a public law claim to include an action for 'damages', but makes no express provision for restitutionary remedies[2]. The obvious procedure is therefore a single private law action, and this will probably do[3].

1   See above, para 18.2.
2   CPR 1998, Pt 54 especially r 54.3 (covering the same ground as the old RSC Ord 53). 'Damages' are defined in the official glossary as 'A sum of money awarded by the court as compensation to the claimant'. There has been a Law Commission proposal, not implemented, that there should be express reference to restitution: *Administrative Law: Judicial review and statutory appeals* (Law Com no 226, HC 669, 1994), paras 8.5–8.8.
3   See eg *British Steel v Customs and Excise Comrs* [1997] 2 All ER 366. See Bamforth 'Restitution and the scope of judicial review' [1997] PL 603.

Compromise, or submission to an honest claim

18.33   It is surprisingly unclear when, if ever, a defence of compromise or submission is allowed. In private law, compromise is encouraged – indeed, the legal system cannot operate at all unless most claims settle, rather than requiring a court hearing. However, in public law this now seems to give an undue advantage to the state. Attitudes have changed, to be sure. At one time, a claimant had but a single chance to go to court. Having paid when confronted with the alternative of legal proceedings, they were regarded as having surrendered their day in court for good. They paid to close the transaction, and cannot later re-open it. That rule has now certainly gone, but it is not clear what has taken its place. In *Woolwich*, Lord Goff thought that an initial refusal to go to court might still sometimes doom a claim: 'If he chooses to give way and pay, rather than obtaining the decision of the court on the question whether the money is due, his payment is not recoverable'[1]. But as Goff plainly did not think that rule fitted the facts in front of him, even though Woolwich did indeed 'give way and pay', his meaning is not altogether clear.

1   *Woolwich Equitable Building Society v IRC* [1993] AC 70 at 165, [1992] 3 All ER 737 at 754, per Lord Goff, citing *William Whiteley Ltd v R* (1909) 101 LT 741, [1908–1910] All ER Rep 639.

18.34   Presumably the defence is narrow, if indeed it exists at all. The sort of case which seems to call out for such a defence, is where the very point of law on which the state was ultimately found to have acted illegally was raised and argued by the claimant; where the claimant's arguments were met, not by brute use of economic or coercive power, but by rational argument on the part of state officials; and where the claimant, having heard those arguments, decided to pay rather than to fight further. Even there, however, the argument from compromise is being used to convert an illegal demand into a legal one, and possibly the courts may feel that this is not legitimate. It is therefore entirely possible that the defence will never be available.

'Settled view of the law' or 'disruption of public finances'

18.35   To correct a single erroneous payment is usually unlikely to put undue strain on the state's finance. However, where the point of law involved is of wider significance, such as in cases involving the interpretation of tax statutes, then the ramifications of correcting an error may be considerable. So it has been suggested that where payment was made on the basis of a settled view of the law taken by the authorities, or where correcting their error would unduly disrupt public finances, then no remedy should lie.

The argument is not morally attractive, as it points to the problems caused by the state's own error as the reason why nothing should be done to correct that error. The argument may also be seen as encouraging the state to take a lax view of the law, in the knowledge that nothing will be done if an error is later proved. It is perhaps for these reasons that the argument has consistently been rejected[1]. Nonetheless, there could be situations where the cost of rectifying the error is so much greater than the harm done by the error, that the argument would have to be taken seriously. It is therefore unlikely to go away. Possibly it might revive in the form of a call for prospective application of the law: so that a claimant who points out an error would be able to recover, but otherwise the remedy would only be available to those who paid *after* the ruling which pointed out the error. This solution was directly rejected in *Kleinwort Benson*, but is likely to rear its head again.

1   *Kleinwort Benson Ltd v Lincoln City Council* [1999] 2 AC 349 at 382, [1998] 4 All ER 513 at 538, per Lord Goff.

Change of position and estoppel

18.36   As defences of change of position and of estoppel are available in analogous private law cases[1], it is not surprising that there have been attempts to apply them here. Indeed, in one of the swaps cases Hobhouse J was prepared to assume that the change of position defence applied, though on the facts he did not find it established[2]. The difficulty is however that these defences, if successful, seem to turn an unlawful payment into a lawful one, or at least one that is irrecoverable, simply because one of the parties *acted as if* it were lawful. In other words, the policy of reversing ultra vires payments is ignored simply because the recipient spends the money. Will this be permitted?

1   On change of position generally, see below, para 21.37ff; and on estoppel generally see below, para 21.16ff.
2   *Kleinwort Benson Ltd v South Tyneside Metropolitan Borough Council* [1994] 4 All ER 972 at 984–987. See also *R v Tower Hamlets London Borough Council, ex p Chetnik Developments Ltd* [1988] AC 858 at 882, [1988] 1 All ER 961 at 974, per Lord Goff.

18.37   When the point was directly raised, Clarke J held that the defence must be rejected. While he made no ruling that the defence would *never* be available, nonetheless his reasons seem to be of general application in any public case. There can be no reliance on an unlawful transaction: so neither change of position nor estoppel can validate an unlawful transaction. He added that the point cannot be evaded by saying that the defendant is relying *on the payment* rather than *on the transaction under which the payment was paid*. So a bank could not resist a claim for reimbursement of money paid under a swap by showing that it had passed on all the money to another bank under a 'hedging' swap[1].

Some have criticised this result, arguing that Clarke J was wrong to reject the distinction between relying on the payment and relying on the unlawful transaction[2]. However, the real issue seems to be about the strength of the public policy behind the ultra vires rule. Is it really so strong that it completely overrules the ordinary policy of protecting security of receipt? On current evidence, the answer is Yes, and so neither change of position nor estoppel has much role to play in this area. However, it is hard to believe that, when the relevant policy considerations are looked at more closely, the policy of ultra vires will *always* be stronger. A more discretionary approach seems indicated.

1   *South Tyneside Metropolitan Borough Council v Svenska International plc* [1995] 1 All ER 545.
2   See especially Nolan 'Change of position in anticipation of enrichment' [1995] Lloyds Maritime and Commercial Law Quarterly 313; Birks 'Private law' in Birks and Rose (eds) *Lessons of the swaps litigation* (2000), pp 28–35; Jewell, 'Change of position' in Birks and Rose (eds) *Lessons of the swaps litigation* (2000), p 273.

'Passing on' or 'mitigation'

18.38   It is sometimes possible to show that the claimant, after making the unlawfully-demanded payment, was able to recoup it from other sources, and so ended up no worse off. This is particularly likely to be so in relation to a tax like VAT, which is *meant* to be passed on by payers to their customers. Or again, many of the swaps cases involved risk-averse banks who purchased 'hedging' swaps, so that every payment they made to the local authority was balanced by a payment from the hedging bank. Some eminent tribunals have accepted the defence[1], and it is an open question whether English law will eventually do so.

However, the defence is a curious one, for it does nothing to get over the illegality of the payment or of the ultra vires decision that lay behind it. Nor does it alter the point that *someone* has unfairly lost out, and that the defendant gained as a result of that loss. It merely suggests that, whoever lost, it was not the claimant. In relation to VAT, the statutory scheme for refunds allows the tribunal some lee-way in the remedy, and it seems that it is sometimes used to identify the real loser and to pay the refund to them, though the difficulties of calculation are considerable[2]. If however it is not possible to return the money to the real loser, the arguments over whether to allow the defence are finely balanced. Administrative convenience favours refusing a remedy, but granting it may provide a useful incentive to identify and complain of revenue errors[3]. More generally, however, the defence of 'passing on' has gained little acceptance, having been rejected in various cases[4]. And the rather similar plea of 'mitigation of loss' in the swaps cases also met with rejection[5].

1   See *Air Canada v British Columbia* (1989) 59 DLR (4th) 161, criticised by Michell 'Restitution, "passing on", and the recovery of unlawfully demanded taxes: Why *Air Canada* doesn't fly' (1995) 53 University of Toronto Faculty of Law Review 130. See also *Amministrazione delle Finanze dello Stato v SpA San Giorgio* [1983] ECR 3595 at 3612–3614 (EU member states may, but need not, adopt such a defence, though if they do they cannot place impossible procedural hurdles in the way of those it affects). See also Woodward '"Passing on" the right to restitution' (1985) 39 University of Miami Law Review 873.
2   See the Value Added Tax Act 1994, s 80, as amended by Finance Act 1997, s 46. See also the Finance Act 1989, s 29(3) (excise duty). For an example of the defence see *Marks and Spencer plc v Customs and Excise Comrs* [2000] STC 16. For criticism see Peacock 'Unjust and unfair?' *Tax Journal* (8 May 2000) p 18.
3   Cf Virgo 'Restitution of overpaid VAT' [1998] British Tax Review 582.
4   *Kleinwort Benson Ltd v Birmingham City Council* [1997] QB 380, [1996] 4 All ER 733, following *Comr of State Revenue (Victoria) v Royal Insurance Australia Ltd* (1994) 182 CLR 51.
5   *Kleinwort Benson Ltd v Birmingham City Council* [1997] QB 380 at 392, [1996] 4 All ER 733 at 741–742, per Evans LJ.

Limitation

18.39   Finally, it is clear that there must be some limit of time beyond which no claim can be made. Statute suggests that the period is six years from the time the claim could first have been made[1]. As the money was, in theory, usually reclaimable as soon as it is paid, the period is therefore six years from that time. Some have suggested that if the true basis of recovery is 'failure of consideration', then recovery would lie not from the time of payment, but from whatever later time the consideration can be said to have failed[2]. But as the 'failure' in public law cases has to be taken to be the illegality of the basis for the transaction, which was there all along, there seems to be nothing in the point.

Difficult questions arise in cases where the relevant period catches some only of a long series of payments under the swap[3].

1 See the Limitation Act 1980, s 5; *Kleinwort Benson Ltd v South Tyneside Metropolitan Borough Council* [1994] 4 All ER 972 at 978, per Hobhouse J. On limitation generally see below, para 21.63ff.
2 Birks 'Private law' in Birks and Rose (eds) *Lessons of the swaps litigation* (2000), p 42.
3 See Rose 'Lapse of time: Limitation' in Birks and Rose (eds) *Lessons of the swaps litigation* (2000), p 348.

18.40   A certain amount of confusion has been caused by another provision of the Limitation Acts, which provides that for a claim for 'relief from the consequences of a mistake', time does not begin to run until the mistake could reasonably have been discovered[1]. This was given a wide interpretation in the *Kleinwort Benson* case, so that payments made on the basis of an old and well-established precedent were recoverable when that precedent was overruled, time beginning to run only from the date of the overruling. Yet this seems to make the law unacceptably generous to claimants. This part of the decision came only by a majority, and even the lords in the majority seemed to think it left the law in an unsatisfactory state[2]. As it is, there is a certain amount of confusion. Most commentators seem to assume that this only applies where the claim was, or could have been, based on the case law about 'mistakes', which raises awkward questions about the nature and scope of that doctrine. However, this is not what the statute says – it demands only that the claim is for 'relief from the consequences of a mistake', not that the claimant could have, or did, put their claim in any particular way[3]. And it should not lightly be assumed that 'mistake' is defined for this purpose in the same way as for other purposes.

1 See the Limitation Act 1980, s 32(1)(c). See above, para 17.88ff, and below, para 21.69ff.
2 *Kleinwort Benson Ltd v Lincoln City Council* [1999] 2 AC 349 at 389, [1998] 4 All ER 513 at 544, per Lord Goff. This is ironic, given that Goff had earlier pointed out that the chaos likely to be caused by a broad right of recovery could be staved off by the use of short limitation periods, though this 'may be too strong medicine for our taste': *Woolwich Equitable Building Society v IRC* [1993] AC 70 at 174, [1992] 3 All ER 737 at 761.
3 The great unanswered question here is whether an 'action ... for relief from the consequences of a mistake', as referred to in the legislation, has to be one based on legal principles which are specific to mistake. The only authority on the matter is the decision of Pearson J in *Phillips-Higgins v Harper* [1954] 1 QB 411, [1954] 1 All ER 116 (unsuccessfully appealed on another point, see [1954] QB 420, [1954] 2 All ER 51).

F   Conclusion

18.41   The *Woolwich* case is of undoubted significance, and no doubt the law will develop significantly in years to come. The real difficulty will be to keep it in its proper perspective. The principle of keeping public authorities within their powers is of the highest importance, but it surely does not follow that every ultra vires action necessitates the return of sums paid under it; private law slowly earned the error of that, and public law will eventually learn it as well. A more nuanced approach is needed. However, what shape that more sophisticated law will take cannot yet be said to be clear. Looked at broadly, it seems that the means used for restraining liability in private law have been tried here, and have failed. The public-law-specific defences that must be developed are only slowly taking shape.

18.42   The swaps cases generally illustrate the weakness of the current approach. The courts reacted to the illegality with blind hostility, often upholding claims for no better reason than that they would have refused them had the transaction been legal. Next-to-nothing was done to identify those who bore responsibility for this expensive fiasco – the parties have simply trotted out the convenient line that they were all 'mistaken', and the courts have made no attempt to identify those whose job it should have been to prevent such mistakes. Nor do we know who really suffered as a result, for the courts were reluctant to investigate the banks' use of 'hedging' swaps to cushion their losses. As it is, the only possible way of justifying the result is as some broad-brush punishment on the parties, upsetting their financial plans to teach them a lesson. But this lesson is an arbitrary and eccentric one, especially as it must in many cases have rewarded illegal behaviour by allowing one party to reverse a swap under which they were a substantial loser. It is an odd sort of punishment that showers money on some of the parties supposedly punished.

18.43   When all is said and done, we have no clear judicial statement as to why the ordinary rule in cases of illegality was not applied in the swaps cases: Why, in other words, the loss was not allowed to lie precisely where it fell, except where one party could be shown to be more guilty than the other. Perhaps, with the development of the law, some such coherent statement will be forthcoming; or perhaps the general right of recovery, which the swaps cases seem to establish, will be seen as a gigantic aberration. It is much too soon to say.

CHAPTER 19

Discharge of Contract for Breach

Greg Tolhurst

A   Introduction

Background

19.1   The purpose of this chapter is to discuss the rules governing claims for restitution following discharge of contract for breach or repudiation. A right to restitution in this area is explicable by reference to the principle against unjust enrichment. It therefore makes sense to structure this chapter by reference to the elements of unjust enrichment, namely, receipt of a benefit, receipt of that benefit 'at the expense of' the claimant and the existence of a ground or basis for restitution rendering receipt or retention of the benefit unjust[1].

[1]   In this chapter the words 'benefit' and 'enrichment' are used interchangeably. However, an 'enrichment' may have a narrower meaning than 'benefit' because, arguably a person is only enriched if they have received something that can be assessed by reference to a monetary value. The law of unjust enrichment is not so restricted and if this meaning of 'enrichment' were to be adopted, then the word 'benefit' would better encapsulate the case law. Cf Beatson *Use and Abuse of Unjust Enrichment* (1991), ch 2. See further on the distinction between enrichment and benefit, Fuller and Perdue 'The Reliance Interest in Contract Damages' (1936) 46 Yale Law Journal 52 at 72.

19.2   Although restitution following discharge of contract for breach or repudiation is explicable by reference to unjust enrichment, this area is naturally subject to the continuing evolution of this principle. Currently there is no general consensus as to when restitution following discharge of contract should be allowed. Within this debate there appears to be two principal areas of dispute. First, there is disagreement over what amounts to a 'benefit'[1]. Second, there is disagreement over the bases for restitution[2]. Both of these areas of dispute, however, are not limited to restitution following discharge of contract for breach or repudiation. Third, it has been suggested that a party who is not in breach of contract should be limited to their claim in damages, and should not have an alternative claim for restitution[3].

[1]   See below, para 19.6.
[2]   See below, para 19.8ff.
[3]   See generally Rafferty 'Contracts Discharged Through Breach: Restitution For Services Rendered by the Innocent Party' (1999) 37 Alberta Law Review 51. Cf Garner 'The Role of Subjective Benefit in the Law of Unjust Enrichment' (1990) 10 OJLS 42 at 55. See below, especially at para 19.103.

RELEVANCE OF THE CONTRACT AND OF PRINCIPLES OF DISCHARGE

19.3   Prior to the consideration of a claim for restitution, the contract must be construed, to determine whether it assumes a particular remedial response following the breach or repudiation. Wherever the contract provides a complete remedial regime it is not appropriate to consider a separate claim for restitution[1].

No detailed treatment of the doctrines of breach and repudiation of contract will be given in this chapter, as this is more properly dealt with in contract texts[2]. However, because of the importance discharge has on restitutionary claims, a few points should be noted.

First, current law dictates that until a contract is discharged or rescinded, no claim for restitution can be considered[3].

Second a contract will generally only be discharged for breach or repudiation when the innocent party elects to terminate the contract. Without an express or implied term, a frustrating event or a statutory provision, discharge is not automatic.

Third, when a contract is terminated for breach or repudiation, it is discharged as to future rights and obligations only[4]. On one view, any rights that have accrued at the time of discharge, whether conditionally or unconditionally, survive the discharge of the contract[5]. However, it is suggested that the better view is that the only rights that survive discharge are those that have unconditionally accrued prior to termination[6]. Therefore if an unperformed primary obligation has accrued prior to discharge, but has not unconditionally accrued because (for example) it was conditional upon some ultimate performance by the other party, then that obligation will not survive discharge.

1 *Pan Ocean Shipping Co Ltd v Creditcorp Ltd, The Trident Beauty* [1994] 1 WLR 161.
2 See Carter *Breach of Contract* (2nd edn, 1991); Furmston (ed) *Law of Contract* (1999), ch 7, especially 7D.
3 See *Dimskal Shipping Co SA v International Transport Workers Federation, The Evia Luck* [1992] 2 AC 152 at 165, per Lord Goff; *Miles v Wakefield Metropolitan District Council* [1987] AC 539 at 561, per Lord Templeman; *Gilbert & Partners (a firm) v Knight* [1968] 2 All ER 248; *Pavey & Matthews Pty Ltd v Paul* (1987) 162 CLR 221 at 256, per Deane J; *Update Constructions Pty Ltd v Rozelle Child Care Centre Ltd* (1990) 20 NSWLR 251 at 275, per Priestley JA; *Christiani & Nielsen Pty Ltd v Goliath Portland Cement Co Ltd* (1993) 2 Tas LR 122. Academic opinions for this rule differ slightly in their reasoning, see Goff and Jones *Law of Restitution* (5th edn, 1998), pp 45, 47, 403, 405, and 418; Birks *An Introduction to the Law of Restitution* (revised edn, 1989), pp 46 and 47; Friedmann 'Valid, Voidable, Qualified and Non-Existing Obligations: An Alternative Perspective on the Law of Restitution' in Burrows (ed) *Essays on the Law of Restitution* (1991), pp 247 and 248; Burrows *Law of Restitution* (1993), pp 250 and 251; Mason and Carter *Restitution Law in Australia* (1995) paras 315, 901–902, and 909; Carter 'Restitution and Contract Risk' in McInnes (ed) *Restitution: Developments in Unjust Enrichment* (1996), p 142. For an alternative analysis see Beatson 'Restitution and Contract: Non Cumul?' (2000) 1 Theoretical Inquiries in Law 83, and Beatson 'The Temptation of Elegance: Concurrence of Restitutionary and Contractual Claims' in Swadling and Jones (eds) *The Search for Principle* (1999), p 143. See further Smith 'Concurrent Liability in Contract and Unjust Enrichment: The Fundamental Breach Requirement' (1999) 115 LQR 245; Mead 'Restitution Within Contract' (1991) 11 Legal Studies 172. Historically, and prior to the modern principles of discharge of contract, a contract had to be rescinded before restitution was possible, see *Planché v Colburn* (1831) 8 Bing 14, 131 ER 305; on which see below, para 19.90.
4 *Johnson v Agnew* [1980] AC 367 at 396; *McDonald v Dennys Lascelles Ltd* (1933) 48 CLR 457 at 476–477. Note, however, that in respect of personal property discharge may revest title, see *R V Ward Ltd v Bignall* [1967] 1 QB 534 at 550, per Diplock LJ; *Kwei Tek Chao v British Traders and Shippers Ltd* [1954] 2 QB 459 at 487–488, per Devlin J; *McDougall v Aeromarine of Emsworth Ltd* [1958] 1 WLR 1126 at 1134, per Diplock J; *Berger & Co Inc v Gill & Duffus SA* [1984] AC 382 at 395, per Lord Diplock. See further below, para 19.33.
5 See *Hyundai Heavy Industries Co Ltd v Papadopoulos* [1980] 1 WLR 1129 at 1141, per Lord Edmund-Davies and *Stocznia Gdanska SA v Latvian Shipping Co* [1998] 1 WLR 574 at 597, per Lord Lloyd. See also Carter 'Shipbuilding Contracts: Not Quite the Final Chapter' (1998) 13 Journal of Contract Law 156 at 162–163.
6 *McDonald v Dennys Lascelles Ltd* (1933) 48 CLR 457 at 476, per Dixon J; *Johnson v Agnew* [1980] AC 367 at 396; *Photo Production Ltd v Securicor Transport Ltd* [1980] AC 827 at 849, per Lord Diplock; *Port Jackson Stevedoring Pty Ltd v Salmond & Spraggon (Aust) Pty Ltd, The New York Star* [1981] 1 WLR 138 at 145 per Lord Wilberforce; *Berger & Co Inc v Gill & Duffus SA* [1984] AC 382 at 390, per Lord Diplock; *Lombard North Central plc v Butterworth* [1987] QB 527 at 535, per

Mustill LJ; *Bank of Boston Connecticut v European Grain & Shipping Ltd, The Dominique* [1989] 1 AC 1056 at 1098–1099, per Lord Brandon; *Hurst v Bryk* [2002] 1 AC 185 at 193, per Lord Millett.

19.4   However, when it is said that unconditional accrued obligations survive the discharge of a contract, this does not mean that it is possible for the innocent party to call for the performance of those obligations. Usually such a demand would be inconsistent with the election to terminate. There is therefore some force in the idea that upon discharge of contract all unperformed primary obligations are discharged[1]. An exception would arise in the case of a sale of goods by instalments, where the price for a particular instalment is paid in advance. In that case, the innocent party can continue to call for those goods to be delivered after discharge. Of course where the unconditional right is a debt that has been earned, payment of that debt can be enforced after discharge. In the normal case, however, the primary right to call for performance and the primary obligation to perform are replaced by a secondary right to damages and a secondary obligation to pay damages. The enforcement of a damages claim is consistent with termination.

Two types of restitutionary claim have historically dominated this area. The first is a claim for the return of money paid, and the second is a claim for reasonable remuneration for services performed or goods supplied[2].

1   See *Photo Production Ltd v Securicor Transport Ltd* [1980] AC 827 at 849, per Lord Diplock.
2   However, today, claims in respect of sale of goods have been subsumed by contract under the sale of goods legislation. Where no price is set under a contract for the sale of goods, the buyer must pay a reasonable price, see the Sale of Goods Act 1979, s 8(2). An action for such a reasonable price is a contract action. Similarly, in a contract for services where no price is fixed, a reasonable charge is payable, see the Supply of Goods and Services Act 1982, s 15(1).

B   Claims for the recovery of money

19.5   A claim for the recovery of money paid generally turns on whether or not there has been a total failure of consideration. This is the most crucial and difficult element of the claim. In terms of unjust enrichment, the requirement of total failure of consideration forms the basis of the claim, that is, the unjust factor.

Benefit

19.6   Where, prior to the discharge of a contract for breach or repudiation, a party receives a payment made under the contract then that party will have received a benefit for the purposes of unjust enrichment. Such a benefit is an 'incontrovertible benefit'[1]. The basis for this conclusion is that no reasonable person in receipt of money would deny that they have received a benefit, since money is a universal medium of exchange. The receipt of an incontrovertible benefit therefore prevents the payee having recourse to subjective devaluation[2]. Importantly, the conclusion that a benefit has been received in such circumstances is not simply based on the fact that the payee is in receipt of all or part of the agreed performance[3]. Although the term 'incontrovertible benefit' is the creation of restitution commentators and not that of the courts[4], its use (if not its scope[5]), does not appear to be too controversial[6].

1   See further below, para 19.78. It is said that this concept is not a straightforward adoption of an objective test for benefit; rather it tempers 'the greater absurdities of a subjective approach': Birks *An Introduction to the Law of Restitution* (revised edn, 1989), p 116.

2   Birks *An Introduction to the Law of Restitution* (revised edn, 1989), pp 109, 116–128. See also Skelton *Restitution and Contract* (1998), pp 12–14. See further para 19.62.
3   *BP Exploration Co (Libya) Ltd v Hunt (No 2)* [1979] 1 WLR 783 at 799, per Robert Goff J. See further para 19.85. On the case itself see below, para 20.10ff.
4   See however *BP Exploration Co (Libya) Ltd v Hunt (No 2)* [1979] 1 WLR 783 at 799, per Robert Goff J; *Procter & Gamble Philippine Manufacturing Corpn v Peter Cremer Gmbh & Co, The Manila* [1988] 3 All ER 843 at 855, per Hirst J; *Strang Patrick Stevedoring Pty Ltd v Owners of the MV Sletter* (1992) 38 FCR 501 at 522 and 529, per Cooper J; *Monks v Poynice Pty Ltd* (1987) 11 ACLR 637 at 640, per Young J; *Cadorange Pty Ltd v Tanga Holdings Pty Ltd* (1990) 20 NSWLR 26 at 35, per Young J; *Peel (Regional Municipality) v Canada* (1992) 98 DLR (4th) 140 at 159, per McLachlin J. See further McInnes 'The Canadian Principle of Unjust Enrichment: Comparative Insights Into the Law of Restitution' (1999) 37 Alberta Law Review 1 at 32–34.
5   See McInnes 'The Structure and Challenges of Unjust Enrichment' in McInnes (ed) *Restitution: Developments in Unjust Enrichment* (1996), p 21.
6   See Goff and Jones *Law of Restitution* (5th edn, 1998), pp 22–25. Cf *Bridgewater v Griffiths* [2000] 1 WLR 524 at 532.

'At the expense of'

19.7   It is a necessary element of any claim for restitution based on unjust enrichment for the claimant to show that the payment he or she made under the contract is causally connected to the gain of the defendant. This element justifies the claimant's claim against the defendant[1]. Subject to a few exceptions[2], the law appears to require the enrichment of the defendant to be directly at the expense of the claimant[3]. In claims made within the context of this chapter, this element generally causes no difficulty because the payment made by the claimant is usually made to (or at the direction of) the other party to the contract who is usually the defendant[4]. It may be noted, however, that although in claims for the recovery of payments made the claimant's loss will equate to the defendant's gain, this is not necessary for this element to be made out. What is necessary is that the loss and gain be shown to be causally connected.

1   See Virgo *Principles of the Law of Restitution* (1999), ch 5; Grantham and Rickett *Enrichment and Restitution in New Zealand* (2000), pp 63 and 64.
2   See Virgo *Principles of the Law of Restitution* (1999), ch 5; Grantham and Rickett *Enrichment and Restitution in New Zealand* (2000), p 64.
3   However, the law appears to be taking a commercial approach to this requirement of the enrichment having to be received directly at the expense of the claimant, see *Banque Financière de la Cité v Parc (Battersea) Ltd* [1999] 1 AC 221. See further above, para 8.47ff.
4   See further Birks 'At the Expense of the Claimant: Direct and Indirect Enrichment in English Law' (2000) Oxford University Comparative Law Forum 1 (at http://ouclf.iuscomp.org).

Bases for restitution

TOTAL FAILURE OF CONSIDERATION – MEANING

19.8   The principal basis for the recovery of money paid under a contract which is discharged for breach or repudiation is total failure of consideration[1]. In this context, the failure of consideration concept is concerned with whether the claimant received any part of the promised counter performance[2]. It needs to be emphasised, however, that once the defendant has commenced performance, then the claimant may be said to have received that performance. The use of the word 'receive' does not require the claimant to be in possession of some objective benefit ultimately due under the contract as many acts of performance may not confer such a benefit. Perhaps it may be easier to place the emphasis on the defendant's side and ask whether or not the defendant has done any act in actual performance of the contract[3].

1   Failure of consideration is not a new concept. It had been recognised prior to the recognition of unjust enrichment and prior to the formulation of the modern rules on discharge of contract, see Stoljar 'The Doctrine of Failure of Consideration' (1959) 75 LQR 53 and *Roxborough v Rothmans of Pall Mall Australia Ltd* [2001] HCA 68 at paras 101–109, per Gummow J. The first modern authoritative case to apply it to a discharged contract was *Fibrosa Spolka Akcjna v Fairbairn Lawson Combe Barbour Ltd* [1943] AC 32. Prior to this there was an insistence that the contract be avoided ab initio, see *Chandler v Webster* [1904] 1 KB 493 (overruled in *Fibrosa*). See further below, para 20.19.

2   *Comptor d'Archat et de Vente du Boerenbond Belge SA v Luis de Ridder Ltda, The Julia* [1949] AC 293 at 316 and 317, per Lord Simonds. Cf as to unenforceable contracts the possible requirement that the defendant must not be ready and willing to perform, see *Thomas v Brown* (1876) 1 QBD 714.

3   See *Stocznia Gdanska SA v Latvian Shipping Co* [1998] 1 WLR 574 at 588, per Lord Goff ('[F]ailure of consideration does not depend upon the question whether the promisee has or has not *received* anything under the contract ... In truth, the test is not whether the promisee has received a specific benefit, but rather whether the promisor has performed any part of the contractual duties in respect of which payment is due'). Cf *Baltic Shipping Co v Dillon, The Mikhail Lermontov* (1993) 176 CLR 344 at 350, per Mason CJ ('If the incomplete performance results in the innocent party receiving and retaining any substantial part of the benefit expected under the contract, there will not be a total failure of consideration'). See also *Rover International Ltd v Cannon Film Sales Ltd (No 3)* [1989] 1 WLR 912 at 923, per Kerr LJ.

19.9   Various expressions have been used to describe the concept of failure of consideration. These include, failure of the 'agreed return'[1] and failure to receive any part of the 'bargained for benefit'[2]. In the context of discharged contracts, the preferred formula, so far as case law is concerned, is perhaps 'failure of performance'[3]. These various expressions have been fashioned in part to prevent confusion between the failure of consideration concept and the doctrine of consideration in the formation of contracts[4]. The most famous statement of that distinction was made in *Fibrosa Spolka Akcjna v Fairbairn Lawson Combe Barbour Ltd*[5], where Viscount Simon LC said[6]:

> When one is considering the law of failure of consideration and of the quasi-contractual right to recover money on that ground, it is, generally speaking, not the promise which is referred to as the consideration, but the performance of the promise ... If this were not so, there could never be any recovery of money, for failure of consideration, by the payer of the money in return for a promise of future performance, yet there are endless examples which show that money can be recovered, as for a complete failure of consideration, in cases where the promise was given but could not be fulfilled.

1   Mason and Carter *Restitution Law in Australia* (1995), paras 207 and 303.

2   See *Stocznia Gdanska SA v Latvian Shipping Co* [1998] 1 WLR 574 at 599–600, per Lord Lloyd; *Rover International Ltd v Cannon Film Sales Ltd (No 3)* [1989] 1 WLR 912 at 923, Kerr LJ. See also *Baltic Shipping Co v Dillon, The Mikhail Lermontov* (1993) 176 CLR 344 at 351, per Mason CJ. See further *David Securities Pty Ltd v Commonwealth Bank of Australia* (1992) 175 CLR 353 at 381–383; *Marsh & McLennan Pty Ltd v Stanyers Transport Pty* [1994] 2 VR 232.

3   See *Fibrosa Spolka Akcjna v Fairbairn Lawson Combe Barbour Ltd* [1943] AC 32 at 48, per Viscount Simon LC; *Stocznia Gdanska SA v Latvian Shipping Co* [1998] 1 WLR 574 at 588, per Lord Goff (with whom Lord Hoffmann, Lord Hope and Lord Hutton agreed). See also *Baltic Shipping Co v Dillon, The Mikhail Lermontov* (1993) 176 CLR 344 at 350–351, per Mason CJ (with whom Brennan and Toohey JJ agreed) and at 389, per McHugh J.

4   For a recent example of where it was suggested these concepts had been confused see *Goss v Chilcott* [1996] AC 788 at 797, per Lord Goff (explaining this confusion in the reasoning of the judge at first instance). See also *Rover International Ltd v Cannon Film Sales Ltd (No 3)* [1989] 1 WLR 912 at 923, per Kerr LJ.

5   [1943] AC 32.

6   [1943] AC 32 at 48.

19.10   The most recent expression devised to prevent confusion between consideration in contract formation and failure of consideration is 'failure of basis'. The submission is that in the phrase 'failure of consideration', 'the word "consideration" denotes the basis of the transfer, and failure of contractual reciprocation is merely a common instance of such a failure of basis'[1]. The concluding words of this quote also show that 'failure of basis' has not been put forward by commentators solely for the purpose of ending the abovementioned confusion. It is, in part, devised to allow failure of consideration to apply or to continue to apply where there is no agreed return[2]. It also forms part of a proposal enabling failure of consideration to be used as a basis for restitution in claims for reasonable remuneration[3]. In terms of its application, the 'failure of basis' proposal is said to focus on 'the reason for the transfer'[4]. The restitutionary right is said to arise when the reason for the transfer is undermined[5] or fails to sustain itself[6].

1   Birks 'Failure of Consideration' in Rose (ed) *Consensus ad idem: Essays in the law of contract in honour of Guenter Treitel* (1996), pp 190 and 191; Birks *Restitution – The Future* (1992), p 10. See also *Fibrosa Spolka Akcyjna v Fairbairn Lawson Combe Barbour Ltd* [1943] AC 32 at 68, per Lord Wright; *Baltic Shipping Co v Dillon, The Mikhail Lermontov* (1993) 176 CLR 344 at 389, per McHugh J, *Roxborough v Rothmans of Pall Mall Australia Ltd* (2002) 76 ALJR 203 at para 104, per Gummow J. Other commentators adopt the expression 'failure of basis', but do not describe its operation in the same way, see eg Jackman *The Varieties of Restitution* (1998), p 44 ('[total failure of consideration insists] on a "total failure" of the reason which brought the transaction about. It is in this sense that "total failure of consideration" is a ground which vitiates the voluntariness of a payment, for the intention to engage in a transaction in which a payment is made is defeated when the reason for, or basis of, the transaction fails to materialise'); Virgo *Principles of the Law of Restitution* (1999), p 325 ('consideration for the purposes of the law of restitution refers to the condition which formed the basis for the plaintiff transferring a benefit to the defendant'); Grantham and Rickett *Enrichment and Restitution in New Zealand* (2000), pp 151 and 152 (the authors of this text in adopting 'failure of basis', correctly it is submitted, draw attention to both receipt and retention of an enrichment; they state, 'As a broad proposition, the basis upon which an enrichment was conferred fails when the condition or basis stipulated in respect of the defendant's receipt and retention of the enrichment do not materialise or are not sustained'). See further Fung *Pre-Contractual Rights and Remedies: Restitution and Promissory Estoppel* (1999), para 3.4.2.
2   See *Roxborough v Rothmans of Pall Mall Australia Ltd* (2002) 76 ALJR 203 at para 16, per Gleeson CJ Gaudron and Hayne JJ, and at para 94, per Gummow J. See further para 19.12.
3   See below, paras 19.99–19.102.
4   Birks *An Introduction to the Law of Restitution* (revised edn, 1989), p 223.
5   Burrows *Law of Restitution* (1993), p 251.
6   Birks *An Introduction to the Law of Restitution* (revised edn, 1989), p 223.

19.11   This explanation of the concept does call for special mention, because its impact on contracts discharged for breach or repudiation is not clear[1]. Generally, a contractual right may be enforced when the time for performance of the related obligation accrues. The basis or reason for any transfer or payment under a contract lies simply in the fact that the time for performance has accrued. Given that discharge operates in futuro, it is difficult to see how it can be said that the initial right to call for payment (assuming it has properly accrued, and payment can be legitimately called for) is undermined or fails to sustain itself when there is a failure to receive 'contractual reciprocation'[2]. That right would only be discharged if at the time of termination the payment had not been made and if it had not been earned. Upon discharge, it is the obligation to perform and earn the payment (and not the right to receive payment) that is discharged, and which gives rise to the failure of consideration. What is therefore 'undermined' is the title to retain. However, that is a separate issue from the basis or reason for the payment being made[3]. It would appear that if the current explanation of 'failure of basis' is strictly applied, then in some cases it may result in the recovery of payments made prior to discharge of contract falling outside of unjust enrichment as its requirements would not be met. Arguably, recovery would then have to be explained on the basis of contract and an implied term[4].

1   See further paras 19.3 and 19.4.
2   Cf Birks *An Introduction to the Law of Restitution* (revised edn, 1989), p 223.
3   See further para 19.31.
4   There is some support for this, see para 19.26.

RELEVANCE OF FAILURE OF CONSIDERATION TO CLAIMS FOR RESTITUTION

19.12   It is not entirely clear why failure of consideration became a principle of quasi-contract. There is no doubt that it was relevant to contract. In the seventeenth century, if a claimant wished to enforce the defendant's promise, he or she would have to aver performance where the defendant had bargained for the performance of the claimant's promise, as opposed to merely bargaining for the claimant's promise[1]. Where the defendant's obligation was dependent on prior or contemporaneous performance by the claimant, it was reasoned that there was no obligation to perform if the failure of the claimant to discharge his or her promise amounted to a failure of consideration[2]. This reasoning was not relevant in the case of independent promises[3]. Similar reasoning may have led to failure of consideration being transferred to quasi-contract[4]. Thus where a claimant sought the recovery of a payment made, it was necessary to establish that the payment had been made in respect of a promise, the performance of which was dependent on the receipt of the defendant's performance. Where the promises were independent promises, there could be no claim for restitution, unless the contract was in fact void. It is therefore difficult (historically) to divorce failure of consideration from contract. In addition, restitution and damages were considered to be mutually exclusive remedies[5], restitution required the contract to be rescinded[6] and it was reasoned that rescission could only take place if there was a total failure of consideration[7].

1   See Carter *Breach of Contract* (2nd edn, 1991), para 122.
2   See eg *Universal Cargo Carriers Corpn v Citati* [1957] 2 QB 401 at 431, per Devlin J ('To bring a contract to an end by breach of warranty there had to be a failure of consideration'); *Cehave NV v Bremer Handelsgesellschaft mbH, The Hansa Nord* [1976] QB 44 at 84, per Ormrod LJ.
3   See *Nichols v Raynbred* (1614) Hob 88, 88 ER 238. See also Simpson *A History of the Common Law of Contract* (1975), p 462.
4   See Jackson *History of Quasi-Contract In English Law* (1936), pp 85 and 86. Although accepting its contractual aspect, Stoljar (citing *Martin v Sitwell* (1691) 1 Show 156 at 157, 89 ER 509 at 510, per Holt CJ) suggests that 'failure of consideration' was used in the specialised sense of forming a basis for the recovery of payments from very early times, see Stoljar 'The Doctrine of Failure of Consideration' (1959) 75 LQR 53 at 53–54. See further *Roxborough v Rothmans of Pall Mall Australia Ltd* (2002) 76 ALJR 203 at paras 94 and 101–104, per Gummow J.
5   See generally *Dutch v Warren* (1720) 1 Stra 406, 93 ER 598; *Moses v MacFerlan* (1760) 2 Burr 1005, 97 ER 676; *Towers v Barrett* (1786) 1 Term Rep 133, 99 ER 1014; *Greville v Da Costa* (1797) Peake Add Cas 113, 170 ER 213; *Hunt v Silk* (1804) 5 East 449, 102 ER 1142; *Beed v Blandford* (1828) 2 Y & J 278, 148 ER 924; *Street v Blay* (1831) 2 B & Ad 456, 109 ER 1212; *Fitt v Cassanet* (1842) 4 Man & G 898, 134 ER 369; *Blackburn v Smith* (1848) 2 Ex Ch 783, 154 ER 707; *Freeman v Jeffries* (1869) LR 4 Ex 189; *Heilbutt v Hickson* (1872) LR 7 CP 438 at 451, per Bovill CJ; *Boston Deep Sea Fishing & Ice Co v Ansell* (1888) 39 Ch D 339 at 364–365, per Bowen LJ; *Boyd and Forrest v Glasgow and South-Western Rly Co* 1915 SC (HL) 20; and see *Hurst v Bryk* [2002] 1 AC 185 at 193, per Lord Millett. See also Atiyah *Rise and Fall of Freedom of Contract* (1979), pp 488 and 489.

6   A contract could not be rescinded if it remained open in the sense that an express warranty remained to be tried; typically this was where the seller supplied unsound or unmerchantable goods as opposed to supplying no goods at all, see *Weston v Downes* (1778) 1 Doug KB 23, 99 ER 19; *Towers v Barrett* (1786) 1 Term Rep 133, 99 ER 1014; *Payne v Whale* (1806) 7 East 274, 103 ER 105; *Hulle v Heightman* (1802) 2 East 145, 102 ER 324 (cf the note on this latter case in *Greville v Da Costa* (1797) Peake Add Cas 113 at 115, 170 ER 213). Moreover, it was thought that a contract could not be rescinded if property had passed under it, see *Street v Blay* (1831) 2 B & Ad 456, 109 ER 1212. Stoljar has suggested that the effect of the early case law was that restitution was limited to where the parties mutually agreed to rescind the contract, where the contract was entered into on a sale or return basis and later, where the contract was wholly executory on the part of the seller, and where the seller delivered either the wrong or worthless goods, see Stoljar *Law of Quasi-Contract* (2nd edn, 1989), pp 225 and 226; Stoljar 'The Doctrine of Failure of Consideration' (1959) 75 LQR 53 at 55–65 and 70. Originally, where a buyer wanted to recover money paid after the seller had executed the contract but provided unsound goods, the buyer could return the goods but the action was one for damages in special assumpsit, see *Fielder v Starkin* (1788) 1 Hy Bl 16, 126 ER 11.

7   See eg *Franklin v Miller* (1836) 4 Ad & El 599 at 605–606, 111 ER 912 at 914–915, per Littledale J ('It is a clearly recognised principle that if there is only partial failure of performance by one party to the contract, for which there may be a compensation in damages, the contract is not put an end to'). See also *Boone v Eyre* (1779) 1 Hy Bl 273n, 126 ER 160. See further Stoljar 'Dependent and Independent Promises' (1957) 2 Sydney Law Review 217 at 243; Stoljar 'The Doctrine of Failure of Consideration' (1959) 75 LQR 53; and *Withers v Reynolds* (1831) 2 B & Ad 882, 109 ER 1370.

TOTAL FAILURE OF CONSIDERATION AND CONSTRUCTION

19.13   The determination of what amounts to consideration in the case of contracts discharged for breach or repudiation is determined by construction[1]. It is therefore imperative in every case to ask, 'what was the promised performance'[2]. If the defendant has commenced performance, there can be no total failure of consideration. It is rare for the claimant to have contracted for no more than the defendant's promise, but if that is the case, once that promise is given there can be no failure of consideration. Usually, however, even where a party contracts on the basis of the other party's promise, the contract will still encapsulate some performance obligation and the retention of advance payments will be conditional upon receipt of that performance[3]. In some instances, the claimant may contract to simply receive a right such as a right to participate in some future earnings. If that is the case and the right is received, there can be no failure of consideration if it turns out that the right is not as profitable as first thought[4].

1   See *Whincup v Hughes* (1871) LR 6 CP 78 at 83, per Willes J, and at 85, per Montague Smith J.
2   See eg *Hunt v Silk* (1804) 5 East 449, 102 ER 1142 (this case may be viewed as one where there was no recovery of a payment when the claimant enjoyed the occupation of premises without ever entering into a formal lease, because allowing the claimant the opportunity to occupy the premises was an act in performance of the agreement – historically the case arose at a time when restitution and damages were considered mutually exclusive, and restitution first required the rescission of the contract, as this was the only way to get rid of the contract for the purposes of claiming restitution – at this level the case is an example of an inability to rescind as there was no total failure of performance. It is an issue of construction, upon which views may differ, as to whether the giving of mere possession amounts to an act in performance or, historically, whether receipt of possession prevented rescission, see *Blackburn v Smith* (1848) 2 Ex Ch 783, 154 ER 707; *Beed v Blandford* (1828) 2 Y & J 278, 148 ER 924; *Spence v Crawford* [1939] 3 All ER 271 at 284, per Lord Thankerton, and at 290, per Lord Wright; *Ahram Steamship Co v Westville Shipping Co* [1923] AC 773 at 782, per Lord Atkinson; *Rowland v Divall* [1923] 2 KB 500; *Pulbrook v Lawes* (1876) 1 QBD 284 at 289, per Blackburn J; *Knowles v Bovill* (1870) 22 LT 70 (on construction the claimant paid money for an application to be made to prolong a patent; he took the chance of the application failing; however, he did not pay money on the chance that the application may or may not be made; the application was not made and he was entitled to recover money paid); *Terrex Resources NL v Magnet Petroleum Pty* (1988) 1 WAR 144 (payments made by reference to a percentage of exploration costs – that exploration having been carried out – were not paid for

exploration but as the price for an interest in an oil exploration permit which was not forthcoming, so that the payments made were recoverable); *Marsh & McLennan Pty Ltd v Stanyers Transport Pty Ltd* [1994] 2 VR 232 (insurer paid out on risk not covered by policy; insured sued broker claiming restitution on the basis of failure of consideration, the promised consideration it was argued being the acceptance by the insurer of the risk; held, the payment by the insurer was acceptance of the risk); *Watney v Mass* (1954) 54 SRNSW 203 (W and M entered into a contract on the basis that W would pay £1500 and M would form a company and allot W 1500 shares; W paid £1,500 into a joint account and M, with the consent of W, withdrew sums to repair her ship which was to be used in the business, and was to form an asset of the company; the company was not formed prior to the termination of the contract by the claimant, and the claimant claimed the monies spent on the repair of the ship; it was held by majority that there was a total failure of consideration in the failure to incorporate the company and allot the shares – see further *Johnson v Goslett* (1856) 18 CB 728, 139 ER 1557; on appeal 3 CBNS 569, 140 ER 863; *Nockels v Crosby* (1825) 3 B & C 814, 107 ER 935; *Wilkinson v Lloyd* (1845) 7 QB 27, 115 ER 398) – it made no difference that the claimant had agreed or acquiesced in the defendant applying the monies in preparing the ship as that did not amount to a benefit accruing to the claimant in the performance of the contract; it was acknowledged that if the money was spent in the performance of the contract then even if the claimant derived no objective benefit from it there would be no total failure of consideration; Owen J (dissenting) thought recovery is based on there being a total failure of consideration and an absence of assent – the further requirement of an absence of assent was also referred to in *Ashpitel v Sercombe* (1850) 5 Ex Ch 147 at 162, 155 ER 63 at 70, per Patteson J. See also *Linz v Electric Wire Co of Palestine Ltd* [1948] AC 371; *Shaw v Ball* (1962) 63 SRNSW 910; *Hewlett v Allen & Sons* [1892] 2 QB 662; *Phillips v School Board for London* [1898] 2 QB 447. As to the ability of a principal to recover money entrusted to an agent for a particular purpose which is not carried out, see *Parry v Roberts* (1835) 3 Ad & El 118, 111 ER 358; *Ehrensperger v Anderson* (1848) 3 Exch 148, 154 ER 793; *Bostock v Jardine* (1865) 3 H & C 700, 159 ER 707; *Hill v Smith* (1844) 12 M & W 618, 152 ER 1346; *Martin v Pont* [1993] 3 NZLR 25. See further *Bowstead and Reynolds on Agency* (16th ed, 1996), paras 6–097 to 6–099.

3   See para 19.31.
4   *Newitt v Leitch* (1997) 6 Tas R 396.

TOTAL FAILURE OF CONSIDERATION AND COLLATERAL BENEFITS

19.14   Generally, the fact that a claimant may have received a benefit will not prevent a claim based on total failure of consideration if that benefit does not, on construction, form part of the agreed return[1]. Such benefits may be conveniently referred to as 'collateral benefits'[2]. For example, in *Rowland v Divall*[3] the defendant sold a motor car for £334 to the claimant, a car dealer, who repainted it and resold it for £400 to a third party. As it turned out, the defendant never had title to the car (nor a right to sell the car) and never received title prior to discharge. The claimant repaid the third party, and then proceeded to bring an action against the defendant for the return of money paid, on the basis of total failure of consideration. The claimant was successful, and it did not matter that the claimant had enjoyed the intermediate possession of the car. Nor did it matter that the claimant could not return the car, as the police had repossessed it for the true owner[4]. The better, or at least the accepted, explanation of this case would appear to be that on construction the claimant contracted for title to the car, and he received no part of that promised performance[5]. Clearly, title would have included a right to possession, but all the claimant enjoyed was actual possession, there was no transfer of a lawful right to possession[6]. The failure of the claimant to return the car to the defendant was excused on the basis that it was the defendant's lack of 'title'[7] or 'right to sell'[8] that gave rise to that failure. Moreover, the mere fact that the claimant had used and sold the car did not prevent there being a total failure of consideration.

1   Where the claimant is in receipt of an incontrovertible benefit or freely accepts such a benefit, the defendant may have a counter claim for reasonable remuneration, see generally above, para 13.45ff.

2 See Virgo *Principles of the Law of Restitution* (1999), p 337.
3 (1923) 2 KB 500, 129 LT 757. See further *Morley v Attenborough* (1849) 3 Ex Ch 500, 154 ER 943; *Eichholz v Bannister* (1864) 17 CBNS 708, 144 ER 284. See also Stoljar 'The Doctrine of Failure of Consideration' (1959) 75 LQR 53 at 67.
4 In fact the true owner had insured the car against theft and received a payment from the insurance company; the insurance company then sold the car to the claimants for £260: see *Rowland v Divall* (1923) 129 LT 757.
5 [1923] 2 KB 500 at 507, per Atkin LJ. See *Rover International Ltd v Cannon Film Sales Ltd* [1989] 1 WLR 912 at 924, per Kerr LJ; *Baltic Shipping Co v Dillon, The Mikhail Lermontov* (1993) 176 CLR 344 at 351, per Mason CJ, and at 389–390, per McHugh J; *David Securities Pty Ltd v Commonwealth Bank of Australia* (1992) 175 CLR 353 at 382–383.
6 See also *Argens v Whitcomb* 147 P 2d 501 (1944).
7 [1923] 2 KB 500 at 505, per Scrutton LJ.
8 [1923] 2 KB 500 at 507, per Atkin LJ.

19.15   It has been suggested that it would have been just as logical to come to a different conclusion as to the construction of the contract. For example, it has been argued that in such a contract the true object is to transfer the use and enjoyment of the goods free of third party claims, and that object is achieved if no third party brings a claim[1]. If this argument were accepted, the use of the goods would prevent there being a total failure of consideration. Arguably, this would not have been applicable in *Rowland* itself, as the claimant there purchased the goods solely for the purpose of resale[2]. A further criticism which has been made of the decision in *Rowland* and the series of cases applying the rule in that case[3] is that it can give rise to a level of injustice within the area of sale and hire-purchase of goods[4]. That injustice may arise because the principle in *Rowland* is not dependent upon the type of goods sold, it takes no account of the situation where the goods have been consumed[5], and it takes no account of whether the true owner has or will commence an action and if so, against whom will that action be commenced[6]. It is suggested that, in the case of sales, each of these criticisms is problematic. First, the idea that a person contracts for the mere use and enjoyment of goods appears contrary to the essence of sale. Second, without evidence of an incontrovertible benefit or free acceptance[7], it is difficult to see how the claimant is benefited when the defendant has not performed the contract. Third, it appears nonsensical to suggest the claimant has received some benefit when his or her use of the goods amounts to a conversion.

1 See Atiyah Adams and MacQueen *Sale of Goods* (10th edn, 2001), p 108.
2 See Treitel *Remedies for Breach of Contract* (1988), p 387; Treitel *Law of Contract* (10th edn, 1999), p 981.
3 See *Karflex Ltd v Poole* [1933] 2 KB 251 (hire-purchase); *Butterworth v Kingsway Motors Ltd* [1954] 1 WLR 1286 (sale); *Warman v Southern Counties Car Finance Corpn Ltd* [1949] 2 KB 576 (hire-purchase); *Barber v NSW Bank plc* [1996] 1 WLR 641 (conditional sale). The effect on hire-purchase agreements may appear harsh, if the recovery of hire payments is allowed on the basis that the hirer is required to have a right to sell at the time of contract even though the buyer gets lawful use of the goods in the period to which the hire payments relate (and assuming the use is at the expense of the defendant): see *Karflex Ltd v Poole* [1933] 2 KB 251 at 263, per Goddard J (note, however, in this case it was held that the contract in question contained as express term requiring the claimants to have that right at the time of contract (cf *Richards v Alliance Acceptance Co Ltd* (1976) 2 NSWLR 96; *Australian Guarantee Corpn Ltd v Ross* [1983] 2 VR 319); it may be that the position is the same with conditional sales, see *Barber v NWS Bank* [1996] 1 WLR 641, and Ulph 'Title Obligations and *Barber*: Too Many Short Cuts?' [1997] Lloyds Maritime and Commercial Law Quarterly 12; however, in that case it was conceded that it was an express term of the contract that the bank would have title at the date of contract; the term in question stated that upon payment of instalments 'the property in the Goods shall pass to the customer but until such time the property in the goods shall remain vested in the [Bank]'; the Court of Appeal thought the concession was properly made; moreover, it was held that this clause raised what would have been an agreement to sell (under which the seller is only required to have a right to sell at the time property is to pass, see the Sale of Goods Act 1979, s 12(1)) to the level of a sale

under which the seller must have the right to sell at the time of contract, see further Bridge *Sale of Goods* (1997), p 389). Cf *Yeoman Credit v Apps* [1962] 2 QB 508 (no recovery of payments made where the complaint was based on the condition of the goods received (which the defendant continued to use for a period) and not on any defect in the claimant's title; the defendant was able to terminate the contract despite his initial affirmation in continuing to use the defective goods as the breach was a continuing one; Holroyd Pearce stated (at 521): 'This is not a case like *Rowland v Divall* where title was lacking and the defendant never had lawful possession. Here the defendant had the possession of the car and its use ... Admittedly, the use was of little (if any) value, but ... that use, coupled with possession, and his continuance of the hiring agreement ... debars the defendant from saying there was a total failure of consideration'). See also *Linz v Electric Wire Co of Palestine Ltd* [1948] AC 371.

4   See Atiyah Adams and MacQueen *Sale of Goods* (10th edn, 2001), pp 106–109; Treitel *Remedies for Breach of Contract* (1988), pp 102, 387 and 388; Bridge 'The Title Obligations of the Seller of Goods' in Palmer and McKendrick (eds) *Interests in Goods* (2nd edn, 1998), pp 318–328.
5   See Atiyah Adams and MacQueen *Sale of Goods* (10th edn, 2001), p 107, and cf Treitel *Law of Contract* (10th edn, 1999), p 983.
6   See Atiyah Adams and MacQueen *Sale of Goods* (10th edn, 2001), p 107; Treitel *Law of Contract* (10th edn, 1999), p 983.
7   See generally above, para 13.44ff.

19.16   A number of other points about the decision in *Rowland* should also be noted. First, the principle flowing from the case appears to apply even if one party in the chain gets in title which would normally then be fed through to the claimant[1]. This constriction on the feeding of title would presumably be limited to the case where the subject contract is discharged prior to that earlier party getting in title[2]. This result has led some commentators to suggest that the failure of consideration in *Rowland* was a consequence of discharge, in the sense that it prevented good title being transferred[3]. The feeding of title prior to discharge, although not negating the prior breach of contract arising from not having the right to sell at the time of contract, should negate any failure of consideration. Second, in *Rowland*, Atkin LJ suggested that there could be no 'sale' where the seller has no right to sell[4]. It is doubtful that by this statement he meant to suggest that there could be no contract for the sale of goods when the seller has no right to sell[5]. However, this statement was made in answer to the argument that the claimant had accepted the goods and in that context one could take the view that Atkin LJ's answer was that there was no contract and therefore no issue of acceptance. It is suggested, however, that what he meant was that the implied condition that the seller will have a right to sell never sinks to the level of a warranty[6]. Third, an issue arises in such cases as to whether the claimant's claim today should be subject to counter-restitution so that the claimant must make some allowance for his or her intermediate use and enjoyment of the goods[7]. The Law Commission has looked at this issue, and ultimately determined that there should be no such allowance[8]. Thus for the moment, until counter-restitution is generally accepted (along with partial failure of consideration), this remains the position[9]. However, it may be added that where a claimant does not have a right to sell or hire, then any enrichment of the defendant (through wrongful use of the goods) is not at the claimant's expense, but rather at the expense of the person who had such right[10]. In such a case no issue of counter-restitution could arise.

1   See *Butterworth v Kingsway Motors Ltd* [1954] 1 WLR 1286.
2   See *Patten v Thomas Motors Pty Ltd* [1965] NSWR 1457, 66 SRNSW 458; *Butterworth v Kingsway Motors Ltd* [1954] 1 WLR 1286 at 1295, per Pearson J. Cf *Barber v NWS Bank* [1996] 1 WLR 641 at 647, per Sir Roger Parker (title not obtained prior to discharge).
3   Mason and Carter *Restitution Law in Australia* (1995) para 1121. See also Bridge 'The Title Obligations of the Seller of Goods' in Palmer and McKendrick (eds) *Interests in Goods* (2nd ed, 1998), p 319.
4   [1923] 2 KB 500 at 506–507.

5 See Goode *Commercial Law* (2nd edn, 1995), p 207; Battersby and Preston '"Title" and "Owner" used in the Sale of Goods Act 1893' (1972) 35 MLR 268; Battersby 'A Reconsideration of "Property" and "Title" in the Sale of Goods Act' [2001] Journal of Business Law 1.
6 Cf Bridge *Sale of Goods* (1998), pp 391–393.
7 See Atiyah Adams and MacQueen *Sale of Goods* (10th edn, 2001), pp 108 and 109; Treitel *Remedies for Breach of Contract* (1988), pp 102 and 387.
8 Law Com no 160 *Sale and Supply of Services* (Cm 137, 1987), paras 6.1–6.5. For an outline of the history of investigations by the Law Commission on this point see Atiyah Adams and MacQueen *Sale of Goods* (10th edn, 2001), p 108; Bridge 'The Title Obligations of the Seller of Goods' in Palmer and McKendrick (eds) *Interests in Goods* (2nd edn, 1998), pp 324–27.
9 Valuation of any counter-restitution is also problematic. Clearly assessment by reference to a reasonable rental value would not be fair. See further Treitel *Law of Contract* (10th edn, 1999), p 983.
10 See *Argens v Whitcomb* 147 P 2d (1944).

TOTAL FAILURE OF CONSIDERATION AND RELIANCE

19.17   The mere fact a defendant has acted in reliance on a payment is not alone sufficient to resist a claim based on total failure of consideration if that reliance does not form part of the agreed performance. For example, in *Fibrosa Spolka Akcyjna v Fairbairn Lawson Combe Barbour Ltd*[1], restitution of payments made was allowed despite work having commenced on the making of the goods which were the subject matter of the contract of sale. The reason for this result was that on construction, the contract was a contract for sale and nothing else[2]. The work carried out and the expenses incurred were not acts in performance of the contract, but rather acts which were necessary for performance but ultimately antecedent to actual performance. The result would have been different if, for example, the contract was construed as a contract to 'design, build and deliver'[3].

1 [1943] AC 32 at 49–50, 54–55, and 71–72 (cf at 76). Cf as to frustration under statute, above, para 20.3ff, and see *Cantiare San Rocco SA v Clyde Shipbuilding & Engineering Co Ltd* [1924] AC 226.
2 See also *McDougall v Aeromarine of Emsworth Ltd* [1958] 1 WLR 1126 at 1129, per Diplock J; *Reid v Macbeth and Gray* [1904] AC 223; *Appleby v Myers* (1867) LR 2 CP 651 at 659. See further *Terrex Resources NL v Magnet Petroleum Pty Ltd* (1988) 1 WAR 144 at 148, per Burt CJ; *Rover International Ltd v Canon Film Sales Ltd* [1989] 1 WLR 912 at 924, per Kerr LJ.
3 See *Hyundai Heavy Industries Co Ltd v Papadopoulos* [1980] 1 WLR 1129; *Salvage Association v CAP Financial Services Ltd* [1995] FSR 654 (and see *Salvage Association v CAP Financial Services Ltd* (9 July 1993, unreported, CA). Cf para 19.16, n 3.

19.18   Some doubt as to the irrelevance of reliance expenditure was raised in *The Mikhail Lermontov*[1]. In that case Mason CJ said that it is 'material' to ascertain whether the payee is 'required by the contract' to perform work and incur expense before completing performance[2]. This reference to incurring expense prior to 'completing' performance is perhaps innocent enough, in that it may be construed as referring to expenditure incurred in performance of the contract. However, he went on to cite *Hyundai Heavy Industries v Papadopoulos*[3], for the proposition that where the payee is required to perform work and incur expense before completing performance, it would be 'unreasonable to hold that the payee's right to retain the payment is *conditional upon performance* of the contractual obligations', unless the contract 'manifests a contrary intention'[4]. McHugh J regarded *Hyundai*[5] as a case where the right to be paid was 'an unconditional right'[6]. It was he said, an example supporting the general proposition that 'if the payee has performed work or services or incurred expense prior to the completion of the contract' the payer cannot claim to recover money paid because such payments should be treated as having been made unconditionally[7].

1   *Baltic Shipping Co v Dillon, The Mikhail Lermontov* (1993) 176 CLR 344.
2   *Baltic Shipping Co v Dillon, The Mikhail Lermontov* (1993) 176 CLR 344 at 352. See further Beatson *Use and Abuse of Unjust Enrichment* (1991), p 60.
3   [1980] 1 WLR 1129.
4   *Baltic Shipping Co v Dillon, The Mikhail Lermontov* (1993) 176 CLR 344 at 352–3 (emphasis added).
5   [1980] 1 WLR 1129. See para 19.23.
6   *Baltic Shipping Co v Dillon, The Mikhail Lermontov* (1993) 176 CLR 344 at 391.
7   *Baltic Shipping Co v Dillon, The Mikhail Lermontov* (1993) 176 CLR 344 at 391.

19.19   It is suggested that these statements should not be taken to mean that a payer will be deprived of a right of recovery merely because the payee incurred some expenses, nor that it is sufficient to deprive the payer of their right to recovery if the payer could have anticipated that the payee would have incurred some expense in preparing to perform[1]. Even where it is necessary for a payee to incur expense this alone should not deprive the payer of his or her right of recovery[2]. In regards to the judgment of Mason CJ, given his initial statement, it is suggested that the words 'conditional upon performance' in the latter statement should read 'conditional upon complete or substantial performance'.

1   See *Terrex Resources NL v Magnet Petroleum Pty Ltd* (1988) 1 WAR 144 at 147–148, per Burt CJ. Cf Beatson *Use and Abuse of Unjust Enrichment* (1991), pp 60, 64, and 71.
2   For example, in a contract for the sale of goods where the seller needs to acquire the goods from a third party, the mere fact that the seller pays the third party will not deprive the buyer of a right of recovery, because prima facie the purchase from the third party is not an act in the performance of the contract with the buyer.

TOTAL FAILURE OF CONSIDERATION AND DISCHARGE OF CONTRACT

19.20   Whether or not there is a total failure of consideration is determined at the time of discharge. Prior to discharge, the mere fact that a party has not performed on time will not give rise to a right of recovery based on failure of consideration, because until discharge there may be a tender and acceptance of late performance. Therefore, whether or not it is correct to speak of a failure of consideration simply because performance has not occurred on time, it is clear that failure of consideration cannot ground recovery until discharge[1]. It follows that there is some logic in the notion that discharge itself causes failure of consideration[2].

1   See Burrows *Law of Restitution* (1993), p 250.
2   See *Baltic Shipping Co v Dillon, TheMikhail Lermontov* (1993) 176 CLR 344 at 352, per Mason CJ.

19.21   In addition to discharge being necessary before a claim for restitution can be considered, the effects of discharge are also important. It was noted above that the better view appears to be that, upon discharge, all obligations that have not unconditionally accrued are discharged[1]. This point is not always made clear. However, it is an important issue to resolve prior to the consideration of any claim for restitution, because it can negate the need to resort to restitution to defend a claim for performance brought by the other party to the contract. In *Stocznia Gdanska SA v Latvian Shipping Co*[2], the buyers' defence to the sellers' claim for payment was that nothing in fact was due, since they could recover any instalments paid on the basis of total failure of consideration[3]. This argument is aimed at avoiding circuity of action. Lord Goff had some reservations about this argument, but was content to approach the matter on that basis, as both parties thought that failure of consideration was the relevant issue, and it was consistent with the approach of the majority in *Hyundai Heavy Industries Co Ltd v Papadopoulos*[4]. It is suggested that such reservations were well founded[5]. The better approach is, to first determine whether the initial conditional right to payment had become unconditional at the time of discharge. If not, then that conditional right will not survive discharge. The answer to this question lies in whether or not the payment had been earned by the time of discharge. This will occur where the obligation has unconditionally accrued as a matter of contractual intent and where the enforcement of the primary obligation is not inconsistent with the election to terminate the contract. References to failure of consideration are not helpful in this regard. More fundamentally, it is up to the claimant to prove he or she has earned the payment, rather than for the defendant to argue that there is no obligation to pay[6].

1   See above, para 19.3.
2   [1998] 1 WLR 574 (the facts are set out below, para 19.26).
3   [1998] 1 WLR 574 at 587.
4   [1980] 1 WLR 1129.
5   Cf [1998] 1 WLR 574 at 597, per Lord Lloyd.
6   See Carter *Breach of Contract* (2nd edn, 1991), ch 12.

19.22   Another example arose in *Rover International Ltd v Cannon Film Sales Ltd (No 3)*[1]. Here Cannon sued Proper to recover an instalment which had fallen due under a contract, under which Proper had agreed to pay a license fee to exhibit certain films owned by Canon. Only two out of three instalments of the license fee were paid prior to the discharge of the contract. However, the contract was terminated prior to the time when Cannon would have been required to supply films and, moreover, Cannon had not at that time supplied any films to Proper. Therefore, the mere fact that Proper's primary obligation to pay had accrued by the time of discharge did not mean that payment had to be made after discharge, because at that time it had not been unconditionally earned by Cannon. Nevertheless, counsel argued the case on the basis that Proper did not have to pay, because if they did they could recover it on the basis of total failure of consideration.

1   [1989] 1 WLR 912.

19.23   Perhaps the most well known and problematic case on this point is *Hyundai Heavy Industries Co Ltd v Papadopoulos*[1]. In that case shipbuilders were contracted to 'build, launch, equip and complete' a vessel. Payment was to be made in instalments, and the price included 'all costs and expenses for designing and supplying all necessary drawings for the Vessel'. The first instalment was duly paid; however, the second instalment was not, and the shipbuilders terminated the contract under an express provision, and successfully sued the buyer's guarantors. No issue arose as to the repayment of the first instalment, as there was an express provision allowing the builder to keep payments made.

Three members of the House of Lords suggested that the buyers would have been liable to pay the second instalment if the guarantors did not exist. The reasoning of these three members was not, however, uniform. It was argued on the basis of *Dies v British and International Mining*[2], that if the buyer in that case was entitled to recover the advance payment, then the buyers in the instant case could not be liable to make the payment that had fallen due but remained unpaid, because if they did make the payment they would be entitled to its immediate repayment but for the express term allowing the builders to keep payments made.

Viscount Dilhorne distinguished this case from *Dies* on the basis that this was not simply a contract for sale, but rather a contract to 'build, launch, equip and complete, the vessel' and was therefore more like a building contract[3]. He concluded that the buyer would have been obligated to pay because in such contracts discharge 'did not affect accrued rights to payments of instalments of the contract price unless the contract provided that it was to do so'[4]. He makes no mention of those rights having to be unconditionally accrued to survive discharge, nor does he emphasise the relevance of performance. Therefore, he was either of the opinion that the obligation to pay was independent of performance, or thought that rights need only be conditionally accrued to survive discharge.

Lord Edmund-Davies held that a party in breach is not released from primary obligations already due at the time of discharge[5]. He thought that rule was based on sound commercial reasons. Although he referred to statements made by Dixon J in *McDonald v Dennys Lascelles Ltd*[6], he appears to have not placed much weight in Dixon J's references to rights having to be 'unconditionally' accrued to survive discharge[7]. Moreover, although drawing an analogy between the subject contract and contracts of hire, he did not emphasise the importance of the right having to be earned to be enforceable after discharge.

Lord Fraser was the only member of the Court to emphasise the relevance of performance[8]. He distinguished *Dies* on the basis that it was a simple contract of sale, which did not require the vendor to perform any work or incur any expense on the subjects of sale[9]. In this case the performance of the contract required the incurring of various expenses prior to the ultimate delivery of the ship. Although there was no evidence of any such performance, and although the buyers had not actually enjoyed any benefit from the work performed, he thought the court had to assume that the builder had carried out its part of the contract prior to cancellation in the absence of evidence to the contrary. That assumption therefore went not only to assuming some partial performance, but that the right to be paid had been unconditionally earned. Lords Russell and Keith doubted the correctness of holding the buyer liable to pay after discharge.

1   [1980] 1 WLR 1129.
2   [1939] 1 KB 724. The fact of this case are discussed below, para 19.28.
3   Cf *McDougall v Aeromarine of Emsworth Ltd* [1958] 1 WLR 1126 at 1129, per Diplock J ('although a shipbuilding contract is in form a contract for the construction of the vessel, it is in law a contract for the sale of goods'). See also *Reid v Macbeth and Gray* [1904] AC 223 and *Appleby v Myers* (1867) LR 2 CP 651 at 659. Arguably, because the instalments in *Hyundai* were not apportioned to work done, the obligation to perform was really an entire obligation, which, not being fully performed, the builders could not sue to recover payments that had fallen due, but remained unpaid at the time of discharge; cf [1980] 1 WLR 1129 at 1142, per Lord Edmund-Davies, and at 1148, per Lord Fraser (suggesting that it was very likely the small prepayments bore some relationship to costs because they increased in proportion to the contract price).
4   [1980] 1 WLR 1129 at 1134.
5   [1980] 1 WLR 1129 at 1141.
6   (1933) 48 CLR 457 at 477: 'When a party to simple contract, upon breach by the other contracting party of a condition of the contract, elects to treat the contract as no longer binding on him, the contract is not rescinded as from the beginning. Both parties are discharged from the further performance of the contract, but rights are not divested or discharged which have already been unconditionally acquired. Rights and obligations which arise from the partial execution of the contract and causes of action which have accrued from its breach alike continue unaffected'.
7   Cf *Rover International Ltd v Cannon Film Sales Ltd (No 3)* [1989] 1 WLR 912 at 930, per Kerr LJ.
8   In *Baltic Shipping Co v Dillon, The Mikhail Lermontov* (1993) 176 CLR 344 at 391, McHugh J regarded *Hyundai* as a case where the right to be paid was 'an unconditional right'. Moreover, he

was of the opinion that Lord Frazer considered the right to payment to be an unconditional right. However, in this regard it may be noted that McHugh J (at 391) took the view that other than in the case of a payment to obtain title to land or goods all payments should be regarded as having been made unconditionally or no longer the subject of a condition if the payee has performed work or services or incurred expenses prior to the completion of the contract; cf para 19.31. He appears to place no weight in the distinction between a payee commencing some performance in respect of a payment and fully or substantially carrying out that performance so as to earn the payment.

9   If a contract is characterised as a mere contract of sale then even though the seller may have to incur expenses in manufacturing the goods for sale those expenses would not be acts in the performance of a contract of sale, see *Fibrosa Spolka Akcyjna v Fairbairn Lawson Combe Barbour Ltd* [1943] AC 32. See further para 19.17.

19.24   Commenting on *Hyundai* in *Stocznia Gdanska SA v Latvian Shipping Co*[1], Lord Goff[2] and Lord Lloyd[3] said that they did not understand Lord Edmund-Davies to be taking a different approach to Viscount Dilhorne and Lord Fraser. In the result, the preferred interpretation of the case must be that either the right to payment was an unconditional right (as per Viscount Dilhorne) or it had been unconditionally earned as (per Lord Fraser). However, it is suggested that the initial argument based on *Dies* was misconceived. The better approach was not to question the builder's right to payment by reference to any defence the buyers had, but rather to simply question that right to payment. The issue put simply, was whether or not the right to payment had been unconditionally earned at the time of discharge. If not, the builder had no right to call for the payment. If it had been earned there was no issue of restitution or failure of consideration to be considered.

1   [1998] 1 WLR 574.
2   [1998] 1 WLR 574 at 590. Lord Hoffmann, Lord Hope and Lord Hutton agreed.
3   [1998] 1 WLR 574 at 599.

CONTRACTUAL TERMS MODIFYING THE RIGHT TO RESTITUTION

19.25   The recovery of payments on the basis of a total failure of consideration may be excluded by the contract parties. This may be achieved in a number of ways. The parties may expressly provide for the remedial consequences of any breach[1]. In addition, the parties may enter into a contract under which all payments are expressly or impliedly retained unconditionally in the sense of not being dependant upon any performance by the other party[2]. Closely related to this is where the counter-performance is merely the other party's promise to perform[3]. Such contracts are rare, but in such instances failure of consideration and consideration in formation equate[4]. However, in many cases where there is a contract based on an exchange of promises, there is still some ultimate performance obligation and the retention of any advance payments may be conditional upon receipt of that performance[5]. The same result may be achieved by incorporating a provision for forfeiture[6].

1   See *Pan Ocean Shipping Co Ltd v Creditcorp, The Trident Beauty* [1994] 1 WLR 161.
2   Cf para 19.31. See *Fibrosa Spolka Akcyjna v Fairbairn Lawson Combe Barbour Ltd* [1943] AC 32 at 67, per Lord Wright, and at 74, per Lord Roche. See eg *Vagres Compania Maritima SA v Nissho-Iwai American Corpn, The Karin Vatis* [1988] 2 Lloyd's Rep 330; *Ellis Shipping Corpn v Voest Alpine Intertrading, The Lefthero* [1991] 2 Lloyd's Rep 599 (reversed on another point [1992] 2 Lloyd's Rep 109); *Bank of Boston Connecticut v European Grain and Shipping Ltd, The Dominique* [1989] AC 1056 (express provisions negating the general rule that freight is earned on delivery by, for example, deeming freight to be unconditionally earned upon loading or signing of bills of lading – generally where freight is payable upon delivery, the obligation to carry goods is an entire obligation; thus a failure to deliver (as opposed to short delivery or delivery of damaged goods) will prevent the carrier recovering freight, see *Metcalfe v Britannia Ironworks Co* (1877) 2 QBD 423 at 428, per Bramwell LJ and see generally *Appleby v Myers* (1867) LR 2 CP 651 at 661, per

Blackburn J). Cf *Antclizo Shipping Corpn v Food Corporation of India, The Antclizo (No 2)* [1992] 1 Lloyd's Rep 558. See further Carver *Carriage by Sea* (13th edn, 1982), paras 1691–1695. Generally, an advance on account of freight to be earned is not recoverable if the delivery of goods is prevented by a frustrating act. Moreover, an advance of freight due but not paid is still payable if the contract is frustrated after the date on which the freight is due, see generally *Andrew v Moorhouse* (1814) 5 Taunt 435, 128 ER 758; *Byrne v Schiller* (1871) LR 6 Ex Ch 20 and 319; *Oriental Steamship Co Ltd v Taylor* [1893] 2 QB 518; *A Coker & Co v Limerick Steamship Co* (1918) 87 LJKB 767; *De Silvale v Kendall* (1815) 4 M & S 37, 105 ER 749; *Saunders v Drew* (1832) 3 B & Ad 445, 110 ER 160; *Greeves v West India & Pacific Steamship Co Ltd* (1870) 22 LT 615; *Fibrosa Spolka Akcyjna v Fairbairn Lawson Combe Barbour Ltd* [1943] AC 32 at 67, per Lord Wright, and at 79, per Lord Porter. This general rule has been stated in wider language, for example in *Allison v Bristol Marine Insurance Co Ltd* (1875) 1 App Cas 209 at 253 (a case concerned with a ship that was lost) Lord Selborne said that it is a 'peculiar rule of English mercantile law, that an advance of account of freight to be earned made at the commencement of the voyage ... is, in the absence of any stipulation to the contrary, an irrevocable payment at the risk of the shipper of the goods and not a loan repayable by the borrower if freight to that amount be not earned'. See also *Re Child, ex p Nyholm* (1873) 29 LT 634; *Civil Service Co-operative Society Ltd v General Steam Navigation Co* [1903] 2 KB 756.

3   Cf para 19.31.
4   See *Workman Clark & Co Ltd v Brazileño* [1908] 1 KB 968 at 976–977, per Lord Alverstone CJ.
5   See para 19.31.
6   In the case of a deposit such a provision will be implied. See para 19.41.

19.26   In addition to restitution for unjust enrichment, a right to restitution may flow from an express or implied contractual term. Drawing a line between these two avenues of recovery can at times be problematic. One area of some difficulty concerns the recovery of conditional payments, that is, payments made on the basis of receiving some future performance. The starting point is the statement of Dixon J in *McDonald v Dennys Lascelles Ltd* where he said:

> When a contract stipulates for payment of part of the purchase money in advance, the purchaser relying only on the vendor's promise to give him a conveyance, the vendor is entitled to enforce payment before the time has arrived for conveying the land; yet his title to retain the money has been considered not to be absolute but conditional upon the subsequent completion of the contract[1].

A difficulty arises from Dixon J's last statement. This has been interpreted as meaning that recovery of payments made prior to discharge might be based simply on the conditional nature of the payment[2]. That is, recovery is contractual. One example is the House of Lords' decision in *Stocznia Gdanska SA v Latvian Shipping Co*[3]. This case concerned six contracts to 'design, build, complete and deliver' six ships. The buyers were to pay 20 per cent of the price after receiving notice that the keel had been laid. The contract gave the seller the right to terminate if payments were not made, to retain any instalments paid, and, on termination, to sell the vessel whether completed or not. Keels were laid for vessels 1 and 2, but the buyers failed to pay and the seller terminated these contracts. It then renumbered the keels, gave notice for payment under the third and fourth contracts, terminated those contracts when payment was not forthcoming, and renumbered the keels again and gave notice for payment under the fifth and sixth contracts. It then exercised its right of sale, appropriating the keels to a contract with a third party. As well as damages the seller claimed the 20% instalments under all six contracts.

1   (1933) 48 CLR 457 at 477.
2   See Beatson *Use and Abuse of Unjust Enrichment* (1991), ch 3. See also Jackman *The Varieties of Restitution* (1998) pp 57–60 and 85–86; Jaffey 'The Restitutionary Conditional Transfer Analysis and the Death of Contract' [1998] Edinburgh Law Review 23; Jaffey *Nature and Scope of Restitution* (2000), ch 2.
3   [1998] 1 WLR 574.

19.27   The House of Lords dismissed the instalment claims in respect of keels 3 to 6 simply on the basis that they had not fallen due. In regards to keels 1 and 2, it was not disputed that the debts had fallen due; however, the buyers argued that they could in any case recover the instalments on the basis of total failure of consideration[1]. Lord Goff, distinguished this type of contract from one of sale and, citing *Dies v British and International Mining*[2] and *McDonald v Dennys Lascelles Ltd*[3], said that in sale contracts 'it has been held that the buyer's remedy is contractual, the seller's title to retain the money being conditional upon his completing the contract'[4].

1   See further para 19.21.
2   [1939] 1 KB 724.
3   (1933) 48 CLR 457 at 475–479.
4   [1998] 1 WLR 574 at 589.

19.28   In *Dies* the purchaser of a quantity of rifles and ammunition for a total price of £270,000 paid £100,000 in advance. No goods were delivered prior to discharge by the seller for the buyer's repudiation. The amount of the payments made, less a sum of £13,500 by way of liquidated damages, was held to be recoverable. Stable J approached his decision on the basis that it was 'not the consideration that failed but the party to the contract'[1]. He added that if the 'language used in the contract is neutral, the general rule is that the law confers' the right to recover money paid[2]. It was thus up to the defendant to then point to some language in the contract from which the inference could be drawn that it could keep the payments made[3].

1   [1939] 1 KB 724 at 744.
2   [1939] 1 KB 724 at 743. See further *Else (1982) Ltd v Parkland Holdings Ltd* [1994] 1 BCLC 130 at 136–137.
3   [1939] 1 KB 724 at 743.

19.29   The contractual approach was also recognised by the High Court of Australia in *The Mikhail Lermontov*[1]. In this case, a passenger on a cruise ship sued to recover compensation and restitution when the voyage was cut short by the sinking of the ship. She had paid the whole fare in advance, but the cruise had lasted only eight of the promised 14 days.

Only Deane and Dawson JJ treated total failure of consideration as the basis for recovery under the concept of unjust enrichment.

Mason CJ, with whom Brennan and Toohey JJ agreed, recognised that a claim to recover a payment under a discharged contract may succeed on either of two alternative bases: the intention of the parties, as expressed in the terms of the contract; or the concept of failure of consideration. He considered it to be a sufficient basis for the recovery of money paid in advance that the 'defendant's right to retain the payment is conditional upon the performance of his or her obligations under the contract'[2].

McHugh J said that where a contractual payment in made 'conditionally upon the performance of a promise by the payee, the right to retain the moneys after discharge of the contract is dependent on whether the promise has been performed'[3]. He went on, that where 'the promise has not been performed, there has been a total failure of consideration by reason of the nonfulfilment of the condition'[4]. Taken together these sentences are not without difficulty, but it would appear that he thought recovery flowed from the contract, that is, the conditional nature of the right to retain, rather than from a distinct obligation imposed by law.

Gaudron J was of the view that where the contract is not entire, recovery depends on non-fulfilment of a condition, not total failure of consideration. She added that if a contract is an entire contract, whereby the right to retain a payment is conditional upon subsequent completion of performance, then a right to have money refunded would arise unless there is complete performance because there is then necessarily a failure of consideration[5].

The majority of the High Court therefore took the view that recovery may be based simply upon the conditional nature of the payer's obligation. Moreover, the majority placed some reliance on the decision in *Dies*. Mason CJ thought the best explanation for that case was that the payment was a mere part payment the right to which depended upon performance of the contract, and thus was conditional[6]. McHugh J also appears to analyse the case on the basis of a conditional right[7]. Gaudron J seems to have regarded the case as involving a condition similar in kind to that present in *McDonald*[8].

1   *Baltic Shipping Co v Dillon, The Mikhail Lermontov* (1993) 176 CLR 344.
2   (1993) 176 CLR 344 at 351.
3   (1993) 176 CLR 344 at 389.
4   (1993) 176 CLR 344 at 389.
5   (1993) 176 CLR 344 at 386.
6   (1993) 176 CLR 344 at 352.
7   (1993) 176 CLR 344 at 390.
8   (1993) 176 CLR 344 at 386.

19.30   In terms of the law, *Stocnizia* and *The Mikhail Lermontov* probably put this matter beyond doubt. However, an issue arises as to whether or not *Dies* and *McDonald* are authority for the principles for which they were relied on.

The decision in *Dies*[1] is problematic and has long been the subject of criticism[2]. Stable J stated that upon termination the contract was not rescinded, but rather 'ceased to impose any obligation of further performance'[3]. Later, he appears to reason that unless a contract is rescinded there can be no failure of consideration[4]. This then led to his now famous statement that in the case before him it 'was not the consideration that failed but the party to the contract'[5]. It would therefore appear that Stable J either confused the idea of consideration in the formation of contract with that of failure of consideration, or he was simply drawing on authority from a time in which restitution and damages were seen as mutually exclusive remedies, and which required the contract to be rescinded before there could be any claim to restitution[6].

Moreover, as noted above, Stable J said that if the 'language used in the contract is neutral, the general rule is that the law confers' the right to recover[7]. His use of the word 'confer' is as much open to the interpretation that he meant an imposed restitutionary right rather than a contractual right. However, it must be noted that at another point in his judgment he did, somewhat confusingly state that the foundation of buyer's right to recover 'derived from the *terms* of the contract and the *principle of law* applicable, to recover back his money'[8].

It may be noted that the claimant in *Dies* was the party in breach of contract. He was therefore attempting to enforce a primary right rather than a secondary right. If the law 'confers' the right to recovery, and it is not based on a term of the contract or a restitutionary right based on unjust enrichment, the interpretation of this case as contractual would amount to a return to 'implied contract' theory.

In the result, either the confusion of doctrine or the resort to doctrine which no longer represents the law, should render *Dies* as being of little authority for the propositions it puts forward.

1   See further para 19.28.
2   See Salmond and Williams *Principles of the Law of Contracts* (2nd edn, 1945), p 568ff. Cf Goff and

Jones *Law of Restitution* (5th edn, 1998), p 537. See further Jones *Restitution in Public and Private Law* (1991), p 104; Beatson *Use and Abuse of Unjust Enrichment* (1991), p 53ff.
3   [1939] 1 KB 724 at 732.
4   [1939] 1 KB 724 at 744.
5   [1939] 1 KB 724 at 744.
6   See para 19.12. It may also be noted that *Chandler v Webster* [1904] 1 KB 493 was still good law at the time of the decision in *Dies*.
7   [1939] 1 KB 724 at 743.
8   [1939] 1 KB 724 at 744 (emphasis added).

19.31   Turning then to *McDonald*, it may be noted that Dixon J said that the right of recovery is implied in law. Given the time of his judgment, it is not a big jump today to change that reference to 'imposed by law'[1]. The alternative is that he meant a contractual term implied in law. However, this point was made by Dixon J to contrast the position at common law and the position in equity. That is, where there is an express or implied provision for forfeiture, recovery depends on equitable principles[2]. Where there is no such provision he said that recovery is based on an implication made at law, which it is suggested was a reference to a quasi-contractual basis of recovery.

In addition, Dixon J was dealing with a contract for the sale of land where the price was payable in instalments. In such a contract, the buyer contracts for the vendor's promise to transfer title. This allows for the vendor to bring an action to recover an instalment that has fallen due, and has not been paid prior to the vendor actually transferring title[3]. This is why Dixon J made reference to 'the purchaser relying on the vendor's promise to give him a conveyance'. That statement reflects his construction of the contract. It follows that his later statement dealing with recovery, namely that the vendor's title to retain any payment was 'conditional upon the subsequent completion of the contract', cannot have been a statement that was concerned with the construction of the contract (that is, the presumed intention of the parties) because that would amount to having two inconsistent interpretations of the contract. It must then follow that he understood the right of recovery to be based on an imposed obligation, that is, an 'implication made at law'[4].

There is therefore a difference between the right to recover a payment from a payer prior to discharge, and the right to recover a payment from a payee after discharge. In addition, it is important to note that the initial right to receive payment was not conditional on performance. Retention was characterised as conditional because of the imposed restitutionary response. Dixon J was not using the word 'conditional' in the sense that it is often used to characterise performance obligations[5]. In terms of the intentions of the parties, this was a contract that involved an unconditional right. The fact that in such a contract failure of consideration still operates evidences the difficulty in categorising failure of consideration as being based solely on qualified intent[6]. It is suggested that failure of consideration was operative and formed the basis of recovery because, although the right to receive the payment was unconditional as a matter of intent, the contract still involved the performance of an act in addition to the vendor's mere promise to convey title and this provided the reason for making retention 'conditional' as a matter of law[7].

1   In fact Dixon J made a similar statement in *Steele v Tardiani* (1946) 72 CLR 386 at 405, in circumstances where he was clearly concerned with restitution, namely, a quantum meruit claim. See para 19.75.
2   See further para 19.42.
3   See *Reynolds v Fury* [1921] VLR 14.
4   See also *Fibrosa Spolka Akcjna v Fairbairn Lawson Combe Barbour Ltd* [1943] AC 32 at 65, per Lord Wright: 'The right ... to claim repayment of money paid in advance must in principle ... attach at

the moment of dissolution. The payment was originally conditional. The condition of retaining it is eventual performance. Accordingly, when that condition fails, the right to retain the money must simultaneously fail. It is not like a claim for damages for breach of the contract, nor is it a claim under the contract. It is in theory and is expressed to be a claim to recover money, received to the use of the plaintiff'.

5   See also *Pan Ocean Shipping Co Ltd v Creditcorp Ltd, The Trident Beauty* [1994] 1 WLR 161 at 165, per Lord Goff: 'in a case like the present [the classification of a payment as conditional means] no more than that the payment is not final since under the contract there is an obligation, express or implied, to repay ... any part of the hire payable which has not been earned'.
6   Cf Birks *An Introduction to the Law of Restitution* (revised edn, 1989), ch 7.
7   See further Kremer 'The Action for Money Had and Received' (2001) 17 Journal of Contract Law 93.

19.32   There is no doubt that the contract may expressly or impliedly govern the right to repayment[1]. Given the decision in *Stocnizia* the law would appear to be that a contractual right of recovery is the principle form of recovery in the case of 'conditional' payments especially as regards sale contracts. It is also accepted that if the contract expressly or impliedly sets out the remedial regime to be applied in the circumstances, there can be no resort to unjust enrichment[2]. However, recovery under the contract should be based on either an express or implied term. Although in *Stocznia* Lord Goff did not state that the right to recovery must come from a distinct express or implied term, it is suggested that his statements on other occasions evidence that such a term is required[3].

1   See eg *Cargill International SA v Bangladesh Sugar & Food Industries Corpn* [1998] 1 WLR 461 and *Comdel Commodities Ltd v Siporex Trade SA* [1997] 1 Lloyd's Rep 424 at 431, per Potter LJ.
2   See *Pan Ocean Shipping Co Ltd v Creditcorp Ltd, The Trident Beauty* [1994] 1 WLR 161.
3   *Pan Ocean Shipping Co Ltd v Creditcorp Ltd (The 'Trident Beauty')* [1994] 1 WLR 161 at 164. See also Beatson *Use and Abuse of Unjust Enrichment* (1991), ch 3; Burrows *Law of Restitution* (1993), p 274; Beatson and Tolhurst 'Debt, Damages and Restitution' [1998] CLJ 253.

TOTAL FAILURE OF CONSIDERATION AND RESTORATION OF BENEFITS RECEIVED

19.33   A total failure of consideration may arise even though the claimant has received part of the promised performance if the effect of discharge is such that a revesting of that performance occurs. For example, where a buyer rejects non-conforming goods prior to accepting them and recovers the price paid[1]. Arguably such cases evidence the ability of the law to give effect to counter-restitution, which in turn eliminates the need to maintain the requirement of *total* failure of consideration. Alternatively it may be that recovery in such cases is based on total failure of consideration whereby the return of the goods by the buyer effectively creates the total failure of consideration. It is suggested that such an analysis is problematic. Any use of the goods (falling short of acceptance of the goods) should amount to receipt of part of the promised performance and prevent there being a total failure of consideration. Moreover, given that such use would be lawful, arguably these cases provide stronger reasons for denying complete restitution than the *Rowland v Divall* line of cases[2].

1   See *Kwei Tek Chao v British Traders and Shippers Ltd* [1954] 2 QB 459; *Rogers v Parish (Scarborough) Ltd* [1987] 2 All ER 232. See also *Bernstein v Pamson Motors (Golders Green) Ltd* [1987] 2 All ER 220; *Bragg v Villanova* (1923) 40 TLR 154; *Heilbutt v Hickson* (1872) LR 7 CP 438; *Millar's Machinery Co Ltd v David Way & Son* (1935) 40 Com Cas 204. In such a case the recovery of payments made may simply form part of a damages award for wasted expenditure, even though there is no total failure of consideration, see *The Salvage Association v CAP Financial Services Ltd* [1995] FSR 654 (and see *Salvage Association v CAP Financial Services Ltd* (9 July 1993, unreported), CA. See further *Giles v Edwards* (1797) 7 Term Rep 181, 101 ER 920 discussed at para 19.36, n 2.
2   See above, para 19.14.

TOTAL FAILURE OF CONSIDERATION AND FAULT

19.34   Failure of consideration operates independently of fault[1]. For this reason it is a favoured ground for restitution amongst restitution scholars, because it is thought that autonomous unjust enrichment should as much as possible operate independently of fault[2]. The one decision that appears to link failure of consideration and fault is that of Stable J in *Dies v British and International Mining*[3]. In his judgment, Stable J suggested that where the claimant is in breach of contract, it is 'not the consideration that [fails] but the party to the contract'[4]. Although Stable J went on to hold that the party in breach there could recover either by virtue of the terms of the contract or some principle of law[5], the statement appears to suggest that conduct may prevent a person relying on failure of consideration.

1   See *Mayson v Clouet* [1924] AC 980; *McDonald v Dennys Lascelles Ltd* (1933) 48 CLR 457 at 478, per Dixon J.
2   See Birks *Restitution – The Future* (1992), pp 9 and 59–60. See also *Banque Financiére de la Cité v Parc (Battersea) Ltd* [1999] 1 AC 221 at 227, per Lord Steyn. Cf paras 19.93 and 19.105.
3   [1939] 1 KB 724.
4   [1939] 1 KB 724 at 744.
5   See para 19.30.

19.35   In addition, in *The Mikhail Lermontov*[1], Mason CJ in discussing *Dies* said that there can be no failure of consideration 'when the plaintiff's unwillingness or refusal to perform the contract on his or her part is the cause of the defendant's non-performance'[2]. He went on to suggest that because of this, the success of the claimant in breach in *Dies* was based on either the conditional nature of the payment or 'on the ground that the seller accepted the plaintiff's repudiation and thus itself effected the discharge of contract'[3].

It is submitted that, to the extent the above comments suggest failure of consideration is conduct sensitive, they cannot be reconciled with prior authorities[4].

1   *Baltic Shipping Co v Dillon, The Mikhail Lermontov* (1993) 176 CLR 344. See also Jackman *The Varieties of Restitution* (1998), pp 57–62.
2   *Baltic Shipping Co v Dillon, The Mikhail Lermontov* (1993) 176 CLR 344 at 352.
3   *Baltic Shipping Co v Dillon, The Mikhail Lermontov* (1993) 176 CLR 344 at 352, citing Birks *An Introduction to the Law of Restitution* (revised edn, 1989), p 237. McHugh J expressly recognised that recovery based on failure of consideration is independent of fault (176 CLR 390, citing Birks *An Introduction to the Law of Restitution* (revised edn, 1989), p 238).
4   See above, paras 19.21–19.23.

TOTAL FAILURE OF CONSIDERATION AND ENTIRE OBLIGATIONS

19.36   One persistent dichotomy with failure of consideration arises in respect of entire obligations. Where a contract embodies an entire obligation, that is, where the liability to pay the contract price or render the agreed counter performance only accrues upon the complete performance of the other party's obligations, then, if for any reason the contract is discharged prior to the substantial performance of that obligation, the price would not have been earned, and therefore no action will lie for it[1]. On the other hand, if in such a contract payment is required to be made in advance, and the payee carries out any part of the agreed performance, then the payer cannot claim the return of the payment on the basis of failure of consideration, unless discharge allows for a return or revesting of the performance rendered[2]. The reason for this latter result is the law's insistence on *total* failure of consideration[3].

That this dichotomy represents the current state of the law in Australia was confirmed by the High Court in *The Mikhail Lermontov*[4]. At first glance these divergent results appear odd, and there is a certain logic and appeal in the argument that if the obligation is entire and has not been (substantially) performed, then the payee has no right to retain any payment made. However, this very argument was rejected in *The Mikhail Lermontov*[5]. It would appear that although such an approach may accurately reflect contract risk, the result of that approach is too harsh to be adopted. *The Mikhail Lermontov* concerned a claim by a passenger who had paid her fare in advance and the cruise was cut short by the sinking of the ship through negligent navigation. The High Court, apart from Gaudron J, thought that the contract was entire or involved an entire obligation. It was held that as she had received the benefit of part of the cruise there could be no recovery on the basis of total failure of consideration. In the result, however, she had her action for damages which was both an appropriate and sufficient basis of redress. This dichotomy is more readily the bearer of rough justice where the contract is frustrated, or where the claim is being made by the party in breach.

1   Cf para 19.79.
2   See para 19.33, and see *Baltic Shipping Co v Dillon, The Mikhail Lermontov* (1993) 176 CLR 344 at 377–388, per Deane and Dawson JJ. An exception arises in sale of goods where the claimant may be in a position to reject the performance rendered by the defendant and thus recover an advance payment on the ground of failure of consideration; cf para 19.33. See also *Giles v Edwards* (1797) 7 Term Rep 181, 101 ER 920 (the claimant paid in advance for the defendant's promise to sell all the defendant's cordwood; the defendant was to cord the timber and the claimant was to re-cord it after which it became the property of the claimant; the obligation of the defendant was construed as being entire; in the result the defendant breached the contract as he corded only a small amount of timber and the claimant re-corded a small proportion of that corded by the defendant; the claimant was successful in obtaining restitution of the amount paid in advance on the ground of failure of consideration – although not recorded, presumably the claimant was permitted to and did reject the timber re-corded, if not the case is at odds with the general flow of cases in this area as it would appear the claimant received and accepted some part of the contracted performance in which case full recovery on the ground of failure of consideration would appear to have been allowed due to the conduct of the defendant in failing to perform its obligations under the contract – however, Stoljar has analysed the case on the basis that the performance was so slight that it was treated as wholly executory on the part of the seller, see Stoljar 'The Doctrine of Failure of Consideration' (1959) 75 LQR 53 at 62).
3   Where the contract is severable and it is possible to allocate a payment to a severable part of that contract to which no performance has been received, see *Fibrosa Spolka Akcyjna v Fairbairn Lawson Combe Barbour Ltd* [1943] AC 32 at 64–65; *China National Foreign Trade Transportation Corporation v Evlogia Shipping Co SA of Panama, The Mihalios Xilas* [1979] 1 WLR 1018 at 1024, per Lord Diplock, and at 1036, per Lord Scarman; *Baltic Shipping Co v Dillon, The Mikhail Lermontov* (1993) 176 CLR 344 at 374–375, per Deane and Dawson JJ. See further para 19.75.
4   *Baltic Shipping Co v Dillon, The Mikhail Lermontov* (1993) 176 CLR 344. Cf *DO Ferguson & Associates v Sohl* (1992) 62 BLR 95.
5   Note, however, Gaudron J thought ((1993) 176 CLR 344 at 386) that if there is anything less than full performance of an entire contract there is 'necessarily a total failure of consideration', entitling a payer to recover.

PARTIAL FAILURE OF CONSIDERATION[1]

19.37   Generally, the requirement that failure of consideration be total has been rigorously applied by the courts[2]. However, there have been signs in recent cases of a move towards adopting a concept of partial failure of consideration which, when combined with the recognition of counter-restitution following discharge of contract[3], may bring about a more just result in some cases[4]. In *David Securities Pty Ltd v Commonwealth Bank of Australia*[5], Mason CJ, Deane, Toohey, Gaudron and McHugh JJ suggested[6]:

... where consideration can be apportioned or where counter-restitution is relatively simple, insistence on total failure of consideration can be misleading and confusing ...

In *The Mikhail Lermontov*[7], Mason CJ stated that there cannot be a total failure of consideration if the incomplete performance results in the other party receiving and retaining 'any substantial part of the benefit expected under the contract'[8]. However, he also described[9] the 'receipt and retention by the plaintiff of any part of the bargained-for benefit' as precluding recovery, 'unless the contract otherwise provides or the circumstances give rise to a fresh contract'. The latter statement accurately expresses the traditional view. Given this latter statement, it is doubtful that he was suggesting that a broader view of failure of consideration may be taken by focusing on whether a 'substantial part' of the agreed performance has or has not been rendered. However, there is force in the notion that the corollary to the principle that substantial performance is sufficient to enable a party to recover the contract price under an entire contract is that a substantial failure of the agreed performance is a sufficient basis for restitution.

1   See Birks 'Failure of Consideration' in Rose (ed) *Consensus ad idem: Essays in the law of contract in honour of Guenter Treitel* (1996), p 179; McKendrick 'Total Failure of Consideration and Counter-Restitution: Two Issues or One' in Birks (ed) *Laundering and Tracing* (1995), ch 8.

2   See *Whincup v Hughes* (1871) LR 6 CP 78. Cf Atiyah *Rise and Fall of Freedom of Contract* (1979) p 488. See also Stoljar 'The Doctrine of Failure of Consideration' (1959) 75 LQR 53 and Stoljar *Law of Quasi-Contract* (2nd edn, 1989), pp 225 and 226. Stoljar suggests that the common law accepted the notion of counter-restitution, but its development was cut short by the requirement that the contract must be rescinded for restitution to be granted; rescission could not take place if the contract remained open, that is, if an express warranty remained to be tried, or if property had passed under the contract. Moreover, he has shown that the common law also adopted a notion of partial failure of consideration (see eg *Hicks v Hicks* (1802) 3 East 16, 102 ER 502), but that in time it insisted upon total failure of consideration because money had and received became the action to recover a payment made for a worthless article and because of the restrictive approach it took to the requirement of rescission as evidenced in cases such as *Hunt v Silk* (1804) 5 East 449; 102 ER 1142, see Stoljar 'The Doctrine of Failure of Consideration' (1959) 75 LQR 53 at 73. See also Ibbetson *A Historical Introduction to the Law of Obligations* (1999), pp 272 and 273.

3   See paras 19.16 and 19.98. There is no doctrinal impediment to adopting counter-restitution in the case of discharged contracts, if it is recognised that it is a principle relevant to preventing unjust enrichment rather than a principle used to distinguish between discharge and rescission of contract, see Carter 'Discharged Contracts: Claims for Restitution' (1997) 11 Journal of Contract 130 at 131.

4   In the context of sale of goods, if a buyer pays in advance and there is a short delivery, the buyer may accept that delivery and recover that part of the money paid which represents the goods not delivered, see *Biggerstaff v Rowatt's Wharf Ltd* [1896] 2 Ch 93 at 101, per Lindley LJ, at 103, per Lopes LJ, and at 105, per Kay LJ; *Behrend & Co Ltd v Produce Brokers Co Ltd* [1920] 3 KB 530; *Copping v Commercial Flour & Oatmeal Milling Co Ltd* (1933) 49 CLR 332; *Ebrahim Dawood Ltd v Heath (Est 1927) Ltd* [1961] 2 Lloyd's Rep 512. See also *Cox v Prentice* (1815) 3 M & S 344, 105 ER 641; *Devaux v Connolly* (1849) 8 CB 640, 137 ER 658; and see Stoljar 'The Doctrine of Failure of Consideration' (1959) 75 LQR 53 at 65. Moreover, as noted above (para 19.33) in sale of goods, a buyer may reject non-conforming goods and bring about a failure of consideration by effecting counter-restitution. Of course the parties themselves may expressly or impliedly allow for recovery in cases where there is a partial failure of consideration, see *Pan Ocean Shipping Ltd v Creditcorp Ltd, The Trident Beauty* [1994] 1 WLR 161 at 164–165, per Lord Goff, explaining the decision in *CA Stewart & Co v Phs Van Ommeren (London) Ltd* [1918] 2 KB 560.

5   (1992) 175 CLR 353. See also *Roxborough v Rothmans of Pall Mall Australia Ltd* (2002) 76 ALJR 203 at paras 105–109, per Gummow J, and cf at para 173, per Kirby J.

6   (1992) 175 CLR 353 at 383. See also the comments of Deane J in *Commonwealth of Australia v Amann Aviation Pty Ltd* (1991) 174 CLR 64 at 117.

7   *Baltic Shipping Co v Dillon, The Mikhail Lermontov* (1993) 176 CLR 344.

8   (1993) 176 CLR 344 at 350.

9   (1993) 176 CLR 344 at 351.

19.38   The most important decision reflecting a move towards the acceptance of partial failure of consideration is *Goss v Chilcott*[1]. In this case a solicitor by the name of Haddon wished to borrow money from the claimant finance company[2] of which he was a director. It was arranged that Mr and Mrs Goss[3], the defendants, would borrow the money from the claimant and then lend the same sum to Haddon. Haddon would then make the loan repayments through the defendants. In order to secure the loan, the defendants executed a mortgage in favour of the claimant. The loan was to be repaid over three months. However, finding himself in some difficulty making payment, Haddon, as agent for the claimant and without the knowledge or consent of the mortgagors, altered the mortgage so that the loan was to be repaid over 12 months.

Haddon made two payments[4] which the claimant appropriated to interest. No further payments were made, and the claimant demanded payment of principal and interest from the defendants. The defendants claimed their personal obligation to repay the loan had merged into the mortgage and that the alteration to the mortgage, without their consent, resulted in the mortgage being discharged under the rule in *Pigot's* case[5]. Moreover, as two payments had been made, they argued that the claimant was not entitled to restitutionary relief there being merely a partial failure of consideration. Only the second argument is relevant here.

1   [1996] AC 788.
2   The claimant was in fact the liquidator of the finance company.
3   Mrs Goss was Haddon's sister.
4   The first being for $914.25NZ and the second for $2,625NZ.
5   (1614) 11 Co Rep 26b, 77 ER 1177.

19.39   The New Zealand Court of Appeal held that although the claimant could not claim under the mortgage, it was entitled to rely simply on the advance and the agreement to repay in three months[1]. The reasoning as explained by Lord Goff, delivering the advice of the Privy Council, rested on two grounds:

> ... first, that the discharge of the defendants' liability under the mortgage instrument did not preclude the [claimant] from characterising the payment from the [claimant] to the defendants as an advance repayable in three months which had not been repaid, so that there remained a debt owing by the defendants to the [claimant]; and second, that the mortgage instrument was preceded by an oral agreement to repay the loan which survived the discharge of the defendants from liability under the mortgage instrument[2].

In the appeal to the Privy Council, counsel for the claimant felt unable to uphold the decision of the Court of Appeal that the advance could be claimed as a debt notwithstanding the discharge of the mortgage and, in addition, felt unable to uphold the Court of Appeal's decision based on the prior oral agreement for the advance. This left only an argument based on restitution.

1   Reported as *Chilcott v Goss* [1995] 1 NZLR 263.
2   [1996] AC 788 at 795. On this reasoning, the claimant was entitled to recover the advance, but not the rate of interest agreed to under the mortgage.

19.40   Lord Goff suggested that if the defendants had been discharged from their obligations due to the variation of the mortgage before any money had been paid then there would have been no difficulty in the claimant recovering the amount of the advance on the basis of total failure of consideration. Moreover, the Privy Council held that it made no difference that two instalments of interest had been paid. Lord Goff said[1]:

The function of the interest payments was to pay for the use of the capital sum over the period for which the loan was outstanding, which was separate and distinct from the obligation to repay the capital sum itself. In these circumstances it is ... both legitimate and appropriate for present purposes to consider the two separately ... [S]ince no part of the capital sum had been repaid, the failure of consideration for the capital sum would plainly have been total. But even if part of the capital sum had been repaid, the law would not hesitate to hold that the balance of the loan outstanding would be recoverable on the ground of failure of consideration; for at least in those cases in which apportionment can be carried out without difficulty, the law will allow partial recovery on this ground: see *David Securities Pty Ltd v Commonwealth Bank of Australia*[2].

The common law has for some time accepted that where a contract is severable it is possible to recover a payment if it is made in respect of a part of the contract to which there has been a total failure of consideration[3]. This approach helps alleviate some of the harshness of the total failure of consideration principle and can perhaps explain the severance of principal and interest. However, in the passage extracted it is clear that if the facts required them to do so, the Privy Council was prepared to take the further step[4] of apportioning the promised performance[5] and, moreover, that apportionment seems to be based on a principle of law rather than intention. If this suggestion is taken up, it will overcome one of the common law's reasons for insisting on total failure of consideration, that is, the inability to apportion payments. The other reason for insisting on total failure of consideration was, as noted above[6], that a claim for restitution first required the contract to be rescinded which was not possible if the claimant had received any part of the counter performance[7]. Clearly, this latter reason for insisting on total failure of consideration is no longer relevant to claims following discharge of contract for breach or repudiation.

1   [1996] AC 788 at 797–798. It was not possible to tell whether the second interest instalment was due before the defendants were discharged from their obligations under the mortgage. If the interest payment had fallen due at this time then it would not have been recoverable by the defendants as there was no total failure of consideration in respect of the payment. However, if the interest payment had not fallen due it would, prima facie at least, have been recoverable. In each case, however, the question of the defendants' right to recover interest paid was distinct from the right of the claimant to recover the capital sum. It was also dependent upon whether the payments were made before the date when the contractual obligation of the defendants to repay the loan was discharged (the date the mortgage was altered). There were no findings with respect to that issue. It may, however, be noted that in the more recent decision of *Stocznia Gdanska SA v Latvian Shipping Co* [1998] 1 WLR 574, although the question did not directly arise for decision, Lord Goff noted (at 590) that although the rule requiring failure of consideration to be total 'had been subject to considerable criticism in the past ... in a comparatively recent Report (Law Com no 121 (1983)) ... the Law Commission had declined to recommend a change in the rule'.

2   (1992) 175 CLR 353 at 383. A defence of change of position, on the basis that the defendants allowed the money to be paid to Haddon, was also rejected. In making its final order the Privy Council noted that, prima facie, the claimant was entitled to restitution of the principal sum advanced ($30,000). However, there would remain the problem of restitution (in favour of the defendants) of the interest payments ($3,539.25). In the end, however, the Privy Council did not have to resolve this issue. There was no appeal against the order of the Court of Appeal which had given judgment in favour of the claimant for the sum of $26,460.75. This sum had been arrived at by deducting the two instalments of interest from the principal sum. It must be remembered, however, that the Court of Appeal considered the two instalments as repayments of capital not interest. That court had held that the defendant never orally agreed to pay interest and because the interest clauses in the mortgage were no longer enforceable the payments were to be treated as repayments of principal.

3   See *Fibrosa Spolka Akcyjna v Fairbairn Lawson Combe Barbour Ltd* [1943] AC 32 at 65; *Baltic Shipping Co v Dillon, The Mikhail Lermontov* (1993) 176 CLR 344 at 375. See also *Rugg v Minett* (1809) 11 East 210, 103 ER 985; *Whincup v Hughes* (1871) LR 6 CP 78 at 81, per Bovill CJ; *Copping v Commercial Flour & Oatmeal Milling Co Ltd* (1933) 49 CLR 332 at 343, per Dixon J; *Roxborough v Rothmans of Pall Mall Australia Ltd* [2001] HCA 68 at paras 17–21, per Gleeson CJ,

Gaudron and Hayne JJ. See further *DO Ferguson & Associates v Sohl* (1992) 62 BLR 95 (in this case a builder repudiated a contract prior to completion of work and left the building site having been paid £26,738.75; the builder sued to recover the balance of payments due at a particular date; the defendant counter claimed for damages and for the recovery of any amount overpaid to the builder; the Court of Appeal upheld the decision of the trial judge allowing the defendant to recover £4,673 as an amount overpaid to the builder; this conclusion was reached by valuing the work done by the builder at £22,065.75 and holding that as regards amounts paid in excess of this there had been a total failure of consideration; although the defendant did not allege that the contract was entire it is not clear from the judgments at first instance or on appeal how payments were apportioned to work done; it would appear the court simply valued the incomplete work, deducted that value from the contract price (together with a sum in respect of defective work) and declared that there had been a total failure of consideration as regards any amount paid in excess of that figure; given this reasoning the case appears to be more an example of apportionment which is a true exception to total failure of consideration; however the Court of Appeal clearly based their decision on total failure of consideration which suggests their ultimate reasoning was based on severability; it may also be noted that the defendant was able to complete the work for less than the contract price and was only awarded nominal damages for breach of contract; the Court rejected an argument that the defendant in such circumstances should have been left with only his or her claim for damages). See also above, para 19.36, n 4.

4   Assuming there is no legal or policy impediment to apportionment, see *Deposit & Investment Co Ltd v Kaye* (1962) 63 SRNSW 453. See also *Ellis v Rowbotham* [1900] 1 QB 740.

5   See also *Devaux v Conolly* (1849) 8 CB 640, 137 ER 658. Cf *Whincup v Hughes* (1871) LR 6 CP 78 at 81, per Bovill CJ, and at 86, per Montague Smith J.

6   See above, para 19.12.

7   See *Franklin v Miller* (1836) 4 Ad & E 599 at 605, 111 ER 912 at 914, per Littledale J. See further para 19.12.

DEPOSITS, INSTALMENTS, FORFEITURE AND RELIEF AGAINST FORFEITURE

19.41   There is an implied right of forfeiture of a deposit on discharge for breach by the buyer[1]. Where the breach and subsequent discharge (prior to receiving any part of the contract performance) is due to the conduct of the vendor, the purchaser may recover any deposit paid[2]. However, it is still an open question whether this right flows from an implied term of the contract, or whether recovery is restitutionary based on failure of consideration. The weight of authority favours a restitutionary analysis[3] although much will depend on the view one takes of the nature of a deposit[4].

1   See *Howe v Smith* (1884) 27 Ch D 89; *Mason v Clouet* [1924] AC 980; *McDonald v Dennys Lascelles Ltd* (1933) 48 CLR 457; *Stratton Motor Co v Mattimoe* (11 February 1994, unreported), CA. The better view would appear to be that a deposit is forfeited even if it was due but remained unpaid at the time of discharge, see Carter *Breach of Contract* (2nd edn, 1991), paras 1251–1254, and see *Hinton v Sparkes* (1868) LR 3 CP 161.

2   *Stickney v Keeble* [1915] AC 386; *Re Stone and Saville's Contract* [1963] 1 WLR 163; *Foran v Wight* (1989) 168 CLR 385.

3   See *Howe v Smith* (1884) 27 Ch D 89; *Stickney v Keeble* [1915] AC 386; *Mason v Clouet* [1924] AC 980; *McDonald v Dennys Lascelles Ltd* (1933) 48 CLR 457; *Re Stone and Saville's Contract* [1963] 1 WLR 163; *Foran v Wight* (1989) 168 CLR 385.

4   See Carter *Breach of Contract* (2nd edn, 1991), paras 1251–1254.

19.42   In addition to the implied forfeiture of deposits, a contract may contain an express term forfeiting instalment payments upon breach by the buyer. Such a provision precludes the buyer from resorting to failure of consideration to recover any instalments paid. The reverse is also true, that is, if there is no provision for forfeiture the claimant must seek recovery at common law on the basis of failure of consideration, he or she cannot resort to relief against forfeiture[1].

1   *McDonald v Dennys Lascelles Ltd* (1933) 48 CLR 457 at 478, per Dixon J; *Mayson v Clouet* [1924] AC 980; *Stockloser v Johnson* [1954] 1 QB 476 at 483 per Somervell LJ, and at 489–490, per Denning LJ.

19.43   Generally, relief against forfeiture is concerned with relief against the forfeiture of some interest in real or personal property. Historically the courts have claimed jurisdiction to grant such relief 'where it is possible to state that the object of the transaction and of the insertion of the right to forfeit is essentially to secure the payment of money'[1], or where the forfeiture results from fraud, accident, mistake or surprise[2]. In *Shiloh Spinners Ltd v Harding*[3], Lord Wilberforce referred to a third head of jurisdiction suggesting that the court 'should reaffirm the right of courts of equity in appropriate and limited cases to relieve against forfeiture for breach of covenant or condition where the primary object of the bargain is to secure a stated result which can effectively be attained when the matter comes before the court, and where the forfeiture provision is added by way of security for the production of that result'[4]. However, he noted that his comments were not meant to establish or recognise any general power to relieve against bargains. He said that 'it remains true today that equity expects men to carry out their bargains and will not let them buy their way out by uncovenanted payment'[5]. The result is that although the heads of jurisdiction appear settled, the extent to which a court will exercise its discretion to grant relief against forfeiture and the factors it will take into account in determining whether it will exercise its discretion are not as clear.

1   *Shiloh Spinners Ltd v Harding* [1973] AC 691 at 722, per Lord Wilberforce. It is on this basis that relief is given in cases of late payment of money due under a mortgage or rent due under a lease.
2   *Shiloh Spinners Ltd v Harding* [1973] AC 691 at 722, per Lord Wilberforce.
3   [1973] AC 691.
4   [1973] AC 691 at 723. Recently in *On Demand Information plc v Michael Gerson (Finance) plc* [2001] 1 WLR 155, this head of jurisdiction was referred to as the basis for the jurisdiction to grant relief against forfeiture of a finance lease; the lease was validly terminated by the lessor when the lessee went into receivership; it was held by majority that relief could not be granted because the goods which were the subject of the lease had been sold and it was thought that relief would have effectively been relief from forfeiture in relation to a sum of money obtained on sale: see below para 19.52, n 1. (This point is not affected by the recent appeal to the Lords, [2002] UKHL 13, [2002] 1 All ER (Comm) 641, where it was held that the sale under RSC Ord 29, r 4 did not affect substantive rights and, although it prevented an order for relief against forfeiture being granted, if prior to the sale the claimant could have successfully claimed such relief, it was still eligible for a remedy.) In *Shiloh Spinners*, Lord Simon ([1973] AC 691 at 726–727) went further stating that 'equity has an unlimited and unfettered jurisdiction to relieve against contractual forfeitures and penalties. What have sometimes been regarded as fetters to the jurisdiction are, in my view, more properly to be seen as considerations which the court will weigh in deciding how to exercise an unfettered jurisdiction ... Prominent but not exclusive among such considerations is the desirability that contractual promises should be observed and contractual rights respected, and even more the undesirability of the law appearing to condone flagrant and contemptuous disregard of obligations'. See also *Mardorf Peach & Co Ltd v Attica Sea Carriers Corpn of Liberia, The Laconia* [1977] AC 850 at 873–874, per Lord Simon. This view was rejected in *Scandinavian Trading Tanker Co v Flota Petrolera Ecuatoriana, The Scaptrade* [1983] 2 AC 694 at 700. See also *Union Eagle Ltd v Golden Achievement Ltd* [1997] AC 514.
5   [1973] AC 691 at 723.

19.44   Deposits   Arguably, successful claims to recover deposits and instalments where they have been 'forfeited' under either express or implied contractual provisions for retention on breach is based on relief against forfeiture[1]. If that view is adopted, then relief against forfeiture in this circumstance may be concerned with the prevention or reversal of an unjust enrichment[2].

1   See *McDonald v Dennys Lascelles Ltd* (1933) 48 CLR 457 at 478, per Dixon J: 'Although the parties might by express agreement give the vendor an absolute right at law to retain the instalments in the event of the contract going off, yet in equity such a contract is considered to involve a forfeiture ... The view adopted in *Re Dagenham (Thames) Dock Co, ex p Hulse* (1873) 8 Ch App 1022, seems to have been that relief should be granted, not against the forfeiture of the

instalments, but against the forfeiture of the estate under a contract which involved the retention of the purchase money: and this may have been the ground upon which Lord Moulton proceeded in *Kilmer v British Columbia Orchard Lands Ltd* [1913] AC 319, notwithstanding the explanation of that case given in *Steedman v Drinkle* [1916] 1 AC 275 and *Brickles v Snell* [1916] 2 AC 599. However, these cases establish the purchaser's right to recover the instalments, other than the deposit, although the contract is not carried into execution'. Cf Rossiter *Penalties and Forfeiture* (1992) p 113.

2   See *Stockloser v Johnson* [1954] 1 QB 476 at 492, per Denning LJ; *Stern v McArthur* (1988) 165 CLR 489 at 526–527, per Deane and Dawson JJ; *Union Eagle Ltd v Golden Achievement Ltd* [1997] AC 514 at 523, per Lord Hoffman; *Lexane Pty Ltd v Highfern Pty Ltd* [1985] 1 Qd R 446 at 455, per McPherson J. See also *Clancy v Salienta Pty Ltd* [2000] NSWCA 248. Academic opinion differs as to whether relief against forfeiture is concerned with preventing or reversing an unjust enrichment, see eg Birks *An Introduction to the Law of Restitution* (revised edn, 1989), p 214; Burrows *Law of Restitution* (1993), p 273; Mason and Carter *Restitution Law in Australia* (1995), para 1142; Virgo *Principles of the Law of Restitution* (1999), pp 354 and 355.

19.45   In the case of contracts for the sale of land, relief against the forfeiture of a deposit may be given if the forfeiture results from fraud, accident, mistake or surprise[1]. A broader view, however, suggests that relief may be available in respect of excessive deposits on the basis that they are penal in nature, and forfeiture would be unconscionable[2]. Unless referring to the equitable jurisdiction to give relief against penalties, on its face this approach appears to blur the common law distinction between liquidated damages and penalties and the equitable jurisdiction to grant relief against forfeiture. A provision which is classified as a penalty operates upon breach and 'is in the nature of a punishment for non-observance of a contractual stipulation'[3]. A forfeiture 'involves the loss or determination of an estate or interest in property or a proprietary right'[4]. However, certain provisions for payment fall between these two definitions[5]. One example is a provision allowing a vendor, upon breach by the buyer, to retain any instalments paid. In such a case the instalments are not payable on breach and, upon payment, the payee clearly obtains title to the money.

The classification of deposits is also problematic and is further complicated because they have three functions. First they form part of the contract price, second they are an earnest of performance, and third they are a form of security. However, in regards to both provisions for the forfeiture of instalments and deposits, both are forfeited on breach, and this creates a degree of commonality between forfeitures and penalties[6]. It is therefore not difficult to see why the view may be taken that provisions allowing for a party to retain instalments or deposits raises issues of forfeiture[7], and that relief falls to be decided upon whether or not the instalments or deposit is in the nature of a penalty and whether the vendor's conduct may be said to be unconscionable.

1   See *Stern v McArthur* (1988) 165 CLR 489 at 526, per Deane and Dawson JJ.
2   *Stockloser v Johnson* [1954] 1 QB 476 at 490. See also *Smyth v Jessep* [1956] VLR 230; *Saunders v Leonardi* (1976) 1 BPR 9409. Cf *Mussen v Van Diemen's Land Co* [1938] Ch 253; *Galbraith v Mitchenall Estates Ltd* [1965] 2 QB 473; *Re Hoobin* [1957] VR 341. See further *Tropical Traders Ltd v Goonan (No 2)* [1965] WAR 174; *Coates v Sarich* [1964] WAR 2.
3   *Legione v Hateley* (1983) 152 CLR 406 at 446, per Mason and Deane JJ.
4   See n 3.
5   See *Jobson v Johnson* [1989] 1 WLR 1026.
6   See further Rossiter *Penalties and Forfeiture* (1992), pp 107 and 108.
7   See *McDonald v Dennys Lascelles Ltd* (1933) 48 CLR 457 at 478, per Dixon J.

19.46   One line of authority has taken the view that the question as to whether or not the provision for forfeiture is penal is different from the determination as to whether an amount payable on breach is a penalty[1]. Arguably, this must follow in the case of a deposit because its threefold function dictates that its calculation need not necessarily be a pre-estimate of damage[2]. On this view a deposit will be considered to be penal in nature if it is extravagant, which in this context means that it is not a reasonable earnest of money[3]. This is apparently determined at the time of contract[4]. However, to obtain relief it is also necessary to determine whether forfeiture would involve unconscionable conduct. The existence of unconscionable conduct on the part of the vendor is determined at the time of forfeiture.

1   See *Smyth v Jessup* [1956] VLR 230; *Else (1982) Ltd v Parkland Holdings Ltd* [1994] 1 BCLC 130 at 139, per Evans LJ, at 141, per Russell LJ, and cf at 146, per Hoffmann LJ: 'The effect of [*Stockloser v Johnson*] was in my judgment that retention of instalments which have been paid under the contract so as to become the absolute property of the vendor does not fall within the penalty rule and is subject only to the jurisdiction for relief against forfeiture. The position will be different when the money has been deposited as a security for due performance of the party's obligation and has not become the absolute property of the other party'. See also *Hinton v Sparkes* (1868) LR 3 CP 161; *Lock v Bell* [1931] 1 Ch 35; *Yardley v Saunders* [1982] WAR 231 at 237, per Kennedy J. Cf *Public Works Comr v Hills* [1906] AC 368. See further Law Commission *Penalty Clauses and Forfeiture of Money Paid* Working Paper No 61 (1975) paras 65–66 and 68; Rossiter *Penalties and Forfeiture* (1992), pp 108 and 109; *McGregor on Damages* (16th ed, 1997), paras 544–557.
2   See *NLS Pty Ltd v Hughes* (1966) 120 CLR 583 at 589, per Barwick CJ. In fact a deposit may be forfeited even if the vendor has suffered no loss.
3   See *Workers Trust & Merchant Bank Ltd v Dojap Investments Ltd* [1993] AC 573 at 579, and see *Linggi Plantations Ltd v Jagatheeson* [1972] 1 MLJ 89. See also Lanyon 'Equity and the Doctrine of Penalties' (1996) 9 Journal of Contract Law 234 at 246–250.
4   See further Rossiter *Penalties and Forfeiture* (1992), pp 110 and 117, who advocates that the penal nature of a deposit should be judged at the time of breach. He also suggests that the requirement of unconscionability adds nothing to the requirement that the forfeiture be penal. It may be added that in this regard he views relief against the 'forfeiture' of a deposit as best explained by reference to equity's jurisdiction to relieve against penalties. In regards to instalments of the purchase price he advocates that the general common law penalty rules should be applied requiring the penal nature to be determined at the time of contract.

19.47   Another view, however, suggests that there is little difference between a sum payable on breach, and a sum forfeited on breach so that recovery in both instances should be governed by the same set of rules[1]. Recently in *Workers Trust & Merchant Bank Ltd v Dojap Investments Ltd*[2], the Privy Council held that relief against forfeiture of a deposit may be granted simply on the basis that it is penal. In that case relief was granted in respect of a deposit that amounted to 25% of the purchase price. Moreover, the Privy Council did not allow for the forfeiture of an amount that would have been reasonable[3]. Although the court here stated that a deposit will be an impermissible penalty if it is not a reasonable earnest of money, its reasoning suggests that application of this principle is not completely divorced from considerations relevant to the common law distinction between liquidated damages and penalties. Thus it was stated[4]:

> In general, a contractual provision which requires one party in the event of his breach of the contract to pay or forfeit a sum of money to the other party is unlawful as being a penalty, unless such provision can be justified as being a payment of liquidated damages, being a genuine pre-estimate of the loss which the innocent party will incur by reason of the breach[5]. One exception to this general rule is the provision for the payment of a deposit by the purchaser on a contract for the sale of land. Ancient law has established that the forfeiture of such a deposit (customarily 10% of the contract price) does not fall within the general rule and can be validly forfeited even though the amount of the deposit bears no reference to the anticipated loss to the vendor flowing from the breach of contract ...
>
> This exception is anomalous ...
>
> However, the special treatment afforded to deposits is plainly capable of being abused if the parties to a contract, by attaching the label 'deposit' to any penalty, could escape the general rule which renders penalties unenforceable ...

It is not possible for the parties to attach the incidents of a deposit to the payment of a sum of money unless such sum is reasonable as earnest money ...

In order to be reasonable a true deposit must be objectively operating as 'earnest money' not as a penalty ...

However, although their Lordships are satisfied that the practice of a limited class of vendors cannot determine the reasonableness of a deposit, it is more difficult to define what the test should be. Since a true deposit may take effect as a penalty, albeit one permitted by law, it is hard to draw a line between a reasonable, permissible amount of penalty and an unreasonable, impermissible penalty. In their Lordships' view the correct approach is to start from the position that, without logic but by long continued usage ... the customary deposit has been 10%. A vendor who seeks to obtain a larger amount by way of forfeitable deposit must show special circumstances which justify such a deposit ...

[The] evidence indicates that far from the amount of the deposit having been fixed upon as a reasonable amount of earnest, the amount was substantially influenced by fiscal considerations having nothing to do with encouragement to perform the contract ...

[The attorney for the bank] accepted that the amount of the deposit was far in excess of what would have been required to cover the maximum out of pocket expenses which would have attended completion ...

The question therefore arises whether the court has jurisdiction to relieve against the express provision of the contract that the deposit of 25% was to be forfeited. Although there is no doubt that the court will not order the payment of a sum contracted for (but not yet paid) if satisfied that such sum is in reality a penalty, it was submitted that the court could not order, by way of relief, the repayment of sums already paid to the defendant in accordance with the terms of the contract which, on breach, the contract provided should be forfeit ...

In the view of their Lordships, since the 25% deposit was not a true deposit by way of earnest, the provision for its forfeiture was a plain penalty. There is clear authority that in a case of a sum paid by one party to another under the contract as security for the performance of that contract, a provision for its forfeiture in the event of non-performance is a penalty from which the court will give relief by ordering repayment of the sum so paid, less any damage actually proved to have been suffered as a result of non-completion ...

Accordingly there is jurisdiction in the court to order repayment of the 25% deposit.

1   See Law Commission *Penalty Clauses and Forfeiture of Money Paid* Working Paper No 61 (1975), paras 53, 65–66, and 68. See also *Coates v Sarich* [1964] WAR 2 at 14–15, per Hale J.
2   [1993] AC 573. See further Harpum 'Deposits as Penalties' [1993] CLJ 389; Carter 'Two Privy Council Cases' (1993) 6 Journal of Contract Law 266.
3   Cf the position in Australia where relief will be given only to the extent that a deposit is penal, see Mason and Carter *Restitution Law in Australia* (1995), para 1137.
4   [1993] AC 573 at 578–582.
5   This sentence appears to reverse the usual onus of proof; in addition it declares such a provision unlawful rather than stating that relief may be given if certain factors are made out; generally the law assumes such provisions to be valid unless determined otherwise.

19.48   In addition to the above, there is a statutory provision dealing with the recovery of deposits in contracts for the sale of land. The Law of Property Act 1925, s 49(2), provides[1]:

Where the court refuses to grant specific performance of a contract, or in any action for the return of a deposit, the court may, if it thinks fit, order the repayment of any deposit.

The important aspect of this provision it that relief is discretionary and, despite some earlier authority to the contrary[2], it now appears that the courts are prepared to recognise the wide language of the provision and use it to order repayment 'in any circumstances which make this the fairest course between the two parties'[3]. That is, the discretion will be exercised when justice requires[4].

1   See also Unfair Terms in Consumer Contracts Regulations 1999 SI 1999/2083, Sch 2, Pt II, para 1(d). See further Treitel *Law of Contract* (10th edn, 1999), p 942. In Australia see Conveyancing Act 1919 (NSW) s 55(2A); Property Law Act 1958 (Vic) s 49(2); and see Rossiter *Penalties and Forfeiture* (1992), pp 117 and 118; and Carter and Harland *Contract Law in Australia* (3rd edn, 1996), para 2334.
2   See the discussion in Treitel *Law of Contract* (10th edn, 1999), p 939.
3   *Universal Corpn v Five Ways Properties Ltd* [1979] 1 All ER 552 at 555, per Buckley LJ. See also *Country and Metropolitan Homes Surrey Ltd v Topclaim Ltd* [1997] 1 All ER 254; *Dimsdale Developments (South East) Ltd v De Haan* (1983) 47 P & CR 1.
4   *Schindler v Pigault* (1975) 30 P & CR 328 at 336, per Megarry VC.

19.49   Instalments   In respect of instalments of the contract price, the law does not imply provisions for forfeiture. Therefore, such a provision must be expressly provided for[1]. Where such a provision exists and where an instalment is 'forfeited', an issue then arises as to the proper basis for recovery of such a payment. On one view, recovery is based on the jurisdiction to grant relief against forfeiture. If correct, then relief against forfeiture may, in part, be informed by the principle against unjust enrichment. On another view, relief against forfeiture is limited to granting relief against the forfeiture of proprietary interests, and is limited to giving the claimant further time to perform. Therefore restitution of 'forfeited' instalments must be based on some other ground, such as the rules against penalties. If the correct basis for recovery is relief against forfeiture then, although as noted earlier the heads of jurisdiction are settled, there still remains the issue as to when a court will exercise it discretion to grant relief against forfeiture[2].

1   *Mayson v Clouet* [1924] AC 980. See also *Cargill International SA v Bangladesh Sugar & Food Industries Corpn* [1998] 1 WLR 461.
2   See *On Demand Information plc v Michael Gerson (Finance) plc* [2001] 1 WLR 155. (This point is not affected by the recent appeal to the Lords, [2002] UKHL 13, [2002] 1 All ER (Comm) 641.)

19.50   Australian courts have exercised the jurisdiction to grant relief against forfeiture (by way of specific performance) of an interest in land where the vendor has terminated the contract for breach of an essential time stipulation[1]. Prior to discharge, relief (by way of specific performance) is properly given against the forfeiture of a proprietary interest because, prior to completion, the purchaser has a beneficial interest commensurate with his or her right to specific performance[2]. However, if the contract has been discharged and specific performance is granted, it would appear that relief against forfeiture is given as a preliminary to reinstate the contract prior to ordering specific performance[3]. In *Legione v Hateley*[4], Mason and Deane JJ[5] overcame this circularity problem by suggesting that a purchaser's equitable interest is commensurate with his or her ability to obtain specific performance, in a broad sense which would include the purchaser's ability to protect its interest by injunction[6]. Gibbs CJ and Murphy J[7] on the other hand took a broader approach to the jurisdiction, and overcame the circularity problem by simply stating that specific performance may be given if it will not cause injustice and will prevent injustice[8].

1   See *Pitt v Curotta* (1931) 31 SRNSW 477; *Berry v Mahoney* [1933] VLR 314; *McDonald v Dennys Lascelles Ltd* (1933) 48 CLR 457 at 478; *Real Estate Securities Ltd v Kew Golf Links Estate Pty Ltd* [1935] VLR 114; *Tropical Traders Ltd v Goonan* (1964) 111 CLR 41; *Legione v Hateley* (1983) 152 CLR 406; *Stern v McArthur* (1988) 165 CLR 489.
2   See Meagher Gummow and Lehane *Equity: Doctrines and Remedies* (3rd edn, 1992), para 1828.
3   See *Stern v McArthur* (1988) 165 CLR 489 at 537, per Gaudron J. See below, para 19.51.
4   (1983) 152 CLR 406.

5   (1983) 152 CLR 406 at 445–446.
6   Cf Meagher 'Sir Frederick Jordon's Footnote' (1999) 15 Journal of Contract Law 1; Gummow 'Forfeiture and Certainty: The High Court and the House of Lords' in Finn (ed) *Essays in Equity* (1985), pp 36 and 37.
7   (1983) 152 CLR 406 at 429.
8   See further *Ciavarella v Balmer* (1983) 153 CLR 438; *Stern v McArthur* (1988) 165 CLR 489; and see the discussion in Meagher Gummow and Lehane *Equity: Doctrines and Remedies* (3rd ed, 1992) para 1828–1829.

19.51   However, in Australia, it would appear that exceptional circumstances are required to give relief against forfeiture as a preliminary to specific performance, where the breach is of an essential time stipulation[1]. Such circumstances are made out where the vendor has engaged in unconscionable conduct. It is unconscionable conduct that forms the basis of the jurisdiction to grant such relief[2]. Arguably, because relief here is given after the valid discharge of the contract, the relief is not given in respect of the forfeiture of an interest in the land, but rather against the loss of instalments[3]. If relief against the loss of instalments can be given by way of specific performance, it would be strange if a court could not, instead of ordering specific performance, order restitution of the instalments. On this basis, the recovery of instalments (in this circumstance) would be based on relief against forfeiture.

1   See *Legione v Hateley* (1983) 152 CLR 406; *Stern v McArthur* (1988) 165 CLR 489 at 503, per Mason CJ, and cf at 526, per Deane and Dawson JJ.
2   See *Stern v McArthur* (1988) 165 CLR 489 at 526–527, per Deane and Dawson JJ ('The general underlying notion is that which has been long identified as underlying much of equity's traditional jurisdiction to grant relief against unconscionable conduct, namely, that a person should not be permitted to use or insist upon his legal rights to take advantage of another's special vulnerability or misadventure for the unjust enrichment of himself'), see also at 537–539, per Gaudron J, cf at 503, per Mason CJ (taking a narrower view of unconscionabilty said, 'to accept the respondents' submission and extend relief against forfeiture to instances in which no exceptional circumstances are established would be to eviscerate unconsionability of its meaning. The doctrine is a limited one that operates only where the vendor has, by his conduct, caused or contributed to a situation in which it would be unconscionable on the *vendor's* part to insist on the forfeiture of the purchaser's interest') and per Brennan J at 516 and 519–520. See further *Legione v Hateley* (1983) 152 CLR 406; *O'Dea v Allstates Leasing System (WA) Pty Ltd* (1983) 152 CLR 359 at 391–392, per Brennan J; *Hill v Terry* [1993] 2 Qd R 640; *CSS Investments Pty Ltd v Lopiron* (1987) 16 FCR 15. Cf *Yardley v Saunders* [1962] WAR 231 at 237. See further Rossiter *Penalties and Forfeiture* (1992), pp 179–184.
3   Gummow has persuasively argued that since the contract is discharged, the relief given by way of specific performance cannot be relief against forfeiture but rather an exercise and recognition of equity's wider jurisdiction to relieve against fraud, accident, mistake and surprise. '[T]he true issue [is] whether there may be an equity to prevent the defendant/vendor in a specific performance suit from raising against the plaintiff/purchaser the defence that the contract is already discharged at law for breach by the plaintiff who thus has left no legal rights upon which equity may operate in its auxiliary jurisdiction': Gummow 'Forfeiture and Certainty: The High Court and the House of Lords' in Finn (ed) *Essays in Equity* (1985), pp 33 and 34. Such an equity may arise where it would be unconscionable for the vendor to rely on his or her strict legal rights.

19.52   In England, it is clear that, at least in cases for the sale of land, if the claimant is ready and willing to perform, and the provision for forfeiture was aimed at securing the payment of money, then he or she may obtain relief against forfeiture by way of specific performance of the contract[1]. Where the contract has been properly discharged for breach of an essential time stipulation by the buyer, then exceptional circumstances are required for relief to be given by way of specific performance[2]. However, although the basis for the relief remains unclear, such a claimant may be given relief (that is restitution) in respect of money paid[3]. The reason for generally refusing relief by way of specific performance is based on the need for certainty in commercial transactions[4]. However, there appears to be no commensurate concern with declaring amounts payable on breach to be penalties.

1   See also *On Demand Information plc v Michael Gerson (Finance) plc* [2001] 1 WLR 155 where the
    Court of Appeal recognised jurisdiction to grant relief against forfeiture of a finance lease on the
    basis that the object of the bargain was to produce a stated result and the forfeiture provision was
    added to secure that result. The lease was validly terminated by the lessor. Relief was refused as
    the goods had been sold by the receiver of the lessee (see above, para 19.43, n 4) (This point is not
    affected by the recent appeal to the Lords, [2002] UKHL 13, [2002] 1 All ER (Comm) 641.) The
    result was a windfall for the lessor as it kept the instalments and the proceeds of sale whereas
    under the contract a large proportion of the proceeds of sale were to go to the lessee. What was
    not fully considered, however, was the ability of the court in that circumstance to then order
    restitution of any part of the instalments – given that relief in respect of instalments in the case of
    contracts for the sale of land has as its focus placing the parties into the position they were in
    before entry into the contract, this would appear to be a legitimate area to investigate.
2   *Union Eagle Ltd v Golden Achievement Ltd* [1997] AC 514 (in this case the purchasers were ready
    and willing to perform and in fact had tendered the purchase money only 10 minutes after the
    time set for completion; for this trivial breach and the vendor's decision to exercise its strict legal
    rights, the purchasers lost their deposit – see further Abedian and Furmston 'Relief Against
    Forfeiture after Breach of an Essential Time Stipulation in the Light of *Union Eagle Ltd v Golden
    Achievements Ltd*' (1998) 12 Journal of Contract Law 189). See also *Scandinavian Trading Tanker
    Co v Flota Petrolera Ecuatoriana, The Scaptrade* [1983] 2 AC 694; *Sport International Bussum Bv v
    Inter-Footwear Ltd* [1984] 1 WLR 776. See further *Steedman v Drinkle* [1916] 1 AC 275; *Brickles v
    Snell* [1916] 2 AC 599. Cf *Re Dagenham (Thames) Dock Co, ex p Hulse* (1873) 8 Ch App 1022;
    Kilmer v British Columbia Orchard Lands Ltd [1913] AC 319 and see Harpum 'Relief Against
    Forfeiture and the Purchaser of Land' [1984] CLJ 134; Nicholson 'Breach of an Essential Time
    Stipulation and Relief Against Forfeiture' (1983) 57 Australian Law Journal 632; Lang
    'Forfeiture of Interests in Land' (1984) 100 LQR 427.
3   See generally *Steedman v Drinkle* [1916] 1 AC 275; *Brickles v Snell* [1916] 2 AC 699. Cf *Starside
    Properties Ltd v Mustapha* [1974] 2 All ER 567.
4   This goes to the exercise of jurisdiction rather than the existence of the jurisdiction.

19.53   Another issue that remains unclear is where the claimant cannot claim
specific performance, or is otherwise not able and willing to perform, but wishes
to recover payments forfeited under the contract. As noted above, the relevant
issues are whether in such circumstances relief (that is, restitution) should be
given, and if so, is the relief an exercise of the jurisdiction to grant relief against
forfeiture or an application of rules against penalties?

19.54   In England (assuming an accepted head of jurisdiction can be
identified), there are two views as to when a court will exercise its discretion to
grant relief against forfeiture. The first view suggests that relief is limited to
allowing the purchaser further time to perform, but requires the purchaser to be
willing and able to perform. For example, in *Stockloser v Johnson*, Romer LJ said:

> ... it appears to me that the cases establish that if a purchaser defaults in punctual
> payment of instalments of purchase-money the court will, in a proper case, relieve
> the purchaser from his contractual liability to forfeit instalments (apart from the
> deposit) already paid to the extent of giving him a further chance and further time to
> pay the money which is in arrear if he is able and willing to do so; but the cases do
> not, in my judgment, show that the court will relieve such a purchaser to any
> further extent than this[1].

The effect of Romer LJ's statement, in a case where the contract is discharged
and where the purchaser is not able to perform the contract, is that relief (by way
of restitution) will only be granted under the broader head of equitable
jurisdiction to relieve against fraud, accident, mistake or surprise[2].

1   [1954] 1 QB 476 at 499. See also *Mussen v Van Diemen's Land Co* [1938] Ch 253 at 265–266, per
    Farwell J; *Cornwall v Henson* (1899) 2 Ch 710.
2   See Meagher Gummow and Lehane *Equity: Doctrines and Remedies* (3rd edn, 1992), para 1827.
    See also *Starside Properties Ltd v Mustapha* [1974] 1 WLR 816 at 822, per Edmund Davies LJ.

19.55   In the same case[1], Somervell LJ and Denning LJ (in obiter) expressed a broader view which was not limited to situations where the contract remained on foot, and which did not limit the claimant who is not able to perform to obtaining relief only where there is fraud, accident, mistake or surprise[2]. Somervell LJ (with whom Denning LJ agreed)[3] said[4]:

> Any penalty provision is, of course, in one sense a term of the contract, and all the plaintiff was seeking to do in the numerous cases in which equity gave relief was to enforce the bargain. There is however, I agree, a difference between cases, for example, where a special penalty is added to normal interest and cases like the present where a purchaser has possession on the one hand and instalments are being paid on the other. All I am concerned to say is that in my opinion the cases do not establish (1) that relief could never be given unless the plaintiff could show that he is financially in a position to complete and would be willing to do so if the defendant were himself prepared to waive the breach and complete the contract, or (2) that after rescission no relief can be given unless there is fraud or sharp practice.

Denning LJ added that[5]:

> The difficulty is to know what are the circumstances which give rise to this equity ... Two things are necessary: first the forfeiture clause must be of a penal nature, in this sense, that the sum forfeited must be out of all proportion to the damage, and, secondly, it must be unconscionable for the seller to retain the money.
>
> [I]n a proper case there is an equity of restitution which a party in default does not lose simply because he is not able and willing to perform the contract. Nay, that is the very reason why he needs equity. The equity operates, not because of the claimant's default, but because it is in the particular case unconscionable for the seller to retain the money. In short, he ought not unjustly enrich himself at the claimant's expense. This equity of restitution is to be tested, I think, not at the time of the contract, but by the conditions existing when it is invoked.

1   See also *Steedman v Drinkle* [1916] 1 AC 275 (contract discharged by vendor and relief against forfeiture of instalments paid was granted on the basis that the right to retain them was penal; however, specific performance was refused). See further *Pitt v Curotta* (1931) 31 SRNSW 477.

2   [1954] 1 QB 476 at 485, per Somervell LJ, and at 492, per Denning LJ (the importance of the contract not being discharged was limited to claims for specific performance); see above, para 19.50.

3   [1954] 1 QB 476 at 490.

4   [1954] 1 QB 476 at 487–488 (explaining away the narrow view taken by Farwell J in *Mussen v Van Diemen's Land Co* [1938] Ch 253 at 266 of *Steedman v Drinkle* [1916] 1 AC 275 (namely that it was based on readiness and willingness to perform and the only reason specific performance was not ordered was that the respondent refused to agree and the terms of the contract made such an order impossible), and noting Farwell J's references to the relevance of unconscionable conduct).

5   [1954] 1 QB 476 at 490 and 492 (citing *Steedman v Drinkle* [1916] 1 AC 275 and disagreeing with the explanation of that case given by Farwell J in *Mussen v Van Diemen's Land Co* [1938] Ch 253 to the effect that the basis of the decision in *Steedman* was that the purchasers were ready and willing to perform – Denning LJ thought that readiness and willingness were essential to specific performance but not relief from forfeiture of sums paid which was the relief granted in *Steedman v Drinkle*. He said: 'The basis of the decision in *Steedman v Drinkle* was, I think, that the vendor had somewhat sharply exercised his right to rescind the contract and retake the land, and it was unconscionable for him also to forfeit the sums already paid').

19.56   In the case itself the majority held that the claim failed on the basis that forfeiture was not unconscionable[1]. Commentators differ as to which statement represents the better view[2]. The narrow view, which appears in part to rest on the maxim that a person who seeks equity must do equity, commands strong support[3]. However, it has been noted that the position of the promisor is merely one factor to be taken into account[4], and the relevance of readiness and willingness to a claim for restitution of payments made (as opposed to a claim to enforce the contract) appears misplaced[5]. It has also been suggested that the view of Romer LJ rests 'on the principle that the law should not interfere with contracts freely made'[6]. In this regard, of course, the concern is not with the mere restitution of payments made, but the general issue of granting relief against forfeiture where a contract has been validly discharged. At present all that can be said is that this issue remains open[7]. If the fate of the claimant requiring restitution of payments forfeited upon discharge properly rests on relief against forfeiture, then the result will ultimately depend upon whether a wide[8] or narrow[9] view is adopted of the discretion to grant relief and the form in which relief may be granted. This may be guided by whether or not it is accepted that relief against forfeiture is in part informed by the principle against unjust enrichment[10]. However, one apparently strong factor limiting relief against forfeiture by way of specific performance concerns the extent to which the court will allow relief against forfeiture to intrude into the certainty of commercial transactions[11]. Arguably that concern would also be just as relevant to recovery of payments made if such recovery is based on relief against forfeiture.

1   [1954] 1 QB 476 at 484, per Somervell LJ, and at 492 per Denning LJ. This was also their explanation of *Mussen v Van Diemen's Land Co* [1938] Ch 253, see [1954] 1 QB 476 at 487, per Somervell LJ, and at 492, per Denning LJ.

2   See Goff and Jones *Law of Restitution* (5th edn, 1998), pp 545 and 546; Treitel *Law of Contract* (10th edn, 1999), pp 939–941; Meagher Gummow and Lehane *Equity: Doctrines and Remedies* (3rd edn, 1992) para 1826–1830; Beatson *Use and Abuse of Unjust Enrichment* (1991), ch 3; Harpum 'Relief Against Forfeiture and the Purchaser of Land' [1984] CLJ 134. See further *Legione v Hateley* (1983) 152 CLR 406 at 443–444, per Mason and Deane JJ; *Scandinavian Trading Tanker Co AB v Flota Petrolera Ecuatoriana* [1983] 2 AC 694 at 702–703; *O'Dea v Allstates Leasing System (WA) Pty Ltd* (1983) 152 CLR 359 at 392; *Esanda Finance Corpn Ltd v Plessing* (1989) 166 CLR 131 at 151.

3   See *Galbraith v Mitchenall Estates Ltd* [1965] 2 QB 473; *Else (1982) Ltd v Parkland Holdings Ltd* [1994] 1 BCLC 130 at 146, per Hoffmann LJ (cf at 139, per Evans LJ, and at 141, per Russell LJ); *Union Eagle Ltd v Golden Achievement Ltd* [1997] AC 514; *Re Hoobin* [1957] VR 341. Cf *Afovos Shipping Co SA v Pagnan & Lli, The Afovos* [1980] 2 Lloyd's Rep 469 (reversed [1982] 1 WLR 848 (CA), [1983] 1 WLR 195, HL); *Shiloh Spinners Ltd v Harding* [1973] AC 691 at 726–727, per Lord Simon of Glaisdale; *Elson v Prices Tailors Ltd* [1963] 1 WLR 287; *Siporex Trade SA v Comdel Commodities Ltd* [1986] 2 Lloyd's Rep 428; *Smyth v Jessup* [1956] VLR 230; *Saunders v Leonardi* (1976) 1 BPR 9409. See also *Starside Properties Ltd v Mustapha* [1974] 1 WLR 816. See further Meagher Gummow and Lehane *Equity: Doctrines and Remedies* (3rd edn, 1992), para 1827.

4   Beatson *Use and Abuse of Unjust Enrichment* (1991), pp 76 and 77.

5   Carter *Breach of Contract* (2nd edn, 1991), para 1259.

6   See Treitel *Law of Contract* (10th edn, 1999), p 940. See also *Bridge v Campbell Discount Co Ltd* [1962] AC 600 at 626, per Lord Radcliffe.

7   See *Scandinavian Trading Tanker Co v Flota Petrolera Ecuatoriana, The Scaptrade* [1983] 2 AC 694 at 702; *Workers Trust and Merchant Bank v Dojap Investments* [1993] AC 573 at 582, per Lord Browne-Wilkinson.

8   See *Shiloh Spinners Ltd v Harding* [1973] AC 691 at 726–727, per Lord Simon of Glaisdale; *BICC plc v Burndy Corpn* [1985] Ch 232 at 251–252, per Dillon LJ, cf at 253, per Kerr LJ. See also *On Demand Information plc v Michael Gerson (Finance) plc* [2001] 1 WLR 155 (appealed on grounds not relevant here, [2002] UKHL 13, [2002] 1 All ER (Comm) 641).

9   See *Scandinavian Trading Tanker Co v Flota Petrolera Ecuatoriana, The Scaptrade* [1983] 2 AC 694 at 702, per Lord Diplock. See also *Sport International Bussum Bv v Inter-Footwear Ltd* [1984] 1 WLR 776; *Else (1982) Ltd v Parkland Holdings Ltd* [1994] 1 BCLC 130 at 145, per Hoffman LJ; *Union Eagle Ltd v Golden Achievement Ltd* [1997] AC 514 at 519, per Lord Hoffmann.

10 See *Stockloser v Johnson* [1954] 1 QB 476 at 492, per Denning LJ; *Union Eagle Ltd v Golden Achievement Ltd* [1997] AC 514 at 523, per Lord Hoffman; *Stern v McArthur* (1988) 165 CLR 489 at 526–527, per Deane and Dawson JJ; *Lexane Pty Ltd v Highfern Pty Ltd* [1985] 1 Qd R 446 at 455, per McPherson J.

11 See *Scandinavian Trading Tanker Co v Flota Petrolera Ecuatoriana, The Scaptrade* [1983] 2 AC 694 at 703–704, per Lord Diplock; *Sport International Bussum Bv v Inter-Footwear Ltd* [1984] 1 WLR 776 at 788; *Union Eagle Ltd v Golden Achievement Ltd* [1997] AC 514 at 523, per Lord Hoffmann. See also *On Demand Information plc v Michael Gerson (Finance) plc* [2001] 1 WLR 155 (appealed on grounds not relevent here, [2002] UKHL 13, [2002] 1 All ER (Comm) 641).

19.57   Moreover, if relief against forfeiture is the proper remedial response to recover instalments, and if relief against forfeiture is to continue to be seen as providing relief against the forfeiture of a proprietary interest, then it will be necessary to accept that contractual rights are sufficiently proprietary for this purpose[1]. Although contractual rights are considered sufficiently proprietary for the purpose of assignment, as between the parties a contract is perhaps considered more obligation than property[2]. At present, English courts have continued to adopt the view that relief against forfeiture is only concerned with the forfeiture of interests in property, and although this has been extended to personal property (such as an interest under a goods lease[3]), there appears at present little scope to extend it further[4].

1   See *Jobson v Johnson* [1989] 1 All ER 621. Cf *Scandinavian Trading Tanker Co v Flota Petrolera Ecuatoriana, The Scaptrade* [1983] 2 AC 694 at 702, per Lord Diplock. See also *Sport International Bussum BV v Inter-Footwear Ltd* [1984] 1 WLR 776, and cf *BICC plc v Burndy Corpn* [1985] Ch 232 at 251–252, per Dillon LJ.
2   Cf 'The Unity of Contract Law' in Benson (ed) *Theory of Contract Law* (2001), ch 4.
3   See *On Demand Information plc v Michael Gerson (Finance) plc* [2001] 1 WLR 155 (appealed on grounds not relevant here, [2002] UKHL 13, [2002] 1 All ER (Comm) 641).
4   Cf *Transag Haulage Ltd v Leyland DAF Finance plc* [1994] 2 BCLC 88, but see the explanation of this case in *On Demand Information plc v Michael Gerson (Finance) plc* [2001] 1 WLR 155 at 170, per Robert Walker LJ. (This point is not affected by the recent appeal to the Lords, [2002] UKHL 13, [2002] 1 All ER (Comm) 641, but see para 29, per Lord Millett.)

19.58   The alternative view is to simply apply the penalty rules. In *Legione v Hateley*, Mason and Deane JJ, after setting out definitions of and distinctions between penalties and forfeiture, said:

> There is, however, a real distinction between 'penalty' and 'forfeiture' and it is unfortunate that the terms have been frequently used in a way which blurs it. The claims made by the purchasers in *Steedman v Drinkle* and *Brickles v Snell* were for relief against the 'forfeiture' of instalments of purchase money ... In this situation, despite the use of the word 'forfeit', relief is granted on the footing that the contractual provision entitling the vendor to retain instalments is in substance a penalty, or in the nature of a penalty, because it is designed to ensure payment of the entire purchase price and it exceeds the damage which he suffers by reason of the purchaser's default[1].

More recently in *Union Eagle Ltd v Golden Achievement Ltd*[2], Lord Hoffmann, delivering the judgment of the Privy Council said:

> The purchaser's loss of the right to specific performance may be said to amount to a forfeiture of the equitable interest which the contract gave him in the land. But this forfeiture is different in its nature from, for example, the vendor's right to retain a deposit or part payments of the purchase price. So far as these retentions exceed a genuine pre-estimate of damage or a reasonable deposit they will constitute a penalty which can be said to be essentially to provide security for payment of the full price. No objectionable uncertainty is created by the existence of a restitutionary form of relief against forfeiture, which gives the court a discretion to order repayment of all or part of the retained money. But the right to rescind the contract, though it involves termination of the purchaser's equitable interest, stands upon a rather different footing. Its purpose is, upon breach of an essential term, to restore to the vendor his freedom to deal with his land as he pleases[3].

There is considerable strength in this approach. Provisions allowing a vendor to retain instalments upon breach by the purchaser are incorporated into contracts as a means of ensuring that payments will be made. In many cases, such clauses pay no regard to the damage suffered by the vendor. In such cases it may be entirely adequate to grant the claimant relief by way of restitution of payments made rather than relief by way of keeping the contract on foot or resurrecting the contract. This is particularly the case where the purchaser is not ready, willing and able to perform. In addition, such an approach appears more doctrinally acceptable, given circumstances where either the contract is validly discharged or where no interest in realty or personalty is involved. Finally, the quotations set out above do not suggest that relief here is anything other than an exercise of equity's jurisdiction to relieve against penalties[4]. Arguably the common law rules as to penalties are entirely appropriate in regards to instalments; however, in the case of deposits, relief must be based on equity's jurisdiction to give relief against penalties[5]. It may be noted, however, in *AMEV-UDC Finance Ltd v Austin*, Mason and Wilson JJ appear to accept that the common law's envelopment of the penalties doctrine has left little residual equitable jurisdiction to relieve against penalties[6]. If correct, and if recovery of deposits is not based on relief against forfeiture, then the recovery of deposits must be treated as being sui generis, because the common law penalty rules do not give a court the level of discretion required. Perhaps this is what the Privy Council was getting at in *Workers Trust*[7].

1   (1983) 152 CLR 406 at 445. See Rossiter *Penalties and Forfeiture* (1992), pp 113 and 114.
2   [1997] AC 514.
3   [1997] AC 514 at 520.
4   See also *O'Dea v Allstates Leasing System (WA) Pty Ltd* (1983) 152 CLR 359 at 391, per Brennan J: 'Although a stipulation as to the price payable for the sale or hiring of goods is not itself in the nature of a penalty, a stipulation which provides for the forfeiture on breach by the buyer or hirer of both the price and the consideration for which it is payable is in the nature of a penalty and equity will relieve against it. The foundation of the jurisdiction to relieve against forfeiture is that the stipulation for the forfeiture is really in the nature of a penalty'.
5   See Rossiter *Penalties and Forfeiture* (1992), pp 113–118.
6   (1986) 162 CLR 170. Cf Lanyon 'Equity and the Doctrine of Penalties' (1996) 9 Journal of Contract Law 234.
7   See above, para 19.47.

C   Claims in respect of non-monetary benefits

19.59   The result of claims made for reasonable remuneration following discharge of contract for breach or repudiation tend to be fairly predictable. Where the claim is made by the party in breach it will usually fail. Where, however, the claim is brought by an innocent party it will usually succeed. Despite this simple demarcation, explaining the case law in this area by reference to the principle against unjust enrichment is problematic, and it is made even more difficult when there is an exception to results just mentioned.

In this section, as in the last, the case law is discussed by reference to the elements of unjust enrichment. Most of the discussion focuses on the issue of benefit. It is here that most of the difficulties arise in explaining the case law by reference to the principle against unjust enrichment.

Benefit – (i) where the claimant is in breach

19.60   Where a defendant contracts for the claimant to perform an entire obligation, then, if the contract is discharged for breach by the claimant at a time when the claimant has only partially performed, the claimant will have no claim to the contract price, and generally will not be able to recover a reasonable remuneration for the work done or services performed[1]. In this section, it is suggested that such claims generally fail because the claimant fails to prove that the defendant has been enriched.

1   When the claimant has express or implied rights under the contract to claim for work done, there is no need to resort to restitution, see *Roberts v Havelock* (1832) 3 B & Ad 404, 110 ER 145.

19.61   Whether or not a contract encapsulates an entire obligation is a matter of construction. Important indicators of entire obligations include the price being payable in a lump sum[1], progress payments not being apportioned to work done, retention monies being held until completion[2] and where payment is not due until the completion of work. However, these are indicators only, and courts lean against construing contracts as encapsulating entire obligations[3]. For example, in *Cutter v Powell*[4], an agreement to pay a sailor well in excess of the common rate evidenced an intention to only pay if the sailor completed the voyage which he failed to do as he died during the voyage. Without such an agreement it has been suggested that a modern court is likely to take the view that the forfeiture which operates against the part performer together with the enrichment of the recipient 'is too high a price to pay for an incentive to contract performance'[5]. On the other hand, the Law Commission has suggested that the courts have been too quick to presume that a contract encapsulates an entire obligation where payment is postponed under a lump sum contract[6].

1   See *Sumpter v Hedges* [1898] 1 QB 673. Cf *Hoenig v Isaacs* [1952] 2 All ER 176 at 180, per Denning LJ.
2   *Hoenig v Isaacs* [1952] 2 All ER 176 at 181, per Denning LJ.
3   *Hoenig v Isaacs* [1952] 2 All ER 176 at 180, per Denning LJ. In 1867 Blackburn J said: 'Bricks built into a wall become part of the house; thread stitched into a coat which is under repair or planks or nails or pitch worked into a ship, under repair, become part of the coat, or the ship; and therefore, generally and in the absence of something to show to the contrary intention, the bricklayer, or tailor, or shipwright, is to be paid for the work and materials he has done and provided, although the work is not complete. It is not material whether in such a case the non-completion is because the shipwright did not choose to go on with the work ... or because in consequence of a fire he could not go on with it ... But, though this is the prima facie contract between those who enter into contracts for doing work and supplying materials, there is nothing to render it either illegal or absurd in the workman to agree to complete the whole, and be paid when the whole is complete and not till then' (*Appleby v Myers* (1867) LR 2 CP 651). See also the Apportionment Act 1870 and para 19.81.
4   (1795) 6 TR 320, 101 ER 573.
5   Waddams 'Restitution for the Part Performer' in Reiter and Swan *Studies in Contract Law* (1980), p 63.
6   Law Commission *Law of Contract: Pecuniary Restitution on Breach of Contract* Law Com no 121 (1983), paras 2.1, 2.11, 2.16, 2.24, 2.32, 2.35 and 2.66–2.69.

'SUBJECTIVE DEVALUATION'

19.62   In terms of unjust enrichment theory, the reason why a claimant in breach of contract generally fails in their claim for restitution is because the defendant can subjectively devalue the claimant's provision of services even where such provision is in partial performance of the contract[1]. That is, even if the claimant's partial performance results in the receipt of an objective benefit, the defendant can maintain the position that that benefit was not what he or she agreed to pay for, and it is therefore of no benefit to him or her[2]. Thus, the claimant fails to prove an enrichment.

In a broader sense, subjective devaluation is based on the premise that a person cannot be enriched unless they had an opportunity to reject the benefit received[3]. The broader view overlaps with free acceptance which is discussed below[4]. However, it may be noted at this point that the onus of proof for each of these is distinct, as the function of free acceptance is to prevent recourse to subjective devaluation[5].

The adoption of a subjective approach to the notion of enrichment, which is encapsulated in the idea of 'subjective devaluation', gives effect to the general principle that bargains are to be upheld. Without an overriding factor the claimant should not be able to rely on an objective benefit to circumvent the bargain struck by the parties.

1   On subjective devaluation see Birks *An Introduction to the Law of Restitution* (revised edn, 1989), pp 109–114. See also *Ministry of Defence v Ashman* [1993] 40 EG 144 at 147, per Hoffmann LJ.
2   See further para 19.67.
3   See *Ministry of Defence v Ashman* [1993] 40 EG 144 at 147, per Hoffmann LJ. See also the discussion in Virgo *Principles of the Law of Restitution* (1999), pp 64–67.
4   See below, para 19.65.
5   See further Virgo *Principles of the Law of Restitution* (1999), pp 84 and 85.

'INCONTROVERTIBLE BENEFIT', FREE ACCEPTANCE AND 'BARGAINED-FOR BENEFIT'

19.63   In certain circumstances, a claimant in breach of contract will succeed in claiming reasonable remuneration. That is, circumstances may arise which remove the claimant's right to remuneration from the exact conditions of the contract, by preventing the defendant from resorting to subjective devaluation. The first such circumstance is where the defendant is incontrovertibly benefited[1]. The two principal (and alternative) arguments put forward to explain the rest of the cases that allow the party in breach to successfully claim restitution are 'free acceptance' and 'bargained-for benefit'. The existence of successful actions by claimants in breach of contract shows that, simply because a person contracts on the basis of an entire obligation, does not mean they have necessarily contracted out of any right to restitution. However, except for certain instances of incontrovertible benefit, any claim is to a large extent dependent upon the conduct of the defendant[2].

1   See above, para 19.64.
2   See Goff and Jones *Law of Restitution* (5th edn, 1998), pp 513 and 514. See further para 19.73.

19.64   As noted earlier, a receipt of money is a clear example of incontrovertible benefit[1]. In the case of a non-monetary enrichment, an incontrovertible benefit may arise where the alleged 'benefit' is later realised in money[2] or where the claimant confers 'a benefit on the defendant which was necessary to the defendant in the sense that he would have had to seek it himself or would have sought it if he had not been deprived of the opportunity'[3], for example, the discharge of a necessary expense[4]. However, it has also been suggested that a payment in the face of the defendant's factual necessity (rather than legal necessity) may also suffice[5]. Goff and Jones suggest that a defendant should be considered incontrovertibly benefited if a reasonable person would conclude that, in consequence of the claimant's actions, he or she has made a realisable financial gain[6]. Burrows suggests that a defendant should be considered incontrovertibly benefited where a court 'regards it as reasonably certain that he will realise the positive benefit'[7].

A detailed description and critique of 'free acceptance' and 'bargained-for benefit' is beyond the scope of this chapter. However, a few points may be noted for what follows.

1   See above, para 19.6.
2   Cf *Steele v Tardiani* (1946) 72 CLR 386 at 394, per Latham CJ; *Forman & Co Pty Ltd v The Liddesdale* [1900] AC 190. See further para 19.104.

3   Birks *An Introduction to the Law of Restitution* (revised edn, 1989), p 117.
4   See *Monks v Poynice Pty Ltd* (1987) 11 ACLR 637 at 640. See further Birks *An Introduction to the Law of Restitution* (revised edn, 1989), p 120.
5   Birks *An Introduction to the Law of Restitution* (revised edn, 1989), pp 118 and 119.
6   Goff and Jones *Law of Restitution* (5th edn, 1998), pp 22 and 23. See also *Marston Construction Co Ltd v Kigass Ltd* (1989) 15 Con LR 116 at 129, per Judge Bowsher QC.
7   Burrows *Law of Restitution* (1993), p 10.

19.65   Although later refining the concept[1], Birks has proposed that a 'free acceptance occurs where a recipient knows that a benefit is being offered to him non-gratuitously and where he, having the opportunity to reject, elects to accept'[2]. It therefore focuses on the conduct of the defendant. The main elements are an opportunity to reject[3], knowledge of a non-gratuitous intent[4] and a failure to reject the benefit in circumstances whereby responsibility is shifted to the defendant[5]. There is no requirement that the defendant actually value the benefit[6], as free acceptance is merely aimed at preventing recourse to subjective devaluation, and probably assumes the existence of an objective benefit[7]. However, free acceptance does not necessarily require an increase in the wealth of the defendant[8], or for the objective benefit to be vested in the defendant[9]. Moreover, pure services may be the subject of a free acceptance even though they leave no marketable residuum[10]. In addition, at least in the context of a discharged contract, it is not sufficient evidence of enrichment that the performance rendered was requested. If that were not the case then, unless 'request' is limited to cases where the claimant has fully carried out the required performance, (which is never going to be the case where the claim is made by the party in breach) any act done, so long as it was in part performance of the contract, would amount to an enrichment – which is not the law[11]. Given the existence of cases that may be explained by reference to free acceptance, it would appear that a request is neither necessary nor sufficient to justify a claim in the context of this section[12].

1   Birks 'In Defence of Free Acceptance' in Burrows (ed) *Essays on the Law of Restitution* (1991), ch 5. See also Birks *Restitution – The Future* (1992), pp 53–58. Much of Birks' reasoning for refining this definition flows from his adoption of failure of consideration as a general basis for restitution which is not limited to claims for the repayment of money. The adoption of failure of consideration overcame what he saw as a limitation on free acceptance, namely that it required an initial unconscientious receipt which will not exist in many requested and unrequested provision of services cases. This allowed him to broaden his notion of enrichment and instead of explaining away failed claims on the basis of a lack of evidence of enrichment they could be explained on the ground that there was no failure of consideration, that is, no basis for restitution. It is suggested later that failure of consideration should not be and has not been extended in this manner and for the purposes of this chapter, Birks' original formulation of free acceptance in adopted: see para 19.99. However, in regards to the requirement of an unconscientious receipt, it may be noted that the concept of 'acceptance' in the context of sale of goods applies even though the buyer may intend to pay for the goods at the moment of initial receipt. The issue as to whether a buyer must pay for non-conforming goods depends on whether it has accepted the goods in the sense of electing to retain the goods. Arguably if the focus in relation to sale of goods is not limited to receipt but encompasses retention, there is no overwhelming reason to so limit claims for reasonable remuneration for services. See further para 19.66.
2   Birks *An Introduction to the Law of Restitution* (revised edn, 1989), p 265. Goff and Jones suggest that a person 'will be held to have benefited from the services rendered if he, as a reasonable man, should have known that the plaintiff who rendered the services expected to be paid for them, and yet he did not take a reasonable opportunity open to him to reject the proffered services. Moreover, in such a case, he cannot deny that he has been *unjustly* enriched': Goff and Jones *Law of Restitution* (5th edn, 1998), p 18. The great merit of this description, it is suggested, is that it allows acceptance to be determined as matter of law from the facts of the case rather than being linked or limited to unconscionable or reprehensible conduct.
3   Birks *An Introduction to the Law of Restitution* (revised edn, 1989), p 280. See *Sumpter v Hedges* [1898] 1 QB 673 at 676, per Collins LJ; *Leigh v Dickeson* (1884) 15 QBD 60 at 64–65, per Brett

MR; *Boyd and Forrest v Glasgow and South-Western Rly Co* 1915 SC (HL) 20 at 25–26, per Lord Atkinson. Examples where there was no opportunity to reject include *Cutter v Powell* (1795) 6 Term Rep 320; *Forman & Co Pty Ltd v The Liddesdale* [1900] AC 190; *Whitaker v Dunn* (1887) 3 TLR 602; *Munro v Butt* (1858) 8 E & B 738, 120 ER 275. Cf *Steele v Tardiani* (1946) 72 CLR 386.

4 Birks *An Introduction to the Law of Restitution* (revised edn, 1989), p 281. See *Way v Latilla* [1937] 3 All ER 759 at 763, per Lord Atkin; *Liebe v Molloy* (1906) 4 CLR 347 at 354, per Griffith CJ; *Update Constructions Pty Ltd v Rozelle Child Care Centre Ltd* (1990) 20 NSWLR 251 at 272, per Priestley JA. See further *Lawford v Billericay RDC* [1903] 1 KB 772; *Falcke v Scottish Imperial Insurance Co* (1886) 34 Ch D 234 at 249, per Bowen LJ.

5 Birks *An Introduction to the Law of Restitution* (revised edn, 1989), p 283. See generally *Lamb v Bunce* (1815) 4 M & S 275, 105 ER 836; *Weatherby v Banham* (1832) 5 C & P 228, 172 ER 950. The extent of action required to reject the performance proffered will depend on the facts; see *Wiluszynski v Tower Hamlets London Borough Council* [1989] ICR 493 (although no claim for restitution was made here, the decision is instructive).

6 See *Brenner v First Artists' Management Pty Ltd* [1993] 2 VLR 221. It has been suggested that if free acceptance is evidenced, that is not the end of the enrichment issue. It is still possible for the defendant to prove 'that he has not been enriched because he was indifferent or perverse or because he had "more important things on which to spend his money"': see Jones 'The Law of Restitution: The Past and the Future' in Burrows (ed) *Essays on the Law of Restitution* (1991), p 5.

7 See Virgo *Principles of the Law of Restitution* (1999), p 85.

8 See para 19.65, n 10.

9 See further Law Com no 121 *Law of Contract: Pecuniary Restitution on Breach of Contract* (1983), para 2.47. Where the contract is divisible and the claimant in breach has substantially or fully performed a severable part, they will have a claim under the contract in respect of that part: see *Roberts v Havelock* (1832) 3 B & Ad 404, 110 ER 145. See also *Hoenig v Isaacs* [1952] 2 All ER 176 at 180, per Denning LJ; *Taylor v Laird* (1856) 25 LJ Ex 329; *Button v Thompson* (1869) LR 4 CP 330; *Warburton v Heyworth* (1880) 6 QBD 1. It is suggested that in such circumstances the claimant should be limited to their contract claim. Full or substantial performance should not be equated with free acceptance in contracts discharged for breach or repudiation.

10 Cf Beatson *Use and Abuse of Unjust Enrichment* (1991), ch 2. See also Grantham and Rickett *Enrichment and Restitution in New Zealand* (2000), p 61 (the authors here suggest that claims in respect of pure services leaving no market residuum are best interpreted as actions for compensation rather than restitution because they do not constitute restorable enrichments; however, they accept that where services result in a marketable end product this may be the subject of a restitution claim but the enrichment is the end product and the quantification of that enrichment must be based on the value of the end product and not the value of the services; there is no doubt that the law could have taken a course whereby claims for the value of services were treated as compensatory claims; moreover, the position taken by the authors is both a logical and inevitable result of their thesis that restitution involves a restoration; however, there are numerous authorities where despite services resulting in an end product the restitutionary claim was quantified by reference to the value of the services rendered; it therefore appears that the law has adopted a course whereby services may count as an enrichment and if that is the case with services resulting in an end product there is no reason to leave out services which leave no market residuum). See further para 19.107.

11 See further Goff and Jones *Law of Restitution* (5th ed, 1998), p 18.

12 Cf as to claims brought by the party not in breach, para 19.90.

19.66   The role of acceptance in unjust enrichment in England is still unclear[1]. However, the concept does form part of Australian law[2]. In addition, although the phrase 'free acceptance' has not been used historically[3], its elements have been mentioned in various decisions[4].

Free acceptance is both a test for enrichment and a ground for restitution[5]. According to Birks' reformulation of the concept[6], it satisfies the benefit requirement because, if made out, it prevents the defendant having recourse to subjective devaluation, on the basis that such recourse would be unconscionable. As an unjust factor, free acceptance focuses on the defendant's conduct and state of mind, that is, the unconscientiousness of receipt[7].

The alternative principle was put forward by Burrows[8]. He has argued that for a successful claim there must first be evidence of an objective benefit by which he means *actual receipt* of something that can be realised in money. The mere commencement of performance will not suffice, except in the case of pure services[9]. Once an objective benefit is in evidence, then subjective devaluation may be rebutted if the defendant bargained for the objective benefit, 'thereby manifesting a positive desire, and willingness to pay for it'[10]. In his view the receipt of even part of the bargained-for performance must count at law as a benefit for the purposes of unjust enrichment[11]. Burrows goes a step further, and suggests that even where no objective benefit has been received, but the defendant subjectively values the performance, the 'bargained-for' benefit test may be used to subjectively overvalue something that has no objective value. Although he does not advocate this step, he suggests that it can be used to explain those cases where restitution has been granted despite the defendant not being in receipt of an objective benefit.

It is suggested that despite its formulation still being uncertain, free acceptance is better at explaining and predicting the results in cases than the bargained-for benefit test. The latter test encapsulates Burrows' view that certain cases (especially those not allowing recovery despite acts of partial performance[12], which still represent the law), should be overruled. One of the criticisms Burrows levels at 'free acceptance' is that its dual role of determining the existence of an enrichment, as well as being a basis for restitution makes it the 'odd man out'[13]. However, the alternative 'bargained-for benefit' test has its genesis as an expression used to explain the concept of failure of consideration[14]. This forms part of Burrows' larger scheme, to broaden the application 'failure of consideration' as a ground for restitution[15]. However, it appears that Burrows has suggested that a defendant will have received a benefit if they have received *any part* of the agreed performance[16] (whether or not there was any agreement to pay for that part performance), and a defendant is liable to make restitution if in that circumstance they have not given any part of the agreed performance. Thus it would appear that he has given consideration (in the sense used in the 'failure of consideration' concept) a dual role.

1   See *Craven-Ellis v Cannons Ltd* [1936] 2 KB 403 at 410, per Greer LJ. Cf *Way v Latilla* [1937] 3 All ER 759 at 765, per Lord Atkin; *Bridgewater v Griffiths* [2000] 1 WLR 524 at 532, per Burton J. See, however, the reference to Bullen and Leake *Precedents of Pleadings* (3rd edn, 1868) at para 19.75 suggesting 'acceptance' has been relevant to quasi-contract for over a century.

2   *Pavey & Matthews Pty Ltd v Paul* (1987) 162 CLR 221 at 227–228, per Mason and Wilson JJ, and at 257 and 262–263, per Deane J; *Horton v Jones* (1934) 34 SRNSW 356 at 367–368, per Jordan CJ; *Hansen v Mayfair Trading Co Pty Ltd* [1962] WAR 148; *Update Constructions Pty Ltd v Rozelle Child Care Centre Ltd* (1990) 20 NSWLR 251; *Strang Patrick Stevedoring Pty Ltd v Owners of MV Sletter* (1992) 38 FCR 501; *Brenner v First Artists' Management Pty Ltd* [1993] 2 VR 221; *Iezzi Constructions Pty Ltd v Watkins Pacific (Qld) Pty Ltd* [1995] 2 Qd R 350. See also Mason and Carter *Restitution Law in Australia* (1995), paras 216–218 and 933–934, Byrne 'Benefits – For Services Rendered' in McInnes (ed) *Restitution: Developments in Unjust Enrichment* (1996), ch 5; cf Garner 'Benefits – For Services Rendered: Commentary' in McInnes (ed) *Restitution: Developments in Unjust Enrichment* (1996), ch 6; McInnes 'Free Acceptance in the Australian Law of Restitution' (1996) 24 ABLR 238.

3   See Birks 'In Defence of Free Acceptance' in Burrows (ed) *Essays on the Law of Restitution* (1991), pp 105–109. Cf Burrows 'Free Acceptance and the Law of Restitution' (1988) 104 LQR 576 (reprinted as Burrows *Understanding the Law of Obligations* (1998), ch 4).

4   See above, para 19.65, nn 3–5. It may be noted that in the context of sale of goods, the original rule was that if the seller tendered goods which the buyer was entitled to reject, because they were not of the contract description, a decision by the buyer to accept the goods led to liability in quasi-contract, not contract, see *Mondel v Steel* (1841) 8 M & W 858 at 870–871, 151 ER 1288 at 1293; *Munro v Butt* (1858) 8 E & B 738 at 752, 120 ER 275 at 280. The sale of goods legislation replaced the quasi-contractual basis with the right to recover a contract debt. Cf the position where there is a major discrepency between the goods contracted for and the goods accepted, see *Suisse Atlantique Société d'Armement Maritime SA v NV Rotterdamsche Kolen Centrale* [1967] 1 AC 361 at 404; Reynolds 'Warranty, Condition and Fundamental Term' (1963) 79 LQR 534 at 550. Acceptance here may result in a new contract or application of restitutionary principles.

5 See Birks *An Introduction to the Law of Restitution* (revised edn, 1989), pp 115 and 116 for a discussion on why these dual roles may require two separate sets of requirements.
6 See para 19.65, n 1.
7 See above para 19.65, n 1, arguably it could be extended to retention. See above para 19.65, n 1, and query whether it should focus on unconscionable conduct.
8 Burrows 'Free Acceptance and the Law of Restitution' (1988) 104 LQR 576 (reprinted as Burrows *Understanding the Law of Obligations* (1998), ch 4). For further criticism of free acceptance see Beatson *Use and Abuse of Unjust Enrichment* (1991), ch 2; Garner 'The Role of Subjective Benefit in the Law of Unjust Enrichment' (1990) 10 OJLS 42; Simester 'Unjust Free Acceptance' [1997] Lloyds Maritime and Commercial Law Quarterly 103; Grantham and Rickett *Enrichment and Restitution in New Zealand* (2000), ch 11.
9 Burrows *Law of Restitution* (1993), pp 8 and 9.
10 Burrows *Law of Restitution* (1993), p 12.
11 Burrows *Law of Restitution* (1993), pp 12 and 262. Garner has identified a gap in logic here. Although a person could not deny that they have been benefited if they receive full performance, it does not follow that they could not deny receiving a benefit in the case of partial performance: 'The Role of Subjective Benefit in the Law of Unjust Enrichment' (1990) 10 OJLS 42 at 53.
12 See para 19.68.
13 Burrows 'Free Acceptance and the Law of Restitution' (1988) 104 LQR 576 at 598 (reprinted in Burrows *Understanding the Law of Obligations* (1998), p 97). See also Burrows *Law of Restitution* (1993), p 13.
14 See *Stocznia Gdanska SA v Latvian Shipping Co* [1998] 1 WLR 574 at 599–600, per Lord Lloyd; *Rover International Ltd v Cannon Film Sales Ltd (No 3)* [1989] 1 WLR 912 at 923, per Kerr LJ. See further, *Baltic Shipping Co v Dillon, The Mikhail Lermontov* (1993) 176 CLR 344 at 351, per Mason CJ; *David Securities Pty Ltd v Commonwealth Bank of Australia* (1992) 175 CLR 353 at 381–383.
15 See para 19.19.
16 Assuming performance satisfies his requirement of an objective benefit.

THE PRIMACY OF CONSTRUCTION – *SUMPTER V HEDGES*

19.67   The leading case in respect of claims brought by a party in breach is *Sumpter v Hedges*[1]. In that case, the claimant builder abandoned work after only partially completing construction on the defendant's land under a lump sum building contract. The contract price was £565. The work completed had a value of £333, and part of the price had been paid by instalments. No claim could have been brought under the contract, as it was an entire contract and the claimant had not completely performed the necessary condition precedent to recover the price. The claimant's claim for reasonable remuneration was refused, although he was successful in his claim in respect of loose materials he had left on the property, and which the defendant has used to finish the job[2].

At the time the decision was handed down, the theory of implied contract governed restitutionary claims. The court's reason for refusing the claim was that there was no evidence of a fresh contract to pay for the work done[3]. However, if the strict reasoning of the case is put aside but the result taken as correct, then the lesson to be learned from the case, so far as modern restitution is concerned, would appear to be that in determining whether or not a defendant (who is innocent of breach of contract) has received a benefit, the construction of the contract is important. If the contract involves an entire obligation, then partial performance of that obligation by the party in breach will not in itself mean that the defendant is enriched. The reason for this appears to be that, despite the existence of an objective benefit, the defendant can subjectively devalue that benefit. That is, the law allows the defendant to resort to the terms of the contract to argue that the benefit received is not what he or she agreed to pay for. Moreover, on the broader view of subjective devaluation[4], clearly in this case, except in regards to the use of the loose materials, the defendant had no opportunity to reject the work done.

This last point is important, because it was argued by counsel that the facts in *Sumpter v Hedges* were distinct from earlier authority[5], as the defendant had completed the structure. This was put forward as evidence of a fresh contract to pay for the work done. This argument was rejected, on the basis that the mere retaining of possession of land was not sufficient evidence to infer a fresh contract[6]. Moreover, it was said that the fact the defendant completed the works afforded no grounds for such an inference, as the defendant was not bound to keep an unfinished building on his land[7]. Collins LJ said that it was only 'where the circumstances are such as to give an option to the defendant to take or not to take the benefit of the work done' that such an inference may arise[8].

1   [1898] 1 QB 673. See also *Spain v Arnott* (1817) 2 Stark 256, 171 ER 638; *Huttman v Boulnois The Younger* (1826) 2 C & P 510, 172 ER 231; *Turner v Robinson* (1833) 5 B & Ad 789, 110 ER 982; *Ridgway v Hungerford Market Co* (1835) 3 AD & El 171; *Lamburn v Cruden* (1841) 2 Man & G 253, 133 ER 741; *Lilley v Elwin* (1848) 11 QB 742, 116 ER 652; *Hopper v Burness* (1876) 1 CPD 137; *Whitaker v Dunn* (1887) 3 TLR 602; *Wheeler v Stratton* (1911) 105 LT 786. In the context of frustration, see *Appleby v Myers* (1867) LR 2 CP 651.
2   See para 19.73.
3   [1898] 1 QB 673 at 674, per AL Smith LJ, at 675, per Chitty LJ, and at 676, per Collins LJ. See further Carter 'Discharged Contracts: Claims for Restitution' (1997) 11 Journal of Contract Law 130 at 132 and 133.
4   See para 19.62.
5   *Munro v Butt* (1858) 8 E & B 738, 120 ER 275. See also *Whitaker v Dunn* (1887) 3 TLR 602.
6   [1898] 1 QB 673 at 675–676, per Chitty LJ. See also *Pattinson v Luckley* (1875) LR 10 Ex Ch 330 at 334, per Bramwell B, and *Munro v Butt* (1858) 8 E & B 738, 120 ER 275. It would be different in the case of a chattel which can be readily rejected. See further *Boyd and Forrest v Glasgow and South-Western Rly Co* 1915 SC (HL) 20 at 25–26, per Lord Atkinson.
7   [1898] 1 QB 673 at 676, per Collins LJ.
8   [1898] 1 QB 673 at 676, per Collins LJ. Interestingly, Collins LJ (at 676) also said that if the builder had 'merely broken his contract in some way so as not to give the defendant the right to treat him as having abandoned the contract, and the defendant has then proceeded to finish the work himself, the plaintiff might perhaps have been entitled to sue on a quantum meruit on the ground that the defendant had taken the benefit of the work done'. See further Stoljar 'Substantial Performance in Building and Works Contracts' (1954–1956) 3 WALR 293 at 303, and *Williamson v Murdoch* (1912) 14 WALR 54.

19.68   To change the result in *Sumpter v Hedges* at a doctrinal level, should it be considered too harsh[1], would require the adoption of a more objective assessment of benefit. Burrows, as his 'bargained-for benefit' test would indicate, has advocated such a move. He suggests that *Sumpter v Hedges* should not be followed, as it could not be denied that the defendant was enriched by being saved an expense in relation to the buildings[2]. That is, the innocent party received part of what he bargained for and thus can be presumed to have been negatively benefited, even if the expense saved was not necessary. This presumption would be rebutted 'if at the time of the dispute it was as expensive to complete the building as the original full contract price ... Similarly if the defendant says that the half building is of no use to him and does not in fact go on to make use of it ... the presumption ... could be rebutted'[3]. In turn, he suggests that the basis for restitution in such a case would be failure of consideration[4]. The counter argument, that to allow restitution in such circumstances would encourage breach of contract, he suggests ignores the fact that the claimant is still liable to pay expectation damages. Moreover, he argues that such a damages claim should be capable of being set off against the claim for restitution[5].

Birks originally adhered to the construction argument set out above[6], but later (after accepting failure of consideration as a ground for restitution in claims for reasonable remuneration)[7] made the concession that 'it is easier to conclude that one who asked for a whole house to be built cannot conscientiously say that three-quarters of a house should be regarded as valueless to him ... In other words, the claimant builder in *Sumpter v Hedges* should not be regarded as having lost on the ground that the defendant was not enriched'[8]. Birks views the decision as correct, but on the basis that no ground for restitution existed[9].

1   Cf *Munro v Butt* (1858) 8 E & B 738 at 754, 120 ER 275 at 280 ('there is neither hardship not injustice in the rule with its qualifications: it holds men to their contracts; it admits, from circumstances, the substitution of new contracts').
2   Burrows 'Free Acceptance and the Law of Restitution' (1988) 104 LQR 576 at 589–590 (reprinted in Burrows *Understanding the Law of Obligations* (1998), ch 4, pp 87 and 88). See also Burrows *Law of Restitution* (1993), pp 276 and 277.
3   Burrows *Law of Restitution* (1993), p 277. See further Derham *Set off* (2nd edn, 1996), paras 1.7.1–1.7.2.
4   See below, para 19.99. However, instalments of the purchase price had been made which would have prevented recovery on the basis of total failure of consideration.
5   Burrows *Law of Restitution* (1993), p 277.
6   Birks *An Introduction to the Law of Restitution* (1989), pp 231 and 233.
7   See para 19.100.
8   Birks 'In Defence of Free Acceptance' in Burrows (ed) *Essays on the Law of Restitution* (1991), p 140.
9   Birks 'In Defence of Free Acceptance' in Burrows (ed) *Essays on the Law of Restitution* (1991), pp 113 and 114. See further para 19.100.

19.69   There is therefore a difference of opinion as to whether *Sumpter v Hedges* should remain the law, and if it should, whether the claim failed on the issue of enrichment or due to a lack of a basis for restitution. Clearly, for the moment, *Sumpter v Hedges* represents the law. Moreover, it is suggested that the real problem for the claimant in that case, so far as the modern law of unjust enrichment is concerned, is a lack of evidence of benefit. By allowing the defendant to subjectively devalue the performance rendered, the allocation of risk between the parties is upheld, as there was no agreement to pay for the work done. Without an overriding reason, that allocation of risk should not be circumvented by the law of unjust enrichment[1]. It is suggested that the level of intervention into that risk allocation advocated by Burrows goes too far. However, one area where there may be sufficient injustice to intervene is where the claimant's performance falls short of substantial performance, but only a small amount is required to be expended to bring the claimant's performance into accordance with the contract, and where that amount is expended by the defendant in that manner. However, even in that case the claimant has merely performed part of the contract, and partial performance alone does not prevent recourse to subjective devaluation. Perhaps the better approach here is to relax the doctrine of substantial performance. It may be noted in this regard that Goff and Jones also favour a refining of the result in *Sumpter v Hedges*, to allow for recovery where the value of the benefit conferred is out of all proportion to the loss suffered by the innocent party[2].

1   See *Munro v Butt* (1858) 8 E & B 738 at 754, 120 ER 275 at 280, per Lord Campbell LJ. Cf para 19.36. See further Mason 'Restitution in Australian Law' in Finn (ed) *Essays on Restitution* (1990), pp 43–45 (suggesting that an entire contract may only prohibit recovery under the contract at contract rates in default of entire or substantial performance).
2   Goff and Jones *Law of Restitution* (5th edn, 1998), p 553.

19.70   It should also be noted that the result in *Sumpter v Hedges* was not as harsh as may appear. Despite being a lump sum contract, substantial instalments of the price were paid, and these were not recoverable[1]. Moreover, most substantial contracts make provision for progress payments. Any reform of this rule will mainly affect small contracts where the employer's only real sanction and bargaining tool is that they can refuse to pay if the contractor does not complete the job[2].

1   See the discussion in Treitel *Law of Contract* (10th edn, 1999), p 760, n 17.
2   See Davenport's 'Note of Dissent' in Law Com 121 *Law of Contract: Pecuniary Restitution on Breach of Contract* (1983), pp 36 and 37, cf paras 2.29–2.31. The Law Commission itself was of the view that the weakening of the employer's bargaining position was exaggerated as they are entitled to damages for failure to complete and for inconvenience. This is a remarkable position for a law reform body to take, namely, to leave the employer (usually a householder) with a remedy that requires them to commence court proceedings which, due to the costs involved, they will invariably not do and take away from them what is in effect a self help remedy, that is, withhold payment. See further para 19.71.

19.71   Reform of *Sumpter v Hedges*   Academic commentators have not been alone in their concern about the result in cases like *Sumpter v Hedges*. The application by the courts of substantial performance to entire obligations perhaps evidences a judicial concern[1]. The Law Commission has also advocated a change in the law[2]. In its report, *Law of Contract: Pecuniary Restitution on Breach of Contract*, Law Com no 121 (1983), it recommended that in the case of advance payments made to a party in breach, the law should remain as is, so that the claimant can only recover if there is a total failure of consideration[3]. However, in the case of non-monetary benefits provided in performance of the contract, the Commission concluded that 'a new remedy should be provided for the party in breach (including, of course, his assignees) where he or a third party acting on his behalf has conferred a benefit on the innocent party by his incomplete or defective performance of an entire contract'[4]. In valuing the defendant's enrichment it was recommended that the contract price be put aside[5]. However, once that valuation process is carried out, the sum awarded is reduced, if necessary, so as not to exceed 'such proportion of the sum payable on completion as is equal to the proportion that what has been done under the contract bears to what was promised to be done'[6]. It was also recommended that the sum payable be decreased or extinguished by the damages which the other party may be entitled to[7]. Moreover, the Law Commission was of the view that the parties could contract out of this remedy by clearly placing the risk on the party in breach. However, merely expressing the consideration as a lump sum, or postponing payment until completion, was not sufficient evidence of such an intention[8]. The recommendations were intended to apply to each severable part of a contract, where each such part encapsulates an entire obligation[9]. However, the proposals were not intended 'to apply to severable parts of contracts where the instalments became due on specific dates (or on the happening of specific events), where the instalments are fixed regardless of the amount or value of the work done, or where the amount to be paid is related to the work which actually has been done'[10].

1   See below, para 19.79.
2   For a discussion on the Law Commission's preliminary views in its Working Paper No 65, see Birks *An Introduction to the Law of Restitution* (revised edn, 1989), pp 259 and 260. On the report itself see Burrows 'Law Commission Report on *Pecuniary Restitution on Breach of Contract*' (1984) 47 MLR 76.
3   Law Com 121 *Law of Contract: Pecuniary Restitution on Breach of Contract* (1983), paras 3.8–3.11.
4   Law Com 121 *Law of Contract: Pecuniary Restitution on Breach of Contract* (1983), para 2.33. As to when a benefit is conferred under the recommendations see above, paras 2.47–2.49.
5   Law Com 121 *Law of Contract: Pecuniary Restitution on Breach of Contract* (1983), para 2.52. The Commission recommended that where the cost of the services exceeds the value of the end product only the value of the end product should be recoverable where there has been a breach. It was reasoned that the party in breach should carry this loss. However, where the end product is worth more than the cost of the services it was said that 'there should be an upper limit so that the

party in breach cannot be better off as a result of the partial performance than he would have been had he completely performed the contract ... [W]hat is being valued is the benefit obtained ... Since our purpose in providing a remedy is to reflect the enrichment of the innocent party, it is the relevant measure of compensation and the value of the benefit should not be based on the contract price'.

6 Law Com no 121 *Law of Contract: Pecuniary Restitution on Breach of Contract* (1983), para 2.53.
7 Law Com no 121 *Law of Contract: Pecuniary Restitution on Breach of Contract* (1983), para 2.56. See also paras 2.61–2.65 as to the relevance of exclusion clauses in determining the amount of damages to be set off. As to the date when value is to be assessed, see para 2.56.
8 Law Com no 121 *Law of Contract: Pecuniary Restitution on Breach of Contract* (1983), paras 2.35 and 2.66–2.69.
9 Law Com no 121 *Law of Contract: Pecuniary Restitution on Breach of Contract* (1983), para 2.77.
10 Law Com no 121 *Law of Contract: Pecuniary Restitution on Breach of Contract* (1983), para 2.80. See also paras 2.81 and 2.82 as to retention funds.

19.72   The basis of the Law Commission's reasoning was that the current legal position was capable of giving a result that has a penal flavour. Thus it should not be lightly assumed that this is what the parties intended merely by agreeing to a postponement of payment. The Commission recommended that such a provision:

... should not by itself preclude the party in breach from recovering an amount which reflects any enrichment which the innocent party has obtained as a result of having had a benefit conferred on him under the contract by the partial performance. [However,] any change in the present law which would entitle the builder to make a claim in respect of the work he has done would, in effect, only entitle him to recover money from the householder where the latter received a significant benefit which exceeds the loss which he has suffered as a result of the breach[1].

1 Law Com no 121 *Law of Contract: Pecuniary Restitution on Breach of Contract* (1983), paras 2.28 and 2.31.

EXCEPTIONS TO CONSTRUCTION – THE ACTIONS OR CONDUCT OF THE DEFENDANT

19.73   As noted above[1], a defendant will be prevented from subjectively devaluing the claimant's provision of services if they have accepted the services rendered, or if they have been incontrovertibly benefited.

Clearly, in cases such as *Sumpter v Hedges*, because the work is carried out on the defendant's land, and is a fixture, it is difficult to find evidence of any conduct of the defendant that would equate to free acceptance[2]. The defendant has no opportunity to reject the work[3]. However, in that case the owner was required to pay for the loose materials the builder had left on the site, and which the owner chose to use in order to complete the buildings. This claim can be rationalised on the basis of free acceptance[4]. In *Forman & Co Pty Ltd v The Liddesdale*[5], the claimants, an Australian company, contracted with the agent of a ship owner to effect certain repairs after the ship had run aground off Western Australia. The owner had authorised the agent to organise the ship to be repaired, but limited that authority to that required to repair the stranding damage, and later further limited the agent's authority to a certain amount[6]. In an action for payment[7], the claimant pointed out that they had carried out work equivalent to or better than that required by the contract, and that this had been done on the agent's authority. It was held that they were aware of the agent's limited authority, and as the contract was entire and they had not entirely performed it, they could not recover under the contract[8]. Moreover, the fact the ship owner had taken the ship and later sold it did not amount to a ratification of the agent's act. Clearly the owner had no opportunity to reject the work done on its own ship. Usually, in practice, it will be easier to prove that the defendant had an opportunity to reject in the case of goods supplied in partial performance of a contract, than in the case of work or services performed[9].

1   See above, para 19.19.
2   See also in the context of frustration *Appleby v Myers* (1867) LR 2 CP 651 at 659.
3   See also *Gilbert & Partners (a firm) v Knight* [1968] 2 All ER 248.
4   However, it would appear that acceptance arose from the defendant's retention of the materials rather than the initial receipt of them, cf para 19.66.
5   [1900] AC 190.
6   Further restrictions were that 20 days payment had to be accepted and details of repairs had to be approved by Lloyds' agent.
7   The claimants claimed the contract price, a sum for extra work at scheduled rates and a sum for extra work not specified in the contract but carried out at the behest of the agent.
8   [1900] AC 190 at 205: 'There is no doubt that many repairs were executed according to the contract; but the cost cannot be recovered, because the contract is an entire one, and in its entirety has never been performed ... It seems hard that the plaintiffs should not be paid for work which they have done; but such is the effect of contracting to work for a lump sum and failing to do the work'.
9   However, as noted earlier (above, para 19.66, n 4), the common law position whereby a buyer accepting goods that it was entitled to reject was liable in quasi-contract, has been replaced by legislation so that the action is now contractual, see the Sale of Goods Act 1979, s 30. As regards short delivery, in Goff and Jones *Law of Restitution* (5th edn, 1998), pp 549–5, the authors note the problem of basing such recovery on the notion of acceptance where the buyer consumes the goods tendered in short delivery in the expectation of complete delivery under an entire contract; such a buyer must pay either at the contract rate or a reasonable sum (see s 8) for the goods delivered but it is not clear how it can be said that he or she necessarily accepted them). See also Guest (ed) *Benjamin's Sale of Goods* (5th edn, 1997), paras 8–040 and 8–043.

19.74   Perhaps the clearest modern example of an exception to construction is that of *Steele v Tardiani*[1], a decision of the High Court of Australia. The respondent Italian internees were released from internment on condition that they accept employment with the appellant. Their job was to cut timber to a certain length and diameter. The respondents sued the appellant for the balance of monies owed under the contract for work and labour done. The appellant disputed the alleged rate of pay, the amount of timber claimed to have been cut, and the cutting specifications proffered by the respondent. In addition, he argued that the wood was not cut in accordance with the specifications as he understood them. The trial judge preferred the evidence of the respondents on all these matters except that regarding the cutting specifications[2]. It followed that he found the respondents had not cut the timber in accordance with the contract.

The trial judge held that the respondents were in breach of contract in not cutting the wood in compliance with the specifications. Therefore, they had no claim for the contract price. However, he awarded the respondents a fair price for the wood cut on the basis that the appellant had accepted the benefit of the respondent's work by taking possession of it and selling it.

1   (1946) 72 CLR 386.
2   The trial judge did not accept the respondents' claim that they had cut 2,000 tons of timber but arrived at the figure of 1,500 tons which was well in excess of what the appellant claimed had been cut.

19.75   The Full Court disagreed with some of the findings of the trial judge. They thought the contract was to cut wood to various lengths and diameters, and to that extent, the respondents had substantially performed the contract and had an action for the contract price.

The High Court reaffirmed the decision of the trial judge. Therefore, the respondent had no claim under the contract and, in the language of the day, had to produce evidence from which an inference of a fresh contract could be drawn. Latham CJ, accepted as a correct statement of law a section from Bullen and Leake *Precedents of Pleadings* which provided:

> Where work is done by one party under a special contract, but not according to its terms, the other may refuse to accept it; but if he does accept it and takes the benefit of it, he may be sued for the value in this [common indebitatus] count [for work done][1].

Latham CJ agreeing with Dixon J thought there was ample evidence from which an inference of a fresh contract could be drawn[2].

Dixon J distinguished this case from that of *Sumpter v Hedges*. This was not a contract for a single piece of work, requiring the whole to be substantially performed before any contract claim could arise. The contract was infinitely divisible. However, each divisible part contained an entire obligation[3]. As none of these obligations had been substantially performed there was no contractual claim. To recover under a quantum meruit, he thought it necessary for the respondents to 'show circumstances removing their right to remuneration from the exact conditions of the special contract ... It is not enough that the work has been beneficial to [the appellant] by turning standing timber into the more valuable form of firewood'[4]. He then cited the decision of Scrutton LJ in *Steven v Bromley & Son*[5] for the principle that a contract may be implied in respect of work done outside the terms of a contract if the benefit of the work is 'taken', in circumstances where the defendant had a choice to take or accept the work or not.

In determining whether there was such a 'taking', Dixon J thought that the trial judge had found that the appellant did not refuse to pay merely because the timber was not cut to size. In fact, that point was not taken until cross-examination. However, he thought the trial judge had based his decision on his findings that the appellant knew the respondents were not cutting the timber correctly and allowed them to continue cutting it without objection. Moreover, notwithstanding such knowledge, he later promised to pay them once the wood was delivered to a buyer. He also allowed them to leave his employment, without informing them that he would not pay them unless they further reduce the diameter of the wood they had cut. He said[6]:

> In such circumstances, it would be proper to treat the failure in complete performance as possessing little importance to the defendant and as acquiesced in by him, with the consequence that the subsequent sale of the firewood might rightly be regarded by the learned judge as a taking of the benefit of the work and so, as involving either a dispensation from precise performance or an implication at law of a new obligation to pay the value of the work done. The actual finding made by the judge at the trial is general, but as it is consistent with his Honour's having proceeded on the foregoing views of the facts, which are open on the evidence, I do not think the defendant should succeed in his attack upon the conclusion that he is bound to pay a fair and reasonable rate of remuneration.

The reference to an 'implication at law' here can be read as 'imposed by law'. Dixon J used similar wording in *McDonald v Denny's Lascelles Ltd*[7], where it is suggested, he was simply using the language of quasi-contract.

It should be noted that before the High Court, it was not accepted that the appellant had to pay because he had sold the wood that had been cut. If that were the case, then *Steele v Tardiani* may be only an example of an incontrovertible benefit arising from the conduct of the defendant. In this regard it should be noted that Latham CJ said:

It was ... rightly argued that the claimants could not put the defendant in the position of having to pay ... merely because he used or sold that firewood. Such use or sale is not in itself evidence of a new contract. The claimants could not impose a new contract upon the defendant upon the basis that, unless he left the firewood to decay upon the ground, he became bound to pay them as if he employed them on other than the contractual terms[8].

Dixon J with whom McTiernan J agreed, was of the same opinion[9].

1   (3rd edn, 1868), p 41.
2   (1946) 72 CLR 386 at 394.
3   (1946) 72 CLR 386 at 401.
4   (1946) 72 CLR 386 at 401.
5   (1919) 2 KB 722 at 727.
6   (1946) 72 CLR 386 at 405.
7   (1933) 48 CLR 457 at 478. See above, para 19.31.
8   (1946) 72 CLR 386 at 394.
9   (1946) 72 CLR 386 at 403–404.

19.76   In terms of restitution theory, *Steele's* case appears to be best explained by reference to the elements of free acceptance. Dixon J clearly spoke of the requirement that there be evidence of circumstances removing the claimant's right to remuneration from the exact conditions of the contract[1]. The defendant had a clear choice or option whether or not to accept the work provided, and voluntarily and consciously accepted that work. There is nothing in the language of the court that adopts the bargained-for benefit test. Moreover, if none of the wood which was the subject of the restitution claim was cut to size, then arguably the bargained-for benefit test would not be satisfied here, and could not explain the result in the case.

1   Generally this requires the work performed to be work outside the contract. If the work falls within that which is promised under the contract, no restitutionary claim can be made as the contract governs recovery, see *Liebe v Molloy* (1906) 4 CLR 347 at 354, per Griffith CJ; *Update Constructions Pty Ltd v Rozelle Child Care Centre Ltd* (1990) 20 NSWLR 251 at 272, per Priestley JA; *Gilbert & Partners v Knight* [1968] 2 All ER 248. It follows that in the case of services, part performance will rarely ever create a situation where free acceptance may be proven because usually there will have been no opportunity to reject.

19.77   There is some further support for the approach taken in *Steele's* case in *Miles v Wakefield Metropolitan District Council*[1]. In that case, a superintendent registrar of births, deaths and marriages, as part of certain industrial action, refused to carry out civil weddings on Saturday mornings. The claimant, however, continued to go to work on Saturday and perform other duties, despite the fact that the defendant Council told him that if he refused to perform marriages on those days, he should not come in at all. The Council deducted $^3/_{37}$ ths from the claimant's salary, being in respect of the three hours he was to work on Saturdays in his 37 hour week. The claimant sued for the unpaid salary, and failed. However, both Lords Brightman[2] and Templeman[3] thought that if, instead of refusing to perform the services, the industrial action took the form of a 'go slow', then although the claimant would not be entitled to wages under the contract, he would be entitled to be paid on a quantum meruit basis for work performed and accepted. In this case, both Lord Brightman and Lord Templeman thought there was no acceptance. However, Lord Brightman suggested that recovery based on a quantum meruit would be upheld even if the acceptance arose out of necessity rather than choice[4]. The case is not strong authority, because Lord Bridge disagreed[5], and Lords Brandon and Oliver left the issue open. Moreover, it would appear that the contract of employment was not discharged. This latter point makes the decision problematic, not only in terms of restitution but also contract. How could the employer refuse to pay if they did not terminate the contract?

1   [1987] AC 539. See also Birks *An Introduction to the Law of Restitution* (revised edn, 1989), p 241.
2   [1987] AC 539 at 553.
3   [1987] AC 539 at 561.
4   [1987] AC 539 at 553. Cf Goff and Jones *Law of Restitution* (5th edn, 1998), p 548. Perhaps by this he meant that where a party expressly or impliedly contracts out of its right to reject, it will be easier to prove acceptance.
5   [1987] AC 539 at 552.

19.78   As noted above[1], any actions or conduct of a defendant that give rise to an incontrovertible benefit will also prevent recourse to subjective devaluation[2]. However, it may be noted that in both *Steele v Tardiani* and *Forman & Co Pty Ltd v The Liddesdale*[3], the mere fact the received performance was realised in money did not advance the restitutionary claim. In each case, the defendant had no choice but to realise the claimant's performance. Therefore, it may not be correct to define 'incontrovertible benefit' simply in terms of a realisation of some performance[4]. It may be that the factual circumstances surrounding realisation, and the timing of that realisation, will be important in determining whether an incontrovertible benefit exists. Alternatively, and perhaps more logically, the position may be that realisation of the claimant's performance will give rise to an incontrovertible benefit, but whether or not that benefit is unjustly received will depend on the circumstances. The most important circumstance may be whether or not the defendant had a choice to realise the performance.

1   See above, para 19.64.
2   The meaning of 'incontrovertible benefit' in respect of non-monetary benefits is discussed above, para 19.64.
3   See above, para 19.73. See also *Wheeler v Stratton* (1911) 105 LT 786. Cf *Greenwood v Bennett* [1973] QB 195.
4   Cf para 19.64.

EXCEPTIONS TO CONSTRUCTION – SUBSTANTIAL PERFORMANCE

19.79   The doctrine of substantial performance dictates that a party under a contract may recover the price for performance if they have substantially performed their obligations[1]. This is a claim for the contract price rather than for restitution, and therefore it has little to do with unjust enrichment[2]. However, it is mentioned here for two reasons.

First, there have been cases where this doctrine has been applied to entire obligations[3]. If correct, this means that this doctrine is an exception to construction. An alternative analysis posited to explain these cases is that the entire obligation only relates to the quantity of the work to be done and not the quality of the work. Thus if the defect in performance relates to quality, the doctrine of substantial performance may be applied[4].

Second, if the law is that a person who has a right to claim the contract price cannot raise a claim for restitution[5], then whether or not there has been substantial performance in any given case becomes something of a condition precedent to a claim for restitution.

1   See *Boone v Eyre* (1779) 1 Hy Bl 273n, 126 ER 160. What amounts to substantial performance is dependant upon the facts of each case. One logical test formulated by Denning LJ in *Hoenig v Isaacs* [1952] 2 All ER 176, that the contract will have been substantially performed if the innocent party is not entitled to elect to terminate the contract for breach or has elected not to terminate for breach has not been picked up by later cases.

2   Cf Stoljar 'Substantial Performance in Building Contracts' (1954–56) 3 University of Western Australia Law Review 293, and Waddams 'Restitution for the Part Performer' in Reiter and Swan (eds) *Studies in Contract Law* (1980) p 157. See also *Farnsworth v Garrard* (1807) 1 Camp 38, 170 ER 867; *Chapel v Hickes* (1833) 2 Cr & M 214, 149 ER 738. Cf *Thornton v Place* (1832) 1 Mood & R 218, 174 ER 74; *Cutler v Close* (1832) 5 C & P 337, 172 ER 1001.

3   See *Bolton v Mahadeva* [1972] 1 WLR 1009, and cf *Hoenig v Isaacs* [1952] 2 All ER 176. Strangely, it has been held to be inapplicable to severable contracts, see *Miles v Wakefield Metropolitan District Council* [1987] AC 539; *Wiluszynski v Tower Hamlets London Borough Council* [1989] ICR 493 and cf *Steele v Tardiani* (1946) 72 CLR 386 at 401.

4   Treitel *Law of Contract* (10th edn, 1999), p 730.

5   See further paras 19.65, n 9, 19.83, 19.85 and 19.89.

19.80   Substantial performance is not a complete answer to the apparent rough justice that can result from the approach the law takes to entire obligations. It is possible for a court to hold that there has been no substantial performance even though the cost to the respondent in making the work done accord with the contract is minimal[1]. As noted above[2], if substantial performance itself is not relaxed, there is an argument that a restitutionary claim should be allowed to fill this gap at least where the recipient of the work done does put it in proper order and takes the benefit of the work carried out by the claimant.

1   For example in *Bolton v Mahadeva* [1972] 1 WLR 1009, Bolton agreed to install a heating system for £560. The system installed did not operate satisfactorily and Bolton was held to have not substantially performed and thus had no right to the contract price even though the cost of putting the system right was only £174.50. Therefore, Mahadeva had only to spend a small amount to retain the benefit of Bolton's work.

2   See above, paras 19.69–19.71.

EXCEPTIONS TO CONSTRUCTION – APPORTIONMENT LEGISLATION[1]

19.81   Section 2 of the Apportionment Act 1870 provides:

From and after the passing of this Act all rents, annuities, dividends, and other periodical payments in the nature of income (whether reserved or made payable under an instrument in writing or otherwise) shall, like interest on money lent, be considered as accruing from day to day, and shall be apportionable in respect of time accordingly.

The operation of this Act may be excluded by the parties[2]. The reference to a 'periodical payment' would mean that the provision cannot be used to reverse a case like *Sumpter v Hedges*, where the contract is a 'lump sum' contract.

The reference to 'annuities' includes 'salaries and pensions', and presumably would include 'wages'[3]. Arguably the provision could be used by an employee to recover a proportionate part of their salary or wages, where payment is due at the end of a certain period, and where they only work for a portion of that time[4]. Moreover, although current authority appears to be against it[5], this provision may reverse the common law position[6] that a properly dismissed employee (or an employee leaving in breach of contract) could not recover wages earned but not payable at the date of dismissal[7].

1   See Treitel *Law of Contract* (10th edn, 1999), pp 763–765.

2   See the Apportionment Act 1870, s 7.

3   See the Apportionment Act 1870, s 5. See *Moriarty v Regent's Garage & Engineering Co Ltd* [1921] 1 KB 423 (reversed on other grounds [1921] 2 KB 766); *Re William Porter & Co Ltd* [1937] 2 All ER 361 at 363, per Simonds J. See also Glanville Williams 'Partial Performance of Entire Contracts' (1941) 57 LQR 373 at 382.

4   See *Moriarty v Regent's Garage Co* [1921] 1 KB 423 (reversed on other grounds [1921] 2 KB 766). See also Treitel *Law of Contract* (10th edn, 1999), p 764. Cf Matthews 'Salaries in the Apportionment Act 1870' (1982) 2 Legal Studies 302.

5   See the discussion of the authorities in Treitel *Law of Contract* (10th edn, 1999), pp 764 and 765.
6   For a statement of the common law rule, see *Boston Deep Sea Fishing & Ice Co v Ansell* (1888) 39 Ch D 339 at 364–365, per Bowen LJ. See also Glanville Williams 'Partial Performance of Entire Contracts' (1941) 57 LQR 373 at 375 and 383. The basis of the common law rule was not the idea of forfeiture. An employee dismissed for misconduct could not recover because they had not carried out work for the relevant period. See further Goff and Jones *Law of Restitution* (5th edn, 1998), p 548 and see *Spain v Arnott* (1817) 2 Stark 256, 171 ER 638; *Huttman v Boulnois The Younger* (1826) 2 C & P 510, 172 ER 231; *Turner v Robinson* (1833) 5 B & Ad 789, 110 ER 982; *Ridgway v Hungerford Market Co* (1835) 3 Ad & E 171, 111 ER 378; *Lamburn v Cruden* (1841) 2 Man & G 253, 133 ER 741; *Lilley v Elwin* (1848) 11 QB 742, 116 ER 652. Cf *Guy v Nichols* (1694) Comb 265, 90 ER 468.
7   See Treitel *Law of Contract* (10th edn, 1999), pp 764 and 765. See also Goff and Jones *Law of Restitution* (5th edn, 1998), p 548; Glanville Williams 'Partial Performance of Entire Contracts' (1941) 57 LQR 373 at 381–383. See further Matthews 'Salaries in the Apportionment Act 1870' (1982) 2 Legal Studies 302; *Boston Deep Sea Fishing & Ice Co v Ansell* (1888) 39 Ch D 339 at 364–365, per Bowen LJ. Cf *Moriarty v Regent's Garage Co* [1921] 1 KB 423 at 435, per Lush J (suggesting, but not ruling, that a lawfully dismissed employee or an employee leaving in breach of contract could not rely on the Act) (cf at 448–449, per McCardie J), and see Law Com no 121 *Law of Contract: Pecuniary Restitution on Breach of Contract* (1983), para 2.21 (also doubting the Act varies the common law rule). See para 19.77 as to the position of an employee who is not dismissed and who has not properly performed his or her duties.

RESTITUTION AND DEVIATION

19.82   It has been suggested that where a cargo-owner terminates a contract of carriage for deviation[1], but where the shipowner continues the voyage and delivers the goods on time and in good condition at the agreed port, then, although the shipowner cannot recover the agreed freight, it can obtain a reasonable remuneration[2].

The result in this line of cases is probably sui generis. It is important to note that the carrier is not being granted restitution on the basis that they have performed the contract. Once the cargo owner elects to terminate the contract, the completion of the voyage by the carrier is not an act of performance. It is for this reason that the carrier cannot obtain the contract price. In contracts discharged for breach or repudiation, mere contract performance should not be seen as giving rise to the receipt of a benefit for the purposes of unjust enrichment. What is required is for the defendant to be in receipt of an incontrovertible benefit or to have freely accepted the services rendered.

The difficulty of explaining the basis of the restitutionary claim in this line of cases is that the carrier, in deciding to complete the voyage, was acting as a mere volunteer[3]. It is difficult to see how it could be said the cargo-owner was incontrovertibly benefited. Free acceptance is also problematic because the cargo owner, despite electing to terminate the contract, really had no choice but to take possession of its own goods upon arrival. Presumably the bargained-for benefit test is also not satisfied because the election to terminate the contract meant that the carrier's decision to complete the voyage was not bargained for. Therefore, perhaps the result is, as noted above, sui generis and based on the harshness or unconscionability of leaving the carrier without a remedy[4].

1   The better view appears to be that a deviation does not automatically discharge the contract, see *Hain Steamship Co Ltd v Tate & Lyle Ltd* [1936] 2 All ER 597 at 601, per Lord Atkin.
2   See *Hain Steamship Co Ltd v Tate & Lyle Ltd* [1936] 2 All ER 597 at 612, per Lord Wright MR, and at 616, per Lord Maugham. See also *Joseph Thorley Ltd v Orchis Steamship Co Ltd* [1907] 1 KB 660 at 667, per Collins MR, and at 669, per Fletcher Moulton LJ; *United States Shipping Board v JJ Masters & Co* (1922) 10 Ll L Rep 573 at 575, per Bankes LJ; *Atlantic Shipping & Trading Co Ltd v Louis Dreyfus & Co* [1922] 2 AC 250 at 257–258, per Lord Dunedin. Cf *United States Shipping Board v Bunge y Born Ltda* (1925) 31 Com Cas 118; *Chandris v Isbrandtsen-Moller Co Inc* [1951] 1 KB 240 at 250; *Société Franco Tunisienne D'Armement v Sidermar SPA* [1961] 2 QB 278 at 313,

per Pearson J (overruled on other grounds *Ocean Tramp Tankers Organisation v V/O Soyfracht, The Eugenia* [1964] 2 QB 226).
3 This was the basis upon which Scrutton LJ in the Court of Appeal would have refused a claim for reasonable remuneration, see *Tate & Lyle Ltd v Hain Steamship Co Ltd* (1934) 39 Com Cas 259 at 272 (overruled [1936] 2 All ER 597).
4 See Goff and Jones *Law of Restitution* (5th edn, 1998), p 551 who point out that where delivery is made at a port other than the agreed port the weight of authority (dicta) suggests that a quantum meruit claim will only succeed if the cargo owner requested carriage to the new port of discharge, see *Hopper v Burness* (1876) 1 CPD 137; *Hain Steamship Co v Tate and Lyle Ltd* [1936] 2 All ER 597 at 612, per Lord Wright, at 616, per Lord Maugham.

Benefit – (ii) where the claimant is not in breach

19.83   Where an innocent party has fully or substantially performed their obligations under an enforceable contract, they will have a right to be paid the contract price[1]. On one view, where the innocent party can bring an action for the price, they should be restricted to that claim, and not be allowed to bring an alternative claim for restitution[2]. This view has the merit of upholding the parties' bargain[3].

1 Assuming there is an agreed contract price, see *Home Management Maintenance Pty Ltd v Doyle* (1992) 107 FLR 225.
2 See *Morrison-Knudsen Co Inc v British Columbia Hydro and Power Authority* (1978) 85 DLR (3d) 186 and *United States for the Use and Benefit of Harkol Inc v Americo Construction Co Inc* 168 F Supp 760 (1958). Cf *Dey v Hill* 181 P 462 (1919). See also paras 19.65, n 9, 19.79 and 19.89.
3 Cf Skelton *Restitution and Contract* (1998), p 49.

19.84   Burrows has disagreed with this view[1]. He points out that a party fully performing by paying the contract price in advance is not restricted to a claim for damages, but can claim restitution on the basis of failure of consideration[2]. Moreover, he suggests that it would be illogical to deny restitution in cases of substantial or full performance and to allow such claims in cases of partial performance[3].

1 See also *Heyman v Darwins Ltd* [1942] AC 356 at 397, per Lord Porter: 'What then, is the effect of such repudiation if it is accepted? In such a case the injured party may sue on the contract forthwith whether the time for performance is due or not, or, if he has *wholly* or partially performed his obligation, he may in certain cases neglect the contract and sue upon a quantum meruit' (emphasis added).
2 Burrows *Law of Restitution* (1993), pp 270 and 271.
3 Burrows *Law of Restitution* (1993), pp 270 and 271. See also Skelton *Restitution and Contract* (1998), pp 69 and 70.

19.85   Subject to the determination of whether or not the contract price places a ceiling on restitutionary claims, there is generally no advantage in bringing a restitutionary claim in cases where full performance has been rendered, as the action in debt is procedurally more efficient[1]. Whether or not the contract price should place a ceiling on any restitutionary claim is dealt with below[2]. However, if restitutionary claims in these circumstances are available, how is the enrichment issue to be explained? Views may differ as to whether resort to subjective devaluation is prevented on the basis of free acceptance[3], bargained-for benefit[4], incontrovertible benefit, constructive acceptance[5] or limited acceptance[6]. Another view may be that full performance itself prevents resort to subjective devaluation[7]. There is little doubt that a person receiving full contractual performance could not deny that they have been enriched. However, it is suggested that the better view is that such claims should not be recognised. Where the claimant can claim the contract price, it is submitted that the law should limit the claimant to their contractual remedies. In such situations primacy must be given to the institution of contract[8]. Claims for restitution should generally be limited to where there is free acceptance or incontrovertible benefit. This explains away Burrow's objection based on claims for the recovery of money. In such cases the defendant receives an incontrovertible benefit[9]. As noted earlier, full or substantial performance alone should not be seen as giving rise to a free acceptance[10]. In the context of sale of goods, other than in the case of goods sold on a sale or return basis, the acceptance of goods (that is, acceptance in circumstances where the buyer has a right to reject) is relevant as a concept only where the seller has not properly performed by delivering the wrong quantity of goods, or goods that do not conform to the contract. Where the seller has properly performed, then generally no issue of acceptance (in the sense of there being an option to retain) arises and the buyer must pay the price. That is, the buyer here has a duty to accept the goods in the sense of taking receipt of the goods.

1 One advantage of bringing a restitutionary claim is that certain rights of set off available to the defendant in a debt or damages claim may not be available in a claim for restitution.
2 See above, paras 19.112–19.120.
3 Birks *An Introduction to the Law of Restitution* (revised edn, 1989), p 230.
4 Burrows *Law of Restitution* (1993), p 302. See also Virgo *Principles of the Law of Restitution* (1999), pp 93 and 94 (subjective revaluation).
5 See *Pavey & Matthews Pty Ltd v Paul* (1987) 162 CLR 221 at 257, per Deane J and *Foran v Wight* (1989) 168 CLR 385 at 438, per Deane J.
6 Birks *An Introduction to the Law of Restitution* (revised edn, 1989), pp 240 and 241. See further para 19.89.
7 See Birks 'Restitution after Ineffective Contracts: Issues for the 1990s' (1990) 2 Journal of Contract Law 227 at 230. See also *Home Management Maintenance Pty Ltd v Doyle* (1992) 107 FLR 225 and *Pavey & Matthews Pty Ltd v Paul* (1987) 162 CLR 221 (neither case, however, involved a contract discharged for breach or repudiation).
8 It may also be argued that the claimant who is in receipt of full contractual performance under a valid and enforceable contract may be taken to have contracted out of any restitutionary claim, see Garner 'The Role of Subjective Benefit in the Law of Unjust Enrichment' (1990) 10 OJLS 42 at 52.
9 However, the adoption of the bargained-for benefit test logically leads to the result Burrows argues for.
10 See above, para 19.65, n 9.

19.86   In regards to Burrow's second argument, namely that it would be illogical to deny restitution in cases of substantial or full performance and yet allow such claims in cases of partial performance, it will be suggested below that in those cases of partial performance where restitution has been granted and where there is no evidence of an incontrovertible benefit or free acceptance, they should be departed from.

19.87   In practice restitutionary claims in this area arise because the claimant has not fully or substantially performed at the time they elect to terminate the contract for the breach or repudiation by the other party. In these circumstances, the claim in restitution is usually successful[1], and therefore for the purposes of unjust enrichment the defendant must have received a benefit. However, because the claimant has not fully performed his or her obligations, prima facie the defendant should be able to subjectively devalue the performance rendered. Some factor is therefore required to prevent recourse to subjective devaluation. Clearly, the requirements of free acceptance and incontrovertible benefit will rarely if ever be satisfied.

1 See *Segur v Franklin* (1934) 34 SRNSW 67 at 72, per Jordon CJ.

19.88 The criterion put forward to analyse the cases is that of 'limited acceptance'[1]. Like free acceptance, limited acceptance is evidenced by reference to the conduct of the defendant[2]. However, in the case of limited acceptance, it is the defendant's conduct in breaching the contract that prevents them having resort to the construction of the contract to subjectively devalue the work or services of the claimant. In these circumstances the law does not seem to require the existence of any objective benefit. Moreover, it would appear that the defendant may not raise as a defence to the claim for restitution that the claimant was also in breach of contract[3].

Clearly, a claimant not in breach may claim damages for breach of contract instead of, or in addition to, his or her restitutionary claim[4]. This will of course be subject to the rules preventing double recovery[5].

1 See below, para 19.89.
2 See above, para 19.65.
3 See *Renard Constructions (ME) Pty Ltd v Minister for Public Works* (1992) 26 NSWLR 234.
4 See *Segur v Franklin* (1934) 34 SRNSW 67 at 72, per Jordon CJ.
5 See below, para 19.121.

LIMITED ACCEPTANCE AND OBJECTIVE BENEFITS

19.89 As noted above, to organise the case law in this area by reference to unjust enrichment, it is necessary to create a further criterion preventing recourse to subjective devaluation. Birks has suggested that in claims brought by parties not in breach, there is a limited acceptance by the defendant which is sufficient to prevent recourse to subjective devaluation[1]. By 'limited acceptance' he means that the defendant was prepared to freely accept the entire performance, and therefore in a limited sense must be taken to accept 'that work which would be necessary to achieve the complete performance'[2]. One problem with this formulation is that it appears to be based on the notion that full performance will give rise to a free acceptance[3]. Another view suggests that what is occurring in those cases where the claimant's part performance has at least resulted in some objective benefit[4] or some increase in the assets of the defendant, is that the acceptance is effectively deemed[5]. The notion behind this deeming is that the defendant cannot deny that he or she has received a benefit in circumstances where, had it not been for the defendant's breach, the claimant would have fully performed[6]. This is a form of estoppel. For example, where a builder partly performs work, and is later prevented from finishing the work by the employer refusing entry onto the property, then, despite the contract's being a lump sum contract, the builder is able to claim a reasonable remuneration for the value of work done and materials supplied[7]. However, in many cases it may not be the defendant's breach that prevents the claimant fully performing, but rather the claimant's decision to terminate the contract.

1 Birks *An Introduction to the Law of Restitution* (revised edn, 1989), p 127.
2 Birks *An Introduction to the Law of Restitution* (revised edn, 1989), p 232.
3 Cf para 19.83.
4 See eg *Ettridge v Vermin Board of the District of Murat Bay* [1928] SASR 124 (see also at [1930] SASR 210); *Chandler Bros Ltd v Boswell* [1936] 3 All ER 179; *Renard Constructions (ME) Pty Ltd v Minister for Public Works* (1992) 26 NSWLR 234. See also *Lusty v Finsbury Securities Ltd* (1991) 58 BLR 66. See further *Appleby v Myers* (1867) LR 2 CP 651 at 659.
5 Mason and Carter *Restitution Law in Australia* (1995) para 1167. See also *Slowey v Lodder* (1901) 20 NZLR 321 at 358, per Williams J (affirmed as *Lodder v Slowey* [1904] AC 442).
6 See *Munro v Butt* (1858) 8 E & B 738 at 753–754, 120 ER 275 at 286, per Lord Campbell CJ.
7 See *Slowey v Lodder* (1900) 20 NZLR 321 (affirmed as *Lodder v Slowey* [1904] AC 442).

19.90   More difficult are those cases where there is no objective benefit or no increase in the assets of the defendant. The leading case in *Planché v Colburn*[1]. Here the defendant commissioned the claimant to write a chapter on 'Costume and Ancient Armour' for a periodical publication entitled *The Juvenile Library*. Due to poor sales of earlier instalments of the publication, the defendant abandoned the project, and refused to pay the claimant, at a time when the claimant had carried out some research (by attending a collection of ancient armour), made some drawings, and partially completed the manuscript. However, no part of the manuscript was ever delivered. The defendants attempted to show that the claimant had entered into a fresh contract, which may have allowed his work to be published separately. This was rejected by the jury, who awarded the claimant damages. That verdict was sought to be set aside on the basis that the claimant could not recover under the contract without delivering any of the work, nor could he recover under the common counts for work and labour while the contract was still on foot.

1   (1831) 8 Bing 14, 131 ER 305, 5 C & P 58, 172 ER 876. See also *Prickett v Badger* (1856) 1 CBNS 296, 140 ER 123. See further *Brooks Robinson Pty Ltd v Rothfield* [1951] VLR 405 (quantum meruit claim for work and labour in building a cocktail cabinet; prior to full performance the claimant terminated the contract for breach by the defendant and was successful in claiming restitution although it would appear from the report that the claimant kept possession of the cabinet).

19.91   Tindal CJ agreed that no quantum meruit claim could be brought while the contract was on foot. However, that was not the case here, as the defendant had abandoned the contract, and the jury had found that no new contract had been entered into. Under these circumstances, he thought the claimant was right to be awarded a sum for his labour. The defendant could not insist on delivery, because they would then publish it in a way not consistent with the basis upon which it was written, that is, for a young audience, and publication in some other form could damage the reputation of the author.

It may be noted that, although it is not clear whether the jury awarded damages or restitution, it does seem clear that Tindal CJ (with whom Gaselee J concurred) was of the opinion that the jury awarded a quantum meruit[1]. Moreover, later cases have viewed the case as a restitution case[2].

1   See further *Planché v Colburn* (1831) 5 C & P 58 at 59, 172 ER 876 at 877: 'The second count stated, that the defendants were indebted to the plaintiff in £100 for work and labour, care, and diligence, in and about the composing and writing a certain work for them, and in an about the making of certain drawings, and also for journies and attendances relating to the business. The third count was similar except that it was on a quantum meruit ... Tindale CJ – I do not think it turns upon the second count, but upon the quantum meruit in the third count'.
2   See eg *Slowey v Lodder* (1901) 20 NZLR 321 at 362 (affirmed as *Lodder v Slowey* [1904] AC 442) (cf (1901) 20 NZLR 321 at 346, per Edwards J at first instance); *Brenner v First Artists' Management Pty Ltd* [1993] 2 VR 221 at 258; *Iezzi Constructions Pty Ltd v Watkins Pacific (Qld) Pty Ltd* [1995] 2 QdR 350 at 361, per McPherson JA; *Prickett v Badger* (1856) 1 CBNS 296, 140 ER 123; *Bartholomew v Markwick* (1864) 15 CBNS 711, 143 ER 964. See also Kull 'Rationalizing Restitution' (1995) 83 California Law Review 1191 at 1204–1205 (who analyses the case as one of restitution not damages on the basis that the obligation to pay only arose upon complete performance, thus there was no breach of contract under the law existing at the time as the pre-condition for the defendant's performance had not yet occurred). Cf *Hochester v De La Tour* (1853) 2 E & B 678 at 693, 118 ER 922 at 927; *Inchbald v Western Neilgherry Coffee, Tea and Cinchona Plantation Co Ltd* (1864) 17 CBNS 733, 144 ER 293.

19.92   Later, in *De Barnardy v Harding*[1], the claimant sued for reasonable remuneration when the defendant repudiated a contract, under which the claimant was to sell tickets to view the funeral of the Duke of Wellington, and was to be paid a percentage of the value of the tickets he sold. At the time of repudiation, the claimant had incurred some expenses in advertising and in employing staff. However, he had not sold any tickets[2]. The trial judge ordered the jury to find for the defendant, on the basis that the claimant should have sued in respect of the breach of contract, and not on a quantum meruit. On appeal it was held that when one party refuses to perform or is incapable of performing the contract, the other party may sue for breach of contract or 'rescind' the contract, and sue on a quantum meruit for work actually done.

1   (1853) 8 Ex Ch 822, 155 ER 1586.
2   The defendant had told the claimant that he would sell the tickets himself and so the claimant sent all applicants for tickets to the defendant. The defendant may therefore have received a benefit (which did not flow from the mere performance of the contract) and arguably accepted that benefit.

19.93   Attempts to synthesize these cases with the principle against unjust enrichment have proved problematic. The principal objection against allowing restitution in cases like *Planché* is that the claimant will recover even though he or she retains possession of any objective benefit created. Burrows accepts the decision in *De Barnardy*, as that was a contract to provide services, and under his bargained-for benefit test, an enrichment occurs when performance of the services commences. He argues that the claimant in *Planché* should be limited to a damages claim, and the case should be interpreted in this way[1]. The reason for this is that the contract there was a contract for services to provide an end result, namely, the delivery of a manuscript. Thus under the bargained-for benefit test, until part of the manuscript was delivered there was no enrichment[2].

1   See also Kull 'Rationalizing Restitution' (1995) 83 California Law Review 1191 at 1205.
2   Burrows *Law of Restitution* (1993), p 267. Cf Beatson *Use and Abuse of Unjust Enrichment* (1991), ch 2. See also Garner 'Benefits – For Services Rendered: Commentary' in McInnes (ed) *Restitution: Developments in Unjust Enrichment* (1996), p 112.

19.94   However, to the extent the claimants in both cases were successful in claiming restitution, and to the extent that these cases are still part of the law, it is necessary to formulate a test for enrichment to bring these cases within the principle against unjust enrichment. Admittedly, such an explanation must be technical and highly artificial.

One could take the view that a defendant is enriched when the claimant executes acts which are part of the contractual performance, whether or not they are of any objective value[1]. However, that on its own would not distinguish these successful claims from those unsuccessful claims brought by a party in breach who has partly performed[2]. In addition, there is nothing in *Planché* to suggest that the claimant will have a claim only if he or she has executed acts in performance of the contract, as opposed to mere acts of reliance. Prima facie, the claimant is protected, even though he or she has only executed acts in reliance – which is at odds with claims based on failure of consideration[3].

Birks suggests that limited acceptance operates in this type of situation so as to prevent the defendant having recourse to subjective devaluation[4]. He suggests this 'may be a test of enrichment which will work against a defendant whose resort to subjective devaluation appears unconscientious in the light of his own conduct in relation to the receipt of the benefit'[5]. However, the point has also been made that if decisions like *Planché* are to be considered cases of restitution for unjust enrichment, it is not only the acceptance that is deemed, but also the benefit[6]. Having a mechanism to prevent recourse to subjective devaluation serves no purpose if the defendant is not in receipt of anything with which to devalue. In short, in this line of cases, it is difficult to pinpoint any enrichment in the defendant[7].

1   See *Brenner v First Artists' Management Pty Ltd* [1993] 2 VR 221 at 258, per Byrne J: 'where a person requests another to do something, it is not unreasonable for the law to conclude that the former sees some benefit in its performance, however wrong this view may be on an objective basis and for the law to act upon the perception of the recipient'. See further McMeel *Modern Law of Restitution* (2000), p 142.
2   See above, para 19.67.
3   See above, para 19.17. See also Goff and Jones *Law of Restitution* (5th edn, 1998), p 21.
4   Birks *An Introduction to the Law of Restitution* (revised edn, 1989), p 232.
5   Birks *An Introduction to the Law of Restitution* (revised edn, 1989), p 232. See also Birks 'In Defence of Free Acceptance' in Burrows (ed) *Essays on the Law of Restitution* (1991), pp 140 and 141.
6   See Mason and Carter *Restitution Law in Australia* (1995), para 1166; Goff and Jones *Law of Restitution* (5th edn, 1998), p 532.
7   See *Iezzi Constructions Pty Ltd v Watkins Pacific (Qld) Pty Ltd* [1995] 2 QdR 350 at 359, per Fitzgerald P (here a subcontractor was successful in its claim for restitution against a contractor in breach of contract when the subcontractor's near full performance produced little actual benefit to the contractor, 'only a valueless right to be paid' for the subcontractor's work by the insolvent proprietor).

19.95   If restitution continues to be available in such cases, it is imperative that restitution for unjust enrichment does not come to be used as a tool for protecting reliance loss. Such loss can be adequately protected by contract. In *De Barnardy v Harding*, unless some case for free acceptance can be made out of the fact the claimant sent all ticket applications to the defendant after the defendant repudiated the contract[1], it is difficult to see the claim being for anything other than a claim for reliance loss as the contract was a contract to sell tickets. In *Planché's* case, if the contract there was to merely write a manuscript, then the act of writing would be an act of performance rather than an act of reliance. The result would be different if the contract was to deliver a manuscript[2]. If the contract were to both write and deliver a manuscript, then the act of writing without delivery would amount to an act of performance[3].

1   See above, para 19.92, n 2.
2   In practice, this is the most likely construction. See further *Luxor (Eastbourne) Ltd v Cooper* [1941] AC 108 at 141, per Lord Wright; *McDougall v Aeromarine of Emsworth Ltd* [1958] 1 WLR 1126; *Reid v Macbeth and Gray* [1904] AC 223; and cf *Hyundai Heavy Industries Co Ltd v Papadopoulos* [1980] 1 WLR 1129.
3   For example, in *ACME Process Equipment Co v United States* 347 F 2d 509 (1965) (overruled on another point 385 US 138 (1966)), the claimant was contracted to 'furnish and deliver' rifles to the defendant. The claimant sued the defendant claiming restitution after the defendant allegedly wrongfully cancelled the contract. The defendant argued that the contract was simply for the purchase of completed rifles being a contract for the 'production and delivery of finished articles': (347 F 2d at 529). Thus any work done short of delivery of a finished product could only be compensated for by an award of reliance damages. The court, however, construed the contract as an agreement to 'manufacture and deliver' the rifles and held that where a contract of this nature was breached restitution was available and, moreover, it was not limited to the reasonable value of the goods actually delivered prior to cancellation: (347 F 2d at 529–530). That is, acts of manufacture that did not result in delivery prior to the cancellation of the contract were included in the valuation of the restitutionary claim as they amounted to acts of performance. The court added that restitution was permitted in such circumstances 'as an alternative remedy for breach of contract in an effort to restore the innocent party to its pre-contract status quo, and not to prevent the unjust enrichment of the breaching party ... It is when the plaintiff is the party in default that his recovery may be limited by the amount of the benefit to the defendant': (347 F 2d 530). The court further held that the claimant's recovery was the reasonable market value of his or her services rather than the reasonable value of those services to the defendant. The claimant argued that the reasonable value of its services was best measured by the costs it had incurred in performance. The court agreed subject to the defendant showing that the costs incurred were excessive. This matter was referred back to the Trial Commissioner.

CONCLUSIONS

19.96   In the result, if (as current law would suggest) restitution in these cases is to be allowed[1], and if that claim is to be based upon unjust enrichment, then for the moment it is suggested that the notion of limited acceptance is the best explanation so far put forward. As a criterion of enrichment, it must be admitted that this test is highly artificial, as it ultimately bases the issue of enrichment on the conduct of the defendant in breaching the contract. Although that may be an acceptable basis for restitution, it should not be a test of enrichment. The availability of a claim for damages should be seen as allowing the law to insist on a more stringent enrichment requirement before granting restitution in such cases. However, such objections do not carry as much weight, as long as 'limited acceptance' is not viewed as a positive test for identifying an enrichment, but rather a criterion for preventing recourse the subjective devaluation. In that regard its focus on the conduct of the defendant is in line with free acceptance and incontrovertible benefit[2]. Ultimately, however, the factor that sets cases of limited acceptance apart from those of free acceptance and incontrovertible benefit and its weakness as a criterion for preventing recourse to subjective devaluation is the ability to mount a successful claim without the defendant being in receipt of anything. Perhaps limited acceptance would not be as objectionable if the law insisted that the defendant be in receipt of an objective benefit in any case.

1   See *Heyman v Darwins Ltd* [1942] AC 356 at 397, per Lord Porter; *Slowey v Lodder* (1901) 20 NZLR 321 at 356, per Williams J (affirmed as *Lodder v Slowey* [1904] AC 442); *Segur v Franklin* (1934) 34 SRNSW 67 at 72, per Jordon CJ; *Prickett v Badger* (1856) 1 CBNS 296, 140 ER 123; *Appleby v Myers* (1866) LR 1 CP 615 at 622; on appeal LR 2 CP 651 at 659; *Newton Woodhouse v Trevor Toys Ltd* (20 December 1991, unreported), CA per Glidewell LJ.
2   See above, paras 19.73 and 19.78.

19.97   It is suggested that the better approach would be to leave the party not in breach to their claim in damages, unless they can prove that there has been a free acceptance or the defendant is in receipt of an incontrovertible benefit[1]. As for cases like *Planché* and *De Barnardy*, it must be kept in mind that at the time these cases were was decided, restitution and damages were seen as mutually exclusive remedies[2]. The claimant could either rescind the contract ab initio and claim restitution or affirm it and claim damages. To the extent that these cases were successful claims in restitution, this was predicated on the contract being rescinded. Today under modern principles of discharge, restitution and damages in this context are not inconsistent remedies. Therefore, there is no reason why it should be thought imperative that these cases must be fitted within a modern statement of restitution for unjust enrichment[3].

1   See *Ranger v Great Western Rly Co* (1854) 5 Hl Cas 72 at 95–97, 10 ER 824 at 833–834, per Lord Cranworth (obiter suggesting the claimant only has a remedy in damages) (cf the remarks of the Privy Council in *Lodder v Slowey* [1904] AC 442 at 451, agreeing with the Court of Appeal in that case that *Ranger* merely decided that the appellants had no claim to equitable relief). See also *Inchbald v Western Neilgherry Coffee, Tea and Cinchona Plantation Co Ltd* (1864) 17 CBNS 733, 144 ER 293 (claimant sued for damages and for work and labour, however, the Court treated the case as one for breach of contract and were silent on the issue of restitution). Goff and Jones suggest that restitution here should be limited to situations where a damages claim would fail, for example where the cost of performance is greater than contract expectation, see Goff and Jones *Law of Restitution* (5th edn, 1998), p 20. See further Kull 'Restitution as Remedy for Breach of Contract' (1994) 67 South California Law Review 1465. There may be an argument in such cases that the defendant should be taken to have been enriched where they take the claimant's performance and complete it themselves (see eg *Slowey v Lodder* (1901) 20 NZLR 321 (affirmed as *Lodder v Slowey* [1904] AC 442), however if adopted it may be difficult to keep such cases distinct from the *Sumpter v Hedges* line of cases, see above, para 19.73.

2   See above, para 19.12.
3   See Carter 'Discharged Contracts: Claims for Restitution' (1997) 11 Journal of Contract Law 130.

'At the expense of '

19.98   In the area of restitution following discharge for breach or repudiation, this element does not cause any great difficulty. However, if for any reason it cannot be made out, the claim must fail. For example in *Rowland v Divall*[1], the defendant sold the claimant a car which it later transpired the defendant had no title to. The claimant was successful in claiming recovery of money paid. If the defendant had counter-claimed for an amount in respect of the use the claimant had made of the car in the intervening period, that claim could have been met with the argument that any benefit received by the claimant was at the expense of the true owner, and not the defendant.

1   [1923] 2 KB 500. See further para 19.16.

Bases for restitution

INTRODUCTION

19.99   Some scholars have suggested that failure of consideration should be extended beyond the recovery of payments, so as to also ground recovery for reasonable remuneration[1]. This extension is aimed at bringing about symmetry between claims for the recovery of money and claims for reasonable remuneration[2]. Birks argues, 'if I pay money for a car which I never get, I can recover that money as paid for a consideration which has failed. If, vice versa, I transfer a car for money which I do not get, I must in principle be able to recover the value of the car on the same ground, since otherwise different law would apply without there being any sufficient reason for the difference'[3].

1   See above, para 19.10. See also Virgo *Principles of the Law of Restitution* (1999), p 327 (citing *Pulbrook v Lawes* (1876) 1 QBD 284) and 350; McMeel *Modern Law of Restitution* (2000), p 123.
2   See *Pearce v Brain* [1929] 2 KB 310 (a case concerning specific restitution) at 315, per Swift J: 'I cannot distinguish between recovery of a specific chattel under a void contract and the recovery of money if the latter cannot be recovered, neither can the former. In order to succeed here it is incumbent on the plaintiff to show a complete failure of consideration'.
3   Birks *An Introduction to the Law of Restitution* (revised edn, 1989), p 227. With respect, however, a different law does apply. It is generally recognised in sale of goods law that in the example given the seller has an action for the price as they have fully or substantially performed their obligations under the contract.

19.100   Proponents of this view generally adopt a broader approach to the issue of enrichment, and seek to explain the case law by reference to the basis for unjust enrichment. That is, they suggest that failed claims turned on the unjust factor and not the enrichment factor. For example, Birks has suggested that in a case like *Sumpter v Hedges*[1], if the enrichment issue is made out[2] but on construction the builder was to forfeit the work done if he did not fully complete, then it is 'true that [his] restitutionary claim based on failure of consideration is defeated for the reason, obvious once that construction has been adopted, that the consideration has not failed. The consideration in such a case is that the value to be forfeited shall serve as a sanction against non-performance, so that, when the sanction attaches, the consideration cannot be said to fail. The only hope of such parties is recourse to relief from penalties and forfeiture'[3]. It is suggested, however, that the weakness in this explanation is that the proposed construction could never be sustained. As noted above[4], except in the case of deposits, the law does not imply provisions for forfeiture.

1   [1898] 1 QB 673. See above, para 19.67.
2   See above, para 19.68.
3   See Birks 'In Defence of Free Acceptance' in Burrows (ed) *Essays on the Law of Restitution* (1991), pp 113 and 114.
4   See above, para 19.42.

19.101   On the other hand, Burrows has argued that *Sumpter v Hedges* was wrongly decided, because on his construction the claimant could ground its claim on failure of consideration. Moreover, the defendant had received part of what it bargained for, thus satisfying his test for the existence of an enrichment[1]. He sees no danger in this approach, so long as there is recognition of the innocent party's right to set off its claim for damages for breach of contract against the claim for restitution[2].

1   Burrows *Law of Restitution* (1993), pp 267 and 276.
2   Burrows *Law of Restitution* (1993), p 272.

19.102   However, where no amount is due under the contract in respect of some particular performance, it is difficult to see how it can be said that there is a failure of consideration, because at the time of discharge there is no agreed return performance for that performance rendered by the claimant[1]. That is, until full or substantial performance is rendered, the part performance is neither received nor retained conditionally. It is different in the case of advance payments, because unless retention is unconditional there is always an agreed return for the payment, and if the contract is discharged prior to any part of that agreed return being rendered (whether the time for performance of that agreed return has accrued or not) there is a total failure of consideration, as the defendant's retention of the payment is conditional. At present, failure of consideration has not been adopted by the courts as a basis for restitution in respect of claims for services. For the reasons given, it is suggested that is should not be so adopted.

1   Opinions on this point, however, appear to differ. Birks has argued that in a case such as *Appleby v Myers* (1867) LR 2 CP 651, where the claimants were to erect machinery on the defendant's premises with payment not being due until the work was completed and where the contract was frustrated after installation had commenced the claimants should be able to rely on failure of consideration. He suggests that the real problem for the claimants in that case was the issue of enrichment, see Birks *An Introduction to the Law of Restitution* (revised edn, 1989), pp 230 and 231.

CLAIMANT IN BREACH

19.103   As noted above[1], in the apparently rare instances where a claimant in breach can evidence the defendant's free acceptance of the performance rendered, then not only is the enrichment issue made out but so to is the basis for restitution. That is, free acceptance operates both to prevent recourse to subjective devaluation and as a basis for restitution. As an unjust factor, free acceptance is said to focus on the defendant's conduct and state of mind, and is concerned with the unconscientiousness of the defendant's receipt of the claimant's performance[2].

1   See above, para 19.66.
2   See para 19.65.

19.104   Where a claimant in breach is able to evidence the receipt by the defendant of an incontrovertible benefit, theoretically the claimant must still identify a basis for restitution. In many instances, where the defendant realises the rendered performance so as to constitute an incontrovertible benefit, it may be too late to rely on free acceptance as a basis for restitution. That is, if free acceptance is properly limited to requiring an initial unconscientious receipt[1]. In any case, it would be rare for the requirements of free acceptance to be made out. Ultimately there is little authority on this point in the case of contracts discharged for breach or repudiation. However, at least in the case of an incontrovertible benefit derived from the defendant realising the claimant's performance, there is nothing fictional in describing the defendant's receipt of the incontrovertible benefit in terms of acceptance (or limited acceptance), even if the initial receipt of the claimant's contractual performance was not unconscionable. That is, if the focus of acceptance is on retention rather than receipt. It was suggested above[2], that even where a defendant realises some performance of the claimant's, that will not give rise to a successful claim if the defendant had no other choice. The requirement of a choice here suggests that acceptance has a role to play. It may be that, where such realisation does amount to an incontrovertible benefit, that realisation will be sufficient to render the retention without accounting to the claimant unconscionable. However, theoretically the enrichment issue must be kept distinct from the basis for restitution. In that regard, as noted above, perhaps the better approach is to view the realisation as giving rise to an incontrovertible benefit, but recognising that it is only when the defendant had a choice to realise the claimant's performance that the incontrovertible benefit will be an unjust enrichment.

1   See Birks 'In Defence of Free Acceptance' in Burrows (ed) *Essays on the Law of Restitution* (1991), ch 5. Cf above, para 19.65 as to whether or not such a requirement need be retained.
2   See above, para 19.78.

CLAIMANT NOT IN BREACH

19.105   It was noted above that where a party not in breach brings a claim for reasonable remuneration, that claim is generally successful. Birks has suggested that the basis for restitution in such cases is that of limited acceptance[1]. However, it is in these cases that reference to notions of acceptance do appear strained as acceptance appears to be deemed. Subject to some reservations, this deeming may be acceptable in relation to preventing recourse to subjective devaluation, however, this does not appear satisfactory when used as a basis for restitution. It has been suggested that the unjust requirement is perhaps more correctly based on the defendant's wrongful breach of contract, and this would appear a more plausible basis for the claim[2].

1   See above, para 19.89.
2   Mason and Carter *Restitution Law in Australia* (1995), para 1167. See also *Segur v Franklin* (1934) 34 SRNSW 67 at 72, per Jordon CJ.

D   Valuation of claims[1]

19.106   Restitution following discharge of contract for breach or repudiation falls within the subtractive sense of 'at the expense of'. It is an application of autonomous restitution. Although the loss to the claimant must be causally related to the gain of the defendant, they need not equate in terms of valuation[2].

The aim of the valuation exercise is to provide a fair and just remedy for the benefit received by the defendant[3]. Generally, however, in claims for the repayment of money based of total failure of consideration, the claimant's loss will, in terms of valuation, equate to the defendant's gain, and the defendant will be required to repay an equivalent amount to that which he or she received[4].

1 See Hunter 'Measuring the Unjust Enrichment in a Restitution Case' (1989) 12 Sydney Law Review 76.
2 Cf McInnes '"At the Plaintiff's Expense": Quantifying Restitutionary Relief' [1998] CLJ 472.
3 See *Pavey & Mathews Pty Ltd v Paul* (1987) 162 CLR 221 at 263–264, per Deane J.
4 See further Smith 'Three-Party Restitution: A Critique of Birks's Theory of Interceptive Subtraction' (1991) 11 OJLS 481 at 482–483.

Claims for reasonable remuneration

19.107   The better view appears to be that reasonable remuneration should generally be valued by reference to the market rate for the services provided or goods supplied at the time of acceptance[1]. This will generally be the time the services are rendered, or the goods are supplied[2]. It is suggested that in the case of a contract for services which produce an end product (and which is not a contract of sale[3]) what should be valued, unless there is a statutory provision to the contrary, is the provision of the services themselves, and not the value of the end product[4]. In this way, the risk that the end product is worthless lies with the party who ordered it. This does not mean that one is providing a remedy valued by reference to the claimant's loss rather than the defendant's gain. If the identified enrichment is the provision of services, the remedy must be a reasonable sum for the provision of those services, and not a sum representing the value of any end product[5].

1 See *Council of the City of Sydney v Woodward* [2000] NSWCA 201 (adopting a similar statement from Mason and Carter *Restitution Law in Australia* (1995), para 2722). The above statement of course assumes there is a market rate, see *Stinchcombe v Thomas* [1957] VR 509; *Brenner v First Artists' Management Pty Ltd* [1993] 2 VR 221. See generally *BP Exploration Co (Libya) Ltd v Hunt (No 2)* [1979] 1 WLR 783 at 805 (affirmed [1983] 2 AC 352); *Flett v Deniliquin Publishing Co Ltd* [1964–5] NSWR 383 at 386. Custom may dictate that remuneration be on a different basis such as on a commission basis, see *Scott v Pattison* [1923] 2 KB 723; *Way v Latilla* [1937] 3 All ER 759 at 764; *Brenner v First Artists' Management Pty Ltd* [1993] 2 VR 221. Note that reasonable remuneration will include an element of profit.
2 See *Batis Maritime Corpn v Petroleos Del Mediterraneo SA, The Batis* [1990] 1 Lloyd's Rep 345. See also *Scaduto v Orlando* 381 F 2d 587 at 595 (1967). See further Goff and Jones *Law of Restitution* (5th edn, 1998), pp 28 and 31.
3 See generally *Robinson v Graves* [1935] 1 KB 579; *Clay v Yates* (1856) 1 H & N 73, 156 ER 1123.
4 See *BP Exploration Co (Libya) Ltd v Hunt (No 2)* [1982] 1 All ER 925 at 940, per Robert Goff J (who agreed that generally it is the services that count as the enrichment but in this case felt constrained by the relevant statutory provision to hold otherwise). See also *Brenner v First Artists' Management Pty Ltd* [1993] 2 VR 221. Cf *Pavey & Matthews Pty Ltd v Paul* (1987) 162 CLR 221 at 263, per Deane J (valuation based on a reasonable rate for the services should not be applied in the case of unsolicited services where that would result in an award that would far exceed the enhanced value of the defendant's property).
5 Cf Virgo *Principles of the Law of Restitution* (1999), pp 68 and 98.

19.108   It follows from has been said that valuation is concerned with valuing the enrichment, or more accurately, the extent to which the enrichment is unjust. It is not necessarily concerned with the value of the enrichment to the defendant, nor is it generally concerned with the actual costs incurred by the claimant[1] in providing the services, whether those costs are above or below the market rate[2]. If this general rule is to give way to a more subjective valuation based on the special position, understanding or agreement of the parties, then the party arguing for that valuation should carry the onus of proof[3].

In assessing the claim, the court will take into account the extent to which the claimant has already been remunerated[4]. It should also be noted that the mere fact that the claimant may have passed on some or all of his or her loss to a third party is not taken into account in assessing his or her loss[5]. Finally, where an order for restitution is made, the court may also order simple interest[6].

1   It would appear such costs are a relevant consideration though, see *Batis Maritime Corporation v Petroleos Del Mediterraneo SA, The Batis* [1990] 1 Lloyd's Rep 345; *Greenmast Shipping Co SA v Jean Lion et Cie SA, The Saronikos* [1986] 2 Lloyd's Rep 277. See also *ACME Process Equipment Co v United States* 347 F 2d 509 (1965).

2   See *Renard Constructions (ME) Pty Ltd v Minister for Public Works* (1992) 26 NSWLR 234 at 276, per Meagher JA (rejecting the argument that because restitution is now based on unjust enrichment the defendant should be required to pay whatever is the value of the services to him or her on the basis that this necessarily equates to the enrichment); *Brenner v First Artists' Management Pty Ltd* [1993] 2 VR 221. See further *BP Exploration Co (Libya) Ltd v Hunt (No 2)* [1979] 1 WLR 783 at 805 (affirmed [1983] 2 AC 352); *Flett v Deniliquin Publishing Co Ltd* [1964–1965] NSWR 383 at 386. Cf McInnes '"At the Plaintiff's Expense": Quantifying Restitutionary Relief' [1998] CLJ 472. Another view suggests that the general rule should be that the claimant cannot recover more than his or her loss and the defendant cannot be made liable for more than his or her gain. A further and related view suggests that where the claimant is in breach of contract his or her award should be the lesser of the reasonable value of the services provided, the increased value of the defendant's assets and a rateable proportion of the contract price, see Goff and Jones *Law of Restitution* (5th edn, 1998), pp 32 and 554.

3   See *Home Management Maintenance Pty Ltd v Doyle* (1992) 107 FLR 225. In *Pavey & Matthews Pty Ltd v Paul* (1987) 162 CLR 221 at 263–264, Deane J suggested that 'it would be contrary to the general notions of restitution and unjust enrichment if what constitutes fair and just compensation for the benefit accepted by the other party were to be ascertained without regard to any identifiable real detriment sustained by that other party by reason of the failure of the first party'. In that case the contract was unenforceable by reason of the failure by the claimant to satisfy certain statutory writing requirements. See also Goff and Jones *Law of Restitution* (5th edn, 1998), pp 28 and 29 and *BP Exploration Co (Libya) Ltd v Hunt (No 2)* [1979] 1 WLR 783 at 805–806 (affirmed [1983] 2 AC 352). See further *Council of the City of Sydney v Woodward* [2000] NSWCA 201 (this case was concerned with valuing the reasonable remuneration for the design of a water sculpture; the claimant was not permitted to recover on a reasonable cost basis but rather on a budgeted cost basis as this was his normal charging method; he was not permitted to vary this method in the appeal when that would have permitted him to increase his costs to a level which the evidence showed was always in excess of that which the defendant intended to expend; moreover, the court adopted as a budgeted costs basis the figures put forward by certain quantity surveyors as it was clear the defendant never intended to set a budget for the sculpture that was as high as that set by the claimant's budgeted cost basis).

4   See *Pavey & Matthews Pty Ltd v Paul* (1987) 162 CLR 221.

5   See *Woolwich Equitable Building Society v IRC* [1993] AC 70 at 177–178, per Lord Goff; *Kleinwort Benson Ltd v Birmingham City Council* [1997] QB 380 at 394, per Saville LJ, and at 400, per Morritt LJ; *Kleinwort Benson Ltd v South Tyneside Metropolitan Borough Council* [1994] 4 All ER 972 at 985, per Hobhouse J. See also *Comr of State Revenue v Royal Insurance Australia Ltd* (1994) 182 CLR 51 at 75, per Mason CJ; *Roxborough v Rothmans of Pall Mall Australia Ltd* [2001] HCA 68 at paras 22–29, per Gleeson CJ Gaudron and Hayne JJ, at paras 68–69 per Gummow J, and at paras 125–143 per Kirby J. It would appear, however, that Canada has accepted a 'passing on' defence, see *Air Canada v British Columbia* (1989) 59 DLR (4th) 161 and see McInnes 'The Canadian Principle of Unjust Enrichment: Comparative Insights Into the Law of Restitution' (1999) 37 Alberta Law Review 1 at 20–23. See further Rose 'Passing On' in Birks (ed) *Laundering and Tracing* (1995), ch 10.

6   See the Supreme Court Act 1981 s35A. See also *BP Exploration Co (Libya) Ltd v Hunt (No 2)* [1979] 1 WLR 783 at 835–837, per Robert Goff J ([1981] 1 WLR 232, CA, [1983] 2 AC 352, HL); *Council of the City of Sydney v Woodward* [2000] NSWCA 201. As to compound interest see *Westdeutsche Landesbank Girozentrale v Islington London Borough Council* [1994] 1 WLR 938 (void contract). See further below, para 21.70ff.

Relevance of the contract price in determining the reasonable value of services

19.109   In contracts discharged for breach or repudiation, the contract price is relevant in determining the reasonable value of services provided and may in some circumstances set a reasonable sum[1]. In the case of a free acceptance, the contract price can only ever be evidence of a reasonable remuneration, as the defendant will have accepted work or services that are not in accordance with the contract.

1   See *British Exploration Co (Libya) Ltd v Hunt (No 2)* [1979] 1 WLR 783 at 805–806, per Robert Goff J ([1981] 1 WLR 232, CA, [1983] 2 AC 352, HL); *Steele v Tardiani* (1946) 72 CLR 386 at 405, per Dixon J; *Pavey & Matthews Pty Ltd v Paul* (1987) 162 CLR 221.

19.110   Arguably the contract price or a rateable proportion of the contract price should govern recovery where the enrichment is arrived at by deemed or limited acceptance[1], that is, where ultimately the claimant is receiving an award referable to some contractual performance[2]. However, if the notion of a pro rata price is adopted[3], it must be evaluated realistically. Merely because a claimant has only performed say 25% of the required performance will not necessarily equate with an award of 25% of the price. It may be that the first 25% percent of performance carried the greatest costs for the claimant, and the pro rata award must recognise this. There may be other terms or factors affecting the price at certain times during the contract that would also have to be taken into account. In short, the contract must be construed within its matrix of facts, to determine exactly the agreed internal allocation of risks between the parties at the relevant time[4]. It is, however suggested that the better view and the more practical view here is still that the claimant, who is generally the party innocent of any breach of contract, should obtain relief valued by the market rate for the services provided, with the contract price being evidence of a reasonable value, and in any case setting an ultimate ceiling on recovery[5]. The basis for this result, rather than a proportion of the contract price is that the contract price, is based on full performance. It does not necessarily encapsulate the presumed intention of the parties as to the allocation of risk if there is something less than full performance[6]. There is usually nothing to suggest that the claimant would have agreed to the prorated price for the work done[7]. In addition, an award based on a proportion of the contract price may allow the defendant to profit from the breach of contract in a way that was only agreed if he or she fully performed. Finally, an approach based on a proportion of the contract price may tend to over-emphasise the costs incurred by the claimant, rather than the extent to which the defendant is unjustly enriched.

1   See above, para 19.89.
2   Cf para 19.94 as to whether some of the cases are really awarding reliance loss. See *Steele v Tardiani* (1946) 72 CLR 386, and para 19.74.
3   See eg *Kehoe v Mayor of Borough of Rutherford* 27 A 912 (1893).
4   See Skelton *Restitution and Contract* (1998), pp 66–67, 76 and 78–83.
5   See below, para 19.112.
6   See Jones *Restitution in Public and Private Law* (1991), pp 119 and 120.
7   See further Beatson *Use and Abuse of Unjust Enrichment* (1991), p 14. See also *Newton Woodhouse v Trevor Toys Ltd* (20 December 1991, unreported), CA, per Beldam LJ, and see para 19.115, n 4.

Valuation and incontrovertible benefits

19.111   Where the defendant is held to have been incontrovertibly benefited, then restitution should be valued by reference to the defendant's actual enrichment, that is, the amount of the payment received[1], the amounts realised on the sale of the claimant's performance, or (on another view) the amount realisable on the claimant's performance[2]. The valuation of a claim based on an incontrovertible benefit where the claimant has realised the defendant's performance should take place at the time the benefit is realised[3].

1 See above, para 19.6.
2 See paras 19.64 and 19.78. See *BP Exploration Co (Libya) Ltd v Hunt (No 2)* [1979] 1 WLR 783 at 805, per Robert Goff J; *William Lacey (Hounslow) Ltd v Davis* [1957] 1 WLR 932. See also Garner 'Benefits – For Services Rendered: Commentary' in McInnes (ed) *Restitution: Developments in Unjust Enrichment* (1996), p 113. Cf Goff and Jones *Law of Restitution* (5th edn, 1998), pp 31 and 32.
3 See Mason and Carter *Restitution Law in Australia* (1995), para 1418. If it is accepted an incontrovertible benefit may arise when the claimant's performance is readily realisable, valuation should occur at the time the claim arises.

The contract price as a ceiling on recovery

19.112   It was noted above that the general rule as to valuation is that an award for reasonable remuneration will equate to the market rate of the services provided by the claimant. Therefore, although the contract price or a rateable proportion of the contract price may be evidence of a reasonable rate, it is not necessarily conclusive. An issue therefore arises in the context of this chapter as to whether the contract price should in any case form a ceiling on recovery.

19.113   There is no doubt that the weight of current authority comes down firmly in favour of the contract price not placing a ceiling on claims for restitution[1]. However, the important earlier authorities such as *Slowey v Lodder*[2] and *Boomer v Muir*[3] are predicated on the view that upon discharge the contract is rescinded, and therefore ceases to exist for all purposes. In addition, where the claim for restitution is against a party in breach of contract, the cases appear to place some weight on the conduct of the defendant. That is, a party in breach forfeits his or her rights to resort to the contract where from his or her view point the contract was advantageous[4].

1 See eg *Slowey v Lodder* (1901) 20 NZLR 321, CA; affd [1904] AC 442, PC; *Boomer v Muir* 24 P 2d 570 (1933); *Scaduto v Orlando* 381 F 2d 587 (1967); *United States v Algernon Blair Inc* 479 F 2d 638 (1973); *Brooks Robinson Pty Ltd v Rothfield* [1951] VLR 405; *Murdock-Bryant Construction Inc v Pearson* 703 P 2d 1206 (1984) at 1217; *Renard Constructions (ME) Pty Ltd v Minister for Public Works* (1992) 26 NSWLR 234; *Iezzi Constructions Pty Ltd v Watkins Pacific (Qld) Pty Ltd* [1995] 2 Qd R 350. See also *Heyman v Darwins Ltd* [1942] AC 356 at 397–398, per Lord Porter. Cf *Dey v Hill* 181 P 462 (1919); *Kehoe v Mayor of Borough of Rutherford* 27 A 912 (1893). See further on the American position Hunter and Carter 'Quantum Meruit and Building Contracts Part II' (1990) 2 Journal of Contract Law 189. On the position in Canada see Rafferty 'Contract Discharged Through Breach: Restitution for Services Rendered by the Innocent Party' (1999) 37 Alberta Law Review 51 at 65–72. See further Skelton *Restitution and Contract* (1998), pp 50–61.
2 (1901) 20 NZLR 321, CA; affd [1904] AC 442, PC.
3 24 P 2d 570 (1933).
4 See *Boomer v Muir* 24 P 2d 570 at 577 (1933); *United States for the Use of Coastal Steel Erectors Inc v Algernon Blair Inc* 479 F 2d 638 at 640 (1973). See also *Renard Constructions (ME) Pty Ltd v Minister of Public Works* (1992) 26 NSWLR 234.

19.114   The leading modern authority, *Renard Constructions (ME) Pty Ltd v Minister of Public Works*[1], cannot be so easily dismissed. This case concerned a construction contract that was terminated by a building contractor, for breach by the defendant. The contract price was approximately $209,000. However, the contractor was successful in electing to bring a claim for restitution, and recovered approximately $285,000. Meagher JA gave the leading judgment on this point. He relied on such cases as *Lodder v Slowey* and *Boomer v Muir*, despite recognising that they were based on discharge having the effect of rescinding the contract[2]. Nevertheless, he thought that in addition to authority, it was also correct in principle to ignore the contract price. He reasoned that the innocent party has an option of suing either in damages for breach of contract or on a quantum meruit for work done. If that election is recognised it must also be recognised that that choice may lead to different results[3]. He thought that 'it would be extremely anomalous if the defaulting party when sued on a quantum meruit could invoke the contract which he has repudiated in order to impose a ceiling on amounts otherwise recoverable'[4]. However, he accepted that the contract price may be evidence of the reasonableness of the amount claimed. He made no comment as to whether the position is the same when the claimant is the party in breach.

1   (1992) 26 NSWLR 234. This case was applied in *Iezzi Constructions Pty Ltd v Watkins Pacific (Qld) Pty Ltd* [1995] 2 Qd R 350. See further *Council of the City of Sydney v Woodward* [2000] NSWCA 201.
2   (1992) 26 NSWLR 234 at 277. Cf *Brooks Robinson Pty Ltd v Rothfield* [1951] VLR 405.
3   (1992) 26 NSWLR 234 at 277.
4   (1992) 26 NSWLR 234 at 278.

19.115   The legal position in England (outside of the point that the contract price is evidence of the value of services rendered) remains unclear[1]. For example, *Lodder v Slowey* is not a binding decision for English courts and, as noted, its reasoning does not stand up against the modern law of discharge. Moreover, the argument that the contract price sets a ceiling on recovery was rejected by the Court of Appeal in *Rover International Ltd v Cannon Film Sales Ltd*[2]. However, that case involved a contract that was void. Prior to *Rover*, in *BP Exploration (Libya) Co v Hunt (No 2)*[3], Robert Goff J, at first instance, appeared to offer some support for the contract price acting as a ceiling on recovery in discharged contracts[4].

1   See Skelton *Restitution and Contract* (1998), p 53ff for a discussion of the various competing remarks in a number of cases on this point.
2   [1989] 1 WLR 912 at 927–928, per Kerr LJ, and at 934, per Dillon LJ (the Court of Appeal held that Cannon could not argue that the contract price set a ceiling on recovery when it had argued that Rover was not entitled to payment under the contract because the contract was void).
3   [1979] 1 WLR 783 (affirmed [1981] 1 WLR 232 (CA); affirmed [1983] 2 AC 352).
4   See also *Ranger v Great Western Rly Co* (1854) 5 HL Cas 72 at 96, 10 ER 824 at 834, per Lord Cranworth (obiter). Cf the remarks of the Privy Council in *Lodder v Slowey* [1904] AC 442 at 451 agreeing with the Court of Appeal in that case to the effect that *Ranger* merely decided that the appellants had no claim to equitable relief); *Newton Woodhouse v Trevor Toys Ltd* (20 December 1991, unreported), CA, per Glidewell LJ (if the contract price did not form a ceiling 'it could result in substantial injustice if a contractor who was losing money heavily on a contract became entitled to payment for the past work on a more favourable basis than the contract provided and when his losses were not caused by the employer's breach'. Cf also: it may be unjust 'to permit a party in breach of contract to retain the benefit of work carried out by a contractor who has quoted a price on the assumption that he will have the opportunity of completing the whole of the work. In such a case it could well be that valuing the work performed pro rata at the contract rate may unjustly enrich the employer at the expense of the contractor ... It must therefore be questionable whether a straight line apportionment of the labour charges to the work actually performed would adequately compensate the plaintiff ... [T]here may be cases in which the contractor ought to be allowed to claim for work done before repudiation of the contract by the employer on a basis other than that agreed for a pro rata apportionment of the whole of the work': per Beldam LJ.

19.116   Academic opinion on this issue is not uniform. Beatson has argued that doctrinally there is no place for the contract price to form a ceiling, if there is evidence of a true enrichment[1]. Burrows has argued that the contract price should not form a ceiling on recovery. He disagrees with the argument that to allow recovery in excess of the contract price would allow claimant's to escape bad bargains. He points out that claims for the recovery of money based on total failure of consideration have never been successfully defended on the basis that the claimant in some cases may be escaping a bad bargain[2]. Burrows' position appears in part driven by his view that, once the contract is discharged, a restitutionary claim will not impinge upon the allocation of risk under the contract, because the contract is inneffective. He maintains the position that a claim in restitution is independent of contract[3]. However, he suggests that the contract price is relevant in determining the value of the benefit received by the defendant[4]. He suggests that except where the defendant is incontrovertibly benefited the defendant is generally capable of arguing that he or she was not willing to pay the market value of services rendered. That is, he or she can subjectively devalue those services to a level he or she was willing to pay, namely the contract rate or price or pro rata contract price. This would then form the limit on recovery[5].

Birks rejects the need for a rule requiring the contract price to set a ceiling on a claim for restitution. Like Burrows he does not think the parties' allocation of risk is relevant on discharge[6]. He agrees with Burrows that there can be no place for a contract ceiling where the enrichment is constituted by an incontrovertible benefit. Moreover, he too places emphasis on the position of claims for the recovery of money where no deduction is made if the bargain was a losing one[7]. However, he accepts the notion of a valuation ceiling whereby a recipient can resort to the circumstances surrounding his or her acceptance to limit the enrichment[8].

On the other hand, both Goff and Jones, and Mason and Carter, suggest that where the quantum meruit claim is made by the party not in breach and where the enrichment is derived from no more than work or services carried out in performance of the contract, the claimant should never recover more than the contract price[9].

1   Beatson *Use and Abuse of Unjust Enrichment* (1991), pp 12–15. Moreover, he argues (pp 13–14) that on a more practical level 'there are several reasons for rejecting the contract price as limit whether by restricting recovery to a rateable proportion of the contract price or in absolute terms, although the case for rejecting the contract price as an overall limit is not as persuasive'. The first reason he gives is that the contract remedy may not adequately achieve its purpose, namely protect expectation. Second, he makes the point that prorating may be difficult and unfair. Third, he argues that to limit restitution to the contract price gives the contract breaker part of his or her contractual expectations which he or she should only be entitled to if they are ready and willing to perform. Finally, he suggests that limiting restitution to the contract price creates a disequilibrium between the innocent party who has done a small proportion of the work and one who has done the bulk of the work.
2   See eg *Bush v Canfield* 2 Conn 485 (1818).
3   Burrows *Law of Restitution* (1993), p 269.
4   Burrows *Law of Restitution* (1993), pp 268–270.
5   See further Skelton *Restitution and Contract* (1998).
6   Birks 'Restitution after Ineffective Contracts: Issues for the 1990s' (1990) 2 Journal of Contract Law 227 at 232: 'Recovery of the prepayment does not subvert the distribution of risks effected by the bargain. That is shown by the fact that according to the law of contract itself the bargain is discharged. That is dogmatic shorthand for a more cumbersome truth: the commitment of each party to the risks inherent in the bargain is initially conditional, and the risks never run if that conditionality is neither purified nor waived'.
7   Birks 'In Defence of Free Acceptance' in Burrows (ed) *Essays on the Law of Restitution* (1991), p 136: 'if the restitutionary claim to recover money after a failure of consideration is upheld

without any deduction to reduce recovery to the lesser amount which the plaintiff, if his bargain was a losing one, would have recovered in contractual damages, it is flatly inconsistent to argue that a restitutionary claim in respect of non-money benefits should be subject to the contract ceiling'.

8 Birks 'In Defence of Free Acceptance' in Burrows (ed) *Essays on the Law of Restitution* (1991), p 136.

9 Goff and Jones *Law of Restitution* (5th edn, 1998) pp 533–534, Mason and Carter *Restitution Law in Australia* (1995), para 1430. See also Jones 'Restitution: Unjust Enrichment as a Unifying Concept in Australia' (1988) 1 Journal of Contract Law 8 at 13–14. See further Hunter and Carter 'Quantum Meruit and Building Contracts Part II' (1990) 2 Journal of Contract Law 189 at 199–200; Kull 'Restitution as Remedy for Breach of Contract' (1994) 67 South California Law Review 1465. Cf Jackman *The Varieties of Restitution* (1998), p 85.

19.117 It would appear that the three main arguments against the contract price setting a ceiling on recovery are: that restitution is independent of contract; that there is no upsetting of contract risk allocation, because the contract must be discharged prior to any restitutionary claim being considered; and that no deduction is made in claims for the recovery of money based on failure of consideration when the bargain is a losing one.

It is suggested that each of these arguments cannot be sustained. The first two are closely related and can be dealt with together. The idea that restitution is independent of contract, and therefore need not pay any heed to the terms of a discharged contract, must be wrong, because the practical effect of that reasoning (awarding a sum in excess of the contract price) fundamentally impacts on the institution of contract where restitution is being given for enrichments which flow from acts carried out in performance of a contract. It must be recognised that the independence of unjust enrichment must at times yield to overriding policy considerations. It does not exist in a vacuum, but rather as an integral part of the law of obligations. In addition, it is an error to suggest that the allocation of risk under a contract is no longer operative once a contract is discharged. In fact, the allocation of risk under a contract may have one of its most important roles to play upon discharge. Where risk allocation is being discussed, it is important to distinguish total failure of consideration cases where the claimant has paid money in performance of the contract and earned some return performance, and quantum meruit cases where the claimant has carried out acts in performance of the contract but has not earned any agreed return under the contract. In the former, the allocation of risk vis-à-vis the claimant is not operative whereas in the latter it is.

19.118 As regards the recovery of money based on failure of consideration, the short answer is that the defendant is incontrovertibly benefitted. Therefore, no deduction should be made on the ground that the contract was a losing one for the claimant[1]. Moreover, where the defendant to such proceedings is in breach of contract, to allow such a deduction would allow him or her to profit from their breach. Therefore, the contract price should not place a ceiling on recovery in such circumstances. The claimant simply recovers the value of the enrichment at the time the defendant received the incontrovertible benefit[2]. Thus in claims for the recovery of payment on the basis of total failure of consideration, the claimant always recovers the amount he or she paid, and not the reasonable market value of that payment at the time of judgment[3]. As noted, recovery based on total failure of consideration does not upset the allocation of risk set by the parties, as that allocation is accepted by the claimant on the basis that the defendant has performed[4], whereas recovery based on total failure of consideration is based on the fact that the defendant has done nothing. The allocation of risk is therefore not operative. To take account of whether or not the contract would have been a losing one for the claimant seems to confuse restitution with compensation.

1 See *Bush v Canfield* 2 Conn 485 (1818); *Wilkinson v Lloyd* (1845) 7 QB 27, 115 ER 398. That this is the position in the United States has recently been confirmed by the Supreme Court of the United States in *Mobil Oil Exploration & Producing Southeast Inc v United States* 530 US 604 (2000). Cf McKendrick 'Total Failure of Consideration and Counter-Restitution: Two Issues or One?' in Birks (ed) *Laundering and Tracing* (1995), pp 227–229.
2 See above, para 19.6.
3 Cf the old case of *Dutch v Warren* (1720) 1 Stra 406, 93 ER 598 (where in an action for money had and received a jury awarded the claimant not the amount he had paid for the transfer of certain shares but the value of those shares at the time the transfer should have taken place, the price had fallen by this time. See also the discussion of this case in *Moses v MacFerlan* (1760) 2 Burr 1005, 97 ER 676; 1 Black & W 220, 96 ER 120. See further Stoljar 'The Doctrine of Failure of Consideration' (1959) 75 LQR 53 at 57.
4 See Law Com no 121 *The Law of Contract: Pecuniary Restitution on Breach of Contract* (1983), para 3.9. Cf Skelton *Restitution and Contract* (1998), pp 34 and 35; and McKendrick 'Total Failure of Consideration and Counter-Restitution: Two Issues or One?' in Birks (ed) *Laundering and Tracing* (1995), pp 227–229.

19.119   In addition to enrichments proven by reference to an incontrovertible benefit not being subject to the contract price as a ceiling on recovery, the same must also follow as regards free acceptance. Where a defendant has freely accepted the services provided by the claimant, it provides the circumstances for removing the claimant's right to remuneration from the exact conditons of the contract. It is generally only made out where the services provided are outside the contract. It must follow that recovery therefore cannot be limited by the contract price, as there will be no contract price for those services.

19.120   The only category left is where restitution is awarded in respect of services, and those services were provided in part performance of a contract, that is, generally where the enrichment is proven by deemed or limited acceptance[1]. Here the contract price should set a ceiling on recovery[2]. Arguably, in such cases the breach of contract is the true basis for restitution[3], and in that circumstance there appears little reason to ignore the contract price, because liability in restitution is simply not independent of contract[4]. Any other result would lead to the incongruity that a party who has only partially performed at the time of discharge would be in a more advantageous position than a party who has substantially or fully performed, as the former is not limited to claiming the contract price if their claim for restitution is successful[5].

1 See above, paras 19.89 and 19.94.
2 See *Kehoe v Mayor of Borough of Rutherford* 27 A 912 (1893); and *Ranger v Great Western Rly Co* (1854) 5 HL Cas 72 at 94, per Lord Cranworth.
3 See above, para 19.105.
4 See Carter 'Discharged Contracts: Claims for Restitution' (1997) 11 Journal of Contract Law 130 at 145. See above, para 19.117. Cf *Heyman v Darwins Ltd* [1942] AC 356 at 397–398, per Lord Porter.
5 See Mason and Carter *Restitution Law in Australia* (1995), para 1430; and Beatson *Use and Abuse of Unjust Enrichment* (1991), p 13.

Damages and restitution

19.121   Where an innocent party has a claim in restitution, they will also have a claim for damages in respect of the breach of contract. These are not inconsistent remedies, and so the claimant does not have to make an election between them. However, the rule against double recovery dictates that a claimant cannot both recover full damages and full restitution in respect of any particular loss[1]. It follows that an award of restitution in respect of some unjust enrichment will not prevent a claim in damages in respect of some other distinct or additional loss, and it would appear that damages may at times include a restitutionary component[2]. Moreover, where the claimant is the party in breach, that claim does not prevent the defendant from bringing a claim for damages and, in some instances, the claim for restitution may be taken into account in the claim for damages[3].

1   See *Heywood v Wellers* [1976] QB 446; *Millar's Machinery Co Ltd v David Way and Son* (1935) 40 Com Cas 204; *Beale v Taylor* [1967] 1 WLR 1193. See further Mason and Carter *Restitution Law in Australia* (1995), para 1410.

2   *Baltic Shipping Co v Dillon, The Mikhail Lermontov* (1993) 176 CLR 344 at 359, per Mason CJ; see also at 379–380, per Deane and Dawson JJ.

3   Cf *McDonald v Dennys Lascelles Ltd* (1933) 48 CLR 457 at 479 (in the case of a contract for the sale of land where the price was payable in instalments, it was not possible to deduct from the instalments paid the amount of loss occasioned by the purchaser's abandonment of the contract. The whole had to be repaid and a counterclaim made for damages).

CHAPTER 20

Frustration of Contract

Steve Hedley

A Introduction

20.1   Where events occur which render the parties' contract inapplicable to the facts as they have emerged, then the contract ceases to govern the parties' mutual rights, and is said to be 'frustrated'. This may occur because of a radical change of circumstances, which invalidates the assumptions on the basis of which the parties contracted; or because changes to the law have made further performance of the contract illegal. It will be assumed in this chapter that the parties' contract has indeed been frustrated, and that (if it is necessary to do so) the precise instant of frustration can be ascertained. The doctrine of frustration is considered in greater detail in works on the law of contract[1].

1   See eg Furmston (ed) *Law of Contract* (1999), ch 7E.

20.2   The general effect of frustration is to leave the loss where it falls. '[E]ach party is left in the position he was in when the event occurred, and legal rights already accrued under the contract are unaffected'[1]. In other words, the court must ascertain the contractual rights of the parties immediately before the frustrating event: and the rights that have accrued *at that point* are prima facie the only rights the contract has created, or can ever create. So if one party has rendered a performance (full or partial) to the other party before frustration, then whether they are entitled to remuneration depends on whether they have earned it under the contract at the instant before the frustrating event. If remuneration is then due, it remains due despite the frustration; if it is not then due, it never will be due[2]. That is the basic rule. However, there are three sources of liability despite this:

- benefits transferred before frustration can lead to an award under the Law Reform (Frustrated Contracts) Act 1943[3];
- in cases where the Act does not apply, remedies are more limited, but a party who has transferred money and recovered nothing in return may sometimes recover it[4];
- benefits transferred after the frustrating event may in appropriate cases be remunerated on the basis of 'free acceptance' or a fresh contract[5].

These three cases will be considered in turn. The resulting law is thought satisfactory by few, and there has been much discussion of possible alternatives[6].

1   *Joseph Constantine Steamship Line Ltd v Imperial Smelting Corpn Ltd* [1942] AC 154 at 170, [1941] 2 All ER 165 at 175–176, per Viscount Maugham.
2   See discussion by Robert Goff J in *BP Exploration Co (Libya) v Hunt (No 2)* [1979] 1 WLR 783 at 808. Note that the Law Reform (Frustrated Contracts) Act 1943, s 1(2), may affected accrued rights; below, para 20.5.

3   See below, para 20.3ff.
4   See below, para 20.19ff.
5   See below, para 20.22ff.
6   See especially Stewart and Carter 'Frustrated contracts and statutory adjustment: The case for a reappraisal' [1992] CLJ 66; Stewart 'The South Australian Frustrated Contracts Act' (1992) 5 Journal of Contract Law 220.

B   The Law Reform (Frustrated Contracts) Act 1943[1]

20.3   The Act applies generally to frustrated contracts; there are a few excluded cases, which are considered below[2]. The Act itself states that it applies whenever the contract 'has become impossible of performance or been otherwise frustrated, and the parties thereto have for that reason been discharged from the further performance of the contract'[3]. This suggests a broad view of frustration.

1   The Act followed on the 7th Interim Report of the Law Revision Committee (1939, Cmnd 6009), and the decision of the House of Lords in *Fibrosa Spolka Akcyjna v Fairbairn Lawson Combe Barbour Ltd* [1943] AC 32, [1942] 2 All ER 122, on which see below, para 20.19. See generally McKendrick 'Frustration, restitution, and loss apportionment' in Burrows (ed) *Essays on the law of restitution* (1991), p 147.
2   See below, para 20.18.
3   See the Law Reform (Frustrated Contracts) Act 1943, s 1(1).

20.4   A contract is either frustrated or it is not, and there is no such thing as partial frustration[1]. Nonetheless, the Act recognises that it may sometimes be appropriate to split a contract into those parts that have been performed and those that have not, granting contractual remedies for the former part but a restitutionary remedy for the latter. More precisely, 'Where it appears to the court that a part of any contract to which this Act applies can be properly severed from the remainder of the contract, being a part wholly performed before the time of discharge, or so performed except for the payment in respect of that part of the contract of sums which are or can be ascertained under the contract, the court shall treat that part of the contract as if it were a separate contract and had not been frustrated and shall treat the foregoing section of this Act as only applicable to the remainder of that contract'[2].
     The general effect of the Act is to provide a limited right to recover the value of benefits transferred under the contract. However, the Act treats money differently from other benefits.

1   The case of *Minnevitch v Café de Paris (Londres) Ltd* [1936] 1 All ER 884 is sometimes said to be an example of partial frustration. A band was employed to play at a restaurant on successive nights, but the restaurant manager cancelled their performance during a short period of national mourning. It was held that the manager was entitled to do so, though the obligation revived on subsequent evenings. However, in my view the case is better seen as turning on construction rather than as representing 'partial frustration'.
2   See the Law Reform (Frustrated Contracts) Act 1943, s 2(4).

The remedy for return of money paid – s 1(2)

20.5   Where money is paid to the other party before the frustrating event, the effect of the Act is that the sum can be reclaimed in accordance with s 1(2). The subsection also provides that a sum which was payable before the frustrating event ceases to be payable. (Though if it was payable in respect of performance in fact rendered by the other party, no doubt the court would avoid recovery by severing that part of the contract from the rest[1].) Read literally, the Act has no application where a sum is paid after frustration but in ignorance that it has occurred. Such a sum was doubtless recoverable, but this is arguably at common law rather than under the Act[2].

1 On severance see above, para 20.4.
2 And so the sum is not subject to the deduction to be discussed in the next paragraph, though the defence of change of position may sometimes lead to a similar result. On change of position see below, para 21.37ff.

20.6   However, where the payee incurred expenses before the time of discharge, then the payee may seek a deduction from the amount that must be refunded to the payor. It is for the payee to establish that a deduction should justly be made, and its extent[1]. In ascertaining the sum to be deducted, the court should ignore any insurance monies paid in respect of the frustrating event, unless the insurance was required either by an express term of the frustrated contract, or by some enactment[2]. The total amount of the expenses is the maximum possible deduction. The expenses must have been incurred 'before the time of discharge ... in, or for the purpose of, the performance of the contract'[3]. However, 'expenses' are not limited to disbursements or sums outgoing: they can include reasonable sums for overheads, and in respect of work or services performed personally[4]. And on the literal wording of the Act at least, they may include sums expended before the contract was made.

1 *Gamerco SA v ICM/Fair Warning (Agency) Ltd* [1995] 1 WLR 1226 at 1235, citing *Lobb v Vasey Housing Auxiliary (War Widows Guild)* [1963] VR 239, under the (very similar) Victorian Frustrated Contracts Act 1959.
2 See the Law Reform (Frustrated Contracts) Act 1943, s 1(5).
3 See the Law Reform (Frustrated Contracts) Act 1943, s 1(3)(a).
4 See the Law Reform (Frustrated Contracts) Act 1943, s 1(4).

20.7   In the leading case the claimants (pop promoters) agreed with the defendants (a rock group) to organise an open-air concert in Madrid starring the defendants. Four days before the concert, however, the stadium was declared unsafe, and, no alternative venue being available, the concert was cancelled. By that point, the claimants had paid over to the defendants US$412,500 as an advance. Both parties had incurred other expenses, the precise extent of which was unclear, but which in the case of the claimants certainly exceeded US$450,000. The claimants were plainly entitled to recover their payment, but need they make any deduction? Garland J held not. It was for the defendants to establish that a deduction should be made, and if so, its extent. In some circumstances, the right approach would be to split the sum between the two parties, but that would not be appropriate where (as here) the parties' losses seemed very unequal. The object of making a deduction would be 'to do justice in a situation which the parties had neither contemplated nor provided for, and to mitigate the possible harshness of allowing all loss to lie where it has fallen'[1]. It seems clear that the main factor influencing Garland J was the defendants' inability to quantify their loss, or to go beyond mere unsupported estimates of it:

> As I have made clear, I would have welcomed assistance on the true measure of the defendants' loss ... The defendants undoubtedly suffered some loss but they have wholly failed to quantify it and, on the evidence available to me, I would decline to pluck a figure from the air[2].

1 Some academic writers, by contrast, have argued that the provisions embody some distinct purpose or policy, hard though it is to discern what it is. See Burrows *Law of Restitution* (1993), pp 284–287.

2   *Gamerco SA v ICM/Fair Warning (Agency) Ltd* [1995] 1 WLR 1226 at 1237. For criticism see
    Carter and Tolhurst 'Gigs 'n' restitution: Frustration and the statutory adjustment of payments
    and expenses' (1996) 10 Journal of Contract Law 264.

The remedy in respect of other benefits – s 1(3)

20.8   Where benefits other than money have been transferred from one party
to the other, an award may be justified under s 1(3). In some cases where both
money and other benefits have been transferred, remedies under both
subsections may be appropriate. In such a case, the correct approach is first to
ascertain the remedy, if any, under s 1(2), and then to consider whether an
additional remedy under s 1(3) is merited[1]. The award under s 1(2) is then a
relevant circumstance in assessing the remedy under s 1(3)[2].

1   This is the single point on which the Court of Appeal in *BP Exploration Co (Libya) Ltd v Hunt (No
    2)* criticised the order of Robert Goff J on liability, though it made no difference on the facts. See
    [1981] 1 WLR 232 at 241, per Lawton LJ.
2   See the Law Reform (Frustrated Contacts) Act 1943, s 1(3)(a), concluding words.

20.9   The subsection provides a structured discretion. Firstly, the court must
place a figure on the extent to which the transferor has been benefited. Secondly,
the court must place a figure on the award which it considers will do justice as
between the parties. The court must then award the lower of these two figures.
Put differently, the court has a discretion to award the claimant such sum as
seems just, but cannot award more than the amount by which it considers that
the defendant has been benefited by the claimant's performance. No doubt in
some cases it will appear to the court that justice would only be done by the
award of a higher figure; but if so, the court has no power under s 1(3) to award
that higher figure.

20.10   There is very little case law on this provision. In the leading case[1], BP
made a contract with Hunt, who owned an oil concession in Libya, for joint
exploitation of that concession. BP were to make certain payments and transfers
of oil to Hunt. The concession would then be jointly owned, and oil from it split
equally. BP were to pay for drilling, extraction and transport of the oil. If and
when the oil came on stream, in principle it was to be half BP's and half Hunt's.
However, BP were entitled to be reimbursed for their expenses, at a rate of $1.25
for every $1 expended; $\frac{3}{8}$ of Hunt's share of oil, when actually produced, was to
go to BP in satisfaction of this debt, until the whole was repaid. This agreement
was acted on, BP expending large sums on works, including the construction of a
500km pipeline to carry the oil. But at a point after the oil came on stream, but
before BP had been fully reimbursed, the Libyan authorities expropriated the
concession, paying a relatively small amount in compensation to Hunt. BP
subsequently sought a remedy from Hunt under the Act.

1   *BP Exploration Co (Libya) Ltd v Hunt (No 2)* [1979] 1 WLR 783 (Robert Goff J), [1981] 1 WLR
    232 (CA), [1983] 2 AC 352 (HL).

20.11   The subsequent litigation applied the 1943 Act in order to determine
how much BP could recover from Hunt. Various issues arose, which are
considered below. In summary, Robert Goff J at first instance reasoned as follows.
An award should be made under s 1(3). In principle, the value of the benefit
received by Hunt was the enhanced value of the concession. However, in the
light of the frustrating event, a better measure of the benefit was the value of oil,

and other benefits actually received by Hunt, such as cash and oil received direct from BP, and sums paid in compensation by the Libyan government[1]. However, it was wrong to treat Hunt as the mere passive recipient of generosity from BP: half of all of these benefits could justly be attributed to Hunt's ownership of the undeveloped concession. The benefit under s 1(3) was therefore calculated by ascertaining Hunt's net cashflow for each year of the operation, and his benefit was valued at half the total. This came to about US$84m. The 'just sum' was taken to be the amount that BP had expended on the project (net of all benefits they received from it): this came to US$35m. The award under s 1(3) was therefore US$35m, the lower of the two sums.

1   As noted above (para 20.8) Robert Goff J included all the benefits in the s 1(3) calculation. This was held to be wrong, as s 1(2) should have been applied first – though in the event it made no difference.

20.12   Robert Goff J's judgment in the case is elaborate, and considers many sub-issues, to which reference will be made below. However, there is an inherent difficulty in applying it as a precedent. Robert Goff J approached the substantial difficulties he faced as problems of statutory interpretation, to be resolved by careful consideration of the wording of the Act and its underlying policy basis, which he took to be the principle against unjust enrichment. The Court of Appeal, however, while making no substantial correction to Robert Goff J's award[1], nonetheless did not agree that it was *required* by the Act. His approach was perfectly legitimate: 'it cannot be said that the judge went wrong ... ' However, it did not follow that it was the only possible approach. '[T]here could be more than one way of assessing a just sum ... [There is] nothing in the Act to indicate that its purpose was to enable the judge to apportion loss or profits, or to put the parties in the positions which they would have been in if that contract had been fully performed or if it had never been made'[2]. As to unjust enrichment: 'We get no help from the use of words which are not in the statute'[3]. So the Court of Appeal ruled that Robert Goff J's approach is legitimate, but not that it was required by the Act, or that other approaches (even to identical facts) might not be equally legitimate[4].

Accordingly, the court must assess two figures: the amount by which the defendant has been 'benefited', and the 'just sum' which in principle the defendant should pay. The remedy under s 1(3) is then for the lower of the two figures.

1   But see below, para 20.16.
2   [1981] 1 WLR 232 at 242–243.
3   [1981] 1 WLR 232 at 243. The proposition that the Act reflects principles of unjust enrichment is accepted by some commentators (eg McKendrick 'The consequences of frustration – The Law Reform (Frustrated Contracts) Act 1943' in McKendrick (ed) *Force majeure and frustration of contract* (2nd edn, 1995), p 223), and denied by others (eg Haycroft and Waksman 'Frustration and restitution' [1984] Journal of Business Law 207; Virgo *Principles of the law of restitution* (1999), p 376).
4   For criticism of the extent of the discretion thus apparently vested in the judges, see Goff and Jones *Law of Restitution* (5th edn, 1998), p 562.

20.13   Plainly the definition of 'benefit' gives the court a measure of flexibility. In *Hunt*, Robert Goff J canvassed various possible meanings in relation to the facts before him. In many cases, he said, the right approach would be to assess the fair market value of what the claimant had provided for the defendant. Certainly this would be so in most cases involving prospecting: the benefit of discovering oil on another's land is not the value of the oil itself (which was there all along) but, rather, the reasonable value of the prospector's services. However, given the precise turn the facts took, it was more appropriate here to look to the end-product of the services, the 'benefit' consisting of the amount by which the defendant was better off as a result of the services. As noted above, Hunt was not the passive recipient of generosity from BP, but was an equal partner in the entire operation; accordingly, only half of the value of benefits obtained could be taken into account for the purposes of s 1(3)[1].

1   See above, para 20.11.

20.14   Was this benefit to be valued as the enhanced value of the oil concession, or rather as the amounts obtained by the concession's exploitation? In choosing the latter measure, Robert Goff J noted that the Act specifically required him to take into account the effect of the frustrating event on the benefit. And it is true that the subsection specifically says that this is relevant[1], as well as expenses paid by the defendant, and sums paid or payable to the claimant in performance of the contract[2]. However, there is some ambiguity here. The subsection says that these are relevant facts, but does not state how, or in precisely what way. On purely semantic grounds, it is certain arguable that they are meant to be relevant to the ascertainment of the just sum *but not to the ascertainment of the benefit*. Therefore, several commentators take the view that Robert Goff J erred here, and should not have taken account of the expropriation of the concession when valuing the benefit – though he could have treated it as one factor relevant to the assessment of the just sum[3]. While on as a matter of strict grammar these commentators have a point, nonetheless it seems more just to treat the actual benefit surviving the frustration as the upper limit of the award. Certainly no very clear reason has been given why the benefit conferred should be treated as solely at the defendants' risk.

1   See the Law Reform (Frustrated Contracts) Act 1943, s 1(3)(b). Note however an exception in relation to the benefit of insurance which was required neither by the contract nor by statute: s 1(5).
2   See the Law Reform (Frustrated Contracts) Act 1943, s 1(3)(a).
3   See eg Virgo *Principles of the law of restitution* (1999), pp 382–384.

20.15   The Act gives little general guidance on the assessment of benefits, but some detailed points are as follows:

- The benefit need not have been conferred on the defendant personally. If the defendant contracts for benefits to be conferred on a third party, then the actual conferment of those benefits, as per the contract, may be a benefit under the Act if the court thinks it just so to treat them[1].
- The benefit can include reasonable overheads, and a reasonable sum for work performed personally by the claimant[2].
- It seems that the benefit must be assessed without regard to the time value of money. So benefits valued at £1m when conferred are valued at that figure for all purposes, however long afterwards the claim is made. This was said by both Robert Goff J[3] and the Court of Appeal[4] to be required by the Act, even where (as in *Hunt*) the contract itself recognises the time value of money[5]. However, the reasoning – that s 1(2) ignores the time value of money, and the two subsections must be interpreted in a parallel fashion – is not compelling. The Act itself says nothing expressly on the point.

1   See the Law Reform (Frustrated Contracts) Act 1943, s 1(6).
2   See the Law Reform (Frustrated Contracts) Act 1943, s 1(4).
3   [1979] 1 WLR 783 at 803–804.
4   [1981] 1 WLR 232 at 244, expressly adopting the reasoning of Robert Goff J.

5   The contract recognised it by providing that BP should be reimbursed $1.25 for every $1 expended.

20.16   The assessment of the 'just sum' again gives a broad degree of flexibility. The Court of Appeal specifically rejected the argument that the Act requires any particular approach, or is motivated by any particular philosophy. On the facts, Robert Goff J placed considerable weight on the terms of the contract itself, declaring the guiding principle to be that the claimant should receive remuneration for work actually done, at the contractual rate. The Court of Appeal accepted this as a legitimate approach, and it is hard to disagree. However, it is equally hard to agree that this is a solution which will be right in very many cases. Firstly, if the courts are right to deny recognition to the time value of money, then the Act does not *allow* the court to apply the precise contractual measure as defined by the parties themselves. There is a measure of artificiality in applying the parties' agreement while ignoring such a vital matter. Secondly, frustration by definition involves circumstances for which the parties themselves made no adequate provision in their contract. It must therefore be a matter of fine judgment whether it will be appropriate to give any weight to their agreement in the circumstances which happened.

20.17   Viewed broadly, it seems awkward to argue that the subsection requires any particular philosophy. Some commentators have argued that it does in fact do so, whether that policy is styled 'loss apportionment' or 'unjust enrichment'. But it is hard to see how such general policies are of much use. It is particularly difficult to see how 'unjust enrichment' can be the basis both of the 'benefit' *and* of the 'just sum', since the draftsman evidently envisaged that these two quantities would usually be different.

The Act therefore has little to say on the assessment of the 'just sum'. As noted earlier, however, the Act states that expenses incurred by the defendant, and amounts paid or payable to the claimant in or for the purposes of the contract, are to be taken into account[1], as is the effect of the frustration on the benefit[2].

1   See the Law Reform (Frustrated Contracts) Act 1943, s 1(3)(a).
2   See the Law Reform (Frustrated Contracts) Act 1943, s 1(3)(b).

Excluded cases

20.18   In various cases, the operation of the Act is stated to be wholly or party excluded.

- While there is no such thing as 'partial frustration', nonetheless the court has a discretion to sever one part of the contractual performance, provided either that it is fully performed, or that the only thing remaining to be done under it is the payment of (ascertained or ascertainable) sums of money. If the court chooses to sever, then the case is treated as if there were two distinct contracts, only one of which is frustrated[1].
- The court must give effect to any contractual provision meant to have effect in the event of frustration. The Act then applies only to the extent that it is consistent with that provision[2].

- Various categories of contract are stated by the Act to be free from its provisions, presumably either on the ground that other statutory provisions provide an adequate remedy, or that the parties to them are likely to be sophisticated enough to provide their own remedy. These contracts are:
  - (a) **Contracts for the carriage of goods by sea, and charterparties** – However, the Act applies to time charters and demise charters[3].
  - (b) **Contracts of insurance**[4] – Therefore the common law rule remains, that insurers have earned their premium as soon as the period covered by the insurance has begun[5].
  - (c) **Sales of specific goods** – Where the contract terminates on the perishing of the goods. Most such cases will be within Sale of Goods Act 1979, s 7 (which makes the contract void, unless the risk had passed to the buyer), but the Act is excluded in any event[6].

1 See above, para 20.4. See the Law Reform (Frustrated Contracts) Act 1943, s 2(4).
2 See the Law Reform (Frustrated Contracts) Act 1943, s 2(3). For an unsuccessful attempt to invoke this provision see *BP Exploration Co (Libya) Ltd v Hunt (No 2)* [1983] 2 AC 352, HL.
3 See the Law Reform (Frustrated Contracts) Act 1943, s 2(5)(a).
4 See the Law Reform (Frustrated Contracts) Act 1943, s 2(5)(b). However, the clause exempts the effect of s 1(5), on which see above, para 20.6.
5 See eg *Tyrie v Fletcher* (1777) 2 Cowp 666, 98 ER 1297.
6 See the Law Reform (Frustrated Contracts) Act 1943, s 2(5)(c).

C   Common law principles on effect of frustration

20.19   Accordingly, in a few limited cases the Act does not apply, and any remedy will be on the common law principles which held sway before the Act was passed.

At common law, money paid by the claimant to the defendant is recoverable if the consideration for the payment has totally failed[1]. At one time it was thought that this principle was of no relevance to cases of frustration. It was argued that any payment under a contract is a payment in return for the obligations placed on the other, and so the consideration has not *wholly* failed if the other was *for a time* subject to those obligations, even if they subsequently dissipated through frustration[2]. However, the House of Lords ruled in 1943 that claimants could fairly be said to have suffered a total failure of consideration if in fact they received no part of what they bargained for[3]. In cases where the common law still applies, therefore, there is a remedy analogous to that under s 1(2), but not subject to a deduction for the defendant/payee's expenses. In principle the claim might be reduced or eliminated by reference to a change of position by the payee, but probably that defence can only apply to changes of position *after* receipt of the money, and so cannot cover pre-frustration expenses[4].

1 For this principle in a different context see above, para 19.14ff.
2 See especially *Chandler v Webster* [1904] 1 KB 493.
3 *Fibrosa Spolka Akcyjna v Fairbairn Lawson Combe Barbour Ltd* [1943] AC 32.
4 On the defence of change of position generally see below, para 21.37ff, and on anticipatory reliance see especially para 21.47.

20.20   Mere partial failure of consideration is not, in principle, a ground of recovery[1]. However, a similar result may sometimes be achieved through a splitting or 'apportionment' of the contract. If the claimant pays in advance for a year's work, but the contract is frustrated after only a month's work has been done, then obviously viewed overall the failure of consideration is only partial.

However, if the court could be persuaded to regard the contract as 12 successive contracts, each for a month's work, then it can fairly be said that $^{11}/_{12}$ of the money *was* paid on a consideration which wholly failed. The difficult question is as to when this apportionment can fairly be said to have taken place. Subject to contrary intention 'expressly stipulated' in the contract[2], statute deems it to have taken place in the following cases: 'rents, annuities, dividends, and other periodical payments in the nature of income [and] interest on money lent'[3]. Apportionment may also be inferred from the construction of the contract. An extreme case was where money was lent on security, a part was re-paid, but then the security became invalid through fraudulent third-party interference with the deed creating it. The Privy Council were prepared to rule that capital sums not re-paid could be said to have been paid on a total failure of consideration[4]. However, this seems to stretch the notion of *total* failure to its limit, or if not beyond it. The line between those obligations which can be apportioned, and those which cannot ('entire obligations') is considered above[5].

1   See eg *Whincup v Hughes* (1871) LR 6 CP 78 (lump sum paid for six-year apprenticeship; master dies after one year). These facts would today be within the scope of s 1(2), see above, para 20.5ff.
2   See the Apportionment Act 1870, s 7.
3   See the Apportionment Act 1870 s 2. See in more detail (including definitions of key terms in the Act) above, para 19.81ff.
4   *Goss v Chilcott* [1996] AC 788, [1997] 2 All ER 110; on which see above, para 19.38.
5   See above, para 19.60ff.

20.21   At common law there is no equivalent to the Act's s 1(3), and no remedy in respect of non-money benefits conferred before the frustrating event[1]. The question is therefore whether, at the instant before the frustrating event, the claimant had earned the contractual remuneration or any part of it. If not, no remedy is available. So where a contract to install machinery was frustrated by a fire sweeping through the premises, the engineers had no remedy beyond sums already earned by that stage of the work[2]. Or again, where a second mate was engaged for a voyage on terms that he would be paid only on its completion, his estate was not entitled to anything for his efforts when he died during the voyage[3].

1   But compare the Scots law: *Cantiare San Rocco SA v Clyde Shipbuilding and Engineering Co Ltd* [1924] AC 226.
2   *Appleby v Myers* (1867) LR 2 CP 651, [1861–1873] All ER Rep 452. Assuming that frustration was found on those facts today, the 1943 Act in principle gives a remedy, but the complete destruction of the work might reduce the award under s 1(3) to zero. See above, para 20.14.
3   *Cutter v Powell* (1795) 6 Term Rep 320, 101 ER 573. In principle the Apportionment Act 1870 gives a remedy on those facts today, subject to whether there was any intention to exclude it.

D   Benefits conferred after frustration

20.22   Once a contract has been frustrated, it can no longer generate claims for breach or for remuneration. And the 1943 Act provides no remedy in respect of benefits transferred after frustration. In most circumstances, however, the parties will be aware of the frustrating circumstances. Accordingly, liability may sometimes be based on a fresh contract, or on principles of incomplete contracts[1].

1   See above, ch 13.

20.23   But what if the parties were not aware, at the time of performance, that the contract was in fact frustrated? This can easily happen if the frustrating circumstances only slowly came to the parties' attention, or if they were aware only of a deepening crisis, even though a court in retrospect thinks the contract frustrated at that point.

Can a claimant who has conferred benefits on the other party, on a contractual basis, later seek remuneration for them if the contract turns out to have been frustrated? Such authority as there is suggests that the answer is Yes. In *The Massalia*[1] Pearson J held that a voyage charter from India to Genoa was frustrated by the closure of the Suez Canal, which blocked the most direct route. He was prepared to award a quantum meruit for the vessel's efforts in carrying the goods via the Cape of Good Hope, which doubled the overall length of the journey. However, the Court of Appeal subsequently ruled that his decision on frustration was wrong[2], and accordingly Pearson J's ruling is only of limited authority. It is weakened further by his heavy reliance on the deviation cases[3], which, as discussed above, are somewhat anomalous[4].

1 *Société Franco Tunisienne d'Armement v Sidermar SpA, The Massalia* [1961] 2 QB 278, [1960] 2 All ER 529. The 1943 Act did not apply, as the facts involved a voyage charter: see above, para 20.18.
2 *Ocean Tramp Tankers Corpn v V/O Sovfracht, The Eugenia* [1964] 2 QB 226, [1964] 1 All ER 161. See also *Davis Contractors Ltd v Fareham UDC* [1956] AC 696 at 715–716, [1956] 2 All ER 145 at 162, per Viscount Simonds.
3 Especially *Hain Steamship Co Ltd v Tate & Lyle Ltd* [1936] 2 All ER 597.
4 See above, para 19.82.

Part V

General Considerations

CHAPTER 21

General Defences and Interest

Craig Rotherham[1]

A   Introduction

21.1   Any writer of a general account of defences in restitution faces two related dilemmas, each of which is, in the current state of theory, hard if not impossible to resolve.

First, it is difficult to keep a balance between the general and the particular. There is a certain amount that can be said generally about defences, but also much that is specific to particular contexts. So, for example, the defence that a restitutionary claim has been compromised is supposedly quite general, but in practice occurs almost exclusively in the context of mistake.

Second, it is not always clear what is a defence, and what is an element of liability. So for some writers 'change of position' is a defence, whereas to others it amounts to a denial that the defendant should be regarded as enriched, and is accordingly best dealt with under liability. Or again, some prefer to assert that there is a defence of 'ministerial receipt', others regard any such defence as a mere denial of liability, and others still regard it as a peculiarity of the rules on agency.

1   With contributions from Steve Hedley.

21.2   It is clear that no one strategy will satisfy everyone. The strategy adopted here is as follows. This chapter concerns itself with six defences: bona fide purchase, estoppel, 'ministerial receipt', change of position, res judicata, and limitation. Some of these topics are also treated elsewhere in particular contexts[1]. Various other defences are (either as a practical matter, or for theoretical reasons) confined to particular areas, and have been treated there: officiousness (recoupment[2]), compromise (contribution[3], mistake[4] and public law cases[5]), and passing on (public law[6]). 'Illegality', a multifarious term, has a chapter to itself[7] as well as incidental references at various points[8].

The chapter concludes with a section in the availability of interest in restitutionary actions.

1   Bona fide purchase is also discussed in the context of mistake (above, para 17.57ff); estoppel is also discussed in relation to public law claims (above, paras 18.36 and 18.37); 'ministerial receipt' is also discussed in relation to receipt of trust property (above, para 5.64); change of position is also discussed in relation to proprietary claims (above, para 4.45ff) and public law claims (above, paras 18.36 and 18.37); and limitation is also discussed in relation to mistake (above, para 17.85ff) and to public law claims (above, para 18.39 and 18.40).
2   See above, para 6.22.
3   See above, paras 7.51 and 7.52.
4   See above, para 17.71ff.
5   See above, paras 18.33 and 18.34.
6   See above, para 18.38.

7   See above, ch 14.
8   See references to it in the context of contribution (above, para 7.61) and mistake (above, para 17.81ff).

B   Bona fide purchase of a legal interest[1]

21.3   The doctrine of bona fide purchase provides an exception to the principle that a buyer cannot acquire a better title than that enjoyed by the seller – the principle encapsulated in the maxim *nemo dat non quod habet*. The doctrine has the effect of extinguishing an owner's property rights and enables the bona fide purchaser to rely on his possessory title to prevail against the rest of the world. In this way, the bona fide purchase doctrine makes good defects in title. In addition to operating as a defence to a cause of action, the doctrine may be pleaded by a purchaser who is bringing an action based on his title. In these circumstances, the purchaser may assert his possessory title and then use the doctrine of bona fide purchase to defeat the objection by the defendant that he has a better title than that enjoyed by the claimant.

1   For recent academic analyses of the area see: Barker 'After Change of Position: Good Faith Exchange in the Modern Law of Restitution' in Birks (ed) *Laundering and Tracing* (1995), p 191; Swadling 'Property, Restitution and the Defence of Bona fide Purchase' in Swadling (ed), *The Limits of Restitutionary Claims – A Comparative Analysis* (1997); Fox 'Bona fide Purchase and the Currency of Money' [1996] CLJ 547; Key 'Bona fide Purchase as a Defence in the Law of Restitution [1994] Lloyds Maritime and Commercial Law Quarterly 421.

The defence at law

21.4   The doctrine of bona fide purchase is not generally available at common law. It does not, for example, provide a defence to actions based on a right to possession to chattels[1]. Claimants can bring an action for conversion against an innocent purchaser provided they have a better right to immediate possession of the chattel in question. Where there is a series of sales after a chattel has been converted, innocent purchasers who are liable for conversion must sue back down the chain of sale, bringing an action for breach of contract against the vendor who sold them the chattel in question.

1   Of course, important statutory exceptions have been enacted. See for example the protection afforded to bona fide purchasers from buyers and sellers in possession under the Sale of Goods Act 1979, ss 24 and 25.

21.5   In contrast, the defence is available in respect of money[1]. This is true whether the claim is for trover based on a right to immediate possession[2] or for money had and received based on a personal right to restitution[3]. Given its limited availability, the justification of the defence rests not on the merits of protecting an innocent purchaser as a matter of individual justice but rather on the public interest in ensuring the security of commercial transactions.

1   The common law also offered protection to certain bona fide purchasers of negotiable instruments – protection that was codified in the Bills of Exchange Act 1882, s 29(1), which protects those characterised as holders in due course. However, it is difficult to regard the defence as applying generally in respect of bills of exchange following the controversial holding in *Jones v Waring and Gillow Ltd* [1926] AC 670, where a bona fide payee of cheques that were accepted in discharge of an existing debt was not protected as a holder in due course.
2   See for example *Miller v Race* (1758) 1 Burr 452, 97 ER 398.
3   *Holiday v Sigil* (1826) 2 C & P 176, 172 ER 81; *United Australia Ltd v Barclays Bank Ltd* [1941] AC 1. Fox 'Bona fide Purchase and the Currency of Money' [1996] CLJ 547.

21.6   It is not clear whether good title will be acquired at common law even if the circumstances were such that it could be said that the purchaser had constructive notice of the owner's rights. Some scholars conclude that constructive notice is a creature of equity and is irrelevant at common law[1]. In their view, the common law recognition of the defence developed quite separately from equity's treatment of the issue. The result is apparent in the approach taken to the statutory protection of holders of bills of exchange in due course, whereby a defence is provided to those who have received a bill in good faith, regardless of any negligence on their part[2]. According to this view, the Bills of Exchange Act 1882 codified the common law and demonstrates that constructive notice has no part to play in the operation of the defence at law.

A different view was taken by Denning J in *Nelson v Larholt*[3]. He argued that the principle that 'The rightful owner can recover the amount from anyone who takes the money with notice ... has been evolved by the courts of law and equity side by side'[4]. In that case, the defence was denied to a defendant bank which had received cheques that a fraudulent executor had drawn on his testator's estate, in circumstances that were such 'that any reasonable person would have been put on inquiry'[5].

While Denning J's reading of the historic development of the defence is difficult to sustain, there is no reason why the common law approach to the defence should not evolve to mirror that taken in equity. While some argue that such an approach would be disastrous to commerce, it is by no means obvious that an objective approach to the matter would be more expensive to administer than one that turns on the proof of subjective states of mind. Moreover, it is accepted that an arduous standard of inquiry is not expected for commercial transactions[6]. Thus, liability is likely to ensue only where there was something special about a transaction. This was true in *Nelson v Larholt*, where the bank knew that the executor was drawing cheques on his testator's estate. It would be arbitrary if, because of a variable approach to the application of the defence of bona fide purchase, the defendant's liability were to depend on whether the action was brought at law or in equity.

1   See for example Fox 'The Transfer of Legal Title to Money' [1996] RLR 60 at 62; Goff and Jones *Law of Restitution* (5th edn, 1998), p 842.
2   See the Bills of Exchange Act 1882, s 29(1).
3   [1948] 1 KB 339.
4   [1948] 1 KB 339 at 343.
5   [1948] 1 KB 339 at 344.
6   See below, para 21.9.

21.7   Consideration need not be adequate[1], although where money is acquired at a substantial undervalue, it may be difficult for defendants to satisfy the court of their honesty. *Lipkin Gorman v Karpnale Ltd* stands as authority for the proposition that a promise that is not legally enforceable will not suffice for the purposes of the defence, even if the defendant subsequently fulfilled the promise. Thus in *Lipkin Gorman*, because gambling contracts are void under the Gaming Act 1845, the defendant casino was not regarded as having purchased money that it received in exchange for gambling chips. Instead the casino had to rely on the defence of change of position to reduce its liability to the extent that it had acted to its detriment in honouring the chips when they were cashed[2].

1   *Bassett v Nosworthy* (1673) Cas temp Finch 102, 23 ER 55.
2   *Lipkin Gorman v Karpnale Ltd* [1991] 2 AC 548.

21.8   It is unlikely that a purely executory promise will be sufficient for the purposes of the defence. In particular, it was suggested in *Lipkin Gorman v*

Karpnale Ltd that an executory promise to account for the money in question will not enable a defendant to raise the defence[1]. If, by being excused of an executory obligation, the defendant would be in no worse a position than he was before the transaction in question, it would be unreasonable to excuse him of liability.

1   *Lipkin Gorman v Karpnale Ltd* [1991] 2 AC 548 at 562, per Lord Templeman, and at 577, per Lord Goff. As Smith has noted, this conclusion has striking implications: *Law of Tracing* (1997), p 389. The bank would, if it received the claimant's property directly, be liable to an action in conversion and, as a result, unable to avail itself of the defences of change of position or ministerial defence for any payments it made after its receipt of the initial payment. However, it will be relatively rare that this will be the case. Where a bank receives the traceable proceeds of the claimant's property, the claimant cannot sue for conversion and the bank's liability would be for money had and received for which the defences of bona fide purchase and change of position will be available. See [1991] 2 AC at 573, per Lord Goff.

The defence in equity

21.9   One who acquires legal title for value and without notice takes free of any equitable claims against the title. Bona fide purchase is available in equity as a defence to any claim based on an equitable proprietary right, regardless of the nature of the assets in question. The burden of proof is on the claimant to establish the defence. Whatever the position is at law, in equity the defendant must generally establish, not merely that he was in good faith, but that he had no notice, actual or constructive, of the claimant's equitable interest[1]. It is often stated that the requirement of constructive notice has no place in commercial transactions[2]. A better view is that, while the requirement is one of general application, whether a purchaser will be taken to have constructive notice of another's equitable rights will depend upon the inquiries it is customary to make in a particular context. Generally, it will be inappropriate to expect the sort of inquiries that are required in the context of conveyances of land to be made in other commercial dealings[3].

1   *Carl-Zeiss-Stiftung v Herbert Smith (No 2)* [1969] 2 Ch 276.
2   See *Manchester Trust v Furness, Withy & Co Ltd* [1895] 2 QB 539 at 545, per Lindley LJ; *Greer v Downs Supply Co* [1927] 2 KB 28; *Panchaud Frères SA v Establissements General Grain Co* [1970] 1 Lloyd's Rep 53.
3   See *El Ajou v Dollar Land Holdings plc* [1993] 3 All ER 717 at 739, per Millett J; *Macmillan Inc v Bishopsgate Investment Trust (No 3)* [1995] 1 WLR 978 at 1000, per Millett J. See Fox 'Constructive Notice and Knowing Receipt' [1998] CLJ 391.

21.10   Historically, the doctrine was no doubt favoured, both for its capacity to protect the interests of innocent purchasers, and for its role in promoting the security of exchange transactions[1]. Given that the change of position defence now provides a more sensitive device for balancing the interests of owners and innocent purchasers, the primary justification for the bona fide purchase defence must now be based in terms of the protection of the market[2].

1   Palmer *Law of Restitution* (1978), vol 1, para 16.5(b).
2   See Barker 'After Change of Position: Good Faith Exchange in the Modern Law of Restitution' in Birks (ed) *Laundering and Tracing* (1995), p 193.

The operation of the defence

THE EFFECT OF THE DEFENCE

21.11   A bona fide purchaser has a complete defence against any action based on the claimant's title, whether the remedy sought is personal or proprietary[1]. In addition, the defence relieves the defendant of any personal liability to make restitution for the value of the property in question. Thus in equity it precludes, not only a claim for a constructive trust or lien, but also any personal action based on the receipt of the claimant's property or its traceable proceeds[2]. Similarly at common law, bona fide purchase provides a defence to actions for conversion based on the claimant's right of immediate possession to property received by the defendant and to actions for money had and received that are based on a personal right to restitution[3].

1   This reflects the approach favoured in American law, where the *Restatement of Restitution* (1937), para 172 states that: '[t]he bona fide purchaser is not only entitled to retain the property free of trust but he is under no personal liability for its value'.
2   For a recent example of a case in which a claim for personal relief based on receipt was met with the defence, see *Macmillan Inc v Bishopsgate Investment Trust Ltd (No 3)* [1995] 1 WLR 978, considered below, para 22.32.
3   *Miller v Race* (1758) 1 Burr 452, 97 ER 398.

TITLE LOST EVEN AGAINST SUBSEQUENT RECIPIENTS WHO ARE NOT BONA FIDE PURCHASERS

21.12   The effect of a bona fide purchase of title is not merely to provide the particular purchaser with a defence to any action brought by a claimant with an interest in the asset in question. Rather, such a transaction extinguishes permanently any adverse proprietary rights. Following a bona fide purchase of the legal title, a party who enjoyed an interest in the property will be unable to enforce that interest, not only against the initial purchaser, but also against a subsequent purchaser of the property with actual notice of the interest[1].

1   *Wilkes v Spooner* [1911] 2 KB 473 at 477.

THE APPLICATION OF THE DEFENCE TO PAYMENTS MADE IN SATISFACTION OF DEBTS

21.13   The defence may be pleaded by a creditor who has accepted payment in discharge for all or part of a debt[1]. This reflects a desire to privilege creditors' security of receipt of such payments. The discharge of the debt is viewed as consideration given by the creditor in return for the debtor's payment. For example, it is well established that the defence is available to a bank meet an action by a claimant where the bank received the money in question from its customer or another party in discharge of its customer's overdraft[2]. There is equally authority that a claimant will not be able to recover from a defendant in respect of a mistaken payment made by the claimant himself where the payment was accepted in discharge of a valid debt owed by the claimant, or another on behalf of whom the claimant was acting as agent[3]. While some commentators view this as a separate defence[4], there seems little reason to differentiate it from other applications of the bona fide purchase defence[5].

1   The same position is taken in the United States in *Restatement of Restitution* (1937), para 173.
2   *Northern Counties of England Fire Insurance Co v Whipp* (1884) 26 Ch D 482 at 495; *Thomson v Clydesdale Bank Ltd* [1893] AC 282.
3   *Aiken v Short* (1856) 35 LJ Ex 321, 1 H & N 210, 156 ER 1180; *Barclays Bank Ltd v WJ Simms, Son & Cooke (Southern) Ltd* [1980] QB 677 at 695, per Robert Goff J; *Lloyds Bank v Independent Insurance Co Ltd* [2000] QB 110; *David Securities Pty Ltd v Commonwealth Bank of Australia* (1992) 175 CLR 353.
4   See for example Barker 'After Change of Position: Good Faith Exchange in the Modern Law of Restitution' in Birks (ed) *Laundering and Tracing* (1995), p 200. A separate defence of discharge for value is recognised in American law. See the *Restatement of Restitution* (1937), para 14; Palmer *Law of Restitution* (1978), vol 1, paras 16.5 and 16.6. For the most part, where the defence of

discharge for value applies, the defence of bona fide purchase would also be available. However, the former defence has a wider application in allowing a defence against a legal owner for those who purchase chattels from a seller without legal title – a context in which the common law does not permit a defence of bona fide purchase. This produces the rather odd result that, while purchasers who furnish money as consideration are denied a defence, those who provide consideration by accepting the chattels in question in return for discharging a debt are not required to make restitution. As Palmer recognises, the House of Lords' decision in *Jones v Waring and Gillow Ltd* [1926] AC 670 suggests that no such separate defence is recognised in English law.

5   See McMeel *Modern Law of Restitution* (2000), p 419; and above, para 17.57ff.

C   Bona fide purchase of an equitable interest

The effect on prior equitable interests

21.14   Where priorities are equal, the party that acquired his or her interest first prevails. The orthodoxy in English law is that equitable interests are defeated only by a bona fide purchase of the *legal* title. As a result, a prior equitable interest is good against subsequent bona fide purchasers of an equitable interest in the asset in question, unless the holder of the earlier interest is estopped from asserting that right[1]. On the other hand, Australian courts have shown a willingness to judge the relative merits of competing equitable claims, rather than rigidly giving priority to the earlier interest. On this view, mere carelessness on the part of the holder of the earlier right may allow a bona fide purchaser of an equitable interest to prevail[2].

1   *Macmillan Inc v Bishopsgate Investment Trust plc (No 3)* [1995] 1 WLR 978 at 1000, per Millett J, *Westdeutsche Landesbank Girozentrale v Islington London Borough Council* [1996] AC 669 at 704, per Lord Browne-Wilkinson.
2   *Heid v Reliance Finance* (1982) 154 CLR 326 at 341, per Mason and Deane JJ; Cope *Proprietary Claims and Remedies* (1997), pp 104–106.

The effect on mere equities

21.15   A mere equity, such as a right of rescission, is regarded as a lesser right than an equitable interest. As a result, because the equities are not equal, a mere equity will not prevail against the holder of an equitable interest merely because it was first in time. Instead, a mere equity is liable to be lost to a bona fide purchaser of an equitable interest[1].

1   *Phillips v Phillips* (1862) 4 De GF & J 208, 45 ER 1164; *LAC Investments v Hotel Terrigal Pty* (1965) 113 CLR 265. See Birks 'Property and Unjust Enrichment: Categorical Truths' [1997] NZLR 623 at 638. See also above, para 5.31ff.

D   Estoppel

21.16   A limited defence to restitution actions has traditionally been available as a result of claimants being estopped from asserting matters necessary to the establishment of their cause of action. The defence is difficult to satisfy, as a claimant will not be prevented from obtaining relief merely because he made a mistake in transferring a benefit to the defendant and in so doing caused the defendant to alter his position to his detriment. Generally, to be estopped, a claimant must have made a representation that led the defendant into changing his position so that it would be inequitable to require restitution. Alternatively, in the absence of a representation, a claimant may be estopped where his conduct is such that his mistake can be characterised as breaching a duty to the defendant.

Thus, the defence focuses as much upon the conduct of the claimant as it does on the defendant's change of circumstances. Defendants who alter their position in circumstances where there was no reason for questioning their entitlement to a benefit cannot raise an estoppel in the absence of some disentitling conduct on the part of the claimant.

Defendant led to believe that he was entitled to a benefit

21.17   Beyond the mere payment of money by mistake, the claimant must do something further to cause the defendant to believe that he is entitled to the payment in question. Sometimes, in the absence of an actual representation, an omission may be enough.

First, on occasion, courts have found that a failure to address a mistake amounted to implied representation that the defendant was entitled to the benefit in issue. This was the case in *Holt v Markham*[1], where the defendant was an air force officer who had been paid more than he was entitled to receive. The claimants discovered the error and wrote to the defendant informing him that there had been an overpayment, but misstated the reasons why he was not entitled to the payment. The defendant contacted the claimants, suggesting that they were in error, but heard nothing in response for some time. In the meantime, the defendant invested the money badly and lost it. The Court of Appeal found for the defendant on two lines of reasoning. First, the members of the Court all indicated that the mistake was one of law rather than fact[2]. Obviously, after *Kleinwort Benson Ltd v Lincoln City Council*[3], this would no longer be a ground for denying an action. Secondly, the Court also found that the claimants' failure to respond to the defendant's letter in a timely fashion amounted to an implied representation that the money had been properly paid. In the light of the defendant's subsequent reliance on this representation, the claimants were estopped from seeking to recover the money paid over by mistake[4].

1   [1923] 1 KB 504.
2   [1923] 1 KB 504 at 510, per Bankes LJ, at 511, per Warrington LJ, and at 516, per Scrutton LJ. Scrutton LJ remarks were obiter, as he chose to rest his decision on the grounds of estoppel.
3   [1999] 2 AC 349; on which see above, para 17.40ff.
4   [1923] 1 KB 504 at 510–511, per Bankes LJ, at 512–513, per Warrington LJ, and at 514, per Scrutton LJ.

21.18   Secondly, even without making an explicit representation that the defendant was entitled to the benefit in question, a claimant may be estopped from seeking restitution where his conduct in mistakenly transferring a benefit amounts to a breach of a duty to take care to ensure the accuracy of such transactions[1]. However, it is not clear when the court will impose such a duty. Arguably, it should arise where the defendant has little or no means of readily verifying his precise entitlement to the benefit in question. Thus, it was suggested obiter in *Avon County Council v Howlett*[2] that the local government owed a duty of accuracy to its employees when paying their salary[3].

1   See Virgo *Principles of the Law of Restitution* (1999), p 697.
2   [1983] 1 WLR 605.
3   [1983] 1 WLR 605 at 612, per Eveleigh LJ, and at 621, per Slade LJ. *Skyring v Greenwood* (1825) 4 B & C 281, 107 ER 1064, might also be seen as reflecting this principle.

Reliance by the defendant

21.19   Obviously enough, a defendant will have a defence based on estoppel only if he can establish that he relied on the claimant's representation or breach of duty. The point is illustrated by *United Overseas Bank v Jiwani*[1], where the court found that the defendant did not actually believe that he was entitled to the money paid to him by mistake. MacKenna J found that, in changing his position, the defendant was acting, not in reliance on his belief in his entitlement to the payment, but rather in the expectation that the defendant would not discover the error. Consequently, the claimant was not estopped from demanding restitution.

1   [1976] 1 WLR 964.

Change of circumstances

21.20   A claimant will be estopped only where the defendant has changed his position so that it would be inequitable for the claimant to assert his right to restitution. This requirement is easily enough satisfied where the defendant can point to specific expenditure that he otherwise would not have made which has resulted in a depletion of the value of his estate. This was true in *Holt v Markham*[1], where the defendant dissipated the money received from the claimant by investing it badly. Equally, defendants may be able to rely on a less stark change of circumstances, as *Avon County Council v Howlett*[2] illustrates. The defendant and his wife were able to rely on the defence, on the ground that over the course of time they had adjusted their lifestyle in response to mistaken payments, and so spent more money than they otherwise would have.

1   [1923] 1 KB 504; above, para 21.17.
2   [1983] 1 WLR 605.

Consequences of estoppel

21.21   Estoppel has been criticised because it is an all or nothing defence. Defendants who have suffered a substantial detriment are excused of any liability to make restitution, even if they could make partial restitution without being prejudiced[1]. This is largely the result of the conceptual basis for the defence[2]. Estoppel operates by preventing the claimant from denying that the assumption upon which the defendant acted was a correct one. As long as estoppel is regarded in this way purely as a rule of evidence, it must take effect by precluding the claimant's action altogether. There has been some support for recognising, as part of the substantive law, a unitary doctrine of estoppel that incorporates the previously isolated doctrines of estoppel by representation and proprietary estoppel[3]. This would make it easier to argue for a flexible approach, and so in appropriate cases to allow estoppel to reduce a claim rather than to eliminate it completely.

This view has gained approval in Australia[4] and was advocated by Lord Denning MR in *Amalgamated Investment & Property Co Ltd v Texas Commerce International Bank Ltd*[5]. However, it was rejected in this context by Slade LJ in *Avon County Council v Howlett*[6]. Nonetheless, the recent Court of Appeal decision in *National Westminster Bank plc v Somer International (UK) Ltd*[7] offers some support for the view that, at least in exceptional circumstances, estoppel can operate to reduce rather than entirely preclude liability[8].

1 *Avon County Council v Howlett* [1983] 1 WLR 605; *Greenwood v Martins Bank Ltd* [1932] 1 KB 371; *Skyring v Greenwood* (1825) 4 B & C 281, 107 ER 1064; *Holt v Markham* [1923] 1 KB 504.
2 *Avon County Council v Howlett* [1983] 1 WLR 605 at 624, per Slade LJ.
3 For an academic analysis, see Fung and Ho 'Change of Position and Estoppel' (2001) 117 LQR 14.
4 See for example *Waltons Stores (Interstate) v Maher* (1988) 164 CLR 387 and *Commonwealth of Australia v Verwayen* (1990) 170 CLR 394.
5 [1982] QB 84 at 122.
6 [1983] 1 WLR 605 at 624.
7 [2001] EWCA Civ 970, [2002] 1 All ER 198.
8 [2001] EWCA Civ 970, [2002] 1 All ER 198 at 210 and 215, per Potter LJ, at 218, per Clarke LJ, and at 220, per Peter Gibson LJ. See below, para 21.24ff.

Role of the defence in the modern law of restitution

21.22   In the light of the recent recognition of the change of position defence in the English law of restitution[1], it is hardly surprising that the continuing role of estoppel has come into question. The issue was raised in *Lipkin Gorman v Karpnale Ltd*[2]. There, Lord Goff suggested that the strict pre-conditions for establishing the defence and its harsh effects in circumstances in which the defendant's change of position was only partial, 'provide a strong indication that, in many cases, estoppel is not an appropriate concept to deal with the problem'[3]. The issue has arisen in Canada, where the Canadian Supreme Court recognised the change of position defence a decade and a half before the House of Lords did the same[4]. Thus, in *RBC Dominion Securities Inc v Dawson*, the Newfoundland Court of Appeal concluded that estoppel should no longer be available as a defence to restitution actions[5].

1 See below, para 21.37ff.
2 [1991] 2 AC 548. On this case see above, para 17.40ff.
3 [1991] 2 AC 548 at 579.
4 *Rural Municipality of Storthoaks v Mobil Oil Canada* (1975) 55 DLR (3d) 1.
5 (1994) 111 DLR (4th) 230.

21.23   It is likely that a similar view will ultimately prevail in English law. In *Derby v Scottish Equitable*[1], Walker LJ suggested that, given that the doctrine was well established in English law, the complete abolition of estoppel as a defence to restitution actions was a matter for the House of Lords[2]. Nonetheless, it seems that this view will not prevent estoppel rapidly withering away in this context. On the facts of the case before him, Walker LJ was prepared to rely an earlier suggestion that the defence might be denied 'where the sums sought to be recovered were so large as to bear no relation to any detriment which the recipient could possibly have suffered'[3].

1 [2001] EWCA Civ 369, [2001] 3 All ER 818.
2 [2001] EWCA Civ 369, [2001] 3 All ER 818 at 830. See also *Philip Collins Ltd v Davis* [2000] 3 All ER 808 at 826, per Parker J, an earlier discussion of the issue.
3 *Avon County Council v Howlett* [1983] 1 WLR 605 at 625, per Slade LJ. A similar view was taken by Cumming-Bruce LJ, [1983] 1 WLR 605 at 608, and Eveleigh LJ, [1983] 1 WLR 605 at 611. See *Derby v Scottish Equitable* [2001] EWCA Civ 369, [2001] 3 All ER 818 at 829–830, per Walker LJ.

21.24   Subsequently the Court of Appeal in *National Westminster Bank plc v Somer International (UK) Ltd*[1] purported to apply Walker LJ's reasoning in this respect to prevent the defendant escaping liability for anything more than the extent of its change of position, which represented $^1/_{17}$ of the overpayment made by the claimant. Some confusion appears to have developed in this area. The statements of the members of the Court of Appeal in *Avon County Council v Howlett*[2] are somewhat ambiguous. Nonetheless, they apparently assume that, because estoppel was necessarily an all or nothing defence, where it would be wholly inequitable for the defendant to escape all liability, the defence of estoppel would be denied altogether. In *Derby v Scottish Equitable*[3], Walker LJ followed this logic in limiting the defendant to the defence of change of position. However, in *National Westminster Bank plc v Somer International (UK) Ltd*, the Court of Appeal assumed that the exception considered in *Avon CC v Howlett* had the effect of allowing estoppel to operate to reduce partially the defendant's liability[4]. This interpretation seems to have been necessary to do justice in this case because, unlike in *Scottish Equitable v Derby*, there is no suggestion in the decision that the defendant pleaded change of position as an alternative defence.

1 [2002] 1 All ER 198.
2 [1983] 1 WLR 605 at 625, per Slade LJ, at 609, per Cumming-Bruce LJ, and at 611, per Eveleigh LJ.
3 [2001] EWCA Civ 369, [2001] 3 All ER 818.
4 See [2002] 1 All ER 198 at 210 and 215, per Potter LJ, at 218, per Clarke LJ, and at 220, per Peter Gibson LJ.

21.25   A further basis for limiting the use of estoppel was recognised by Walker LJ in *Derby v Scottish Equitable*. Without deciding the case on this basis, Walker LJ noted the attraction of the argument that the availability of the change of position defence logically precludes the operation of estoppel[1]. The change of position defence ensures that a defendant who is able to plead the defence has not suffered any detriment as a result of being required to make restitution to the claimant. It is arguable that defendants who are entitled to avail themselves of the defence will not be able to establish the requirements for estoppel by representation that they have altered their circumstances to their detriment in reliance on the representation in question.

1 [2001] EWCA Civ 369, [2001] 3 All ER 818 at 830–831.

E   Benefits passed on by agents to their principals – 'ministerial receipt'[1]

21.26   An agent will have a defence to an action for restitution where he received the benefit in question from the claimant on behalf of his principal, and accounted to his principal for that benefit in circumstances in which the agent was not aware of any impropriety[2]. While the defence is often labelled 'ministerial receipt', this is something of a misnomer, as receipt itself is not sufficient to found the defence. Rather, the basis of the defence lies in the fact that the benefit has been passed on to the principal so that the agent can no longer be said to be enriched.

1 See also para 5.64 above.
2 For a recent analysis of the principles underlying this area see Swadling 'The Nature of Ministerial Receipt' in Birks (ed) *Laundering and Tracing* (1995), p 243.

The effect of ministerial receipt at law and in equity

21.27   A distinction is often made between the operation of the defence at law and in equity. According to this view, in equity, in contrast to the position taken at law, there is no requirement that an agent has passed the benefit in question on to his principal[1]. The better view is that this is a misconception and that, strictly speaking, the defence has no application in equity. The privileged position of agents in equity results from the structure of the cause of action for knowing receipt, whereby defendants are liable only if they receive property for their benefit. The liability of those who receive property as mere agents can be for knowing assistance alone[2]. This is evident in cases in which the defendant is a bank: provided a bank receives a sum as an agent and credits the account of its customer, its receipt will not be treated as beneficial. However, a bank will be treated as having received a benefit if it sets-off the sum received against sums owed by its customer[3]. Thus, equity has taken the view that, where the customer's account is credited, the bank's customer is the proper claimant in an action for primary liability for receipt of the benefit in question. Moreover, if a bank has credited its customer's account, the position of the claimant should not be undermined by this approach. In any event, the bank may be secondarily liable if it dishonestly assisted its customer's receipt of the benefit in question[4]. Thus, strictly speaking, proof of receipt as an agent does not serve to establish a defence to an action for knowing receipt, but rather to demonstrate that the claimant has not satisfied the requirements of the cause of action.

1   *Agip (Africa) Ltd v Jackson* [1990] Ch 265.
2   *Agip (Africa) Ltd v Jackson* [1990] Ch 265 at 288, per Millett J; Millett 'Tracing the Proceeds of Fraud' (1991) 107 LQR 71 at 76. See also above, para 5.63ff.
3   *Thomson v Clydesdale Bank Ltd* [1893] AC 282.
4   *Royal Brunei Airlines v Tan* [1995] 2 AC 378. Secondary liability for assistance is apparently subject to a higher standard of liability than that required for primary liability for receipt. See *BCCI v Akindele* [2001] Ch 437, and more generally above, ch 5.

The basis of the defence

21.28   The basis of the defence can be explained in various ways. It has been said that an agent is not liable because he is 'a mere conduit pipe and the money is taken as having been paid to the principal rather than the agent'[1]. This might suggest that, on the basis of trite agency principles, in cases of disclosed agency the principal is the proper party to sue. On the one hand, this is consistent with the denial of the defence in cases of undisclosed agency[2]. For, where the agency is undisclosed, upon discovering the identity of the principal, the party who has dealt with the agent has the choice of suing either the agent or the principal[3]. However, agency alone cannot explain the defence given to agents. First, the fact that one who contracts with an agent whose principal is disclosed cannot sue the agent on the contract, does not indicate that he should not be able to recover from the agent should he have a right to restitution arising from the payment. Secondly, claimants are not denied recovery against any agents, but only those who have passed the benefit on in good faith.

1   *Continental Caoutchouc v Gutta Perchas Co v Kleinwort Sons and Co* (1904) 20 TLR 403 at 405, per Collins MR.
2   *Sadler v Evans* (1766) 4 Burr 1984 at 1986, 98 ER 34 at 35, per Lord Mansfield; *Oates v Hudson* (1851) 6 Ex 346 at 348, 155 ER 576 at 577, per Parke B; *Gurney v Womersley* (1854) 4 E & B 133, 119 ER 51; *Baylis v Bishop of London* [1913] 1 Ch 127 at 133, per Cozens-Hardy MR; *Agip (Africa) Ltd v Jackson* [1990] Ch 265 at 288, per Millett J.
3   This is true both where the agency is completely undisclosed (see eg *Clarkson Booker Ltd v Andjel* [1964] 2 QB 775), and where the fact of the agency is revealed but the identity of the principal is not (see *Thomson v Davenport* (1829) 9 B & C 78, 109 ER 30).

21.29   The defence has alternatively been explained on the basis of estoppel, in that if the claimant knew the agent was acting as such, he has authorised the transfer of the benefit to the principal and is estopped from bringing a restitutionary claim[1]. The risk of injustice that arises from estoppel providing a complete defence, regardless of the extent of the defendant's change of position, is not a concern in this context. For an agent is relieved of liability only to the extent that he has passed the benefit on to his principal.

1   Swadling 'The Nature of Ministerial Receipt' in Birks (ed) *Laundering and Tracing* (1995), p 257.

21.30   Yet even if estoppel apparently provides a workable explanation of the treatment of agents, in light of the apparent demise of estoppel as a defence to restitution actions, it is worth asking whether this area of the law might be absorbed into the general defence recognised in *Lipkin Gorman v Karpnale Ltd*[1]. One obstacle to such an analysis is presented by the denial of the defence in the case of undisclosed agents. However, this might be regarded as an exception to the general rule that can be explained on the basis of an estoppel arising against the agent as a result of an implied representation that he was dealing in his own right. Ultimately, the developing change of position defence is flexible enough to explain any limitations placed on agents in this context.

1   [1991] 2 AC 548. See above, paras 21.22–21.25.

Receipt as an agent

21.31   Defendants will be able to avail themselves of the defence only if they had authority, actual or apparent, to receive the benefit on behalf of their principal. The defence is available only where a defendant was purporting to act as an agent. It is not be available to those whose agency is undisclosed[1]. The reason for this is clear enough: if the claimant was dealing with a defendant on the basis that the transaction in question was for the defendant's own benefit, the claimant would expect that he would be able to have recourse to the defendant in the event that anything were to go wrong. In the light of this, it would be unfair to allow the agent a defence on the basis that he has passed the benefit on to his principal. Instead, the agent should be liable and be left to seek an indemnity from his principal. It is possible that a defence might be made available to undisclosed agents in this context following the recognition of a general change of position defence. However, the better view is that undisclosed agents should continue to bear the risk of any change of position.

1   *Gurney v Womersley* (1854) 4 E & B 133, 119 ER 51; *Baylis v Bishop of London* [1913] 1 Ch 127.

21.32   It is less clear whether the defence is available where the defendant has indicated that he was acting in the capacity as an agent but the identity of his principal was undisclosed. In *Agip (Africa) Ltd v Jackson*[1] Millett J suggested that the defence would avail only agents who received property on the behalf of a *named* principal[2]. However, in *Gowers v Lloyds & National Provincial Foreign Bank Ltd*[3], the Court of Appeal allowed the defence in circumstances where even the agent was unaware of the identity of his principal[4].

1   [1990] Ch 265.
2   [1990] Ch 265 at 288.
3   [1938] 1 All ER 766.
4   Swadling 'The Nature of Ministerial Receipt' in Birks (ed) *Laundering and Tracing* (1995), p 252.

THE TRANSFER OF THE BENEFIT TO THE PRINCIPAL

21.33   As mentioned, it is required that an agent must have accounted to his principal for the benefit in question before the defence can be raised. Thus Lord Ellenborough remarked, 'I take it to be clear, that an agent who receives money for his principal is liable as a principal so long as he stands in his original situation; and until there has been a change of circumstances by his having paid over the money to his principal, or done something equivalent to it'[1]. The transfer of the benefit in question may take place in a number of ways. Most obviously, this requirement will be satisfied where the agent simply passes on a payment to his principal. However, the defence will equally be allowed where agents have paid the money over to a third party with their principal's authority in order, for example, to discharge a debt owed by the principal[2]. Similarly, the defence may be pleaded where agents set off the amount received against a debt owed to them by their principal[3]. On the other hand, the defence will not be made out where an agent has merely credited the principal's account[4].

1   *Cox v Prentice* (1815) 3 M & S 344 at 348, 105 ER 641 at 642.
2   *Holland v Russell* (1863) 4 B & S 14, 122 ER 365.
3   *Kleinwort Sons and Co v Dunlop Rubber Co* (1907) 97 LT 263 at 265, per Lord Atkinson. See below, para 21.35.
4   *Buller v Harrison* (1777) 2 Cowp 565, 98 ER 1243; *Cox v Prentice* (1815) 3 M & S 344, 105 ER 641; *Colonial Bank v Exchange Bank of Yarmouth, Nova Scotia* (1885) 11 App Cas 84.

BONA FIDES

21.34   An agent who extracted the payment in question from the claimant by fraud, duress or another wrong will not be able to raise the defence of ministerial receipt against a claimant[1]. In addition, an agent will not be able to rely on the defence if he was knowingly a party to a wrong that gives rise to a right of restitution[2]. Nor will the defence be available if the agent was aware of the wrong at the time he received the payment[3]. Similarly, the defence will not avail an agent who, after receiving the payment, became aware of the grounds for the claimant's restitution claim before passing the money on to his principal[4].

1   *Snowdon v Davis* (1808) 1 Taunt 359, 127 ER 872; cf *Owen & Co v Cronk* [1895] 1 QB 265.
2   *Townson v Wilson* (1808) 1 Camp 396, 170 ER 997.
3   *Agip (Africa) Ltd v Jackson* [1990] Ch 265 at 288, per Millett J.
4   *Buller v Harrison* (1777) 2 Cowp 565, 98 ER 1243; *Agip (Africa) Ltd v Jackson* [1990] Ch 265 at 288, per Millett J.

The relevance of detriment

21.35   It has been argued by some that detriment to the agent is not a necessary requirement of the defence[1]. This would amount to a striking conclusion that would make it difficult to understand the defence either as an instance of the change of position defence or as an example of estoppel. The doubt has largely focused on the fact that the defence has been thought to be available where an agent sets off the payment in question against a debt owed to him by the principal[2]. It is quite right to say that such steps will not invariably be to the defendant's detriment. However, often they will, as an agent's chances of being paid may have been jeopardised by the opportunity that he has lost to pressure his principal to settle his account, or to set off other sums that he has received on his principal's behalf against the debt in question. It would cause too much uncertainty if an agent had to prove that this was so in any particular case. The need for parties in these situations, to have a clear understanding of their rights, demands that the law treat the opportunity lost by the agent as a sufficient detriment for the purposes of the defence of ministerial receipt.

1   Virgo *Principles of the Law of Restitution* (1999), p 706.
2   *Continental Caoutchouc and Gutta Percha Co v Kleinwort Sons and Co* (1904) 90 LT 474; *Kleinwort Sons and Co v Dunlop Rubber Co* (1907) 97 LT 263 at 265, per Lord Atkinson.

The effect of the defence

21.36   The defence reduces an agent's liability only to the extent that the benefit has actually been passed on to the principal[1]. This is strong indication that the defence is better regarded as an example of the change of position defence than as an instance of estoppel.

1   See for example *Australia and New Zealand Banking Group Ltd v Westpac Banking Corpn* (1988) 164 CLR 662.

F   Change of position

The development of the defence

21.37   There was early support for some form of a change of position defence in *Sadler v Evans*[1], where Lord Mansfield was prepared to recognise a broad common law defence to an action for money had and received. His Lordship, perhaps rather unhelpfully, concluded that '[t]he defence is any equity that will rebut the action'[2]. However the defence was subsequently rejected. In *Baylis v Bishop of London*[3], the Court of Appeal concluded that the defence was not available in a case where the recipient had, in good faith, given the money to the needy. Similarly, the defence was rejected in equity by the House of Lords in *Ministry of Health v Simpson*[4], where various charities had spent money on improving realty.

1   (1766) 4 Burr 1984, 98 ER 34.
2   (1766) 4 Burr 1984 at 1986, 98 ER 34 at 35.
3   [1913] 1 Ch 127.
4   [1951] AC 251.

21.38   The failure to recognise the defence had consequences for the availability of restitutionary actions. Courts were understandably reluctant to require defendants to make restitution in circumstances where they had, in good faith, acted to their detriment in reliance on their entitlement to the benefit in question. As a result, courts on occasion were tempted to find causes of action more difficult to sustain than they otherwise might have. The problem with the law in this area is that, without any mechanism to distribute rather than simply shift loss, it has traditionally required one party to carry the entire burden of the claimant's loss. An example of the consequences of this state of affairs is provided by the manner in which the courts, in determining liability for receipt of another's property in equity, drifted unpredictably between different degrees of knowledge in response to the facts of particular cases[1].

1   See above, para 5.49ff.

21.39   The defence was eventually recognised in English law by the House of Lords in *Lipkin Gorman v Karpnale Ltd*[1]. A partner at the claimant firm of solicitors gambled the traceable proceeds of the claimant's money at the defendant's casino. Their Lordships held that the defendant could not rely on the defence of bona fide purchase because the unenforceability of gambling contracts meant that, as a matter of law, the defendant could not be said to have provided consideration for the claimant's money[2]. However, the defendant was allowed to rely on the defence of change of position. As a result, the defendant was permitted to take account of the money it had paid out to the solicitor when he cashed his chips at the Casino. Thus, the defendant was liable only for the net benefit that it ultimately obtained at the expense of the claimant.

1   [1991] 2 AC 548.
2   [1991] 2 AC 548 at 563, per Lord Templeman, and at 577, per Lord Goff.

21.40   Lord Goff indicated that the defence was 'available to a person whose position has so changed that it would be inequitable in all the circumstances to require him to make restitution, or alternatively to make restitution in full'[1]. He noted that the recognition of the defence would enable the courts to take a liberal approach to actions to reverse unjust enrichment in the knowledge that there was a mechanism to protect innocent recipients from the consequences of their detrimental reliance on the validity of the transfer in question[2]. However, their Lordships did not seek to elaborate fully the parameters of the defence. Instead, Lord Goff indicated that he was, 'most anxious that, in recognising this defence to actions of restitution, nothing should be said at this stage to inhibit the development of the defence on a case by case basis, in the usual way'[3].

1   [1991] 2 AC 548 at 580.
2   [1991] 2 AC 548 at 581.
3   [1991] 2 AC 548 at 580.

Conditions for establishing the defence

A CHANGE OF POSITION IN RELIANCE ON THE BENEFIT RECEIVED AT THE CLAIMANT'S EXPENSE

21.41   **The defence as a response to disenrichment**   Not all expenditure incurred in reliance upon the defendant's receipt of a benefit at the claimant's expense will be characterised as sufficient to render it inequitable for a defendant to be required to make restitution. The availability of the defence is often explicable on the basis that a defendant is no longer enriched as a result of dissipating the benefit in question or spending a similar amount in reliance on his entitlement to that benefit. The issue largely concerns the extent to which the defendant's expenditure results in an increase in the market value of the defendant's estate. Thus, in *Lipkin Gorman v Karpnale Ltd*, Lord Templeman contrasted two ways in which defendants might alter their position in reliance on their receipt of a benefit at the expense of the claimant. He concluded that a defendant who changed his position by purchasing a car would be enriched only to the extent of the value of the car at the date the action was brought. He compared this with a defendant who altered his position by spending money on a holiday. To the extent of that expenditure, the latter defendant would no longer be enriched, and so would be excused of any liability[1].

1   [1991] 2 AC 548 at 560.

21.42   The defence as a response to the unfairness of making a defendant account for an enrichment   Extraordinarily, there may be situations in which, even though a defendant's change of position has resulted in an appreciation in the market value of his estate, it would be inequitable to require the defendant to make restitution. This may be the case where a defendant has incurred expenditure augmenting an existing asset to which he is liable to attach special worth. In these circumstances, it may be true that the expenditure has left the defendant with a surviving enrichment as a result of having increased the value of the asset in question. However, this needs to be balanced against the reality that the defendant is unlikely to realise that value because the asset is one that he is not likely to sell lightly.

These issues arose to some extent in *Re Diplock*[1], where one of the claimants was an innocent recipient of money wrongfully distributed by the administrators of Diplock's estate, which it had used to improve its realty. The Court of Appeal held that it would have been inequitable to grant a charge over the defendant's land to secure the claimant's personal claims[2]. Two objections may be made to ordering restitution in these circumstances. First, there is a danger that a defendant who has neither sufficient assets to meet its obligation to make restitution to the claimant out of other assets nor is in a position to mortgage the property in question might be forced to sell the property. Secondly, even if a defendant would be able to make restitution without selling the asset, if he would not have chosen to have altered the asset had he not received the benefit in question, he might legitimately complain that he would be left worse off by being required to make restitution.

1   [1948] Ch 465. See above, para 4.27ff.
2   [1948] Ch 465 at 548.

21.43   Changes of positions in the nature of sacrificed opportunities In *National Westminster Bank plc v Somer International (UK) Ltd*[1], Potter LJ apparently accepted the opinion expressed academically that the defence might not be available where the defendant's change of position does not involve increases in expenditure, but rather takes the form of passing up an opportunity to earn income or acquire assets. Potter LJ suggested that this was a justification for the continued use of estoppel as defence to restitutionary actions[2]. However, this perspective is in conflict with Walker LJ's earlier discussion of the change of position defence in *Derby v Scottish Equitable*[3]. In an account of the different types of change of position for which the defence would be available, Walker LJ noted that a defendant:

> may make some decision which involves no immediate expenditure, but is nevertheless causally linked to the receipt. Voluntarily giving up his job, at an age when it would not be easy to get new employment, is the most obvious example[4].

The idea that the change of position defence should not be available for forgone opportunities is inconsistent with the flexibility that has been favoured by the courts since the inception of the defence a little over a decade ago. An indication of this tendency can be found in the Privy Council's rejection of the idea that the defence was not available for anticipatory changes of position[5]. Thus, Lord Templeman, in *Dextra Bank & Trust Co Ltd v Bank of Jamica*[6], dismissed such an artificial restriction by observing that 'what is in issue is the justice or injustice of enforcing a restitutionary claim in respect of a benefit conferred'[7]. It is worth bearing in mind that Lord Goff was anxious in introducing the defence in *Lipkin Gorman v Karpnale Ltd* 'that nothing should be said at this stage to inhibit the development of the defence on a case by case basis, in the usual way'. Thus, it is strange to suggest that the defence is not available in these circumstances when there has yet to have been a case that has turned on the issue. There is nothing in the doctrinal logic of the defence nor any sound reason of policy to limit the defence to changes of position that involve expenditure. Rather the defence should be available for any bona fide change of position made in reliance on the receipt of a benefit at the expense of the claimant.

1 [2002] 1 All ER 198.
2 [2002] 1 All ER at 215.
3 [2001] EWCA Civ 369, [2001] 3 All ER 818. See above, paras 21.22–21.26.
4 [2001] EWCA Civ 369, [2001] 3 All ER 818 at 827.
5 See below, para 21.47.
6 [2002] 1 All ER (Comm) 193.
7 [2002] 1 All ER (Comm) 193 at 203.

21.44   The requirement of a causal link   To give rise to a defence, there must be some causal link between the receipt of the payment and a change of position by the defendant. It is not enough that the defendant has suffered a downturn in his fortunes since receiving the payment in question. Thus, in *Derby v Scottish Equitable*, the fact that the defendant's general financial difficulties, arising from the future separation or divorce from his wife, were irrelevant because the defendant could not demonstrate that they were causally connected to the benefit mistakenly paid by the claimant[1].

1 [2001] EWCA Civ 369, [2001] 3 All ER 818 at 827–828, per Walker LJ, and at 831, per Simon Brown LJ.

21.45   The burden of proving a change of position lies on the defendant[1]. The problems of proof that arise in this area are apparent in *Philip Collins Ltd v Davis*[2]. The defendants were backing musicians who were mistakenly overpaid hundreds of thousands of pounds as royalties for their contribution to an album released by Collins. After realising the mistake in 1997, the claimant claimed the right to set off the overpayments against any future royalties. The defendants argued that they had changed their position so that it would be inequitable to require them to make restitution. Parker J accepted that the defendants had adjusted their expenditure to reflect their income. However, there were clearly real problems in establishing the precise extent of any change of position. Parker J observed that:

> ... the court should beware of applying too strict a standard. Depending on the circumstances, it may well be unrealistic to expect the defendant to produce conclusive evidence of change of position, given that when he changed his position he can have no expectation that he might thereafter have to prove that he did so, and the reason why he did so, in a court of law[3].

If anything, the defendants were too convincing for their own good in detailing their expenditure after receiving the benefits in question. Ultimately, Parker J thought that, despite having spent the money received from the claimant, the defendants could not completely escape liability to make restitution. In his view, their propensity to live beyond their means was such that they might well have incurred much of the expenditure in question even if they had to go into debt to do so[4]. Parker J favoured a rough compromise, reducing the defendants' liability by half.

1 *Philip Collins Ltd v Davis* [2000] 3 All ER 808 at 827, per Parker J.

2 [2000] 3 All ER 808.
3 [2000] 3 All ER 808 at 827. This view was endorsed by Walker LJ in *Derby v Scottish Equitable* [2001] EWCA Civ 369, [2001] 3 All ER 818 at 827–828.
4 [2001] EWCA Civ 369, [2000] 3 All ER 808 at 828–830.

21.46   Payment of debts and change of position   Generally, defendants will not be able to establish a defence on the basis they changed position by paying off debts earlier than they otherwise would have[1]. For, were restitution to be ordered after such expenditure, the defendant's net balance of assets and liabilities would be returned to the position it was prior to the receipt of the benefit from the claimant. The only difference would be that the defendant would become liable to the claimant, rather than to the creditor who was paid as a result of the change of position in question[2]. The point is illustrated by *Derby v Scottish Equitable*[3], where the defendant used a mistaken overpayment received from the claimant to pay off $^2/_3$ of a mortgage[4]. The defendant had the benefit of lower mortgage payments for a period and could have remortgaged the house if he had difficulty raising the amount of restitution that he was obliged to repay.

1 *RBC Dominion Securities Inc v Dawson* (1994) 111 DLR (4th) 230; *Derby v Scottish Equitable* [2001] EWCA Civ 369, [2001] 3 All ER 819.
2 This is also the justification given for allowing a claimant whose payment has been used to repay a defendant's debt to acquire the rights of the creditor by subrogation. See *Butler v Rice* [1910] 2 Ch 277 at 282–283, per Warrington J, and above, para 8.45ff. Indeed, subrogation should be available to a claimant after a defendant has innocently changed his position by paying a debt. However, subrogation will bring advantages over a more direct restitutionary claim only if it would allow the claimant to take the benefit of any secured rights enjoyed by the creditor.
3 [2001] EWCA Civ 369, [2001] 3 All ER 818.
4 [2001] EWCA Civ 369, [2001] 3 All ER 818 at 828.

21.47   Reliance in anticipation of a benefit   There is authority for the view that the defence is unavailable in circumstances in which the defendant changed position in anticipation of receiving a benefit. In *South Tyneside Metropolitan Borough Council v Svenska International plc*[1], Clarke J concluded that, in these circumstances, the defendant had relied, not on the receipt of an enrichment, but rather on the validity of a void transaction. The insistence that the availability of the defence depends upon the precise timing of events is liable to work injustice, and few commentators supported this conclusion[2]. A strong indication that this position will not be followed was provided by the Privy Council in *Dextra Bank & Trust Co Ltd v Bank of Jamaica*[3]. The Privy Council was reluctant to recognise Dextra's claim, rather oddly characterising the bank's error as a misprediction that a loan would result, rather than an actionable mistake[4]. Nevertheless, in giving the judicial committee's advice, Lord Templeman considered the application of the change of position defence to the facts. The Bank of Jamaica changed its position before receiving the benefit in question, thus raising the issue of 'anticipatory reliance'. His Lordship stated that 'what is in issue is the justice or injustice of enforcing a restitutionary claim in respect of a benefit conferred'[5]. He concluded there was no relevant distinction to be drawn on the basis of whether the detrimental reliance proceeded or followed the transfer in respect of which the claimant seeks restitution[6].

1 [1995] 1 All ER 545.
2 See for example Nolan 'Change of Position' in Birks (ed) *Laundering and Tracing* (1995), p 135; Jewell 'Change of Position' in Birks and Rose (eds), *Lessons of the Swaps Litigation* (2000), p 273.
3 [2002] 1 All ER (Comm) 193.
4 [2002] 1 All ER (Comm) 193 at 202.
5 [2002] 1 All ER (Comm) 193 at 204.
6 [2002] 1 All ER (Comm) 193 at 204.

21.48   Change of position without reliance?   What happens if the defendant's position has altered, not by the defendant doing anything positive in reliance on the validity of the receipt, but rather as a result of the property being lost, stolen, destroyed or depreciating in value? While, in the absence of a change of position, the claimant is entitled to demand restitution, it would be unreasonable to require an innocent recipient effectively to underwrite the risk of the loss of the enrichment received at the claimant's expense[1]. This was the view taken in the United States in the *Restatement of Restitution*[2]. While a case that turns on this matter has yet to come before an English court, the same approach is favoured by most commentators[3], and there is little reason to think that the courts will take a different view. Indeed, Harrison J in the first instance decision in *Derby v Scottish Equitable* favoured a broad approach to the defence that would extend protection to defendants who had the benefit they received stolen from them – a view that was noted with apparent approval by Robert Walker LJ in the Court of Appeal[4]. Certainly the manner in which the defence was framed in *Lipkin Gorman* is broad enough to accommodate its availability in such circumstances[5].

1   See Smith 'Restitution: The Heart of Corrective of Justice' (2001) 79 Texas Law Review 2115 at 2149.
2   See para 142(3). See Palmer *Law of Restitution* (1978) vol 1, para 528.
3   Goff and Jones *Law of Restitution* (5th edn, 1998), p 822; Burrows *Law of Restitution* (1993), p 427.
4   [2001] EWCA Civ 369, [2001] 3 All ER 818 at 827.
5   [1991] 2 AC 548 at 580, per Lord Goff.

GOOD FAITH

21.49   The defendant must have changed his position in good faith: a subjective requirement of honesty[1]. It follows that the defence will not be available to conscious wrongdoers. It probably also means that the defence has no application in cases of receipt in equity, as defendants will be personally liable only if their receipt or use of the property in question was unconscionable[2] – a state of mind that presumably precludes characterising the defendant as bona fide. While it has been suggested that the development of a change of position defence should encourage the courts to make liability in this context strict subject to defences[3], this has yet to happen.

1   *Lipkin Gorman v Karpnale Ltd* [1991] 2 AC 548 at 580, per Lord Goff.
2   *Bank of Credit and Commerce International (Overseas) Ltd v Akindele* [2001] Ch 437. See above, para 5.52ff.
3   See for example Birks 'Misdirected Funds: Restitution from the Recipient' [1989] Lloyds Maritime and Commercial Law Quarterly 296; Lord Nicholls 'Knowing Receipt – The Need for a New Landmark' in Cornish, Nolan, O'Sullivan and Virgo (eds) *Restitution past present and future – Essays in honour of Gareth Jones* (1998), p 231. For a more cautious view see Gardner 'Knowing Assistance and Knowing Receipt: Taking Stock' (1996) 112 LQR 56.See above, para 5.54ff.

21.50   In *Lipkin Gorman v Karpnale Ltd*, Lord Goff indicated that the defence of change of position would not be available to one who is guilty of a tort[1]. If the defence is denied to those who are liable for strict torts, this has nothing to do with the requirement of good faith. For example, it is probable that the defence would be denied to innocent purchasers who are sued for conversion. The action has never been regarded as restitutionary and it would be odd to allow the defence of change of position when the more obviously appropriate defence of bona fide purchase has not been made available.

1   [1991] 2 AC 548 at 580.

21.51   Presumably the defence will not generally be available to those who have committed equitable wrongs. However, the Court of Appeal decision in *Cheese v Thomas*[1] suggests that this might not always be the case. The court had accepted that the claimant was entitled to relief because the defendant could not rebut the presumption raised in the circumstances that the claimant's decision to participate with the defendant in the joint purchase of a property was induced by undue influence. The issue then became whether the defendant ought to repay in full the value of the claimant's contribution, despite a fall in the value of the property in question. The court concluded that, given that the defendant had acted in good faith, the parties should share the loss resulting from the decline in the housing market in proportion to their relative contributions to the purchase[2]. While the court treated the matter as an exercise of its inherent equitable jurisdiction to adjust the terms of rescission to do practical justice, it clearly has much in common with the change of position defence[3]. On the other hand, it might be asked whether one who cannot displace a presumption of undue influence should really be excused of liability to make restitution.

1   [1994] 1 All ER 35.
2   [1994] 1 WLR 129 at 136, per Nicholls VC.
3   Chen-Wishart (1994) 110 LQR 173.

THE RELEVANCE OF FAULT

21.52   Will the defence be available if the defendant acted in good faith, but was careless in that he ought to have known that the benefit was transferred in circumstances that gave the claimant a right to restitution? The position taken in the United States by the commentators of the *Restatement* was that the defence would be available only where the defendant 'was no more at fault for his receipt, retention or dealing with the subject matter than was the claimant'[1]. It might be thought to be rather harsh that a defendant should be required to bear the entire loss simply because he was somewhat more careless than was the claimant. A different approach was favoured by the legislatures of New Zealand and Western Australia which, in providing a defence for those who have changed their position in reliance on a mistaken payment, have allowed the courts to apportion relief in accordance with the parties' relative fault[2]. However, there seems little chance of either approach gaining favour in this jurisdiction.

1   *Restatement of Restitution* (1937), para 142(2).
2   See the Judicature Act 1908, s 94B (NZ) (introduced by the Judicature Amendment Act 1958); and the Property Law Act 1969, s 125(1) (WA).

21.53   The Privy Council considered the matter in *Dextra Bank & Trust Co Ltd v Bank of Jamaica*[1]. Both the claimant's mistake and the defendant's change of position were caused by the parties being duped by intermediaries and a fraudulent insider at the defendant bank. While the claimant paid the defendant in the belief that it was advancing a loan, the defendant paid money into accounts operated by the intermediaries in the belief that it was financing a currency exchange. The Privy Council concluded that the fact that the defendant was in good faith was sufficient for it to be fully excused of any responsibility to make restitution to the extent that it had changed its position[2]. As a decision of the Privy Council in response to an appeal from Jamaica, *Dextra* is obviously not binding on English courts. Moreover, its remarks on change of position must be regarded as obiter, given that the Judicial Committee found that the claimant did not have a valid cause of action[3]. However, the Privy Council's unequivocal rejection of the relevance of fault is liable to be followed by English courts. Nevertheless, the reasons adduced in Lord Templeman's advice are far from convincing.

1   [2002] 1 All ER (Comm) 193.
2   [2002] 1 All ER (Comm) 193 at 207.
3   [2002] 1 All ER (Comm) 193 at 202.

21.54   Lord Templeman noted that fault did not preclude claimants from claiming restitution for mistake. In the light of this, he thought it strange that a defendant who had changed his position in reliance on the validity of a mistaken payment 'should find his conduct examined to ascertain whether he had been negligent, and still more so that the plaintiff's conduct should likewise be examined for the purposes of assessing the relative fault of the parties'[1]. Yet, on reflection, this hardly seems strange at all. In the absence of a change of position, claimants' fault should be irrelevant as all that is sought is a restoration of the status quo. Once there is a change of position, fault might be thought relevant because the status quo cannot be restored: there is a loss that has to be borne by one of the parties or shared by both of them. Certainly, other defences to restitution claims take account of the parties' fault. Thus, our law allows estoppel as a defence only where a claimant, by making a representation or breaching a duty owed to the defendant, has caused the defendant to change his position to his detriment[2]. Similarly, the defendant's fault is taken into account in the application of the defence of bona fide purchaser by its denial to those who had constructive notice of a claimant's interest[3].

1   [2002] 1 All ER (Comm) 193 at 207.
2   See above, para 21.16.
3   See above, para 21.9.

21.55   Lord Templeman dismissed the position taken in the *Restatement of Restitution*[1], relying on a suggestion that American Courts had disregarded the provision which indicates that the defence is unavailable when the defendant had been more at fault than the claimant[2]. Yet that view was based principally on cases that provide for recovery for mistake despite the claimant's carelessness, and it is difficult to see that these do anything to support the claim about the judicial response to defendants' carelessness. In addition, Lord Templeman relied on Birks's view that cases decided in New Zealand pursuant to the Judicature Act 1908, s 94B, have demonstrated 'how hopelessly unstable' the defence is 'when it is used to reflect relative fault'[3]. It is hardly obvious that this is so. The legislative provision in question has generated very little case law[4], which rather suggests that parties are able to second guess quite readily judicial intuitions about appropriate apportionment.

1   See above, para 21.52.
2   [2002] 1 All ER (Comm) 193 at 206, referring to Dawson 'Restitution without Enrichment' (1981) 61 Boston University Law Review 563 at 571–572.
3   [2002] 1 All ER (Comm) 193 at 207, referring to Birks 'Change of Position and Surviving Enrichment' in Swadling (ed) *Limits of Restitutionary Claims: A Comparative Analysis* (1997), p 41. Birks made his remarks in relation to the application of the provision in *Thomas v Houston Corbett & Co* [1969] NZLR 151.
4   See *Thomas v Houston Corbett & Co* [1969] NZLR 151; *Westpac Banking Corpn v Rae* [1992] 1 NZLR 338; *National Bank of New Zealand Ltd v Waitaki International Processing (NI) Ltd* [1999] 2 NZLR 211.

21.56   Certainly more thought might have been given to the merits of an approach that allowed apportionment on the basis of relative fault, given that this is the solution favoured by the legislature in the law of tort[1]. In addition, apportionment was favoured by the Court of Appeal in *Cheese v Thomas*, where it required the parties to share the loss resulting from a depreciation in value of an asset acquired in a voidable transaction[2]. It is hardly clear that the result in *Dextra*, where the loss arising as a result of the two parties being duped by intermediaries was borne by one of the parties alone, was the most just outcome available. A rule that apportions liability pursuant to relative fault is likely to be the optimal norm for encouraging efficient investment in the avoidance of such events[3]. Moreover where, as in *Dextra*, the defendant is an institution, there are strong economic arguments for denying the change of position defence altogether that make it particularly difficult to support allowing careless defendants to be fully excused of liability[4].

1 See the Law Reform (Contributory Negligence) Act 1945, s 1(1).
2 [1994] 1 WLR 129. See above, paras 21.51.
3 See Dagan 'Mistakes' (2001) 79 Texas Law Review 1795 at 1815–1817.
4 See Beatson and Bishop 'Mistaken Payments in the Law of Restitution' in Beatson *Use and Abuse of Unjust Enrichment: Essays on the Law of Restitution* (1991), p 144; Dagan 'Mistakes' (2001) 79 Texas Law Review 1795 at 1820.

21.57   Even if apportionment on the basis of relative fault were thought too unstable an approach, serious consideration ought to be given to denying the defence to a defendant who ought to have been aware of the claimant's rights. Difficulties in assessing a defendant's state of mind at the time he changed his position are likely to mean that a subjective standard will make life unduly difficult, both for counsel deciding whether to go to court, and for judges asked to rule on the matter[1].

1 Nolan 'Change of Position' in Birks (ed) *Laundering and Tracing* (1995), p 158.

VINDICATION OF PROPRIETARY RIGHTS[1]

21.58   As has already been mentioned, in *Foskett v McKeown*[2] Lord Millett argued that, because tracing is concerned with the transmission of property rights and not with the reversal of unjust enrichment, a proprietary claim contingent upon tracing was not subject to the change of position defence[3]. It has also been noted that this view is difficult to reconcile with *Re Diplock* and dicta in subsequent cases[4].

1 See above, ch 4.
2 [2001] 1 AC 102.
3 [2001] 1 AC 102 at 108 and 109, per Lord Browne-Wilkinson, at 115, per Lord Hoffman, and at 127 and 129, per Lord Millett.
4 See *Lipkin Gorman v Karpnale Ltd* [1991] 2 AC 548 at 581, per Lord Goff; *Boscawen v Bajwa* [1995] 4 All ER 769 at 776–777, per Millett LJ; above, para 4.45.

21.59   Contrary to Lord Millett's analysis, it cannot be presumed that actions must necessarily be characterised as providing solely for either restitution or the vindication of property rights. When the question is whether the change of position defence should be available, Lord Millett's analysis is liable to lead to circular logic. Given that the best indication of whether an action is conditioned by considerations of unjust enrichment is the availability of the change of position defence, the availability of the defence cannot be determined by asking whether the action is concerned with the reversal of unjust enrichment.

21.60   The line drawn by Lord Millett might be thought to indicate that the change of position defence will not available where a claimant is entitled to a proprietary remedy because this would, by definition, be characterised as involving the vindication of property rights[1]. If so, this might have rather striking results. On some analyses, proprietary relief is available in the context of mistaken payments[2]. If this is so, it is hardly obvious that it should be thought to follow that the change of position defence should be denied.

1   For reasoning of this kind, see for example Virgo *Principles of the Law of Restitution* (1999), p 596.
2   See for example *Chase Manhattan Bank v Israel-British Bank* [1981] Ch 105 at 118–120, per Goulding J; and *Westdeutsche Landesbank Girozentrale v Islington London Borough Council* [1996] AC 669 at 714–715, per Lord Browne-Wilkinson. See above, para 3.38ff.

21.61   If the defence were available in respect to proprietary remedies, it is easy enough to see how it would be applied with equitable charges over bank accounts or liens over other assets, where the extent of the personal liability secured by the lien or charge would simply be reduced[1]. On the other hand, it is less obvious how the defence would operate in the context of rights of ownership generated by resulting or constructive trusts. Presumably, where the claimant has a right over a particular asset, the award could be made on terms, so that the claimant would have to pay the defendant a monetary sum before being entitled to the transfer of the asset[2].

1   Nolan 'Change of Position' in Birks (ed) *Laundering and Tracing* (1995), p 179.
2   Birks 'Property and Unjust Enrichment: Categorical Truths' [1997] NZLR 623 at 634.

G   Res judicata

21.62   *Res judicata* is a plea that the parties' mutual rights have already been adjudicated on by a competent court, and so cannot be put in issue again. Some famous examples in earlier centuries involve conflicts in jurisdiction between different tribunals[1], thankfully usually irrelevant in the modern legal system. But the principle was relevant in a recent case where compensation was given to the Bricklayers' Guild in Dublin, when a nineteenth century hall was demolished to make way for a road-widening scheme. The compensation was assessed at a high figure, to allow the Guild to re-instate the hall away from the road; but when this unexpectedly turned out to be impossible, the City demanded the bulk of their money back. Nonetheless it was held that, the appropriate tribunal having assessed a figure in compensation, it was not open to either party to undermine the award by a plea of mistake falling short of fraud[2].

1   Most famously in *Moses v Macferlan* (1760) 2 Burr 1005, 97 ER 676.
2   *Dublin Corpn v Building and Allied Trade Union* [1996] 1 IR 468, noted by O'Dell (1997) 113 LQR 245.

H   Limitation[1]

21.63   The law on limitation is confused and confusing, and ripe for reform. The basic period for most restitutionary claims is six years from the point when the action first arose. However, this is not stated in any one section, but only piecemeal. The six year period is stated to apply to any claim 'to recover any sum recoverable by virtue of any enactment'[2], to actions in tort[3], and to actions by beneficiaries in respect of a breach of trust or for trust property[4]. It also applies to actions 'founded in simple contract'[5], which is accepted to include actions based on contracts 'implied in law', and therefore actions in common law restitution[6].

1 See generally Rose 'Lapse of time: Limitation' in Birks and Rose (eds) *Lessons of the swaps litigation* (2000), p 348.
2 See the Limitation Act 1980, s 9. It is not entirely clear whether this catches claims under the Law Reform (Frustrated Contracts) Act 1943 (above, para 20.3ff) and/or the Misrepresentation Act 1967; its meaning is highly obscure. See discussion in McGee *Limitation periods* (3rd edn, 1998), paras 4.014–4.021; Oughton 'Contract, specialty or "sum recoverable by virtue of any enactment": A limitation conundrum' (2001) 20 Civil Justice Quarterly 150.
3 See the Limitation Act 1980, s 2. Note also that the end of the right to sue in tort for lost goods also terminates the claimant's title to those goods: s 3.
4 See the Limitation Act 1980, s 21.
5 See the Limitation Act 1980, s 5. See also s 23 (claims for an account are subject to the same limit as the duty on which they are based).
6 *Re Diplock, Diplock v Wintle* [1948] Ch 465 at 514, per curiam, commenting on the predecessor provision to s 5 (Limitation Act 1939, s 2(1)(a)); see to the same effect *Westdeutsche Landesbank Girozentrale v Islington London Borough Council* [1994] 4 All ER 890 at 942–943, per Hobhouse J.

21.64   The limitation period starts as soon as the cause of action is complete. So if a wrongful payment was in principle recoverable as soon as it was made, then time runs from the date of the payment, whereas a claim to recover money on a total failure of consideration runs from the date the consideration failed. It may sometimes matter precisely which statutory provision is invoked, even if all the potentially relevant provisions have a six year period. If the defendant takes the claimant's chattel (thereby committing the tort of conversion) and then sells it, the claimant suing for proceeds, does the six years run from the commission of the tort, or from the receipt of the proceeds? It has been held that the action for proceeds is sufficiently distinct from the action in tort to have its own period, and so the latter solution has been adopted[1].

1 *Chesworth v Farrar* [1967] 1 QB 407 (based on a provision in the 1939 Act which does not feature in the modern law, though dicta support the point in the text). For criticism see Birks *An Introduction to the Law of Restitution* (revised edn, 1989), pp 348 and 349.

21.65   Some particular types of claim have their own periods, different from the six-year norm:

- a two-year period is prescribed for claims under the Civil Liability (Contribution) Act 1978[1] and claims for salvage[2];
- a 12-year period applies to claims in respect of the personal estate of a deceased person[3];
- claims that a trustee was personally involved in a fraudulent breach of trust, or that a trustee still has the trust property or its proceeds, are not subject to any limitation period[4].

1 See the Limitation Act 1980, s 10.
2 See the Maritime Conventions Act 1911, s 8. This is a difficult provision. See McGee *Limitation periods* (3rd edn, 1998), ch 24.
3 See the Limitation Act 1980, s 22.
4 See the Limitation Act 1980, s 21(1). Unreasonable delay will defeat a claim.

21.66   Some equitable claims, such as claims for rescission and most claims for breach of fiduciary duty, are not expressly caught by any of the periods mentioned in the legislation. The test is then one of whether the claimant has been guilty of unreasonable delay ('laches'). In principle the court can take into account any factor it chooses in determining this question, though the starting-point is the six-year period applicable to most other claims, which applies by analogy. The main considerations are, on the claimant's side, why the delay in bringing the claim was so great, and on the defendant's side, what prejudice has been caused by the delay[1].

1 See eg *Allcard v Skinner* (1887) 36 Ch D 145; *Lindsay Petroleum Co v Hurd* (1874) LR 5 PC 221.

21.67   A recent case, which might have made a revolution here, has quietly been sidelined. In *Nelson v Rye*, a pop musician was suing his former manager, claiming that the manager had not passed on all fees received for the musician's services. The ordinary six-year period had passed, but the claimant pointed out that his manger was a fiduciary, and argued that therefore the period did not apply. This was because no period is expressly mentioned in the legislation as generally applicable to fiduciaries. Alternatively, he argued that the remedy for breach of fiduciary duty was the imposition of a constructive trust on the errant fiduciary, and therefore the case was within the provision for breach of trust, where the legislation expressly says that there is no limitation period[1]. Laddie J accepted these arguments[2].

1   See the Limitation Act 1980, s 21(1); above, para 21.65.
2   *Nelson v Rye* [1996] 1 WLR 1378.

21.68   However this result, which in effect exempted claimants from the law on limitation periods so long as they can re-cast their claim as one based on breach of fiduciary duty, has been firmly rejected in later cases, on various grounds.

• Firstly, while the manager was a fiduciary, it did not follow that *every* breach of his contract was a breach of fiduciary duty. Breach of fiduciary duty usually implies dishonesty. So a mere failure to render a proper account, while it would be a breach of contract, would not ordinarily be a breach of fiduciary duty as well[1].

• Secondly, where a fiduciary duty merely reproduced a common law duty (such as the duty of a manager under their contract) then equity would apply the common law period by analogy. The claimant could not change the length of the period merely by a simple re-classification of the claim[2], even where dishonesty is alleged[3].

• Thirdly, while it was true that the remedy sought was traditionally described as the 'imposition of a constructive trust', this was usually mere shorthand for saying that there was a personal liability to account, closely analogous to that imposed on a trustee. It was not in any other sense a claim involving a trust. So the special provisions relating to trusts could only be invoked if the defendant was in some substantive respect a trustee, either because there was some pre-existing trust, or because the defendant had taken it on himself to act as trustee[4].

So where the substance of the matter was that there was a simple breach of contract, the trust provisions did not apply merely because the court might remedy it by the imposition of a constructive trust[5]. In the event, the courts have, here as elsewhere, fought off an attempt to disrupt settled common law rules by re-framing the claim as an equitable one[6].

1   *Coulthard v Disco Mix Club Ltd* [2000] 1 WLR 707.
2   *Paragon Finance plc v DB Thakerar plc* [1999] 1 All ER 400.
3   *Cia de Seguros Imperio v Heath (REBX) Ltd* [2001] 1 WLR 112. For a note on the first instance ruling (with which the CA agreed) see McGee and Scanlan 'Fiduciary duties and limitation periods' (2001) 20 Civil Justice Quarterly 171.
4   See eg *James v Williams* [2000] Ch 1.
5   *Coulthard v Disco Mix Club Ltd* [2000] 1 WLR 707.
6   See generally Hemsworth '"Constructive trusts" and "constructive trustees" – What's in a name?' (2000) 19 Civil Justice Quarterly 154.

21.69   The ordinary operation of the limitation period is delayed in certain cases. Any part-payment of a debt, or signed acknowledgement that it is still owing, resets the clock to the start of the period[1]. If at the start of the period the claimant is under age, or is suffering from a mental disability, then time does not begin to run until the claimant either acquires full competence or dies[2]. There is also a provision for delaying the onset of the period until the claimant should first reasonably have suspected the truth: cases of fraud[3], deliberate concealment of evidence[4], or where 'the action is for relief from the consequences of a mistake'[5].

Controversially, this last provision was recently extended by the House of Lords to cover cases of mistake of law. So if the claimant pays money in the belief that it is due, and then an unexpected new precedent rules definitively that it was never owing, then time begins to run on the claim only from the date of the new precedent. It does not matter how far in the past the mistaken payment was[6].

This is certainly undesirable in theory, though in practice this undesirable result does not often appear. Nonetheless, it is one more argument for reform. The Law Commission has suggested that the general rule in limitation law should be for a three-year period, but running from the date at which the cause of action could first reasonably have been discovered. There would be a long-stop of ten years, after which in general no action would lie[7].

1 See the Limitation Act 1980, ss 29–31. This applies only to actions for 'any debt or other liquidated pecuniary claim'. Surprisingly, and probably wrongly, this has been held to cover a claim in quantum meruit: *Amantilla Ltd v Telefusion plc* (1987) 9 Contr LR 139.
2 See the Limitation Act 1980, s 28. The period is then six years, for any type of claim.
3 See the Limitation Act 1980, s 32(1)(a); eg *GL Baker Ltd v Medway Building and Supplies Ltd* [1958] 1 WLR 1216.
4 See the Limitation Act 1980, s 32(1)(b).
5 See the Limitation Act 1980, s 32(1)(c); eg *Peco Arts Inc v Hazlitt Gallery Ltd* [1983] 1 WLR 1315 (money paid under a fundamentally mistaken contract).
6 *Kleinwort Benson Ltd v Lincoln City Council* [1999] 2 AC 349. See also above, para 17.88ff.
7 Law Commission *Limitation of Actions* (CP No 151, 1998). See also above, para 17.91ff.

I   Interest

21.70   Simple interest can be awarded in any restitution case. The general statutory provision only applies to cases of 'debt or damages'[1], but it is assumed that this will be given a meaning wide enough to include most restitutionary claims. Awards of interest are at the discretion of the court, not merely as to whether an award should be made at all, but also as to the rate of interest and as to the period covered. The general rule is that interest runs from the date when the cause of action arose, until the date at which the claimant obtains judgment in their favour[2]. Judgment in the claimant's favour marks the cut-off point for the award of interest (but there is separate provision for interest on judgment debts[3]).

1 See the Supreme Court Act 1981, s 35A (inserted by the Administration of Justice Act 1982, s 15 and Sch 1, Pt I).
2 See eg *Woolwich Equitable Building Society v IRC* [1993] AC 70, [1992] 3 All ER 737; on which see above, para 18.3ff.
3 See the Judgments Act 1838, 1&2 Vict c 110, s 17. The rate is usually assumed to be 8%.

21.71   However, the guiding principle is that interest is awarded to remedy the unfairness of keeping the claimant out of their money, and it is open to the defendant to demonstrate that justice would be done by taking into account only a lesser period. So if the claim is an unusual one, which the defendant had no reason to anticipate, interest may be held to run only when they had notice that a claim was being made. Or if the claimant unreasonably delayed the litigation, the period covered by the delay may be disregarded for the purpose of assessing interest[1].

1   See discussion in *BP Exploration (Libya) Ltd v Hunt (No 2)* [1979] 1 WLR 783 at 846–847, per Robert Goff J.

21.72   Compound interest is more limited, the discretion to grant it being traditionally confined to cases of fraud and of breach of fiduciary duty[1]. This has been criticised, as a claimant who is being kept out of their money will often have to make good the loss by commercial borrowing, which will of course be at a compound rate. Matters came to a head in the *Westdeutsche* case, where the issue was whether an action to recover £2.5m paid to a local authority under an invalid swap carried compound interest. The payor bank argued that compound interest could be awarded in an appropriate case in any sort of claim; or that, if it was necessary to bring themselves within the more traditional categories of claim, the local authority's duty to return the money could be styled a fiduciary duty. They observed that they could only make good the money in the interim by borrowing at commercial rates, where interest would of course be compounded.

Nonetheless, these arguments failed, and simple interest only was awarded, from the date of the defendant's receipt of the money[2]. The Lords unanimously rejected any argument that there was a fiduciary duty – the claim was on a simple personal liability at common law – and a majority insisted that the traditional categories were binding. The existence of these categories had earlier been affirmed both by decisions of the Lords themselves[3] and (in effect) by Parliament's failure to provide for compound interest at common law[4], despite implementing other reforms as to interest[5]. For the courts to get rid of them would be too adventurous an exercise in judicial legislation.

1   See eg *Wallersteiner v Moir (No 2)* [1975] QB 373, [1975] 1 All ER 849.
2   *Westdeutsche Landesbank Girozentrale v Islington London Borough Council* [1996] AC 669, [1996] 2 All ER 961. See Rose 'Interest' in Birks and Rose (eds) *Lessons of the swaps litigation* (2000), p 291.
3   Especially in *President of India v La Pintada Compania Navigacion SA* [1985] AC 104, [1984] 2 All ER 773.
4   On the claim itself see above, para 18.19ff.
5   See eg Late Payment of Commercial Debts (Interest) Act 1998. For argument for a broader remedy see Ridge 'Just feel-good words? Recent Australian developments towards a restitutionary cause of action for pre-judgement interest' (2000) 28 Australian Business Law Review 275. For conflict of laws aspects see Virgo 'Interest, constructive trusts and the conflict of laws' [2000] RLR 122.

CHAPTER 22

Conflict of Laws

Joanna Bird

A   Introduction

22.1   The conflict of laws is that part of the law which deals with issues that arise when a legal dispute contains a foreign element. A foreign element may be introduced into a legal dispute in a myriad of ways: for example, a party to a dispute may be a resident of a foreign state; some or all of the facts relevant to the dispute may have occurred in another or a number of other countries; or the parties themselves may have expressed a wish that their dispute be resolved by the courts of a foreign state or the laws of a foreign state.

22.2   Given the prevalence of international transactions in the modern world, and the ease with which assets can be moved through jurisdictions, many restitution disputes must involve such foreign elements. Nevertheless, there is relatively little relevant legislation or case law. The lack of legislative or judicial attention has not been matched by academic indifference. The vast array of complex legal issues that can arise when restitution meets the conflicts of laws, and the huge areas of uncertainty created by the lack of legislative or judicial treatment, have in recent years at least enlivened scholarly interest. Accordingly, there is a substantial and growing body of academic discussion of restitution and the conflict of laws[1].

1   See for example: Panagopoulos *Restitution in Private International Law* (2000); Rose (ed) *Restitution and the Conflict of Laws* (1995); Collins (ed) *Dicey and Morris on The Conflict of Laws* (13th edn, 2000), r 200, ch 34; North and Fawcett *Cheshire and North's Private International Law* (13th edn, 1999), ch 20; Burrows *Law of Restitution* (1993), pp 490–500; Zweigert and Müller-Gindullis 'Quasi Contract' in Lipstein (ed) *International Encyclopedia of Comparative Law* (1974), vol III, ch 30; Lee 'Restitution, Public Policy and the Conflict of Laws' (1998) 20 University of Queensland Law Journal 1; Leslie 'Unjustified Enrichment in the Conflict of Laws' (1998) 2 Edinburgh Law Review 233; Bennett 'Choice of Law Rules in Claims of Unjust Enrichment' (1990) 39 ICLQ 136; Blaikie 'Unjust Enrichment in the Conflict of Laws' [1984] Juridical Review 112; Cohen 'Quasi Contract and the Conflict of Laws' (1956) 31 Los Angeles Bar Bulletin 71; Ehrenzweig 'Restitution in the Conflict of Laws' (1961) 36 New York University Law Review 1298; Gutteridge and Lipstein 'Conflicts of Law in Matters of Unjustifiable Enrichment' (1941) 7 CLJ 80.

22.3   The two main issues that arise when a legal dispute has a foreign element are: where should the dispute be heard, and what law should be applied to the dispute. These issues are respectively described as 'jurisdiction' and 'choice of law'. This chapter will deal with both issues. The relevant case, statutory and convention law and the various academic theories will be discussed and analysed. However, in light of the paucity of judicial consideration, most conclusions as to the current state of the law will necessarily be tentative.

B   Jurisdiction

Introduction

22.4   The English rules of jurisdiction are technical and complex. It is only possible here to give the briefest outline, highlighting issues that may arise when a party wishes to commence a claim for restitution in an English court[1].

1 For a more detailed treatment of the English law on jurisdiction see North and Fawcett *Cheshire and North's Private International Law* (13th edn, 1999), chs 10–14; and Briggs and Rees *Civil Jurisdiction and Judgments* (2nd edn, 1997).

22.5   The jurisdiction of English courts to adjudicate on claims in restitution may be affected by the Brussels Convention[1], the Lugano Convention[2], the Modified Convention[3], the common law, and the Civil Procedure Rules. Thus, the first task is to determine where one looks for the relevant jurisdictional rules in any given situation.

1 European Community Convention on Jurisdiction and the Enforcement of Judgments in Civil and Commercial Matters, in Civil Jurisdiction and Judgments Act 1982, Schs 1 and 2. The Convention is given the force of law in the United Kingdom by s 2.
2 European Community and European Free Trade Association Convention on Jurisdiction and the Enforcement of Judgments in Civil and Commercial Matters, in Civil Jurisdiction and Judgments Act 1982, Sch 3C. The Convention is given the force of law in the United Kingdom by s 3A.
3 This is not an international or regional treaty. It is a modified version of the Brussels Convention which is used to allocate jurisdiction within the United Kingdom: Civil Jurisdiction and Judgments Act 1982, s 16. The Modified Convention is in the Civil Jurisdiction and Judgments Act 1982, Sch 4.

22.6   In civil and commercial matters[1], such as the vast majority of restitution claims[2], the starting point is always the Brussels Convention[3]. In such matters, the Brussels Convention applies to allocate jurisdiction whenever the defendant is domiciled[4] in a European Union State[5], or if the provisions of Articles 16 to 18 of that Convention allocate jurisdiction to a European Union State. Likewise, if the defendant in a civil or commercial matter is domiciled in a European Free Trade Association (EFTA) State, or if Articles 16 to 17 of the Lugano Convention allocate jurisdiction to an EFTA State, then the Lugano Convention governs jurisdiction.

1 Article 1 of the Brussels Convention provides that: 'This Convention shall apply in civil and commercial matters whatever the nature of the court or tribunal. It shall not extend, in particular, to revenue, customs or administrative matters'. Article 1 then lists a number of matters, such as social security and arbitration, that are explicitly excluded from the scope of the Convention. 'Civil and commercial' essentially covers private law, as opposed to public law, matters: *LTU GmbH v Eurocontrol* (Case No 29/76) [1976] ECR 1541 and *Netherlands State v Rüffer* (Case 814/79) [1980] ECR 3807. For further discussion see North and Fawcett *Cheshire and North's Private International Law* (13th edn, 1999), pp 190–195.
2 It is arguable that an action to recover payment pursuant to an ultra vires demand by a public authority, especially where the payment is a purported tax, is not a civil and commercial matter. (On such claims see above, ch 18.) See Panagopoulos *Restitution in Private International Law* (2000), pp 190–192 where it is argued that such an action falls within the Convention, provided that the claimant does not need to establish the ultra vires nature of the demand in the same action as he or she seeks restitution.
3 Briggs and Rees *Civil Jurisdiction and Judgments* (2nd edn, 1997), pp 3–5.
4 Defined in Brussels Convention, art 52, and Civil Jurisdiction and Judgments Act 1982, ss 41–46.
5 Defined in arts 2 and 3.

22.7   The Modified Convention allocates jurisdiction within the United Kingdom, in two situations[1]. Firstly, if application of the Brussels Convention leads to the conclusion that jurisdiction is given to the United Kingdom (either because the defendant is domiciled in the United Kingdom, or because the United Kingdom has exclusive jurisdiction under Art 16), the rules in the Modified Convention determine whether jurisdiction is given to the courts of England and Wales, Scotland, or Northern Ireland. Secondly, the Modified Convention also applies to allocate jurisdiction within the United Kingdom, in civil and commercial matters which are entirely internal to the United Kingdom, such as where an English bank brings an action against a Scottish local authority for restitution of moneys paid under a void contract[2].

1 Civil Jurisdiction and Judgments Act 1982, ss 16 and 17.
2 See eg *Kleinwort Benson Ltd v Glasgow City Council* [1999] 1 AC 153; considered below, para 22.11ff.

22.8 In all remaining situations, the common law and the Civil Procedure Rules prescribe the limits of the jurisdiction of English courts.

Brussels Convention

22.9 The Brussels Convention is based on the proposition that persons domiciled in a Contracting State, that is, a European Union State, should generally be sued in the courts of that State. This means that the United Kingdom courts have jurisdiction in restitution actions brought against a person domiciled in the United Kingdom[1]. Conversely, it means that the United Kingdom Courts will only have jurisdiction over defendants domiciled in a Contracting State other than the United Kingdom if the action comes within the exceptions to the general principle in sections 2 to 6 of Title II of the Convention[2]. Those exceptions that are most likely to be invoked in restitution actions are examined below[3].

1 See Article 2. The Modified Convention (below, para 22.17ff) then applies to allocate jurisdiction to the courts of the various parts of the United Kingdom.
2 See Article 3.
3 See below, paras 22.10–22.16. It must be noted that a claimant in an action for restitution may be able to establish exceptional jurisdiction on bases other than those mentioned. For example, under art 18 United Kingdom courts would have jurisdiction in restitution disputes if the defendant submitted to the jurisdiction of the United Kingdom courts.

ARTICLE 5

22.10 Article 5 gives jurisdiction in certain categories of disputes to the courts of places which are assumed to have a particularly close connection with those disputes[1]. This jurisdiction is concurrent with that of the courts for the place of the defendant's domicile. Article 5(4) gives jurisdiction in:

> ... a civil claim for damages or restitution which is based on an act giving rise to criminal proceedings, [to] the court seised of those proceedings, to the extent that that court has jurisdiction under its own law to entertain civil proceedings.

However, claimants seeking to obtain restitution in courts other than those of the defendant's domicile are most likely to resort to Art 5(1) or 5(3), neither of which specifically mentions restitution.

1 For decisions based on this article, see for example *Handelskwekerij GJ Bier BV v Mines de Potasse d'Alsace SA* (Case 21/76) [1976] ECR 1735, para 11; *Somafer SA v Saar-Ferngas AG* (Case 33/78) [1978] ECR 2183, para 7; *Martin Peters Bauunternehmung GmbH v Zuid Nederlandse Aanemers Vereniging* (Case 34/82) [1983] ECR 987, para 6.

22.11   Article 5(1) provides that the defendant may be sued:

> ... in matters relating to a contract, in the courts for the place of performance of the obligation in question[1].

The European Court of Justice has yet to consider whether claims for restitution can be brought under this provision. However, in *Kleinwort Benson Ltd v Glasgow City Council*[2], a bare majority of the House of Lords held that a claim for restitution of money paid under a void contract did not fall within the (identical) provision in the Modified Convention. Whilst the reasoning of the majority judges differs in certain respects[3], there are a number of common points. In compliance with the direction in Civil Jurisdiction and Judgments Act 1982, s 16(3)(a), to have regard to relevant principles and decisions of the European Court of Justice when interpreting the Modified Convention, all three majority judges were heavily influenced by decisions of the European Court of Justice on the scope of Art 5(1) of the Brussels Convention and, in fact, sought to anticipate the decision that that Court would have reached if the action had arisen in the context of the Brussels Convention[4]. They all noted that European Court jurisprudence[5] establishes that, because Art 5 represents a derogation from the basic principle that the defendant should be sued in the courts of his or her domicile, it should be interpreted restrictively[6]. Finally, all three members of the majority derived the scope of Art 5(1), at least in part, by reference to the connecting factor, 'the place of performance of the obligation in question'. European Court of Justice decisions show that the obligation in question is the contractual obligation[7] that forms the basis of the claimant's claim[8]. Therefore, the majority in the House of Lords concluded that a claim for restitution of money paid under a contract, which both parties accept was void ab initio, cannot fall within Art 5(1), because it is not based upon a performance of a particular contractual obligation[9].

1   Note that Art 5(1) then goes on to define 'the place of performance of the obligation in question' in individual employment contracts.
2   [1999] 1 AC 153.
3   For an analysis of the decisions and the differences between them see Dickinson 'Restitution and the Conflict of Laws in the House of Lords' [1998] RLR 104 at 107–111.
4   [1999] 1 AC 153 at 163, per Lord Goff, at 178–179, per Lord Clyde, and at 187, per Lord Hutton.
5   *Kalfelis v Bankhause Schröder, Munchmeyer, Hengst and Co* (Case 189/87) [1988] ECR 5565, para 19.
6   [1999] 1 AC 153 at 164, per Lord Goff, at 179, per Lord Clyde, and at 188 and 195, per Lord Hutton.
7   It should be noted that, in Art 5(1) 'contract' has an autonomous European Community meaning, independent of its meaning in national law: *Jakob Handte and Co GmbH v Traitements Mecano-chimiques des Surfaces SA* (Case C–26/91) [1992] ECR, I-3967, para 10.
8   *Ets A de Bloos SPRL v Societe en commandite par actions Bouyer* (Case 14/76) [1976] ECR 1497, para 15; *Custom Made Commercial Ltd v Stawa Metallbau GmbH* (Case C–288/92) [1994] ECR I-2913, para 23.
9   [1999] 1 AC 153 at 167, per Lord Goff, at 181–182, per Lord Clyde, and at 189, per Lord Hutton.

22.12   However, the decision in *Kleinwort Benson* is not the death knell for attempts to bring restitution actions under Art 5(1) of the Brussels Convention. Firstly, the decision has been criticised[1], and there is clearly room to debate whether the European Court of Justice will reach the same decision when a similar case is before it. Secondly, even if the decision is correct, it does not follow that all claims for restitution fall outside the article. In fact, Lord Goff in *Kleinwort Benson* accepted that a claim for restitution of money paid under a broken contract, on the basis of failure of consideration, probably falls within Art 5(1)[2]. The same result must follow in relation to restitution for the wrong of breach of contract[3]. In both these situations, the claimant sues in relation to the non-performance or breach of a contractual obligation. Finally, it must be acknowledged that the relatively broad interpretation of Art 5(1) of the Lugano Convention in *Agnew v Länsförsäkringsbolagens AB*[4] sits uneasily with *Kleinwort Benson*. In *Agnew*, a majority of the House of Lords accepted that a claim that a reinsurance contract should be avoided for material non-disclosure was a 'matter relating to a contract' for the purposes of Art 5(1) and that the pre-contractual obligation to make a fair disclosure of the risk was the 'obligation in question' for the purposes of Art 5(1). It has been suggested that this decision will lead to *Kleinwort Benson* being confined to its facts and, accordingly, a claim for restitution of money paid under a voidable (as opposed to void ab initio) contract will now be considered to fall within Art 5(1)[5]. The 'post-contractual' obligation to give restitution of money paid under the avoided contract will be construed as the 'obligation in question'. However, this suggestion is hard to reconcile with the fact that the majority in *Agnew* did not consider that its decision in anyway threatened the validity of the decision in *Kleinwort Benson*.

1 Peel 'Jurisdiction over Restitutionary Claims' [1998] Lloyds Maritime and Commercial Law Quarterly 22; Virgo 'Jurisdiction over Unjust Enrichment Claims' (1998) 114 LQR 386; North and Fawcett *Cheshire and North's Private International Law* (13th edn, 1999) pp 202–203. Cf Dickinson 'Restitution and the Conflict of Laws in the House of Lords' [1998] RLR 104; Pitel 'Jurisdiction over Restitutionary Claims' [1998] CLJ 19.
2 [1999] 1 AC 153 at 171.
3 As 'contract' has an autonomous Community meaning, Art 5(1) may extend to restitution for breaches of equitable wrongs which arise from the agreement of the parties: Briggs and Rees *Civil Jurisdiction and Judgments* (2nd edn, 1997), pp 116 and 117.
4 [2001] 1 AC 223.
5 Briggs (2000) 71 British Yearbook of International Law 451.

22.13   The claimant in *Kleinwort Benson* also sought to rely on Art 5(3), which gives jurisdiction:

> ... in matters relating to tort, delict or quasi-delict, [to] the courts for the place where the harmful event occurred.

The argument was based on the decision of the European Court of Justice in *Kalfelis v Bankhaus Schröder, Munchmeyer, Hengst and Co*, that:

> ... the term 'matters relating to tort, delict or quasi-delict' within the meaning of Art 5(3) of the Convention must be regarded as an independent concept covering all actions which seek to establish the liability of a defendant and which are not related to a 'contract' within the meaning of Article 5(1)[1].

In other words, the claimant argued that, if the matter did not fall within Art 5(1), it must fall within Art 5(3)[2]. The House of Lords unanimously dismissed this argument, seeing it as based on a misreading of the decision in *Kalfelis*. Lords Goff and Hutton also noted that Art 5(3) was inappropriate because, in general, restitution is not based on a harmful event[3].

1 (Case 189/87) [1988] ECR 5565 at 5585.
2 [1999] 1 AC 153 at 160.
3 [1999] 1 AC 153 at 172, per Lord Goff, and at 196, per Lord Hutton.

22.14   Clearly, this decision does not prevent recourse to Art 5(3) by a claimant who seeks restitution of profits made as a result of a tort[1]. Restitution for the wrong of tort is based on a harmful event. The same argument must apply to claims for restitution of profits made as a result of an equitable wrong, provided the equitable wrong falls within the autonomous Community concept of 'tort, delict or quasi-delict'. Although this point has not been decided, the better view is that equitable wrongs which arise from the unilateral conduct of the defendant, as opposed to the breach of an agreement between the claimant and defendant, must fall within the scope of Art 5(3)[2]. Finally, it has also been suggested that other types of restitutionary claim which are linked to particular conduct by the defendant, such as duress or misappropriation of property, may also come within Art 5(3)[3].

1   On which see above, ch 12. It is inconceivable that the English law notion that a claimant who seeks restitution of profits made by a tortfeasor 'waives the tort' and sues on the basis of some other cause of action, would be allowed to infect interpretation of the Brussels Convention. On this notion see above, para 12.2ff.
2   Briggs and Rees *Civil Jurisdiction and Judgments* (2nd edn, 1997), pp 116 and 117.
3   Dickinson 'Restitution and the Conflict of Laws in the House of Lords' [1998] RLR 104 at 117.

ARTICLE 16

22.15   Article 16 confers exclusive jurisdiction, regardless of the defendant's domicile, in limited circumstances. At first glance, Art 16(1)(a) seems likely to be determinative of jurisdiction in those proprietary restitution claims brought with the object of establishing a right in immovable property. It gives exclusive jurisdiction:

> ... in proceedings which have as their object rights in rem in immovable property or tenancies of immovable property, [to] the courts of the Contracting State in which the property is situated[1].

However, in *Webb v Webb*[2] the European Court of Justice gave Art 16(1)(a) a restrictive interpretation, likely to severely limit its applicability to restitution claims. In 1971, a father provided the funds for the purchase a flat in France in the name of his son. Both the father and son used the flat as a holiday home, but the father paid the bulk of the outgoings. In 1990, the father sought, from the English court, a declaration that the son held the property on resulting trust for the father, and an order requiring the son to execute the documents necessary to vest legal title in the father. The son argued that the claim came within Art 16(1) and, accordingly, the French courts had exclusive jurisdiction.

The European Court of Justice rejected the son's argument. The Court made it clear that the crucial question under Art 16(1) is not whether the claimant's ultimate purpose is to obtain a right in rem in immovable property. The claimant's action must be based on an existing right in rem in the property, rather than a right in personam. According to the court, the father's claim fell outside this requirement because he 'does not claim that he already enjoys rights directly relating to the property which are enforceable against the whole world, but seeks only to assert rights as against the son'[3]. The court also supported its decision by reference to the policy behind Art 16(1). The grant of exclusive jurisdiction to the courts of the State in which the property is situated is justified 'because actions concerning rights in rem in immovable property often involve disputes frequently necessitating checks, inquiries and expert assessments which must be carried out on the spot'[4]. The father's claim in this case clearly required none of these local inquiries or assessments. As the court pointed out[5], the nature of the legal dispute would have been identical if the father had purchased a yacht in the son's name.

1   Note that Art 16(1)(b) contains an exception in relation to short term private tenancies.
2   Case C–294/92 [1994] ECR I-1717.
3   [1994] ECR I-1717, para 15.

4   [1994] ECR I-1717, para 17.
5   [1994] ECR I-1717, para 18.

22.16   The court's assertion that the father's claim was not based on a right in rem because he was making a claim against the son, rather than the whole world, is open to criticism[1]. The father made a claim against the son only because that was all he was required to do to get what he wanted, legal title to the property. However, the father made this claim on the basis that he was the existing holder of a right in the flat that could be asserted against (a sizeable portion of) the whole world; the father's right could have been asserted against anyone other than a bona fide purchaser for value of the flat. It is difficult, in these circumstances, to describe the basis or foundation of the father's claim as a right in personam. As Briggs points out[2], the intriguing issue is whether an action in which the claimant relied upon his right in the property against a third party, who had acquired an interest in the property from the son with notice, would fall within Art 16(1). The liability of a knowing recipient of trust property is based on constructive trust and is generally considered to be restitutionary[3]. Given the lack of relationship between the claimant and the third party in such a situation, it seems extraordinary to describe the claim as personal and outside Art 16(1). On the other hand, a conclusion that the claim against the resulting trustee son is personal, but that against the constructive trustee third party is proprietary seems 'strongly counter-intuitive'[4].

1   Briggs 'Trusts of Land and the Brussels Convention' (1994) 110 LQR 526.
2   (1994) 110 LQR 526 at 529–530.
3   On this type of claim, see above, para 5.49ff.
4   (1994) 110 LQR 526 at 530.

Lugano Convention and Modified Convention

22.17   As noted above[1], the Lugano Convention applies in respect of EFTA States and the Modified Convention allocates jurisdiction within the United Kingdom. While there are some differences of substance between these Conventions and the Brussels Convention[2], both Conventions essentially mirror the Brussels Convention, and allocate jurisdiction by reference to the same principles. Subject to the qualification to be made immediately below, the discussion in relation to Arts 5 and 16 of the Brussels Convention above[3] applies equally in relation to the Lugano Convention and the Modified Convention.

1   See above, paras 22.6 and 22.7.
2   For an overview of the differences see North and Fawcett *Cheshire and North's Private International Law* (13th edn, 1999), pp 276, 277, 281 and 282.
3   See above, para 22.10.

22.18   The only qualification is that, because the European Court of Justice is not the final arbiter on questions of interpretation of either the Lugano Convention or the Modified Convention, there is a risk of different interpretations. Every attempt has been made to ensure that this does not happen. Protocol 2 to the Lugano Convention provides that the courts of each EFTA Contracting State shall 'pay due account to the principles laid down by any relevant decision delivered by courts of the other Contracting States concerning provisions' of the Lugano Convention[1]. In order to enhance this process, the Protocol also provides that the Contracting States agree to set up a system of exchange of relevant judgments[2]. In *Agnew v Länsförsäkringsbolagens AB* Lord Hope observed that[3]:

... we must do our best to arrive at an interpretation of the relevant articles of the Lugano Convention which is compatible with that which would be given to the equivalent provisions in the Brussels Convention by the Court of Justice.

Section 16(3) of the Civil Jurisdiction and Judgments Act 1982 requires United Kingdom courts to have regard to the European Court of Justice's principles and decisions on the Brussels Convention when interpreting the Modified Convention. On the whole, the House of Lords' approach to the interpretation of the Modified Convention in *Kleinwort Benson Ltd v Glasgow City Council*[4] shows that it is particularly concerned to ensure uniformity of interpretation. However, there is one worrying note in the decision of Lord Goff. He implied that Art 5(1) of the Modified Convention may not be interpreted to include claims for restitution on basis of failure of consideration following breach of contract, even if Art 5(1) of the Brussels Convention is so interpreted by the European Court of Justice[5]. Lord Goff considered the inclusion of such restitution actions within the scope of Art 5(1) of the Modified Convention to be 'problematical', presumably because English law treats such claims as part of the law of restitution, rather than the law of contract. It is hoped that future the English courts will look for the meaning of terms used in the Modified Convention, including the term 'matters relating to a contract', in European Union law, not English domestic law.

1   See Art 1, Protocol 2 of the Lugano Convention. This provision is given the force of law in the United Kingdom by Civil Jurisdiction and Judgments Act 1982, s 3B(1).
2   See Art 2, Protocol 2 of the Lugano Convention.
3   [2001] 1 AC 223 at 248.
4   [1999] 1 AC 153. See above, para 22.11ff.
5   [1999] 1 AC 153 at 171.

Common law and the Civil Procedure Rules

Introduction

22.19   If the Brussels, Lugano or Modified Conventions do not determine jurisdiction, then an English court will have jurisdiction (in non-admiralty cases[1]) in three situations[2]. Firstly, an English court will have jurisdiction if the originating process was served on the defendant whilst the defendant was physically present in the jurisdiction[3]. Secondly, the common law, like the Brussels Convention[4], recognises that a court has jurisdiction over a defendant who has submitted to the court's jurisdiction[5]. Finally, the court may exercise jurisdiction if the defendant has been served with originating process outside the jurisdiction in accordance with the Civil Procedure Rules[6].

1   Actions in rem against a ship will not be considered. For jurisdiction in such actions see North and Fawcett *Cheshire and North's Private International Law* (13th edn, 1999), pp 325–332.
2   Note that even if the court has jurisdiction under these rules, it has a discretion to decline to exercise that jurisdiction. See North and Fawcett *Cheshire and North's Private International Law* (13th edn, 1999), pp 313–322 and 333–359.
3   See North and Fawcett *Cheshire and North's Private International Law* (13th edn, 1999), pp 286–295.
4   See art 18, Brussels Convention.
5   See North and Fawcett *Cheshire and North's Private International Law* (13th edn, 1999), pp 295 and 296.
6   Part 6, section III, Civil Procedure Rules. These rules were introduced by The Civil Procedure (Amendment) Rules 2000, SI 2000/221 (L.1), and came into force on 2 May 2000. They replace RSC Ord 11.

22.20   In the first two situations, the legal or factual nature of the claimant's claim is irrelevant. All that matters is the defendant's physical location at a particular time, or the defendant's willingness to appear in front of the English courts. However, the validity of service outside the jurisdiction under the Civil Procedure Rules may be affected by the nature of the claim. Service outside the jurisdiction will only be effective if the proceedings fall within one of the heads of jurisdiction in CPR 1998, Pt 6.20, which are designed to identify those claims which have a sufficiently close connection to England to justify a grant of jurisdiction to English courts. A number of the heads of jurisdiction relate to specific causes of action, or to certain factual circumstances surrounding the proceedings. Those heads of jurisdiction that may be relevant to a claim for restitution are now considered.

However, first it must be noted that service out of the jurisdiction is not as of right. Even if the proceedings fall squarely within one of the heads of jurisdiction in CPR 1998, Pt 6.20, the claimant requires permission from the court in order to serve outside the jurisdiction[1].

1   See CPR 1998, Pt 6.21. Note that under CPR 1998, Pt 6.21(2A) the 'court will not give permission unless it is satisfied that England and Wales is the proper place in which to bring the claim'. This ensures a connection between the claim and the jurisdiction.

CPR 1998, Pt 6.20(15) – Claims for restitution[1]

22.21   The new civil procedure rules, introduced in 2000, make explicit provision for claims in restitution. CPR 1998, Pt 6.20(15) provides that originating process may be served out of the jurisdiction if:

> ... a claim is made for restitution where the defendant's alleged liability arises out of acts committed within the jurisdiction.

The language of this paragraph appears to be broad enough to encompass both restitution on the basis of unjust enrichment by subtraction and restitution for wrongs[2]. Thus, the only real issue that needs to be determined is: when will it be said that the defendant's alleged liability arises out of acts committed in England. The old RSC Ord 11, r 1(1)(t), which dealt with the liability of constructive trustees, also required that the 'defendant's alleged liability arises out of acts committed ... within the jurisdiction'. In *Polly Peck International plc v Nadir*[3], Hoffmann LJ held that this requirement was satisfied:

> ... if a substantial part of the acts, viewed as a whole, ... which give rise to the alleged liability, took place within the jurisdiction.

Glidewell LJ said a claim fell within the sub-rule (t) if:

> ... one or more substantial and effective acts ... took place within the jurisdiction, even though some other substantial and effective act, necessary to establish liability, took place outside the jurisdiction.

It is hoped that this expansive interpretation would be applied to paragraph (15). The alternative interpretation, confining application of the provision to the situation where *all* the acts necessary to establish liability took place within the jurisdiction[4], would severely limit the impact of paragraph (15).

1   For a discussion of the issues raised by the paragraph see Panagopoulos *Restitution in Private International Law* (2000), pp 235–241.
2   On this distinction see above, para 1.23.
3   (1993) Times, 22 March, (1993) Independent, 31 March, CA.
4   See Panagopoulos *Restitution in Private International Law* (2000), p 237.

CPR 1998, Pt 6.20(5), (6) and (7) – Claims made in respect of a contract

22.22   Prior to the introduction of CPR 1998, Pt 6.20(15), those seeking restitution could only serve outside the jurisdiction if they could fit their claim within one of the heads of jurisdiction designed to accommodate proceedings in contract, tort or constructive trust. The introduction of paragraph (15) has greatly minimised the need for such contortions, but it has certainly not done away with them. Where liability in restitution does not arise out of 'acts committed within the jurisdiction' as required by paragraph (15), claimants will still be tempted to squeeze their claims into one of the other heads of jurisdiction in CPR 1998, Pt 6.20. The most likely candidates will be paragraphs (5) and (6), which provide for service out of the jurisdiction with the permission of the court if:

    (5) a claim is made in respect of a contract where the contract –
    (a) was made within the jurisdiction;
    (b) was made by or through an agent trading or residing within the jurisdiction;
    (c) is governed by English law; or
    (d) contains a term to the effect that the court shall have jurisdiction to determine any claim in respect of the contract.
    (6) a claim is made in respect of a breach of contract committed within the jurisdiction.

22.23   In the past, courts have been prepared to treat restitution (or what they describe as 'quasi-contract'), as equivalent to contract for the purposes of the rules for service outside the jurisdiction[1]. However, the courts' reasoning in the relevant cases is based on the 'implied contract' theory of restitution; that is, the obligation of the defendant to make restitution to the claimant is treated as a contractual obligation implied by law[2]. It is suggested that, as the implied contract theory has now been entirely abandoned[3], this line of authority is unlikely to be applied in the future. Courts are likely to conclude that the inclusion of paragraph (15) enables them to abandon the accumulated fictions involved in the implied contract theory. Moreover, such a development is consistent with the well established principle that heads of jurisdiction should be construed strictly, and in favour of the foreign defendant[4].

1 *Bowling v Cox* [1926] AC 751; *Rousou's (a bankrupt) Trustee v Rousou* [1955] 1 WLR 545; *Re Jogia (a bankrupt)* [1988] 1 WLR 484.
2 See above, para 1.9.
3 *Westdeutsche Landesbank Girozentrale v Islington London Borough Council* [1996] AC 669.
4 *The Siskina (Cargo Owners) v Distos Compania Naviera SA* [1979] AC 210 at 254–255, per Lord Diplock.

22.24   However, abandonment of the 'implied contract' theory does not foreclose an argument that a claim in restitution, which arises out of a contractual relationship, is a claim 'made in respect of a contract' or 'made in respect of a breach of contract' for the purposes of paragraphs (5) or (6). The phrase 'made in respect of a contract' is very broad and, on its face, does not require that the claimant's claim be based on a contractual right. It is not stretching the English language to say that a claim for restitution of money paid under a contract, which is subsequently terminated for breach or some other reason, is made in respect of a contract or a breach of contract. Additionally, a claim for restitution of profits made by contract-breaker seems to fall squarely within paragraph (6).

22.25   On the other hand, the courts may be less willing to accept that restitution of money transferred under a contract which is later held to be void or non-existent is 'a claim made in respect of a contract'. In such a situation, the claimant is seeking restitution precisely because there is *no* contract in respect of which a claim can be made. This construction of the rule is supported by a line of authority which holds that, where the claimant sought relief on the basis that there was no contract between the parties, the predecessors to paragraphs (5) and (6) were unavailable[1]. For example, in *Finnish Marine Insurance Co Ltd v Protective National Insurance Co*[2] the claimant argued that its agents had entered into contracts without its authority, and sought a declaration that it was not a party to any contract with the defendant. Adrian Hamilton QC held that this claim did not fall within the contract head of jurisdiction, which applied, inter alia, if the claim was brought to 'otherwise affect a contract'[3], because there was no contract to be affected[4]. Later authority reached the opposite conclusion, supporting the grant of leave to serve outside the jurisdiction even though the claimant alleged there was no contract[5]. To a certain extent, the new Civil Procedure Rules put an end to this debate by introducing paragraph (7), a new head of jurisdiction which provides for service out of the jurisdiction if:

> ... a claim is made for a declaration that no contract exists where, if the contract was found to exist, it would comply with the conditions set out in paragraph (5).

The inclusion of this paragraph implies that restitution claims consequent upon the non-existence of a contract do not fall within paragraph (5). Thus, the only issue is whether paragraph (7) is broad enough to encompass both a claim for a declaration of non-existence and a claim for relief, such as restitution, consequent upon such a declaration[6].

1   See Briggs 'Jurisdiction under Traditional Rules' in Rose (ed) *Restitution and the Conflict of Laws* (1995), pp 53 and 54; and Panagopoulos *Restitution in Private International Law* (2000), p 252.
2   [1990] 1 QB 1078.
3   See RSC Ord 11, r 1(1)(d).
4   [1990] 1 QB 1078 at 1083–1084.
5   See *DR Insurance Co v Central National Insurance Co* [1996] 1 Lloyd's Rep 74 at 79–80, per Martin Moore-Bick QC.
6   See Panagopoulos *Restitution in Private International Law* (2000), p 253. Note that, if the defendant's alleged liability arises out of acts committed within the jurisdiction, the claim will clearly fall within paragraph (15).

CPR 1998, Pt 6.20(8) – Claims made in tort

22.26   Paragraph (8) of CPR 1998, Pt 6.20 provides that originating process may be served outside the jurisdiction with the permission of the court if:

> ... a claim is made in tort where–
> (a) damage was sustained within the jurisdiction; or
> (b) the damage sustained resulted from an act committed within the jurisdiction.

A claim for restitution of profits made by a tortfeasor[1] or, indeed, an equitable wrongdoer[2], may fall within this paragraph. The first issue is whether restitution for torts or equitable wrongs can be said to be 'a claim in tort'. There is debate as to whether this phrase refers to a tort as a matter of English domestic law or as a matter of English conflict of laws[3]. However, the better view is that a claim will be considered to be one in tort, for the purposes of paragraph (8), if it is a tort according to the English conflict of laws[4]. This debate is actually irrelevant if the claimant's claim is for restitution of profits made by a tortfeasor. On either view, such a claim satisfies the requirement of 'a claim in tort'. Below it is concluded that restitution for torts is categorised as a tort for the purposes of both English domestic law and English conflict of laws[5]. However, the outcome of the debate is crucial for the claimant seeking restitution for an equitable wrong. If paragraph (8) requires a tort according to English domestic law, then the claimant will not be able to serve under this head of jurisdiction. However, if 'a claim in tort' requires a tort according to English conflict of laws, then the claimant has some basis for hope. As outlined below[6], the correct characterisation of restitution for equitable wrongs is a matter of considerable controversy. However, there is a view that it should be characterised as tort for the purposes of English conflict of laws.

1   See above, ch 12.
2   See above, ch 10.
3   Briggs and Rees *Civil Jurisdiction and Judgments* (2nd edn, 1997), pp 230–232.
4   Briggs and Rees *Civil Jurisdiction and Judgments* (2nd edn, 1997), p 232.
5   See below, paras 22.56–22.62.
6   See n 5.

22.27   Still more difficulties may be encountered by claimants seeking to serve outside the jurisdiction under para (8) in order to obtain restitution of profits made by a wrongdoer. The two connecting factors in the paragraph both assume that the claimant has suffered 'damage', but it is not a pre-requisite to a claim for restitution for wrongs that the claimant has suffered damage[1]. In fact the lack of damage, or the difficulty of establishing such damage, may be the very reason why the claimant is seeking restitution, rather than compensation. It has been argued that the particular wrong committed against the claimant may be viewed as 'damage'[2]. While such an interpretation would give English courts jurisdiction over claims with which they had a substantial connection, it is contrary to the generally accepted meaning of 'damage', and difficult to sustain in the face of the principle that the heads of jurisdiction are to be interpreted restrictively[3].

1   Panagopoulos *Restitution in Private International Law* (2000) pp 257–258.
2   See n 1.
3   *The Siskina (Cargo Owners) v Distos Compania Naviera SA* [1979] AC 210 at 254–255, per Lord Diplock.

22.28   The connecting factor in sub-paragraph (a) will be satisfied if 'some significant damage has been sustained in England'[1]. Likewise, it is not necessary to show that all acts necessary to cause the damage occurred in England for the purposes of paragraph (b). It is sufficient if the damage resulted 'from substantial and efficacious acts committed within the jurisdiction'[2].

1   *Metall und Rohstoff AG v Donaldson Lufkin and Jenrette Inc* [1990] 1 QB 391 at 437, per Slade LJ (speaking per curiam).
2   See n 1.

CPR 1998, Pt 6.20(10) – Claims relating to property

22.29   Under Paragraph (10) of CPR 1998, Pt 6.20, English courts may grant permission for service outside the jurisdiction if:

> ... the whole subject matter of a claim relates to property located within the jurisdiction.

The wording of this head of jurisdiction is extremely broad. It encompasses both movable and immovable property. Moreover, unlike Art 16(1) of the

Brussels Convention[1], there is no basis on which it could be interpreted to exclude claims based on equitable proprietary interests. A restitutionary claim by a father seeking a declaration that his son, who is domiciled in Australia, holds an apartment in London on resulting trust for the father and an order for transfer of the legal title, would fall within the paragraph[2].

1   See above, paras 22.15 and 22.16.
2   Contrast *Webb v Webb* (Case C–294/92) [1994] ECR I-1717; above, paras 22.15 and 22.16.

CPR 1998, Pt 6.20(14) – Claims against constructive trustees

22.30   CPR 1998, Pt 6.20(14) provides that a claim form may be served out of the jurisdiction if:

> ... a claim is made for a remedy against the defendant as constructive trustee where the defendant's alleged liability arises out of acts committed within the jurisdiction.

Claims in both restitution for unjust enrichment by subtraction and restitution for wrongs may lead to the imposition of a constructive trust on the defendant. For example, claims based on receipt of trust property[1] or dishonest assistance in a breach of trust[2] or breach of fiduciary duty[3] may be pursued in England under paragraph (14) provided the relevant acts were committed in England. As stated above[4], it is sufficient to satisfy the connecting factor in this paragraph if a substantial part of the acts required to establish liability took place in England.

1   See above, para 5.49ff.
2   See above, para 5.4ff.
3   See above, ch 9.
4   See *Polly Peck International plc v Nadir* 17 March 1993 (Court of Appeal), (1993) Times, 22 March, (1993) Independent 31 March; and above, para 22.21.

C   Choice of law

Characterisation

Introduction

22.31   A choice of law rule identifies the legal system which governs the resolution of issues falling within the ambit of that particular rule. The central issue in this section is: what is the choice of law rule for restitution? However, before attempting to determine this rule, it is necessary to identify the legal issues to which such a rule will be applied. That is, it is necessary to identify the ambit of the rule. This process is called characterisation.

22.32   Characterisation poses notoriously difficult conceptual problems[1]. Consequently, it has given rise to abundant academic literature[2] but is rarely analysed by courts[3]. Fortuitously, one of the most recent judicial discussions of the process of characterisation arose in the context of a restitution case, *Macmillan Inc v Bishopsgate Investment Trust plc (No 3)*[4].
    Macmillan Inc, a company incorporated in Delaware, and effectively jointly owned by the public and the Maxwell family, agreed that shares which it held in Berlitz International Inc (a New York corporation) should be transferred to Bishopsgate Investment Trust plc. Bishopsgate was incorporated in England, and was wholly owned and controlled by the Maxwell family. Macmillan intended

that Bishopsgate should hold the shares as a bare trustee, and Bishopsgate signed a declaration to this effect. Robert Maxwell had other plans. In breach of trust, Bishopsgate repeatedly used the shares as security for debts owed by the Maxwell family's private companies. At the time of Robert Maxwell's disappearance and the collapse of his business empire, a number of the shares were held as security by Swiss Volksbank, Crédit Suisse and Lehman Bros International Ltd. These banks acquired their initial security interests either by the deposit of share certificates and executed blank transfers in London, or by means of book entries in New York[5]. The defendants, Swiss Volksbank, Crédit Suisse and Shearson Lehman Brothers Holding plc, which had acquired Lehman Bros International's interest in the shares, eventually perfected their security and became the registered legal owners of the shares.

Macmillan claimed that these facts gave rise to a cause of action in restitution[6], and sought a declaration that it was still beneficially entitled to the Berlitz shares, a declaration that the defendants held the shares on constructive trust for it, restoration of the shares, and compensation for breach of constructive trust[7].

1   This is especially so in relation to restitution. In Collins (ed) *Dicey and Morris on The Conflict of Laws* (13th edn, 2000), p 1487 it is observed that 'in some ways, the definition of the territory governed by [the restitution choice of law rule] is the most difficult aspect of choice of law for restitution'.
2   Collins (ed) *Dicey and Morris on The Conflict of Laws* (13th edn, 2000), p 33, n 1.
3   Collins (ed) *Dicey and Morris on The Conflict of Laws* (13th edn, 2000), p 37. See also Forsyth 'Characterisation Revisited: An Essay in the Theory and Practice of the English Conflict of Laws' (1998) 114 LQR 141 at 141, which describes the approach of the English courts as 'pragmatic' or, perhaps, 'atheoretical'.
4   [1996] 1 WLR 387. Note that Staughton and Aldous LJJ's acceptance of the proposition that the claim was restitutionary is controversial. Auld LJ appeared to be skeptical: see [1996] 1 WLR at 407–409. See also Swadling 'A Claim in Restitution?' [1996] Lloyds Maritime and Commercial Law Quarterly 63; Stevens 'Restitution or Property? Priority and Title to Shares in the Conflict of Laws' (1996) 59 MLR 741 at 744–745; and Bird 'Restitution's Uncertain Progress' [1995] Lloyds Maritime and Commercial Law Quarterly 308. It is possible that the judges only accepted the claimant's assertion that its claim was in restitution because it was ultimately irrelevant to the outcome of the case: see [1996] 1 WLR at 398, per Staughton LJ, and at 417–418, per Aldous LJ. On the other hand, Millett J at first instance appeared to have no doubt that the claim was one in restitution: *Macmillan Inc v Bishopsgate Investment Trust plc (No 3)* [1995] 1 WLR 978 at 988.
5   In order to facilitate the fraud, a number of the shares were deposited with the Depository Trust Company in New York, a paperless transfer system.
6   This claim is controversial: see nn 4 and 5.
7   Macmillan also claimed in conversion against Crédit Suisse.

22.33   As the case involved a number of foreign elements, the court had to decide what law should be applied. Macmillan contended that its claim should be characterised as restitutionary. Thus, the choice of law rule for restitution should be applied, which pointed to English law. The defendants' response to Macmillan's claim was that they were bona fide purchasers for value, without notice of Macmillan's interests. Therefore, they argued, the appropriate choice of law rule was the one that governed the validity of this defence to the claimant's claim. That is, the defendants claimed that the court must characterise the issue in dispute, not the claimant's cause of action. Here the issue in dispute was one of priority of competing property interests in shares. The defendants argued that the choice of law rule for priority disputes in relation to shares pointed to the law of New York.

22.34   In order to resolve this dispute, the Court of Appeal had to come to terms with the two central dilemmas in the process of characterisation:

- Exactly what is it that the court should characterise in order to isolate the appropriate choice of law rule? Does the court characterise the claimant's cause of action, the issue in dispute, the facts of the dispute, or the relevant rules of law? and
- By reference to what legal system should the court undertake the process of characterisation?

WHAT DOES THE COURT CHARACTERISE?

22.35   The members of the Court of Appeal unanimously agreed that what must be characterised is the legal issue or issues before the court[1]. In the case before them, the only issue was whether the defendants were bona fide purchasers for value without notice of Macmillan's interests. This issue was characterised as one of priority of proprietary interests in the shares. The Court of Appeal concluded that the relevant choice of law rule dictated that such an issue is determined by reference to the lex situs, that is, the law of the place where the shares were situated[2]. The Berlitz shares were situated in New York. Accordingly, New York law, which was more favourable to the defendants, applied. Under New York law, the defendants had acquired a title to the shares which defeated the interests of Macmillan in the shares.

1   See [1996] 1 WLR 387 at 399, per Staughton LJ, at 406, per Auld LJ, and at 418, per Aldous LJ.
2   See below, para 22.44ff.

22.36   In a thoughtful article prompted by *Macmillan v Bishopsgate*, Forsyth has argued that it is rules of law, not legal issues, which are characterised[1]. On his analysis, the task of the court in *Macmillan v Bishopsgate* was to characterise the rules of law which the parties put forward as relevant to the settlement of their dispute. The defendants pointed to the New York law which defined the level of notice of others' interests that would prevent a purchaser of shares from obtaining unencumbered legal title to the shares. Macmillan, on the other hand, sought to rely on the equivalent English rule, which, unsurprisingly, was more favourable to it. These rules of law are characterised as rules in relation to property in shares[2]. The choice of law rule for property in shares points to the lex situs of the shares, that is, the law of New York. Therefore, the New York law applied and the English law did not.

1   Forsyth 'Characterisation Revisited: An Essay in the Theory and Practice of the English Conflict of Laws' (1998) 114 LQR 141.
2   (1998) 114 LQR 141 at 156–177.

22.37   When Forsyth's argument is expressed in this way, it becomes clear that (as he himself points out[1]), characterisation by reference to the legal issue is much the same as characterisation of a rule of law. Legal issues, or indeed, causes of action, do 'not exist in the abstract'[2]. Legal issues can only be articulated by reference to rules of law and they are dictated by those rules of law. That is, identifying and characterising the relevant legal issues in the dispute between the claimant and defendant is another way of identifying and characterising the legal rules relevant to that dispute. In fact, Auld LJ acknowledged this. He stated:

> It follows from what I have said that the proper approach is to look beyond the formulation of the claim and to identify according to the lex fori the true issue or issues thrown up by the claim and defence. This requires a parallel exercise in classification of the relevant rule of law[3].

1   (1998) 114 LQR 141 at 148–150.
2   (1998) 114 LQR 141 at 149.
3   [1996] 1 WLR 387 at 407. Note also that Staughton LJ (at 392) appears to approve the discussion in Collins (ed) *Dicey and Morris on The Conflict of Laws* (12th edn, 1993), p 44, which talks of characterising a rule of law.

WHAT LAW GOVERNS THE CHARACTERISATION PROCESS?

22.38   In *Macmillan v Bishopsgate*, Auld LJ also confronted the other enduring characterisation dilemma: what legal system does the court use to characterise the legal issue or rule of law. The two contenders are the lex fori[1] and the lex causae[2]. However, each of these has obvious inadequacies. If the legal issue or rule that is to be characterised has no equivalent in the forum's legal system, then charcterisation by reference to the lex fori may so distort the relevant foreign law that the law applied by the court bears no resemblance to a law applied anywhere[3]. Characterisation by reference to the lex fori will also lead to inconsistent results in different fora. If characterisation is conducted by reference to the lex fori, thc outcome of a claim by a German, who has paid a sum of money to an Englishman under a void contract, for example, may vary according to the forum in which the dispute is heard. If the contract contains a non-exclusive jurisdiction clause in favour of the German courts, the German party could bring an action for return of the money in either Germany or England[4]. If the action were brought in Germany, the German court would characterise the issue as contract, and observe the contract choice of law rule in the Rome Convention on the Law Applicable to Contractual Obligations (the Rome Convention). Accordingly, if the contract nominates German law as the governing law, the German court would apply German law. As the Rome Convention does not apply in England to 'the consequences of nullity of the contract'[5], an English court, characterising according to its own law, would characterise the issue in the case as one of restitution, and apply the choice of law rule appropriate to that characterisation. If the relevant choice of law rule pointed to a law other than German, inconsistent results may follow. This is clearly contrary to the main goal of the conflict of laws, which is the attainment of uniform results regardless of the venue of litigation.

1   Law of the forum, that is, the law of the court hearing the case.
2   Law of the cause, which in this context is the legal system from which the law or issue being characterised originates.
3   Collins (ed) *Dicey and Morris on The Conflict of Laws* (13th edn, 2000), pp 35 and 36.
4   See Brussels Convention arts 2 and 17 (as interpreted in *Kurz v Stella Musical Verangstaltungs GmbH* [1992] Ch 196 at 202–206).
5   See the Contracts (Applicable Law) Act 1990, s 2(2); on which see below paras 22.46ff and 22.75ff.

22.39   The alternative solution is to characterise the issue or rule by reference to the legal system from which it comes. However, this solution also has inherent shortcomings. It may result in a conclusion that two or more contradictory rules from different legal systems should be applied or in a conclusion that there are no applicable laws relevant to an issue. Additionally, the conclusion that a foreign law should dictate the scope of English choice of law rules is problematic. In fact, it is probably unrealistic to assume that a judge is capable of totally abandoning his or her own legal concepts in favour of those from a foreign legal system. It seems likely that any attempt to characterise by reference to the lex causae would be distorted by local bias[1].

1   Forsyth 'Characterisation Revisited: An Essay in the Theory and Practice of the English Conflict of Laws' (1998) 114 LQR 141 at 152.

22.40   As with much of the conflict of laws, there is no one logically correct solution to this dilemma. What is required is a good dose of pragmatism and common sense. With this in mind, the best solution appears to be Kahn-Freund's notion of an 'enlightened lex fori'. Kahn-Freund accepted that a court should characterise by reference to its own legal system, but argued that, when doing so, the court should used enlightened definitions of domestic law categories, which take into account international conceptions of legal categories[1]. An 'enlightened lex fori' means that an English court could characterise, for example, a claim for *negotiorum gestio* even though English law recognises no equivalent cause of action[2]. When asked to characterise the issues in relation to such a claim, the English would 'take a wide view of the concept of restitution ... , looking at the characterisation adopted by foreign legal systems which have this cause of action'[3]. In *Macmillan v Bishopsgate*, Auld LJ appeared to endorse the idea of characterisation by reference to an enlightened lex fori. He said:

> Subject to what I shall say in a moment, characterisation or classification is governed by the lex fori ... However, classification of an issue and rule of law for this purpose, the underlying principle of which is to strive for comity between competing legal systems, should not be constrained by particular notions or distinctions of the domestic law of the lex fori, or that of the competing system of law, which may have no counterpart in the other's system. Nor should the issue be defined too narrowly so that it attracts a particular domestic rule under the lex fori which may not be applicable under the other system ... [4]

1   Kahn-Freund *General Problems of Private International Law* (1976), pp 228–231. See also Falconbridge's *via media*: Falconbridge *Essays on the Conflict of Laws* (2nd edn, 1954), pp 56–68.
2   See also above, para 16.7.
3   North and Fawcett *Cheshire and North's Private International Law* (13th edn, 1999), pp 676.
4   [1996] 1 WLR 387 at 407. Staughton LJ did not explicitly label the law by which he characterised the issue. His approval (at 392) of the discussion of characterisation in Collins (ed) *Dicey and Morris on The Conflict of Laws* (12th edn, 1993), pp 34–47 indicates that he saw the process of characterisation as one of refining the English conflict of laws rules, something which must be done by reference to English law. Aldous LJ simply noted (at 417) that the parties agree that the characterisation of the issue was to be determined according to English law: [1996] 1 WLR 387 at 417.

22.41   The analysis of characterisation in *Macmillan v Bishopsgate* and, in particular, in the judgment of Auld LJ, is extremely welcome. However, we should not pretend that it solves all characterisation problems. The process of characterisation will still occasionally result in both distortion of foreign law by English courts and inconsistent results. For example, the notion that the legal consequences of a void contract is part of the law of restitution, not contract, is probably so entrenched in English law, that a plea that English courts take a more international view of characterisation in this situation would be futile. In fact, it is likely that an English court would take the view that the Contracts (Applicable Law) Act 1990, s 2(2), mandates characterisation in this situation by reference to an unenlightened domestic law. Section 2(2) provides that Art 10(1)(e) of the Rome Convention does not have the force of law in the United Kingdom. Article 10(1)(e) provides that the law applicable to a contract under the Convention shall govern 'the consequences of nullity of the contract'. The United Kingdom entered a reservation in respect of Art 10(1)(e) because in English and Scottish law the consequences of nullity of a contract are dealt with by the law of restitution, rather than the law of contract, and therefore, it would be inappropriate for such a matter to be dealt with in a convention that is confined to contract[1]. Conversely, a German Court would presumably take the view that Art 10(1)(e) forecloses any argument that a claim to recover sums paid under a void contract should be characterised as anything other than contract. Inconsistent characterisations are ensured.

1 Giuliano-Lagarde *Report on the Convention on the Law Applicable to Contractual Obligations* 1980 OJ C 282/33; Burrows *Law of Restitution* (1993), p 491; North 'The EEC Convention on the Law Applicable to Contractual Obligations (1980): Its History and Main Features' in North (ed) *Contract Conflicts* (1982), p 16.

WHAT IS COVERED BY THE RESTITUTION CHOICE OF LAW RULE?

22.42   The result of the analysis of characterisation in *Macmillan v Bishopsgate* is that the restitution choice of law rule may well not be used to determine the law applicable to every, or indeed any, issue that arises in what English lawyers describe as restitution cases. Many of the issues that arise in such cases will be determined by reference to other, more established, choice of law rules, either because, although the cause of action is according to English lawyers restitutionary, the particular issues in dispute are not so characterised, or because the enlightened, more international version of English law used to characterise the issues, leads to a different characterisation. There are many illustrations of this, apart from *Macmillan v Bishopsgate*[1]. For example, in *City of Gotha v Sotheby's (No 2)*, Moses J accepted that the claimant's claim under the Torts (Interference with Goods) Act 1977 was 'a restitutionary proprietary claim to protect and enforce rights deriving from the plaintiffs' ownership of the painting', *The Holy Family with Saints John and Elizabeth* by Joachim Wtewael[2]. However, the central issues in the case were whether title to the painting had passed to certain bodies at certain times, and whether the claimant's claim was statute barred. Neither of these issues is characterised as restitutionary.

1 See above, para 22.32ff.
2 (1998) Times, 8 October. The judgment is on line at http://www.iuscomp.org/gla/judgments/foreign/gotha1.htm.

22.43   The other clear lesson from *Macmillan v Bishopsgate* is that the process of determining exactly what issues will fall within the scope of the restitution choice of law rule is particularly troublesome. This is because such a task must be carried out by reference to English law, albeit an enlightened version of English law, and in English law the boundaries of restitution are still being mapped. Moreover, restitution cuts across many of the traditional dividing lines in English law, such as the line between common law and equitable actions, and the line between the law of obligations and the law of property. Even within the law of obligations, there is room for debate as to whether certain issues fall within the law of restitution, tort or contract. Some of the more contentious areas will be considered below.

22.44   Issues at the border of restitution and property   There is a tendency in English courts to describe as 'restitutionary' actions in which the claimant seeks to vindicate his or her persisting property right in an asset that is in the possession of someone else[1]. The academic commentators are divided on the accuracy of this description[2]. Regardless of the role of such claims in the domestic law of restitution, it now seems likely that they should not be characterised as restitution for the purposes of the conflict of laws. This conclusion flows from *Macmillan v Bishopsgate*[3]. Even taking into account the fact that a court must characterise the relevant *issue*, not the cause of action, the methodology of the Court of Appeal in *Macmillan v Bishopsgate* was not consistent with acceptance of the claimant's argument that its cause of action was, for the purposes of the conflicts of laws, restitution. As Briggs has observed[4], if the claimant's cause of action were restitutionary, then orthodox conflict of laws analysis would require that the validity of the defendant's defence of bona fide purchaser be treated as an incidental question, and determined by reference to the choice of law rule for restitution. This is so, even if English law would ordinarily apply a different law to issues in relation to a bona fide purchaser's proprietary rights. Thus, the analysis of the court in *Macmillan v Bishopsgate* supports the view that, whatever the role of proprietary restitution in domestic English law, such claims are not characterised as restitutionary under the enlightened, more international, version of English law that is applied when characterising for the purposes of conflict of laws. This is largely because other legal systems do not share this idiosyncratic English notion of proprietary restitution. That this is the import of *Macmillan v Bishopsgate* is made crystal clear by Auld LJ, who asserted:

> The 'receipt-based restitutionary claim' is a notion of English domestic law that may not have a counterpart in many other legal systems, and is one that it may not be appropriate to translate into the English law of conflict[5]. In my view, it would be wrong to attempt to graft this equitable newcomer onto the class of cases where English courts will intervene to enforce an equity in respect of property abroad. Adrian Briggs made the point ... 'It is a commonplace that conceptual divisions in domestic law do not necessarily translate into the conflict of laws ... To take a distinction which is struggling to define itself within the domestic law of restitution and then project this into the realm of choice of law may be unwise'[6].

1   *Macmillan v Bishopgate* [1995] 1 WLR 978, above, para 22.32ff; *Tribe v Tribe* [1996] Ch 107, above, para 14.38ff; Stevens 'Restitution or Property? Priority and Title to Shares in the Conflict of Laws' (1996) 59 MLR 741 at 745. See also Grantham and Rickett 'Restitution, Property and Mistaken Payments' [1997] RLR 83, which discusses a New Zealand case, *National Bank of New Zealand Ltd v Waitaki International Processing (NI) Ltd* [1997] 1 NZLR 724, which categorised an action to vindicate a persisting property right as restitutionary.
2   See articles referred to above, para 22.32, n 4. Also, note, at a more fundamental level there is even a dispute about whether a claim to recover physical property falls within restitution. Birks and others maintain that property, not restitution, is the basis of any claim in which the claimant relies on a persisting legal proprietary interest: Birks *An Introduction to the Law of Restitution* (revised edn, 1989), pp 13–16. Burrows *Law of Restitution* (1993), pp 362–369, on the other hand, believes that the retention by the defendant of the claimant's property, without the claimant's consent, gives rise to a cause of action in restitution, even if the claimant has retained title to the property.
3   See above, para 22.32ff. See also Collins (ed) *Dicey and Morris on The Conflict of Laws* (13th edn, 2000), p 1488; North and Fawcett *Cheshire and North's Private International Law* (13th edn, 1999), p 673; Leslie 'Unjustified Enrichment in the conflict of Laws' (1988) 2 Edinburgh Law Review 233 at 235; Stevens 'The Choice of Law Rules of Restitutionary Obligations' in Rose (ed) *Restitution and the Conflict of Laws* (1995), pp 182–186.
4   Briggs (1996) 67 BYBIL 604 at 606.
5   Sic. Presumably 'conflict of law' was meant.
6   [1996] 1 WLR 387 at 407, quoting Briggs 'Restitution meets the conflict of laws' [1995] RLR 94 at 97. See also per Aldous LJ (at 418) who notes that the choice of law rule for restitution in *Dicey and Morris* 'is concerned with what has been called unjustified enrichment, not a case like the present where the defendants gave value for the shares and the dispute is whether the legal titles they obtained have priority over that of the plaintiffs'.

22.45   Issues at the border of restitution and contract   Although restitution claims often arises in a contractual context in English domestic law, the line between contract and restitution is clearly defined. The law of restitution can only be relied upon by contractual parties if the contract is ineffective, that is, if the contract has come to a premature end, or has been held to be unenforceable or void. The law of contract determines when the contract is ineffective. Once it is ineffective, one or both of the parties may be able to seek restitution of benefits conferred under the contract on the basis of restitution. However, the line between contract and restitution is not drawn in the same place in other legal systems[1]. Accordingly, subject to the comments below, there is a good argument that when characterising restitution claims arising out of ineffective contracts for the purpose of the conflict of laws, English courts should to some extent bow to foreign opinion on the appropriate dividing line between contract and restitution.

1   For example, in German law the return of benefits conferred under contracts which have been terminated on the ground of breach or frustration is governed by the law of contract, not restitution: Zweigert and Kötz *Introduction to Comparative Law* (3rd edn, 1998), pp 542 and 543.

22.46   Fortunately, however, much of the debate as to the degree to which characterisation in this context 'should not be constrained by particular notions or distinctions of the domestic law'[1] is now irrelevant. To a large extent, the characterisation of restitution claims arising out of ineffective contracts is now dictated by the Rome Convention and the Contracts (Applicable Law) Act 1990[2]. The Contracts (Applicable Law) Act 1990, s 2, provides that the Rome Convention, with the exception of Arts 7(1)[3] and 10(1)(e)[4], has the force of law in the United Kingdom. Accordingly, English courts are bound by the choice of law rule and characterisation in that Convention. The Convention applies to 'contractual obligations'. This term must be given an independent, international definition[5]. It is not to be confined by English domestic law and, in particular, it is not limited by the common law notion that a claim to recover benefits conferred under an ineffective contract is governed by restitution, not contract, law. Article 10(1)(c) requires the application of the contract choice of law rule to actions in relation to 'the consequences of breach'[6]. Thus, an English court cannot characterise as 'restitutionary issues' relating to a claim to recover benefits conferred under a contract terminated for breach. on the basis of (for example), failure of consideration[7]. Likewise, an action to recover restitution of profits gained by a contract-breaker[8] would fall within Art 10(1)(c). Additionally, it is arguable, although less certain, that actions to recover contractual overpayments[9], or benefits conferred under a contract which is subsequently frustrated[10], are covered by Art 10(1)(b) and (d) respectively and, hence, also governed by the contract choice of law rule in the Convention[11].

1   *Macmillan v Bishopsgate* [1996] 1 WLR 387 at 407.
2   See above, para 22.38.
3   This article deals with the effect of mandatory laws of a country with which the situation has a close connection.
4   This article deals with the consequences of nullity of a contract.
5   See Art 18. See Lasok and Stone *Conflict of Laws in the European Community* (1987), pp 345–348.
6   See Collins (ed) *Dicey and Morris on The Conflict of Laws* (13th edn, 2000), p 1487. Note that North and Fawcett *Cheshire and North's Private International Law* (13th edn, 1999), p 673 conclude that the Rome Convention does not apply in this situation, because it is only concerned with contractual obligations. However, this conclusion is based on the assumption that 'contractual obligations' has an English definition. Such an assumption is contrary to Art 18.
7   On which see above, para 19.8ff.
8   On which see above, ch 11.
9   On which see above, para 17.37ff.
10 See above, ch 20.
11 Collins (ed) *Dicey and Morris on The Conflict of Laws* (13th edn, 2000), p 1487.

22.47   Conversely, the UK reservation in relation to Art 10(1)(e)[1] has probably foreclosed any argument that the consequences of nullity of a contract should be characterised by English courts as anything other than restitutionary[2].

1   See above, para 22.41.
2   North and Fawcett *Cheshire and North's Private International Law* (13th edn, 1999), p 673.

22.48   Of course, the Rome Convention and the Contracts (Applicable Law) Act 1990 have not disposed of all characterisation issues that will arise at the dividing line between contract and restitution. However, the way in which the choice of law rule for restitution is drafted is such that the remaining areas of difference between common law and other legal systems are of less importance. As outlined below[1], the law which governs the contract is (on one view) determinative of or (on another) strongly influential on the choice of the law which governs restitution of benefits conferred under the contract. Hence, the problems caused by different definitions of the scope of the two areas are substantially minimised. Whether restitution of a benefit conferred under a contract is characterised as restitution or contract, the governing law may well be the same.

1   See below, paras 22.74–22.83.

22.49   The synchronisation of the choice of law rule for restitution with the choice of law rule for contract also reduces the impact of the United Kingdom's reservation to Art 10(1)(e) of the Rome Convention[1]. Even though the courts of the United Kingdom will characterise restitution of benefits conferred under void contracts as restitution and apply a restitution choice of law rule, while the remainder of the European Community will apply the contract choice of law rule to such claims, the outcome of the claims should not vary according to the forum in which they are heard. This can be illustrated by reference to the example above, of a claim for restitution of benefits conferred under a void contract, containing a choice of law clause in favour of Germany[2]. Article 10(1)(e) will require a German court hearing this claim to determine the parties' rights by reference to German law. An English court would characterise the issues as restitutionary, and determine the parties' rights by reference to the legal system to which the restitution choice of law rule points. It is likely, although not certain, that the English choice of law rule for restitution will point to German law.

1   On which see above paras 22.41ff and 22.47ff.
2   See above, paras 22.38 and 22.46.

22.50   Contribution[1]   Contribution between parties liable to a third person is yet another contentious area[2]. Contribution claims can be framed in a number of ways[3]. The most important legal bases of such claims are contract, restitution and statutory right. The claimant may rely on an implied or express right to contribution in a contract between the claimant and the defendant. A contribution claimant may also seek restitution on the basis that the defendant has been unjustly enriched at his or her expense. Finally, and most likely, the claimant may rely on a statutory right to contribution.

1   On contribution see above, ch 7.
2   For a more detailed analysis than is possible here see Takahashi *Claims for Contribution and Reimbursement in an International Context* (2000), ch 3.
3   Takahashi *Claims for Contribution and Reimbursement in an International Context* (2000), pp 7–20.

22.51   The most logical solution to the characterisation of issues in relation to contribution is to characterise according to the legal basis on which the relevant claim is brought[1]. Therefore, the issue of whether a claimant is entitled to claim contribution under a contract should be characterised as contractual[2]. Likewise, the issue of whether contribution is allowed under the common law of restitution should be characterised as restitution[3].

1   Takahashi *Claims for Contribution and Reimbursement in an International Context* (2000), p 53.
2   Collins (ed) *Dicey and Morris on The Conflict of Laws* (13th edn, 2000), p 1488.
3   The Civil Liability (Contribution) Act 1978 (above, para 7.47ff) does not apply to claims between co-debtors. Such claims are most likely to be based on restitution: Takahashi *Claims for Contribution and Reimbursement in an International Context* (2000), p 60. Collins (ed) *Dicey and Morris on The Conflict of Laws* (13th edn, 2000), p 1505, illustration 2, also suggest such claims between co-debtors should be characterised as restitution.

22.52   However, this approach leaves the characterisation of issues in relation to statutory contribution claims undecided. A court faced with the task of characterising such issues would have to examine the nature of the statutory right on which the claimant relies. Unfortunately, frequently the nature of such rights is not obvious. The majority of judges who have addressed the issue concluded that statutory contribution rights are sui generis[1]. This is of little assistance. As was said in relation to a claim under New South Wales legislation allowing contribution between joint tortfeasors[2]:

> There is much to be said for the view expressed by Sholl J in *Gilchrist v Dean*[3], that such a claim is 'a very special kind of action'. But, for the purposes of private international law, there are not special rules for each 'very special kind of action' provided by legislation as part of the general body of the law relating to civil liability. Each such 'very special kind of action' must be fitted in to whichever of the broad classifications of private international law is most appropriate[4].

1   See for example *Gilchrist v Dean* (1958) 2 FLR 175 at 181; *Harvey v RG O'Dell Ltd* [1958] 2 QB 78 at 107, per McNair J; *Plozza v South Australian Insurance Co Ltd* [1963] SASR 122 at 126, per Hogarth J; *Ronex Properties Ltd v John Laing Construction* [1983] QB 398 at 406, per Donaldson LJ. Takahashi *Claims for Contribution and Reimbursement in an International Context* (2000), p 10 concludes that Civil Liability (Contribution) Act 1978 is to some extent restitutionary, but that 'the restitutionary nature is not unequivocal ... A contribution claim under the 1978 Act can, therefore, be seen as sui generis'.
2   See the Law Reform (Miscellaneous Provisions) Act 1946.
3   (1958) 2 FLR 175 at 181.
4   *Baldry v Jackson* [1977] 1 NSWLR 494 at 499.

22.53   The judicial and academic authorities do not assist those attempting this task of determining which broad classification is the most appropriate. They are extraordinarily divided[1]. As the issue is entirely open, it is tentatively concluded that, whilst it is accepted that statutory claims do not neatly fit into any established choice of law category, they most closely resemble restitution, and this characterisation is to be preferred[2].

1   For a description of relevant English Australian and American case law, as well as various academic views, see Takahashi *Claims for Contribution and Reimbursement in an International Context* (2000), pp 50–66.
2   Collins (ed) *Dicey and Morris on The Conflict of Laws* (13th edn, 2000), p 1488 supports a restitution characterisation.

22.54   In England, however, the characterisation of contribution claims appears to be of little importance. In *Arab Monetary Fund v Hashim (No 9)*[1] Chadwick J took the view that no question of choice of law arises when a claim is brought in an English Court under the Civil Liability (Contribution) Act 1978.

The Act applies, regardless of any foreign elements, to allow contribution between two parties who are, or would be, liable to a third in respect of the same damage if sued in an English court (by reference to foreign or English law)[2]. The only filter on actions which can be brought in English courts under the Act is found in the laws of jurisdiction: the English court must have jurisdiction over the party from whom contribution is sought. There need be no other connection to England. This generous invitation to forum shoppers has been criticised[3].

1   (1994) Times 11 October.
2   See above, para 7.47.
3   Briggs 'The International Dimension to Claims for Contribution' [1996] Lloyds Maritime and Commercial Law Quarterly 437; Takahashi *Claims for Contribution and Reimbursement in an International Context* (2000), pp 71–77.

22.55   It should be noted that *Arab Monetary Fund v Hashim (No 9)* is not inconsistent with the proposition that an English court should characterise issues in relation to liability under foreign contribution statutes as restitution. Chadwick J accepts that, if the Civil Liability (Contribution) Act 1978 does not apply, a party may well be able to rely upon a foreign contribution law in an English court. Moreover, he even implies that restitution may be the appropriate characterisation in such a situation[1].

1   See Chadwick J's apparent approval of *Stewart v Honey* [1972] 2 SASR 585 at 592, in which it was said: 'The right of indemnity or contribution between tortfeasors should probably be classified for juristic purposes as quasi-contractual ... The proper law of a quasi-contract, at least in a case where the obligation is not one supervening on any real contract, is probably the law of the place with which the circumstances giving rise to the obligation have the most real connection'.

22.56   Restitution for wrongs   Issues in relation to claims for restitution of profits gained as a result of a breach of contract must be characterised as contractual. They fall within Art 10(1)(c) of the Rome Convention, which provides that the law applicable to contract governs the 'consequences of breach'[1].

1   See above, para 22.46.

22.57   Characterisation of issues which arise when a claimant seeks restitution for tort or equitable wrongs[1] is more complex. This is largely because the categorisation of these actions in domestic law is unclear. Theories on the juridical nature of restitution for wrongs divide into three approximate groups.

According to the first theory, restitution for wrongs belongs within the law of wrongs[2]. The cause of action is the wrong, that is, either tort, contract or equitable wrong. Restitution is the remedial response and the law of restitution for wrongs merely describes when this remedial response is available for the wrong. Generally, the cause of action will alternatively give rise to other remedial responses, such as compensation.

Other scholars and jurists also talk of restitution for wrongs as merely an alternative remedy for a wrong, but maintain that, when a claimant seeks restitution for a wrong, his or her cause of action is in restitution, not in the wrong[3]. According to this theory, however, the essential elements of this restitutionary cause of action are identical to those of the wrong. The only additional element may be that the wrong involved must be one that the law recognises as giving rise to restitution. For example, in *United Australia Ltd v Barclays Bank Ltd*[4], the House of Lords considered that the claimant's choice between suing in tort for compensation and seeking restitution for the tort, was merely 'a choice between possible remedies'[5] and that the claimant could not seek restitution for a tort without establishing the tort[6]. However, their Lordships also referred to the cause of action pursued by a claimant seeking restitution for a tort as being other than tort[7].

The third theory[8] claims that the cases referred to as restitution for wrongs should be assimilated into the law of restitution because they are analytically no different from that part of restitution which is generally referred to as unjust enrichment by subtraction. In them the defendant is unjustly enriched by subtraction from the claimant and the circumstances are such that the law will allow restitution. The elements of the cause of action in these cases are not identical to those of either tort, breach of contract or equitable wrong; restitution for wrongs is not parasitic on these civil wrongs.

1   This term is used to denote equitable actions such as knowing assistance in a breach of trust, breach of confidence and breach of fiduciary duty.
2   See Birks *An Introduction to the Law of Restitution* (revised edn, 1989), p 316; and Smith 'The Province of the Law of Restitution' (1992) 71 Canadian Bar Review 672 at 683. See also Birks *Restitution – The Future* (1992), p 1; and Birks 'Civil Wrongs: A New World' in *Butterworths Lectures: 1990–1991* (1992), especially pp 68–74.
3   Goff and Jones *Law of Restitution* (5th edn, 1998), p 773; Fridman *Restitution* (2nd edn, 1992), pp 355 and 356; Palmer *Law of Restitution* (1978), p 51; *Restatement of the Law of Restitution (1st)* (1937), 525.
4   [1941] AC 1. On this case see above, para 12.7.
5   [1941] AC 1 at 13, per Viscount Simon LC. See also [1941] 1 AC at 18 and 19, per Viscount Simon LC, at 29, per Lord Atkin, and at 34, per Lord Romer.
6   [1941] AC 1 at 18 and 19, per Viscount Simon LC, and at 35, per Lord Romer.
7   [1941] AC 1 at 19, per Viscount Simon LC, at 30, per Lord Atkin, at 35, per Lord Romer, and at 48 and 54, per Lord Porter.
8   Beatson *Use and Abuse of Unjust Enrichment: Essays in the Law of Restitution* (1991), pp 25–28 and 206–243. Maddaugh and McCamus *Law of Restitution* (1990), p 507, n 4 agree 'in essence' with Beatson's view that restitution for wrongs is independent of tort, and Goff and Jones *Law of Restitution* (5th edn, 1998), p 775 describe his theory as 'jurisprudentially most attractive'. See also Hedley 'The Myth of Waiver of Tort' (1984) 100 LQR 653, in which it is argued that tort is not part of the cause of action relied upon in the waiver of tort cases.

22.58   Of the three theories, the first is the most convincing and theoretically satisfying. It neatly explains why, for example, cases of mistake and breach of fiduciary duty appear so different, even though the remedial response is the same in both, and it allows a unified approach to all civil wrongs cases. Furthermore, it is consistent with the few cases in which restitutionary damages have been awarded for torts[1].

The second theory above is supported by the language used in the 'waiver of tort' cases[2] and the fact that in cases such as *Chesworth v Farrar*[3] procedural bars to tort cases have been held not to apply to 'waiver of tort'. However, it is important not to be led astray by what may merely be loose language. At the time when the 'waiver of tort' cases were decided, the law of restitution was in an inchoate stage and the language of restitution was inconsistent and confused. Furthermore, *Chesworth v Farrar*[4] and other similar cases can be dismissed as examples of the occasions on which judges ignore doctrine in order to achieve a convenient result.

The problems inherent in the third theory appear to be overwhelming. It has little, if any, case support. It also requires an unappealingly elastic view of the concept of subtraction. For example, it is very hard to accept that there is in fact a subtraction from the claimant in a case such as *Boardman v Phipps*[5]. Moreover, the third theory requires acceptance that the claimant may recover from the defendant more than the value subtracted from him. This is contrary to what is generally considered to be one of the basic features of the cause of action in restitution[6]. Finally, the unjust factor involved appears to be wrongful acquisition of the claimant's benefit. 'Wrongful' does not appear to be defined independently of the law of wrongs, and thus the claim still appears to be parasitic on the law of wrongs.

1   *Ministry for Defence v Ashman* [1993] 40 EG 144 (affirmed in *Ministry for Defence v Thompson* [1993] 40 EG 148), in which Kennedy and Hoffmann LJJ clearly see restitution and compensation as alternative remedies for trespass. See also *Swordheath Properties Ltd v Tabet* [1979] 1 WLR 285; *Penarth Dock Engineering Company Ltd v Pounds* [1963] 1 Lloyd's Rep 359; *Strand Electric and Engineering Co Ltd v Brisford Entertainments Ltd* [1952] 2 QB 246, per Denning LJ. In the latter case, Denning LJ states (at 255) that the claim for restitutionary damages 'resembles, therefore, an action for restitution rather than an action of tort' (emphasis added), but this is not inconsistent with Birks' and Smith's theory. See generally above, para 12.37ff.
2   *Oughton v Seppings* (1830) 1 B & Ad 241, 109 ER 776; *United Australia Ltd v Barclays Bank Ltd* [1941] AC 1; *Chesworth v Farrar* [1967] 1 QB 407.
3   [1967] 1 QB 407.
4   [1967] 1 QB 407. In this case, the conclusion that the claim was in 'quasi-contract', not tort, enabled Edmund Davies J to avoid the effect of legislation which provided that 'a cause of action in tort' against a deceased person's estate is barred unless commenced within six months of the deceased person's personal representative taking out representation.
5   [1967] 2 AC 46; on which see above, para 9.39ff.
6   Burrows *Law of Restitution* (1993), pp 20 and 21.

22.59   Assuming the first theory is to be preferred, issues of liability in cases of restitution for tort should be characterised as tort. As has been observed, the categorisation of restitution for torts in domestic law is not definitive for the purposes of characterisation in the conflict of laws[1]. However, it is the starting point[2]. More important, however, is that fact that if the first theory is correct, there is no policy justification for characterising issues in relation to restitution for tort by reference to anything other than the tort. Characterisation of an issue should not vary according to the remedy sought by the claimant. The claimant's entitlement to recover in respect of trespass, for example, should not be determined by reference to one legal system when he or she seeks compensation or an injunction, but by reference to another if he or she seeks restitution. Of course, the availability of the remedies may be determined by a different legal system from that which determines the underlying liability[3]. However, the underlying liability should be determined by reference to the same legal system, regardless of the remedy sought. In fact, if the choice of law rule did differ according to the remedy sought, a claimant would have a perfect opportunity for forum shopping; in many cases, it would be a simple matter to alter the remedy sought by reference to the most favourable choice of law rule. The majority of commentators support characterisation of restitution for tort as tortious[4], and as there is a lack of relevant case law, it seems that all English courts should be free to adopt this principled approach.

1   See above, paras 22.38–22.41. See also North and Fawcett *Cheshire and North's Private International Law* (13th edn, 1999), p 694.
2   See also Collins (ed) *Dicey and Morris on The Conflict of Laws* (13th edn, 2000), p 1487, which observes that: 'Although there is no strict need for the rules of the conflict of laws to mirror in every detail the emerging structure of the domestic law of restitution, it is obviously preferable that there should be reasonable harmony between them'.
3   See below, paras 22.105 and 22.106.
4   See Panagopoulos *Restitution in Private International Law* (2000), pp 82–84; Collins (ed) *Dicey and Morris on The Conflict of Laws* (13th edn, 2000), pp 1487, 1488, 1491, 1492, 1498 and 1499; Clarkson and Hill *Jaffey on the Conflict of Laws* (1997), p 275; Stevens 'The Choice of Law Rules of Restitutionary Obligations' in Rose (ed) *Restitution and the Conflict of Laws* (1995), pp 187 and 188. Burrows *Law of Restitution* (1993), pp 492–494 rejects the application of the tort choice of law rule to restitution for tort cases; but this position appears to be driven by the unsatisfactory

nature of the then common law tort choice of law rule, and the resulting undesirability of extending it further than is absolutely necessary. His support for the approach advocated in this chapter is suggested by his advocacy of application of the contract choice of law rule to issues of restitution for breach of contract (p 494).

22.60 Characterisation of restitution for equitable wrongs is more problematic[1]. The analysis above leads to the conclusion that, as a matter of principle, a claim in which the claimant seeks restitution for equitable wrongs should be characterised in the same way as a claim in which the claimant seeks some other remedy for that equitable wrong. Unfortunately, however, it is not clear how equitable wrongs should be characterised. The commentators have come up with a number of suggestions. Barnard suggests that issues in relation to equitable wrongs should be placed in their own category of 'equitable wrongs'[2]. *Dicey and Morris* suggest that restitution for equitable wrongs should be characterised as restitutionary[3]; however, they also conclude that the choice of law rule governing restitution for equitable wrongs should not necessarily be the same as the choice of law rule which applies to other restitution actions[4]. This seems to be much the same as characterising restitution for equitable wrongs as something other than restitutionary. Stevens argues that equitable wrongs should be assimilated with tort for the purposes of the conflict of laws[5]. Finally, Panagopoulos suggests that equitable wrongs should be dispersed into a number of categories: breaches of trust should be characterised as trust; breaches of consensual fiduciary relationships should be characterised as contractual, and all other equitable wrongs (including breaches of non-consensual fiduciary relationships) should be characterised as tort[6].

1 On equitable wrongs see above, ch 9.
2 Barnard 'Choice of Law in Equitable Wrongs: A Comparative Analysis' [1992] CLJ 474. See also Bird 'Choice of Law' in Rose (ed) *Restitution and the Conflict of Laws* (1995), p 76.
3 Collins (ed) *Dicey and Morris on The Conflict of Laws* (13th edn, 2000), p 1499.
4 Collins (ed) *Dicey and Morris on The Conflict of Laws* (13th edn, 2000), pp 1499 and 1500.
5 'The Choice of Law Rules of Restitutionary Obligations' in Rose (ed) *Restitution and the Conflict of Laws* (1995), pp 188 and 189.
6 Panagopoulos *Restitution in Private International Law* (2000), pp 87–91.

22.61 Whilst there is not an abundance of relevant case law, there now appears to be a line of (not necessarily satisfactorily reasoned) cases in which it is assumed that restitution for equitable wrongs should be characterised as restitution[1]. The most recent case in this line is *Kuwait Oil Tanker Co SAK v Al Bader*[2]. The claim was essentially in tort. The claimants alleged, and the court agreed, that the defendants dishonestly conspired to defraud them of large sums of money. However, so as to be entitled to compound interest, the claimants also alleged that the defendants had breached fiduciary duties owed to the claimants and were liable to account for profits gained as constructive trustees[3]. This latter claim is one for restitution for an equitable wrong, and the Court of Appeal, without any discussion of alternatives, accepted that it should be characterised as restitution for the purposes of the conflict of laws.

1 See *Thahir v PT Pertambangan Minyak dan Gas Bumi Negara (Pertamina)* [1994] 3 SLR 257; *Arab Monetary Fund v Hashim* [1996] 1 Lloyd' Rep 589; *Arab Monetary Fund v Hashim (No 9)* (1994) Times, 11 October, Chadwick J).
2 [2000] 2 All ER (Comm) 271, CA.
3 On interest see above, para 21.70ff. The court accepted that the claimant had established the breach of fiduciary duty but insisted that the defendants were not liable as constructive trustees. The court said that where directors who owe fiduciary duties to a company misappropriate that company's funds, they are 'treated by the law as if they were actual trustees of the funds'.

22.62   On the other hand, in *Arab Monetary Fund v Hashim (No 9)* Chadwick J was prepared to analogise equitable wrongs with tort and apply the tort choice of law rule to restitution for equitable wrongs[1]. Additionally, there are Australian cases which are consistent with characterisation by reference to the underlying wrong, rather than the remedy sought. However, they do not adopt a tortious characterisation. In *United States Surgical Corpn v Hospital Products International*[2] and *A-G (UK) v Heinemann Publishers Australia Pty Ltd*[3], the claimants sought the restitutionary remedy of account of profits, as well as other remedies, for the equitable wrong of breach of fiduciary duty. In the latter case, the claimant also relied on a breach of confidence. There is nothing in any of the judgments which indicates restitutionary or tortious characterisation should be adopted, nor is there anything which suggests that the characterisation of issues in relation to equitable wrongs differs depending on whether the claim is for restitution or some other remedy[4]. However, it must be accepted that in both cases the discussion of conflict of laws issues was both tentative and obiter.

1   (1994) Times, 11 October.
2   [1982] 2 NSWLR 766. This case went on appeal to the New South Wales Court of Appeal ([1983] 2 NSWLR 157) and the High Court of Australia ((1984) 156 CLR 41). Neither appellate court made observations as to the choice of law rule for equitable wrongs.
3   (1987) 10 NSWLR 86. This judgment went on appeal to the High Court of Australia: (1988) 165 CLR 30. The High Court did not discuss the choice of law rule for equitable obligations.
4   For further discussion of these cases see Bird 'Choice of Law' in Rose (ed) *Restitution and the Conflict of Laws* (1995), pp 93 and 94.

Choice of law rule

CHOICE OF LAW RULE FOR RESTITUTION FOR UNJUST ENRICHMENT BY SUBTRACTION

22.63   Academic approaches   Those attempting to devise a choice of law rule for restitution are confronted by an array of structural issues. For example, they must decide whether English law should adopt a traditional choice of law rule, whereby a connecting factor points to the relevant law, or whether it should favour a 'proper law' approach, looking on a case by case basis for the legal system with which the obligation to make restitution has its closest connection[1]. If they opt for the former approach, they then have to decide whether they need a number of sub-rules, each with its own connecting factor, and, if so, how those sub-rules should divide the subject of restitution. Additionally, they have to decide whether to incorporate an element of flexibility, by means of an exception. A 'proper law' approach is, of course, so inherently flexible that an exception would be redundant. However, if it is to be more than an 'incantation of the formula'[2], there must be some indication of the factors which will point to the law with which the issue is most closely connected, and of their relative weight[3]. Unsurprisingly, given the number of permutations available, the academic literature displays a variety of different choice of law rules. Only a sample will be outlined here[4].

1   The phrase 'proper law' is used in a number of different senses, and its use in relation to restitution has been justifiably criticised: see Dickinson, 'Restitution and incapacity: a choice of law solution?' [1997] RLR 66 at 68, and Maher 'Unjustified Enrichment and Choice of Law: *Baring Bros & Co Ltd v Cunninghame District Council*' [1997] Juridical Review 190 at 190. Nevertheless, it is here used to denote the system of law to which the obligation to make restitution has its closest and most real connection, much like the common law choice of law rule for contract refers to the system of law 'with which the transaction has its closest or most real connexion': *Bonython v Commonwealth* [1951] AC 201 at 219, per Lords Simonds. According to Collins (ed) *Dicey and Morris on The Conflict of Laws* (13th edn, 2000), p 1490, the 'general

approach of the English conflict of laws rules has been to subject claims in the law of obligations to the law with which the obligation has its closest and most real connection'.

2   Millett J has said 'It is impossible to quarrel with the contention that the governing law should be the law which has 'the closest and most real connection with the transaction.' In the present case, however, the incantation of the formula is not particularly helpful. It is merely to state the question, not to solve it': *Macmillan Inc v Bishopsgate Investment Trust plc (No 3)* [1995] 1 WLR 978 at 991.

3   Dickinson 'Restitution and incapacity: a choice of law solution?' [1997] RLR 66 at 67–68.

4   For a comprehensive list of relevant academic discussion see above, para 22.2, n 1. For summaries of the different approaches also see North and Fawcett *Cheshire and North's Private International Law* (13th edn, 1999), pp 676–685; and Bird 'Choice of Law' in Rose (ed) *Restitution and the Conflict of Laws* (1995), pp 99–136.

22.64   The early writers favoured a choice of law rule with a single connecting factor to govern all unjust enrichment claims. For example Beale[1], Gutteridge and Lipstein[2], and the *Restatement on the Conflicts of Laws (1st)*[3] all proposed that the law of the place of receipt of enrichment should govern restitution[4]. Ehrenzweig supported application of the law of the forum to all restitution claims, on the basis that restitution is founded on considerations of justice and public policy, and a court must apply its own principles of justice and public policy[5].

1   Beale *A Treatise on the Conflict of Laws* (1935), pp 1429 and 1430.

2   Gutteridge and Lipstein 'Conflicts of Law in Matters of Unjustifiable Enrichment' (1941) 7 CLJ 80 at 89–90 and 92–93. It is interesting to note that Lipstein appears to have changed his opinion subsequent to the publication of this article. Lipstein was the author of the choice of law rule for quasi-contract in Morris (ed) *Dicey: The Conflict of Laws* (6th edn, 1949), pp 754–756, which is almost identical to the current r 200 (see Collins (ed) *Dicey and Morris on The Conflict of Laws* (13th edn, 2000), p 1485): see Collier 'The Draft Convention and Restitution or Quasi-Contract' in Lipstein (ed) *Harmonisation of Private International Law by the EEC* (1978), p 87 and Blaikie 'Unjust Enrichment in the Conflict of Laws' [1984] Juridical Review 112 at 119, n 37.

3   (1934). See rr 452 and 453.

4   More recently, Leslie has endorsed the law of the place of enrichment, albeit subject to a proper law exception: Leslie 'Unjustified Enrichment in the Conflict of Laws' [1998] 2 Edinburgh Law Review 233 at 236–241.

5   Ehrenzweig 'Restitution in the Conflict of Laws' (1961) 36 New York University Law Review 1298. For an analysis of the role of the public policy, and therefore the lex fori, in restitution conflict of laws cases, see Lee 'Restitution, Public Policy and the Conflict of Laws' (1998) 20 University of Queensland Law Journal 1. For a critique of Ehrenzweig's approach see Bird 'Choice of Law' in Rose (ed) *Restitution and the Conflict of Laws* (1995), pp 102–106.

22.65   However, most commentators now accept that, in light of the diverse factual and legal contexts in which claims for unjust enrichment arise, a single connecting factor is inadequate[1]. The current approaches tend to involve either a number of sub-rules, with an exception[2], or the flexibility of the 'proper law'. For example, *Dicey and Morris*, r 200 provides:

(1)   The obligation to restore the benefit of an enrichment obtained at another person's expense is governed by the proper law of the obligation.

(2)   The proper law of the obligation is (*semble*) determined as follows:

(a)   If the obligation arises in connection with a contract, its proper law is the law applicable to the contract;

(b)   If it arises in connection with a transaction concerning an immovable (land), its proper law is the law of the country where the immovable is situated (lex situs);

(c)   If it arises in any other circumstances, its proper law is the law of the country where the enrichment occurs[3].

A simple reading of this rule suggests that the editors of *Dicey and Morris* favour a set of rigid sub-rules, and that the first paragraph is mere surplusage[4].

However, as has been observed, the commentary in the recent editions demonstrates that the current editors of *Dicey and Morris* lean towards a proper law approach, in which the court's task is to look for the law which has the most significant connection to the claim[5]. The sub-rules in paragraph 2 are intended merely to give '*guidance* as to the choice of law which will follow from that general principle in *certain* particular cases'[6]. Thus the *Dicey and Morris* choice of law rule is equivalent to that proposed by Blaikie, who supports a proper law approach and argues the three sub-rules in clause 2 of *Dicey and Morris* Rule should be 'regarded as a list of examples of ways in which the proper law of the obligation to restore might be discovered'[7].

1   Zweigert and Müller-Gindullis 'Quasi Contract' in Lipstein (ed) *International Encyclopedia of Comparative Law* (1974), vol III, ch 30; Collier 'The Draft Convention and Restitution or Quasi-Contract' in Lipstein (ed) *Harmonisation of Private International Law by the EEC* (1978), pp 84 and 85; Blaikie 'Unjust Enrichment in the Conflict of Laws' [1984] Juridical Review 112 at 122.
2   Bird 'Choice of Law' in Rose (ed) *Restitution and the Conflict of Laws* (1995), pp 135 and 136.
3   Collins (ed) *Dicey and Morris on The Conflict of Laws* (13th edn, 2000), p 1485.
4   However, even in the earlier editions, the commentary indicated clause 2(c) was not a hard and fast rule: Collins (ed) *Dicey and Morris on The Conflict of Laws* (11th edn, 1987), p 1354.
5   *Baring Bros & Co Ltd v Cunninghame District Council* [1997] CLC 108 at 120, referring to Collins (ed) *Dicey and Morris on The Conflict of Laws* (12th edn, 1993). The relevant section of the commentary in Collins (ed) *Dicey and Morris on The Conflict of Laws* (13th edn, 2000) is the same and, in fact, the 13th edition gives stronger support for the flexible proper law approach: see n 6.
6   Collins (ed) *Dicey and Morris on The Conflict of Laws* (13th edn, 2000), p 1486 (emphasis added). This sentence appears for the first time in the 13th edition. See also pp 1497 and 1498, which stress that cls 2(a) and (c) do not state an inflexible rule, and will not always isolate the law with which the obligation to make restitution has its closest connection.
7   'Unjust Enrichment in the Conflict of Laws' [1984] Juridical Review 112 at 125.

22.66   Zweigert and Müller-Gindullis place greater emphasis on the law governing the underlying transaction, legal relationship or factual situation[1]. They divide restitution into unjustifiable enrichment and *negotiorum gestio*. In general terms, they suggest that a restitution claim which arises in the context of a legal relationship between the parties should be governed by the law which governed the relationship. Those restitution claims which arise without reference to a legal relationship are governed by the law which governs the shift of assets from the claimant to the defendant, that is, the law governing the transfer of the asset[2]. They suggest a hierarchy of rules for categories of *negotiorum gestio*, the first one of which looks to the law of the relationship between the parties[3].

1   Zweigert and Müller-Gindullis 'Quasi Contract' in Lipstein (ed) *International Encyclopedia of Comparative Law* (1974) vol III, ch 30.
2   Zweigert and Müller-Gindullis 'Quasi Contract' in Lipstein (ed) *International Encyclopedia of Comparative Law* (1974) vol III, ch 30, 12 and 14–17.
3   Zweigert and Müller-Gindullis 'Quasi Contract' in Lipstein (ed) *International Encyclopedia of Comparative Law* (1974) vol III, ch 30, 19–21.

22.67   Finally, reference should be made to *Restatement (2nd)*, para 221[1]. It resembles the 'proper law' approach of Blaikie and the more recent editions of *Dicey and Morris*, in that it requires the court to apply the law of the state which 'has the most significant relationship to the occurrence and the parties'. It also refers to a list of localising factors to assist this choice. Paragraph 221 provides:

(1)   In actions for restitution, the rights and liabilities of the parties with respect to the particular issue are determined by the local law of the state which, with respect to that issue, has the most significant relationship to the occurrence and the parties under the principles stated in para 6[2].

(2)   Contacts to be taken into account in applying the principles of §6 to determine the law applicable to an issue include:

(a)   the place where a relationship between the parties was centered, provided that the receipt of enrichment was substantially related to the relationship,

(b)   the place where the benefit or enrichment was received,

(c)   the place where the act conferring the benefit or enrichment was done,

(d)   the domicil, residence, nationality, place of incorporation and place of business of the parties, and

(e)   the place where a physical thing, such as land or a chattel, which was substantially related to the enrichment, was situated at the time of the enrichment.

These contacts are to be evaluated according to their relative importance with respect to the particular issue.

1   *Restatement of the Law (2nd): the Conflict of Laws* (1971).
2   Paragraph 6 provides, inter alia, that the factors relevant to the choice of the applicable law include: the needs of the interstate and international systems; relevant policies of the forum; relevant policies of other interested states and the relative interests of those states in the determination of the particular issue; protection of justified expectations; the basic policies underlying the particular field of law; certainty, predictability and uniformity of result; and ease in the determination and application of the law to be applied.

22.68   It is important not to overstate the differences in the modern academic choice of law rules. In the majority of cases, they will point to the same governing law. However, at the margins, there are differences. For example, various rules differ on the question of the relevance of the law governing the underlying contract, particularly where that law is chosen by the parties, if a party seeks restitution of benefits conferred under a void contract[1]. More fundamentally, perhaps, while most of the modern rules tolerate a degree of flexibility, they lie at different points on the continuum between certainty and predictability, on the one hand, and flexibility and justice in the individual case, on the other[2].

1   This was the issue in *Baring Bros & Co Ltd v Cunninghame District Council* [1997] CLC 108 (see below, para 22.70) and the varying approaches to the issue are canvassed in the judgment. Note however that since that judgment *Dicey and Morris* has changed its stance on this issue. The 12th edition rejected reference to the chosen law: Collins (ed) *Dicey and Morris on The Conflict of Laws* (12th edn, 1993), p 1473. However, the 13th edition accepts that 'in certain cases it will be appropriate to allow an expressly chosen law to govern the restitutionary claim': p 1492.
2   Bird 'Choice of Law and Restitution of Benefits conferred under a Void Contract' [1997] Lloyds Maritime and Commercial Law Quarterly 182 at 188–192.

22.69   Judicial approach   It is not yet possible to isolate a dominant judicial approach to the choice of law rule for restitution. The rule in *Dicey and Morris* has been referred to, with varying degrees of enthusiasm, on a number of occasions[1]. However, it would be inaccurate to assert that this amounts to judicial endorsement of that rule[2].

1   For examples see Collins (ed) *Dicey and Morris on The Conflict of Laws* (13th edn, 2000), p 1486, and in particular the cases referred to in nn 8 and 9. See also *Arab Monetary Fund v Hashim (No 9)* (1994) Times, 11 October, Chadwick J) and *Kuwait Oil Tanker Co SAK v Al Bader* [2000] 2 All ER (Comm) 271, CA.
2   The commentary in Collins (ed) *Dicey and Morris on The Conflict of Laws* (13th edn, 2000), p 1486, n 8, accepts that the clearest approval of the rule comes from Evans J in *Arab Monetary Fund v Hashim* [1993] 1 Lloyd's Rep 543. However, even in that judgment Evans J stressed (at 566) that he preferred to base his decision on the law governing the claimant's restitution claim on wider grounds than the *Dicey and Morris* rule. Chadwick J did much the same thing in *Arab Monetary*

Fund v Hashim (No 9) (1994) Times, 11 October, Chadwick J): after stating the rule with approval, he went on to apply a slightly different rule, in which the governing law was the law of the underlying relationship between the parties. Moreover, an assessment of the judicial acceptance of the *Dicey and Morris* rule is complicated by the fact that the rule appears to have undergone subtle metamorphoses at the hands of different editors. The current rule dates back to the 6th edition of the text: Morris (ed) *Dicey: The Conflict of Laws* (6th edn, 1949), pp 754–756. The wording of clause 2(a) was, however, altered in the 12th edition. Since the 12th edition, this clause has referred to 'the law applicable to the contract', rather than 'the proper law of the contract': see Collins (ed) *Dicey and Morris on The Conflict of Laws* (12th edn, 1993), p 1471. This was presumably intended to indicate that the proper law of the contract did not govern restitution claims if that proper law was chosen by the parties. This stance was taken in the 12th edition (see Collins (ed) *Dicey and Morris on The Conflict of Laws* (12th edn, 1993), pp 1473 and 1474) and appears to have been abandoned in the 13th edition. The 13th edition (Collins (ed) *Dicey and Morris on The Conflict of Laws* (13th edn, 2000), p 1492) accepts that in appropriate cases an expressly chosen law can govern a restitution claim. Additionally, the recent editions show a shift towards a greater acceptance of flexibility: see above, para 22.65.

22.70   Probably the greatest impediment to an assessment of the judicial approach to the restitution choice of law rule is the fact that, on the rare occasions on which the issue has been raised, it has seldom received detailed analysis. The one recent case that does canvas the issue thoroughly is *Baring Bros & Co Ltd v Cunninghame District Council*[1]. The Outer House of the Court of Session had to decide what law governed Baring Brothers' claim to restitution of money it had paid to Cunninghame District Council under an interest rate swap contract which was void ab initio. After an impressive review of the relevant literature, Lord Penrose stated that his preferred choice of law rule for restitution is the proper law rule adopted by Blaikie[2]. He summarised it as follows:

> on the flexible approach one may reasonably accept two propositions: (a) that the restitutionary or quasi-contractual obligation is governed by the proper law of that obligation; and (b) that the proper law of the obligation is the law of the country with which, in the light of the whole facts and circumstances, the critical events have their closest and most real connection[3].

1   [1997] CLC 108 (Sc).
2   See above, para 22.65.
3   [1997] CLC 108 at 127.

22.71   Yet this means little without an indication of those facts, in the scenario giving rise to the claimant's claim, which indicate a connection between that claim and a particular legal system, and the relative weight that should be given to those facts[1]. Lord Penrose gave some indication of the relevant facts and their weight. The parties' attempt to enter into a contract governed by English law, and the fact that the contract was connected with the London financial market, were clearly important indicators of a connection to the English legal system. On the other hand, Lord Penrose dismissed the relevance of both the domicile of the parties and the place of enrichment because, on the facts of the particular case, they were purely matters of chance[2]. However Lord Penrose did not (nor, one assumes, does he think it possible to) lay down a definitive list of relevant facts and their relative weight.

1   See above, para 22.63. See also Dickinson 'Restitution and incapacity: a choice of law solution?' [1997] RLR 66 at 67–68.
2   [1997] CLC 108 at 127.

22.72   The obvious drawback of the proper law approach adopted by Lord Penrose is the uncertainty it creates. A rule requiring a court to identify 'the law of the country with which, in the light of the whole facts and circumstances, the critical events have their closest and most real connection'[1] is not far removed from an open-ended judicial discretion. However, it may well be that at this early stage in the development of choice of law for restitution, lawyers must be content to see certainty sacrificed to flexibility in this way[2]. Hopefully, when courts have had more experience of these cases, the flexibility of the proper law approach may begin to give way to some more certain rules, capable of delivering predictable results.

1   [1997] CLC 108 at 127.
2   Cf Dickinson 'Restitution and incapacity: a choice of law solution?' [1997] RLR 66 at 70; Bird 'Choice of Law and Restitution of Benefits conferred under a Void Contract' [1997] Lloyds Maritime and Commercial Law Quarterly 182 at 189–192.

22.73   Relevant factors   If the choice of law rule for restitution requires identification of the law with which the restitution claim has its closest and most real connection, it is important to know what facts in the scenarios giving rise to restitutionary liability will indicate such a connection and the weight that should be given to those facts[1]. Alternatively, if the choice of law rule for restitution divides restitution into various subsets, each with its own connecting factor, then lawyers need to know what those connecting factors are, and to what subset of restitution claims they apply. Some of the relevant facts or connecting factors are now considered.

1   See above, paras 22.63 and 22.71.

22.74   Relevant factors: Law of the contract   Restitution claims frequently arise in the wake of a failed contract[1], and many commentators have suggested that the governing law of the failed contract should have some role in the choice of law rule for those restitution claims[2]. However, the exact nature of that role and, indeed, the legitimacy of looking to the law of the failed contract at all, are amongst the most contentious issues in this area of law. Before considering the various debates, it is worthwhile looking at the main justifications for referring to the governing law of the failed contract, when searching for the law which governs restitution claims.

1   This term is used to refer to a contract which is void, terminated, non-existent or otherwise ineffective.
2   Collins (ed) *Dicey and Morris on The Conflict of Laws* (13th edn, 2000), pp 1485 and 1493–1497; Bird 'Choice of Law' in Rose (ed) *Restitution and the Conflict of Laws* (1995), pp 119–130; Brereton 'Restitution and Contract' in Rose (ed) *Restitution and the Conflict of Laws* (1995), pp 142–147; Blaikie 'Unjust Enrichment in the Conflict of Laws' [1984] Juridical Review 112 at 126; Zweigert and Müller-Gindullis 'Quasi Contract' in Lipstein (ed) *International Encyclopedia of Comparative Law* (1974), vol III, ch 30, para 11–17; *Restatement of the Law (2nd): the Conflict of Laws* (1971) comment d, 730; Wolff *Private International Law* (2nd edn, 1950), pp 499–501; Rabel *The Conflict of Laws – A Comparative Study* (1950), vol 3, pp 372, 373 and 380–383.

22.75   The principal justification is that such reference is in conformity with the parties' expectations[1]. The governing law of the failed contract is the law which the parties chose to govern their contractual relationship[2] or, if they do not make such a choice, the law of the country with which the contract is most closely connected[3]. It seems reasonable to assume that persons who have attempted to enter into a contract, and who have chosen a law to govern that contract, expect that law to govern all issues arising out of that contract. That is, they will expect it to govern both the contractual relationship between them and the fall-out if they are unsuccessful in creating such a relationship. They are unlikely to draw a distinction between the contractual and restitutionary issues that might arise out of what, to them, is a single relationship[4]. Even if the governing law of the contract is 'the law of the country with which the contract is most closely connected'[5], rather than a chosen law, it seems unlikely that the parties would expect different laws to apply to the contractual and restitutionary issues arising out of that contract. Whilst from the point of view of strict legal theory the question of whether a contract is void or otherwise fails falls in a different category to the question of what the consequences of that finding are, from all other points of view it is part of the same problem.

1   Bird 'Choice of Law' in Rose (ed) *Restitution and the Conflict of Laws* (1995), pp 123 and 124; Brereton 'Restitution and Contract' in Rose (ed) *Restitution and the Conflict of Laws* (1995), pp 156 and 157; Lasok and Stone *Conflict of Laws in the European Community* (1987), p 371.
2   See Art 3(1) of the Rome Convention.
3   See Art 4(1) of the Rome Convention.
4   Bird 'Choice of Law' in Rose (ed) *Restitution and the Conflict of Laws* (1995), p 124; Brereton 'Restitution and Contract' in Rose (ed) *Restitution and the Conflict of Laws* (1995), p 144.
5   Rome Convention, art 4(1).

22.76   It may be that the parties have absolutely no expectation as to which law will govern contractual or other issues arising out of their attempt to create a contractual relationship. In these circumstances, the proper law of the failed contract (that is, the law most closely connected to the failed contract) is also likely to be the law which is most closely connected to the restitutionary claim consequent on that failure, and which has the greatest interest in regulation of that restitutionary claim. Restitution and contract lawyers in the United Kingdom draw a clear line of demarcation between the issues of what avoids or terminates a contract, and whether payments made under a void or terminated contract can be recovered[1]. However, from a practical perspective, the two issues are intimately related; very few of the legal problems encountered by those lawyers are likely to raise the latter but not the former issue. Accordingly, it is difficult to see why the two issues should be governed by different laws. The reality is that restitution actions which arise out of failed contracts are, in a sense, merely contractual remedies[2], and the law which declares that the contract has failed is the most suitable to regulate the consequences of that finding[3].

1   See eg the *Kleinwort Benson* case; discussed above, para 22.12ff.
2   Bird 'Choice of Law' in Rose (ed) *Restitution and the Conflict of Laws* (1995), p 124; Zweigert and Müller-Gindullis 'Quasi Contract' in Lipstein (ed) *International Encyclopedia of Comparative Law* (1974), vol III, ch 30, 14.
3   Zweigert and Müller-Gindullis 'Quasi Contract' in Lipstein (ed) *International Encyclopedia of Comparative Law* (1974) vol III, ch 30, 11.

22.77   These arguments for the application of the proper law of the failed contract to restitution claims arising out of the failed contract do not justify the application of that law where the contract has been avoided because of a fundamental mistake. Likewise, they would not support application of that law to restitution claims following rescission of a contract because of vitiating factors such as misrepresentation or duress[1]. In these circumstances there is no true meeting of minds. That is, there is in fact no genuine attempt to enter into contractual relations, and no genuine agreement as to the law which governs the underlying contract. However, leaving these situations aside, there appear to be sound arguments of principle justifying reference to the governing law of the contract.

1   On duress see above, para 10.51ff.

22.78   There is also a raft of secondary reasons which favour application of the proper law of the failed contract. It is convenient to have all issues which arise out of what is essentially a single relationship governed by one law[1]. In most cases, although not all[2], the law which determines that the contract has failed will be the governing law of the contract. For example, if a party brought a claim for restitution of amounts paid under contract which it alleged should be avoided for duress, the court would have to decide whether the contract was voidable by reference to the governing law of the contract[3]. It would be inconvenient to apply a different law to determine whether amounts paid under the contract can be recovered. Legal systems may have an internal balance, which is destroyed if one part of what is essentially a single problem is dealt with by one legal system and another by a different legal system. Certainty and consistency in the application of legal rules would be enhanced if restitution claims were determined by reference to the governing law of the underlying contract because the choice of law rule for contract is both certain and, to a substantial degree, consistent across jurisdictions[4]. Finally, as stated above,[5] the characterisation problems referred to above would be minimised if the restitution choice of law rule pointed to the same law as the contract choice of law.

1   *Restatement of the Law (2nd): the Conflict of Laws* (1971), 730; Collier 'The Draft Convention and Restitution or Quasi-Contract' in Lipstein (ed) *Harmonisation of Private International Law by the EEC* (1978), p 88; Lasok and Stone *Conflict of Laws in the European Community* (1987), p 371.
2   For example, the question of whether a contract is void for lack of capacity is governed by the personal law of the relevant party: see Dickinson 'Restitution and the conflict of laws' [1996] Lloyds Maritime and Commercial Law Quarterly 556 at 570–571; 'Restitution and incapacity: a choice of law solution?' [1997] RLR 66 at 70–71. This point is illustrated by *Baring Bros & Co Ltd v Cunninghame District Council* [1997] CLC 108, on which see above, para 22.70.
3   See Art 8 of the Rome Convention; *Dimskal Shipping Co v International Transport Workers Federation, The Evia Luck* [1992] 2 AC 152.
4   Bird 'Choice of Law' in Rose (ed) *Restitution and the Conflict of Laws* (1995), p 123.
5   See above, paras 22.48 and 22.49.

22.79   However, in spite of these arguments, the role of the governing law of the failed contract in the restitution choice of law rule is highly contentious. The first issue is whether it is legitimate to consider the governing law of the failed contract at all. A restitution claim arising out a contractual relationship between the parties can only succeed if, according to its governing law, the contract has ceased to exist or never existed. Therefore, some argue that the application of the governing law of the contract is illogical; one cannot refer to the governing law of a contract that has ceased to exist or never existed[1].

1   Glanville Williams *Law Reform (Frustrated Contracts) Act, 1943* (1944), p 19; Gutteridge and Lipstein 'Conflicts of Law in Matters of Unjustifiable Enrichment' (1941) 7 CLJ 80 at 86. See also *Baring Bros & Co Ltd v Cunninghame District Council* [1997] CLC 108 at 123. Note also that Lipstein appears to have later changed his mind: see above, para 22.64, n 2.

22.80   However, this argument misconceives both the effect of the legal conclusion that the contract has ceased to exist or never existed, and the nature of the governing law of the contract. A finding that as a matter of law a contract is at an end, or is void ab initio, does not mean that the parties never attempted to enter into consensual relations, or never reached agreement on certain points. A legal finding does not erase factual events. The NSW Supreme Court recognised this when it rejected an argument that the court should ignore an exclusive jurisdiction clause because one party argued that the contract was void ab initio for material non-disclosure[1]. Giles J said[2]:

Sometimes words are used to the effect that a contract avoided ab initio is taken never to have existed ... The words are sufficient for most purposes, but they should not be taken literally ... Avoidance ab initio means that the parties are to be restored substantially to the positions they would have been in had there not been a contract, but it remains that there was a contract ... The law works out the consequences of the avoidance ab initio ... One working-out is that the contract may remain on foot so far as it contains an arbitration clause and ... so far as it contains an exclusive jurisdiction clause. Nothing in the concept of avoidance ab initio compels the conclusion that the former existence of the contract is denied, or that it cannot be recognised for the purpose of working out the consequences of its avoidance.

Likewise, one can assert that nothing in the finding that a contract is at an end, or is void ab initio, compels the conclusion that the governing law of the contract cannot be considered for the purposes of determining the governing law of restitution claims arising from the contract. The governing law of a contract is not a concrete portion of the contract which is destroyed along with the contract; it is an indication of the law with which the entire relationship between the contractual parties is most closely connected[3] and, especially where there is an express or implied choice as to the governing law, it is also evidence of the law which the parties intend to apply to legal claims arising out of their relationship, including claims which arise as a result of the failure of the contract. Provided that it is not held that the contract never existed because there was no meeting of minds, the same argument applies where the putative governing law of the contract leads to the conclusion that the contract never existed[4].

1   *FAI General Insurance Co Ltd v Ocean Marine Mutual Protection and Indemnity Association* (1997) 41 NSWLR 559, [1998] Lloyd's Rep IR 24. See also *Ferris v Plaister* (1994) 34 NSWLR 474.
2   (1997) 41 NSWLR 117.
3   *Alaskan Airlines v United Airlines* 902 F 2d 1400 at 1403 (9th Cir, 1990).
4   Zweigert and Müller-Gindullis 'Quasi Contract' in Lipstein (ed) *International Encyclopedia of Comparative Law* (1974), vol III, ch 30, 12; Bennett 'Choice of Law Rules in Claims of Unjust Enrichment' (1990) 39 ICLQ 126 at 162.

22.81   Even amongst those commentators who accept the legitimacy of the role of the law of the contract, there is vigorous disagreement about the exact nature of that role. There are essentially two points of disagreement. Firstly, there is dispute about the validity of determining a restitution claim by reference to a law chosen by the parties. Some argue that, as liability in restitution is non-consensual and imposed by law, it is improper to determine restitution claims by reference to the law the parties have chosen to govern their contract. Instead, it is claimed, the choice of law rule for restitution claims should look to the law with which the contract is objectively most closely connected, ignoring any express or implied choice of law[1]. A number of comments can be made about this objection. Firstly, there is no doubt that the obligation to make restitution is imposed by law. So too is the obligation to pay damages for breach of contract or the finding that a contract is frustrated[2]. Nevertheless, no-one has objected to the application of a chosen law to these issues. Secondly, it is inaccurate to state, as does the 12th edition of *Dicey and Morris*, that 'the relation out of which the restitutionary obligation arises does not depend on the volition of the parties'[3]. In the context under consideration, the restitutionary obligation arises out of the voluntary, but unsuccessful, attempt to create a contractual relationship. The parties may not be in a contractual relationship, but they are in a voluntary relationship. Thirdly, reference to the law chosen by the parties in their void contract involves a presumption that, in most cases, the parties intended a certain legal system would apply to their entire relationship – not, as Blaikie alleges, a 'presumption of an intention that restitution should take place'[4]. Where the parties to a contract have no intention as to restitutionary liability arising between them, they may still have an intention or expectation as to the legal system that will govern their whole relationship, including any unanticipated claims. Finally, even if the parties do not have an intention as to the law which will govern their relationship, the law which decided that the contract was void, whether it is a chosen law or not, is the law which is most closely concerned with the consequences of that decision[5].

1   Collins (ed) *Dicey and Morris on The Conflict of Laws* (12th edn, 1993), p 1473; Blaikie 'Unjust Enrichment in the Conflict of Laws' [1984] Juridical Review 112 at 123. Collins (ed) *Dicey and Morris on The Conflict of Laws* (13th edn, 2000), p 1492 accepts that in appropriate cases an expressly chosen law can govern a restitution claim.
2   Brereton 'Restitution and Contract' in Rose (ed) *Restitution and the Conflict of Laws* (1995), p 157.
3   Collins (ed) *Dicey and Morris on The Conflict of Laws* (12th edn, 1993), p 1473.
4   Blaikie 'Unjust Enrichment in the Conflict of Laws' [1984] Juridical Review 112 at 123.
5   See *Restatement of the Law (2nd): the Conflict of Laws* (1971) 729–30; and above, para 22.76.

22.82   The second point of disagreement concerns whether the law of the contract is more or less definitive, governing nearly all restitution claims arising out of the contract, or whether it is merely one of a number of factors to be taken into account in the search for the law governing the restitution claim. The earlier editions of *Dicey and Morris* treated the law of the contract as definitive, but the more recent editions tend towards a more flexible approach[1]. The law of the contract has always been given a very influential role in the choice of law rule for restitution in the *Restatement*[2]. Under the Blaikie rule, it is one factor to be taken into account[3].

1   See above, para 22.65. Note also that in the choice of law rule drafted by Bird, subject to a flexible exception, the law of the contract applies 'when there is or was a contractual relationship between the parties, or both parties were under the mistaken assumption that there was such a relationship between them, and the enrichment would not have occurred but for that real or supposed contract': Bird 'Choice of Law' in Rose (ed) *Restitution and the Conflict of Laws* (1995), p 135.
2   *Restatement of the Law Second: the Conflict of Laws* (1971) comment d, 729–730.
3   'Unjust enrichment in the Conflict of Laws' [1984] Juridical Review 112 at 122–124.

22.83   The case law is not decisive but there is a tendency is to support a non-definitive role for the governing law of the failed contract, regardless of whether that law is chosen or not[1].

1   This is the approach in *Baring Bros & Co Ltd v Cunninghame District Council* [1997] CLC 108. It is consistent with *Arab Monetary Fund v Hashim (No 9)* (1994) Times, 11 October, Chadwick J), *Arab Monetary Fund v Hashim* [1993] 1 Lloyd's Rep 543 (Evans J), [1996] 1 Lloyd's Rep 589, CA; and *Kuwait Oil Tanker Co SAK v Al Bader* [2000] 2 All ER (Comm) 271, CA.

22.84   Relevant factors: Law of the non-contractual relationship
Claims to restitution may arise in the context of a non-contractual relationship, such as an agency relationship, or the relationship between a director and the company. Such relationships come within para 221(2)(a) of the *Restatement* which refers to:

... the place where a relationship between the parties was centered, provided that the receipt of enrichment was substantially related to the relationship[1].

In the scheme of the *Restatement* this contact is the one which 'as to most issues, is given the greatest weight'[2].

1   See also Zweigert and Müller-Gindullis 'Quasi Contract' in Lipstein (ed) *International Encyclopedia of Comparative Law* (1974), vol III, ch 30, 20; and Bird 'Choice of Law' in Rose (ed) *Restitution and the Conflict of Laws* (1995), pp 130–133 and 135.
2   Comment d, 730.

22.85   Whilst the law of the relationship between the parties, especially if that relationship is non-contractual, is a novel concept in English conflict of laws, its relevance to the choice of law for restitution has been given support by Chadwick J. In *Arab Monetary Fund v Hashim (No 9)* he said:

> Where the underlying obligation[1] arises out of the relationship of employment or agency or the holding of an office, the proper law of the underlying obligation is the law which governs that relationship[2].

This approach has been endorsed by the Court of Appeal[3]. The arguments in support of the law of the relationship are much the same as those which favour of the law of the contract[4].

1   The obligation in the case was the obligation of a fiduciary to account for misappropriated property. Chadwick J characterised this obligation as restitutionary: see above, para 22.61.
2   (1994) Times, 11 October.
3   *Kuwait Oil Tanker Co SAK v Al Bader* [2000] 2 All ER (Comm) 271, CA.
4   See above, paras 22.74–22.83.

22.86   Relevant factors: Place of enrichment[1]   The law of the place of receipt of the enrichment was proposed as a general choice of law rule by Beale[2], Gutteridge and Lipstein[3], the *Restatement on the Conflicts of Laws (1st)*[4] and, subject to a proper law exception, Leslie[5]. Others have suggested that the law of the place of receipt of the enrichment be applied to only some cases of unjust enrichment. For example, sub-rule 200(2)(c) in *Dicey and Morris* provides that, where the obligation to make restitution arises, neither in connection with a contract nor a transaction concerning land, 'its proper law is the law of the country where the enrichment occurs'[6]. This sub-rule has been approved in *Arab Bank New York Ltd v Barclays Bank*[7], *Re Jogia (a bankrupt)*[8], *El Ajou v Dollar Land Holdings Ltd*[9], *Hongkong and Shanghai Banking Corpn v United Overseas Bank*[10] and *Thahir v PT Pertambangan Minyak dan Gas Bumi Negara (Pertamina)*[11].

1   Commentators have also suggested that other places related to the chain of events giving rise to the claim for restitution are relevant to the choice of law rule for restitution. Cohen proposed the law of the place of impoverishment as a general choice of law rule for restitution: Cohen 'Quasi Contract and the Conflict of Laws' (1956) 31 Los Angeles Bar Bulletin 71. The commentary in Collins (ed) *Dicey and Morris on The Conflict of Laws* (13th edn, 2000), p 1502 accepts that in some situations the place of impoverishment is relevant. Burrows *Law of Restitution* (1993), p 492 proposed application of the law of the place of impoverishment and the place of enrichment, if they coincide. *Restatement of the Law Second: the Conflict of Laws* (1971), para 221(2)(c) refers to the 'place where the act conferring the benefit or enrichment was done' as one of the factors to be taken into account in ascertaining the applicable law. The commentary emphasises that this law will apply where there is no prior relationship between the parties, and where the place of enrichment cannot be identified, or is unrelated to the facts of the cause of action: comment d, 732–733.
2   Beale *A Treatise on the Conflict of Laws* (1935), pp 1429 and 1430.
3   Gutteridge and Lipstein 'Conflicts of Law in Matters of Unjustifiable Enrichment' (1941) 7 CLJ 80 at 89–90 and 92–93.
4   (1934). See rr 452 and 453.
5   Leslie 'Unjustified Enrichment in the Conflict of Laws' [1998] 2 Edinburgh Law Review 233 at 236–241.
6   Collins (ed) *Dicey and Morris on The Conflict of Laws* (13th edn, 2000), p 1485. See also Zweigert and Müller-Gindullis 'Quasi Contract' in Lipstein (ed) *International Encyclopedia of Comparative Law* (1974), vol III, ch 30, 16; and Bird 'Choice of Law' in Rose (ed) *Restitution and the Conflict of Laws* (1995), pp 113–116 and 135.
7   [1952] 2 TLR 920 at 924, per Parker J. However, note that the approval is obiter, and the rule is misapplied, because the case would appear to call for the application of sub-rule (2)(a). In the Court of Appeal, Jenkins LJ, the only judge to consider the issue, states that the law which invalidates the original contract should apply: [1953] 2 QB 527 at 572.
8   [1988] 1 WLR 484. However, it is questionable whether the claim in this case should have been dealt with under sub-rule 201(2)(c), rather than sub-rule 201(2)(a).

9   [1993] 3 All ER 717 at 736, per Millett J.
10 [1992] 2 SLR 495.
11 [1994] 3 SLR 257. See also *Sumitomo Bank Ltd v Thahir* [1993] 1 SLR 735.

22.87   However, the current editors of *Dicey and Morris* appear to prefer an approach in which the place of enrichment is merely one factor relevant to the identification of the proper law of the obligation to make restitution. The commentary in the current edition describes the place of enrichment as a 'starting point for the identification of the proper law'[1], in those cases neither connected with a contract nor a transaction concerning land. This approach is similar to that in *Baring Bros & Co Ltd v Cunninghame District Council*[2]. It is also resembles the *Restatement (2nd)*. The place where the enrichment is received is one of the contacts in the *Restatement*, para 221(2). The commentary states that this contact will generally be most important when there is no prior relationship between the parties[3].

1   Collins (ed) *Dicey and Morris on The Conflict of Laws* (13th edn, 2000), p 1501.
2   [1997] CLC 108 at 127; above, para 22.70ff.
3   Comment d, 732.

22.88   The place of enrichment has an obvious factual connection to the obligation to make restitution. Although the liability in restitution for unjust enrichment by subtraction requires both an impoverishment and an enrichment, the enrichment is the focus of the principle against unjust enrichment, and is at the heart of the action[1].

1   Contra Cohen 'Quasi Contract and the Conflict of Laws' (1956) 31 Los Angeles Bar Bulletin 71 at 78.

22.89   The place of enrichment will be least relevant where the obligation to make restitution arises in the context of a prior relationship. However, the prior relationship is likely to have a more meaningful connection to the obligation to make restitution than the place of enrichment and, moreover, the parties may expect the law of that relationship to apply[1]. This is illustrated by *Arab Monetary Fund v Hashim*[2]. In that case, the Court of Appeal held that the law of Abu Dhabi applied to the claimant's claims to recover a bribe from its employee, Hashim. Hashim had been enriched in either Switzerland or England: the bribe was paid into a Swiss bank account, and a substantial part was subsequently dispersed to England. Nevertheless, Abu Dhabi was clearly most closely connected to the obligation to make restitution because it was the place where the building transaction which gave rise to the bribe was centred, where Hashim was based, where the claimant's headquarters were located and (most importantly) it was the state whose law governed the relationship between the claimant and Hashim. Moreover, the parties may well have expected Abu Dhabi law to govern any legal claims which arose out of their relationship. Switzerland, on the other hand, had no connection to the parties and the claim for unjust enrichment, other than the fact that it was where Hashim's enrichment was originally deposited. Likewise, England was merely the place to which Hashim transferred his enrichment, and the place where the bribers organised the mechanics of payment.

1   Zweigert and Müller-Gindullis 'Quasi Contract' in Lipstein (ed) *International Encyclopedia of Comparative Law* (1974), vol III, ch 30, 7; Blaikie 'Unjust Enrichment in the Conflict of Laws' [1984] Juridical Review 112 at 120–121; Bennett 'Choice of Law Rules in Claims of Unjust Enrichment' (1990) 39 ICLQ 126 at 149.
2   [1996] 1 Lloyd's Rep 589. See also [1993] 1 Ll 543.

22.90   The place of enrichment may also be irrelevant and unconnected with the obligation to make restitution because it is transitory or trivial. This is especially so in the modern world, where money may be moved quickly[1], or retained in locations for reasons which have nothing to do with the basis of the claim, such as taxation or secrecy. Moreover, the place of enrichment can be manipulated. For example, in *Arab Monetary Fund v Hashim* the claimant suggested that the place of enrichment was deliberately kept outside Abu Dhabi[2]. In *Baring Bros & Co Ltd v Cunninghame District Council* Lord Penrose dismissed the relevance of the place of enrichment to the identification of the proper law of the Council's obligation to make restitution because it was purely casual. As there were payments on both sides of the swaps contract, the place of enrichment 'might oscillate between the locations of the parties' centres of administration'[3].

1   See *Hongkong and Shanghai Banking Corpn v United Overseas Bank* [1992] 2 SLR 495 especially at 500.
2   [1993] 1 Lloyd's Rep 543 at 566.
3   [1997] CLR 108 at 127. On the case see above, para 22.70ff.

22.91   Finally, it should be noted that the place of enrichment may be difficult to locate[1]. This problem is not peculiar to unjust enrichment. In all branches of the conflict of laws, it is frequently difficult to locate the relevant locus on which choice of law or jurisdictional rules are pinned[2]. Essentially, the various loci are often inappropriate in all but the simplest legal problems. The acts which give rise to legal liability and their consequences are seldom as concrete or tangible as the notion of 'locus' assumes.

1   Morris 'The Choice of Law Clause in Statutes' (1946) 63 LQR 170 at 182; Blaikie 'Unjust Enrichment in the Conflict of Laws' [1984] Juridical Review 112 at 120; Bennett 'Choice of Law Rules in Claims of Unjust Enrichment' (1990) 39 ICLQ 126; Bird 'Choice of Law' in Rose (ed) *Restitution and the Conflict of Laws* (1995), pp 110 and 114–116.
2   See eg *Distillers Co (Biochemicals) v Thompson* [1971] AC 458; *GJ Bier Handelswekerij v Mines de potasse d'Alsace BV* [1976] ECR 1735; *Diamond v Bank of London and Montreal Ltd* [1979] QB 333; *Castree v ER Squibb and Sons* [1980] 1 WLR 1248; *Brinkibon Ltd v Stahag Stahl und Stahlwarenhandelsgesellschaft* [1983] 2 AC 34; *The Albaforth* [1984] 2 Lloyd's Rep 91; *Shenavai v Kreischer* [1987] ECR 239; *Metall und Rohstoff AG v Donaldson Lufkin and Jenrette Inc* [1990] 1 QB 391; *Dumez France and Tracoba v Hessiche Landesbank* [1990] ECR 49; Law Com No 193, para 3.6.

22.92   Relevant factors: Situs   The *Restatement (2nd)* lists 'the place where a physical thing, such as land or a chattel, which was substantially related to the enrichment, was situated at the time of the enrichment' as one of the relevant contacts[1]. The commentary stresses that generally this factor is of greater importance when the 'physical thing' in question is land[2]. Clause 200(2)(b) of *Dicey and Morris* calls for application of the lex situs to unjust enrichment claims which arise 'in connection with a transaction concerning an immovable'[3].

1   Paragraph 221(2)(e).
2   Comment d, 733.
3   Collins (ed) *Dicey and Morris on The Conflict of Laws* (13th edn, 2000), p 1485.

22.93   The case law in favour of this factor is not overwhelming. Both *Dicey and Morris*[1] and the *Restatement (2nd)*[2] cite *Batthyany v Walford*[3] as authority. On the death of Prince Batthyany Strattman, the claimant came into possession of lands in Austria and Hungary, which had been in the Prince's possession and which, under Austrian and Hungarian law, were the subject of a *fidei commiss*. Under Austrian and Hungarian law, the possessor of a *fidei commiss* was obliged to hand the property to its successor in the same state as it was received, and failure to do so resulted in liability to the successor for any deterioration. Liability would not accrue if the possessor proved that the deterioration occurred without fault on its behalf. In an action against the executrix of the Prince's estate in England, the claimant sued in respect of the Prince's liability for the deterioration of the property. The Court of Appeal, perhaps questionably[4], characterised the claim as one in implied contract, or what today would be called restitution. The court then proceeded to assume, without any real discussion of the issue, that the claimant's claim must be adjudicated in the courts of Austria and Hungary, under their law. However, given the relatively undeveloped nature of both the law of conflicts and the law of restitution at the time of this decision, and the lack of reasoning in the judgments on the issue of choice of law, the case is of limited value.

1   Collins (ed) *Dicey and Morris on The Conflict of Laws* (13th edn, 2000), p 1497.
2   *Restatement of the Law Second: the Conflict of Laws* (1971), 734.
3   (1887) 36 Ch D 269.
4   Bennett 'Choice of Law Rules in Claims of Unjust Enrichment' (1990) 39 ICLQ 126 at 141–142.

22.94   Some support for the relevance of the situs of property can also be found in the American cases. For example, in *Gold v Wolpert*[1] the claimant was a real estate broker and the defendants were the purchasers and seller of land. The claimant had introduced the defendants, but they concluded contracts for the sale of the land without his assistance, and did not pay him commission. He brought an action to recover the value of his services. The court held that the action would be governed by Arkansas, Louisiana, Tennessee or New York law. The only connection Louisiana and Tennessee had to the action was that parcels of the land in question were situated in both states.

In *First Wisconsin Trust Co v Shroud*[2], mortgagees of property located in Indiana mistakenly understated the amount required to discharge a mortgage. After the discharge of the mortgage and discovery of the mistake, the mortgagees sought recovery of amounts still due on the mortgage. The court applied Indiana law, the lex situs, but it also noted that a number of other contacts pointed to Indiana.

1   876 F 2d 1327 (7th Cir, 1989).
2   916 F 2d 394 (7th Cir, 1990).

22.95   The arguments of principle in favour of the situs of property are more persuasive than its case law support. Application of the lex situs to the transfer of movables is often justified on the basis that the parties intend that law to apply[1]. This may also be true in relation to some cases of restitution which arise in connection with property. However, the strength of this argument should not be overstated. In the context of a consensual relationship, such as a contract, between the parties, it seems likely that the parties intend or expect the law of that relationship, rather than the lex situs, to govern restitution claims between them. For example, if two parties enter into a contract, which is governed by English law, to transfer property in Scotland, they probably intend that English law should govern, for example, restitution of the contract price. Outside the context of a consensual relationship, it cannot be said with certainty that both parties have any intention or expectation as to the applicable law.

1   North and Fawcett *Cheshire and North's Private International Law* (13th edn, 1999), p 940.

22.96   The lex situs has an interest in the use and ownership of property, especially land, within its jurisdiction[1]. Therefore, if the claimant seeks or asserts an interest in property, especially land, on the basis of a restitution claim, the lex situs will have an interest in the determination of the claim: the claim may affect the use or ownership of land. The lex situs probably also has an interest, although admittedly a lesser one, in the personal restitutionary claimswhich arise in connection with property[2].

1   North and Fawcett *Cheshire and North's Private International Law* (13th edn, 1999), p 929.
2   Such as for mistaken improvements of property (see for example *Greenwood v Bennett* [1973] 1 QB 195) or necessitous interventions in relation to property (see for example *Great Northern Rly Co v Swaffield* (1874) LR 9 Exch 132, above, paras 16.19).

22.97   The primary reason given for the application of the lex situs to questions of transfer of property in land is that, as only the lex situs can control how land within its jurisdiction is transferred, it would be ineffective to apply any other law[1]. This reasoning appears to suggest that any restitution claim which purports to result in a transfer of an interest in land must be governed by the lex situs. However, against this is must be noted that most proprietary restitution claims involve assertions of an equitable interest in property and English courts take the view that such an interest may be enforced by an order in personam against the defendant, which does not require enforcement in the courts of the situs[2]. Accordingly, it is not essential that the lex situs be applied.

1   North and Fawcett *Cheshire and North's Private International Law* (13th edn, 1999), p 929.
2   *Webb v Webb* [1991] 1 WLR 1410 at 1417–1418, per Paul Baker QC. See also *Webb v Webb* (1992) Financial Times, 11 March, CA.

22.98   Relevant factors: Domicile or residence of the parties   Some continental commentators have suggested that restitution should be governed by the personal law of the parties, if common, or, alternatively, that of the defendant[1]. This choice of law rule has been adopted by some continental courts, at least in relation to some cases of restitution[2]. Burrows also suggested that the personal law should be taken into account in ascertaining the applicable law, when the claimant's loss and the defendant's gain have occurred in different jurisdictions[3]. 'Domicil, residence, nationality, place of incorporation and place of business of the parties' are listed as relevant contacts in the *Restatement (2nd)*[4] but the commentary notes that '[t]heir importance depends largely upon the extent to which they are grouped with other contacts'[5]. Finally, in *Baring Bros & Co Ltd v Cunninghame District Council* Lord Penrose implied that in some situations the personal law of the parties and, in particular, that of the defendant, may be relevant to the identification of the law with which the circumstances have their closest and most real connection[6].

1   See Gutteridge and Lipstein 'Conflicts of Law in Matters of Unjustifiable Enrichment' (1941) 7 CLJ 80 at 86–87.
2   Zweigert and Müller-Gindullis 'Quasi Contract' in Lipstein (ed) *International Encyclopedia of Comparative Law* (1974), vol III, ch 30, 8.
3   Burrows *Law of Restitution* (1993), p 492.
4   Paragraph 221(2)(d).
5   Comment d, 733.
6   [1997] CLC 108 at 127. On *Baring* see above, para 22.70ff.

22.99   There are arguments in favour of the relevance of the parties' domicile or residence. However, none of them are particularly strong.

It is argued that restitution is governed by considerations of justice and public policy, and that a person should be held liable only on the basis of the considerations of justice and public policy found in his or her own law[1]. Similarly, it is said that, as the defendant may become liable involuntarily, his or her personal law should apply[2]. The premise of the former argument is weak; restitution is no more based on considerations of justice and public policy than other areas of the law of obligation, such as tort[3]. Moreover, both arguments appear to rest on the mistaken view that people carry their own laws with them, no matter where they are, and no matter what activities they are engaged in.

It could also be argued that the parties expect their personal law to apply. However, a consideration of the circumstances in which restitution claims arise leads to the conclusion that, even if the parties have an expectation about the governing law, they probably do not expect that the personal law applies. Where the restitution claim arises out of a prior relationship between the parties, the parties may well expect the law which applies to that relationship, not the personal law, to govern the claim[4]. This is especially so when, as will often be the case, the parties are unaware of each other's personal law[5]. Even where there is no prior relationship between the parties, it is not obvious that the parties expect their personal law, rather than some other law (such as the law of the place of enrichment) to apply.

1   This sentiment is evident in *American Surety Co of NY v Wrightson* (1910) 103 LT 663 at 665. See also Blaikie 'Unjust Enrichment in the conflict of Laws' [1984] Juridical Review 112 at 118.
2   See Zweigert and Müller-Gindullis 'Quasi Contract' in Lipstein (ed) *International Encyclopedia of Comparative Law* (1974), vol III, ch 30, 8.
3   See Bird 'Choice of Law' in Rose (ed) *Restitution and the Conflict of Laws* (1995), pp 102 and 103.
4   Blaikie 'Unjust Enrichment in the Conflict of Laws' [1984] Juridical Review 112 at 118.
5   Gutteridge and Lipstein 'Conflicts of Law in Matters of Unjustifiable Enrichment' (1941) 7 CLJ 80 at 89.

22.100   For both practical and logical reasons, courts are likely to ignore the domicile or residence of the parties when attempting to identify the law governing a restitution claim. There may well be more than one personal law[1]. This may be an obstacle even if, as is usual, the personal law of the defendant only is considered relevant; there may be more than one defendant. The overwhelming objection to the personal law is that it will frequently have no connection to the claim for restitution[2]. In all disputes, and especially commercial ones, the personal law will probably be entirely fortuitous. In *Baring Bros & Co Ltd v Cunninghame District Council*, Lord Penrose dismissed the relevance of the personal law to the case before him because there was no natural creditor or debtor in the swaps transaction; the fact that Baring Brothers, rather than the Council, was the claimant was purely a matter of chance[3].

1   Gutteridge and Lipstein 'Conflicts of Law in Matters of Unjustifiable Enrichment' (1941) 7 CLJ 80 at 89; Cohen 'Quasi Contract and the Conflict of Laws' (1956) 31 Los Angeles Bar Bulletin 71 at 73; Blaikie 'Unjust Enrichment in the Conflict of Laws' [1984] Juridical Review 112 at 118.
2   Cohen 'Quasi Contract and the Conflict of Laws' (1956) 31 Los Angeles Bar Bulletin 71 at 73.
3   [1997] CLC 108 at 127.

CHOICE OF LAW RULE FOR RESTITUTION FOR WRONGS[1]

22.101   Breach of Contract   Article 10(1)(c) of the Rome Convention[2] provides that the law applicable to a contract under the choice of law rules in the Convention shall govern 'the consequences of breach'. It was argued above that issues in relation to the liability of a contract breaker to give restitution of profits gained as a result of a breach must fall within this provision[3]. Therefore, the applicable choice of law rule for restitution for breach of contract is that set out in the Rome Convention. In summary, that rule provides for application of the law chosen by the parties to govern their contract[4] or, in the absence of choice, the law with which the contract is most closely connected[5]. There are rebuttable presumptions in relation to the law with which the contract is most closely connected[6], and special provisions for consumer[7] and employment[8] contracts.

1 On restitution for wrongs see above, chs 10–12.
2 This Convention is given the force of law in the United Kingdom: Contracts (Applicable Law) Act 1990, s 2.
3 See above, paras 22.46 and 22.56.
4 See art 3.
5 See art 4(1).
6 See art 4(2)–(5).
7 See art 5.
8 See art 6.

22.102   Tort   It was argued above that issues in relation to the liability of a tortfeasor to give restitution of profits gained as a result of a tort should be characterised by reference to the underlying tort[1]. Assuming this is correct, the choice of law rule for restitution for torts, other than defamation, is laid down by the Private International Law (Miscellaneous Provisions) Act 1995, Pt III. Under the Act, the general rule is that 'the applicable law is the law of the country in which the events constituting the tort or delict in question occur'[2]. The Act also contains rules for determining the country in which the events occurred[3], and a flexible exception to the general rule when 'it is substantially more appropriate' for the applicable law to be the law of another country[4]. Restitution of profits made as a result of defamation would be governed by the common law double actionability rule[5].

1 See above, paras 22.57–22.59.
2 See the Private International Law (Miscellaneous Provisions) Act 1995, s 11(1).
3 See the Private International Law (Miscellaneous Provisions) Act 1995, s 11(2).
4 See the Private International Law (Miscellaneous Provisions) Act 1995, s 12.
5 Defamation is excluded from the scope of Pt III of the Private International Law (Miscellaneous Provisions) Act: see s 13. For the choice of law rule for defamation see Collins (ed) *Dicey and Morris on The Conflict of Laws* (13th edn, 2000), r 205, pp 1560–1572.

22.103   Equitable wrongs   The choice of law rule applicable to restitution for equitable wrongs is far more problematic, because, as discussed above, the characterisation of such a claim is a matter of great uncertainty[1]. A number of cases have adopted a restitutionary characterisation and, therefore, applied a restitution choice of law rule[2]. Some of those cases[3] explicitly approved the approach of Chadwick J in *Arab Monetary Fund v Hashim (No 9)*[4]. In that case, Chadwick J said that when a claimant seeks restitution, on the basis of constructive trust, for breach of duty owed by the defendant to the claimant, the court should ask itself the following questions:

(i) what is the proper law which governs the relationship between the defendant and the person for whose benefit those powers have been conferred, (ii) what under that law, are the duties to which the defendant is subject in relation to those powers, (iii) is the nature of those duties such that they would be regarded by an English court as fiduciary duties and (iv) if so, is it unconscionable for the defendant to retain those assets.

Chadwick J also said that this approach is consistent with the restitution choice of law rule in *Dicey and Morris*[5]. Assuming that sub-rule 2(a) of that rule encompasses the law of the relevant relationship, this is an accurate assessment[6].

1 See above, paras 22.60–22.52.
2 See above, paras 22.63–22.100.

3   See *Kuwait Oil Tanker Co SAK v Al Bader* [2000] 2 All ER (Comm) 271; *Grupo Torras SA v Al-Sabah* [1999] CLC 1469 at 1668–1670; *Dubai Aluminium Co Ltd v Salaam* [1999] 1 Lloyd's Rep 415 at 453.
4   (1994) Times, 11 October.
5   Collins (ed) *Dicey and Morris on The Conflict of Laws* (13th edn, 2000), r 200, p 1485; above. para 22.65ff.
6   However, the approach is also not far removed from that in *Paramasivam v Flynn* (1998) 160 ALR 203 and Chadwick J's preferred approach in *Arab Monetary Fund v Hashim (No 9)* (1994) Times, 11 October, both of which are outlined below, para 22.104.

22.104   There are, however, a number of alternative approaches. In *Arab Monetary Fund v Hashim (No 9)*[1] Chadwick J was prepared to apply the tort choice of law rule to issues in relation to a claim for restitution arising out of dishonest assistance in a breach of trust. A number of Australian cases favour application of the law of the forum to equitable claims, on the basis that equity acts in personam[2]. The most recent of these cases is *Paramasivam v Flynn*[3], in which the Full Federal Court declared that, with some possible exceptions which are considered below, application of the law of the forum to actions for breach of fiduciary duty is supported by both principle and the balance of authority. However, the court also stated[4]:

> ... where the circumstances giving rise to the asserted duty or the impugned conduct (or some of it) occurred outside the jurisdiction, the attitude of the law of the place where the circumstances arose or the conduct was undertaken is likely to be an important aspect of the factual circumstances in which the court determines whether a fiduciary relationship existed and, if so, the scope and content of the duties to which it gave rise.

It must be noted that the claimant in *Paramasivam v Flynn* was not seeking restitution.

The final alternative is application of the contract choice of law rule. In *Paramasivam v Flynn* the court indicated that fiduciary relationships which arise out of a contract and the fiduciary relationship owed by a director or officer to a foreign corporation should not be governed by the law of the forum. Instead, the court suggested that the former relationship may be governed by the law of contract. The court made no comment in relation to the governing law of the latter fiduciary relationship[5].

1   (1994) Times, 11 October.
2   *National Commercial Bank v Wimbourne* (1978) 5 BPR [97423] at 11,982; *United States Surgical Corpn v Hospital Products International* [1982] 2 NSWLR 766; *A-G (UK) v Heinemann Publishers Australia Pty Ltd* (1987) 10 NSWLR 86 at 151, per Kirby P, and at 192, per McHugh JA; *Paramasivam v Flynn* (1998) 160 ALR 203. Note that Collins (ed) *Dicey and Morris on The Conflict of Laws* (13th edn, 2000), p 1499 dismissed the notion that equitable claims are governed by the lex fori because equity acts in personam, stating that 'this almost certainly means no more than that a court may order equitable remedies in accordance with its own procedural law over a defendant subject to its personal jurisdiction in respect of rights which have been found to arise under the law identified by its choice of law rules'.
3   (1998) 160 ALR 203 at 217.
4   (1998) 160 ALR 203 at 217.
5   (1998) 160 ALR 203 at 217.

22.105   Law governing the issue of availability of restitutionary remedies   Some issues relating to remedies are characterised as procedural for the purposes of the conflict of laws, and matters of procedure are governed by the *lex fori*[1]. Thus, the question arises whether laws which allow, or dictate, a restitutionary remedy for a civil wrong are merely procedural, so that the availability of such a remedy is always determined by the lex fori. That is, the question is whether the claimant's entitlement to restitutionary damages for the wrong should be determined by the lex fori, on the basis that it is a procedural issue, or in accordance with the law governing the defendant's liability for the underlying wrong, on the basis that entitlement to such a remedy is a matter of substance, governed by the law which governs the main issue of liability.

1 Collins (ed) *Dicey and Morris on The Conflict of Laws* (13th edn, 2000), pp 157–160 and 170–172.

22.106 Whilst traditionally English lawyers have given 'procedure' an expansive definition, the current trend is to narrow the range of matters characterised as procedural, and confine procedure to those matters which a court would find too inconvenient to apply any other law[1]. In light of this, as a matter of legal principle the correct analysis is to characterise the issue of the availability of restitutionary remedies as a matter of substance, rather than procedure; it is hard to see why an English court would have difficulty in applying such laws. Support for this analysis can be gleaned from a number of sources. The High Court of Australia has recently declared, that for the purposes of characterisation in the conflict of laws, 'all questions about the kinds of damages, or amount of damages that may be recovered' should be treated as substantive[2]. In *Chaplin v Boys*[3] Lord Pearson concluded that matters relating to heads of damages are substantive, because otherwise a claimant may recover under the law of the forum when he would have no cause of action under the relevant foreign law. That is, if the only damage in question were recoverable under the law of the forum but not under the foreign law, there would be no cause of action under the foreign law; yet, if the law of the forum were to apply, the claimant would be granted recovery. In these circumstances it is impossible, he said, to describe the difference between the two laws as one of procedure. Likewise, if under the relevant foreign law the wrong in question did not give rise to restitutionary remedies, but it did under the law of the forum, and, while the defendant had made a profit, the claimant suffered no loss, then the same result would follow: the claimant has no cause of action under the relevant foreign law, but can recover under the forum law. If heads of damages are a matter of substance, then a fortiori the issue of whether restitutionary remedies are available is one of substance, to be determined by the law governing liability. Finally, the analysis advanced here is further supported by the fact that the availability of exemplary damages is considered to be a matter of substance[4]. The availability of exemplary damages is clearly analogous to the availability of restitutionary damages.

On the other hand, it must be acknowledged that the oft-quoted passage from *Arab Monetary Fund v Hashim (No 9)*[5] gives an expansive definition to matters of procedure in the context of restitution for wrongs. According to Chadwick J, the governing law determines the nature of the duties arising out of the relationship between the parties, but the law of the forum determines whether those duties are of a type that give rise to restitutionary proprietary remedies.

1 Collins (ed) *Dicey and Morris on The Conflict of Laws* (13th edn, 2000), p 157.
2 *John Pfeiffer Pty Ltd v Rogerson* (2000) 172 ALR 625 at 651.
3 [1971] AC 356 at 394–395.
4 *Waterhouse v Australian Broadcasting Corpn* (1989) 86 ACTR 1 at 19; Collins (ed) *Dicey and Morris on The Conflict of Laws* (13th edn, 2000), p 1533.
5 (1994) Times, 11 October. See above, para 22.103.

INDEX